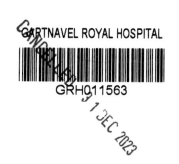

LIBRARY

Learning
Resource Centre

HANDBOOK OF AUTISM AND PERVASIVE DEVELOPMENTAL DISORDERS

HANDBOOK OF AUTISM AND PERVASIVE DEVELOPMENTAL DISORDERS

VOLUME 1: DIAGNOSIS, DEVELOPMENT, AND BRAIN MECHANISMS

Fourth Edition

Edited by

FRED R. VOLKMAR, SALLY J. ROGERS, RHEA PAUL,
AND KEVIN A. PELPHREY

Published by John Wiley & Sons, Inc., Hoboken, New Jersey
Published simultaneously in Canada

Library of Congress Cataloging-in-Publication Data:

Handbook of autism and pervasive developmental disorders / edited by Fred R. Volkmar, Sally J. Rogers, Rhea Paul, and Kevin A. Pelphrey.–Fourth edition.
   p. ; cm.
   Autism and pervasive developmental disorders
   Includes bibliographical references and indexes.
   ISBN 978-1-118-10702-7 (v. 1 : cloth : alk. paper)
   ISBN 978-1-118-10703-4 (v. 2 : cloth : alk. paper)
   ISBN 978-1-118-14068-0 (set : cloth : alk. paper)
   ISBN 978-0-471-69442-7 (ebk.)
   ISBN 978-1-118-28219-9 (ebk.)
   I. Volkmar, Fred R., editor of compilation. II. Rogers, Sally J., editor of compilation. III. Paul, Rhea, editor of compilation.
IV. Pelphrey, Kevin Archer, editor of compilation. V. Title: Autism and pervasive developmental disorders.
   [DNLM: 1. Child Development Disorders, Pervasive. WS 350.8.P4]
   RJ506.A9
   618.92′85882—dc23
                                                                                          2013034363

Printed in the United States of America

10 9 8 7 6 5 4 3 2 1

Contents

VOLUME 2: ASSESSMENT, INTERVENTIONS, AND POLICY

IV   ASSESSMENT   581

Contributors

George M. Anderson, PhD
Child Study Center
Yale University School of Medicine
New Haven, Connecticut

Karla K. Ausderau, PhD
Kinesiology Department
University of Wisconsin–Madison
Madison, Wisconsin

Grace T. Baranek, PhD, OTR/L, FAOTA
Department of Allied Health Sciences
University of North Carolina at Chapel Hill
Chapel Hill, North Carolina

Erin E. Barton, PhD, BCBA-D
School of Education and Human Development
University of Colorado, Denver

Nirit Bauminger-Zviely, PhD
School of Education
Bar-Ilan University
Ramat-Gan, Israel

Scott Bellini, PhD
Social Skills Research Clinic
School Psychology Program
Indiana University
Bloomington, Indiana

Raphael A. Bernier, PhD
Center on Human Development and Disability
University of Washington
Seattle, Washington

Stefanie Bodison, OTD, OTR/L, C/NDT
Division of Occupational Science
  and Occupational Therapy
University of Southern California
Los Angeles, California

Leah Langford Booth, MS, CCC-SLP
Child Study Center
Yale University School of Medicine
New Haven, Connecticut

Kristen Bottema-Beutel, PhD
Department of Special Education
Vanderbilt University
Nashville, Tennessee

Brian A. Boyd, PhD
University of North Carolina at Chapel Hill
Chapel Hill, North Carolina

Jane Thierfeld Brown, EdD
University of Connecticut
School of Law
Hartford, Connecticut

Ariane Buescher, MSc
Personal Social Service Research Unit
London School of Economics and Political Science
London, United Kingdom

Alice S. Carter, PhD
Department of Psychology
University of Massachusetts, Boston
Boston, Massachusetts

Manuel F. Casanova, MD
Department of Psychiatry
University of Louisville
Louisville, Kentucky

Ya-Chih Chang, PhD
Center for Autism Research and Treatment
University of California
Los Angeles, California

Katarzyna Chawarska, PhD
Child Study Center
Yale University School of Medicine
New Haven, Connecticut

Frank Cicero, PhD, BCBA
Eden II Programs
Staten Island, New York

Elaine E. Coonrod, PhD
TEACCH Autism Program
University of North Carolina at Chapel Hill
Chapel Hill, North Carolina

Christina Corsello, PhD
Autism Discovery Institute
San Diego, California

Naomi Ornstein Davis, PhD
Department of Psychiatry
Duke University Medical Center
Durham, North Carolina

Whitney J. Detar, PhD
Graduate School of Education
University of California, Santa Barbara
Goleta, California

Oana de Vinck-Baroody, DO
Developmental-Behavioral Pediatrics
Yale School of Medicine
New Haven, Connecticut

Peter Doehring, PhD
ASD Roadmap
Chadds Ford, Pennsylvania

Shaunessy M. Egan, MS Ed, BCBA
Center for Children with Special Needs
Glastonbury, Connecticut

Ruth Blennerhassett Eren, EdD
Professor of Special Education
Southern Connecticut State University
New Haven, Connecticut

Donia Fahim, PhD, Cert. MRCSLT
Hunter College
City University of New York
New York, New York

Kate E. Fiske, PhD, BCBA-D
Douglass Developmental Disabilities Center
Rutgers, The State University of New Jersey
New Brunswick, New Jersey

Eric Fombonne, MD
Department of Psychiatry
McGill University
Montreal, Quebec, Canada

Solandy Forte, MSW, BCBA
Center for Children with Special Needs
Glastonbury, Connecticut

Megan Freeth
Psychology Department
University of Sheffield
Western Bank, Sheffield, United Kingdom

Lauren Gardner, PhD
Boling Center for Developmental Disabilities
University of Tennessee Health Science Center
Memphis, Tennessee

Peter F. Gerhardt, EdD
Organization for Autism Research
Arlington, Virginia

Mark P. Groskreutz, PhD
Southern Connecticut State University
New Haven, Connecticut

Rebecca Grzadzinski
Teachers College
Columbia University
New York, New York

Abha R. Gupta, MD
Department of Pediatrics
Yale University School of Medicine
New Haven, Connecticut

Laura J. Hall, PhD
Department of Special Education
San Diego State University
San Diego, California

Antonia Hamilton, PhD
School of Psychology
University of Nottingham
Nottingham, United Kingdom

Jan S. Handleman (deceased)

Sandra L. Harris, PhD
Douglass Developmental Disabilities Center
Rutgers, The State University of New Jersey
New Brunswick, New Jersey

Irva Hertz-Picciotto, PhD
Division of Environmental and
    Occupational Health
and
MIND Institute
UC Davis Medical Center
University of California, Davis
Davis, California

Alison Presmanes Hill, MS, PhD
Department of Pediatrics
Oregon Health & Sciences University
Beaverton, Oregon

R. Peter Hobson, MD
Institute of Child Health
University College London
London, United Kingdom

Patricia Howlin, MSc, PhD
St. George's Hospital Medical School
University of London
London, United Kingdom

Kara A. Hume, PhD
FPG Child Development Institute
University of North Carolina at Chapel Hill
Carrboro, North Carolina

Lisa V. Ibañez
University of Washington Autism Center
Seattle, Washingon

Brooke Ingersoll, PhD
Department of Psychology
Michigan State University
East Lansing, Michigan

William R. Jenson, PhD
Department of Educational Psychology
University of Utah
Salt Lake City, Utah

Connie Kasari, PhD
Center for Autism Research and Treatment
University of California at Los Angeles
Los Angeles, California

So Hyun Kim, PhD
Child Study Center
Yale University School of Medicine
New Haven, Connecticut

Martin Knapp
London School of Economics and Political Science
King's College London
London, United Kingdom

Lynn Kern Koegel, PhD
Koegel Autism Center
University of California, Santa Barbara
Goleta, California

Robert L. Koegel, PhD
Koegel Autism Center
University of California, Santa Barbara
Goleta, California

Elizabeth Lanter, PhD, CCC-SLP
Department of Communication Sciences
and Disorders
Radford University
Radford, Virginia

Jennifer Leung, MD
Department of Pediatrics
Yale University School of Medicine
New Haven, Connecticut

Lauren M. Little, PhD
Department of Allied Health Sciences
University of North Carolina at Chapel Hill
Chapel Hill, North Carolina

James W. Loomis, PhD
Center for Children with Special Needs
Glastonbury, Connecticut

Catherine Lord, PhD
Center for Autism and the Developing Brain
Weill Cornell Medical College
White Plains, New York

Kristen Lyall, ScD
MIND Institute
UC Davis Medical Center
University of California, Davis
Davis, California

Megan C. Lyons, MS, CCC-SLP
Child Study Center
Yale University School of Medicine
New Haven, Connecticut

Suzanne L. Macari, PhD
Child Study Center
Yale University School of Medicine
New Haven, Connecticut

David S. Mandell, ScD
University of Pennsylvania School of Medicine
Philadelphia, Pennsylvania

Kimberly Markoff, MSEd
St. John's Pavilion
Springfield, Illinois

Andrés Martin, MD, MPH
Child Study Center
Yale University School of Medicine
New Haven, Connecticut

Megan P. Martins, PhD, BCBA-D
Center for Development & Disability
University of New Mexico Health Sciences Center
Albuquerque, New Mexico

Gary S. Mayerson, JD
Mayerson & Associates
New York, New York

Erik Mayville, PhD, BCBA-D
Institute for Educational Planning
Connecticut Center for Child Development
Milford, Connecticut

Carla A. Mazefsky, PhD
Department of Psychiatry
University of Pittsburgh
Pittsburgh, Pennsylvania

Iain McClure, MB, BS
University of Edinburgh
Edinburgh, United Kingdom

James C. McPartland, PhD
Child Study Center
Yale University School of Medicine
New Haven, Connecticut

Judith Meyers, PhD
The Child Health and Development Institute
of Connecticut, Inc.
Farmington, Connecticut

Amber R. Miller, BA
Graduate School of Education
University of California, Santa Barbara
Goleta, California

Elizabeth Milne
Psychology Department
University of Sheffield
Sheffield, United Kingdom

Pat Mirenda, PhD
Centre for Interdisciplinary Research
    and Collaboration in Autism
The University of British Columbia
Vancouver, British Columbia

Stewart Mostofsky
Laboratory for Neurocognitive and
    Imaging Research
Kennedy Krieger Institute
Baltimore, Maryland

Elizabeth C. Nulty, MS, BCBA
Center for Children with Special Needs
Glastonbury, Connecticut

Leona Oakes, BA
Strong Center for Developmental Disabilities
University of Rochester Medical Center
Rochester, New York

Samuel L. Odom, PhD
Frank Porter Graham Child Development
    Institute
University of North Carolina
Chapel Hill, North Carolina

Robert E. O'Neill
Department of Special Education
University of Utah
Salt Lake City, Utah

Mark J. Palmieri, PsyD, BCBA-D
School Consultation Services
Center for Children with Special Needs
Glastonbury, Connecticut

L. Diane Parham, PhD
Occupational Therapy Graduate Program
University of New Mexico
Albuquerque, New Mexico

Rhea Paul, PhD, CCC-SLP
Department of Speech-Language Pathology
Sacred Heart University
Fairfield, Connecticut

Kevin A. Pelphrey, PhD
Child Study Center
Yale University School of Medicine
New Haven, Connecticut

Lauren Pepa, BA
Douglass Developmental Disabilities Center
Rutgers, The State University of New Jersey
New Brunswick, New Jersey

Marie-Christine Potvin, PhD, OTR, ATP
Center on Disability and Community Inclusion
University of Vermont
Burlington, Vermont

Kelly Powell, MA
Child Study Center
Yale University School of Medicine
New Haven, Connecticut

Michael D. Powers, PsyD
Center for Children with Special Needs
Glastonbury, Connecticut
and
Child Study Center
Yale University School of Medicine
New Haven, Connecticut

Patricia A. Prelock, PhD
College of Nursing and Health Sciences
University of Vermont
Burlington, Vermont

Keith C. Radley, III, PhD
Department of Psychology
University of Southern Mississippi
Hattiesburg, Mississippi

Rajani Ramachandran, PhD
University of Calicut
Kerala, India

Brian Reichow, PhD
Child Study Center
Yale University School of Medicine
New Haven, Connecticut

Sally J. Rogers, PhD
UC Davis Medical Center
University of California, Davis
and
MIND Institute
Sacramento, California

Jessica L. Rohrer, MS, BCBA
Center for Children with Special Needs
Glastonbury, Connecticut

Justin Rowberry, Major, USAF
Developmental and Behavioral Pediatrics
Mike O'Callaghan Federal Medical Center
Nellis AFB, Nevada

**Michael Rutter, CBE, MD, FRCP,
    FRCPsych, FRS**
Social, Genetic and Developmental
    Psychiatry Centre
Institute of Psychiatry
King's College, London
London, United Kingdom

Maura G. Sabatos-DeVito, MS
Department of Psychology,
    Developmental Program
University of North Carolina at Chapel Hill
Chapel Hill, North Carolina

Micheal P. Sandbank, MEd
Department of Special Education
Vanderbilt University
Nashville, Tennessee

**Liliane Beaudoin Savard, PT, DPT,
    PCS, PLLC**
Zippy Life Physical Therapy
Montpelier, Vermont

Lawrence Scahill, MSN, PhD
School of Nursing
and
Child Study Center
Yale University School of Medicine
New Haven, Connecticut

Rebecca J. Schmidt, PhD, MS
Department of Public Health Sciences
MIND Institute
UC Davis Medical Center
University of California, Davis
Davis, California

Elizabeth Schoen Simmons, MS, CCC-SLP
Child Study Center
Yale University School of Medicine
New Haven, Connecticut

Katelyn Selver, BA
Strong Center for Developmental Disabilities
Department of Pediatrics
University of Rochester Medical Center
Rochester, New York

Elizabeth Sheppard, PhD
Psychology Department
University of Nottingham Malaysia Campus
Selangot Darul Ehsan, Malaysia

Frederick Shic, PhD
Child Study Center
Yale University School of Medicine
New Haven, Connecticut

Tristram Smith, PhD
Strong Center for Developmental Disabilities
Department of Pediatrics
University of Rochester Medical Center
Rochester, New York

Laurie Snider, PhD, OTR(C)
School of Physical and Occupational Therapy
McGill University
Montreal, Canada

Wendy L. Stone, PhD
UW Autism Center
University of Washington
Seattle, Washington

Helen Tager-Flusberg, PhD
Department of Anatomy and Neurobiology
Boston University School of Medicine
Boston, Massachusetts

Anita Thapar, MBBCh, PhD, FRCPsych, FMedSci
MRC Centre for Neuropsychiatric Genetics
    and Genomics
and
Institute of Psychological Medicine and
    Clinical Neurosciences
Cardiff University School of Medicine
Cardiff, Wales, United Kingdom

Caitlin S. Tillberg
Frank H. Netter School of Medicine
Quinnipiac University
North Haven, Connecticut

Rachael M. Tillman, BA
Child Study Center
Yale University School of Medicine
New Haven, Connecticut

Katherine D. Tsatsanis, PhD
Child Study Center
Yale University School of Medicine
New Haven, Connecticut

Nita Vaswani, DO
Child Study Center
Yale University School of Medicine
New Haven, Connecticut

Laurie Vismara, PhD
Psychiatry and Behavioral Sciences
University of California, Davis
and
MIND Institute
Sacramento, California

Giacomo Vivanti, PhD
Department of Psychology
Olga Tennisson Autism Research Centre
La Trobe University
Melbourne, Australia

Fred R. Volkmar, MD
Child Study Center
Yale University School of Medicine
New Haven, Connecticut

Allison Wainer, MA
Department of Psychology
Michigan State University
East Lansing, Michigan

Christine Wenzel, BA, MA
Center for Students with Disabilities
University of Connecticut
Storrs, Connecticut

Alexander Westphal, MD
Department of Psychiatry
Yale University School of Medicine
New Haven, Connecticut

Susan W. White, PhD
Virginia Tech Autism Center
Virginia Tech
Blacksburg, Virginia

Lisa A. Wiesner, MD
Pediatrics and Adolescent Medicine
Orange, Connecticut

Tiffany Woynaroski, MS, SLP
Vanderbilt Kennedy Center
Nashville, Tennessee

Daniel Y.-J. Yang, PhD
Child Study Center
Yale University School of Medicine
New Haven, Connecticut

Paul Yoder, PhD
Vanderbilt Kennedy Center
Nashville, Tennessee

Katharine E. Zuckerman, MD, MPH
Division of General Pediatrics and
    Child and Adolescent Health
    Measurement Initiative
Oregon Health and Sciences University
Portland, Oregon

Preface

The pace of autism research has increased dramatically since the previous edition of this *Handbook* appeared. In that year, 2005, there were approximately 800 peer-reviewed scientific papers on autism, while in 2012 this number had increased to over 2,600. This marked increase in research productivity poses important challenges for editors of a comprehensive handbook devoted to autism. Inevitably, some difficult choices have to be made in balancing coverage of research, intervention, theory, and social policy.

In the 70 years since Kanner's initial description of autism, the condition has attracted interest from clinicians and researchers alike. As a disorder that impacts core aspects of socialization, it has posed important challenges for theories of developmental psychology and neurobiology as well as for clinical practice in diagnosis and intervention, and studies of diagnostic validity and treatment. Essentially every theory relating to child development—cognitive, social, behavioral, affective, neurobiological—has been applied to understanding this enigmatic condition. Autism has served as a paradigmatic disorder for research on the essential preconditions for normal social-cognitive maturation—expression and recognition of emotions, intersubjectivity, sharing the focus of interest with other people, the meaning and uses of language, forming attachments, and relating empathetically to others.

In developing this new edition, we have been mindful of the considerable progress made in the field as well as areas where knowledge remains limited. Great advances have been made, for example, in understanding the social brain, in genetics, and in basic aspects of neurobiology. Other advances have also been made in the areas of intervention and there is a new and growing convergence between research findings and evidence-based practice. On the other hand, there are many areas where knowledge remains limited—for example, work on aging in autism is almost nonexistent.

As with other areas of science, we believe that autism scholarship and service will advance when we adopt, as much as possible, rigorous standards of scientific research. Our aim with this fourth edition is to provide a comprehensive account of current work in the field. In many instances, authors have kindly revised earlier contributions in light of current research; in other cases, we have solicited new contributors and chapters. Our goal for these volumes is to provide timely overviews in key areas that can help researchers, clinicians, and policy makers.

We are acutely aware that investigators and clinicians, working alongside families and advocates, have learned so much, often with limited resources. The knowledge summarized in these volumes speaks to the commitment of these individuals in understanding and caring for children with autism. We hope that these volumes document their achievements and inspire their future efforts.

We thank a number of colleagues who have critiqued early versions of chapters or who helped us select chapter authors or focus chapter topics. These include Brian Reichow, Roger Jou, William Nordhaus, Peter Doehring, Abha Ghupta, Carlisle Runge, Iain McClure, Christopher McDougle, Linda Mayes, George Anderson, and Dean Sutherland. We also thank a number of individuals for secretarial and administrative support: at the Child Study Center Lori Klein, Emily Hau, and Rosemary Serra, and from UC Davis MIND Institute, we would like to thank Diane Larzelere. We are also grateful to our editor at Wiley, Patricia Rossi, who has helped us consistently strive for excellence.

Diagnosis, Epidemiology, Course

This section of the *Handbook* is concerned with issues of diagnosis and classification, the broader autism phenotype, epidemiology, and outcome. These topics share many points of connection. The past 20 years have been a time of remarkable progress for the field as a whole. On the other hand, new findings have emerged that stretch traditional boundaries of diagnosis and raise important new questions for future research.

The first chapter is concerned with issues in diagnosis and classification. Changes in nomenclature can impact longitudinal and epidemiological studies. It is important to realize that there must be a balance of research and clinical needs. For the latter it is the diagnostic process that becomes critically important (i.e., when the unique constellation of strengths and vulnerabilities of the individual in the context of his or her family and culture must be addressed). As noted in this chapter, the past few years have witnessed significant changes in approaches to diagnosis, with several official systems now extant. It remains to be seen how these changes will translate into changes in clinical practice and research; for example, see Huerta, Bishop, Duncan, Hus, and Lord (2012) and Volkmar, Reichow, and McPartland (2012) for differing views.

Ingersol and Wainer focus on the broader phenotype of autism and note that despite considerable interest in this as a topic, research findings remain rather conflicting, although there is a general consensus that social difficulties remain the major point of connection to more strictly diagnosed autism/autism spectrum disorder (Bernier, Gerdts, Munson, Dawson, & Estes, 2012; Ingersoll, 2010).

There is also some relevant work on communication difficulties (particularly those of a social nature) and some work on repetitive behaviors, as well as specific cognitive abilities and risk for specific mental health problems. Integration of findings into genetic studies may be a particularly fruitful area in years tocome.

Fombonne and colleagues review recent work on the epidemiology of autism/autism spectrum disorder. As they point out, an extensive body of work is now available so that recent studies suggest that perhaps 1 child in 150 may have autism or a related condition. As they note, although there has been considerable interest in a secular increase in the incidence of autism and although the data are somewhat limited, it does appear that this reflects changing diagnostic concepts as well as awareness of entitlements, in some countries, for services (Fombonne, 2005; Yeargin-Allsopp, Boyle, Braun, & Trevathan, 2008). Research now underway may clarify these issues, particularly in relation to the diagnostic changes discussed in the first chapter.

In the final chapter in this section, Howlin provides a very helpful summary of current knowledge regarding outcome. As she notes, this area represents rather a moving target, with earlier detection, better treatments, and changes in diagnostic concepts all potentially impacting outcome. In the United States, several key landmarks are readily identified—for example, the passage of Public Law 94–152 mandating provision of education to all children with disabilities and the National Research Council's 2001 report on intervention (National Research Council, 2001), among others. The growing awareness of both the general public and health care providers (see Chapters 44 and 49) also has played a role in potential changes in outcome. As Howlin also observes, knowledge of adult outcome focuses almost entirely on outcome in early adult life, with an almost total lack of work on autism in the elderly (Piven & Rabins, 2011).

REFERENCES

Bernier, R., Gerdts, J., Munson, J., Dawson, G., & Estes, A. (2012). Evidence for broader autism phenotype characteristics in parents from multiple-incidence autism families. *Autism Research*, *5*(1), 13–20.

Fombonne, E. (2005). Epidemiology of autistic disorder and other pervasive developmental disorders. *Journal of Clinical Psychiatry*, *66*(Suppl. 10), 3–8.

Huerta, M., Bishop, S. L., Duncan, A., Hus, V., & Lord, C. (2012). Application of *DSM-5* criteria for autism spectrum disorder to three samples of children with *DSM-IV* diagnoses of pervasive developmental disorders. *American Journal of Psychiatry*, *169*(10), 1056–1064.

Ingersoll, B. (2010). Broader autism phenotype and nonverbal sensitivity: Evidence for an association in the general population. *Journal of Autism and Developmental Disorders*, *40*(5), 590–598.

National Research Council. (2001). *Educating young children with autism*. Washington, DC: National Academies Press.

Piven, J., & Rabins, P. (2011). Autism spectrum disorders in older adults: Toward defining a research agenda. *Journal of the American Geriatrics Society*, *59*(11), 2151–2155.

Volkmar, F. R., Reichow, B., & McPartland, J. (2012). Classification of autism and related conditions: Progress, challenges, and opportunities. *Dialogues in Clinical Neuroscience*, *14*(3), 229–237.

Yeargin-Allsopp, M., Boyle, C., Braun, K. V. N., & Trevathan, E. (2008). The epidemiology of developmental disabilities. In P. J. Accardo (Ed.), *Capute and Accardo's neurodevelopmental disabilities in infancy and childhood: Vol. 1. Neurodevelopmental diagnosis and treatment* (pp. 61–104). Baltimore, MD: Paul H. Brookes.

CHAPTER 1

Autism and the Autism Spectrum: Diagnostic Concepts

FRED R. VOLKMAR, BRIAN REICHOW, ALEXANDER WESTPHAL,
AND DAVID S. MANDELL

It has now been 70 years since Kanner's classic (1943) description of the syndrome of infantile autism. Over this time, and particularly over the past two decades, there has been an explosion of work. In this chapter we provide an overview of relevant diagnostic concepts, current and prior approaches to diagnosis, areas of controversy, and where knowledge is lacking. The major focus in this

chapter is on autism and those conditions included in the Pervasive Developmental Disorders category in the *Diagnostic and Statistical Manual of Mental Disorders*, fourth edition (*DSM-IV*; American Psychiatric Association [APA], 1994). Chapter 2 focuses on the issue of the broader autism phenotype in greater detail; it is appropriate to begin here with a short review of general issues in diagnosis and classification. We should note that when we refer to autism we are referring to the more

From the Child Study Center and Department of Psychiatry, Yale University School of Medicine (Drs. Volkmar and Westphal); A.J. Pappanikou Center for Excellence in Developmental Disabilities, University of Connecticut Health Center (Dr. Reichow), and Department of Psychiatry of the Children's Hospital of Philadelphia Center for Autism Research (Dr. Mandell). The authors thank the Associates of the Child Study Center, the Hillibrand Foundation, and Slifka Foundation for their support. This publication was made possible in part by CTSA Grant

Number UL1 RR024139 or KL2 RR024138 or TL1 RR024137 (as appropriate) from the National Center for Research Resources (NCRR) and the National Center for Advancing Translational Science (NCATS), components of the National Institutes of Health (NIH), and NIH Roadmap for Medical Research. Its contents are solely the responsibility of the authors and do not necessarily represent the official view of NIH.

specific diagnosis employed in *DSM-IV* and the *Clinical Descriptions and Diagnostic Guidelines* (*ICD-10*; World Health Organization, 1992) (i.e., autistic disorder); we will use the terms *pervasive developmental disorder* (PDD—the *DSM-IV* and *ICD-10* terms for the entire category to which autism was assigned but including conditions like Asperger's disorder) and *autism spectrum disorder* (ASD—the new *DSM-5* term) interchangeably, although we will also discuss the potential of there being differences between the two.

ISSUES IN DIAGNOSIS AND CLASSIFICATION

Systems for classification have many different uses and orientations. They enhance communication, further research and clinical work, and help in planning and social policy. It is clear that for a classification system to work well it must be clear, broadly accepted, and straightforward to use. Changes in diagnostic concepts should be carefully made since diagnostic stability is important. Official diagnostic systems should be logical and comprehensive, encompass developmental change, and avoid issues of cultural, social, or gender bias. A range of approaches are used and each has its strengths and limitations (see Taylor & Rutter, 2008, for a recent review).

It is important to emphasize a diagnosis is only one part of an entire *diagnostic process* (Cohen, 1976). The latter will include a much fuller description of the clinical situation and will highlight areas of strength and weakness that should be considered in designing an intervention program. Official diagnostic systems must strike a careful balance between being two broad or narrow. Diagnostic systems lose their value if they are either overly broad or overly narrow. There are intrinsic tensions in balancing research and clinical needs, for example, in the case of a single gene disorder it might be important to have, for some purposes, a strict definition. On the other hand, for service provision broader views may be more appropriate. Other issues include the degree to which (or not)

impairment is a defining feature, for example, for a condition like Tourette's syndrome a father may have had recurrent vocal and motor tics for years but never been impaired as a result, *but* his child may have much significant difficulties; on the other hand, some individuals with significant social disability may see their problems more as a lifestyle/personality type and as such may want to not feel stigmatized by being said to have a disorder (see Rutter, 2011, for a discussion of this issue specific to autism and disorders on the autism spectrum). These various tensions are legitimate ones but also are often underappreciated (Volkmar & Klin, 2005).

Dimension approaches to classification have important advantages in that they provide more nuanced information. Their use is exemplified in measures like blood pressure, IQ, or adaptive skills where specific dichotomous points may be used to define disorder or risk. There are some risks in this as well, of course, in that the difference between an IQ of 68 and one of 70 is relatively small but can have major implications for adult services. With the advent of better diagnostic assessments in autism the use of such approaches has advanced research (although there are also tensions around this approach as well). An example of a different developmental approach was using predictions of normative social ability (as assessed by the Vineland Adaptive Behavior scale [Sparrow, Cicchetti, & Balla, 2005]) were made based on a skill levels expected based on either chronological or mental age and found to be highly predictive of autism (Volkmar et al., 1987).

The role of theory in guiding classification schemes is much debated, although the recent trend, starting with *DSM-III*, has been to focus on a theoretical, phenomenological approach. This reflected awareness that highly theoretical systems are not always generally shared. Since 1980 the trend is for use of the research diagnostic criteria approach (Spitzer, Endicott, & Robbins, 1978). Using this approach work on establishing validity of proposed categories has focused on issues like genetic or family findings (e.g., higher rates of autism in family members), drug response, epidemiology, course, developmental and cognitive correlates, and biological findings (Taylor & Rutter, 2008).

All conditions do, of course, have developmental correlates. For those like autism and ASD these factors have great importance. An understanding of developmental issues can enrich our understanding of clinical phenomenon, for example, the echolalia frequently observed in autism has some similarities to that seen in typically developing children learning to speak but can be more prolonged and problematic and likely reflects one aspect of a more general "gestalt learning style" (Volkmar & Wiesner, 2009). Early understanding of autism (viewed through a theoretical lens) often viewed echolalia as an attempt by the child to avoid interaction, but we now know this to be mistaken. Indeed when a previously mute child begins to echo we see this as a sign of progress. The use of multiaxial classification schemes (Rutter et al., 1969) has been important. Similarly in *DSM-5* (APA, 2013) the greater use of dimensions for diagnostic criteria may have some important advantages.

A challenge for all diagnostic systems is the problem of *comorbidity* (Rutter, 1994a; Volkmar & Woolston, 1997), that is, of having more than one condition at a time. This issue was highlighted for child psychiatry in Rutter's pioneering study on the Isle of Wight (Rutter, Tizard, Yule, Graham, & Whitmore, 1976) but has become a more active topic of discussion and debate since *DSM-IV* and *ICD-10* adopted somewhat differing approaches to the problem. Angold and colleagues (Angold, Costello, & Erkanli, 1999) noted the great need for research in this area—particularly in epidemiological samples, given that there may be important implications of comorbidity for treatment and course. For older individuals, particularly the higher functioning, associated depression or anxiety problems may be targets of intervention.

The role of etiology in treatment also presents some challenges for diagnosis. Even in a condition like Trisomy 21 (Down syndrome), considerable phenotypic heterogeneity is seen with some individuals having IQs in the normal range. The Down syndrome example is also a good one in that it illustrates that a condition can impact multiple areas of medicine (psychiatry, neurology, cardiology, hematology). Issues of etiology are very complicated in psychiatry where clearly many factors impact the final expression of the disorders studied. For example, Rett's disorder was included as a PDD in *DSM-IV* (APA, 1994) not so much because it was a form of autism (although Rett had originally speculated on this [Rett, 1966]) and there may be a time of social withdrawal as the syndrome onsets. However, the subsequent presentation and course is very different (Van Acker, Loncola, & Van Acker, 2005) but because it was sufficiently distinctive as to need to be included somewhere (Rutter, 1994b). Interestingly with *DSM-5* it will no longer be included, in part, because a single gene etiology has been discovered. This will become more of a challenge for diagnostic systems in the future where genetic contributions will be identified, but even here the actual phenotypic expression may be significant and, in reality, most psychiatric, developmental, and emotional disorders will be influenced by a range of factors.

Like all things, classification systems can be misused (Hobbs, 1975). A common mistake is the confusion of a person with a label. A single label cannot capture the fullness of the individual. Dichotomous categories can also minimize the tremendous range of syndrome expression. In autism and the ASDs other kinds of information (on communicative and cognitive abilities and adaptive skills) is needed. Another major source of misuse results from the reification of a label into explanation. A final misuse of labels is their potential for stigmatization. If a diagnostic label is mistaken for an explanation, areas of ignorance may be covered over and the search for underlying causes may end prematurely.

Diagnostic systems help to organize the clinical and research work. For autism and disorders on the autism spectrum, they have facilitated an explosion of research. Diagnostic systems can always be improved, although there is a need to balance any change with the potential difficulties in interpreting earlier work, disrupting ongoing studies, and, potentially, complicating service provision.

DEVELOPMENT OF AUTISM AS A DIAGNOSTIC CONCEPT

Kanner's Report

Children with autism may have been seen before Kanner's work (e.g., Wolff, 2004), although it was his genius to provide an overarching clinical description (Kanner, 1943). He reported on 11 children with "autistic disturbances of affective contact" and prefigured many of the important research questions for the next decade. He was careful to frame in his description in a developmental context the suspicion that early infantile autism was an inborn disorder where infants were cut off from the social world. His use of the word *autism* to convey this self-contained quality was very evocative although, unfortunately, also a source of some confusion (i.e., with schizophrenia).

In addition to autism Kanner noted one other feature that he felt was essential. He referred to this as "insistence on sameness" or "resistance to change" and referred to the difficulties children had in dealing with change in the nonsocial world. While seemingly the same, the terms *insistence on sameness* and *resistance to change* have some subtle differences especially when one includes, as did Kanner, repetitive movements/interests (e.g., stereotyped hand flapping). In Kanner's view these repetitive movements/interests were one manifestation of the desire for sameness. This category has changed, in some ways, over the years and remains an area of active (if somewhat limited) research.

Kanner's paper anticipated some areas of current research, for example, approaches to studying social development in very young infants and those at genetic risk. He also prefigured one of the major challenges for theory building in that his report suggested we need to understand the *lack* of social interest and the seeming *over*engagement in the nonsocial world (Klin, Jones, Schultz, & Volkmar, 2005).

In addition to the two central features mentioned, a number of other unusual features have now been the focus of research for some decades. Kanner noted that although children with autism

did well on some parts of IQ tests, these were the parts that were nonverbal and memory based while symbolization, abstraction, and understanding of meaning were areas of challenge. He noted that three of the children he described were mute and that the others had language characterized echolalia and literalness, as well as an idiosyncratic language and difficulties in use of pronouns.

Kanner's report, while remarkably enduring, also served to mislead work in some ways. Noteworthy false leads included an observation by Kanner of the high levels of professional success of parents. This then led a number of early investigators to focus on the role of parents in pathogenesis. Subsequently, it has seemed very clear that there is not a social class bias in autism (Wing, 1980) and that genetic factors have a major contribution (El-Fishawy & State, 2010).

Kanner originally speculated that autism was not a manifestation of known medical conditions, but subsequent research has clearly shown associations with some disorders—notably epilepsy (Volkmar & Nelson, 1990) and several strongly genetic conditions (e.g., Fragile X syndrome and tuberous sclerosis; see Chapter 17). Early attempts were made to subtype by distinguishing between "primary" and "secondary" autism depending on the presence of associated medical conditions. This work led to the potential delineation of many types of autism (Gillberg & Coleman, 1996), although much of this work was based on case reports; other studies questioned many of the reported associations (Rutter, Bailey, Bolton, & Le Couteur, 1994). With the discovery of a number of genes potentially involved in the pathogenesis of autism is, somewhat paradoxically, the case that we may return to the concept of autism rather than a single unifying construct (El-Fishawy & State, 2010).

Kanner noted that certain nonverbal and memory skills appeared to be preserved in the face of major verbal difficulties. It was also the case that individuals with autism with unusual abilities in some area (drawing, memory, calendar calculation) also were observed (Hermelin, 2001), contributing to the difficulties in understanding the potential major impact of autism for intellectual development. This led many early investigators to assume that poor performance on the rest of the IQ test was due to lack of motivation or negativism; over time it became clear that intellectual disability was frequently observed with a pattern of highly variable, sometimes striking, discrepancies in subscores.

Another area of confusion arose from Kanner's use of the word *autism*—a term borrowed from Bleuler's self-centered and idiosyncratic thinking in schizophrenia (Bleuler, 1911). Kanner's use of the term was quite different, but given broad views of schizophrenia and childhood psychosis, many clinicians began to view autism as a form, perhaps the earliest manifestation, of schizophrenia (Bender, 1969). In contrast to schizophrenia in adults, however, the autism of autism referred to difficulties in social interaction primarily, rather than in thought content, and was a failure of development, not a regression or retreat into some fantasy world. Beginning with the pioneering work of Kolvin (1971) and Rutter (Rutter, 1972), the view of autism as being a form of schizophrenia or psychosis was seriously questioned given differences in onset and course, clinical features, and family history.

From Kanner to *DSM-III*

Following Kanner's description there was a slow increase in interest in the condition with the first follow-up studies providing some support for its validity as a diagnostic concept (see Chapter 4). Other developments in psychiatric diagnosis, such as the use of multiple axes and research diagnostic criteria, had a major impact on new approaches to diagnosis. Two important attempts in the late 1970s were made and prefigured the inclusion of autism in *DSM-III* in 1980.

Rutter (1978) synthesized Kanner's original report and subsequent research in a highly influential definition that emphasized four essential features: (1) a distinctive form of social impairment not just due to any associated intellectual disability, (2) language skills also not just due to associated intellectual disability, (3) difficulties with change and other unusual behaviors

consistent with Kanner's concept of insistence on sameness, and (4) early onset (by age 30 months). Another influential approach was that of the National Society of Autistic Children (NSAC) definition, which appeared in 1977 (Ritvo & Freeman, 1977). The NSAC definition emphasized disturbances in (1) rates and sequences of development; (2) responses to sensory stimuli; (3) speech, language-cognition, and nonverbal communication; and (4) the capacity to relate appropriately to people, events, and objects. It also underscored the neurobiological basis of autism. The growing body of work on the validity of autism and approaches definition led to its first recognition in the third edition of the *Diagnostic and Statistical Manual* (*DSM-III*; APA, 1980).

From *DSM-III* to *DSM-IV*

DSM-III (APA, 1980) was a landmark in psychiatric diagnosis with its atheoretical approach that emphasized valid, reliable descriptions of clinical conditions. For the first time autism was included in the diagnostic manual (as Infantile Autism) along with several other disorders in a new *class* of disorder—the Pervasive Developmental Disorders. Other conditions included were criteria for residual infantile autism, childhood onset pervasive developmental disorder (COPDD), and residual COPDD and for a subthreshold condition (atypical PDD; over time the latter became pervasive developmental disorder not otherwise specified (PDD-NOS).

The new category term Pervasive Developmental Disorder was coined by the developers as a new and a theoretical term suggesting areas of multiple impairments. In retrospect it might have been better to say "autism and related conditions" or "autism spectrum disorders" for the category, but it was broadly accepted by clinicians and researchers alike.

In many respects *DSM-III* represents a major advance in that it officially recognized autism as a disorder category, adopted a multi-axial approach, and elaborated criteria that could be used for research and clinical work. Given that this was the first time autism had been so recognized, it is not surprising that some problems were quickly identified (Volkmar, Cohen, & Paul, 1986).

The definition of infantile autism in *DSM-III* was, in many ways, just that—a definition of the disorder as it first presented. Criteria were presented monothetically (i.e., all had to be present), and the defining social criterion was that of *pervasive* deficits in social interaction. However, over time social skills do develop albeit often at a much slower rate and in unusual ways (Wing & Gould, 1979). This was addressed by including a category for residual autism where the criteria had once been met. This had several disadvantages. It essentially required a thorough developmental history (potentially a problem for adults) and seemed to suggest that individuals grew out of autism rather than changed over time. Consistent with Rutter (1978), an age of onset of no later than 30 months was specified. However, there was an awareness that a small number of children developed an autistic-like disorder after age 30 months (Kolvin, 1971). Although some work had been done on Heller's syndrome (disintegrative psychosis/childhood disintegrative disorder), the *DSM-III* COPDD category was not meant to be precisely analogues to this. Somewhat paradoxically, the COPDD definition was more flexibly formulated than that for autism with polythetic criteria.

Atypical PDD was included to be analogous to other disorders in *DSM-III*, that is, a subthreshold category was generally included for each class of conditions given that often a clinician had to deal with (and provide service to) individuals whose problems did not precisely map on to the more strictly defined conditions but were close to them in terms of presentation and/or service needs. This issue was more complicated than first appreciated given Rank's (1949, 1955; Rank & McNaughton, 1949) earlier use of the term *atypical personality development*—suggesting an unintended, although probably substantive, overlap with the *DSM-III* category.

A few other issues arose with the *DSM-III* criteria for autism. They emphasized gross deficits in language development rather than communication.

Given the consensus that evidence that autism was different from schizophrenia, an exclusionary rule was adopted, that is, the two categories of disturbance could not both be present. Given how common schizophrenia is in the general population as individuals enter later adolescence and adulthood, it was a bit odd to assume that having autism protected one from also developing schizophrenia. In fact although diagnosis can be complicated some such cases are observed but at probably no higher than the population rate in persons with autism (Volkmar & Cohen, 1991). Other sources of controversy had to do with the multi-axial placement of autism. As a result of these various concerns, a number of steps were taken to approve the diagnostic approach in a revision: *DSM-III-R* (APA, 1987).

What began as a simple revision of *DSM-III* quickly became a major renovation with major changes for autism (see Spitzer & Siegel, 1990; Waterhouse, Wing, Spitzer, & Siegel, 1992). There was also some tension regarding these changes given the need to balance the rationale for revision with the impact that rapid change has on research and clinical work. Given the criticisms of *DSM-III*, a decision was made to move to an approach more reminiscent of that employed by Lorna Wing and colleagues (Wing & Gould, 1979), who were interested in both the range of syndrome expression and changes over development. As a practical matter, this view was somewhat broader than that of *DSM-III*. For *DSM-III-R* difficulties in three major areas were included and features with specified more developmentally oriented criteria in each of the three domains. This gave more flexibility in use as a polythetic approach was used so that only some rather than all criteria were needed for a diagnosis. Age of onset was dropped as an essential feature, although onset before or after age 3 could be specified. A national field trial was conducted (Spitzer & Siegel, 1990) and a set of 16 proposed criteria for autistic disorder were used. The change in name reflected the desire to avoid an overemphasis on the infantile aspect of autism.

In retrospect this field trial faced some important challenges, for example, cases could be rated based on review of record rather than on actual contact with the case and the comparison cases included cases with diagnoses that would not usually reasonably be thought of as relevant to a diagnosis of autism (e.g., cases of conduct disorder). The final scoring rule required that of the 16 criteria, at least 8 had to be present (at least two symptoms from the social domain and one each from the communication and restricted activities categories). Other changes in *DSM-III-R* had to do with a terminology change for all subthreshold categories to "not otherwise specified" (NOS), and individuals with autism were no longer excluded from also exhibiting schizophrenia.

Issues with *DSM-III-R* arose from the more complex criteria set as well as from the inclusion of specific examples within the actual criteria (thus appearing to some to require the presence of the example mentioned). In the end it appeared that *DSM-III-R* had a relatively high false positive rate and overdiagnosed autism in individuals with severe intellectual disabilities. A further complication was the major differences that *DSM-III-R* had with the pending revision of *ICD-10*.

DSM-IV and *ICD-10*

In the end, and particularly for autism and related disorders, the revision process for *DSM-IV* and *ICD-10* were closely related (Volkmar et al., 1994). For autism this reflected a major effort toward convergence with the hope of facilitating research and service. The relationship of the international (*ICD*) and American (*DSM*) systems are complex. At some level they are very fundamentally related since by formal agreement the systems must share a common approach to diagnostic coding. On other hand, there are also some important and major differences (Volkmar & Schwab-Stone, 1996).

One major difference has to do with the intended use of the guide. Since the time of *DSM-III* (and indeed now) the framers have desired a single book useful to clinicians and researchers. *ICD-10* takes a different approach with different books for these two sets of users (one of clinical descriptions and the other of research criteria). There are other

differences as well in areas like the approach to comorbidity and relative emphasis on history versus contemporaneous examination.

The initial draft of the *ICD-10* research definition of autistic disorder included 20 criteria and also recognized a number of new disorders in the PDD class. Asperger's syndrome, Rett's, childhood disintegrative disorder, and atypical autism were recognized along with autistic disorder. The ability to correlate cross walk between *ICD-10* and *DSM-III-R* seemed problematic. Furthermore, initial studies of the draft *ICD-10* approach (e.g., Volkmar, Cicchetti, Cohen, & Bregman, 1992) suggested better convergence with the diagnoses of experienced clinicians with *ICD-10*.

Work on the development of a fourth edition of *DSM* began shortly after *DSM-II* appeared. The relatively rapid revision process reflected various factors, including the concern of significant difference for the two approaches. A revision process was implemented with the *DSM-IV* work group reviewing available research and outlying areas of consensus as well as controversy. Issues like clinical utility, reliability, and descriptive validity of categories and criteria were considered. Coordination with the *ICD-10* revision was felt to be important (Frances et al., 1991). Steps taken as part of *DSM-IV* included a series of commissioned literature reviews, data reanalyses, and, in some cases, field trials. These reviews appeared several years before the final *DSM-IV* product so that a broader audience could both be informed but also comment on the issues and process (e.g., see Rutter & Schopler, 1992; Szatmari, 1992a, 1992b; Tsai, 1992; Volkmar et al., 1992). These literature reviews favored, on balance, a move to the *ICD-10* approach with more explicitly defined subtypes. There was general agreement that whenever possible convergence of the *DSM* and *ICD* systems was to be desired if areas of general consensus could be established (see Rutter & Schopler, 1992).

The *DSM-IV* field trial for autism was undertaken in collaboration with *ICD-10* revision process with a goal of attempting to have consensus on a reasonably robust definition of autism, with a good balance of sensitivity and specificity. This field trial took place over the space of a year and involved 21 sites, and 125 raters participated from around the world, providing data on nearly 1,000 cases. Raters ranged in experience level and range of professional backgrounds, and reliability data were obtained. In general the preference was for cases to be rated on the basis of contemporaneous examination, although for conditions that were less common, it was recognized that this might not be the case. In about half of cases the clinician had had previous contact with the case, and typically multiple sources of information were available with raters judging the quality of information available to them as either excellent or good in about 75% of cases (see Volkmar et al., 1994).

A standard system of coding was used with an explicit indication from the rater of his or her clinical diagnosis (based on his or her best judgment) and explicit ratings of criteria from *DSM-III* and *DSM-III-R* and potential criteria for *ICD-10* and *DSM-IV*. This form also included proposed criteria for Asperger's syndrome, Rett's syndrome, and childhood disintegrative disorder, based on the draft of *ICD-10* (see Volkmar et al., 1994).

Results of the *DSM-IV* field trial can be quickly summarized (see Table 1.1). When considered together the *DSM-III* diagnoses of infantile autism and residual autism had a reasonable balance of sensitivity and specificity relative to clinician diagnosis (although it was recognized that the use of the residual autism category entailed other problems). As expected the *DSM-III-R* criteria set had a higher sensitivity but lower specificity and a relatively high rate of false positive cases, particularly in cases with significant intellectual disability. As might be expected given its focus on research, the *ICD-10* draft definition had higher specificity.

The issue of age of onset was explored. Had onset by 36 months been added as an essential feature to *DSM-III-R*, the sensitivity of that system would have increased. Interrater reliability was assessed using chance-corrected statistics, with interrater reliability of individual diagnostic criteria generally in the good to excellent range. Experienced evaluators generally exhibited excellent agreement among themselves (and were more

TABLE 1.1   Sensitivity (Se)/Specificity (Sp) by IQ Level

By IQ Level	N	DSM-III[a] Se	DSM-III[a] Sp	DSM-III-R Se	DSM-III-R Sp	ICD-10[b] Se	ICD-10[b] Sp
<25	64	.90	.76	.84	.39	.74	.88
25–39	148	.88	.76	.90	.60	.88	.92
40–54	191	.79	.76	.93	.74	.84	.83
55–69	167	.86	.78	.84	.77	.78	.89
70–85	152	.79	.81	.88	.81	.74	.96
>85	218	.78	.83	.78	.78	.78	.91
Overall		.82	.80	.86	.83	.79	.89

[a]"Lifetime" diagnosis (current IA or "residual" IA).
[b]Original *ICD-10* criteria and scoring.
Adapted from "Field Trial for Autistic Disorder in *DSM-IV*," by F. R. Volkmar et al., 1994, *American Journal of Psychiatry, 151,* 1361–1367. Used with permission.

likely to agree with each other than with less experienced raters). Rater experience, regardless of discipline, had the greatest impact on reliability. Other analyses explored issues of internal consistency and temporal stability. Statistical approaches like signal detection analysis and factor analysis were employed. Given the concern that *ICD-10*'s research version was too detailed to be used in *DSM-IV*, a series of analyses were undertaken to see if any items (e.g., with low base rates or strong developmental associations) might be eliminated. The potential *ICD-10* criterion of having unusual attachments (to objects rather than people) was highly specific but relatively low frequency and, of course, most applicable in somewhat only to the younger children. A slimmed down *ICD-10* criteria set was noted to work reasonably well with good coverage over the range of age and levels of cognitive ability.

A number of cases with clinical diagnoses of nonautistic forms of PDD had been included in the field trial, and, on balance, there was data suggesting it reasonable to include these. In the end there was general (although not total) convergence of the *ICD-10* research definition and *DSM-IV* both in terms of categories and criteria. The *ICD-10* diagnostic criteria for these various conditions are presented in Table 1.2.

During the final editing of *DSM-IV* what might seem to have been minor changes were introduced. For example, in *DSM-IV* the definition of

TABLE 1.2   *ICD-10* Diagnostic Guidelines

Pervasive Developmental Disorders

A group of disorders characterized by qualitative abnormalities in reciprocal social interactions and in patterns of communication, and by a restricted, stereotyped, repetitive repertoire of interests and activities. These qualitative abnormalities are a pervasive feature of the individual's functioning in all situations.

Use additional code, if desired, to identify any associated medical condition and mental retardation.

F84.0   Childhood autism

A type of pervasive developmental disorder that is defined by: (a) the presence of abnormal or impaired development that is manifest before the age of 3 years, and (b) the characteristic type of abnormal functioning in all the three areas of psychopathology: reciprocal social interaction, communication, and restricted, stereotyped, repetitive behaviour. In addition to these specific diagnostic features, a range of other nonspecific problems are common, such as phobias, sleeping and eating disturbances, temper tantrums, and (self-directed) aggression.

Autistic disorder
Infantile:
• autism
• psychosis
Kanner's syndrome

Excludes: autistic psychopathy (F84.5)

F84.1   Atypical autism

A type of pervasive developmental disorder that differs from childhood autism either in age of onset or in failing to fulfil all three sets of diagnostic criteria. This subcategory should be used when there is abnormal and impaired development that is present only after age 3 years, and a lack of sufficient demonstrable abnormalities in one or two of the three areas of psychopathology required for the diagnosis of autism (namely, reciprocal social interactions, communication, and restricted, stereotyped, repetitive behaviour) in spite of characteristic abnormalities in the other area(s). Atypical autism arises most often in profoundly retarded individuals and in individuals with a severe specific developmental disorder of receptive language.

Atypical childhood psychosis
Mental retardation with autistic features

Use additional code (F70-F79), if desired, to identify mental retardation.

F84.2   Rett's syndrome

A condition, so far found only in girls, in which apparently normal early development is followed by partial or complete loss of speech and of skills in locomotion and use of hands, together with deceleration in head growth, usually with an onset between 7 and 24 months of age. Loss of purposive hand movements, hand-wringing stereotypies, and hyperventilation are characteristic. Social and play development are arrested but social interest tends to be maintained. Trunk ataxia and apraxia start to develop by age four years and choreoathetoid movements frequently follow. Severe mental retardation almost invariably results.

F84.3   Other childhood disintegrative disorder

A type of pervasive developmental disorder that is defined by a period of entirely normal development before the onset of the disorder, followed by a definite loss of previously acquired skills in several areas of development over the course of a few months. Typically, this is accompanied by a general loss of interest in the environment, by stereotyped, repetitive motor mannerisms, and by autistic-like abnormalities in social interaction and communication. In some cases the disorder can be shown to be due to some associated encephalopathy but the diagnosis should be made on the behavioural features.

Dementia infantilis
Disintegrative psychosis
Heller's syndrome
Symbiotic psychosis

Use additional code, if desired, to identify any associated neurological condition.

Excludes: Rett's syndrome (F84.2)

F84.4   Overactive disorder associated with mental retardation and stereotyped movements

An ill-defined disorder of uncertain nosological validity. The category is designed to include a group of children with severe mental retardation (IQ below 35) who show major problems in hyperactivity and in attention, as well as stereotyped behaviours. They tend not to benefit from stimulant drugs (unlike those with an IQ in the normal range) and may exhibit a severe dysphoric reaction (sometimes with psychomotor retardation) when given stimulants. In adolescence, the overactivity tends to be replaced by underactivity (a pattern that is not usual in hyperkinetic children with normal intelligence). This syndrome is also often associated with a variety of developmental delays, either specific or global. The extent to which the behavioural pattern is a function of low IQ or of organic brain damage is not known.

F84.5   Asperger's syndrome

A disorder of uncertain nosological validity, characterized by the same type of qualitative abnormalities of reciprocal social interaction that typify autism, together with a restricted, stereotyped, repetitive repertoire of interests and activities. It differs from autism primarily in the fact that there is no general delay or retardation in language or in cognitive development. This disorder is often associated with marked clumsiness. There is a strong tendency for the abnormalities to persist into adolescence and adult life. Psychotic episodes occasionally occur in early adult life.

Autistic psychopathy
Schizoid disorder of childhood

F84.8   Other pervasive developmental disorders

F84.9   Pervasive developmental disorder, unspecified

From *Diagnostic Criteria for Research*, World Health Organization, 1993. Reprinted with permission.

PDD-NOS had been changed unintentionally from *DSM-III-R*—where some problems with social interaction *and* in communication or restricted interests had to be present in *DSM-IV*, this *and* was the changed to an *or*, contributing to confusion about an already poorly defined condition (Luteijn et al., 2000). The text originally proposed for Asperger's disorder (and certain aspects of the definition) were substantially changed in the final push for publication. In *DSM-IV-R* (APA, 2000), the PDD-NOS definition was corrected, and while the text for Asperger's was markedly changed (essentially to what had first been proposed), the criteria (as was true in the entirety of *DSM-IV-R*) could not be. Although, as always, having its limitation *DSM-IV* proved remarkably enduring and, for autism, was associated with a vast increase in research and with development of new dimensional assessment instruments explicitly keyed to it (see Lord & Corsello, 2005).

DSM-5 and Autism

A new edition, *DSM-5* (APA, 2013), was released in May of 2013, set to address both the challenges in diagnosing mental disease, and the advances that have been made in the 20 years since the last version (e.g., Rutter, 2011). Significant changes to the overall structure, including the elimination of subthreshold categories and the decision to rely, as much as possible (e.g., Regier, Narrow, Kuhl, & Kupfer, 2010), on standardized diagnostic instruments and neuropsychiatric findings for the source of defining the included disorders, were made. One of the disorders receiving a great amount of both scientific (e.g., Ritvo, 2012; Singer, 2012; Wing, Gould, & Gillberg, 2011) and media scrutiny and attention (Baron-Cohen, 2009; Carey, 2012) has been autism spectrum disorder (ASD), which has proposed major changes in the structure of the diagnostic category and to the diagnostic criteria themselves (Lord & Jones, 2012). A range of other concerns have been raised as well (Jones, 2012).

Several changes have been made in *DSM-5*. The five distinct pervasive developmental disorders of the *DSM-IV* (i.e., autistic disorder, Asperger's syndrome, Rett's disorder, childhood disintegrative disorder, pervasive developmental disorder, not otherwise specified [PDD-NOS]) have been discarded in favor over an overarching category of ASD. The second most apparent change is the collapse of the symptom triad (social, communication, behavioral) into a dyad by combining the social and communication domains. A third significant change is the proposed requirement that all three social-communication symptoms be met and an increase from one to two (or zero to two in the case of the change from PDD-NOS to ASD) repetitive and behavioral symptoms be present. A fourth major change is that the criteria (symptoms) can now be met currently or by history, which is a departure from the previous criteria that symptoms were currently manifested. The *DSM-5* also has a note that if an individual has a well-documented *DSM-IV* diagnosis of autistic disorder, Asperger's disorder, or PDD-NOS, he or she should continue to receive a diagnosis of ASD under *DSM-5*. Finally, the *DSM-5* has moved away from the axial system of *DSM-IV* and now contains specifiers, which are intended to provide an "opportunity to define a more homogeneous subgrouping of individuals with the disorder who share certain features . . . and to convey information that is relevant to the management of the individual's disorder" (APA, 2013, pp. 21–22). The system of specifiers for ASD includes a functional severity level across a three-level scale (requiring support, requiring substantial support, and requiring very substantial support). This severity scale is rated by the clinician separately for the social communication and restricted, repetitive behavior domains. The specifiers also provide information related to the presence of accompanying intellectual disability and/or language impairment and associations with other known medical or genetic conditions; environmental factors; neurodevelopmental, mental, or behavioral disorders; and catatonia. The specifiers are not mutually exclusive or jointly exhaustive; thus more than one specifier can be given (e.g., ASD with intellectual impairment without language impairment).

Some aspects of the changes will provide needed clarity, such as the move to a better description of the class of disorder (autism spectrum disorder to replace pervasive developmental disorder) and the addition of severity dimensions in combination with the categorical diagnosis. However, it is not known at the time of this writing how well the newer criteria will work in standard practice (Tsai, 2012). Accordingly important questions remain to be addressed. The remainder of this section highlights some of the ongoing debate and early evaluations of the potential impact of these revisions.

The most apparent change from *DSM-IV* to *DSM-5* is the change of the overall categorical name from pervasive developmental disorder (and its five subcategories) to the singular ASD category and diagnosis. As with many changes, there are likely positive implications and some implications that could have negative consequences. While the removal of Rett's syndrome, which has been found to have a single gene etiology since its inclusion in *DSM-IV*, is sensible on face value; the elimination of it creates a potentially problematic precedent given the expanding genetic research at this critical time and the isolation of this disorder's single gene etiology, possibly providing great insight into genetic vulnerability of related disorders. The removal of childhood disintegrative disorder, which has also seen increased genetic research and leads into its etiology, also might have significant implications in the attempts to unravel the etiology of autism. As stated earlier, the entire *DSM-5* has removed subthreshold categories, so the elimination of PDD-NOS was somewhat of a formality, although the increased number of symptoms that must be present to receive an ASD diagnosis is likely to cause difficulties for some individuals who have benefited from services once received under this diagnosis. The removal of Asperger's

syndrome has been most frequently discussed (e.g., Baron-Cohen, 2009; Ghaziuddin, 2010; Kaland, 2011). Although some research has shown clinicians have difficulty reliably distinguishing between Asperger's syndrome, high functioning autism, and PDD-NOS (e.g., Lord et al., 2012; Sharma, Woolfson, & Hunter, 2012), other studies have shown distinct neuropsychological profiles that potentially differentiate the disorders (Klin, Volkmar, Sparrow, Cicchetti, & Rourke, 1995; Lincoln, Courchesne, Allen, Hanson, & Ene, 1998; Ozonoff & Griffith, 2000). Collapsing individuals with Asperger's into a broader ASD category has the potential to obscure important clinical distinctions (e.g., patients with Asperger's syndrome with more intact verbal skills might benefit more from certain types of psychotherapy than individuals with high-functioning autism with severely impaired verbal skills). Moreover, although subtypes such as Asperger's disorder have not been shown to have distinct etiologies, it might in fact have one that the scientific community has yet to uncover (Ghanizadeh, 2011). A second disorder, social communication disorder (SCD), has been included in the *DSM-5*; however, the relation between it and ASD is not clear (e.g., although ASD must be ruled out in the diagnostic criteria, prevalence estimates of ASD have included SCD, and on face value, the criteria seem very similar to our current conceptualizations of PDD-NOS and possibly Asperger's syndrome). Another remaining question is whether the World Health Organization (WHO), which is revising their diagnostic criteria, the International Classification of Disease, will include subtypes of disorders or move as *DSM* has done into one broad umbrella category meant to encompass all subtypes.

Another significant change is the move away from a triad of symptom domains to a dyad. This decision was based on a factor analysis (e.g., Lord et al., 2012; Norris, Lecavalier, & Edwards, 2012) of data derived from the two gold standard diagnostic instruments (i.e., the Autism Diagnostic Observation Schedule [ADOS] and the Autism

Diagnostic Interview–Revised [ADI-R]), which showed the social and communication domains tended to cluster together. First, the social and communication features were collapsed into a single category. Given the closely interrelatedness of social and communicative behaviors, this seems sensible, but as executed, problems might arise, which are discussed in more detail later. The second symptom domain includes items consistent with Kanner's insistence on sameness/restricted interests, with the addition of a sensory sensitivity symptom (Lord et al., 2012; Lord & Jones, 2012), which was excluded from the *DSM-IV* due to poor specificity.

The move to the symptom dyad also brought changes in the number and combinations of symptoms required to meet the diagnostic threshold; that is, there are now much fewer combinations in the *DSM-5* than in the *DSM-IV* (11 and 2,027, respectively). This decrease is the direct effect of two related changes. The first change involved the combination of the communication and social criteria, which, by reducing the number of categories, reduces the number of levels in a factorial. The second factor is the monothetic approach used for the social-communication domain, where instead of two or four and one of four criteria required for the social and communication domains, respectively, in the *DSM-IV* for autistic disorder (two of four social and zero communication in the case of Asperger's syndrome and one of four social in the case of PDD-NOS), three of three criteria are required for the in the *DSM-5*. A polythetic approach was retained for the repetitive and restrictive behavioral domain, although the number of symptoms needing to be met was increased from one of four (zero of four potentially in PDD-NOS) in the *DSM-IV* to two of four for the *DSM-5*. Collectively, these changes result in there being 11 symptom combinations possible for ASD in *DSM-5*, down from greater than 2,000 possible combinations in the *DSM-IV*, suggesting that although the name of the disorder confers a broader spectrum, the actual spectrum of autism might have less variability under the new criteria and harken back to what will closely resemble

Kanner's classic autism (Volkmar, Reichow, & McPartland, 2012).

Given the potential impact of the changes in diagnostic criteria, a number of studies have evaluated the draft *DSM-5* criteria by comparing them to the current diagnostic systems (*DSM-IV* and *ICD-10*). In this section, we will review a selection of the studies supporting the changes and those that have raised concerns, and then conclude this section with a discussion of issues that must be considered moving forward. Table 1.3 provides the *DSM-5* diagnostic criteria for autism spectrum disorder.

Research Providing Preliminary Support of the New ASD *DSM-5* Criteria

There have been multiple examinations of sensitivity and specificity of the proposed *DSM-5* ASD criteria. The initial set of data supporting the new criteria were shown in a study using a large data set of siblings (some with and others without ASD) (Frazier et al., 2012). The results showed that in this sample of children (ages 2 to 18) the sensitivity of *DSM-5* was higher than *DSM-IV*, with slightly lower specificity, which Frazier et al. noted could be improved by relaxing diagnostic threshold (e.g., only requiring two of three social-communication symptoms). The most significant support for the new diagnostic criteria of ASD comes from a study that utilized data from a large series of well-characterized cases using the two gold standard research diagnostic instruments, the ADOS and ADI-R (Huerta, Bishop, Duncan, Hus, & Lord, 2012). The results suggested when both instruments were used were maximized and in acceptable ranges. Their data showed very few cases diagnosed under *DSM-IV* would fail to meet the new *DSM-5* criteria. However, if only one instrument was used, specificity fell. The authors noted this study was not a field trial and that these results were obtained under optimal conditions. Mazefsky, McPartland, Gasteb, and Minshew (2012) compared *DSM-IV* and *DSM-5* diagnosis also using the ADOS and ADI-R research instruments. They found that nearly all high-functioning cases continued to meet criteria for ASD in *DSM-5*

TABLE 1.3 *DSM-5* **Diagnostic Criteria for Autism Spectrum Disorder**

Diagnostic Criteria	299.00 (F84.0)

A. Persistent deficits in social communication and social interaction across multiple contexts, as manifested by the following, currently or by history (examples are illustrative, not exhaustive; see text):

1. Deficits in social-emotional reciprocity, ranging, for example, from abnormal social approach and failure of normal back-and-forth conversation; to reduced sharing of interest, emotions, or affect; to failure to initiate or respond to social interactions.
2. Deficits in nonverbal communicative behaviors used to social interaction, ranging, for example, from poorly integrated verbal and nonverbal communication; to abnormalities in eye contact and body language or deficits in understanding and use of gestures; to a total lack of facial expressions and nonverbal communication.
3. Deficits in developing, maintaining, and understanding relationships, ranging, for example, from difficulties adjusting behavior to suit various social contexts; to difficulties in sharing imaginative play or in making friends; to absence of interest in peers.

Specify current severity:

Severity is based on social communication impairments and restricted, repetitive patterns of behavior

B. Restricted, repetitive patterns of behavior, interests, or activities, as manifested by at least two of the following, currently or by history (examples are illustrative, not exhaustive; see text):

1. Stereotyped or repetitive motor movements, use of objects, or speech (e.g., simple motor stereotypies, lining up toys or flipping objects, echolalia, idiosyncratic phrases).
2. Insistence on sameness, inflexible adherence to routines, or ritualized patterns of verbal or nonverbal behavior (e.g., extreme distress at small changes, difficulties with transitions, rigid thinking patterns, greeting rituals, need to take same route or eat same food every day).
3. Highly restricted, fixated interests that are abnormal in intensity or focus (e.g., strong attachment to or preoccupation with unusual objects, excessively circumscribed or perseverative interests).
4. Hyper- or hyporeactivity to sensory input or unusual interest in sensory aspects of the environment (e.g., apparent indifference to pain/temperature, adverse response to specific sounds or textures, excessive smelling or touching of objects, visual fascination with lights or movement).

Specify current severity:

Severity is based on social communication impairments and restricted, repetitive patterns of behavior

C. Symptoms must be present in the early developmental period (but may not become fully manifested until social demands exceed limited capacities, or may be masked by learned strategies in later life).
D. Symptoms cause clinically significant impairment in social, occupational, or other important areas of current functioning.
E. These disturbances are not better explained by intellectual disability (intellectual developmental disorder) or global developmental delay. Intellectual disability and autism spectrum disorder frequently co-occur; to make comorbid diagnoses of autism spectrum disorder and intellectual disability, social communication should be below that expected of general developmental level.

Note: Individuals with a well-established *DSM-IV* diagnosis of autistic disorder, Asperger's disorder, or pervasive developmental disorder not otherwise specified should be given the diagnosis of autism spectrum disorder. Individuals who have marked deficits in social communication, but whose symptoms do not otherwise need criteria for autism spectrum disorder, should be evaluated for social (pragmatic) communication disorder.

Specify if:

With or without accompanying intellectual impairment

With or without accompanying language impairment

Associated with a known medical or genetic condition or environmental factor (Coding note: Use additional code to identify the associated medical or genetic condition.)

Associated with another neurological, mental, or behavioral disorder (Coding note: Use additional code[s] to identify the associated neurodevelopmental, mental, or behavioral disorder[s].)

With catatonia (refer to the criteria for catatonia associated with another mental disorder, pp. 119–120, for definition) (**Coding note:** Use additional cost 293.89 [F06.1] catatonia associated with autism spectrum disorder to indicate the presence of the comorbid catatonia).

From the *Diagnostic and Statistical Manual*, 5th edition, pp. 50–55. American Psychiatric Association, 2013, Arlington, VA: American Psychiatric Publishing. Reprinted with permission.

when both instruments were used, but sensitivity decreased when only the parent instrument used and went lower still if only the individual assessment was available. The final set of data supporting the new diagnostic criteria were provided in the *DSM-5* field trial (Regier et al., 2013), which showed good sensitivity but questionable specificity. However, the methods of the field trial have been questioned (Frances, 2012; Jones, 2012), and the results for ASD were based on a small number of cases seen in clinical, not real-world, settings. It is unclear if the results will generalize to everyday clinical practice in which there is a high likelihood that no research instruments will be used in an evaluation.

Studies Showing Potential Difficulties for *DSM-5* ASD Criteria

There have been more studies published suggesting the new *DSM-5* criteria might be more restrictive (i.e., exclude cases currently meeting diagnostic criteria), especially those with average to above average levels of cognition. The first study with critical findings of *DSM-5* ASD criteria was published by Mattila et al. (2011) using an earlier draft of *DSM-5* to examine the impact of the changes using an epidemiological sample of 8-year-old children in Finland. In their study, 110 children were seen for follow-up after screening positive on the Autism Spectrum Screening Questionnaire (ASQ). Their results showed *DSM-5* to be less sensitive than *DSM-IV*, with individuals who had higher IQs being less likely to meet the new diagnostic criteria.

Very similar findings were found by McPartland, Reichow, and Volkmar (2012) using data from the *DSM-IV* field trial (Volkmar et al., 1994). In their study, sensitivity and specificity were evaluated by cross-walking *DSM-IV* criteria to the proposed *DSM-5* criteria. Although they found the specificity of the new criteria to be high and superior to the old criteria, sensitivity varied dramatically by clinical group, varying from acceptable levels for autism, to very poor levels for Asperger's disorder and PDD-NOS. McPartland et al. also found sensitivity varied significantly by cognitive ability,

with moderate levels of sensitivity for individuals with IQ < 70 and poor levels of sensitivity for individuals with IQ ≥ 70.

Similar findings have been found by a number of other studies. Worley and Matson (2012) compared symptoms of ASD in several hundred children using *DSM-IV* and *DSM-5*. They found a significant proportion of children currently meeting diagnostic criteria would not meet the newer criteria. In their attempt to show ways to improve the proposed criteria of *DSM-5*, Matson, Hattier, and Williams (2012) showed, as proposed, the criteria would exclude a significant proportion of toddlers who exhibited significant impairment. Gibbs, Aldridge, Chandler, Witzlsperger, and Smith (2012) compared *DSM-IV-TR* and *DSM-5* diagnosis in a sample of 132 children, finding that many children who had been diagnosed with autism or a related PDD under *DSM-IV* would not meet the new criteria, with the greatest number of those excluded having received a PDD-NOS diagnosis under *DSM-IV-TR*. A similar pattern was found by Taheri and Perry (2012), who conducted a case review of over 100 cases of children diagnosed with autism or a related PDD under *DSM-IV*. Wilson and colleagues (2013) compared *DSM-IV*, *ICD-10*, and *DSM-5* in a sample of 150 adults with ASD who were more cognitively able. Their study is unique in that it is the first study that attempted to quantify the proportion of individuals who do not meet ASD criteria but might meet criteria for SCD. They found just over half of the sample meeting *ICD-10* criteria for a PDD would meet *DSM-5* criteria for ASD. However, they found nearly 20% of those not meeting criteria for ASD met *DSM-5* criteria for SCD. Finally, another very recent study of the new *DSM-5* criteria in toddlers (Barton, Robins, Jashar, Brenna, & Fein, in press) suggests yet other problems for its use in toddlers. Barton et al. evaluated the new criteria in a large group of toddlers and noted that this age group, in particular, may be impacted by the more stringer requirements of *DSM-5*. They suggested that modification of scoring would improve it for this population. Together all this work suggests several practical issues and problems, for example, impact on service eligibility (and in the cases of toddlers particularly in a group most in need of service) as well on research. Prospective, longitudinal, and epidemiologically focused projects would appear to be some of those most likely to face challenge.

RELATED DIAGNOSTIC CONCEPTS

Asperger's Disorder

First described the year after autism by Hans Asperger (1944), this condition was little researched until its inclusion in *DSM-IV* and *ICD-10*. Asperger's original report provided a description of verbally precocious but socially impaired boys. His use of the word *autism* in his name for the condition (frequently translated to "autistic psychopathy" but probably better translated as "autistic personality disorder") suggested an obvious similarity to Kanner's (1943) description. Despite their verbal precocity, the boys were socially isolated, intellectualized their feelings, and engaged in long-winded conversations about topics of special interest. Typically these special interests revolved around collecting information about a specific, often esoteric, topic that dominated the individual's conversation and family life. Asperger made the important point that this significantly interfered with the child's development and also negatively impacted family life. He mentioned as well that motor clumsiness was usual and that there often were similar traits in fathers. His report attracted relatively little attention until Wing published her description of the condition and a series of case studies (1981). Subsequent work was hampered by a lack of consistent definitions, although it did suggest some areas of potential difference from autism, for example, relative to neuropsychological profiles. Work in the area was also complicated given a plethora of terms from various disciplines similarly used to describe verbally able but socially impaired individuals (see McPartland, Klin, & Volkmar, in press). As noted previously, a decision was made to include Asperger's in

DSM-IV and *ICD-10* although the final definition proved somewhat controversial (Volkmar & Klin, 2000).

Subsequent to *DSM-IV*'s appearance, work on Asperger's increased dramatically and the concept received considerable attention from the lay press and educators. Unfortunately, controversy about best approaches to definition complicated interpretation of available research. Studies using a strict approach often found differences in neuropsychological profiles as well as in rates of other comorbid conditions and family history (e.g., Klin, Pauls, Schultz, & Volkmar, 2005). Research interest centered on the possibility that the constellation of marked social vulnerability in the face of good language (but poor communication) skills might represent a different pathway from autism into serious social disability. Similarly, preserved verbal skills suggested a potential area for intervention not usually emphasized in programs for individuals with autism (Klin et al., 2005). Several studies also suggested that cases frequently exhibited a neuropsychological profile consistent with nonverbal learning disability. Overlap with the right hemisphere syndrome/developmental disabilities of the right hemisphere syndrome or with semantic-pragmatic disorder have also been suggested (Volkmar et al., in press). The condition has been of interest to researchers and clinicians given better verbal abilities. There clearly is some possibility that autism and Asperger's are etiologically related given case reports of both conditions in members of the same family. As noted earlier, the decision to eliminate Asperger's in *DSM-5* has been controversial (see also Rutter, 2011).

Available research suggests that many individuals with Asperger's will now (or at least going forward) no longer have an ASD diagnosis; in some cases the SCD diagnosis may apply, although difficulties exhibited are broader than just social communication. High rates of anxiety and depression have been reported as children age into adolescence and young adulthood (McPartland et al., in press). Given the sometimes high levels of intellectual ability, the level of social disability can be quite striking. As with higher functioning autism, prosodic differences and difficulties with register (voice loudness) are frequent, although some suggestion of difference has also been noted (Shriberg et al., 2001).

If relatively stringently defined, the disorder is less common than autism, although, of course, if broadly defined (and essentially equated with PDD-NOS) the numbers increase dramatically. Males are more likely than females to exhibit the condition—at a much higher rate than is typical in autism, although this issue is complex since girls may be impacted in more subtle ways.

Pervasive Developmental Disorder Not Otherwise Specified (PDD-NOS)

PDD-NOS and the *ICD-10* equivalent of atypical autism have been used as a residual (i.e., sub-threshold) category for persons whose difficulties suggest an autism/autism spectrum diagnosis but do not meet criteria. Unintentionally, the concept has some overlap with the atypical personality development (Rank, 1949). As a practical matter it refers to a large group of children (probably about 1 in 100–150 or so) who have problems in social interaction and either communication or restricted interests and behaviors. The concept is closely related to the concept of the broader autism phenotype (see Chapter 2 and also Towbin, 2005).

Not surprisingly there is considerable diagnostic heterogeneity. In the past attempts have been made to define specific subgroups/subtypes (Towbin, 2005). Given its frequency, the condition has been remarkably little studied but has been used to justify services, and likely many cases are included in epidemiological and similar studies based on school records. The *ICD-10* approach provides greater specificity for indicating (through code numbers) the nature of the subthreshold condition, that is, failing onset, behavioural criteria.

Clinically it is usually the case that children with the condition have unusual sensitivities and atypical affective responses suggestive of autism (along with social difficulties) although typically they have better cognitive and language abilities

than in autism. In the past the concept has, at times, been equated with Asperger's disorder, although *DSM-IV* and *ICD-10* explicitly did not allow this. As noted previously in the *DSM-IV* field trial, cases with clinical diagnosis of Asperger disorder differed from those with PDD-NOS with significantly more social difficulties in individuals with Asperger disorder. As noted previously although the term *autism spectrum* in *DSM-5* suggests that it might include cases of PDD-NOS, it appears likely that this will not be the case with the clear majority of cases likely to lose the diagnosis or, possibly, to receive a new social communication disorder one.

Rett's Disorder

This disorder is a progressive condition originally reported by Andreas Rett in 1966 that initially was apparently confined to girls. It was viewed by Rett as a form of autism although it appeared that the more autistic-like phase was relatively brief, confined largely to early childhood (Hagberg, 1992). Efforts were also made to produce consensus guidelines for this relative rare (1 in 15,000 to 22,000) condition (see Van Acker et al., 2005). The decision to include Rett's in the PDD category in *DSM-IV* was somewhat controversial but it appeared important to include it somewhere (see Gillberg, 1994; Rutter, 1994b). Subsequent to its inclusion a specific genetic etiology has been found associated with a defect in the gene MECP2—a regulator gene on the X chromosome (Zoghbi, 1988).

In *DSM-5* Rett's disorder could be listed as an associated condition if an ASD diagnosis was justified but the disorder itself will no longer be listed given its genetic etiology. Given the likelihood, over time, that specific genes will be found to be involved in various forms of autism, this seems an unfortunate precedent.

Childhood Disintegrative Disorder and Regressive Autism

Regression of developmental milestones has been associated with autism since Leo Kanner first reported where one of his cases seemed to have "gone backward mentally gradually for the last two years" (Kanner, 1943, p. 225). However many years before Kanner's description, Theodor Heller, an Austrian educator and researcher, described a group of children who developed normally, then had rapid losses of adaptive function, including social skills and language, and developed "strange stereotypies of expression and movement" (Heller, 1908; Westphal, Schelinski, Volkmar, & Pelphrey, 2013, p. 225, 2013).

Over the years a number of terms have been used to refer to this condition, including *childhood disintegrative disorder*, *disintegrative psychosis*, and *Heller's syndrome*. To date only a few hundred cases of late regression of the type that defines disintegrative disorder have been described in the literature, and there are only a handful of research studies exploring the condition. The available data suggest that children with childhood disintegrative disorder (CDD) have significantly worse adaptive and cognitive outcomes than their counterparts with other ASDs. This observation along with a distinctive pattern of onset have been taken to support including it as a distinctive condition (Volkmar & Rutter, 1995).

Regression in CDD generally occurs in children between 3 and 4 years of age but has occurred in older children (Malhotra & Gupta, 2002; Volkmar & Cohen, 1989). During the acute regression, behavioral changes often occur that are unique to the period. Kurita, Osada, and Miyake (2004) found that 80% of a cohort of 10 children with childhood disintegrative disorder showed fearfulness during the period of regression. During the same period, Malhotra and Gupta (2002) reported elevated rates of hyperactivity (67%), aggression (42%), tantrums (42%), sleep problems (33%), and loss of motor skills (33%) in a similar cohort. Both Heller's original description, and the follow-up study of a cohort of children with childhood disintegrative disorder seen at Yale Child Study Center had bouts of severe anxiety preceding skill loss (Westphal, Schelinski, Volkmar, & Pelphrey, 2013).

Biological distinctions would help to address the question of whether there is value to maintaining a distinction between late regression and other forms of ASD. But progress has been limited by the rarity of the phenomenon.

DSM-IV and *ICD-10* included the condition separate from autism, but the decision in *DSM-5* was to include it as part of the ASD concept. The presumption in *DSM-5* is that the factors that distinguish CDD from other ASDs are differences of degree, rather than of kind, thus better described by as a single spectrum disorder. Although some cases would clearly meet ASD criteria, others, with later onset, might be judged not to given the requirement for onset in the early developmental period. There is no grandfathering of CDD cases into ASD and no specification for a modifier for late onset (although a modified is available for ASD associated with catatonia). Unfortunately with the elimination of the diagnostic category of Childhood Disintegrative Disorder from the *DSM*, research on this rare condition may become more difficult.

Other Diagnostic Concepts

A number of other diagnostic concepts have been proposed. Many of these have attracted some, although not usually extensive, research interest. Mahler's concept of symbiotic psychosis (Mahler, 1965) was proposed for children who seemed to fail in the task of separating their psychological selves from a hypothesized, early fusion with their mothers. This concept, deeply rooted in psychoanalytic theory, is now largely of historical interest (as is the notion of a normal autistic phase of development). In contrast, another psychoanalyst, Beate Rank, proposed the notion of atypical personality development (Rank, 1949) to describe a range of difficulties in early development, including problems in social interaction, environmental responses, and social development. In some ways her notion prefigured the concept of atypical PDD/PDD-NOS recognized in *DSM-III*. Some work on the concept was conducted (e.g., Dahl, Cohen, & Provence, 1986). Other concepts have included the disorder of attention and motor planning (DAMP) syndrome—a condition hypothesized to lie at the boundary of autism and attention deficit disorder

(Hellgren, Gillberg, Gillberg, & Enerskog, 1993). As noted previously, the concept of PDD-NOS will now be eliminated in *DSM-5* with (apparently) many cases falling outside the boundaries of the proposed autism spectrum concept (McPartland et al., 2012).

COMORBIDITY

As with other disorders, particularly those of early onset, issues around comorbidity with other disorders are complex and have been the focus of some research in recent years. This issue raises complicated problems for classification and, historically, has tended to be resolved rather differently in the *ICD* and *DSM* (the former including some comorbid conditions while generally not encouraging multiple diagnoses and the latter encouraging multiple diagnoses) (see Rutter, 1997; Volkmar & Woolston, 1997). Clearly having any serious disability would be expected to increase risk for other problems. Additional complications for autism have to do with aspects of diagnosis both in more able and less able individuals. Disentangling some aspects of comorbidity depends on the availability of relevant, epidemiologically representative samples and assessment instruments. These issues are most complex in nonverbal individuals. As in intellectual disability research, autism has sometimes overshadowed other difficulties (Rutter, 1997; Volkmar & Klin, 2005). The issue of comorbidity is relevant to both treatment and research. For example, the use of new pharmacological treatments perhaps in combination with new behavioral treatments might be of interest. From the research side the potential for marking potential subgroups in relation to genetic and other mechanisms is also important.

Much of the relevant literature on this topic is based on case reports; the problem with this is not whether any disorder is *ever* seen with autism but whether it is seen at higher than expected rates (Rutter, 1997). A host of conditions including hyperactivity, obsessive compulsive phenomena,

self-injury, tics, and affective symptoms have been reported to co-occur with autism (see Volkmar & Klin, 2005). Probably the strongest data arise with more cognitively able and older individuals since more typical assessments can be used. In this population there has appeared to be an increased risk for anxiety and mood (McPartland, Klin, & Volkmar, in press; White & Schry, 2011). Other disorders, for example, schizophrenia, do not appear to be present at increased in samples of individuals with autism (Volkmar & Cohen, 1991).

Diagnostic difficulties, even in more able individuals, should not, however, be minimized. Baron-Cohen (1989) has observed that simply equating repetitive behaviors with obsessions and compulsions more typical in obsessive-compulsive disorder (OCD). Similarly reports of association with Tourette's syndrome might be of interest given the growing body of work on the pathophysiology of this condition.

In recent years there has been concern about the potential association of autism with additional problems such as attention deficit disorder (ADD) and attention-deficit/hyperactivity disorder (ADHD) and the potential implications for treatment. Although the initial impression that stimulant medications were not well tolerated in autism has been modified, there does appear to be greater risk for adverse reactions (Aman, Farmer, Hollway, & Arnold, 2008; Jahromi et al., 2009). The issue may be more relevant (and complicated) for individuals with the broader autism phenotype (see Chapter 2). The relative dearth of research in older individuals, particularly adults, has complicated work in this area. The topic remains an important one and has some potential for helping us potentially identify more robust endophenotypes.

BARRIERS TO SERVICE

Knowledge regarding the best ways to care for individuals with autism spectrum disorders has grown tremendously over the past decades (see Chapter 42). Diagnosis can be made reliably by experienced clinicians in children as young as 24 months of age (National Collaborating Centre for Women's and Children's Health, 2011). Psychosocial treatments have proven efficacious in addressing core deficits of the disorder (Reichow, Steiner, & Volkmar, 2012), especially in young children (Reichow, Barton, Boyd, & Hume, 2012). Studies of medications find a number helpful in addressing ancillary, often-impairing symptoms (Dove et al., 2012; Huffman, Sutcliffe, Tanner, & Feldman, 2011). And a growing literature shows the importance and effectiveness of supportive services for individuals with ASD and their families, including respite care, vocational training, and sibling and parent support and counseling services.

Despite increasing scientific support for a host of interventions to improve the lives of individuals with ASD and their families, access to evidence-based care often is limited or nonexistent. Many experience significant barriers to obtaining timely and appropriate services. Among those who do receive care, the interventions to which they have access often deviate significantly from the evidence base. Barriers to receiving care can be categorized as those relating to the perceived needs of the individual with ASD, parents'/caregivers' beliefs and resources, the training and practices of the professionals providing care, and the policies of the systems that guide and pay for care. We briefly describe the barriers associated with each of these areas.

System-level policies and practices. The needs of individuals with ASD often uneasily straddle multiple systems. In the United States, the large majority of individuals with autism less than 22 years of age is served primarily by the education system and receives most intervention in schools (Shattuck & Grosse, 2007). The legally defined mission of the education system is to provide a "free and appropriate public education" in the least restrictive environment necessary to students' needs (Individuals with Disabilities Education Act, 2004). The Supreme Court has clarified that "appropriate" does not mean optimal and that schools are not responsible for providing ideal services designed to maximize functioning. Therefore many individuals with ASD must turn to the health system to receive interventions to address core systems, as well as care to address the many other physical and psychiatric symptoms that often accompany ASD (Nazeer & Ghaziuddin, 2012). While the goal of the health system is to maximize functioning, public and private health care payers have made a sometimes-arbitrary distinction between rehabilitative services (designed to restore functioning) and habilitative services (designed to develop new skills), arguing that the education system should be responsible for covering habilitative care. This inconsistency and uncertainty regarding what systems are responsible for paying for or providing which types of care, as well as the additional challenges of coordinating care between these two systems, can create challenges to obtaining appropriate services (Shattuck & Grosse, 2007). An additional challenge is that many education and health-care services are regulated at the county or state level, meaning that there are geographic disparities in many types of care, depending on how education and health care for individuals with ASD are funded (Mandell, Morales, Xie, Lawer, et al., 2010; Mandell, Morales, Xie, Polsky, et al., 2010; Stahmer & Mandell, 2007). For example, some but not all states have Medicaid waivers (Cidav, Marcus, & Mandell, 2012) or private insurance mandates that increase the availability of health care for children with ASD (Bouder, Spielman, & Mandell, 2009; Stein, Sorbero, Goswami, Schuster, & Leslie, 2012).

Professional training and practice. The workforce trained in evidence-based care for individuals with ASD has not kept pace with the dramatic growth in the prevalence of this disorder (Rispoli, Neely, Lang, & Ganz, 2011; Spencer, Turkett, Vaughan, & Koenig, 2006). Even when local policy and regulation support payment for care, individuals with ASD and their families may not be able to find professionals who can provide indicated care (Self, Coufal, & Parham, 2010). While this challenge is an issue for many psychiatric and developmental disorders, it is of particular concern in autism, where evidence-based diagnostic practices and therapeutic interventions often are multifaceted and complex to implement (Stahmer & Aarons, 2009). Payment rarely is tied to the use of evidence-based practices or to outcomes, meaning that there is little financial incentive for practitioners to stay up-to-date or to monitor outcomes in in a systematic way (Dingfelder & Mandell, 2010). To be fair, the evidence base for behavioral and pharmacological interventions for autism is limited, even for younger children, and sometimes nonexistent for adolescents and adults. Practitioners therefore may have difficulty identifying and receiving training and ongoing support in appropriate practices.

Caregivers' beliefs and resources. In the study of barriers to care, most attention has been paid to how family characteristics are associated with care, focusing primarily on sociodemographic characteristics, and focusing even more particularly on how these characteristics are associated with age of diagnosis. Later age of diagnosis has been found among poorer families, families from traditionally underserved minority groups, and rural families (Daniels & Mandell, in press-a, in press-b). A few more recent studies have found similar disparities in factors associated with quality general pediatric care (Chiri & Warfield, 2012; Magaña, Parish, Rose, Timberlake, & Swaine, 2012), transition planning within the health care and education systems (Cheak-Zamora, Yang, Farmer, & Clark, 2013), and use post–high school services (Shattuck, Wagner, Narendorf, Sterzing, & Hensley, 2011). Of particular note and urgency to the field, while many studies have examined the association of these relatively unmalleable factors with disparities, studies have not yet gone deeper to understand what factors mediate the association between, for example, ethnicity and service use. A number of factors have been hypothesized, including interpretation of symptoms, varying beliefs about the cause and course of ASD, and different beliefs about and interactions with the health-care and education systems (Mandell & Novak, 2005). A critical area for research and practice is to develop family and system-level interventions to address these disparities.

DIAGNOSING ASD IN 2013 AND BEYOND

The development of various diagnostic concepts and studies discussed in this chapter highlight important considerations as the field redefines what is now considered one of the most prevalent neurodevelopmental disorders. Though the *DSM-5* proposes the transition to an autism spectrum, the alterations in diagnostic criteria paradoxically seems, in some ways, to harken back to a condition with the more severe, pervasive difficulties seen in classic autism associated with cognitive delay. Studies of the newly proposed criteria have already appeared, with studies both lending support and suggesting the changes might be problematic. All of the studies have methodological limitations and more work is needed. For the future a high priority should be more studies that thoroughly and prospectively evaluate the new criteria with respect to current diagnostic conceptualizations are needed.

Major changes in clinical practice, such as altering who qualifies or fails to qualify for a diagnosis, can influence access to services. The proposed introduction of new diagnostic labels, such as SCD, may further complicate service eligibility and access. In addition to affecting service access, diagnostic labels provide a framework for organizing and interpreting research. The possibility that the term *ASD* could soon refer to a different group of individuals may prevent direct comparisons between participants in prior and future research and limits generalization of past results. Additional concerns arise when considering that the *DSM* and *ICD*, which is also currently undergoing revision, might not have the same level of congruence with respect to the diagnostic criteria that was achieved with the *DSM-IV* and *ICD-10*, whose criteria are nearly identical. Finally, and possibly most significant, is the fact that we do not know how these new criteria behave in real-world settings (e.g., pediatrician's office, being seen by a clinical psychologist in a community practice), where the majority of diagnoses of ASD are made. It is seems likely that we are entering a period where several, somewhat different, diagnostic approaches will be used. All of these issues present significant challenges for moving the field forward in the future; hopefully consensus can be reached and we can continue, as a field, to be as productive in the next 10 years as in the past decade.

CROSS-REFERENCES

Issues of the broader autism phenotype are discussed in Chapter 2. Epidemiology is addressed in Chapter 3. Aspects of screening, diagnostic instruments, and multidisciplinary assessments are discussed in Chapters 24, 25, and 26. Chapter 44 focuses on cultural issues.

REFERENCES

Aman, M. G., Farmer, C. A., Hollway, J., & Arnold, L. E. (2008). Treatment of inattention, overactivity, and impulsiveness in autism spectrum disorders. *Child & Adolescent Psychiatric Clinics of North America*, *17*(4), 713–738.

American Psychiatric Association. (1980). *Diagnostic and statistical manual of mental disorders* (3rd ed.). Washington, DC: Author.

American Psychiatric Association, (1987). *Diagnostic and statistical manual of mental disorders* (3rd ed., rev.). Washington, DC: Author.

American Psychiatric Association. (1994). *Diagnostic and statistical manual of mental disorders* (4th ed.). Washington, DC: Author.

American Psychiatric Association. (2000). *Diagnostic and statistical manual of mental disorders* (4th ed., text rev.). Washington, DC: Author.

American Psychiatric Association. (2013). *Diagnostic and statistical manual of mental disorders* (5th ed.). Arlington, VA: American Psychiatric Publishing.

Angold, A, Costello, E., & Erkanli, A. (1999). Comorbidity. *Journal of Child Psychology & Psychiatry*, *40*(1), 57–87.

Asperger, H. (1944). Die "autistichen Psychopathen" im Kindersalter. *Archive fur psychiatrie und Nervenkrankheiten*, *117*, 76–136.

Baron-Cohen, S. (1989). Do autistic children have obsessions and compulsions? *British Journal of Clinical Psychology*, *28*(Pt 3), 193–200.

Baron-Cohen, S. (2009, November 9). The short life of a diagnosis. *New York Times*.

Barton, M. L., Robins, D., Jashar, D., Brenna, L., & Fein, D. (in press). Sensitivity and specificity of proposed DSM-5 criteria for autism spectrum disorder in toddlers. *Journal of Autism and Developmental Disorders*.

Bender, L. (1969). A longitudinal study of schizophrenic children with autism. *Hospital and Community Psychiatry*, *20*(8), 230–237.

Bleuler, E. (1911). *Dementia praecox oder Gruppe der Schizophrenien* (J. Zinkin, Trans.). New York, NY: International Universities Press.

Bouder, J., Spielman, S., & Mandell, D. (2009). Brief report: Quantifying the impact of autism coverage on private insurance premiums. *Journal of Autism and Developmental Disorders*, *39*(6), 953–957.

Carey, B. (2012, January 19). New definition of autism may exclude many, study suggests. *New York Times*.

Cheak-Zamora, N., Yang, X., Farmer, J., & Clark, M. (2013). Disparities in transition planning for youth with autism spectrum disorder. *Pediatrics*, *131*(3), 447–454.

Chiri, G., & Warfield, M. (2012). Unmet need and problems accessing core health care services for children with autism spectrum disorder. *Maternal and Child Health Journal*, *16*(5), 1081–1091.

Cidav, Z., Marcus, S., & Mandell, D. (2012). Age-related variation in health service use and associated expenditures among children with autism. *Journal of Autism and Developmental Disorders* [electronic publication ahead of print].

Cohen, D. J. (1976). The diagnostic process in child psychiatry. *Psychiatric Annals*, *6*(9), 29–56.

Dahl, E. K., Cohen, D. J., & Provence, S. (1986). Clinical and multivariate approaches to the nosology of pervasive developmental disorders. *Journal of the American Academy of Child Psychiatry*, *25*(2), 170–180.

Daniels, A., & Mandell, D. (in press-a). Compliance with American Academy of Pediatrics' well-child care guidelines and the early detection of autism. *Journal of Autism and Developmental Disorders*.

Daniels, A., & Mandell, D. (in press-b). Explaining differences in age at autism spectrum disorder diagnosis: A critical review. *Autism*.

Dingfelder, H., & Mandell, D. (2010). Applying diffusion of innovation theory to the dissemination of efficacious interventions for children with autism. *Journal of Autism and Developmental Disorders* [electronic publication ahead of press].

Dove, D., Warren, Z., McPheeters, M., Taylor, J., Sathe, N., & Veenstra-VanderWeele, J. (2012). Medications for adolescents and young adults with autism spectrum disorders a systematic review. *Pediatrics*, *130*(4), 717–726.

El-Fishawy, P., & State, M. W. (2010). The genetics of autism: Key issues, recent findings, and clinical implications. *Psychiatric Clinics of North America*, *33*(1), 83–105.

Frances, A. (2012). Better safe than sorry. *Australian and New Zealand Journal of Psychiatry*, *46*(8), 695–696.

Frances, A., Wakefield Davis, W., Kline, M., Pincus, H., First, M., & Widiger, T. A. (1991). The DSM-IV field trials: Moving towards an empirically derived. *European Psychiatry 1991*, *6*(6), 307–314.

Frazier, T. W., Youngstrom, E. A., Speer, L., Embacher, R., Law, P., Constantino, J., . . . Eng, C. (2012). Validation of proposed DSM-5 criteria for autism spectrum disorder. *Journal of the American Academy of Child & Adolescent Psychiatry*, *51*(1), 28–40.e23.

Ghanizadeh, A. (2011). Can retaining Asperger syndrome in *DSM V* help establish neurobiological endophenotypes? *Journal of Autism and Developmental Disorders*, *41*(1), 130. doi: http://dx.doi.org/10.1007/s10803-010-1028-5

Ghaziuddin, M. (2010). Should the *DSM V* drop Asperger syndrome? *Journal of Autism and Developmental Disorders*, *40*(9), 1146–1148.

Gibbs, V., Aldridge, F., Chandler, F., Witzlsperger, E., & Smith, K. (2012). An exploratory study comparing diagnostic outcomes for autism spectrum disorders under DSM-IV-TR with the proposed DSM-5 revision. *Journal of Autism and Developmental Disorders*, *42*(8), 1750–1756. doi: http://dx.doi.org/10.1007/s10803-012-1560-6

Gillberg, C. (1994). Debate and argument: Having Rett syndrome in the ICD-10 PDD category does not make sense. *Journal of Child Psychology & Psychiatry & Allied Disciplines*, *35*(2), 377–378.

Gillberg, C., & Coleman, M. (1996). Autism and medical disorders: A review of the literature. *Developmental Medicine & Child Neurology*, *38*(3), 191–202.

Hagberg, B. (1992). The Rett syndrome: An introductory overview 1990. *Brain & Development*, *14*(Suppl), S5–S8.

Heller, T. (1908). Dementia Infantilis. *Zeitschrift fur die Erforschung und Behandlung des Jugenlichen, Schwachsinns*, *2*, 141–165.

Hellgren, L., Gillberg, C., Gillberg, I. C., & Enerskog, I. (1993). Children with deficits in attention, motor control and perception (DAMP) almost grown up: General health at 16 years. *Developmental Medicine & Child Neurology*, *35*(10), 881–892.

Hermelin, B. (2001). *Bright splinters of the mind: A personal story of research with autistic savants*. London, England: Jessica Kingsley.

Hobbs, N. (1975). *Issues in the classification of children*. San Francisco, CA: Jossey-Bass.

Huerta, M., Bishop, S. L., Duncan, A., Hus, V., & Lord, C. (2012). Application of DSM-5 criteria for autism spectrum disorder to three samples of children with DSM-IV diagnoses of pervasive developmental disorders. *American Journal of Psychiatry*, *169*(10), 1056–1064. doi: 10.1176/appi.ajp.2012.12020276

Huffman, L., Sutcliffe, T., Tanner, I., & Feldman, H. (2011). Management of symptoms in children with autism spectrum disorders: A comprehensive review of pharmacologic and complementary-alternative medicine treatments. *Journal of Developmental & Behavioral Pediatrics*, *32*(1), 56–68.

Individuals with Disabilities Education Act 636 (d) (2). (2004).

Jahromi, L. B., Kasari, C. L., McCracken, J. T., Lee, L. S. Y., Aman, M. G., McDougle, C. J., . . . Posey, D. J. (2009). Positive effects of methylphenidate on social communication and self-regulation in children with pervasive developmental disorders and hyperactivity. *Journal of Autism and Developmental Disorders*, *39*(3), 395–404.

Jones, K. D. (2012). A critique of the *DSM-5* field trials. *Journal of Nervous and Mental Disease*, *200*(6), 517–519.

Kaland, N. (2011). Brief report: Should Asperger syndrome be excluded from the forthcoming *DSM-V*? *Research in Autism Spectrum Disorders*, *5*(3), 984–989. doi: http://dx.doi.org/10.1016/j.rasd.2011.01.011

Kanner, L. (1943). Autistic disturbances of affective contact. *Nervous Child*, *2*, 217–250.

Klin, A., Jones, W., Schultz, R. T., & Volkmar, F. R. (2005). The enactive mind—from actions to cognition: Lessons from autism. In F. R. Volkmar, R. Paul, A. Klin, & D. Cohen (Eds.), *Handbook of autism and pervasive developmental disorders: Vol. 1. Diagnosis, development, neurobiology, and behavior* (3rd ed., pp. 682–703). Hoboken, NJ: Wiley.

Klin, A., Pauls, D., Schultz, R., & Volkmar, F. (2005). Three diagnostic approaches to Asperger syndrome: Implications for research. *Journal of Autism and Developmental Disorders*, *35*(2), 221–234.

Klin, A., Volkmar, F., Sparrow, S., Cicchetti, D., & Rourke, B. P. (1995). Validity and neuropsychological characterization of Asperger syndrome: Convergence with nonverbal learning disabilities syndrome. *Journal of Child Psychology & Psychiatry & Allied Disciplines*, *36*(7), 1127–1140.

Kolvin, I. (1971). Studies in childhood psychoses. I. Diagnostic criteria and classification. *British Journal of Psychiatry*, *118*, 381–384.

Kurita, H., Osada, H., & Miyake, Y. (2004). External validity of childhood disintegrative disorder in comparison with autistic disorder. *Journal of Autism and Developmental Disorders*, *34*(3), 355–362.

Lincoln, A., Courchesne, E., Allen, M., Hanson, E., & Ene, M. (1998). Neurobiology of Asperger syndrome: Seven case studies and quantitative magnetic resonance imaging findings. In E. Schopler, G. B. Mesibov, & L. J. Kunc (Eds.), *Asperger syndrome or high functioning autism?* (pp. 145–166). New York, NY: Plenum Press.

Lord, C., & Corsello, C. (2005). Diagnostic instruments in autism spectrum disorders. In F. Volkmar, A. Klin, R. Paul, & D. J. Cohen (Eds.)., *Handbook of autism and pervasive developmental disorders* (3rd ed., pp. 730–771). Hoboken, NJ: Wiley.

Lord, C., & Jones, R. M. (2012). Annual research review: Re-thinking the classification of autism spectrum disorders. *Journal of Child Psychology and Psychiatry*, *53*(5), 490–509.

Lord, C., Petkova, E., Hus, V., Gan, W., Lu, F., Martin, D. M., . . . Risi, S. (2012). A multisite study of the clinical diagnosis of different autism spectrum disorders. *Archives of General Psychiatry*, *69*(3), 306–313. doi: http://dx.doi.org/10.1001/archgenpsychiatry.2011.148

Luteijn, E. F., Serra, M., Jackson, S., Steenhuis, M. P., Althaus, M., Volkmar, F., & Minderaa, R. (2000). How unspecified are disorders of children with a pervasive developmental disorder not otherwise specified? A study of social problems in children with PDD-NOS and ADHD. *European Child & Adolescent Psychiatry*, *9*(3), 168–179.

Magaña, S., Parish, S., Rose, R., Timberlake, M., & Swaine, J. (2012). Racial and ethnic disparities in quality of health care among children with autism and other developmental disabilities. *Intellectual and Developmental Disabilities*, *50*(4), 287–299.

Mahler, M. S. (1965). On early infantile psychosis: The symbiotic and autistic syndromes. *Journal of the American Academy of Child Psychiatry*, *4*(4), 554–568.

Malhotra, S., & Gupta, N. (2002). Childhood disintegrative disorder: Re-examination of the current concept. *European Child & Adolescent Psychiatry*, *11*(3), 108–114.

Mandell, D., Morales, K., Xie, M., Lawer, L., Stahmer, A., & Marcus, S. (2010). Age of diagnosis among

Medicaid-enrolled children with autism, 2001–2004. *Psychiatric Services*, *61*(8), 822–829.

Mandell, D., Morales, K., Xie, M., Polsky, D., Stahmer, A., & Marcus, S. (2010). County-level variation in the prevalence of medicaid-enrolled children with autism spectrum disorders. *Journal of Autism and Developmental Disorders*, *40*(10), 1241–1246.

Mandell, D., & Novak, M. (2005). The role of culture in families' treatment decisions for children with autism spectrum disorders. [Review]. *Mental Retardation and Developmental Disabilities Research Reviews*, *11*(2), 110–115.

Matson, J. L., Hattier, M. A., & Williams, L. W. (2012). How does relaxing the algorithm for autism affect DSM-V prevalence rates? *Journal of Autism and Developmental Disorders*, *42*(8), 1549–1556.

Mattila, M., Kielinen, M., Linna, S., Jussila, K., Ebeling, H., Bloigu, R.,... Moilanen, I. (2011). Autism spectrum disorders according to DSM-IV-TR and comparison with DSM-5 draft criteria: An epidemiological study. *Journal of the American Academy of Child & Adolescent Psychiatry*, *50*(6), 583–592.e511.

Mazefsky, C. A., McPartland, J. C., Gasteb, H. Z., & Minshew, N. (2012). Brief report: Comparability of DSM-IV and DSM-5 ASD in research samples. *Journal of Autism and Developmental Disorders*, *43*(5), 1235–1242.

McPartland, J., Klin, A., & Volkmar, F. (in press). *Asperger syndrome: Assessing and treating high functioning autism spectrum disorders*. New York, NY: Guilford Press.

McPartland, J. C., Reichow, B., & Volkmar, F. R. (2012). Sensitivity and specificity of proposed DSM-5 diagnostic criteria for autism spectrum disorder. *Journal of the American Academy of Child & Adolescent Psychiatry*, *51*(4), 368–383.

National Collaborating Centre for Women's and Children's Health. (2011, September). *Autism: Recognition, referral, diagnosis and management of adults on the autism spectrum—draft 2011*. London, England: National Institute for Health and Clinical Excellence.

Nazeer, A., & Ghaziuddin, M. (2012). Autism spectrum disorders: Clinical features and diagnosis. *Pediatric Clinics of North America*, *59*(1), 19–25.

Norris, M., Lecavalier, L., & Edwards, M. C. (2012). The structure of autism symptoms as measured by the Autism Diagnostic Observation Schedule. *Journal of Autism and Developmental Disorders*, *42*(6), 1075–1086.

Ozonoff, S., & Griffith, E. M. (2000). Neuropsychological function and the external validity of Asperger syndrome. In A. Klin & F. R. Volkmar (Eds.), *Asperger syndrome* (pp. 72–96). New York, NY: Guilford Press.

Rank, B. (1949). Adaptation of the psychoanalytic technique for the treatment of young children with atypical development. *American Journal of Orthopsychiatry 19*(1), 130–139.

Rank, B. (1955). Intensive study and treatment of preschool children who show marked personality deviations, or "atypical development," and their parents. In G. Caplan (Ed.), *Emotional problems of early childhood* (pp. 491–501). Oxford, England: Basic Books.

Rank, B., & MacNaughton, D. (1949). A clinical contribution to early ego development. In A. Freud, H. Hartmann, & E. Kris (Eds.), *The psychoanalytic study of the child* (Vol. 3/4, pp. 53–65). Oxford, England: International Universities Press.

Regier, D. A., Narrow, W. E., Kuhl, E. A., & Kupfer, D. J. (Eds.). (2010). *The conceptual evolution of DSM-5*. Arlington, VA: American Psychiatric Publishing.

Regier, D. A., Narrow, W. E., Clarke, D. E., Kraemer, H. C., Kuramoto, S. J., Kuhl, E. A., & Kupfer, D. J. (2013). *DSM-5* field trials in the United States and Canada, Part II: Test-retest reliability of selected categorical diagnoses. *American Journal of Psychiatry*, *170*(1), 59–70.

Reichow, B., Barton, E. E., Boyd, B. A., & Hume, K. (2012). Early intensive behavioral intervention (EIBI) for young children with autism spectrum disorders (ASD). *Cochrane Database of Systematic Reviews*, *2012*(10), CD009260. doi: 10.1002/14651858.CD009260

Reichow, B., Steiner, A. M., & Volkmar, F. (2012). Social skills groups for people aged 6 to 21 with autism spectrum disorders (ASD). *Cochrane Database of Systematic Reviews*, *2012*, Issue 7. Art. No.: CD008511. doi: 10.1002/14651858.CD008511.pub2

Rett, A. (1966). Uber ein eigenartiges hirntophisces Syndroem bei hyperammonie im Kindersalter. *Wein Medizinische Wochenschrift*, *118*, 723–726.

Rispoli, M., Neely, L., Lang, R., & Ganz, J. (2011). Training paraprofessionals to implement interventions for people autism spectrum disorders: A systematic review. *Developmental Neurorehabilitation*, *14*(6), 378–388.

Ritvo, E. R. (2012). Postponing the proposed changes in *DSM 5* for autistic spectrum disorder until new scientific evidence adequately supports them. *Journal of Autism and Developmental Disorders*, *42*(9), 2021–2022. doi: http://dx.doi.org/10.1007/s10803-012-1613-x

Ritvo, E. R., & Freeman, B. J. (1977). National Society for Autistic Children definition of the syndrome of autism. *Journal of Pediatric Psychology*, *2*(4), 142–145.

Rutter, M. (1972, October). Childhood schizophrenia reconsidered. *Journal of Autism & Childhood Schizophrenia*, *2*(4), 315–337.

Rutter, M. (1978). Diagnosis and definitions of childhood autism. *Journal of Autism and Developmental Disorders*, *8*(2), 139–161.

Rutter, M. (1994a). Comorbidity: Meanings and mechanisms. *Clinical Psychology: Science & Practice*, *1*(1), 100–103.

Rutter, M. (1994b). Debate and argument: There are connections between brain and mind and it is important that Rett syndrome be classified somewhere. *Journal of Child Psychology and Psychiatry and Allied Disciplines*, *35*(2), 379–381.

Rutter, M. (1997). Comorbidity: Concepts, claims and choices. *Criminal Behaviour & Mental Health*, *7*(4), 265–285.

Rutter, M. (2011). Research review: Child psychiatric diagnosis and classification: Concepts, findings, challenges and potential. *Journal of Child Psychology and Psychiatry and Allied Disciplines*, *52*(6), 647–660. doi: http://dx.doi.org/10.1111/j.1469-7610.2011.02367.x

Rutter, M., Bailey, A., Bolton, P., & Le Couteur, A. (1994). Autism and known medical conditions: Myth and substance. *Journal of Child Psychology and Psychiatry and Allied Disciplines*, *35*(2), 311–322.

Rutter, M., Lebovici, S., Eisenberg, L., Sneznevskij, A. V., Sadoun, R., Brooke, E., & Lin, T. Y. (1969). A tri-axial classification of mental disorders in childhood: An international study. *Journal of Child Psychology and Psychiatry and Allied Disciplines, 10*(1), 41–61.

Rutter, M., & Schopler, E. (1992). Classification of pervasive developmental disorders: Some concepts and practical considerations. *Journal of Autism and Developmental Disorders, 22*(4), 459–482.

Rutter, M., Tizard, J., Yule, W., Graham, P., & Whitmore, K. (1976). Research report: Isle of Wight studies, 1964–1974. *Psychological Medicine, 6*(2), 313–332.

Self, T., Coufal, K., & Parham, D. (2010). Allied healthcare providers' role in screening for autism spectrum disorders. *Journal of Allied Health, 39*(3), 165–174.

Sharma, S., Woolfson, L. M., & Hunter, S. C. (2012). Confusion and inconsistency in diagnosis of Asperger syndrome: A review of studies from 1981 to 2010. *Autism, 16*(5), 465–486.

Shattuck, P., & Grosse, S. (2007). Issues related to the diagnosis and treatment of autism spectrum disorders. *Mental Retardation and Developmental Disabilities Research Reviews, 13,* 129–135.

Shattuck, P., Wagner, M., Narendorf, S., Sterzing, P., & Hensley, M. (2011). Post–high school service use among young adults with an autism spectrum disorder. *Archives of Pediatrics & Adolescent Medicine, 165*(2), 141–146.

Shriberg, L. D., Paul, R., McSweeny, J. L., Klin, A., Cohen, D. J., & Volkmar, F. R. (2001). Speech and prosody characteristics of adolescents and adults with high-functioning autism and Asperger syndrome. *Journal of Speech Language & Hearing Research, 44*(5), 1097–1115.

Singer, E. (2012). Diagnosis: Redefining autism. *Nature, 491,* S12–S13.

Sparrow, S. S., Cicchetti, D. V., & Balla, D. A. (2005). *Vineland Adaptive Behavior Scales: Second edition (Vineland II) Survey Interview Form/Caregiver Rating Form.* Livonia, MN: Pearson.

Spencer, K., Turkett, A., Vaughan, R., & Koenig, S. (2006). School-based practice patterns: A survey of occupational therapists in Colorado. *American Journal of Occupational Therapists, 60*(1), 81–91.

Spitzer, R. L., Endicott, J. E., & Robbins, E. (1978). Resarch Diagnostic Criteria. *Archives of General Psychiatry, 35,* 773–782.

Spitzer, R. L., & Siegel, B. (1990, November). The *DSM-III-R* field trial of pervasive developmental disorders. *Journal of the American Academy of Child & Adolescent Psychiatry, 29*(6), 855–862.

Stahmer, A., & Aarons, G. (2009). Attitudes toward adoption of evidence-based practices: A comparison of autism early intervention providers and children's mental health providers. *Psychological Services, 6*(3), 223–234.

Stahmer, A., & Mandell, D. (2007). State infant/toddler program policies for eligibility and services provision for young children with autism. *Administration and Policy in Mental Health and Mental Health Services Research, 34*(1), 29–37.

Stein, B., Sorbero, M., Goswami, U., Schuster, J., & Leslie, D. (2012). Impact of a private health insurance mandate on public sector autism service use in Pennsylvania. *Journal of the American Academy of Child & Adolescent Psychiatry, 51*(8), 771–779.

Szatmari, P. (1992a). A review of the DSM-III-R criteria for autistic disorder. *Journal of Autism and Developmental Disorders, 22*(4), 507–523.

Szatmari, P. (1992b). The validity of autistic spectrum disorders: A literature review. *Journal of Autism and Developmental Disorders, 22*(4), 583–600.

Taheri, A., & Perry, A. (2012). Exploring the proposed DSM-5 criteria in a clinical sample. *Journal of Autism and Developmental Disorders, 42*(9), 1810–1817. doi: http://dx.doi.org/10.1007/s10803-012-1599-4

Taylor, E., & Rutter, M. (2008). Classification. In M. Rutter, D. Bishop, D. Pine, S. Scott, J. Stevenson, E. Taylor, & A. Thapr (Eds.), *Rutter's child and adolescent psychiatry* (5th ed., pp. 18–31). London, England: Blackwell.

Towbin, K. (2005). Pervasive developmental disorder not otherwise specified. In F. R. Volkmar, R. Paul, A. Klin, & D. J. Cohen (Eds.), *Handbook of autism and pervasive developmental disorders* (3rd ed., pp. 165–200). Hoboken, NJ: Wiley.

Tsai, L. (1992). Is Rett syndrome a subtype of pervasive developmental disorder? *Journal of Autism and Developmental Disorders, 22,* 551–561.

Tsai, L. Y. (2012). Sensitivity and specificity: *DSM-IV* versus *DSM-5* criteria for autism spectrum disorder. *American Journal of Psychiatry, 169*(10), 1009–1011. doi: 10.1176/appi.ajp.2012.12070922

Van Acker, Richard, Loncola, Jennifer A., & Van Acker, Eryn Y. (2005). Rett syndrome: A pervasive developmental disorder. In F. R. Volkmar, A. Klin, R. Paul, & D. J. Cohen (Eds.), *Handbook of autism and pervasive developmental disorders* (3rd ed., Vol. 1, pp. 126–164). Hoboken, NJ: Wiley.

Volkmar, F. R., Cicchetti, D. V., Cohen, D. J., & Bregman, J. (1992). Brief report: Developmental aspects of *DSM-III-R* criteria for autism. *Journal of Autism and Developmental Disorders, 22*(4), 657–662.

Volkmar, F. R., & Cohen, D. J. (1989). Disintegrative disorder or "late onset" autism. *Journal of Child Psychology & Psychiatry & Allied Disciplines, 30*(5), 717–724.

Volkmar, F. R., & Cohen, D. J. (1991). Comorbid association of autism and schizophrenia. *American Journal of Psychiatry, 148*(12), 1705–1707.

Volkmar, F. R., Cohen, D. J., & Paul, R. (1986). An evaluation of *DSM-III* criteria for infantile autism. *Journal of the American Academy of Child Psychiatry, 25*(2), 190–197.

Volkmar, F. R., & Klin, A. (2000). Diagnostic issues in Asperger syndrome. In A. Klin & F. R. Volkmar (Eds.), *Asperger syndrome.* (pp. 25–71). New York, NY: Guilford Press.

Volkmar, F. R., & Klin, A. (2005). Issues in the classification of autism and related conditions. In F. R. Volkmar, A. Klin, R. Paul, & D. J. Cohen (Eds.), *Handbook of autism and pervasive developmental disorders* (3rd ed., Vol. 1, pp. 5–41). Hoboken, NJ: Wiley.

Volkmar, F. R., Klin, A., & McPartland, J. (in press). Asperger's disorder: An overview. In J. McPartland, A. Klin, & F. R. Volkmar (Eds.), *Asperger syndrome: Assessing and treating high-functioning autism spectrum disorders* (2nd ed.). New York, NY: Guilford Press.

Volkmar, F. R., Klin, A., Siegel, B., Szatmari, P., Lord, C., Campbell, M., . . . Kline, W. (1994). Field trial for autistic disorder in DSM-IV. *The American Journal of Psychiatry, 151*(9), 1361–1367.

Volkmar, F. R., & Nelson, D. S. (1990). Seizure disorders in autism. *Journal of the American Academy of Child & Adolescent Psychiatry, 29*(1), 127–129.

Volkmar, F. R., Reichow, B., & McPartland, J. (2012). Classification of autism and related conditions: progress, challenges, and opportunities. *Dialogues in Clinical Neuroscience, 14*(3), 229–237.

Volkmar, F. R., & Rutter, M. (1995). Childhood disintegrative disorder: Results of the DSM-IV autism field trial. *Journal of the American Academy of Child & Adolescent Psychiatry, 34*(8), 1092–1095.

Volkmar, F. R., & Schwab-Stone, M. (1996). Annotation: Childhood disorders in DSM-IV. *Journal of Child Psychology & Psychiatry & Allied Disciplines, 37*(7), 779–784.

Volkmar, F. R., Sparrow, S. S., Goudreau, D., Cicchetti, D. V., Paul, R., & Cohen, D. J. (1987). Social deficits in autism: An operational approach using the Vineland Adaptive Behavior Scales. *Journal of the American Academy of Child & Adolescent Psychiatry, 26*(2), 156–161.

Volkmar, F., & Wiesner, L. (2009). *A practical duide to autism.* Hoboken, NJ: Wiley.

Volkmar, F. R., & Woolston, J. L. (1997). Comorbidity of psychiatric disorders in children and adolescents. In S. Wetzler & W. C. Sanderson (Eds.), *Treatment strategies for patients with psychiatric comorbidity.* An Einstein psychiatry publication, No. 14 (pp. 307–322). New York, NY: Wiley.

Waterhouse, L., Wing, L., Spitzer, R., & Siegel, B. (1992). Pervasive developmental disorders: From *DSM-III* to *DSM-III-R. Journal of Autism and Developmental Disorders, 22*(4), 525–549.

Westphal, A., Schelinski, S., Volkmar, F. R., & Pelphrey, K. (2013). Revisiting regression in autism: Heller's dementia infantilis. Includes a translation of Über Dementia Infantilis. *Journal of Autism and Developmental Disorders, 43*(2), 265–271.

White, S. W., & Schry, A. R. (2011). Social anxiety in adolescents on the autism spectrum. In C. A. Alfano & D. C. Beidel (Eds.), *Social anxiety in adolescents and young adults: Translating developmental science into practice* (pp. 183–201). Washington, DC: American Psychological Association.

Wilson, C. E., Gillan, N., Spain, D., Robertson, D., Roberts, G., Murphy, C. M., . . . Murphy, D. G. (2013, March 16). Comparison of ICD-10R, *DSM-IV-TR* and *DSM-5* in an adult autism spectrum disorder diagnostic clinic. *Journal of Autism and Developmental Disorders.* [Epub ahead of print]

Wing, L. (1980). Childhood autism and social class a question of selection? *British Journal of Psychiatry, 137,* 410–417.

Wing, L. (1981). Asperger's syndrome: A Clinical Account. *Psychological Medicine, 11*(1), 115–129.

Wing, L., & Gould, J. (1979). Severe impairments of social interaction and associated abnormalities in children: Epidemiology and classification. *Journal of Autism & Developmental Disorders, 9*(1), 11–29.

Wing, L., Gould, J., & Gillberg, C. (2011). Autism spectrum disorder in *DSM-V*: Better or worse than *DSM-IV? Research in Developmental Disabilities, 32,* 768–773.

Wolff, S. (2004). The history of autism. *European Child & Adolescent Psychiatry, 13*(4), 201–208.

World Health Organization (1992). *Clinical descriptions and diagnostic guidelines.* Geneva, Switzerland: Author.

World Health Organization. (1993). *Diagnostic criteria for research* (10th ed.). Geneva, Switzerland: Author.

Worley, J. A., & Matson, J. L. (2012). Comparing symptoms of autism spectrum disorders using the current *DSM-IV-TR* diagnostic criteria and the proposed *DSM-V* diagnostic criteria. *Research in Autism Spectrum Disorders, 6*(2), 965–970. doi: http://dx.doi.org/10.1016/j.rasd.2011.12.012

Zoghbi, H. (1988). Genetic aspects of Rett syndrome. *Journal of Child Neurology, 3*(Suppl), S76–78.

CHAPTER 2

The Broader Autism Phenotype

BROOKE INGERSOLL AND ALLISON WAINER

HISTORICAL PERSPECTIVE OF THE BROADER AUTISM PHENOTYPE

In Kanner's (1943) original description of autism he noted that many of the family members of the young patients that he examined exhibited personalities that were similar in quality to the core features of the disorder, noting, "For the most part, the parents, grandparents, and collaterals are preoccupied with abstractions of a scientific, literary, or artistic nature, and limited in general interest in people" (p. 250). Although Kanner originally suspected that autism had a biological cause, interpretations of this observation in the 1950s and 1960s led to the unfortunate theory of refrigerator mothers, whose cold, analytical, and rejecting behavior led to the ultimate withdrawal of the infant into autism (e.g., Bettelheim, 1967). Pioneering twin research in the 1970s provided the first evidence that autism had a genetic component (Folstein & Rutter, 1977). In their seminal study of 21 same-sexed twin pairs, Folstein and Rutter found that the concordance rate for autism in dizygotic (DZ) twins was 0% while the concordance rate in monozygotic (MZ) twins was 36%. When they

examined milder cognitive abnormalities, including delayed speech, low IQ, and academic difficulties, the concordance rate in DZ twins rose to 10%, while it jumped to 82% in MZ twins. They concluded that autism is a heritable condition, and that what is inherited extends to a milder form of nonautistic cognitive impairment. Since this initial paper, a number of twin studies including ones using contemporary criteria for autism have found higher rates of autism and subthreshold symptoms in MZ compared to DZ twins (Bailey, Palferman, Heavey, & Le Couteur, 1998), with heritability estimates around .80 (Ronald & Hoekstra, 2011). These milder cognitive and language symptoms in family members of individuals with autism are thought to represent an intermediate phenotype or endophenotype for the disorder that has come to be known as the broader autism phenotype (BAP).

Early work on the BAP using family histories demonstrated that relatives of probands with autism exhibited elevated rates of cognitive, language, learning, and psychiatric problems (e.g., Bartak, Rutter, & Cox, 1975; Bolton et al., 1994; Bolton, Pickles, Murphy, & Rutter, 1998; Piven, Palmer, Jacobi, Childress, & Arndt, 1997). Like autism spectrum disorder (ASD), these traits were more pronounced in males than in females (e.g., Baron-Cohen, Wheelwright, Skinner, Martin, & Clubley, 2001). As research on the BAP has progressed, there has been an increased focus on understanding specific personality and cognitive profiles that characterize the BAP in family members, as well as the identification of behavioral and neurophysiological markers. In addition, studies using recently developed quantitative measures of the BAP have demonstrated that these traits are continuously distributed and extend beyond family members into the general population (Constantino & Todd, 2003; Hoekstra, Bartels, Verweij, & Boomsma, 2007; Hurst, Mitchell, Kimbrel, Kwapil, & Nelson-Gray, 2007; Stewart & Austin, 2009). As such, there are a growing number of studies that have examined the BAP in the general population in an attempt to better characterize the phenotype. These quantitative measures have also allowed for increased sensitivity in behavioral and molecular genetic studies of autism and autistic traits, and a growing number of genetic studies are considering the BAP in their designs. These recent advances have contributed to a better understanding of autism as well as its lesser variants.

This chapter will provide an overview of research on the BAP that has been conducted in family members, as well as the general population. It will begin with a discussion of methodological issues in the assessment of the BAP and then describe the domains thought to characterize the BAP. It will end with a brief discussion of the etiological significance of the BAP.

Assessment of the Broader Autism Phenotype

Unlike ASD, which has specific diagnostic criteria, there are no well-accepted criteria for the BAP. A number of different features have been proposed to characterize the BAP, and across studies, the BAP has been defined in multiple ways. For example, some studies have considered difficulties in a single area of functioning that parallels the features of autism (e.g., social functioning) to be indicative of

the BAP in family members (Losh et al., 2009), while others have required two or more deficits on standardized measures of the BAP (e.g., Hurley, Losh, Parlier, Reznick, & Piven, 2007), more closely mirroring the criteria of ASD. The lack of standardized criteria for the BAP has made comparisons across studies more challenging. In addition, the use of different measurement tools and varied methodological approaches across studies has complicated attempts to define the core features of the BAP. An appreciation of these differences is important when evaluating findings from the extant literature. Despite these challenges, results across studies have tended to converge more often than not and several recent reviews have suggested similar core features of the BAP (Gerdts & Bernier, 2011; Losh, Adolphs, & Piven, 2011; Sucksmith, Roth, & Hoekstra, 2011).

Measurement Tools

Unlike the Autism Diagnostic Observation Schedule (ADOS; Lord, Rutter, DiLavore, & Risi, 2002) and Autism Diagnostic Interview—Revised (ADI-R; Lord, Rutter, & Le Couteur, 1994) for ASD, there are no universally accepted instruments for assessing the BAP. Thus, the measurement tools used have varied greatly across studies. These tools vary in their approach to classification, the characteristics assessed, the informant, and the method of administration, all of which can influence study findings. One of the earliest and most commonly used tools is the Autism Family History Interview (AFHI; Bolton et al., 1994). The AFHI is a standardized clinical interview that asks the informant detailed questions regarding his or her own and his or her relatives' personality and behavior in domains that parallel the defining symptoms of ASD (i.e., social, communication, and rigid/repetitive interests and behavior). Questions pertain to the individual's functioning during both childhood and adulthood. Based on the interview, a case vignette is created that includes all relevant information, and vignettes are rated based on predetermined criteria by trained raters blind to the informant's family of origin. The ratings are then used to determine whether the individual exhibits the BAP (BAP+) or not (BAP−). The AFHI has strong interrater reliability (Bolton et al., 1994), and studies have found that a greater number of family members of autistic probands are BAP+ than family members of controls (e.g., Bolton et al., 1994). Although this approach is efficient in that information can be obtained about multiple family members during a single interview, the use of a single informant can introduce bias.

An extension of this approach has been the use of structured interviews and observational ratings that assess specific features of the BAP. The Modified Personality Assessment Schedule–Revised (M-PAS-R; Piven et al., 1994), which was adapted from the Personality Assessment Schedule (Tyrer, 1988), a structured interview for identifying personality disorders, has been used to assess specific personality profiles associated with the BAP. Research comparing parents of children with ASD to parents of children with Down syndrome on this measure found that ASD parents were rated higher than controls on three personality dimensions: aloof, untactful, undemonstrative (Piven et al., 1994). Similarly, the Friendship Interview (FI; Santangelo & Folstein, 1995) was developed to assess one aspect of social functioning, the number and quality of an individual's friendships. Research using this measure has found that parents of children with ASD report fewer and lower quality friendships than parents of controls (Santangelo & Folstein, 1995). Finally, the Pragmatic Rating Scale (PRS; Landa et al., 1992) is an observational tool that rates the individual's pragmatic skills based on a conversational sample. Parents of children with ASD have been shown to have more difficulty with pragmatic language than parents of controls on this measure (Landa et al., 1992; Losh, Childress, Lam, & Piven, 2008). These measures have also been combined in an attempt to further characterize the BAP in family measures. The features of aloof personality and hypersensitivity to criticism (M-PAS-R), speech abnormalities (PRS), and friendship score (FI) were found to best differentiate parents of children with ASD from parents of children with Down syndrome. The presence of two or more of these features is

considered indicative of the BAP (Piven, Palmer, Landa, et al., 1997).

The Broader Phenotype Autism Symptom Scale (BPASS; Dawson et al., 2007) is a combined parent interview and observational rating scale that was developed for use in genetic studies of ASD in multiplex families. Unlike the previous tools that provide a qualitative measure of the BAP, the BPASS provides a quantitative measure of autistic traits in four domains—social motivation, social expressiveness, conversational skills, and flexibility/range of interests—in affected children, their parents, and unaffected siblings. Nonverbal behavior, such as eye contact, is assessed via direct observation, whereas restricted behaviors are assessed via parent interview. An initial evaluation of the psychometric properties of the BPASS suggests that it has acceptable to good interrater reliability and internal consistency. Scores for affected children and their parents showed overlapping distributions, suggesting the BPASS captured variability in traits across groups (Dawson et al., 2007). Subsequent studies have found the social motivation and flexibility domains to be highly heritable in multiplex families (Sung et al., 2005), and that parents from multiplex autism families (those with two or more children with ASD) score higher on the BPASS than parents from simplex autism families, developmentally delayed families, or typical families, although no differences were found between parents in the latter three groups (Bernier, Gerdts, Munson, Dawson, & Estes, 2012).

Each of these instruments has adequate reliability as well as face validity for providing an index of the features thought to comprise the BAP. However, administration of the interviews and observational ratings is lengthy and requires substantial training to achieve reliability. As such, there has been a movement toward the development of questionnaires that can be completed at a significantly reduced cost. These measures provide the opportunity to examine the BAP dimensionally, and a number of these tools have been used to demonstrate that BAP traits are continuously distributed in the general population (e.g., Constantino & Todd, 2003, 2005; Hurst, Mitchell, et al., 2007). With some exception, most of these scales were designed to identify ASD or language impairment rather than the BAP; thus, their ability to appropriately capture the BAP is somewhat unclear.

The most commonly used rating scale for assessing the BAP is the Autism Spectrum Quotient (AQ; Baron-Cohen, Wheelwright, Skinner, et al., 2001). The AQ is a self-report questionnaire that was originally developed to identify ASD among adults with normal intelligence. It contains five theoretically defined subscales of autistic behavior: social skills, attention switching, attention to detail, communication, and imagination. A number of studies have used the AQ as an index of BAP, both in relatives of individuals with ASD as well as the general population. These studies have found that parents of children with ASD score higher on several subscales of the AQ than parents without children with ASD (Wheelwright, Auyeung, Allison, & Baron-Cohen, 2010; Woodbury-Smith, Robinson, Wheelwright, & Baron-Cohen 2005) and that autistic traits measured on the AQ are normally distributed in the population (Hurst, Mitchell, et al., 2007) and heritable (Hoekstra et al., 2007). Finally, a number of studies that have used the AQ as a measure of the BAP in the general population have found an association between AQ scores and measures of social functioning (Ingersoll, 2010; Jobe & White, 2007; Kunihira, Senju, Dairoku, Wakabayashi, & Hasegawa, 2006), personality structure (Austin, 2005; Wakabayashi, Baron-Cohen, & Wheelwright, 2006), and related psychopathology (Hurst, Nelson-Gray, Mitchell, & Kwapil, 2007; Kunihira et al., 2006).

Another questionnaire that has been used in BAP research is the Social Responsiveness Scale (SRS; Constantino, 2002), formally the Social Reciprocity Scale (Constantino, Przybeck, Friesen, & Todd, 2000). The SRS is a parent/teacher questionnaire that was developed for distinguishing children with ASDs from children with typical development and other psychiatric disorders. The original published instrument was developed for children ages 4 to 17; however, the SRS has been adapted for use with adults (SRS-A) by changing the wording on several items (Constantino & Todd,

2005), and a newer version for individuals ages 2 to adult has recently been published. The SRS focuses on reciprocal social behaviors which have been found to be impaired in ASD, but includes items related to all three ASD symptom domains. It has five theoretically defined subscales: social awareness, social cognition, social communication, social motivation, and autistic mannerisms. A number of studies that have used the SRS as an index of the BAP have shown that siblings of children with ASD score higher on the SRS than siblings of children with non-ASD psychopathology (Constantino et al., 2006) and that autistic traits measured on the SRS are continuously distributed and heritable in the general population (Constantino & Todd, 2003, 2005). Finally, several studies have found that self-reported autistic symptoms on the SRS were associated with a number of psychiatric problems and interpersonal difficulties in nonclinical samples (e.g., Kanne, Christ, & Reiersen, 2009).

The Children's Communication Checklist–2 (CCC-2; Bishop, 2003) is a questionnaire that was originally designed to assess language and communication deficits in children (Bishop, 1998). This parent-report questionnaire asks about children's communication in everyday situations. Research using the CCC-2 found that siblings of children with ASD were rated more poorly on a number of language features than non-ASD siblings (Bishop, Maybery, Wong, Maley, & Hallmayer, 2006). A recent study on an extension of this measure for adults, the Communication Checklist–Adult Version (CC-A; Whitehouse & Bishop, 2009; Whitehouse, Coon, Miller, Salisbury, & Bishop, 2010), found that parents of children with ASD showed more impairment on the social engagement scale of the CC-A (but not pragmatic scale) than parents of children without ASD, suggesting that these questionnaires may be able to assess the social communication features of the BAP.

Both the Childhood Asperger Syndrome Test (CAST; Scott, Baron-Cohen, Bolton, & Brayne, 2002) and the Social and Communication Disorders Checklist (Skuse, Mandy, & Scourfield, 2005) have been used as a measure of autistic traits in school-aged children in population-based twin samples. The SCDC is a 12-item parent-report measure that measures social-cognitive traits associated with ASD in school-aged children of normal intelligence. The CAST is a 31-item parent-report measure developed to identify Asperger's syndrome in school-aged children. Research using these measures indicates that autistic traits are continuously distributed and heritable in the general population (Ronald, Happé, & Plomin, 2008; Skuse et al., 2005). However, the extent to which the SCDC or CAST measure the BAP as conceptualized in family members is not yet clear.

Unlike the previous questionnaires, which were originally developed to identify individuals with ASD or language impairment, the Broad Autism Phenotype Questionnaire (BAPQ) was specifically designed as a self-report measure of the BAP in relatives of individuals with ASD (Hurley et al., 2007). As such, it has good convergent validity with direct clinical assessment of the BAP using the MPAS-R and PRS (Hurley et al., 2007). A psychometric evaluation of the BAPQ found it to have strong test-retest and interrater reliability in parents of children with ASD, and parents of individuals with ASD scored higher on this measure than parents of controls (Hurley et al., 2007). The BAPQ has a proposed cut-off score for the BAP based on best-estimate ratings (self- and informant-report), but the measure has also been used dimensionally. Recent work on the BAPQ has shown scores correlate in meaningful ways with self-report measures of interpersonal problems and related psychopathology in nonclinical samples (Ingersoll, Hopwood, Wainer, & Donnellan, 2011; Wainer, Block, Donnellan, & Ingersoll, 2013).

Since there are no standard definitions of the BAP, the sensitivity and specificity of these tools assessing the BAP has not been established. In addition, there has been limited research comparing assessments methods; thus it is unclear the degree to which the different measures assess overlapping or independent information, or whether one tool is better than another at identifying features of the BAP. There is some evidence that the BAPQ corresponds well with the M-PAS-R/PRS (Hurley et al., 2007) in its ability to identify BAP+ cases

among parents of individuals with ASD. A recent study comparing three self-report questionnaires of the BAP (AQ, SRS, BAPQ) in the general population found moderate correlations (.55–.66) between measures (Ingersoll, Hopwood, et al., 2011). However, the BAPQ was the only measure with a replicable factor structure that reflected the proposed structure of the BAP (aloofness, pragmatic problems, and rigidity). As a more complete picture of the BAP emerges, it is important that the ability of these measurement tools to assess its core features be evaluated, both in family members and the general population.

Study Design

The most common methodological approach to studying the BAP has been the family history method in which the relatives of individuals with ASD are examined. Early studies focused exclusively on family members in an attempt to develop an initial picture of the BAP (e.g., Bolton et al., 1994; Landa et al., 1992; Piven et al., 1994; Wolff, Narayan, & Moyes, 1988). As this research progressed, researchers began including control groups in their designs to determine the extent to which these profiles were unique to relatives of individuals with ASD. These studies have differed in their selection of control groups, and these differences have the potential to influence the results and interpretations the findings. For example, some studies have used family members of individuals with no history of developmental problems (e.g., Ingersoll, Meyer, & Becker, 2011; Losh et al., 2009). It has been noted that these studies cannot effectively rule out the possibility that increased rates of some BAP features in first-degree family members (e.g., depression) are the result of the stressors of raising a child with a disability (Bailey et al., 1998). To control for this potential confound, a number of studies have used control groups of family members of an individual with a disability. A majority of these studies has used Down syndrome, a nonheritable form of developmental delay, as the control. However, others have used disabilities that are heritable (e.g., specific language impairment [SLI], schizophrenia) and could also result in phenotypic expression in family members. Relatives of individuals with heritable conditions that share features with ASD (e.g., SLI) might be expected to also exhibit phenotypes that overlap with the BAP. In these cases, associated phenotypes could be missed. Indeed, studies that have used an SLI control group have been less likely to find evidence of higher rates of language impairment in relatives of ASD probands (e.g., Whitehouse, Barry, & Bishop, 2007) than studies using relatives of individuals with typical development or Down syndrome as controls (e.g., Bolton et al., 1994; Schmidt et al., 2008).

It has been suggested that that the rate of the BAP in first degree relatives (as defined by a BAP score of 2 or more on the M-PAS-R/PRS/FI measure) is 57% (Piven, Palmer, Landa, et al., 1997). Thus, many family members would not be expected to express the BAP. For this reason, some studies have chosen to compare BAP+ and BAP– groups on a particular characteristic. These studies might be expected to find larger effects than studies that compare average differences between autism relatives and controls. These issues highlight the importance of consideration of the control group when interpreting the results of these studies.

Another methodological difference has been the method of ascertainment of the ASD probands. Most family history studies have relied on clinic-referred samples. Given their small to moderate size, these studies allow for detailed assessment of family members and confirmation of diagnosis in the probands. However, these studies can introduce bias, especially when cases are not well matched on important variables such as gender, age, ethnicity, and socioeconomic status. More recently, there have been several studies that have employed population-based samples (e.g., Litchenstien, Carlstrom, Rastam, Gillberg, & Anckarsater, 2010; Rosenberg et al., 2009). These studies have the advantage of being able to control for referral bias. However, given the large sample sizes, information is usually obtained from a single informant and information about diagnoses in the probands are usually based on parent-report or medical records rather than direct assessment. Finally, most studies have examined first degree relatives (parents or siblings); however, some studies have included second- and third-degree relatives. Traits of the BAP might be expected to be expressed more strongly in first-degree relatives than in more distant family members (Bolton et al., 1998), and thus the degree of relationship of the relatives included in the study needs to be considered.

A special type of family studies are *high-risk infant* or *baby sibs* studies. These prospective longitudinal studies, which capitalize on the 20-fold higher recurrence rate of ASD in siblings (Rogers, 2009), are designed to identify early markers of ASD. These studies recruit high-risk infants in families in which there is an older child with ASD and low-risk infants in families with no ASD history. Infants in both groups are periodically assessed on a variety of measures of early development beginning in the first year of life through the age at which a valid ASD diagnosis can be provided.

A number of studies comparing risk groups have found that high-risk infants show less developed language (e.g., Ben-Yizhak et al., 2011), social skills (e.g., Cassel et al., 2007; Nadig et al., 2007), and motor skills (e.g., Iverson & Wozniak, 2007) than low-risk infants. These results are consistent with family history studies with older siblings and have been interpreted as evidence for the BAP. However, the age of the infants at the time of comparison and the length of the follow-up period can significantly affect the results. Specifically, studies in which the data are analyzed before the children reach an age at which a valid ASD diagnosis can be made (e.g., 36 months) are likely to include children who will eventually develop ASD. Thus, differences between groups may be driven by a small number of children in the high-risk group who eventually develop ASD rather than the BAP. In order to address this issue, more recent studies have waited to analyze early data until the children reach the age of diagnosis, and then removed the children who meet criteria for ASD from the sample.

This approach has the distinct advantage of being able to examine the emergence of the BAP in very young children. A limitation of this approach, however, is that the high-risk sample has rarely been followed past the age of 3 or 4 (when a reliable ASD diagnosis can be made). It is unclear if early developmental differences in the high-risk group persist over time or whether they ameliorate with development. The few studies that have followed children to school age have found differing results. Gamliel, Yirmiya, Jaffe, Manor, and Sigman (2009) found that high-risk siblings (without ASD) continued to show deficits in cognitive and language skills and demonstrated academic difficulties at age 7, findings that mirrored family history studies with older siblings. However, Warren et al. (2012) found that group differences in cognitive, language, and social development that were present at age 3 (Stone, McMahon, Yoder, & Walden, 2007) were no longer present when the children were 5, suggesting that early developmental differences observed in high-risk siblings may resolve over time. However, subtle differences in executive functioning, social cognition, and repetitive behaviors were found when the children were 5, providing some support for the BAP in their sample and suggesting that the manifestation of the BAP may change with development.

A third methodological approach to studying the BAP has been to examine autistic traits in the general population, rather than focusing on family members. These studies, many of which have been conducted with convenience samples (e.g., college students), have examined the relationship between the degree of BAP traits and a behavior of interest (e.g., Jobe & White, 2007; Wainer, Ingersoll, & Hopwood, 2011). These studies have relied primarily on self- or informant-report questionnaires of the BAP and have defined the BAP dimensionally (i.e., examined correlations between BAP traits and the behavior of interest), although some studies have compared individuals with high and low BAP scores on the behavior of interest (e.g., Jobe & White, 2007).

Given their use of rating scales and nonclinical samples, these studies are easy to conduct and allow for the recruitment of large numbers of participants, including some population-based and

large twin samples (see Ronald & Hoekstra, 2011, for review). This advantage has led to a substantial increase in this type of design over the past few years. Studies of the BAP in the general population have replicated many of the findings seen in family members. In addition, they have demonstrated associations between BAP traits and a performance on other behavioral, personality, cognitive, and emotional measures shown to be impaired in ASD. Thus, this approach has the distinct advantage of being able to advance the study of the phenotype more quickly. However, it is not yet clear whether the BAP in family members is the same as the BAP in individuals without a family history of ASD (Losh et al., 2011). Heritability estimates for autistic traits in the general population are similar to heritability estimates for autism (Ronald & Hoekstra, 2011), although this does not prove that they are due to similar genetic influences. One large twin study (3,419 pairs) that included a representative proportion of children with ASD found that heritability estimates were similar for the whole sample, as well as those at the extreme for autistic traits (Ronald et al., 2006). This study suggests that there is a genetic link between autistic traits seen at the extreme end of the distribution (i.e., ASD and BAP) and variation in the general population. If further research can demonstrate that BAP traits are inherited similarly in families with and without a history of ASD, this method holds significant promise for population-based genetic studies of autistic symptomatology by increasing the scale at which this work can be done (Ronald & Hoekstra, 2011).

DOMAINS OF THE BAP

Social Behavior

A deficit in reciprocal social behaviors is considered a core feature of ASD (American Psychiatric Association [APA], 2000). Thus, much of the literature on the BAP has explored the expression of subclinical autism traits and difficulties in global social functioning. Indeed, deficits in markers of early social behavior can be some of the earliest indicators of broader autism characteristics (e.g., Cassel et al., 2007; Goldberg et al., 2005). Early social behavioral deficits that have been noted in some ASD siblings include responding to one's name (Nadig et al., 2007), social smiling (Toth, Dawson, Meltzoff, Greenson, & Fein, 2007), requesting behaviors (Cassel et al., 2007; Goldberg et al., 2005), and eye gaze duration and movements (Ibañez, Messinger, Newell, Lambert, & Sheskin, 2008; Merin, Young, Ozonoff, & Rogers, 2007). Importantly, the majority of these studies are not longitudinal, and therefore it is difficult to determine how long these group differences persist. Moreover, because of the lack of information about which high-risk siblings go on to demonstrate BAP characteristics or ASD, the relationship between these early deficits and the expression of the BAP is still somewhat unclear.

There is also accumulating evidence that the expression of BAP characteristics in older relatives is related to problems in social functioning. A number of studies have suggested high rates of social difficulties in both first- (Bolton et al., 1994) and second-degree (Piven, Palmer, Jacobi, et al., 1997) ASD relatives. Siblings, especially brothers, of individuals with ASD have also been found to demonstrate reduced social responsiveness as measured by the SRS (Constantino et al., 2006; Constantino, Zhang, Frazier, Abbacchi, & Law, 2010). ASD parents report more problems with social skills (Wheelwright et al., 2010) and social engagement (Whitehouse et al., 2010) than parents of typically developing children and adults from the general population, respectively. Additionally, ASD parents have been shown to demonstrate less interest in purely social interactions, and report having fewer and lower quality friendships than parents of children with Down syndrome and non-clinical control parents (Losh et al., 2008; Piven, Palmer, Landa, et al., 1997).

To date, only a few studies have explored the link between social problems and the BAP in nonclinical samples. In general, the expression of greater levels of BAP characteristics is related to more global interpersonal problems in the general population (Wainer et al., 2011). With respect to specific kinds of social difficulties, Jobe and White (2007) found that greater levels of subclinical ASD traits were associated with fewer and shorter friendships, higher levels of loneliness, and less motivation to seek out and maintain friendships. Building off this work, a recent study examined the degree to which expression of BAP characteristics influences the quality and experience of friendships (Wainer et al., 2013). This study found individuals who demonstrate more BAP characteristics tend to derive less satisfaction from relationships and engage in behaviors that do not typically promote positive interpersonal interactions; yet these same individuals tend to also experience loneliness and social isolation. Finally, there is some evidence to suggest that the BAP may influence other types of social interactions and relationships, including the quality and satisfaction of romantic relationships (Pollmann, Finkenauer, & Begeer, 2010), particularly among men. Taken together, studies in both ASD family members as well as in nonclinical samples indicate that the expression of BAP characteristics and difficulties with social functioning are closely connected.

Language Abilities

Given that ASD is also characterized by deficits in language and communication skills, many investigators have explored the relationship between the BAP and milder forms of impairment in these areas. An elevated rate of speech and language disorders in parents and siblings of children with ASD was first noted by Bartak and colleagues (1975). Since then, a number of studies have examined the degree to which specific language deficits comprise the BAP. Research that has examined structural language deficits has been somewhat mixed. For example, there is some evidence to suggest that early language problems can be found in siblings and adult relatives of individuals with ASD (e.g., Bolton et al., 1994; Fombonne, Bolton, Prior, Jordan, & Rutter, 1997; Piven, Palmer, Landa, et al., 1997; Toth et al., 2007). Interestingly, although ASD mothers reported high rates of developmental language problems (Piven, Palmer, Jacobi, et al., 1997), they did not perform any worse than control parents on direct measures of language abilities (Piven & Palmer, 1997). Moreover, ASD parents who were categorized as BAP+ reported more histories of early language and literacy problems than those categorized as BAP– parents; yet, the BAP+ parents did not demonstrate worse structural language abilities, such as phonological processing (Bishop et al., 2004). Findings from these studies suggest that reports of early language problems in ASD family members do not necessarily correspond to language problems in the adult expression of the BAP. In further support of this contention, work by Whitehouse and colleagues (2007) found that while parents of children with specific language impairment demonstrated difficulties with structural language skills, there were no differences in such abilities between parents of children with ASD and parents of typically developing children. It is important to note that some research has indeed demonstrated a link between language ability and the BAP in adult family members; in contrast to the work done by Bishop and colleagues (2004), a later study found that parents of children with ASD demonstrated worse phonological processing relative to parents of typically developing children (Schmidt et al., 2008). To date, there has not been any systematic research evaluating structural language abilities in individuals with the BAP in the general population. However, results from the extant literature on ASD family members suggest that although the rate of early language problems may be elevated in this population, it remains unclear as to whether structural language impairments are related to the expression of the BAP.

In contrast to structural language deficits, there appears to more consistent evidence to suggest that the BAP is related to problems with the social use of language, or pragmatics. Pragmatic language includes the supralinguistic aspects of language, such as conversational turn taking and topic maintenance, as well as nonverbal features such as eye contact, gestures, facial expressions, and vocal prosody (Seidman, Yirmiya, Milshtein, Ebstein,

& Levi, 2012). Indeed, a number of studies have found that problems with pragmatic language are more common in both sibling and adult family members of individuals with ASD. Results from informant-based family history studies (e.g., Bolton et al., 1994) and from direct observational assessment (Landa et al., 1992; Piven, Palmer, Landa, et al., 1997; Ruser et al., 2007) support the contention that pragmatic language problems are more common among relatives of autistic probands as compared to relatives of children with Down syndrome (Bolton et al., 1994). Moreover, self-reports of pragmatic language abilities have been found to differentiate BAP+ ASD parents from BAP– ASD parents and from control parents (Hurley et al., 2007). Additionally, parents of children with ASD report increased levels of pragmatic language problems relative to parents of children with specific language impairments (Whitehouse et al., 2007); however, results from direct assessment of pragmatic language abilities have not always replicated these findings (Ruser et al., 2007). While research evaluating pragmatic language abilities and the BAP in nonclinical samples is limited, initial findings suggest a meaningful relationship between the two. A conjoint factor analysis across the BAPQ, AQ, and SRS, three commonly used self-report measures of the BAP, revealed that pragmatic language difficulties is one of three empirically derived dimensions that characterize the BAP in the general population (Wainer et al., 2011). Taken together, this research suggests that problems with pragmatic language are characteristic of, and/or closely related to, the BAP in ASD family members and the general population.

In addition to the language difficulties described here, there is evidence to suggest that early emerging communication difficulties may also be related to the BAP. High-risk sibling studies have suggested the presence of early language delay in approximately 20% of ASD younger siblings (Chuthapisith, Ruangdaraganon, Sombuntham, & Roongpraiwan, 2007; Constantino et al., 2010), as well as lower rates of social communication including the use of gestures and words, pointing to request and/or show objects to others, and responding to social smiling (Toth et al., 2007). Indeed, Ben-Yizhak and colleagues (2011) found that ASD baby siblings of performed worse on items related to semantic-pragmatic language skills on the ADOS (Lord et al., 2002) than did typically developing infants. Moreover, there is evidence to suggest that ASD infant siblings show lower rates of early social communicative behaviors that often precede, and are associated with, language development, such as joint attention (Cassel et al., 2007; Landa & Garrett-Mayer, 2006; Presmanes, Walden, Stone, & Yoder, 2007; Sullivan et al., 2007). ASD infant siblings have been found to be less likely than controls to initiate (Cassel et al., 2007; Landa & Garrett-Mayer, 2006) and respond to joint attention (Presmanes et al., 2007). Although joint attention deficits are associated with language development similarly in high- and low-risk infant siblings (Malesa et al., 2013), by 63 months, high-risk siblings do not show lower scores on standardized language assessments than low-risk siblings (Warren et al., 2012). Importantly, these tests examine structural language use and thus are not optimal for examining pragmatic language. Given data across studies, it appears that the language profile of the BAP may be best characterized as an early delay in joint attention resulting in slightly delayed language acquisition among a proportion of high-risk siblings. This early language delay appears to ameliorate in the preschool years; however, problems with pragmatic language, associated with the BAP, may persist through adulthood.

Restricted, Repetitive Behaviors and Interests

The final domain included in the triad of impairments that characterize ASD is the presence of restricted, repetitive, and stereotyped behaviors and interests. There is some evidence to suggest that difficulties with such behavioral patterns are manifest at lower levels of autistic trait expression as well. ASD infant siblings have been found to engage in more stereotyped and repetitive nonfunctional play relative to low-risk infants (Christensen et al., 2010). ASD parents have

been found to demonstrate increased levels of behavioral rigidity, perfectionism, and stereotyped behaviors (e.g., Losh et al., 2008; Murphy et al., 2000; Piven, Palmer, Jacobi, et al., 1997). Moreover, ASD parents have been shown to display a tendency toward single-mindedness, particularly when related to areas of special interests (Narayan, Moyes, & Wolff, 1990), and to rate themselves higher than controls in a preference for nonsocial activities (e.g., solitary activities) and in strong detail-processing skills/interests (e.g., memory for exact factual information) (Briskman, Happé, & Frith, 2001).

Baron-Cohen and colleagues have proposed that individuals high in autistic traits have a preference for activities that involve systematizing, or the tendency to analyze, understand, predict, control, and construct rule-based systems, and an avoidance of activities that require empathizing, or the ability to identify another person's emotions and thoughts (Baron-Cohen, 2002; Wheelwright et al., 2006). Consistent with this hypothesis, Baron-Cohen and colleagues (1998) have found that ASD parents are more likely to be engaged in highly technical professions where such traits are valued and considered beneficial, such as engineering, physics, and mathematics. Likewise, there is evidence from work in the general population that science and mathematics majors display more subclinical autism traits than do humanities and social science students (Baron-Cohen et al., 1998). Research in nonclinical college student samples has also indicated a relationship between the BAP and particular preferences/interests. For example, students high on the BAP, especially with respect to pragmatic language difficulties, tend to show an elevated interest in activities related to finance, vehicles, and collecting, while those students high on the BAP, especially with respect to aloofness, show a preference for solitary activities (Wainer et al., 2011). These findings suggest that exhibiting BAP-related characteristics may influence interests and preferences, as well as the type of activities that one engages in. Altogether, this literature indicates that the BAP is related to a mild expression of restricted and repetitive behaviors and interests in ASD family members, as well as in nonclinical populations.

Personality Features

Some of the earliest research exploring the construct of the BAP examined the personality profiles related to the expression of subclinical autism characteristics (e.g., Piven, Palmer, Landa, et al., 1997). Since these first studies, a growing body of literature has found that specific personality traits tend to be associated with the BAP in relatives of individuals with ASD, as well as in the general population. Indeed, there is evidence to suggest that adult relatives of children with autism display greater levels of personality traits such as aloofness, shyness, unresponsiveness, suspiciousness, rigidity, hypersensitivity to criticism, impulsiveness, anxiousness, self-consciousness, and eccentricity, relative to parents of children with Down syndrome (Lainhart et al., 2002; Losh et al., 2008; Murphy et al., 2000; Piven, Palmer, Landa, et al., 1997). For example, using direct personality assessment (the M-PAS-R), Piven, Palmer, Landa, et al. (1997) found that parents in multiple incidence autism families were more likely to demonstrate the personality characteristics of aloof, anxious, hypersensitivity to criticism, and rigid. Murphy and colleagues (2000) have suggested that such personality characteristics associated with the BAP in family members cluster into groups of features representing impairments in social functioning (withdrawn or difficult) and anxiety-related characteristics (tense).

More recently, studies have investigated the personality profile of individuals with the BAP in the general population. Specifically, there has been an interest in examining the relationship between the BAP and major personality dimensions such as the five-factor model of personality. Using the AQ as a measure of the BAP in the general population, researchers have found that greater levels of autistic traits are related to lower levels of extraversion and agreeableness and higher levels of neuroticism (Austin, 2005; De Pauw, Mervielde, Van Leeuwen, & De Clercq, 2010; Wakabayashi et al., 2006). Research utilizing a BAP score derived across the

AQ, SRS, and BAPQ has replicated these findings in a college student sample (Wainer et al., 2011). As such, there is evidence to suggest that specific personality characteristics and personality profiles are highly related to the expression of the BAP in clinical and nonclinical populations.

Cognition

Given that cognitive and intellectual impairment is a common condition in individuals with ASD, researchers have examined relationship between general cognitive functioning and the BAP. Some of the earliest research suggested that ASD siblings demonstrated below average cognitive functioning (August, Stewart, & Tsai, 1981; Minton, Campbell, & Green, 1982). Subsequent work did not replicate these early findings (Fombonne et al., 1997; Szatmari et al., 1993), but rather indicated intellectual abilities in the average to high average range in ASD siblings, as well as ASD parents (e.g., Dawson et al., 2007; Freeman et al., 1989; Szatmari et al., 1993). More recent research with younger siblings has also failed to find differences in general cognitive development and functioning between siblings of typically developing children and high-risk ASD siblings (Warren et al., 2012; Yirmiya, Gamliel, Shaked, & Sigman, 2007). Given the limited evidence for an association between the BAP and global intellectual impairment in ASD family members, this link has not be evaluated in the general population. Yet, based on the available literature there does not seem to be a significant relationship between general cognitive ability and the BAP.

Several studies, however, have suggested that more specific cognitive deficits or cognitive profiles are part of expression of the BAP (e.g., Fombonne et al. 1997; Hughes, Leboyer, & Bouvard 1997; Piven & Palmer, 1997). The majority of research in this area has focused on exploring cognitive factors such as weak central coherence, poor social cognition, and impaired executive functioning, all of which have been linked with the etiology of ASD (Best, Moffat, Power, Owens, & Johnstone, 2008). With the exception of some social cognition investigations, the vast majority of this work has been conducted with ASD family members and not yet with nonclinical populations.

Weak Central Coherence

Several investigators have suggested that a tendency to focus on smaller details at a cost to processing more global perspectives, or weak central coherence, may explain the cognitive processing deficits observed in individuals with ASD (Gerdts & Bernier, 2011). As such, there has been interest in examining such a cognitive processing model in individuals who express subclinical autistic traits as well. Importantly, findings from empirical evaluations of this relationship are mixed; a small number of studies have explored central coherence in ASD family members and the majority of findings have supported the tendency toward weak central coherence in ASD parents but not siblings (Briskman et al., 2001; Happé, Briskman, & Frith, 2001). When compared to parents of children with dyslexia and those of typically developing children, ASD parents, particularly fathers, displayed a unique cognitive profile in which detail-focused processing was favored over integrative gestalt processing (Happé et al., 2001). A follow-up study indicated that ASD parents who showed preferences for nonsocial activities also tended to display a detail-focused processing style (Briskman et al., 2001). However, not all studies with ASD parents have replicated these positive findings. For example, Losh and colleagues (2009) found that weak central coherence, as measured by the Embedded Figures task and Block Design, did not consistently differentiate BAP+ from BAP− ASD parents, nor did it distinguish ASD parents from controls. Research exploring the relationship between weak central coherence and subclinical autistic traits in nonclinical samples has demonstrated mixed findings as well. For example, Kunihira and colleges (2006) did not find a relationship between central coherence tendencies and the expression of the BAP in university students. However, Best and colleagues (2008) found that poorer performance on central coherence tasks, such as Block Design, was related to higher levels

of autistic traits on the Social Communication Questionnaire (SCQ; Berument, Rutter, Lord, Pickles, & Bailey, 1999), a parent-report screener for ASD. It is important to note that participants in the Kunihira et al. (2006) study were typically developing, while participants in the Best et al. (2008) study all demonstrated learning difficulties. Thus, it is possible that the relationship observed in the Best et al. (2008) study reflected more broad cognitive difficulties, rather than a specific relationship between subclinical autistic traits and central coherence. Results from the literature summarized earlier, therefore, suggest that the strength of the link between weak central coherence and the expression of the BAP is ambiguous.

Executive Functioning

Difficulties with executive functions, such as planning, organization, and cognitive flexibility, have been linked to ASD (Rajendran & Mitchell, 2007). Yet, empirical findings supporting a relationship between impaired executive functioning and the expression of the BAP are mixed (Sucksmith et al., 2011). Hughes and colleagues (1997) demonstrated that relative to parents of children with learning disabilities and parents of typically developing children, ASD parents tended to experience impaired executive functioning, particularly around planning skills and cognitive flexibility. Similarly, Piven and Palmer (1997) demonstrated that parents from multi-incidence autism families displayed deficits on the Tower of Hanoi task, providing further evidence for poor planning and cognitive flexibility in this population. However, other studies have failed to replicate these positive findings (e.g., Losh et al., 2009; Pilowsky, Yirmiya, Gross-Tsur, & Shalev, 2007; Schmidt et al., 2008). Losh and colleagues (2009) demonstrated that there were no differences in planning, cognitive flexibility, or cognitive control between ASD parents and controls, while Pilowsky and colleagues (2007) did not find differences in cognitive planning and flexibility between ASD siblings, siblings of children with intellectual disability, and siblings of children with a developmental language delay. There is also mixed evidence for the relationship between the

BAP and other executive functions including working memory (e.g., Koczat, Rogers, Pennington, & Ross, 2002; Mosconi et al., 2010; Noland, Reznick, Stone, Walden, & Sheridan, 2010; Wong, Maybery, Bishop, Maley, & Hallmayer, 2006), generativity/fluency (e.g., Delorme et al., 2007; Dichter, Lam, Turner-Brown, Holtzclaw, & Bodfish, 2009; Pilowsky et al., 2007, Wong et al., 2006). Most recently, investigators have evaluated executive functioning skills in high-risk ASD siblings and found that ASD siblings demonstrated poorer performance on high-level executive functioning tasks, particularly with respect to auditory attention, inhibition, and rapid processing, relative to low-risk control siblings (Warren et al., 2012).

There is also mixed evidence with respect to a relationship between executive functioning and the expression of the BAP in the general population. As was the case with the cognitive domains discussed previously, Kunihira and colleagues (2006) failed to find a significant relationship between college student's cognitive flexibility, as measured by the Wisconsin Card Sorting Test, and AQ scores. In contrast, Best and colleagues (2008) found that a greater number of autistic traits in adolescents and young adults with learning disorders was related to difficulties with cognitive flexibility, as measured by the ability to reverse an ambiguous figure. As previously discussed, the observed relationship between autistic traits and several cognitive domains, including executive functioning, in this particular sample may be due a cognitive processing style in those with learning problems, rather than reflective of a BAP-related cognitive profile. Altogether, research exploring the link between executive functioning skills and BAP characteristics is inconclusive, and thus it remains unclear as to whether or not impairments in executive function are specific to, and indicative of, the BAP.

Social Cognition

There is accumulating evidence indicating that deficits in social cognition are common in individuals with autism. Thus, several researchers have explored social cognition as is relates to the expression of the BAP in ASD family members, and more recently in the general population. In particular, much of this research has focused on *theory of mind*, or the ability to process information from another's perspective. In general, research has not revealed differences on theory of mind tasks between ASD younger siblings and siblings of typically developing children (e.g., Shaked, Gamliel, & Yirmiya, 2006). Yet, work with ASD parents has demonstrated a relationship between difficulties with theory of mind and the expression of the BAP in adults (Baron-Cohen & Hammer, 1997; Di Michele, Mazza, Cerbo, Roncone, & Casacchia, 2007). In particular, ASD parents tend to perform poorly on theory of mind tasks such as the Reading the Mind in the Eyes test (Baron-Cohen, Wheelwright, Hill, Raste, & Plumb, 2001) in which they are asked to identify complex psychological states using information from just the eye region of the face. Indeed, performance on the Eyes test was found to differentiate ASD parents classified as BAP+ from those classified as BAP−, as well as from control parents (Losh et al., 2009). The small number of studies that have examined the relationship between theory of mind and the BAP in nonclinical populations have demonstrated mixed results. For example, there was no association between AQ scores and performance on the Eyes test in a sample of Japanese college students (Kunihira et al., 2006). However, Best and colleagues (2008) found that the performance of adolescents and young adults with learning disabilities on another theory of mind task (False Belief Task), predicted the status of parent reports of autistic symptomotology on the SCQ. Again, given that all of these participants had learning difficulties, it is unclear as to whether or not this relationship reflects more general cognitive difficulties or a BAP-specific cognitive characteristic. Yet, quite recently, Miu, Pana, and Avram (2012) demonstrated that high AQ scores in adults from the general population were related to increased latency on the Eyes test, suggesting that higher levels of autistic traits may be associated with decreased efficiency in theory of mind abilities.

Additional social-cognitive skills, such as the ability to process information from faces, has also been explored with respect to the expression of the BAP in family members (Bölte & Poustka, 2003; Palermo, Pasqualetti, Barbati, Intelligente, & Rossini, 2006; Wallace, Sebastian, Pellicano, Parr, & Bailey, 2010). There is evidence to suggest that both parents and siblings of individuals with ASD show poorer performance on basic tests of facial affect recognition, particularly for the emotions of sadness and disgust, relative to control participants (Palermo et al., 2006; Wallace et al., 2010). Moreover, there is also some evidence indicating that facial affect recognition abilities are poorer in parents with multiple children with ASD relative to parents with a single child with ASD (Bölte & Poustka, 2003), which may suggest different modes of genetic transmission of broader autism traits (Sucksmith et al., 2011). Losh and colleagues (2009) demonstrated that ASD parents with the BAP do significantly poorer than ASD parents without the BAP and control parents when asked to make judgments about the emotional content of complex scenes based on facial information. Similar results have been found in nonclinical samples. For example, Ingersoll (2010) found that difficulties identifying emotions from facial expressions were related to more autistic characteristics as measured by the AQ in a college student sample. Moreover, results indicated an inverse relationship between explicit knowledge of social nonverbal cues and the expression of subthreshold symptoms of autism. As such, these bodies of literature suggest that subclinical symptoms of autism in ASD family members and the general population may be related in meaningful ways to deficits in or difficulties with certain aspects of social cognition, particularly reading emotional cues from facial expressions.

There has also been interest in exploring social cue processing and the expression of the BAP. In particular, much of this research has focused on understanding eye gaze processing in relatives of individuals with ASD. Fathers of autistic probands have been found to respond more slowly to the direction of eye gaze on a Posner cuing paradigm than control fathers (Scheeren & Stauder, 2008).

Additionally, adult relatives of individuals with ASD have been shown to be less sensitive to detecting direct eye gaze (as opposed to averted gaze), than nonclinical controls (Wallace et al., 2010). Dalton, Nacewicz, Alexander, and Davidson (2007) found similar patterns in ASD siblings such that they spent less time than controls fixating on the eye region of photos of human faces. As such, there is emerging evidence to suggest that problems orienting toward and processing eye gaze may be other social cognitive difficulties related to the BAP.

Psychiatric Profiles

There is also evidence from ASD family members, as well as from work with nonclinical samples, to suggest that certain psychopathological constructs may highly related to the BAP. Indeed, it has been suggested that some characteristics of the BAP in ASD family members overlap with those of schizoid personality disorder (Wolff et al., 1988). In one such study, Wolff and colleagues (1988) found that parents of autistic probands, particularly fathers, were more likely to demonstrate schizoid traits. Additionally, the expression of autistic and schizophrenic symptoms have been found to overlap on a continuum (Constantino & Todd, 2003; Mason, Claridge, & Jackson, 1995), and there is some evidence to suggest that ASD parents showed an increased rate of schizophrenia relative to controls (Daniels et al., 2008).

Several studies have suggested higher rates of anxiety and affective disorders in ASD family members relative to control groups (Yirmiya & Shaked, 2005). For example, both social phobia and obsessive-compulsive disorder have been found to be higher in relatives of individuals with ASD (e.g., Bolton et al., 1998; Piven & Palmer, 1999; Wilcox, Tsuang, Schnurr, & Baida-Fragoso, 2003). There is support for increased rates of such disorders, particularly OCD, in both first-degree (Bolton et al., 1998) and second-degree (Micali, Chakrabarti, & Fombonne, 2004) relatives of individuals with ASD. Moreover, there is evidence to suggest that parents, especially fathers, of children with autism with higher rates of repetitive behaviors are more likely to demonstrate obsessive-compulsive behaviors or have a diagnosis of OCD (Hollander, King, Delaney, Smith, & Silverman, 2003). Finally, a number of studies have found rates of depression to be higher in relatives of individuals with ASD (e.g., Bolton et al., 1998; Ingersoll et al., 2011; Micali et al., 2004). Importantly, although depression appears to aggregate in families of children with ASD, it does not consistently correlate with the behavioral patterns observed in the BAP (Bolton et al., 1998; Micali et al., 2004; Piven & Palmer, 1999). As such, some researchers have suggested that elevated rates of depression in ASD parents may be a direct result of the stress associated with raising a child with ASD (e.g., Dumas, Wolf, Fisman, & Culligan, 1991; Hastings et al., 2005); however, extensive family history interviews reveal that the majority of ASD parents reported having their first depressive episode before the birth of their child with ASD (Bolton et al., 1998; Micali et al., 2004; Piven & Palmer, 1999). This suggests that increased rates of depression in ASD family members is not due solely to having a child with ASD. Additional research is required in order to better elucidate the relationship between depression and the expression of BAP characteristics in ASD family members.

Recent research has begun to explore whether the relationship between the expression of the BAP and other forms of psychiatric conditions extends to the general population. There is evidence to suggest that the BAP and its facets are associated with social phobia, OCD, depression, schizotypy, and schizoid personality disorder in a college student population (Wainer et al., 2011). Another study found that the expression of autism spectrum traits overlapped with the expression of symptoms schizotypy, particularly in the areas of social/interpersonal functioning and communication/disorganization, in a large undergraduate sample (Hurst, Nelson-Gray, et al., 2007). Such results suggest a potential overlap between the BAP and schizophrenia spectrum characteristics (Russell-Smith, Maybery, & Bayliss, 2011), which is not necessarily surprising given the similarity

in diagnostic criteria for ASD and schizotypy, as well as schizophrenia. The observed relationship between these the BAP and schizophrenia spectrum traits suggests that while these are conceptualized as two distinct phenotypes, additional research in this area is needed in order to better differentiate these two constructs (Sugihara, Tsuchiya, & Takei, 2008).

Neurocognitive Underpinnings

A growing body of research has focused on identifying specific neurofunctional and neuroanatomical profiles that may account for the behavioral abnormalities observed in ASD. As such, there has also been interest in evaluating whether these neurological profiles characterize relatives of autistic probands as well.

fMRI Studies

Many of these studies have utilized fMRI technology to explore neurological activation patterns in ASD relatives. Using fMRI, differences between ASD relatives and control groups have been detected on visual attention tasks; Baron-Cohen and colleagues (2006) found that ASD parents showed less activation in the right middle occipital gyrus and left lingual gyrus, while Belmonte, Gomot, and Baron-Cohen (2010) found atypical cerebellar activity in autistic probands as well as their unaffected brothers. Other studies have used fMRI to explore facial and facial affect processing abilities in ASD relatives. There is evidence to suggest decreased activation in the right hemisphere of the fusiform gyrus, as a result of impaired facial processing, in ASD probands and their siblings, relative to typically developing controls (Dalton et al., 2007). Likewise, ASD siblings have been found to show less activation in the fusiform face area and superior temporal sulcus when responding to emotional facial expressions (Spencer et al., 2011). ASD parents have been shown to demonstrate reduced activation in the mid temporal gyrus and inferior frontal gyrus during the Reading the Mind in the Eyes task (Baron-Cohen et al., 2006). As such, there is some evidence to suggest that ASD family members show decreased activation in areas of the brain related to visual and facial processing.

EEG Studies

Electrophysiological studies using event related potentials (ERP) have also been utilized to explore the neurological underpinnings of the BAP. Elsabbagh and colleagues (2009) found that individuals with ASD, as well as their high-risk siblings, demonstrated slower and less persistent responses in the P-400 component in response to direct eye gaze, relative to controls. Another ERP study found that ASD parents demonstrated a delay in the face-related N170 component when looking at faces, but not at objects (Dawson et al., 2005). These initial investigations suggest that ASD family members may be delayed and less persistent in their neurological responses to social, particularly face-related, stimuli.

Structural MRI Studies

Other studies have utilized structural MRI technology in order to examine the neuroanatomy of ASD relatives. There is accumulating evidence to suggest abnormal growth and volume in gray and white brain matter, particularly in the amygdala, frontal lobes, and temporal lobes, in individuals with ASD (Amaral, Schumann, & Nordahl, 2008; Courchesne et al., 2007; Schumann et al., 2010). Yet, findings from research looking at differences in white and gray matter of ASD family members have been less consistent. There is some evidence to suggest reduced white matter in individuals with ASD and their siblings, relative to controls (Barnea-Goraly, Lotspeich, & Reiss, 2010; Kates et al., 2004). In comparison to controls, ASD siblings have been shown to display decreased amygdala volume (Dalton et al., 2007). Other research has found elevated gray matter in the cerebellum and inferior and medial frontal gyri (Peterson et al., 2006) and increased hippocampal volumes (Rojas et al., 2004) in ASD parents relative to typical controls, while work by Palmen and colleagues (2005) did not reveal any neuroanatomical differences between ASD parents and controls. As such, the extent to which ASD relatives demonstrate neurostructural differences from the general population remains unclear.

Correlational Research

Importantly, the research described here has focused primarily on identifying neurofunctional and neuroanatomical profiles of ASD family members. However, this research typically has not assessed the relationship between these profiles and the expression of autistic traits. Indeed, only a few studies have explored how these neurological characteristics may be related to the actual expression of autistic traits in ASD family members. One such area has focused on the relationship between macrocephaly and BAP traits given the accumulating evidence for the general macrocephaly in individuals with ASD (e.g., Davidovitch, Patterson, & Gartside, 1996). Research has both supported (Fidler, Bailey & Smalley, 2000; Miles, Hadden, Takahashi, & Hillman, 2000) and refuted (Palmen et al., 2005) the presence of macrocephaly in ASD family members. Indeed, Elder, Dawson, Toth, Fein, and Munson (2008) found that those ASD infant siblings who demonstrated a rapid head circumference growth in the first year of life, followed by a slowing of growth in the second year, demonstrated more autistic-like traits. Constantino and colleagues (2010) did not find a similar relationship between rate of head growth and the expression of ASD traits in ASD infant siblings. Thus, within the current literature, it has been difficult to find consistent differences in neuroanatomy and neurofunctioning in ASD family members, as well as to determine how such differences relate, either directly or indirectly, to the expression of the BAP. See Table 2.1.

Summary of Findings and Future Directions

Taken together, the research indicates that the BAP is comprised of a number of characteristics seen in individuals with ASD, but to a lesser extent. There is evidence that individuals who express the BAP show subtle deficits in social functioning. In early development, these deficits are characterized by lower social responsiveness in terms of responding to name, requesting behaviors, social smiling,

TABLE 2.1   Summary of Research Findings on the Broader Autism Phenotype

Domain	Sample	Behaviors (Example references)	Key Findings	Summary and Considerations
Social Behaviors				Evidence for a strong relationship between the BAP and social functioning, particularly in adults
	High-risk ASD infant siblings	Responding to one's name (Nadig et al., 2007)	Increased rates of deficits in early social behaviors in high-risk siblings	Relationship between early social behavioral deficits and expression of BAP is still unclear
		Social smiling (Toth et al., 2007)		
		Requesting behaviors (Cassel et al., 2007; Goldberg et al., 2005)		
		Eye gaze duration and movements (Ibañez et al., 2008; Merin et al., 2007)		
	ASD siblings	Social responsiveness (Constantino et al., 2006, 2010)	Reduced social responsiveness in ASD siblings, especially brothers	
		Social impairments (Bolton et al., 1994)	Increased rates of social impairments	
	ASD parents	Social skills (Wheelwright et al., 2010)	Increased rates of social deficits	
		Social engagement (Whitehouse et al., 2010)	Increased problems with social skills and social engagement	
		Social deficits (Piven, Palmer, Jacobi, et al., 1997)	Decreased interest in social interactions	
		Social relationships (Losh et al., 2008; Piven, Palmer, Landa, et al., 1997)	Fewer and lower quality friendships	
	Nonclinical adults	Interpersonal problems (Wainer et al., 2011)	Greater levels of BAP characteristics associated with more interpersonal problems	
		Friendships (Jobe & White, 2007; Wainer et al., 2013)	Greater levels of BAP characteristics associated with fewer, shorter, and less satisfying friendships	
			Greater levels of BAP characteristics associated with more loneliness and social isolation and less social motivation	
Language Abilities				Evidence for difficulties in early social communication/language development and th BAP
				Evidence for relationship between the BAP and pragmatic language difficulties
				Relationship between the BAP and structural language problems is still ambiguous

	Group	Finding (reference)	Summary
	High-risk ASD infant siblings	Early language delay (Chuthapisith et al., 2007; Constantino et al., 2010)	Early language delay in approximately 20% of ASD younger siblings	Differences between high- and low-risk siblings on structural language abilities not present later in development
		Use of gestures and words (Toth et al. 2007)	Fewer social communicative behaviors including use of gestures and words, pointing to request/show, responding to a social smile, and initiating and responding to joint attention	Later differences between groups on pragmatic language abilities is less clear
		Pointing to request/show (Toth et al., 2007)		
		Joint attention (Cassel et al., 2007; Landa & Garrett-Mayer, 2006; Presmanes et al., 2007; Sullivan et al., 2007)		
		Semantic-pragmatic language abilities (Ben-Yizhak et al., 2011)	Poorer semantic-pragmatic language skills	
	ASD siblings	Speech and language disorders/problems (e.g., Bartak et al., 1975)	Increased reports of early language problems	
		Pragmatic language abilities (Bolton et al., 1994)	Increased reports of pragmatic language problems	
	ASD parents	Speech and language disorders/problems (e.g., Bartak et al., 1975; Piven, Palmer, Jacobi, et al., 1997)	Increased reports early language and literacy problems	Relationship between structural language problems and the BAP in adult relatives is unclear
		Structural language abilities (Bishop et al., 2004; Whitehouse et al., 2007)	Greater BAP traits associated with more reports of early language problems	Strong evidence for experience of pragmatic language difficulties in adult relatives, but relationship between BAP characteristics and expression of pragmatic language problems is less clear
		Pragmatic language abilities (e.g., Hurley et al., 2007; Landa et al., 1992; Whitehouse et al., 2007)	Mixed evidence for structural language deficits (e.g., phonological processing)	
			Increased rates self-reported pragmatic language problems	
			Greater BAP traits associated with more self-reports of pragmatic language problems	
			Mixed evidence for objective pragmatic language problems	
	Nonclinical adults	Pragmatic language abilities (Wainer et al., 2011)	Pragmatic language problems was found to be one of three dimensions characterizing the BAP in a nonclinical sample	Pragmatic language difficulties may be a core feature of the expression of the BAP in the general population
Restricted Repetitive Behaviors and Interests	High-risk ASD infant siblings	Play behaviors and interests (Christensen et al., 2010)	Increased rates of stereotyped and repetitive nonfunctional play	Some evidence to suggest a relationship between the BAP and mild restricted repetitive behaviors and interests

(continued)

TABLE 2.1 (*Continued*)

Domain	Sample	Behaviors (Example references)	Key Findings	Summary and Considerations
	ASD parents	Personality characteristics (Losh et al., 2008; Murphy et al., 2000; Narayan et al., 1990; Piven, Palmer, Landa, et al., 1997)	Increased rates of behavioral rigidity, perfectionism, stereotyped behaviors, and single-mindedness	BAP is related to a mild expression of restricted and repetitive behaviors and interests in ASD parents
		Activity preferences and Interests (Briskman et al., 2001)	Increased preference for nonsocial activities and increased detail-processing skills/interests	
		Career preferences (Baron-Cohen et al., 1998)	More likely to be involved in scientific and mathematical professions	
	Nonclinical adults	Career/study preferences (Baron-Cohen et al., 1998)	Science and mathematics majors display more subclinical autism traits	Evidence that BAP-related characteristics influence interests and preferences in the general population
		Activity preferences and interests (Wainer et al., 2011)	Greater BAP traits associated with elevated interest in finance, vehicles, collecting, and solitary activities	
Personality Features	ASD parents	General personality characteristics (Lainhart et al., 2002; Losh et al., 2008; Murphy et al., 2000; Piven, Palmer, Landa, et al., 1997)	Increased rates of aloofness, anxiousness, shyness, unresponsiveness, suspiciousness, rigidity, hypersensitivity to criticism, impulsiveness, anxiousness, self-consciousness, and eccentricity	
	Nonclinical adults	Five factor model of personality (Austin, 2005; De Pauw et al., 2010; Wainer et al., 2011; Wakabayashi et al., 2006)	Greater levels of BAP characteristics associated with decreased extraversion and agreeableness and increased neuroticism	
Cognitive Functioning Intellectual Functioning	High-risk ASD infant siblings	Early cognitive development (Warren et al., 2012; Yirmiya et al., 2007)	No impairments in general cognitive development or functioning were observed	Limited evidence for a relationship between BAP and global intellectual impairment
	ASD siblings	General intellectual functioning (e.g., August et al., 1981; Fombonne et al., 1997; Minton et al., 1982; Szatmari, et al., 1993)	Early research indicated below average cognitive functioning	
			More recent work has consistently found intellectual abilities in the average to high average range	
	ASD parents	General intellectual functioning (e.g., Dawson et al. 2007; Freeman et al., 1989)	Intellectual abilities within the average range	

46

	Group	Measure (source)	Finding	Summary
Central Coherence	ASD siblings	Central coherence (Briskman et al., 2001; Happé et al., 2001)	No observed tendency toward weak central coherence	Limited evidence for relationship between the BAP and weak central coherence
	ASD parents	Central coherence (Briskman et al., 2001; Happé et al., 2001)	Mixed evidence for tendency toward weak central coherence	
	Nonclinical adults	Central coherence (Kunihira et al., 2006)	No observed tendency toward weak central coherence	
	Adolescents with learning difficulties	Central coherence (Best et al., 2008)	Greater levels of BAP traits associated with weak central coherence	These findings may reflect more broad cognitive difficulties, rather than a specific relationship between autistic traits and central coherence
Executive Functions	High-risk ASD infant siblings	Executive functions (Warren et al., 2012)	Poorer performance on high-level executive functioning tasks	Relationship between executive functioning skills and expression of BAP characteristics is ambiguous
	ASD siblings	Executive functions (Pilowsky et al., 2007)	No observed difficulties in cognitive planning or cognitive flexibility	
	ASD parents	Executive functions (e.g., Hughes et al., 1997; Losh et al., 2009; Piven & Palmer 1997; Schmidt et al., 2008)	Mixed evidence for difficulties with cognitive planning, cognitive flexibility, working memory, and generativity/fluency	
	Nonclinical adults	Executive functions (Kunihira et al., 2006)	No observed relationship between BAP traits and cognitive flexibility	
	Adolescents with learning difficulties	Executive functions (Best et al., 2008)	Greater expression of ASD traits associated with poorer cognitive flexibility	Unclear as to whether these difficulties reflect BAP-specific characteristics or more global cognitive difficulties
Social Cognition	ASD siblings	Theory of mind (Shaked et al., 2006)	No observed impairments in theory of mind	Evidence for different difficulties with social cognition skills depending on the specific population
		Facial affect recognition (Wallace et al., 2010)	Poorer recognition of negative emotions from faces	Evidence for difficulties in facial affect recognition and eye gaze processing, but not theory of mind impairments in ASD siblings
		Eye gaze processing (Dalton et al., 2007)	Less time fixating on the eye region of photos of human faces	
	ASD parents	Theory of mind (Baron-Cohen, Wheelwright, Hill, et al., 2001; Losh et al., 2009)	Increased difficulties with theory of mind; Greater number of BAP traits associated with poorer theory of mind abilities	Evidence for relationship between expression of BAP and difficulties with theory of mind and facial affect recognition

(continued)

TABLE 2.1 (*Continued*)

Domain	Sample	Behaviors (Example references)	Key Findings	Summary and Considerations
		Facial affect recognition (Bölte & Poustka, 2003; Losh et al., 2009; Palermo et al., 2006; Wallace et al., 2010)	Poorer recognition of negative emotions from faces	Evidence for decreased eye gaze sensitivity in ASD parents
		Eye gaze processing (Scheeren & Stauder, 2008; Wallace et al., 2010)	Greater number of ASD traits associated with facial emotion recognition	
			Less sensitive to eye gaze	
	Nonclinical adults	Theory of mind (Kunihira et al., 2006; Miu et al., 2012)	Mixed evidence for difficulties in theory of mind abilities	Evidence for the relationship between the BAP and facial affect recognition difficulties
		Facial affect cognition (Ingersoll, 2010)	Greater expression of ASD traits linked to poorer facial affect recognition	The relationship between the BAP and theory of mind abilities in the general population remains unclear
	Adolescents with learning difficulties	Theory of mind (Best et al., 2008)	Poorer theory of mind abilities associated with greater reports of ASD characteristics	Unclear as to whether these difficulties reflect BAP-specific characteristics or more global cognitive difficulties
				Evidence that more tense and difficult personality profiles are related to the BAP
Psychiatric Profiles	ASD parents	Anxiety disorders (Bolton et al., 1998; Piven & Palmer, 1999; Wilcox et al., 2003)	Increased rate of anxiety disorders (e.g., social phobia, OCD) in ASD relatives	Evidence that certain psychopathological traits and disorders are related to the expression of the BAP
		Affective disorders (Bolton et al., 1998; Ingersoll, Meyer, & Becker, 2011; Micali et al., 2004; Yirmiya & Shaked, 2005)	Increased rate of affective disorders in ASD relatives	Evidence for elevated levels of anxiety disorders in ASD relatives
		Schizoid Personality Disorder (Wolff et al., 1988)	Depression aggregates in ASD families, but does not correlate with behavioral indicators of the BAP	Evidence for overlap between schizophrenia spectrum traits and BAP traits
		Schizophrenia spectrum (Constantino & Todd, 2003; Mason et al., 1995)	Increased levels of schizoid traits in ASD relatives, especially fathers	Relationship between the BAP and depression is still unclear
			Expression of autistic and schizophrenic traits overlap on a continuum	
	Nonclinical adults	Anxiety (Wainer et al., 2011)	Greater expression of BAP characteristics associated with increased levels anxiety, depression, schizoid traits and schizotypy traits	Evidence that the expression of the BAP and other forms of psychopathology extend to the general population
		Depression (Wainer et al., 2011)		
		Schizoid Personality Disorder (Wainer et al., 2011)		

Neurocognitive Underpinnings			
	Schizophrenia spectrum (Hurst, Nelson-Gray, et al., 2007; Wainer et al., 2011)		Evidence for slower and diminished neurological reactions to social stimuli
			Relationship between neurodevelopment, neuroanatomy, and BAP is less clear
High-risk ASD infant siblings	Neurological responses (Elsabbagh et al., 2009)	Slower and less persistent neurological responses to direct eye gaze	
	Neurodevelopment (Constantino et al., 2010; Elder et al., 2008)	Mixed evidence for relationship between atypical neurodevelopmental trajectory and expression of ASD traits	
ASD siblings	Neurological activation patterns (Belmonte et al., 2010; Dalton et al., 2007)	Atypical neurological activation on visual attention tasks	
	Neuroanatomy (Barnea-Goraly, et al., 2010; Dalton et al., 2007; Kates et al., 2004)	Decreased neurological activation on facial processing tasks	
		Reduced white matter	
		Decreased amygdala volume	
ASD parents	Neurological activation patterns (Baron-Cohen et al., 2006)	Reduced neurological activation on facial processing/theory of mind tasks	
	Neurological responses (Dawson et al., 2007)	Delayed neurological responses to social stimuli	
	Neuroanatomy (Palmen et al., 2005; Peterson et al., 2006; Rojas et al., 2004)	Elevated gray matter	
		Increased hippocampal volumes	
		Mixed evidence for the relationship between BAP and macrocephaly	

49

and gaze shifting. In adulthood, difficulties with social functioning are manifest by less desire for close relationships and fewer and lower quality friendships. The BAP is also associated with subtle deficits in language functioning. In young children, these deficits are seen in reduced joint attention and early language delay. In school-aged children and adults, deficits are seen primarily in pragmatic language. While there is less research on restricted and repetitive interests in the BAP, there does appear to be some evidence for repetitive play in infant siblings and special interests in adults, although more research on this aspect of the profile is needed.

Individuals with the BAP also exhibit increased rigidity, and show a personality profile characterized by lower extroversion and agreeableness and higher neuroticism. While previous reports of impaired intellectual functioning have not been supported, there is evidence that individuals with the BAP exhibit subtle deficits in specific cognitive skills. In particular, there seems to be evidence of reduced sensitivity to facial expressions of emotion and decreased ability to attribute mental states to others, while the evidence of deficits in executive functioning and weak central coherence have been less clear. Finally, there is evidence of increased rates of psychiatric disorders in individuals with the BAP, specifically anxiety and depression.

Our understanding of the BAP has been drawn from studies that have employed a variety of measures of the BAP and different methodological designs, and used different populations. The fact that in many cases, the results from these varied approaches have tended to converge is promising; however, there still remain a number of findings that have failed to replicate in the literature. The extent to which these discrepancies are due to the use of different methodological approaches is not yet known. Research that can examine the correspondence between findings at different levels of analysis (e.g., self-report measures, behavioral observations, neurological findings) will be particularly informative in this regard.

Future research is needed regarding the genetic etiology of both the BAP and ASD. Findings from

several studies have indicated that BAP traits are higher in multiplex families (families with two or more children with ASD) than simplex families (families with a single child with ASD) (Szatmari et al., 2000; Virkud, Todd, Abbacchi, Zhang, & Constantino, 2009). These results are suggestive of differential modes of genetic transmission of autistic traits in simplex and multiplex families (e.g., Sucksmith et al., 2011). Additional research with simplex and multiplex families is needed to examine this hypothesis.

The recent development of questionnaires that measure BAP traits dimensionally have provided evidence that BAP traits are continuously distributed and extend beyond family members to individuals in the general population. Preliminary data suggest similar levels of heritability of autistic traits among individuals with ASD and the general population (Ronald & Hoekstra, 2011). However, additional research is needed to determine the extent to which autistic traits in the general population and family members are due to similar genetic processes. If so, population-based studies using measures of the BAP have the potential to dramatically enhance the power to detect candidate genes that may be involved in the expression of ASD.

CROSS-REFERENCES

Chapter 1 focuses on issues of diagnosis, Chapter 3 on epidemiology, and Chapter 17 on genetic aspects of autism and related conditions.

REFERENCES

Amaral, D. G., Schumann, C. M., & Nordahl, C. W. (2008). Neuroanatomy of autism. *Trends in Neurosciences, 31*(3), 137–145.

American Psychiatric Association. (2000). *Diagnostic and statistical manual of mental disorders* (4th ed., text rev.). Washington, DC: Author.

August, G. J., Stewart, M. A., & Tsai, L. (1981). The incidence of cognitive disabilities in the siblings of autistic children. *British Journal of Psychiatry, 138*, 416–422.

Austin, E. J. (2005). Personality correlates of the broader autism phenotype as assessed by the Autism Spectrum Quotient (AQ). *Personality and Individual Differences, 38*(2), 451–460.

Bailey, A., Palferman, S., Heavey, L., & Le Couteur, A. (1998). Autism: The phenotype in relatives. *Journal of Autism and Developmental Disorders, 28*(5), 369–392.

Barnea-Goraly, N., Lotspeich, L. J., & Reiss, A. L. (2010). Similar white matter aberrations in children with autism and their unaffected siblings. *Archives of General Psychiatry, 67*(10), 1052–1060.

Baron-Cohen, S. (2002). The extreme male brain theory of autism. *Trends in Cognitive Science, 6*, 248–254.

Baron-Cohen, S., Bolton, P., Wheelwright, S., Short, L., Mead, G., Smith, A., & Scahill, V. (1998). Autism occurs more often in families of physicists, engineers, and mathematicians. *Autism, 2*, 296–301.

Baron-Cohen, S., & Hammer, J. (1997). Parents of Children with Asperger syndrome: What is the cognitive phenotype? *Journal of Cognitive Neuroscience, 9*(4), 548–554.

Baron-Cohen, S., Ring, H., Chitnis, X., Wheelwright, S., Gregory, L., Williams, S., . . . Bullmore, E. (2006). fMRI of parents of children with Asperger Syndrome: A pilot study. *Brain and Cognition, 61*, 122–130.

Baron-Cohen, S., Wheelwright, S., Hill, J., Raste, Y., & Plumb, I. (2001). The "reading the mind in the eyes" test revised version: A study with normal adults, and adults with Asperger syndrome or high-functioning autism. *Journal of Child Psychology and Psychiatry, 42*(2), 241–251.

Baron-Cohen, S., Wheelwright, S., Skinner, R., Martin, J., & Clubley, E. (2001). The Autism-Spectrum Quotient (AQ): Evidence from Asperger syndrome/high-functioning autism, males and females, scientists and mathematicians. *Journal of Autism and Developmental Disorders, 31*(1), 5–17.

Bartak, L., Rutter, M., & Cox, A. (1975). A comparative study of infantile autism and specific developmental receptive language disorder: I. The children. *British Journal of Psychiatry, 126*, 127–145.

Belmonte, M. K., Gomot, M., & Baron-Cohen, S. (2010). Visual attention in autism families: "Unaffected" sibs share atypical frontal activation. *Journal of Child Psychology and Psychiatry, 51*(3), 259–276.

Ben-Yizhak, N., Yirmiya, N., Seidman, I., Alon, R., Lord, C., & Sigman, M. (2011). Pragmatic language and school related linguistic abilities in siblings of children with autism. *Journal of Autism and Developmental Disorders, 41*, 750–760.

Bernier, R., Gerdts, J., Munson, J., Dawson, G., & Estes, A. (2012). Evidence from broader autism phenotype characteristics in parents from multiple-incidence autism families. *Autism Research, 5*, 13–20.

Berument, S. K., Rutter, M., Lord, C., Pickles, A., & Bailey, A. (1999). Autism screening questionnaire: Diagnostic validity. *The British Journal of Psychiatry, 175*, 444–451.

Best, C. S., Moffat, V. J., Power, M. J., Owens, D. G. C., & Johnstone, E. C. (2008). The boundaries of the cognitive phenotype of autism: Theory of mind, central coherence and ambiguous figure perception in young people with autistic traits. *Journal of Autism and Developmental Disorders, 38*(5), 840–847.

Bettelheim, B. (1967). *The empty fortress: Infantile autism and the birth of the self*. New York, NY: Free Press.

Bishop, D. V. M. (1998). Development of the Children's Communication Checklist (CCC): A method for assessing qualitative aspects of communicative impairment in children. *Journal of Child Psychology Psychiatry, 39*, 879–891.

Bishop, D. V. M. (2003). *The Children's Communication Checklist version 2 (CCC-2)*. London, England: Psychological Corporation.

Bishop, D. V. M., Maybery, M., Wong, D., Maley, A., & Hallmayer, J. (2006). Characteristics of the broader phenotype in autism: A study of siblings using the Children's Communication Checklist-2. *American Journal of Medical Genetics. Part B, Neuropsychiatric Genetics, 141B*, 117–122.

Bishop, D. V. M., Maybery, M., Wong, D., Maley, A., Hill, W., & Hallmayer, J. (2004). Are phonological processing deficits part of the broad autism phenotype? *American Journal of Medical Genetics Part B (Neuropsychiatric Genetics), 128B*, 54–60.

Bölte, S., & Poustka, F. (2003). The recognition of facial affect in autistic and schizophrenic subjects and their first-degree relatives. *Psychological Medicine, 33*, 907–915.

Bolton, P., Macdonald, H., Pickles, A., Rios, P., Goode, S., Crowson, M., . . . Rutter, M. (1994). A case control family history study of autism. *Journal of Child Psychology and Psychiatry, 35*(5), 877–900.

Bolton, P. F., Pickles, A., Murphy, M., & Rutter, M. (1998). Autism, affective and other psychiatric disorders: Patterns of familial aggregation. *Psychological Medicine, 28*, 385–395.

Briskman, J., Happé, F., & Frith, U. (2001). Exploring the cognitive phenotype of autism: Weak "central coherence" in parents and siblings of children with autism: II. Real-life skills and preferences. *Journal of Child Psychology and Psychiatry, 42*(3), 309–316.

Cassel, T. D., Messinger, D. S., Ibañez, L. V., Haltigan, J. D., Acosta, S. I., & Buchman, A. C. (2007). Early social and emotional communication in the infant siblings of children with autism spectrum disorders: an examination of the broad phenotype. *Journal of Autism and Developmental Disorders, 37*, 122–132.

Christensen, L., Hutman, T., Rozga, A., Young, G. S., Ozonoff, S., Rogers, S. J., . . . Sigman, M. (2010). Play and developmental outcomes in infant siblings of children with autism. *Journal of Autism and Developmental Disorders, 40*, 946–957.

Chuthapisith, J., Ruangdaraganon, N., Sombuntham, T., & Roongpraiwan, R. (2007). Language development among the siblings of children with autistic spectrum disorder. *Autism, 11*(2), 149–160.

Constantino, J. N. (2002). *The social responsiveness scale*. Los Angeles, CA: Western Psychological Services.

Constantino, J. N., Lajonchere, C., Lutz, M., Gray, T., Abbacchi, A., McKenna, K., . . . Todd, R. D. (2006). Autistic social impairment in the siblings of children with pervasive developmental disorders. *The American Journal of Psychiatry, 163*, 294–296.

Constantino, J. N., Przybeck, T., Friesen, D., & Todd, R. D. (2000). Reciprocal social behavior in children without pervasive developmental disorders. *Developmental and Behavioral Pediatrics, 21*(1), 2–11.

Constantino, J. N., & Todd, R. D. (2003). Autistic traits in the general population: A twin study. *Archives of General Psychiatry, 60*(5), 524–530.

Constantino, J. N., & Todd, R. D. (2005). Intergenerational transmission of subthreshold autistic traits in the general population. *Biological Psychiatry*, *57*(6), 655–660.

Constantino, J. N., Zhang, Y., Frazier, T., Abbacchi, A. M., & Law, P. (2010). Sibling recurrence and the genetic epidemiology of autism. *American Journal of Psychiatry*, *167*(11), 1349–1356.

Courchesne, E., Pierce, K., Schumann, C. M., Redcay, E., Buckwalter, J. A., Kennedy, D. P., & Morgan, J. (2007). Mapping early brain development in autism. *Neuron*, *56*, 399–413.

Dalton, K. M., Nacewicz, B. M., Alexander, A. L., & Davidson, R. J. (2007). Gaze-fixation, brain activation, and amygdala volume in unaffected siblings of individuals with autism. *Biological Psychiatry*, *61*, 512–520.

Daniels, J. L., Forssen, U., Hultman, C. M., Cnattingius, S., Savitz, D. A., Feychting, M., & Sparen, P. (2008). Parental psychiatric disorders associated with autism spectrum disorders in the offspring. *Pediatrics*, *121*(5), e1357–e1362.

Davidovitch, M., Patterson, B., & Gartside, P. (1996). Head circumference measurements in children with autism. *Journal of Child Neurology*, *11*, 389–393.

Dawson, G., Estes, A., Munson, J., Schellenberg, G., Bernier, R., & Abbott. R. (2007). Quantitative assessment of autism symptom-related traits in probands and parents: Broader phenotype autism symptom scale. *Journal of Autism and Developmental Disorders*, *37*, 523–536.

Dawson, G., Webb, S. J., Wijsman, E., Schellenberg, G., Estes, A., Munson, J., & Faja, S. (2005). Neurocognitive and electrophysiological evidence of altered face processing in parents of children with autism: Implications for a model of abnormal development of social brain circuitry in autism. *Development and Psychopathology*, *17*, 679–697.

De Pauw, S. S. W., Mervielde, I., Van Leeuwen, K. G., & De Clercq, B. J. (2010). How temperament and personality contribute to the maladjustment of children with autism. *Journal of Autism and Developmental Disorders*, *41*(2), 196–212.

Delorme, R., Goussé, V., Roy, I., Trandafir, A., Mathieu, F., Mouren-Siméoni, M. C.,...Leboyer, M. (2007). Shared executive dysfunctions in unaffected relatives of patients with autism and obsessive compulsive disorder. *European Psychiatry*, *22*, 32–38.

Dichter, G. S., Lam, K. S. L., Turner-Brown, L. M., Holtzclaw, T. N., & Bodfish, J. W. (2009). Generativity abilities predict communication deficits but not repetitive behaviors in autism spectrum disorders. *Journal of Autism and Developmental Disorders*, *39*, 1298–1304.

Di Michele, V., Mazza, M., Cerbo, R., Roncone, R., & Casacchia, M. (2007). Deficits in pragmatic conversation as manifestation of genetic liability in autism. *Clinical Neuropsychiatry*, *4*, 144–151.

Dumas, J. E., Wolf, L. C., Fisman, S. N., & Culligan, A. (1991). Parenting stress, child behavior problems, and dysphoria in parents of children with autism, Down syndrome, behavior disorders, and normal development. *Exceptionality*, *2*, 97–110.

Elder, L. M., Dawson, G., Toth, K., Fein, D., & Munson, J. (2008). Head circumference as an early predictor of autism symptoms in younger siblings of children with autism spectrum disorder. *Journal of Autism and Developmental Disorders*, *38*, 1104–1111.

Elsabbagh, M., Volein, A., Csibra, G., Holmboe, K., Garwood, H., Tucker, L.,...Johnson, M. H. (2009). Neural correlates of eye gaze processing in the infant broader autism phenotype. *Biological Psychiatry*, *65*, 31–38.

Fidler, D. J., Bailey, J. N., & Smalley, S. L. (2000). Macrocephaly in autism and other pervasive developmental disorders. *Developmental Medicine and Child Neurology*, *42*(11), 737–740.

Folstein, S., & Rutter, M. (1977). Infantile autism: A genetic study of 21 twin pairs. *Journal of Child Psychology and Psychiatry*, *18*(4), 297–321.

Fombonne, E., Bolton, P., Prior, J., Jordan, H., & Rutter, M. (1997). A family study of autism: Cognitive patterns and levels in parents and siblings. *Journal of Child Psychology and Psychiatry*, *38*, 667–683.

Freeman, B. J., Ritvo, E. R., Mason-Brothers, A., Pingree, C., Yokota, A., Jenson, W. R.,...Schroth, P. (1989). Psychometric assessment of first degree relatives of 62 autistic probands in Utah. *American Journal of Psychiatry*, *146*(3), 361–364.

Gamliel, I., Yirmiya, N., Jaffe, D. H., Manor, O., & Sigman, M. (2009). Developmental trajectories in siblings of children with autism: cognition and language from 4 months to 7 years. *Journal of Autism and Developmental Disorders*, *39*, 1131–1144.

Gerdts, J., & Bernier, R. (2011). The broader autism phenotype and its implications on the etiology and treatment of autism spectrum disorders. *Autism Research and Treatment*, Article ID 545901, 1–19.

Goldberg, W. A., Jarvis, K. L., Osann, K., Laulhere, T. M., Straub, C., Thomas, E.,...Spence, M. A. (2005). Brief report: Early social communication behaviors in the younger siblings of children with autism. *Journal of Autism and Developmental Disorders*, *35*(5), 657–664.

Happé, F., Briskman, J., & Frith, U. (2001). Exploring the cognitive phenotype of autism: Weak "central coherence" in parents and siblings of children with autism: I. Experimental tests. *Journal of Child Psychology and Psychiatry*, *42*, 299–307.

Hastings, R. P., Kovshoff, H., Brown, T., Ward, N. J., Espinosa, F. D., & Remington, B. (2005). Coping strategies in mothers and fathers of preschool and school-age children with autism. *Autism*, *9*, 377–391.

Hoekstra, R. A., Bartels, M., Verweij, C. J. H., & Boomsma, D. I. (2007). Heritability of autistic traits in the general population. *Archives of Pediatrics and Adolescent Medicine*, *161*(4), 372–377.

Hollander, E., King, A., Delaney, K., Smith, C. J., & Silverman, J. M. (2003). Obsessive-compulsive behaviors in parents of multiplex autism families. *Psychiatry Research*, *117*, 11–16.

Hughes, C., Leboyer, M., & Bouvard, M. (1997). Executive function in parents of children with autism. *Psychological Medicine*, *27*, 209–220.

Hurley, R. S. E., Losh, M., Parlier, M., Reznick, J. S., & Piven, J. (2007). The broad autism phenotype questionnaire. *Journal of Autism and Developmental Disorders*, *37*(9), 1679–1690.

Hurst, R. M., Mitchell, J. T., Kimbrel, N. A., Kwapil, T. K., & Nelson-Gray, R. O. (2007). Examination of the reliability and factor structure of the Autism Spectrum Quotient (AQ) in a non-clinical sample. *Personality and Individual Differences*, *43*(7), 1938–1949.

Hurst, R. M., Nelson-Gray, R. O., Mitchell, J. T., & Kwapil, T. R. (2007). The relationship of Asperger's characteristics and schizotypal personality traits in a non-clinical adult sample. *Journal of Autism and Developmental Disorders, 37*(9), 1711–1720.

Ibañez, L. V., Messinger, D. S., Newell, L., Lambert, B., & Sheskin, M. (2008). Visual disengagement in the infant siblings of children with an autism spectrum disorder (ASD). *Autism, 12*(5), 473–485.

Ingersoll, B. (2010). Broader autism phenotype and nonverbal sensitivity: Evidence for an association in the general population. *Journal of Autism and Developmental Disorders, 40,* 590–598.

Ingersoll, B., Hopwood, C. J., Wainer, A., & Donnelan, M. B. (2011). A comparison of three self-report measures of the broader autism phenotype in a non-clinical sample. *Journal of Autism and Developmental Disorders, 41,* 1646–1657.

Ingersoll, B., Meyer, K., & Becker, M. W. (2011). Increased rates of depressed mood in mothers of children with ASD associated with the presence of the broader autism phenotype. *Autism Research, 4,* 143–148.

Iverson, J. M., & Wozniak, R. H. (2007). Variation in vocal-motor development in infant siblings of children with autism. *Journal of Autism and Developmental Disorders, 37,* 158–170.

Jobe, L. E., & White, S. W. (2007). Loneliness, social relationships, and a broader autism phenotype in college students. *Personality and Individual Differences, 42*(8), 1479–1489.

Kanne, S. M., Christ, S. E., & Reiersen, A. M. (2009). Psychiatric symptoms and psychosocial difficulties in young adults with autistic traits. *Journal of Autism and Developmental Disorders, 39*(6), 827–833.

Kanner, L. (1943). Autistic disturbances of affective contact. *Nervous Child, 2,* 217–225.

Kates, W. R., Burnette, C. P., Eliez, S., Strunge, L. A., Kaplan, D., Landa, R., ... Pearison, G. D. (2004). Neuroanatomic variation in monozygotic twin pairs discordant for the narrow phenotype for autism. *American Journal of Psychiatry, 161*(3), 539–546.

Koczat, D. L., Rogers, S. J., Pennington, B. F., & Ross, R. G. (2002). Eye movement abnormality suggestive of a spatial working memory deficit is present in parents of autistic probands. *Journal of Autism and Developmental Disorders, 32,* 513–518.

Kunihira, Y., Senju, A., Dairoku, H., Wakabayashi, A., & Hasegawa, T. (2006). "Autistic" traits in non-autistic Japanese populations: Relationships with personality traits and cognitive ability. *Journal of Autism and Developmental Disorders, 36*(4), 553–566.

Lainhart, J. E., Ozonoff, S., Coon, H., Krasny, L., Dinh, E., Nice, J., & McMahon, W. (2002). Autism, regression, and the broader autism phenotype. *American Journal of Medical Genetics, 113*(3), 231–237.

Landa, R., & Garrett-Mayer, E. (2006). Development in infants with autism spectrum disorders: A prospective study. *Journal of Child Psychology and Psychiatry, 47*(6), 629–638.

Landa, R., Piven, J., Wzorek, M. M., Gayle, J. O., Chase, G. A., & Folstein, S. E. (1992). Social language use in parents of autistic individuals. *Psychological Medicine, 22*(1), 245–254.

Lichtenstein, P., Carlstrom, E., Rastam, M., Gillberg, C., & Anckarsater, H. (2010). The genetics of autism spectrum disorders and related neuropsychiatric disorders in childhood. *American Journal of Psychiatry, 167*(11), 1357–1363.

Lord, C., Rutter, M., DiLavore, P. C., & Risi, S. (2002). *Autism diagnostic observation schedule.* Los Angeles, CA: Western Psychological Services.

Lord, C., Rutter, M., & Le Couteur, A. (1994). Autism Diagnostic Interview—Revised: A revised version of a diagnostic interview for caregivers of individuals with possible pervasive developmental disorders. *Journal of Autism and Developmental Disorders, 24,* 659–685.

Losh M., Adolphs, R., & Piven, J. (2011). The broad autism phenotype. In G. Dawson, D. Amaral, & D. Geschwind (Eds.), *Autism spectrum disorders* (pp. 457–476). Oxford, England: Oxford University Press.

Losh, M., Adolphs, R., Poe, M. D., Couture, S., Penn, D., Baranek, G. T., & Piven, J. (2009). Neuropsychological profile of autism and the broad autism phenotype. *Archives of General Psychiatry, 66*(5), 518–526.

Losh, M., Childress, D., Lam, K., & Piven, J. (2008). Defining key features of the broad autism phenotype: A comparison across parents of multiple- and single-incidence autism families. *American Journal of Medical Genetics. Part B, Neuropsychiatric Genetics, 147B,* 424–433.

Malesa, E., Foss-Feig, J., Yoder, P., Warren, Z., Walden, T., & Stone, W. (2013). Predicting language and social outcomes at age 5 for later-born siblings of children with autism spectrum disorders. *Autism, 17,* 558–570.

Mason, O., Claridge, G., & Jackson, M. (1995). New scales for the assessment of schizotypy. *Personality and Individual Differences, 18,* 7–13.

Merin, N., Young, G. S., Ozonoff, S., & Rogers, S. J. (2007). Visual fixation patterns during reciprocal social interaction distinguish a subgroup of 6-month-old infants at-risk for autism from comparison infants. *Journal of Autism and Developmental Disorders, 37,* 108–121.

Micali, N., Chakrabarti, S., & Fombonne, E. (2004). The broad autism phenotype: Findings from an epidemiological survey. *Autism, 8*(1), 21–37.

Miles, J. H., Hadden, L. L., Takahashi, T. N., & Hillman, R. E. (2000). Head circumference is an independent clinical finding associated with autism. *American Journal of Medical Genetics, 95*(4), 339–350.

Minton, J., Campbell, M., & Green, W. H. (1982). Cognitive assessment of siblings of autistic children. *Journal of the American Academy of Child Psychiatry, 21*(3), 315–321.

Miu, A. C., Pana, S., & Avram, J. (2012). Emotional face processing in neurotypicals with autistic traits: Implications for the broad autism phenotype. *Psychiatry Research.* doi:10.1016/j.psychres.2012.01.024

Mosconi, M. W., Kay, M., D'Cruz, A. M., Guter, S., Kapur, K., Macmillan, C., ... Sweeney, J. A. (2010). Neurobehavioral abnormalities in first-degree relatives of individuals with autism. *Archives of General Psychiatry, 67*(8), 830–840.

Murphy, M., Bolton, P. F., Pickles, A., Fombonne, E., Piven, J., & Rutter, M. (2000). Personality traits of the relatives of autistic probands. *Psychological Medicine, 30*(6), 1411–1424.

Nadig, A. S., Ozonoff, S., Young, G. S., Rozga, A., Sigman, M., & Rogers, S. J. (2007). A prospective study of response to name in infants at risk for autism. *Archives of Pediatrics & Adolescent Medicine, 161*, 378–383.

Narayan, S., Moyes, B., & Wolff, S. (1990). Family characteristics of autistic children—a further report. *Journal of Autism and Developmental Disorders, 20*(4), 523–535.

Noland, J. S., Reznick, J. S., Stone, W. L., Walden, T., & Sheridan, E. H. (2010). Better working memory for non-social targets in infant siblings of children with autism spectrum disorder. *Developmental Science, 13*(1), 244–251.

Palermo, M. T., Pasqualetti, P., Barbati, G., Intelligente, F., & Rossini, P. M. (2006). Recognition of schematic facial displays of emotion in parents of children with autism. *Autism, 10*(4), 353–364.

Palmen, S. J. M. C., Pol, H. E. H., Kemner, C., Schnack, H. G., Sitskoorn, M. M., Appels, M. C. M., . . . Van Engeland, H. (2005). Brain anatomy in non-affected parents of autistic probands a MRI study. *Psychological Medicine, 35*, 1411–1420.

Peterson, E., Schmidt, G. L., Tregellas, J. R., Winterrowd, E., Kopelioff, L., Hepburn, S., . . . Rojas, D. C. (2006). A voxel-based morphometry study of gray matter in parents of children with autism. *NeuroReport, 17*(12), 1289–1292.

Pilowsky, T., Yirmiya, N., Gross-Tsur, V., & Shalev, R. S. (2007). Neuropsychological functioning of siblings of children with autism, siblings of children with developmental language delay, and siblings of children with mental retardation of unknown genetic etiology. *Journal of Autism and Developmental Disorders, 37*, 537–552.

Piven, J., & Palmer, P. (1997). Cognitive deficits in parents from multiple-incidence autism families. *Journal of Child Psychology and Psychiatry, 38*(8), 1011–1021.

Piven, J., & Palmer, P. (1999). Psychiatric disorder and the broad autism phenotype: evidence from a family study of multiple incidence autism families. *American Journal of Psychiatry, 156*(4), 557–563.

Piven, J., Palmer, P., Jacobi, D., Childress, D., & Arndt, S. (1997). Broader autism phenotype: Evidence from a family history study of multiple-incidence autism families. *American Journal of Psychiatry, 154*, 185–190.

Piven, J., Palmer, P., Landa, R., Santangelo, S., Jacobi, D., & Childress, D. (1997). Personality and language characteristics in parents from multiple-incidence autism families. *American Journal of Medical Genetics, 74*(4), 398–411.

Piven, J., Wzorek, M., Landa, R., Lainhart, J., Bolton, P., Chase, G., & Folstein, S. (1994). Personality characteristics of the parents of autistic individuals. *Psychological Medicine, 24*, 783–795.

Pollmann, M. M. H., Finkenauer, C., & Begeer, S. (2010). Mediators of the link between autistic traits and relationship satisfaction in a non-clinical sample. *Journal of Autism and Developmental Disorders, 40*(4), 470–478.

Presmanes, A. G., Walden, T. A., Stone, W. L., & Yoder, P. J. (2007). Effects of different attentional cues on responding to joint attention in younger siblings of children with autism spectrum disorders. *Journal of Autism and Developmental Disorders, 37*, 133–144.

Rajendran, G., & Mitchell, P. (2007). Cognitive theories of autism. *Developmental Review, 27*(2), 224–260.

Rogers, S. J. (2009). What are infant siblings teaching us about autism in infancy? *Autism Research, 2*, 125–137.

Rojas, D. C., Smith, J. A., Benkers, T. L., Camou, S. L., Reite, M. L., & Rogers, S. J. (2004). Hippocampus and amygdala volumes in parents of children with autistic disorder. *The American Journal of Psychiatry, 161*(11), 2038–2044.

Ronald, A., Happé, F., Bolton, P., Butcher, L. M., Price, T. S., Wheelwright, S., Baron-Cohen, S., & Plomin, R. (2006). Genetic heterogeneity between the three components of the autism spectrum: A twin study. *Journal of the American Academy of Child & Adolescent Psychiatry, 45*, 691–699.

Ronald, A., & Hoekstra, R. A. (2011). Autism spectrum disorders and autistic traits: A decade of new twin studies. *American Journal of Medical Genetics Part B, 156*, 255–274.

Ronald, A., Happé, F., & Plomin, R. (2008). A twin study investigating the genetic and environmental aetiologies of parent, teacher and child ratings of autistic-like traits and their overlap. *European Child and Adolescent Psychiatry, 17*, 473–483.

Rosenberg, R. E., Law, J. K., Yenokyan, G., McGready, J., Kaufmann, W. E., Law, P. A. (2009). Characteristics and concordance of autism spectrum disorders among 277 twin pairs. *Archives of Pediatrics & Adolescent Medicine, 163*, 907–914.

Ruser, T. F., Arin, D., Dowd, M., Putnam, S., Winklosky, B., Rosen-Sheidley, B., . . . Folstein, S. (2007). Communicative competence in parents of children with autism and parents of children with specific language impairment. *Journal of Autism and Developmental Disorders, 37*(7), 1323–1336.

Russell-Smith, S. N., Maybery, M. T., & Bayliss, D. M. (2011). Relationships between autistic-like and schizotypy traits: An analysis using the autism spectrum quotient and Oxford-Liverpool inventory of feelings and experiences. *Personality and Individual Differences, 51*, 128–132.

Santangelo, S. L., & Folstein, S. E. (1995). Social deficits in the families of autistic probands. *American Journal of Human Genetics, 57*(4), supplement 89.

Scheeren, A. M., & Stauder, J. E. A. (2008). Broader autism phenotype in parents of autistic children: reality or myth? *Journal of Autism and Developmental Disorders, 28*, 276–287.

Schmidt, G. L., Kimel, L. K., Winterrowd, E., Pennington, B. F., Hepburn, S. L., & Rojas, D. C. (2008). Impairments in phonological processing and nonverbal intellectual function in parents of children with autism. *Journal of Clinical and Experimental Neuropsychology, 30*(5), 557–567.

Schumann, C. M., Bloss, C. S., Barnes, C. C., Wideman, G. M., Carper, R. A., Akshoomoff, N., . . . Courchesne, E. (2010). Longitudinal magnetic resonance imaging study of cortical development through early childhood in autism. *Journal of Neuroscience, 30*(12), 4419–4427.

Scott, F. J., Baron-Cohen, S., Bolton, P., & Brayne, C. (2002). The CAST (childhood Asperger syndrome test): Preliminary development of a UK screen for mainstream primary-school age children. *Autism, 6*, 9–31.

Seidman, I., Yirmiya, N., Milshtein, S., Ebstein, R. P., & Levi, S. (2012). The broad autism phenotype questionnaire: Mothers versus fathers of children with an autism spectrum disorder. *Journal of Autism and Developmental Disorders*, 42(5), 837–846.

Shaked, M., Gamliel, I., & Yirmiya, N. (2006). Theory of mind abilities in young siblings of children with autism. *Autism*, 10(2), 173–187.

Skuse, D. H., Mandy, W. P. L., & Scourfield, J. (2005). Measuring autistic traits: Heritability, reliability and validity of the social and communication disorders checklist. *The British Journal of Psychiatry*, 187, 568–572.

Spencer, M. D., Holt, R. J., Chura, L. R., Suckling, J., Calder, A. J., Bullmore, E. T., & Baron-Cohen, S. (2011). A novel functional brain imaging endophenotype of autism: The neural response to facial expression of emotion. *Translational Psychiatry*, 1, e19.

Stewart, M. E., & Austin, E. J. (2009). The structure of the Autism-Spectrum Quotient (AQ): Evidence from a student sample in Scotland. *Personality and Individual Differences*, 47(3), 224–228.

Stone, W. L., McMahon, C. R., Yoder, P. J., & Walden, T. A. (2007). Early social-communicative and cognitive development of younger siblings of children with autism spectrum disorders. *Archives of Pediatrics & Adolescent Medicine*, 161(4), 384–390.

Sucksmith, E., Roth, I., & Hoekstra, R. A. (2011). Autistic traits below the clinical threshold: Re-examining the broader autism phenotype in the 21st century. *Neuropsychological Review*, 21, 360–389.

Sugihara, G., Tsuchiya, K. J., & Takei, N. (2008). Distinguishing broad autism phenotype from schizophrenia-spectrum disorders. *Journal of Autism and Developmental Disorders*, 38, 1998–1999.

Sullivan, M., Finelli, J., Marvin, A., Garrett-Mayer, E., Bauman, M., & Landa, R. (2007). Response to joint attention in toddlers at risk for autism spectrum disorder a prospective study. *Journal of Autism and Developmental Disorders*, 37, 37–48.

Sung, Y., Dawson, G., Munson, J., Estes, A., Schellenberg, G. D., & Wijsman, E. M. (2005). Genetic investigation of quantitative traits related to autism: use of multivariate polygenic models with ascertainment adjustment. *American Journal of Human Genetics*, 76, 68–81.

Szatmari, P., Jones, M. B., Tuff, L., Bartolucci, G., Fisman, S., & Mahoney, W. (1993). Lack of cognitive impairment in first degree relatives of pervasive developmental disorder probands. *Journal of the American Academy of Child & Adolescent Psychiatry*, 32, 1264–1273.

Szatmari, P., MacLean, J. E., Jones, M. B., Bryson, S. E., Zwaigenbaum, L., Bartolucci, G., . . . Tuff, L. (2000). The familial aggregation of the lesser variant in biological and non-biological relatives of PDD probands a family history study. *Journal of Child Psychology and Psychiatry*, 41, 579–586.

Toth, K., Dawson, G., Meltzoff, A. N., Greenson, J., & Fein, D. (2007). Early social, imitation, play, and language abilities of young non-autistic siblings of children with autism. *Journal of Autism and Developmental Disorders*, 37, 145–157.

Tyrer, P. (1988). Personality assessment schedule. In PDDMa (Ed.), *Course*. London, England: Butterworth and Company.

Virkud, Y. V., Todd, R. D., Abbacchi, A., Zhang, Y., & Constantino, J. N. (2009). Familial aggregation of quantitative autistic traits in multiplex versus simplex autism. *American Journal of Medical Genetics. Part B, Neuropsychiatric Genetics*, 150B, 328–334.

Wainer, A. L., Block, N., Donnellan, M. B., & Ingersoll, B. (2013). The broader autism phenotype and friendships in non-clinical dyads. *Journal of Autism and Developmental Disorders*, 43, 2418–2425.

Wainer, A. L., Ingersoll, B. R., & Hopwood, C. J. (2011). The structure and nature of the broader autism phenotype in a non-clinical sample. *Journal of Psychopathology and Behavioral Assessment*, 33(4), 1646–1657.

Wakabayashi, A., Baron-Cohen, S., & Wheelwright, S. (2006). Are autistic traits an independent personality dimension? A study of the Autism-Spectrum Quotient (AQ) and the NEO-PI-R. *Personality and Individual Differences*, 41(5), 873–883.

Wallace, S., Sebastian, C., Pellicano, E., Parr, J., & Bailey, A. (2010). Face processing abilities in relatives of individuals with ASD. *Autism Research*, 3(6), 345–349.

Warren, Z. E., Foss-Feig, J. H., Malesa, E. E., Less, E. B., Taylora, J. L., Newsom, C. R., . . . Stone, W. L. (2012). Neurocognitive and behavioral outcomes of younger siblings of children with autism spectrum disorder at age five. *Journal of Autism and Developmental Disorders*, 42, 409–418.

Wheelwright, S., Auyeung, B., Allison, C., & Baron-Cohen, S. (2010). Defining the broader, medium and narrow autism phenotype among parents using the Autism Spectrum Quotient (AQ). *Molecular Autism*, 1, 1–10.

Wheelwright, S., Baron-Cohen, S., Goldenfeld, N., Delaney, J., Fine, D., Smith, R., . . . Wakabayashi, A. (2006). Predicting autism spectrum quotient (AQ) from the systemizing quotient-revised (SQ-R) and empathy quotient (EQ). *Brain Research*, 1079(1), 47–56.

Whitehouse, A. J. O., Barry, J. G., & Bishop, D. V. M. (2007). The broader language phenotype of autism: A comparison with specific language impairment. *Journal of Child Psychology and Psychiatry*, 48(8), 822–830.

Whitehouse, A. J. O., & Bishop, D. V. M. (2009). *The Children's Communication Checklist—Adult Version (CC-A)*. London, England: Pearson.

Whitehouse, A. J. O., Coon, H., Miller, J., Salisbury, B., & Bishop, D. V. M. (2010). Narrowing the broader autism phenotype: A study using the Communication Checklist—Adult Version (CC-A). *Autism*, 14(6), 559–574.

Wilcox, J. A., Tsuang, M. T., Schnurr, T., & Baida-Fragoso, N. (2003). Case–control family study of lesser variant traits in autism. *Neuropsychobiology*, 47(4), 171–177.

Wolff, S., Narayan, S., & Moyes, B. (1988). Personality characteristics of parents of autistic children: A controlled study. *Journal of Child Psychology and Psychiatry*, 29(2), 143–153.

Wong, D., Maybery, M., Bishop, D. V. M., Maley, A., & Hallmayer, J. (2006). Profiles of executive function in parents and siblings of individuals with autism spectrum disorders. *Genes, Brain, and Behavior*, 5, 561–576.

Woodbury-Smith, M. R., Robinson, J., Wheelwright, S., & Baron-Cohen. S. (2005). Screening adults for Asperger syndrome using the AQ: A preliminary study of its diagnostic validity in clinical practice. *Journal of Autism and Developmental Disorders, 35*, 331–335.

Yirmiya, N., Gamliel, I., Shaked, M., & Sigman, M. (2007). Cognitive and verbal abilities of 24- to 36-month-old siblings of children with autism. *Journal of Autism and Developmental Disorders, 37*, 218–229.

Yirmiya, N., & Shaked, M. (2005). Psychiatric disorders in parents of children with autism: A meta-analysis. *Journal of Child Psychology and Psychiatry, 46*(1), 69–83.

CHAPTER 3

Epidemiology of Autism Spectrum Disorders

ALISON PRESMANES HILL, KATHARINE E. ZUCKERMAN,
AND ERIC FOMBONNE

INTRODUCTION

Epidemiological surveys of autism were first initiated in the mid-1960s in England (Lotter, 1966, 1967) and have since been conducted in over 20 countries. In this chapter, we provide a comprehensive review of the findings and methodological features of published epidemiological surveys concerned with the prevalence of autism spectrum disorders (ASDs[1]) since 1966. This chapter builds upon previous reviews (Elsabbagh et al., 2012; Fombonne, 2003a, 2003b, 2005, 2009a; Fombonne, Quirke, & Hagen, 2011; French, Bertone,

Hyde, & Fombonne, 2013; J. G. Williams, Brayne, & Higgins, 2006) and includes the results of pertinent studies since published. The specific questions addressed in this chapter are as follows: (1) What is the range of prevalence estimates for autism and related ASDs? (2) How should the time trends observed in the current prevalence rates of ASDs be interpreted? and (3) What are the correlates of ASDs in epidemiological surveys?

Systematic Review Methodology

Search Strategies

Epidemiological reports included in Tables 3.1 through 3.4 in this chapter were identified from previous reviews of epidemiological surveys

[1]Autism spectrum disorder (ASD) is the modern term that replaces the former pervasive developmental delay (PDD).

(Elsabbagh et al., 2012; Fombonne, 2003a, 2003b, 2005, 2009a; Fombonne et al., 2011; French et al., 2013; J. G. Williams et al., 2006) and through systematic searches using major scientific literature databases (Medline, PsycINFO, Embase, PubMed). Where multiple surveys based on the same or overlapping populations were evident, the publication listed in the tables is the most detailed and comprehensive account. For example, surveys conducted by the U.S. Centers for Disease Control (CDC; 2007a, 2007b, 2009, 2012) as part of the Autism and Developmental Disabilities Monitoring (ADDM) Network are each included in Table 3.4, although additional accounts for individual states are available elsewhere (e.g., Nicholas et al., 2008; Pinborough-Zimmerman et al., 2012; Rice et al., 2010; Zahorodny et al., 2012).

Inclusion and Exclusion Criteria

The following criteria were set a priori to select epidemiological surveys included in Tables 3.1 through 3.4:

- The full article was published in English. Several studies published in other languages (e.g., from China) are also available for consideration and have been reviewed elsewhere (for a recent review, see Elsabbagh et al., 2012).
- The minimum population was 5,000; studies involving smaller populations were excluded. Emerging evidence from smaller studies around the world is largely consistent with the findings discussed here; the interested reader is encouraged to review studies conducted in Brazil: Paula, Ribeiro, Fombonne, and Mercadante (2011); in Sweden: Arvidsson et al. (1997), Kadesjo, Gillberg, and Hagberg (1999), Gillberg, Steffenburg, Börjesson, and Andersson (1987), Gillberg, Schaumann, and Gillberg (1995); in the UK: Tebruegge, Nandini, and Ritchie (2004); and elsewhere for more information.
- The survey included independent validation of caseness by professionals. Studies that relied on questionnaire-based approaches (e.g., Ghanizadeh, 2008) or on parental report (e.g., Blumberg et al., 2013) for ASD diagnosis are not presented in tables, but are referenced in text where relevant. In addition, surveys that imposed further non-ASD criteria were excluded (e.g., presence of additional disability: N. Li, Chen, Song, Du, & Zheng, 2011; singleton births: Grether, Anderson, Croen, Smith, & Windham, 2009; Leonard et al., 2011).
- The following information categories were included or could be ascertained based on information from the survey: the country and area where the survey was conducted, the size of the population base on which the prevalence estimate was ascertained, the age range of the participants, the number of children affected, the diagnostic criteria used in case definition, and the prevalence estimate (number per 10,000). Where available, we also report the proportion of subjects with IQ within the normal range and gender ratios.

Overall, 81 studies published between 1966 and early 2013 met criteria and were selected. Of these, 54 studies provided information on rates specific to autistic disorder (AD), 18 studies on Asperger's disorder (later referred to as Asperger's syndrome; AS), and 13 studies on childhood disintegrative disorder (CDD). A total of 48 studies provided estimates on ASDs combined, of which 24 also provided rates for specific ASD subtypes (14 provided rates for both AD and AS; 10 provided rates for AD but not AS). Surveys were conducted in 23 different countries (including 17 in the United Kingdom, 16 in the United States, and 7 in Japan). The results of over half of the studies ($n = 55$) were published after 2000, with most studies relying on school-aged samples. Finally, a very large variation in the size of the population surveyed was evidenced (range: 5,007 to 4.3 million; median: 50,210; mean: 275,300), with some recent studies conducted by the CDC relying on samples of several hundreds of thousands of individuals.

Study Design and Methodological Issues

Epidemiology is concerned with the study of the repartition of diseases in human population and of the factors that influence it. Epidemiologists use several measures of disease occurrence. Incidence rate refers to the number of new cases (numerator) of a disease occurring over a specified period in those at risk of developing the disease in the population (denominator, in person × years). Cumulative incidence is the proportion of those who were free of the disease at the beginning of the observation period and developed the disease during that period. Measures of incidence are required to properly estimate several variables such as morbidity due to a disease, possible changes over time, and the risk factors underlying disease status. Prevalence is a measure used in cross-sectional surveys (in which there is no passage of time) and reflects the proportion of subjects in a given population who, at that point in time, suffer from the disease. To date, most epidemiological studies of ASDs have been cross-sectional, reflecting the complications involved in conducting a survey when the timing of diagnosis lags behind onset of symptoms and is likely to be influenced by a range of factors potentially unrelated to risk (discussed further in "Correlates of ASDs"). As a result, the most commonly reported measures of ASD population frequency have been prevalence rates (point prevalence or period prevalence), with a few recent exceptions (e.g., Campbell, Reynolds, Cunningham, Minnis, & Gillberg, 2011; Hertz-Picciotto & Delwiche, 2009; Manning et al., 2011; van der Ven et al., 2012). In designing a prevalence study, three major features are critical for the planning and logistics of the study as well as for the interpretation of its results: case definition, case identification (or case ascertainment), and case evaluation methods (Fombonne, 2007).

Case Definition

Over time, the definition of autism has changed, as illustrated by the numerous diagnostic criteria that were used in both epidemiological and clinical settings (see Table 3.1). Starting with the narrowly defined Kanner's autism (1943), definitions progressively broadened in the criteria from that proposed by Rutter (1970), and subsequent International Classification of Diseases, ninth revision

(*ICD-9*; World Health Organization [WHO], 1977); *Diagnostic and Statistical Manual of Mental Disorders*, third edition (*DSM-III*; American Psychiatric Association [APA], 1980); and *DSM-III-R* (APA, 1987), and more recently in the two more major nosographies used worldwide; *ICD-10* (WHO, 1992) and *DSM-IV* (APA, 1994). The earliest diagnostic criteria reflected the more qualitatively severe forms of autism's behavioral phenotype, usually associated with severe delays in language and cognitive skills. It was only in the 1980s that less severe forms of autism were recognized, either as a qualifier for autism occurring without intellectual disability (i.e., high-functioning autism), or as separate diagnostic categories (Pervasive Developmental Disorders Not Otherwise Specified [PDD-NOS] or Autism Spectrum Disorders [ASD]) within a broader class of autism spectrum disorders denominated "pervasive developmental disorders" (PDDs, an equivalent to ASDs) in current nosographies. Although Asperger had described it in the literature as early as 1944, Asperger's disorder only appeared in official nosographies in the 1990s, with unclear validity, particularly with respect to its differentiation from high-functioning autism. Other ASD subtypes that were described in *DSM-III* subsequently disappeared (e.g., Autism–Residual State).

While there is generally high interrater reliability regarding diagnosis of ASDs and commonality of concepts across experts, some differences still persist between nomenclatures about the terminology and operationalized criteria of ASDs. For example, *DSM-IV* (APA, 1994) has a broad category of PDD-NOS, sometimes referred to loosely as "atypical autism," whereas *ICD-10* (WHO, 1992) has several corresponding diagnoses for clinical presentations that do not allow an autistic disorder diagnosis and include Atypical Autism (F84.1, a diagnostic category that existed already in *ICD-9*), Other PDD (F84.8), and PDD—Unspecified (F84.9). As a result, studies that refer to "atypical autism" must be carefully interpreted, and equivalence with the *DSM-IV* concept of PDD-NOS should not be assumed. As no diagnostic criteria are available for these milder forms of the autism phenotype, the resulting boundaries of the spectrum of ASDs are left uncertain. Whether or not this plays a role in more recent epidemiological studies is difficult to ascertain, but the possibility should be considered in assessing results for subsequent epidemiological surveys.

Case Identification/Ascertainment

When an area or population has been identified for a survey, different strategies have been employed to find individuals matching the case definition retained for the study. Some studies have relied solely on existing service providers databases (Chien, Lin, Chou, & Chou, 2011; Croen, Grether, Hoogstrate, & Selvin, 2002; Davidovitch, Hemo, Manning-Courtney, & Fombonne, 2012), on special educational databases (Fombonne, Zakarian, Bennett, Meng, & McLean-Heywood, 2006; Gurney et al., 2003; Lazoff, Zhong, Piperni, & Fombonne, 2010; Maenner & Durkin, 2010), or on national registers (Al-Farsi et al., 2011; Parner et al., 2012; Samadi, Mahmoodizadeh, & McConkey, 2011) for case identification. These studies have the common limitation of relying on a population group that was readily accessible to the service provider or agencies, rather than sampling from the population at large. As a result, individuals with the disorder who are not in contact with these services are not included as cases, leading to an underestimation of the prevalence proportion. This is a particularly important issue when estimating prevalence using such methods in communities with recognized limitations in available services.

Other investigations have relied on a multistage approach to identify cases in underlying populations (e.g., CDC, 2012; Idring et al., 2012; Kim et al., 2011). The aim of the first screening stage of these studies is to cast a wide net in order to identify subjects possibly affected with an ASD, with the final diagnostic status being determined at subsequent stages. This process often consists of sending letters or brief screening scales requesting school and health professionals and/or other data sources to identify possible cases of autism. Few of these investigations rely on systematic sampling techniques that would ensure a near complete coverage of the target population. Moreover, such investigations differ in several key aspects with regard to the initial screening stage. First, the thoroughness of the coverage of all relevant data sources vary enormously from one study to another. In addition, the surveyed areas are not comparable in terms of service development, reflecting the specific educational or health care systems of each country and of the period of investigation. Second, the inclusion information sent out to professionals invited to identify children varies from a few clinical descriptors of autism-related symptoms or diagnostic checklists rephrased in nontechnical terms, to more systematic screening strategies based on questionnaires or rating scales of known reliability and validity. Third, uneven participation rates in the first screening stages provide another source of variation in the screening efficiency of surveys, although refusal rates tend, on average, to be very low.

To illustrate the effects of differential participation rates in the first screening stage, two hypothetical scenarios are illustrated in Figure 3.1, both of which are based on a true ASD prevalence of 150/10,000 and a sensitivity of 100% for the screening process and total accuracy in the diagnostic confirmation. In Scenario A, we assume a 60% participation rate for ASD and non-ASD cases in the first screening stage, resulting in a total of 90 participating ASD cases that screen positive. With a 70% participation rate for both ASD and non-ASD cases in the final diagnostic stage, we would identify and confirm a total of 63 ASD cases in the second phase. Weighting back phase 2 data, we would obtain an unbiased prevalence estimate of 1.5% (or 150/10,000) in this scenario. In Scenario B, we equally assume an average 60% participation rate, but with a higher 80% participation rate for ASD cases, reflecting a scenario in which individuals with ASD are more likely to participate in the first screening stage than non-ASD cases. Thus, with the same average participation rates in the first screening (60%) and the final diagnostic stages (70%), we identify and confirm a total of 84 ASD cases and calculate a biased prevalence estimate of 2% (200/10,000), an estimate that is 0.5% higher

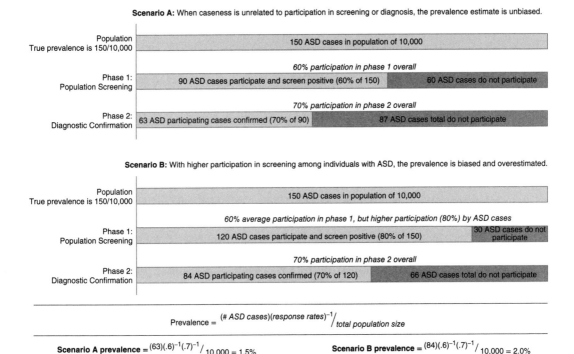

Scenario A: When caseness is unrelated to participation in screening or diagnosis, the prevalence estimate is unbiased.

Population
True prevalence is 150/10,000

150 ASD cases in population of 10,000

60% participation in phase 1 overall

Phase 1:
Population Screening

90 ASD cases participate and screen positive (60% of 150) | 60 ASD cases do not participate

70% participation in phase 2 overall

Phase 2:
Diagnostic Confirmation

63 ASD participating cases confirmed (70% of 90) | 87 ASD cases total do not participate

Scenario B: With higher participation in screening among individuals with ASD, the prevalence is biased and overestimated.

Population
True prevalence is 150/10,000

150 ASD cases in population of 10,000

60% average participation in phase 1, but higher participation (80%) by ASD cases

Phase 1:
Population Screening

120 ASD cases participate and screen positive (80% of 150) | 30 ASD cases do not participate

70% participation in phase 2 overall

Phase 2:
Diagnostic Confirmation

84 ASD participating cases confirmed (70% of 120) | 66 ASD cases total do not participate

$$\text{Prevalence} = \frac{(\# \, ASD \, cases)(response \, rates)^{-1}}{total \, population \, size}$$

Scenario A prevalence $= \frac{(63)(.6)^{-1}(.7)^{-1}}{10,000} = 1.5\%$ **Scenario B prevalence** $= \frac{(84)(.6)^{-1}(.7)^{-1}}{10,000} = 2.0\%$

Figure 3.1   Impact of differential participation rates in screening on ASD prevalence estimates: Two hypothetical scenarios.

than the true prevalence. The bias arises for two reasons: (1) participation in screening is associated with case status (here, with ASD cases more likely to participate than non-cases); and (2) as investigators typically have no such information, weights used for prevalence estimation were not adjusted correspondingly, resulting in the upward bias in the estimate.

Another possible scenario (not illustrated) is one in which individuals with ASD are less likely to participate than noncases, leading to underestimation of prevalence. For example, Posserud, Lundervold, Lie, and Gillberg (2010) reported an ASD prevalence of 72/10,000 in their identified sample and estimated a prevalence of 128/10,000 in nonresponders (based on teacher ratings during the screening phase), indicating increased refusal rates among those with more ASD symptoms. On the other hand, Webb et al. (2003) reported increased refusal rates among individuals with fewer ASD symptoms. Unfortunately, few studies have been able to estimate the extent to which willingness

or refusal to participate is associated with final caseness, so it is not known what effect differential participation rates at different phases in population surveys may have on estimates of prevalence.

The sensitivity of the screening methodology is also difficult to gauge in autism surveys, as the proportion of children truly affected with the disorder but not identified in the screening stage (the false negatives) remains generally unmeasured. Few studies provided an estimate of the reliability of the screening procedure. The usual approach, which consists of randomly sampling screened negative subjects in order to estimate the proportion of false negatives and adjusting the estimate accordingly, has not been used in these surveys. The main reason is that due to the relatively low frequency of the disorder, it would be both imprecise and very costly to undertake such estimations. This may gradually change in view of recent prevalence studies suggesting that autism can no longer be regarded as a rare condition. However, prevalence estimates must be understood as underestimates of "true" prevalence rates, with the magnitude of this underestimation unknown in each survey.

To provide a concrete illustration of this, the surveys conducted by the CDC in the United States (2007a, 2007b, 2009, 2012) rely, for case ascertainment, on scrutinizing educational and medical records. Children not accessing such services cannot be identified. Although some recent surveys that systematically screen the normal school population might detect a large pool of unidentified cases (Kim et al., 2011), it remains to be seen if this applies to most populations and requires change in sampling approaches for surveying autism. Of note, the CDC methodology identifies ASD cases without prior official ASD diagnosis (21% of identified cases in 2008; CDC, 2012), suggesting that underidentification is a widespread phenomenon.

Case Evaluation

When the screening phase is completed, subjects identified as positive go through a more in-depth diagnostic evaluation to confirm their case status. Similar considerations about the methodological variability across studies apply to these more intensive assessment phases. In the studies reviewed, participation rates in second-stage assessments were generally high (over 80%). The source of information used to determine diagnosis usually involves a combination of data from different informants (parents, teachers, pediatricians, other health professionals, etc.) and data sources (medical records, educational sources), with an in-person assessment of the person with autism being offered in some but not all studies. Obviously, surveys of very large populations, such as those conducted in the United States by the CDC ADDM Network (e.g., 2012) or in national registers (e.g., Idring et al., 2012), did not include a direct diagnostic assessment of all subjects by the research team. However, these investigators could generally confirm the accuracy of their final caseness determination by undertaking, on a randomly selected subsample, a more complete diagnostic workup (Rice et al., 2007). The CDC surveys have established a methodology for surveys of large populations that relies on screening of the population using multiple data sources, a standardized procedure for abstracting records, and a systematic review and scoring system for the data gathered in the screening phase. In the less obvious cases, this information is then combined with input from experienced clinicians with known reliability and validity. This methodology is adequate for large samples, and is likely to be used in the future for surveillance efforts. Several recent studies have adopted the evaluation approach for population-based autism surveillance developed by the CDC, highlighting the utility of these methods for facilitating multisource active surveillance in the United States (Windham et al., 2011) and for establishing the validity of registry-based ASD diagnoses in Denmark (94% of registered cases confirmed; Lauritsen et al., 2010).

When subjects were directly examined, the assessments were conducted with various diagnostic instruments, ranging from a typical unstructured examination by a clinical expert (but without demonstrated psychometric properties), to the use of batteries of standardized measures by trained research staff. The Autism Diagnostic Interview (Le Couteur et al., 1989) and/or the Autism Diagnostic Observation Schedule (Lord et al., 2000) have been increasingly used in the most recent surveys (e.g., Isaksen, Diseth, Schjolberg, & Skjeldal, 2012; Kim et al., 2011; Mattila et al., 2011).

Keeping in mind the range and limitations of case definition, identification, and evaluation methods employed in the studies we report, we now turn to the available evidence from epidemiological surveys.

PREVALENCE ESTIMATES

Autistic Disorder

Prevalence estimates for autistic disorder are summarized in Table 3.1. There were 54 studies (including 12 in the United Kingdom, 8 in the United States, and 6 in Japan), with over half of them published since 2001. The sample size varied from 5,007 to 4.95 million, with a median

TABLE 3.1   Prevalence Surveys of Autistic Disorder (AD)

Year	Authors	Country	Area	Population	Age	Number Affected	Diagnostic Criteria	% With Normal IQ	Gender Ratio (M:F)	Prevalence Rate/10,000	95% CI
1966	Lotter	UK	Middlesex	78,000	8–10	32	Rating scale	15.6	2.6 (23:9)	4.1	2.7; 5.5
1970	Brask	Denmark	Aarhus County	46,500	2–14	20	Clinical	—	1.4 (12:7)	4.3	2.4; 6.2
1970	Treffert	United States	Wisconsin	899,750	3–12	69	Kanner	—	3.06 (52:17)	0.7	0.6; 0.9
1976	Wing, Yeates, Brierly, and Gould	UK	Camberwell	25,000	5–14	17[a]	24-item rating scale of Lotter	30	16 (16:1)	4.8[b]	2.1; 7.5
1982	Hoshino, Kumashiro, Yashima, Tachibana, and Watanabe	Japan	Fukushima-Ken	609,848	0–18	142	Kanner's criteria	—	9.9 (129:13)	2.33	1.9; 2.7
1983	Bohman, Bohman, Bjorck, and Sjoholm	Sweden	County of Västerbotten	69,000	0–20	39	Rutter criteria	20.5	1.6 (24:15)	5.6	3.9; 7.4
1984	McCarthy, Fitzgerald, and Smith	Ireland	East	65,000	8–10	28	Kanner	—	1.33 (16:12)	4.3	2.7; 5.9
1986	Steinhausen, Gobel, Breinlinger, and Wohlloben	Germany	West Berlin	279,616	0–14	52	Rutter	55.8	2.25 (36:16)	1.9	1.4; 2.4
1987	Burd, Fisher, and Kerbeshan	United States	North Dakota	180,986	2–18	59	DSM-III	—	2.7 (43:16)	3.26	2.4; 4.1
1987	Matsuishi et al.	Japan	Kurume City	32,834	4–12	51	DSM-III	—	4.7 (42:9)	15.5	11.3; 19.8
1988	Bryson, Clark, and Smith	Canada	Part of Nova Scotia	20,800	6–14	21	New RDC	23.8	2.5 (15:6)	10.1	5.8; 14.4
1988	Tanoue, Oda, Asano, and Kawashima	Japan	Southern Ibaraki	95,394	7	132	DSM-III	—	4.07 (106:26)	13.8	11.5; 16.2
1989	Cialdella and Mamelle	France	Rhône	135,180	3–9	61	DSM-III like	—	2.3	4.5	3.4; 5.6
1989	Ritvo et al.	United States	Utah	769,620	3–27	241	DSM-III	34	3.73 (190:51)	2.47	2.1; 2.8
1989	Sugiyama and Abe	Japan	Nagoya	12,263	3	16	DSM-III	—	—	13.0	6.7; 19.4
1991	Gillberg, Steffenburg, and Schaumann	Sweden	South-West Göteborg, Bohuslän	78,106[c]	4–13	74	DSM-III-R	18	2.7 (54:20)	9.5	7.3; 11.6
1992	Fombonne and du Mazaubrun	France	4 régions 14 départements	274,816	9 and 13	154	Clinical/ICD-10 like	13.3	2.1 (105:49)	4.9	4.1; 5.7
1992	Wignyosumarto, Mukhlas, and Shirataki	Indonesia	Yogyakarita (SE of Jakarta)	5,120	4–7	6	CARS	0	2.0 (4:2)	11.7	2.3; 21.1

(continued)

TABLE 3.1 (*Continued*)

Year	Authors	Country	Area	Population	Age	Number Affected	Diagnostic Criteria	% With Normal IQ	Gender Ratio (M:F)	Prevalence Rate/10,000	95% CI
1996	Honda, Shimizu, Misumi, Niimi, and Ohashi	Japan	Yokohama	8,537	5	18	ICD-10	50.0	2.6 (13.5)	21.08	11.4; 30.8
1997	Fombonne, du Mazaubrun, Cans, and Grandjean	France	3 départements	325,347	8–16	174	Clinical ICD-10 like	12.1	1.81 (112:62)	5.35	4.6; 6.1
1997	Webb, Lobo, Hervas, Scourfield, and Fraser	UK	South Glamorgan, Wales	73,301	3–15	53	DSM-III-R	—	6.57 (46:7)	7.2	5.3; 9.3
1998	Sponheim and Skjeldal	Norway	Akershus County	65,688	3–14	25	ICD-10	36.0[d]	2.10 (17:8)	3.8	1.9; 5.1
1999	Taylor et al.	UK	North Thames	490,805*	0–16	427	ICD-10	—	—	8.7	7.9; 9.6
2000	Baird et al.	UK	South-East Thames	16,235	7	45[e]	ICD-10	60	14 (42:3)	27.7[e]	20.7; 37.1*
2000	Kielinen, Linna, and Moilanen	Finland	North (Oulu et Lapland)	152,732	3–18	187*	ICD-10, DSM-IV	50.2	—	12.2	10.6; 14.1*
2000	Powell et al.	UK	West Midlands	58,974*	1–5	46	Clinical, ICD-10, DSM-IV	—	—	7.8	5.8; 10.5
2001	Bertrand et al.	United States	Brick Township, New Jersey	8,896	3–10	36	DSM-IV	36.7	2.2 (25:11)	40.5	28.0; 56.0
2001	Chakrabarti and Fombonne	UK (Midlands)	Staffordshire	15,500	2.5–6.5	26	ICD-10, DSM-IV	29.2	3.3 (20:6)	16.8	10.3; 23.2
2001	Davidovitch, Holtzman, and Tirosh	Israel	Haiffa	26,160	7–11	26	DSM-III-R, DSM-IV	—	4.2 (21:5)	10.0	6.6; 14.4
2001	Magnússon and Saemundsen	Iceland	Whole Island	43,153	5–14	57	ICD-9, ICD-10	13.5	4.2	13.2	9.8; 16.6
2002	Croen, Grether, Hoogstrate, and Selvin	United States	Northern California (DDS: 1987–1994)	4,950,333	5–12	5,038	"Full syndrome autism"—CA Dept. of Developmental Services	62.8[f]	4.47 (4116:921)	11.0	10.7; 11.3
2003	Lingam et al.	UK	North East London	186,206	5–14	278	ICD-10	—	5.8 (278:48)	14.9	13.3; 16.8*
2005	Barbaresi, Katusic, Colligan, Weaver, and Jacobsen	United States	Olmstead County, Minnesota	37,726	0–21	112	DSM-IV	—	—	29.7	24.6; 35.7*
2005	Chakrabarti and Fombonne	UK (Midlands)	Staffordshire	10,903	4–6	24	ICD-10, DSM-IV	33.3	3.8 (19:5)	22.0	14.4; 32.2
2005	Honda, Shimizu, and Rutter[g]	Japan	Yokohama	32,791	5	123	ICD-10	25.3	2.5 (70:27)	37.5	31.0; 45.0

Year	Author	Country	Location	N	Age	Cases	Diagnostic criteria				
2006	Baird et al.	UK	South Thames, London	56,946	9–10	81	ICD-10	47	8.3 (~72:9)	38.9	29.9; 47.8
2006	Fombonne, Zakarian, Bennett, Meng, and McLean-Heywood	Canada	Montreal Island, Quebec	27,749	5–17	60	DSM-IV	—	5.7 (51:9)	21.6	16.5; 27.8
2006	Gillberg, Cederlund, Lamberg, and Zeijlon	Sweden	Göteborg	32,568	7–12	115	DSM-III, DSM-IV, Gillberg's criteria for AS	—	3.6 (90:25)	35.3	29.2; 42.2
2007	Croen, Najjar, Fireman, and Grether	United States	Northern California (1995–1999)	132,844	5–10	277	ICD-09-CM	—	4.1	20.9	18.5; 23.5*
2007	Latif and Williams	UK	Wales	39,220	0–17	50	Kanner	—	—	12.7	9.0; 17.0
2007	Oliveira et al.	Portugal	Mainland and Azores	67,795	6–9	115	DSM-IV	17	2.9	16.7	14.0; 20.0
2008	Montiel-Nava and Pena	Venezuela	Maracaibo	254,905	3–9	287	DSM-IV-TR	—	4.1 (231:56)	11	10; 14
2008	E. Williams, Thomas, Sidebotham, and Emond	UK	South West (Avon)	14,062	11	30	ICD-10	86.7	5.0 (25:5)	21.6	13.9; 29.3
2009	van Balkom et al.	Netherlands	Aruba (Caribbean)	13,109	0–13	25	DSM-IV	36.0	7.3 (22:3)	19.1	12.3; 28.1
2010	Fernell and Gillberg	Sweden	Stockholm	23,566	6	75	DSM-IV, DSM-IV-TR, ICD-10	11	6.5	32	26; 37
2010	Lazoff, Zhong, Piperni, and Fombonne	Canada	Montreal	23,635	5–17	60	DSM-IV	—	5.8(58:10)	25.4	19.0; 31.8
2011	Kim et al.	S. Korea	Goyang City	55,226	7–12	27	DSM-IV	55.6	4.4	94	56; 134
2011	Mattila et al.	Finland	Northern Ostrobothnia County	5,484	8	18	DSM-IV-TR including ADOS and ADI	61	2	41	26; 64
2011	Parner et al.[h]	Australia	Western Australia (1994–1999)	152,060	0–10	516	DSM-IV, DSM-IV-TR	—	4.4	39.3	—
2011	Windham et al.[i]	United States	San Francisco Bay Area (DDS: 1994, 1996)	162,402	0–8	477	"Full syndrome autism"—CA Dept. of Developmental Services	—	6.4 (493:77)	29	26.9; 32.1*
2012	Isaksen, Diseth, Schjolberg, and Skjeldal	Norway	Oppland and Hedmark	31,015	6–12	42	ICD-10 including ADOS and ADI	—	3.2	14	10; 18

(continued)

TABLE 3.1 (*Continued*)

Year	Authors	Country	Area	Population	Age	Number Affected	Diagnostic Criteria	% With Normal IQ	Gender Ratio (M:F)	Prevalence Rate/10,000	95% CI
2012	Kočovská, Biskupsto, et al.[j]	Denmark	Faroe Islands	7,128	15–24	15	*DSM-IV/ICD-10*	—	2 (10:5)	21	12; 35
2012	Nygren, Cederlund, Sandberg, Gillstedt, and Arvidsson	Sweden	Göteborg	5,007	2	26	*DSM-IV-TR*	—	5.5	52	35.5; 76.0*
2012	Parner et al.[k]	Denmark	National Register (1980–2003)	1,311,736	6–29	2,446	*ICD-8, ICD-9, ICD-10*	—	4.4	18.65*	17.9; 19.4*

*Calculated by the authors.

[a]This number corresponds to the sample described in Wing and Gould (1979).

[b]This rate corresponds to the first published paper on this survey and is based on 12 subjects among children aged 5 to 14 years.

[c]For the Göteborg surveys by Gillberg and colleagues (Gillberg, 1984; Gillberg, Steffenburg, & Schaumann 1991; Steffenburg & Gillberg, 1986), a detailed examination showed that there was overlap between the samples included in the three surveys; consequently only the 1991 survey has been included in this table.

[d]In this study, mild mental retardation was combined with normal IQ (approximately IQ > 50), whereas moderate and severe mental retardation were grouped together (IQ < 50).

[e]This prevalence was calculated by the authors after removing the $n = 5$ cases that also met criteria for Asperger's.

[f]This proportion is likely to be overestimated and to reflect an underreporting of mental retardation to the California Department of Developmental Services.

[g]This figure was calculated by the author and refers to prevalence data (not cumulative incidence) presented in the paper (the M:F ratio is based on a subsample).

[h]Note that this is an updated prevalence estimate: previous estimates have been reported by Nassar et al. (2009; birth years: 1983–1999; prevalence: 20.8/10,000;) and Leonard et al. (2011; birth years: 1984–1999; singletons; prevalence: 21/10,000) using the same register in Western Australia.

[i]Note that there is partial overlap between this sample and that reported by Croen, Grether, Hoogstrate, and Selvin (2002); because of the minimal overlap between these two sample populations (birth year: 1994), both prevalence estimates are included in this table.

[j]Note that this is an updated prevalence estimate: a previous estimate of 16/10,000 was reported by Ellefsen, Kampmann, Billstedt, Gillberg, and Gillberg (2007) based on the same geographical area with the same cohort.

[k]Note that this is an updated prevalence estimate: previous estimates have been reported by Lauritsen, Pedersen, and Mortensen (2004; birth years: 1971–2000; prevalence: 11.8/10,000) and by Parner et al. (2011; birth years: 1994–1999; prevalence: 21.8/10,000) using the same national register in Denmark.

of 56,090 (mean: 233,300) subjects in the surveyed populations. Age ranged from 0 to 29 years, with a median age of 8.5 years (mean: 8.4 years). The number of subjects identified with autistic disorder ranged from 6 to 5,038 (median: 55; mean: 234). Males consistently outnumbered females in the 48 studies where gender differences were reported, with a male/female ratio ranging from 1.3:1 to 16:1, leading to an average male/female ratio of 4.3:1.

There was a 134-fold variation in prevalence estimates for autistic disorder, with rates ranging from 0.7 to 94 per 10,000 (median: 13.5; mean: 18). Prevalence rates were negatively correlated with sample size (Spearman's r: -0.55; $p <$ .0001), with small-scale studies reporting higher prevalence rates. There was a significant positive correlation between prevalence rate and publication year (Spearman's r: .78; $p < $ .0001), with higher rates in more recent surveys. Therefore, a current estimate for the prevalence of autistic disorder must be derived from more recent surveys with an adequate sample size. In 31 studies published since 2000, the mean prevalence was 26.1/10,000 (median: 21.6/10,000). After exclusion of the two studies with the smallest and largest sample sizes, the results were very similar (mean: 25.7/10,000; median: 21.6/10,000). Thus, the best current estimate for the prevalence of autistic disorder is 26/10,000.

Of the 54 studies, 27 reported the proportion of subjects with IQ within the normal range (median: 33.3%; interquartile range: 17.5%–50.1%). Over time, there were minor associations between the year of publication of the survey and the sample male/female ratio (Spearman's r: 0.31; $p = $ .03) and the proportion of subjects without mental retardation (Spearman's r: 0.32; $p = $ .1). Taken in conjunction with the much stronger increase over time in prevalence rates, these results suggest that the increase in prevalence rates is not entirely accounted for by the inclusion of milder forms (i.e., less cognitively impaired) of autistic disorder, albeit this might have contributed to it to some degree.

Asperger's Syndrome

Epidemiological studies of Asperger's syndrome are sparse, due to the fact that it was acknowledged as a separate diagnostic category in both *ICD-10* and *DSM-IV* only in the early 1990s. Three epidemiological surveys (not featured in the current analysis due to relatively small population sizes) *specifically* investigated AS prevalence (Ehlers & Gillberg, 1993; Kadesjo et al., 1999, Mattila et al., 2007). However, only a handful of cases were identified in these surveys, with the resulting estimates varying greatly. In addition, it remains unclear if these subjects would have also met criteria for autistic disorder and how prevalence rates would be affected if hierarchical rules were followed to diagnose both disorders. For example, Mattila et al. (2007) reported that 4 out of 10 children previously diagnosed with AS were reassigned to a diagnosis of high-functioning autism following *DSM-IV/ICD-10* criteria. One survey of high-functioning ASDs in Welsh mainstream primary schools yielded a relatively high (uncorrected) prevalence estimate of 14.5/10,000, but no rate was available specifically for AS (Webb et al., 2003).

Other recent surveys have examined samples with respect to the presence of both autistic disorder and Asperger's syndrome. Eighteen studies published since 1998 provide usable data (Table 3.2). The median population size was 25,690, and the median age 8.3 years. Numbers of children identified with AS varied from 2 to 419 (median: 26; mean: 59). There was a 173-fold variation in estimated prevalence of AS (range: 0.3 to 52/10,000; median: 7.2/10,000; mean: 12.3/10,000). For the majority of studies (15 out the 18 total), the number of children with autistic disorder was higher than that of children with AS. In these studies, the ratio of children with AD to those with AS exceeded 1 (median: 3.0; mean: 5.8), indicating that the rate of AS was consistently *lower* than that for autism (Table 3.2). Unusually high rates of AS relative to autistic disorder were obtained in three studies with

TABLE 3.2 Asperger's Syndrome (AS) in Recent Autism Surveys

					Assessment		Autistic Disorder		Asperger Syndrome		
Year	Authors	Population	Age	Informants	Instruments	Diagnostic Criteria	N	Prevalence Rate/10,000	N	Prevalence Rate/10,000	AD/AS Ratio
1998	Sponheim and Skjeldal	65,688	3–14	Parent Child	Parental Interview + direct observation, CARS, ABC	ICD-10	25	3.8	2	0.3	12.5
1999	Taylor et al.	490,000	0–16	Record	Rating of all data available in child record	ICD-10	427	8.7	71	1.4	6.0
2000	Baird et al.	16,235	7	Parents Child Other data	ADI-R Psychometry	ICD-10 DSM-IV	45	27.7	5	3.1	9.0
2001	Chakrabarti and Fombonne	15,500	2.5–6.5	Child Parent Professional	ADI-R, 2 weeks multidisciplinary assessment, Merrill-Palmer, WPPSI	ICD-10, DSM-IV	26	16.8	13	8.4	2.0
2003	Lingam et al.	186,206	5–14	Disability Register	Review of medical records	ICD-10	278	14.9	94	5.0	3.0
2004	Lauritsen, Pedersen, and Mortensen[a]	643,220*	1–10	National Registry	Available data	ICD-8, ICD-10	759	11.8	419	4.7	1.8
2005	Chakrabarti and Fombonne	10,903	4–6	Child Parent Professional	ADI-R, 2 weeks multidisciplinary assessment, Merrill-Palmer, WPPSI	ICD-10, DSM-IV	24	22.0	12	11.0	2.0
2006	Fombonne, Zakarian, Bennett, Meng, and McLean-Heywood	27,749	5–17	School registry	Clinical	DSM-IV	60	21.6	28	10.1	2.1
2007	Latif and Williams	39,220	0–17	?	Clinical	Kanner, Gillberg AS criteria	50	12.7	139	35.4	0.36
2008	Montiel-Nava and Pena	254,905	3–9	Child Parent Professional	School and/or medical records, CARS, ADOS	DSM-IV-TR	287	11.0	39	1.52[b]	7.4

Year	Author	N	Age	Source	Method	Criteria					
2008	E. Williams et al.	14,062	11	Medical records and educational registry	Clinical	ICD-10	30	21.6	23	16.6	1.3
2009	Nassar et al.[c]	419,917	0–21	Record	Available data (1983–1999)	DSM-III, DSM-IV, DSM-IV-TR	700	20.8	40	1.0	17.5
2009	van Balkom et al.	13,109	0–13	Clinic series	Review of medical records	DSM-IV	25	19.1	2	1.5	12.5
2010	Fernell and Gillberg	23,566	6	Parent	Clinical	DSM-IV, DSM-IV-TR, ICD-10	75	32	14	6	5.4
2010	Lazoff, Zhong, Piperni, and Fombonne	23,635	5–17	School registry	Review of educational records	DSM-IV	60	25.4	23	9.7	2.6
2011	Mattila et al.	5,484	8	Parent Child Professional	Clinical, ADOS-G, ADI-R	DSM-IV-TR	18	41	11	25	1.64
2012	Isaksen, Diseth, Schjolberg, and Skjeldal	31,015	6–12	Parent Child Professional	Clinical, ADOS-G, ADI-R	ICD-10	42	14	89	28	0.47
2012	Kočovská, Biskupsto, et al.[d]	7,128	15–24	Parent Child Professional	DISCO, WISC-R, ASSQ	ICD-10 Gillberg AS criteria	15	21	37	52	0.41

* Calculated by the authors.

[a] Note that a subsequent survey by Parner et al. (2012) using an overlapping sample provided updated prevalence estimates for AD and ASD but not for AS; those estimates are included in Tables 3.1 and 3.4 instead of Lauritsen et al. (2004).

[b] The authors note that this is likely an underestimation due to the case ascertainment methods employed.

[c] Note that a subsequent survey by Parner et al. (2011) using an overlapping sample provided updated prevalence estimates for AD and ASD but not for AS; those estimates are included in Tables 3.1 and 3.4 instead of Nassar et al. (2009).

[d] Note that this is an updated prevalence estimate; Ellefsen et al. (2007) initially reported prevalence for AS of 16/10,000 based on a survey of the same geographical area with the same cohort.

a median and mean AD/AS ratio of 0.4 (Isaksen et al., 2012; Kočovská, Biskupsto, et al., 2012; Latif & Williams, 2007). Isaksen et al. (2012) noted that the increased rates might reflect the catch-all status of AS as a diagnostic category, or that some clinicians may lack the expertise required to differentiate AS from other ASD subtypes. In the Faroe Islands survey, Kočovská, Biskupsto, et al. (2012) followed up with the same cohort from an earlier 2002 population survey (Ellefsen, Kampmann, Billstedt, Gillberg, & Gillberg, 2007). In addition to identifying 23 newly diagnosed cases, the authors noted diagnostic stability in those previously identified with ASDs overall, yet considerable variability in the stability of diagnostic subtypes (previous AS prevalence estimate: 26/10,000; updated: 52/10,000). In Latif and Williams (2007), AS prevalence estimates appeared to be inflated due to the inclusion of high-functioning autism in the AS definition. The epidemiological data on AS are therefore of dubious quality, reflecting uncertainties around inclusion of AS in recent nosographies as well as the lack of proper measurement strategies that can ensure a reliable difference between AS and autistic disorder.

Childhood Disintegrative Disorder

Thirteen surveys provided data on childhood disintegrative disorder (Table 3.3). In 5 of these, only one case was reported; no case of CDD was identified in 5 other studies. Prevalence estimates ranged from 0 to 9.2/100,000, with a median rate of 1.5/100,000. The pooled estimate, based on 11 identified cases and a surveyed population of about 570,000 children, was 1.9/100,000. Gender was reported in 10 of the 11 studies, and males appear to be overrepresented with a male/female ratio of 9:1. The upper limit of the confidence interval associated to the pooled prevalence estimate (3.5/100,000) indicates that CDD is a rare condition, with about 1 case occurring for every 189 cases of autistic disorder.

Prevalence for Combined ASDs

A new objective of more recent epidemiological surveys has been to estimate the prevalence of all

disorders falling onto the autism spectrum, thereby prompting important changes in the conceptualization and design of surveys. However, before reviewing the findings of these studies conducted since 2000, we first examine how findings of the first generation of epidemiological surveys of a narrow definition of autism also informed our understanding of the modern concept of autism spectrum disorders.

Unspecified ASDs in Earlier Surveys

In previous reviews, we documented that several studies performed in the 1960s and 1970s had provided useful information on rates of syndromes similar to autism but not meeting the strict diagnostic criteria for autistic disorder then in use (Fombonne, 2003a, 2003b, 2005). At the time, different labels were used by authors to characterize these clinical pictures, such as the *triad of impairments* involving deficits in reciprocal social interaction, communication, and imagination (Wing & Gould, 1979), autistic mental retardation (Hoshino, Kumashiro, Yashima, Tachibana, & Watanabe, 1982), borderline childhood psychoses (Brask, 1970), or autistic-like syndromes (Burd, Fisher, & Kerbeshan, 1987). These syndromes would fall within our currently defined autistic spectrum, probably with diagnostic labels such as atypical autism and/or PDD-NOS. In 8 of 12 surveys providing separate estimates of the prevalence of these developmental disorders, higher rates for the atypical forms were actually found compared to those for more narrowly defined autistic disorder (see Fombonne, 2003a). However, this atypical group received little attention in previous epidemiological studies; these subjects were not defined as "cases" and were not included in the numerators of prevalence calculations, thereby underestimating systematically the prevalence of what would be defined today as the spectrum of autistic disorders. For example, in the first survey by Lotter (1966), the prevalence would rise from 4.1 to 7.8/10,000 if these atypical forms of autism had been included in the case definition. Similarly, in Wing, Yeates, Brierly, & Gould's study (1976), the prevalence was 4.9/10,000 for autistic disorder,

TABLE 3.3 Prevalence Surveys of Childhood Disintegrative Disorder (CDD)

Year	Authors	Country	Area	Population	Age	Number Affected	Diagnostic Assessment	Gender ratio (M:F)	Prevalence Rate/100,000	95% CI
1987	Burd, Fisher, and Kerbeshan	United States	North Dakota	180,986	2–18	2	Structured parental interview and review of all data available—*DSM-III* criteria	2:—	1.11	0.13; 3.4
1998	Sponheim and Skjeldal	Norway	Akershus County	65,688	3–14	1	Parental interview and direct observation (CARS, ABC)	—	1.52	0.04; 8.5
2001	Chakrabarti and Fombonne	UK (Midlands)	Staffordshire	15,500	2.5–6.5	1	ADI-R, 2 weeks multidisciplinary assessment, Merrill-Palmer, WPPSI-*ICD-10*/*DSM-IV*	1:—	6.45	0.16; 35.9
2001	Fombonne, Simmons, Ford, Meltzer, and Goodman	UK	England and Wales	10,438	5–15	0	Parental interview and direct observation, *DSM-IV*, *ICD-10*	—	0	—
2001	Magnússon and Saemundsen	Iceland	Whole Island	85,556	5–14	2	ADI-R, CARS, and psychological tests—mostly *ICD-10*	2:—	2.34	0.3; 8.4
2005	Chakrabarti and Fombonne	UK (Midlands)	Staffordshire	10,903	4–6	1	ADI-R, 2 weeks multidisciplinary assessment, Merrill-Palmer, WPPSI-*ICD-10*/*DSM-IV*	1:—	9.17	0; 58.6
2006	Fombonne, Zakarian, Bennett, Meng, and McLean-Heywood	Canada	Montreal Island, Quebec	27,749	5–17	1	*DSM-IV*, special needs school survey	1:—	3.6	0; 20
2006	Gillberg, Cederlund, Lamberg, and Zeijlon	Sweden	Göteborg	102,485	7–24	2	*DSM-IV*, review of medical records of local diagnostic center	1:1	2	0.5; 7.1
2007	Ellefsen, Kampmann, Billstedt, Gillberg, and Gillberg	Denmark	Faroe Islands	7,689	8–17	0	DISCO, Vineland, WISC-R, *ICD-10*/*DSM-IV*	—	0	—
2008	Kawamura, Takahashi, and Ishii	Japan	Toyota	12,589	5–8	0	*DSM-IV*, population based screening at 18 and 36 months	—	0	—
2008	E. Williams, Thomas, Sidebotham, and Emond	UK	South West (Avon)	14,062	11	0	*ICD-10*, educational and medical record review	—	0	—
2009	van Balkom et al.	Netherlands	Aruba (Caribbean)	13,109	0–13	0	Clinic medical record review	—	0	—
2010	Lazoff, Zhong, Piperni, and Fombonne	Canada	Montreal	23,635	5–17	1	*DSM-IV*, special needs school survey	1:0	4.23	0.7; 24
POOLED ESTIMATES				**570,389**		**11**		**9:1**	**1.9**	**1.1; 3.5**

but the prevalence for the whole ASD spectrum was in fact 21.1/10,000 after the figure of 16.3/10,000 (Wing & Gould, 1979), corresponding to the triad of impairments, was added. The progressive recognition of the importance and relevance of these less typical clinical presentations has led to changes in the design of more recent epidemiological surveys (see later discussion) that now use case definitions that incorporate a priori these milder phenotypes.

Newer Surveys of ASDs

The results of surveys that estimated the prevalence of the whole spectrum of ASDs are summarized in Table 3.4. Of the 48 studies listed, 24 also provided separate estimates for autistic disorder and other ASD subtypes; the other 24 studies provided only an estimate for the combined ASD rate. All selected surveys were published since 2000, with the majority (58%) published since 2008. The studies were performed in 17 different countries (including 13 in the United Kingdom and 11 in the United States, of which 4 were conducted by the CDC). Sample sizes ranged from 5,007 to 4.3 million (median: 56,110; mean: 273,200).

Ages of the surveyed populations ranged from 0 to 98 (median: 8; mean: 9). One recent study was specifically conducted on adults and provided the only estimate (98.2/10,000) thus far available for adults (Brugha et al., 2011). Two recent surveys specifically focused on toddlers (Nygren et al., 2012) and preschoolers (Nicholas, Carpenter, King, Jenner, & Charles, 2009) provided estimates of approximately 80 per 10,000. In the 45 remaining surveys, the average median and modal age was 8 years (mean: 8.2).

The diagnostic criteria used in 42 studies reflected the reliance on modern diagnostic schemes (10 studies used *ICD-10*, 24 the *DSM-III*, *DSM-IV*, or *DSM-IV-TR*; both schemes being used simultaneously in 8 studies). Assessments were often performed with standardized diagnostic measures (i.e., Autism Diagnostic Interview–Revised [ADI-R] and Autism Diagnostic Observation Schedule [ADOS]) that match well the more dimensional approach retained for case definition. In 24 studies where IQ data were reported, the proportion

of subjects within the normal IQ range varied from 0% to 100% (median: 55.4%; mean: 53.2%), a proportion that is higher than that for autistic disorder and reflects the lesser degree of association, or lack thereof, between intellectual impairment and milder forms of ASDs. Overrepresentation of males was the rule in the 42 studies reporting gender ratios, with male/female ratio ranging from 1.8:1 to 15.7:1 (median: 4.3:1; mean: 4.9:1).

Overall, the number of individuals affected by ASD ranged from 16 to 9,556 across studies (median: 215; mean: 948). There was a 189-fold variation in prevalence that ranged from a low of 1.4/10,000 to a high of 264/10,000 (see Figure 3.2). There was also substantial variation in confidence interval width (the difference between the upper and lower 95% limits of the interval), which indicates variation in sample sizes and in the precision achieved in each study (range: 0.5–146; mean interval width: 23.6). However, some degree of consistency in the ASD prevalence estimates is found in the center of this distribution, with a median rate of 61.6/10,000 and a mean rate of 66/10,000 (interquartile range: 43–80/10,000). Prevalence was negatively correlated with sample size (Spearman's r: $-.40$, $p = .005$), with small-scale studies reporting higher prevalence. There was also a significant positive correlation between ASD prevalence estimates and year of publication (Spearman's r: .29, $p = .04$), indicative of higher rates in more recent surveys.

Of note, five studies since 2000 reported ASD prevalences higher than 100/10,000 (median: 116.1/10,000; mean: 157.8/10,000) (Baird et al., 2006; CDC, 2012; Idring et al., 2012; Kawamura et al., 2008; Kim et al., 2011; see Figure 3.2). Baird et al. (2006) and Kim et al. (2011) both employed proactive case finding techniques, relying on multiple and repeated screening phases, involving both different informants at each phase and surveying the same cohorts at different ages, which certainly enhanced the sensitivity of case identification. Multisource active surveillance techniques, as employed in the Stockholm Youth Cohort (Idring et al., 2012) and by the CDC's ADDM Network (2012), also improve identification of individuals

TABLE 3.4 Prevalence Surveys of ASDs Since 2000

Year	Authors	Country	Area	Population	Age	Number Affected	Diagnostic Criteria	% with Normal IQ	Gender Ratio (M:F)	Prevalence Rate/10,000	95% CI
2000	Baird et al.	UK	South East Thames	16,235	7	94	ICD-10	60	15.7 (83:11)	57.9	46.8; 70.9
2000	Powell et al.	UK	West Midlands	58,654*	1–5	122	Clinical, ICD-10, DSM-IV	—	—	20.8	17.3; 24.9
2001	Bertrand et al.	United States	New Jersey	8,896	3–10	60	DSM-IV	51	2.7 (44:16)	67.4	51.5; 86.7
2001	Chakrabarti and Fombonne	UK	Stafford	15,500	2.5–6.5	96	ICD-10	74.2	3.8 (77:20)	61.9	50.2; 75.6
2001	Fombonne, Simmons, Ford, Meltzer, and Goodman	UK	England and Wales	10,438	5–15	27	DSM-IV, ICD-10	55.5	8.0 (24:3)	26.1	16.2; 36.0
2002	Scott, Baron-Cohen, Bolton, and Brayne	UK	Cambridge	33,598	5–11	196	ICD-10	—	4.0 (—)	58.3*	50.7; 67.1*
2003	Yeargin-Allsopp et al.	United States	Atlanta, GA	289,456	3–10	987	DSM-IV	31.8	4.0 (787:197)	34.0	32; 36
2003	Gurney et al.	United States	Minnesota (2001–2002)	787,308*	6–11	4,094	Receipt of MN special education services	—	—	52.0[a]	50.4; 53.6*
2003	Lingam et al.	UK	North East London	186,206	5–14	567	ICD-10	—	4.8 (469:98)	30.5*	27.9; 32.9*
2004	Icasiano, Hewson, Machet, Cooper, and Marshall	Australia	Barwon	45,153*	2–17	177	DSM-IV	53.4	8.3 (158:19)	39.2	33.8; 45.4*
2005	Chakrabarti and Fombonne	UK	Stafford	10,903	4–6	64	ICD-10	70.2	6.1 (55:9)	58.7	45.2; 74.9
2006	Baird et al.	UK	South Thames (1990–1991)	56,946	9–10	158	ICD-10	45	3.3 (121:37)	116.1	90.4; 141.8
2006	Fombonne, Zakarian, Bennett, Meng, and McLean-Heywood	Canada	Montreal	27,749	5–17	180	DSM-IV	—	4.8 (149:31)	64.9	55.8; 75.0
2006	Harrison, O'Hare, Campbell, Adamson, and McNeillage	UK	Scotland	134,661	0–15	443[b]	ICD-10, DSM-IV	—	7.0 (369:53)	44.2	39.5; 48.9
2006	Gillberg, Cederlund, Lamberg, and Zeijlon	Sweden	Göteborg	32,568	7–12	262	DSM-III, DSM-IV, Gillberg's criteria for AS	—	3.6 (205:57)	80.4	71.3; 90.3
2006	Ouellette-Kuntz et al.	Canada	Manitoba and Prince Edward Island	227,526	1–14	657	DSM-IV		4.1 (527:130)	28.9*	26.8; 31.2*
2007	Croen, Najjar, Fireman, and Grether	United States	Northern California (1995–1999)	132,844	5–10	593	ICD-9-CM	—	5.5 (501:92)	45	41.2; 48.4*
2007a	CDC	United States	6 states	187,761	8	1,252	DSM-IV-TR	38 to 60[c]	2.8 to 5.5	67.0	63.1; 70.5*
2007b	CDC	United States	14 states	407,578	8	2,685	DSM-IV-TR	55.4[d]	3.4 to 6.5	66.0	63; 68

(continued)

73

TABLE 3.4 (*Continued*)

Year	Authors	Country	Area	Population	Age	Number Affected	Diagnostic Criteria	% with Normal IQ	Gender Ratio (M:F)	Prevalence Rate/10,000	95% CI
2007	Latif and Williams	UK	South Wales	39,220	0–17	240	ICD-10, DSM-IV, Kanner's and Gillberg's criteria	—	6.8 (—)	61.2	53.9; 69.4*
2008	Wong and Hui	China	Hong Kong Registry	4,247,206	0–14	682	DSM-IV	30	6.6 (592:90)	16.1	14.9; 17.3*
2008	Montiel-Nava and Pena	Venezuela	Maracaibo	254,905	3–9	430	DSM-IV-TR	—	3.3 (329:101)	17	13; 20
2008	Kawamura, Takahashi, and Ishii	Japan	Toyota	12,589	5–8	228	DSM-IV	66.4	2.8 (168:60)	181.1	159.2; 205.9*
2008	E. Williams, Thomas, Sidebotham, and Emond	UK	Avon	14,062	11	86	ICD-10	85.3	6.8 (75:11)	61.9	48.8; 74.9
2009	Baron-Cohen et al.	UK	Cambridgeshire	8,824	5–9	83	ICD-10	—	—	94[e]	75; 116
2009	Nicholas et al.	United States	South Carolina	8,156	4	65	DSM-IV-TR	44.2	4.7	80	61; 99
2009	van Balkom et al.	Netherlands	Aruba	13,109	0–13	69	DSM-IV	58.8	6.7 (60:9)	52.6	41.0; 66.6
2009	CDC	United States	11 states	308,038	8	2,757	DSM-IV	59	4.5	90	86; 93
2010	Fernell and Gillberg	Sweden	Stockholm	24,084	6	147	DSM-IV, DSM-IV-TR, ICD-10	33	5.1 (123:24)	62	52; 72
2010	Lazoff, Zhong, Piperni, and Fombonne	Canada	Montreal	23,635	5–17	187	DSM-IV	—	5.4 (158:29)	79.1	67.8; 90.4
2010	Barnevik-Olsson, Gillberg, and Fernell	Sweden	Stockholm	113,391	6–10	250	DSM-IV	0	—	22	19.4; 25.0*
2010	Maenner and Durkin	United States	Wisconsin	428,030	Elementary school-aged	3,831	DSM-IV like criteria for WI special education services (by school district)	—	—	90	86.7; 92.4*
2010	Posserud, Lundervold, Lie, and Gillberg	Norway	Bergen	9,430	7–9	16	DSM-IV, ICD-10 Included DAWBA and DISCO	—	7 (14:2)	87[f]	—
2011	Al-Farsi et al.	Oman	National Register	528,335	0–14	113	DSM-IV-TR	—	2.9 (84:29)	1.4	1.2; 1.7
2011	Brugha et al.	UK	England	7,333	16–98	72	ADOS	100	3.8	98.2	30; 165
2011	Kim et al.	S. Korea	Goyang City	55,266	7–12	201	DSM-IV	31.5	3.8	264	191; 337
2011	Mattila et al.	Finland	Northern Ostrobothnia County	5,484	8	37	DSM-IV-TR included ADOS-G and ADI-R	65	1.8	84	61; 115
2011	Parner et al.[g]	Australia	Western Australia (1994–1999)	152,060	0–10	678	DSM-IV, DSM-IV-TR	—	4.1	51	47; 55.3

Year	Authors	Country	Source		Age	Cases	Criteria				
	..., Mahmoodizadeh, and McConkey	Iran	National Register	1,326,354	5	826	ADI-R	—	4.3	6.4	5.84; 6.70
2011	Chien, Lin, Chou, and Chou	Taiwan	National Health Research Institute	229,457*	0–18	659	ICD-9	—	3.7	28.7	26.6; 31*
2011	Windham et al.[h]	United States	San Francisco Bay Area (1994,1996)	80,249	9	374	"Full syndrome autism"—CA Dept. of Developmental Services, receipt of CA special education services, or DSM-IV	—	6.2 (324:50)	47	42; 52
2012	CDC	United States	14 states	337,093	8	3,820	DSM-IV	38	4.6	113	110; 117
2012	Davidovitch, Hemo, Manning-Courtney, and Fombonne	Israel	Maccabi HMO Registry	423,524	1–12	2,034	DSM-IV	—	5.2	48	45.9; 50.1
2012	Idring et al.	Sweden	Stockholm County Register	444,154	0–17	5,100	ICD-09, ICD-10, DSM-IV	57.4	2.6	115	112; 118
2012	Isaksen, Diseth, Schjolberg, and Skjeldal	Norway	Oppland and Hedmark	31,015	6–12	158	ICD-10 included ADOS-G and ADI-R	—	4.27 (128:30)	51	43; 59
2012	Kočovská, Biskuptso, et al.[i]	Denmark	Faroe Islands	7,128	15–24	67	ICD-10, DSM-IV, Gillberg's criteria	—	2.7* (49:18)	94	73; 119
2012	Nygren, Cederlund, Sandberg, Gillstedt, and Arvidsson	Sweden	Göteborg	5,007	2	40	DSM-IV-TR	63*	4 (32:8)	80	57; 109
2012	Parner et al.[j]	Denmark	National Register (1980–2003)	1,311,736	6–29	9,556	ICD-8, ICD-9, ICD-10	—	4.1	72.9*	71.4; 74.3*

* Calculated by the authors.

[a] This is the prevalence for children aged 6–11 in the 2001–2002 school year.

[b] Estimated using a capture-recapture analysis, the number of cases used to calculate prevalence was estimated to be 596.

[c] Specific values for % with normal IQ and confidence intervals are available for each state prevalence.

[d] Average across seven states.

[e] Rate based on Special Education Needs register. A figure of 99/10,000 is provided from a parental and diagnostic survey. Other estimates in this study vary from 47 to 165/10,000 deriving from various assumptions made by the authors.

[f] This was the prevalence estimate based on the identified sample; when adjusted for nonresponders, the prevalence was estimated to be even higher (87/10,000).

[g] Note that this is an updated prevalence estimate: Previous estimates have been reported by Nassar et al. (2009; birth years: 1983–1999; prevalence: 23.4/10,000) and Leonard et al. (2011; birth years: 1984–1999; singletons; prevalence: 30/10,000) using the same register in Western Australia.

[h] Data for 1996 birth cohort; overall prevalence for both 1994 and 1996 cohorts was 47/10000 although other specific values differed slightly. This study population may overlap to some degree with Croen et al. (2007), where 1995–1999 births only at Kaiser Permanente Northern California (KPNC) were examined; KPNC was one of three types of health-based sources used in Windham et al. (2011).

[i] Note that this is an updated prevalence estimate: a previous estimate of 53.3/10,000 was reported by Ellefsen, Kampmann, Billstedt, Gillberg, and Gillberg (2007) based on a survey of the same geographical area with the same cohort.

[j] Note that this is an updated prevalence estimate: a previous estimate was reported by Lauritsen, Pedersen, and Mortensen (2004; birth years: 1971–2000; prevalence: 34.4/10,000) and Parner et al. (2011; birth years: 1994–1999; prevalence: 68.5/10,000) using the same national register in Denmark.

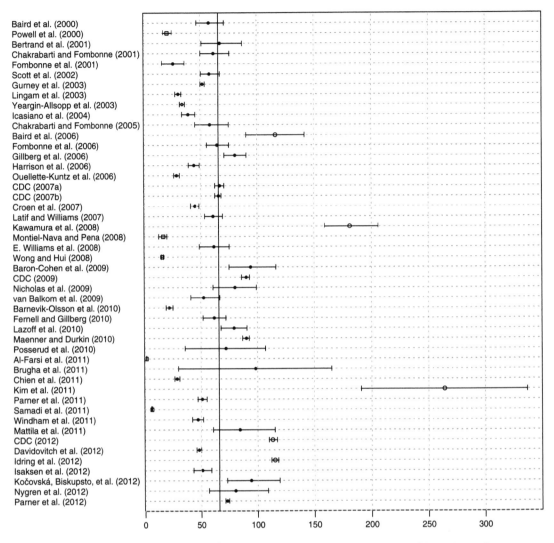

Figure 3.2   Prevalence estimates for ASD from Table 3.4 (rate per 10,000 and 95% confidence interval).

with ASD. The CDC's 2012 prevalence estimate of 113 per 10,000 reflects the highest estimate to date across all of the previous ADDM Network reports (2007a, 2007b, 2009). One factor associated with the prevalence increase in the CDC monitoring survey was improved quality and quantity of information available through records, indicative of greater awareness about ASD among community professionals. As surveillance efforts continue, it is likely that awareness and services will develop in states that were lagging behind, resulting in a predictable increase in the average prevalence

for the United States as time elapses. These CDC findings apply to other countries as well, and prevalence estimates from any study should always be regarded in the context of the imperfect sensitivity of case ascertainment that results in downward biases in prevalence proportions in most surveys.

By contrast, the five studies reporting the lowest ASD prevalence estimates (Al-Farsi et al., 2011; Montiel-Nava & Pena, 2008; Powell et al., 2000; Samadi et al., 2011; Wong & Hui, 2008) probably underestimated the true population rates (see Figure 3.2). In three surveys (Al-Farsi et al.,

2011; Samadi et al., 2011; Wong & Hui, 2008), case finding depended on enrollment to a National Registry, a method usually associated with lower sensitivity for case finding. Similarly, both the UK (Powell et al., 2000) and Venezuelan surveys (Montiel-Nava & Pena, 2008) relied on review of school and/or medical records for case ascertainment, which are also associated with decreased sensitivity in prevalence surveys. Moreover, both the Omani and Iranian surveys (Al-Farsi et al., 2011; Samadi et al., 2011) attributed the low prevalence estimates to underdiagnosis, limited service access, and cultural factors, all of which likely contributed to underestimation of ASD prevalence in these populations.

Overall, results of recent surveys agree that an average figure of 66/10,000 can be used as the current estimate for the spectrum of ASDs. The convergence of estimates around 60 to 90 per 10,000 for all ASDs combined, conducted in different regions and countries by different teams, is striking especially when derived from studies with improved methodology. The prevalence figure of 66/10,000 (equivalent to 6.6/1,000 or .66%) translates into 1 child out of 152 with an ASD diagnosis. This estimate is now the best estimate for the prevalence of ASDs currently available. However, this represents an average and conservative figure, and it is important to recognize the substantial variability that exists between studies and within studies, across sites or areas. In the studies reviewed here, 19 of the 48 studies reported ASD prevalence rates higher than 66/10,000, with some recent studies reporting rates even 2 to 4 times higher (Kawamura et al., 2008; Kim et al., 2011).

TIME TRENDS IN PREVALENCE AND THEIR INTERPRETATION

The debate on the hypothesis of a secular increase in rates of autism has been obscured by a lack of clarity in the measures of disease occurrence used by investigators, or in the interpretation of their meaning. In particular, it is crucial to differentiate prevalence from incidence. Whereas prevalence is useful to estimate needs and plan services, only incidence rates can be used for causal research. Both prevalence and incidence estimates will increase when case definition is broadened and case ascertainment is improved. Time trends in rates can therefore only be gauged in investigations that hold these parameters under strict control over time. These methodological requirements must be borne in mind while reviewing the evidence for a secular increase in rates of ASDs, or testing for the "epidemic" hypothesis. The epidemic hypothesis emerged in the 1990s when, in most countries, increasing numbers were diagnosed with ASDs leading to an upward trend in children registered in service providers' databases that was paralleled by higher prevalence rates in epidemiological surveys. These trends were interpreted as evidence that the actual population incidence of ASDs was increasing (what the term *epidemic* means). However, alternative explanations for the rise in numbers of children diagnosed with ASDs should be ruled out first before supporting this conclusion, and include the following.

Use of Referral Statistics

Increasing numbers of children referred to specialist services or known to special education registers have been taken as evidence for an increased incidence of ASDs. Upward trends in national registries, medical, and educational databases have been seen in many different countries (Gurney et al., 2003; Madsen et al., 2002; Shattuck, 2006; Taylor et al., 1999), all occurring in the late 1980s and early 1990s. However, trends over time in *referred* samples are confounded by many factors such as referral patterns, availability of services, heightened public awareness, decreasing age at diagnosis, and changes over time in diagnostic concepts and practices.

Failure to control for these confounding factors was obvious in previous reports (Fombonne, 2001), such as the widely quoted reports from California Developmental Database Services (CDDS; 1999, 2003). Additionally, the decreasing age at diagnosis results in itself to increasing numbers of young children being identified in official statistics (Wazana, Bresnahan, & Kline, 2007) or referred to specialist medical and educational services. Earlier identification of children from the prevalence pool may therefore result in increased service activity that may lead to a misperception by professionals of an epidemic. However, it is important to note that an increase in referrals does not necessarily mean increased *incidence*. Studies based solely on cases registered for services cannot rule out that the proportion of cases within the general population who registered with services has changed over time.

As an illustration, in Figure 3.3, we contrast two methods for surveying ASD using hypothetical data: one based on sampling from the total population, and the other relying solely on service access counts. Here, assuming a constant incidence

and prevalence of 100/10,000 between Time 1 and Time 2 (meaning there is no epidemic), population surveys at two time points result in prevalence estimates that are not only accurate but also stable over time, showing no prevalence change in the target population. However, if prevalence is estimated based only on service access counts where the number of ASD individuals accessing services increases from 20% to 60% within a certain time interval, prevalence would be underestimated at both time points, yet would appear to rise 200% in that time interval while the underlying true incidence and prevalence remained stable. This type of pattern of results was recently reported based on special education data in Wisconsin (Maenner & Durkin, 2010), in which ASD prevalence rates appeared to level off between 2002 and 2008 in school districts with initially high baseline

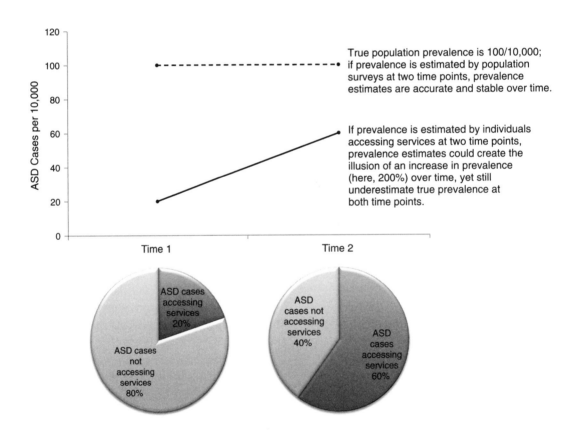

Figure 3.3   Impact on prevalence estimates and trends of two methods for surveying ASD: population sampling, or reliance of service access counts (hypothetical data).

prevalence rates (~120/10,000), whereas school districts with the lowest baseline rates experienced significant increases in prevalence over the same time period (e.g., in one district rates rose from 5 to 70/10,000; corresponding to a 1300% increase in 6 years). As illustrated in Figure 3.3, in order to accurately estimate prevalence and gauge time trends, data over time are needed both on referred subjects and on nonreferred (or referred to other services) subjects.

The Role of Diagnostic Substitution

One possible explanation for increased numbers of a diagnostic category is that children presenting with the same developmental disability may receive one particular diagnosis at one time and another diagnosis at a subsequent time. Such diagnostic substitution (or switching) may occur when diagnostic categories become increasingly familiar to health professionals and/or when access to better services is ensured by using a new diagnostic category.

The strongest evidence of diagnostic switching contributing to the prevalence increase was produced in all U.S. states in a complex analysis of Department of Education Data in 50 U.S. states (Shattuck, 2006), indicating that a relatively high proportion of children previously diagnosed as having mental retardation were subsequently identified as having an ASD diagnosis. Shattuck showed that the odds of being classified in the autism category increased by 1.21 during 1994–2003. Concurrently, the odds of being classified in the learning disability (LD) (odds ratio: OR = 0.98) and the mental retardation (MR) categories (OR = 0.97) decreased significantly. Shattuck (2006) further demonstrated that the growing prevalence of autism was directly associated with decreasing prevalence of LD and MR within states, and that a significant downward deflection in the historical trajectories of LD and MR occurred when autism became reported in the United States as an independent category in 1993–1994. Finally, Shattuck (2006) showed that, from 1994 to 2003, the mean increase for the combined category of

Autism + Other Health Impairments + Trauma Brain Injury + Developmental Delay was 12/1,000, whereas the mean decrease for MR and LD was 11/1,000 during the same period. One exception to these ratios was California, for which previous authors had debated the presence of diagnostic substitution between MR and autism (Croen, Grether, Hoogstrate, et al., 2002; Eagle, 2004).

The previous investigations have largely relied on ecological, aggregated data that have known limitations. Using individual level data, a newer study reexamined the hypothesis of diagnostic substitution in the California DDS dataset (King & Bearman, 2009) and showed that 24% of the increase in caseload was attributable to such diagnostic substitution (from the mental retardation to the autism category). It is important to keep in mind that other types of diagnostic substitution are likely to have occurred as well for milder forms of the ASD phenotype, from various psychiatric disorders (including childhood schizoid personality disorders; Wolff & Barlow, 1979) that have not been studied yet (Fombonne, 2009b). For example, children currently diagnosed with Asperger's disorder were previously diagnosed with other psychiatric diagnoses (i.e., obsessive-compulsive disorder, school phobia, social anxiety, etc.) in clinical settings before the developmental nature of their condition was fully recognized.

Evidence of diagnostic substitution within the class of developmental disorders has also been provided in UK-based studies. Using the General Practitioner Research Database, Jick and Kaye (2003) demonstrated that the incidence of specific developmental disorders (including language disorders) decreased by about the same amount that the incidence of diagnoses of autism increased in boys born from 1990 to 1997. Another UK study (Bishop, Whitehouse, Watt, & Line, 2008) showed that up to 66% of adults previously diagnosed as children with developmental language disorders would meet diagnostic criteria for a broad definition of ASD. This change was observed for children diagnosed with specific language impairments, but even more so for those diagnosed with pragmatic language impairments.

Comparison of Cross-Sectional Epidemiological Surveys

Epidemiological surveys of autism each possess unique design features that could account almost entirely for between-studies variation in rates. Therefore, time trends in rates of autism are difficult to gauge from published prevalence rates. The significant aforementioned correlation between prevalence rate and year of publication for autistic disorder could merely reflect increased efficiency over time in case identification methods used in surveys as well as changes in diagnostic concepts and practices (Bishop et al., 2008; Kielinen, Linna, & Moilanen, 2000; Magnússon & Saemundsen, 2001; Shattuck, 2006; Webb, Lobo, Hervas, Scourfield, & Fraser, 1997). In studies using capture-recapture methods, it is apparent that up to a third of prevalent cases may be missed by an ascertainment source, even in recently conducted studies (Harrison et al., 2006). Evidence that method factors could account for most of the variability in published prevalence estimates comes from a direct comparison of eight recent surveys

conducted in the United Kingdom and the United States (Fombonne, 2005). In each country, four surveys were conducted around the same year and with similar age groups. As there is no reason to expect large variations in between-area differences in rates, prevalence estimates should therefore be comparable within each country. However, there was a 6-fold variation in rates for UK surveys, and a 14-fold variation in U.S. rates. In each set of studies, high rates derived from surveys where intensive population-based screening techniques were employed, whereas lower rates were obtained from studies relying on passive administrative methods for case finding. Since no passage of time was involved, the magnitude of these gradients in rates can only be attributed to differences in case identification methods across surveys.

Even more convincing evidence comes from the survey by the CDC on 337,093 U.S. children aged 8 in 2008, where an average prevalence of 113/10,000 was reported across 14 U.S. states (CDC, 2012). One striking finding in this report is the almost 4.5-fold variation in prevalence rates by state (range: 48–212 per 10,000; see Figure 3.4).

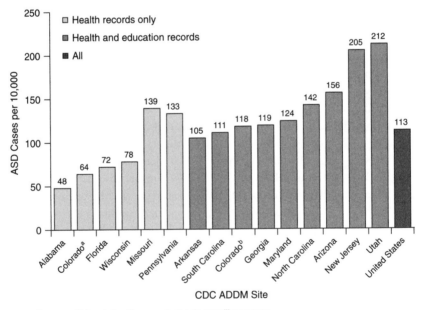

ªExpanded Colorado health source type only surveillance area.
ᵇColorado health and education source type surveillance area.

Figure 3.4 Estimated prevalence of ASDs among children aged 8 years in the United States by ADDM site and type of records access (CDC, 2012).

Across individual states, Alabama had the lowest rate of 48/10,000, whereas Utah and New Jersey had the highest rates (212 and 205 per 10,000, respectively; CDC, 2012). It would be surprising if there were truly this much state-to-state variability in the number of children with autism in the United States. These substantial differences most certainly reflected ascertainment variability across sites in a study that was otherwise performed with the same methods, at the same time, on children of the same age, and within the same country.

On average, estimated ASD prevalence was significantly lower in states that had access to health data sources only compared to that of states where educational data was also available (89 versus 144 out of 10,000, respectively). This is exemplified by data from Colorado, in which two prevalence estimates were available: one based on six counties with access to health data sources only (64 per 10,000), and the other based on a single county with access to both health and education records (118 per 10,000). Thus, within one state, there was a 1.8-fold variation in prevalence estimates depending on the availability of records (CDC, 2012). Although differences in prevalence estimates across states cannot be attributed solely to records access (e.g., service availability and other state-specific factors are also likely to contribute), this is a factor that is consistently associated with higher prevalence rates in the ADDM Network. The 2012 CDC report also included the highest proportion of identified children with a previously documented ASD classification for any ADDM surveillance year (79%), offering evidence that community providers are increasingly likely to identify and document ASDs. Taken together with the higher proportion of children with ASD diagnosed by 36 months of age and the increased identification among children without intellectual disability, these factors suggest that improved sensitivity in case ascertainment within the ADDM Network has contributed substantially to the increase in prevalence. Thus, no inference on trends in the incidence of ASDs can be derived from a simple comparison of prevalence rates over time, since studies conducted at different periods are likely to differ even more with respect to their methodologies.

Repeat Surveys in Defined Geographical Areas

Repeated surveys, using the same methodology and conducted in the same geographical area at different points in time, can potentially yield useful information on time trends provided that methods are kept relatively constant. The Göteborg studies (Gillberg, 1984; Gillberg, Steffenburg, & Schaumann, 1991) provided three prevalence estimates that increased over a short period of time from 4.0 (1980) to 6.6 (1984) and 9.5/10,000 (1988), the gradient being even steeper if rates for the urban area alone are considered (4.0, 7.5, and 11.6/10,000, respectively) (Gillberg et al., 1991). However, comparison of these rates is not straightforward, as different age groups were included in each survey. Second, the increased prevalence in the second survey was explained by improved detection among those with intellectual delays, and that of the third survey by cases born to immigrant parents. That the majority of the latter group was born abroad suggests that migration into the area could be a key explanation. Taken in conjunction with a change in local services and a progressive broadening of the definition of autism over time that was acknowledged by the authors (Gillberg et al., 1991), these findings do not provide evidence for an increased incidence in the rate of autism. Similarly, studies conducted in Japan at different points in time in Toyota (Kawamura, Takahashi, O., & Ishii, 2008) and Yokohama (Honda, Shimizu, Misumi, Niimi, & Ohashi, 1996; Honda, Shimizu, & Rutter, 2005) showed rises in prevalence rates that their authors interpreted as reflecting the effect of both improved population screening of preschoolers and a broadening of diagnostic concepts and criteria.

Two separate surveys of children born between 1992 and 1995 and between 1996 and 1998 in Staffordshire, United Kingdom (Chakrabarti & Fombonne, 2001, 2005), were performed with rigorously identical methods for case definition and case identification. The prevalence for combined ASDs was comparable and not statistically different in the two surveys (Chakrabarti & Fombonne, 2005), suggesting no upward trend in overall rates of ASDs, at least during the short time interval between studies.

Comparisons between successive CDC ADDM surveillance years also shed light on time trends using consistent methodology. In the 2008 surveillance year (prevalence: 113/10,000; CDC, 2012), 11 sites also contributed to the 2006 surveillance year (prevalence: 90/10,000; CDC, 2009). Of those, seven sites identified a higher prevalence in 2008 compared to 2006, whereas three sites were similar across both years, and one site (Alabama) reported a lower prevalence in 2008 compared to 2006, with rates increasing on average 23% during 2006–2008. In comparing the 2008 surveillance year to 2002, 12 out of 13 sites that contributed to both reports identified significantly higher prevalence in 2008 than in 2002 (with the exception of Arkansas), with rates increasing on average 78% during 2002–2008. Nevertheless, CDC researchers concluded that increases in ASD prevalence over successive surveillance years were influenced by a number of factors, including increased awareness and access to services, making it impossible to determine whether any proportion of the observed increase is attributable to a true increase in ASD in the population.

Birth Cohorts

In large surveys encompassing a wide age range, increasing prevalence rates among most recent birth cohorts could be interpreted as indicating a secular increase in ASD incidence, provided that alternative explanations can confidently be eliminated. This analysis was used in two large French surveys (Fombonne & du Mazaubrun, 1992; Fombonne, du Mazaubrun, Cans, & Grandjean, 1997). The surveys included birth cohorts from 1972 to 1985 (735,000 children, 389 of whom had autism), and when pooling the data of both surveys, age-specific rates showed no upward trend (Fombonne et al., 1997).

An analysis of special educational data from Minnesota showed a 16-fold increase in the number of children identified with an ASD from 1991–1992 to 2001–2002 (Gurney et al., 2003). The increase was not specific to autism since, during the same period, an increase of 50% was observed for all disability categories (except severe intellectual deficiency), especially for the category including attention-deficit/hyperactivity disorder (ADHD). The large sample size allowed the authors to assess age, period, and cohort effects. Prevalence increased regularly in successive birth cohorts; for example, among 7-year-olds, the prevalence rose from 18/10,000 in those born in 1989, to 29/10,000 in those born in 1991, and to 55/10,000 in those born in 1993, suggestive of birth cohort effects. Within the *same* birth cohorts, age effects were also apparent since for children born in 1989 the prevalence rose with age from 13/10,000 at age 6, to 21/10,000 at age 9, and 33/10,000 at age 11. As argued by Gurney et al. (2003), this pattern is not consistent with that expected from a chronic nonfatal condition diagnosed during the first years of life. Their analysis also showed a marked period effect that identified the early 1990s as the period where rates started to increase in all ages and birth cohorts. Gurney et al. (2003) further argued that this phenomenon coincided closely with the inclusion of ASDs in the federal Individuals with Disabilities Educational Act (IDEA) funding and reporting mechanism in the United States. A similar interpretation of upward trends had been put forward by Croen, Grether, Hoogstrate, et al. (2002) in their analysis of the California DDS data, and by Shattuck (2006) in his well-executed analysis of trends in the Department of Education data in all U.S. states.

Using hypothetical data, increasing prevalence rates across and within birth cohorts are illustrated in Figure 3.5. As reported in several studies (e.g., Gurney et al., 2003; Keyes et al., 2012; Nassar et al., 2009), we portray an increase in the prevalence of ASD by year of birth across three hypothetical successive birth cohorts (a cohort effect; Figure 3.5a). Within each birth cohort, followed longitudinally, prevalence rates also increase as children age

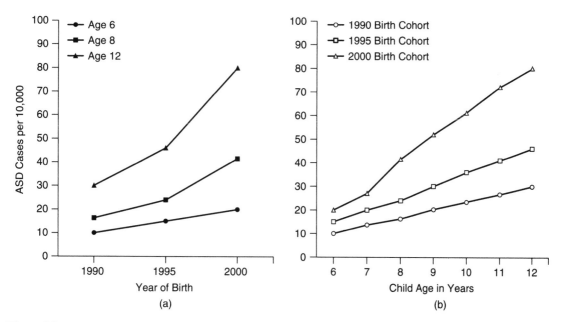

Figure 3.5   Time trends in ASD prevalence rates across and within birth cohorts (hypothetical data).

(Figure 3.5b): For children in the 2000 birth cohort, based on previous ASD prevalence estimates, age 6 prevalence is 20/10,000, whereas at age 12, we may expect prevalence of 80/10,000 for the same birth cohort. Increasing prevalence rates with age within birth cohorts cannot reflect the onset of ASD in later childhood and early adolescence. It is more likely that observed increases in prevalence reflect underdiagnosis in the preschool years as well as changes in public awareness, service availability, and diagnostic concepts and practices.

A similar scenario was recently reported in a Faroe Islands survey in which researchers followed up on a 2002 population study (Ellefsen et al., 2007). In the follow-up study, Kočovská, Biskupsto, et al. (2012) observed a substantially increased ASD prevalence of 94/10,000 in individuals aged 15 to 24 years, compared to 53.3/10,000 in almost the exact same sample at ages 8 to 17 (Ellefsen et al., 2007). If treated as two separate cross-sectional studies separated by 7 years, we might interpret this pattern of results as a rise in incidence. However, because the sample was almost exactly the same cohort as in the first study, the researchers suggest the rising prevalence in this study reflects newly identified cases that were

simply missed before, and suggest that the apparent rise may be due to lack of awareness for the clinical presentation of ASD in females, which accounted for the majority of missed cases in the follow-up study.

Implications of Upcoming Changes to Diagnostic Criteria

The changes now occurring in the DSM with the new fifth edition (*DSM-5*; APA, 2013) may impact prevalence estimates in the future and, if so, will make it more difficult to compare past and future surveys and interpret time trends. *DSM-5* proposes a single new category of Autism Spectrum Disorders, conceptually equivalent to the previous diagnostic class of PDDs. However, fewer diagnostic criteria have been retained (7 instead of 12) that are combined in two clusters of social communication deficits (three criteria; all must be met) and restricted patterns of behaviors and interests (two of the four criteria must be met). The removal of the loosely defined PDD-NOS from *DSM-IV-TR* (APA, 2000) will likely increase the specificity of the ASD diagnostic category, and the removal of Asperger Disorder as a separate category is consistent with research that has generally failed to provide evidence for the discriminant validity of this diagnostic concept vis-à-vis forms of autistic disorder that are not associated with severe language impairments or intellectual deficits. Concerns have been raised that subjects with a previous *DSM-IV* diagnosis of PDD may fail to meet the more stringent diagnostic criteria for ASD in *DSM-5*, thereby losing access to services and support systems that require a diagnosis for eligibility. Nine studies have recently been published that examined the relationship between *DSM-5* and *DSM-IV* or *ICD-10* using clinical or research samples of various origins (Frazier et al., 2012; Gibbs, Aldridge, Chandler, Witzlsperger, & Smith, 2012; Huerta, Bishop, Duncan, Hus, & Lord, 2012; Matson, Belva, Horovitz, Kozlowski, & Bamburg, 2012; Matson, Hattier, & Williams, 2012; Mattila et al., 2011; McPartland, Reichow, & Volkmar, 2012; Taheri & Perry, 2012; Worley & Matson, 2012). The proportion of subjects who met criteria for ASD in *DSM-5* ranged from a low 46% (Mattila et al., 2011) to a high 91% (Huerta et al., 2012). It is important to recognize that by design these proportions could only be lower or equal to 100%. Due to the fact that past diagnostic information was collected at a time when *DSM-5* was not available, it is very possible that the new information required in *DSM-5* (e.g., with a new diagnostic emphasis on sensory processing deficits) was simply not available for rescoring *DSM-5*. Equally, the studies were constrained in sampling children with a *DSM-IV* PDD diagnosis and could not therefore estimate which proportion of children who did not meet criteria for *DSM-IV* would have met those for *DSM-5* should data on children failing *DSM-IV* criteria had been available.

The impact of *DSM-5* changes on epidemiological estimates remains to be fully assessed in the context of epidemiological surveys. Only one study has thus far shed light on this issue. Kim et al. (submitted) reanalyzed the survey data of the South Korean study (Kim et al., 2011) and reapplied both *DSM-IV* and *DSM-5* criteria to a population based sample of cases identified in the original survey. The authors used the *DSM-5* ASD category as well as the new diagnostic category

of Social Communication Disorder (SCD) that has been added to ASD largely in anticipation of children with few repetitive behaviors and a PDD-NOS diagnosis in *DSM-IV* now meeting criteria for SCD rather than ASD in *DSM-5*. Indeed, the prevalence estimate for *DSM-5* ASD in the South Korean survey was 17% lower (2.20%) than that with *DSM-IV* (2.64%); 99% of subjects with a *DSM-IV* diagnosis and 92% of those with an Asperger Disorder diagnosis met *DSM-5* criteria for ASD, and all others met criteria for SCD. For PDD-NOS, 63% met criteria for ASD and an additional 32% for SCD. When *DSM-5* ASD and SCD were considered together, there was no significant change in the prevalence estimate. More studies are on their way that will provide further examination of the impact on prevalence estimates of narrowing the ASD definition in *DSM-5*.

Conclusion on Time Trends

As it stands now, the recent upward trend in rates of *prevalence* cannot be directly attributed to an increase in the *incidence* of the disorder, or to an epidemic of autism. There is good evidence that changes in diagnostic criteria, diagnostic substitution, changes in the policies for special education, and the increasing availability of services are responsible for the higher prevalence figures. It is also noteworthy that the rise in number of children diagnosed occurred at the same time in many countries (in the early 1990s), when radical shifts occurred in the ideas, diagnostic approaches, and services for children with ASDs. Alternatively, this might, of course, reflect the effect of environmental influences operating simultaneously in different parts of the world. However, there has been no proposed and legitimate environmental risk mechanism to account for this worldwide effect. Moreover, due to the relatively low frequency of autism and ASDs, statistical power is a significant limitation in most investigations, and variations of small magnitude in the incidence of the disorder are very likely to go undetected. Equally, the possibility that a true increase in the incidence of ASDs has also partially contributed to the upward trend in prevalence rates cannot, and should not, be eliminated based on available data. It remains to be seen how changes to diagnostic criteria introduced in the *DSM-5* will impact estimates of ASD prevalence.

CORRELATES OF ASDs IN EPIDEMIOLOGICAL SURVEYS

Studies of associations between ASDs and socioeconomic status (SES), race/ethnicity, and immigrant status have shown variable results and face numerous technical challenges. In general, studies that base diagnosis rates on developmental service utilization may undercount minority and low SES children. Underprivileged children have less health services access overall (Shi & Stevens, 2005) and particularly low mental health services access (Kataoka, Zhang, & Wells, 2002), which can lead to underidentification of ASD. In contrast, children with more educated, wealthier, or more health-literate parents may have resources to make their way to ASD diagnostic services and, therefore, an ASD diagnosis (Tsai, Stewart, Faust, & Shook, 1982). Cross-sectional studies based on parent report of ASD are problematic for the same reason, as parent report of ASD is more likely among families who have adequate access to ASD-related services. Undercounting of minorities may additionally occur in the context of multistage, population-based research. Minority and low SES families may participate in such research studies at disproportionately low rates, due to higher rates of distrust of scientific researchers (Rajakumar, Thomas, Musa, Almario, & Garza, 2009) or less access to research opportunities. They also may be excluded from studies or incorrectly assessed if forms are not available in appropriate languages or if a language-congruent assessor is not available (Laing & Hamhi, 2003). Finally, because ASD is a relatively rare event, population-based studies of ASD prevalence may have relatively small numbers of low SES, minority, or immigrant children meeting case criteria, making data difficult to interpret (e.g., Powell et al., 2000; Sponheim & Skjedal, 1998).

Socioeconomic Status

Socioeconomic status can be defined variously, the most common methods being parental education, income, parental occupation, or some combination of these factors. Over 20 studies have investigated associations between these factors and ASD prevalence.

Many recent U.S.-based studies suggest an association between higher SES (as assessed by one of these factors) and higher ASD prevalence. Several recent studies have used CDC ADDM data combined with imputed sociodemographic data from U.S. Census tracts to show a link between parental income/education and ASD diagnosis. Using 2007 data from New Jersey, Thomas et al. (2012) showed that the ASD prevalence ratio between the highest income tract (>$90,000 USD) and the lowest income tract (<$30,000 USD) was 2.2. In addition, children in the higher income tracts were more likely to have a higher number of professional evaluations and a lower age of diagnosis, suggesting a referral bias or an underdiagnosis of children at the lower end of the SES spectrum. Using CDC ADDM data from all 14 participating states, Durkin et al. (2010) developed a composite SES indicator that took into account both parental education and household income. This study found a dose-response relationship between SES and ASD prevalence, regardless of gender and data source. SES-based differences in prevalence were significantly weaker when children with a previous ASD diagnosis (as opposed to a new diagnosis in context of the study) were excluded, a finding that suggests that prior access to ASD diagnostic services may explain some of the difference. Both of these studies benefit from a population-based data collection framework; however, they are limited in that no individual level SES data was available.

Similarly, Bhasin and Schendel (2007) conducted a population-based case-control study, directly measuring maternal education and imputing household income from census tract data in Atlanta, Georgia. Higher median family income was significantly associated with autism overall. Both markers of higher SES (higher maternal education and higher median family income) were significantly associated with autism without intellectual disability (ID) but not autism with ID, suggesting that, in addition to biases based on service access, diagnostic substitution may be occurring more frequently among children with higher SES. Leonard et al. (2011) observed a similar finding in Western Australian children born from 1984 to 1999. The prevalence of ASD without ID was significantly increased among children whose mothers had more economic resources.

One criticism of these recent studies, particularly the studies based in the United States, is that SES has been confounded by inequitable health services access, and that in a setting where health services access is more equitable, the effects of SES might be lessened or even reversed. In a Denmark population-based case-control study, Larsson et al. (2005) found that the risk of ASD was actually higher among children with less parental wealth in bivariate analyses, but that after adjusting for other demographic factors, there was no association of either parental education or wealth with ASD; similar results were found in adjusted analysis performed in China (N. Li et al., 2011). In a Swedish case-control study by Rai, Lewis, et al. (2012), children in families with lower income and whose parents had manual occupations were at higher risk for ASD diagnosis after multivariate adjustment. In England, which also has national health insurance, Brugha et al. (2011) found that ASD adults with higher educational attainment had lower rates of autism after multivariate adjustment; however, it is likely that an ASD diagnosis may have reduced the subjects' educational attainment. In contrast, in an Israeli study, where access to and coverage of ASD-related services was reported to be excellent, Davidovitch et al. (2012) found lower prevalence of ASD in children who lived in low-income versus higher-income communities, or whose families did not purchase supplemental private insurance.

Overall, many recent large-scale studies have shown an association between ASD prevalence and SES, although it appears that these differences were due to decreased access to diagnostic services among children with lower SES, or diagnostic substitution between ID and ASD among children with higher SES. In settings where health care is more accessible, these effects seem to lessen or even reverse. To date, no plausible biological mechanism has been proposed or supported that might explain SES-related differences in ASD prevalence. The fact that older studies either did not show SES associations (e.g., Gillberg & Schaumann, 1982; Ritvo et al., 1989; Tsai et al., 1982) or showed variability based on referral source (Wing, 1980) or autism subtype (Sanua, 1987) also support the fact that SES differences are due to differences in ASD ascertainment as opposed to an underlying biological or psychosocial mechanism.

Race/Ethnicity

Many studies of racial/ethnic minorities show lower rates of ASD compared to White or European populations, although these differences appear to be narrowing in more current studies. The evidence is strongest for African American and Hispanic populations in the United States. Several recent studies are highlighted here, although other recent studies show similar findings (Liptak et al., 2008; Mandell et al., 2009). Since minority race and ethnic status often correlates with lower SES and worse health care access, studies attempting to assess the effects of race/ethnicity on ASD diagnosis should control for SES and health care accessibility factors in their analyses.

Using administrative data from Texas school districts, Palmer, Walker, Mandell, Bayles, and Miller (2010) showed that the number of autism diagnoses in a school district was inversely proportional to the number of Hispanic school children in that district, after adjusting for number of pediatricians, child psychologists, and neurologists by county, as well as county median household income. A strength of this approach is that it did attempt to adjust for SES as well as differential services availability, as well as comorbid ID and learning disabilities on a population level. Interestingly, these factors better explained variability in ASD diagnoses among White non-Hispanic children than Hispanic children, suggesting that SES and access factors alone do not explain lower diagnosis rates in Hispanics, at least on a population level. However, this ecological study did not measure individual-level access factors (e.g., insurance adequacy) or factors such as provider bias that may also impact ASD diagnostic rates.

The most recent CDC ADDM data also suggest an overall lower rate of ASD among non-Hispanic Black (102/10,000) and Hispanic children (79/10,000) compared to White children (120/10,000) in the 14 U.S. states that participated in the study. However, there was considerable variability among the states, with some states reporting higher rates of ASD among Hispanics than among Whites, for example, suggesting that administrative records may have had systematic biases in some states. In addition, when the surveillance data from 2008 was compared to previous waves of data collection, Hispanic and African American populations had greater increases in diagnosis rates (respectively, 29% and 42%; although continued overall rates of underdiagnosis) than non-Hispanic White children (16%; CDC, 2012). Pedersen et al. (2012) examined racial/ethnic differences more thoroughly using several waves of ADDM data in Arizona, which has a large Hispanic population. That study also found a lower rate of ASD in Hispanic children compared to non-Hispanic White children. ASD prevalence increased in both populations over the study years, and the gap in prevalence between racial/ethnic groups decreased. The authors speculated that much of this difference might be attributable to underutilization and lack of access to ASD services by Hispanic families. They also speculated that these differences might reflect the "Hispanic paradox" or "healthy immigrant" effect, in which Hispanic immigrants to the United States have lower rates of multiple adverse health outcomes despite multiple SES and health-care access risk factors (Franzini, Ribble, & Keddie, 2001). However, the fact that differences in diagnostic rates are narrowing rather rapidly suggests that changes in awareness and utilization of services may be more likely than inherent genetic or developmental differences by race/ethnicity.

Windham et al. (2011) used a large administrative sample from multiple sources in Northern California, to show a lower prevalence of ASD among children of Hispanic and Black mothers compared to children of White non-Hispanic mothers, after adjusting for maternal education and age, with similar decreases in racial differences over the study years. However, the observed racial variation was attenuated by adjustment for SES and varied significantly by data source, suggesting that variable health services utilization may have affected ASD rates.

Finally, in a U.S. population-based study using parent report of ASD diagnosis, Kogan et al. (2009) found lower rates of ASD diagnosis in non-Hispanic Black and multiracial children when compared to White children, after adjusting for parental education and income. This study also noted a disproportionately high number of Black children whose parents reported a past diagnosis of ASD that subsequently resolved, which runs contrary to most epidemiologic data about ASD lifetime trajectories. This finding suggests that low rates of ASD among Black children may be due to racial differences in parent health beliefs about ASD. This study found no significant difference in ASD diagnoses by Hispanic versus non-Hispanic ethnicity; however, follow-up analysis of the same dataset by Schieve et al. (2012) showed that there were significantly lower rates of ASD among Hispanic children with foreign-born parents compared to White children. Schieve et al. concluded that by failing to take into account the heterogeneity of Hispanic children with ASD, previous studies that grouped all Hispanics together may have been biased toward a null result. The authors felt that the findings were likely related to differences in parental awareness and access to care stemming from a lower level of acculturation for this subgroup. They also speculated that the findings might reflect the healthy immigrant effect.

In studies outside of the United States, reports about racial/ethnic differences in ASD prevalence have been more mixed, and most studies are not adjusted for SES, which makes it difficult to assess the unique effect of race/ethnicity from other confounders. In addition these studies are difficult to interpret since what constitutes a minority race or ethnicity is quite variable by country. In Israel, Davidovitch et al. (2012) found a lower prevalence of ASD among Arab Israelis in rural settlements and in ultra-Orthodox Jews than in the general Israeli population, although prevalence was not adjusted for SES differences. Findings from a 1999–2003 census report in Stockholm, Sweden (Barnevik-Olsson, Gillberg, & Fernell, 2010), revealed that the prevalence rate of autism (autism and PDD-NOS/autistic-like condition) with learning disability was higher in Somali versus non-Somali Swedish children. The study did not adjust for SES differences between these mothers and other Swedish mothers. The authors hypothesized that lower levels of vitamin D in immigrant Somali mothers may have affected fetal brain development and possibly led to autism and other concerning behavioral characteristics; however, the study did not measure vitamin D in any of the participants (see Kočovská, Fernell, Billstedt, Minnis, & Gillberg, 2012, for a recent review on the role of vitamin D in ASD). Several older, unadjusted studies also suggest a higher prevalence of ASD among recent Swedish immigrants, although these immigrants' countries of origins were so mixed that it is difficult to interpret this information in terms of ethnic or racial differences (Gillberg et al., 1987; Gillberg et al., 1991; Gillberg et al., 1995).

Overall, most recent studies about racial/ethnic differences in ASD diagnosis do suggest that race/ethnicity affects diagnostic rates above and beyond SES alone, at least in U.S.-based populations. However, given that the racial/ethnic effects are present in several traditionally underserved racial/ethnic groups, are quite variable by data source and study type, and have narrowed over time, they are most likely explained by differential health services utilization, parental health beliefs, and acculturation. Little high-quality data is available about the effects of race/ethnicity in non-U.S. settings.

Migration and Prenatal Exposure to Stressful Events

Migration has historically been implicated as a possible risk factor for autism, based on observed higher rates of autism among immigrant populations in some epidemiological surveys (Barnevik-Olsson et al., 2010; Gillberg et al., 1987; Gillberg et al., 1991; Gillberg et al., 1995; Wing, 1980). However, evidence for an association between migration and ASD has been inconsistent, with some recent studies reporting increased ASD risk among immigrant populations (e.g., Hultman, Sparen, & Cnattingius, 2002; Keen, Reid, & Arnone, 2010; Lauritsen, Pedersen, & Mortensen, 2005) and others reporting equivalent and even decreased ASD risk in some populations (Croen, Grether, & Selvin, 2002; Gillberg et al., 1987; Hultman et al., 2002; Lauritsen et al., 2005). Most of the early claims about migration as a possible correlate of autism derived from post hoc observations of very small samples and were not subjected to rigorous statistical testing. However, recent studies have attempted to reexamine the association between migration and ASDs. For example, in a recent study using a population-based Swedish cohort, Magnusson et al. (2012) found that children of migrant parents were at increased risk for ASD with intellectual disability compared to children of Swedish-born parents. However, the reverse was true for ASD without intellectual disability: Children of Swedish-born parents were at significantly higher risk than children of migrant parents, particularly those from countries with low human development indices. The authors suggest that the most plausible explanation for this pattern of findings is the underdiagnosis of ASD in migrant children with high cognitive abilities; for these children, the more subtle social deficits associated with ASD may be overlooked or misattributed to language or cultural differences. In addition, because case ascertainment was based on service use, migrant families may have been less aware of or less likely to seek services in the community in the absence of clear developmental or cognitive delays. However, the researchers also suggest that we cannot dismiss the possibility of environmental factors associated with migration and acting in utero that may contribute to ASD.

One environmental factor associated with migration that has been posited to contribute to ASD risk is prenatal exposure to stressful life events, due to the fact that migration itself is likely to be a stressful event as it may occur when families flee armed conflict or other extreme conditions in their home country (e.g., Magnusson et al., 2012). Using a population-based cohort of approximately 1.5 million singleton children in Denmark, J. Li et al. (2009) examined whether prenatal exposure to maternal bereavement (loss of a child, spouse, parent, or sibling during or up to 1 year prior to pregnancy) was associated with increased risk of ASD (*ICD-8/ICD-10* criteria). J. Li et al. (2009) found no evidence of an effect of maternal bereavement on autism risk, even after accounting for the timing, nature, and severity of the exposure, although maternal bereavement was rare even in the total population (experienced by 2.5%). Similarly, in a recent study utilizing population-based cohorts in Sweden and England, Rai, Golding, et al. (2012) also found no evidence for an association between prenatal exposure to stressful life events, including deaths, serious accidents, and diagnosis of serious illnesses in first-degree relatives, and ASD risk, although again these events were extremely rare (experienced by 1% of the population). Thus, the hypothesis of an association between migration, as well as exposure to other prenatal stressful events, with ASD remains largely unsupported by the empirical results. However, it should be noted that even with large-scale population-based cohorts, these events were extremely rare.

Implications and Unmet Research Needs

Overall, the research findings related to low SES, minority, and immigrant populations primarily point to problems of underdiagnosis due to

problems in access to health care services and health literacy. Evidence for a biological difference based on SES, race/ethnicity, or immigration is weak, as is the case for multiple other chronic health conditions among children and adults (Pearce, Foliaki, Sporle, & Cunningham, 2004). In order to obtain an accurate depiction of ASD prevalence in underserved populations, investigators will need to specifically reach out to these populations to ensure equal participation, and also oversample these groups so that sample sizes are adequate. In addition there is a need for validated screening and diagnostic tools in multiple languages to ensure that diagnoses, when they occur, are accurate. Finally, key variables in these analyses such as parental education, income, and race/ethnicity need to be directly measured as opposed to imputed from census tract data.

CONCLUSION

Epidemiological surveys of autism and ASDs have now been conducted in many countries. Methodological differences regarding case definition and finding procedures make between survey comparisons difficult to perform. However, from recent studies, a best estimate of (66/10,000) (equivalences = 6.6/1,000 or .66% or 1 child in about 152 children) can be confidently derived for the prevalence of ASD. Current evidence does not strongly support the hypothesis of a secular increase in the incidence of autism, but power to detect time trends is seriously limited in existing datasets. While it is clear that prevalence estimates have increased over time, this increase most likely represents changes in the concepts, definitions, service availability, and awareness of autistic-spectrum disorders in both the lay and professional public. To assess whether the incidence has increased, methodological factors that account for an important proportion of the variability in rates must be stringently controlled for. New survey methods have been developed for use in multinational comparisons; ongoing surveillance programs are currently under way and will soon provide more meaningful data to evaluate this hypothesis. The possibility that a true change in the underlying incidence has contributed to higher prevalence figures remains to be adequately tested. Meanwhile, the available prevalence figures carry straightforward implications for current and future needs in services and early educational intervention programs.

CROSS-REFERENCES

Chapter 1 addresses diagnostic issues; Chapter 2 focuses on the broader autism phenotype, Chapter 24 and 25 on screening and assessment instruments, and Chapter 49 on social policy and services planning.

REFERENCES

Al-Farsi, Y., Al-Sharbati, M., Al-Farsi, O., Al-Shafaee, M., Brooks, D., & Waly, M. (2011). Brief report: Prevalence of autistic spectrum disorder in the Sultanate of Oman. *Journal of Autism and Developmental Disorders, 41*(6), 821–825.

American Psychiatric Association. (1980). *Diagnostic and statistical manual of mental disorders* (3rd ed.). Washington, DC: Author.

American Psychiatric Association. (1987). *Diagnostic and statistical manual of mental disorders* (3rd ed., rev.). Washington, DC: Author.

American Psychiatric Association. (1994). *Diagnostic and statistical manual of mental disorders*. (4th ed.). Washington, DC: Author.

American Psychiatric Association. (2000). *Diagnostic and statistical manual of mental disorders* (4th ed., text rev.). Washington, DC: Author.

American Psychiatric Association. (2013). *Diagnostic and statistical manual of mental disorders* (5th ed.). Arlington, VA: American Psychiatric Publishing.

Arvidsson, T., Danielsson, B., Forsberg, P., Gillberg, C., Johansson, M., & Kjellgren, G. (1997). Autism in 3–6 year-olds in a suburb of Göteborg, Sweden. *Autism, 2*, 163–173.

Baird, G., Charman, T., Baron-Cohen, S., Cox, A., Swettenham, J., Wheelwright, S., & Drew, A. (2000). A screening instrument for autism at 18 months of age: A 6-year follow-up study. *Journal of the American Academy of Child & Adolescent Psychiatry, 39*, 694–702.

Baird, G., Simonoff, E., Pickles, A., Chandler, S., Loucas, T., Meldrum, D., & Charman, T. (2006). Prevalence of disorders of the autism spectrum in a population cohort of children in South Thames: The special needs and autism project (SNAP). *Lancet, 368*(9531), 210–215.

Barbaresi, W. J., Katusic, S. K., Colligan, R. C., Weaver, A. L., & Jacobsen, S. J. (2005). The incidence of autism in Olmsted County, Minnesota, 1976–1997: Results from a population-based study. *Archives of Pediatrics and Adolescent Medicine, 159*(1), 37–44.

Barnevik-Olsson, M., Gillberg, C., & Fernell, E. (2010). Prevalence of autism in children of Somali origin living in Stockholm: Brief report of an at-risk population. *Developmental Medicine & Child Neurology, 52*, 1167–1168.

Baron-Cohen, S., Scott, F. J., Allison, C., Williams, J., Bolton, P., Matthews, F. E., & Brayne, C. (2009). Prevalence of autism-spectrum conditions: UK school-based population study. *British Journal of Psychiatry, 194*(6), 500–509.

Bertrand, J., Mars, A., Boyle, C., Bove, F., Yeargin-Allsopp, M., & Decoufle, P. (2001). Prevalence of autism in a United States population: The Brick Township, New Jersey, investigation. *Pediatrics, 108*(5), 1155–1161.

Bhasin, T. K., & Schendel, D. (2007). Sociodemographic risk factors for autism in a U.S. metropolitan area. *Journal of Autism and Developmental Disorders, 37*(4), 667–677.

Bishop, D. V., Whitehouse, A. J., Watt, H. J., & Line, E. A. (2008). Autism and diagnostic substitution: Evidence from a study of adults with a history of developmental language disorder. *Developmental Medicine & Child Neurology, 50*(5), 341–345.

Blumberg, S., Bramlett, M., Kogan, M., Schieve, L., Jones, J., & Lu, M. C. (2013). Changes in prevalence of parent-reported autism spectrum disorder in school-aged U.S. children: 2007 to 2011–2012. *National Health Statistics Reports, 65*, 1–12.

Bohman, M., Bohman, I., Bjorck, P., & Sjoholm, E. (1983). Childhood psychosis in a northern Swedish county: Some preliminary findings from an epidemiological survey. In M. Schmidt & H. Remschmidt (Eds.), *Epidemiological approaches in child psychiatry* (pp. 164–173). Stuttgart: Georg Thieme Verlag.

Brask, B. (1970). *A prevalence investigation of childhood psychoses.* Paper presented at the Nordic Symposium on the Care of Psychotic Children, Oslo, Norway.

Brugha, T. S., McManus, S., Bankart, J., Scott, F., Purdon, S., Smith, J., . . . Meltzer, H. (2011). Epidemiology of autism spectrum disorders in adults in the community in England. *Archives of General Psychiatry, 68*(5), 459–466.

Bryson, S. E., Clark, B. S., & Smith, I. M. (1988). First report of a Canadian epidemiological study of autistic syndromes. *Journal of Child Psychology & Psychiatry and Allied Disciplines, 29*(4), 433–445.

Burd, L., Fisher, W., & Kerbeshan, J. (1987). A prevalence study of pervasive developmental disorders in North Dakota. *Journal of the American Academy of Child & Adolescent Psychiatry, 26*, 700–703.

California Department of Developmental Services. (1999, March 1). *Changes in the population of persons with autism and pervasive developmental disorders in California's Developmental Services System: 1987 through 1998.* Report to the Legislature March 1, 1999, 19 pages. Retrieved from http://www.dds.ca.gov

California Department of Developmental Services. (2003, April). *Autism spectrum disorders: Changes in the California caseload—an update 1999 through 2002.* Retrieved from http://www.dds.ca.gov/Autism/docs/AutismReport2003.pdf

California Department of Developmental Services (2007, December). Table 34. Retrieved from http://www.dds.ca.gov /FactsStats/docs/Dec07_QRTTBLS.pdf

Campbell, D. B., Reynolds, L., Cunningham, J., Minnis, H., & Gillberg, C. G. (2011). Autism in Glasgow: Cumulative incidence and the effects of referral age, deprivation and geographic location. *Child: Care, Health and Development*, 1–7.

Centers for Disease Control. (2007a). Prevalence of autism spectrum disorders—Autism and developmental disabilities monitoring network, six sites, United States, 2000. *Morbidity and Mortality Weekly Report Surveillance Summary*, 56(1), 1–11.

Centers for Disease Control. (2007b). Prevalence of autism spectrum disorders—Autism and developmental disabilities monitoring network, 14 sites, United States, 2002. *Morbidity and Mortality Weekly Report Surveillance Summary*, 56(1), 12–28.

Centers for Disease Control. (2009). Prevalence of autism spectrum disorders—Autism and developmental disabilities monitoring network, United States, 2006. *Morbidity and Mortality Weekly Report Surveillance Summary*, 58, 1–14.

Centers for Disease Control. (2012). Prevalence of autism spectrum disorders—Autism and developmental disabilities monitoring network, 14 sites, United States, 2008. *Morbidity and Mortality Weekly Report Surveillance Summary*, 61(3), 1–19.

Chakrabarti, S., & Fombonne, E. (2001). Pervasive developmental disorders in preschool children. *Journal of the American Medical Association*, 285(24), 3093–3099.

Chakrabarti, S., & Fombonne, E. (2005). Pervasive developmental disorders in preschool children: Confirmation of high prevalence. *American Journal of Psychiatry*, 162(6), 1133–1141.

Chien, C., Lin, C., Chou, Y., & Chou, P. (2011). Prevalence and incidence of autism spectrum disorders among national health insurance enrollees in Taiwan from 1996 to 2005. *Journal of Child Neurology*, 26(7), 830–834.

Cialdella, P., & Mamelle, N. (1989). An epidemiological study of infantile autism in a French department (Rhone): A research note. *Journal of Child Psychology & Psychiatry and Allied Disciplines*, 30(1), 165–175.

Croen, L. A., Grether, J. K., & Selvin, S. (2002). Descriptive epidemiology of autism in a California population: Who is at risk? *Journal of Autism and Developmental Disorders*, 32, 217–224.

Croen, L. A., Grether, J. K., Hoogstrate, J., & Selvin, S. (2002). The changing prevalence of autism in California. *Journal of Autism and Developmental Disorders*, 32(3), 207–215.

Croen, L. A., Najjar, D. V., Fireman, B., & Grether, J. K. (2007). Maternal and paternal age and risk of autism spectrum disorders. *Archives of Pediatrics and Adolescent Medicine*, 161(4), 334–340.

Davidovitch, M., Hemo, B., Manning-Courtney, P., & Fombonne, E. (2012). Prevalence and incidence of autism spectrum disorder in an Israeli population. *Journal of Autism and Developmental Disorders*, 43(4), 785–793.

Davidovitch, M., Holtzman, G., & Tirosh, E. (2001, March). Autism in the Haifa area: An epidemiological perspective. *Israeli Medical Association Journal*, 3, 188–189.

Durkin, M. S., Maenner, M. J., Meaney, F. J., Levy, S. E., DiGuiseppi, C., Nicholas, J. S., ... Schieve, L. A. (2010). Socioeconomic inequality in the prevalence of autism spectrum disorder: Evidence from a U.S. cross-sectional study. *PLoS One*, 5(7), e11551. doi:10.1371/ journal.pone.0011551

Eagle, R. S. (2004). Commentary: Further commentary on the debate regarding increase in autism in California. *Journal of Autism and Developmental Disorders*, 34(1), 87–88.

Ehlers, S., & Gillberg, C. (1993). The epidemiology of Asperger syndrome: A total population study. *Journal of Child Psychology & Psychiatry and Allied Disciplines*, 34(8), 1327–1350.

Ellefsen, A., Kampmann, H., Billstedt, E., Gillberg, I. C., & Gillberg, C. (2007). Autism in the Faroe Islands: An epidemiological study. *Journal of Autism and Developmental Disorders*, 37(3), 437–444.

Elsabbagh, M., Divan, G., Koh, Y.-J., Kim, Y. S., Kauchali, S., Marcin, C., ... Fombonne, E. (2012). Global prevalence of autism and other pervasive developmental disorders. *Autism Research*, 5, 160–179.

Fernell, E., & Gillberg, C. (2010). Autism spectrum disorder in Stockholm preschoolers. *Research in Developmental Disabilities*, 31(3), 680–685.

Fombonne, E. (2001). Is there an epidemic of autism? *Pediatrics*, 107, 411–413.

Fombonne, E. (2003a). Epidemiological surveys of autism and other pervasive developmental disorders: An update. *Journal of Autism and Developmental Disorders*, 33(4), 365–382.

Fombonne, E. (2003b). The prevalence of autism. *Journal of the American Medical Association*, 289(1), 1–3.

Fombonne, E. (2005). Epidemiology of autistic disorder and other pervasive developmental disorders. *Journal of Clinical Psychiatry*, 66 (Suppl. 10), 3–8.

Fombonne, E. (2007). Epidemiology. In A. Martin & F. Volkmar (Eds.), *Lewis's child and adolescent psychiatry: A comprehensive textbook* (4th ed., pp. 150–171). Philadelphia, PA: Lippincott, Williams, & Wilkins.

Fombonne, E. (2009a). Epidemiology of pervasive developmental disorders. *Pediatric Research*, 65(6), 591–598.

Fombonne, E. (2009b). Commentary: On King and Bearman. *International Journal of Epidemiology*, 38(5), 1241–1242.

Fombonne, E., & du Mazaubrun, C. (1992). Prevalence of infantile autism in four French regions. *Social Psychiatry & Psychiatric Epidemiology*, 27(4), 203–210.

Fombonne, E., du Mazaubrun, C., Cans, C., & Grandjean, H. (1997). Autism and associated medical disorders in a French epidemiological survey. *Journal of the American Academy of Child & Adolescent Psychiatry*, 36(11), 1561–1569.

Fombonne, E., Quirke, S., & Hagen, A. (2011). Epidemiology of pervasive developmental disorders. In D. G. Amaral, G. Dawson, & D. H. Geschwind (Eds.), *Autism spectrum disorders* (pp. 90–111). New York, NY: Oxford University Press.

Fombonne, E., Simmons, H., Ford, T., Meltzer, H., & Goodman, R. (2001). Prevalence of pervasive developmental disorders in the British nationwide survey of child mental health. *Journal of the American Academy of Child & Adolescent Psychiatry*, 40(7), 820–827.

Fombonne, E., Zakarian, R., Bennett, A., Meng, L., & McLean-Heywood, D. (2006). Pervasive developmental disorders in Montreal, Quebec, Canada: Prevalence and links with immunizations. *Pediatrics*, *118*(1), e139–150.

Franzini, L., Ribble, J. C., & Keddie, A. M. (2001). Understanding the Hispanic paradox. *Ethnicity and Disease*, *11*(3), 496–518.

Frazier, T. W., Youngstrom, E. A., Speer, L., Embacher, R., Law, P., Constantino, J., . . . Eng, C. (2012). Validation of proposed *DSM-5* criteria for autism spectrum disorder. *Journal of the American Academy of Child & Adolescent Psychiatry*, *51*, 28–40.

French, L., Bertone, A., Hyde, K., & Fombonne, E. (2013). Epidemiology of autism spectrum disorders. In J. D. Buxbaum & P. R. Hof (Eds.), *The Neuroscience of Autism Spectrum Disorders* (pp. 3–24). Oxford, England: Elsevier.

Ghanizadeh, A. (2008). A preliminary study on screening prevalence of pervasive developmental disorder in school children in Iran. *Journal of Autism and Developmental Disorders*, *38*(4), 759–763.

Gibbs, V., Aldridge, F., Chandler, F., Witzlsperger, E., & Smith, K. (2012). Brief report: An exploratory study comparing diagnostic outcomes for autism spectrum disorders under *DSM-IV-TR* with the proposed *DSM-5* revision. *Journal of Autism and Developmental Disorders*, *42*, 1750–1756.

Gillberg, C. (1984). Infantile autism and other childhood psychoses in a Swedish urban region: Epidemiological aspects. *Journal of Child Psychology & Psychiatry and Allied Disciplines*, *25*(1), 35–43.

Gillberg, C., Cederlund, M., Lamberg, K., & Zeijlon, L. (2006). Brief report: "The autism epidemic." The registered prevalence of autism in a Swedish urban area. *Journal of Autism and Developmental Disorders*, *36*(3), 429–435.

Gillberg, C., & Schaumann, H. (1982). Social class and infantile autism. *Journal of Autism and Developmental Disorders*, *12*(3), 223–228.

Gillberg, C., Schaumann, H., & Gillberg, I. C. (1995). Autism in immigrants: Children born in Sweden to mothers born in Uganda. *Journal of Intellectual Disability Research*, *39*, 141–144.

Gillberg, C., Steffenburg, S., Börjesson, B., & Andersson, L. (1987). Infantile autism in children of immigrant parents: A population-based study from Göteborg, Sweden. *British Journal of Psychiatry*, *150*, 856–858.

Gillberg, C., Steffenburg, S., & Schaumann, H. (1991). Is autism more common now than ten years ago? *British Journal of Psychiatry*, *158*, 403–409.

Grether, J. K., Anderson, M. C., Croen, L. A., Smith, D., & Windham, G. (2009). Risk of autism and increasing maternal and paternal age in a large North American population. *American Journal of Epidemiology*, *170*(9), 1118–1126.

Gurney, J. G., Fritz, M. S., Ness, K. K., Sievers, P., Newschaffer, C. J., & Shapiro, E. G. (2003). Analysis of prevalence trends of autism spectrum disorder in Minnesota. *Archives of Pediatrics & Adolescent Medicine*, *157*(7), 622–627.

Harrison, M. J., O'Hare, A. E., Campbell, H., Adamson, A., & McNeillage, J. (2006). Prevalence of autistic spectrum disorders in Lothian, Scotland: An estimate using the "capture-recapture" technique. *Archives of Disease in Childhood*, *91*(1), 16–19.

Hertz-Picciotto, I., & Delwiche, L. (2009). The rise in autism and the role of age at diagnosis. *Epidemiology*, *38*(5), 84–90.

Honda, H., Shimizu, Y., Misumi, K., Niimi, M., & Ohashi, Y. (1996). Cumulative incidence and prevalence of childhood autism in children in Japan. *British Journal of Psychiatry*, *169*, 228–235.

Honda, H., Shimizu, Y., & Rutter, M. (2005). No effect of MMR withdrawal on the incidence of autism: A total population study. *Journal of Child Psychology & Psychiatry and Allied Disciplines*, *46*(6), 572–579.

Hoshino, Y., Kumashiro, H., Yashima, Y., Tachibana, R., & Watanabe, M. (1982). The epidemiological study of autism in Fukushima-Ken. *Folia Psychiatrica et Neurologica Japonica*, *36*, 115–124.

Huerta, M., Bishop, S. L., Duncan, A., Hus, V., & Lord, C. (2012). Application of *DSM-5* criteria for autism spectrum disorder to three samples of children with *DSM-IV* diagnoses of pervasive developmental disorders. *American Journal of Psychiatry*, *169*, 1056–1064.

Hultman, C. M., Sparen, P., & Cnattingius, S. (2002). Perinatal risk factors for infantile autism. *Epidemiology*, *13*, 417–423.

Icasiano, F., Hewson, P., Machet, P., Cooper, C., & Marshall, A. (2004). Childhood autism spectrum disorder in the Barwon region: A community based study. *Journal of Paediatrics & Child Health*, *40*(12), 696–701.

Idring, S., Dheeraj, R., Dal, H., Dalman, C., Sturm, H., Zander, E., . . . Magnusson, C. (2012). Autism spectrum disorder in the Stockholm youth cohort: Design, prevalence and validity. *PLoS ONE 7*: e41280. doi: 10.1371/journal.pone.004 1280

Isaksen, J., Diseth, T. H., Schjolberg, S., & Skjeldal, O. H. (2012). Observed prevalence of autism spectrum disorders in two Norwegian counties. *European Journal of Paediatric Neurology*, *16*(6), 592–598.

Jick, H., & Kaye, J. A. (2003). Epidemiology and possible causes of autism. *Pharmacotherapy*, *23*(12), 1524–1530.

Kadesjo, B., Gillberg, C., & Hagberg, B. (1999). Brief report: Autism and Asperger syndrome in seven-year-old children: A total population study. *Journal of Autism and Developmental Disorders*, *29*(4), 327–331.

Kanner, L. (1943). Autistic disturbances of affective contact. *The Nervous Child*, *2*, 217–250.

Kataoka, S. H., Zhang, L., & Wells, K. B. (2002). Unmet need for mental health care among U.S. children: variation by ethnicity and insurance status. *American Journal of Psychiatry*, *159*, 1548–1555.

Kawamura, Y., Takahashi, O., & Ishii, T. (2008). Reevaluating the incidence of pervasive developmental disorders: Impact of elevated rates of detection through implementation of an integrated system of screening in Toyota, Japan. *Psychiatry & Clinical Neurosciences*, *62*(2), 152–159.

Keen, D. V., Reid, F. D., & Arnone, D. (2010). Autism, ethnicity, and maternal immigration. *British Journal of Psychiatry*, *196*, 274–281.

Keyes, K. M., Susser, E., Cheslack-Postava, K., Fountain, C., Liu, K., & Bearman, P. S. (2012). Cohort effects explain the increase in autism diagnosis among children born from 1992 to 2003 in California. *International Journal of Epidemiology*, *41*, 495–503.

Kielinen, M., Linna, S.-L., & Moilanen, I. (2000). Autism in northern Finland. *European Child & Adolescent Psychiatry*, *9*, 162–167.

Kim, Y. S., Fombonne, E., Koh, Y. J., Kim, S. J., Cheon, K., & Leventhal, B. (submitted). *Comparison of prevalence of DSM 5 ASD, SCD, and DSM IV PDD in a total population study.*

Kim, Y. S., Leventhal, B. L., Koh, Y. J., Fombonne, E., Laska, E., Lim, E. C.,... Grinker, R. R. (2011). Prevalence of autism spectrum disorders in a total population sample. *American Journal of Psychiatry* [Epub ahead of print] PubMed PMID: 21558103.

King, M., & Bearman, P. (2009). Diagnostic change and the increase in prevalence of autism. *International Journal of Epidemiology, 38*(5), 1224–1234.

Kočovská, E., Biskupsto, R., Gillberg, I. C., Ellefsen, A., Kampmann, H., Stora, T.,... Gillberg, C. (2012). The rising prevalence of autism: A prospective longitudinal study in the Faroe Islands. *Journal of Autism and Developmental Disorders, 42*(9), 1959–1966.

Kočovská, E., Fernell, E., Billstedt, E., Minnis, H., & Gillberg, C. (2012). Vitamin D and autism: Clinical review. *Research in Developmental Disabilities, 33*, 1541–1550.

Kogan, M. D., Blumberg, S. J., Schieve, L. A., Boyle, C. A., Perrin, J. M., Ghandour, R. M.,... van Dyck, P. C. (2009). Prevalence of parent-reported diagnosis of autism spectrum disorder among children in the U.S., 2007. *Pediatrics, 124* (5), 1395–1403.

Laing, S. P., & Hamhi, A. (2003). Alternative assessment of language and literacy in culturally and linguistically diverse populations. *Language, Speech, & Hearing Services in Schools, 34*, 44.

Larsson, H. J., Eaton, W. W., Madsen, K. M., Vestergaard, M., Olesen, A. V., Agerbo, E.,... Mortensen, P. B. (2005). Risk factors for autism: perinatal factors, parental psychiatric history, and socioeconomic status. *American Journal of Epidemiology, 161*, 916–925.

Latif, A. H., & Williams, W. R. (2007). Diagnostic trends in autistic spectrum disorders in the South Wales valleys. *Autism, 11*(6), 479–487.

Lauritsen, M. B., Jorgensen, M., Madsen, K. M., Lemcke, S., Toft, S., & Grove, J. (2010). Validity of childhood autism in the Danish psychiatric central register: Findings from a cohort sample born 1990–1999. *Journal of Autism and Developmental Disorders, 40*, 139–148.

Lauritsen, M. B., Pedersen, C. B., & Mortensen, P. B. (2004). The incidence and prevalence of pervasive developmental disorders: A Danish population-based study. *Psychological Medicine, 34*, 1339–1346.

Lauritsen, M. B., Pedersen, C. B., & Mortensen, P. B. (2005). Effects of familial risk factors and place of birth on the risk of autism: A nationwide register-based study. *Journal of Child Psychology & Psychiatry, 46*, 963–971.

Lazoff, T., Zhong, L., Piperni, T., & Fombonne, E. (2010). Prevalence rates of PDD among children in a Montreal School Board. *Canadian Journal of Child Psychiatry, 55*(11), 715–720.

Le Couteur, A., Rutter, M., Lord, C., Rios, P., Robertson, S., Holdgrafer, M., & McLennan, J. (1989). Autism diagnostic interview: A standardized investigator-based instrument. *Journal of Autism and Developmental Disorders, 19*, 363–387.

Leonard, H., Glasson, E., Nassar, N., Whitehouse, A., Bebbington, A., Bourke, J.,... Stanley, F. (2011). Autism and intellectual disability are differentially related to sociodemographic background at birth. *PLoS ONE, 6*(3): e17875. doi:10.1371/journal.pone.0017875

Li, J., Vestergaard, M., Obel, C., Christensen, J., Precht, D. H., Lu, M., & Olsen, J. (2009). A nationwide study on the risk of autism after prenatal stress exposure to maternal bereavement. *Pediatrics, 123*, 1102–1107.

Li, N., Chen, G., Song, X., Du, W., & Zheng, X. (2011). Prevalence of autism-caused disability among Chinese children: A national population-based survey. *Epilepsy & Behavior, 22*, 786–789.

Lingam, R., Simmons, A., Andrews, N., Miller, E., Stowe, J., & Taylor, B. (2003). Prevalence of autism and parentally reported triggers in a north east London population. *Archives of Disease in Childhood, 88*, 666–670.

Liptak, G. S., Benzoni, L. B., Mruzek, D. W., Nolan, K. W., Thingvoll, M. A., Wade, C. M., & Fryer, G. E. (2008). Disparities in diagnosis and access to health services for children with autism: data from the National Survey of Children's Health. *Journal of Developmental & Behavioral Pediatrics, 29*(3), 152–160.

Lord, C., Risi, S., Lambrecht, L., Cook, E. H., Jr., Leventhal, B. L., DiLavore, P. C.,... Rutter, M. (2000). The Autism Diagnostic Observation Schedule-Generic: A standard measure of social and communication deficits associated with the spectrum of autism. *Journal of Autism and Developmental Disorders, 30*(3), 205–223.

Lotter, V. (1966). Epidemiology of autistic conditions in young children: I. Prevalence. *Social Psychiatry, 1*, 124–137.

Lotter, V. (1967). Epidemiology of autistic conditions in young children: II. Some characteristics of the parents and children. *Social Psychiatry, 1*(4), 163–173.

Madsen, K. M., Hviid, A., Vestergaard, M., Schendel, D., Wohlfahrt, J., Thorsen, P.,... Melbye, M. (2002). A population-based study of measles, mumps, and rubella vaccination and autism. *New England Journal of Medicine, 347*(19), 1477–1482.

Maenner, M. J., & Durkin, M. S. (2010). Trends in the prevalence of autism on the basis of special education data. *Pediatrics, 126*(5), 1018–1025.

Magnusson, C., Rai, D., Goodman, A., Lundberg, M., Idring, S., Svensson, A.,... Dalman, C. (2012). Migration and autism spectrum disorder: Population-based study. *British Journal of Psychiatry, 201*, 109–115.

Magnússon, P., & Saemundsen, E. (2001). Prevalence of autism in Iceland. *Journal of Autism and Developmental Disorders, 31*(2), 153–163.

Mandell, D. S., Wiggins, L. D., Carpenter, L. A., Daniels, J., DiGuiseppi, C., Durkin, M. S.,... Kirby, R. S. (2009). Racial/ethnic disparities in the identification of children with autism spectrum disorders. *American Journal of Public Health, 99*(3), 493–498.

Manning, S. E., Davin, C. A., Barfield, W. D., Kotelchuck M., Clements, K., Diop, H.,... Smith, L. A. (2011). Early diagnoses of autism spectrum disorders in Massachusetts birth cohorts, 2001–2005. *Pediatrics, 127*(6), 1043–1051.

Matson, J. L., Belva, B. C., Horovitz, M., Kozlowski, A. M., & Bamburg, J. W. (2012). Comparing symptoms of autism spectrum disorders in a developmentally disabled adult population using the current *DSM-IV-TR* diagnostic criteria and the proposed *DSM-5* diagnostic criteria. *Journal of Developmental & Physical Disabilities, 24,* 403–414.

Matson, J. L., Hattier, M. A., & Williams, L. W. (2012). How does relaxing the algorithm for autism affect *DSM-V* prevalence rates? *Journal of Autism and Developmental Disorders, 42,* 1549–1556.

Matsuishi, T., Shiotsuki, M., Yoshimura, K., Shoji, H., Imuta, F., & Yamashita, F. (1987). High prevalence of infantile autism in Kurume city, Japan. *Journal of Child Neurology, 2,* 268–271.

Mattila, M.-L., Kielinen, M., Jussila, K., Linna, S.-L., Bloigu, R., Ebeling, H., & Moilanen, I. (2007). An epidemiological and diagnostic study of Asperger syndrome according to four sets of diagnostic criteria. *Journal of the American Academy of Child & Adolescent Psychiatry, 50*(6), 636–646.

Mattila, M.-L., Kielinen, M., Linna, S. L., Jussila, K., Ebeling, H., Bloigu, R., . . . Moilanen, I. (2011). Autism spectrum disorders according to DSM-IV-TR and compared with DSM-V draft criteria: An epidemiological study. *Journal of the American Academy of Child & Adolescent Psychiatry, 46*(5), 583–592.

McCarthy, P., Fitzgerald, M., & Smith, M. (1984). Prevalence of childhood autism in Ireland. *Irish Medical Journal, 77,* 129–130.

McPartland, J. C., Reichow, B., & Volkmar, F. R. (2012). Sensitivity and specificity of proposed *DSM-5* diagnostic criteria for autism spectrum disorder. *Journal of the American Academy of Child & Adolescent Psychiatry, 51,* 368–383.

Montiel-Nava, C. & Pena, J. (2008). Epidemiological findings of pervasive developmental disorders in a Venezuelan Study. *Autism, 12,* 191–202.

Nassar, N., Dixon, G., Bourke, J., Bower, C., Glasson, E., de Klerk, N., & Leonard, H. (2009). Autism spectrum disorders in young children: Effects of changes in diagnostic practices. *International Journal of Epidemiology, 38*(5), 1245–1254.

Nicholas, J. S., Carpenter, L. A., King, L. B., Jenner, W., & Charles, J. M. (2009). Autism spectrum disorders in preschool-aged children: Prevalence and comparison to a school-aged population. *Annals of Epidemiology, 19,* 808–814.

Nicholas, J. S., Charles, J. M., Carpenter, L. A., King, L. B., Jenner, W., & Spratt, E. G. (2008). Prevalence and characteristics of children with autism-spectrum disorders. *Annals of Epidemiology, 18*(2), 130–136.

Nygren, G., Cederlund, M., Sandberg, E., Gillstedt, F., & Arvidsson, T. (2012). The prevalence of autism spectrum disorders in toddlers: A population study of 2-year-old Swedish children. *Journal of Autism and Developmental Disorders, 42*(7), 1491–1497.

Oliveira, G., Ataide, A., Marques, C., Miguel, T. S., Coutinho, A. M., Mota-Vieira, L., . . . Vicente, A. M. (2007). Epidemiology of autism spectrum disorder in Portugal: Prevalence, clinical characterization, and medical conditions. *Developmental Medicine & Child Neurology, 49*(10), 726–733.

Ouellette-Kuntz, H., Coo, H., Yu, C. T., Chudley, A. E., Noonan, A., Breitenbach, M., . . . Holden, J. J. A. (2006). Prevalence of pervasive developmental disorders in two Canadian provinces. *Journal of Policy and Practice in Intellectual Disabilities, 3*(3), 164–172.

Palmer, R. F., Walker, T., Mandell, D., Bayles, B., & Miller, C. S. (2010). Explaining low rates of autism among Hispanic schoolchildren in Texas. *American Journal of Public Health, 100*(2), 270–272.

Parner, E. T., Baron-Cohen, S., Lauritsen, M. B., Jorgensen, M., Schieve, L. A., Yeargin-Allsopp, M., & Obel, C. (2012). Parental age and autism spectrum disorders. *Annals of Epidemiology, 22,* 143–150.

Parner, E. T., Thorsen, P., Dixon, G., de Klerk, N., Leonard, H., Nassar, N., . . . Glasson, E. J. (2011). A comparison of autism prevalence trends in Denmark and Western Australia. *Journal of Autism and Developmental Disorders, 41,* 1601–1608.

Paula, C. S., Ribeiro, S., Fombonne, E., & Mercadante, M. T. (2011). Prevalence of pervasive developmental disorder in Brazil: A pilot study. *Journal of Autism and Developmental Disorders, 41,* 1738–1742.

Pearce, N., Foliaki, S., Sporle, A., & Cunningham, C. (2004). Genetics, race, ethnicity, and health. *British Medical Journal, 328,* 1070–1072.

Pedersen, A., Pettygrove, S., Meaney, J., Mancilla, K., Gotschall, K., Kessler., . . . Cunniff, C. (2012). Prevalence of autism spectrum disorders in Hispanic and non-Hispanic white children. *Pediatrics, 129*(3), 629–635.

Pinbrough-Zimmerman, J., Bakian, A. V., Fombonne, E., Bilder, D., Taylor, J., & McMahon, W. M. (2012). Changes in the administrative prevalence of autism spectrum disorders: Contribution of special education and health from 2002–2008. *Journal of Autism and Developmental Disorders, 42*(4), 521–530.

Posserud, M., Lundervold, A. J., Lie, S. A., & Gillberg, C. (2010). The prevalence of autism spectrum disorders: Impact of diagnostic instrument and non-response bias. *Social Psychiatry and Psychiatric Epidemiology, 45*(3), 319–327.

Powell, J., Edwards, A., Edwards, M., Pandit, B., Sungum-Paliwal, S., & Whitehouse, W. (2000). Changes in the incidence of childhood autism and other autistic spectrum disorders in preschool children from two areas of the West Midlands, UK. *Developmental Medicine & Child Neurology, 42,* 624–628.

Rai, D., Golding, J., Magnusson, C., Steer, C., Lewis, G., & Dalman, C. (2012). Prenatal and early life exposure to stressful life events and risk in autism spectrum disorder: Population-based studies in Sweden and England. *PLoS ONE, 7,* e38893. doi:10.1371/journal.pone.0038893

Rai, D., Lewis, G., Lundberg, M., Araya, R., Svensson, A., Dalman, C., . . . Magnusson, C. (2012). Parental socioeconomic status and risk of offspring autism spectrum disorders in a Swedish population-based study. *Journal of the American Academy of Child & Adolescent Psychiatry, 51*(5), 467–476.

Rajakumar, K., Thomas, S. B., Musa, D., Almario, D., & Garza, M. A. (2009). Racial differences in parents' distrust of medicine and research. *Archives of Pediatrics & Adolescent Medicine, 163,* 108–114.

Rice, C. E., Baio, J., Braun, K. V. N., Doernberg, N., Meaney, F. J., & Kirby, R. S. (2007). A public health collaboration for the surveillance of autism spectrum disorders. *Pediatric & Perinatal Epidemiology, 21,* 179–190.

Rice, C., Nicholas, J., Baio, J., Pettygrove, S., Lee, L.-C., Braun, K. V. N., . . . Yeargin-Allsopp, M. (2010). Changes in autism spectrum disorder prevalence in 4 areas of the United States. *Disability & Health Journal, 3*(3), 186–201.

Ritvo, E., Freeman, B., Pingree, C., Mason-Brothers, A., Jorde, L., Jenson, W., . . . Ritvo, A. (1989). The UCLA-University of Utah epidemiologic survey of autism: Prevalence. *American Journal of Psychiatry, 146*, 194–199.

Rutter, M. (1970). Autistic children: Infancy to adulthood. *Seminars in Psychiatry, 2*(4), 435–450.

Samadi, S. A., Mahmoodizadeh, A., & McConkey, R. (2011). A national study of the prevalence of autism among five-year-old children in Iran. *Autism, 16*, 5–14.

Sanua, V. (1987). Infantile autism and parental socioeconomic status a case of bimodal distribution. *Child Psychiatry & Human Development, 17*(3), 189–198.

Schieve, L., Boulet, S., Blumberg, S., Kogan, M. D., Yeargin-Allsopp, M., Boyle, C., . . . Rice, C. (2012). Association between parental nativity and autism spectrum disorder among US-born non-Hispanic white and Hispanic children, 2007 national survey of children's health. *Disabilities & Health Journal, 5*(1), 18–25.

Scott, F. J., Baron-Cohen, S., Bolton, P., & Brayne, C. (2002). Brief report: Prevalence of autism spectrum conditions in children aged 5–11 years in Cambridgeshire, UK. *Autism, 6*(3), 231–237.

Shattuck, P. T. (2006). The contribution of diagnostic substitution to the growing administrative prevalence of autism in US special education. *Pediatrics, 117*(4), 1028–1037.

Shi, L., & Stevens, G. (2005). Disparities in access to care and satisfaction among U.S. children: The roles of race/ethnicity and poverty status. *Public Health Reports, 120*(4), 431–441.

Sponheim, E., & Skjeldal, O. (1998). Autism and related disorders: Epidemiological findings in a Norwegian study using ICD-10 diagnostic criteria. *Journal of Autism and Developmental Disorders, 28*, 217–227.

Steffenburg, S., & Gillberg, C. (1986). Autism and autistic-like conditions in Swedish rural and urban areas a population study. *British Journal of Psychiatry, 149*(1), 81–87.

Steinhausen, H.-C., Gobel, D., Breinlinger, M., & Wohlloben, B. (1986). A community survey of infantile autism. *Journal of the American Academy of Child Psychiatry, 25*, 186–189.

Sugiyama, T., & Abe, T. (1989). The prevalence of autism in Nagoya, Japan: A total population study. *Journal of Autism and Developmental Disorders, 19*, 87–96.

Taheri, A., & Perry, A. (2012). Exploring the proposed *DSM-5* criteria in a clinical sample. *Journal of Autism and Developmental Disorders, 42*, 1810–1817.

Tanoue, Y., Oda, S., Asano, F., & Kawashima, K. (1988). Epidemiology of infantile autism in southern Ibaraki, Japan: Differences in prevalence in birth cohorts. *Journal of Autism and Developmental Disorders, 18*, 155–166.

Taylor, B., Miller, E., Farrington, C., Petropoulos, M.-C., Favot-Mayaud, I., Li, J., & Waight, P. A. (1999, June 12). Autism and measles, mumps, and rubella vaccine: No epidemiological evidence for a causal association. *Lancet, 353*, 2026–2029.

Tebruegge, M., Nandini, V., & Ritchie, J. (2004). Does routine child health surveillance contribute to the early detection of children with pervasive developmental disorders? An epidemiological study in Kent, UK. *BMC Pediatrics, 4*, 4.

Thomas, P., Zahorodny, W., Peng, B., Kim, S., Jani, N., Halperin, W., & Brimacombe, M. (2012). The association of autism diagnosis with socioeconomic status. *Autism, 16*, 201–213.

Treffert, D. A. (1970). Epidemiology of infantile autism. *Archives of General Psychiatry, 22*, 431–438.

Tsai, L., Stewart, M. A., Faust, M., & Shook, S. (1982). Social class distribution of fathers of children enrolled in Iowa program. *Journal of Autism and Developmental Disorders, 12*, 211–221.

van Balkom, I. D. C., Bresnahan, M., Vogtländer, M. F., van Hoeken, D., Minderaa, R., Susser, E., . . . Hoek, H. W. (2009). Prevalence of treated autism spectrum disorders in Aruba. *Journal of Neurodevelopmental Disorders, 1*, 197–204.

van der Ven, E., Termorshuizen, F., Laan, W., Breetvelt, E. J., van Os, J., & Selten, J. P. (2012). An incidence study of diagnosed autism spectrum disorders among immigrants to the Netherlands. *Acta Psychiatrica Scandinavica, 1–7*.

Wazana, A., Bresnahan, M., & Kline, J. (2007). The autism epidemic: Fact or artifact? *Journal of the American Academy of Child & Adolescent Psychiatry, 46*(6), 721–730.

Webb, E., Lobo, S., Hervas, A., Scourfield, J., & Fraser, W. (1997). The changing prevalence of autistic disorder in a Welsh health district. *Developmental Medicine & Child Neurology, 39*, 150–152.

Webb, E., Morey, J., Thompsen, W., Butler, C., Barber, M., & Fraser, W. I. (2003). Prevalence of autistic spectrum disorder in children attending mainstream schools in a Welsh education authority. *Developmental Medicine & Child Neurology, 45*(6), 377–384.

Wignyosumarto, S., Mukhlas, M., & Shirataki, S. (1992). Epidemiological and clinical study of autistic children in Yogyakarta, Indonesia. *Kobe Journal of Medical Sciences, 38*(1), 1–19.

Williams, E., Thomas, K., Sidebotham, H., & Emond, A. (2008). Prevalence and characteristics of autistic spectrum disorders in the ALSPAC cohort. *Developmental Medicine & Child Neurology, 50*(9), 672–677.

Williams, J. G., Brayne, C. E., & Higgins, J. P. (2006). Systematic review of prevalence studies of autism spectrum disorders. *Archives of Disease in Childhood, 91*(1), 8–15.

Windham, G. C., Anderson, M. C., Croen, L. A., Smith, K. S., Collins, J., & Grether, J. K. (2011). Birth prevalence of autism spectrum disorders in the San Francisco Bay Area by demographic and ascertainment source characteristics. *Journal of Autism and Developmental Disorders, 41*(10), 1362–1372.

Wing, L. (1980). Childhood autism and social class a question of selection? *British Journal of Psychiatry, 137*, 410–417.

Wing, L., & Gould, J. (1979). Severe impairments of social interaction and associated abnormalities in children: Epidemiology and classification. *Journal of Autism and Developmental Disorders, 9*, 11–29.

Wing, L., Yeates, S., Brierly, L., & Gould, J. (1976). The prevalence of early childhood autism: Comparison of administrative and epidemiological studies. *Psychological Medicine, 6*, 89–100.

Wolff, S., & Barlow, A. (1979). Schizoid personality in childhood: A comparative study of schizoid, autistic and normal children. *Journal of Child Psychology & Psychiatry*, *20*(1), 29–46.

Wong, V. C., & Hui, S. L. (2008). Epidemiological study of autism spectrum disorder in China. *Journal of Child Neurology*, *23*(1), 67–72.

World Health Organization. (1977). *The ICD-9 classification of mental and behavioural disorders: Clinical descriptions and diagnostic guidelines*. Geneva, Switzerland: Author.

World Health Organization. (1992). *The ICD-10 classification of mental and behavioural disorders: Clinical descriptions and diagnostic guidelines*. Geneva, Switzerland: Author.

Worley, J. A., & Matson, J. L. (2012). Comparing symptoms of autism spectrum disorders using the current *DSM-IV-TR* diagnostic criteria and the proposed *DSM-V* diagnostic criteria. *Research in Autism Spectrum Disorders*, *6*, 965–970.

Yeargin-Allsopp, M., Rice, C., Karapurkar, T., Doernberg, N., Boyle, C., & Murphy, C. (2003). Prevalence of autism in a U.S. metropolitan area. *Journal of the American Medical Association*, *289*(1), 49–5.

Zahorodny, W., Shenouda, J., Howell, S., Rosato, N. S., Peng, B., & Mehta, U. (2012, December 17). Increasing autism prevalence in metropolitan New Jersey. *Autism*, 1–15.

CHAPTER 4

Outcomes in Adults With Autism Spectrum Disorders

PATRICIA HOWLIN

Recent epidemiological studies of autism have confirmed that prevalence rates for adults parallel those in children (i.e., approximately 1% of the population; Brugha et al., 2011). However, whereas there are many thousands of papers on children with autism, only a tiny proportion of studies involve adults and fewer still have systematically investigated the progress of individuals with autism as they move through adolescence and into adulthood. This chapter focuses on the prognosis for individuals with autism and variables related to outcome. The impact of intervention programs for adults, especially those related to supported employment, is also assessed. Finally, data on mental health and factors associated with deterioration in adulthood are explored.

STUDIES OF OUTCOME IN ADULT LIFE

Information on life for adults with autism comes from a variety of sources. These include impressive autobiographical accounts by higher functioning individuals (e.g., Gerland, 2003; Grandin, 2006; Willey, 1999; Lawson, 2002; Williams, 1992; and many others); early clinical descriptions (e.g., Creak, 1963; Eisenberg & Kanner, 1956); and studies that have traced development from childhood to adulthood. One of the earliest of these, a follow-up of 96 individuals first seen as children and then reassessed in their 20s and 30s, was by Kanner himself (1973). The majority of his patients had remained highly dependent, living with parents, in sheltered communities, in state institutions for people with intellectual disabilities, or in psychiatric hospitals. Outcome was more positive for those with better developed communication skills, and among this group just over half were functioning relatively well. Eleven individuals had jobs and one was at college; seven lived independently, and one man (a successful music composer) was married with a child.

The first systematic studies of development from childhood to adulthood were conducted by

Rutter and his colleagues (Lockyer & Rutter, 1969, 1970; Rutter, Greenfeld, & Lockyer, 1967; Rutter & Lockyer, 1967). They followed up 38 individuals who had been diagnosed with autism as children in the 1950s or 1960s. At follow-up, when aged on average 16 years, more than half were in long-term hospital care. Of the 11 who still lived with their parents, 7 had no outside occupation and only 3 had paid jobs. The authors divided their cohort into those who, overall, were rated as having a "Good" or "Very Good" social adjustment (14%); those with a "Fair" outcome (25%), and those who were considered to have a "Poor" or "Very Poor" outcome (61%). These classifications of outcome, in terms of social competence, have subsequently been used by several other authors. Although in some studies, particularly those conducted pre-2000, ratings are mainly subjective, later reports have attempted to derive a more objective rating based on composite scores for levels of independence, occupational status and friendships/social relationships (see Henninger & Taylor, 2013).

Howlin and Moss (2012) conducted a systematic review of follow-up studies of adults with autism from the time of the original studies of Rutter through 2011. Criteria for inclusion in the review were as follows: sample size ≥ 10; mean age of participants at follow-up ≥ 16 years; mixed IQ range (i.e., at least some participants with an IQ > 70). Cohorts in which *all* participants had intellectual disability were not included since it is well established that individuals with autism who also have severe intellectual disabilities almost invariably remain very dependent as adults (Howlin, Goode, Hutton, & Rutter, 2004). The review identified 23 studies (Tables 4.1 and 4.2) meeting inclusion criteria. Table 4.1 describes the sample characteristics and adult social outcomes in the studies reviewed by Howlin and Moss (2012), together with additional data from a recent study by Howlin, Moss, Savage, and Rutter (2013); Table 4.2 provides specific data on independent living, employment, relationships, and friendships. The average age of the adults studied was around 27 years (range 16 to 64). Although, as is evident from

these tables, the findings related to outcome were very variable, only a minority of individuals (average 21%) was rated as having a good outcome in adulthood, with the range varying widely from 0% to 48%. Overall, 46% of participants were judged to have a Poor or Very Poor outcome (although figures range from 12% to 78%), and the remaining 32% (range 11% to 75%) were rated as Fair. With regard to factors related to social independence, almost half (46%) of the individuals in the cohorts studied were still living with their parents; around 30% were in some form of residential placement; and 9% were in hospital care. Only a minority (18%) was living independently or semi-independently. Fewer than half (45%) were in employment or full-time tertiary education, although, again, the numbers varied widely from study to study. Even among those in employment, jobs were generally low level and poorly paid.

In their review, Howlin and Moss (2012) also examined changes in outcome among cohorts studied in the latter half of the past century, and those who were included in more recent outcome research. Given that the prospects for children with autism have improved markedly in recent years, with many children being diagnosed and provided with specialist educational provision well before the age of 5, the expectation was that outcome in the earlier studies would be significantly poorer than for more recent cohorts. Disappointingly, however, even in studies conducted in the past decade, the percentage of individuals assessed as having a Good/Very Good outcome, or as living independently or semi-independently, was under 20%. However, fewer adults were continuing to live with their parents, and a much smaller proportion than in studies conducted pre-2000 was in any form of hospital or institutionalized care. Nevertheless, because the severity of their behavior problems had made it impossible for them to move into community-based provision, some individuals continued to require hospital (Howlin et al., 2004).

Few of the studies reviewed reported on marriage rates or quality of friendships but, as is apparent from Table 4.2, the numbers of individuals with close friends, or in long-term relationships were

TABLE 4.1   Overall Outcomes Reported in Follow-Up Studies of Adults With ASD

Author (studies 1960–2000)	Diagnosis	N	Mean age (range)	Mean IQ (range)	Outcome %[a] Poor/Very Poor	Fair	Good/ Very Good
Lockyer and Rutter (1969); Rutter and Lockyer (1967)	Infantile autism	63	16 years	62[b]	61%	25%	14%
Lotter (1974)	Autism	29	ns (16–18 years)	71 (55–90)	62%	24%	14%
Rumsey, Rapoport, and Sceery[c] (1985)	Infantile autism	14	28 years (18–39 years)	9 had VIQ > 80	29%	35%	35%
Tantam (1991)	Asperger's syndrome	85	24 years (ns)	ns	—	—	—
Gillberg and Steffenberg (1987)	Infantile autism	23	20 years (16–23 years)	mixed	44%	48%	4%
Szatmari, Bartolucci, Bremner, Bond, and Rich (1989)	Autism, childhood schizophrenia/ psychosis	16	26 years (17–34 years)	92 (68–110)	31%	31%	38%
Kobayashi, Murata, and Yoshinaga (1992)	Autism	197	22 years (18–33 years)	mixed	46%	27%	27%
Ballaban-Gil, Rapin, Tuchman, and Shinnar (1996)	Autistic disorder	99	18 years (12–30 years)	mixed	—	—	—
Larsen and Mourisden (1997)	Autism and Asperger's syndrome	18	36 years[2] (ns)	mixed	45%	28%	28%
Studies post-2000							
Howlin, Mawhood, and Rutter (2000)	Autism	19	24 years (21–27 years)	ns (70–117)	74%	11%	16%
Engström, Ekström, and Emilsson (2003)	Asperger's syndrome, high functioning autism	16	31 years (23–46 years)	ns	12%	75%	12%
Howlin, Goode, Hutton, and Rutter (2004)	Autism	67	29 years (21–49 years)	PIQ 75 (51–137)	58%	19%	23%
Billstedt, Gillberg, and Gillberg (2005, 2011)	Autistic disorder and atypical autism	108	ns (17–40 years)	ns	78%	21%	0%
Cederlund, Hagberg, Billstedt, Gillberg, and Gillberg (2008)	Autism and Asperger's syndrome	140	23 years (16–36 years)	≥ 70	39%	47%	14%
Eaves and Ho (2008)	ASD	47	24 years (ns)	mixed	47%	32%	21%
Hutton, Goode, Murphy, Le Couteur, and Rutter (2008)	Autism	135	35 years (21–57 years)	> 30	—	—	
Mazefsky, Folstein, and Lainhart (2008)	Autistic disorder	17	21 years (18–32 years)	29% ≥ 70			
Farley et al. (2009)	Autism	41	33 years (22–46 years)	89 (50–140)	17%	34%	48%
Hofvander et al. (2009)	Autistic disorder, Asperger's syndrome, PDD-NOS	122	ns (16-60 years)	ns (normal IQ)	—	—	—
Marriage, Wolverton, and Marriage (2009)	Autism spectrum disorder	33	21 years (19–37 years)	≥ 70	ns	ns	15%
Whitehouse, Watt, Line, and Bishop (2009)	Autism spectrum disorder	11	22 years (16–28 years)	ns	—	—	—

(continued)

TABLE 4.1   (*Continued*)

Author (studies 1960–2000)	Diagnosis	N	Mean age (range)	Mean IQ (range)	Outcome %[a] Poor/Very Poor	Fair	Good/ Very good
Gillespie-Lynch et al. (2012)	Autism	20 (from 70 at origin)	26.6	DQ 54 at first assessment	50%	20%	30%
Taylor and Seltzer (2011)	ASD	241	20–35 yrs	ns			
Howlin, Moss, Savage, and Rutter (2013)	Autism	60	44 years (29–64 years)	70 (<30–139)	60%		

Note. ns = no data; — = Outcome category not used or outcome not specified or insufficient data.
[a]Summary ratings based on authors' own classification where provided. Otherwise "Good" = moderate to high levels of independence in job (or student) and/or living (may be at home with minimal supervision); some friends/acquaintances. "Fair" = some degree of independence or job, may require moderate levels of support and supervision but does not need specialist residential accommodation; no close friends but may have some acquaintances. "Poor" = requires specialist residential accommodation or hospital provision (or parental home with close supervision majority of the time); no friends or acquaintances.
[b]IQ and/or age-based on a subsample because data not available for all participants (e.g., died).
[c]Outcome scores based on employment and living status as only data available

TABLE 4.2   Specific Achievements in Adolescence and Adulthood Reported in Follow-Up Studies

Study	Semi/ Independent	With Parents	Residential Placement	Hospital Care	Employed (any type) or Education	Long-Term Relationship/ Married	Some Friends
Rutter, Greenfeld, and Lockyer (1967)	ns	ns	ns	44%	24%	—	—
Lotter (1974)	ns	ns	ns	48%	21%	—	—
Rumsey, Rapoport, and Sceery (1985)	21%	64%	7%	7%	79%	—	—
Tantam (1991)	1%	41%	53%	0%	13%	3%	—
Gillberg and Steffenberg (1987)	4%	61%	35%	0%	—	—	—
Szatmari, Bartolucci, Bremner, Bond, and Rich (1989)	31%	63%	6%	0%	88%	25%	—
Kobayashi, Murata, and Yoshinaga (1992)	5%[a]	93%[a]	2%[a]	2%	22%	—	—
Ballaban-Gil, Rapin, Tuchman, and Shinnar[b] (1996)	—	—	24%	—	27%	—	—
Larsen and Mourisden (1997)	44%	22%	33%	0%	56%	22%	—
Howlin, Mawhood, and Rutter (2000)	16%	32%	47%	5%	32%	5%	21%
Engström, Ekström, and Emilsson (2003)	56%	6%	31%	6%	31%	38%	—
Howlin, Goode, Hutton, and Rutter (2004)	10%	38%	38%	12%	34%	4%	27%
Billstedt, Gillberg, and Gillberg (2005; 2011)	4%	—	—	—	—	1%	—
Cederlund, Hagberg, Billstedt, Gillberg, and Gillberg (2008)	16%	—	—	—	6%	11%	—
Eaves and Ho (2008)	8%	56%	35%	0%	56%	33%	10%
Hutton, Goode, Murphy, Le Couteur, and Rutter (2008)	10%	27%	60%	3%	16%	—	—
Mazefsky, Folstein, and Lainhart (2008)	0%	41%	47%	12%	94%	—	—
Farley et al. (2009)	29%	56%	15%	0%	66%	20%	—
Hofvander et al.[c] (2009)	50%	—	—	—	43%	16%	—
Marriage, Wolverton, and Marriage (2009)	—	—	—	—	—	—	—
Whitehouse, Watt, Line, and Bishop (2009)	—	—	—	—	91%	0%	36%
Gillespie-Lynch et al. (2012)	15%	50%	35%		65%		25%
Taylor and Seltzer (2011)		70%	~30% (data unclear)				
Howlin, Moss, Savage, and Rutter (2013)	22%	22%	53%	3%	45%	7%	

Note. ns = no data; — = information not provided/insufficient data available to calculate scores.
[a]Information based on employed participants (n = 43).
[b]Information based on adult subgroup only (n = 45).
[c]Information based on individuals > 23 years old (n not specified).

generally very low. There are no systematic data on the quality of these relationships, although personal accounts document many of the adaptations that are necessary in order to make marriages/close relationships work (Aston, 2001; Newport & Newport, 2002; Slater-Walker & Slater-Walker, 2002). Similarly, there is no systematic research on the difficulties faced by parents with autism in bringing up children of their own. Although family genetic studies indicate the increased risk to individuals with autism of having affected children themselves (Kumar & Christian, 2009; Pinto et al., 2010), precise data on the incidence of autism among offspring are lacking, as is information on the quality of child-rearing in these families. Personal accounts (and clinical experience) suggest that many individuals with ASD (autism spectrum disorder) are able to parent well despite their own difficulties (Willey, 1999). However, others can experience major problems and adequate support for these families is rarely available (Lawson, 2002).

CHILDHOOD PREDICTORS OF ADULT OUTCOME

Individual Characteristics

The variability in outcome among individuals with autism was noted in the very earliest follow-up studies of Eisenberg and Kanner (Eisenberg & Kanner, 1956; Kanner, 1943; Kanner & Eisenberg, 1956), and there have been many subsequent attempts to identify childhood variables that best predict functioning in later life (see Levy & Perry, 2011). Rutter and colleagues (Lockyer & Rutter, 1969; Rutter & Lockyer, 1967; Rutter et al., 1967) were among the first to demonstrate the prognostic importance of IQ, and it is now well established that very few individuals with a childhood IQ below 70 are able to live independently as adults (e.g., Eaves & Ho, 2008; Farley et al. 2009; Gillberg & Steffenberg, 1987; Howlin et al., 2004). Nevertheless, IQ is not the only determining factor, and many individuals with a high IQ in childhood still do poorly in adulthood. Thus, it seems that while only individuals with a childhood IQ of at least

70–75 do well in adulthood, even amongst those with an IQ above this level, outcome can still be very poor (Howlin et al., 2004).

The development of at least some useful language by the age of 5 to 6 years is another important prognostic indicator (Howlin, Mawhood, & Rutter, 2000; Howlin et al., 2004; Lockyer & Rutter, 1969; Rutter & Lockyer, 1967; Rutter et al., 1967; Szatmari, Bartolucci, Bremner, & Rich, 1989; Venter, Lord, & Schopler, 1992). Although there are some accounts of children who develop speech considerably later and then go on to make good progress, on the whole, individuals who have not acquired speech by the time they enter elementary school tend to have a much poorer outcome in adulthood.

The relationship between later outcome and severity of autistic symptoms in early childhood is less well established. There is some evidence that overall symptom severity at diagnosis is predictive of later functioning (e.g., DeMyer et al., 1973; Rutter et al., 1967); other studies suggest that the severity of repetitive and stereotyped behaviors in childhood is of particular prognostic importance (e.g., Venter et al., 1992); still others have found that the extent of impairment in social skills in early childhood is the most significant predictor of adult outcome (Howlin, Moss, Savage, & Rutter, 2012; Kamp-Becker, Ghahreman, Smidt, & Remschmidt, 2009).

Many other individual characteristics also play an important role. For example, Gillespie-Lynch et al. (2012) found that joint attention skills in the first 5 years of life were strong predictors of social functioning over 20 years later. Gender is another factor that appears to be related to outcome, with a number of studies suggesting that outcome in females tends to be poorer than in males (Holtmann, Bölte, & Poutska, 2007; Howlin et al., 2012; Lord, Schopler, & Revicki, 1982). However, in most outcome studies the number of females involved is small and the differences found are often statistically insignificant. There is also some evidence that, on average, females tend to be of lower IQ and at greater risk of conditions such as epilepsy, two factors that, of themselves, are also associated with a poorer outcome (Howlin et al.,

2013). There is almost no research on the impact of other individual characteristics such as personality, temperament, or on the role of family factors such as parental mental health or child-rearing practices. Although some early studies suggested that socioeconomic factors and quality of family life were predictive of outcome (e.g., DeMyer et al., 1973; Lotter, 1974), there is little evidence of a direct causal relationship between an impoverished or disruptive family background. Nevertheless, as with any other disorder, increased family disruption or stress may be associated with higher rates of behavioral problems (Totsika, Hastings, Emerson, Lancaster, & Berridge, 2011).

The Impact of Early Intervention

Kanner (1973) and Rutter (Lockyer & Rutter, 1969; Rutter & Lockyer, 1967; Rutter et al., 1967) were among the first to highlight the importance of adequate early education for children with autism. In the original follow-up studies of Rutter and colleagues, most children had never attended full-time school and many spent their adult years in institutional care. By the 1980s, however, most children with autism in developed countries were in full-time education and few would ever be placed in hospital care (Venter et al., 1992). However, the quality of education varies widely and what constitutes "effective education" remains undetermined. A number of studies suggest that eclectic approaches to education are less effective than early, highly intensive Applied Behavior Analysis (ABA)-based programs (Magiati, Tay, & Howlin, 2012) but, to date, there is no evidence to support suggestions that access to such intervention in early childhood results in significantly less need for specialist services in later adolescence or adulthood (c.f. claims by Chasson, Harris, & Neely, 2007; Jacobson, Mulick, & Green 1998; Motiwal, Gupta, Lilly, Ungar, & Coyte, 2006).

INTERVENTIONS IN ADULTHOOD

Several recent studies have highlighted the paucity of research on adults with autism (c.f. Piven, Rabins, & the Autism in Older Adults Working Group, 2011). For example, Mukaetova-Ladinska, Perry, Baron, and Povey (2012) noted the relatively tiny number of adult autism studies in comparison with the many thousands of articles on children. A recent review of almost 150 articles on intervention research in autism identified fewer than 2% of participants aged over 20 years (Edwards, Watkins, Lotfizadeh, & Poling, 2012). Similarly, Shattuck et al. (2012), in a review of papers on adults with ASD published between 2000 and 2010, found that out of approximately 11,000 studies, only 23 directly addressed intervention services. The generally poor quality of adult intervention research has also been noted in recent systematic reviews (e.g., National Institute for Health and Clinical Excellence, 2012), and this is paralleled by the relatively poor quality of services for adults compared with provision for children. Thus, Taylor and Seltzer (2011) found that day services for adults with autism were significantly poorer than services for young people of school age, and the standard was particularly low for adults of normal intellectual ability.

Lack of adequate research on and funding for effective interventions for adults with autism is particularly important given that access to support networks in adulthood can have a greater impact on outcome and quality of life than factors such as the individual's IQ (Renty & Roeyers, 2006; Venter et al., 1992). The study by Farley and colleagues (2009), for example, demonstrates how good community support can influence outcome. Social integration among the young adults described in this study was much more positive than that reported for other cohorts of similar ability. Participants were more likely to be in work and to have married or formed close relationships, and around half were rated as having Good or Very Good outcomes. What distinguished this cohort from other follow-up studies was the fact that almost all the individuals involved had grown up and continue to live in communities belonging to the Church of the Latter-day Saints in Utah. This, the Mormon society, offers its members lifelong support and the inclusion of individuals with disabilities is also a strong cultural value.

Nevertheless, at the present time, the evidence base for most interventions for adults remains very weak. Although the behavioral literature contains many examples of operant based approaches that can be used to modify behavioral difficulties, or increase functional skills in individuals with autism and severe intellectual disabilities, few well-controlled studies of effective treatments or services for more able adults exist. There are some studies demonstrating the potential effectiveness of supported employment programs (see later section) and a small number of controlled studies that have investigated the effects of training in social and emotional awareness (e.g., Golan, Baron-Cohen, & Hill, 2006; Turner-Brown, Perry, Dichter, Bodfish, & Penn, 2008). McClannahan, MacDuff, and Krantz (2002) also describe the potential benefits of a broad based behavioral intervention program for adults. The majority of adults with ASD, however, have *no* access to specialist intervention services and, unless they are supported by intellectual disability or mental health services, provision is both limited and inadequate (Taylor & Seltzer, 2011), often resulting in a reduction in progress after leaving school. Perhaps because of this lack of support, rates of mental health problems and medication use tend to be higher in adults (including those of normal intelligence) than in children. Esbensen, Greenberg, Seltzer, and Aman (2009), for example, found that medication use increased steadily with age, with 88% of adults in their survey being on at least one medication and 40% taking three or more different types of medication. Moreover, once medication started it was likely to continue over time.

Supported Employment for People With Autism

The need for specialist schemes to help people with autism find and keep employment has been highlighted in a number of recent studies. Ganz (2007) and Knapp, Romeo, and Beecham (2009) have documented the high life-time costs of autism in terms of lost productivity and the annual costs of services and support. Brugha et al., (2011), in a prevalence study of adults

with ASD, also found that individuals with ASD, including those of normal IQ, were significantly less likely to be in work and far more likely to be economically and socially disadvantaged than their peers.

In their review of adult outcome studies, Howlin and Moss (2012) noted the low rates of employment reported. Among the 1,561 individuals included in these studies (average age 24 years), the median proportion in any form of educational or work placement was 33%. In many cohorts, particularly those including individuals of low cognitive ability, employment rates were typically below 25%, and across all studies the majority of jobs found were low level and poorly paid. Moreover, despite many improvements in educational provision and specialist intervention programs *for children* over recent years, there was no indication of comparable improvement in rates of employment. Thus, the average proportion in employment in the years 1997–2000 and 2001–2011 showed almost no change.

Nonspecialist employment services for people with intellectual disabilities rarely meet the needs of individuals with autism. Cimera and Cowan (2009) and Hurlbutt and Chalmers (2004) note the difficulties involved in finding employment for people with autism via generic vocational rehabilitation programs (higher costs, greater complexity of disorders, communication difficulties, and physical and mental health problems) compared with job-finding for individuals with intellectual disability. Mawhood and Howlin (1999) also found that only a minority of job seekers with autism found employment via generic employment services. Although over the past two decades, a growing number of supported employment schemes have been developed specifically for individuals with autism, research in this field remains limited (Cimera & Cowan, 2009). For example, among papers on services for adults with autism published between 2000 and 2010, Shattuck et al. (2012) identified only 16 that were specifically related to work. In the United Kingdom, the National Institute for Health and Clinical Excellence Guideline Group for Adults with ASD (2012) found only a very limited

TABLE 4.3 Employment Training for Individuals With ASD—Review of Published Papers (sample size >3)

Author/Date/Country	Client Characteristics N/Sex/ Age/Diagnosis	Training Procedures	Outcome
Burt, Fuller, and Lewis, 1991; United States	4 (3 male) 21–29 years ASD, borderline to normal IQ	Work training program (behavioral and social skills) Support in workplace	3X clerical work 1 laundry work (though subsequently lost job)
Keel, Mesibov, and Woods, 1997	100, 16–48 years Autism (42% have LD)	TEACCH support program in the workplace	96% placed in work (food, 38%; clerical, 15%; warehouse, 11%; custodial, 11%; lab/technical, 9%; manufacturing, 4%; other, 12%) 69% in individual job placements. Average 28 hours per week
Mawhood and Howlin, 1999	30, 18–55 years ASD, mean IQ 104	Support in workplace	63% of supported group vs. 25% of nonsupported group in work; 86% vs. 2% of jobs admin/computing/clerical. Supported group had significant increase in wages; amount of support reduced significantly over time. No improvements in self esteem, independent living, or friendships.
García-Villamisar, Ross, and Wehman, 2000; García-Villamisar, Wehman, and Navarro, 2002; García-Villamisar and Hughes, 2007; Spain and Germany	55 (42 male); mean age 21 years Autism, mean IQ 57	Support in workplace	Service industry work (retail, waiting, and agriculture). Supported employment group showed less pathology, better quality of life, and enhanced cognitive skills compared to sheltered workshop group.
Lattimore, Parsons, and Reid, 2002, 2003; Lattimore and Parsons, 2006; Lattimore, Parsons, and Reid, 2009	19 (male) 25–44 years Autism, severe LD/nonverbal	Intensive behavioral task training on and off worksite and support in workplace	Acquired assembly type tasks
McClannahan et al., 2002	15, LD and autism; no further information	Behavioral intervention to increase work skills and decrease problem behaviors	73% in work; mostly part-time and hotel/catering work; low rates of pay
Howlin, Alcock, and Burkin, 2005	117 (95 male) 18–55 years ASD, mean IQ 110	Support in workplace	Significant reduction in benefits; increase in salary 63% jobs admin/computing/clerical. High satisfaction in both employees with ASD and employers
Schaller and Yang, 2005	815 (700 male) 15–64 years No further information	Rehabilitation services (in competitive and supported employment)	Job retention higher in the supported group, but wages and working hours less. Job finding and job placement significantly related to success.
Hillier et al., 2007; United States	9 (8 male) 18–36 years ASD, mean IQ 111	Support in workplace	2X clerical; 2X supermarket; 1 bookstore; 4 food service 7 remained in work by end of project; job satisfaction high; 4-fold increase in income levels.
Allen, Wallace, Greene, Bowen, and Burke, 2010; Allen, Wallace, Renes, and Bowen, 2010; United States	7 (male) 16–25 years ASD/PDD NOS; borderline to normal IQ	Video modeling and script	Brief sessional work dressed as mascot (cartoon figure) in retail outlet.
Burke, Andersen, Bowen, Howard, and Allen (2010); United States	6 (male) 18–27 years ASD, borderline to normal IQ	Video modeling and script. Cues for action using iPhone	Brief sessional work dressed as mascot (cartoon figure) to accompany fire protection officer.
Cimera, Wehman, West, and Burgess, 2012	215 in supported employment vs. 215 in sheltered workshops prior to employment	Support in workplace	No group differences in rates of employment but workshop group earned significantly less and support costs were significantly higher.

104

number of peer reviewed papers on employment (see Table 4.3), most of which were characterized by very small sample size and a generally qualitative, rather than quantitative approach to data analysis. Only four studies (Cimera, Wehman, West, & Burgess, 2012; Howlin, Alcock, & Burkin, 2005; Keel, Mesibov, & Woods 1997; Schaller & Yang, 2005) had a sample size > 50, and only three case-control studies were reported. Mawhood and Howlin (1999) compared supported employment with generic state- provided employment services for individuals with disabilities; Cimera et al. (2012) and García-Villamisar, Wehman, and Navarro (2002) compared sheltered workshop with supported employment schemes. These studies found the supported employment model to be superior to alternative across a range of different variables, including job level, pay, and quality of life.

As is evident from Table 4.3, many of the jobs obtained via these supported employment programs were unskilled, poorly paid (and sometimes of dubious value; e.g., training people with autism to parade as cartoon characters in retail outlets; Allen, Wallace, Green, Bowen, & Burke, 2010; Allen, Wallace, Renes, & Bowen, 2010). Nevertheless, supported employment can also help to find appropriate, adequately paid work for higher ability people with autism and can have a significant impact on their lives. For example, Howlin and colleagues (Howlin et al., 2005; Mawhood & Howlin, 1999) report on the success of a scheme that was particularly designed for individuals with autism of normal IQ. Despite the fact that many participants had been unemployed for several years or had experienced frequent job breakdowns in the past, two thirds of those enrolled in the program found work during a 2-year period. Only 25% of individuals in the control group (who were in receipt of nonspecialist disability services) found work during the same period. Moreover, over 80% of jobs in the supported group were in administration or computing and levels of satisfaction were high, among both the participants with autism and their employers. A further follow-up of this program, which is supported by the National Autistic Society

in the United Kingdom, demonstrated that these initial achievements continued over subsequent years. Almost 200 jobs were found during the 8-year follow-up period, a 68% success rate, with salaries increasing significantly after enrolment in the program. Despite their potential effectiveness, specialist employment services for people with autism remain expensive and can be difficult to implement (Cimera & Cowan, 2009), and recent research efforts have focused on identifying the key elements associated with successful schemes. These include detailed assessment of clients' profiles of skills and difficulties to ensure that job placements are appropriate and that the person with autism has the ability to work alongside others and to cope with change and the social demands of the post (Mawhood & Howlin, 1999). It is also essential to be able to identify a wide range of employers and job possibilities in order to place clients appropriately (Schaller & Yang, 2005). Several studies describe the various behavioral strategies that can be used to develop and maintain job related and social skills, and decrease behaviors that may be a barrier to work (e.g., Hume, Loftin, & Lantz, 2009; Hume & Odom, 2007; Lattimore & Parsons, 2006; Lattimore, Parsons, & Reid, 2002, 2003, 2009; McClannahan et al., 2002). Help to understand and cope with the social demands of the job is also crucial for success (Lawer, Brusilovsky, Seltzer, & Mandell, 2009). Clement-Hiest, Siegel, and Gaylord-Ross (1992) note the importance of training in work related and social skills in simulated work settings, and then in work experience placements, *before* individuals leave school. If these basic skills have not been taught as part of the school curriculum, this transitional training stage will be required prior to entry into work.

Once appropriate employment opportunities have been found and the basic skills required established, in situ support is needed to ensure that these skills are effectively transferred to and maintained in the workplace. There are no fixed guidelines concerning the hours of support needed to help clients achieve independent work skills, and for some individuals with severe intellectual impairments, there may be a need for continuous monitoring of behavior by job coaches (e.g., Smith, Belcher & Juhrs, 1995). For more able individuals, Mawhood and Howlin (1999) found that guidance from the support worker was generally needed on a full-time basis for the first 2–4 weeks of employment. The amount of support could then be gradually decreased, reducing to an average of around 5 hours per month after 4 months. However, a support worker could always be contacted at any time, by either the employer or employee with autism, should problems arise.

Finally, education and information for potential and existing employers and advice for work colleagues or supervisors on how to deal with or avoid problems are crucial. Making potential employers aware of the qualities of individuals with ASD and the advantages they can bring to the workplace (honesty, hard work, reliability, attention to detail, willingness to do routine jobs that other workers may dislike, and much more) is particularly important. Employers and work colleagues also need support and help in ensuring that the workplace is ASD friendly. These include the need to provide a relatively quiet, nondistracting place to work; explicit and written guidelines about the quality, quantity, and timeliness of jobs to be completed; visual rather than verbal instructions; clear and instant feedback if performance is not satisfactory; explanations about the unwritten social rules of the workplace (for example, which areas in the canteen are set aside for the senior staff and which for junior employees); and gradual introduction of change to established work practices (e.g., when giving the person with ASD greater autonomy or a more supervisory role; for full details see Fausett, 2005).

In summary, although supported employment schemes are initially expensive, they have made it possible for individuals who have never had paid work, who have lost previous jobs because of interpersonal or behavioral difficulties, or who have only ever had inappropriate work experiences, to find jobs where they are using their skills and receiving real pay for real work. Moreover, the costs, in terms of both time and money, decline steadily over time, offering benefits to individuals with ASD, their families, and society as a whole.

MENTAL HEALTH

Estimates of mental health difficulties in adults with ASD vary considerably, with some studies suggesting that up to 84% of individuals suffer from some form of diagnosable mental illness (see Lainhart, 1999; Levy & Perry, 2011; Stewart, Barnard, Pearson, Hasan, & O'Brien, 2006, for reviews). However, these data are often derived from clinical samples of individuals referred to psychiatric services; cohorts selected from general epidemiological or follow-up studies suggest rather lower rates (of around 25% to 30%; Brugha et al., 2011; Howlin et al., 2013; Hutton, Goode, Murphy, Le Couteur, & Rutter, 2008; Szatmari et al., 1989). Underwood, McCarthy, and Tsakanikos (2010) also found that adults with an intellectual disability and ASD were at no greater risk of psychiatric disorders than those without ASD.

There is also great variation in reported rates of specific mental health difficulties, although mood disorders, particularly anxiety and depression, tend to be the problems most often reported. A review by Lainhart (1999) found that rates of depression across studies ranged from 4% to 58% and of anxiety disorders from 7% to 84%. Stewart et al. (2006) also noted the variability in rates for depression, but the highest rate that they identified was 34%. Amongst anxiety-related disorders, generalized anxiety disorder, obsessive-compulsive disorder, and/ or social phobia tend to be the most frequently reported, although again rates vary greatly (from 2% to 65%; Moss, 2011). Reported rates for schizophrenia tend to be much lower (from < 1 to 7%; Moss, 2011) and, overall, are no higher than in the general population (i.e., approximately 1.1% of the U.S. adult population; National Institute of Mental Health, 2010).

Factors Associated With Mental Health in Adulthood

As in the general population, mental health difficulties can have a deleterious effect on functioning in adulthood (Billstedt et al., 2005; Ghaziuddin & Zafar, 2008; Seltzer, Shattuck, Abbeduto, & Greenberg, 2004; Stewart et al., 2006). Cederlund,

Hagberg, and Gillberg (2010), for example, found that no young people who scored ≥ 16 on the Beck Depression Inventory were living independently. Hofvander et al. (2009) also found that adults with autism and a comorbid mental health diagnosis were less likely to be in a long-term relationship; more likely to be living with parents or in group homes; and more likely to be unemployed. However, Farley et al. (2009) found little association between mental health problems and adult outcome.

There has been a number of studies exploring factors that predispose to mental health problems in autism, again with rather variable results. It has been suggested that individuals with an IQ in the normal range are *more* likely than those with a low IQ to experience mental health problems (Ghaziuddin, 2005; Ghaziuddin, Ghaziuddin, & Greden, 2002; Sterling, Dawson, Estes, & Greenson, 2008). Thus, their cognitive and language abilities may mean that unachievable expectations are placed on them, despite their often profound social difficulties. Second, they are often acutely aware that their difficulties prevent them from succeeding as well as their peers in areas such as employment and relationships. Hedley and Young (2006), for example, found that awareness of the dissimilarity between themselves and their peers was related to increased reporting of depressive symptoms in individuals with Asperger syndrome. However, Sturmey (1998) notes that rates of mental health difficulties may be just as high in individuals of low IQ, but that communication problems make the identification of mental health disorders in this group much more difficult. Hutton et al. (2008) found that psychiatric disorders occurred equally in low and high IQ groups, a finding also supported by Simonoff et al. (2008) in their study of children.

Data on other possible risk factors, such as severity of autistic symptomatology, age, or social deprivation are very limited, although environmental factors related to major life transitions, loss, inadequate support, or social isolation do seem to be related to onset in many cases (Hutton et al., 2008). Moreover, finding effective treatments can prove very difficult; response to medication can be unpredictable and paradoxical, and the benefits of cognitive behavioral therapies for adults with ASD who also have significant mental health problems have yet to be demonstrated.

MORTALITY AND LIFE EXPECTANCY

There are no systematic data on life expectancy in autism, but there is some indication that death rates are higher than in the general population. Two studies conducted in the past decade (Mouridsen, Bronnum-Hansen, Rich, & Isager, 2008, of 341 adults in Denmark; Shavelle, Strauss, & Pickett 2001, using a data base of 13,000 individuals in California) concluded that mortality rates were around twice as high as expected. Gillberg, Billstedt, Sundh, and Gillberg (2010) reported even higher rates (5.6 times higher than expected) in their Swedish cohort of 120 adults with autism. Death rates appear to be particularly elevated among women (Gillberg et al., 2010; Mouridsen et al., 2008; Shavelle et al., 2001), in individuals with epilepsy (Pickett, Xiu, Tuchman, Dawson, & Lajonchere, 2011), and in those with severe-profound intellectual disabilities. Among this latter group there was a threefold increase in mortality, and deaths were often related to inadequate institutional care, poor medical supervision, or infection (Ballaban-Gil, Rapin, Tuchman, & Shinner, 1996; Kobayashi, Murata, & Yoshinaga, 1992; Larsen & Mouridsen, 1997). Consequently, Mouridsen et al. (2008) stress the need for care staff to be much better trained in dealing with the physical conditions associated with ASD (Shavelle et al., 2001). However, death rates are also elevated in individuals who do not have intellectual impairments, with drowning being reported as a cause of death in several studies. In contrast, death due to smoking, alcohol, traffic, and work accidents is suggested as being less common than in nonautistic peer groups (Shea & Mesibov, 2005).

Suicide

Anecdotal reports of suicide by more able individuals with ASD have been noted in a number of adult studies (e.g., Tantam, 1991; Wing, 1981; Wolff &

McGuire, 1995), although no systematic data are available. Suicide attempts, when they occur, may be related to difficulties in coping with change. For example, in Wing's (1981) group of 18 individuals with Asperger syndrome, three had attempted suicide, including one young man who had become very distressed by minor changes in his work routine and had tried to drown himself. Fortunately, he failed because he was a good swimmer, and when he tried to strangle himself, the attempt also failed because, as he said, "I am not a very practical person." Tantam (1991) described the case of one man who threw himself into the river Thames because the government refused to abolish British Summer Time, and he believed that watches were damaged by the necessity of being altered twice a year.

Epilepsy

Although lifetime prevalence estimates vary, between 11% and 39% of individuals with autism have been reported to develop epilepsy (Amiet et al., 2008; Tuchman, Moshe, & Rapin, 2009; Tuchman & Rapin, 2002). This is a significantly higher rate than in the general population (Kurtz, Tookey, & Ross, 1998), and age of onset (in early teens) is also atypical. The presence of seizures is related to lower IQ, sex (risk higher in females), poorer language skills, greater behavioral disturbance, and higher mortality rates. In a recent study of 150 individuals diagnosed with autism in childhood, and followed up after 21 years of age, Bolton et al. (2011) found that epilepsy developed in 22%, with generalized tonic-clonic seizures predominating (88% of all epilepsy cases). However, in over half of those with seizures, fits occurred weekly or less frequently and were well controlled with anti-convulsants. Howlin et al. (2013) also found relatively low rates (18%) of epilepsy in a cohort of adults who were all of normal nonverbal intelligence (PIQ $\geq$ 70) as children. Those who had developed epilepsy were significantly more likely to have shown a deterioration in cognitive ability from child to adulthood, but age of onset of epilepsy was not directly related to onset of

cognitive decline, suggesting that some form of brain dysfunction was the cause of both.

DETERIORATION IN ADULTHOOD

The transition to adulthood can be a time of upheaval and challenges for many young people, and in a number of follow-up studies of people with autism there have been accounts of an increase in disruptive behaviors in adolescence. Lockyer and Rutter (1970), for example, noted that 5 out of 64 individuals followed up into adulthood showed a marked deterioration in their communication skills over time, coupled with progressive inertia, and general cognitive decline. Three of these cases had also developed epilepsy. Gillberg and Steffenburg (1987) reported that around a third of their sample of 23 individuals presented with a temporary (1 to 2 years) aggravation of symptoms, such as hyperactivity, aggressiveness, destructiveness, and ritualistic behaviors. In another five cases, the symptoms had persisted, resulting in continuing deterioration, increased inertia, loss of language skills, and slow intellectual decline. This pattern was more likely to occur in females than in males. Von Knorring and Häglöf (1993) also noted that of the 4 individuals in their sample of 34 who showed a mildly deteriorating course, 3 were women. Ballaban-Gil et al. (1996) noted that ratings of problem behaviors had increased in almost 50% of their adult sample, although the nature of these is not defined. In a Japanese follow-up of 201 young adults, Kobayashi and his colleagues (1992) found that 31% showed a worsening of symptoms, mainly after the age of 10 years, but there was no difference in the proportions of males and females who experienced a loss of skills. Larsen and Mouridsen (1997), in a comparative study of autism and Asperger syndrome, reported that three of the nine cases with Asperger syndrome and two of the nine with autism had shown deterioration, mainly occurring in late puberty. In both of these latter studies, the pattern of deterioration described was very similar to that outlined by Rutter and by Gillberg and Steffenberg.

In one of the very few systematic investigations of deterioration over time, Hutton et al. (2008) examined the emergence of new problems in adulthood among 125 individuals. Over a third were reported to have developed new behavioral or psychiatric problems, including psychosis, obsessive-compulsive disorder, anxiety, depression, tics, social withdrawal, phobias, and aggression. These difficulties typically emerged in the late teens to early 20s with most people developing symptoms prior to the age of 30. The increase in mental health problems was not associated with epilepsy or cognitive decline, but the risk was greater in women and individuals with a lower *verbal* IQ in childhood. Marked deterioration in cognitive abilities occurred mostly among individuals in long-term hospital placements.

Although it is clear that some individuals with autism do show an increase in problems as they grow older, in most follow-up studies the most characteristic trajectory is one of improvement over time. This was reported in the early follow-up studies of Rutter and his group and by Kanner himself, who noted that for some individuals, particularly those who become more aware of their difficulties and ways to overcome them, mid-adolescence was often a period of marked improvement (Kanner, 1973). Although a third of the individuals in the Kobayashi et al. (1992) study had shown some increase in problems during adolescence, over 40% were rated as showing considerable improvement, generally between 10 and 15 years. Even in the Ballaban-Gil study (1996), where reports of behavioral disturbance were higher than in other cohorts, 51% had improved or shown no deterioration in behavior from childhood to adulthood. Many other studies, both retrospective and prospective, indicate that change over time is more likely to be positive than negative. Studies using standardized assessment instruments such as the Autism Diagnostic Interview–Revised (ADI-R; Lord, Rutter, & Le Couteur, 1994) or the Autism Diagnostic Observation Schedule—Generic (ADOS-G; Lord, Rutter, Di Lavore, & Risi, 2000) have found the severity and frequency of many symptoms decrease significantly with time (Gilchrist, Green, Cox, Rutter, &

Le Couteur, 2001; Howlin, 2003; Piven, Harper, Palmer, & Arndt, 1996). In a study of more than 400 individuals with autism from 10 to 53 years of age, Seltzer et al. (2003) found clear evidence of improvement on ADI-R scores from childhood to adolescence and adulthood. Verbal and nonverbal communication had improved, as had scores on the Reciprocal Social Interaction domain. Scores on *all* the items in the Restricted, Repetitive Behaviors, and Interests domain had also decreased from childhood to adulthood. Similar improvements have been reported in individuals with severe learning disabilities Thus, Beadle-Brown, Murphy, Wing, Shah, and Holmes (2000) reported improvements in scores on the Handicaps, Behaviors, and Skills schedule (HBS; Wing & Gould, 1978) for 146 young adults with severe learning disabilities and/or autism over a period of 12 years (age at initial assessment 2 to 18 years; age at follow-up, 13 to 30 years). Although there was no marked change in IQ, self-care skills (toileting, feeding, grooming, washing, dressing, etc.) had improved significantly, and there had also been progress in certain areas related to educational achievement (e.g., reading, writing, numbers, money, and time). Expressive and receptive language scores had also increased. Improvements were most evident in individuals with milder intellectual impairment; less change was observed in participants who had an IQ below 55 (or who were untestable).

Follow-up studies with a focus on more able individuals have also documented steady improvements over time. For example, in the studies of Howlin and colleagues (Howlin et al. 2000; Mawhood, Howlin, & Rutter, 2000), of 19 young men followed up from 7 to 23 years of age, verbal ability on formal IQ tests had increased significantly and, in terms of general social competence, almost one third of the group had moved from a rating of Poor functioning in childhood to a Good rating as adults. Among older adults, however, improvement may be less marked. In a 40-year follow-up of 60 individuals (mean age 44 years), all of normal performance IQ when diagnosed as children, Howlin et al., 2013) found that although all participants continued to meet criteria for

ASD in at least two core domains of the ADI-R severity of autism symptoms had decreased over time and repetitive and stereotyped behaviors, in particular, had declined. IQ remained remarkably stable in most individuals and language skills had also improved. Nevertheless, few participants had received any specialist support in adulthood and only 11 individuals (18%) were rated as having a Good or Very Good outcome and social outcomes in mid–later adulthood were often poorer than they had been in early adulthood. The findings suggest that, at an individual level, the majority of children with ASD who are of normal intellectual ability tend to show improvements in many areas as they grow older. At a societal level, however, there is a failure to provide the support structures needed to foster social inclusion.

In a large-scale study of 241 adolescents and adults (mean age 22 years), Shattuck and colleagues (2012) also found a significant improvement in severity of autism symptoms (especially repetitive behaviors) and in maladaptive behaviors over a 4-year period. The older individuals in the study (aged 31 and older) exhibited fewer maladaptive behaviors than the adolescents and had shown more improvement in these behaviors over time. Overall, improvements were most likely to occur in individuals who were not intellectually impaired. A retrospective study by Piven et al. (1996) of 38 high-IQ adolescents and adults autistic individuals aged 13 to 28 years also documented improvements over the years although, in contrast to Shattuck's findings, improvements tended to be greater in communication and social behaviors than in ritualistic/repetitive behaviors. Five of 38 participants who met criteria for autistic disorder at age 5 years no longer met criteria although all five continued to have substantial impairment.

Although some individuals do show an increase in behavioral or mental health difficulties in their late teens or early adult years there is some evidence to suggest that the onset of such problems is related to environmental factors. These include the lack of a structured or stimulating environment once they leave school; difficulties in coping with college or work or other significant life changes (move to residential care; loss of parents or other relatives; siblings leaving home; Howlin, 2004). However, overall the proportion of adults who show marked deterioration in all aspects of their functioning is small, and regression appears to be the exception rather than the rule.

ASSESSING QUALITY OF LIFE IN AUTISM

Implicit in almost all adult outcome studies is the assumption that a "good outcome" means living independently of family, having paid employment that is appropriate for an individual's intellectual and academic level, and having friends and close relationships. However, Halpern (1993) pointed out that these goals are not necessarily appropriate for individuals with intellectual disabilities, and the same applies to individuals with ASD. Even for those of higher intelligence, independent living, without adequate support, can actually mean a life that is lonely, isolated, and devoid of interest and stimulation. Inappropriate employment (even if the job appears to be within the individual's *intellectual* competence) can result in intolerable levels of stress, especially if there are excessive demands on flexibility or social skills. Moreover, not all individuals with autism do want close friendships. In recent interviews with adults with autism and their families, as part of a long-term follow-up study of adult outcomes (Howlin et al., 2013) the wish of many individuals and their families was not necessarily for independent accommodation, but for a range of residential settings that offered space, security, and stimulation, with support as and when required. In particular, concerns that that there might be no adequate services to care for the individual with autism when parents were no longer living were a major source of anxiety for many. Although the majority of adults wanted employment of some sort, many felt that they could not cope with full-time work or with jobs that made too many demands either intellectually or socially. Jobs that were part time, routine, and did not require too much social involvement were what many were seeking, even if such work seemed inappropriate for their intellectual level. With regard to close friend-ships, although some individuals wished for close relationships or marriage and a family, this was by no means the case for all. Indeed some individuals expressed the wish that "neurotypicals" would stop imposing upon them their own views of "a good life." Not all wanted friends, or the demands that close relationships entail. What was wanted, by many individuals and families, was a much wider range of social support networks and access to appropriate levels of support that varied according to individual needs, and was flexible enough to deal with changing circumstances. Thus, at times, even for high-functioning individuals, there might be a need for a relatively intense level of support; at other times regular monitoring to check that all was well might be all that was required.

In that study, too, it was found that living independently was not necessarily a positive expe-rience. One 40-year-old man, for example, although living independently in his own apartment, was in accommodation that was dirty and shabby; he had no social contacts apart from occasional visits from his brother, and his life generally was very restricted and unstimulating. His environment contrasted unfavorably with that of a middle-aged woman living in a medium-sized residential setting. She had limited autonomy and no close friends, but the home was very attractive both internally and externally, had excellent facilities and close links to the local community, and residents had access to many different outside activities. Although far from independent, she was obviously very happy and extremely well settled.

Billstedt et al. (2011) question the appropri-ateness of traditional quality of life measures for people with autism and highlight the need for measures that focus on the autism-friendly aspects of living conditions. They found that high levels of dependency—that is, living in specialist residential accommodation—was not incompatible with a high-quality of life, as long as staff were knowl-edgeable about autism and residents were provided with occupational, educational, and leisure pro-grams that were structured, individualized, and suited to their capacity levels. Renty and Roeyers

(2006) also found that quality of life in more able individuals with autism was related more to the perceived level of support available to them than to individual characteristics such as age or intellectual ability (see also Henninger & Taylor, 2013).

IMPLICATIONS FOR FUTURE RESEARCH

In a recent review of adult outcome studies Hen-ninger and Taylor (2013) raise the issue of how accurately existing research data will reflect out-comes for the current generation of children and young people with autism. The findings on outcome reported above are based on groups of individuals who were growing up at a time when specialist programs for children with autism were very limited, and when only more severely affected children were likely to be given a diagnosis. In outcome studies conducted before 1980, almost no individuals had received full-time education; very few lived independently or had jobs and, as adults, over half of were placed in long-stay hospitals or institutions for people with severe intellectual disabilities. Over the past two decades, access to early diagnosis, preschool intervention, specialist educational support in both school and college, and supported employment programs has greatly increased. It is also evident that early intervention programs, particularly focusing on behavioral approaches, positive parent–child interactions, joint attention, and play can lead to important developmental and communication gains in at least some children (Dawson et al., 2010). Whether these early improvements will be reflected in the adult lives of the current generation of people with ASD has yet to be demonstrated, but identification of factors that can significantly improve outcome will be an essential focus of future research.

The other crucial area for future research is what happens to individuals with autism as they approach old age. Almost all current adult outcome studies have focused on individuals in their 20s to 40s. Knowledge about the aging process in ASD is almost nonexistent, and systematic information about the physical and mental health needs of elderly people with ASD is lacking. For example, it is not known whether rates of dementia are likely to be higher or lower in this group than in the population as a whole. It is also evident that many individuals remain highly dependent on their families well into adulthood. How they will cope when parents are no longer able to support them has major implications for society as a whole.

CROSS-REFERENCES

Issues of diagnosis are discussed in Chapter 1. Chapter 8 focuses on adults with autism. Chapter 36 addresses recreational activities, Chapter 38 discusses employment, Chapter 39 addresses post-secondary educational services, and Chapter 48 addresses economic issues.

REFERENCES

Allen, K. D., Wallace, D. P., Greene, D. J., Bowen, S. L., & Burke, R. V. (2010). Community-based vocational instruction using videotaped modeling for young adults with autism spectrum disorders performing in air-inflated mascots. *Focus on Autism & Other Developmental Disabilities*, *25*(3), 186–192.

Allen, K. D., Wallace, D. P., Renes, D., & Bowen, S. L. (2010). Use of video modeling to teach vocational skills to adolescents and young adults with autism spectrum disorders. *Education and Training of Children*, *33*(3), 339–349.

Amiet, C., Gourfinkel-An, I., Bouzamondo, A., Tordjman, S., Baulac, M., Lechat, P., ... Cohen, D. (2008). Epilepsy in autism is associated with intellectual disability and gender: Evidence from a meta-analysis. *Biological Psychiatry*, *64*, 577–582.

Aston, M. (2001). *The other half of Asperger syndrome*. London, England: National Autistic Society.

Ballaban-Gil, K., Rapin, I., Tuchman, R., & Shinnar, S. (1996). Longitudinal examination of the behavioral, language, and social changes in a population of adolescents and young adults with autistic disorder. *Pediatric Neurology*, *15*, 217–223.

Beadle-Brown, J., Murphy, G., Wing, L., Shah, A., & Holmes, N. (2000). Changes in skills for people with intellectual disability: A follow-up of the Camberwell Cohort. *Journal of Intellectual Disability Research*, *44*, 12–24.

Billstedt, E., Gillberg, I. C., & Gillberg, C. (2005). Autism after adolescence: Population-based 13- to 22-year follow-up study of 120 individuals with autism diagnosed in childhood. *Journal of Autism and Developmental Disorders*, *35*, 351–360.

Billstedt, E., Gillberg, I. C., & Gillberg C. (2011). Aspects of quality of life in adults diagnosed with autism in childhood: A population-based study. *Autism*, *15*, 7–20.

Bolton, P. F., Carcani-Rathwell, I., Hutton J., Goode S., Howlin, P., & Rutter M. (2011). Features and correlates of epilepsy in autism. *British Journal of Psychiatry*, *198*, 289–294.

Brugha, T. S., McManus, S., Bankart, J., Scott, F., Purdon, S., Smith, J., ... Meltzer, H. (2011). The epidemiology of autism spectrum disorders in adults in the community in England. *Archives of General Psychiatry*, *68*, 459–466.

Burke, R. V., Andersen, M. N., Bowen, S. L., Howard, M. R., & Allen, K. D. (2010). Evaluation of two instruction methods to increase employment options for young adults with autism spectrum disorders. *Research in Developmental Disabilities*, *31*(6), 1223–1233.

Burt, D. B., Fuller, S. P., & Lewis, K. R. (1991). Brief report: Competitive Employment of adults with autism. *Journal of Autism and Developmental Disorders*, *21*, 237–242.

Cederlund, M., Hagberg, B., & Gillberg, C. (2010). Asperger syndrome in adolescent and young adult males. Interview, self- and parent assessment of social, emotional, and cognitive problems. *Research in Developmental Disabilities*, *31*, 287–298.

Cederlund, M., Hagberg, B., Billstedt, E., Gillberg, I. C., & Gillberg, C. (2008). Asperger syndrome and autism: A comparative longitudinal follow-up study more than 5 years after original diagnosis. *Journal of Autism and Developmental Disorders*, *38*, 72–85.

Chasson, G. S., Harris, G. E., & Neely, W. J. (2007). Cost comparison of early intensive behavioral intervention and special education for children with autism. *Journal of Child and Family Studies*, *16*, 401–413.

Cimera, R. E., & Cowan, R. J. (2009). The costs of services and employment outcomes achieved by adults with autism in the US. *Autism*, *13*, 285–302.

Cimera, R. E., Wehman, P., West, M., & Burgess, S. (2012). Do sheltered workshops enhance employment opportunities for adults with autism spectrum disorder. *Autism*, *16*(10), 87–94.

Clement-Heist, K., Siegel, S., & Gaylord-Ross, R. (1992, February). Simulated and in situ vocational social skills training for youths with learning disabilities. *Exceptional Children*, 336–345.

Creak, E. M. (1963). Childhood Psychosis: A review of 100 cases. *British Journal of Psychiatry*, *109*, 84–89.

Dawson, G., Rogers, S., Munson, J., Smith, M., Winter, J., Greenson, J., ... Varley, J. (2010). Randomized, controlled trial of an intervention for toddlers with autism: The Early Start Denver Model. *Pediatrics*, *125*, 17–23.

DeMyer, M. K., Barton, S., DeMyer, W. E., Norton, J. A., Allen, J., & Steele, R. (1973). Prognosis in autism: A follow-up study. *Journal of Autism and Child Schizophrenia*, *3*, 199–246.

Eaves, L. C., & Ho, H. H. (2008). Young adult outcome of autism spectrum disorders. *Journal of Autism and Developmental Disorders*, *38*, 739–747.

Edwards, T. L., Watkins, E. E., Lotfizadeh, A. D., & Poling, A. (2012). Intervention research to benefit people with autism: How old are the participants? *Research in Autism Spectrum Disorders*, *6*, 96–99.

Eisenberg, L., & Kanner, L. (1956). Childhood schizophrenia; symposium, 1955. VI, Early infantile autism, 1943–55. *American Journal of Orthopsychiatry, 26*, 556–566.

Engström, I., Ekström, L., and Emilsson, B. (2003). Psychosocial functioning in a group of Swedish adults with Asperger syndrome or high-functioning autism. *Autism, 7*(1), 99–100.

Esbensen, A. J., Greenberg, J. S., Seltzer, M. M., & Aman, M. G. (2009). A longitudinal investigation of psychoactive and physical medication use among adolescents and adults with autism spectrum disorders. *Journal of Autism and Developmental Disorders, 39*, 1339–1349.

Farley, M. A., McMahon, W. M., Fombonne, E., Jenson, W. R., Miller, J., Gardner, M., . . . Coon, H. (2009). Twenty-year outcome for individuals with autism and average or near-average cognitive abilities. Autism Research, 2, 109–118.

Fausett, M. (2005). *Employing people with Asperger syndrome—a practical guide*. London, England: The National Autistic Society.

Ganz, M. L. (2007). The lifetime distribution of the incremental societal costs of autism. *Archives of Pediatric & Adolescent Medicine, 161*(4), 343–349.

García-Villamisar, D., & Hughes C. (2007). Supported employment improves cognitive performance in adults with autism. *Journal of Intellectual Disability Research, 51*(2), 142–150.

García-Villamisar, D., Ross, D., & Wehman, P. (2000). Clinical differential analysis of persons with autism in a work setting. *Journal of Vocational Rehabilitation 14*, 183–185.

García-Villamisar, D., Wehman, P., & Navarro, M. D. (2002). Changes in the quality of autistic people's life that work in supported and sheltered employment: A five year follow-up study. *Journal of Vocational Rehabilitation, 17*, 300–312.

Gerland, G. (2003). *A real person: Life on the outside*. London, England: Jessica Kingsley.

Ghaziuddin, M. (2005). *Mental health aspects of autism and Asperger syndrome*. London, England: Jessica Kingsley.

Ghaziuddin, M., Ghaziuddin, N., & Greden, J. (2002). Depression in persons with autism: implications for research and clinical care. *Journal of Autism and Developmental Disorders, 32*, 299–306.

Ghaziuddin, M., & Zafar, S. (2008). Psychiatric comorbidity of adults with autism spectrum disorders. *Clinical Neuropsychiatry, 5*, 9–12.

Gilchrist, A., Green, J., Cox, A., Rutter, M., & Le Couteur, A. (2001). Development and current functioning in adolescents with Asperger syndrome: A comparative study. *Journal of Child Psychology and Psychiatry, 42*, 227–240.

Gillberg, C., Billstedt, E., Sundh, V., & Gillberg, C. (2010). Mortality in autism: A prospective longitudinal community based study. *Journal of Autism and Developmental Disorders, 40*, 352–357.

Gillberg, C., & Steffenburg, S. (1987). Outcome and prognostic factors in infantile autism and similar conditions: A population-based study of 46 cases followed through puberty. *Journal of Autism and Developmental Disorders, 17*, 273–287.

Gillespie-Lynch, K., Sepeta, L., Wang, Y., Marshall, S., Gomez, L., Sigman, M., & Hutman, T. (2012). Early childhood predictors of the social competence of adults with autism. *Journal of Autism and Developmental Disorders. 42*(2), 161–174.

Golan, O., Baron-Cohen, S., & Hill, J. (2006). The Cambridge Mindreading (CAM) Face-Voice Battery: Testing complex emotion recognition in adults with and without Asperger syndrome. *Journal of Autism and Developmental Disorders, 36*(2), 169–183.

Grandin, T. (2006). *Thinking in Pictures*. London, England: Bloomsbury.

Halpern, A. S. (1993). Quality of life as a conceptual framework for evaluating transition outcomes. *Exceptional Children, 59*(6), 486–498.

Hedley, D., & Young, R. (2006). Social comparison processes and depressive symptoms in children and adolescents with Asperger syndrome. *Autism, 10*(2), 139–153.

Henninger, N. A., & Taylor, J. L. (2013). Outcomes in adults with autism spectrum disorders: An historical perspective. *Autism, 17*, 103–116.

Hillier, A., Campbell, H., Mastriani, K., Izzo, M. V., Kool-Tucker, A. K., Cherry, L., & Beversdorf, D. (2007). Two-year evaluation of a vocational support program for adults on the autism spectrum. *Career Development for Exceptional Individuals, 30*(1), 35–47.

Hofvander, B., Delorme, R., Chaste, P., Nydén, A., Wentz, E., Ståhlberg, O., . . . Leboyer, M. (2009). Psychiatric and psychosocial problems in adults with normal-intelligence autism spectrum disorders. *Biomed Central Psychiatry, 9*, 35.

Holtmann, M., Bölte, S., & Poustka, F. (2007). Autism Spectrum Disorders: Sex differences in autistic behaviour domains and coexisting psychopathology. *Developmental Medicine and Child Neurology, 49*, 361–366.

Howlin, P. (2003). Outcome in high functioning adults with autism with and without early language delays: Implications for the differentiation between autism and Asperger syndrome. *Journal of Autism and Developmental Disorders, 33*, 3–13.

Howlin, P. (2004). *Autism and Asperger syndrome: Preparing for adulthood* (2nd ed). London, England, and New York, NY: Routledge.

Howlin, P., Alcock, J., & Burkin, C. (2005). An 8 year follow-up of a specialist supported employment service for high-ability adults with autism or Asperger syndrome. *Autism, 9*(5), 533–549.

Howlin, P., Goode, S., Hutton, J., & Rutter, M. (2004). Adult outcome for children with autism. *Journal of Child Psychology and Psychiatry, 45*, 212–229.

Howlin, P., Mawhood, L., & Rutter, M. (2000). Autism and developmental receptive language disorder—a follow-up comparison in early adult life. II: Social, behavioural, and psychiatric outcomes. *Journal of Child Psychology and Psychiatry, 41*, 561–578.

Howlin, P., & Moss, P. (2012). Adults with autism spectrum disorders. *Canadian Journal of Psychiatry, 57*(5), 275–283.

Howlin, P., Moss, P., Savage, S., & Rutter, M. (2013). Social outcomes in mid to later adulthood among individuals diagnosed with autism as children. *Journal of the American Academy of Child & Adolescent Psychiatry, 52*(6), 572–581.

Hume, K., Loftin, R., & Lantz, J. (2009) Increasing independence in autism spectrum disorders a review of 3 focused interventions. *Journal of Autism and Developmental Disorders, 39*, 1329–1338.

Hume K., & Odom, S. (2007). Effects of an Individual work system on the independent functioning of students with autism. *Journal of Autism and Developmental Disorders*, *37*, 1166–1180.

Hurlbutt, K., & Chalmers, L. (2004). Employment and adults with Asperger syndrome. *Focus on Autism & Other Developmental Disabilities*, *19*, 215–222.

Hutton, J., Goode, S., Murphy, M., Le Couteur A., & Rutter, M. (2008). New-onset psychiatric disorders in individuals with autism. *Autism*, *12*, 373–390.

Jacobson, J. W., Mulick, J. A., & Green, G. (1998). Cost-benefit estimates for early intensive behavioral intervention for young children with autism—general model and single state case. *Behavior Intervention*, *13*, 201–226.

Kamp-Becker, I., Ghahreman, M., Smidt, J., & Remschmidt, H. (2009). Dimensional structure of the autism phenotype: relations between early development and current presentation. *Journal of Autism and Developmental Disorders*, *39*, 557–571.

Kanner, L. (1943). Autistic disturbances of affective contact. *Nervous Child*, *2*, 217–250.

Kanner, L. (1973). *Childhood psychosis: Initial studies and new insights*. New York: Winston/Wiley.

Kanner, L., & Eisenberg, L. (1956). Early infantile autism. *American Journal of Orthopsychiatry*, *26*, 55–65.

Keel, J. H., Mesibov, G., & Woods, A. V. (1997). TEACCH-Supported employment programme. *Journal of Autism and Developmental Disorders*, *27*, 3–10.

Knapp, M., Romeo, R., & Beecham, J. (2009). Economic cost of autism in the UK. *Autism*, *13*(3), 317–336.

Kobayashi, R., Murata, T., & Yoshinaga, K. (1992). A follow-up study of 201 children with autism in Kyushu and Yamaguchi areas, Japan. *Journal of Autism and Developmental Disorders*, *22*, 395–411.

Kumar, R. A., & Christian, S. L. (2009). Genetics of autism spectrum disorders. *Current Neurology and Neuroscience Reports*, *9*, 188–197.

Kurtz, Z., Tookey, P., & Ross, E. (1998), Epilepsy in young people: 23 year follow up of the British National Child Development Study. *British Medical Journal*, *7128*, 339–342.

Lainhart, J. E. (1999). Psychiatric problems in individuals with autism, their parents and siblings. *International Review of Psychiatry*, *11*, 278–298.

Larsen, F. W., & Mouridsen, S. E. (1997). The outcome in children with childhood autism and Asperger syndrome originally diagnosed as psychotic: A 30-year follow-up study of subjects hospitalized as children. *European Child and Adolescent Psychiatry*, *6*, 181–190.

Lattimore, L. P., & Parsons, M. B. (2006). Enhancing job-site training of supported workers with autism a re-emphasis on simulation. *Journal of Applied Behavior Analysis*, *39*(1), 91–102.

Lattimore, L. P., Parsons, M. B., & Reid, D. H. (2002). A pre-work assessment of task preferences among adults with autism beginning a supported job. *Journal of Applied Behavior Analysis*, *35*(1), 85–88.

Lattimore, L. P., Parsons, M. B., & Reid, D. H. (2003). Assessing preferred work among adults with autism beginning jobs; identification of constant and alternating job preferences. *Behavioral Intervention*, *18*, 161–177.

Lattimore, L. P., Parsons, M. B., & Reid, D. H. (2009). Rapid training of a community job skill to nonvocal adults with autism: an extension of intensive teaching. *Behavior Analysis & Practice*. *2*(1), 34–42.

Lawer, L., Brusilovsky, E., Seltzer, M. S., & Mandell, D. (2009). Use of vocational rehabilitative services among adults with autism. *Journal of Autism and Developmental Disorders*, *39*, 487–494.

Lawson, W. (2002). *Life behind glass*. London, England: Jessica Kingsley.

Levy, A., & Perry, A. (2011). Outcomes in adolescents and adults with autism a review of the literature. *Research in Autism Spectrum Disorders*. Doi:10.1016/jrasd2011.01.023

Lockyer, L., & Rutter, M. (1969). A five- to fifteen-year follow-up study of infantile psychosis. III. Psychological aspects. *British Journal of Psychiatry*, *115*, 865–882.

Lockyer, L., & Rutter, M. (1970). A five to fifteen year follow-up study of infantile psychosis. IV. Patterns of cognitive abilities. *British Journal of Social and Clinical Psychology*, *9*, 152–163.

Lord, C., Rutter, M., Di Lavore, P. C., & Risi, S. (2000). *Autism Diagnostic Observation Schedule (ADOS)*. Los Angeles, VA: Western Psychological Services.

Lord, C., Rutter, M., & Le Couteur, A. (1994). Autism Diagnostic Interview-Revised: A revised version of a diagnostic interview for carers of individuals with possible pervasive developmental disorders. *Journal of Autism and Developmental Disorders*, *24*, 659–685.

Lord, C., Schopler, E., & Revicki, D. (1982). Sex differences in autism. *Journal of Autism and Developmental Disorders*, *12*, 317–330.

Lotter, V. (1974). Social adjustment and placement of autistic children in Middlesex a follow-up study. *Journal of Autism and Childhood Schizophrenia*, *4*, 11–322.

Magiati, I., Tay, X. W., & Howlin, P. (2012). Early comprehensive interventions for children with autism spectrum disorders: A critical synthesis of recent review findings. *Neuropsychiatry*, *2*(6), 543–570.

Marriage, S., Wolverton, A., & Marriage, K. (2009). Autism spectrum disorder grown up: A chart review of adult functioning. *Journal of the Canadian Academy of Child and Adolescent Psychiatry*, *18*, 322–328.

Mawhood, L., Howlin, P., & Rutter, M. (2000). *Journal of Child Psychology and Psychiatry*, *41*(5), 547–559.

Mawhood L., & Howlin P. (1999). Outcome of a supported employment scheme for high-functioning adults with autism or AS. *Autism*, *3*(3), 229–254.

Mazefsky, C. A., Folstein, S. E., & Lainhart J. E. (2008). Over-representation of mood and anxiety disorders in adults with autism and their first-degree relatives: what does it mean? *Autism Research*, *1*, 193–197.

McClannahan, L. E., MacDuff, G. S., & Krantz, P. J. (2002). Behavior analysis and intervention for adults with autism. *Behavior Modification*, *26*, 9–26.

Moss, P. (2011). *Social and mental health outcomes in adults with autism and their siblings*. Unpublished PhD thesis, King's College, London, England.

Motiwala, S. S., Gupta, S., Lilly, M. B., Ungar, W. J., & Coyte, P. C. (2006). The cost-effectiveness of expanding intensive behavioural intervention to all autistic children in Ontario. *Healthcare Policy, 1*, 135–151.

Mouridsen, S. E., Bronnum-Hansen, H., Rich, B., & Isager, T. (2008). Mortality and causes of death in autism spectrum disorders: An update. *Autism, 12*, 413–414.

Mukaetova-Ladinska, E. B., Perry, E., Baron, M., & Povey, C. (2012). Ageing in people with autistic spectrum disorder. *International Journal of Geriatric Psychiatry, 27*(2), 109–118.

National Institute for Health and Clinical Excellence Guideline Group for Adults with ASD. (2012, June). Autism: Recognition, referral, diagnosis and management of adults on the autism spectrum. *CG 142.*

National Institute of Mental Health. (2010). National Institute of Mental Health: Schizophrenia. [Online]. Retrieved from http://www.nimh.nih.gov/health/topics/schizophrenia/index .shtml

Newport, J., & Newport, M. (2002). *Autism-Asperger's & sexuality: Puberty and beyond.* Arlington, TX: Future Horizons.

Pickett, J., Xiu, R., Tuchman, G., Dawson, G., & Lajonchere, C. (2011). Mortality in individuals with autism, with and without epilepsy. *Journal of Child Neurology, 26*(8), 932–939.

Pinto, D., Pagnamenta, A. T., Klei, L., Anney, R., Merico, D., Regan, R., . . . Betancur, C. (2010). Functional impact of global rare copy number variation in autism spectrum disorders. *Nature, 466*, 368–372.

Piven, J., Harper, J., Palmer, P., & Arndt, S. (1996). Course of behavioural change in autism: A retrospective study of high-IQ adolescents and adults. *Journal of the American Academy of Child & Adolescent Psychiatry, 35*, 523–529.

Piven, J., Rabins, P., & the Autism in Older Adults Working Group (2011). Autism spectrum disorders in older adults: Towards defining a research agenda. *Journal of the American Geriatric Society, 59*(11), 2151–2155.

Renty, J., & Roeyers, H. (2006). Quality of life in high functioning adults with autism spectrum disorder. *Autism, 10*, 511–524.

Rumsey, J. M., Rapoport, J. L., & Sceery, W. R. (1985). Autistic children as adults: Psychiatric, social, and behavioral outcomes. *Journal of the American Academy of Child & Adolescent Psychiatry, 24*, 465–473.

Rutter, M., Greenfeld, D., & Lockyer, L. (1967). A five to fifteen year follow-up study of infantile psychosis. II. Social and behavioural outcome. *British Journal of Psychiatry, 113*(504), 1183–1199.

Rutter, M., & Lockyer, L. (1967). A five to fifteen year follow-up study of infantile psychosis. I. Description of sample. *British Journal of Psychiatry, 113*, 1169–1182.

Schaller, J., & Yang, N. K. (2005). Competitive employment for people with autism: Correlates of successful closure in competitive and supported employment. *Rehabilitation Counseling Bulletin, 49*(1), 4–16.

Seltzer, M. M., Krauss, M. W., Shattuck, P. T., Orsmond, G., Swe, A., & Lord, C. (2003). The symptoms of autism spectrum disorders in adolescence and adulthood. *Journal of Autism and Developmental Disorders, 33*, 565–581.

Seltzer, M. M., Shattuck, P., Abbeduto, L., & Greenberg, J. S. (2004). Trajectory of development in adolescents and adults with autism. *Mental Retardation and Developmental Disabilities Research Reviews, 10*, 234–247.

Shattuck, P. T., Roux, A. M., Hudson, L. E., Lounds-Taylor, J., Maenner, M., & Trani, J.-F. (2012). Services for adults with an autism spectrum disorder. *Canadian Journal of Psychiatry, 57*(5), 284–291.

Shavelle, R. M., Strauss, D. J., & Pickett, J. (2001). Causes of death in autism. *Journal of Autism and Developmental Disorders, 31*, 569–576,

Shea, V., & Mesibov, G. B. (2005). Adolescents and adults with autism. In F. R. Volkmar, R. Paul, A. Klin, & D. Cohen (Eds.), *Handbook of autism and pervasive developmental disorders* (3rd ed., pp. 288–311). Hoboken, NJ: Wiley.

Simonoff, E., Pickles, A., Charman, T., Chandler, S., Loucas, T., & Baird, G. (2008). Psychiatric disorders in children with autism spectrum disorders: prevalence, comorbidity, and associated factors in a population-derived sample. *Journal of the American Academy of Child & Adolescent Psychiatry, 47*, 921–929.

Slater-Walker, G., & Slater-Walker, C. (2002). *An Asperger marriage.* London, England: Jessica Kingsley.

Smith, M., Belcher, R., & Juhrs, P. (1995). *A guide to successful employment for individuals with autism.* Baltimore, MD: Paul H. Brookes.

Sterling, L., Dawson, G., Estes, A., & Greenson, J. (2008). Characteristics associated with presence of depressive symptoms in adults with autism spectrum disorder. *Journal of Autism and Developmental Disorders, 38*, 1011–1018.

Stewart, M. E., Barnard, L., Pearson, J., Hasan, R., & O'Brien, G. (2006). Presentation of depression in autism and Asperger syndrome: A review. *Autism, 10*, 103–116.

Sturmey, P. (1998). Classification and diagnosis of psychiatric disorders in persons with developmental disabilities. *Journal of Developmental and Physical Disabilities, 10*, 317–330.

Szatmari, P., Bartolucci, G., Bremner, R., Bond, S., & Rich, S. (1989). A follow-up study of high-functioning autistic children. *Journal of Autism and Developmental Disorders, 19*, 213–225.

Tantam, D. (1991). Asperger's syndrome in adulthood. In U. Frith (Ed.), *Autism and Asperger syndrome* (pp. 147–183). Cambridge, England: Cambridge University Press.

Taylor, J. L., & Seltzer, M. M. (2011). Employment and post-secondary educational activities for young adults with autism spectrum disorders during the transition to adulthood. *Journal of Autism and Developmental Disorders, 41*(5), 566–574.

Totsika, V., Hastings, R. P., Emerson, E., Lancaster, G. A., & Berridge, D. A. (2011). A population-based investigation of behavioural and emotional problems and maternal mental health: Associations with autism spectrum disorder and intellectual disability. *Journal of Child Psychology and Psychiatry Autism and Developmental Disorders, 52*(1), 91–99.

Tuchman, R., Moshe, S. L., & Rapin, I. (2009). Convulsing toward the pathophysiology of autism. *Brain Development, 31*, 95–103.

Tuchman, R., & Rapin, I. (2002). Epilepsy in autism. *Lancet Neurology, 1*, 352–358.

Turner-Brown, L. M., Perry, T. D., Dichter, G. S., Bodfish, J. W., & Penn, D. L. (2008). Brief report: Feasibility of social cognition and interaction training for adults with high functioning autism. *Journal of Autism and Developmental Disorders, 38*, 1777–1784.

Underwood, L., McCarthy, J., & Tsakanikos, E. (2010). Mental health of adults with autism spectrum disorders and intellectual disability. *Current Opinion in Psychiatry, 23*, 421–426.

Venter, A., Lord, C., & Schopler, E. (1992). A follow-up study of high-functioning autistic children. *Journal of Child Psychology and Psychiatry, 33*, 489–507.

von Knorring, A.-L., & Häglöf, B. (1993). Autism in northern Sweden: A population based follow-up study: Psychopathology. *European Child and Adolescent Psychiatry, 2*, 91–97.

Whitehouse, A. J., Watt, H. J., Line, E. A., & Bishop, D. V. (2009). Adult psychosocial outcomes of children with specific language impairment, pragmatic language impairment and autism. *International Journal of Language and Communication Disorders, 44*, 511–528.

Willey, L. H. (1999). *Pretending to be normal: Living with Asperger's syndrome*. London, England: Jessica Kingsley.

Williams, D. (1992). *Nobody nowhere*. London, England: Corgi Books.

Wing, L. (1981). Asperger's syndrome: A clinical account. *Psychological Medicine, 11*, 115–29.

Wing, L., & Gould, J. (1978). Systematic recording of behaviors and skills of retarded and psychotic children. *Journal of Autism and Childhood Schizophrenia, 8*, 79–97.

Wolff, S., & McGuire, R. J. (1995). Schizoid personality in girls: A follow-up study. What are the links with Asperger's syndrome? *Journal of Child Psychology and Psychiatry, 36*, 793–818.

Development and Behavior

Section II provides a history of the research in development across all the main domains of childhood carried out in autism spectrum disorder (ASD). It also gives us the most current findings, and how the current knowledge adds to, refutes, or alters previous concepts and beliefs. The understanding of autism as a developmental disorder, resulting from and reflecting differences in most areas of childhood development, has been a mainstream approach for many years now. Yet, it is still common to see some approach ASD from an orientation more akin to adult brain injury than to infant development. The developmental lens cautions us that brain networks and processes, areas of expertise and mechanics, are all shaped by experience, and that the adult brain reflects the lifetime experience of the person. Differences that are found in adults with autism compared to adults with other or no diagnoses may or may not reflect the biology of autism, but they must reflect the lifetime of experiences of that adult. The developmental perspective helps us appreciate areas of strength and relative strength in people with ASD, and it establishes common grounds among people with and without disability. It also casts adult behavior and skills as the later point in a trajectory beginning very early in life, and so helps us appreciate all the points on that trajectory that can have influence on the endpoint. The chapters in this section on development provide us with the most updated literature on the developmental science of ASD, written by the scientists who are producing much of the most important developmental work in ASD.

In Chapter 5, Chawarska and colleagues provide a strong synopsis of the most recent findings from the fast-moving filed of longitudinal infant siblings studies. This area of science has provided corrections for many previously held ideas about the onset and course of ASD. Diagnosis of ASD in the youngest children has increased due to the existence of better measures and data suggesting stability of symptoms throughout the toddler and preschool years. It appears we can be successful identifying altered patterns of brain function in response to social and sensory stimuli in 6-month-olds. Questions concerning the narrowness of the prodrome of ASD are thoughtfully considered in this chapter.

In Chapter 6, Bauminger reviews current developmental research in autism in the school years and points out the growing social, psychiatric, and cognitive-academic complexities and expectations that mark this period of life and result in an ever-widening social-communicative gap between children with ASD and their typically developing peers. Difficulties in interpreting others' inner emotional and mental states create additional barriers to satisfying peer relations, and the partial understanding many children with ASD have in these areas add challenges to their social partners, resulting in their positions in the periphery of peer networks. Children with ASD often report loneliness and victimization and are helped in these areas more by peer mediators than by adults. However, cognitive difficulties in learning, abstraction, and executive function create an additional set of stressors for children with ASD in the school years.

Interventions need to support social and cognitive learning and foster friendship development.

Koegel and colleagues (Chapter 7) address developments that present new challenges to adolescents with ASD. While the issues that highlighted the earlier school years continue, new school challenges involve independent motivation and management of academic learning outside of school. Future planning for teens with ASD needs to focus on transitions to vocational preparation or college. Including a well-developed pathway to careers rather than college is a problem for adolescents throughout the American education system. The use of intervention strategies and provision of needed supports will assure that the next generation of adults with ASD have far more opportunities for competitive employment, independent living, and satisfying adult lives than do the current generation of adults with ASD, a topic addressed by Mazefsky and White in Chapter 8.

Adults with ASD are receiving more attention than in previous decades, exemplified by the increased attention to adults seen in this edition of the handbook compared to previous editions. While ASD diagnoses tend to be stable in adulthood and ASD symptoms may even improve, declines in adaptive behavior performance not seen in other groups with developmental disorders raise much concern. Outcomes for adults with ASD as a group have been disappointing, with far less competitive employment, independent living, and satisfying adult lives than is seen in other groups with similar intellectual and language abilities. The lack of well-developed intervention approaches and support systems for adults with ASD in inclusive community settings will draw more and more attention as the numbers of adults with ASD in communities increase due to rising prevalence.

Social development is the most affected area of impairment for people with ASD, and Carter provides a helpful review in Chapter 9. An exciting addition to the descriptions of social characteristics seen in autism has been the use of new technologies for assessing and studying social behavior. Eye tracking, fMRI, and EEG, among others, have provided new aids for understanding social differences

in ASD. As with other areas of development in ASD, there is no one prototypic pattern of social development. All of the core social symptoms seen early in autism—lack of eye contact, social engagement, imitation, joint attention—improve in response to interventions, which demonstrates the plasticity of even core symptoms in ASD.

Social development is closely tied to language and communication development, covered in Chapter 10 by Kim and colleagues. The profiles of language and communication ability and their developmental trajectories vary widely among people with ASD. In the past decade, classic language impairments involving phonology, vocabulary, syntax, and morphology have been seen within a subgroup of children with ASD that are virtually identical to those seen in children without ASD. Another discovery is the presence of communication and receptive understanding deficits in infants who do not yet have ASD but will later develop ASD. A third important recent finding in this domain is the shrinking subgroup of nonverbal people with ASD, likely reflecting several factors, one of which is probably the availability of early intervention services to young children with ASD. The chapter thoroughly reviews all aspects of communication and language usage in ASD using an up-to-date lens that also addresses brain mechanisms.

Unlike the clearly articulated theories, tools, concepts, and terms in the study of communication and language, the area of play is far less articulated in all domains, observe authors Kasari and Chang (Chapter 11), and single-subject designs dominate the research landscape. However, as with language and social development, even though play is affected in a primary way in ASD, play skills can be stimulated via effective intervention approaches, and children with ASD can make great progress in constructive and symbolic play development. These authors provide a very helpful table of studies that will aid both academicians and clinicians.

Chapter 12, on imitation, by Vivanti and Hamilton, delves into the very interesting research work on the mirror neuron system (MNS) and hypothesized links between the MNS and autism. This new line of theorizing is thoughtfully reviewed here. These authors help draw attention to the complexities involved in a seemingly simple act of imitating another and provide a heuristic neuropsychological model for characterizing the multiple aspects of imitation and the multiple areas that could be impaired while also thoroughly reviewing the conflicting studies of imitation performance in persons with ASD and helping to integrate the findings into a whole.

A thorough review of the neuropsychological research is provided in Chapter 13 by Tsatsanis and Powell, including review of sensory-perceptual function, attention, memory abilities, executive functions, and intellectual ability. The authors provide helpful summaries of the most current findings in each of these areas, and they provide appropriate cautions concerning the fundamental disparities in subject selection that occur in neuropsychological studies (the majority of studies are based on older participants with fewer challenges to intellectual and language function than occurs in many or most people with ASD).

Hobson's chapter on emotion cautions the reader to consider the conceptual boundaries that we use to (artificially) separate cognitive, conative, and emotional domains. He carefully separates difficulties with social relatedness from capacities for relationships, and he cautions us not to equate difficulties with emotional perception with theory of mind problems, nor to assume that people with ASD do not respond emotionally to a wide range of stimuli. He cautions us to remember that experiences shape minds, and that neural differences seen in ASD may reflect the cumulative effects of a life lived with ASD rather than a starting state.

Chapters 15 and 16, on motor development (Bodison and Mostofsky) and sensory development (Baranek and colleagues), finish off this section. The chapter on motor development reminds us that motor learning is a primary learning system for young children and across the lifespan, that there is considerable evidence of multiple motor impairments in ASD, including difficulties with motor learning, and that motor learning consists of many processes and multiple neural control systems. They highlight three processes well studied in ASD: goal-directed reaching, postural stability, and motor learning; and they provide for understanding the integration of sensory and motor processes for learning that applies very well to findings from studies involving ASD. In their chapter, Baranek and colleagues integrate and synthesize what is known about sensory responses, processing, and development in ASD in an exceptionally well-organized, systematic, and informative way. The authors describe both what is known, and how much is not known about the pathogenesis, mechanisms, interventions, and functional impacts of sensory differences seen in ASD.

CHAPTER 5

ASD in Infants and Toddlers

KATARZYNA CHAWARSKA, SUZANNE MACARI, FRED R. VOLKMAR,
SO HYUN KIM, AND FREDERICK SHIC

Autism spectrum disorder (ASD) is a complex neurodevelopmental disorder characterized by severe impairments in social communication and social interaction and a range of restricted, repetitive patterns of behaviors, interests, or activities. Despite the fact that the onset of ASD occurs in most cases before the age of 2 years, until relatively recently, ASD was usually not diagnosed until several years later. However, advances in research on early syndrome expression and reports stressing the efficacy of early intervention have made the transition toward earlier diagnosis both possible and imperative (Chawarska, Klin, & Volkmar, 2008; Chawarska & Volkmar, 2005; Lord & Risi, 2000; National Research Council, 2001; Paul, 2007; Wetherby, Prizant, & Schuler, 2000). Early identification of ASD also provides an opportunity to study the disorder before confounding effects of treatment, development of compensatory strategies, and comorbid disorders have begun to impact its manifestation. In this chapter, we provide a review of research regarding the symptoms of autism in infancy and early childhood with a particular focus on the new and rapidly advancing area of research on the prodromal stage of ASD.

The authors gratefully acknowledge the support of the National Institute of Child Health and Human Development (grants P01 HD35482, P01 HD042127, P01 HD03008), the National Institute of Mental Health (U54 MH066594. P50 MH081756, R01MH087554, R03 MH092617, R03MH086732, R03 MH092618), as well as the National Alliance of Autism Research and Autism Speaks research grants. The authors thank Emily Prince for her help in the preparation of this chapter.

SYMPTOMS OF ASD IN EARLY CHILDHOOD

Developmental Perspective

Infancy is a period of rapid growth and change; thus, the presence or absence of a behavior typical for a certain narrowly defined developmental period may become clinically significant only a few months later. For instance, sensory exploration of objects is adaptive prior to the first birthday, but may signify developmental problems when it persists into the second year of life (see Chapter 16, this *Handbook*, this volume) and is not replaced by functional and symbolic forms of play. Similarly, the physical act of reaching to pursue a desirable object is typical under the age of 9 months and soon thereafter becomes synchronized with eye contact and socially directed vocalizations as an index of emerging intentional communication (Bates, 1979); a persistent lack of such synchronization signals a disruption in the development of social communication in the second year of life. Moreover, some early symptoms of ASD such as lack of response to bids for joint attention become less diagnostically useful over time as children begin to benefit from intervention programs targeting these specific deficits. Thus, in the search for diagnostic markers of ASD in the first 2 years of life, one must carefully consider the developmental context and timetables.

Onset of Symptoms

Studies of parental recognition of developmental abnormalities in autism suggest that at least 80% to 90% of parents recognize that their child's behavior is atypical by the age of 24 months, though the age at which recognition occurs varies widely (Baghdadli, Picot, Pascal, Pry, & Aussilloux, 2003; Chawarska, Paul, et al., 2007; De Giacomo & Fombonne, 1998; Rogers & DiLalla, 1990). Among parents of toddlers presenting for a first diagnosis of ASD before the age of 3 years, approximately 20% reported having concerns in the first 10 months, that is, during the period of development dominated by nonverbal dyadic social interactions, 40% noted abnormalities during the period notable for the emergence of joint attention skills and first words (11 to 17 months) and another 40% or so at or after 18 months, the period marked by emergence of complex and integrated social, communication, and symbolic skills (Chawarska,

Paul, et al., 2007). The sources of such variability are not well understood, but are likely to involve variation in parental ability to recognize atypical social behaviors and delays as well as differences in their patterns of onset and presence of co-occurring motor, cognitive, and language delays or medical problems (Baghdadli et al., 2003; De Giacomo & Fombonne, 1998). Not surprisingly, in toddlers with autism and pervasive developmental disorder not otherwise specified (PDD-NOS), the first concerns are related to social and speech delays (Chawarska, Paul, et al., 2007; De Giacomo & Fombonne, 1998). However, parents of children with autism reported more concerns regarding motor development and the presence of unusual sensory and stereotypic behaviors than parents of children diagnosed with PDD-NOS. In contrast, regulatory problems related to feeding, eating, and overall activity level were more frequent in the PDD-NOS group than in the autism group (Chawarska, Paul, et al., 2007).

Patterns of Onset

Although the initial observations of cases of autism suggested the presence of social abnormalities from birth (early onset) (Kanner, 1943/1968), further clinical observations revealed the possibility that symptoms may emerge after a period of more or less typical development (late onset) either as a result of a loss of skills (regression) (Eisenberg & Kanner, 1956; Kurita, 1985; Lord, Shulman, & DiLavore, 2004; Ozonoff et al., 2011; Tuchman & Rapin, 1997; Volkmar & Cohen, 1989) or a failure to progress (plateau) (Kalb, Law, Landa, & Law, 2010; Ozonoff et al., 2011; Siperstein & Volkmar, 2004). Research regarding the relation between reported patterns of onset and developmental profiles or longer-term outcomes have been inconsistent, with more recent longitudinal studies reporting largely negative results (Chawarska, Klin, Paul, & Volkmar, 2007; Landa, Gross, Stuart, & Bauman, 2012; Ozonoff, Heung, Byrd, Hansen, & Hertz-Picciotto, 2008; Ozonoff et al., 2010; Shumway et al., 2011; Werner, Dawson, Munson, & Osterling, 2005). The categorical conceptualization of onset patterns has recently been challenged in a study more closely examining the emergence of ASD-specific deficits in infant siblings of children with ASD (high-risk infants; see "Prodomal Symptoms of ASD in the First Year of Life," later in this chapter) between 6 and 36 months (Ozonoff et al., 2010). Growth curve analysis suggested that some behaviors (e.g., eye contact and social smiling) show a gradual decrease in frequency from 6 to 18 months, whereas others (e.g., social vocalizations) fail to increase at the rate observed in typical controls. These findings suggest that the models of onset might be better captured by a multidimensional rather than a categorical approach, as it is plausible that the departure from typical trajectories in specific domains may follow different patterns (i.e., plateau or regression) and take place during different developmental periods. Thus, as the evidence from the ongoing prospective longitudinal studies accumulates, the current conceptualization of patterns of onset in ASD may need to be revised. This approach may prove to be more fruitful with regard to identifying mechanisms underlying core deficits in ASD.

EARLY DIAGNOSIS

The past several years have brought significant improvements in the conceptualization and assessment of early symptoms of ASD (Chawarska et al., 2008). These advances have been reflected in revisions of existing diagnostic instruments, as well as in the reformulation of the diagnostic criteria in the fifth edition of the *Diagnostic and Statistical Manual* (*DSM-5*; American Psychiatric Association [APA], 2013).

Diagnostic Criteria for Infants and Toddlers

Although the *DSM-IV* (APA, 1994) diagnostic criteria for autism and related disorders had very good sensitivity and specificity in general and covered a range of syndrome expression across a broad spectrum of intellectual disability (Volkmar et al., 1994),

applicability to the youngest children with autism was limited (Lord, 1995; Stone et al., 1999). Very few children under the age of 3 were included in the *DSM-IV* field trial, and thus, some of the diagnostic criteria did not apply to this age group (e.g., failure to develop peer relationships, impaired conversational skills, and stereotyped language). Furthermore, in the past two decades since *DSM-IV*, great progress has been made in understanding the phenotypic presentation of ASD in the first 3 years of life, with results suggesting a nuanced developmental course dependent on a child's individual chronological and mental age. Recognizing these considerations, developmental levels have been taken into consideration in the recently published *DSM-5* ASD criteria (APA, 2013). The *DSM-5* advances the conceptualization of autism as representing a broad spectrum of disorders (hence, the new category of autism spectrum disorder), and encompassing previously differentiated diagnostic labels of Autistic Disorder, Pervasive Developmental Disorder Not Otherwise Specified (PDD-NOS), Childhood Disintegrative Disorder, and Asperger Syndrome under a single umbrella of ASD. The symptoms of ASD have been grouped into two domains: Social Communication and Social Interaction (SCSI) and Restricted, Repetitive Behaviors, Interests, and Activities (RRBIA), a model of latent structure of symptoms of autism strongly supported by empirical work both on older children (Frazier et al., 2012; Gotham et al., 2008; Gotham, Risi, Pickles, & Lord, 2007; Mandy, Charman, & Skuse, 2012) as well as toddlers (Georgiades, Szatmari, Boyle, et al., 2013; Guthrie, Swineford, Wetherby, & Lord, 2013). For a child to be diagnosed with ASD, all three criteria in the SCSI domain and two out of four criteria in the RRBIA domain have to be met. For each of the two domains, it is necessary to specify the level of support required given the severity of ASD symptoms. Moreover, it is also required to specify whether the ASD symptoms are accompanied by intellectual disability or language impairment, and whether they are associated with any known medical (e.g., epilepsy) or genetic condition (e.g., Rett syndrome or fragile X syndrome) or environmental factors (e.g., very low birth weight or exposure to valproic acid). Comorbid disorders such as attention-deficit/hyperactivity disorder (ADHD), anxiety, sleep disorder, or disruptive behavior should be noted in the diagnostic formulation as well (see Volkmar, Reichow, Westphal, & Mandell, Chapter 1 of this *Handbook*, for more in-depth discussion of issues in the diagnosis of ASD).

Preliminary retrospective analyses evaluating the sensitivity and specificity of the provisional *DSM-5* criteria when applied to children under the age of 4 years suggested high sensitivity (.90 to .98) and improved specificity (.40 to .53) compared to *DSM-IV* (Huerta, Bishop, Duncan, Hus, & Lord, 2012). Inclusion of information from two sources: parent report (Autism Diagnostic Interview [ADI]) and direct observation (Autism Diagnostic Observation Schedule [ADOS]) increased the specificity of the diagnostic classification. Barton and colleagues (Barton, Robins, Jashar, Brennan, & Fein, 2013) investigated whether further modification of the *DSM-5* criteria could be employed for children under the age of 3 to improve specificity. Both studies report high sensitivity and moderate specificity of the *DSM-5* criteria for young children. Notably, both studies accounted for symptoms recorded only in the ADOS and ADI. Considering that both instruments are based largely on the *DSM-IV* criteria, it is possible that some of the *DSM-5* criteria might not be captured precisely by the instruments (Huerta et al., 2012). Furthermore, exclusive reliance on the two measures does not fully reflect actual clinical diagnostic decision-making practices where information from multiple sources, including developmental and language testing as well as medical and developmental history, is typically considered, contributing to improved diagnostic precision. Further studies, however, will be necessary to evaluate performance of the *DSM-5* classification criteria in children under the age of 3 within the context of prospective rather than retrospective data collection.

Stability and Change of Syndrome Expression

Best Estimate Diagnosis

Due to a lack of biological markers, ASD is currently diagnosed solely by a constellation of behavioral features. Considering marked heterogeneity as well as rapid changes in syndrome expression in the first 3 years of life, the diagnostic process involves consideration of multiple sources of information (Kim & Lord, 2012; Risi et al., 2006), including results of diagnostic tests such as the Autism Diagnostic Observation Schedule–2 (ADOS-2; Lord, Rutter, et al., 2012), Autism Diagnostic Observation Schedule–Toddler (ADOS-T) (Lord, Luyster, et al., 2012), and the Autism Diagnostic Interview–Revised (ADI-R; Rutter, Le Couteur, & Lord, 2003) (see Lord, Corsello, & Grzadzinski, Chapter 25 of this *Handbook*, Volume 2); assessment of developmental skills (e.g., Mullen Scales of Early Learning [Mullen Scales] [Mullen, 1995] and Bayley Scales of Infant and Toddler Development, third edition [Bayley Scales] [Bayley, 2006]), language and communication (e.g., Communication and Symbolic Behaviors Scale [CSBS] [Wetherby & Prizant, 2002] and Preschool Language Scale–5 [PLS-5] [Zimmerman, Violette, Steiner, & Pond, 2011]), and adaptive functioning (Vineland Adaptive Behaviors Schedule–Revised [Vineland-II] [Sparrow, Balla, & Cicchetti, 2005]); and review of the child's medical and family history. Genetic, audiological, or neurological exams are often necessary evaluating potential presence of associated conditions (e.g., fragile X syndrome, hearing loss, or seizure disorder) (Action, 1999; American Speech-Language-Hearing Association, 2006; see also Chapter 22 of this *Handbook*, by Volkmar & colleagues, on medical care in autism). A vast majority of prospective longitudinal studies indicate very high (82%–100%) short-term (Chawarska, Klin, et al., 2007; Chawarska, Klin, Paul, Macari, & Volkmar, 2009; Cox et al., 1999; Eaves & Ho, 2004; Guthrie, Swineford, Nottke, & Wetherby, 2013) as well as long-term stability (Charman et al., 2005; Lord et al., 2006; Turner, Stone, Pozdol, & Coonrod, 2006) of best estimate ASD diagnosis. Thus, there is overwhelming evidence suggesting that symptoms of ASD can be identified in a majority of clinic-referred children with ASD in the second year of life and that the diagnostic classification is likely to be stable into school age. However, despite these advances, a majority of children are not diagnosed until late preschool age or school age. Among the key factors affecting age at diagnosis are inadequate screening practices (Sices, Feudtner, McLaughlin, Drotar, & Williams, 2003), as well as ethnic (Mandel, Ittenbach, Levy, & Pinto-Martin, 2007), cultural (Daley, 2004), and socioeconomic factors (Mandell, Listerud, Levy, & Pinto-Martin, 2002; Mandell, Novak, & Zubritsky, 2005). Decreasing the gap between symptom onset and the age of diagnosis and initiation of treatment for all children with ASD constitutes one of the most pressing challenges in the field.

Developmental Trajectories

Despite the overall high stability of the best estimate diagnosis of ASD, marked changes in verbal, nonverbal, adaptive, and social-communicative skills have been reported in children before the age of 3 (Charman et al., 2005; Chawarska et al., 2009; Lord et al., 2006; Magiati, Charman, & Howlin, 2007; Magiati, Moss, Charman, & Howlin, 2011). This phenomenon is particularly pronounced with regard to verbal skills where the vast majority of the affected toddlers in the second year of life show severe language delays, but by the age of 3, the variability amongst them increases as some children catch up with typical peers, whereas others continue to struggle with the acquisition of communicative speech. The limited stability of verbal and nonverbal abilities in toddlers with autism before the second birthday is exemplified by modest correlations between verbal ($r = .35$) and nonverbal ($r = .47$) Mullen Scales scores from the second to the third year of life (Chawarska et al., 2009). Interestingly, in toddlers with less severe social impairments who are diagnosed with PDD-NOS, the stability appears somewhat higher with correlations of .70 and .73 for verbal and nonverbal skills, respectively (Chawarska et al., 2009). Despite the high variability in the rate of progress over time in verbal and nonverbal domains, the severity of autism symptoms and impairments in adaptive social functioning appear relatively stable (Anderson, Oti, Lord, & Welch, 2009; Gotham, Pickles, & Lord, 2012; Magiati et al., 2011). For instance, in a cohort followed from 2 to 10 years, a majority of children showed persistent severe or moderate levels of social impairment and social adaptation over time, and only a small minority

of the affected children exhibited a marked drop in their autism severity (Gotham et al., 2012) and increases in their adaptive social functioning levels (Anderson et al., 2009). However, emerging evidence suggests that in more recently ascertained cohorts the proportion of children exhibiting lessening of symptom severity over time might be higher, in some cases resulting in changes in diagnostic classification from ASD to non-ASD (Chawarska et al., 2009; Kleinman et al., 2008; Lord, Luyster, Guthrie, & Pickles, 2012). This may be due more generally to the increased availability of effective intensive intervention for toddlers (Dawson et al., 2010; Howlin, Magiati, & Charman, 2009; Kasari, Gulsrud, Freeman, Paparella, & Hellemann, 2012; Kasari, Gulsrud, Wong, Kwon, & Locke, 2010; Koegel, Koegel, Fredeen, & Gengoux, 2008; Magiati et al., 2011; Smith, Groen, & Wynn, 2000; Wetherby & Woods, 2008) (see Rogers & Vismara, Chapter 29 of this *Handbook*, Volume 2, for review of research on early intervention in ASD). Moreover, given the improvements in screening and precision of diagnostic procedures, it is likely that more toddlers who are higher-functioning, moderately affected, and therefore, more amenable to treatment are being identified in the second year of life (see Ibañez, Stone, & Coonrod, Chapter 24 of this *Handbook*, Volume 2, on screening).

Predictors of Outcome

Outcome in ASD has been typically defined along several dimensions, including verbal and nonverbal skills, severity of core symptoms, or educational placement. Predictors of outcome in older children are often shared across domains and include age at entry into treatment, receptive language skills, IQ, severity of autism symptoms, and levels of adaptive behaviors (Flanagan, Perry, & Freeman, 2012; Harris & Handleman, 2000; Magiati et al., 2011; Remington et al., 2007; Smith et al., 2000). Considering that neither IQ nor expressive language ability can be measured reliably in young and thereby largely preverbal children with ASD, there has been a more extensive focus on behavioral precursors of more advanced cognitive and communicative skills (Charman et al., 2005). Given the centrality of joint attention skills to the development of social cognition and communication in typical development, it is not surprising that the ability to initiate and to respond to joint attention bids has been identified as a strong predictor of subsequent levels of social functioning and language in ASD (Kasari et al., 2012; Sigman & Ruskin, 1999; Yoder & Stone, 2006; Yoder, Stone, Walden, & Malesa, 2009). The rate of communicative bids at 2 years was strongly associated with adaptive communication and socialization scores several years later (Charman et al., 2005; Shumway & Wetherby, 2009). Diversity of play schemes and functional play skills has been associated with the development of nonverbal cognitive and adaptive skills (Kasari et al., 2012; Sigman & McGovern, 2005; Vivanti, Dissanayake, Zierhut, & Rogers, 2012) and better vocal and motor imitation in young children predicts later nonverbal skills (Thurm, Lord, Lee, & Newschaffer, 2007; Vivanti et al., 2012). Moreover, the number and types of stimuli that function as reinforcers have also been identified as strong predictors of later adaptive functioning in toddlers with ASD receiving intensive behavioral interventions (Klintwall & Eikeseth, 2012). Amongst other factors associated with outcomes are the child's age at entry into treatment (Kasari et al., 2012; Rogers et al., 2012), quality of parental involvement in parent-mediated interventions (Kasari et al., 2010), frequency of parental child-directed speech synchronous with the child's interests and activities (McDuffie & Yoder, 2010; Perryman et al., 2012), and parental stress levels (Osborne, McHugh, Saunders, & Reed, 2008), along with other factors related to the treatment itself such as treatment intensity (Eldevik et al., 2010) and therapist allegiance to treatment (Klintwall, Gillberg, Bölte, & Fernell, 2012).

More recently, efforts have been made to identify novel factors associated with outcome including attentional and physiological responses to various classes of social stimuli. In one such study, vagal activity combined with looking time responses to child-directed speech at 3 years of age predicted communication indices at 4 years in toddlers with ASD (Watson, Baranek, Roberts, David, & Perryman, 2010). Vivanti and colleagues (2012)

reported predictive associations between responses to an eye-tracking task capturing understanding of goals of others and gains in receptive language over a 1-year period. Campbell, Shic, Macari, and Chawarska (2013) found that 14- to 24-month-old toddlers who, during a brief eye-tracking experiment exhibited limited attention to eye contact and child-directed speech cues, showed very limited progress in skill acquisition and poor levels of functioning at the age of 3 years despite intensive early intervention, raising the question of whether spontaneous attention to social cues in toddlers might constitute a marker of amenability to treatment. Further work will be necessary to elucidate how the heterogeneity in any one of these novel individual characteristics may differentially mediate the response to various treatment methods and varying degrees of treatment intensity. A number of other parameters that may mediate response to intervention, including physiological markers as well as familial and other environmental factors, still remain to be identified.

SYMPTOMS OF ASD IN THE SECOND AND THIRD YEARS OF LIFE

In the second year, typically developing infants undergo a rapid growth of skills encompassing social interactions, imaginative play, and verbal as well as nonverbal communication. Though more subtle behavioral signs of ASD may be apparent earlier in life in some children, for most children later diagnosed with ASD, the second year of life is the time when the developmental trajectories of toddlers with ASD begin to diverge rapidly from those of typically developing children, triggering parental concerns and the search for professional advice (Chawarska, Paul, et al., 2007; De Giacomo & Fombonne, 1998; Rogers & DiLalla, 1990).

Core Symptoms

Early studies of syndrome expression in toddlers relied heavily on parental reports, both retrospective (Hoshino et al., 1982; Ornitz, Guthrie,

& Farley, 1978) and prospective (Baird et al., 2000; Baron-Cohen, Cox, Baird, Sweettenham, & Nighingale, 1996; Lord, 1995). However, with improved detection of ASD early in life through advances in early screening and increased community awareness of ASD, as well as the development of direct observational scales such as the ADOS (Lord, Rutter, DiLavore, & Risi, 2000; Lord, Luyster, Gotham, et al., 2012; Lord, Rutter, et al., 2012) and the Autism Observation Scale for Infants (AOSI) (Bryson, Zwaigenbaum, McDermott, Rombough, & Brian, 2008) as well as experimental measures of social engagement and communication, more recent accounts have been based on direct assessment of ASD-specific features.

Reciprocal Social Communication and Social Interaction

Core symptoms in this domain include persistent deficits that manifest across multiple contexts encompassing deficits in (1) social-emotional reciprocity, (2) nonverbal communication, and (3) developing, maintaining, and understanding relationships with others (APA, 2013). To be diagnosed with ASD, a child must exhibit deficits in all three areas. In early development, many of the social and communicative impairments characteristic of ASD are expressed in the absence of spoken language or robust representational skills (e.g., Chawarska et al., 2009; Chawarska, Klin, et al., 2007; Guthrie, Swineford, Nottke, et al., 2013; Lord, Luyster, Guthrie, et al., 2012; Luyster et al., 2009). Thus, ASD-specific deficits in toddlers are defined primarily with regard to elementary face-to-face (dyadic) and shared attention (triadic) interaction, communication, and play skills.

Toddlers with ASD struggle with reciprocal social and emotional exchanges (Bishop, Luyster, Richler, & Lord, 2008; Charman et al., 1997; Chawarska, Klin, et al., 2007; Lord, 1995; Stone, Ousley, Yoder, Hogan, & Hepburn, 1997). They exhibit limited eye contact and, when they do make eye contact, the eye contact is usually poorly integrated with other social-communicative overtures. Although they may initiate some social overtures,

these overtures are more likely to serve the purpose of seeking comfort or help rather than initiating shared games and activities. Their range of affective expressions is typically limited, and they have difficulties communicating their emotional states by directing facial expressions to others (e.g., frowning and making eye contact with a parent). Moreover, toddlers with ASD show a limited capacity to derive salient information from the affective expressions of others (Cornew, Dobkins, Akshoomoff, McCleery, & Carver, 2012; Dawson et al., 2004; Sigman, Arbelle, & Dissanayake, 1995) or from gaze and gestural cues (Landa, Holman, & Garrett-Mayer, 2007; Shumway & Wetherby, 2009; Sullivan et al., 2007; Wetherby, Watt, Morgan & Shumway, 2007). Impairments in imitation of others, including their body movements, actions with objects, facial expressions, and vocalizations, have also been found in toddlers with ASD (Charman et al., 1997; Rogers, Hepburn, Stackhouse, & Wehner, 2003; Rowberry et al., under review; Stone, Ousley, Yoder, et al., 1997; Young et al., 2011) (see Vivanti & Hamilton, Chapter 12 in this *Handbook*, for more details). These impairments are not only closely related to the other core symptoms of ASD (Rogers et al., 2003) but also have negative implications for the development of peer interactions during toddlerhood (Nadel, Guerini, Peze, & Rivet, 1999).

Toddlers with ASD also exhibit marked impairments in nonverbal communication. They communicate less frequently than their nonaffected peers and the majority of their communicative bids serve to convey needs (protoimperative communication) rather than to share experiences with others (protodeclarative communication) (Dawson, Meltzoff, Osterling, Rinaldi, & Brown, 1998; Landa et al., 2007; Mundy & Crowson, 1997; Shumway & Wetherby, 2009; Sigman & Ruskin, 1999; Woods & Wetherby, 2003). Although the ability to respond to and initiate joint attention bids in ASD increases over time, especially in highly structured contexts (Leekam, Hunnisett, & Moore, 1998; Leekam, López, & Moore, 2000), children with autism have difficulties using these skills adaptively and spontaneously in more naturalistic situations (Baron-Cohen, Baldwin, & Crowson, 1997; Baron-Cohen, Campbell, Karmiloff-Smith, Grant, & Walker, 1995; Leekam, Baron-Cohen, Perrett, Milders, & Brown, 1997). Moreover, the sequence of joint attention acquisition appears to differ from that observed in typical development, which may be suggestive of the development of alternative compensatory strategies in young children with ASD (Carpenter, Pennington, & Rogers, 2002; Kasari et al., 2012). In the absence of language in early development, gestures serve as one of the key means of communication. However, gesture use in toddlers with ASD is significantly impaired, both in terms of rate of gestural communication (Cox et al., 1999; Shumway & Wetherby, 2009), total inventory of gestures (Landa et al., 2007; Mitchell et al., 2006), and types of gestures, especially showing and pointing (Shumway & Wetherby, 2009; Stone, Ousley, Yoder, et al., 1997). These results have significant implications for the development of communication skills since the inventory of gestures at 2 years has been found to uniquely contribute to receptive language outcome at 3 years (Watt, Wetherby, & Shumway, 2006). Unusual forms of communication are also observed, such as using an adult's hand as a tool (Stone, Ousley, Yoder, et al., 1997). When language eventually emerges in toddlers with ASD it is usually later than expected and often marked by abnormal features such as unusual intonation, as well as immediate and delayed echolalia (see Kim, Paul, Tager-Flusberg, & Lord, Chapter 10 of this *Handbook*).

Difficulties in peer interaction may manifest as a limited response to or active avoidance of peers or initiation of overtures that are inappropriate considering the child's developmental level (e.g., indiscriminate approaches toward strangers). These difficulties, when combined with deficits in reciprocal social and emotional exchanges including imitation, further limit the toddler's opportunities for social interactions and joint play (see Kasari & Chang, Chapter 11 of this *Handbook*, on play in ASD). Furthermore, while play skills in toddlers with ASD do advance over time, the play routines are often rigid, repetitive, and organized around specific topics (e.g., makes and models of cars) and are usually not conducive to carrying on successful reciprocal exchanges with peers.

Restricted, Repetitive Behaviors, Interests, and Activities

The current *DSM-5* criteria specify four key areas of impairment, including (1) stereotyped or repetitive movements, speech, or use of objects; (2) insistence on sameness and inflexible adherence to routines or ritualized patterns of verbal or nonverbal behavior; (3) highly restricted interests of abnormal intensity; and (4) hyper- or hyporeactivity to sensory input. Initial observations and parental reports suggested that RRBIAs may be relatively rare in toddlers or preschoolers with ASD (Cox et al., 1999; Stone et al., 1999; Ventola et al., 2006). However, more recent work suggests that RRBIAs are already quite prevalent in the second year of life, according to parent report (Richler, Bishop, Kleinke, & Lord, 2007) and direct observation (Barber, Wetherby, & Chambers, 2012; Chawarska, Klin, et al., 2007; Kim & Lord, 2010; Watt, Wetherby, Barber, & Morgan, 2008; Wetherby et al., 2004). Studies focused on RRBIAs in young children suggest that even though some repetitive behaviors are present in infants and children without ASD (Evans et al., 1997; Sallustro & Atwell, 1978; Thelen, 1979), toddlers with ASD demonstrate significantly more severe and/or frequent repetitive actions with objects, motor mannerisms, sensory interests, as well as nonspeech vocalizations and stereotyped language compared to children with developmental delays and typically developing children (Barber et al., 2012; Kim & Lord, 2010; Schoen, Paul, & Chawarska, 2011; Sheinkopf, Mundy, Oller, & Steffens, 2000; Watt et al., 2008; Wetherby et al., 2004). On the other hand, in very young children, insistence on sameness appears less prevalent, though modest increases in difficulties with changes in routine have been reported in toddlers with ASD compared with both typical and delayed controls (Richler et al., 2007). Lastly, circumscribed interests comprising behaviors such as intense, focused hobbies and strong preoccupations with odd topics, have not been consistently observed in children under the age of 3 except for unusually strong interests in certain objects (Kim & Lord, 2010).

Specific Areas of Functioning

Social Attention: Behavioral Studies

One of the important roles that attention plays in everyday life is the selection of socially or task-relevant aspects of the environment for further processing (James, 1890/1950). Studies of older individuals with autism suggest that their spontaneous visual attention to people in general and to faces in particular is diminished as compared with developmentally delayed groups (Volkmar & Mayes, 1990). A similar trend has been observed in toddlers with ASD (Dawson et al., 1998; Swettenham et al., 1998). For instance, 20-month-old toddlers with autism spent a greater proportion of their play focused on objects and a smaller proportion of time orienting spontaneously to people and monitoring their behavior as compared with the control groups (Swettenham et al., 1998). Limited social monitoring has been reported as early as at 12 months in infants later diagnosed with ASD in the context of an object-oriented interaction (Ozonoff et al., 2010) and the distress-response paradigm (Hutman, Chela, Gillespie-Lynch, & Sigman, 2012; Hutman et al., 2010).

Social Attention: Eye-Tracking Studies

Several eye-tracking studies have examined the attentional responses to a range of complex social stimuli in toddlers with ASD with the aim of identifying processes that may compromise the development of social attention in ASD (Chawarska, Macari, & Shic, 2012; Jones, Carr, & Klin, 2008; Shic, Bradshaw, Klin, Scassellati, & Chawarska, 2011). These studies suggest that when toddlers with ASD view adults trying to engage them either through simple social games (e.g., peek-a-boo; Jones et al., 2008) or through direct eye contact and child-directed speech (Chawarska et al., 2012), they tend to look at faces less than control participants, a pattern similar to that seen

in adolescents with ASD (Klin, Jones, Schultz, Volkmar, & Cohen, 2002). They also are less likely to look at objects attended to by others (Bedford et al., 2012) and show decreased monitoring of the activities of others (Shic et al., 2011). Thus, in the second year of life, deficits in spontaneous social monitoring in ASD have already begun to extend beyond simple attention to faces. It is possible that these deficits represent the sequelae of limited attention toward faces and people earlier in life; however, it is also possible that the deficits are more fundamentally related and share a common underlying mechanism.

Moreover, extant evidence suggests that unlike in typically developing individuals (Langton, Law, Burton, & Schweinberger, 2008; Lavie, Ro, & Russell, 2003; Ro, Friggel, & Lavie, 2007), in toddlers with ASD, social stimuli are not prioritized for processing in the attentional system; that is, they have a limited capacity to engage and hold the attention of the affected children. When tested in a variation of the attention-cueing paradigm (Hood, Willen, & Driver, 1998), toddlers with ASD disengaged their attention from faces faster than developmentally delayed and typically developing controls, which signifies limited depth of engagement with these socially relevant stimuli (Chawarska, Klin, & Volkmar, 2003; Chawarska, Volkmar, & Klin, 2010). In typical individuals, limited depth of attentional engagement with faces typically results in less effective encoding of their invariant features (Bloom & Mudd, 1991; Coin & Tiberghien, 1997). Consistent with this finding, toddlers with ASD show poor face recognition skills compared to developmentally delayed and typically developing controls (Chawarska & Shic, 2009), a deficit that appears to be specific to faces but not to objects (Bradshaw, Shic, & Chawarska, 2011).

In summary, evidence to date suggests that by 2 years of age, attention toward socially relevant phenomena is disrupted in toddlers with ASD, an effect that will likely impair further acquisition of critical social-emotional and communicative skills and as well as development of nonsocial cognition. Further work will need to critically examine the underlying motivational or perceptual biases that lead to early atypicalities in social attention, as well as the developmental course and resultant impact of early atypical social attention on social, cognitive, and adaptive outcomes later in life.

Adaptive Functioning

Studies of adaptive functioning, or the development and application of abilities serving to achieve personal independence and social sufficiency (Cicchetti & Sparrow, 1990), suggest that compared with mental age- or IQ-matched controls, school-age children with autism children have lower overall adaptive functioning scores (Lord & Schopler, 1989) and present with greater variability in the profile of adaptive skills (Burack & Volkmar, 1992; Kanne et al., 2011; Klin, Volkmar, & Sparrow, 1992; Volkmar et al., 1987). In particular, children with ASD show deficits in socialization that are more pronounced than deficits in other areas of adaptive behaviors or cognitive ability (Volkmar, Carter, Sparrow, & Cicchetti, 1993). A similar pattern of deficits in the development of adaptive behaviors has been reported in toddlers with ASD. Compared to chronological age- and mental age–matched controls, 2-year-old children with ASD had significantly lower communication, socialization, and daily living skills scores (Paul, Fuerst, Ramsay, Chawarska & Klin, 2011; Ray-Subramanian, Huai, & Weismer, 2011; Stone et al., 1999). Their scores in these areas were significantly lower than their overall mental level, suggesting marked difficulties in translating their cognitive potential into real-life functioning. Thus, similar to older children, toddlers with autism exhibit syndrome-specific patterns of developmental and adaptive skills that suggest adaptive communication and socialization are unique and specific areas of vulnerability in early development in ASDs.

Attachment

Attachment, or the affective bond between a child and a mothering figure (Ainsworth, Blehar, Waters, & Wall, 1978), has been extensively studied in children with ASD. The results of numerous studies of older children using the Strange Situation paradigm provide limited evidence of syndrome-specific deficits in this area (Capps, Sigman, & Mundy, 1994; Naber et al., 2007; Rogers, Ozonoff, & Maslin-Cole, 1993; Waterhouse & Fein, 1998). These findings appear counterintuitive considering numerous reports regarding parental perception of their children's impoverished affective bond with their parents, as well as the presence of attachments to unusual transitional objects (Volkmar, Cohen, & Paul, 1986). A meta-analysis of 10 studies of attachment in preschoolers with ASD (Rutgers, Bakermans-Kranenburg, van IJzendoorn, & Berckelaer-Onnes, 2004) reported that across all studies, 53% of the children showed evidence of secure attachment, significantly lower than the rates of secure attachment in comparison groups. Moderators included diagnosis and mental ability, with both greater severity of social impairments and severity of intellectual disability adversely affecting the ability of a parent–child dyad to establish a secure emotional attachment. Many studies have used Ainsworth and colleagues' (1978) original four-category classification system, but assessments of attachment using alternative methods such as the Richters attachment security rating (Richters, Waters, & Vaughn, 1988) or the Brief Attachment Screening Questionnaire (Bakermans-Kranenburg, van IJzendoorn, & Juffer, 2003), a modification of the Attachment Q-Sort (Waters, 1995), have revealed significantly less secure attachment in toddlers with ASD compared to children with other impairments and typical controls (Naber et al., 2007; Rutgers et al., 2007; van IJzendoorn et al., 2007). Thus it appears that conflicting reports of attachment in ASD could be attributed to a measurement issue, with finer-grained measures showing consistent ASD-specific differences.

Temperament

Temperament is defined as constitutionally based attentional, emotional, and activity-related dimensions that emerge beginning in early infancy and serve as the foundation for personality development (Goldsmith et al. 1987; Rothbart & Bates, 1998; Rothbart & Derryberry, 1981). A majority of studies of temperament in ASD has been conducted in younger siblings of children with ASD, who, due to familial factors, are at increased risk for developing the disorder themselves. The studies suggest unique temperamental profiles in infants with ASD compared with both low-risk and high-risk controls (Clifford, Hudry, Elsabbagh, Charman, & Johnson, 2013; Garon et al., 2009; Zwaigenbaum et al., 2005). As early as 12–14 months of age, infants later diagnosed with ASD were described by their parents as displaying elevated distress reactions, longer durations of attending to objects (Zwaigenbaum et al., 2005), less frequent smiling and laughter, diminished cuddliness, and increased perceptual sensitivity (Clifford et al., 2013). By 24 months, children with ASD were reported to exhibit more sadness and shyness, lower soothability, less enjoyment of calm activities, diminished cuddliness (Clifford et al., 2013), reduced ability to shift attention to social cues, lower inhibitory control, and less positive anticipation (Garon et al., 2009; Zwaigenbaum et al., 2005) than their nonaffected high-risk and low-risk peers. Data on temperamental characteristics in clinic-referred toddlers with ASD between 18 and 36 months of age is largely consistent with the reports of high-risk toddlers with ASD (Koller, Campbell, Macari, & Chawarska, under review). Parents of 114 young children with autism reported that their children had less positive anticipation, greater difficulty responding to verbal cues to shift attention, decreased preference for quiet activities, and less inhibitory control than did the parents of both typically developing and developmentally delayed age-matched controls. Temperamental features of toddlers with milder autism symptoms (PDD-NOS; $N = 52$) were largely intermediate between the autism and developmentally delayed groups. At the same time, toddlers with both ASD and non-ASD developmental delays shared difficulties in attention focusing, affect regulation, and awareness of minor perceptual stimuli, as well as greater expression of anger, and more social fear. Temperamental features in the second and third year of life, including attention shifting and perceptual sensitivity, uniquely contributed to autism severity at ages 3–5 years, above and

beyond variance predicted by developmental level or symptom severity. These studies show a burgeoning interest in biologically based dimensions that shed light on noncore facets of the ASD phenotype that are potentially relevant to broadly defined heterogeneity of syndrome expression and comorbid features.

Summary

In the absence of biological markers, best estimate clinical diagnosis continues to constitute a gold standard in diagnosis of ASDs not only in school-age children but also in toddlers. Considering the heterogeneity of the early syndrome expression and rapid developmental changes observed within the first 3 years of life, the diagnostic process requires simultaneous consideration of several sources of information including the child's medical history, developmental level, adaptive functioning, and verbal and nonverbal communication, in addition to the direct assessment of the core symptoms of ASD. Both short- and long-term stability of early clinical diagnosis is very high. However, there is marked variability amongst toddlers with ASD with regard to not only severity of social impairments but also rates of progress over time. Amongst the factors affecting long-term outcomes in toddlers with ASD are age, understanding of language, cognitive level, and social adaptation both at the time of the first diagnosis and at entry into treatment. Amongst more specific features associated with positive outcomes in toddlers are emerging joint attention skills, interest in functional play, imitation skills, and diversity of and responsivity to reinforcers in treatment contexts. Considering the importance of enhancing the frequency and type of learning opportunities for very young children with ASD, parental variables such as stress levels, interaction style, and involvement in the treatment have been recently implicated as associated with outcome as well. Findings regarding individual differences in syndrome expression and developmental trajectories of affected children highlight the need for the development of new methodologies, including new experimental paradigms, measurement techniques, and analytic approaches, in order to better identify more phenotypically homogenous subgroups of toddlers, a goal that would facilitate the discovery of the underlying biological mechanisms of ASD. Work on identifying predictive moderators of outcome in ASD brings us closer to the understanding of mechanisms underlying specific impairments, and ultimately, to the ability to match individual children to appropriate treatment approaches that accommodate their unique profiles of skills and disabilities in service of optimizing their long-term outcomes and enhancing their quality of life.

PRODROMAL SYMPTOMS OF ASD IN THE FIRST YEAR OF LIFE

Understanding predictors and mechanisms of emergence of ASD is a critical step in the search for early markers and preventive interventions. In recent years, these objectives propelled a wave of research on preonset (prodromal) symptoms in the first year of life.

Retrospective Studies

Early studies of prodromal signs of ASD in the first year relied primarily on retrospective information including parental report, case studies, and videotape analysis.

Parent Report

Retrospective studies suggest that the early symptoms may include both social difficulties as well as regulatory problems. Parents of preschoolers with autism reported that compared with developmentally delayed controls, their children, as infants, failed to exhibit anticipation of being picked up, affection toward familiar people, reaching for a familiar person, and playing simple interactive games with others (Klin et al., 1992). Children later diagnosed with autism were often described by parents as either extremely difficult or very passive in infancy, with symptoms of irritability, low soothability, and erratic physiological patterns (Rogers & DiLalla, 1990).

Case Studies

Kanner (1943/1968) noted that while abnormalities of speech and stereotyped behaviors emerge over time, the "autistic aloneness" may be present from birth. Infants later diagnosed with ASD have been described as exhibiting extreme self-sufficiency with the ability to occupy themselves for long periods of time, difficulties in adjusting body posture while being held and in assuming an anticipatory posture in preparation for being picked up (Kanner, 1943/1968), limited eye contact and social responsivity (Dawson, Osterling, Meltzoff, & Kuhl, 2000; Klin et al., 2004; Sparling, 1991), as well as limited motor and vocal imitation (Dawson et al., 2000). Tremulousness and excessive startle response in the perinatal period (Sparling, 1991), arousal regulation difficulties, sleep difficulties, unusual sensitivity to stimuli, and oral-motor problems have been reported as well (Dawson et al., 2000).

Video Analysis

In the absence of prospective data, analysis of home movies of infants later diagnosed with autism gained popularity in the 1990s. The studies typically returned positive results both in comparison to typically developing infants (Maestro et al., 2002; Osterling & Dawson, 1994; Werner, Dawson, Osterling, & Dinno, 2000) and developmentally delayed infants (Baranek, 1999; Osterling, Dawson, & Munson, 2002). Compared to typically developing controls, 6-month-old infants later diagnosed with ASD showed diminished attention and affective responses to people, were less likely to anticipate others' aims (Maestro et al., 2002), and exhibited atypical postural characteristics (Esposito, Venuti, Maestro, & Muratori, 2009). When 9- to 12-month-old infants with autism were compared to developmentally delayed peers, they were less likely to respond when their name was called (Baranek, 1999; Osterling et al., 2002), and exhibited limited attention to people (Osterling et al., 2002). No differences between the groups were found with regard to gaze aversion, response to social touch and affective expressions, attention to objects, pointing, participation in social games, and imitation within this age range (Baranek, 1999; Osterling et al., 2002).

Prospective Infant Sibling Studies

Due to genetic liability, younger siblings of children with ASD are at an increased risk for developing the disorder themselves. Following their development prospectively allows for examination of the syndrome's emergence in *status nascendi* and thus facilitate identification of the earliest prognostic signs and treatment targets (Rogers, 2009; Tager-Flusberg, 2010; Yirmiya & Charman, 2011; Zwaigenbaum et al., 2009). Current estimates of the recurrence rate amongst younger siblings of children with ASD ranges from 6.9% (Grønborg, Schendel, & Parner, 2013) to 10% (Constantino, Zangh, Frazier, Abbacchi, & Law, 2010), to 18% (Ozonoff et al., 2010), depending on the mode of sample ascertainment. A significant minority of high-risk infants are also likely to develop milder deficits in social and communication domains or atypical repetitive or rigid behaviors; these patterns of development are often referred to as the broader autism phenotype (Bailey, Palferman, Heavey, & Le Couteur, 1998; Constantino, et al., 2010; Georgiades, Szatmari, Zwaigenbaum, et al., 2013; Messinger et al., 2013; Murphy et al., 2000; Schwichtenberg, Young, Sigman, Hutman, & Ozonoff, 2010, see Ingersoll & Wainer, Chapter 2 in this *Handbook*, on the broader autism phenotype). The past decade brought an explosion of prospective longitudinal studies on development of high-risk infant siblings. Considering our focus on prodromal symptoms of ASD and developmental trajectories of affected infants, the following section includes only the studies in which diagnostic outcomes were available at the age of 2 years or thereafter, rather than studies more broadly comparing high- and low-risk infants. While in some studies, infants who later develop ASD are compared to low-risk controls and non-ASD high-risk infants, in others, the latter group is further differentiated into high-risk infants who exhibit delays and atypical features as well as high-risk infants who follow typical developmental

patterns. No studies thus far have compared infants who later develop ASD with low-risk, developmentally delayed infants. Depending on the comparison groups, interpretation of both positive and negative results may vary.

Prodromal Symptoms of ASD in the First 6 Months of Life in Infants at Risk

Early Social-Communicative Skills

Theoretical considerations and findings from retrospective studies suggest that prodromal symptoms of ASD are likely to include behaviors that constitute the basis for engagement in reciprocal face-to-face interactions. Such behaviors include attention to people and their faces, as well as presence of eye contact and socially directed smiling and vocalizations, all of which are universally impaired in toddlers with ASD (Chawarska et al., 2009; Chawarska, Klin, et al., 2007; Lord, Luyster, Guthrie, et al., 2012; Lord et al., 2006). Given that they are expressed robustly in typically developing infants by 6 months of age, such behaviors have been considered promising candidates for prodromal features of ASD. Several studies evaluated dyadic social responses of infants who were later diagnosed with ASD during face-to-face interactions with a parent (Rozga et al., 2011) or in the context of object- or task-focused interactions with an examiner (Ozonoff et al., 2010). No differences were found in social smiling, affective expressions, gaze direction (Young, Merin, Rogers, & Ozonoff, 2009), and social vocalizations (Ozonoff et al., 2010; Rozga et al., 2011) between those diagnosed later with ASD and non-ASD siblings or low-risk controls at the age of 6 months. It is plausible that this pattern of results reflects the natural history of ASD, with social deficits emerging on the behavioral level around or after the first birthday. However, it is also plausible that similar to parents of children with other developmental disabilities (Doussard-Roosevelt, Joe, Bazhenova, & Porges, 2003; Lemanek, Stone, & Fishel, 1993), sensing vulnerability in their child, parents of children with ASD employ a variety of implicit strategies (e.g., more direct interactive style) to elicit more social responses in their children (Wan et al., 2012). A recent study where aspects of face-to-face interaction were manipulated experimentally by inclusion of child-directed speech, play with objects, or anticipatory games, and the use of implicit cues for engagement was explicitly controlled, suggested that 6-, 9-, and 12-month-old infants later diagnosed with ASD attended less to the interactive partner when she spoke to them, but not when she used toys or perceptually salient games, such as peek-a-boo, to engage their attention (Kim et al., 2013). Thus, the extant, albeit limited, evidence suggests that overt symptoms of ASD might not be readily observable at 6 months; though in certain conditions where the attention of infants is less supported by an interactive partner, subtle differences between siblings who later develop ASD and unaffected siblings begin to emerge.

Verbal, Nonverbal, and Motor Skills

Considering the high prevalence of developmental delays in toddlers with ASD, verbal, nonverbal, and motor functioning has been examined closely in 6-month-old high-risk infants. However, as a group, infants later diagnosed with ASD appear to have no major developmental delays in the areas of nonverbal functioning, language, or motor skills as captured by the Mullen Scales of Early Learning (Chawarska, Macari, & Shic, 2013; Landa & Garrett-Mayer, 2006; Ozonoff et al., 2010; Zwaigenbaum et al., 2005). More recently, subtle motor deficits including poor postural control have been observed at 6 months (Flanagan, Landa, Bhat, & Bauman, 2012), possibly foreshadowing the motor difficulties described in older children with ASD (Fournier, Hass, Naik, Lodha, & Cauraugh, 2010) (see also Bodison & Mostofsky, Chapter 15 of this *Handbook*, on motor control and motor learning processes). Future studies will examine if such early manifesting motor features are specific to those who later develop ASD or whether they are shared with infants who later develop developmental delays (Ozonoff, Young, et al., 2008).

Social Attention

Considering that development is an experience-dependent process (Greenough, Black, & Wallace, 2002), it has been hypothesized that early atypical social experiences driven by the limited ability to detect and prioritize social stimuli for processing may play a formative role in the development of social cognition and communication in infants and toddlers with ASD. Several studies have examined elementary (e.g., attention capture) and more complex (e.g., spontaneous monitoring) aspects of social attention using eye-tracking methods. Six- to 10-month-olds with a later diagnosis of ASD show typical attention capture by faces presented in an array of objects (Elsabbagh, Gliga, et al., 2013) as well as gaze following, another relatively low-level and early emerging aspect of social attention (Bedford et al., 2012). These findings are consistent with reports regarding attention capture by faces in toddlers with ASD (O'Loughlin, Macari, Shic, & Chawarska, 2012) and orienting to gaze cues (Chawarska et al., 2003) in toddlers with ASD and add to the growing evidence that selected elementary attentional functions related to the processing of social stimuli may be intact in infants and toddlers with ASD.

In contrast, two recent eye-tracking studies reported on deficits in attention to complex dynamic social stimuli (Chawarska et al., 2013; Shic, Macari, & Chawarska, 2013). The paradigms captured the infants' endogenous strategies for selecting and attending to targets in the environment they find most relevant in the context of a free-viewing paradigm. While Shic and colleagues (2013) compared scanning strategies in response to static as well as dynamic smiling or speaking faces, Chawarska and colleagues (2013) examined attention to a person engaged in several activities (e.g., making a sandwich or addressing the viewer). Consistent with other behavioral and eye-tracking studies (Rozga et al., 2011; Young et al., 2009), 6-month-old infants who later developed ASD made context-specific adjustments to their scanning patterns similar to their typically and atypically developing high- and low-risk peers. That is, they attended to the actress's face when she spoke and to her hands when she made a sandwich (Chawarska et al., 2013), or looked at the mouth of a speaker more frequently than the mouth in a static photograph (Shic et al., 2013). However, in both studies the infants spent more time looking away from the social scenes, suggesting that one of the prodromal features of ASD is likely to consist of a general deficit in regulation of visual attention to faces and social scenes. When the infants did look at the social scenes, they spent less time fixating on the actress's face (Chawarska et al., 2013) and looked less at the speaker's mouth (Shic et al., 2013), suggesting a limited ability to sustain attention toward the interactive bids of others. Consistent with the interactive specialization hypothesis, which, in broad terms, suggests that in the postnatal period many brain regions are poorly specialized, but undergo fine-tuning to more specific classes of stimuli in an experience-dependent fashion (Greenough et al., 2002; Johnson, Grossmann, & Kadosh, 2009; Nelson, de Haan, & Thomas, 2006), the limited salience of social stimuli in ASD observed in early infancy may hinder the specialization process that rapidly advances in nonaffected infants, resulting in the progressive divergence between social cognitive skills in the affected and nonaffected groups over time.

Another important area of inquiry is attention disengagement from ongoing stimuli. Early deficits in the ability to flexibly shift attention between competing aspects of the visual scene could have implications for development of social and nonsocial cognition. Although toddlers with ASD have been found to disengage from faces faster than non-affected peers (Chawarska et al., 2003; Chawarska et al., 2010), suggesting limited depth of processing of these highly socially relevant stimuli, it has been hypothesized that in response to other classes of stimuli, they may have difficulties shifting their attention to other targets in a flexible manner (Landry & Bryson, 2004). Research on disengagement of attention in siblings at high risk suggests

that although 7-month-old infants later diagnosed with ASD show no deficits in disengagement of attention from a range of stimuli, by 14 months, the deficits begin to emerge (Elsabbagh, Fernandes, et al., 2013, but see Elison et al., 2013). Further work on factors affecting attentional engagement and disengagement in young children with ASD and how they are related to the core symptoms is needed. This work, however, suggests that the search for prodromal signs of ASD might need to be extended beyond the social communicative domains into more broadly defined nonsocial perception, attention, and learning.

Neurophysiological and Neuroanatomical Features

Investigations into neuroanatomical and neurophysiological prodromal features of ASD represent an emerging and exciting area of inquiry. In one such study, nonaffected high- and low-risk infants showed differential electrophysiological responses to direct and averted gaze stimuli, but infants later diagnosed with ASD failed to make such a distinction, suggesting a lack of sensitivity to subtle gaze cues at the neural level, which may not manifest readily on the behavioral level (Elsabbagh et al., 2012). Neuroanatomical studies suggest that young children with ASD exhibit enlarged total brain volume (Courchesne, Carper, & Akshoomoff, 2003; Hazlett et al., 2005; Hazlett et al., 2011; Sparks et al., 2002). This enlargement is likely to result from an atypical acceleration of head size growth occurring in the first year of life (Campbell, Chang, & Chawarska, under review; Chawarska et al., 2011; Courchesne et al., 2003; Raznahan et al., 2013). Recent work suggests that head overgrowth is accompanied by accelerated growth in height and weight (Dissanayake, Bui, Huggins, & Loesch, 2006; Fukumoto et al., 2011; Mraz, Green, Dumont-Mathieu, Makin, & Fein, 2007), and thereby constitutes a part of the early generalized overgrowth (EGO) phenomenon in ASD (Campbell et al., under review; Chawarska et al., 2011). This phenomenon is present in a minority of children later diagnosed with ASD, but those who do experience early atypical physical growth patterns may have more severe symptoms of autism and lower verbal and nonverbal skills at the age of 4 years (Campbell et al., under review). Examination of growth patterns in ASD offers promise for identifying biomarkers that could aid in stratifying children with ASD into more homogenous, clinically meaningful subgroups and identifying novel treatment targets. The first direct evidence regarding atypical neural development in infants who later exhibit symptoms of ASD suggest that at 6 months these infants show a pattern of atypical white matter development, and their subsequent developmental trajectory is different from other high-risk asymptomatic infants (Wolff et al., 2012). These findings represent the first step toward understanding the neural processes that underlie the emergence of ASD symptoms in the first years of life.

Prodromal Symptoms of ASD at 12 Months in Infants at Risk

Social Interaction, Communication, and Repetitive Behaviors

By 12 months, infants later diagnosed with ASD begin to display clear signs of vulnerabilities in several core developmental areas. Atypicalities appear in the domains of social communication and responsivity to social cues including reduced eye contact, social smiling, orienting to name, requesting, and initiation of joint attention, which map onto those observed later toddlers with frank symptoms of ASD (Nadig et al., 2007; Ozonoff et al., 2010; Rozga et al., 2011; Zwaigenbaum et al., 2005). Moreover, those later diagnosed with ASD exhibited reduced speech-like vocalizations (Paul et al., 2011), a smaller inventory of communicative gestures (Mitchell et al., 2006), and limited response to another person's distress (Hutman et al., 2010). Atypical object exploration including spinning and unusual visual inspection of objects was also found at this age in those later diagnosed with ASD compared to those with developmental delays and typical development (Ozonoff, Macari,

et al. 2008). Finally, repetitive motor movements, specifically arm waving, differentiated infants with ASD at 12 months from other high- and low-risk infants (Loh et al., 2007).

With regard to the severity of ASD-specific symptoms at 12 months of age, approximately 40% of the infants who were later diagnosed with ASD already exhibited severe symptoms as measured by the Autism Diagnostic Observation Schedule–Toddler version (Lord, Luyster, Gotham, et al., 2012) that persisted into the 2nd year of life (Macari et al., 2012). The remaining 60% of infants later diagnosed with ASD demonstrated mild initial symptoms that increased in severity over time. However, a significant minority of infants who did not ultimately receive a diagnosis of ASD exhibited delays and atypical features in key diagnostic areas at 12 months as measured by the ADOS-T (Macari et al., 2012) or the AOSI (Georgiades, Szatmari, Zwaigenbaum, et al., 2013). This suggests that the genetic vulnerability to ASD is expressed in a variable manner, with many high-risk infants showing a range of autism-related symptoms early in life. It is possible that these early atypicalities in high-risk infants without an ASD outcome are illustrative of the broader autism phenotype (see Chapter 2 on the broader autism phenotype), although the continuity of specific abnormalities over time remains to be examined.

Verbal and Nonverbal Skills

Delays in nonverbal cognitive skills are typically not very pronounced at the group level among 12-month-old infants later diagnosed with ASD (Macari et al., 2012; Ozonoff et al., 2010). However, differences begin to emerge in the areas of language and fine motor development, though such delays are not specific to infants who later develop ASD. Although 12-month-old infants with ASD exhibit lower scores on receptive and expressive language scales of the Mullen Scales of Early Learning (Mullen, 1995) compared to typical controls (Mitchell et al., 2006; Zwaigenbaum et al., 2005), similar deficits were observed amongst high-risk infants without ASD but with a broad range of developmental delays and atypical features (Landa & Garrett-Mayer, 2006; Macari et al., 2012). In addition to language delays, subtle fine motor delays were noted at 12 months in infants with ASD, which is particularly interesting given reported predictive associations between the early development of fine motor and later expressive language skills at the age of 3 years (LeBarton & Iverson, 2013).

Summary

Prospective studies of infants at risk for ASD hold great potential to contribute to the discovery of behavioral and biological markers of the disorder before overt symptoms reach clinically significant levels. Should such markers be found to play a role in the causal path to the disorder, the discovery would facilitate identification of novel treatment targets and therapeutic approaches. Such treatments, whether behavioral or pharmacological, could be implemented before the full-blown syndrome emerges, and, by capitalizing on early brain plasticity, lead to radical changes in the developmental outcomes of the affected children (see Chapter 29 in this *Handbook*, Volume 2, for more details on interventions for infants and toddlers). Results from prospective studies thus far suggest that at the age of 6 months, overt behavioral signs of ASD are likely to be subtle. However, emerging evidence suggests that ASD-related vulnerabilities may be observed at the level of both brain structure development and function. Evidence from eye-tracking studies suggests that those later diagnosed with ASD exhibit limited visual engagement with interactive partners, presumably affecting experience-dependent fine-tuning of social brain networks. The consistency between deficits observed in social attention in 6-month-old high-risk infants with ASD and those noted in 2-year-old clinic-referred toddlers with ASD are encouraging and suggests that at least in some areas of functioning, there is continuity across cohorts and over developmental epochs with regard to certain phenotypic features defining the disorder. By 12 months, robust behavioral signs begin to emerge in infants later diagnosed with

ASD, manifesting in the core areas that define ASD. Interestingly, many of the siblings who do not develop the disorder also show patterns of delays and atypical features at this age, which may either wane over time or lead to development of other, associated developmental problems. Work on understanding the complex interplay between risk and protective factors amongst infants with familial risk for the disorder is essential.

As the search for prodromal markers of ASD in the first months of life continues, several issues will require further attention. Amongst them is the question of representativeness of the behavioral and biological findings from multiplex cases (families with more than one child with ASD) to the population of children in families with only one affected child (simplex case) in whom the disorder might arise through, at least partially, different genetic mechanisms (Sanders et al., 2012; Sebat et al., 2007; see Rutter & Thapar, Chapter 17, on the genetics of autism spectrum disorders for details about genetic bases of ASD). Consequently, future studies will need to verify whether the phenotypic characteristics of the infants in multiplex families are consistent with those observed in simplex cases as well. In search of early markers or intermediate phenotypes, there may also be need to consider whether the search for prodromal features of ASD has been focused too narrowly on the social domain. Considering the complex interplay between the development of social and nonsocial cognition early on, it is likely that early signs might be expressed across domains including more broadly defined attentional, learning, and regulatory functions. Such deficits very early in development are likely to have profound effects on learning and development of social cognition later in life and on the emergence of comorbid conditions that profoundly affect the adaptive functioning of older individuals with ASD.

CONCLUSION AND FUTURE DIRECTIONS

Early detection and treatment of ASD remains one of the key priorities of National Institutes of

Health as well as numerous private foundations (Interagency Autism Coordinating Committee [IAAC], 2012). In the past decade, research on early manifestations and treatment of ASD has increased exponentially. Direct observational and experimental studies both from clinic-referred samples as well as prospective studies of infants at risk have extended and refined the earlier findings based on retrospective parent report and analysis of videotape diaries. Still, much work remains to be done. Despite advances in early diagnosis, many children with ASD are not identified until late preschool or early school age. Despite the development of empirically validated treatments for ASD early in life, many children have limited access to such services. Ameliorating the effects of race, ethnicity, and socioeconomic status on the age at which children gain access to early intervention constitutes one of the key challenges in the field of ASD. Considering the high variability of both the phenotypic expression of the syndrome early in development and rates of progress over time, identification of more homogeneous subtypes within the autism spectrum would facilitate the search for underlying neural and genetic mechanisms and identification of factors affecting amenability to treatment. These in turn would facilitate the development of treatments tailored to specific profiles of skills and deficits, leading to interventions that can optimize the outcome of children with ASD and improve the quality of their lives. Further refinement of the understanding prodromal signs of ASD in the first year of life and their role in the etiology of ASD, as well as identification of predictors of outcome will be crucial for advancing preventative treatments and discovery of the undoubtedly complex causal pathways to ASD.

CROSS-REFERENCES

Chapter 1 addresses diagnostic issues and Chapter 2 the broader autism phenotype. Chapters 6, 7, and 8 focus on autism in school-age children, adolescents, and adults. Chapter 29 discusses interventions for young children with autism.

REFERENCES

Action, A. O. (1999). Practice parameters for the assessment and treatment of children, adolescents, and adults with autism and other pervasive developmental disorders. *Journal of the American Academy of Child & Adolescent Psychiatry*, *38*(12 Suppl), 32S–54S.

Ainsworth, M. S., Blehar, M. C., Waters, E., & Wall, S. (1978). Patterns of attachment: A psychological study of the strange situation. *Child Development*, *41*(1), 49–67.

American Psychiatric Association. (1994). *Diagnostic and statistical manual of mental disorders* (4th ed.). Washington, DC: Author.

American Psychiatric Association. (2013). *Diagnostic and statistical manual of mental disorders* (5th ed.). Arlington, VA: American Psychiatric Publishing.

American Speech-Language-Hearing Association. (2006). *Guidelines for speech-language pathologists in diagnosis, assessment, and treatment of autism spectrum disorders across the life span*. Rockville, MD: Author.

Anderson, D. K., Oti, R. S., Lord, C., & Welch, K. (2009). Patterns of growth in adaptive social abilities among children with autism spectrum disorders. *Journal of Abnormal Child Psychology: An Official Publication of the International Society for Research in Child and Adolescent Psychopathology*, *37*(7), 1019–1034.

Baghdadli, A., Picot, M. C., Pascal, C., Pry, R., & Aussilloux, C. (2003). Relationship between age of recognition of first disturbances and severity in young children with autism. *European Child & Adolescent Psychiatry*, *12*(3), 122–127.

Bailey, A., Palferman, S., Heavey, L., & Le Couteur, A. (1998). Autism: The phenotype in relatives. *Journal of Autism and Developmental Disorders*, *28*(5), 369–392.

Baird, G., Charman, T., Baron-Cohen, S., Cox, A., Swettenham, J., Wheelwright, S., & Drew, A. (2000). A screening instrument for autism at 18 months of age: A 6-year follow-up study. *Journal of the American Academy of Child & Adolescent Psychiatry*, *39*(6), 694–702.

Bakermans-Kranenburg, M. J., van IJzendoorn, M. H., & Juffer, F. (2003). Less is more: Meta-analyses of sensitivity and attachment interventions in early childhood. *Psychological Bulletin*, *129*(2), 195–215.

Baranek, G. T. (1999). Autism during infancy: A retrospective video analysis of sensory-motor and social behaviors at 9–12 months of age. *Journal of Autism and Developmental Disorders*, *29*(3), 213–224.

Barber, A. B., Wetherby, A. M., & Chambers, N. W. (2012). Brief report: Repetitive behaviors in young children with autism spectrum disorder and developmentally similar peers: A follow up to Watt et al. (2008). *Journal of Autism and Developmental Disorders*, *42*(9), 2006–2012.

Baron-Cohen, S., Baldwin, D. A., & Crowson, M. (1997). Do children with autism use the speaker's direction of gaze strategy to crack the code of language? *Child Development*, *68*(1), 48–57.

Baron-Cohen, S., Campbell, R., Karmiloff-Smith, A., Grant, J., & Walker, J. (1995). Are children with autism blind to the mentalistic significance of the eyes? *British Journal of Developmental Psychology*, *13*(4), 379–398.

Baron-Cohen, S., Cox, A., Baird, G., Sweettenham, J., & Nighingale, N. (1996). Psychological markers in the detection of autism in infancy in a large population. *British Journal of Psychiatry, 168*(2), 158–163.

Barton, M., Robins, D., Jashar, D., Brennan, L., & Fein, D. (2013). Sensitivity and Specificity of Proposed DSM-5 Criteria for Autism Spectrum Disorder in Toddlers. *Journal of Autism and Developmental Disorders, 43*(5), 1184–1195. doi:10.1007/s1080-013-1817-8

Bates, E. (1979). *The emergence of symbols: Cognition and communication in infancy*. New York, NY: Academic Press.

Bayley, N. (2006). *Bayley Scales of Infant and Toddler Development–Third Edition (Bayley-III)*. San Antonio, TX: Harcourt Assessment.

Bedford, R., Elsabbagh, M., Gliga, T., Pickles, A., Senju, A., Charman, T., Johnson, M. H., & the BASIS Team. (2012). Precursors to social and communication difficulties in infants at-risk for autism: Gaze following and attentional engagement. *Journal of Autism and Developmental Disorders, 42*(10), 2208–2218.

Bishop, S. L., Luyster, R., Richler, J., & Lord, C. (2008). Diagnostic assessment. In K. Chawarska, A. Klin, & F. R. Volkmar (Eds.), *Autism spectrum disorders in infants and toddlers: Diagnosis, assessment, and treatment* (pp. 23–49). New York, NY: Guilford Press.

Bloom, L. C., & Mudd, S. A. (1991). Depth of processing approach to face recognition: A test of two theories. *Journal of Experimental Psychology: Learning, Memory, and Cognition, 17*(3), 556–565.

Bradshaw, J., Shic, F., & Chawarska, K. (2011). Brief report: Face-specific recognition deficits in young children with autism spectrum disorders. *Journal of Autism and Developmental Disorders, 41*(10), 1429–1435. doi:10.1007/s10803-010-1150-4

Bryson, S. E., Zwaigenbaum, L., McDermott, C., Rombough, V., & Brian, J. (2008). The Autism Observation Scale for Infants: Scale development and reliability data. *Journal of Autism and Developmental Disorders, 38*(4), 731–738.

Burack, J. A., & Volkmar, F. R. (1992). Development of low- and high-functioning autistic children. *Journal of Child Psychology & Psychiatry & Allied Disciplines, 33*(3), 607–616.

Campbell, D., Chang, J., & Chawarska, K. (under review). Early generalized overgrowth in infants with ASD: Prevalence, associations with gender and clinical outcomes.

Campbell, D., Shic, F., Macari, S., & Chawarska, K. (2013, July). Gaze patterns in response to dyadic bids at 2 years predict functioning at 3 years in autism spectrum disorders: A subtyping analysis. *Journal of Autism and Developmental Disorders*. [Epub ahead of print]

Capps, L., Sigman, M., & Mundy, P. (1994). Attachment security in children with autism. *Development & Psychopathology, 6*(2), 249–261.

Carpenter, M., Pennington, B. F., & Rogers, S. J. (2002). Interrelations among social-cognitive skills in young children with autism. *Journal of Autism and Developmental Disorders, 32*(2), 91–106.

Charman, T., Swettenham, J., Baron-Cohen, S., Cox, A., Baird, G., & Drew, A. (1997). Infants with autism: An investigation of empathy, pretend play, joint attention, and imitation. *Developmental Psychology, 33*(5), 781–789.

Charman, T., Taylor, E., Drew, A., Cockerill, H., Brown, J.-A., & Baird, G. (2005). Outcome at 7 years of children diagnosed with autism at age 2: Predictive validity of assessments conducted at 2 and 3 years of age and pattern of symptom change over time. *Journal of Child Psychology and Psychiatry, 46*(5), 500–513.

Chawarska, K., Campbell, D., Chen, L., Shic, F., Klin, A., & Chang, J. (2011). Early generalized overgrowth in boys with autism. *Archives of General Psychiatry, 68*(10), 1021–1031.

Chawarska, K., Klin, A., Paul, R., Macari, S., & Volkmar, F. (2009). A prospective study of toddlers with ASD: Short-term diagnostic and cognitive outcomes. *Journal of Child Psychology and Psychiatry, 50*(10), 1235–1245.

Chawarska, K., Klin, A., Paul, R., & Volkmar, F. (2007). Autism spectrum disorder in the second year: Stability and change in syndrome expression. *Journal of Child Psychology and Psychiatry, 48*(2), 128–138.

Chawarska, K., Klin, A., & Volkmar, F. (2003). Automatic attention cueing through eye movement in 2-year-old children with autism. *Child Development, 74*(4), 1108–1122.

Chawarska, K., Klin, A., & Volkmar, F. (2008). *Autism spectrum disorders in infants and toddlers: Diagnosis, assessment, and treatment*. New York, NY: Guilford Press.

Chawarska, K., Macari, S., & Shic, F. (2012). Context modulates attention to social scenes in toddlers with autism. *Journal of Child Psychology and Psychiatry, 53*(8), 903–913.

Chawarska, K., Macari, S., & Shic, F. (2013). Decreased spontaneous attention to social scenes in 6-month-old Infants later diagnosed with autism spectrum disorders. *Biological Psychiatry.* doi:http://dx.doi.org/10.1016/j.biopsych.2012.11.022

Chawarska, K., Paul, R., Klin, A., Hannigen, S., Dichtel, L. E., & Volkmar, F. (2007). Parental recognition of developmental problems in toddlers with autism spectrum disorders. *Journal of Autism and Developmental Disorders, 37*(1), 62–72.

Chawarska, K., & Shic, F. (2009). Looking but not seeing: Atypical visual scanning and recognition of faces in 2- and 4-year-old children with autism spectrum disorder. *Journal of Autism and Developmental Disorders, 39*(12), 1663–1672.

Chawarska, K., & Volkmar, F. R. (2005). Autism in infancy and early childhood. In F. R. Volkmar, R. Paul, A. Klin, & D. Cohen (Eds.), *Handbook of autism and pervasive developmental disorders: Diagnosis, development, neurobiology, and behavior* (3rd ed., Vol. 1, pp. xxv, 703).

Chawarska, K., Volkmar, F., & Klin, A. (2010). Limited attentional bias for faces in toddlers with autism spectrum disorders. [Research Support, N.I.H., Extramural]. *Archives of General Psychiatry, 67*(2), 178–185.

Cicchetti, D. V., & Sparrow, S. S. (1990). Assessment of adaptive behavior in young children. In J. H. Johnson & J. Goldman (Eds.), *Developmental assessment in clinical child psychology: A handbook*, Pergamon general psychology series (Vol. 163, pp. 173–196). New York, NY: Pergamon Press.

Clifford, S. M., Hudry, K., Elsabbagh, M., Charman, T., & Johnson, M. H. (2013). Temperament in the first 2 years of life in infants at high-risk for autism spectrum disorders. *Journal of Autism and Developmental Disorders, 43*(3), 673–686.

Coin, C., & Tiberghien, G. (1997). Encoding activity and face recognition. *Memory, 5*(5), 545–568.

Constantino, J. N., Zhang, Y., Frazier, T., Abbacchi, A. M., & Law, P. (2010). Sibling recurrence and the genetic epidemiology of autism. *American Journal of Psychiatry, 167*(11), 1349–1356.

Cornew, L., Dobkins, K., Akshoomoff, N., McCleery, J., & Carver, L. (2012). Atypical social referencing in infant siblings of children with autism spectrum disorders. *Journal of Autism and Developmental Disorders, 42*(12), 2611–2621. doi:10.1007/s10803-012-1518-8

Courchesne, E., Carper, R., & Akshoomoff, N. (2003). Evidence of brain overgrowth in the first year of life in autism. *JAMA: Journal of the American Medical Association, 290*(3), 337–344.

Cox, A., Klein, K., Charman, T., Baird, G., Baron-Cohen, S., Swettenham, J.,...Wheelwright, S. (1999). Autism spectrum disorders at 20 and 42 months of age: Stability of clinical and ADI-R diagnosis. *Journal of Child Psychology & Psychiatry & Allied Disciplines, 40*(5), 719–732.

Daley, T. (2004). From symptom recognition to diagnosis: Children with autism in urban india. *Social Science and Medicine, 58*, 1323–1335.

Dawson, G., Meltzoff, A. N., Osterling, J., Rinaldi, J., & Brown, E. (1998). Children with autism fail to orient to naturally occurring social stimuli. *Journal of Autism and Developmental Disorders, 28*(6), 479–485.

Dawson, G., Osterling, J., Meltzoff, A. N., & Kuhl, P. (2000). Case study of the development of an infant with autism from birth to two years of age. *Journal of Applied Developmental Psychology, 21*(3), 299–313.

Dawson, G., Rogers, S., Munson, J., Smith, M., Winter, J., Greenson, J.,...Varley, J. (2010). Randomized, controlled trial of an intervention for toddlers with autism: The Early Start Denver Model. [Comparative Study Randomized Controlled Trial Research Support, N.I.H., Extramural]. *Pediatrics, 125*(1), e17–e23.

Dawson, G., Toth, K., Abbott, R., Osterling, J., Munson, J., Estes, A., & Liaw, J. (2004). Early social attention impairments in autism: Social orienting, joint attention, and attention to distress. *Developmental Psychology, 40*(2), 271–283.

De Giacomo, A., & Fombonne, E. (1998). Parental recognition of developmental abnormalities in autism. *European Child & Adolescent Psychiatry, 7*(3), 131–136.

Dissanayake, C., Bui, Q. M., Huggins, R., & Loesch, D. Z. (2006). Growth in stature and head circumference in high-functioning autism and Asperger disorder during the first 3 years of life. *Development and Psychopathology, 18*(2), 381–393.

Doussard-Roosevelt, J. A., Joe, C. M., Bazhenova, O. V., & Porges, S. W. (2003). Mother–child interaction in autistic and nonautistic children: Characteristics of maternal approach behaviors and child social responses. *Development and Psychopathology, 15*(2), 277–295.

Eaves, L. C., & Ho, H. H. (2004). The very early identification of autism: Outcome to age 4 1/2–5. *Journal of Autism and Developmental Disorders, 34*(4), 367–378.

Eisenberg, L., & Kanner, L. (1956). Early infantile autism, 1943–55. *American Journal of Orthopsychiatry, 26*, 556–566.

Eldevik, S., Hastings, R. P., Hughes, J. C., Jahr, E., Eikeseth, S., & Cross, S. (2010). Using participant data to extend the evidence base for intensive behavioral intervention for children with autism. *American Journal on Intellectual and Developmental Disabilities, 115*(5), 381–405.

Elison, J. T., Paterson, S. J., Wolff, J. J., Reznick, J. S., Sasson, N. J., Gu, H.,...Piven, J. (2013). White matter microstructure and atypical visual orienting in 7-month-olds at risk for autism. *American Journal of Psychiatry.* doi:10.1176/appi.ajp.2012.12091150

Elsabbagh, M., Fernandes, J., Jane Webb, S., Dawson, G., Charman, T., Johnson, M. H., & British Autism Study of Invant Siblings Team. (2013). Disengagement of visual attention in infancy is associated with emerging autism in toddlerhood. *Biological Psychiatry, 74*(3), 189–194.

Elsabbagh, M., Gliga, T., Pickles, A., Hudry, K., Charman, T., Johnson, M. H., & BASIS Team. (2013). The development of face orienting mechanisms in infants at-risk for autism. *Behavioural Brain Research, 251*, 147–154.

Elsabbagh, M., Mercure, E., Hudry, K., Chandler, S., Pasco, G., Charman, T.,...Johnson, M. H. (2012). Infant neural sensitivity to dynamic eye gaze is associated with later emerging autism. *Current Biology, 22*(4), 338–342.

Esposito, G., Venuti, P., Maestro, S., & Muratori, F. (2009). An exploration of symmetry in early autism spectrum disorders: Analysis of lying. *Brain and Development, 31*(2), 131–138. doi:http://dx.doi.org/10.1016/j.braindev.2008.04.005

Evans, D. W., Leckman, J. F., Carter, A., Reznick, J. S., Henshaw, D., King, R. A., & Pauls, D. (1997). Ritual, habit, and perfectionism: The prevalence and development of compulsive-like behaviour in normal young children. *Child Development, 68*(1), 58–68.

Flanagan, H. E., Perry, A., & Freeman, N. L. (2012). Effectiveness of large-scale community-based intensive behavioral intervention: A waitlist comparison study exploring outcomes and predictors. *Research in Autism Spectrum Disorders, 6*(2), 673–682.

Flanagan, J. E., Landa, R., Bhat, A., & Bauman, M. (2012). Head lag in infants at risk for autism: A preliminary study. *American Journal of Occupational Therapy, 66*(5), 577–585.

Fournier, K., Hass, C., Naik, S., Lodha, N., & Cauraugh, J. (2010). Motor coordination in autism spectrum disorders: A synthesis and meta-analysis. *Journal of Autism and Developmental Disorders, 40*(10), 1227–1240. doi: 10.1007/s10803-010-0981-3

Frazier, T. W., Youngstrom, E. A., Speer, L., Embacher, R., Law, P., Constantino, J.,...Eng, C. (2012). Validation of proposed DSM-5 criteria for autism spectrum disorder. *Journal of the American Academy of Child & Adolescent Psychiatry, 51*(1), 28–40. doi:http://dx.doi.org/10.1016/j.jaac.2011.09.021

Fukumoto, A., Hashimoto, T., Mori, K., Tsuda, Y., Arisawa, K., & Kagami, S. (2011). Head circumference and body growth in autism spectrum disorders. *Brain and Development, 33*(7), 569–575. doi:http://dx.doi.org/10.1016/j.braindev.2010.09.004

Garon, N., Bryson, S. E., Zwaigenbaum, L., Smith, I. M., Brian, J., Roberts, W., & Szatmari, P. (2009). Temperament and its relationship to autistic symptoms in a high-risk infant sib cohort. *Journal of Abnormal Child Psychology, 37*(1), 59–78.

Georgiades, S., Szatmari, P., Boyle, M., Hanna, S., Duku, E., Zwaigenbaum, L., . . . Pathways in A.S.D.S.T. (2013). Investigating phenotypic heterogeneity in children with autism spectrum disorder: A factor mixture modeling approach. *Journal of Child Psychology and Psychiatry, 54*(2), 206–215. doi:10.1111/j.1469-7610.2012.02588.x

Georgiades, S., Szatmari, P., Zwaigenbaum, L., Bryson, S., Brian, J., Roberts, W., . . . Garon, N. (2013). A prospective study of autistic-like traits in unaffected siblings of probands with autism spectrum disorder. *JAMA Psychiatry, 70*(1), 42–48.

Goldsmith, H. H., Buss, A. H., Plomin, R., Rothbart, M. K., Thomas, A., Chess, S., . . . McCall, R. B. (1987). Roundtable: What is temperament? Four approaches. *Child Development, 58*(2), 505–529.

Gotham, K., Pickles, A., & Lord, C. (2012). Trajectories of autism severity in children using standardized ADOS scores. *Pediatrics, 130*(5), e1278–e1284.

Gotham, K., Risi, S., Dawson, G., Tager-Flusberg, H., Joseph, R., Carter, A., . . . Lord, C. (2008). A replication of the Autism Diagnostic Observation Schedule (ADOS) revised algorithms. *Journal of the American Academy of Child & Adolescent Psychiatry, 47*(6), 642–651.

Gotham, K., Risi, S., Pickles, A., & Lord, C. (2007). The Autism Diagnostic Observation Schedule: Revised algorithms for improved diagnostic validity. [Research Support, N.I.H., Extramural]. *Journal of Autism and Developmental Disorders, 37*(4), 613–627.

Greenough, W. T., Black, J. E., & Wallace, C. S. (2002). Experience and brain development. In M. Johnson, Y. Munakata, & et al. (Eds.), *Brain development and cognition: A reader* (2nd ed., pp. 186–216). Malden, MA: Blackwell.

Grønborg, T. K., Schendel, D. E., & Parner, E. T. (2013). Recurrence of autism spectrum disorders in full- and half-siblings and trends over time: A population-based cohort study. *JAMA Pediatrics.* Published online.

Guthrie, W., Swineford, L. B., Nottke, C., & Wetherby, A. M. (2013). Early diagnosis of autism spectrum disorder: Stability and change in clinical diagnosis and symptom presentation. *Journal of Child Psychology and Psychiatry, 54*(5), 582–590. doi:10.1111/jcpp.12008

Guthrie, W., Swineford, L. B., Wetherby, A. M., & Lord, C. (2013). Comparison of DSM-IV and DSM-5 factor structure models for toddlers with autism spectrum disorder. *Journal of the American Academy of Child & Adolescent Psychiatry, 52*(8), 797–805.

Harris, S. L., & Handleman, J. S. (2000). Age and IQ at intake as predictors of placement for young children with autism: A four- to six-year follow-up. *Journal of Autism and Developmental Disorders, 30*(2), 137–142.

Hazlett, H. C., Poe, M., Gerig, G., Smith, R. G., Provenzale, J., Ross, A., . . . Piven, J. (2005). Magnetic resonance imaging and head circumference study of brain size in autism. *Archives of General Psychiatry, 62*(12), 1366–1376.

Hazlett, H., Poe, M., Gerig, G., Styner, M., Chappell, C., Smith, R., . . . Piven, J. (2011). Early brain overgrowth in autism associated with an increase in cortical surface area before age 2 years. *Archives of General Psychiatry, 68*(5), 467–476. doi:10.1001/archgenpsychiatry.2011.39

Hood, B. M., Willen, J., & Driver, J. (1998). Adult's eyes trigger shifts of visual attention in human infants. *Psychological Science, 9*(2), 131–134.

Hoshino, Y., Kumashiro, H., Yashima, Y., Tachibana, R., Watanabe, M., & Furukawa, H. (1982). Early symptoms of autistic children and its diagnostic significance. *Folia Psychiatrica et Neurologica, 36*, 367–374.

Howlin, P., Magiati, I., & Charman, T. (2009). Systematic review of early intensive behavioral interventions for children with autism. *American Journal on Intellectual and Developmental Disabilities, 114*(1), 23–41.

Huerta, M., Bishop, S. L., Duncan, A., Hus, V., & Lord, C. (2012). Application of DSM-5 criteria for autism spectrum disorder to three samples of children with DSM-IV diagnoses of pervasive developmental disorders. *American Journal of Psychiatry, 169*(10), 1056–1064.

Hutman, T., Chela, M. K., Gillespie-Lynch, K., & Sigman, M. (2012). Selective visual attention at twelve months: Signs of autism in early social interactions. *Journal of Autism and Developmental Disorders, 42*(4), 487–498.

Hutman, T., Rozga, A., DeLaurentis, A. D., Barnwell, J. M., Sugar, C. A., & Sigman, M. (2010). Response to distress in infants at risk for autism: A prospective longitudinal study. *Journal of Child Psychology and Psychiatry, 51*(9), 1010–1020.

Interagency Autism Coordinating Committee. (2012, December). IACC strategic plan for autism spectrum disorder (ASD) research—2012 update. Retrieved from the U.S. Department of Health and Human Services Interagency Autism Coordinating Committee website: http://iacc.hhs .gov/strategic-plan/2012/index.shtml

James, W. (1890/1950). *The principles of psychology.* New York, NY: Dover.

Johnson, M. H., Grossmann, T., & Kadosh, K. C. (2009). Mapping functional brain development: Building a social brain through interactive specialization. *Developmental Psychology, 45*(1), 151–159.

Jones, W., Carr, K., & Klin, A. (2008). Absence of preferential looking to the eyes of approaching adults predicts level of social disability in 2-year-old toddlers with autism spectrum disorder. *Archives of General Psychiatry, 65*(8), 946.

Kalb, L., Law, J. K., Landa, R., & Law, P. (2010). Onset patterns prior to 36 months in autism spectrum disorders. *Journal of Autism and Developmental Disorders, 40*(11), 1389–1402. doi: 10.1007/s10803-010-0998-7

Kanne, S. M., Gerber, A. J., Quirmbach, L. M., Sparrow, S. S., Cicchetti, D. V., & Saulnier, C. A. (2011). The role of adaptive behavior in autism spectrum disorders: Implications for functional outcome. *Journal of Autism and Developmental Disorders, 41*(8), 1007–1018.

Kanner, L. (1943/1968). Autistic disturbances of affective contact. *Acta Paedopsychiatrica: International Journal of Child & Adolescent Psychiatry, 35*(4–8), 98–136.

Kasari, C., Gulsrud, A., Freeman, S., Paparella, T., & Hellemann, G. (2012). Longitudinal follow-up of children with autism receiving targeted interventions on joint attention and play. *Journal of the American Academy of Child & Adolescent Psychiatry, 51*(5), 487–495. doi:http://dx.doi.org/10.1016/j.jaac.2012.02.019

Kasari, C., Gulsrud, A., Wong, C., Kwon, S., & Locke, J. (2010). Randomized controlled caregiver mediated joint engagement intervention for toddlers with autism. *Journal of Autism and Developmental Disorders*, *40*(9), 1045–1056. doi:10.1007/s10803-010-0955-5

Kim, S. H., & Lord, C. (2010). Restricted and repetitive behaviors in toddlers and preschoolers with autism spectrum disorders based on the autism diagnostic observation schedule (ADOS). *Autism Research*, *3*(4), 162–173.

Kim, S. H., & Lord, C. (2012). Combining information from multiple sources for the diagnosis of autism spectrum disorders for toddlers and young preschoolers from 12 to 47 months of age. *Journal of Child Psychology and Psychiatry*, *53*(2), 143–151.

Kim, S., Macari, S., Shic, F., Dowd, A., O'Loughlin, K., . . . Chawarska, K. (2013, May). Atypical social attention patterns in 6-month-old infants later diagnosed with ASD during a face-to-face dyadic interaction. Oral presentation at the International Meeting for Autism Research (IMFAR), San Sebastian, Spain.

Kleinman, J. M., Robins, D. L., Ventola, P. E., Pandey, J., Boorstein, H. C., Esser, E. L., . . . Fein, D. (2008). The Modified Checklist for Autism in Toddlers: A follow-up study investigating the early detection of autism spectrum disorders. *Journal of Autism and Developmental Disorders*, *38*(5), 827–839.

Klin, A., Chawarska, K., Paul, R., Rubin, E., Morgan, T., Wiesner, L., & Volkmar, F. (2004). Autism in a 15-month-old child. *American Journal of Psychiatry*, *161*(11), 1981–1988.

Klin, A., Jones, W., Schultz, R., Volkmar, F. R., & Cohen, D. J. (2002). Visual fixation patterns during viewing of naturalistic social situations as predictors of social competence in individuals with autism. *Archives of General Psychiatry*, *59*(9), 809–816.

Klin, A., Volkmar, F. R., & Sparrow, S. S. (1992). Autistic social dysfunction: Some limitations of the theory of mind hypothesis. *Journal of Child Psychology & Psychiatry & Allied Disciplines*, *33*(5), 861–876.

Klintwall, L., & Eikeseth, S. (2012). Number and controllability of reinforcers as predictors of individual outcome for children with autism receiving early and intensive behavioral intervention: A preliminary study. *Research in Autism Spectrum Disorders*, *6*(1), 493–499.

Klintwall, L., Gillberg, C., Bölte, S., & Fernell, E. (2012). The efficacy of intensive behavioral intervention for children with autism: A matter of allegiance? *Journal of Autism and Developmental Disorders*, *42*(1), 139–140.

Koegel, L. K., Koegel, R. L., Fredeen, R. M., & Gengoux, G. W. (2008). Naturalistic behavioral approaches to treatment. In K. Chawarska, A. Klin, & F. Volkmar (Eds.), *Autism spectrum disorders in infants and toddlers: Diagnosis, assessment, and treatment* (pp. 207–242). New York, NY: Guilford Press.

Koller, J., Campbell, D., Macari, S., & Chawarska, K. (under review). Temperament in toddlers with ASD.

Kurita, H. (1985). Infantile autism with speech loss before the age of thirty months. *Journal of the American Academy of Child Psychiatry*, *24*(2), 191–196.

Landa, R., & Garrett-Mayer, E. (2006). Development in infants with autism spectrum disorders: A prospective study. [Original]. *Journal of Child Psychology and Psychiatry*, *47*(6), 629–638.

Landa, R. J., Gross, A. L., Stuart, E. A., & Bauman, M. (2012). Latent class analysis of early developmental trajectory in baby siblings of children with autism. *Journal of Child Psychology and Psychiatry*, *53*(9), 986–996. doi:10.1111/j.1469-7610.2012.02558.x

Landa, R. J., Holman, K. C., & Garrett-Mayer, E. (2007). Social and communication development in toddlers with early and later diagnosis of autism spectrum disorders. *Archives of General Psychiatry*, *64*(7), 853–864.

Landry, R., & Bryson, S. E. (2004). Impaired disengagement of attention in young children with autism. *Journal of Child Psychology and Psychiatry*, *45*(6), 1115–1122.

Langton, S. R., Law, A. S., Burton, A., & Schweinberger, S. R. (2008). Attention capture by faces. *Cognition*, *107*(1), 330–342.

Lavie, N., Ro, T., & Russell, C. (2003). The role of perceptual load in processing distractor faces. *Psychological Science*, *14*(5), 510–515.

LeBarton & Iverson, J. (2013). Fine motor skills predict expressive language in infant siblings of children with autism. *Developmental Science*, *16*(6), 815–827.

Leekam, S., Baron-Cohen, S., Perrett, D., Milders, M., & Brown, S. (1997). Eye-direction detection: A dissociation between geometric and joint attention skills in autism. *British Journal of Developmental Psychology*, *15*(1), 77–95.

Leekam, S. R., Hunnisett, E., & Moore, C. (1998). Targets and cues: Gaze-following in children with autism. *Journal of Child Psychology and Psychiatry*, *39*(7), 951–962.

Leekam, S. R., López, B., & Moore, C. (2000). Attention and joint attention in preschool children with autism. *Developmental Psychology*, *36*(2), 261.

Lemanek, K. L., Stone, W. L., & Fishel, P. T. (1993). Parent–child interactions in handicapped preschoolers: The relation between parent behaviors and compliance. *Journal of Clinical Child Psychology*, *22*(1), 68–77.

Loh, A., Soman, T., Brian, J., Bryson, S. E., Roberts, W., Szatmari, P., . . . Zwaigenbaum, L. (2007). Stereotyped motor behaviors associated with autism in high-risk infants: A pilot videotape analysis of a sibling sample. *Journal of Autism and Developmental Disorders*, *37*(1), 25–36.

Lord, C. (1995). Follow-up of two-year-olds referred for possible autism. *Journal of Child Psychology & Psychiatry & Allied Disciplines*, *36*(8), 1365–1382.

Lord, C., Luyster, R., Gotham, K., Guthrie, W., Risi, S., & Rutter, M. (2012). *Autism Diagnostic Observation Schedule–toddler module manual*. Los Angeles, CA: Western Psychological Services.

Lord, C., Luyster, R., Guthrie, W., & Pickles, A. (2012). Patterns of developmental trajectories in toddlers with autism spectrum disorder. *Journal of Consulting and Clinical Psychology*, *80*(3), 477–489. doi:10.1037/a0027214

Lord, C., & Risi, S. (2000). Diagnosis of autism spectrum disorders in young children. In A. M. Wetherby & B. Prizant (Eds.) *Autism spectrum disorders: A transactional developmental perspective*. Communication and language intervention series (Vol. 9, pp. 11–30). Baltimore, MD: Paul H. Brookes.

Lord, C., Risi, S., DiLavore, P. S., Shulman, C., Thurm, A., & Pickles, A. (2006). Autism from 2 to 9 years of age. *Archives of General Psychiatry*, *63*(6), 694–701.

Lord, C., Rutter, M., DiLavore, P. C., & Risi, S. (2000). *Autism Diagnostic Observation Schedule*. Los Angeles, CA: Western Psychological Services.

Lord, C., Rutter, M., DiLavore, P. C., Risi, S., Gotham, K., & Bishop, S. (2012). *Autism Diagnostic Observation Schedule: ADOS-2*. Los Angeles, CA: Western Psychological Services.

Lord, C., & Schopler, E. (1989). The role of age at assessment, developmental level, and test in the stability of intelligence scores in young autistic children. *Journal of Autism and Developmental Disorders*, *19*(4), 483–499.

Lord, C., Shulman, C., & DiLavore, P. (2004). Regression and word loss in autistic spectrum disorders. *Journal of Child Psychology and Psychiatry*, *45*(5), 936–955.

Luyster, R., Gotham, K., Guthrie, W., Coffing, M., Petrak, R., Pierce, K., ... Lord, C. (2009). The Autism Diagnostic Observation Schedule—Toddler Module: A new module of a standardized diagnostic measure for autism spectrum disorders. *Journal of Autism and Developmental Disorders*, *39*(9), 1305–1320.

Macari, S., Campbell, D., Gengoux, G., Saulnier, C., Klin, A., & Chawarska, K. (2012). Predicting developmental status from 12 to 24 months in infants at risk for autism spectrum disorder: A preliminary report. *Journal of Autism and Developmental Disorders*, *42*(12), 2636–2647.

Maestro, S., Muratori, F., Cavallaro, M. C., Pei, F., Stern, D., Golse, B., & Palacio-Espasa, F. (2002). Attentional skills during the first 6 months of age in autism spectrum disorder. *Journal of the American Academy of Child & Adolescent Psychiatry*, *41*(10), 1239–1245.

Magiati, I., Charman, T., & Howlin, P. (2007). A two-year prospective follow-up study of community-based early intensive behavioural intervention and specialist nursery provision for children with autism spectrum disorders. *Journal of Child Psychology and Psychiatry*, *48*(8), 803–812.

Magiati, I., Moss, J., Charman, T., & Howlin, P. (2011). Patterns of change in children with autism spectrum disorders who received community based comprehensive interventions in their pre-school years: A seven year follow-up study. *Research in Autism Spectrum Disorders*, *5*(3), 1016–1027.

Mandell, D. S., Ittenbach, R. F., Levy, S. E., & Pinto-Martin, J. A. (2007). Disparities in diagnosed received prior to a diagnosis of autism spectrum disorder. *Journal of Autism and Developmental Disorders*, *37*(9), 1795–1802.

Mandell, D. S., Listerud, J., Levy, S., & Pinto-Martin, J. (2002). Race differences in the age at diagnosis among Medicaid-eligible children with autism. *Journal of the American Academy of Child & Adolescent Psychiatry*, *41*(12), 1447–1453. doi:10.1097/00004583-200212000-00016

Mandell D. S., Novak M. M., & Zubritsky C. D. (2005). Factors associated with age of diagnosis among children with autism spectrum disorders. *Pediatrics*, *116*(6), 1480–1486.

Mandy, W. P. L., Charman, T., & Skuse, D. H. (2012). Testing the construct validity of proposed criteria for *DSM-5* autism spectrum disorder. *Journal of the American Academy of Child & Adolescent Psychiatry*, *51*(1), 41–50.

McDuffie, A., & Yoder, P. (2010). Types of parent verbal responsiveness that predict language in young children with autism spectrum disorder. *Journal of Speech, Language & Hearing Research*, *53*(4), 1026–1039. doi:10.1044/1092-4388(2009/09-0023)

Messinger, D., Young, G., Ozonoff, S., Dobkins, K., Carter, A., Zwaigenbaum, L., ... Constantino, J. N. (2013). Beyond autism: A baby siblings research consortium study of high-risk children at three years of age. *Journal of the American Academy of Child & Adolescent Psychiatry*, *52*(3), 300–308.

Mitchell, S., Brian, J., Zwaigenbaum, L., Roberts, W., Szatmari, P., Smith, I., & Bryson, S. (2006). Early language and communication development of infants later diagnosed with autism spectrum disorder. *Journal of Developmental & Behavioral Pediatrics* *27*(Suppl 2), S69–S78.

Mraz, K. D., Green, J., Dumont-Mathieu, T., Makin, S., & Fein, D. (2007). Correlates of head circumference growth in infants later diagnosed with autism spectrum disorders. *Journal of Child Neurology*, *22*(6), 700–713.

Mullen, E. (1995). *Mullen Scales of Early Learning*: AGS Edition. Circle Pines, MN: American Guidance Serivce.

Mundy, P., & Crowson, M. (1997). Joint attention and early social communication: Implications for research on intervention with autism. *Journal of Autism and Developmental Disorders*, *27*(6), 653–676.

Murphy, M., Bolton, P., Pickles, A., Fombonne, E., Piven, J., & Rutter, M. (2000). Personality traits of the relatives of autistic probands. *Psychological Medicine*, *30*(6), 1411–1424.

Naber, F. B., Swinkels, S. H., Buitelaar, J. K., Bakermans-Kranenburg, M. J., van IJzendoorn, M. H., Dietz, C., ... van Engeland, H. (2007). Attachment in toddlers with autism and other developmental disorders. *Journal of Autism and Developmental Disorders*, *37*(6), 1123–1138.

Nadel, J., Guerini, C., Peze, A., & Rivet, C. (1999). The evolving nature of imitation as a format for communication. In J. Nadel & G. Butterworth (Eds.), *Imitation in infancy*. Cambridge studies in cognitive perceptual development (pp. 209–234). Cambridge, England: Cambridge University Press.

Nadig, A., Ozonoff, S., Young, G. S., Rozga, A., Sigman, M., & Rogers, S. J. (2007). Prospective study of response to name in infants at risk for autism. *Archives of Pediatrics and Adolescence Medicine*, *161*(4), 378–383.

National Research Council. (2001). *Educating children with autism: Committee on Educational Interventions for Children With Autism* (C. Lord & J. P. McGee, Eds.). Washington, DC: National Academies Press, Division of Behavioral and Social Sciences and Education.

Nelson, C. A., de Haan, M., & Thomas, K. M. (2006). *Neuroscience of cognitive development: The role of experience and the developing brain*. Hoboken, NJ: Wiley.

O'Loughlin, K., Macari, S., Shic, F., & Chawarska, K. (2012, May). *Attention capture by and preference for faces with direct gaze in toddlers with ASD, DD, and TD*. Poster presented at the 2012 International Meeting for Autism Research, Toronto, Canada.

Ornitz, E. M., Guthrie, D., & Farley, A. J. (1978). The early symptoms of childhood autism. In G. Serban (Ed.), *Cognitive defects in the development of mental illness* (pp. 24–42). New York, NY: Brunner/Mazel.

Osborne, L. A., McHugh, L., Saunders, J., & Reed, P. (2008). Parenting stress reduces the effectiveness of early teaching interventions for autistic spectrum disorders. *Journal of Autism and Developmental Disorders, 38*(6), 1092–1103.

Osterling, J. A., & Dawson, G. (1994). Early recognition of children with autism: A study of first birthday home videotapes. *Journal of Autism and Developmental Disorders, 24*(3), 247–257.

Osterling, J. A., Dawson, G., & Munson, J. A. (2002). Early recognition of 1-year-old infants with autism spectrum disorder versus mental retardation. *Development & Psychopathology, 14*(2), 239–251.

Ozonoff, S., Heung, K., Byrd, R., Hansen, R., & Hertz-Picciotto, I. (2008). The onset of autism: Patterns of symptom emergence in the first years of life. *Autism Research, 1*(6), 320–328.

Ozonoff, S., Iosif, A., Baguio, F., Cook, I. D., Hill, M. M., Hutman, T., ... Young, G. S. (2010). A prospective study of the emergence of early behavioral signs of autism. *Journal of the American Academy of Child & Adolescent Psychiatry, 49*(3), 258–268.

Ozonoff, S., Iosif, A., Young, G. S., Hepburn, S., Thompson, M., Colombi, C., ... Rogers, S. J. (2011). Onset patterns in autism: Correspondence between home video and parent report. *Journal of the American Academy of Child & Adolescent Psychiatry, 50*(8), 796–806.e791. doi:http://dx.doi.org/10.1016/j.jaac.2011.03.012

Ozonoff, S., Macari, S., Young, G. S., Goldring, S., Thompson, M., & Rogers, S. J. (2008). Atypical object exploration at 12 months of age is associated with autism in a prospective sample. *Autism, 12*(5), 457–472.

Ozonoff, S., Young, G. S., Goldring, S., Greiss-Hess, L., Herrera, A. M., Steele, J., ... Rogers, S. J. (2008). Gross motor development, movement abnormalities, and early identification of autism. *Journal of Autism and Developmental Disorders, 38*(4), 644–656.

Paul, R. (2007). Communication and its development in autism spectrum disorders. In F. R. Volkmar (Ed.), *Autism and pervasive developmental disorders* (2nd ed., pp. 129–155). New York, NY: Cambridge University Press.

Paul, R., Fuerst, Y., Ramsay, G., Chawarska, K., & Klin, A. (2011). Out of the mouths of babes: vocal production in infant siblings of children with ASD. *Journal of Child Psychology and Psychiatry, 52*(5), 588–598. doi:10.1111/j.1469-7610.2010.02332.x

Perryman, T. Y., Carter, A. S., Messinger, D. S., Stone, W. L., Ivanescu, A. E., & Yoder, P. J. (2012). Brief report: Parental child-directed speech as a predictor of receptive language in children with autism symptomatology. *Journal of Autism and Developmental Disorders.* doi:10.1007/s10803-012-1725-3

Ray-Subramanian, C. E., Huai, N., & Weismer, S. E. (2011). Brief report: Adaptive behavior and cognitive skills for toddlers on the autism spectrum. *Journal of Autism and Developmental Disorders, 41*(5), 679–684.

Raznahan, A., Wallace, G. L., Antezana, L., Greenstein, D., Lenroot, R., Thurm, A., ... Giedd, J. N. (2013). Compared to what? Early brain overgrowth in autism and the perils of population norms. *Biological Psychiatry, 74*(8), 563–575.

Remington, B., Hastings, R. P., Kovshoff, H., degli Espinosa, F., Jahr, E., Brown, T., ... Ward, N. (2007). Early intensive behavioral intervention: Outcomes for children with autism and their parents after two years. *American Journal on Mental Retardation, 112*(6), 418–438.

Richler, J., Bishop, S. L., Kleinke, J. R., & Lord, C. (2007). Restricted and repetitive behaviors in young children with autism spectrum disorders. *Journal of Autism and Developmental Disorders, 37*(1), 73–85.

Richters, J. E., Waters, E., & Vaughn, B. E. (1988). Empirical classification of infant-mother relationships from interactive behavior and crying during reunion. *Child Development, 59*(2), 512–522.

Risi, S., Lord, C., Gotham, K., Corsello, C., Chrysler, C., Szatmari, P., ... Pickles, A. (2006). Combining information from multiple sources in the diagnosis of autism spectrum disorders. *Journal of the American Academy of Child & Adolescent Psychiatry, 45*(9), 1094–1103.

Ro, T., Friggel, A., & Lavie, N. (2007). Attentional biases for faces and body parts. *Visual Cognition, 15*(3), 322–348.

Rogers, S. J. (2009). What are infant siblings teaching us about autism in infancy? *Autism Research, 2*(3), 125–137.

Rogers, S. J., & DiLalla, D. L. (1990). Age of symptom onset in young children with pervasive developmental disorders. *Journal of the American Academy of Child & Adolescent Psychiatry, 29*(6), 863–872.

Rogers, S. J., Estes, A., Lord, C., Vismara, L., Winter, J., Fitzpatrick, A., ... Dawson, G. (2012). Effects of a brief Early Start Denver Model (ESDM)–based parent intervention on toddlers at risk for autism spectrum disorders: A randomized controlled trial. *Journal of the American Academy of Child & Adolescent Psychiatry, 51*(10), 1052–1065. doi:http://dx.doi.org/10.1016/j.jaac.2012.08.003

Rogers, S. J., Hepburn, S. L., Stackhouse, T., & Wehner, B. (2003). Imitation performance in toddlers with autism and those with other developmental disorders. *Journal of Child Psychology and Psychiatry, 44*(5), 763–781.

Rogers, S. J., Ozonoff, S., & Maslin-Cole, C. (1993). Developmental aspects of attachment behavior in young children with pervasive developmental disorders. *Journal of the American Academy of Child & Adolescent Psychiatry, 32*(6), 1274–1282.

Rothbart, M. K., & Bates, J. E. (1998). Temperament. In W. Damon (Series Ed.) & N. Eisenberg (Vol. Ed.), *Handbook of child psychology: Vol. 3. Social, emotional, and personality development* (5th ed., pp. 105–176). New York, NY: Wiley.

Rothbart, M. K., & Derryberry, D. (1981). Development of individual differences in temperament. In M. E. Lamb & A. L. Brown (Eds.), *Advances in developmental psychology* (Vol. 1, pp. 37–86). Hillsdale, NJ: Erlbaum.

Rowberry, J., Macari, S., Chen, G., Campbell, D., Weitzman, C., Leventhal, J. M., & Chawarska, K. (under review). Screening for autism spectrum disorders at 12 months in high-risk infants.

Rozga, A., Hutman, T., Young, G. S., Rogers, S. J., Ozonoff, S., Dapretto, M., & Sigman, M. (2011). Behavioral profiles of affected and unaffected siblings of children with autism:

Contribution of measures of mother-infant interaction and nonverbal communication. *Journal of Autism and Developmental Disorders, 41*(3), 287–301.

Rutgers, A. H., Bakermans-Kranenburg, M. J., van IJzendoorn, M. H., & Berckelaer-Onnes, I. A. (2004). Autism and attachment: A meta-analytic review. *Journal of Child Psychology and Psychiatry, 45*(6), 1123–1134.

Rutgers, A. H., van IJzendoorn, M. H., Bakermans-Kranenburg, M. J., Swinkels, S. H., van Daalen, E., Dietz, C., . . . van Engeland, H. (2007). Autism, attachment and parenting: A comparison of children with autism spectrum disorder, mental retardation, language disorder, and non-clinical children. *Journal of Abnormal Child Psychology, 35*(5), 859–870.

Rutter, M., Le Couteur, A., & Lord, C. (2003). ADI-R: Autism Diagnostic Interview–Revised. Los Angeles, CA: Western Psychological Services.

Sallustro, F., & Atwell, C. W. (1978). Body rocking, head banging, and head rolling in normal children. *The Journal of Pediatrics, 93*(4), 704–708.

Sanders, S. J., Murtha, M. T., Gupta, A. R., Murdoch, J. D., Raubenson, M. J., Willsey, A. J., . . . State, M. W. (2012). De novo mutations revealed by whole-exome sequencing are strongly associated with autism. *Nature, 485*(7397), 237–241.

Schoen, E., Paul, R., & Chawarska, K. (2011). Phonology and vocal behavior in toddlers with autism spectrum disorders. *Autism Research, 4*(3), 177–188

Schwichtenberg, A. J., Young, G. S., Sigman, M., Hutman, T., & Ozonoff, S. (2010), Can family affectedness inform infant sibling outcomes of autism spectrum disorders? *Journal of Child Psychology and Psychiatry, 51*(9), 1021–1030.

Sebat, J., Lakshmi, B., Malhotra, D., Troge, J., Lese-Martin, C., Walsh, T., . . . Wigler, M. (2007). Strong association of de novo copy number mutations with autism. *Science, 316*(5823), 445–449. doi:10.1126/science.1138659

Sheinkopf, S. J., Mundy, P., Oller, D. K., & Steffens, M. (2000). Vocal atypicalities of preverbal autistic children. *Journal of Autism and Developmental Disorders, 30*(4), 345–354.

Shic, F., Bradshaw, J., Klin, A., Scassellati, B., & Chawarska, K. (2011). Limited activity monitoring in toddlers with autism spectrum disorder. *Brain Research, 1380*, 246–254.

Shic, F., Macari, S., & Chawarska, K. (2013). Speech disturbs face scanning in 6-month olds who develop autism spectrum disorder. *Biological Psychiatry.* [Epub ahead of print]

Shumway, S., Athurm, U., Swedo, S. E., Deprey, L., Barnett, L. A., Amaral, D. G., . . . Ozonoff, S. (2011). Brief report: Symptom onset patterns and functional outcomes in young children with autism spectrum disorders. *Neurology, 77*(12), 1727–1732.

Shumway, S., & Wetherby, A. M. (2009). Communicative acts of children with autism spectrum disorders in the second year of life. *Journal of Speech, Language & Hearing Research, 52*(5), 1139–1156. doi: 10.1044/1092-4388(2009/07-0280)

Sices, L., Feudtner, C., McLaughlin, J., Drotar, D., & Williams, M. (2003). How do primary care physicians identify young children with developmental delays? A national survey. *Journal of Developmental and Behavioral Pediatrics, 24*(6), 409–417.

Sigman, M., Arbelle, S., & Dissanayake, C. (1995). Current research findings on childhood autism. *Canadian Journal of Psychiatry—Revue Canadienne de Psychiatrie, 40*(6), 289–294.

Sigman, M., & McGovern, C. W. (2005). Improvement in cognitive and language skills from preschool to adolescence in autism. *Journal of Autism and Developmental Disorders 35*(1), 15–23.

Sigman, M., & Ruskin, E. (1999). Continuity and change in the social competence of children with autism, Down syndrome, and developmental delays. *Monographs of the Society for Research in Child Development, 64*(1), v–114.

Siperstein, R., & Volkmar, F. (2004). Brief report: Parental reporting of regression in children with pervasive developmental disorders. *Journal of Autism and Developmental Disorders, 34*(6), 731–734.

Smith, T., Groen, A. D., & Wynn, J. W. (2000). Randomized trial of intensive early intervention for children with pervasive developmental disorder. *American Journal on Mental Retardation, 105*(4), 269–285.

Sparks, B. F., Friedman, S. D., Shaw, D. W., Aylward, E. H., Echelard, D., Artru, A. A., . . . Dager, S. R. (2002). Brain structural abnormalities in young children with autism spectrum disorder. *Neurology, 59*(2), 184–192.

Sparling, J. W. (1991). A prospective case report of infantile autism from pregnancy to four years. *Journal of Autism and Developmental Disorders, 21*(2), 229–236.

Sparrow, S. S., Balla, D. A., & Cicchetti, D. V. (2005). *Vineland Adaptive Behavior Scales* (2nd ed.). Circle Pines, MN: American Guidance Service.

Stone, W. L., Lee, E. B., Ashford, L., Brissie, J., Hepburn, S. L., Coonrod, E. E., & Weiss, B. H. (1999). Can autism be diagnosed accurately in children under 3 years? *Journal of Child Psychology & Psychiatry & Allied Disciplines, 40*(2), 219–226.

Stone, W. L., Ousley, O. Y., Yoder, P. J., Hogan, K. L., & Hepburn, S. L. (1997). Nonverbal communication in two- and three-year-old children with autism. *Journal of Autism and Developmental Disorders, 27*(6), 677–696.

Sullivan, M., Finelli, J., Marvin, A., Garrett-Mayer, E., Bauman, M., & Landa, R. (2007). Response to joint attention in toddlers at risk for autism spectrum disorder: A prospective study. *Journal of Autism and Developmental Disorders, 37*(1), 37–48.

Swettenham, J., Baron-Cohen, S., Charman, T., Cox, A., Baird, G., Drew, A., Rees, L., & Wheelwright, S. (1998). The frequency and distribution of spontaneous attention shifts between social and nonsocial stimuli in autistic, typically developing, and nonautistic developmentally delayed infants. *Journal of Child Psychology & Psychiatry & Allied Disciplines, 39*(5), 747–753.

Tager-Flusberg, H. (2010). The origins of social impairments in autism spectrum disorder: Studies of infants at risk. *Neural Networks, 23*(8–9), 1072–1076.

Thelen, E. (1979). Rhythmical stereotypies in normal human infants. *Animal Behaviour, 27*(3), 699–715.

Thurm, A., Lord, C., Lee, L.-C., & Newschaffer, C. (2007). Predictors of language acquisition in preschool children with autism spectrum disorders. *Journal of Autism and Developmental Disorders, 37*(9), 1721–1734.

Tuchman, R. F., & Rapin, I. (1997). Regression in pervasive developmental disorders: Seizures and epileptiform electroencephalogram correlates. *Pediatrics*, *99*(4), 560–566.

Turner, L. M., Stone, W. L., Pozdol, S. L., & Coonrod, E. E. (2006). Follow-up of children with autism spectrum disorders from age 2 to age 9. *Autism*, *10*(3), 243–265.

van IJzendoorn, M. H., Rutgers, A. H., Bakermans-Kranenburg, M. J., Swinkels, S. H., van Daalen, E., Dietz, C., . . . van Engeland, H. (2007). Parental sensitivity and attachment in children with autism spectrum disorder: Comparison with children with mental retardation, with language delays, and with typical development. *Child Development*, *78*(2), 597–608.

Ventola, P., Kleinman, B., Pandey, J., Barton, M., Allen, S., Green, J., . . . Fein, D. (2006). Agreement among four diagnostic instruments for autism spectrum disorders in toddlers. *Journal of Autism and Developmental Disorders*, *36*(7), 839–847.

Vivanti, G., Dissanayake, C., Zierhut, C., & Rogers, S. (2012). Brief report: Predictors of outcomes in the early start Denver model delivered in a group setting. *Journal of Autism and Developmental Disorders*, 1–8. doi:10.1007/s10803-012-1705-7

Volkmar, F. R., Carter, A., Sparrow, S. S., & Cicchetti, D. V. (1993). Quantifying social development in autism. *Journal of the American Academy of Child & Adolescent Psychiatry*, *32*(3), 627–632.

Volkmar, F. R., & Cohen, D. J. (1989). Disintegrative disorder or "late onset" autism. *Journal of Child Psychology & Psychiatry & Allied Disciplines*, *30*(5), 717–724.

Volkmar, F. R., Cohen, D. J., & Paul, R. (1986). An evaluation of *DSM-III* criteria for infantile autism. *Journal of the American Academy of Child Psychiatry*, *25*(2), 190–197.

Volkmar, F. R., Klin, A., Siegel, B., Szatmari, P., Lord, C., Campbell, M., . . . Kline, W. (1994). Field trial for autistic disorder in DSM-IV. *American Journal of Psychiatry*, *151*(9), 1361–1367.

Volkmar, F. R., & Mayes, L. C. (1990). Gaze behavior in autism. *Development and Psychopathology*, *2*(1), 61–69.

Volkmar, F. R., Sparrow, S. S., Goudreau, D., Cicchetti, D. V., Paul R., & Cohen, D. J. (1987). Social deficits in autism: An operational approach using the Vineland Adaptive Behavior Scales. *Journal of the American Academy of Child & Adolescent Psychiatry*, *26*(2), 156–161.

Wan, M. W., Green, J., Elsabbagh, M., Johnson, M., Charman, T., & Plummer, F. (2012). Parent–infant interaction in infant siblings at risk of autism. *Research in Developmental Disabilities*, *33*(3), 924–932. doi:10.1016/j.ridd.2011.12.011

Waterhouse, L., & Fein, D. (1998). Autism and the evolution of human social skills. In F. R. Volkmar (Ed.), *Autism and pervasive developmental disorders* (pp. 242–267). Cambridge, England: Cambridge University Press.

Waters, E. (1995). Appendix A: The Attachment Q-Set (Version 3.0). *Monographs of the Society for Research in Child Development*, *60*, 234–246.

Watson, L. R., Baranek, G. T., Roberts, J. E., David, F. J., & Perryman, T. Y. (2010). Behavioral and physiological responses to child-directed speech as predictors of communication outcomes in children with autism spectrum disorders.

Journal of Speech, Language and Hearing Research, *53*(4), 1052.

Watt, N., Wetherby, A. M., Barber, A., & Morgan, L. (2008). Repetitive and stereotyped behaviors in children with autism spectrum disorders in the second year of life. *Journal of Autism and Developmental Disorders*, *38*(8), 1518–1533.

Watt, N., Wetherby, A., & Shumway, S. (2006). Prelinguistic predictors of language outcome at 3 years of age. *Journal of Speech, Language and Hearing Research*, *49*(6), 1224.

Werner, E., Dawson, G., Munson, J., & Osterling, J. (2005). Variation in early developmental course in autism and its relation with behavioral outcome at 3–4 years of age. *Journal of Autism and Developmental Disorders*, *35*(3), 337–350.

Werner, E., Dawson, G., Osterling, J., & Dinno, N. (2000). Brief report: Recognition of autism spectrum disorder before one year of age: A retrospective study based on home videotapes. *Journal of Autism and Developmental Disorders*, *30*(2), 157–162.

Wetherby, A. M., & Prizant, B. M. (2002). *Communication and Symbolic Behavior Scales: Developmental Profile*. Baltimore, MD: Paul H. Brookes.

Wetherby, A. M., Prizant, B. M., & Schuler, A. L. (2000). Understanding the nature of communication and language impairments. In A. M. Wetherby & B. M. Prizant (Eds.), *Autism spectrum disorders: A transactional developmental perspective*. Communication and language intervention series (Vol. 9, pp. 109–141). Baltimore, MD: Paul H. Brookes.

Wetherby, A. M., Watt, N., Morgan, L., & Shumway, S. (2007). Social communication profiles of children with autism spectrum disorders late in the second year of life. *Journal of Autism and Developmental Disorders*, *37*(5), 960–975.

Wetherby, A., & Woods, J. (2008). Developmental Aproaches to Treatment. In K. Chawarska, A. Klin, & F. Volkmar (Eds.), *Autism spectrum disorders in infants and toddlers: Diagnosis, assessment, and treatment* (pp. 170–206). New York, NY: Guilford Press.

Wetherby, A. M., Woods, J., Allen, L., Cleary, J., Dickinson, H., & Lord, C. (2004). Early indicators of autism spectrum disorders in the second year of life. *Journal of Autism and Developmental Disorders*, *34*(5), 473–493.

Wolff, J. J., Hongbin, G., Gerig, G., Elison, J. T., Styner, M. Gouttard, S., . . . the IBIS Network. (2012). Differences in white matter fiber tract development present from 6 to 24 months in infants with autism. *American Journal of Psychiatry*, *169*(6), 589–600. doi:10.1176/appi.ajp.2011.11091447

Woods, J. J., & Wetherby, A. M. (2003). Early identification of and intervention for infants and toddlers who are at risk for autism spectrum disorder. *Language, Speech, and Hearing Services in Schools*, *34*(3), 180.

Yirmiya, N., & Charman, T. (2011). The prodrome of autism: Early behavioral and biological signs, regression, peri- and post-natal development and genetics. *Journal of Child Psychology and Psychiatry*, *51*(4), 452–458.

Yoder, P., & Stone, W. L. (2006). A randomized comparison of the effect of two prelinguistic communication interventions on the acquisition of spoken communication in preschoolers with ASD. *Journal of Speech, Language, and Hearing Research*, *49*(4), 698–711.

Yoder, P., Stone, W. L., Walden, T., & Malesa, E. (2009). Predicting social impairment and ASD diagnosis in younger siblings of children with autism spectrum disorder. *Journal of Autism and Developmental Disorders*, *39*(10), 1381–1391.

Young, G. S., Merin, N., Rogers, S. J., & Ozonoff, S. (2009). Gaze behavior and affect at 6 months: Predicting clinical outcomes and language development in typically developing infants and infants at risk for autism. *Developmental Science*, *12*(5), 798–814. doi:10.1111/j.1467-7687.2009.00833.x

Young, G. S., Rogers, S., Hutman, T., Rozga, A., Sigman, M., & Ozonoff, S. (2011). Imitation from 12 to 24 months in autism and typical development: A longitudinal Rasch analysis. *Developmental Psychology*, *47*(6), 1565–1578.

Zimmerman, I. L., Violette, G., Steiner, B. S., & Pond, R. E. (2011). *Preschool Language Scale* (5th ed.). San Antonio, TX: Psychological Corporation.

Zwaigenbaum, L., Bryson, S., Lord, C., Rogers, S., Carter, A., Carver, L., ... Yirmiya, N. (2009). Clinical assessment and management of toddlers with suspected autism spectrum disorder: insights from studies of high-risk infants. [Research Support, N.I.H., Extramural Review]. *Pediatrics*, *123*(5), 1383–1391.

Zwaigenbaum, L., Bryson, S., Rogers, T., Roberts, W., Brian, J., & Szatmari, P. (2005). Behavioral manifestations of autism in the first year of life. *International Journal of Developmental Neuroscience*, *23*(2–3), 143–152.

CHAPTER 6

School-Age Children With ASD

NIRIT BAUMINGER-ZVIELY

INTRODUCTION

The transition to school from the early childhood years of toddlerhood and preschool poses new social and cognitive-academic challenges for children with autism spectrum disorders (ASD). The preschool setting offers a relatively predictable, manageable, and protective social environment that includes few teachers and peers, with a few key adults addressing the child's needs, whereas the school setting is a significantly more complex and demanding social and academic environment characterized by frequent changes in daily routine and an abundance of interactions with various adults and peers (e.g., Fabes, Martin, & Hanish, 2009). In typical development (TYP), the peer group gains special importance in the school years. Social behaviors gradually become less straightforward, thereby demanding much more effort to decipher and perform. In particular, the spontaneous authentic behaviors and emotions that peers exhibit at younger ages are gradually replaced by mediated or inhibited behaviors and hidden emotions, requiring children to acquire deeper social and emotional understanding and knowledge in order to comprehend interpersonal situations and participate in them effectively (e.g., Fabes et al., 2009). In a like manner, more advanced language and pragmatic skills are required to take part in and make sense of peer behaviors. Adding to this, executive function capabilities such as cognitive flexibility, planning, and problem-solving skills are all necessary to cope efficiently with both the social and academic demands of school (e.g., Fabes et al., 2009). In light of the core deficits found in children with ASD in these areas (e.g., peer interaction, social communication, social cognition, executive functioning), the social-emotional and cognitive-academic demands of school can pose serious difficulties.

Indeed, Staar, Szatmari, Bryson, and Zwaigenbaum (2003) traced an increase in difficulties in the social domain (based on the Autism Diagnostic Interview; Rutter, Le Couteur, & Lord, 2003) in school-age children with ASD (age 6–8 years) compared to preschoolers (age 4–6 years), and an even more robust increase in social difficulties for higher functioning children on the spectrum (Asperger syndrome). Both school-age groups showed greater impairment than their younger counterparts—in their range and appropriateness of facial expressions and in their greeting behaviors. The older children with Asperger also showed a decline with age in their level of sharing behaviors, appropriate social responses, and vocal expressions. This overall decline in social functioning measures may reflect these children's increasing difficulty in meeting the greater social expectations for the early school years due to their sociocognitive and sociocommunicative skill deficits.

Two findings of Klin et al. (2007) for cognitively high-functioning children with ASD (HFASD; i.e., IQ >70) are of particular interest in this regard. First, these researchers demonstrated that in two independent samples of school-age children and adolescents with HFASD (7–18 years), socialization scores based on the Vineland Adaptive Behavior Scale (VABS; Sparrow, Balla, & Cicchetti, 1984) were two to three standard deviations below IQ, and a similar but smaller gap between IQ and adaptive functioning emerged for the VABS communication domain (one to two standard deviations). Second, age was negatively linked with both VABS domains, suggesting that the gap increases with age between individuals with HFASD and their typical peers, both in communicative and social abilities. This suggests that older children and adolescents with ASD become increasingly more impaired relative to their age-mates with TYP.

Links between the social and academic domains were found in school-age children with HFASD (Estes, Rivera, Bryan, Cali, & Dawson, 2011). Children with higher social skills at age 6 years demonstrated higher levels of academic achievement, specifically in word reading, at age 9 years. However, 60% of the sample showed lower academic achievement than would be predicted based solely on their intellectual ability, indicating the complicating effects of the autism-related deficits and/or the presence of additional specific disabilities in academic domains. Also, Montes and Halterman's (2006) nationwide survey of U.S. children from kindergarten (age 5–6 years) through eighth grade (age 13–14 years) revealed that children with ASD and children without ASD were equally likely to attend public schools, but the former were significantly less likely to receive A and B grades compared to the latter (43% vs. 74%, respectively). Furthermore, children with ASD were more likely to carry multiple diagnoses compared to children without ASD, mainly learning disabilities (67% vs. 8%), attention deficit disorders (54% vs. 7%), and speech impairments (58% vs. 4%). Psychiatric comorbidities like depression and anxiety were found to increase in frequency in the school years for children with ASD, comprising 5.6% of ages 4–6 years, 48.4% of ages 7–10 years, and 46.0% of ages 11–17 years (McPheeter, Davis, Navarre, & Scott, 2011). Children with HFASD seemed to be at a greater risk for these two psychiatric disorders than children with lower cognitive functioning on the autism spectrum (LFA; IQ <70), probably because those with stronger cognitive abilities understood and were distressed by their deficits (Mayes, Calhoun, Murray, Ahuja, & Smith, 2011). Perhaps higher functioning children are easier to diagnose because they are able to report about their psychiatric symptoms.

However, it is important to note that despite the overall significant difficulties elicited by the transition to school and its heightened social and academic demands, areas of growth were also identified during middle childhood for children with ASD, especially in cognitive and linguistic functioning. For example, L. M. Turner, Stone, Pozdol, and Coonrod (2006) found that 9-year-old children with ASD who were first diagnosed before age 3 (*n* = 25) demonstrated improvements over time in cognitive and language skills. Cognitive scores increased for most children (68% showed an increase of 15 points); at age 2 years 84% of the children showed significant cognitive delay (two or more standard deviations below the mean), whereas at age 9 half the children revealed average to higher cognitive scores. Likewise, at age 2 years 60% of the children showed very low expressive language capabilities, whereas at age 9 years 88% revealed at least some functional language; a substantial minority (32%) could engage in conversations with an unfamiliar examiner (using the Autism

Diagnostic Observation Schedule [ADOS]; Lord et al., 2000); and only 12% were nonverbal.

In this chapter, I describe areas of ability and disability among school-age children with ASD, referring to ages 6–12 years but at times due to topic's importance also to a wider age range including younger children and adolescents (on the condition that the samples' mean chronological age [CA] was within the 6- to 12-year range). After briefly providing general information about ASD prevalence in the school years, this chapter will discuss the disorder's core deficits and abilities that hold important implications for the social and academic functioning of children with ASD, in the areas of social functioning (sociocognitive capabilities and sociocommunicative skills), repetitive behaviors, and cognitive-academic characteristics. The chapter will conclude with future directions for research.

SCHOOL-AGE ASD PREVALENCE AND GENERAL CHARACTERISTICS

Surveys of the U.S. population of school-age children with ASD (at age 8) have shown a significant 78% increase in recent years, from 2002 to 2008, growing from 1:150 to 1:88 (Centers for Disease Control and Prevention [CDC], 2012). A careful look at the ASD prevalence rates for boys (1:54 in the United States, 1:66 in the United Kingdom) and for girls (1:252 in the United States; 1:208 in the United Kingdom) emphasizes the need to plan services to meet the needs of almost 2% of the school-age population (CDC, 2012 in the United States; Baron-Cohen et al., 2009 in the United Kingdom). With regard to cognitive functioning in school-age children with ASD, 38% show an intellectual deficit (IQ <70, LFA), 24% fall in the borderline range of intellectual abilities (IQ = 71–85); 62% do not reveal an intellectual deficit (IQ >70; HFASD); and 38% have an IQ over 85 (CDC, 2012). The boy-to-girl ratio differs somewhat in ASD groups with different cognitive functioning levels, ranging from 6:1 to 15:1 for children with HFASD (IQ >70) and ranging from

2:1 to 6.5:1 for low-functioning (IQ <70) children (Johnson & Myers, 2007).

In a recent U.S. national survey examining treatment services for school-age children with ASD (ages 6–11 years), Pringle, Colpe, Blumberg, Avila, and Kogan (2012) found that most children received social skills training (60.1%) and speech or language therapy (68.4%), followed by 51.3% receiving occupational therapy and 40.2% receiving behavioral intervention. Furthermore, more than half of school-age children and adolescents with ASD use psychotropic medications (Pringle et al., 2012). To sum up, prevalence studies demonstrate that school-age children with ASD form a substantial and sizable group of children with varying degrees of cognitive functioning, who merit consideration of their specific needs based on their abilities and disabilities, as detailed next.

SOCIAL FUNCTIONING

The core social deficits in autism pertain to these children's sociocognitive and their sociocommunicative capabilities.

Sociocognitive Skills

Sociocognitive capabilities such as social attention, social-emotional knowledge, and theory of mind (ToM) abilities establish the foundation for peer relations. This section will review the atypical development of sociocognitive skills that characterizes school-age children with ASD (e.g., see extensive review in Bauminger-Zviely, 2013).

Social Attention

Social interaction starts with children's ability to be attuned to others' faces, read their expressions, listen to their verbalizations, observe their body gestures, and integrate all these stimuli into a meaningful interaction. The social attention processes necessary at different developmental stages are hampered in ASD (e.g., as shown by Elison, Sasson, Turner-Brown, Dichter, & Bodfish, 2012, for a large age range of 2.60–17.25 years). Elison et al.'s research suggested that the essence of these children's difficulty in social attention lies in their disproportional visual attention to nonsocial objects (e.g., trains, vehicle, road signs) relative to social stimuli (e.g., happy facial expression of males and females of various ages). Several researchers also found reduced eye gaze toward human faces in ASD versus TYP, for example, when Riby and Hancock (2009) presented children (CA = 12.4 years) with faces that were artificially embedded into pictures of natural scenes (e.g., harbor with boats, mountains behind a village) or were inserted into scrambled pictures containing objects. Children with TYP (CA = 10.4 years) were found to pay more attention to human faces when these faces were a distracter that slowed down their given task (searching for a butterfly from among human and nonhuman pictures), but children with ASD (CA = 12.11 years) did not reveal this preference for human faces (Riby, Brown, Jones, & Hanley, 2012).

It seems that level of cognitive functioning plays an important role in social attention capabilities. In Riby and Hancock's (2009) study, children with lower cognitive functioning directed fewer gazes toward faces than children with higher cognitive functioning. Interestingly, Riby et al. (2012) found that children with ASD who had higher cognitive functioning showed higher degrees of face distraction than their lower functioning counterparts, resembling the distractibility of the children with TYP. Studies focusing on HFASD indicate other subtle group differences. For example, Wilson, Brock, and Palermo's (2010) study of visual fixation using an eye-tracking procedure found that children with HFASD resembled their peers with TYP (CA = 10.13 years) in their strong bias to orient toward social stimuli (people) before orienting toward nonsocial stimuli (pelican, ice cream van). However, the children with TYP were quicker to fixate on the people and fixated their look primarily on people and secondarily on objects throughout the trial, whereas children with HFASD fixated equally between people and objects, and overall they looked less at faces compared with the TYP group.

Interestingly, attention capabilities may differ according to the social stimulus's complexity. Indeed, van der Geest, Kemner, Camfferman, Verbaten, and van Engeland (2002) and van der Geest, Kemner, Verbaten, and van Engeland (2002) reported no impairment in attention focused on static facial or emotional stimuli among children with HFASD (CA = 10.6 years) compared to age-matched peers with TYP. In the van der Geest, Kemner, Camfferman, et al. (2002) study, the two groups revealed similar gaze behaviors when viewing cartoon-like static scenes that included human figures. In the van der Geest, Kemner, Verbaten, et al. (2002) study, the HFASD group resembled the TYP group when viewing still photos of human faces displaying emotional states. In contrast, Evers, Noens, Steyaert, and Wagemans (2011) found that children with HFASD demonstrated a specific visual perception difficulty compared to children with TYP (CA = 7–11 years) when the task required attention toward a complex social static stimuli rather than a simple one (matching a larger versus smaller number of human faces) or attention toward dynamic (animated) human faces expressing emotions versus static human faces. Other research that included older children with HFASD (e.g., adolescents and young adults) reported greater difficulty in visually fixating on dynamic social interactions versus fixating on still photographs of such interactions, as well as less fixation on the eye region than TYP (e.g., Klin, Jones, Schultz, Volkmar, & Cohen, 2002).

In sum, social attention processes may be influenced by level of cognitive functioning and by the complexity of stimuli, but overall these processes are impaired in school-age children with ASD. This deficit may hold significance for other important aspects of social cognition, such as how children make sense of others' mental states, as described next.

ToM

Deficits in mentalizing other minds (ToM) in terms of others' thoughts, feelings, desires, and intentions have been suggested as a major characteristic of ASD and as an explanatory mechanism for these children's difficulties in social functioning (see review in Baron-Cohen, 2000). Various verbal and nonverbal tasks and paradigms have been applied to assess ToM in school-age children with ASD. For example, the false-belief (FB) paradigm is frequently used to assess children's (true) belief versus their awareness of someone else's different false belief (e.g., Bauminger & Kasari, 1999; Lind & Bowler, 2009; Matthews et al., 2012; Peterson, Garnett, Kelly, & Attwood, 2009; Peterson, Slaughter, & Paynter, 2007; White, Hill, Happé, & Frith, 2009). FB may refer to first-order attributions ("X believes that P") or second-order attributions ("X believes that Y believes that P"). Peterson et al. (2009) found associations between first-order laboratory measures of FB on misleading-appearance tasks (e.g., a box of crayons containing candy, a pen that looks like a carrot) and children's mindreading in everyday interactions and conversations. Children with ASD (CA = 9.61 years) who passed the FB task versus those who failed were better at applying mindreading in everyday interactions and conversation, but even those FB passers still functioned in everyday skills below younger children with TYP (CA = 6.06 years). In another study, Peterson et al. (2007) showed that first-order FB scores (unexpected-location tasks) contributed significantly, beyond age and verbal skills, to age-referenced social maturity (rated as group entry, self-assertion, peer leadership, interactive social play, coping with disruptive peers, tolerance, and sensitivity) in children with autism (CA = 8.02), Asperger (CA = 8.58), and TYP (CA = 8.33 and 4.68). Children with autism scored below both age-matched and younger children with TYP, in both ToM and social maturation. Children with Asperger performed better on ToM than children with autism, but showed a lower proportion of FB passers compared with TYP and were rated as socially immature by their teachers.

Lind and Bowler (2009) stressed the fact that, differently from children with TYP (CA = 10.50 years), school-age children with ASD (CA = 10.42 years, verbal mental age [VMA] = 6.77 years) use verbal compensatory mechanisms to solve first-order FB unexpected-location tasks.

Using the second-order FB ice cream van story (Perner & Wimmer, 1985), Bauminger and Kasari (1999) also found that verbal and full IQ correlated with performance on the FB and justification questions, but only for the group with HFASD (CA = 10.74 years) and not for age-mates with TYP. Interestingly, group differences in this study emerged only for justifications' relevancy; children with HFASD gave more irrelevant or incorrect justifications when asked to provide explanation to the belief question, probably due to deficits in social understanding (Bauminger & Kasari, 1999). Lastly, Matthews et al. (2012) explained heterogeneity in first-order FB tasks by considering early experience in social interaction. He found that early onset ASD (CA = 9.47 years) had poorer FB capabilities than their younger counterparts with TYP (CA = 5.76 years) and regressive ASD (CA = 8.88 years), who fall in between early onset and TYP.

A number of researchers have implemented advanced ToM tasks for the more able (IQ > 70) school-age children with ASD. Happé's (1994) original strange stories (SSs) were developed to assess understanding of lies, white lies, double bluff, persuasion, and misunderstanding by explaining why a character says something that is not literally true, thereby attributing mental states like desires, beliefs, or intentions (e.g., Brent, Rios, Happé, & Charman, 2004). In a revised SS, White et al. (2009), used a control scenario without mental states (stories on nature) to assess whether the source of the difficulties lay in attributing mental states or in comprehending text. Another type of task was developed by Baron-Cohen, Wheelwright, Scahill, Lawson, and Spong (2001), the nonverbal Reading the Mind in the Eyes ToM task, which requires children to recognize emotional states from a person's eyes (e.g., Brent et al., 2004). A third popular paradigm involves attributing mental states to computerized, animated, interacting geometric triangular figures (e.g., Salter, Seigal, Claxton, Lawrence, & Skuse, 2008). Finally, Peterson, Wellman, and Slaughter, (2012) used an assessment based on a revision of Wellman and Liu's (2004) five-step ToM model of increasingly complex skills, the steps of which include (1) diverse desires (different people want different things), (2) diverse beliefs (different people have contrasting, potentially true beliefs about the same thing), (3) knowledge access (not seeing leads to not knowing), (4) FB (standard first-order misleading-container task), and (5) hidden emotion (people can feel a different emotion from the one they display) and understanding of nonliteral communication such as sarcasm and irony.

Unsurprisingly, in all these various studies of advanced ToM, children with ASD performed more poorly than their age-mates with TYP overall. This included lower performance on the Eyes task (e.g., Brent et al., 2004), on the original SS mentalizing task—where children with ASD provided more inappropriate mental-state responses to explain characters' intentions (e.g., Brent et al., 2004); on the revised SS (White et al., 2009), mainly on the mentalizing stories; and on the revised developmental ToM scale (Peterson et al., 2012), with special difficulty in understanding nonliteral communication (sarcasm).

Interestingly, in Peterson et al. (2012), children with autism also showed an atypical developmental sequence of ToM development, in which FB was found to be harder than hidden emotion, rather than the opposite as found for children with TYP. With regard to children's ability to use mentalizing language (e.g., "surprising," "mocking," "seducing" to tap the intentions of animated interacting geometric triangles), Salter et al. (2008) found that children with HFASD (CA = 10.37 years) were comparable to age-mates with TYP, although the HFASD group's description of the event in the animation was significantly less appropriate, emphasizing lack of social understanding rather than difficulties in tapping the figures' intentions (mentalizing). In a like manner, Pexman et al. (2011) reported intact ability to mentalize about others' beliefs but poor social understanding of these beliefs' social function. Children with HFASD (CA = 10.96 years) were able to identify ironic speech—they understood that speakers who make ironic criticisms hold a belief that is different from their words and that the speaker's intent is to

criticize—but as in Salter et al., (2008), children in Pexman et al. (2011) could not understand the broader social function of irony, such as the speaker's humorous intent. Thus, taking the findings altogether, ToM capabilities are not intact in school-age children with ASD, and difficulties in ToM are also accompanied by a deficit in broader social understanding, another sociocognitive deficit characterizing ASD, described next.

Social-Emotional Knowledge

In addition to being attuned to ongoing social interactions, children must also make interpretations of these interactions' social and emotional stimuli. Making sense of social and emotional behavior requires accurate processing of social information, a "bank of knowledge" about social norms and rules, and emotion recognition and understanding capabilities.

Crick and Dodge (1994) proposed a social information processing (SIP) model to explain the mental processes involved in understanding social interactions. This model includes six main stages: encoding social and emotional stimuli, interpreting the encoded stimuli, searching for possible social or emotional responses, evaluating them, and choosing the best social solution to be enacted. Few studies have examined the SIP model in school-age children with ASD. Meyer, Mundy, van Hecke, and Durocher (2006), for example, found that children with Asperger syndrome (CA = 10.1 years) made more encoding errors (added information that was not in the vignettes) and suggested more passive responses and fewer assertive responses in the solution elicitation stage than children with TYP (CA = 10.2 years). Similarly, differences in encoding also emerged in Embregts and van Nieuwenhuijzen (2009), where children with HFASD (CA = 12.54 years) focused more on negative information in the scenario than did children with TYP (CA = 10.54 years). Group differences also emerged on assertive responses at the evaluation stage, where children with HFASD evaluated assertive responses less positively and considered themselves less capable of acting assertively than did the TYP group. As in the Meyer et al. study, both groups understood that aggressive and submissive responses were inadequate.

The encoding stage is affected mostly by the child's attentional focus, based on the aforementioned difficulties in social attention; therefore, lower performance at the encoding stage is not surprising. The difficulties these children revealed on response elicitation and evaluation seem to be related to their lower social understanding capabilities. Indeed, children with ASD also show difficulties in judging the social appropriateness of videotaped social behaviors. Loveland, Pearson, Tunali-Kotoski, Ortegon, and Gibbs (2001) exposed children ($M = 9.12$) to four types of video scenarios: verbally appropriate (e.g., admiring a picture that someone offers to show), nonverbally appropriate (e.g., cooperating in making a sandwich), verbally inappropriate (e.g., when introduced, saying, "Is your father dead?"), and nonverbally inappropriate (e.g., hitting someone). The ASD group was less accurate at identifying examples of inappropriate social behavior than their peers with TYP, particularly for verbal inappropriateness. However, this group difference did not emerge when identifying appropriate behavior. Also, the ASD group had more difficulty providing explanations for the inappropriateness of verbal social behaviors than of nonverbal ones. Nah and Poon (2011) presented similar results for a series of socially inappropriate events in a comic strip (i.e., putting a leg on a table in public to see what was causing an itch). No group differences emerged for rating socially inappropriate behaviors, but children with HFASD (CA = 10.40 years) exhibited a specific difficulty in providing justifications for their responses. They provided inappropriate, bizarre, or inadequate ("I don't know") justifications instead of appropriate social justifications that would reflect social awareness. These studies attest to a core deficit in social understanding and knowledge, even in the face of some implicit awareness of behavioral norms. Emotional understanding poses another area of difficulty for children with HFASD, due to their limited social-emotional awareness and ToM capabilities.

Emotional Understanding

Various emotional understanding capabilities were examined in school-age children with ASD, including the ability to tell about and understand one's own personal emotional experience (e.g., Bauminger, 2004; Bauminger & Kasari, 2000; Losh & Capps, 2006; Rieffe, Terwogt, & Kotronopoulou, 2007); the ability to identify and recognize emotions in others and in social situations (e.g., Golan, Baron-Cohen, & Golan, 2008; Heerey, Keltner, & Capps, 2003); and the ability to demonstrate higher order emotional knowledge such as the understanding of the multidimensionality of the emotional experience by acknowledging mixed and hidden emotions as well as by suggesting coping strategies for emotional regulation (e.g., Barbaro & Dissanayake, 2007; Bauminger, 2004; Begeer, Terwogt, Rieffe, Stegge, & Koot, 2007; Dennis, Lockyer, & Lazenby, 2000; Jaedicke, Storoschuk, & Lord, 1994; Rieffe et al., 2007; Rieffe, Terwogt, & Stockmann, 2000).

Access to *one's own* emotional experience is closely linked with children's ability for self-introspection and for recalling events pertaining to the self—two capabilities considered lacking in ASD (e.g., Losh & Capps, 2006; see also expansion on this issue in Chapter 14 of this volume). Children with ASD (CA = 10.3 years) demonstrate deficits in recalling personal incidents of negative basic emotions like sadness, fear, or anger (Rieffe et al., 2007). A specific difficulty emerged in Losh and Capps (2006) in the ability of children with ASD (CA = 7–13 years, $M = 11.1$) to provide personal narration of complex emotions, which was most pronounced for self-conscious social emotions like pride, embarrassment, and guilt that require expression of awareness or concern for others' evaluations (versus complex nonsocial emotions like curiosity or surprise and versus simple emotions like disgust). On the whole, when asked to give an example of a time when they experienced a complex emotion like pride, these children provided examples of basic emotions such as receiving a video game, which likely illustrates joy or pleasure. Several other studies documented children's difficulty in providing examples or explanations for social emotions that are directly linked with interpersonal relations, such as loneliness and jealousy (e.g., Bauminger, 2004; Bauminger & Kasari, 2000). Compared to children with TYP, children with ASD less frequently reported both affective loneliness, which reflects a desire for or absence of close intimate relationships (children with HFASD, CA = 10.74 years; Bauminger & Kasari, 2000), and affective jealousy as assessed by ratings like "When a kid from my class is going to play with another kid from class, and not with me, I feel sad" (children with ASD, CA = 11.14 years; Bauminger, 2004). To sum up, personal narration of emotional accounts are not intact in school-age children with ASD, and specific difficulties emerge for socially complex emotions, for linking emotions and interpersonal relations, and also for basic negative emotions.

The majority of research on emotion recognition or understanding *in others* did not specifically focus on school-age children with ASD, but those studies with such a focus portrayed difficulties, mainly in children's understanding of complex self-conscious emotions. For example, using color photos of a male actor expressing nine different emotions, Heerey et al. (2003) asked children to identify non-self-conscious emotions (anger, contempt, disgust, happiness, fear, sadness, and surprise) and self-conscious emotions (embarrassment and shame). Children with TYP (CA = 10.51 years) outperformed children with ASD (CA = 10.70 years) only with regard to the self-conscious emotions (significantly for embarrassment and nearing significance for shame). Interestingly, group differences were no longer significant after controlling for ToM capabilities, which stresses their importance for understanding complex emotions. In addition, Golan et al. (2008) found that children with HFASD (CA = 8–12 years) showed difficulty compared to their peers with TYP in recognizing complex emotions (guilt, loneliness) and mental states (bothered, friendly) in social contexts, including facial expressions, body language, actions, as well as auditory input (prosody, verbal, content). Altogether, for school-age children with ASD, identification of

emotions is presumably more difficult for complex self-conscious affects than for basic ones and for emotions expressed within social contexts rather than those assessed with simulated materials.

Studies that examined *higher-order emotion understanding capabilities* in school-age children with ASD yielded interesting findings. First, these children showed a more unidimensional than multidimensional perception of emotions (e.g., Rieffe et al., 2007). When asked about stories of social interaction entailing several concurrent emotions, children with ASD (CA = 10.2 years) detected fewer emotions than their age-mates with TYP and had difficulty recognizing the simultaneous presence of two negative emotions (anger, sadness). Also, children with ASD reveal less sophisticated understanding of the source of emotional experiences, with problems in acknowledging the influence of mood on emotions (e.g., Begeer et al., 2007) and in providing explanations for the causes of simple (happy, sad, afraid, angry) emotions (Jaedicke et al., 1994).

Second, their understanding of hidden emotions may be impaired. Dennis et al. (2000) found that children with ASD (CA = 9.6 years) had difficulties in identifying deceptive emotions—which require consideration of protagonists' hidden beliefs (e.g., hiding tummyache from mother)—as well as in explaining the reasons for the deception (i.e., because the child wants to go to the playground). Both the identification of the deceptive emotions and their explanation necessitate awareness of protagonists' mental states (e.g., beliefs). However, Barbaro and Dissanayake (2007) presented conflicting results using a different methodology where children only had to name deceptive emotions but did not have to justify the protagonist's emotions. In Barbaro and Dissanayake (2007), children (CA = 8.01 years) were told that a puppet really feels X but does not want anyone to know how he feels, so he hides his emotion. They were asked to say how the puppet really feels; how he tries to look on his face (deceptive emotions); and how other story characters in the story thought he felt (understanding mental states). After controlling for VMA, there were no group differences (HFASD/TYP).

A possible integration of these two studies taken together, would suggest that the children with ASD showed less sophistication or maturity in understanding the rules for social and emotional displays, than do TYPs.

Overall, difficulties in emotional understanding in school-age children with ASD encompass various capabilities, including identifying one's own emotional experience (e.g., complex self-conscious social emotions and negative emotions); identifying emotions in others (e.g., self-conscious emotions and emotions in social interactions); and showing a less sophisticated and unidirectional perspective of emotions. These capabilities are all part of the aforementioned broader sociocognitive deficit in social understanding and ToM. Social attention, ToM, and social-emotional understanding, all impaired in ASD, are necessary to form adequate social interactions and to develop mature social relationships, and doing so without a full set of social-cognitive tools poses a real challenge for school-age children with ASD.

Social Interactions and Relationships

The second major aspect of social functioning is the ability to interact efficiently with peers and adults as well as to develop ongoing social relationships with adults and peers (e.g., attachment to a caregiver, friendship with peers). This section will describe the prevalence and nature of social interactive skills in school-age children with ASD, including play, conversation, and recreational capabilities, as well as children's friendship experiences and relationships within the family.

Prevalence of Social Interactions

Specific failure to develop developmentally appropriate peer relationships is considered a diagnostic characteristic of ASD by the new *Diagnostic and Statistical Manual of Mental Disorders*, fifth edition (*DSM-5*; American Psychiatric Association [APA], 2013). Indeed, observational studies (e.g., Bauminger, Shulman, & Agam, 2003; Hauck, Fein, Waterhouse, & Feinstein, 1995; Jackson et al. 2003; Kasari, Locke, Gulsrud, & Rotheram-Fuller,

2011; Pan, 2009) as well as research that implemented social network paradigms and sociometric evaluations (e.g., Chamberlain, Kasari, & Rotheram-Fuller, 2007; Kasari et al., 2011; Rotheram-Fuller, Kasari, Chamberlain, & Locke, 2010) all demonstrated low rates of naturally occurring social involvement in daily peer interactions for school-age children with ASD.

To pinpoint the effect of autism symptomology beyond the effect of low cognitive functioning (LFA), two studies compared social interactions in children with LFA and children with intellectual disability (ID) during two naturalistic school situations: lunchtime and free play during recess. Hauck et al. (1995), who focused on peer initiations, found that children with ASD (CA = 9.58 years) initiated bids of social interaction to their peers one third as often as children with ID (CA = 9.16 years). Likewise, in Jackson et al. (2003), children with ASD produced fewer positive responses, more "no responses" to peers, and less engagement in sustained play than children with ID; however, rates of simple conversation were similar between the groups. Interestingly, children with ASD showed more intact interactions with adults than with peers, producing more positive initiations (Huack et al.) and responses (Jackson et al.) toward adults than peers. For the same social settings (lunch time and free play during recess), a slightly higher frequency of naturalistic social interactions with peers was observed in Bauminger et al. (2003) for school-age children with HFASD (CA = 11 years); they spent half the time as their matched counterparts with TYP in social interaction. Similarly, Macintosh and Dissanayake (2006) found that children with HFASD and Asperger (CA = 8 years) were less able than TYP to participate in ongoing schoolyard social exchanges, particularly when interactions included three or more partners.

Studies that implemented social network paradigms and/or sociometric evaluations, mainly by collecting reports from the target child and his or her peers in inclusive settings, provide support for the observational data. Children with ASD were nominated as peripheral to social relationships with peers (i.e., having only tenuous connections to one or two peers) or as secondary (i.e., involved in the classroom social network, but not the most nominated students in the class), and they received fewer reciprocal friendship nominations (e.g., Chamberlain et al., 2007; Kasari et al., 2011; Rotheram-Fuller et al., 2010). Importantly, according to Kasari et al. (2011), only a minority of children was found to be socially isolated with no connections at all (13%). Interestingly, another minority was found to be nuclear—most frequently nominated by peers (8%). To sum up, sociometric evaluations support observational findings indicating that school-age children with ASD tend to become involved in peer interactions, but to a much lesser degree and centrality compared to children with TYP. Low frequency may result from low quality of social interaction, as described in the following.

Nature of Social Interaction

Three types of spontaneous social initiations were examined in school-age children with LFA (Hauck et al., 1995): (1) positive—social initiations that enable positive-adaptive social interaction (i.e., give affection; give information; greet; initiate play; initiate joint attention; seek aid/information verbally and nonverbally); (2) low-level behaviors that may hold hidden communicative intent without the ability to transform them into active interaction (i.e., imitation; echolalia; looking; moving into proximity; neutral physical contact; ritualized interaction); and (3) negative—behaviors that result in nonadaptive and often aggressive interactions (i.e., aggression, provocation). Children's verbal and nonverbal attention-seeking behaviors as well as avoidant behaviors (e.g., moving out of proximity) were also examined. Children with LFA (like their peers with ID), showed a profile of social initiations including mostly positive and low-level interactions and very infrequent attention-seeking, negative, and avoidant behaviors. Although many interactions for both groups were positive, the LFA group engaged in more ritualized behaviors and the ID group engaged in more playful initiations. Findings for specific behaviors revealed that children with LFA made fewer play initiations toward

peers and fewer imitations of peers' play compared to children with ID.

Bauminger et al. (2003) used a modified version of Hauck et al.'s (1995) observational scale to examine spontaneous social interaction in school-age children with HFASD versus age-mates with TYP. The modified scale included not only initiations but also responses in the three overall categories (positive, low-level, and negative), and more complex social behaviors were added. Behaviors added to the positive category included eye contact combined with a smile, social communicative behaviors ("Let's play"), sharing experiences and objects, expressed affection, talk that reflected an interest in another, requests, and providing help. In the low-level category, functional communication was added to tap intentions to fulfill one's own need with no clear social intention. Overall findings yielded an identical global profile of initiations and responses for the two groups' social interactions (HFASD/TYP), even if behaviors appeared at a lower frequency in HFASD. That is, most social behaviors were positive, followed by low-level, and to a much lesser extent the rarely observed negative behaviors. Group differences appeared only for positive and low-level interactions: The HFASD group showed a significantly lower frequency of all positive-adaptive behaviors except eye contact (which was at a similar frequency between groups). However, significantly more instances of low-level, merely functional communication appeared in the HFASD group than in the TYP group.

A deeper look at the specific behavioral profile for each group revealed that children with HFASD mainly showed passive low-level social behaviors such as eye contact (not combined with a smile) and close proximity, whereas children with TYP used a broader repertoire of more active and communicative behaviors such as eye contact and smile, affection, object sharing, experience sharing, social communication, talk that reflects interest in another, and helping. Another recent study on school-age children with ASD (CA = 7.9 years) versus those with TYP (Forde, Holloway, Healy, & Brosnan, 2011) revealed less spontaneous communication (i.e., not prompted by another peer/adult) and more elicited social communication (i.e., prompted by another) during academic lessons (e.g., reading, mathematics, and drama) and during classroom free-play activities (e.g., watching DVDs, playing video games).

Hence, based on these studies, social interactions in children with ASD appear to occur not only less frequently but also differently in quality compared to children with TYP or ID. Particular attention should be paid to the low-level interaction behavioral category, for two reasons: (1) Children with ASD who spontaneously produce this type of behavior (i.e., close proximity) fairly often might think that they initiated an interaction that was not reciprocated by peers and may misjudge it as rejection. (2) Some of these behaviors are socially inappropriate (e.g., echolalia, rituals), denoting an active-but-odd interaction style (Wing & Gould, 1979) where children actively seek interactions with others but in an unusual way that may lead to unproductive spontaneous interactions with peers.

Collaboration, Play, and Conversation

ASD researchers have examined the ability to coordinate and co-regulate actions with a peer in a collaborative task (Stoit et al., 2011) as well as children's play and conversational behaviors (e.g., Capps, Kehres, & Sigman, 1998; Kasari et al., 2011; Macintosh & Dissanayake, 2006; Nadig, Lee, Singh, Bosshart, & Ozonoff, 2010). Stoit et al., for example, found that joint engagement and co-regulation of actions with a peer is limited in children with ASD (CA = 11.6 years) compared to children with TYP; when solving a computerized balancing task together with another child that required using one hand each to balance a ball on a bar, they revealed impairments in predicting the partner's response; in synchronizing their response to the partner's initiation (causing the ball to drop quickly after movement onset), and they did not delay the timing of their lift initiation to accommodate the partner.

Play and conversational behaviors—considered key components of peer interaction—are also not intact in school-age children with ASD. Macintosh and Dissanayake's (2006) study of schoolyard

play behavior found that children with HFASD showed fewer episodes of simple play (play or activity with a common focus or goal but with no structure or rules) than children with TYP, although no group differences appeared in the frequency of complementary play (involving adoption of role/pretend character including games with clear rules or structure). This finding highlights a specific difficulty in unstructured activities, where children must operate social knowledge and creativity to create shared actions and play with peers. Difficulty in more advanced joint social play behaviors was also demonstrated in Kasari et al.'s (2011) observation of school playground behavior in children with ASD from first through fifth grades (CA = 6–11 years). Joint engaged actions with peers were of low frequency (18.6%), and another 20% of children's time was spent playing in structured games with rules. A significant amount of time was spent in solitary/unengaged activity (33.4%) or in low-level noninteractive parallel games (aware and unaware) and mere looking at other children's play activities (28%).

Inadequate conversational skills were found in school-age children with ASD (CA = 11.9 years) versus children with development delay (DD; CA = 9.4 years) matched on MA (8.9 and 7.4 years, respectively) during snack time in a semistructured conversation with a familiar adult (Capps et al., 1998). Children with ASD more often failed to respond to questions, repeated prior comments and questions verbatim, and provided more bizarre or idiosyncratic comments than the DD group. They also less often extended an ongoing topic of conversation by offering new relevant information; they produced fewer narratives of personal experience; and their narratives as a whole tended to be minimalistic and focused on the immediate physical environment, whereas the narratives of the DD group were always relevant to ongoing dialogue and included meaningful personal events. The more simplistic conversational behaviors like one-word utterances and yes/no replies did not differ between groups. Interestingly, only one nonverbal behavior during conversation differed between groups: Children with ASD nodded less than DD while listening, whereas smile, appropriate affect, and use of gesture were similar between groups.

In a recent study, Nadig et al. (2010) showed that when children with HFASD (CA = 11 years) talked about their own peculiar areas of interest with an adult, the discourse was less reciprocal, including fewer contingent utterances and more monologue-style speech than the talk of age-mates with TYP (CA = 10.10 years). Difficulties also emerged on ending a conversation appropriately; children with HFASD more frequently walked away from a conversation without coherently ending it by making a friendly closure that accounted for the other person's perspective (e.g., Rubin & Lennon, 2004). In sum, children with ASD experience difficulties in navigating the communication demands of social conversation, and these difficulties may be partly explained by their sociocognitive deficits in social knowledge and ToM (e.g., Capps et al., 1998).

Recreational and Leisure Activities

Recreational activities are important for peer interaction as well as for children's well-being (e.g., Potvin, Snider, Prelock, Kehayia, & Wood-Dauphinee, 2012). Although not extensively examined in school-age children with ASD, two recent studies described these behaviors in school-age children with LFA (CA = 9.99 years; Solish, Perry, & Minnes, 2010) and with HFASD (CA = 9.25 years; Potvin et al., 2012). Parent reports in Solish et al. included three subscales: social, recreational, and leisure activities. Children with LFA were reported by parents as participating in significantly fewer social and recreational activities but showing a similar frequency of leisure activities compared to peers with TYP. These leisure activities were mostly home based as well as more passive and solitary activities like watching TV, reading, playing computer and video games, using the Internet, and going for walks.

More specifically, the profile of social activities for the LFA group showed a high frequency of going to the park and out to meals (89.2% and 77.3%, respectively); a medium frequency of birthday parties and movies (50.8% each), going to the

mall (46.2%), and talking on the phone (44.6%); and a low frequency of playing at a friend's house (26.2%), having friends over (23.3%), sleepovers (15.4%), and chatting on the computer (13.8%). Thus, most of the low-frequency social activities involved peer interaction. Overall, recreational activities appeared at low frequencies for the children with LFA; the most frequent of these activities were swimming lessons (27.7%), horseback riding (15.4%), music, and soccer (12.3% each). Other activities were reported at very low frequencies: hockey, baseball, skating, and skiing lessons were all below 10%, and other team sports, gymnastics, karate, dancing, and art lessons were all reported below 5%.

The partner for the various activities differed between the groups. Children with LFA participated in fewer social and recreational activities with peer partners than children with TYP and in fewer recreational activities with peer partners than children with ID. Moreover, children with ASD participated in more social activities with parents than did children with TYP. Altogether, children with ASD were the least involved in activities with peers.

Similarly to Solish et al.'s (2010) parent reports for children with LFA, Potvin et al.'s (2012) study of self-reports in HFASD indicated that recreational activities more frequently occurred close to home and either included solitary activities or family members, which differed from the activities of peers with TYP. Diversity of activity was also significantly higher in the TYP group, especially for physical activities (e.g., bicycling, team and nonteam sports, track and field, water sports). Yet, interestingly, no significant group differences emerged overall for the social domain (e.g., going to parties and movies, hanging out, talking on the phone) or for expressed enjoyment from and preference for being involved in recreational activities. Also, surprisingly, pretend play was higher in frequency for the HFASD group than the TYP group. As expected, playing computer or video games was the most frequent activity reported for all of the participants with HFASD. The surprising results for social activities and pretend play may be explained by the methodology—reported desired activities rather than actual ones—and another study comparing parental and self-reports may shed light on these discrepancies. However, this may also coincide with other findings reported here showing that ASD and more specifically HFASD do not relinquish social activities but rather lack sufficient knowledge for effective participation.

Friendship

In contrast to mere peer interaction, friendship poses higher requirements from children to co-regulate another person's perspectives and behaviors in order to develop an ongoing, durable, and stable set of reciprocal interactions (lasting a minimum of 6 months) that result in intimate and close bonding. Friendship formation is an enormous challenge for children with ASD due to their difficulties in intersubjectivity and ToM (e.g., Baron-Cohen, 2000; Rogers & Bennetto, 2001). Indeed, school-age children have significantly fewer reciprocal friendships compared to children with TYP (e.g., Chamberlain et al., 2007; Kasari et al., 2011; Rotheram-Fuller et al., 2010), children with ID (e.g., Solish et al., 2010), and children with other special education needs (e.g., Rowley et al., 2012). In Solish et al. (2010), 53.3% of children with ASD had no friend versus only 21.4% of children with ID and only 1.2% of children with TYP. Yet, even if to a lesser extent, friendship does exist in some school-age children with ASD, eliciting questions about its quality. Not many studies have explored quality of friendship in school-age ASD, but the few that did so yielded both similarities and differences compared with friendships in TYP. Self-reports on friendship quality found that friendships in ASD were not seen as more conflictual than those of their age-mates with TYP, but group differences favoring the TYP group did emerge on intimacy, help, companionship, and affective closeness (e.g., Bauminger, Solomon, Aviezer, Heung, Gazit et al., 2008; Chamberlain et al., 2007; Kasari et al., 2011).

Observational studies on friendship in school-age with ASD are scarce. A binational study that Bauminger et al. (2008) executed from Israel along with Rogers and Solomon from the United States extensively explored the quality of friendship by comparing children's interactions with their friends in three semistructured social situations—construction, drawing, and free play during break—in HFASD versus TYP groups (CA = 9.66 and 10.16 years, respectively; range: 8–12 years). Overall, TYP dyads outperformed HFASD dyads in the behavioral manifestations of friendship and in the dyadic qualities of interaction, as follows: The children with HFASD showed poorer cooperative skills, less positive affect, and less skillful conversational skills, as well as a more rigid conversation style. With regard to play complexity, the children with HFASD exhibited a higher frequency of mere parallel play and a lower frequency of constructive play. The qualities of the dyadic interactions containing a child with HFASD were less socially oriented, cohesive, harmonious, and responsive, as well as less enjoyable and close. All these differences support clinical as well as theoretical perspectives on friendship as a challenging social relationship for the child with HFASD.

However, interesting similarities also emerged between the HFASD and TYP friendship dyads on several complex social behaviors such as the incidence of prosocial behaviors, sharing, and eye contact with a smile, possibly suggesting that friendship may nonetheless offer an advantageous framework for enhancing social skills among children with HFASD. Indeed, in a recent study on preschoolers with HFASD conducted in my laboratory (Bauminger & Agam Ben Artzi, 2012), interactions with a friend demonstrated better qualities compared to interactions with a nonfriend (e.g., positive affect, complex forms of social and collaborative pretend play, shared fun, and reciprocity), but this was not yet examined for school-age children.

Interestingly, for those school-age children with HFASD who form friendships, the friendships are relatively long lasting, ranging from about 6 months to 4 years, and they comprise mainly same-age, same-sex pairs (e.g., Bauminger, Solomon, Aviezer, Heung, Gazit et al., 2008; Kasari et al., 2011). Children with HFASD may form "mixed" friendships with peers who have TYP and may also form "nonmixed" friendships with peers who have a disability (most likely HFASD), but quality was shown to differ between these two friendship types (e.g., Bauminger, Solomon, Aviezer, Heung, Brown et al., 2008). Nonmixed dyads showed the lowest friendship quality (versus mixed and TYP-only friendships), as manifested in their highest frequency of parallel play and lowest frequency of engagement in goal-directed activity, sharing, and positive affect. Also, nonmixed dyads were less responsive and cohesive, exhibited a lower positive social orientation, and showed less complex levels of play. Nevertheless, despite the lower friendship quality observed for nonmixed dyads when interacting with a friend, the nonmixed friendships appeared more symmetric in the degree to which each partner assumed dominant or subordinate roles, such as leader and follower, whereas children with HFASD in mixed friendships had fewer leadership opportunities. Thus, even if it seems that a friend with TYP is important for the development of more complex social behaviors, a friend with ASD may be equally important for self-perception. An extensive review on friendship is beyond the scope of this chapter; interested readers can refer to Bauminger-Zviely (2013).

Family Relationships

Parent–child relationships have been extensively examined for younger children with ASD, but not so for older. To the best of my knowledge, only one study has examined security of attachment in school-age children with ASD. Using self-reports, Bauminger, Solomon, and Rogers (2010b) found that half of the children with HFASD (54.4%; CA = 8–12 years) perceived themselves as securely attached to their mother, thereby corroborating data from younger children with ASD (e.g., Rutgers, Bakermans-Kranenburg, van IJzendoorn, & van Berckelaer-Onnes, 2004). Despite the fact that 71% of the TYP group reported secure attachment to the mother, the two groups did not significantly differ in proportion of secure attachments; however, they did differ on the quality of parent–child relationships: Children with HFASD perceived their relationships with their mothers as less open to communication and less trustful compared to the TYP group. Thus, as for the younger children, it seems that for mid-childhood school-age children too, security of attachment does not provide the complete narrative of the relationships with caregivers.

One important aspect that may affect child–parent quality of relations is parental stress (especially mothers'), which has been shown to be particularly high in parents of children with ASD, compared to parents of children with TYP or with other disabilities like Down syndrome, cerebral palsy, or ID (e.g., see review in Hayes & Watson, 2012). A recent study showed that autism severity (per the ADOS; Lord et al., 2000) adversely affected the overall quality of parent–child relationships (CA = 7.4 years) during semistructured play interactions, and specifically contributed to the dimensions of coordination, communication, emotional expression, responsivity, and mood, resulting in nonsatisfactory parent–child interactions (e.g., Beurkens, Hobson, & Hobson, 2012). In another study (Bauminger, Solomon, & Rogers, 2010a), parental stress was related to the severity of both internalizing and externalizing behaviors in children with HFASD (CA = 9.66 years).

Following attachment theory, parents' internal working models of attachment may be transmitted to their child and may affect the child's capacity for social relationships. Recent research showed this for school-age children (CA = 4–16 years, most between 6 to 13 years) with ASD (Seskin et al., 2010). Parents who themselves were securely attached had children with more developed social skills and a greater capacity to engage in developmentally appropriate social interactions, such as initiating and responding in two-way presymbolic gestural communication; organizing two-way social problem-solving communication; and engaging in imaginative thinking, symbolic play, and verbal communication. Altogether, studies that explored child–parent quality of relationships for school-age children are quite limited, and future studies would do well to untangle these relationships for this age group, due to their importance for children's development and well-being. Studies have accentuated the importance of the families' emotional and social support networks as well as participation in parental support groups as factors promoting positive psychological adjustment in the parents of children with ASD (e.g., Benson, 2012; Clifford & Minnes, 2012). This, in turn, may render positive effects on the quality of child–parent relationships.

Siblings

The effect of siblings with TYP on the proband with ASD has not been extensively examined, especially for the school years. Some evidence has shown the important contribution of siblings with TYP to probands' socialization capabilities (per the VABS; Sparrow et al., 1984), with a more robust effect for younger siblings than for older siblings (e.g., Brewton, Nowell, Lasala, & Goin-Kochel, 2012). In a like manner, siblings with TYP were found to provide effective opportunities for probands to experience and acquire various interactive and play skills. Two studies that included spontaneous observations of the proband–sibling interaction in routine social activities at home (Knott, Lewis, & Williams, 1995, 2007) highlighted that, even if to a lower extent compared to children with Down syndrome, probands with ASD engaged in a wide range of interactive play behaviors with their siblings, ranging from simple rough and tumble to sophisticated play with a toy theater, and they were actively involved in the interaction for 66% of the time spent together (Knott et al., 1995), which significantly surpasses the percentage of time spent in social interactions with peers, as described earlier. These interactive behaviors of the proband continued to grow over a 1-year period, but mainly due to greater initiations on the part of the siblings with TYP (Knott et al., 2007), indicating that these siblings with TYP may play an important role in scaffolding and supporting social interactive skills in probands with ASD, despite the probable asymmetry of the interactions. This asymmetry may evolve into an overprotective relationship that might also have a negative side. For example, in a recent study (O'Brien, Slaughter, & Peterson, 2011), having an older sibling was found to be disadvantageous for ToM development in probands

with ASD (CA = 3.67–12.67 years; M = 6.67), even after controlling for the effects of age, VMA, executive function, and ASD severity. This may be due to apparent overcompensation on the part of the older sibling with TYP for their younger proband with ASD during social interactions, and as such may hinder the latter's opportunities for sociocognitive growth. Further discussion of siblings' effects of the proband with ASD is beyond the focus of this chapter; see Chapter 40, this *Handbook*, Volume 2, for elaboration.

Internal and External Components That Contribute to Social Interaction

Contributors to social interaction include children's intrinsic characteristics on the one hand and children's social environment and significant social agents on the other hand. Among intrinsic components found to contribute to social interactions are children's IQ (e.g., above 50 versus below 50, in Stone & Caro-Martinez, 1990), children's adequate vocabulary and ability to use language functionally (e.g., Hauck et al., 1995), and children's speech level (e.g., Stone & Caro-Martinez, 1990). Language age was also found to contribute to conversational contingency and to the ability to provide new information in a conversation. Not surprisingly, lower severity of social impairment (e.g., on the VABS socialization measure; Hauck et al., 1995) was linked with greater social participation, and a higher ability to meet peers for play dates at home (according to parents' report) was linked with more active social participation of the children on the school playground (Frankel, Gorospe, Chang, & Sugar, 2011). Children's more restricted interests were inversely related to the ability to develop verbal exchanges during a conversation (Nadig et al., 2010).

Among the extrinsic components found to contribute to children's degree of participation in social interactions are the social situation's level of structure (e.g., recess versus social activities in physical education; Pan, 2009) and the type of social task (e.g., simple social play versus rule-governed games; Macintosh & Dissanayake, 2006), in favor of the more semistructured social situations and tasks. In terms of partner type, peers with TYP were found to evoke more complex social behaviors in children with ASD, but interactions with an ASD partner are more egalitarian (Bauminger et al., 2003). Thus, inclusive settings are important, but interactions with another child with a disability also hold significance in terms of children's sense of self-worth and ease in the interaction. Interestingly, the presence of a one-on-one aide during school recess resulted in less active involvement of the ASD child (Kasari et al., 2011). Thus, aides' roles during unstructured times should be carefully planned.

Summary of Social Interaction

All in all, school-age children are involved in a wide range of interactions with peers and adults along various social settings and tasks, albeit to a lesser degree and quality than their counterparts with TYP or ID. Their social interaction profile emphasizes the need for interventions in school (see Chapter 35, this *Handbook*, Volume 2), particularly during nonstructured social situations in school (i.e., recess). Such interventions may enable children with ASD to develop more efficient interactive behaviors with their peers and may reduce the high loneliness reported by these children relative to their counterparts with TYP (e.g., Bauminger & Kasari, 2000) as well as their heighted risk for being bullied and ridiculed by peers compared to the risk faced by children with TYP or with other special education needs (e.g., Rowley et al., 2012). Interestingly, Rowley et al. (2012) demonstrated that more socially able children with ASD (CA = 10–12 years) reported greater bullying and victimization than their less socially able counterparts. This may signify, in line with findings described earlier (Wing & Gould, 1979), that the more able children act actively but oddly in their peer interactions and therefore are more vulnerable to peer harassment. Indeed, a recent comparative intervention study for ASD in the schoolyard found that intervention using peer mediators with TYP was more efficient than intervention using adult mediators in terms of reducing isolation on the

playground (e.g., Kasari, Rotheram-Fuller, Locke, & Gulsrud, 2012), suggesting that more such models are greatly needed.

As seen throughout the section on social interaction, one reason for their inadequate social interactions lies in these children's inappropriate (odd), repetitive, and stereotypic interests and preoccupations, as described next.

Restricted, Repetitive Patterns of Behavior, Interests, or Activities

In the new *DSM-5* (APA, 2013), a pattern of restricted, repetitive behaviors (RRBs) is considered the second major deficit in ASD, after the sociocommunicative deficit. This is a broadband domain encompassing abnormal motor stereotypies and sensory difficulties, atypical areas of interest and activities, and insistence on sameness. RRBs are important to consider in ASD due to the fact that they interfere with many aspects of everyday functioning and interactions; thus, they may hinder effective learning from the environment as well as place considerable stress on family functioning (Bishop, Richler, Cain, & Lord, 2007). Indeed, RRBs are not specific to school-age children because they span all developmental and functioning levels, but a recent study (Richler, Huerta, Bishop, & Lord, 2010) presented developmental trajectories of RRBs that are relevant to school-age children (CA = 9 years). In line with other studies (e.g., Bishop, Richler, & Lord, 2006; Cuccaro et al., 2003), RRBs were factored out into two main subtypes: (1) repetitive sensorimotor (RSM) comprising hand or finger mannerisms, such as flicking or twisting fingers; complex body mannerisms, such as spinning in circles; unusual sensory interests, such as peering at objects from the side; and repetitive use of objects, such as lining up toys; and (2) insistence on sameness (IS) comprising difficulties with minor changes in routine, such as insisting on sitting in the same seat in the car; resistance to trivial changes in the environment; refusing to make any changes in room organization; and compulsion and rituals, such as insisting on turning right out of the driveway. The developmental trajectory for

RSM showed that children with a diagnosis of autism at age 2 years revealed more severe RSM behaviors at age 9 compared to children with milder PDD-NOS (pervasive developmental disorder not otherwise specified). Also, higher cognitive ability at age 2 was associated with milder RSM behaviors at age 9 and with greater improvement in these behaviors over time (between 2 to 9), even after controlling for diagnosis. Interestingly, an early communication/social deficit did not correlate with RSM. The developmental pattern differed for IS, in which social/communicative impairments at age 2 were positively associated with concurrent IS behaviors. Milder early impairments were associated with more severe later IS behaviors, but cognitive abilities did not correlate with IS.

In line with Richler and her colleagues' findings, Lam, Bodfish, and Piven (2008) identified the same two subclassifications (RSM and IS) in individuals with ASD between the ages of 20 months and 29 years (CA = 9.02 years), as well as third classification of "circumscribed interest" that included behaviors such as intense, focused hobbies, strong preoccupations with odd topics (such as sewer systems or garage doors), and unusually strong attachment to certain objects. Examination of each subclassification's correlations revealed that RSM was more prevalent in younger children with lower verbal IQ, greater social deficits, greater communication impairments (in verbal subjects), and more severe loss of language. Like in the studies by Richler's group, Lam et al. also found that IS was correlated with social and communication impairment. Interestingly, circumscribed interest was independent of subject characteristics. Also, in Bishop et al. (2006), younger children were more likely to engage in RSM, whereas older children were more likely to exhibit IS (CA = 15 months to 12 years, n = 830). Overall, Bishop et al. also found that RSM behaviors (classified as lower order behaviors including primitive brain processes; M. A. Turner, 1999) were more common in LFA, whereas IS behaviors (classified as high-order, cognitively mediated behaviors; M. A. Turner, 1999) were more common in HFASD, but that both types of behaviors (even if to a lower

extent) were noted across development in every age and IQ group. For example, lower order behaviors such as hand and finger mannerisms were present in 38% of the 6- to 12-year-olds with HFASD, and higher order behaviors like circumscribed interests were present in 27% of the lowest functioning 6- to 12-year-olds. In accordance with these findings, Lam et al. (2008) found that multiple forms of RRBs in an individual were related to more severe ASD social and communicative symptoms.

While relating only to low-order motor behaviors (e.g., rocking, finger posturing, repetitive vocalizations), Joosten, Bundy, and Einfeld (2012) touched upon a relatively neglected topic in RRBs, namely, the identification of underlying motivators for RRBs in children with ASD (CA = 9.7 years). Motivators were divided into intrinsic (i.e., enhanced sensation and decreased anxiety) and extrinsic (i.e., seeking attention, objects, or escape) and were observed and rated by parents and careers along three social settings: free time, transition, and engagement in a task. Transition periods evoked many RRBs in the children with extrinsic motivators; escape and intrinsic anxiety reduction were most strongly linked to this setting. Free time periods mostly elicited sensation seeking, as well as motivators like gaining attention or objects. This study showing that motivators for RRBs may differ based on the situation may hold important implications for intervention planning, emphasizing the possible role of setting in mitigating or increasing RRBs.

Sensory Processing and Motor Dysfunction

As was previously described, sensory processing abnormalities are important aspects of RRBs and are highly prevalent in ASD (e.g., 90% of ages 2.8–11.6 years; Leekam, Nieto, Libby, Wing, & Gould, 2007). Indeed, sensory processing dysfunction, defined as "hyper- or hypo-reactivity to sensory input or unusual interest in sensory aspects of environment," are included as a diagnostic criterion under the broadband domain of RRBs in the new *DSM-5* (APA, 2013).

Sensory abnormalities offer important explanations for social functioning in ASD, for example, atypical sensory processing significantly correlated with social impairment based on the Social Responsiveness Scale (SRS; Constantino & Gruber, 2005) in both children with TYP and with HFASD (Hilton et al., 2012). More specifically, abnormal responses to multisensory, touch, and oral sensory/olfactory stimuli were identified as possible predictors of social severity in ASD (CA = 6–10 years, M = 8.89; Hilton et al., 2012). Sensory profile was also linked with maladaptive functioning measured using the VABS; specifically, atypical taste/smell sensitivity, auditory filtering, and movement sensitivity were associated with less maladaptive behavior in children with ASD (CA = 2.75–9.58 years; M = 7.8; Lane, Young, Baker, & Angley, 2010). Atypical auditory responsiveness—including filtering difficulties, sensory underresponsiveness, and sensory seeking—were associated with academic underachievement; in addition, tactile sensitivity was associated with attention difficulties and hyperactivity. Also, reduced auditory filtering was related with inattention to cognitive tasks in children with HFASD (CA = 6–10 years; Ashburner, Ziviani, & Rodger, 2008). These findings hold significance for class organization and teaching strategies, supporting the importance of visual modalities and the consideration of reducing noise distractions and unpredictable tactile input during academic lessons.

According to a recent meta-analytic study (Ben-Sasson et al., 2009), differences between ASD and TYP were greater for underresponsivity (e.g., unawareness or slow response to sensory input, such as a tendency to walk into things), followed by overresponsivity (e.g., exaggerated, rapid onset and/or prolonged reactions to sensory stimulation, such as distress from loud noises), followed by sensory seeking (e.g., craving of and interest in sensory experiences that are prolonged or intense, such as engaging in rhythmical movements). However, differently from the overall sensory processing abnormality score and from the other two modalities (i.e., overresponsivity and seeking), underresponsivity did not yield a clear developmental trajectory. Overall sensory processing abnormalities, overresponsivity, and sensory seeking each showed an increase in frequency from infancy up to age 6–9 years and then a decrease (e.g., Ben-Sasson et al., 2009), thus the highest increase in frequency was reported for school-age children age 6–9 years (versus infancy—CA = 0.0–3.4; preschool—CA = 3.5–6.4; and adolescents—CA = 9.5+). It seems that school-age children are at risk for experiencing heightened sensory difficulties compared to the other age periods. This may accentuates the special extrinsic demands with which children with ASD must cope when entering the school system, but on the other hand it may also reflect an intrinsic increase in these symptoms in the early school years. Whether this finding reflects innate growth or environmentally based growth in symptomatology currently remains unknown; however, school-age children's special sensitivity in this domain holds important implication for interventionists. Based on another finding of Ben-Sasson et al. (2009) showing greater sensory abnormalities in children with more severe ASD, it seems that school-age children with LFA are at the greatest risk for vulnerability to sensory difficulties.

Sensory-Motor and More General Motor Dysfunctions

Sensory-motor and in ASD have gained increasing attention in recent research due to these dysfunctions' potential contribution to these children's sociocommunicative deficit. These motor impairments may limit children's ability to play in the schoolyard with peers or even to develop speech and thus communicate with other children. Researchers have reported a range of motor dysfunctions in ASD. For example, a recent meta-analysis of 41 studies explored substantial deficits in motor coordination (e.g., movement preparation or planning) including arm movement, gait, and postural stability across ages (from toddlerhood up to young adulthood) in ASD versus TYP, pinpointing a slight reduction in symptoms along development (Fournier, Hass, Naik, Lodha, & Cauraugh, 2010).

Another study (Ming, Brimacombe, & Wagner, 2007) based on retrospective clinical reviews presented a high prevalence of other aspects of motor dysfunction in a large cohort of children with ASD spanning a wide age range (n = 154;

CA = 2–18 years). Specifically, 51% of the sample exhibited hypotonia (reduced resistance during passive movement in the limbs); 34% exhibited oral and muscle motor apraxia (impairment of the ability to execute skilled movements and gestures, despite having the desire and the physical ability to perform them, such as blowing a bubble or licking lips with tongue in the oral apraxia and difficulties in holding a pen in the hand apraxia); only 19% exhibited toe-walking (present, whether intermittent or persistent, sometime during the child's life for at least 6 months); and only 9% exhibited delayed gross-motor millstones (such as independent walking, walking up steps, and jumping up). Interestingly, improvement was observed for all domains with age: Younger children with ASD (CA = 2–6 years) showed a higher frequency of motor impairments than older children (CA = 7–18 years), but age differences were significant only for hypotonia (63% versus 38%, respectively) and neared significance for apraxia (41% versus 27%). Thus, school-age children may be at reduced risk versus young children for experiencing the aforementioned motor impairments, but not free of them. One difficulty in the Ming et al. study is the lack of normative comparisons for each of these motor domains, making it difficult to estimate their exact risk rate for the population of ASD.

Other studies including school-age children with ASD demonstrated motor impairments in various gross- and fine-motor capabilities compared to children with TYP. Impairment in gross-motor skills included difficulties with balance and impaired gait, slower speed and more dysrhythmia with timed movements of hands and feet, greater overflow during performance of timed movements and stressed gait maneuvers (Jansiewicz et al., 2006) and reduced overall coordinated locomotor skills (Staples & Reid, 2010), more specifically difficulties in hopping and galloping (Pan, Tsai, & Chu, 2009). Impairment in fine-motor skills included, for example, poor object-control skills such as ball catching, rolling, batting, and dribbling (Pan et al., 2009; Staples & Reid, 2010). Lastly, a recent study suggested a sensorimotor deficit in children with Asperger (CA = 10.72 years), demonstrating

a link between motor dysfunction (movement performance like bilateral motor coordination) and sensory integration deficit in proprioceptive and vestibular processing, which are considered important for motor performance and for the development of "body schema"—the internalized model of the body in action (Siaperas et al., 2012).

Taking these findings altogether, the difficulties demonstrated by school-age children with ASD in all three domains—RRBs, sensory processing, and motor functioning—appear to affect their ability to form adequate and efficient peer interactions and may also influence these children's academic skills, as seen next.

COGNITIVE-ACADEMIC FUNCTIONING

Cognitive-academic difficulties are not considered a diagnostic criterion of ASD; however, difficulties in this arena are extensive and hold specific implications for understanding children's performance in school, as described here (see also comprehensive review in Bauminger-Zviely & Kimhi, 2013a).

Executive Function (EF)

The higher-order cognitive functions that aid in developing goal-directed behaviors—EF—may provide explanations for how children with ASD process information (e.g., Hill, 2004). EF difficulties have been well documented in children with ASD, specifically in the areas of cognitive planning and flexibility (e.g., see reviews in Hill, 2004, and in Van Eylen et al., 2011, for children and adolescents). Other EF subdomains such as working memory, generativity of novel ideas, and verbal fluency have yielded mixed results for school-age children, and response inhibition was found to be relatively intact (e.g., Ozonoff & Strayer, 2001; Robinson, Goddard, Dritschel, Wisley, & Howlin, 2009; Semrud-Clikeman, Walkowiak, Wilkinson, & Butcher, 2010; Vertè, Geurts, Roeyers, Oosterlaan, & Sergeant, 2006). In children with TYP, EF was found to be linked with various social abilities (e.g. self-regulation, ToM, and social cognition;

see review in Best, Miller, & Jones, 2009) and with various academic capabilities (e.g., math and reading; Best, Miller, & Naglieri, 2011). Also, EF abilities were linked with diverse areas of functioning in school-age children with ASD. For example, EF-behavior regulation (a composite score of inhibition, attention shifting, and emotional control) was linked with total RRBs, self-injury, compulsion, and rituals/sameness. Yet, EF-metacognition (e.g., working memory, planning, monitoring) did not correlate with RRBs (Boyd, McBee, Holtzclaw, Baranek, & Bodfish, 2009). However, the EF-metacognition index was found to predict the VABS adaptive composite score (Sparrow et al., 1984) as well its socialization and communication subdomains, stressing the importance of EF for general sociocommunicative functioning in ASD (e.g., Gilotty, Kenworthy, Sirian, Black, & Wagner, 2002). Lastly, EF was found to positively link with level of participation in school activities (e.g., Zingerevich & LaVesser, 2009). Taken altogether, EF capabilities seem to greatly contribute to various functional domains in school-age children with ASD.

Cognitive Characteristics

As stated previously, recent reports documented that at about 40%–50% of school-age children have co-occurring intellectual deficits (e.g., Charman et al., 2010; Johnson & Myers, 2007). The profile of children with ASD on various intelligence tests has often demonstrated a gap between performance IQ (PIQ) and verbal IQ (VIQ), favoring PIQ, as reflected, for example (e.g., Mayes & Calhoun, 2003), in poor verbal abilities (Comprehension and Vocabulary subtests) versus good visuo-spatial skills (Block Design substests) on the Wechsler Intelligence Scale for Children (WISC) for school ages (Wechsler, 1974). However, it should be noted that other researchers found little PIQ–VIQ discrepancy (e.g., Charman et al., 2010), and in many cases this PIQ–VIQ gap was shown to diminish with age (e.g., Joseph, Tager-Flusberg, & Lord, 2002) and was found to be related with improvement in language ability, especially among

children with HFASD (Sigman & McGovern, 2005). Moreover, the most improvement in cognitive and language functioning was found to occur between the preschool and middle school years (versus middle school and up), with greater gains for HFASD versus LFA, whose language skills did not show improvement after the middle school period (Sigman & McGovern, 2005).

Another important cognitive characteristic of ASD that may render significant influence on children's learning process is their poor capacity for abstraction of information across multiple stimuli or situations (e.g., categorization, concept formation, metaphor understanding). For example, in Ropar and Peebles (2007), children with ASD (CA = 12.11 years, VMA = 8.6 years) preferred to sort books by concrete dimensions of color and size over abstract dimensions like category membership. Another cognitive deficit related to abstraction is these children's lack of generalization capabilities, which hampers their ability to apply previously learned concepts or information to novel stimuli, particularly when the novel information is less similar to the category's prototype (e.g., Froehlich et al., 2012).

Memory and imitation are two other basic cognitive skills that are important for learning and are hampered in school-age children with ASD. Memory deficits are well recognized in ASD versus TYP, spanning verbal, nonverbal, autobiographic, and everyday memory aspects (e.g., Southwick et al., 2011). Furthermore, these children's recall strategies do not sufficiently consider items' relatedness unless cued recall is supplied at the retrieval stage (as opposed to the storage stage; Southwick et al). Also, with increases in task load, individuals with ASD show decreasing verbal and spatial working memory abilities (see review in Bauminger-Zviely & Kimhi 2013a).

Imitation, which is the basic ability that enables learning, whether social or academic, is considered to be deficient in ASD (see review in Williams, Whitten, & Singh, 2004). Yet, some forms of imitation (of action style, Hobson & Hobson, 2008; of gestures, Vivanti, Nadig, Ozonoff, & Rogers, 2008) were found to be more impeded than others, such as simple imitation of actions taken on objects (Hobson & Hobson, 2008). Although considerable variability characterizes motor imitation in ASD, it is a cardinal obstacle that thwarts productive learning. To sum up, the cognitive profile of children with ASD, which includes difficulties in abstraction, memory, and some aspects of motor imitation, all affect these children's academic achievements in major learning domains.

Academic Abilities

Patterns of academic abilities and disabilities in reading, writing, and mathematics have not yet been clearly demarcated in ASD inasmuch as a wide range of academic achievement outcomes has been reported for this population, ranging from significantly above expected levels to far below expected levels (e.g., Estes et al., 2011). In a recent review of academic abilities of children with ASD, Whitby and Mancil (2009) concluded that areas such as basic reading, encoding, and rote skills are less impaired than reading comprehension, written expression, graphomotor skills, processing of complex materials in all academic domains, and problem solving. Furthermore, in many cases, deficits arose when academic requisites shifted from rote tasks to abstract tasks that demanded conceptual understanding.

Indeed, a recent study (Heumer & Mann, 2010) that evaluated *reading abilities* like decoding and comprehension in 384 children with ASD (CA = 10.08 years) in comparison to 100 children with dyslexia (CA = 11.2 years) yielded opposite profiles for the two groups regarding decoding and comprehension. The children with ASD showed good decoding skills but poor comprehension abilities, whereas the opposite profile emerged for the children with dyslexia. Other studies support this reading comprehension deficit in ASD (e.g., see reviews in Nation, Clarke, Wright, & Williams, 2006 and Randi, Newman, & Grigorenko, 2010). To read for understanding, readers must apply a wide array of cognitive abilities, such as inference and attention, motivational strategies, knowledge of vocabulary, and prior knowledge of the topic

(Randi et al., 2010). Randi et al. (2010) pointed out that comprehension difficulties in ASD may stem from problems in integrating information with a coherent context, from general language impairments like difficulty in comprehending linguistic units beyond the word level, and, when reading longer texts, from memory dysfunction.

Underlying cognitive and sociocognitive deficits characterizing ASD such as ToM, EF, and weak central coherence (WCC) may also impair reading comprehension. WCC is a detail-oriented, overlooking-the-forest-for-the-trees cognitive style associated with children with ASD. Due to WCC, readers with ASD may tend to focus on single words rather than global meanings (e.g., Randi et al., 2010). This piecemeal processing may impair children's extraction of global configurations and higher level meanings, thereby resulting in a failure to understand and use contexts efficiently (e.g., Happé & Frith, 2006). Deficits in readers' ability to understand others' perspectives (ToM) may hinder comprehension of even simplistic, mundane texts because in ASD the understanding that communication enhances interpretation of intended meanings is deficient (Hale & Tager-Flusberg, 2005). Tager-Flusberg and Sullivan (1995) found that children with ASD showed difficulty in supplying appropriate mental-state explanations for story events, in comparison to children with TYP. Likewise, Losh and Capps (2003) reported that children with HFASD provided fewer explanations for characters' internal states, in comparison to children with TYP. EF deficits in ASD such as poor cognitive flexibility may hinder readers' ability to shift flexibly between phonological and semantic processing on the one hand and decoding and comprehension strategies on the other (Randi et al., 2010).

Hyperlexia is a term that denotes a disproportionate gap between superior word reading skills and poor reading comprehension skills (Cardoso-Martins & da Silva, 2010; Grigorenko, Volkmar, & Klin, 2003). There appears to be a higher frequency of hyperlexia among children with ASD in comparison to children with TYP or with other clinical disabilities, with 5% to 10%

of children on the spectrum exhibiting hyperlexia (Grigorenko et al., 2003). Many children with hyperlexia are described as having an unusual passion and interest for the printed word, and they may regard reading as a decoding process without emphasis on comprehension (Cardoso-Martins & da Silva, 2010).

Reading and writing are interrelated skills under the broad domain of literacy. *Writing* reflects the ability to form letters and words in order to communicate. It involves motor-graphic (handwriting) as well as cognitive capabilities, including planning, language, and orthographic abilities. In school, writing (like reading) is a cardinal skill, and after proficiency in forming the letters is achieved, a more complex process starts that includes higher order cognitive demands and compositions (Kushki, Chau, & Anagnostou, 2011). Despite its importance, writing skill in ASD is an overlooked topic. In a recent review (of seven papers), children with ASD were found to show poor handwriting skills, specifically lower legibility, poorer letter formation, and poorer handwriting quality than their peers with TYP (Kushki et al., 2011). Moreover, the processes that contribute to handwriting development, such as fine-motor skills, motor control, and visual-motor integration, were found to be impaired in ASD (Kushki et al., 2011). Poor quality of composition skills in narrative and expository texts was found in adults with ASD (CA = 25.75 years; Brown & Klein, 2011). Interestingly, ToM was found to be linked with writing quality and text length across both genres (narrative and expository), but future studies would do well to untangle composition skills in school-age children with ASD. In Myles-Smith et al. (2003), children with Asperger (CA = 11.7 years), given a standardized test of written language skills and handwriting legibility, demonstrated poorer handwriting skills than children with TYP (less legible letters and words). However, informal evaluation of written samples further revealed no group differences in written quantity or in use of grammatical rules, whereas the children with Asperger did have more difficulty producing qualitative writing than their peers with TYP.

Mathematic skills in ASD is an even a more overlooked topic of study than writing or reading. Computational mathematics skills are more intact than skills for solving complex mathematical problems, at least in HFASD (e.g., Whitby & Mancil, 2009). Cihak and Foust (2008) reported that when these students are taught mathematical skills, they can acquire functional activities such as counting, managing time, and money skills. Also, once competent in basic computational math, they can learn to manage banking, purchasing, and budgeting.

Summary

On the whole, the cognitive-academic domain is challenging for school students with ASD, who evidence difficulties mainly with regard to more complex tasks in areas such as information processing, memory, mathematics, reading, and writing. Moreover, abstract learning is more impaired than concrete tasks in ASD. Intervention studies aiming to enhance academic capabilities as well as additional studies that explore the academic profile of children with ASD are greatly needed (for expansion on cognitive-academic strategies and interventions, see Bauminger-Zviely & Kimhi, 2013b).

SUMMARY AND CONCLUSIONS

In this chapter, abilities and disabilities of school-age children with ASD in the sociocognitive, sociocommunicative, RRB, and cognitive-academic domains were described. As seen along the chapter, even if children reveal progress in some areas during the transition to school, such as in language, many areas nevertheless require extensive support. In the social domains, teaching should focus on both social-emotional understanding as well as helping children develop productive peer interactive behaviors. Help in supporting peer friendship and peer interaction seems to be especially important because schoolchildren's social difficulties in peer interaction place them at risk for bullying and victimization by their peers, a circumstance that holds significant implications for their quality of life and well-being (e.g., Cappadocia, Weiss, & Pepler, 2012). More adequate peer interaction, and especially friendship, may possibly lessen the risk for comorbid affective difficulties such as depression or anxiety (e.g., Cappadocia et al., 2012). In the cognitive-academic domains, help should be given with an emphasis on abstract learning, reading comprehension, solving mathematics problems, and supporting handwriting difficulties based on graphomotor challenges. Interventionists should also take into consideration these children's frequent comorbid psychiatric conditions (e.g., learning difficulties, attention-deficit/hyperactivity disorder, anxiety, and depression) as well as their unique characteristics in motor planning and sensory processing, which all affect these children's capabilities for learning both in the academic and the social spheres. Cognitive and sociocognitive underpinnings to the socioacademic deficit such as ToM and EF were also reviewed, as well as their influence on the unique way in which children with ASD process information. School-age children with ASD form a substantial portion (between 1% and 2%) of school-age children in general, with increasing rates along the recent years. All told, currently available research outcomes indicate the need for substantial emphasis on designing appropriate interventions that will support this population's multidimensional deficits in order to increase independence and productive functioning. Interventions aiming to facilitate functioning along the various domains reach beyond the focus of this chapter, but are covered extensively in other chapters in this *Handbook* (see Chapters 33–37, 40, and 47) as well as in Bauminger-Zviely (2013).

CROSS-REFERENCES

Chapter 1 addresses diagnostic issues and Chapter 2 the broader autism phenotype. Chapters 5, 7, and 8 focus on autism in infants and young children, adolescents, and adults. Chapters 30 through 37 address aspects of intervention relevant to school-age children with autism.

REFERENCES

American Psychiatric Association. (2013). *Diagnostic and statistical manual of mental disorders* (5th ed). Arlington, VA: American Psychiatric Publishing.

Ashburner, J., Ziviani, J., & Rodger, S. (2008). Sensory processing and classroom emotional, behavioral, and educational outcomes in children with autism spectrum disorder. *American Journal of Occupational Therapy, 62*, 564–573.

Barbaro, J., & Dissanayake, C. (2007). A comparative study of the use and understanding of self-presentational display rules in children with high functioning autism and Asperger's disorder. *Journal of Autism and Developmental Disorders 37*, 1235–1246.

Baron-Cohen, S. (2000). Theory of mind and autism: A fifteen year review. In S. Baron-Cohen, H. H. Tager-Flusberg, & D. J. Cohen (Eds.), *Understanding other minds: Perspectives from developmental cognitive neuroscience* (pp. 3–20). Oxford, England: Oxford University Press.

Baron-Cohen, S., Scott, F., Allison, C., Williams, J., Bolton, P., Matthews. F., & Brayne, C. (2009). *British Journal of Psychiatry, 194*, 500–509.

Baron-Cohen, S., Wheelwright, S., Scahill, V., Lawson, J., & Spong, A. (2001). Are intuitive physics and intuitive psychology independent? A test with children with Asperger syndrome. *Journal of Developmental and Learning Disorders, 5*, 47–78.

Bauminger, N. (2004). The expression and understanding of jealousy in children with autism. *Development and Psychopathology, 16*, 157–177.

Bauminger, N., & Agam Ben-Artzi., G. (2012). *Young friendship in HFASD and typical development: Friend vs. non-friend comparisons.* Manuscript in preparation.

Bauminger, N., & Kasari, C. (1999). Theory of mind in high-functioning children with autism. *Journal of Autism and Developmental Disorders, 29*, 81–86.

Bauminger, N., & Kasari, C. (2000). Loneliness and friendship in high-functioning children with autism. *Child Development, 71*, 447–456.

Bauminger, N., Shulman, C., & Agam, G. (2003). Peer interaction and loneliness in high functioning children with autism. *Journal of Autism and Developmental Disorders, 33*, 489–507.

Bauminger, N., Solomon, M., Aviezer, A., Heung, K., Brown, J., & Rogers, S. (2008). Friendship in high-functioning children with ASD: Mixed and non-mixed dyads. *Journal of Autism and Developmental Disorders, 38*, 1121–1229.

Bauminger, N., Solomon, M., Aviezer, A., Heung, K., Gazit, L., Brown, J., & Rogers, S. (2008). Friendship manifestations, dyadic qualities of friendship, and friendship perception in high-functioning preadolescents with autism spectrum disorder. *Journal of Abnormal Child Psychology, 36*, 135–150.

Bauminger, N., Solomon, M., & Rogers, S. (2010a). Externalizing and internalizing behaviors in children with ASD. *Autism Research, 3*, 101–112.

Bauminger, N., Solomon, M., & Rogers, S. (2010b). Predicting friendship quality in autism spectrum disorders and typical development. *Journal of Autism and Developmental Disorders, 40*, 751–761.

Bauminger-Zviely, N. (2013). *Social and academic abilities in high-functioning children with autism spectrum disorders.* New York, NY: Guilford Press.

Bauminger-Zviely, N., & Kimhi, Y. (2013a). Cognitive strengths and weaknesses in HFASD. In N. Bauminger-Zviely, *Social and academic abilities in high-functioning children with autism spectrum disorders* (pp. 88–109). New York, NY: Guilford Press.

Bauminger-Zviely, N., & Kimhi, Y. (2013b). Interventions to facilitate cognitive and academic functioning in HFASD. In N. Bauminger-Zviely, *Social and academic abilities in high-functioning children with autism spectrum disorders* (pp. 155–186). New York, NY: Guilford Press.

Begeer, S., Terwogt, M., Rieffe, C., Stegge, H., & Koot, J. M. (2007). Do children with autism acknowledge the influence of mood on behaviour? *Autism, 11,* 503–521.

Ben-Sasson, A., Hen, L., Fluss, L., Cermak, S. A., Engel-Yeger, B., & Gal, E. (2009). A meta-analysis of sensory modulation symptoms in individuals with autism spectrum disorders. *Journal of Autism and Developmental Disorders, 39,* 1–11.

Benson, P. (2012). Network characteristics, perceived social support, and psychological adjustment in mothers of children with autism spectrum disorder. *Journal of Autism and Developmental Disorders.* Advance online publication. doi: 10.1007/s10803-012-1517-9

Best, J. R., Miller, P. H., & Jones, L. L. (2009). Executive functions after age 5: Changes and correlates. *Developmental Review, 29,* 180–200.

Best, J. R., Miller, P. H., & Naglieri, J. (2011). Relations between executive function and academic achievement from ages 5 to 17 in a large, representative national sample. *Learning and Individual Differences, 21,* 327–336.

Beurkens, N., Hobson, J., & Hobson, P. (2012). Autism severity and qualities of parent-child relations. *Journal of Autism and Developmental Disorders.* Advance online publication. doi: 10.1007/s10803-012-1562-4

Bishop, S. L., Richler, J., Cain, A. C., & Lord, C. (2007). Predictors of perceived negative impact in mothers of children with autism spectrum disorders. *American Journal on Mental Retardation, 112,* 450–461.

Bishop, S., Richler, J., & Lord, C. (2006). Association between restricted and repetitive behaviors and nonverbal IQ in children with autism spectrum disorders. *Child Neuropsychology, 12,* 247–267.

Boyd, B. A., McBee, M., Holtzclaw, T., Baranek, G. T., & Bodfish, J. W. (2009). Relationships among repetitive behaviors, sensory features, and executive functions in high functioning autism. *Research in Autism Spectrum Disorders, 3,* 959–966.

Brent, E., Rios, P., Happé, F., & Charman, T. (2004). Performance of children with autism spectrum disorder on advanced theory of mind tasks. *Autism, 8,* 283–299.

Brewton, C., Nowell, K., Lasala, M., & Goin-Kochel, R. (2012). Relationship between the social functioning of children with autism spectrum disorders and their siblings' competencies/problem behaviors. *Research in Autism Spectrum Disorders, 6,* 646–653.

Brown, H. M., & Klein, P. D. (2011). Writing, Asperger syndrome and theory of mind. *Journal of Autism and Developmental Disorders, 41,* 1464–1474.

Cappadocia, M. C., Weiss, J. A., & Pepler, D. (2012). Bullying experiences among children and youth with autism spectrum disorders. *Journal of Autism and Developmental Disorders, 42,* 266–277.

Capps, L., Kehres, J., & Sigman, M. (1998). Conversational abilities among children with autism and children with developmental delays. *Autism, 2,* 325–344.

Cardoso-Martins, C., & da Silva, J. R. (2010). Cognitive and language correlates of hyperlexia: Evidence from children with autism spectrum disorders. *Reading and Writing, 23,* 129–145.

Centers for Disease Control and Prevention. (2012). *Prevalence of autism spectrum disorders (ASDs) among multiple areas of the United States in 2008.* [Community report from the Autism and Developmental Disabilities Monitoring (ADDM) Network]. Retrieved from http://www.cdc.gov/ncbddd/autism/documents/ADDM-2012-Community-Report.pdf

Chamberlain, B., Kasari, C., & Rotheram-Fuller, E. (2007). Involvement or isolation? The social network of children with autism in regular classrooms. *Journal of Autism and Developmental Disorders, 37,* 230–242.

Charman, T., Pickles, A., Simonoff, E., Chandler, S., Loucas, T., & Baird, G. (2010). IQ in children with autism spectrum disorders: Data from the special needs and autism project (SNAP). *Psychological Medicine, 41,* 619–627.

Cihak, D. F., & Foust, J. L. (2008). Comparing number lines and touch points to teach addition facts to students with autism. *Focus on Autism and Other Developmental Disabilities, 23,* 131–137.

Clifford, T., & Minnes, P. (2012). Who participates in support groups for parents of children with autism spectrum disorders? The role of beliefs and coping style. *Journal of Autism and Developmental Disorders.* Advance online publication. doi: 10.1007/s10803-012-1561-5

Constantino, J. N., & Gruber, C. P. (2005). *Social responsiveness scale (SRS) manual.* Los Angeles, CA: Western Psychological Services.

Crick, N. R., & Dodge, K. A. (1994). A review and reformulation of social-information processing mechanisms in children's social adjustment. *Psychological Bulletin, 115,* 74–101.

Cuccaro, M. L., Shao, Y., Grubber, J., Slifer, M., Wolpert, C. M., Donnelly, S. L., . . . Pericak-Vance, M. A. (2003). Factor analysis of restricted and repetitive behaviors in autism using the Autism Diagnostic Interview-R. *Child Psychiatry and Human Development, 34,* 3–17.

Dennis, M., Lockyer, L., & Lazenby, A. L. (2000). How high-functioning children with autism understand real and deceptive emotion. *Autism, 4,* 370–381.

Elison, J. T., Sasson, N. J., Turner-Brown, L. M., Dichter, G. S., & Bodfish, J. W. (2012). Age trends in visual exploration of social and nonsocial information in children with autism. *Research in Autism Spectrum Disorders, 6,* 842–851.

Embregts, P., & van Nieuwenhuijzen, M. (2009). Social information processing in boys with autistic spectrum disorder and mild to borderline intellectual disabilities. *Journal of Intellectual Disability Research, 35,* 922–931.

Estes, A., Rivera, V., Byran, M., Cali, P., & Dawson, G. (2011). Discrepancies between academic achievement and intellectual ability in higher functioning school aged children with autism spectrum disorder. *Journal of Autism and Developmental Disorders, 41*, 1044–1052.

Evers, K., Noens, I., Steyaert, J., & Wagemans, J. (2011). Combining strengths and weaknesses in visual perception of children with an autism spectrum disorder: Perceptual matching of facial expressions. *Research in Autism Spectrum Disorders, 5*, 1327–1342.

Fabes, R. A., Martin, C. L., & Hanish, L. D. (2009). Children's behavior and interactions with peers. In K. H. Rubin., W. M. Bukowski, & B. Laursen (Eds.), *Handbook of peer interactions, relationships, and groups* (pp. 45–62). New York, NY: Guilford Press.

Forde, I., Holloway, J., Healy, O., & Brosnan, J. (2011). A dyadic analysis of the effects of setting and communication partner on elicited and spontaneous communication of children with autism spectrum disorder and typically developing children. *Research in Autism Spectrum Disorders, 5*, 1471–1478.

Fournier, K., Hass, C., Naik, S., Lodha, N., & Cauraugh, J. (2010). Motor coordination in autism spectrum disorders: A synthesis and meta-analysis. *Journal of Autism and Developmental Disorders, 40*, 1227–1240.

Frankel, F., Gorospe, C., Chang, Y., & Sugar, C. (2011). Mothers' reports of play dates and observation of school playground behavior of children having high-functioning autism spectrum disorders. *Journal of Child Psychology and Psychiatry, 52*, 571–579.

Froehlich, A., Anderson, J., Bigler, E., Miller, J., Lange, N., DuBray, M., & Lainhart, J. (2012). Intact prototype formation but impaired generalization in autism. *Research in Autism Spectrum Disorders, 6*, 921–930.

Gilotty, L., Kenworthy, L., Sirian, L., Black, D., & Wagner, A. (2002). Adaptive skills and executive function in autism spectrum disorders. *Child Neuropsychology, 8*, 241–248.

Golan, O., Baron-Cohen, S., & Golan, Y. (2008). The "reading the mind in films" task [child version]: Complex emotion and mental state recognition in children with and without autism spectrum conditions. *Journal of Autism and Developmental Disorders, 38*, 1534–1541.

Grigorenko, E. L., Volkmar, F., & Klin, A. (2003). Hyperlexia: Disability or superability? *Journal of Child Psychology and Psychiatry, 44*, 1079–1091.

Hale, C. M., & Tager-Flusberg, H. (2005). Social communication in children with autism: The relationship between theory of mind and discourse development. *Autism, 9*, 157–178.

Happé, F. (1994). An advanced test of theory of mind: Understanding of story characters' thoughts and feelings by able autistic, mentally handicapped, and normal children and adults. *Journal of Autism and Developmental Disorders, 24*, 129–154.

Happé, F., & Frith, U. (2006). The weak coherence account: Detail-focused cognitive style in autism spectrum disorders. *Journal of Autism and Developmental Disorders, 35*, 5–25.

Hauck, M., Fein, D., Waterhouse, L., & Feinstein, C. (1995). Social initiations by autistic children to adults and other children. *Journal of Autism and Developmental Disorders, 25*, 579–595.

Hayes, S., & Watson, S. (2012). The impact of parenting stress: A meta-analysis of studies comparing the experience of parenting stress in parents of children with and without autism spectrum disorder. *Journal of Autism and Developmental Disorders*. Advance online publication. doi: 10.1007/s10803-012-1604-y

Heerey, E. A., Keltner, D., & Capps, L. M. (2003). Making sense of self-conscious emotion: Linking theory of mind and emotion in children with autism. *Emotion, 3*, 394–400.

Heumer, S. V., & Mann, V. (2010). A comprehensive profile of decoding and comprehension in autism spectrum disorders. *Journal of Autism and Developmental Disorders, 40*, 485–493.

Hill, E. L. (2004). Evaluating the theory of executive dysfunction in autism. *Developmental Review, 24*, 189–233.

Hilton, C., Harper, J., Kueker, R., Lang, A., Abbacchi, A., Todorov, A., & LaVesser, P. (2012). Sensory responsiveness as a predictor of social severity in children with high functioning autism spectrum disorders. *Journal of Autism and Developmental Disorders*. Advance online publication. doi: 10.1007/s10803-010-0944-8

Hobson, R. P., & Hobson, J. A. (2008). Dissociable aspects of imitation: A study in autism. *Journal of Experimental Child Psychology, 101*, 170–185.

Jackson, C., Fein, D., Wolf, J., Jones, G., Hauck, M., Waterhouse, L., & Feinstein, C. (2003). Responses and sustained interactions in children with mental retardation and autism. *Journal of Autism and Developmental Disorders, 33*, 115–121.

Jaedicke, S., Storoschuk, S., & Lord, C. (1994). Subjective experience and causes of affect in high-functioning children and adolescents with autism. *Development and Psychopathology, 6*, 273–284.

Jansiewicz, E., Goldberg, M., Newschaffer, C., Denckla, M., Landa, R., & Mostofsky, S. (2006). Motor signs distinguish children with high functioning autism and Asperger's syndrome from controls. *Journal of Autism and Developmental Disorders, 36*, 613–621.

Johnson, C., & Myers, S. (2007). Identification and evaluation of children with autism spectrum disorders. *Pediatrics, 120*, 1183–1215.

Joosten, A., Bundy, A., & Einfeld, S. (2012). Context influences the motivation for stereotypic and repetitive behaviour in children diagnosed with intellectual disability with and without autism. *Journal of Applied Research in Intellectual Disabilities, 25*, 262–270.

Joseph, R. M., Tager-Flusberg, H., & Lord, C. (2002). Cognitive profiles and social-communicative functioning in children with autism spectrum disorder. *Journal of Child Psychology and Psychiatry, 43*, 807–821.

Kasari, C., Locke, J., Gulsrud, A., & Rotheram-Fuller, E. (2011). Social networks and friendships at school: Comparing children with and without ASD. *Journal of Autism and Developmental Disorders, 41*, 533–544.

Kasari, C., Rotheram-Fuller, E., Locke, J., & Gulsrud, A. (2012). Making the connection: Randomized controlled trial of social skills at school for children with autism spectrum disorders. *Journal of Child Psychology and Psychiatry, 53*, 431–439.

Klin, A., Jones, W., Schultz, R., Volkmar, F., & Cohen, D. (2002). Visual fixation patterns during viewing of naturalistic social situations as predictors of social competence in individuals with autism. *Archives of General Psychiatry, 59*, 809–815.

Klin, A., Saulnier, C. A., Sparrow, S. S., Cicchetti, D. V., Volkmar, F. R., & Lord, C. (2007). Social and communication abilities and disabilities in higher functioning individuals with autism spectrum disorders: The Vineland and the ADOS. *Journal of Autism and Developmental Disorders, 42*, 161–174.

Knott, F., Lewis, C., & Williams, T. (1995). Sibling interaction of children with learning disabilities: A comparison of autism and Down's syndrome. *Journal of Child Psychology and Psychiatry, 36*, 965–976.

Knott, F., Lewis, C., & Williams, T. (2007). Sibling interaction of children with autism: Development over 12 months. *Journal of Autism and Developmental Disorders, 37*, 1987–1995.

Kushki, A., Chau, T., & Anagnostou, E. (2011). Handwriting difficulties in children with autism spectrum disorders: A scoping review. *Journal of Autism and Developmental Disorders, 41*, 1706–1716.

Lam, K., Bodfish, J., & Piven, J. (2008). Evidence for three subtypes of repetitive behavior in autism that differ in familiality and association with other symptoms. *Journal of Child Psychology and Psychiatry, 49*, 1193–1200.

Lane, A., Young, R., Baker, A., & Angley, M. (2010). Sensory processing subtypes in autism: Association with adaptive behavior. *Journal of Autism and Developmental Disorders, 40*, 112–122.

Leekam, S., Nieto, C., Libby, S., Wing, L., & Gould, J. (2007). Describing the sensory abnormalities of children and adults with autism. *Journal of Autism and Developmental Disorders, 37*, 894–910.

Lind, S. E., & Bowler, D. M. (2009). Recognition memory, self-other source memory, and theory of mind in children with autism spectrum disorder. *Journal of Autism and Developmental Disorders, 39*, 1231–1239.

Lord, C., Risi, S., Lambrecht, L., Cook, E. H., Leventhal., B. L., DiLavore, P. C., . . . Rutter, M. (2000). The Autism Diagnostic Observational Schedule—Generic: A standard measure of social and communication deficits associated with the spectrum of autism. *Journal of Autism and Developmental Disorders, 30*, 205–223.

Losh, M., & Capps, L. (2003). Narrative ability in high-functioning children with autism or Asperger's syndrome. *Journal of Autism and Developmental Disorders, 33*, 239–251.

Losh, M., & Capps, L. (2006). Understanding of emotional experience in autism: Insights from the personal accounts of high-functioning children with autism. *Developmental Psychology, 42*, 809–818.

Loveland, K. A., Pearson, D. A., Tunali-Kotoski, B., Ortegon, J., & Gibbs, M. C. (2001). Judgments of social appropriateness by children and adolescents with autism. *Journal of Autism and Developmental Disorders, 31*, 367–376.

Macintosh, K., & Dissanayake, C. (2006). A comparative study of the spontaneous social interactions of children with high-functioning autism and children with Asperger's disorder. *Autism, 10*, 199–220.

Matthews, N., Goldberg, W., Lukowski, A., Osann, K., Abdullah, M., Agnes, R., Thorsen, K., & Spence, M. (2012). Does theory of mind performance differ in children with early-onset and regressive autism? *Developmental Science, 15*, 25–34.

Mayes, S. D., & Calhoun, S. L. (2003). Analysis of WISC-III, Stanford-Binet IV, and academic achievement test scores in children with autism. *Journal of Autism and Developmental Disorders, 33*, 329–341.

Mayes, D. S., Calhoun, S. L., Murray, M. J., Ahuja, M., & Smith, A. S. (2011). Anxiety, depression, and irritability in children with autism relative to other neuropsychiatric disorders and typical development. *Research in Autism Spectrum Disorders, 5*, 474–485.

McPheeter, M. L., Davis, A., Navarre, J. R., & Scott, T. A. (2011). Family report of ASD concomitant with depression or anxiety among US children. *Journal of Autism and Developmental Disorders, 41*, 646–653.

Meyer, J. A., Mundy, P. C., Van Hecke, A. V., & Durocher, J. S. (2006). Social attribution processes and comorbid psychiatric symptoms in children with Asperger syndrome. *Autism, 10*, 383–402.

Ming, X., Brimacombe, M., & Wagner, G. C. (2007). Prevalence of motor impairment in autism spectrum disorders. *Brain and Development, 29*, 565–570.

Montes, G., & Halterman, J. (2006). Characteristics of school-age children with autism. *Developmental and Behavioral Pediatrics, 27*, 379–385.

Myles-Smith, B., Huggins, A., Rome-Lake, M., Hagiwara, T., Barnhill, G. P., Griswold, D. E. (2003). Written language profile of children and youth with Asperger syndrome: From research to practice. *Education and Training in Developmental Disabilities, 38*, 362–369.

Nadig, A., Lee, I., Singh, L., Bosshart, K., & Ozonoff, S. (2010). How does the topic of conversation affect verbal exchange and eye gaze? A comparison between typical development and high-functioning autism. *Neuropsychologia, 48*, 2730–2739.

Nah, Y., & Poon, K. (2011). The perception of social situations by children with autism spectrum disorders. *Autism, 15*, 185–203.

Nation, K., Clarke, P., Wright, B., & Williams, C. (2006). Patterns of reading ability in children with autism spectrum disorder. *Journal of Autism and Developmental Disorders, 36*, 911–919.

O'Brien, K., Slaughter, V., & Peterson, C. (2011). Sibling influences on theory of mind development for children with ASD. *Journal of Child Psychology and Psychiatry, 52*, 713–719.

Ozonoff, S., & Strayer, D. L. (2001). Further evidence of intact working memory in autism. *Journal of Autism and Developmental Disorders, 31*, 257–263.

Pan, C. (2009). Age, social engagement, and physical activity in children with autism spectrum disorders. *Research in Autism Spectrum Disorders, 31*, 22–31.

Pan, C., Tsai, C., & Chu, C. (2009). Fundamental movement skills in children diagnosed with autism spectrum disorders and attention deficit hyperactivity disorder. *Journal of Autism and Developmental Disorders, 39*, 1694–1705.

Perner, J., & Wimmer, H. (1985). John thinks that Mary thinks that: Attribution of second-order beliefs by 5-to 10-year-old children. *Journal of Experimental Child Psychology, 60*, 689–700.

Peterson, C. C., Garnett, M., Kelly, A., & Attwood, T. (2009). Everyday social and conversation applications of theory-of-mind understanding by children with autism-spectrum disorders or typical development. *European Child and Adolescent Psychiatry*, *18*, 105–115.

Peterson, C., Slaughter, V., & Paynter, J. (2007). Social maturity and theory of mind in typically developing children and those on the autism spectrum. *Journal of Child Psychology and Psychiatry and Allied Disciplines*, *48*, 1243–1250.

Peterson, C., Wellman, H., & Slaughter, V. (2012). The mind behind the message: Advancing theory-of-mind scales for typically developing children, and those with deafness, autism, or Asperger syndrome. *Child Development*, *83*, 469–485.

Pexman, P. M., Rostad, K. R., McMorris, C. A., Climie, E. A., Stowkowy, J., & Glenwright, M. R. (2011). Processing of ironic language in children with high-functioning autism spectrum disorder. *Journal of Autism and Developmental Disorders*, *41*, 1097–1112.

Potvin, M., Snider, L., Prelock, P., Kehayia, E., & Wood-Dauphinee, S. (2012). Recreational participation of children with high functioning autism. *Journal of Autism and Developmental Disorders*. Advance online publication. doi: 10.1007/s10803-012-1589-6

Pringle, B., Colpe, L., Blumberg, S., Avila, R., & Kogan, M. (2012). *Diagnostic history and treatment of school-aged children with autism spectrum disorder and special health care needs.* NCHS Data Brief, No. 97. Hyattsville, MD: National Center for Health Statistics.

Randi, J., Newman, T., & Grigorenko, E. L. (2010). Teaching children with autism to read for meaning: Challenges and possibilities. *Journal of Autism and Developmental Disorders*, *40*, 890–902.

Riby, D., Brown, F., Jones, N., & Hanley, M. (2012). Brief report: Faces cause less distraction in autism. *Journal of Autism and Developmental Disorders*, *42*, 634–639.

Riby, D., & Hancock, P. J. B. (2009). Do faces capture the attention of children with Williams syndrome or autism? Evidence from tracking eye-movements. *Journal of Autism and Developmental Disorders*, *39*, 421–431.

Richler, J., Huerta, M., Bishop, S., & Lord, C. (2010). Developmental trajectories of restricted and repetitive behaviors and interests in children with autism spectrum disorders. *Development and Psychopathology*, *22*, 55–69.

Rieffe, C., Terwogt, M. M., & Kotronopoulou, K. (2007). Awareness of single and multiple emotions in high-functioning children with autism. *Journal of Autism and Developmental Disorders*, *37*, 455–465.

Rieffe, C., Terwogt, M. M., & Stockmann, L. (2000). Understanding atypical emotions among children with autism. *Journal of Autism and Developmental Disorders*, *30*, 195–203.

Robinson, S., Goddard, L., Dritschel, B., Wisley, M., & Howlin, P. (2009). Executive functions in children with autism spectrum disorders. *Brain and Cognition*, *71*, 362–368.

Rogers, S. R., & Bennetto, L. (2001). Intersubjectivity in autism: The role of imitation and executive function. In A. M. Wetherby & B. M. Prizant (Eds.), *Autism spectrum disorders: A transactional developmental perspective* (pp. 79–107). Baltimore, MD: Paul H. Brookes.

Ropar, D., & Peebles, D. (2007). Sorting preference in children with autism: The dominance of concrete features. *Journal of Autism and Developmental Disorders*, *37*, 270–280.

Rotheram-Fuller, E., Kasari, C., Chamberlain, B., & Locke, J. (2010). Social involvement of children with autism spectrum disorders in elementary school classrooms. *Journal of Child Psychology and Psychiatry*, *51*, 1227–1234.

Rowley, E., Chandler, S., Baird, G., Simonoff, E., Pickles, A., Loucas, T., & Charman, T. (2012). The experience of friendship, victimization and bullying in children with an autism spectrum disorder: Associations with child characteristics and school placement. *Research in Autism Spectrum Disorders*, *6*, 126–1134.

Rubin, E., & Lennon, L. (2004). Challenges in social communication in Asperger syndrome and high-functioning autism. *Topics in Language Disorders*, *24*, 271–285.

Rutgers, A. H., Bakermans-Kranenburg, M. J., van Ijzendoorn, M. H., & van Berckelaer-Onnes, I. A. (2004). Autism and attachment: A meta-analytic review. *Journal of Child Psychology and Psychiatry*, *45*, 1123–1134.

Rutter, M., Le Couteur, A., & Lord, C. (2003). *The Autism Diagnostic Interview—Revised (ADI-R) manual.* Los Angeles, CA: Western Psychological Services.

Salter, G., Seigal, A., Claxton, M., Lawrence, K., & Skuse, D. (2008). Can autistic children read the mind of an animated triangle? *Autism*, *12*, 347–391.

Semrud-Clikeman, M., Walkowiak, J., Wilkinson, A., & Butcher, B. (2010). Executive functioning in children with Asperger syndrome, ADHD-combined type, ADHD-predominately inattentive type, and controls. *Journal of Autism and Developmental Disorders*, *40*, 1017–1027.

Seskin, L., Feliciano, E., Tippy, G., Yedloutschnig, R., Sossin, M., & Yasik, A. (2010). Attachment and autism: Parental attachment representations and relational behaviors in the parent-child dyad. *Journal of Abnormal Child Psychology*, *38*, 949–960.

Siaperas, P., Ring, H., McAllister, C., Henderson, S., Barnett, A., Watson, P., & Holland, A. (2012). Atypical movement performance and sensory integration in Asperger's syndrome. *Journal of Autism and Developmental Disorders*, *42*, 718–725.

Sigman, M., & McGovern, C. W. (2005). Improvement in cognitive and language skills from preschool to adolescence in autism. *Journal of Autism and Developmental Disorders*, *35*, 15–23.

Solish, A., Perry, A., & Minnes, P. (2010). Participation of children with and without disabilities in social, recreational and leisure activities. *Journal of Applied Research in Intellectual Disabilities*, *23*, 226–236.

Southwick, J. S., Bigler, E. D., Froehlich, A., DuBray, M. B., Alexander, A. L., Lange, S., & Lainhart, J. E. (2011). Memory functioning in children and adolescents with autism. *Neuropsychology*, *25*, 701–710.

Sparrow, S., Balla, D. A., & Cicchetti, D. V. (1984). *Vineland adaptive behavior scales.* Circle Pines, MN: American Guidance Services.

Staar, E., Szatmari, P., Bryson, S., & Zwaigenbaum, L. (2003). Stability and change among high-functioning children with pervasive developmental disorders: A 2-year outcome study. *Journal of Autism and Developmental Disorders*, *33*, 15–22.

Staples, K., & Reid, G. (2010). Fundamental movement skills and autism spectrum disorders. *Journal of Autism and Developmental Disorders*, *40*, 209–217.

Stoit, A., van Schie, H., Riem, M., Meulenbroek, R., Newman-Norlund, R., Slaats-Willemse, D., ... Buitelaar, K. (2011). Internal model deficits impair joint action in children and adolescents with autism spectrum disorders. *Research in Autism Spectrum Disorders*, *5*, 1526–1537.

Stone, W. L., & Caro-Martinez, L. M. (1990). Naturalistic observations of spontaneous communication in autistic children. *Journal of Autism and Developmental Disorders*, *20*, 437–453.

Tager-Flusberg, H., & Sullivan, K. (1995). Attributing mental states to story characters: A comparison of narratives produced by autistic and mentally retarded individuals. *Applied Psycholinguistics*, *16*, 241–256.

Turner, L. M., Stone, W. L., Pozdol, S. L., & Coonrod, E. E. (2006). Follow-up of children with autism spectrum disorders from age 2 to age 9. *Autism*, *10*, 243–265.

Turner, M. A. (1999). Annotation: Repetitive behavior in autism: A review of psychological research. *Journal of Child Psychology and Psychiatry*, *40*, 839–849.

van der Geest, J. N., Kemner, C., Camfferman, G., Verbaten, M. N., & van Engeland, H. (2002). Looking at images with human figures: Comparison between autistic and normal children. *Journal of Autism and Developmental Disorders*, *32*, 69–75.

van der Geest, J. N., Kemner, C., Verbaten, M. N., & van Engeland, H. (2002). Gaze behavior of children with pervasive developmental disorder toward human faces: A fixation time study. *Journal of Child Psychology and Psychiatry*, *43*, 669–678.

Van Eylen, L., Boets, B., Steyaert, J., Evers, K., Wagemans, J., & Noens, I. (2011). Cognitive flexibility in autism spectrum disorder: Explaining the inconsistencies? *Research in Autism Spectrum Disorders*, *5*, 1390–1401.

Vertè, S., Geurts, H. M., Roeyers, H., Oosterlaan, J., & Sergeant, J. A. (2006). Executive functioning in children with an autism spectrum disorder: Can we differentiate within the spectrum? *Journal of Autism and Developmental Disorders*, *36*, 351–372.

Vivanti, G., Nadig, A., Ozonoff, S., & Rogers, S. J. (2008). What do children with autism attend to during imitation tasks? *Journal of Experimental Child Psychology*, *101*, 186–205.

Wechsler, D. (1974). *Wechsler Intelligence Scale for Children—revised*. New York, NY: Psychological Corporation.

Wellman, H. M., & Liu, D. (2004). Scaling of theory-of-mind tasks. *Child Development*, *75*, 523–541.

Whitby, P. J. S., & Mancil, G. R. (2009). Academic achievement profiles of children with high functioning autism and Asperger syndrome: A review of the literature. *Education and Training in Developmental Disabilities*, *44*, 551–560.

White, S., Hill, E., Happé, F., & Frith, U. (2009). Revisiting the strange stories: Revealing mentalizing impairments in autism. *Child Development*, *80*, 1097–1117.

Williams, J., Whitten, A., & Singh, T. (2004). A systematic review of action imitation in autistic spectrum disorder. *Journal of Autism and Developmental Disorders*, *34*, 285–296.

Wilson, C. E., Brock, J., & Palermo, R. (2010). Attention to social stimuli and facial identity recognition skills in autism spectrum disorder. *Journal of Intellectual Disability Research*, *54*, 1104–1115.

Wing, L., & Gould, J. (1979). Severe impairments of social interaction and associated abnormalities in children: Epidemiology and classification. *Journal of Autism and Developmental Disorders*, *9*, 11–29.

Zingerevich, C., & LaVesser, P. (2009). The contribution of executive functions to participation in school activities of children with high functioning autism spectrum disorder. *Research in Autism Spectrum Disorders*, *3*, 429–437.

CHAPTER 7

Issues and Interventions for Autism Spectrum Disorders During Adolescence and Beyond

LYNN KERN KOEGEL, ROBERT L. KOEGEL, AMBER R. MILLER,
AND WHITNEY J. DETAR

PREFACE

Individuals with autism spectrum disorders can benefit from intervention at all ages, and while the bulk of intervention studies are geared toward helping children, an emerging body of evidence is documenting effective, empirically based interventions for adolescents. Further, effective interventions for children with autism spectrum disorders often can be adapted for use beyond childhood. In this chapter, we explore some of the relevant issues and interventions that can be employed in middle school, high school, and beyond, including priming, motivational procedures to improve academics, self-management, video modeling, and peer-mediated interventions. In addition, we discuss assessment issues, employment, and higher education for individuals on the autism spectrum. The chapter discusses interventions that may be applicable to those adolescents and adults with fewer support needs, as well as the transition to a functional curriculum for those adolescents and young adults who require greater supports. We also discuss areas that would benefit from further research.

Preparation of this chapter and the research reported within were supported in part by generous donations from the Eli and Edythe L. Broad Center for Asperger Research, the Douglas Foundation, the Kind World Foundation, and by National Institutes of Health Research Grant No. DC010924 from the NIDCD. Robert and Lynn Koegel are also partners in the private consulting firm, Koegel Autism Consultants.

INTRODUCTION

Adolescence can be a difficult time for any child; however, individuals with autism spectrum disorders (ASDs) may be particularly affected due to higher levels of bullying and victimization by their peers, as well as issues related to curriculum and socialization. In fact, bullying experiences are 4 times more likely to occur among students with ASD than typically developing students (Little, 2002), with more than half reporting being victimized by their peers (S. Carter, 2009). That is, bullying against youth with ASDs is frequent and when it occurs, it is likely to continue over a long period of time (Cappadocia, Weiss, & Pepler, 2012). The cyclical problem of bullying and victimization is especially concerning. Specifically, students with social and communicative difficulties are more likely to be bullied and victimized (Cappadocia et al., 2012), and in turn, children who are bullied are more likely to have negative social and academic outcomes, have poor social and emotional development, and exhibit mental health problems, including depression and anxiety (Grills & Ollendick, 2002; Sterling, Dawson, Estes & Greenson, 2008; White & Schry, 2011). For this reason, it is critical that interventions are developed and implemented that focus on improving socialization, peer acceptance, and independent living for individuals with ASD.

Entering middle school can present new challenges for students. Class schedules are often different, with changes in classrooms frequently required between subjects. These quick transitions, as well as the increased complexity of assignments, require greater organizational skills than previously expected. Furthermore, by middle school, course content and curriculum are more abstract and inferential and are delivered at a faster pace. Students are expected to work independently and demonstrate organization and thoroughness in regard to work habits (Kurth & Mastergeorge, 2010).

As academics are becoming more challenging for students, so are social demands. Adolescents are expected to understand more subtle social nuances and can be subjected to teasing or bullying if they are not keeping up with their peers socially (Green, Gilchrist, Burton, & Cox, 2000). Unfortunately, many adolescents with ASD express a great desire for friendships as they mature, but often lack the requisite social skills to fit in (Church, Alisanski, & Amanullah, 2000). This lack of peer acceptance often leads to very detrimental outcomes including depression, anxiety, and feelings of rejection (Church et al., 2000; Ghaziuddin, Ghaziuddin, & Greden, 2002; Kim, Szatmari, Bryson, Streiner, & Wilson, 2000). That is, these youth are often interested in having friends but may not be skilled at developing and maintaining friendships. Fortunately, a new body of research is emerging on effective, empirically supported interventions to aide teens and young adults with ASD, both academically and socially.

EDUCATIONAL ASSESSMENT

Adolescents with ASD present with a wide range of needs and do not have consistent patterns of strengths and weaknesses. The first step to an effective and individualized treatment plan is a thorough assessment, which can identify vulnerabilities to be targeted and strengths to be utilized. A review of academic achievement profiles of individuals with ASD concluded that "proper assessment and analysis of subtest domains is needed to determine the strengths and weaknesses of a student" (Whitby & Mancil, 2009, p. 557). For example, incorporating areas of strengths or special interests into social groups or academic assignments has been shown to improve responding and decrease problem behaviors. Next, we discuss some specific areas that have been shown to be particularly effective with students with ASD.

Motivational Procedures to Improve Academic Performance

One of the big changes that takes place between elementary and middle school is a shift in the focus of homework. Muhlenbruck, Cooper, Nye, and Lindsay (2000) found evidence to suggest that teachers in early grades use homework most often to develop students' management of time, whereas teachers in later grades more often use homework to prepare for and expand upon material that is covered in class. Thus, adolescents are expected to have the organizational skills necessary to complete their homework, which becomes an essential aspect of their education, in addition to learning new information. It has also been shown that students who require different homework assignments (as opposed to working on the same type of assignment as their classmates) experience an exacerbation of social difficulties, as they may be stigmatized and engage in fewer opportunities to work on homework with classmates (Vaughn, Schumm, & Kouzekanani, 1993). Thus, it is important to ensure that children with ASD have the necessary skills to complete their homework in a way that is similar or identical to their classmates, as the benefits from successful homework completion include academic progress as well as increased social opportunities.

Cooper and Nye (1994) conducted a literature review of homework policies and practices for students with disabilities and found that parental involvement and immediate positive reinforcement were essential components of any homework program for children with disabilities. In a related area, R. L. Koegel, Tran, Mossman, and Koegel (2006) conducted a study that involved both parent involvement and immediate positive reinforcement to improve homework performance in children with ASDs. This multiple-baseline study used the motivational procedures of pivotal response treatment (PRT) during homework time with three children with ASD. While none of the participants in the study were adolescents, similar procedures might be effective with adolescents as well (L. K. Koegel & LaZebnik, 2009). The motivational components of PRT that were employed in the study included the following:

- *Choice* (such as allowing the student to choose writing utensils, order of problems, where to sit, etc.).
- *Natural and direct reinforcers* (such as giving the student a treat that was used to calculate a math problem).
- *Reinforcing attempts* (such as reinforcing trying to write a word even if it contains errors while trying to learn to spell it correctly).

- *Interspersing maintenance and acquisition tasks* (such as mixing simple math problems with new more difficult problems).
- *Contingent reinforcement* (providing reinforcement immediately after successful completion).

The research found that applying PRT procedures to homework resulted in decreased disruptive behavior, improved affect, increased positive comments made by the child, and improved rate of homework completion. In a related study, L. K. Koegel, Singh, and Koegel (2010) found that by incorporating a student's interest into the assignment and providing a natural reinforcer, such as having a student write a story about what he or she would like to do, then providing the opportunity for the student to engage in that activity, increased work productivity and decreased disruptive behavior. Preliminary research suggests that using such motivational procedures may also help adolescents with ASD stay on track academically. While there are a number of other curricular modifications that can be made, such as a reduced number of problems, partial participation in the assignments, and so on, incorporating the motivational components into the activity assures that the core curriculum will be addressed in way that is more enjoyable and motivating for all of the students in the class.

Priming

Wilde, Koegel, and Koegel (1992) describe priming as a method of intervention that previews information or activities that are likely to be difficult for a student with ASD. Parents or specialists can implement priming during the afternoon or evening before the activity occurs. While few systematic studies have assessed how parents or specialists can best implement the procedures, the general recommendations involve presenting academic material in a nondemanding atmosphere. In a repeated reversals design study targeting academics it was shown that priming decreased problem behaviors at school and increased appropriate academic responding (L. K. Koegel, Koegel, Frea, & Green-Hopkins, 2003). This study, and other related work, included both children and adolescents, suggesting that priming can be an effective intervention across a wide age range and across many academic and social areas. In addition to helping academic progress, priming has been shown to be a helpful social intervention. Gengoux (2009) conducted a study in which children with autism received priming for table games. Following priming, all students in the study exhibited increased rates of initiations to peers and social engagement.

The advantages of priming are many. First, the students do not need to be pulled out of class for intervention, as priming is often conducted outside of school hours. Second, it can be a part of an effective home-school coordination program in which all team members—teachers and parents—work cooperatively on behalf of the student. Third, rather than playing catch-up, the student is exposed to the activity prior to when it occurs, which has been shown to prevent disruptive and inappropriate avoidance behaviors that are typically demonstrated with difficult activities. Thus, priming can decrease the need for modification of schoolwork and direct social intervention during class, thereby providing an effective antecedent strategy for adolescents.

Self-Management

Self-management is a well-documented intervention that teaches individuals to evaluate, then to record, and ultimately obtain reinforcement for the presence or absence of a target behavior. Typically, students are first taught to differentiate desirable from undesirable behaviors, then to record (either on paper, using a wrist-counter, or using another counting device) the presence of desirable behaviors or the absence undesirable behaviors. The recording alone appears to result in a decrease in undesirable behaviors (or an increase in desirable behaviors) as a reactive effect, but motivational components are often added so that the individual can earn rewards for exhibiting and recording desirable behaviors. Meta-analyses and literature reviews have consistently found strong empirical support for the use of self-management (e.g., Koyama & Wang, 2011; Lee, Simpson, & Shogren, 2007; Southall & Gast, 2011). In the following section we discuss several studies that use

self-management as an intervention for adolescents with ASD. Self-management has been effectively used in and outside of school settings for academics and social skills.

For example, L. K. Koegel, Koegel, Hurley, and Frea (1992) implemented self-management programs with four children and adolescents with autism, using a multiple baseline design, with a withdrawal phase for two of the four participants. Prior to the start of the self-management program, the participants responded to questions only about half of the time. They were then taught to self-manage appropriate verbal responding to others using a wrist counter in multiple settings: the clinic, home, school, and community. All participants showed an increase in appropriate responding to questions as well as a decrease in disruptive behaviors (which were not directly targeted). This study showed that self-management could be implemented in the participants' natural environments without the presence of an interventionist, making the intervention unlikely to interfere with social functioning and allowing the adolescents independence from constant prompting.

R. L. Koegel and Frea (1993) conducted another study of self-management, which examined its effect upon adolescents' use of five deficient social communicative behaviors: facial expression and affect, eye gaze, nonverbal mannerisms, voice volume, and perseveration of topic. The participants' appropriate pragmatic, prosodic, and social behaviors improved to 100% or near 100% for all treated behaviors and also generalized to untreated behaviors, as well. This study demonstrated that social communicative behaviors could be improved through the use of self-management and found collateral benefits in untargeted areas.

Stahmer and Schreibman (1992) studied the use of self-management to improve appropriate play in three students, two of whom were adolescents, using a multiple-baseline design. Reinforcement was provided after intervals in which appropriate play occurred and was recorded correctly. The reinforcement and the self-management materials were then faded, but the behavioral gains (increases in appropriate play and decreases in self-stimulatory behavior) maintained across all participants. This study suggests that self-management materials and reinforcers may not need to be continued indefinitely: Removal did not result in any decrease of appropriate behavior or increase in inappropriate behavior.

Self-management has also been studied directly in the school setting by Wehmeyer, Yeager, Bolding, Agran, and Hughes (2003). The authors used a multiple-baseline design to assess the effects of self-management with three adolescents with developmental disabilities in the classroom on various behaviors, including disruptive behavior, on-task behavior, and following directions. All behaviors improved following the implementation of the self-management intervention. The behaviors targeted were important for both academic achievement and social functioning, showing that self-management can be used to target both of these areas at once.

In summary, self-management is a highly effective strategy to help adolescents manage and develop a variety of behaviors, including academics and social skills. For adolescents and young adults, self-management is attractive, as it can be programmed to occur in the absence of a treatment provider. This promotes independent functioning, eliminates the need for constant vigilance from an adult, and also recruits the participant as an active agent in the intervention process.

Video Modeling

Video modeling is another effective intervention that has been documented in the ASD literature. Among other reasons, video modeling may be an effective learning modality for individuals with ASD because it capitalizes on visual learning, which is often a strength of individuals with ASD (Bellini & Akullian, 2007).

Several literature reviews and meta-analyses have compiled information about the video-modeling studies conducted in recent years. For example, the National Standards Project described video modeling as an established practice for adolescents (National Autism Center, 2009). Others have reported similar positive results, concluding

that video modeling is an evidence-based intervention, showing effectiveness for treating many behaviors, including communication, social skills, functional skills, and behavioral functioning (Bellini & Akullian, 2007; Gelbar, Anderson, McCarthy, & Buggey, 2012; Wang & Spillane, 2009). In addition, Bellini and Akullian noted that the skills improved through video modeling were typically maintained over time and transferred across persons and settings.

For example, Allen, Wallace, and Renes (2010) used video modeling to teach vocational skills to adolescents and young adults with ASD. This study used a multiple-baseline design with the video model focused on training individuals to perform the job of a retail mascot. Results suggested that all participants were able to learn and perform the job correctly, and supervisors reported that all were consistently meeting performance expectations for the job. Burke, Anderson, Bowen, Howard, and Allen (2010) also used video modeling, as part of an intervention package, to teach individuals to serve the role of a mascot, this time for promoting fire safety. Such studies suggest that video modeling may be a useful strategy in vocational training.

Another example of a video modeling intervention used with adolescents focused on improving social conversation behaviors, such as initiations, in four adolescents and young adults with ASD (Smith, 2011). This study employed a multiple-baseline design and used the self as a model, meaning that the participants were videotaped during conversations and then shown clips of themselves demonstrating examples of the target behaviors as well as clips of behaviors that "need improvement." The participants were provided with an opportunity to self-evaluate their conversational behaviors and generate options for appropriate behaviors for the needs-improvement clips. The intervention resulted in increases in the target behavior of question asking. Further, decreases occurred in untreated awkward pauses in conversation for all four participants, and the skills maintained after the intervention ended for three of the four participants. Overall, this study demonstrated that video modeling can be effective for improving the general flow of conversation between individuals with ASD and their conversational partners.

In conclusion, video modeling is an effective strategy that can be used to target many behaviors. It may be a desirable intervention strategy for many adolescents, as the use of video can be an engaging way to learn new skills. While more research is needed, studies suggest that video-based interventions may target the pivotal area of motivation (Mechling & Cronin, 2006; Schreibman, Whalen, & Stahmer, 2000), may lead to faster and greater acquisition of the target behavior than in-vivo modeling (Charlop-Christy, Le, & Freeman, 2000; Dowrick, 1991; Graetz, Mastropieri, & Scruggs, 2006; McCoy & Hermansen, 2007), and can result in increased generalization and maintenance of skills taught (Charlop & Milstein, 1989).

Peer-Mediated Interventions

One way to promote the acquisition of new skills while providing adolescents with opportunities to interact with peers is through peer-mediated interventions. While the actual intervention components can vary greatly, Chan et al. (2009) found, in a systematic review of the literature, that peer-mediated interventions can be versatile and effective for individuals with ASD and can target a range of symptoms, including social, communication, and academic issues. Peer-mediated interventions can also be particularly useful in inclusive general education classrooms, and the use of typical peers can reduce the need for an aide or paraprofessional (Harrower & Dunlap, 2001).

One such study conducted by Haring and Breen (1992) assessed the impact of a peer network intervention for a 13-year-old with autism. The peer intervention was implemented during unstructured social times between classes and at lunch and involved both peer reinforcement and self-management. Peers were instructed to differentially reinforce the student with ASD's appropriate and inappropriate responses to their initiations. The intervention resulted in increased appropriate social responding, as well as improved peer attitudes and ratings of friendship toward the target student.

This study was expanded upon by Morrison, Kamps, Garcia, and Parker (2001), who assessed a peer-mediated intervention with four adolescents, using a multiple-baseline design. After implementing the intervention, the target behavior (initiations), as well as other untargeted behaviors (response to others' initiations and percent time engaged), increased for each child. These peer-mediated interventions were conducted within the schools and provide evidence that interventions utilizing peers can be effective for treating symptoms of ASD in the school setting.

In addition, a larger scale randomized trial of a peer-mediated intervention was conducted with 85 children, between the ages of 5 and 13, in Belgium with autism or pervasive developmental disorder (Roeyers, 1996). Each peer was matched with a target child, and play opportunities were arranged for 30 minutes during lunch or after school. Each peer was given a small amount of instruction on how to best interact with his or her match, but no training in specific techniques was given. Statistically significant differences were found between the treatment and control groups in the following areas: (a) increased time spent in interaction; (b) increased length of sustained interaction; (c) increased degree of responsiveness to the partner's initiations; (d) increase in the number of initiations made by the target children; and (e) increases in presocial behaviors, such as time spent observing the behavior of the peer, and decreases in interfering behaviors, such as self-stimulation. These gains also generalized to interactions with unfamiliar playmates.

Clearly, peer-mediated interventions can be useful in improving the social interactions of adolescents with ASD. However, the question arises as to whether the use of multiple peers may be more effective (e.g., a peer clique) rather than having one student paired with an adolescent with ASD. E. W. Carter, Cushing, Clark, and Kennedy (2005) addressed this issue using an A-B-A-B design with 3 adolescent students with ASD. When comparing interventions using one peer versus two peers, it was found that conditions including a second peer resulted in higher levels of social interaction and contact with the general curriculum than were observed using only one peer interventionist. E. W. Carter et al. (2005) suggested that because the differences in implementation requirements between one- and two-peer support arrangements are relatively small, improved academic and social outcomes may be provided to students with only minimal additional time and effort required on the part of educators. This research is also supported by the aforementioned study by Haring and Breen (1992) that successfully paired an adolescent with ASD with a peer clique to improve socialization. Researchers speculate that the relationships may be more durable if an entire clique supported the student with autism rather than recruiting only one student who would need to break away from his or her clique to socially support a student with ASD.

Social Events Around the Specialized Interests of the Individual With ASD

A number of publications have described procedures for using the strengths of individuals with autism, such as their restricted or specialized interest (Klin & Volkmar, 2000), as the theme of social activities (Baker, Koegel, & Koegel, 1998). This intervention has been effectively implemented with adolescents in the form of lunch clubs on campus (R. L. Koegel, Fredeen, Kim, Danial, Rubinstein, & Koegel, 2012). Specifically, the intensive/restricted interest of the adolescent with ASD is assessed and then activities are developed around that theme in a way that is mutually interesting to all participants. Research shows that this technique is easy and effective, even with adolescents who spend the majority of their time in isolation. Further, since many of the students with ASD have accumulated very large amounts of information on the thematic topic of the club, they are often considered the most valued member of the peer group. This not only builds upon the student with ASD's strengths, but also may be very high on the reinforcer hierarchy of the student with ASD, thereby providing a competing reinforcer to any other type of inappropriate

behavior that may have been occurring prior to their engagement in the club activities.

TRANSITION TO A FUNCTIONAL CURRICULUM FOR INDIVIDUALS WITH GREATER SUPPORT NEEDS

While early intervention is the most desirable route for individuals with ASD, often eliminating many or all of their later support needs, there are nevertheless some adolescents and young adults who did not have the benefit of early intervention or who progressed slowly through intervention and still need significant support into adulthood. These individuals tend to present with a comorbid diagnosis of autism and intellectual disability (ID). Similar to the social communication patterns of younger children with autism, the adolescent and young adult population that has both autism and significant intellectual disabilities also tends to interact infrequently with others, and when they do interact, it is primarily for behavior regulation (Maljaars, Noens, Jansen, Scholte, & van Berckelaer-Onnes, 2011; L. K. Koegel, Koegel, Shoshan, & McNerney, 1999). Despite these stable patterns of significant social communicative impairment, this is not to suggest that adolescents and adults with autism and ID do not benefit from, and should not receive, intervention. On the contrary, intensive intervention may be even more critical for this group to achieve participation in typical environments. However, for those who remain nonverbal or minimally verbal in adolescence and adulthood, learning expressive verbal communication may be more challenging. For this population, desirable goals may include improving the use of nonverbal behaviors, such as intentional pointing, or improving intentional communication, facilitating voluntary motor planning, and instating or increasing the use of alternative and augmentative communication (AAC) to substitute or enhance verbal expressive communication and to decrease problematic behaviors (Maljaars et al., 2011). AAC strategies may involve manual signs, graphic communication (such as photographs, drawings, written words), and computerized speech-generating devices. In addition to improving communication, AAC devices can also improve emotion recognition and social interactions in individuals with autism and ID (Hopkins et al., 2011).

In addition, a number of studies have documented improvements in self-help areas for individuals diagnosed with autism and ID. For example, students with autism and moderate intellectual disabilities who have difficulty with math can be taught to purchase items independently. A common strategy is the "dollar plus" or "count on" strategy wherein they are taught to add one more dollar instead of having to count out change. When procedures are taken to learn the strategy, then practice it in natural settings, generalization and maintenance have been shown (Cihak & Grim, 2008).

EMPLOYMENT

Creating opportunities and interventions for employment is another area that has been largely neglected. Thus, most individuals with autism and ID remain unemployed throughout their lives, despite the fact that many can learn to work. In addition to the financial benefits of working, research suggests that cognitive skills improve as a result of supported employment, in contrast to unemployment, which typically results in no cognitive improvements. Importantly, adults with autism who work show significantly greater improvements in cognitive areas, thus emphasizing the broad impact of employment (García-Villamisar & Hughes, 2007). In a review of the literature, Matson, Hattier, and Belva (2012) point out the positive correlation between employment and other positive outcomes. However, given the effectiveness of applied behavior analysis (ABA) techniques with a variety of target behaviors, the lack of such publications for assisting with employment is astonishing. This is particularly concerning given the improvements in quality of life and the independence, social, and communication opportunities that employment affords. In addition to cognition, areas such as hygiene, social interaction, social conversation, safety, developing friendships and intimate

relationships, and other appropriate social behaviors are of increased importance once an individual receives gainful employment and interacts in everyday settings on a regular basis with peers (L. K. Koegel, Detar, Fox, & Koegel, in press). Another challenge is the fact that when individuals with autism and ID are employed, most of the programs primarily focus on residential care in group homes and supported employment in quite menial jobs. These programs put little focus on development of meaningful friendships and relationships, and when they do, they are not inclusive with typically developing individuals. Although studies have found that adults with ASD typically require different and more intensive treatment techniques than those used for individuals with other disabilities (Sullivan, 2007; Van Bourgondien & Elgar, 1990; Van Bourgondien & Reichle, 1997; Van Bourgondien & Schopler, 1996), with these specialized interventions, the wealth of employment opportunities available to those without disabilities may become accessible to individuals with ASD and ID. Thus, there is a considerable need for additional programs that focus on employment and the array of social and self-help areas that are associated with gaining and maintaining a job. Additional research in this area will undoubtedly result in improving the quality-of-life issues for adults with ASD and ID.

TRANSITION TO COLLEGE

Another area that has been greatly understudied is higher education for adolescents and young adults on the spectrum, and the resulting gap in access and achievement between typically developing college students and college students with disabilities is very concerning. That is, students with disabilities attend postsecondary school at approximately half the rate of typically developing students (Blackorby & Wagner, 1996; Henderson, 1999a, 1999b, 2001; National Center for Education Statistics [NCES], 1999a, 1999b; Stodden, 2001; Wagner, D'Amico, Marder, Newman, & Blackorby, 1992; Wagner, Newman, Cameto, Garza, & Levine, 2005). Furthermore, even when included in college, students with disabilities graduate at a lesser rate than their typically developing peers (Erickson & Lee, 2008; Murray, Goldstein, Nourse, & Edgar, 2000; National Council on Disability, 2000). Policies providing for accommodations for students with disabilities in college are focused on only a few specific disabilities. While more adults with ASD are attending postsecondary education than in the past, with 5%–40% (depending on the sample) attending and successfully completing some type of college or university (Levy & Perry, 2011; Madaus, 2011), an even larger number of such individuals have unfulfilled desires to attend college. Approximately 66% of the youth with autism had a goal to attend postsecondary education, and 53% specifically wanted to attend a 2- or 4-year college (Wagner et al., 2005).

Access to higher education for students with disabilities is particularly important given its implications for quality of life (Halpern, 1993; Robertson, 2010). We know that individuals who attend and complete higher education or professional job training are more likely to obtain employment than are those who do not (Benz, Doren, & Yvanoff, 1998; Blackorby & Wagner, 1996; Golden & Jones, 2002; National Organization on Disabilities, 1998). Blackorby and Wagner (1996) assert that this gap in employment will continue to grow until equal participation in higher education is achieved between individuals with and without disabilities. Therefore, it is extremely important that students with ASD be supported appropriately in their higher education goals.

The challenge of providing access and accommodations to students with autism in higher education is a relatively new problem with little research guiding effective practices. Transition planning is crucial for increasing numbers of adolescents and young adults with ASD who have a goal to access higher education. Quality-of-life outcomes, including "social entitlements," should be of primary consideration when evaluating transition planning, yet postsecondary education and social services are often neglected (Halpern, 1993). Current best practices in transition preparation include work experience, employment preparation,

family involvement, inclusion in general education, instruction in social skills, practices guided by self-determination, daily-living skills training, and community collaboration (Landmark, Ju, & Zhang, 2010; Test et al., 2009; Test et al., 2010; Test & Grossi, 2011). Although the Americans with Disabilities Act (ADA; 1990, PL 101–336) and Section 504 (1973, PL 102–569) provide for "reasonable accommodations," the burden of self-advocacy often prohibits college students with ASD from attaining the level of accommodations needed. Since the Individuals with Disabilities Education Act (IDEA; 2004) does not apply at this level of education, students and parents encounter the challenge of providing appropriate accommodations without an Individualized Education Plan (IEP). Under the ADA (1990; PL 101–336) and Section 504 (1973; P.L. 102–569), the school is not required to create appropriate academic goals and continually measure the student's progress, which often help adolescents with ASD achieve success in middle and high school.

As a whole, although it is essential that faculty and staff are knowledgeable about meeting the needs of individuals with disabilities, there are few resources for professors on understanding ASD and how to modify advanced curricula. Though most studies find faculty are supportive of students with disabilities in their classrooms and have a desire to accommodate student specific needs (Leyser & Greenberger, 2008; Matthews, Anderson, & Skolnick, 1987; Thompson, Bethea, & Turner 1997), the level of support and actual provision of accommodations depends on the faculty's background and knowledge of support services (Konur, 2006; Leyser & Greenberger, 2008; Vogel, Leyser, Burgstahler, Sligar, & Zecker, 2006; Vogel, Leyser, Wyland, & Brulle, 1999). A study conducted by West et al. (1993) of 761 students with disabilities across 57 schools showed that while many were moderately satisfied with the services their school offered, 86.4% reported encountering barriers to their education because of a lack of understanding and cooperation from university staff, faculty, and other students. Furthermore, faculty often have limited knowledge of the laws that pertain to disability education (Dona & Edmister, 2001; Madaus, 2011). Cook, Rumrill, and Tankersley (2009) indicate that "the success of any college student, particularly in the academic realm, is to some degree determined by the type and quality of interactions that he or she has with his or her instructors" (p. 84). Research on academic interventions or accommodations that faculty could implement should be conducted, as well as efforts to increase awareness of the specific needs of diverse student populations, such as those with ASD.

Some programs are beginning to emerge as effective for college students with ASD. For example, L. K. Koegel, Ashbaugh, Koegel, Detar, and Register (in press) implemented a study that focused on improving socialization in university students with ASD who engaged in no social activities whatsoever. The authors used an intervention that involved participation in clubs and other social activities around the student with ASD's interests. Specifically, a clinician and a student with ASD chose social activities developed around their specialized interests, and peer mentors attended the activities to provide support and encouragement, particularly initially. In addition to the club meetings, weekly intervention sessions addressed social skills and challenges. These sessions focused on trouble shooting, discussing ways in which to initiate a conversation, appropriate pragmatic behavior, how to ask questions during social interactions, and so on. Results showed widespread positive improvements in untargeted areas for the students after they began attending the clubs, including more leisure activities, improved grade point averages, obtaining employment, friendship development, and intimate relationships for some of the students. The results were consistent with other studies suggesting lower comorbid diagnoses (anxiety and depression) and related challenges that are directly caused by a lack of socialization.

SUMMARY

Although the research on intervention for adolescents and adults with ASD is still in its infancy, the literature documents a number of effective interventions for this age group. As well, many effective interventions for children have been shown to be successful with adolescents or adults with little or no modification. In addition to the need for development of new procedures for adolescents and adults, there is also a need to disseminate information about current best practices (Sullivan, 2007).

As a whole, interventions that enhance the strengths of adolescents with ASD must be identified. Further, research that considers the dignity of the adolescent or adult with ASD should be conducted, such as extending the applicability of specific motivational variables (e.g., pivotal response treatment) so that interventions, whether they are communicative, social, or academic, are interesting and tied to real-life positive outcomes. Consequently, in targeting the pivotal areas of motivation, initiations, and self-management, we are likely to see collateral gains in many other areas and increased success in many realms of life (R. L. Koegel & Koegel, 2012). Furthermore, individuals with ASD are often not provided with employment opportunities that could benefit their mental health and improve their cognitive abilities. Research and advocacy in this area is essential.

Further research should also be conducted on using the new technology of video-based interventions with this older population, perhaps especially for social targets. Data on specific outcomes in inclusive peer support models should be obtained to determine the areas and individuals best served by these models. Areas to be addressed in this intervention research should include social conversation skills (such as initiations), friendship-making skills, self-presentation skills, daily living skills, self-management skills, organizational skills, and other targets individualized to each person's needs. Such research should greatly enhance the ability to gain and maintain employment and to improve social relationships.

Next, efforts to individualize accommodations and supports for each student with a disability should be made inherent in higher education disability support programs. This potentially could be done by extending the concept of universal design

(Scott, Loewen, Funckes, & Kroeger, 2003) to include access to social and community environments and activities and thinking beyond simple accommodations for students with ASD. The current model of disability will likely need to integrate several perspectives in order to do so. Diverse students will require diverse resources. Within a disability model that integrates several perspectives, future research will address and modify both environmental variables and behavioral obstructions to full participation in academic, social, and community domains by adolescents/adults with ASDs.

Undoubtedly, effective supports for adolescents with ASD will need to consider the real barriers currently present in the system. First, the slow nature of system policy changes due to lack of funding and resources, and the need for changes in public opinion may present a barrier to implementation of additional supports for individuals with ASD systemwide. Policies enhancing affirmative action may be helpful in reducing the many barriers individuals with disabilities, particularly ASD, encounter on their road to independent and successful participation in society. Furthermore, a changing of the types of support necessary for success is needed, to include individualized social supports and behavioral interventions. As other fields are moving toward developing common standards in accommodations and services, the autism field should do the same to create independence in individuals with ASD. This will necessitate future research in higher education, employment, and independent living. With such supports, adolescents with ADS are likely to gain employment, become contributing members of society, reach their educational and social potential, and overall experience a high quality of adult life.

CROSS-REFERENCES

Chapter 1 addresses diagnostic issues and Chapter 2 the broader autism phenotype. Chapters 5, 6, and 8 focus on autism in infants and young children, school-aged children, and adults, respectively. Chapter 36 addresses promotion of recreational activities, Chapter 38 supporting employment, and Chapter 39 postsecondary educational services.

REFERENCES

Allen, K. D., Wallace, D. P., & Renes, D. (2010). Use of video modeling to teach vocational skills to adolescents and young adults with autism spectrum disorders. *Education and Treatment of Children, 33*(3), 339–349.

Americans With Disabilities Act of 1990, as amended. Retrieved June 14, 2012, from http://www.ada.gov/pubs/ada.htm

Baker, M. J., Koegel, R. L., & Koegel, L. K. (1998). Increasing the social behavior of young children with autism using their obsessive behaviors. *Journal of the Association for Persons with Severe Handicaps, 23*(4), 300–308. doi:10.2511/rpsd.23.4.300

Bellini, S., & Akullian, J. (2007). A meta-analysis of video modeling and video self-modeling interventions for children and adolescents with autism spectrum disorders. *Exceptional Children, 73*(3), 264–287.

Benz, M., Doren, B., & Yovanoff, P. (1998). Crossing the great divide: Predicting productive engagement for young women with disabilities. *Career Development for Exceptional Individuals, 21*(1), 3–16.

Blackorby, J., & Wagner, M. (1996). Longitudinal postschool outcomes of youth with disabilities: Findings from the National Longitudinal Transition Study. *Exceptional Children, 62,* 399–413.

Burke, R. V., Andersen, M. N., Bowen, S. L., Howard, M. R., & Allen, K. D. (2010). Evaluation of two instruction methods to increase employment options for young adults with autism spectrum disorders. *Research in Developmental Disabilities, 31*(6), 1223–1233.

Cappadocia, M. C., Weiss, J. A., & Pepler, D. (2012). Bullying experiences among children and youth with autism spectrum disorders. *Journal of Autism and Developmental Disorders, 42*(2), 266–277.

Carter, E. W., Cushing, L. S., Clark, N. M., & Kennedy, C. H. (2005). Effects of peer support interventions on students' access to the general curriculum and social interactions. *Research and Practice for Persons with Severe Disabilities, 30,* 15–25.

Carter, S. (2009). Bullying of students with Asperger syndrome. *Issues in Comprehensive Pediatric Nursing, 32*(3), 145–154. doi:10.1080/01460860903062782

Chan, J. M., Lang, R., Rispoli, M., O'Reilly, M., Sigafoos, J., & Cole, H. (2009). Use of peer-mediated interventions in the treatment of autism spectrum disorders: A systematic review. *Research in Autism Spectrum Disorders, 3*(4), 876–889. doi:10.1016/j.rasd.2009.04.003

Charlop, M. H., & Milstein, J. P. (1989). Teaching autistic children conversational speech using video modeling. *Journal of Applied Behavior Analysis, 22*(3), 275–285.

Charlop-Christy, M. H., Le, L., & Freeman, K. A. (2000). A comparison of video modeling with in vivo modeling for teaching children with autism. *Journal of Autism and Developmental Disorders, 30*(6), 537–552.

Church, C., Alisanski, S., & Amanullah, S. (2000). The social, behavioral, and academic experiences of children with Asperger syndrome. *Focus on Autism and Other Developmental Disabilities, 15*(1), 12–20.

Cihak, D. F., & Grim, J. (2008). Teaching students with autism spectrum disorder and moderate intellectual disabilities to use counting-on strategies to enhance independent purchasing skills. *Research in Autism Spectrum Disorders, 2*(4), 716–727. doi:10.1016/j.rasd.2008.02.006

Cook, L., Rumrill, P. D., & Tankersley, M. (2009). Priorities and understanding of faculty members regarding college students with disabilities. *International Journal of Teaching and Learning in Higher Education, 21*(1), 84–96.

Cooper, H., & Nye, B. (1994). Homework for students with learning disabilities: The Implications of research for policy and practice. *Journal of Learning Disabilities, 27*(8), 470–479. doi:10.1177/002221949402700802

Dona, J., & Edmister, J. H. (2001). An examination of community college faculty members' knowledge of the Americans with Disabilities Act of 1990 at the fifteen community colleges in Mississippi. *Journal of Postsecondary Education and Disability, 14*(2), 91–103.

Dowrick, P. W. (1991). *Practical guide to using video in the behavioral sciences.* New York, NY: Wiley Interscience.

Erickson, W., & Lee, C. (2008). 2007 Disability Status Report: The United States. Ithaca, NY: Cornell University Rehabilitation Research and Training Center on Disability Demographics and Statistics.

García-Villamisar, D., & Hughes, C. (2007). Supported employment improves cognitive performance in adults with Autism. *Journal of Intellectual Disability Research, 51*(2), 142–150. doi:10.1111/j.1365–2788.2006.00854.x

Gelbar, N. W., Anderson, C., McCarthy, S., & Buggey, T. (2012). Video self-modeling as an intervention strategy for individuals with autism spectrum disorders. *Psychology in the Schools, 49*(1), 15–22. doi:10.1002/pits.20628

Gengoux, G. W. (2009). *Priming for games and cooperative activities with children with autism: Effects on social interactions with typically developing peers.* Santa Barbara: University of California Press.

Ghaziuddin, M., Ghaziuddin, N., & Greden, J. (2002). Depression in persons with autism: implications for research and clinical care. *Journal of Autism and Developmental Disorders, 32*(4), 299–306.

Golden, T. P., & Jones, M. A. (2002, Spring). SSI and postsecondary education support for students with disabilities. *Impact (Newsletter of the Institute on Community Integration) 15*(1). Retrieved from http://digitalcommons.ilr.cornell.edu/edicollect/147

Graetz, J. E., Mastropieri, M. A., & Scruggs, T. E. (2006). Show time: Using video self-modeling to decrease inappropriate behavior. *Teaching Exceptional Children, 38*(5), 43–48.

Green, J., Gilchrist, A., Burton, D., & Cox, A. (2000). Social and psychiatric functioning in adolescents with Asperger syndrome compared with conduct disorder. *Journal of Autism and Developmental Disorders, 30*(4), 279–293.

Grills, A. E., & Ollendick, T. H. (2002). Peer victimization, global self-worth, and anxiety in middle school children. *Journal of Clinical Child and Adolescent Psychology, 31*(1), 59–68.

Halpern, A. (1993). Quality of life as a conceptual framework for evaluating transition outcomes. *Exceptional Children, 59,* 486–498.

Haring, T. G., & Breen, C. G. (1992). A peer-mediated social network intervention to enhance the social integration of persons with moderate and severe disabilities. *Journal of Applied Behavior Analysis, 25*(2), 319–333.

Harrower, J. K., & Dunlap, G. (2001). Including children with autism in general education classrooms: A review of effective strategies. *Behavior Modification. Special Issue: Autism, 25,* 762–784. doi:10.1177/0145445501255006

Henderson, C. (1999a). *College freshmen with disabilities: Statistical year 1998.* Washington, DC: American Council on Education.

Henderson, C. (1999b). *1999 college freshmen with disabilities: A biennial statistical profile.* Washington, DC: American Council on Education, HEATH Resource Center.

Henderson, C. (2001). *College freshmen with disabilities, 2001: A biennial statistical profile.* Washington, DC: American Council on Education, Health Resource Center.

Hopkins, I. M., Gower, M. W., Perez, T. A., Smith, D. S., Amthor, F. R., Wimsatt, F. C., & Biasini, F. J. (2011). Avatar assistant: Improving social skills in students with an ASD through a computer-based intervention. *Journal of Autism and Developmental Disorders, 41*(11), 1543–1555. doi:10.1007/s10803-011-1179-z

Individuals with Disabilities Education Improvement Act of 2004, Pub. L. No. 108–446, 118 Stat. 2647 (2004).

Kim, J. A., Szatmari, P., Bryson, S. E., Streiner, D. L., & Wilson, F. J. (2000). The prevalence of anxiety and mood problems among children with autism and Asperger syndrome. *Autism, 4*(2), 117–132.

Klin, A., & Volkmar, F. R. (2000). Treatment and intervention guidelines for individuals with Asperger syndrome. In A. Klin, S. S. Sparrow, & F. R. Volkmar (Eds.), *Asperger syndrome* (pp. 340–366). New York, NY: Guilford Press.

Koegel, L. K., Ashbaugh, K., Koegel, R. L, Detar, W. J., & Register, A. (in press). Behavioral approaches for the treatment of adults with autism spectrum disorders. In K. Haertl (Ed.), *Adults with intellectual and developmental disabilities: Strategies for occupational therapy.*

Koegel, L. K., Detar, W. J., Fox, A., & Koegel, R. L. (in press). Romantic relationships, sexuality, and autism spectrum disorders. In F. Volkmar, J. McPartland, & B. Reichow (Eds.), *Adolescents and adults with autism spectrum disorders.* New York, NY: Springer.

Koegel, L. K., Koegel, R. L., Frea, W., & Green-Hopkins, I. (2003). Priming as a method of coordinating educational services for students with autism. *Language, 34,* 228–235. doi:10.1044/0161-1461(2003/019)

Koegel, L. K., Koegel, R. L., Hurley, C., & Frea, W. D. (1992). Improving social skills and disruptive behavior in children with autism through self-management. *Journal of Applied Behavior Analysis, 25*(2), 341–353. doi:10.1901/jaba.1992.25-341

Koegel, L. K., Koegel, R. L., Shoshan, Y., & McNerney, E. (1999). Pivotal response intervention II: Preliminary long-term outcomes data. *Journal of the Association for Persons with Severe Handicaps, 24*(3), 186–198. doi:10.2511/rpsd.24.3.186

Koegel, L. K., & LaZebnik, C. (2009). *Growing up on the spectrum: A guide to life, love, and learning for teens and young adults with autism and Asperger's.* New York, NY: Viking.

Koegel, L. K., Singh, A. K., & Koegel, R. L. (2010). Improving motivation for academics in children with autism. *Journal of Autism and Developmental Disorders, 40*(9), 1057–1066. doi:10.1007/s10803-010-0962-6

Koegel, R. L., & Frea, W. D. (1993). Treatment of social behavior in autism through the modification of pivotal social skills. *Journal of Applied Behavior Analysis, 26*(3), 369–377. doi:10.1901/jaba.1993.26-369

Koegel, R. L., Fredeen, R., Kim, S., Danial, J., Rubinstein, D., & Koegel, L. (2012). Using perseverative interests to improve interactions between adolescents with autism and their typical peers in school settings. *Journal of Positive Behavior Interventions, 14*(3), 133–141.

Koegel, R. L., & Koegel, L. K. (2012). *The PRT pocket guide.* Baltimore, MD: Paul H. Brookes.

Koegel, R. L., Tran, Q. H., Mossman, A., & Koegel, L. K. (2006). Incorporating motivational procedures to improve homework performance. In R. L. Koegel & L. K. Koegel (Eds.), *Pivotal response treatments for autism: communication, social, & academic development* (pp. 81–91). Baltimore, MD: Paul H. Brookes.

Konur, O. (2006). Teaching disabled students in higher education. *Teaching in Higher Education, 11*(3), 351–363.

Koyama, T., & Wang, H.-T. (2011). Use of activity schedule to promote independent performance of individuals with autism and other intellectual disabilities: A review. *Research in Developmental Disabilities, 32*(6), 2235–2242.

Kurth, J., & Mastergeorge, A. M. (2010). Individual education plan goals and services for adolescents with autism: Impact of age and educational setting. *Journal of Special Education, 44*(3), 146–160.

Landmark, L. J., Ju, S., & Zhang, D. (2010). Substantiated best practices in transition: Fifteen plus years later. *Career Development for Exceptional Individuals, 33*(3), 165–176.

Lee, S.-H., Simpson, R. L., & Shogren, K. A. (2007). Effects and implications of self-management for students with autism: A meta-analysis. *Focus on Autism and Other Developmental Disabilities, 22*(1), 2–13. doi:10.1177/10883576070220010101

Levy, A., & Perry, A. (2011). Outcomes in adolescents and adults with autism: A review of the literature. *Research in Autism Spectrum Disorders, 5*(4), 1271–1282. doi:10.1016/j.rasd.2011.01.023

Leyser, Y., & Greenberger, L. (2008). College students with disabilities in teacher education: Faculty attitudes and practices. *European Journal of Special Needs Education, 23*(3), 237–237.

Little, L. (2002). Middle-class mother's perceptions of peer and sibling victimization among children with Asperger's syndrome and nonverbal learning disorders. *Issues in Comprehensive Pediatric Nursing, 25*, 43–57.

Madaus, J. W. (2011). The history of disability services in higher education. *New Directions for Higher Education, 154*, 5–15. doi:10.1002/he.429

Maljaars, J., Noens, I., Jansen, R., Scholte, E., & van Berckelaer-Onnes, I. (2011). Intentional communication in nonverbal and verbal low-functioning children with autism. *Journal of Communication Disorders, 44*(6), 601–614. doi:10.1016/j.jcomdis.2011.07.004

Matson, J. L., Hattier, M. A., & Belva, B. (2012). Treating adaptive living skills of persons with autism using applied behavior analysis: A review. *Research in Autism Spectrum Disorders, 6*(1), 271–276.

Matthews, P. R., Anderson, D. W., & Skolnick, B. D. (1987). Faculty attitude toward accommodations for college students with learning disabilities. *Learning Disabilities Focus, 31*(1) 46–46.

McCoy, K., & Hermansen, E. (2007). Video modeling for individuals with autism: A review of model types and effects. *Education and Treatment of Children, 30*(4), 183–213.

Mechling, L. C., & Cronin, B. (2006). Computer-based video instruction to teach the use of augmentative and alternative communication devices for ordering at fast-food restaurants. *Journal of Special Education, 39*(4), 234–245.

Morrison, L., Kamps, D., Garcia, J., & Parker, D. (2001). Peer mediation and monitoring strategies to improve initiations and social skills for students with autism. *Journal of Positive Behavior Interventions, 3*(4), 237–250. doi:10.1177/109830070100300405

Muhlenbruck, L., Cooper, H., Nye, B., & Lindsay, J. J. (2000). Homework and achievement: Explaining the different strengths of relation at the elementary and secondary school levels. *Social Psychology of Education, 3*(4), 295–317.

Murray, C., Goldstein, D. E., Nourse, S., & Edgar, E. (2000). The postsecondary school attendance and completion rates of high school graduates with learning disabilities. *Learning Disabilities Research, 15*, 119–127.

National Autism Center. (2009). *National Standards Project: Addressing the need for evidence-based practice guidelines for autism spectrum disorder. Findings and conclusions.* Retrieved from http://www.nationalautismcenter.org/pdf/NAC%20Standards%20Report.pdf

National Center for Education Statistics. (1999a). *Students with disabilities in postsecondary education a profile of preparation, participation, and outcomes.* Retrieved from http://nces.ed.gov/pubsearch/pubsinfo.asp?pubid=1999187

National Center for Education Statistics. (1999b). *An institutional perspective on students with disabilities in postsecondary education.* NCES 1999-046. Washington, DC: Author.

National Council on Disability. (2000). *Transition and post-school outcomes for youth with disabilities: Closing the gaps to postsecondary education and employment.* Washington, DC: Author.

National Organization on Disabilities (1998). *N.O.D. Harris survey of Americans with disabilities*. Washington, DC: Louis Harris and Associates.

Robertson, S. M. (2010). Neurodiversity, quality of life, and autistic adults: Shifting research and professional focuses onto real-life challenges. *Disability Studies Quarterly, 30*(1). Retrieved from http://www.dsq-sds.org/article/view/1069/1234

Roeyers, H. (1996). The influence of nonhandicapped peers on the social interactions of children with a pervasive developmental disorder. *Journal of Autism and Developmental Disorders, 26*, 303–320.

Scott, S. S., Loewen, G., Funckes, C., & Kroeger, S. (2003). Implementing universal design in higher education: Moving beyond the built environment. *Journal on Postsecondary Education and Disability, 16*(2), 78–89.

Schreibman, L., Whalen, C., & Stahmer, A. C. (2000). The use of video priming to reduce disruptive transition behavior in children with autism. *Journal of Positive Behavior Interventions, 2*(1), 3–11.

Section 504 of the Rehabilitation Act of 1973, P.L. No. 102–569, 29 U.S.C. § 794.

Smith, W. J. (2011). *Improving social conversation in young adults with Asperger's syndrome using video feedback*. Presented at the Improving Social Conversation in Young Adults with Autism Spectrum Disorders Symposium, Applied Behavior Analysis International Annual Convention, Denver, CO.

Southall, C. M., & Gast, D. L. (2011). Self-management procedures: A comparison across the autism spectrum. *Education and Training in Autism and Developmental Disabilities, 46*(2), 155–171.

Stahmer, A. C., & Schreibman, L. (1992). Teaching children with autism appropriate play in unsupervised environments using a self-management treatment package. *Journal of Applied Behavior Analysis, 25*(2), 447–459. doi:10.1901/jaba.1992.25-447

Sterling, L., Dawson, G., Estes, A., & Greenson, J. (2008). Characteristics associated with presence of depressive symptoms in adults with autism spectrum disorder. *Journal of Autism and Developmental Disorders, 38*(6), 1011–1018.

Stodden, R. A. (2001). Postsecondary education supports for students with disabilities: A review and response. *Journal for Vocational Special Needs Education, 23*(2), 4–11.

Sullivan, R. C. (2007). *Autism Society of America position paper on the national crisis in adult services for individuals with autism*. Autism Society of America. Retrieved from http://support.autism-society.org/site/DocServer/Adult_Services_vMay2007.pdf?docID=2601

Test, D. W., Fowler, C. H., Richter, S. M., White, J., Mazzotti, V., Walker, A. R., . . . Kortering, L. (2009). Evidence-based practices in secondary transition. *Career Development for Exceptional Individuals, 32*(2), 115–128.

Test, D. W., & Grossi, T. (2011). Transition planning and evidence-based research. *Journal of Vocational Rehabilitation, 35*, 173–175. doi:10.3233/JVR-2011-0566

Test, D. W., Mazzotti, V. L., Mustian, A. L., Fowler, C. H., Kortering, L., & Kohler, P. (2010). Evidence-based secondary transition predictors for improving postschool outcomes for students with disabilities. *Career Development for Exceptional Individuals, 32*(3), 160–181. doi: 10.1177/0885728809346960.

Thompson, A. R., Bethea, L., & Turner, J. (1997). Faculty knowledge of disability laws in higher education: A survey. *Rehabilitation Counseling Bulletin, 40*(3), 166–166.

Van Bourgondien, M. E., & Elgar, S. (1990). The relationship between existing residential services and the needs of autistic adults. *Journal of Autism and Developmental Disorders, 20*(3), 299–308.

Van Bourgondien, M. E., & Reichle, N. C. (1997). Residential treatment for individuals with autism. In D. J. Cohen & F. R. Volkmar (Eds.), *Handbook of autism and pervasive developmental disorders* (2nd ed., pp. 691–706). New York, NY: Wiley.

Van Bourgondien, M. E., & Schopler, E. (1996). Intervention for adults with autism. *Journal of Rehabilitation, 62*, 65–71.

Vaughn, S., Schumm, J. S., & Kouzekanani, K. (1993). What do students with learning disabilities think when their general education teachers make adaptations? *Journal of Learning Disabilities, 26*(8), 545–555. doi:10.1177/002221949302600808

Vogel, S. A., Leyser, Y., Burgstahler, S., Sligar, S. R., & Zecker, S. C. (2006). Faculty knowledge and practices regarding students with disabilities in three contrasting institutions of higher education. *Journal of Postsecondary Education and Disability, 18*, 109–123.

Vogel, S. A., Leyser, Y., Wyland, S., & Brulle, A. (1999). Students with learning disabilities in higher education: Faculty attitude and practices. *Learning Disabilities Research and Practice, 14*(3), 173–186.

Wagner, M., D'Amico, R., Marder, C., Newman, L., & Blackorby, J. (Eds.). (1992). *What happens next? Trends in postschool outcomes of youth with disabilities*. The second comprehensive report from the National Longitudinal Transition Study of Special Education Students. Menlo Park, CA: SRI International.

Wagner, M., Newman, L., Cameto, R., Garza, N., & Levine, P. (2005). *After high school: A first look at the postschool experiences of youth with disabilities. A Report from the National Longitudinal Transition Study-2 (NLTS2)* Menlo Park, CA: SRI International. Retrieved from www.nlts2.org/reports/2005_04/nlts2_report_2005_04_complete.pdf

Wang, P., & Spillane, A. (2009). Evidence-based social skills interventions for children with autism: A meta-analysis. *Education and Training in Developmental Disabilities, 44*(3), 318–342.

Wehmeyer, M. L., Yeager, D., Bolding, N., Agran, M., & Hughes, C. (2003). The effects of self-regulation strategies on goal attainment for students with developmental disabilities in general education classrooms. *Journal of Developmental and Physical Disabilities, 15*(1), 79–91. doi:10.1023/A:1021408405270

West, M., Kregel, J., Getzel, E. E., Ming, Z., Ipsen, S. M., & Martin, E. D. (1993). Beyond Section 504: Satisfaction and empowerment of students with disabilities in higher education. *Exceptional Children, 59*(5), 456–467.

Whitby, P. J. S., & Mancil, G. R. (2009). Academic achievement profiles of children with high functioning autism and Asperger syndrome: A review of the literature. *Education and Training in Developmental Disabilities*, *44*(4), 551–560.

White, S. W., & Schry, A. R. (2011). Social anxiety in adolescents on the autism spectrum. In C. A. Alfano & D. C. Beidel (Eds.), *Social anxiety disorder in adolescents and young adults: Translating developmental science into practice* (pp. 183–201). Washington, DC: American Psychological Association.

Wilde, L. D., Koegel, L. K., & Koegel, R. L. (1992). *Increasing success in school through priming: A training manual*. Santa Barbara: University of California Press.

CHAPTER 8

Adults With Autism

CARLA A. MAZEFSKY AND SUSAN W. WHITE

INTRODUCTION

It is difficult to draw firm, empirically based conclusions about the developmental course and progression of autism spectrum disorder (ASD) in adults because of changes in our diagnostic practices, lack of longitudinal studies, historically weak long-term symptom monitoring, and use of different tools for assessment and diagnosis over time. As Seltzer et al. (2003) astutely observed, for these reasons we are limited in our ability to make inferences about developmental pathways in people with ASD when using cross-sectional comparisons. We are, in essence, likely to make the faulty assumption that samples are equivalent and therefore comparable (akin to an "apples to mangos" comparison).

The field of ASD research, however, is on the forefront of a zeitgeist—a change toward greater clinical and scientific appreciation of, and curiosity about, ASD in adults. Indeed, this is the first edition of the *Handbook* to include a chapter dedicated

solely to issues relevant to affected adults. An electronic search of the most commonly cited journals in our field, using the words *autism* and *adult* in the title, is quite telling. From 1990 to 1999, 93 peer-reviewed articles were identified. In the following 10-year period (2000–2009), the same search yielded 285 articles. From 2010 to 2012, 199 articles were found—a publication rate far exceeding that of the previous two decades. Greater scientific attention (and, in suit, more research dollars) is now being dedicated to enhancing our knowledge of adult ASD than ever before. In the next several years, we will develop our knowledge base about the unique needs faced by this rapidly expanding population, and advances will be made in our approaches to the assessment, support, and treatment of adults affected by ASD. The field is ripe for innovation and growth. This is not only an exciting venture; it is a necessary one. There is little argument that ASD is much more common than previously recognized, and identification rates have soared in recent history. Those children who were first identified on the front-end of this growth period, in the early 1990s (Gurney et al., 2003), are now firmly in adulthood. The population of adults diagnosed with ASD will surely grow at a pace that will unfortunately exceed our scientific and financial resources.

In this chapter we summarize research on adult outcome and prognosis, including the stability of ASD core and secondary symptoms. We discuss developmental challenges and transitions, identify the most common clinical issues presented by adults with ASD, and summarize the limited available research on adult services and treatment. Although we have tried to be comprehensive in our synthesis of the research to date, some of this, by necessity, is based on clinical experience and observation. Finally, we present specific suggestions for future research.

DEVELOPMENTAL COURSE AND PROGNOSIS

Autism spectrum disorder is chronic, typically identified before the age of 5 (United States Centers for Disease Control and Prevention, 2009) and persisting into adulthood. Although the degree of symptomatic impairment tends to wax and wane over the course of development, there is a general tendency toward improvement, believed to be attributable to developmental factors as well as various treatments delivered over the course of the person's life (Cederlund, Hagberg, Billstedt, Gillberg, & Gillberg, 2008; Howlin, Goode, Hutton, & Rutter, 2004; Seltzer et al., 2003). Despite variable symptomatic improvement, there is a high degree of diagnostic stability from childhood to adulthood (e.g., Billstedt, Gillberg, & Gillberg, 2005; Farley et al., 2009).

Available research at this point indicates that growth trajectories may flatten to some degree post-adolescence. Taylor and Seltzer (2010) assessed 242 adolescents and adults with ASD over a nearly 10-year period and found that the improvement observed in ASD symptoms and maladaptive behaviors seen during adolescence slowed significantly after exiting secondary education (high school). In a recent longitudinal study of community-based adolescents and adults with ASD ($n = 397$), Smith, Maenner, and Seltzer (2012) found that daily living skills improved into early adulthood but then plateaued, a pattern not seen in their comparison sample of adolescents and adults with Down syndrome. Although more research is needed on this topic, a pattern of symptomatic improvement and growth in adaptive behavior through adolescence that then halts (or perhaps even regresses) during young adulthood (Smith et al., 2012; Taylor & Seltzer, 2010) is of great concern and requires further investigation.

Consideration of outcome often goes beyond ASD symptoms and diagnostic status, to include factors such as housing situation or residential placement, whether employment has been obtained, degree of social contact, and overall level of independence. The available evidence suggests widely variable outcomes (e.g., Fountain, Winter, & Bearman, 2012; see Chapter 4 by Patricia Howlin for a thorough discussion of outcome). Studies are inconsistent about the most common living arrangement in adulthood, though it is clear that long-term dependence on caregivers is common (Billstedt, Gillberg, & Gillberg, 2011). Adults with ASD and intellectual disability are also significantly more likely to live in group homes with other adults with disabilities, than are adults with Down syndrome (Esbensen, Bishop, Seltzer, Greenberg, & Taylor, 2010). For higher functioning individuals, independence is often hampered by inability to gain or maintain employment. Even among the minority who live alone, a high proportion requires public or private financial support (Engström, Ekström, & Emilsson, 2003). Young adults without cognitive impairment are less likely than adults with ASD and intellectual disability to have structured daytime activities (Taylor & Seltzer, 2011). As such, adults with ASD who do not have intellectual impairment face a unique set of challenges—they often do not have access to services and supports that might be helpful, yet they struggle to live independently.

The most commonly reported predictors of positive outcome are better cognitive ability and expressive language skills measured at age 5 or beyond (Billstedt et al., 2005; Howlin, Mawhood, & Rutter, 2000). On the other hand, psychiatric comorbidity and the need for psychological or behavioral services are both related to poorer outcomes in adulthood (e.g., Esbensen et al., 2010). Interestingly, the same factors touted as generally protective, namely, cognitive ability and expressive language (Lord & Bailey, 2002; Seltzer, Shattuck, Abbeduto, & Greenberg, 2004), may pose risks for psychiatric problems in adulthood. Sterling, Dawson, Estes, and Greenson (2008) found that, among adults with diagnosed ASD, less severe social impairment and better cognitive function were associated with symptoms of depression. The ability of adults with ASD who are higher functioning and verbal to self-report problems and psychiatric symptoms may, at least partially, explain these findings. In other words, some types of comorbidity (e.g., depression, anxiety) may be less apparent, even when they are present, among lower functioning and less verbal adults. It is also possible that higher functioning individuals truly do experience more psychiatric difficulties than lower functioning individuals. Higher functioning individuals may have more difficulty handling the challenges of adulthood, compared to less able adults with ASD, whose lives are highly orchestrated by others and who tend to receive more ongoing services.

In summary, there is insufficient longitudinal research at this point to have a firm understanding of the developmental course of ASD into adulthood. The ASD diagnosis tends to be stable throughout development; few individuals truly outgrow it or are treated to remission. But improvement, interspersed with periods of worsening in some domains, is common. There is tremendous need for longitudinal studies to examine potential heterotypic continuity (cf. Rutter & Sroufe, 2000) in behavior, or different manifestations over time of the same underlying problem or cause. It is apparent that, when exploring long-term outcomes, we must view outcome and quality of life multidimensionally and also consider the individual person's perspective, including their subjective experience of quality of life. A high-functioning adult with ASD, for instance, may live independently and be gainfully employed but struggle with depression and be severely socially isolated.

TRANSITIONS

The first major transition encountered by young adults with ASD is completion of secondary school. Although individuals with disabilities with an Individualized Education Plan can receive services from public schools until the age of 21 in the United States, IDEA (Individuals with Disabilities Education Act) requires a transition plan to be in place for each by the age of 16. The intent of transition plans is to identify goals agreed upon by the family, individual, and team members (usually a subset of the educational team), as well as the specific skills required to achieve these goals placed in the context of the child's individual strengths and weaknesses, and services and procedures for assisting persons to acquire those skills. While nearly three quarters of individuals with ASD have a transition plan, only approximately one third of individuals with ASD themselves have actually been involved in the planning. This lack of personal input into the plan may pose a barrier to the accomplishment of these plans (Hendricks & Wehman, 2009). Further, although transition plans identify skills to be taught, supporting generalization to the actual environment where they will eventually be applied is not always considered.

A recent study of 66 high school graduates with ASD and a range of intellectual abilities raised concerns about the adequacy of transition plans, especially for more cognitively able individuals with ASD (Taylor & Seltzer, 2011). Overall, Taylor and Seltzer (2011) found that 13.6% went to college, 6.1% went directly into competitive employment, 12.1% participated in supported employment, the majority (56.1%) attended adult day services/sheltered workshops, and 12.1% had no regular activities. However, when broken down by intellectual ability level, nearly a quarter of those without intellectual disability had no regular activities, which suggests that more attention needs to be paid to transition plans for cognitively able individuals with ASD who do not go onto college.

For adults with ASD who participate in higher education, adequate preparation and consideration of student–college fit is essential in ensuring a positive transition (VanBergeijk, Klin, & Volkmar, 2008). Some of the key considerations in achieving a good fit include school/class size, availability of counseling services, opportunities for studies in an area of interest, the school's willingness to allow accommodations, experience supporting students with ASD, and the types of living arrangements available (VanBergeijk et al., 2008). Colleges in the United States are required to provide supports to individuals with disabilities by the Americans with Disabilities Act. However, an individual must self-identify as having a disability to the university in order to receive services. Furthermore, the levels and types of services and supports available vary widely across institutions.

The transition from college into paid employment, or directly from high school to the working world, can be challenging and anxiety provoking for adults with ASD. The following quote from a 35-year-old with Asperger's and superior range IQ about his experience after graduating college provides some insight into the transition: "It was a lot of things one on top of the other . . . feeling like the rug was pulled out from under me sort of. I was always on a path throughout school . . . sort of a program . . . then all of a sudden, there's nothing. I had to figure out what to do with myself and my life for the first time . . . and lo and behold, I couldn't do it. I didn't know how to do it." It is clear that the sudden lack of external structure experienced during this transition can be stressful and overwhelming for individuals with ASD. In addition, college graduates may require explicit instruction in how to apply classroom-based learning in a job setting (VanBergeijk et al., 2008).

The young man just described did not find a job and spiraled into depression, despite graduating from a competitive university and having succeeded with limited support throughout the various stages of his education. Often adults with ASD will require assistance in finding, applying for, and interviewing at potential jobs. Similar to the process of choosing a college, the choices among employment options and opportunities to explore should be built from a careful consideration of the strengths and needs of the adult with ASD. Specifically, it is important to consider the interests of the individual with ASD, the interpersonal and communicative demands of a given job, any unique sensory sensitivities and how that may or may not match well with a potential opportunity, and willingness of the employer to be supportive and accommodating (McGonigle, Allen, & Lubetsky, 2011).

Later in life, transitions of significance may involve the loss of lifelong support systems such as the death of a family member. As discussed previously, individuals with ASD tend to rely heavily on family, especially parents, for emotional and financial support as well as help with daily living needs (e.g., structuring the person's time, reminding the person to take medications as prescribed). We lack research on later life transitions in ASD, but there are many important questions for which we will soon need to provide answers. What can parents of children (or adults) do to help ensure that their son or daughter is prepared for independent or assisted living when the parents pass on? What supports might spouses and partners of people with ASD benefit from, to promote successful long-term relationships?

CLINICAL ISSUES

Identification of ASD in Adulthood

Although diagnosis of ASD typically occurs during early childhood, identification tends to be later for individuals who are cognitively unimpaired. For some individuals, diagnosis does not occur until early adulthood (White, Ollendick, & Bray, 2011). The reasons for such delayed identification are not well understood, but it is likely that the person might use compensatory strategies to cover their deficits (e.g., Bastiaansen et al., 2011), or that problems are minimized, avoided, or managed by parents, until the person is forced to be in situations that require deficient skills (e.g., independent time management, vaguely defined social situations, competing demands and obligations, lack of external structure). In some cases, more prominent psychiatric symptoms may mask or overshadow the ASD diagnosis (Mazefsky, Oswald, et al., 2012). Studies have found relatively high rates of adults with undiagnosed ASD in psychiatric inpatient units as well (Nylander & Gillberg, 2001).

It can be extraordinarily difficult to identify ASD in older individuals, and there are very few diagnostic tools explicitly developed for assessing adults. Diagnosing adults is difficult for many reasons, including limitations in our current cadre of tools (Bastiaansen et al., 2011). Diagnosis requires both a current presentation consistent with diagnostic criteria and also a history that fits what we know about the developmental course of people with ASD. While clinical interviews can elicit current symptoms in adults, clinicians often lack access to developmental history and information. Parents may be unavailable or deceased, or may simply not recall pertinent information (this is especially common in families with multiple children). It is sometimes helpful to ask if someone who knew the person when he was younger (e.g., an older sibling or a parent) can be available for interview. Oftentimes, school report cards (especially the teachers' written observations), picture albums (to observe the child's play and interests), and home movies (often extremely helpful for early language samples and detecting subtle mannerisms) can be enlightening and informative to the assessment process.

Recently, Bastiaansen and colleagues (2011) found the Autism Diagnostic Observation Schedule (ADOS) Module 4 (Lord, Rutter, DiLavore, & Risi, 2002) to be reliable and valid in assessing ASD in adult males. Based primarily on clinical experience, as well as preliminary research, however, we caution against exclusive reliance upon the ADOS for diagnosis of ASD in adults. Farley et al. (2009) and White, Ollendick, et al. (2011) found that some higher functioning adults with an ASD diagnosis did not exceed ASD threshold for ASD on

the ADOS. As Farley postulated, adults who have received (often considerable amounts of) treatment over several years for ASD-related problems, yet who still exhibit considerable difficulty in their day-to-day functioning owing to ASD symptoms, may be missed when the clinician relies solely on the ADOS. The Autism Diagnostic Interview–Revised (ADI-R; Lord, Rutter, & Le Couteur, 1994) can be used for diagnosis with adults, but the heavy focus in the interview on the early childhood years can make the interview cumbersome to complete and threatens validity of the results. It is often very difficult for parents to accurately answer questions about their son or daughter's use of gestures, joint attention, and phrase speech, for example, after a 20-plus year gap.

The number of available measures for diagnosing high-functioning adults with ASD is growing. However, most of these measures have limited research on their psychometric properties to date, and the samples used in their initial validation/reliability studies have been small (Stoesz, Montgomery, Smart, & Hellsten, 2011). Some informant-based questionnaires that are primarily childhood measures, such as the Krug Asperger's Disorder Index (KADI; Krug & Arick, 2003) and the Gilliam Asperger's Disorder Scale (GADS; Gilliam, 2001) are marketed as applicable up to age 22. Yet caution should be exercised as few young adults were included in their initial studies (Stoesz et al., 2011), and it is unclear if measures developed primarily for children would assess the full range of expression and impairment one would expect in an adult with ASD. Most of the specifically adult-focused measures are in their infancy and have some weaknesses. For example, the Autism Spectrum Disorder in Adults Screening Questionnaire (ASDASQ; Nylander & Gillberg, 2001), a brief, nine-item questionnaire that can be completed by someone who knows the adult fairly well, such as his or her psychiatrist, has had little published research on its clinical utility. The Adult Asperger Assessment (AAA; Baron-Cohen, Wheelwright, Robinson, & Woodbury-Smith, 2005) is unique in that it is a clinician-administered interview designed explicitly for adults, but it takes approximately three hours to complete (comparable to, or slightly longer than, the ADI-R), is somewhat more conservative than diagnoses based strictly on *DSM* (*Diagnostic and Statistical Manual of Mental Disorders*) criteria, and notably lacks norms.

There are some promising self-report instruments available. The Autism Spectrum Quotient (AQ; Baron-Cohen, Wheelwright, Skinner, Martin, & Clubley, 2001), a 50-item self-report measure, has been found to possess fairly strong psychometric qualities (for the total score) and be quite useful as a screening measure among adults without cognitive impairment (Baron-Cohen et al., 2001; White, Bray, & Ollendick, 2011; Woodbury-Smith, Robinson, Wheelwright, & Baron-Cohen, 2005). The Social Responsiveness Scale (SRS; Constantino & Gruber, 2005) is one of the most widely used measures in children with extensive evidence supporting its psychometric properties, and an SRS-Adult, that can be completed either as a self- or informant-report, has recently been developed (Constantino, 2012; Constantino & Gruber, 2005). The SRS-Adult items generally mirror the 65-item child version, with some adaptations in wording and content to make it more applicable (Constantino, 2012). An 11-item self-report screening version of the SRS-Adult (Constantino, in press) has been used in several studies to date (Kanne, Christ, & Reiersen, 2009; Reiersen, Constantino, Grimmer, Martin, & Todd, 2008; White, Ollendick, et al., 2011), which have supported its psychometric properties.

A full review and evaluation of the available tools that can be used for screening and diagnosis of ASD in adults is beyond the scope of this chapter (see also Chapter 25 on diagnostic instruments by Cathy Lord, Christina Corsello, and Rebecca Grzadzinski). We have, however, described some of the most frequently used tools and will offer assessment recommendations based on our review. For initial diagnosis of ASD in an adult, it is suggested that clinicians try to complete a developmental history that is as comprehensive as possible (recognizing the aforementioned difficulties), conduct structured behavioral observations of the individual and include established diagnostic tools (e.g., ADOS), and interview the person as well as someone who knows the person well—ideally someone who interacts with him or her on a daily basis. Of course, issues of psychiatric comorbidity must also be considered and parsimony should guide diagnostic clinical decision making. Historical accounts are often needed to determine whether ASD is present among adults with significant psychiatric impairment (e.g., severe chronic depression with social phobia) that may present as possible ASD (Ghaziuddin & Zafar, 2008). This multisource, multimethod approach is consistent with established best practices for clinical evaluation (e.g., Sattler, 2001).

Sex Differences and Identification in Females

Very little is known about the unique expression of ASD in females, especially in adults. Most of what we know of ASD in general is based on research from primarily male samples, owing largely to the high male-to-female (4.3:1) sex ratio (Fombonne, 2003, 2005). Though far from uniformly supporting sex differences, there is growing evidence of clinically relevant yet subtle differences in symptom manifestation between the sexes (e.g., Holtmann, Bölte, & Poustka, 2007; Lai et al., 2011; Mandy et al., 2011; Solomon, Miller, Taylor, Hinshaw, & Carter, 2012). It is possible, for example, that females with ASD may be more adept at developing compensatory strategies during adolescence to accommodate their social deficits because of the importance typically placed on interpersonal, same-sex relationships among girls. The deficits are still present, but are essentially masked. As such, extra caution may need to be taken in assessing possible in ASD in women. Moreover, our diagnostic instruments were developed and normed on primarily male samples, introducing an additional potential source of bias and, potentially, decreased sensitivity in clinical judgments using existing diagnostic tools (Kreiser, 2011).

Psychiatric Comorbidity and Differential Diagnosis

Course and Types of Disorders

As with the general population, risk for certain psychiatric disorders may increase with age (Kessler et al., 2005). In particular for adults with ASD, risk for disorders such as depression and social phobia may increase as awareness of one's own social difficulties and feelings of loneliness increase. There are many potential stressors that are common in adulthood that could increase the likelihood of developing affective problems, such as ongoing social problems, difficulty maintaining employment, loss of the primary caregiver system, limited coping skills, and sometimes acute awareness of being different or not fitting in. Further, studies applying a continuous approach to examining ASD characteristics among nondiagnosed adult samples have found that ASD traits are positively correlated with symptoms of anxiety, depression, and hostility (White, Ollendick, et al., 2011).

In part because of the complexity of differential diagnosis, and also due to different methods and sample characteristics across psychiatric comorbidity studies, reported prevalence rates for psychiatric disorders in ASD have widely varied. However, accumulating evidence does suggest that the majority of the ASD population meets criteria for at least one comorbid psychiatric disorder (Gjevik, Eldevik, Fjæran-Granum, & Sponheim, 2011; Leyfer et al., 2006; Simonoff et al., 2008). Although most psychiatric comorbidity studies have focused on children and adolescents, studies of adults have reported similar or even higher rates of comorbidity (e.g., Bakken et al., 2010; Hofvander et al., 2009).

Anxiety disorders are present in approximately 40% of children with ASD, making it the most common comorbid psychiatric disorder in this population (van Steensel, Bogels, & Perrin, 2011; White, Oswald, Ollendick, & Scahill, 2009). Anxiety is also very problematic among adults with ASD, with estimates of comorbidity hovering around 50% (e.g., Lugnegård, Hallerbäck, & Gillberg, 2011).

Although there are only a few studies with small sample sizes, available evidence suggests that mood disorders may be even more prevalent than anxiety in adulthood (e.g. Ghaziuddin & Zafar, 2008; Hofvander et al., 2009; Lugnegård et al., 2011). For example, two studies found that 70% of adults with ASD had experienced depression at some point (Bakken et al., 2010; Lugnegård et al., 2011), with 50% experiencing recurrent depressive episodes (Lugnegård et al., 2011).

The traditional trajectory of anxiety in childhood leading to, or increasing risk for, later depression in adolescence and adulthood among non-ASD samples (e.g., Costello, Mustillo, Erkanli, Keeler, & Angold, 2003; Moffitt et al., 2007) may be similarly true in ASD and could explain the pattern of higher mood disorder rates in adulthood, should these early findings be replicated. In general, additional research is needed to better understand the pathways leading to the high rates of adulthood psychiatric comorbidity in ASD. On the other hand, rates of some disorders, such as attention-deficit/hyperactivity disorder (ADHD), usually decrease dramatically in adulthood among non-ASD populations (J. C. Hill & Schroener, 1996). There is not enough research yet to say if this is the case for individuals with ASD and ADHD symptoms. Further, ongoing nosological questions about what type of differences in attention and impulsivity should be considered part of the ASD itself (possibly reflecting a different underlying neural circuitry than pure ADHD) may be informed by better understanding the developmental trajectories of these symptoms over the lifespan and how trajectories may differ from non-ASD samples.

Assessment of Psychiatric Comorbidity in Adulthood

Unfortunately there are no gold-standard measures (i.e., with demonstrated clinical utility, psychometric reliability, and construct validity) for the assessment of comorbid problems in adults with ASD that we can recommend. There are few ASD-specific measures available, and those that do exist have limited research to date. Many (not ASD-specific) psychiatric screeners and structured interviews are available and have been utilized with ASD populations. However, most often individuals with ASD were excluded when the psychometric properties of these measures were established. Given the possibility of different presenting symptoms and difficulty differentiating impairment related to the underlying ASD from impairment due to a separate condition, application of non-ASD-specific measures may not be straightforward. A few studies have explored how well certain psychiatric questionnaires work in ASD populations (e.g., Mazefsky, Kao, Conner, & Oswald, 2011; White, Schry, & Maddox, 2012), but at this point there is not sufficient research to recommend any particular instruments.

Self-report psychiatric screeners administered to individuals with ASD may yield valuable information, but clinicians should interpret them cautiously based on clinical judgment and all available information given potential concerns about validity. Questions about validity have been raised because the discrepancy between parent- and child-report is even more pronounced in children and adolescents with ASD than in non-ASD populations (Hurtig et al., 2009; Lopata et al., 2010; Mazefsky, Kao, et al., 2011). Specifically, studies have shown that children with ASD respond in a consistent (e.g., reliable) manner but tend to underreport their symptoms (Mazefsky, Kao, et al., 2011; Russell & Sofronoff, 2005; White et al., 2012). The reasons for the low agreement are not well understood but may be associated with difficulty in providing accurate self-reports due to problems with verbal and nonverbal communication, inability to recognize thoughts and feelings, and poor emotional expression (Capps, Yirmiya, & Sigman, 1992; Leyfer et al., 2006). Given that most of this research has been done with adolescents, more research is needed to clarify whether a similar degree of underreporting on self-report screeners would be found with adults. Understanding of self-report on structured psychiatric interviews is also limited, with evidence from adolescent samples suggesting a tendency to underreport and difficulty providing

course and duration information required for differential diagnosis (Mazefsky, Hughes, Oswald, & Lainhart, 2012). It is also true that individuals with ASD can also be easily led in an interview or misunderstand questions (i.e., interpret too literally).

In lieu of recommending specific measures, one can keep some general guidelines on how to approach the assessment of comorbid disorders in adults with ASD in mind. For episodic disorders such as mood disorders, there should be evidence for increased impairment (e.g., new symptoms or a worsening of baseline behavior/emotions). Therefore, a critical component of a psychiatric comorbidity assessment is establishing a time course and understanding of how the individual is at his or her best. This can be a particular challenge in adulthood when it may be difficult to find a reporter who knows the individual well and knows the individual's history. Given that inappropriate affect and difficulty appropriately modifying emotional reactions can be part of ASD itself (Mazefsky, Pelphrey, & Dahl, 2012), there is a delicate balancing act between being conservative (so as not to misdiagnose ASD symptom manifestations as comorbid disorders) and accurately identifying concerns that require separate attention and treatment.

Magnuson and Constantino (2011) derived a helpful strategy for determining whether one should consider if a depressive disorder is present, which could be applied to other (especially episodic) disorders as well. Briefly, their approach is to start by determining whether traditional *DSM* (American Psychiatric Association [APA], 2000) criteria are met or not met. If not, additional questions one should consider before dismissing the possibility of a comorbid disorder are whether there is a change from baseline, if alternative presentations or behavioral manifestations that have been described in ASD might be present, and whether there are any known predisposing factors or risk factors (e.g., family history, stressful life events, etc.). This strategy would help ensure that comorbid disorders that do not present in the typical fashion are not missed.

The one caveat that we would apply to the aforementioned approach is that it is also critical to consider if the symptoms of concern should be more accurately considered part of the ASD. In other words, when initially determining if standard *DSM* criteria are met, it is important to be careful not to count symptoms that might be better explained by the ASD itself. This is especially essential for nonepisodic disorders (e.g., dysthymia, generalized anxiety disorder, ADHD), which are the most difficult to differentially diagnose. Consideration of all the ways in which ASD may in and of itself produce symptoms that are similar to those of other psychiatric disorders is out of the scope of this chapter (see Mazefsky, Filipink, Link, & Lubetsky, 2011) but some illustrative examples are included in Table 8.1.

Understanding aspects of ASD that may be misinterpreted as psychotic or schizophrenia spectrum is particularly important when working with adults. Many adults with diagnosed or undiagnosed (but present) ASD might have been diagnosed with a psychotic disorder that may not be accurate. Misdiagnosis might be especially likely for those born before the full range of presentation of ASD was appreciated (i.e., prior to the early 1990s), those with stereotyped language and mild degrees of intellectual impairment, or those with lower socioecomonic status or access to resources where ASD specialists are available. There is currently no compelling evidence to support the notion that individuals with ASD are at any greater risk for schizophrenia spectrum disorders (Seltzer et al., 2004). However, some ASD symptoms can easily be misinterpreted as due to psychosis. For example, flat affect, having a limited range of interests, and limited speech (e.g., having speech ability but providing brief or minimal responses) can raise

TABLE 8.1   Examples of Pertinent Baseline Considerations for Various Psychiatric Symptoms

Symptom	Possible ASD-Related Explanations
Depressed mood	General history of restricted or flat affect
Irritability; anger	Temperamental or situational irritability; outbursts related to communication frustrations
Anhedonia; boredom	General history of restricted interests
Insomnia; hypersomnia; decreased need for sleep	General history of sleep problems
Psychomotor agitation	Typical activity level/degree of restlessness
Poor concentration; distractibility	Slow processing time; focusing on details/interests to the exclusion of other information; lack of understanding; hearing problems
Indecision	Ability and opportunities to make independent decisions
Changes in weight/appetite	Medication-related weight changes; history of being a selective eater
Elated mood	History of inappropriate affect (laughing when nothing is funny); tendency to get easily excited by things they like
Racing thoughts; pressured speech	Tendency to be overly verbose; history of prosody problems (speech too fast, loud, etc.); history of tangential speech
Unusual violence	Frequency, quality, and triggers of baseline aggression
Grandiosity	Overattachment to important people or favorite characters from special interests
Engagement in dangerous activities	Level of judgment/cognitive ability
Panic attack	Identifiable situational triggers
Obsessions	Special interests that are enjoyable rather than distressing/intrusive
Compulsions	History of repetitive behaviors that one enjoys (lining things up, etc.)
Social avoidance	Lack of interest; avoidance of sensory aspects of a social environment (e.g., as opposed to avoidance due to fear of embarrassment)
Worry; repetitive questions	Questions to gain knowledge about special interests
Positive psychotic symptoms	Echolalia; self-talk during stress; repetitive speech; poor pragmatics
Negative psychotic symptoms	History of restricted affect and interests; avoidance of social chitchat

Note: Many of the above concepts are from the Autism Comorbidity Interview (ACI; Lainhart, Leyfer, & Folstein, 2003).

questions of negative symptoms of psychotic disorders. Stereotyped and odd speech, echolalia, and repeating things to oneself (either when anxious or to help with processing), off-topic tangents, and so on can present as disorganized speech, conversing with auditory hallucinations, and other positive symptoms of psychotic disorders. Thus, if there is concern about this as a possibility, it is critical to involve a caregiver or other person familiar with the adult to determine if these behaviors represent a change or deterioration before considering a psychotic disorder.

Similarly, it is important to be aware of which disorders are most common and ways in which presentation may differ in ASD. As noted at the beginning of this section, anxiety and depression are among the most common comorbidities. Eating disorders and body dysphoria are garnering more attention as particularly relevant in ASD as well (Wentz, Lacey, Waller, Råstam, Turk, & Gillberg, 2005). Unfortunately the field is still in its infancy in understanding how psychiatric disorders may manifest differently in ASD (e.g., nonconventional presentations). Probably the most relevant work in this area has been done on depression (though in children), suggesting that increases in self-injury or aggression, change to a more morbid quality of special interests, and an increase in repetitive behaviors combined with irritability and tension may signal concern for a possible mood disorder (Magnuson & Constantino, 2011; Mazefsky, Filipink, et al., 2011).

In sum, psychiatric disorders are highly relevant in adulthood, with evidence for a possible increase in prevalence with age. Having a comorbid disorder is often associated with poorer outcomes (Esbensen et al., 2010), and untreated psychiatric symptoms secondary to the ASD can exacerbate social concerns and interfere with other treatments. Given that more targeted treatments are usually more effective than process-oriented or general therapies, it is important to identify comorbid concerns when they are present. However, it is also important to be conservative not to overdiagnose aspects of ASD as additional disorders, which can cause confusion to the patients, their families, and other practitioners,

and also pose significant (medication) treatment implications. Thus the assessment of comorbidity in adults with ASD should incorporate all possible sources of information (and not disregard the possibility in the event of a negative self-report) and include consideration of baseline functioning.

COMMON TREATMENT TARGETS

Similar to children with ASD, adults with ASD are heterogeneous in their most pressing treatment needs. In this section, we highlight some of the areas that are mostly likely problems for which adults with ASD, and their families, seek treatment (above and beyond core symptoms and any comorbid disorders). Many of the childhood treatment foci, such as language and communication, daily living skills, and so on may still be areas of weakness and require attention. However, here we emphasize the treatment needs that are more unique to adulthood. Some topics are covered in more detail in other chapters, as noted.

Employment and Vocational Training

Adults with ASD often work in jobs that are relatively undemanding, or below their technical, academic, and intellectual ability level (Barnhill, 2007). Frequently even when an individual with ASD possesses the skills to complete a job, problems with reciprocal communication and social interaction interfere with their ultimate success in, or even ability to maintain, employment (Barnhill, 2007). This is consistent with findings that adults with ASD who have fewer autism symptoms are more likely to be competitively employed as opposed to participating in supportive employment or adult day services (Taylor & Seltzer, 2011).

Direct training to support employment or to help develop a vocation is often necessary. Peter Gerhardt, Frank Cicero, and Erik Mayville describe employment and vocational training in detail in Chapter 38. Many adults with ASD self-report a need for hands-on assistance with day-to-day challenges and life skills, such as job training, career placement, and on-site coaching (e.g., in the workplace) (White

& Pugliese, 2009). Help with developmental tasks, such as completing job applications or applying for a driving permit, is often needed. These activities often prove very challenging for older adolescents and adults with ASD, yet they are critical to achieving functional independence.

Social and vocational skills training programs can be instrumental in improving quality of life in adulthood. For example, a brief social and vocational skills training program facilitated improvements in relationships with others for adults with ASD self-reported decreased depression and anxiety (Hillier, Fish, Siegel, & Beversdorf, 2011). In addition, ASD-specific supported employment programs can lead to a high rate of job placement and retention for adults with ASD. For example, the Prospects program in the United Kingdom led to 68% of adult clients with ASD finding employment (mostly in administrative, technical, or computing jobs), with high rates of client and employer satisfaction (Howlin, Alcock, & Burkin, 2005).

Postsecondary Education

A relatively large percentage (~50%) of cognitively able young adults with ASD pursue postsecondary education (Taylor & Seltzer, 2011). Unfortunately, however, highly capable young people with ASD have been found to report feeling less satisfied in college, despite doing well academically (White, Ollendick, et al., 2011). In addition, college students with ASD may experience stress and anxiety related to lack of predictability, social stressors, academic demands, and being independent for the first time (Glennon, 2001). Many skills are required for college success, including organizational skills, time management, and so on, that may be weaknesses for the adult with ASD. Jane Thierfield Brown and Christine Wenzel (in Chapter 39) provide a thorough review of the issues facing college students with ASD, as well as recommendations for addressing some of these challenges.

Cognitive and Information Processing Deficits

Even among intellectually able adults with ASD, cognitive and information processing deficits are apparent and limiting. Adults with high-functioning ASD demonstrate a pattern of intact or enhanced performance in attention, simple memory, simple language, and visual-spatial domains and impaired functioning in more complex skills in these same domains and in abstract reasoning and concept formation (Minshew, Goldstein, & Siegel, 1997). The primary weaknesses appear to be in domains that require a high level of integration of information. Processing speed also tends to be significantly impaired relative to IQ. Difficulty in social cognition remains evident in adulthood across a variety of tasks, including making complex judgments of trustworthiness and affective valence identification through motion or subtle variation in facial expressions (Losh et al., 2009).

Identifying and appreciating cognitive and information processing deficits in adulthood is important for several reasons. First, limitations in cognitive and executive functioning may play a central role in the success or failure of higher education and employment efforts. Therefore, they should be considered when determining needed adaptations for higher education and/or the most appropriate work placement. In addition, it can be important to directly target these skills through cognitive remediation programs that have promise for producing significant and meaningful changes even in later adulthood (e.g., Eack et al., 2013).

Social Interaction, Sexuality, and Intimacy

Loneliness and social isolation are common among adults with ASD (Eaves & Ho, 2008). A pervasive inability to recognize and accurately interpret social nuances and subtle communication signals affects interpersonal relationships at all levels—at work, with friends, and with potential partners (White & Pugliese, 2009). Only a small minority of adults with ASD marry. One study indicated that nearly half of adults with ASD have never been in a romantic relationship (Farley et al., 2009). While some parents of adults with ASD report that their child does not seem interested in romantic relationships, romantic and sexual interest is evident for most (Farley et al., 2009). Further, many verbal adults with ASD report being distressed by feelings of isolation and an unfulfilled desire for intimacy (Muller, Schuler, & Yates, 2008). Therefore, teaching skills to develop romantic and other types of close relationships is often an important focus of therapy.

It is also important to consider whether an adult with ASD has achieved even a rudimentary understanding of him- or herself as a sexual being, the sexual response cycle, and human reproduction, both in order to ensure that they are not taken advantage of and to avoid any unintentional offensive or interpersonally violating behavior by the adult with ASD. This would include concepts related to privacy, what type of touching is appropriate and with whom, and so on. Unfortunately there is limited research on what adults with ASD understand related to these topics. A survey of teachers of children with ASD indicated that lower functioning children with ASD seemed to have less knowledge of sexual education and displayed more overt inappropriate sexual behavior (e.g., public masturbation), but that teachers were most concerned about problems related to sexuality for higher functioning children due to their greater involvement in social scenarios with less external structure (Kalyva, 2009). Issues related to inappropriate courting behavior must sometimes be addressed. Young people with ASD have been found to engage in inappropriate courting behavior, including pursuing the target of affection for a longer duration, than people without ASD (Stokes, Newton, & Kaur, 2007).

Maladaptive Behaviors and Involvement With the Law

Although maladaptive behaviors, such as verbal and physical aggression, hostility, destruction of property, and self-injury, may improve (decrease) with age (Shattuck et al., 2007), externalizing behaviors are more common in adults with ASD than in matched controls with intellectual disability (Tsakanikos, Costello, Holt, Sturmey, & Bouras, 2007). Having more maladaptive behaviors in adulthood is related to lower levels of

independence (Esbensen et al., 2010). In addition, those with externalizing behaviors are a greater risk for psychiatric hospitalizations (Tsakanikos et al., 2007). Initial work on patterns of maladaptive behavior in adults indicates that aggression is more common in younger adults and those with moderate to severe intellectual disability, and self-injury is most common in females and those with severe to profound intellectual disability (Cohen et al., 2010). It is possible, however, that aggression and interpersonal hostility are present but in a different manifestation among adults with ASD who are higher functioning.

Identifying factors associated with or leading to greater externalizing behaviors in adulthood could help identify important treatment targets, but unfortunately little research has been done in this area. There are many possible mechanisms that may contribute to problems with aggression and hostility among people with ASD, including deficits in executive functioning such as poor inhibition of the prepotent response (e.g., E. Hill, 2004; Verté, Geurts, Roevers, Oosterlaan, & Sergeant, 2006), a tendency to react emotionally (Sofronoff, Attwood, Hinton, & Levin, 2007), and poor emotion identification and recognition (e.g., Harms, Martin, & Wallace, 2010; Laurent & Rubin, 2004). Psychiatric comorbidity is likely to play a role for some adults with ASD (Cohen et al., 2010).

Social rejection may be yet another contributing factor to problems with hostility and aggression. Among adolescents without ASD, rejection by peers contributes to feelings of anger and to hostile intent, which mediates reactive aggression (Reijntes et al., 2011). Most children and adults with ASD regularly experience negative social feedback, including rejection, social humiliation, and fear of rejection by others, which may mediate hostility and aggression. Indeed, in recent study, a curvilinear relationship was found between rejection fears and aggression among high-functioning children with ASD, a relationship not found in peers with either social phobia or externalizing behavior problems (Pugliese, White, White, & Ollendick, 2012). In adults without ASD, social anxiety was found to partially mediate the relationship between characteristics of ASD and self-reported hostility toward others (White, Kreiser, Pugliese, & Scarpa, 2012).

Reports of involvement in more severe forms of maladaptive behavior such as violent crime are mixed. Most of the research in this area has consisted of case studies and suggests a higher rate of psychiatric comorbidity among those who do commit violent crime (Newman & Ghaziuddin, 2008). While the majority of individuals with ASD do not engage in violent crime (Allen et al., 2008), adults with ASD may become involved with the legal system for a variety of reasons. In a study of adults with ASD, Allen and colleagues (2008) found that many of the predisposing factors (e.g., social naivety, poor understanding of social rules) and precipitating events (e.g., family stress, peer rejection) identified as related to self-reported offending behaviors were related to ASD.

Family Relationships

Behavioral problems, as well as an overall slowing in symptom improvement, can negatively impact the parent–child relationship as well. Specifically, young adults with increasing or persistent maladaptive behaviors have significantly less positive affect, more feelings of burden, and less warmth in the mother–child relationship (Taylor & Seltzer, 2010). Interestingly, Taylor and Seltzer (2010) found that decreases in maternal warmth after graduation from high school were most pronounced in mothers of children with ASD without intellectual disability. The authors suggested that this could be due to failure to achieve high expectations for college or independent living coupled with a greater likelihood to attribute maladaptive behaviors to being more within the child's control as compared to children with intellectual ability.

Overreliance on parents and other family members by adults with ASD poses a weighty challenge and can strain family relationships. The predictability and structure provided by school is often sorely missed by the adults with ASD and their parents alike (Billstedt et al., 2011). Further, often parents, and especially mothers, take on an increased

responsibility for coordinating care after secondary education. A combination of higher stress levels reported by parents of children with ASD, social isolation resulting from the time and energy spent caring for an adult with a disability, and the presence of the broader autism phenotype among family members may all interact to place families and parents at heightened risk for psychological distress (Seltzer et al., 2003).

TREATMENTS AND SERVICES FOR ADULTS

Relatively little research has addressed treatment development or evaluation for adults with ASD, and there is a general lack of services available to this population. This is true for core ASD deficits, such as social disability, as well as associated and comorbid problems. A recent review of published research on services for adults with ASD identified only 23 studies related to treatment or services for adults with ASD (Shattuck et al., 2012). Over the past 10 years or so, preliminary and pilot treatment studies on a range of problems using diverse modalities have been conducted (e.g., self-determination training: Fullerton & Coyne, 1999; music therapy to promote self-esteem and reduce anxiety: Hillier, Greher, Poto, & Dougherty, 2011; problem-solving therapy for college students with ASD: Pugliese, 2012). Here, we review some of the most commonly studied treatment targets and intervention approaches.

Targeted Treatments

Although the ASD-related social disability is related to poor long-term outcomes regardless of relative intellectual or verbal strengths (Segrin & Givertz, 2003; VanBergeijk et al., 2008) and does not improve with age without intervention (Sigman & Ruskin, 1999), there are no empirically supported treatments shown to effectively improve the social functioning of adults with ASD. Most research in this area has been conducted exclusively with people under the age of 13 (Reichow & Volkmar,

2010; Wang & Spillane, 2009). The only published randomized controlled trial (RCT) study to evaluate a manualized social skills training program for adults (PEERS for Young Adults; Laugeson & Frankel, 2010) found that young adults who received PEERS, a structured group-based treatment, self-reported less loneliness and improved social skills knowledge posttreatment (Gantman, Kapp, Orenski, & Laugeson, 2012). In addition, the adults' caregivers reported improved social skills, compared to young adults in the wait-list condition. Turner-Brown, Perry, Dichter, Bodfish, and Penn (2008) modified a cognitive-behavioral treatment program designed initially to improve social-cognitive function in adults with psychosis for use with adults with ASD. In an uncontrolled, pilot study ($n = 11$) they found support for the feasibility (e.g., attendance and participant satisfaction) of the intervention program and evidence for improvement in theory-of-mind skills, but not improvement in actual social skills. An ongoing RCT of cognitive enhancement therapy (CET)—an intervention originally studied in schizophrenia that integrates computer-based cognitive remediation exercises in attention, memory, and problem solving with a small group–based social-cognitive training curriculum—compared to enriched supportive therapy, indicates that adults with ASD enjoy CET and that the application of CET to adults with ASD is both feasible and promising (Eack, 2013; Eack et al., 2013).

Treatment studies to develop adaptive skills (i.e., skills or behaviors related to social interaction, employment, or daily living) in higher functioning adults with ASD have generally found considerable support for efficacy, although methodological limitations such as quasi-experimental designs dampen the strength of the conclusions to be drawn from much of the extant research (Palmen, Didden, & Lang, 2012). Practical and research recommendations include greater incorporation of technology into intervention, to help reduce prompt dependence, and integration of behavioral principles in treatment such as differential reinforcement, provision of corrective (as opposed to

descriptive) feedback, and prompt fading (Palmen et al., 2012).

Effectiveness and optimal delivery of applied behavior analysis, the most supported treatment in the ASD literature, has not been well established in adults on the spectrum. There are many obstacles to the effective application of behavioral treatment for some adults with ASD, such as intense behavioral problems (often seen in adults who are lower functioning), which causes some interventionists to elect not to work clinically with this population due to greater risk of injury and the severity of the behavior, compared to children (who may have intense behaviors, but less physical strength and stature) (see Manente, Maraventano, LaRue, Delmolino, & Sloan, 2010, for review). More research on adapting applied behavior analysis or discrete trials training for adults, both high and lower functioning, with ASD is needed.

Cognitive-behavioral therapy (CBT), a problem-focused approach that is typically brief, has been applied to adults with ASD, primarily to treat comorbid conditions such as depression and anxiety (Gaus, 2007, 2011). Often, techniques such as thought restructuring and emotion monitoring must be modified (e.g., Attwood & Scarpa, 2013) to make them effective for clients with ASD. Most of the literature in this area has been on children, and some with adolescents, with ASD (White, 2012). At this time, we are not aware of any controlled, group trials on the efficacy of CBT for adults with ASD, although there is emerging support for its feasibility and efficacy (e.g., Pugliese & White, 2013). It is common for the comorbid symptoms (e.g., problems with anxiety and depression), as opposed to the ASD itself, to prompt treatment referral (Joshi et al., 2010). In light of the established efficacy of CBT for a range of psychiatric problems in adults without ASD (e.g., Chambless & Ollendick, 2001), more empirical attention is warranted. In addition, given the chronicity of ASD and the long-term dependence typically associated (as discussed earlier), family therapy is often sought to address problems such as stressed parent–adult child relationships and parental worries about the future. Unfortunately, this too is an understudied area.

In a research review of pharmacotherapy in adults with ASD, Broadstock, Doughty, and Eggleston (2007) found just five double-blind RCTs on medication efficacy in adults with ASD, all of which had fairly small samples and brief treatment duration. There is also only one psychiatric inpatient unit specializing in adults with ASD (at Western Psychiatric Institute and Clinic at the University of Pittsburgh), compared to 11 inpatient psychiatry units for children and adolescents with ASD and developmental disabilities.

Supportive Programs and Services

Finding outlets for social integration, including ways to connect with other adults with similar interests, can provide much-needed support and structure. Adults with ASD self-report that they find membership with specialized interest groups (e.g., chess, electronics) and support groups to be important to them (Muller et al., 2008). There are several online forums for people with ASD to meet each other and share concerns and resources. The Global and Regional Asperger Syndrome Partnership (GRASP; www.grasp.org), an organization with the mission of promoting self-advocacy, education, and improved quality of life for adults with ASD, has a strong online presence and self-sustaining, participant-led support groups around the country.

Residential programs are available in some communities, but are not commonplace in the United States. Most such programs have been developed for people with developmental disabilities and are not specific to ASD. These programs usually serve adults with moderate to severe intellectual impairments. Preliminary evidence is supportive, indicating that individualized programming can be provided to facilitate independence (Van Bourgondien, Reichle, & Schopler, 2003). There is growing interest in transitional services, including supported living communities, for higher functioning adults with ASD, to support successful independent living, develop vocational and self-care skills, and promote healthy socialization. Most such services are privately offered and are multifaceted (e.g., family counseling, job placement help, coaching). At this time, we know of no research on this endeavor.

CONCLUSION

Although research on adults with ASD is increasing exponentially, there are few aspects of ASD as it is expressed or experienced among adults that are well understood. At this time, there are generally many more unknowns than knowns. To be able to make firm conclusions, both more research and a different kind of research will be required. Longitudinal studies will be essential to improve our understanding of developmental trajectories into adulthood. A challenge to this research will be the lack of measures that apply across the age range to allow direct comparisons. A combined longitudinal/cross-sectional approach may be particularly informative, by providing an opportunity to also uncover potential cohort effects. For example, children diagnosed in the past 10 years will hopefully have better outcomes (as a result of earlier diagnosis and more intensive and specific treatments) than those initially diagnosed in the 1980s or 1990s. Yet, there will continue to be individual and developmental differences within cohorts. In addition to group designs, another approach that has the potential to uncover potentially important protective factors is to examine success cases (e.g., adults with a high quality of life, those succeeding in higher education) to identify possible moderators and mechanisms of a positive outcome retrospectively.

The list of areas of research that we need to explore related to adulthood in ASD is nearly endless. Clearly a priority area is the dramatic lack of empirically supported interventions, or even any intervention. It is imperative that clinical scientists investigate new and modified treatments—biological/medical as well as psychosocial—for adults with ASD. There is a treatment and service gap for adults with ASD, which is probably most acutely felt among those who are cognitively more able and their loved ones. They age out of the educational system and struggle to find independence within their families and society, and many mental health practitioners feel ill-equipped to address their psychiatric needs. Suggestions for future research in this area include exploration of cost and efficiency of specific services, and how to most effectively coordinate care among providers (Shattuck et al., 2012). Manente et al. (2010) suggest the systematic extension of strategies with demonstrated efficacy in children with ASD to adults with ASD. This is different from many other areas of clinical psychopathology, in which treatments developed initially for adults have been extended downward (e.g., modified to be developmentally appropriate) to children. The need for such upward extension also applies to pharmacological treatment for symptom management in adults with ASD.

More research is needed on the assessment and treatment of psychiatric comorbidity and maladaptive behaviors in ASD, particularly given the impact that these concerns have on outcome and the early research suggesting that they are highly prevalent problems in adulthood. This need is even more pressing when one considers that there is a dramatic dearth of research on psychotropic medication use in adulthood despite the common experience of polypharmacy among adults. Further, adults with ASD who require inpatient psychiatric care are typically served in general psychiatric units by physicians with limited experience in ASD.

More research is needed to understand how to facilitate successful transitions from school to college or work. Most adults with ASD experience the transition from secondary school to either higher education or the work force as abrupt and feel unprepared. Supportive services, such as transitional living facilities to help the young adult develop independent living skills in a graded fashion, are sorely needed. There is some movement in this area, but research is in its infancy. There is also a striking lack of research on late-life transitions as well as a lack of support options available for older

adults with ASD who have been highly dependent on parents who will eventually pass on.

In conclusion, in the next decade, we anticipate that the most growth in the field of ASD research will likely be with adults. Most of life is spent in adulthood, and adults with ASD now make up the majority of the ASD population—a fact that has received little recognition until recently. A greater focus on adulthood is also likely to bring with it a shift away from the focus on etiology and cure that has, by some accounts, dominated ASD research for the past few decades. In other words, instead of the goal to treat to remission that is the case for most Axis I conditions, the goal for adults with ASD will more likely be to optimize outcomes and improve symptom management. Thus, future research with adults with ASD is likely to involve developing coping strategies, strengths building, and societal adaptation. This is a shift that will impact clinical conceptualization and treatment outcome research in terms of how we define a positive outcome and measures we use to gauge growth, change, and success. In addition, with rapid advances in neuroscience technology, we also expect an increase in neuroimaging research focused on neuroplasticity demonstrating that brain changes following intervention can continue to be produced and detected in adulthood.

CROSS-REFERENCES

Chapter 7 focuses on autism in adolescents. Chapter 36 addresses promotion of recreational activities, Chapter 38 supporting employment, and Chapter 39 postsecondary educational services. Chapter 40 addresses family support and Chapter 41 supporting adult independence.

REFERENCES

Allen, D., Evans, C., Hider, A., Hawkins, S., Peckett, H., & Morgan, H. (2008). Offending behavior in adults with Asperger syndrome. *Journal of Autism and Developmental Disorders*, *38*, 748–758.

American Psychiatric Association. (2000). *Diagnostic and statistical manual of mental disorders* (4th ed., text rev.). Washington, DC: Author.

Attwood, T., & Scarpa, A. (2013). Modifications of CBT for use with children and adolescents with high functioning ASD and their common deficits. In A. Scarpa, S. W. White, & T. Attwood (Eds.), *Promising cognitive behavioral interventions for children and adolescents with high functioning autism spectrum disorders*. New York, NY: Guilford Press.

Bakken, T. L., Helverschou, S. B., Eilertsen, D. E., Heggelund, T., Myrbakk, E., & Martinsen, H. (2010). Psychiatric disorders in adolescents and adults with autism and intellectual disability: A representative study in one county in Norway. *Research in Developmental Disabilities, 31*, 1669–1677.

Barnhill, G. P. (2007). Outcomes in adults with Asperger syndrome. *Focus on Autism and Other Developmental Disorders, 22*, 116–126.

Baron-Cohen, S., Wheelwright, S., Robinson, J., & Woodbury-Smith, M. (2005). The Adult Asperger Assessment (AAA): A diagnostic method. *Journal of Autism and Developmental Disorders, 35*, 807–819.

Baron-Cohen, S., Wheelwright, S., Skinner, R., Martin, J., & Clubley, E. (2001). The Autism-Spectrum Quotient (AQ): Evidence from Asperger syndrome/high-functioning autism, males and females, scientists and mathematicians. *Journal of Autism and Developmental Disorders, 31*(1), 5–17. doi:10.1023/A:1005653411471

Bastiaansen, J. A., Meffert, H., Hein, S., Huizinga, P., Ketelaars, C., Pijnenborg, M., . . . de Bildt, A. (2011). Diagnosing autism spectrum disorders in adults: The use of the Autism Diagnostic Observation Schedule (ADOS) Module 4. *Journal of Autism and Developmental Disorders, 41*, 1256–1266. doi: 10.1007/s10803-010-1157-x

Billstedt, E., Gillberg, I. C., & Gillberg, C. (2005). Autism after adolescence: Population-based 13- to 22-year follow-up study of 120 individuals with autism diagnosed in childhood. *Journal of Autism and Developmental Disorders, 35*(3), 351–360. doi: 10.1007/s10803-005-3302-5

Billstedt, E., Gillberg, I. C., & Gillberg, C. (2011). Aspects of quality of life in adults diagnosed with autism in childhood: A population-based study. *Autism, 15*(1), 7–20. doi: 10.1177/1362361309346066

Broadstock, M., Doughty, C., & Eggleston, M. (2007). Systematic review of the effectiveness of pharmacological treatments for adolescents and adults with autism spectrum disorder. *Autism, 11*, 335–348. doi: 10.1177/1362361307078132

Capps, L., Yirmiya, N., & Sigman, M. (1992). Understanding of simple and complex emotions in non-retarded children with autism. *Journal of Child Psychology and Psychiatry, 33*(7), 1169–1182.

Cederlund, M., Hagberg, B., Billstedt, E., Gillberg, I. C., & Gillberg, C. (2008). Asperger syndrome and autism: A comparative longitudinal follow-up study more than 5 years after original diagnosis. *Journal of Autism and Developmental Disorders, 38*, 72–85. doi: 10.1007/s10803-007-0364-6

Chambless, D. L., & Ollendick, T. H. (2001). Empirically supported psychological interventions: Controversies and evidence. *Annual Review of Psychology, 52*, 685–716.

Cohen I., Tsiouris, J., Flory, M., Kim, S. Y., Freedland, R., Heaney, G., . . . Brown, W. (2010). A large scale study of the psychometric characteristics of the IBR Modified Overt Aggression Scale: Findings and evidence for increased self-destructive behaviors in adult females with autism spectrum disorder. *Journal of Autism and Developmental Disorders, 40*, 599–609.

Constantino, J. N. (in press). *Social Responsiveness Scale–adult self-report, brief format.* Los Angeles, CA: Western Psychological Services.

Constantino, J. N. (2012). *Social Responsiveness Scale—second edition (SRS-2).* Los Angeles, CA: Western Psychological Services.

Constantino, J. N., & Gruber, C. P. (2005). *Social Responsiveness Scale (SRS).* Los Angeles, CA: Western Psychological Services.

Costello, E. J., Mustillo, S., Erkanli, A., Keeler, G., & Angold, A. (2003). Prevalence and development of psychiatric disorders in childhood and adolescence. *Archives of General Psychiatry, 60*, 837–844.

Eack, S. M. (2013). Cognitive enhancement therapy. In F. R. Volkmar (Ed.), *Encyclopedia of autism spectrum disorders*. New York, NY: Springer.

Eack, S. M., Greenwald, D. P., Hogarty, S. S., Bahorik, A. L., Litschge, M. Y., Mazefsky, C. A., & Minshew, N. J. (2013, April). Cognitive enhancement therapy for adults with autism spectrum disorder: Results of an 18-month feasibility study. *Journal of Autism and Developmental Disorders.* [Epub ahead of print.]

Eaves, L. C., & Ho, H. H. (2008). Young adult outcome of autism spectrum disorders. *Journal of Autism and Developmental Disorders, 38*, 739–747.

Engström, I., Ekström, L., & Emilsson, B. (2003). Psychosocial functioning in a group of Swedish adults with Asperger syndrome or high functioning autism. *Autism, 7*(1), 99–110.

Esbensen, A. J., Bishop, S. L., Seltzer, M. M., Greenberg, J. S., & Taylor, J. L. (2010). Comparisons between individuals with autism spectrum disorders and individuals with Down syndrome in adulthood. *American Journal of Intellectual and Developmental Disabilities, 115*, 277–290.

Farley, M. A., McMahon, W. M., Fombonne, E., Jenson, W. R., Miller, J., Gardner, M., . . . Coon, H. (2009). Twenty-year outcome for individuals with autism and average or near-average cognitive abilities. *Autism Research, 2*, 109–118. doi: 10.1002/aur.69

Fombonne, E. (2003). Epidemiological surveys of autism and other pervasive developmental disorders: An update. *Journal of Autism and Developmental Disorders, 33*(4), 365–382. Retrieved from http://www.ncbi.nlm.nih.gov/pubmed/12959416

Fombonne, E. (2005). The changing epidemiology of autism. *Journal of Applied Research in Intellectual Disabilities, 18*, 281–294.

Fountain, C., Winter, A. S., & Bearman, P. S. (2012). Six developmental trajectories characterize children with autism. *Pediatrics, 129*, e112–e120. doi:10.1542/peds.2011-1601

Fullerton, A., & Coyne, P. (1999). Developing skills and concepts for self-determination of young adults with autism. *Focus on Autism and Other Developmental Disabilities, 14*, 42–52.

Gantman, A., Kapp, S. K., Orenski, K., & Laugeson, E. A. (2012). Social skills training for young adults with high-functioning autism spectrum disorders: A randomized controlled pilot study. *Journal of Autism and Developmental*

Disorders, *37*(1), 1094–1103. doi: 10.1007/s10803-011-1350-6

Gaus, V. L. (2007). *Cognitive-behavioral therapy for adult Asperger syndrome*. New York, NY: Guilford Press.

Gaus, V. L. (2011). Adult Asperger syndrome and the utility of cognitive-behavioral therapy. *Journal of Contemporary Psychotherapy*, *41*, 47–56.

Ghaziuddin, M., & Zafar, S. (2008). Psychiatric comorbidity of adults with autism spectrum disorders. *Clinical Neuropsychiatry*, *5*, 9–12.

Gilliam, J. E. (2001). *Gilliam Asperger's Disorder Scale (GADS)*. Austin, TX: PRO-ED.

Gjevik, E., Eldevik, S., Fjæran-Granum, T., & Sponheim, E. (2011). Kiddie-SADS reveals high rates of *DSM-IV* disorders in children and adolescents. *Journal of Autism and Developmental Disorders*, *41*, 761–769. doi: 10.1007/s10803-010-1095-7

Glennon, T. J. (2001). The stress of the university experience for students with Asperger syndrome. *Work*, *17*(3), 189–190.

Gurney, J. G., Fritz, M. S., Ness, K. K., Sievers, P., Newschaffer, C. J., & Shapiro, E. G. (2003). Analysis of prevalence trends of autism spectrum disorder in Minnesota. *Archives of Pediatric Adolescent Medicine*, *157*, 622–627.

Harms, M. B., Martin, A., & Wallace, G. L. (2010). Facial emotion recognition in autism spectrum disorders: A review of behavioral and neuroimaging studies. *Neuropsychology Review*, *20*, 290–322.

Hendricks, D., & Wehman, P. (2009). Transition from school to adulthood for youth with autism spectrum disorders: Review and recommendations. *Focus on Autism and Other Developmental Disabilities*, *24*, 77–88. doi:10.1177/1088357608329827

Hill, E. (2004). Executive dysfunction in autism. *Trends in Cognitive Sciences*, *8*, 26–32.

Hill, J. C., & Schoener, E. P. (1996). Age-dependent decline of attention deficit hyperactivity disorder. *American Journal of Psychiatry*, *153*, 1143–1146.

Hillier, A. J., Fish, T., Siegel, J. H., & Beversdorf, D. Q. (2011). Social and vocational skills training reduces self-reported anxiety and depression among young adults on the autism spectrum. *Journal of Developmental and Physical Disabilities*, *23*, 267–276. doi: 10.1007/s10882-011-9226-4

Hillier, A., Greher, G., Poto, N., & Dougherty, M. (2011). Positive outcomes following participation in a music intervention for adolescents and young adults on the autism spectrum. *Psychology of Music*, *40*(2), 201–215. doi: 10.1177/0305735610386837

Hofvander, B., Delorme, R., Chaste, P., Nydén, A., Wentz, E., Ståhlberg, O.,...Leboyer, M. (2009). Psychiatric and psychosocial problems in adults with normal-intelligence autism spectrum disorders. *BMC Psychiatry*, *9*, 1–9.

Holtmann, M., Bölte, S., & Poustka, F. (2007). Autism spectrum disorders: Sex differences in autistic behaviour domains and coexisting psychopathology. *Developmental Medicine and Child Neurology*, *49*(5), 361–366. doi:10.1111/j.1469-8749.2007.00361.x

Howlin, P., Alcock, J., Burkin, C. (2005). An 8 year follow-up of a specialist supported employment service for high-ability adults with autism or Asperger syndrome. *Autism*, *9*, 533–549.

Howlin, P., Goode, J., Hutton, J., & Rutter, M. (2004). Adult outcome for children with autism. *Journal of Child Psychology and Psychiatry*, *45*, 212–229. doi:10.1111/j.1469-7610.2004.00215.x

Howlin, P., Mawhood, L., & Rutter, M. (2000). Autism and developmental receptive language disorder—A follow-up comparison in early adult life. II: Social, behavioral, and psychiatric outcomes. *Journal of Child Psychology and Psychiatry*, *41*(5), 561–578.

Hurtig, T., Kuusikko, S., Mattila, M.-L., Haapsamo, H., Elbeling, H., Iussila, K.,...Moilanen, I. (2009). Multi-informant reports of psychiatric symptoms among high-functioning adolescents with Asperger syndrome or autism. *Autism*, *13*(6), 583–598.

Joshi, G., Petty, C., Wozniak, J., Henin, A., Fried, R., Galdo, M.,...Biederman, J. (2010). The heavy burden of psychiatric comorbidity in youth with autism spectrum disorders: A large comparative study of a psychiatrically referred population. *Journal of Autism and Developmental Disorders*, *40*, 1361–1370. doi: 10.1007/s10803-010-0996-9

Kalyva, E. (2009). Teachers' perspectives of the sexuality of children with autism spectrum disorders. *Research in Autism Spectrum Disorders*, *4*, 433–437. doi: org/10.1016/j.rasd.2009.10.014

Kanne, S. M., Christ, S. E., & Reiersen, A. M. (2009). Psychiatric symptoms and psychosocial difficulties in young adults with autistic traits. *Journal of Autism and Developmental Disorders*, *39*, 827–833. doi: 10.1007/s10803-008-0688-x

Kessler, R. C., Berglund, P., Demler, O., Jin, R., Merikangas, K. R., & Walters, E. E. (2005). Lifetime prevalence and age-of-onset distributions of *DSM-IV* disorders in the national comorbidity survey replication. *Archives of General Psychiatry*, *62*, 593–602. doi:10.1001/archpsyc.62.6.593

Kreiser, N. (2011). *ASD in females: Are we overstating the sex difference in diagnosis?* Unpublished manuscript, Department of Psychology, Virginia Tech, Blacksburg, VA.

Krug, D. A., & Arick, J. R. (2003). *Krug Asperger's Disorder Index*. Austin, TX: PRO-ED.

Lai, M. C., Lombardo, M. V., Pasco, G., Ruigrok, A. N. V., Wheelwright, S. J., Sadek, S. A.,...Baron-Cohen, S. (2011). A behavioral comparison of male and female adults with high functioning autism spectrum conditions. *PloS One*, *6*(6), e20835. doi:10.1371/journal.pone.0020835

Lainhart, J. E., Leyfer, O. T., Folstein, S. E. (2003). *Autism Comorbidity Interview—Present and Lifetime version (ACI-PL)*. Salt Lake City: University of Utah.

Laugeson, E. A., & Frankel, F. (2010). *Social skills for teenagers with developmental and autism spectrum disorders: The PEERS treatment manual*. New York, NY: Routledge.

Laurent, A.C., & Rubin, E. (2004). Challenges in emotional regulation in Asperger syndrome and high-functioning autism. *Topics in Language Disorders*, *24*, 286–297.

Leyfer, O. T., Folstein, S. E., Bacalman, S., Davis, N. O., Dinh, E., Morgan, J., Tager-Flusberg, H., & Lainhart, J. E. (2006). Comorbid psychiatric disorders in children with autism: Interview development and rates of disorders. *Journal of Autism and Developmental Disorders*, *36*, 849–861.

Lopata, C., Thomeer, M. L., Volker, M. A., Toomey, J. A., Nida, R. E., Lee, G. K.,...Rodgers J. D. (2010). RCT of a manualized social treatment for high-functioning autism spectrum disorders. *Journal of Autism and Developmental Disorders, 40*, 1297–1310.

Lord, C., & Bailey, A. (2002). Autism spectrum disorders. In M. Rutter & E. Taylor (Eds.), *Child and adolescent psychiatry* (4th ed., pp.664–681). Oxford, England: Blackwell Scientific.

Lord, C., Rutter, M., DiLavore, P. C., & Risi, S. (2002). *Autism Diagnostic Observation Schedule.* Los Angeles, CA: Western Psychological Services.

Lord, C., Rutter, M., & Le Couteur, A. (1994). Autism Diagnostic Interview—Revised: A revised version of a diagnostic interview for caregivers of individuals with possible pervasive developmental disorders. *Journal of Autism and Developmental Disorders, 24*(5), 659–685. doi:10.1007/BF02172145

Losh, M., Adolphs, R., Poe, M. D., Couture, S., Penn, D., Baranek, G. T., & Piven, J. (2009). Neuropsychological profile of autism and the broad autism phenotype. *Archives of General Psychiatry, 66*, 518–526.

Lugnegård, T., Hallerbäck, M. V., & Gillberg, C. (2011). Psychiatric comorbidity in young adults with a clinical diagnosis of Asperger syndrome. *Research in Developmental Disabilities, 32*, 1910–1917.

Magnuson, K. M., & Constantino, J. N. (2011). Characterization of depression in children with autism spectrum disorders. *Journal of Developmental Behavioral Pediatrics, 32*(4), 332–340.

Mandy, W., Cilvers, R., Chowdhurry, U., Salter, G., Seigal, A., & Skuse, D. (2011). Sex differences in autism spectrum disorder: Evidence from a large sample of children and adolescents. *Journal of Autism and Developmental Disorders.* Retrieved from http://www.springerlink.com/content/j265 180823313456/

Manente, C. J., Maraventano, J. C., LaRue, R. H., Delmolino, L., & Sloan, D. (2010). Effective behavioral intervention for adults on the autism spectrum: Best practices in functional assessment and treatment development. *Behavior Analyst Today, 11*(1), 36–48.

Mazefsky, C. A., Filipink, R., Link, J., & Lubetsky, M. J. (2011). Medical evaluation and co-morbid psychiatric disorders. In M. J. Lubetsky, B. L. Handen, & J. J. McGonigle (Eds.), *Autism spectrum disorder.* New York, NY: Oxford University Press.

Mazefsky, C. A., Hughes, A. J., Oswald, D. P., & Lainhart, J. E. (2012). Lack of correspondence between self- and parent-report on structured psychiatric interview of adolescents with high-functioning autism spectrum disorders. Oral presentation at the International Meeting for Autism Research, Toronto, Canada.

Mazefsky, C. A., Kao, J., Conner, C., & Oswald, D. P. (2011). Preliminary caution regarding the use of psychiatric self-report measures with adolescents with high-functioning autism spectrum disorders. *Research in Autism Spectrum Disorders, 5*, 164–174.

Mazefsky, C. A., Oswald, D. P., Day, T., Eack, S., Minshew, N. J., & Lainhart, J. (2012). ASD a comorbid psychiatric disorder, or both? Psychiatric diagnoses in high-functioning adolescents with ASD. *Journal of Clinical Child and Adolescent Psychology.* doi:10.1080/15374416.2012.686102

Mazefsky, C. A., Pelphrey, K. A., & Dahl, R. E. (2012). The need for a broader approach to emotion regulation research in autism. *Child Development Perspectives, 6*, 92–97. doi: 10.1111/j.1750-8606.2011.00229.x

McGonigle, J., Allen, G., & Lubetsky, M. (2011). Transition-age and adult interventions. In M. Lubetsky, B. Handen, & J. McGonigle (Eds.), *Autism spectrum disorder* (pp. 231–251). New York, NY: Oxford University Press.

Minshew, J., Goldstein, G., & Siegel, D. (1997). Neuropsychologic functioning in autism: Profile of a complex informational processing disorder. *Journal of the International Neuropsychological Society, 3*, 303–316.

Moffitt, T. E., Caspi, A., Harrington, H., Milne, B. J., Melchior, M., Goldberg, D., & Poutlon, R. (2007). Generalized anxiety disorder and depression: Childhood risk factors in a birth cohort followed to age 32. *Psychological Medicine, 37*, 441–452. doi:10.1017/S0033291706009640

Muller, E., Schuler, A., & Yates, G. (2008). Social challenges and supports from the perspective of individuals with Asperger syndrome and other autism spectrum disabilities. *Autism, 12*, 173–190.

Newman, S. S., & Ghaziuddin, M. (2008) Violent crime in Asperger syndrome: The role of psychiatric comorbidity. *Journal of Autism and Developmental Disorders, 38*, 1848–1852.

Nylander, L., & Gillberg, C. (2001). Screening for autism spectrum disorders in adult psychiatric out-patients: A preliminary report. *Acta Psychiatrica Scandinavica, 103*, 428–434.

Palmen, A., Didden, R., & Lang, R. (2012). A systematic review of behavioral intervention research on adaptive skill building in high-functioning young adults with autism spectrum disorder. *Research in Autism Spectrum Disorders, 6*, 602–617. doi:10.1016/j.rasd.2011.10.001

Pugliese, C. E. (2012). *A pilot study examining the feasibility and preliminary efficacy of problem solving therapy in college students with autism spectrum disorders.* Unpublished doctoral dissertation, Virginia Tech, Blacksburg, VA.

Pugliese, C. E., & White, S. W. (2013). Problem-solving therapy in college students with autism spectrum disorders: Feasibility and preliminary efficacy. *Journal of Autism and Developmental Disorders.* doi: 10.1007/s10803-013-1914-8

Pugliese, C., White, B. A., White, S. W., & Ollendick, T. (2012). *Social anxiety predicts aggression in children with high functioning autism spectrum disorders.* Manuscript submitted for publication.

Reichow, B., & Volkmar, F. R. (2010). Social skills interventions for individuals with autism: evaluation for evidence-based practices within a best evidence synthesis framework. *Journal of Autism and Developmental Disorders, 40*(2), 149–166. doi:10.1007/s10803-009-0842-0

Reiersen, A. M., Constantino, J. N., Grimmer, M., Martin, N. G., & Todd, R. D. (2008). Evidence for shared genetic influences on self-reported ADHD and autistic symptoms in young adult Australian twins. *Twin Research and Human Genetics, 11*(6), 579–585. doi: 10.1375/twin.11.6.579

Reijntjes, A., Thomaes, S., Kamphuis, J. H., Bushman, B. J., Orobio de Castro, B., & Telch, M. (2011). Explaining the paradoxical rejection-aggression link: The mediating effects of hostile intent attributions, anger, and decreases in state self-esteem on peer rejection-induced aggression in youth. *Personality and Social Psychology Bulletin, 37*(7), 955–963.

Russell, E., & Sofronoff, K. (2005). Anxiety and social worries in children with Asperger syndrome. *Australian and New Zealand Journal of Psychiatry, 39*(7), 633–638.

Rutter, M. L., & Sroufe, L. A. (2000). Developmental psychopathology: Concepts and challenges. *Development and Psychopathology, 12,* 265–296.

Sattler, J. M. (2001). *Assessment of children: Cognitive applications* (4th ed.). San Diego, CA: Jerome M. Sattler.

Segrin, C., & Givertz, M. (2003). Methods of social skills training and development. In J. O Greene & B. R. Burleson (Eds.), *Handbook of communication and social interaction skills* (135–176). Mahwah, NJ: Erlbaum.

Seltzer, M. M., Krauss, M. W., Shattuck, P. T., Orsmond, G., Swe, A., & Lord, C. (2003). The symptoms of autism spectrum disorders in adolescence and adulthood. *Journal of Autism and Developmental Disorders, 33,* 565–581.

Seltzer, M. M., Shattuck, P., Abbeduto, L., & Greenberg, J. (2004). Trajectory of development in adolescents and adults with autism. *Mental Retardation and Developmental Disabilities Research Reviews, 10,* 234–247.

Shattuck, P. T., Roux, A. M., Hudson, L. E., Taylor, J. L., Maenner, M. J., & Trani, J. F. (2012). Services for adults with autism spectrum disorder. *Canadian Journal of Psychiatry, 57,* 284–291.

Shattuck, P. T., Seltzer, M. M., Greenberg, J. S., Orsmond, G. I., Bolt, D., Kring, S., ... Lord, C. (2007). Change in autism symptoms and maladaptive behaviors in adolescents and adults with an autism spectrum disorder. *Journal of Autism and Developmental Disorders, 37,* 1735–1747.

Sigman, M., & Ruskin, E. (1999). Continuity and change in the social competence of children with autism, Down syndrome, and developmental delays. *Monographs of the Society for Research in Child Development, 64*(1), v–114. Doi: 10.1111/1540-5834.00001

Simonoff, E., Pickles, A., Charman, T., Chandler, S., Loucas, T., & Baird, G. (2008). Psychiatric disorders in children with autism spectrum disorders: Prevalence, comorbidity, and associated factors in a population-derived sample. *Journal of the American Academy of Child & Adolescent Psychiatry, 47,* 921–929.

Smith, E., Maenner, M., & Seltzer, M. (2012). Developmental trajectories in adolescents and adults with autism: The case of daily living skills. *Journal of the American Academy of Child & Adolescent Psychiatry, 51,* 622–631.

Sofronoff, K., Attwood, T., Hinton, S., & Levin, I. (2007). A randomized controlled trial of a cognitive behavioural intervention for anger management in children diagnosed with Asperger Syndrome. *Journal of Autism and Development Disorders, 37*(7), 1203–1214.

Solomon, M., Miller, M., Taylor, S. L., Hinshaw, S. P., & Carter, C. S. (2012). Autism symptoms and internalizing psychopathology in girls and boys with autism spectrum disorders. *Journal of Autism and Developmental Disorders, 48–59.* doi:10.1007/s10803–011–1215-z

Sterling, L., Dawson, G., Estes, A., & Greenson, J. (2008). Characteristics associated with presence of depressive symptoms in adults with autism spectrum disorder. *Journal of Autism and Developmental Disorders, 38,* 1011–1018.

Stoesz, B. M., Montgomery, J. M., Smart, S. L., & Hellsten, L. M. (2011). Review of five instruments for the assessment of Asperger's disorder in adults. *The Clinical Neuropsychologist, 25*(3), 376–401. doi: 10.1080/13854046.2011 .559482

Stokes, M., Newton, N., & Kaur, A. (2007). Stalking, and social and romantic functioning among adolescents and adults with Autism spectrum disorder. *Journal of Autism and Developmental Disorders, 37*(10), 1969–1986.

Taylor, J. L., & Seltzer, M. M. (2010). Changes in the autism behavioral phenotype during the transition to adulthood. *Journal of Autism and Developmental Disorders, 40,* 1431–1446. doi: 10.1007/s10803-010-1005-z

Taylor, J. L., & Seltzer, M. M. (2011). Employment and post-secondary educational activities for young adults with autism spectrum disorders during the transition to adulthood. *Journal of Autism and Developmental Disorders, 41,* 566–574.

Tsakanikos, E., Costello, H., Holt, G., Sturmey, P., & Bouras, N. (2007). Behaviour management problems as predictors of psychotropic medication and use of psychiatric services in adults with autism. *Journal of Autism and Developmental Disorders, 37,* 1080–1085.

Turner-Brown, L. M., Perry, T. D., Dichter, G. S., Bodfish, J. W., & Penn, D. L. (2008). Brief report: Feasibility of social cognition and interaction training for adults with high functioning autism. *Journal of Autism and Developmental Disorders, 38,* 1777–1784. doi: 10.1007/s10803-008-0545-y

United States Centers for Disease Control and Prevention. (2009). Prevalence of autism spectrum disorders—autism and developmental disabilities monitoring network, United States, 2006. *MMWR Surveillance Summaries, 58,* 1–20.

VanBergeijk, E., Klin, A., & Volkmar, F. R. (2008). Supporting more able students on the autism spectrum: College and beyond. *Journal of Autism and Developmental Disabilities, 38,* 1359–1370.

Van Bourgondien, M. E., Reichle, N. C., & Schopler, E. (2003). Effects of a model treatment approach on adults with autism. *Journal of Autism and Developmental Disorders, 33*(2), 131–140.

van Steensel, F., Bögels, S., & Perrin, S. (2011). Anxiety disorders in children and adolescents with autistic spectrum disorders: A meta-analysis. *Behavioral Science Clinical Child and Family Psychology Review, 14,* 302–317. doi: 10.1007/s10567-011-0097-0

Verté, S., Geurts, H. M., Roeyers, H., Oosterlaan, J., & Sergeant, J. A. (2006). Executive functioning in children with an autism spectrum disorder: Can we differentiate within the spectrum? *Journal of Autism and Developmental Disorder, 36,* 351–372.

Wang, P., & Spillane, A. (2009). Evidence-based social skills interventions for children with autism: A meta-analysis. *Education and Training in Developmental Disabilities, 44*(3), 318–342.

Wentz, E., Lacey, J., Waller, G., Råstam, M., Turk, J., & Gillberg, C. (2005). Childhood onset neuropsychiatric disorders in adult eating disorder patients. *European Child & Adolescent Psychiatry, 14*(8), 431–437. doi:10.1007/s00787-005-0494-3

White, S. W. (2012). Growing pains: How psychologists can help to meet the clinical needs of clients with autism spectrum disorders. *Cognitive and Behavioral Practice*, *19*(3), 433–436. doi: 10.1016/j.cbpra.2011.08.001

White, S. W., Bray, B. C., & Ollendick, T. H. (2011). Examining shared and unique aspects of social anxiety disorder and autism spectrum disorder using factor analysis. *Journal of Autism and Developmental Disorders*, *42*(5), 874–884. doi: 10.1008/s10803-011-1325-7

White, S. W., Kreiser, N. L., Pugliese, C. E., & Scarpa, A. (2012). Social anxiety mediates the effect of autism spectrum disorder characteristics on hostility in young adults. *Autism: The International Journal of Research and Practice, 16*. doi: 10.1177/1362361311431951

White, S. W., Ollendick, T. H., & Bray, B. C. (2011). College students on the autism spectrum: Prevalence and associated problems. *Autism*. [Advance online publication.] doi: 10.1177/1362361310393363

White, S. W., Oswald, D., Ollendick, T., & Scahill, L. (2009). Anxiety in children with autism spectrum disorders. *Clinical Psychology Review*, *29*, 216–229.

White, S. W., & Pugliese, C. (2009, March). Growing up with autism: What's ahead and what can scientists and practitioners do to help? *ABCT Developmental Disorders Special Interest Group Newsletter*.

White, S. W., Schry, A. R., & Maddox, B. M. (2012). Brief report: The assessment of anxiety in high-functioning adolescents with autism spectrum disorder. *Journal of Autism and Developmental Disorders*. Advance online publication. doi:10.1007/s10803-011-1353-3.

Woodbury-Smith, M. R., Robinson, J., Wheelwright, S., & Baron-Cohen, S. (2005). Screening adults for Asperger syndrome using the AQ: A diagnostic validity in clinical practice. *Journal of Autism and Developmental Disorders*, *35*(3), 331–335. doi:10.1007/s10803-005-3300-7.

CHAPTER 9

Social Development in Autism

NAOMI ORNSTEIN DAVIS AND ALICE S. CARTER

INTRODUCTION

In 1943, Leo Kanner published his remarkably enduring paper in which he described 11 children who exhibited what Kanner interpreted as a congenital lack of interest in other people. He coined this disengaged social presentation as *autism*, from the Greek *autos*, meaning "self." The children that Kanner observed were highly interested in aspects of the inanimate environment, yet they demonstrated very limited interest in the social environment, including members of their own families. Kanner regarded both the social dysfunction and the unusual responses to the environment to be the two essential features of the syndrome. Subsequent descriptive and diagnostic work has modified Kanner's original description of autism in important ways, but social deviance has continued to be recognized as a significant phenomenological aspect of the syndrome. Throughout the broad range of syndrome expression and evolving diagnostic definitions over time, the social disability of persons with autism remains probably the most striking, and poorly understood, aspect of the

condition (Klin, Jones, Schultz, Volkmar, & Cohen, 2001; Lord, 1993).

Social deficits are observed in persons with autism across the range of developmental and cognitive functioning and over the lifespan (Marriage, Wolverton, & Marriage, 2009; Rimland, 1964; Rutter, 1978; L. E. Smith, Greenberg, Seltzer, & Hong, 2008; Wing, 1976). Indeed, routine social encounters with persons with autism illustrate that social deficits interfere in everyday social interactions despite heterogeneity in social ability. For example, a young, severely affected autistic child may prefer to spend most of his or her time engaged in solitary activities, fail to respond differentially to a strange person, and have relatively little interest in social interaction—even with his or her parents. Similarly, an older individual with autism, even at low level of functioning, may accept bids for social interaction in a passive manner, but rarely initiate social interaction for the sole purpose of shared social enjoyment. In contrast to these examples, higher functioning individuals with autism may show great interest in social interaction across the lifespan. However, they often have a limited capacity to understand or anticipate others' internal emotional states, intentions, and motivations, which makes it very difficult to negotiate the nuances of social interaction in order to connect with others in a normative way (Klin, Jones, Schultz, & Volkmar, 2003). Even adults with autism who are considered to be high functioning continue to experience social difficulty in certain contexts, such as maintaining intimate relationships or social networking in the workplace (Marriage et al., 2009).

Significant progress has been made in the last 30 years in understanding developmental aspects of autism syndrome expression and in formulating broader theoretical views of autistic social dysfunction. With the advent of improved instrumentation and diagnostic tools, the field of social neuroscience has offered a range of methodology that is informing our understanding of social deficits (Insel & Fernald, 2004; McPartland & Pelphrey, 2012). This literature has grown tremendously since the previous edition of this chapter and now includes multiple studies examining elements of brain function associated with the unique social disabilities in autism (McPartland & Pelphrey, 2012). Despite an increase in scientific interest in autism spectrum disorders (ASDs), considerable gaps still exist in our understanding of the factors that influence social interest, social functioning, and social development in the context of autism. Although interest in social interactions can range from high to negligible (Lord, 1993), and although some aspects of social functioning appear to improve over time, it is clear that social behavior in the context of autism is rarely normal (Volkmar, Sparrow, Goudreau, & Cicchetti, 1987; Wing & Gould, 1979).

In this chapter, we aim to selectively review the topic of social development in autism, to identify gaps in current knowledge about social developmental trajectories, and to outline areas of future research in this field. We begin with a review of historical and current beliefs about assessing and diagnosing social dysfunction in the context of the autism. Next, we describe several basic social processes that are deviant in individuals with autism and discuss the developmental course of these social behaviors. In the next section, we review current understanding about factors that may influence developmental changes in the social realm, including findings from longitudinal studies and treatment outcome studies. Finally, we describe additional factors (e.g., clinical features, developmental characteristics) that may mediate or moderate social development in the context of autism and that warrant future investigation.

ASSESSMENT AND CLASSIFICATION OF SOCIAL DYSFUNCTION

While certain aspects of Kanner's original description proved to be false leads for research, his phenomenological report of social experience in autism has proven remarkably enduring. Kanner emphasized that social deviance and delay was a hallmark, if not the hallmark, of autism. He contrasted the social interest of children with autism with that of normally developing infants and concluded that the autistic social dysfunction was distinctive. This emphasis has been continuously reflected in the various official and unofficial guidelines for the diagnosis of autism that have appeared since Kanner's original report. The need for coherent diagnostic guidelines became more critical during the late 1970s as the validity of autism as a diagnostic category became more clearly established. Various attempts, both categorical and dimensional, have been made to specify the nature of the social deficit.

Rutter emphasized that the unusual social development observed in autism was one of the essential features for definition, was distinctive, and was not just a function of associated mental retardation (Rutter, 1978). Early epidemiological studies also highlighted some of the difficulties in assessing social development relative to overall cognitive ability, particularly among the more severely handicapped (Wing & Gould, 1979). By 1980, there was general agreement on the need to include autism in official diagnostic systems like the American Psychiatric Association's *Diagnostic and Statistical Manual*, third edition (American Psychiatric

Association [APA], 1980). The *DSM-III* definition of infantile autism defined the social deficit as "pervasive," although the use of this term was really most appropriate for the youngest and most impaired children, that is, consistent with the name of the category. The term *residual autism* was available for persons who had once exhibited the pervasive social deficit but no longer did so. As a practical matter it was clear that some social skills did emerge over time and imprecision regarding the nature of the social deficit was clearly problematic (Volkmar et al., 1987).

In the subsequent revision of the *DSM-III* (*DSM-III-R*; APA, 1987), the nature of the social deficit in autism was defined with greater attention to developmental variation. Qualitative impairment in social interaction was retained as one of three essential diagnostic features for autistic disorder (in addition to impairments in communication and a restricted range of interests/activities). Within the social domain, an individual had to exhibit at least two items from a list of five criteria to demonstrate a social deficit (see Table 9.1). The *DSM-III-R* criteria also included many examples to clarify the nature of the social deficits that were described. This approach to defining social dysfunction in autism also reflected an awareness of the developmental changes in syndrome expression and recognition that even the social skills that emerged over time were unusual in quality and/or quantity. This developmental perspective was also reflected in the official change of name of the disorder from infantile autism to autistic disorder.

Given the greater number and better specification of criteria for social dysfunction, the *DSM-III-R* system had the major advantage over previous *DSM* versions of suitability for statistical evaluation. For example, Siegel and colleagues reanalyzed clinician ratings of *DSM-III-R* criteria for autism by employing signal detection analysis, an approach designed to identify the most robust criterion or combination of criteria that can reliably be used for diagnosis (Siegel, Vukicevic, Elliott, & Kraemer, 1989). Consistent with Kanner's original impression and subsequent research, this analysis indicated that the social criteria were the most

potent predictors of diagnosis. Unfortunately, however, the broader orientation of *DSM-III-R* also lead to a change in the threshold of diagnosis, with many individuals who previously would not have met criteria for infantile autism classified with a diagnosis of autistic disorder. Major revisions were made in *DSM-IV* (APA, 2000) which paralleled the major changes in the International Classification of Diseases system—*ICD-10*. In both *DSM-IV* and *ICD-10*, qualitative impairments in social interaction was maintained as one of the essential diagnostic features. The *DSM-IV* revision included a reduction in the number of criteria and the detail of these criteria, with problems in at least two of the four areas required for the autistic social dysfunction to be considered present (Table 9.1).

Perspectives on measuring social dysfunction in autism have continued to evolve and were an integral component of the *DSM-5* taskforce discussion. Although the impact of new diagnostic criteria in the *DSM-5* (APA, 2013) cannot yet be evaluated,

TABLE 9.1   History of Social Dysfunction Definitions in Autism Spectrum Disorder

Source	Year	Definition of Social Dysfunction
Rutter	1978	Social delays/deviance that is not just secondary to mental retardation
DSM-III	1980	Pervasive social problems
DSM-III-R	1987	Qualitative impairment in social interaction (at least two of the following): Lack of awareness of others Absent/abnormal comfort seeking Absent/impaired imitation Absent/abnormal social play Gross deficits in ability to make peer friendships
DSM-IV	1994	Qualitative impairment in social interaction (at least two of the following): Market deficits in nonverbal behaviors used in social interaction Absent peer relationship relative to developmental level Lack of shared enjoyment/pleasure Problems in social-emotional reciprocity
DSM-5	2013	Social communication impairment (at least three of the following): Deficits in social-emotional reciprocity Deficits in nonverbal communicative behaviors used for social interaction Deficits in developing and maintaining relationships

the changes generated significant discussion in the scientific and lay communities about how social deficits in autism, and indeed the diagnosis of autism itself, are conceptualized. Specifically, the triad of autism impairment is now reduced into a dyad, such that social and communication impairments will comprise one area of impairment rather than two distinct areas. These changes stem from research that suggests an overlap in symptoms from these two categories, which has been evident from a clinical perspective and has also been confirmed via factor analytic studies show they are part of the same factor (Mahjouri & Lord, 2012). For example, engaging in reciprocal conversation is both a communicative act as well as an act of social engagement. The *DSM-5* criteria provide a smaller number of more general principles regarding social communication with examples that reflect manifestation in individuals with ASD across age and developmental level.

In contrast to existing, norm-referenced tests of cognitive or language ability, the field has lagged behind considerably with respect to established tools for assessment of social functioning. Although diagnostic gold-standard assessments have been developed and are becoming more widely used clinically, there has also been a push for greater use of dimensional measures to defining social dysfunction. Assessment of change over time, as well as intervention effects, requires social assessment tools that are validated for this purpose, yet the field has been lacking in clear guidelines in this area (Cunningham, 2012). Selecting appropriate measures to examine change in social behavior is critical for standardizing assessments and facilitating comparisons across studies of individuals with autism. In the following discussion, some existing tools are reviewed, including rating scales, parent interviews, and observational tools that provide an assessment of social functioning and an ability to compare children's social development to normative peers and over time.

Rating scales can yield helpful information based on normative samples and target the specific areas of impairment affected in autism spectrum disorders. The Social Responsiveness Scale (SRS)

(Constantino & Gruber, 2005) has been utilized in numerous studies to measure quantitatively the social behavior of individuals with autism. Intended uses of the SRS include its function as a screener to identify cases that warrant full assessment and as a research tool to quantify autism spectrum traits (Bölte, Poustka, & Constantino, 2008; Duvall et al., 2007). However, a number of studies have raised concerns that SRS scores are highly correlated with behavior problems, cautioning for careful interpretation of SRS scores given possible lack of specificity for core autism symptoms (Hus, Bishop, Gotham, Huerta, & Lord, 2013). Another rating scale that is widely used to examine social functioning in individuals with autism is the Social Communication Questionnaire (SCQ) (Berument, Rutter, Lord, Pickles, & Bailey, 1999). The SCQ was developed as a diagnostic screener to identify children at risk for autism spectrum disorder and has shown adequate sensitivity and specificity as an initial screener for ASD (Chandler et al., 2007). Other studies have found agreement between the SCQ and similar rating scales, but suggest that the existing cutoff scores may not be adequate for accurate classification depending on age and developmental level (Snow & Lecavalier, 2008; Wiggins, Bakeman, Adamson, & Robins, 2007).

The most commonly used parent interview, the Autism Diagnostic Interview–Revised (ADI-R) (Lord, Rutter, & Le Couteur, 1994), was designed for diagnostic purpose to assign caseness. The ADI-R items identify an individual's typical pattern of social engagement as well as highly unusual social features. Despite the interview's origins as a diagnostic tool, multiple studies have begun to use the scores generated with the ADI as continuous phenotypes to characterize social functioning (Spiker, Lotspeich, Dimiceli, Myers, & Risch, 2002; Wiggins, Robins, Adamson, Bakeman, & Henrich, 2012). As an alternative to an autism-specific interview, the Vineland Adaptive Behavior Scales is another parent interview than can be useful for providing a measure of social dysfunction in the context of autism (Sparrow, Balla, & Cicchetti, 1984). The Vineland is a semistructured parent interview that assesses day-to-day adaptive functioning and personal self-sufficiency in the areas of communication, daily living, and socialization. Studies have shown that children with autism demonstrate much lower than expected social skills relative to their overall cognitive ability or developmental level (Volkmar et al., 1987). Delays in social skills as measured by the Vineland are robust predictors of the diagnosis of autism, even when compared to delays in communication (Gillham, Carter, Volkmar, & Sparrow, 2000; Volkmar, Carter, Sparrow, & Cicchetti, 1993).

Additional tools that can be useful in quantifying dimensions of social functioning and social impairment are observational instruments (see Table 9.2). The most widely used tool is the Autism Diagnostic Observation Schedule (ADOS), a standardized measure that is considered a gold standard for autism diagnosis (Lord, Rutter, DiLavore, & Risi, 2001). Like the ADI, the ADOS was developed originally for categorical purposes (i.e., assess if symptoms are above or below diagnostic threshold), but more recently algorithms have been developed to use scores from the ADOS in a dimensional fashion. The "calibrated severity score" has been developed as a metric to use for comparing assessments over time as well as identifying developmental trajectories (Gotham, Pickles, & Lord, 2009; Shumway et al., 2012). Other observational tools are used less frequently and most often in the context of research. For example, the Autism Observation Scale for Infants (AOSI) is a reliable observational tool comprised of a series of 18 presses to elicit specific social behaviors in 6- to 18-month-old infants (Bryson, Zwaigenbaum, McDermott, Rombough, & Brian, 2008). The STAT (Screening Tool for Autism in Two-Year-Olds) is an interactive, play-based screening measure for autism that assesses play, communication, and imitation skills (Stone, Coonrod, Turner, & Pozdol, 2004). Research has found acceptable agreement between the STAT and the ADOS and suggest its promise as a screening instrument (Stone, McMahon, & Henderson, 2008). In addition, both the AOSI and STAT show promise as tools for screening at-risk siblings of children diagnosed with autism spectrum disorder.

TABLE 9.2　Quantifying Dimensions of Social Functioning and Social Impairment

Scale	Social Items	Ages
Social Responsiveness Scale (SRS)	65-item questionnaire assesses social awareness, information processing, reciprocal social communication, social anxiety	4–18 years
Social Communication Questionnaire (SCQ)	40-item questionnaire assesses communication skills and social functioning in both current (past 3 months) and lifetime forms	4 years through adulthood (mental age over 2 years)
Autism Diagnostic Interview—Revised (ADI-R)	93-item comprehensive interview of symptoms in three functional domains, including language/communication, reciprocal social interaction, and restricted, repetitive behaviors and interests	Children and adults with mental age over 2 years
Autism Diagnostic Observation Schedule, Second Edition (ADOS-II)	Semistructured, standardized observational assessment of communication, social interaction, play, and restricted and repetitive behavior	12 months through adulthood
Vineland Adaptive Behavior Scales, Second Edition (VABS-II)	Semistructured interview and rating forms assess self-sufficiency in multiple domains including socialization, specifically interpersonal relationships, play and leisure time, and coping skills	Birth through 90 years
Autism Observation Scale for Infants (AOSI)	18-item direct observational measure of early emerging social functioning (e.g., reciprocal smiling, social anticipation and imitation)	6–18 months
Screening Tool for Autism in Two-Year-Olds (STAT)	12 activity-based items assess a range of social-communicative behaviors, including play, requesting, directing attention, and motor imitation	24–36 months

DEVELOPMENTAL PROCESSES IN TYPICAL SOCIAL DEVELOPMENT

Infants typically enter the world prewired by evolution with the motivation and capacity to begin establishing an immediate social relationship with their caregivers. In the context of typical development, a series of social milestones typically unfolds, beginning with basic building blocks (e.g., social smiling, sharing eye gaze) and working up to more complex social behaviors (e.g., referencing social partners for information, shared affect in context of intimate relationship) that are critical for functioning in the social world. These behaviors develop initially in the context of interactions with primary caretakers and evolve over time to extend to other social relationships. In contrast to this typical developmental pattern, children with autism show initial deficits in basic skills that limit their social experiences, thereby limiting their ability to acquire more advanced social skills (Vernon, Koegel, Dauterman, & Stolen, 2012). Despite the heterogeneity in the social presentation among individuals with autism, early departures from normative social developmental processes are likely to affect all children with autism, although the individual trajectories may differ (Jones & Klin, 2009). As Jones and Klin suggest, a very young child with autism who engages primarily with the physical environment rather than the social environment will miss out on critical opportunities for social development. Recent research on neural circuits associated with social behavior suggests that this early pattern of social disruption also has the potential to influence subsequent brain development through missed opportunities for experience dependent learning (Pelphrey, Shultz, Hudac, & Vander Wyk, 2011).

Reflecting back on Kanner's original observations, it is clear that Kanner believed that "these children have come into the world with the innate inability to form the usual, biologically provided affective contact with people" (Kanner, 1943, p. 250). Although many of Kanner's initial impressions have been consistent with subsequent research, emerging evidence from studies of infant siblings of children with autism does not support the idea that social deficits are present at birth (Ozonoff et al., 2011; Yirmiya & Ozonoff, 2007). Current science clearly supports the idea that social deviance associated with autism is apparent, in most cases, during the first 1 to 2 years of life based on retrospective parent reports (Ornitz, Guthrie, & Farley, 1977), record review (Fombonne et al., 2004), and observational coding of family videotapes (Osterling, Dawson, & Munson, 2002). In a recent comprehensive review of early signs of autism, Yirmiya and Charman conclude that a picture indicative of prodromal signs of autism is emerging, whereby infants show some social-communication abnormalities toward the end of the first year of life (Yirmiya & Charman, 2010). In fact, studies of infants who are considered at risk for autism based on sibling diagnostic status have shown that symptom onset varies widely, and onset patterns are not good predictors of functional outcomes (Shumway et al., 2011). With improved diagnostic tools and heightened awareness that earlier diagnosis and intervention are beneficial, continued research on infants will allow for greater understanding of the earliest course of social dysfunction in autism and its implications for both intervention and long-term functioning.

In the next section, we focus on specific aspects of social behavior that develop very early in the context of normative development. When these specific social processes are disrupted early in development, later-emerging, more complex skills (e.g., symbolic play, theory of mind) are likely impacted due to disrupted opportunities for social learning (Ingersoll, 2011). Our review of the literature is not comprehensive, but rather is intended to illustrate what is known about basic social processes that are a foundation for the later emerging, more complex social behavior. These processes include eye gaze, imitation, and joint attention.

Eye Gaze

Newborn infants show preference for face-like stimuli and, in the first months of life, typically developing infants demonstrate selective attention to social stimuli and preferential attention to human faces (Spitz, 1965). Mutual gaze is used to establish the earliest social interactions and may be the driving force behind infants' interest in human faces (Gliga & Csibra, 2007). Numerous studies have shown atypical patterns of eye gaze in individuals with autism across the lifespan (Volkmar & Mayes, 1990). Although limited eye contact is considered to be one of the early emerging signs of ASD, more recent research has found early infancy gaze behavior does not predict later diagnostic status in infants at risk for autism (Young, Merin, Rogers, & Ozonoff, 2009). Nonetheless, because of their limited attention to faces, very young children with autism appear to miss out on social cues in the environment that provide a range of information about the attentional and emotional states of others (Chawarska, Volkmar, & Klin, 2010). This type of deviation in use of eye gaze has not been observed among children with developmental delays or who are later diagnosed with mental retardation, and thus appears specific to autism (Yirmiya, Pilowsky, Solomonica-Levi, & Shulman, 1999).

Eye gaze is frequently reported to be abnormal by parents of children with autism. For example, in one retrospective study, 90% of parents of children with autism reported that their child often, very often, or almost always avoided eye contact (Volkmar, Cohen, & Paul, 1986). Several studies have suggested that engaging in direct or indirect eye contact is stressful for children with autism, as measured by skin conductance response, which is an indicator of autonomic arousal (Joseph, Ehrman, McNally, & Keehn, 2008). In fact, more recent work studying individuals with autism with normal-range intelligence suggests that higher autonomic response in response to unfamiliar faces is associated with poorer social skills (Kaartinen et al., 2012). At the same time, contextual influences (e.g., how an adult interacts with the child) can influence eye contact and can even facilitate improvement in children's use of gaze, for example, in more structured situations and when an adult interaction partner follows a child's interests (Dawson, Hill, Spencer, & Galpert, 1990; Kasari, Sigman, & Yirmiya, 1993; Wimpory, Hobson, &

Nash, 2007). Similarly, the nature of task demands may influence amounts of eye contact (Dawson & Galpert, 1990).

Recent advances in eye-tracking and computer-modeling technologies have increased interest in the study of gaze, and studies of gaze are now an integral component of social neuroscience in autism. Early studies suggested that children with autism did not evidence the expected preferential gaze shifting in response to a social cue (Senju, Tojo, Dairoku, & Hasegawa, 2004). Although toddlers with autism do not follow the gaze of others in naturalistic settings, eye-tracking data has shown that they are sensitive to directional cues inherent in eye movement (Chawarska, Klin, & Volkmar, 2003). Additional findings on reaction time to biological and nonbiological movement suggest that different underlying strategies or mechanisms for gaze processing may be present by 2 years of age. In more recent work, Chawarska demonstrated that toddlers with autism do not differ from typically developing and delayed peers in their gaze toward some social scenes; however, significant differences in gaze emerge when toddlers were presented with scenes that included explicit social cues (i.e., clear social bids for attention) (Chawarska, Macari, & Shic, 2012). More work is needed to fully understand the mechanisms that underlie developmental processes involved in gaze shifting among individuals with autism. To this end, novel technology has been recently tested to expand on findings from eye-tracking studies. Noris and colleagues developed a novel tool to track gaze direction and lateral field of viewing and showed that children with autism spectrum disorder differed from typical peers in their downward gaze and use of the lateral field of view (Noris, Nadel, Barker, Hadjikhani, & Billard, 2012). These findings have implications for understanding how well individuals with autism are able to discern relevant social contextual information.

Overall, results from older and more recent studies of eye gaze indicate that a variety of issues must be considered in exploring eye gaze in the context of autism, including difficulty disengaging from competing stimuli, atypical shifts in attention, and strategies of visual exploration (Elison et al., 2013; Noris et al., 2012). Deficits in gaze may be amplified by naturalistic demands to coordinate eye gaze with gestural and verbal systems of expression and understanding. For example, younger children with autism are less likely to use gaze to augment other sources of information about ambiguous interactions (Phillips, Baron-Cohen, & Rutter, 1992), and children with autism have difficulty integrating gaze and other nonverbal behaviors (Buitelaar, van Engeland, de Kogel, de Vries, & van Hooff, 1991).

Imitation

Typically developing infants develop skills in imitation early in development, and numerous authors have outlined the relationship between imitation skills and subsequent symbolic and social communication behaviors (Meltzoff & Moore, 1977; Rogers & Pennington, 1991). The ability of an infant to share experiences with his or her caregiver with regard to an object of reference is an important context for symbolic development (Werner & Kaplan, 1963), and deficits in the areas of imitation have important consequences for other aspects of development. A range of studies has documented that many children with autism display significant deficits across different types of imitation tasks (I. Smith & Bryson, 1994; Williams, Whiten, & Singh, 2004). Infants and children with autism produce fewer spontaneous imitations of the actions of their parents (Dawson & Adams, 1984) and they are less adept at elicited imitation (Charman & Baron-Cohen, 1994). Studies have consistently revealed that younger children with autism have problems in the imitation of simple body movements and those that involve objects (Stone, Lemanek, Fishel, Fernandez, & Altemeier, 1990; Stone, Ousley, & Littleford, 1997). For example, Rogers and colleagues demonstrated that toddlers with autism evidenced delays relative to developmentally delayed and typically developing children in specific types of imitation skills including oral-facial imitation (e.g., extending and wiggling tongue) and imitation of actions on

objects (e.g., patting a squeaky toy with their elbow) (Rogers, Hepburn, Stackhouse, & Wehner, 2003). Deficits in reciprocal social play, characterized by infant games such as peekaboo and patty-cake, which integrate imitation and social dialogue, are also noted by parents of children with autism (Klin, 1992).

As with other social behaviors, imitation skills in children with autism appear to be influenced by factors such as developmental level and context (Dawson & Adams, 1984). Some studies have suggested that specific types of imitation (e.g., oral-facial, object imitation skills) are related to overall developmental level and to an estimate of autism severity (Rogers et al., 2003). High-risk infants who are later diagnosed with autism show atypical development in the area of imitation within the first 12 months (Zwaigenbaum et al., 2005). In addition, a recent longitudinal study of infants at risk for autism and with typical development suggest that infants who are later diagnosed with autism demonstrated delayed imitation development but were not easily distinguished from infants with other types of cognitive delays (Young et al., 2011). Ingersoll differentiated between the types of imitation skills that emerge in different contexts, specifically a structured situation in which imitation is directly elicited versus a social-interactive context. Results indicated that young children with autism were more successful imitators in the structure-elicited context, and that imitation skills in the social-interactive context were correlated with other social abilities including reciprocity and symbolic play (Ingersoll & Meyer, 2011).

Joint Attention

The absence or deviance of normative gaze and other forms of early nonverbal social interchange in children with autism interferes with the emergence of intersubjectivity, which is defined as the co-construction of shared emotional meaning between parent and child (Trevarthen & Aitken, 2001). Failure to achieve intersubjectivity also results in deficits in the development of joint attention, which emerges in the 8- to 12-month age period in the context of typical development (Bakeman & Adamson, 1984). Joint attention is a preverbal social communicative skill that involves sharing with another person the experience of a third object or event (Schaffer, 1984). Two aspects of joint attention are generally discussed in the literature: the ability to use eye contact to establish a shared experience (initiating joint attention) and the capacity to follow gaze or gesture to respond to another person's bid for sharing (responding to joint attention) (Mundy et al., 2007). For example, a typically developing infant will smile and point at a toy he finds interesting, and then alternately look at the toy and to his mother to share his experience of the toy with her. Similarly, a typically developing infant will follow the parent's eye gaze and/or point when the parent turns to show an object of interest in the distance (e.g., a plane off in the distance). The fundamental skill of joint attention in infancy and early toddlerhood is considered a building block for later social skills, and research indicates that infant joint attention in the context of typical development is predictive of preschool social and behavioral competence (Van Hecke et al., 2007).

A wealth of research on social development in autism indicates that triadic exchanges (person-person-object) are consistently impoverished in children with autism as compared to peers of similar cognitive and developmental level (Mundy, 2003). Given that this behavior typically emerges before a diagnosis of autism is typically made (i.e., prior to 12 months), retrospective video studies have provided a methodology for examining early joint attention skills in children who are later diagnosed with autism. In one of the seminal studies using this design, Osterling and Dawson reviewed videotapes of first birthday parties of 22 children (11 with autism and 11 who were developing normally) to assess social, affective, communicative, and joint attention behaviors as well as for symptoms suggestive of autism (Osterling & Dawson, 1994). Results demonstrated group differences such that the children with autism exhibited fewer social and joint attention behaviors and more autistic symptoms. In a subsequent study, children diagnosed with ASD were compared to children with mental retardation and typically developing children on the same measures (Osterling et al., 2002). This study extended earlier findings that children with autism show fewer social and joint attention behaviors and more atypical autism-specific behaviors than both comparison groups, indicating the difficulties were not just a function of developmental delays but rather were central to the diagnosis of autism. Indeed, deficits in joint attention are among the most striking and persistent problems in younger children with autism (Mundy, 1995).

In the context of autism, requisite behaviors such as showing or pointing to objects may account for some of the relative failures in joint attention. When children do show or point, they are much less likely to alternate gaze at the interactive partner and a desired or interesting object/activity than a typically developing child would. Even when joint attention is observed its quality is unusual, with minimal coordination of gaze, vocalizations, and gestures. Further complicating the social interactions of children with autism is that they may also show less positive affect directed toward others in social exchanges and may even avoid positive praise (Kasari, Sigman, Mundy, & Yirmiya, 1990). Thus, rather than evidencing a complete deficit, individuals with autism may demonstrate a pattern of joint attention characterized more by requesting help from another person (e.g., pointing to a box of cookies on a high shelf) rather than calling another person's attention to an object or experience (e.g., showing a parent that one has found an interesting toy) (Bruinsma, Koegel, & Koegel, 2004). Even those children with autism who display an ability to coordinate eye contact with gestures and actions tend not to use it merely to share an awareness or an experience of an object or event, as do normal children and developmentally matched children with mental retardation.

As with other aspects of gaze behavior, developmental relationships and correlates of joint attention have been observed. Children with autism who are functioning at lower developmental levels across other domains typically show lower levels of joint attention (Mundy, Sigman, & Kasari, 1994). Joint attention has been related to language abilities

(Mundy, Sigman, & Kasari, 1990), to gains in language abilities over time (Siller & Sigman, 2002), and to aspects of executive functioning (McEvoy, Rogers, & Pennington, 1993). In a more recent study of rating videotaped parent–child interactions of toddlers/young children with autism, Down syndrome, and typical development, results supported prior findings of less coordinated joint engagement in children with autism (Adamson, Bakeman, Deckner, & Nelson, 2012). It is also important to note that most of these assessments of joint attention have pertained to younger children with autism, and there have been fewer studies of ways to measure joint attention skills in older individuals. The development of measures of joint attention for children and adolescents would allow for meaningful longitudinal study and assessment of intervention effectiveness (Bean & Eigsti, 2012).

DEVELOPMENTAL TRAJECTORY

Over 20 years ago, Rogers and Pennington proposed a developmental cascade model of autism, in which deficits in specific aspects of interpersonal development disrupt the expected course of development in each successive stage (Rogers & Pennington, 1991). This model certainly pertains to the realm of social development in autism. Although basic social behaviors are impaired, they often develop eventually, albeit at a pace and sometimes sequence that differs from that observed in typical development. For example, children with autism have been shown to be delayed relative to their peers in both nonverbal joint attention and in requesting skills, but both sets of skills eventually do develop in most children (Paparella, Goods, Freeman, & Kasari, 2011). Requesting skills appear to develop in the same sequence in autism as in typical development, whereas specific joint attention skills appear to emerge in a different pattern (Paparella et al., 2011). Similarly, Carpenter and colleagues noted that children with autism generally follow a typical sequence of first sharing attention, then following attention, and then directing attention social interactions, but there is more

variability in individual trajectories in children with autism as compared to typical development (Carpenter, Pennington, & Rogers, 2002).

Whereas the period of early childhood has been examined through numerous studies of infants, toddlers, and preschoolers, including at-risk baby siblings, fewer studies have described the longitudinal course of social development in autism from early childhood into adolescence or even adulthood. These types of studies are critical in order to understand how social abilities change over time in the context of autism, and results can inform more tailored intervention needs. Of the longitudinal studies that have been conducted, several studies have documented both continuity in diagnostic status over time as well as a change in symptom profiles over time (Anderson, Oti, Lord, & Welch, 2009; McGovern & Sigman, 2005). In a monograph dedicated to continuity and change in social competence, Sigman and Ruskin followed children with autism, Down syndrome, and other developmental delays from early childhood to the midschool years. They noted sustained deficits in social competence (i.e., social engagement with peers) in the context of autism that was associated with less frequent initiations and also fewer acceptances of peers' bids to play. Longitudinal analysis indicated that early nonverbal communication and play skills during preschool were predictive of peer engagement when children with autism were school-aged (Sigman & Ruskin, 1999). Anderson and colleagues followed a large sample of children with autism from toddlerhood to adolescence with five separate evaluations of their social and behavioral functioning. Their findings support overall growth in adaptive social ability and social skills over time, although they noted considerable variation in social outcomes across their sample (Anderson et al., 2009). Specifically, they found that individuals with lower cognitive ability as well as fewer environmental resources, as defined by maternal education and parent-mediated treatment, were shown to make fewer social gains. Similarly, a small study of 20 participants evaluated longitudinally from early childhood through young adulthood found that early social functioning—specifically, responsiveness to joint attention—was predictive of adult social functioning along with language ability (Gillespie-Lynch et al., 2012). All of these studies suggest that later social outcome can be predicted from specific processes in early development, which may have implications for intervention targets throughout childhood.

Most developmental studies of clinical populations with autism have been limited by small sample sizes or the difficult task of coordinating across many sites (or over many years) to attain a large enough sample size. In contrast, a recent evaluation was published that examined data on almost 7,000 children diagnosed with autism in the state of California between 1992 and 2001 (Fountain, Winter, & Bearman, 2012). Complex trajectory analysis yielded six typical patterns of functioning over time, which demonstrated significant heterogeneity within each domain of functioning. Of particular interest is the finding regarding social behavior, which suggested that about 10% of children could be classified as "bloomers" in the realm of social behavior. Although these children were among the lowest in social development initially, they gained skills at a faster rate such that they attained almost as many skills the high functioning group (Fountain et al., 2012). Such findings indicate the potential for identifying which early factors may serve to maximize outcomes over time.

Some studies have demonstrated gradual improvements in social behavior into adolescence and early adulthood, and these improvements have been shown to coincide with increased social interest (McGovern & Sigman, 2005). In general, however, adolescents with autism participate in far fewer social activities than their typically developing peers (Shattuck, Orsmond, Wagner, & Cooper, 2011) and therefore have fewer opportunities to develop appropriate social skills. There is growing evidence that these adolescents experience more loneliness and poorer friendships than their typically developing peers, despite a desire to foster these relationships (Locke, Ishijima, Kasari, & London, 2010). Locke and colleagues suggest that the gaps between children with autism and their typically developing peers widen during adolescence,

in particular in the context of more complex social environments and the need for strong interpersonal skills to maintain adolescent relationships.

Although the literature on adults with autism is small, there is growing interest in understanding development trajectories throughout the lifespan (Perkins & Berkman, 2012). Many early studies pointed to poor outcomes in adulthood, yet there are a number of studies that demonstrate a minority of individuals with autism are living more independently and experiencing life satisfaction (Howlin, Goode, Hutton, & Rutter, 2004; McMahon & Farley, 2011). Of note, even when individuals are doing better in adulthood, reports from family members indicate ongoing perceived needs in the social realm in the majority of cases (Eaves & Ho, 2008).

INTERVENTION

Prior longitudinal and cross-sectional studies of children with autism have provided a wealth of information about social functioning across developmental stages. Most of these studies have been descriptive, and few were designed to examine the effects of targeted interventions on social development. In addition, many of the earlier studies were conducted at a time when few children with autism were receiving a high level of intervention services to address their developmental problems. For example, the longitudinal data collected by Fountain and colleagues over a period of almost 20 years (1992–2001) likely include children who were receiving varying levels of intervention services and others who did not get systematic treatment (Fountain et al., 2012). In this type of longitudinal study, it is difficult to distinguish change that may be a function of an individual's own developmental process from change that can be attributed to intervention. To better understand the ways in which changes in social functioning may be facilitated, it is important to review findings from intervention studies that have been designed to target a specific social deficit. In this section, we selectively review some of these studies to describe possible avenues of social growth in the context of autism. Overall, results across studies indicate that many individuals with autism are able to make clear improvements and gain skills in each area of social functioning with appropriate intervention.

Gaze Training

Research suggests that gaze behavior can increase even with brief but targeted training. Dawson and Galpert found that young children with autism who engaged in imitative play regularly for 2 weeks with their mothers showed significant increases in gaze at their mothers' faces after the intervention (Dawson & Galpert, 1990). Hopkins et al. (2011) conducted a computerized social skills training that included a segment designed to teach purposeful use of eye gaze, which was rewarded in the game when done successfully. Results indicated that, in combination with two other social tasks (i.e., discriminating faces, recognizing emotions), both low- and high-functioning children with autism spectrum disorder were able to improve social skills at the end of the training (Hopkins et al., 2011). Technological advances may also yield innovative methods for teaching and training eye gaze. For example, Grynszpan and colleagues have developed a virtual reality system that measures eye movement in the context of different social stimuli, under normal and blurred visual field conditions. Results showed impairments in self-monitoring of eye gaze in the autism group, and authors suggest possible use of this technology for treatment (Grynszpan et al., 2012).

Imitation

Studies suggest that young children can benefit from direct intervention in imitation skills. One approach, Reciprocal Imitation Training, has demonstrated efficacy for teaching both object and gesture imitation skills that have generalized to other environments and been maintained over time shown (Ingersoll, 2010). Other interventions have examined different modalities of imitation training and have shown gains in imitation skills

through both reciprocal imitation training and video modeling (Cardon & Wilcox, 2011). Given the early onset of imitation in the context of social development, Ingersoll and colleagues have explored whether teaching targeted imitation skills can lead to more general social improvements. Results of a randomized controlled trial indicated positive effects of an imitation intervention on young children's joint attention skills, but analyses did not support that imitation was the mechanism of action (Ingersoll, 2012).

Joint Attention Intervention

A great number of studies on joint attention have been published in the last 15 years, and the vast majority of these studies have shown positive effects on children with autism (White et al., 2011). Key findings include long-term positive benefits of joint attention training on other behavioral targets, including language skills (Kasari, Gulsrud, Freeman, Paparella, & Hellemann, 2012). Interestingly, gains in joint attention may also result from other types of early intervention, as shown by Lawton and Kasari in their study comparing a joint attention and symbolic play intervention (Lawton & Kasari, 2012). Overall, studies vary considerably in terms of their emphasis on different aspects of joint attention (i.e., response or initiation) and whether they focused directly or indirectly on joint attention (White et al., 2011). As White and colleagues highlight, future research should begin to determine how to best build upon children's developmental capacities and the context of learning in order to maximize outcomes. As with other aspects of autism intervention, some researchers have developed computer-based methods for training joint attention skills. Cheng and Huang described the development and pilot testing of a virtual reality playroom in which joint attention was taught through discrete tasks of pointing, showing, sharing, and interacting with the characters in the computerized task. Although this study used a very small sample, results indicate promise for both gaining joint attention skills and extending these to everyday life (Cheng & Huang, 2012).

Integrated Treatments

The early social developmental skills reviewed here, including gaze, imitation, and joint attention, come together to support other more complex skills, including social use of language, symbolic play, and aspects of social cognition. Interventions that can address this level of complexity of social development may be best poised to yield global improvements in this domain. One program that is supported by a growing research base is the Early Start Denver Model, a parent-mediated treatment that promotes development in social communication skills through play and relationship-focused routines (Rogers & Dawson, 2010). Results of a randomized controlled trial showed significant gains in cognitive ability and adaptive behavior among children who received the intervention as compared to a community intervention (Dawson et al., 2010). Secondary analysis from this trial showed not only improved social behavior in young children with autism who received the intervention, but also normalization in brain activity in response to viewing social stimuli (i.e., faces) (Dawson et al., 2012).

FUTURE DIRECTIONS

Considerable research on social deficits in autism has been conducted since the last publication of this *Handbook*. Improved assessments of social behavior and technologies (e.g., tracking eye gaze, virtual reality), have not only improved knowledge about social development but have informed the development of interventions to treat social deficits. The widespread use of common diagnostic tools and standardized measures has enabled more accurate comparisons across studies. Further, continued earlier detection and improvements in diagnostic measures for very young children, as well as studies focused on the early social development of baby siblings of children already diagnosed with autism, have facilitated research on early social dysfunction.

Consistent with Kanner's earliest descriptions, social dysfunction remains a hallmark feature of autism. At the same time, and in contrast to the early depiction of the absence of social behaviors, it is now clear that there is great variability in social behaviors across individuals with autism. This variability is evident in overall level of social functioning in day-to-day settings, in performance on laboratory-based tasks, and importantly in response to intervention and developmental change over time. Because social impairments remain a primary, if not the central component of autism, future research is needed to better explain the social behaviors that are present for an individual and ways to facilitate social growth. More work is needed to better understand the interrelationships between cognitive and language abilities and social development throughout the lifespan, as young children, who have been most intensively studied, develop into adolescents and adults. Similarly, the impact of comorbid psychiatric problems, which are increasingly recognized in individual with autism, need to be examined with respect to their impact on social development and social interventions. Continued collaboration with experts in neuroscience will no doubt increase understanding of the mechanisms that contribute to social dysfunction and to the possibility for growth and change over time.

CROSS-REFERENCES

Chapter 4 addresses outcomes in autism, Chapter 5 autism in infants and young children, Chapter 12 imitation in autism, and Chapter 14 emotional development. Chapter 29 focuses on intervention in young children and Chapter 30 on comprehensive treatment models for children and youth. Social skills interventions are the focus of Chapter 37.

REFERENCES

Adamson, L. B., Bakeman, R., Deckner, D. F., & Nelson, P. B. (2012). Rating parent–child interactions: Joint engagement, communication dynamics, and shared topics in autism, Down syndrome, and typical development. *Journal of Autism and Developmental Disorders, 42*(12), 2622–2635. doi: 10.1007/s10803-012-1520-1

American Psychiatric Association. (1980). *Diagnostic and statistical manual* (3rd ed). Washington, DC: Author.

American Psychiatric Association. (1987). *Diagnostic and statistical manual of mental disorders* (3rd ed., revised). Washington, DC: Author.

American Psychiatric Association. (2000). *Diagnostic and statistical manual of mental disorders* (4th ed., text rev.). Washington, DC: Author.

American Psychiatric Association. (2013). *Diagnostic and statistical manual of mental disorders* (5th ed). Arlington, VA: American Psychiatric Publishing.

Anderson, D. K., Oti, R. S., Lord, C., & Welch, K. (2009). Patterns of growth in adaptive social abilities among children with autism spectrum disorders. *Journal of Abnormal Child Psychology, 37*(7), 1019–1034. doi: 10.1007/s10802-009-9326-0

Bakeman, R., & Adamson, L. B. (1984). Coordinating attention to people and objects in mother–infant and peer–infant interaction. *Child Development, 55*(4), 1278–1289. doi: 10.2307/1129997

Bean, J. L., & Eigsti, I.-M. (2012). Assessment of joint attention in school-age children and adolescents. *Research in Autism Spectrum Disorders, 6*(4), 1304–1310. doi: 10.1016/j.rasd.2012.04.003

Berument, S. K., Rutter, M., Lord, C., Pickles, A., & Bailey, A. (1999). Autism screening questionnaire: Diagnostic validity. *British Journal of Psychiatry, 175*, 444–451.

Bölte, S., Poustka, F., & Constantino, J. N. (2008). Assessing autistic traits: Cross-cultural validation of the Social Responsiveness Scale (SRS). *Autism Research, 1*(6), 354–363. doi: 10.1002/aur.49

Bruinsma, Y., Koegel, R. L., & Koegel, L. K. (2004). Joint Attention and Children with Autism: A Review of the Literature. *Mental Retardation and Developmental Disabilities Research Reviews, 10*(3), 169–175. doi: 10.1002/mrdd.20036

Bryson, S. E., Zwaigenbaum, L., McDermott, C., Rombough, V., & Brian, J. (2008). The Autism Observation Scale for Infants: Scale development and reliability data. *Journal of Autism and Developmental Disorders, 38*(4), 731–738. doi: 10.1007/s10803-007-0440-y

Buitelaar, J. K., van Engeland, H., de Kogel, K. H., de Vries, H., & van Hooff, J. A. (1991). Differences in the structure of social behaviour of autistic children and non-autistic retarded controls. *Journal of Child Psychology and Psychiatry, 32*(6), 995–1015.

Cardon, T. A., & Wilcox, M. J. (2011). Promoting imitation in young children with autism: A comparison of reciprocal imitation training and video modeling. *Journal of Autism and Developmental Disorders, 41*(5), 654–666. doi: 10.1007/s10803-010-1086-8

Carpenter, M., Pennington, B. E., & Rogers, S. J. (2002). Interrelations among social-cognitive skills in young children with autism. *Journal of Autism and Developmental Disorders, 32*(2), 91–106. doi: 10.1023/a:1014836521114

Chandler, S., Charman, T., Baird, G., Simonoff, E., Loucas, T., Meldrum, D., ... Pickles, A. (2007). Validation of the social communication questionnaire in a population cohort of children with autism spectrum diorders. *Journal of the American Academy of Child & Adolescent Psychiatry, 46*(10), 1324–1332. doi: 10.1097/chi.0b013e31812f7d8d

Charman, T., & Baron-Cohen, S. (1994). Another look at imitation in autism. *Development and Psychopathology, 6*(3), 403–413. doi: 10.1017/s0954579400006015

Chawarska, K., Klin, A., & Volkmar, F. (2003). Automatic attention cueing through eye movement in 2-year-old children with autism. *Child Development, 74*(4), 1108–1122. doi: 10.1111/1467-8624.00595

Chawarska, K., Macari, S., & Shic, F. (2012). Context modulates attention to social scenes in toddlers with autism. *Journal of Child Psychology and Psychiatry, 53*(8), 903–913. doi: 10.1111/j.1469-7610.2012.02538.x

Chawarska, K., Volkmar, F., & Klin, A. (2010). Limited attentional bias for faces in toddlers with autism spectrum disorders. *Archives of General Psychiatry, 67*(2), 178–185. doi: 10.1001/archgenpsychiatry.2009.194

Cheng, Y., & Huang, R. (2012). Using virtual reality environment to improve joint attention associated with pervasive developmental disorder. *Research in Developmental Disabilities, 33*(6), 2141–2152. doi: 10.1016/j.ridd.2012.05.023

Constantino, J. N., & Gruber, C. P. (2005). *Social Responsiveness Scale*. Los Angeles, CA: Western Psychological Services.

Cunningham, A. B. (2012). Measuring change in social interaction skills of young children with Autism. *Journal of Autism and Developmental Disorders, 42*(4), 593–605. doi: 10.1007/s10803-011-1280-3

Dawson, G., & Adams, A. (1984). Imitation and social responsiveness in autistic children. *Journal of Abnormal Child Psychology, 12*(2), 209–225. doi: 10.1007/bf00910664

Dawson, G., & Galpert, L. (1990). Mothers' use of imitative play for facilitating social responsiveness and toy play in young autistic children. *Development and Psychopathology, 2*(2), 151–162. doi: 10.1017/s0954579400000675

Dawson, G., Hill, D., Spencer, A., & Galpert, L. (1990). Affective exchanges between young autistic children and their mothers. *Journal of Abnormal Child Psychology, 18*(3), 335–345. doi: 10.1007/bf00916569

Dawson, G., Jones, E. J. H., Merkle, K., Venema, K., Lowy, R., Faja, S., ... Webb, S. J. (2012). Early behavioral intervention is associated with normalized brain activity in young children with autism. *Journal of the American Academy of Child & Adolescent Psychiatry, 51*(11), 1150–1159. doi: 10.1016/j.jaac.2012.08.018

Dawson, G., Rogers, S., Munson, J., Smith, M., Winter, J., Greenson, J., ... Varley, J. (2010). Randomized, controlled trial of an intervention for toddlers with autism: The Early Start Denver Model. *Pediatrics, 125*(1), e17–e23. doi: 10.1542/peds.2009-0958

Duvall, J. A., Lu, A., Cantor, R. M., Todd, R. D., Constantino, J. N., & Geschwind, D. H. (2007). A quantitative trait locus analysis of social responsiveness in multiplex autism families. *American Journal of Psychiatry, 164*(4), 656–662.

Eaves, L. C., & Ho, H. H. (2008). Young adult outcome of autism spectrum disorders. *Journal of Autism and Developmental Disorders, 38*(4), 739–747.

Elison, J. T., Paterson, S. J., Wolff, J. J., Reznick, J. S., Sasson, N. J., Gu, H., ... Piven, J. (2013). White matter microstructure and atypical visual orienting in 7-month-olds at risk for autism. *American Journal of Psychiatry, 20*(10), 12091150.

Fombonne, E., Heavey, L., Smeeth, L., Rodrigues, L. C., Cook, C., Smith, P. G., . . . Hall, A. J. (2004). Validation of the diagnosis of autism in general practitioner records. *BMC Public Health, 4*, 5.

Fountain, C., Winter, A. S., & Bearman, P. S. (2012). Six developmental trajectories characterize children with autism. *Pediatrics, 129*(5), e1112–e1120. doi: 10.1542/peds.2011-1601

Gillespie-Lynch, K., Sepeta, L., Wang, Y., Marshall, S., Gomez, L., Sigman, M., & Hutman, T. (2012). Early childhood predictors of the social competence of adults with autism. *Journal of Autism and Developmental Disorders, 42*(2), 161–174. doi: 10.1007/s10803-011-1222-0

Gillham, J. E., Carter, A. S., Volkmar, F. R., & Sparrow, S. S. (2000). Toward a developmental operational definition of autism. *Journal of Autism and Developmental Disorders, 30*(4), 269–278. doi: 10.1023/a:1005571115268

Gliga, T., & Csibra, G. (2007). Seeing the face through the eyes: A developmental perspective on face expertise. *Progress in Brain Research, 164*, 323–339.

Gotham, K., Pickles, A., & Lord, C. (2009). Standardizing ADOS scores for a measure of severity in autism spectrum disorders. *Journal of Autism and Developmental Disorders, 39*(5), 693–705. doi: 10.1007/s10803-008-0674-3

Grynszpan, O., Nadel, J., Martin, J.-C., Simonin, J., Bailleul, P., Wang, Y., . . . Constant, J. (2012). Self-monitoring of gaze in high functioning autism. *Journal of Autism and Developmental Disorders, 42*(8), 1642–1650. doi: 10.1007/s10803-011-1404-9

Hopkins, I. M., Gower, M. W., Perez, T. A., Smith, D. S., Amthor, F. R., Wimsatt, F. C., & Biasini, F. J. (2011). Avatar assistant: Improving social skills in students with an ASD through a computer-based intervention. *Journal of Autism and Developmental Disorders, 41*(11), 1543–1555. doi: 10.1007/s10803-011-1179-z

Howlin, P., Goode, S., Hutton, J., & Rutter, M. (2004). Adult outcome for children with autism. *Journal of Child Psychology and Psychiatry, 45*(2), 212–229. doi: 10.1111/j.1469-7610.2004.00215.x

Hus, V., Bishop, S., Gotham, K., Huerta, M., & Lord, C. (2013). Factors influencing scores on the Social Responsiveness Scale. *Journal of Child Psychology and Psychiatry, 54*(2), 216–224. doi: 10.1111/j.1469-7610.2012.02589.x

Ingersoll, B. (2010). Brief report: Pilot randomized controlled trial of reciprocal imitation training for teaching elicited and spontaneous imitation to children with autism. *Journal of Autism and Developmental Disorders, 40*(9), 1154–1160. doi: 10.1007/s10803-010-0966-2

Ingersoll, B. (2011). Recent advances in early identification and treatment of autism. *Current Directions in Psychological Science, 20*(5), 335–339. doi: 10.1177/0963721411418470

Ingersoll, B. (2012). Effect of a focused imitation intervention on social functioning in children with autism. *Journal of Autism and Developmental Disorders, 42*(8), 1768–1773. doi: 10.1007/s10803-011-1423-6

Ingersoll, B., & Meyer, K. (2011). Examination of correlates of different imitative functions in young children with autism

spectrum disorders. *Research in Autism Spectrum Disorders, 5*(3), 1078–1085. doi: 10.1016/j.rasd.2010.12.001

Insel, T. R., & Fernald, R. D. (2004). How the brain processes social information: Searching for the social brain. *Annual Review of Neuroscience, 27*, 697–722.

Jones, W., & Klin, A. (2009). Heterogeneity and homogeneity across the autism spectrum: The role of development. *Journal of the American Academy of Child & Adolescent Psychiatry, 48*(5), 471–473. doi: 10.1097/CHI.0b013e31819f6c0d

Joseph, R. M., Ehrman, K., McNally, R., & Keehn, B. (2008). Affective response to eye contact and face recognition ability in children with ASD. *Journal of the International Neuropsychological Society, 14*(6), 947–955. doi: 10.1017/s1355617708081344

Kaartinen, M., Puura, K., Mäkelä, T., Rannisto, M., Lemponen, R., Helminen, M., . . . Hietanen, J. K. (2012). Autonomic arousal to direct gaze correlates with social impairments among children with ASD. *Journal of Autism and Developmental Disorders, 42*(9), 1917–1927. doi: 10.1007/s10803-011-1435-2

Kanner, L. (1943). Autistic disturbances of affective contact. *Nervous Child, 2*, 217–250.

Kasari, C., Gulsrud, A., Freeman, S., Paparella, T., & Hellemann, G. (2012). Longitudinal follow-up of children with autism receiving targeted interventions on joint attention and play. *Journal of the American Academy of Child & Adolescent Psychiatry, 51*(5), 487–495. doi: 10.1016/j.jaac.2012.02.019

Kasari, C., Sigman, M., Mundy, P., & Yirmiya, N. (1990). Affective sharing in the context of joint attention interactions of normal, autistic, and mentally retarded children. *Journal of Autism and Developmental Disorders, 20*(1), 87–100. doi: 10.1007/bf02206859

Kasari, C., Sigman, M., & Yirmiya, N. (1993). Focused and social attention of autistic children in interactions with familiar and unfamiliar adults: A comparison of autistic, mentally retarded, and normal children. *Development and Psychopathology, 5*(3), 403–414. doi: 10.1017/s0954579400004491

Klin, A. (1992). Listening preferences in regard to speech in four children with developmental disabilities. *Journal of Child Psychology and Psychiatry, 33*, 763–769.

Klin, A., Jones, W., Schultz, R., & Volkmar, F. (2003). The enactive mind, or from actions to cognition: Lessons from autism. In U. Frith & E. Hill (Eds.), *Autism: Mind and brain.* (pp. 127–159). New York, NY: Oxford University Press.

Klin, A., Jones, W., Schultz, R., Volkmar, F., & Cohen, D. (2001). Defining and quantifying the social phenotype in autism. *American Journal of Psychiatry, 159*(6), 895–908.

Lawton, K., & Kasari, C. (2012). Teacher-implemented joint attention intervention: Pilot randomized controlled study for preschoolers with autism. *Journal of Consulting and Clinical Psychology, 80*(4), 687–693. doi: 10.1037/a0028506

Locke, J., Ishijima, E. H., Kasari, C., & London, N. (2010). Loneliness, friendship quality and the social networks of adolescents with high-functioning autism in an inclusive school setting. *Journal of Research in Special Educational Needs, 10*(2), 74–81. doi: 10.1111/j.1471-3802.2010.01148.x

Lord, C. (1993). The complexity of social behavior in autism. In S. Baron-Cohen, H. Tager-Flusberg, & D. Cohen (Eds.),

Understanding other minds: Perspectives from autism (pp. 292–316). Oxford, England: Oxford University Press.

Lord, C., Rutter, M., DiLavore, P. C., & Risi, S. (2001). *Autism Diagnostic Observation Schedule.* Los Angeles, CA: Western Psychological Services.

Lord, C., Rutter, M., & Le Couteur, A. (1994). Autism Diagnostic Interview—Revised: A revised version of a diagnostic interview for caregivers of individuals with possible pervasive developmental disorders. *Journal of Autism and Developmental Disorders, 24*(5), 659–685. doi: 10.1007/bf02172145

Mahjouri, S., & Lord, C. E. (2012). What the DSM-5 portends for research, diagnosis, and treatment of autism spectrum disorders. *Current Psychiatry Reports, 14*(6), 739–747.

Marriage, S., Wolverton, A., & Marriage, K. (2009). Autism spectrum disorder grown up: A chart review of adult functioning. *Journal of the Canadian Academy of Child and Adolescent Psychiatry/Journal de l'Académie canadienne de psychiatrie de l'enfant et de l'adolescent, 18*(4), 322–328.

McEvoy, R. E., Rogers, S. J., & Pennington, B. F. (1993). Executive function and social communication deficits in young autistic children. *Child Psychology & Psychiatry & Allied Disciplines, 34*(4), 563–578. doi: 10.1111/j.1469-7610.1993.tb01036.x

McGovern, C. W., & Sigman, M. (2005). Continuity and change from early childhood to adolescence in autism. *Journal of Child Psychology and Psychiatry, 46*(4), 401–408. doi: 10.1111/j.1469-7610.2004.00361.x

McMahon, W. M., & Farley, M. A. (2011). Can people with ASC live independently as adults? In S. Bölte & J. Hallmayer (Eds.), *Autism spectrum conditions: FAQs on autism, Asperger syndrome, and atypical autism answered by international experts* (pp. 84–86). Cambridge, MA: Hogrefe.

McPartland, J. C., & Pelphrey, K. A. (2012). The implications of social neuroscience for social disability. *Journal of Autism and Developmental Disorders, 42*(6), 1256–1262.

Meltzoff, A. N., & Moore, M. K. (1977). Imitation of facial and manual gestures by human neonates. *Science, 198*(4312), 75–78).

Mundy, P. (1995). Joint attention and social-emotional approach behavior in children with autism. *Development and Psychopathology, 7*(1), 63–82. doi: 10.1017/s0954579400006349

Mundy, P. (2003). Annotation: The neural basis of social impairments in autism: The role of the dorsal medial-frontal cortex and anterior cingulate system. *Journal of Child Psychology and Psychiatry, 44*(6), 793–809.

Mundy, P., Block, J., Delgado, C., Pomares, Y., Van Hecke, A. V., & Parlade, M. V. (2007). Individual differences and the development of joint attention in infancy. *Child Development, 78*(3), 938–954. doi: 10.1111/j.1467-8624.2007.01042.x

Mundy, P., Sigman, M., & Kasari, C. (1990). A longitudinal study of joint attention and language development in autistic children. *Journal of Autism and Developmental Disorders, 20*(1), 115–128. doi: 10.1007/bf02206861

Mundy, P., Sigman, M., & Kasari, C. (1994). Joint attention, developmental level, and symptom presentation in autism. *Development and Psychopathology, 6*(3), 389–401. doi: 10.1017/s0954579400006003

Noris, B., Nadel, J., Barker, M., Hadjikhani, N., & Billard, A. (2012). Investigating gaze of children with ASD in naturalistic settings. *PLoS ONE, 7*(9). doi: 10.1371/journal.pone.0044144

Ornitz, E. M., Guthrie, D., & Farley, A. H. (1977). The early development of autistic children. *Journal of Autism & Childhood Schizophrenia, 7*(3), 207–229. doi: 10.1007/bf01538999

Osterling, J. A., & Dawson, G. (1994). Early recognition of children with autism: A study of 1st birthday home videotapes. *Journal of Autism and Developmental Disorders, 24,* 247–257.

Osterling, J. A., Dawson, G., & Munson, J. A. (2002). Early recognition of 1-year-old infants with autism spectrum disorder versus mental retardation. *Development and Psychopathology, 14*(2), 239–251. doi: 10.1017/s0954579402002031

Ozonoff, S., Young, G. S., Carter, A., Messinger, D., Yirmiya, N., Zwaigenbaum, L.,...Stone, W. L. (2011). Recurrence risk for autism spectrum disorders: A Baby Siblings Research Consortium study. *Pediatrics, 128*(3), e488–e495.

Paparella, T., Goods, K. S., Freeman, S., & Kasari, C. (2011). The emergence of nonverbal joint attention and requesting skills in young children with autism. *Journal of Communication Disorders, 44*(6), 569–583. doi: 10.1016/j.jcomdis.2011.08.002

Pelphrey, K. A., Shultz, S., Hudac, C. M., & Vander Wyk, B. C. (2011). Research review: Constraining heterogeneity: The social brain and its development in autism spectrum disorder. *Journal of Child Psychology and Psychiatry, 52*(6), 631–644. doi: 10.1111/j.1469-7610.2010.02349.x

Perkins, E. A., & Berkman, K. A. (2012). Into the unknown: Aging with autism spectrum disorders. *American Journal on Intellectual and Developmental Disabilities, 117*(6), 478–496. doi: 10.1352/1944-7558-117.6.478

Phillips, W., Baron-Cohen, S., & Rutter, M. (1992). The role of eye contact in goal detection: Evidence from normal infants and children with autism or mental handicap. *Development and Psychopathology, 4*(3), 375–383. doi: 10.1017/s0954579400000845

Rimland, B. (1964). *Infantile autism.* New York, NY: Appleton, Century Crofts.

Rogers, S., & Dawson, G. (2010). *Early Start Denver Model for young children with autism: Promoting language, learning, and engagement.* New York, NY: Guilford Press.

Rogers, S., & Pennington, B. (1991). A theoretical approach to the deficits in infantile autism. *Developmental Psychology, 3,* 137–162.

Rogers, S. J., Hepburn, S. L., Stackhouse, T., & Wehner, E. (2003). Imitation performance in toddlers with autism and those with other developmental disorders. *Journal of Child Psychology and Psychiatry, 44*(5), 763–781. doi: 10.1111/1469-7610.00162

Rutter, M. (1978). Diagnosis and definition. In M. Rutter & E. Schopler (Eds.), *Autism: A reappraisal of concepts and treatment* (pp. 15–36). New York: Plenum Press.

Schaffer, H. R. (1984). *The child's entry into a social world.* Behavioural Development: A Series of Monographs. London, England: Academic Press.

Senju, A., Tojo, Y., Dairoku, H., & Hasegawa, T. (2004). Reflexive orienting in response to eye gaze and an arrow in children with and without autism. *Journal of Child Psychology and Psychiatry, 45*(3), 445–458. doi: 10.1111/j.1469-7610.2004.00236.x

Shattuck, P. T., Orsmond, G. I., Wagner, M., & Cooper, B. P. (2011). Participation in social activities among adolescents with an autism spectrum disorder. *PLoS ONE, 6*(11). doi: 10.1371/journal.pone.0027176

Shumway, S., Farmer, C., Thurm, A., Joseph, L., Black, D., & Golden, C. (2012). The ADOS calibrated severity score: Relationship to phenotypic variables and stability over time. *Autism Research, 5*(4), 267–276. doi: 10.1002/aur.1238

Shumway, S., Thurm, A., Swedo, S. E., Deprey, L., Barnett, L. A., Amaral, D. G., … Ozonoff, S. (2011). Brief report: Symptom onset patterns and functional outcomes in young children with autism spectrum disorders. *Journal of Autism and Developmental Disorders, 41*(12), 1727–1732. doi: 10.1007/s10803-011-1203-3

Siegel, B., Vukicevic, J., Elliott, G. R., & Kraemer, H. C. (1989). The use of signal detection theory to assess *DSM-III-R* criteria for autistic disorder. *Journal of the American Academy of Child & Adolescent Psychiatry, 28*(4), 542–548. doi: 10.1097/00004583-198907000–00013

Sigman, M., & Ruskin, E. (1999). Continuity and change in the social competence of children with autism, Down syndrome, and developmental delays. *Monographs of the Society for Research in Child Development, 64*(1), v–114. doi: 10.1111/1540-5834.00001

Siller, M., & Sigman, M. (2002). The behaviors of parents of children with autism predict the subsequent development of their children's communication. *Journal of Autism and Developmental Disorders, 32*(2), 77–89. doi: 10.1023/a:1014884404276

Smith, I., & Bryson, S. (1994). Imitation and action in autism: A critical review. *Psychological Bulletin, 116*, 259–273.

Smith, L. E., Greenberg, J. S., Seltzer, M. M., & Hong, J. (2008). Symptoms and behavior problems of adolescents and adults with autism: Effects of mother-child relationship quality, warmth, and praise. *American Journal on Mental Retardation, 113*(5), 387–402. doi: 10.1352/2008.113:387-402

Snow, A. V., & Lecavalier, L. (2008). Sensitivity and specificity of the modified checklist for autism in toddlers and the social communication questionnaire in preschoolers suspected of having pervasive developmental disorders. *Autism, 12*(6), 627–644. doi: 10.1177/1362361308097116

Sparrow, S. S., Balla, D., & Cicchetti, D. V. (1984). *Vineland Adaptive Behavior Scales*. Circle Pines, MN: American Guidance Service.

Spiker, D., Lotspeich, L. J., Dimiceli, S., Myers, R. M., & Risch, N. (2002). Behavioral phenotypic variation in autism multiplex families: Evidence for a continuous severity gradient. *American Journal of Medical Genetics, 114*(2), 129–136.

Spitz, R. (1965). *The first year of life*. New York, NY: International Universities Press.

Stone, W. L., Coonrod, E. E., Turner, L. M., & Pozdol, S. L. (2004). Psychometric Properties of the STAT for Early Autism Screening. *Journal of Autism and Developmental Disorders, 34*(6), 691–701. doi: 10.1007/s10803-004-5289-8

Stone, W. L., Lemanek, K. L., Fishel, P. T., Fernandez, M. C., & Altemeier, W. A. (1990). Play and imitation skills in the diagnosis of autism in young children. [Research Support, Non-U.S. Government]. *Pediatrics, 86*(2), 267–272.

Stone, W. L., McMahon, C. R., & Henderson, L. M. (2008). Use of the Screening Tool for Autism in Two-Year-Olds (STAT) for children under 24 months: An exploratory study. *Autism, 12*(5), 557–573. doi: 10.1177/1362361308096403

Stone, W. L., Ousley, O. Y., & Littleford, C. D. (1997). Motor imitation in young children with autism: What's the object? *Journal of Abnormal Child Psychology, 25*(6), 475–485.

Trevarthen, C., & Aitken, K. J. (2001). Infant intersubjectivity: Research, theory, and clinical applications. *Journal of Child Psychology and Psychiatry, 42*(1), 3–48. doi: 10.1111/1469-7610.00701

Van Hecke, A. V., Mundy, P. C., Acra, C. F., Block, J. J., Delgado, C. E. F., Parlade, M. V., … Pomares, Y. B. (2007). Infant joint attention, temperament, and social competence in preschool children. *Child Development, 78*(1), 53–69. doi: 10.1111/j.1467-8624.2007.00985.x

Vernon, T. W., Koegel, R. L., Dauterman, H., & Stolen, K. (2012). An early social engagement intervention for young children with autism and their parents. *Journal of Autism and Developmental Disorders, 42*(12), 2702–2717. doi: 10.1007/s10803-012-1535-7

Volkmar, F. R., Carter, A., Sparrow, S. S., & Cicchetti, D. V. (1993). Quantifying social development in autism. *Journal of the American Academy of Child & Adolescent Psychiatry, 32*(3), 627–632. doi: 10.1097/00004583-199305000-00020

Volkmar, F. R., Cohen, D. J., & Paul, R. (1986). An evaluation of *DSM-III* criteria for infantile autism. *Journal of the American Academy of Child Psychiatry, 25*(2), 190–197. doi: 10.1016/s0002-7138(09)60226-0

Volkmar, F. R., & Mayes, L. C. (1990). Gaze behavior in autism. *Development and Psychopathology, 2*(1), 61–69. doi: 10.1017/s0954579400000596

Volkmar, F. R., Sparrow, S. S., Goudreau, D., & Cicchetti, D. V. (1987). Social deficits in autism: An operational approach using the Vineland Adaptive Behavior Scales. *Journal of the American Academy of Child & Adolescent Psychiatry, 26*(2), 156–161. doi: 10.1097/00004583-198703000-00005

Werner, H., & Kaplan, B. (1963). *Symbol formation*. New York, NY: Wiley.

White, P. J., O'Reilly, M., Streusand, W., Levine, A., Sigafoos, J., Lancioni, G., … Aguilar, J. (2011). Best practices for teaching joint attention: A systematic review of the intervention literature. *Research in Autism Spectrum Disorders, 5*(4), 1283–1295. doi: 10.1016/j.rasd.2011.02.003

Wiggins, L. D., Bakeman, R., Adamson, L. B., & Robins, D. L. (2007). The utility of the Social Communication Questionnaire in screening for autism in children referred for early intervention. *Focus on Autism and Other Developmental Disabilities, 22*(1), 33–38. doi: 10.1177/10883576070220010401

Wiggins, L. D., Robins, D. L., Adamson, L. B., Bakeman, R., & Henrich, C. C. (2012). Support for a dimensional view of autism spectrum disorders in toddlers. *Journal of Autism and Developmental Disorders, 42*(2), 191–200. doi: 10.1007/s10803-011-1230-0

Williams, J. H. G., Whiten, A., & Singh, T. (2004). A systematic review of action imitation in autistic spectrum disorder. *Journal of Autism and Developmental Disorders, 34*(3), 285–299. doi: 10.1023/B:JADD.0000029551.56735.3a

Wimpory, D. C., Hobson, R. P., & Nash, S. (2007). What facilitates social engagement in preschool children with autism? *Journal of Autism and Developmental Disorders, 37*(3), 564–573. doi: 10.1007/s10803-006-0187-x

Wing, L. (1976). *Early childhood autism.* New York, NY: Pergamon Press.

Wing, L., & Gould, J. (1979). Severe impairments of social interaction and associated abnormalities in children: Epidemiology and classification. *Journal of Autism and Developmental Disorders, 9*, 11–29.

Yirmiya, N., & Charman, T. (2010). The prodrome of autism: Early behavioral and biological signs, regression, peri- and post-natal development and genetics. *Journal of Child Psychology and Psychiatry, 51*(4), 432–458. doi: 10.1111/j.1469-7610.2010.02214.x

Yirmiya, N., & Ozonoff, S. (2007). The very early autism phenotype. *Journal of Autism and Developmental Disorders, 37*(1), 1–11. doi: 10.1007/s10803-006-0329-1

Yirmiya, N., Pilowsky, T., Solomonica-Levi, D., & Shulman, C. (1999). Gaze behavior and theory of mind abilities in individuals with autism, Down syndrome, and mental retardation of unknown etiology. *Journal of Autism and Developmental Disorders, 29*(4), 333–341. doi: 10.1023/a:1022167504388

Young, G. S., Merin, N., Rogers, S. J., & Ozonoff, S. (2009). Gaze behavior and affect at 6 months: Predicting clinical outcomes and language development in typically developing infants and infants at risk for autism. *Developmental Science, 12*(5), 798–814. doi: 10.1111/j.1467-7687.2009.00833.x

Young, G. S., Rogers, S. J., Hutman, T., Rozga, A., Sigman, M., & Ozonoff, S. (2011). Imitation from 12 to 24 months in autism and typical development: A longitudinal Rasch analysis. *Developmental Psychology, 47*(6), 1565–1578. doi: 10.1037/a0025418

Zwaigenbaum, L., Bryson, S., Rogers, T., Roberts, W., Brian, J., & Szatmari, P. (2005). Behavioral manifestations of autism in the first year of life. *International Journal of Developmental Neuroscience, 23*(2–3), 143–152. doi: 10.1016/j.ijdevneu.2004.05.001

CHAPTER 10

Language and Communication in Autism

SO HYUN KIM, RHEA PAUL, HELEN TAGER-FLUSBERG, AND CATHERINE LORD

Knowledge about human communication is central to theory and clinical practice in the field of autism. Milestones in language and communication play major roles at almost every point in development in understanding autism. Most parents of autistic children first begin to be concerned that something is not quite right in their child's development because of early delays or regressions in the development of speech (Short & Schopler, 1988). Functional language use by school age has been shown to be related to better long-term outcomes in autism (Paul & Cohen, 1984a). Fluency and flexibility of expressive language are underlying dimensions beneath the distinction between high-functioning and low-functioning autism in school age or adolescence. A history of language delay can be particularly crucial in differentiating autism from other psychiatric disorders in high-functioning adults (Lord & Venter, 1992).

Even though autism is often first recognized because of slow or unusual patterns of speech development, many early aspects of the language deficit associated with it overlap with other disorders (Beitchman & Inglis, 1991; Bishop & Adams, 1989). Thus, though skill in language is important to the functioning of people with autism, delays in expressive language in the early preschool years are not specific to autism (Cantwell, Baker, & Mattison, 1980). When there is a good description of a child's early social history and use of objects, the diagnosis of autism can often be made without reference to language delay at all (Cohen, Sudhalter, Landon-Jimenez, & Keogh, 1993; Lord, Storoschuk, Rutter, & Pickles, 1993; Siegel,

Vukicevic, Elliott, & Kraemer, 1989). Although expressive language level at age 5 was an important discriminator of higher versus lower functioning older children and adults with autism (Rutter, 1970), simple characterization of language history did not add predictive power for outcome within a high-functioning group of adults (Howlin, Goode, Hutton, & Rutter, 2004).

In addition, evidence from numerous sources suggests that the social and linguistic environments of autistic children, most of whom have active, loving, and determined parents and teachers, can be quite different than those of other children. Thus, initial deficits in language acquisition and in social or cognitive factors affecting language may be compounded by experiential differences (Konstantareas, Zajdemann, Homatidis, & McCabe, 1988; Siller & Sigman, 2002). The root of this difference is thought to be the limited nature of the social and linguistic opportunities that these youngsters provide to others (Doussard-Roosevelt, Joe, Bzhevova, & Porges, 2003; Lord, Merrin, Vest, & Kelly, 1983).

The history of autism has included waxing and waning of interest in language and communication, from interpreting language abnormalities as secondary to deficits in social-emotional functioning (Kanner, 1943), to the view that autism impairments are the result of primary linguistic disorder (Rutter, 1970), to an exclusive focus on pragmatic impairments (Baltaxe, 1977), to interest in using language to study other behaviors, particularly higher order cognitive abilities, such as theory of mind (Baron-Cohen, 1993). It is now recognized that language in autism is extremely variable and that there are likely to be subgroups of individuals within the autism spectrum that have distinct language profiles, some of which are similar to those found in other developmental language disorders.

Tager-Flusberg and Joseph (2003) identified two language phenotypes among verbal children with autism: children with normal linguistic abilities (phonological skills, vocabulary, syntax and morphology) and children with autism and impaired language, that is, similar to the phenotype found in specific language impairment. There may also be other subgroups on the autism spectrum that reflect different kinds of language disorder. For example, a significant number of children with autism never acquire speech. It is unlikely that all these children remain mute for the same reason, especially since recent reports suggest that the proportion of nonspeakers within the autistic population is decreasing as early intervention becomes more prevalent (Goldstein, 2002). One potential subgroup within nonspeakers, for instance, may experience *verbal apraxia* or *apraxia of speech*, a neuromotor deficit that affects the ability to produce speech sounds, sound sequences, and prosodic features (Darley, Aronson, & Brown, 1975). If this subgroup exists, however, is likely to account for a small minority of nonspeakers with autism spectrum disorder (ASD; Rogers, 2006). Since little is known about language capacities in nonspeaking children with autism, due to a dearth of communication research on these children without functional language, the causes of failure to acquire speech are primarily speculation at this time. Nonetheless, it is likely that subgroups exist within both the speaking and nonspeaking autistic populations.

THE STUDY OF LANGUAGE DEVELOPMENT IN TYPICAL POPULATIONS

Early Communicative Intent

Often parents recognize the absence of early communication in their young children with autism some time during the second year, when the majority of children the same age begin to have established vocabularies of numerous words (Short & Schopler, 1988). However, nonhandicapped infants show communicative behaviors even from the first weeks and months of life, including recognizing their mother's voice, synchronizing their patterns of eye gaze, movements, facial expressions of affect, and vocal turn-taking (Fernald, 1992).

Infants typically exhibit a variety of communicative behaviors by the end of their first year that, to a knowing observer, are not usually seen in autism. These nonverbal communication patterns have been found to express the same intentions for which words will be used in the coming months, such as requesting objects, rejecting offered actions, calling attention to objects or events, and commenting on their appearance (Bates, 1976; Carpenter Nagell, & Tomasello, 1998).

Another achievement that normally occurs toward the end of the first year is the beginning of the understanding of words. At first, a few words associated with games such as *pat-a-cake* or *so big* will be recognized. Infants gradually become more active responders to these routines (Bruner, 1975). By 12 months, merely saying the words ("Let's play pat-a-cake!" or "Show me your nose") in a familiar context will often elicit a spontaneous action from the child such as clapping or touching the nose.

First Words

Conventional use of language begins around 12 months (see Table 10.1), when toddlers usually say their first recognizable words. At this age, children also show clear evidence of understanding some words or even simple phrases, responding appropriately to specific words outside the context of routine games (Huttenlocher, 1974; Tomasello & Krueger, 1992). During the 12- to 18-month period, there is a gradual increase in both receptive and expressive vocabulary. The words children learn in this period are used to name of objects and people, usually those on which the child acts (e.g., *daddy, mommy, cookie, ball*) and describe relationships among objects (e.g., *all gone, more*) (Fenson et al., 1994). Much like early gestures, first words are often used to express ideas such as appearance ("Uh-oh"), disappearance ("All gone") and recurrence ("More"), related to the child's developing notions of object permanence (Bloom & Lahey, 1978; Gopnik & Meltzoff, 1987).

By the age of 18 months, the word explosion begins, and during this period, words are learned very quickly, often after only a single exposure

without any explicit instruction. This stage marks an important turning point as children start understanding the referential nature of words (Nazzi & Bertoninci, 2003) and are able now to use words to get new information about the world (Halliday, 1975). By 16 to 19 months infants are able to use nonverbal cues, such as an adult's eye gaze, to make quite fine distinctions between an object that an adult is naming and another object that happens to be present (Baldwin, 1991), suggesting that they can now understand the intentions of others within language contexts.

Prior to age 2, most children begin combining words to form two-word telegraphic sentences (Brown, 1973), encoding a small set of meanings. Children talk about objects by naming them and by discussing their locations or attributes, who owns them, and who is doing things to them. They also talk about other people, their actions, their locations, their own actions on objects, and so forth. Objects, people, actions, and their interrelationships preoccupy the young typically developing child. Individual differences exist among typically developing children, but language acquisition is not a random process. There are generally clear links between forms (i.e., gesture, words, syntax) and functions (e.g., why the child is trying to communicate) over time.

The period of 18 to 24 months is also a time of important developments in conversational ability. Children now begin to understand the conversational obligation to answer speech with speech (Chapman, 1981). They reliably ask *and* answer routine questions ("Where's the doggy?" "What's this?" "What's the cow say?") and can now genuinely take their own part in a back-and-forth linguistic exchange.

THE ACQUISITION OF LINGUISTIC STRUCTURES

The preschool period (from 2 to 5 years) is the time during which the child's language evolves from simple telegraphic utterances to fully grammatical

TABLE 10.1   A Summary of Milestones in Typical Language Development

	12 to 15 months	18 months	24 to 36 months	3 to 4 years	4 to 7 years
Semantics	Average expressive vocabulary size at 15 months: 10 words	Average expressive vocabulary size at 18 months: 100 words (±105)	Average expressive vocabulary size at 24 months: 300 words (±75)	Average expressive vocabulary size at 3 years: 900 words	Average expressive vocabulary size at 6 years: 2,500 words
	Average receptive vocabulary size at 15 months: 50 words	Average receptive vocabulary size at 18 months: 300 words	Average receptive vocabulary size at 24 months: 900 words		Average receptive vocabulary size at 6 years: 8,000 words
	Comprehension strategies include attending to objects named, and doing what is usually done	Comprehension strategies include acting on objects in the way mentioned, interpreting sentences as requests for child action	Comprehension strategies include interpreting sentences according to knowledge of probable events	Comprehension strategies include supplying most probable missing information in answer to difficult questions	Comprehension strategies include overreliance on word order to process sentences that use unusual word order, such as passives
Syntax	First productions are singleword *holophrases*; one word carries the force of a whole sentence	Average age of first word combinations: 18 months (normal range: 14 to 24 months)	Average MLU at 24 months: 1.92 (±0.5)	Average MLU at 4 years: 4.4 (±0.9)	Average MLU at 5 years: 5.6 (±1.2)
			Average MLU at 30 months: 2.54 (±0.6)	Grammatical morphemes become more consistent	
		First word combinations express basic semantic relations with consistent word order	Average MLU at 36 months: 3.16 (±0.7)	Mature forms of negatives and questions develop	Use of complex sentences increases from less than 10% to more than 20% of all utterances
Phonology	Most productions have CV or CVCV (consonant vowel/consonant vowel consonant vowel combinations, e.g., "ba" or "mama") form Front stops and nasals are most frequent consonants	Back stops, fricatives, and glides are added to the consonant inventory	9 to 10 different consonants are used in initial position; 5 to 6 in final; stops at all places of articulation are used; liquids appear	Most sounds are produced correctly	Almost all sounds are produced correctly
		CVC syllable shapes begin to be used	Two-syllable words and initial consonant clusters are used by a majority of children	Consonant blends are used	Phonological processes are no longer used; a few distortions on difficult sounds (/s/, /1/, /r/) may persist
		50% of consonants are produced correctly	70% of consonants are consonants are correct; speech is 50% intelligible	Some phonological simplification processes may persist Speech is nearly 100% intelligible	Phonological analysis skills are learned for reading and spelling

(continued)

TABLE 10.1 (*Continued*)

	12 to 15 months	18 months	24 to 36 months	3 to 4 years	4 to 7 years
Pragmatics	Average rate of communications: 1 per minute	Average rate of communications: 2 per minute	Average rate of communications: 5 per minute	Talk about past and future events increases	Language is used to predict, reason, negotiate
	Requests and comments are used; communication is accomplished by combining gestures with speechlike vocalizations	Requests and comments are used; words predominate; gestural /vocal communication decreases	Requests and comments are used; children begin to ask questions and convey new information; word combinations predominate	More options for politeness are acquired New communicative functions (projecting, narrating, imagining, etc.) are expressed	
Play	Conventional, functional play	Symbolic play using self as actor	Pretend play involving others and using multiple schemes	Sequences of events are played out (preparing food, setting table, eating)	Fantasy themes are played out
				Child engages in dialogues, talking for all characters	Child or doll can take multiple roles Elaboration of planning and planning and narrative story lines included in play

MLU = mean length of utterance

CV = consonant vowel

CVCV = consonant vowel consonant vowel

forms. The child also goes through a process of approximating more and more closely the grammar of the language spoken in the home. There is evidence of the child's active role as a hypothesis generator in the frequent occurrence of overgeneralized forms, such as *goed*, *comed*, and *mouses* (Cazden, 1968; Pinker, 1999). These errors are taken as evidence that the child is indeed acquiring a rule-governed system, rather than learning these inflections by imitation or on a word-by-word basis.

As the child's grammar becomes more complex, sentence length increases (Brown, 1973; Loban, 1976; Miller & Chapman, 1981) and children begin to use a variety of sentence forms including statements, negation, and questions. As structures in simple sentences approach the adult model, complex sentences using embedded clauses ("Whoever wins can go first") and conjoined clauses ("Then it broke and we didn't have it any more") emerge (Paul, Chapman, & Wanska, 1980). The abilities to encode ideas grammatically ("Daddy's shoe" versus "Daddy shoe") and to relate ideas within one utterance ("I'll go get it if you give me a bite of your candy"), free the child's language from dependence on nonlinguistic contexts for interpretation.

In addition to changing their use of grammatical form, children between 3 and 5 years of age also change the ideas that they express in their sentences. During preschool years, sentence content expands to allow for reference to events that are remote in time and space. Children begin to use their language in more diverse ways (Dore, 1978) to include imaginative, nonliteral, interpretive, and logical functions.

At this time a variety of more advanced conversational and other discourse skills also emerge and become refined. Children increase their ability to maintain and add new information to the conversational topic; to clarify and request clarification of misunderstood utterances; to make their requests or comment using polite or indirect forms; and to choose the appropriate speech style on the basis of the speaker's role and the listener's status (Bates, 1976).

The Elaboration of Language

Although children have acquired most of the sentence structure of their language by age 5, syntactic development continues into the school years as children learn devices for elaborating their utterances, expressing coreference relations using pronouns (e.g., "When Mom wakes up, she'll help me dress"), and for condensing more information into each sentence by increasing the proportion of dependent clauses (Loban, 1976). Children also gradually learn to use and to comprehend the more complex, optional sentence types in their language, such as passives ("The boy was hit by the car"; Lempert, 1978). They learn to use syntactic cues not only to decode semantic relations within sentences but also to identify the connections between sentence elements and those given previously in the discourse (Paul, 1985). School-aged children gradually acquire the ability to communicate with precision, to take the listener's viewpoint into account in formulating an utterance (Asher, 1978), and to tell more complex well-structured narratives.

Issues From the Study of Language Development in Typical Children

Several issues arise in determining how to fit the different patterns of language development seen in autism into models of normal language acquisition. One source of confusion to parents and professionals is the question of consistency. Both children with autism and, on occasion, typically developing children, may use a new word for a few days but then fail to continue to use this word in appropriate contexts. Are these real words? Does the child have them stored somewhere in the brain to be used if sufficiently motivated? Two questions arise: (1) How do we set standards for what is a reasonable level of consistency? (2) How broad do the contexts have to be in which we can reliably expect a behavior? For example, we might expect a 10-month-old to understand *bubbles* only in the bathtub, but by 18 months, he should be able to say and understand the same word in a variety of different situations. The development of these sorts of standards may be particularly helpful for parents and primary care professionals trying to evaluate the seriousness of a possible communication delay in a very young child.

Another source of confusion is that if one does not have a reasonable level of knowledge regarding the breadth and depth of typical language development, it is fairly easy to fail to notice its absence in autism. For example, a child who occasionally says five words but does so without clear communicative intent is very different from another child who also has only five different words, but uses them to express a range of different meanings (as described earlier) marked in a number of different ways (gesture, words, simple syntax, intonation) throughout each day. There is variability within the normal range in the development of expressive language (Rutter & Lord, 1987), though, on close inspection, individual differences within the normal range do not resemble the kinds of patterns of communication delay seen in autism. It is important that recognition of individual differences does not lead to underestimating communication delays usually seen in autism.

COMMUNICATION AND DEVELOPMENT IN AUTISM

Course and Developmental Change

As noted earlier, there is enormous variation in the timing and patterns of acquisition of language among children with autism. A minority of children, usually children with high-functioning autism (HFA), do not show any significant delays in the onset of language milestones. In contrast, most individuals with autism begin to speak late and develop speech at a significantly slower rate than others (Le Couteur, Bailey, Rutter, & Gottesman, 1989) with words first produced at an average age of 38 months (Howlin, 2003) rather than the typical time of 12–18 months. Because autism is not usually diagnosed until age 3 or 4, there is relatively little information about language in very young children with autism.

Various retrospective studies using parent report and videotapes collected during infancy and the toddler years suggest that by the second year of life the communication of most children with autism is different from other children (Dahlgren & Gillberg, 1989). Several studies have found that, as early as 1 year of age, very young children with autism are less responsive to their names or to someone speaking compared to other children (Lord, 1995; Osterling & Dawson, 1994), and they are also less responsive to the sound of their mother's voice (Klin, 1991) and child-directed speech (Paul, Chawarska, Fowler, Cicchetti, & Volkmar, 2007). In another study (Lord, Pickles, DiLavore, & Shulman, 1996), 2-year-old children judged very likely to have autism had mean expressive and receptive language ages of less than 9 months, in contrast to other skills falling between 16 and 21 months. Not only was their language severely delayed at age 2, but, expressive skills continued to develop at a slower rate through age 5 compared to nonautistic children with developmental delays at similar nonverbal levels.

Studies on siblings of children with ASD have suggested that at as early as 12 months, children later diagnosed with ASD understand significantly fewer phrases and produce fewer gestures (Mitchell et al., 2006). Another study based on siblings of children with ASD found that infants at high risk for ASD at 9 months had a reduced ability to match audiovisual speech information, unlike low-risk infants who were able to detect incongruent audio and visual speech cues (Guiraud et al., 2012). This is particularly notable since audiovisual perception has been found to be related to spontaneous babbling in infants and speech production in preschoolers (Desjardins, Rogers, & Werker, 1997; Patterson & Werker, 1999). Retrospective parental reports also have indicated that, at least by age 18 to 24 months, children with ASD understand fewer phrases than developmentally delayed or typically developing children (Luyster et al., 2005; Mitchell et al., 2006).

About 25% of children with autism are described by their parents as having some words at 12 or 18 months and then losing them (Kurita, 1985).

Regression typically occurs within the first 3 years (e.g., median 23–26 months; Centers for Disease Control and Prevention [CDC], 2007). A large-scale systematic longitudinal study of toddlers by Lord, Shulman, and DiLavore (2004) found that this kind of language regression after a pattern of normal language onset was unique to autism and not found among children with other developmental delays. Generally, the regression is a gradual process in which the children do not learn new words and fail to engage in communicative routines in which they may have participated before. Language loss occurred in these children when they still had relatively small expressive vocabularies, and before the word explosion. Lord and her colleagues found that children who experienced loss of words also lost some social skills, supporting the findings from Goldberg and her colleagues (Goldberg et al., 2003), and that similar losses of social skills occurred in a smaller group of children with autism who had not yet used words at the time of loss (Luyster et al., 2005). This phenomenon is quite different than the regression that is associated with disintegrative disorder (see Chapter 3), which typically occurs at a later time, and involves loss of advanced linguistic skills and communication to no speech. Though the skills children with autism may have had before the regression are often minimal, it is still confusing and heartbreaking for parents to watch their children lose any component of communicative skill, fleeting though it may have been. Studies have demonstrated only a minimal relationship between language regression in autism and later prognosis or outcome, with children who had regressions having, on average, slightly lower verbal IQ scores at school age than children with no history of loss (Richler et al., 2006).

To gauge the developmental timing of language milestones for children with autism we are generally dependent on parental report. Most diagnostic interviews, such as the Autism Diagnostic Interview–Revised (ADI-R; Rutter, Le Couteur, & Lord, 2003) include questions about the age of first words and phrases (see Lord et al., 2004, for examples of regression questions from a modified ADI for toddlers). Past studies based on repeated administrations of the ADI-R revealed that the ages that parents reported these language milestones increased with the age of the child at the time of the interview (Hus, Taylor, & Lord, 2011; Taylor, 2004). This systematic telescoping means that parents of older children with autism are more likely to recall their children's language as being even more delayed than they did when their children were younger.

Both within and across categories of children with ASDs there is significant variability in the rate at which language progresses among those children who do acquire some functional language (Lord et al., 2004). Studies have examined various early predictors of later language development in toddlers and preschoolers with ASD. Findings from both cross-sectional and longitudinal studies have identified joint attention skills (e.g., showing objects to others to share interests, giving objects to request for help; Charman et al. 2003; Dawson et al. 2004; Paul, Chawarska, Cicchetti, & Volkmar, 2008; Sigman and McGovern 2005), imitation (Carpenter, Pennington, & Rogers, 2002; Stone, Ousley, & Littleford, 1997) and play (Mundy, Sigman, Ungerer, Sherman, 1987; Paul et al., 2008) skills, and gesture (Luyster, Kadlec, Carter, & Tager-Flusberg, 2008) as main predictors of language acquisition in ASD. A recent study by Young, Merin, Rogers, and Ozonoff (2009) has also found a significant relationship between a face scanning pattern at 6 months and expressive language skills at 18 months such that a greater amounts of fixation to the mother's mouth during live interaction predicted higher levels of expressive language at outcome and greater rates of growth even though no unique scanning pattern was found in children with autism at this early age. These findings suggest that although gaze behavior at 6 months may not provide early markers for autism as initially conceived, gaze to the mouth in particular may be useful in predicting individual differences in language development. There is also often a significant correlation between IQ and language outcomes. For example, Luyster et al. (2008) have found that best concurrent predictors for both receptive and expressive language in toddlers between 18 and 33 months are gesture use and nonverbal cognitive ability (e.g., nonverbal problem solving skills measured by Mullen Early Scale of Learning; Mullen, 1995) although higher levels of nonverbal IQ are not always associated with higher level language skills (Howlin et al., 2004; Kjelgaard & Tager-Flusberg, 2001). Although few longitudinal studies of language acquisition among verbal children with autism have been conducted, the research suggests that during the preschool years progress within each domain of language (e.g., vocabulary, syntax) follows similar pathways as has been found for typically developing children (e.g., Tager-Flusberg et al., 1990).

Individuals with autism continue to make progress in language, and related developmental domains well beyond the preschool years. Paul, Cohen, & Caparulo (1983), in a longitudinal study of children with aphasic and autistic disorders, showed that comprehension ability at early ages was related to degree of improvement in social relations in late adolescence and early adulthood. Paul and Cohen (1984a) suggested that both comprehension and expressive abilities continue to improve in these populations through adolescence and adulthood, although expressive skills show greater rates of improvement. This pattern may occur because speech is more accessible than comprehension and more often a direct target of remedial efforts. In another series of follow-up studies in Britain, almost all of the participants with autism or developmental language disorders showed substantial improvements in formal aspects of language into adulthood (Cantwell & Baker, 1989). However, the group with autism, who had serious receptive language deficits in early childhood, remained more severely language delayed as a whole (Rutter, Mawhood, & Howlin, 1992). They had more severe behavioral limitations compared to the nonautistic language disordered group, who had a much broader range of outcome, from total independence and good language skill to severe psychiatric disorder and continued expressive language problems.

Some children with autism never acquire functional language; many of these children have very low nonverbal IQ scores. Epidemiological studies indicate that about half the population remains nonverbal by middle childhood (Bryson, Clark, & Smith, 1988); however, recent longitudinal studies of children referred for possible autism at early ages have suggested that the proportion of children with ASD who do not use words to speak is less than 20% (Lord et al., 2004). It has been also reported that about 50–70% of children with ASD by around 8–10 years of age acquire functional phrase speech even though only a small number of these children initially have functional phrase speech by the age of 3–5 (Anderson et al., 2007; Magiati, Moss, Charman, & Howlin, 2011; Turner, Stone, Pozdol, & Coonrod, 2006). Such a statistic is clearly affected by variation in who is studied: What age are the participants with autism? Are they recruited from special education services or clinics or from broader populations? What about the effect of education and treatment? The statistic is also affected by how useful speech is defined: Are single words enough? Simple sentences? How spontaneous do they have to be? How often do they have to be used? How intelligible must they be?

There is some optimism that with more children receiving earlier diagnoses and thus better access to early intensive interventions, especially for language and communication skills, the proportion of children with autism who fail to acquire functional language is diminishing. Nevertheless, as the prevalence rates for ASDs increase, it is not easy to disentangle improvements in language skills across the autism spectrum, from an increase in the diagnosis among higher functioning, more verbal individuals.

Articulation

Among children with autism who speak, articulation is often normal or even precocious (Kjelgaard & Tager-Flusberg, 2001; Pierce & Bartolucci, 1977). However, Bartak, Rutter, and Cox (1975) found articulation development to be somewhat slower than normal. These delays were more transient in a group of high-functioning boys with autism than in language-level matched nonautistic boys with severe receptive-expressive delays in middle childhood (Rutter et al., 1992) and may be the result of later onset of language milestones. Still, Shriberg, Paul, McSweeney, Klin, and Volkmar (2001) reported that one third of speakers with high-functioning autism retained residual speech distortion errors on sounds such as /r/, /l/, and /s/ into adulthood, whereas the rate of these errors in the general population is 1%. Recent studies have also found two main types of language disorders in school-aged children with ASD (mean age of 8 years): severe impairment in expressive phonology (24%) and borderline/normal phonology with impaired comprehension (76%; Rapin, Dunn, Allen, Stevens, & Fein, 2009). It was also found that a minority of children (12%) with high-functioning autism and Asperger's syndrome (AS) from 5 to 13 years presented with standard scores below the normal range on a standardized test of articulation (Cleland, Gibbon, Peppe, O'Hare, & Rutherford, 2010).

Bartolucci, Pierce, Streiner, and Tolkin-Eppel (1976) showed that phoneme frequency distribution and the distribution of phonological error types in a small group of children with autism was similar to children with intellectual disabilities (IDs) and typical children matched for nonverbal mental age. The less frequent the phoneme's use in the language, the greater was the number of errors. Phonological perception among the groups also was similar. These findings indicate that the developmental trajectory for phonological development in autism follows the same path as in other groups of children, although a higher rate of distortion errors is seen in adult speakers.

Two caveats should be noted. First, difficulties in articulation are relatively common in nonautistic children with ID. Even though no relationship was found between scores on language measures or cognitive measures and standard scores from an articulation test (McCann, Peppé, Gibbon, O'Hare, & Rutherford, 2007), the fact that there is no difference between autistic and IQ-matched children with ID does not mean that no children with autism have articulation difficulties. Second, there is a relatively small number of autistic children who are identified as high functioning on the basis of nonverbal tests during preschool but who have extraordinary difficulties in producing intelligible speech. These children are not likely to be included in many studies of language because they are relatively rare. By the time they are 10 or 12 years old, fluent language often becomes an implicit criteria for the category of high functioning.

Word Use

Word use in autism can be observed by asking two rather different questions: (1) Do children with autism use and understand words as belonging to the same categories as other people? (2) Is there anything unusual about how individuals with autism use words? The answer to both questions is *yes*. In the first case, studies have shown that verbal children with autism use semantic groupings (e.g., *bird, boat, food*) in very similar ways to categorize and to retrieve words (Boucher, 1988; Minshew & Goldstein, 1993; Tager-Flusberg, 1985). High-functioning children and adolescents with autism can score quite well on standardized vocabulary tests indicating an unusually rich knowledge of words (Fein & Waterhouse, 1979; Jarrold, Boucher, & Russell, 1997; Kjelgaard & Tager-Flusberg, 2001) and an area of relative strength for some individuals with autism (Whitehouse, Maybery, & Durkin, 2007). At the same time, Tager-Flusberg (1991) found that children with autism often fail to use their knowledge of words in a normal way to facilitate performance on retrieval or organizational tasks.

At the same time, it appears that certain classes of words may be underrepresented in the vocabularies of children with autism. For example, Tager-Flusberg (1992) found that the children participating in a longitudinal language study used hardly any mental state terms, particularly terms for cognitive states (e.g., *know, think, remember, pretend*). These findings were replicated in research including older children with autism (Storoschuk,

Lord, & Jaedicke, 1995; Tager-Flusberg & Sullivan, 1994). Other studies suggest that children with autism have particular difficulties understanding social-emotional terms as measured on vocabulary tests such as the Peabody Picture Vocabulary Test (Eskes, Bryson, & McCormick, 1990; Hobson & Lee, 1989; Van Lancker, Cornelius, & Needleman, 1991). Thus, while overall lexical knowledge may be a relative strength in autism, the acquisition of words that map onto mental state concepts may be specifically impaired in this disorder.

Abnormal use of words and phrases has been described in autism for many years (Rutter, 1970). In samples of high-functioning adolescents and adults, a significant minority has been shown to use words with special meanings (Rumsey, Rapoport, & Sceery, 1985; Volden & Lord, 1991), or "metaphorical language" use, as Kanner (1946) described this unusual phenomenon. In most cases, these words or phrases were modifications of ordinary word roots or phrases that produced slightly odd sounding, but comprehensible terms such as *commendment* for praise or *cuts and bluesers* for cuts and bruises. These terms were not radically different from those used occasionally by children with ID or younger children without ID who were matched on expressive language level, except that they were more frequent in the autistic population. Only subjects with autism produced neologisms or odd phrases for which the root was not fairly obvious, though these too were relatively rare (Volden & Lord, 1991). One interesting finding was that increased language ability was associated with increased (proportions as well as absolute numbers) peculiarities and perseveration in individuals with autism. In a nonautistic children with ID, oddities decreased steadily as expressive language ability improved (Volden & Lord, 1991). Rutter and Lord (1987) suggest that these abnormal uses of words may be functionally similar to the kinds of early word meaning errors made by young typically developing children. It is their persistence in autism that defines them as abnormal, and they may reflect the fact that children with autism are not sensitive to the corrective feedback

provided by their parents because of their social impairments.

Pedantic speech and being overly precise in a rather concrete way are also descriptors frequently used with individuals with HFA (Ghaziuddin, Tsai, & Ghaziuddin, 1992), though these qualities can be very difficult to quantify. Wing (1981), commented on the language of people with HFAs having a bookish quality exemplified by the use of obscure words. She considered pedantic speech to be one of the main clinical features of this disorder (Burgoine & Wing, 1983). Mayes, Volkmar, Hooks, and Cicchetti (1993) found that the presence of peculiar language patterns was one of the best discriminators of pervasive developmental disorder from language disability.

Syntax and Morphology

Relatively few studies have systematically investigated grammatical aspects of language acquisition in autism. The longitudinal study of six autistic boys conducted by Tager-Flusberg and her colleagues found that these children followed the same developmental path as an age-matched comparison group of children with Down syndrome who were part of the study, and as normally developing children drawn from the extant literature (Tager-Flusberg et al., 1990). The children with autism and Down syndrome showed similar growth curves in the length of their utterances (MLU), which is usually taken as a hallmark measure of grammatical development. At the same time, in a follow-up study using the same language samples, Scarborough, Rescorla, Tager-Flusberg, Fowler, and Sudhalter (1991) compared the relationship between MLU and scores on a different index of grammatical development, which charts the emergence of a wide range of grammatical constructions: the Index of Productive Syntax (IPSyn). The main findings were that at higher MLU levels, MLU tended to significantly overestimate IPSyn scores for the subjects with autism, suggesting that for the children with autism the relatively limited growth in IPSyn reflects the tendency to make use of a narrower range of constructions and to ask fewer questions, which accounts for a significant portion of the IPSyn score.

Several studies of English-speaking children with autism investigated the acquisition of grammatical morphology, based on data from spontaneous speech samples. Some of these studies must be interpreted with caution as they included very small numbers of children, who varied widely in age, mental age, and language ability. Two cross-sectional studies found differences between children with autism and a comparison group of typical children or children with ID in the mastery of certain grammatical morphemes (Bartolucci, Pierce, & Streiner, 1980; Howlin, 1984). Bartolucci et al. (1980) found that children with autism were more likely to omit certain morphemes, particularly articles (*a*, *the*), auxiliary and copula verbs, past tense, third-person present tense, and present progressive. Tager-Flusberg (1989) also found that children with autism were significantly less likely to mark past tense than were matched controls with Down syndrome. Bartolucci and Albers (1974) compared children with autism to controls in performance on a task designed to elicit production of present progressive *-ing* and past tense *-ed* for different verbs. The children with autism performed well on the present progressive form, as did the controls. They were, however, significantly impaired on the past tense elicitation trials. This finding was replicated in a recent study of over 60 children with autism who were given tasks to elicit both the past tense and the third-person present tense (Roberts, Rice, & Tager-Flusberg, 2004). The sample was divided into those who had scores within the normal range on standardized language tests and those who were significantly below the mean. Only those with impaired language scores performed poorly on the tense tasks. Across these studies then, marking tense was impaired among children with autism. Roberts et al. (2004) interpret their findings as evidence that a subgroup of children with autism have grammatical deficits that are similar to those reported among children with specific language impairment (cf. Rice, 2004).

Studies of other sentence forms in spontaneous language have generally indicated that children with autism are similar to mental-age matched youngsters in terms of the acquisition of rule-governed syntactic systems (Bartak et al., 1975; Pierce & Bartolucci, 1977; Shulman & Guberman, 2007). Children with autism, ID, or developmental language disorders lag in language development relative to nonverbal mental age. It seems very likely that syntactic development in children with autism is more similar than dissimilar to normal development. It often proceeds at a slower pace and is related to developmental level more than to chronological age, although it may not keep pace with other areas of development (Tager-Flusberg, 1981). For example, Eigsti, Bennetto, and Dadlani (2007) showed significant syntactic delays and increased production of nonmeaningful words (jargon) in a group of children with autism compared to children matched on lexical level and nonverbal mental age with developmental delays and typical development.

Studies of adults with autism (Paul & Cohen, 1984a) suggest that this development eventually reaches a plateau in at least some individuals with autism. Adults with autism did significantly more poorly on measures of syntactic production in free speech than adults with ID matched for nonverbal IQ. The lags shown by children and adolescents with autism are often more severe than those of other children with comparable delays earlier in childhood. In research, these delays are often less obvious because children with autism who are not delayed on nonverbal tests are generally grouped with children with autism who are more severely delayed. Moreover, it is now clear that among children with autism there are different subgroups, some of whom have impaired language while other have normal language, as measured on standardized tests (Tager-Flusberg, 2003). The entire autism group is erroneously compared to a more homogeneous control group of nonautistic children with ID (Lord & Pickles, 1996). These concerns highlight the need for more studies that are longitudinal in design, providing follow-up into late adolescence or adulthood, with a focus on individual variation among participants with ASDs.

Echolalia

One of the most salient aspects of deviant speech in autism is the occurrence of echolalia. Echolalia is the repetition, with similar intonation, of words or phrases that someone else has said. It can be immediate; for example, a child repeats back her teacher's greeting, "Hi, Susie," exactly as it was said to her. It can be delayed, as in the case of a child who approaches his father and says, "It's time to tickle you!" as a signal that he wants to be tickled, repeating a phrase he has heard his parents say in the past.

Echolalia was once viewed as an undesirable, nonfunctional behavior (Lovaas, 1977). However other clinicians, beginning with Fay (1969) and elaborated by Prizant and colleagues (see Chapter 27), have emphasized that often echolalia serves the child specific functions. Prizant and Duchan (1981) highlighted six communicative functions that they found were served by immediate echolalia: turn-taking, assertions, affirmative answers, requests, rehearsal to aid processing, and self-regulation. Delayed echoes can be used communicatively to request re-creations of the scenes with which the remarks were originally associated, such as a child saying "You're okay" in a sympathetic tone of voice if he falls down. They can serve other functions as well. Baltaxe and Simmons (1977) showed that the bedtime soliloquies of an 8-year-old autistic child contained frequent examples of delayed echolalia, which they suggested the child used as a base for analyzing linguistic forms that she was in the process of acquiring, as found among some nonautistic children (Weir, 1962).

Although echolalia is one of the most classic symptoms of autism (Kanner, 1946), not all children with autism echo, nor is echoing seen only in autism. Echoing, particularly immediate repetition, occurs in blind children, in children with other language impairments, in older people with dementia, and, perhaps most importantly, in some normally developing children, as well (Yule & Rutter, 1987).

McEvoy, Loveland, and Landry (1988) found that immediate echolalia was most frequent in children with autism who had minimal expressive language but was not closely associated with chronological or nonverbal mental age. Shapiro (1977) and Carr, Schreibman, and Lovaas (1975) found that children with autism were most likely to echo immediately questions and commands that they did not understand or for which they did not know the appropriate response.

A substantial minority, but not all, of verbal autistic adolescents and adults are described by their parents as having engaged in delayed echolalia at some point in their development (Le Couteur et al., 1989). Echolalia has been offered as evidence of gestalt processing in autism (Frith, 1989). Prizant (1983) proposed that children with autism are especially dependent on the gestalt approach to acquiring language (cf. Peters, 1983) and that this is evident in their reliance on echolalia. Tager-Flusberg and Calkins (1990) investigated whether variations in echolalia were tied to differences in the process by which grammar was acquired in autism, when compared to language-matched groups of typically developing children and young children with Down syndrome. As predicted, the children with autism at the early stages of language development produced the most echolalic and formulaic speech. For all children, echolalia declined quite rapidly over the course of development. To investigate whether children with autism used echolalia as a means for acquiring new grammatical knowledge, Tager-Flusberg and Calkins compared echolalic and noncholalic spontaneous speech drawn from the same language sample, for length of utterances using MLU, and for the complexity of grammatical constructions using IPSyn. If imitation is important in the acquisition of grammatical knowledge, then length and grammatical complexity should be more advanced in echolalic than in spontaneous speech produced at the same developmental point. This hypothesis was not confirmed for any of the children in this study. On the contrary, across all language samples, spontaneous utterances were significantly longer and included more advanced grammatical constructions. These findings suggest that echolalia is not an important process in facilitating grammatical development in autism, though it clearly reflects a different conversational style and plays an important role in children's communication with others, especially when they have very limited linguistic knowledge.

In summary, although immediate and delayed echolalia are salient features of autistic speech, they are neither synonymous with nor unique to this syndrome. Although some echolalia in autism may appear to be nonfunctional or self-stimulatory, both immediate and delayed echolalia can serve communicative purposes for the speaker.

Use of Deictic Terms

Confusion of personal pronouns (e.g., when a child asks for a drink by saying, "Do you want a drink of water?") is another frequently mentioned atypical language behavior associated with autism. As with other aspects of deviant language, pronoun reversal sometimes occurs in children with language disorders other than autism, or in blind children (Fraiberg & Fraiberg, 1977), and it may even be present briefly in the language of some normally developing children (Chiat, 1982). As with echolalia, pronoun reversal errors may not occur in all children with autism, but they are more common in individuals with autism than in any other population (Le Couteur et al., 1989; Lee, Hobson & Chiat, 1994). Interestingly, Tager-Flusberg (1994) found that among small group of young children with autism, all of them went through a stage of reversing pronouns, though as they got older the more linguistically advanced children stopped making these errors. The majority of the time, children used pronouns correctly; reversal errors only averaged 13% of all pronouns produced.

Kanner (1943) originally attributed pronoun reversals to echolalia. Some examples, such as the child who says, "Carry you!" seem to reflect this relationship. Other accounts have considered the linguistic or information-processing demands in having to shift and mark reference (Rice, Wexler, & Cleave, 1995). Within autism difficulty using pronouns is generally viewed as part of a more general difficulty with deixis, the aspect of language that codes shifting reference between the speaker and the listener. For example, in labeling a person by name (e.g., *James*), the label remains the same without regard to who is speaking; whereas, for pronouns, whether James is referred to as "I" or "you" depends on whether he is the speaker or the listener during a particular conversation. Deixis is marked, not only by pronouns, but in various ways in different languages. In English, these include various determiners (for example, whether a speaker uses "this" or "that" depending on previous reference or location of an object) or the selection of verbs (such as "come" and "go") and verb tense.

Most current interpretations of pronoun errors in autism view them as a reflection of the difficulties that children with autism have in conceptualizing notions of self and other as they are embedded in shifting discourse role between speaker and listener (Lee et al., 1994; Tager-Flusberg, 1993). Their difficulty understanding discourse roles is related to impaired social communicative functioning, specifically conceptual perspective-taking (Loveland, 1984), and may be related to their broader social deficits (see Chapter 12).

Suprasegmental Aspects of Language

Paralinguistic features such as vocal quality, intonation, and stress patterns are another frequently noted speech characteristic of individuals with ASDs (Rutter et al., 1992). Odd intonation patterns associated with autism seem to be one of the most immediately recognizable clinical signs of the disorder. However, defining what constitutes autism-related paralinguistic abnormalities so that clinicians can make reliable judgments about them has been quite challenging (Lord et al., 2000; Lord, Rutter, & Le Conteur, 1994; Volkmar et al., 1994). In part, this may be because of the number of different ways in which language can sound unusual.

There are several levels of prosodic function: grammatical, pragmatic, and affective (Merewether & Alpert, 1990). Grammatical prosody includes cues to the type of utterance (e.g., questions end with rising pitch) and different stress patterns used to distinguish different parts of speech (e.g., marking the word *present* with stress on the first syllable if used as a noun). Pragmatic stress may highlight new information or draw the listener's attention to the significance of the message expressed (e.g., "Are *you* the writer of this note?" versus "Are you the *writer* of this note?"). Affective prosody conveys the speaker's feelings or attitudes and may include variations in vocal tone and speech rate. Failure to use and appreciate intonational cues, then, will likely not only affect the emotional tone of a verbal exchange but also hamper its comprehensibility.

Intonational peculiarities frequently are associated with ASDs. The most frequently cited is monotony (see Fay & Schuler, 1980). These patterns were formerly attributed to emotional states thought to be present (or absent) in autistic individuals, and were originally thought to reflect flat affect, the failure to express personality or repressed anger (see Lord & Rutter, 1994). Fay and Schuler (1980) also describe a subset of autistic individuals who used a sing-song rather than flat pattern. Goldfarb, Braunstein, and Lorge (1956) and Pronovost, Wakstein, and Wakstein (1966) found unusually high fundamental frequency levels in autistic speakers. Other voice disorders, such as hoarseness, harshness, and hypernasality, have been identified (Pronovost et al., 1966). Our own clinical observations detected hyponasality in some children with autism. Poor control of volume, with unexplained fluctuations, has also been reported (Pronovost et al., 1966). And Fay (1969) reported frequent whispering among children who echo.

Research on HFA suggests that these abnormalities in intonation and prosody are even more prevalent for children and adults with HFA than for individuals with autism with average or lower than average intelligence and verbal skills. The most systematic direct investigation of prosodic features in HFA was conducted by Shriberg and his colleagues (Shriberg et al., 2001). They analyzed speech samples collected during a diagnostic interview, the Autism Diagnostic Observation Schedule (ADOS),

which was conducted with the adolescent and adult participants with autism. The main findings were that about one third of the participants with HFA had distorted speech and articulation problems and two thirds expressed prosodic abnormalities at grammatical, pragmatic, or affective levels. A number of the study participants had loud, high voices with a nasal tone. Koning and Magill-Evans (2001) investigated whether high-functioning adolescents with autism were able to use nonverbal cues, including facial expression, body gestures, and prosody, to interpret the feelings of people acting in videotaped scenes. They found that the adolescents with HFA were significantly worse than controls in interpreting the emotions, and relied least on prosodic information. These findings suggest that not only are people with HFA impaired in expressive prosody, they also have difficulty comprehending prosodic information expressed by others.

The reasons behind these deficits in suprasegmental features remain obscure. Frith (1969) showed that like typically developing children, children with autism recalled stressed words better than unstressed ones, especially when the stress was placed on content words. On the other hand, children with autism seemed less able than typical children to take advantage of stress cues for meaning (see also Baltaxe, 1984). For example, high-functioning adolescents with ASD (those with IQ score higher than 70) were found to show a different pattern in the perception of prosody compared to typically developing peers such that those with ASD judged speaker's affect based on the rate of the speech rather than the stress (Paul, Augustyn, Klin, & Volkmar, 2005). In addition, Thurber and Tager-Flusberg (1993) found autistic children produced fewer nongrammatical pauses than controls matched on verbal mental age, when telling a story from a wordless picture book. There was no difference in grammatical pauses (i.e., those between phrases). Deviance in intonation seems unlikely to be due solely to simple perceptual or motor deficits. More fundamental aspects of the autistic syndrome reflected in higher level language and communicative behaviors, such as understanding of other persons, related social cognitive deficits, and/or ability to plan and execute a complex action, may contribute to how autistic children learn to use intonation and other paralinguistic features (Paul, Shriberg, et al., 2005).

There seems no doubt that there is something different about the way in which the stream of sound associated with speech is produced in many persons with autism. Ricks and Wing (1976) carried out one of the first studies in this area. They studied parents' identification of the meaning of the prelinguistic vocalizations of autistic children and found that parents of children with autism were unable to understand the preverbal vocalizations of other children with autism, even though they could understand their own child's messages. In contrast, parents of typically developing children could understand vocalizations of typical children who were not their own, as well as those of their own child. These findings were not replicated in a later study by Elliot (1993).

Historically, autistic children have been described as babbling less frequently than other children during early childhood. However, Elliott (1993) found no difference in the frequency with which preverbal, developmentally delayed 2-year-olds, preverbal typically developing 10- to 12-month-olds, and 2-year-olds with autism produced vocalizations in situations that were intended to engage the children socially (e.g., watching a balloon fly around the room); however, a smaller proportion of the children with autism vocalized than in the comparison groups. Moreover, the vocalizations the children with autism did produce were less likely to be paired with other nonverbal communication, such as shifts in gaze or gesture or changes in facial expression than they were for the other children (Hellreigel, Tao, DiLavore, & Lord, 1995). Sheinkopf and his colleagues conducted a detailed examination of the vocal behavior of young preverbal children with autism and a group of comparison children with developmental delays (Sheinkopf, Mundy, Oller, & Steffens, 2000). Although the children with autism did not have difficulty with the expression of well-formed syllables (i.e., canonical babbling), they did display significant impairments in vocal quality (i.e., atypical phonation). Specifically, autistic children produced a greater proportion of syllables with atypical phonation than did comparison children. The atypicalities in the vocal behavior of children with autism were, however, unrelated to individual differences in joint attention skill, suggesting that a multiple process model may be needed to describe early social-communication impairments in children with autism. A recent study also showed that infants and toddlers with ASD produced significantly more atypical nonspeech vocalizations or an excess of high-pitched vocalizations compared to control groups who were matched based on age or language level (Schoen, Paul, & Chawarska, 2011). These results suggest that toddlers with ASD may show less winnowing of the other kinds of sounds not produced by the speech models in their environment, leading to the reduced tendency to tune in and tune up (Shriberg, Paul, Black, & van Santen, 2011) to ambient speech models (Paul, Fuerst, Ramsay, Chawarska, & Klin, 2010).

Taken together, these findings suggest that the source of the difference between the vocalizations of the young children with autism and those of other young, nonverbal children was not just in social intent, but also in a more basic aspect of the form of the vocalization beginning very early in development.

Language Comprehension in Autism

Most research on the language of individuals with autism centers on their productive capacities. In contrast, less attention has been focused on their comprehension skills. This is unfortunate because early response to language, a likely precursor to comprehension, is one of the strongest indicators of autism in very young children (Dahlgren & Gillberg, 1989; Lord, 1995). Charman and his colleagues collected data on early language development from a large group of preschool-aged children with autism using a parent report measure: the MacArthur Communicative Development Inventory (Charman, Drew, Baird & Baird, 2003). They found that comprehension of words was delayed relative to production, though, like typically developing children, in absolute terms the children with autism understood more words than they produced. The continuation of significant delays in comprehension is also one of the strongest differentiators of high-functioning autism from specific language disorders (Rutter et al., 1992).

Bartak and colleagues (Bartak et al., 1975) and Paul and Cohen (1984a) showed that individuals with autism performed more poorly on standardized measures of language comprehension than participants with aphasic or ID at similar nonverbal mental-age levels. Studies of very young children (Paul et al., 2008) suggest that comprehension skills are depressed relative to production in the second year of life, while the gap tends to narrow, with receptive skills moving closer to expressive levels, in the third to fourth year. Studies that have compared receptive and expressive language skills among somewhat older children with autism using standardized tests have found that receptive skills as measured by standard scores tend to be comparable to expressive on vocabulary tests as well as tests of higher order language processing (Jarrold et al., 1997; Kjelgaard & Tager-Flusberg, 2001). Yet, there is a clear clinical impression that among verbal children with autism, comprehension is more significantly impaired (Tager-Flusberg, 1981; Saalasti et al., 2008; Seung, 2007).

It has been also suggested that when a child displays substantially more difficulty with language comprehension than production at early periods of development, it may be a strong indicator of ASD (Paul, Chawarska, & Volkmar, 2008; Paul & Weismer, in press). For example, Paul and colleagues (2008) found that toddlers with ASD showed significantly lower scores on the Receptive Language domain using the Mullen Scales of Early Learning (1995) than late talkers without autism, though no difference emerged between these two groups for the Expressive Language domain. All of these children had nonverbal developmental levels within the normal range but had scores on the Expressive Language domain more than one standard deviation below the mean for their age.

In another study, toddlers with autism were also found to score significantly higher on production of language than comprehension (p <.05; Weismer, Lord, & Esler, 2010). On the other hand, the authors found a reverse pattern for children who had development delay (DD) without autism. These results have been recently replicated, suggesting that the significant impairment in receptive language compared to expressive language is unique for toddlers with ASD even though both toddlers with ASD and late talkers without ASD show similar levels of expressive language (Weismer et al., 2011).

More insight into the mechanisms that underlie the impression of impaired language comprehension in autism comes from experimental studies. Sigman and Ungerer (1981) looked at language comprehension and sensorimotor performance in children with autism with mental ages of about 2 years. They found quite sophisticated performance on object permanence tasks but poor performance on receptive language measures. They suggested that sensorimotor skills play a small role in the acquisition of language. Play skills, on the other hand, were highly related to receptive language level, particularly those forms of play that were directed outward toward dolls. Thus, the more social aspects of cognition, those involving the imaginary creation of a scene with dolls and interactions between people, appear to be more related to the understanding of language than are those involving knowledge about objects, which can be learned with very little social interaction. Tager-Flusberg (1981) investigated sentence comprehension using experimental tasks that assessed the use of different strategies. Children with autism performed at the same level as typical controls in their use of a word order strategy for processing sentences (interpreting noun-verb-noun sequences as agent-action-object), however, they were less likely to use a semantically based probable event strategy, interpreting sentences based on their likelihood of occurring in the real world (e.g., knowing that a mother is more likely to pick up a baby than a baby pick up a mother). Tager-Flusberg (1981) concluded that children with autism have difficulty applying their knowledge about the probabilities of occurrence of events in the world to the task of understanding sentences.

In a partial replication of this study, Gaddes (1984) showed that children with autism were much less consistent in identifying probable events that involved relationships between people (e.g., the mother feeds the baby) than were very young normally developing children with lower or equivalent expressive abilities. This occurred when the relationships were acted out by dolls, even when no comprehension of language was required. Thus, the difficulties may lie in comprehending the situation, and what is probable in it, as well as comprehending the word order that depicts the situation. Paul, Fischer, and Cohen (1988) found that although children with autism used similar strategies in sentence comprehension as other children, they always performed less competently. Together, these findings suggest that, not only may children have limited ability to integrate linguistic input with real-world knowledge, but that, in some cases, they may lack knowledge about social events used by normally developing children to buttress emerging language skills and to acquire increasingly advanced linguistic structures (Lord, 1985).

Another source of difficulty in comprehending language in everyday situations rather than in standardized testing situations may be the ability to integrate nonverbal cues to help interpret linguistic input. Examples include noticing the smile on another's face, the way in which another person touches you, the tone of her voice, as well as the words in order to determine if someone is being affectionate, teasing, or aggressive (Loveland, 1991; Ozonoff, Pennington, & Rogers, 1990; St. James & Tager-Flusberg, 1994).

Similarly, interpretation of an utterance demands an ability to go beyond linguistically given meaning by using and connecting relevant contextual information, with which individuals with ASD have great difficulties. In one study, despite having average language skills, children with high-functioning ASD showed difficulties when answering contextually demanding questions, and especially when giving explanations for their correct answers, suggesting that impairments in language comprehension that

rely on pragmatic cues are evident in individuals with ASD even if their linguistic abilities are at normal level (Loukusa et al., 2007).

Paul and Cohen (1985) looked at the ability of matched groups of participants with autism and ID to understand indirect requests for action (e.g., "Can you color this circle blue?") of varying syntactic complexity. The two groups, with IQs in the mildly to moderately impaired range, performed similarly in a context in which the request intent of the utterance was made explicit (e.g., "I'm going to tell you to do some things. Can you . . . "). However the autism group performed significantly worse when the same requests were presented in an unstructured context with no prefacing cue as to the intention of the utterance. The authors concluded that the individuals with autism are impaired in the ability to determine the speaker's intention without explicit cuing, over and above any syntactic comprehension deficit that might be present. This pattern may be an example of why, in their follow-up of high-functioning autistic individuals, Rutter and colleagues (Rutter et al., 1992) found a strong relationship between language comprehension and social functioning in adulthood, with no similar finding for adults identified as having specific receptive and expressive language impairment as children.

For individuals with autism, understanding language in conversational and other discourse contexts remains a significant challenge because semantic and pragmatic aspects of language are so closely linked to nonverbal social communication and other aspects of social adaptation.

Language Use

Language use, or the pragmatic aspects of language, in autism has been studied from a variety of perspectives. This domain has been the focus of research for the past several decades because problems have been found across all individuals with ASDs. Studies on language use including specific, unusual aspects of language use such as delayed echolalia and neologisms, as well as language used to describe particular phenomena such as mental states or emotions, are discussed elsewhere in the chapter; this section will focus on research on speech acts, referential communication, discourse, and narration.

One of the most interesting characteristics of language use in autism is that it has aspects that are constant across development and aspects that change. As with the development of social behavior (Lord, 1995), some of the changes occur because children improve in their communicative abilities; other changes occur because situational demands for communication are different for children of different ages and for adults and vary with the contexts in which individuals find themselves. Thus, in considering deficits in language use, factors such as what individuals are expected to do, what they are given the opportunity to do, and what they usually do all must be considered. Stone and Caro-Martinez (1990), in an observational study of the spontaneous communication of children with autism of varying abilities placed in special classrooms, found differences in the functions about which the children communicated. These differences were related to chronological age, nonverbal IQ, and whether the children's primary mode of communication was through speech or motor acts. Children who did not talk engaged in more social routines than verbal children. Children with speech were more likely to use language to offer new information. They communicated to a greater number of different people (rather than just the teacher) and were more likely to address communications to peers as well as adults than children without speech. McHale, Simeonsson, Marcus, and Olley (1980) showed that autistic students communicated more in the presence of their teachers than in their absence, and directed their communication only to adults, not to peers.

Across different language levels, children with autism also share important similarities. Despite deficits in spontaneous speech, most children on the autism spectrum do attempt to use their language to communicate even if only in limited ways. Bernard-Opitz (1982) showed that communicative performance of one child with autism varied with different interlocutors and in different settings,

indicating some social awareness in his use of language. However, rate of initiation of spontaneous communications in autism is often described as very low. In the study by Stone and Caro-Martinez (1990), the modal frequency in school was two or three spontaneous communicative acts per child, per hour. Only half of the children ever directed a communication to a peer across multiple observations. Several other investigators have shown autistic children to have less frequent and less varied speech acts in free play or more open-ended situations, even when their responses to highly structured situations were similar to those of control groups (Landry & Loveland, 1989; Mermelstein, 1983; Wetherby & Prutting, 1984). In general, studies of younger children with autism find that they rarely use language for comments, showing off, acknowledging the listener, initiating social interaction, or requesting information. Even among older higher functioning children, language is rarely used to explain or describe events in a conversational context (Ziatas, Durkin, & Pratt, 2003). The speech acts that are missing or rarely used in the conversations of children with autism all have in common an emphasis on social rather than regulatory uses of language (Wetherby, 1986).

There are also similarities in abnormalities in language use across verbal individuals with autism who show a range of expressive language abilities. Difficulties in listening, talking to oneself, problems in following rules of politeness, and making irrelevant remarks occur for many children and adults with autism (Baltaxe, 1977; Rumsey et al., 1985).

Difficulties in social uses of language, especially in conversations and other discourse contexts, have also been widely noted for people with HFA by clinicians and researchers (e.g., Klin & Volkmar, 1997; see Landa, 2000, for review). Paul, Orlovski, Marchinko, and Volkmar (2009) reported on conversational behaviors in 30 adolescents with HFA who were engaged in semistructured conversational interviews with clinicians. Findings revealed that for individuals with HFA, conversational errors were *inconsistent*, rather than constant. Nonetheless, it was possible to distinguish teenagers with

ASD from those with typical development (TD) in terms of the quantity of conversational errors. No TD subject made more than five errors within a 30-minute sample, whereas all subjects with HFA made more than eight errors. The most robust differences observed were in the areas of gaze and intonation, while remaining differences centered on ability to share topics and infer others' informational state. Similarly, Paul and Feldman (1984) reported in a case series presentation that highly verbal adolescents and adults with autism showed difficulties in identifying the topic initiated by the conversational partner and in providing a relevant comment. They had difficulty judging, on the basis of cues in the conversation and on the basis of general knowledge about what listeners could reasonably be expected already to have in their knowledge store, how much information was the right amount to include in an utterance (Lord et al., 1989). For example, when asked the question, "Did you and your sister do anything besides rake leaves over the weekend?" a participant responded, "Yes." This answer, although correct in a strictly syntactic sense, fails to appreciate the listener's real purpose in asking the question. It fails to provide the socially appropriate amount of information in response. On the other hand, another adolescent with autism, when asked how his day had gone, began the account with a description of the exact time when he awakened, the bathroom where he washed his face, and the color of his toothbrush. Similar findings were reported by Surian and his colleagues using a structured experimental task (Surian, Baron-Cohen, & Van der Lely, 1996). Ghaziuddin and Gerstein (1996) included monologue speech as part of their definition of pedantic speech style, which suggests that people with HFA do not engage much in turn-taking during reciprocal conversations with other people, and may also talk too much. Ramberg, Ehlers, Nyden, Johanssen and Gillberg (1996) found that children with HFA were impaired in taking turns during dyadic conversations, providing some support for this view.

Adams and her colleagues (Adams, Green, Gilchrist, & Cox, 2002) compared conversational samples collected from adolescents with HFA and a group of age- and IQ-matched children with severe conduct disorder. Although there were no overall significant group differences in verbosity, the adolescents with HFA tended to talk more during conversational contexts that focused on emotional topics. A few participants with HFA were extremely verbose. The groups were similar in their ability to respond to questions and comments offered by their conversational partner, but a qualitative analysis of responses revealed that the participants with HFA had more pragmatic problems such as providing an inadequate or tangential response, especially when discussing an unusual event or personal narrative.

Children and adolescents with autism perform less well on tasks of referential communication (Loveland, McEvoy, Tunali, & Kelley, 1990), although many can identify another person's visual perspective (Baron-Cohen, 1989; Hobson, 1984). More social and/or more complex aspects of referential communication, such as those that affect narration and discourse, are particularly affected (Hemphill, Picardi, & Tager-Flusberg, 1991). Children with autism often have difficulty dealing with new information (Tager-Flusberg & Andersen, 1991). They produce more noncontingent utterances, with similar patterns to those of language-impaired children but with proportionately more errors (Baltaxe & D'Angiola, 1992). Hurtig, Ensrud, and Tomblin (1980) reported that persistent and perseverative questioning generally did not serve the purpose of requesting information in autistic children, but was communicative, often functioning as a means of initiating interaction or getting attention.

Bishop and her colleagues (Bishop, Hartley, & Weir, 1994) studied a group of children with semantic-pragmatic disorder who had some social and communicative behaviors that overlap with autism and pervasive developmental disorder. They found that, in these more verbally fluent children, there was a higher proportion of utterances that were initiations than responses. This finding seemed to account for how language-impaired children, including some with autism, could be considered talkative, even though the total amount of language they produce is not higher than that of other children.

Paul and Cohen (1984b) studied responses to requests for clarification in adults with autism or ID matched for nonverbal IQ. They found that although the participants with autism were just as likely to respond to requests for clarification, their answers were less specific than those of the nonautistic participants. They were also less likely to add additional information that might be of help to the listener, suggesting that they had difficulty judging what piece of information was relevant.

Paul and colleagues (2009) used conversational probes and role playing to examine the pragmatic abilities of adolescents with HFA and AS. In these more structured conversational situations, as in more naturalistic interviews discussed earlier, subjects with ASD had significantly more difficulty than controls with TD in responding to topics introduced by others and in making comments contingent upon the interlocutor's remark. They also had difficulty gracefully terminating topics. In role-playing situations that required the subject to lead the conversation, teenagers with ASD generally were unable to take assertive conversational role. Paradoxically, then, adolescents with ASD showed difficulty in responding contingently to others' conversational input *and* in appropriately guiding conversations to elicit remarks from an interlocutor. Taken together these results suggest a basic difficulty in establishing and maintaining reciprocity in conversation; in the ability to engage in mutual, cooperative social dialogue.

Studies of the ability of individuals with autism to produce narrative discourse have also provided information about the ways in which persons with autism organize and convey their thoughts to others. In general, studies have found that, commensurate with their language ability, children and adults with autism are able to narrate stories and follow simple scripts for common social events, such as a birthday party. Particular difficulties in making causal statements were found in one study (Tager-Flusberg, 1995), but these findings were not replicated in a later study (Capps, Losh, & Thurber, 2000). Loveland and her colleagues

asked individuals with autism or Down syndrome, matched on chronological and verbal mental age, to retell the story they were shown in the form of a puppet show or video sketch (Loveland et al., 1990). Compared to the controls, the children with autism were more likely to exhibit pragmatic violations including bizarre or inappropriate utterances and were less able to take into consideration the listener's needs. Some of the participants in this study with autism even failed to understand the story as a representation of meaningful events, suggesting that they lacked a cultural perspective underlying narrative (Bruner & Feldman, 1993; Loveland & Tunali, 1993). However, few differences between narrative skills of children with ASD and those with specific language impairment were found, suggesting that difficulties with stories may be common to children with communication impairments (Norbury & Bishop, 2003; Norbury, Gemmell, & Paul, 2013).

Taken together, these studies of pragmatic skills in verbal autistic individuals echo the suggestions of studies of nonverbal communication in young autistic children. Although basic intention to communicate often exists, the autistic person has impaired skill in participating in communicative activities involving joint reference or shared topics. This is particularly true in supplying new information relevant to a listener's purposes. The strategies used by an individual with autism to maintain conversation are less advanced than syntactic ability would predict, as is the ability to infer the interlocutor's implicit intentions.

One difference between individuals with autism and other populations with language impairments has been that, in most groups with language impairment, the more a child talks, the less likely it is that the language will have unusual characteristics. In contrast, two studies with autistic children and adolescents showed that subjects' unusual aspects of language and lack of cohesiveness increased with the amount of speech (Caplan, Guthrie, Shields, & Yudovin, 1994; Volden & Lord, 1991). In autism, difficulties in explaining and predicting behavior seem to be related both to general language deficits and to deficits in specific cognitive functions, such as metarepresentation and using the information at hand (Tager-Flusberg & Sullivan, 1994). Because most, though not all, individuals with autism have significant delays as well as deviance in language, they are doubly handicapped in communication.

Reading

Many children with autism have an early interest in letters and numbers, and some learn to read words without any direct instruction (Loveland & Tunali-Kotoski, 1997). Decoding, or pronouncing written words, and spelling tend to be relative strengths for many individuals with ASD (Lindgren, Folstein, Tomblin, & Tager-Flusberg, 2009). These strengths are especially noteworthy when children with autism are compared to other individuals with histories of language delay, who tend to do especially poorly in reading and writing. Children with autism typically show literacy skills that are on par with their overall developmental level (Loveland & Tunali-Kotoski, 1997; Myles et al., 2002) and can understand simple reading passages at grade level (Ventner, Lord, & Schopler, 1992). Written material has been shown in a variety of studies to provide a helpful medium of intervention for these children. Written scripts, social stories, graphic organizers, reminder cards, and lists are useful in increasing social and communicative behavior for individuals with autism who read (e.g., Gray, 2000; Krantz & McClannahan, 1998; Simmons, Lanter, & Lyons, Chapter 34, this *Handbook*, Volume 2). Nonetheless, these individuals can have relative deficits in comprehension, particularly when longer, more complex texts, such as narratives, are involved (Wahlberg & Magliano, 2004) anddifficulty in structuring narratives (Diehl & Young, 2006).

Even though studies have found relatively intact decoding skills in ASD, a wide variability in word-level reading and reading comprehension skills have been found in ASD (Nation, Clarke, Wright, & Williams, 2006; Williams, Goldstein, & Minshew, 2006). It has been suggested that difficulties with word-level reading and text comprehension may be associated with oral language

competence (Nation et al., 2006). In addition, consistent with typically developing children, poor comprehension of connected text, particularly limitations in inferencing skills, has been suggested to be associated with word recognition and reading comprehension in children with ASD (Norbury & Bishop, 2002) and a limited ability to use written context to modify word reading (Lopez & Leekam, 2003). However, an opposite result was found in adolescents with ASD (Saldana & Frith, 2007), suggesting that it is still not yet clear if limited inferencing skills are associated with the variability found in reading comprehension of individuals with ASD across development. In addition, these studies have consistently suggested that the deficits in reading comprehension observed in individuals with ASD do not go beyond but are on par with the impairments in other areas of language development.

While developmental level-appropriate literacy skills are the norm in autism, there is a subset of children with ASD who show remarkable decoding ability (Grigorenko, Klin, & Volkmar, 2003). These children are often referred to as hyperlexic. They usually begin reading words before they get to school, and are obsessive in their interest in letters, writing, and reading (Nation, 1999). However Grigorenko et al. (2003) point out that hyperlexia is not synonymous with autism. Their review reveals that only 5–10% of children with autism show hyperlexia, although this rate is much higher than that which occurs in otherwise normal development. Moreover, hyperlexia is not specific to autism; it is also seen in a variety of other disabilities including Turner syndrome, Tourette syndrome, and ID. Although hyperlexia is more prevalent in autism than in these disorders, it can occur in conjunction with nonautistic disabilities. The hallmarks of hyperlexia are advanced word recognition in children who otherwise have significant cognitive, linguistic, or social handicaps; a compulsive preoccupation with reading, letters, or writing; and a significant discrepancy between strong word recognition and weak comprehension of what has been read. Children with autism who show hyperlexia are often baffling to families, because their independent, early acquisition of word recognition contrasts so sharply with their severe handicaps in social communication and learning in other areas. Hyperlexia is, to some extent, a savant skill, like other special abilities occasionally seen in children with autism (e.g., drawing, calculation, music, calendar calculation), which fails to connect to general intellectual and functional abilities. Like other savant skills, hyperlexia can be used as a starting point for teaching other, more functional behaviors, but direct instruction and intensive practice will be necessary to move from the unprocessed word calling that is characteristic of this syndrome to more purposeful and communicative uses of reading.

Underlying Mechanisms

Recently, increasingly sophisticated neuroimaging and neurophysiological measures have allowed documentation of anatomical and functional differences in the brain. For instance, recent studies have investigated structural brain abnormalities related to language using MRI.

In the normal population, left cortical regions, especially in key language areas (perisylvian region, planum temporale, and Heschel's gyrus), are enlarged relative to the size of those regions in the right hemisphere. Herbert and her colleagues compared 16 boys with autism (all with normal nonverbal IQ scores) to 15 age-, sex-, and handedness-matched typically developing controls (Herbert et al., 2002). Their main findings were that the boys with autism had significant *reversal* of asymmetry in the inferior lateral frontal cortex, which was 27% larger in the right hemisphere compared to 17% larger in the left hemisphere for the normal controls. There were also significant differences between the autism and control groups in the asymmetry patterns in the planum temporale. While both groups showed a left hemisphere asymmetry, this was more extreme in the autistic boys (25% leftward asymmetry for autism compared to only 5% in the controls). These findings for the planum temporale were not replicated in a study comparing adults with autism and age-matched

normal controls (Rojas, Bawn, Benkers, Reite, & Rogers, 2002). Rojas and his colleagues found that their adults with autism had significantly reduced left hemisphere planum temporale volumes, and no hemispheric asymmetry in this important language region. Perhaps methodological differences can explain these conflicting findings. Rojas et al. (2002) studied adults rather than children, included women in their sample, and their groups were not matched for IQ.

Recent studies have also used the functional magnetic resonance imaging (fMRI) to investigate online language processing in autism. Just, Cherkassky, Keller, and Minshew (2004) investigated brain activation during sentence comprehension. Reliable differences were found between subjects with HFA and TD in activation in the basic language areas of the cortex. Subjects with HFA showed higher activation in Wenicke's (left laterosuperior temporal) region, which is traditionally associated with language comprehension, particularly understanding words, and lower activity in Broca's area (left inferior frontal gyrus), usually associated with production and grammar. Functional connectivity between cortical regions also appeared lower in the subjects with HFA.

Another study using fMRI based on 16 adolescents with HFA has also indicated that when perceiving prosodic cues, activation of neural regions was more generalized in ASD than in typical development, and areas recruited reflect heightened reliance on cognitive control, reading of intentions, attentional management, and visualization, suggesting that speakers with HFA have developed less automaticity in language processing (Eigsti, Schuh, Mencl, Schultz, & Paul, 2011).

Abnormal brain activity in individuals with ASD during semantic processing tasks have been also noted (Braeutigan, Swithenby, & Bailey, 2008; Dunn & Bates, 2005; Gaffrey et al., 2007; Harris et al., 2006; Knaus, Silver, Lindgren, Hadjikhani, & Tager-Flusberg, 2008; McCleery et al., 2010). For example, decreased activation in the left inferior frontal gyrus (LIFG) area has been also noted for adults with ASD for semantic processing at the sentence (Just et al., 2004) and word (Gaffrey et al.,

2007) level based on fMRI. The LIFG plays a key role in the integration process by unifying a broad range of information, such as knowledge about the context and the world, as well as co-speech gestures (Tesink et al., 2009). Therefore, the results on decreased activation in the LIFG in individuals with ASD indicate that the brains of individuals with ASD engage less in integrative processing (as takes place in LIFG), but focus more on lower level lexical processing (Harris et al., 2006). Neural correlates of pragmatic language comprehension difficulties in ASD have been also noted in a few fMRI studies. For instance, children and adults with ASD when making inferences from discourse and comprehending irony showed increased activation in the right inferior frontal gyrus (RIFG; Mason, Williams, Kana, Minshew, & Just, 2008; Wang, Lee, Sigman, & Dapretto, 2006). In these studies, increased activity in the ASD groups fell within networks that were activated for control groups. These results may suggest that individuals with ASD have the higher task demands when interpreting discourse in context compared to matched control groups (Mason et al., 2008; Wang et al., 2006).

Past studies have suggested a link between the impairment in the mirror neuron system (MNS) and language deficits in ASD (Bekkering, 2002; Oberman & Ramachandran, 2007; Perkins, Stokes, McGillivray, & Bittar, 2010; Rogers, 2006). Past studies have found that the mirror neurons (Bekkering, 2002) are activated both when a movement is seen and made and that this resonance may facilitate imitation of motor activities that may have an impact on speech production. Rogers (2006) speculates that specific mirror neurons for sights and sounds associated with speech may exist that could impact the ability to imitate and learn from language input. Children with ASDs, who are known to have special difficulties with vocal imitation (Stone, Lemanek, Fishel, Fernandez, & Altemeier, 1990), may be impacted by deficits in these mirror neuron systems, which might provide one element of etiology of speech delays and deviance in these syndromes. In addition, MNS associated communication have been discovered in the lateral region

of area F5 of Macaques monkeys (homologous to human Broca's area; Ferrari, Gallese, Rizzolatti, & Fogassi, 2003). The authors have suggested that these cells respond to performed or observed actions with communicative intent such as tongue protrusion or lip smacking. Studies based on electroencephalograph (EEG) and fMRI also support the dysfunctions in MNS in individuals with ASD (see Oberman & Ramachandran, 2007, or Perkins et al., 2010, for more detailed reviews).

Further studies are clearly needed to explore the structural abnormalities in brain regions subserving language in both children and adults with autism. These findings from studies exploring the neurobiology of language impairment, combined with advances in molecular genetics, suggest that in the long term, neurobiological approaches contribute significantly to our understanding and treatment of language and communication in autism.

Any robust theoretical model for communication abnormalities in autism must have several characteristics. It needs to describe a course that goes awry very early in development and that has a range of consequences, from severe language disability involving no representational-communication system, to more circumscribed abnormalities primarily affecting the pragmatics of connected discourse. It needs to be related to other social and cognitive functions, but not completely accounted for by other factors. That is, there are children and adults without apparent syntactic and semantic difficulties who share the social difficulties seen in autism (as in individuals with HFA), and there are children and adults with severe to profound ID or with specific language disorders who make substantial improvements in social areas and/or nonverbal cognitive functioning but who remain significantly impaired in spoken language. Thus, it appears that, although outcome and severity of social and cognitive deficits in autism are related to language level, these factors are also independent to some degree.

A complete theoretical account of language impairment ultimately needs to delineate the underlying mechanisms that explain these very different patterns of language acquisition and impairment in autism. It is likely that across different children, different mechanisms may be impaired. For some, communicative deficits are related most closely to social impairments in decoding nonverbal cues and understanding other minds. For other children these social-cognitive impairments may be more severe, leading to the inability to understand language as an intentional symbolic system, which may impede them from even entering the linguistic system as marked by the absence of rudimentary comprehension skills and severe joint attention deficits. Additional mechanisms that may be directly or indirectly linked to language acquisition in children with autism include oral motor skills, imitation, and auditory processing and attentional systems. We are still at the early stages of developing theoretical accounts to explain the individual variation in language outcomes in ASDs that encompass all levels of analysis from genetics to neuropathology to cognition and behavior.

CONCLUSION

Many questions remain to be answered about communication in autism. For example, how is odd intonation related to deficits in communication and social cognition? How do linguistic comprehension deficits relate to the various aspects of deviant language seen in the syndrome? What triggers the initial failure of social cognition and joint attention that seems to be associated with such pervasive communicative difficulties? Like so many other questions about autism, the answers to these are likely to be neither simple nor universally true. A wide and heterogeneous range of communicative behaviors and function are seen in the syndrome. Whatever the biological explanation, communication disorders in autism are most likely affected by deficits in the ability to process information about social situations and how people behave when interacting with each other at every point in development. This deficit must be addressed in any attempt to remediate autistic communicative disorders. In addition, although they are integrally tied to broader cognitive and social deficits, delays

in the ability to understand and produce words and sentences may have an even greater effect on the lives of individuals with autism than they do on persons with other handicaps. The double handicap of delay and deviance in autism means that we cannot assume that either individuals with autism or those who provide their linguistic environments can naturally compensate for these deficits without carefully considered intervention. This intervention must include understanding of how these deficits are manifested in particular children or adults and the communicative contexts in which each individual needs to function.

CROSS-REFERENCES

Chapter 9 addresses social skills in autism. Chapter 12 focuses on imitation and 27 on assessment of communication skills. Treatment models are discussed in Chapters 28 through 37.

REFERENCES

Adams, C., Green, J., Gilchrist, A., and Cox, A. (2002). Conversational behaviour of children with Asperger syndrome and conduct disorder. *Journal of Child Psychology and Psychiatry, 43*, 679–690.

Anderson, D. K., Lord, C., Risi, S., DiLavore, P. S., Shulman, C., Thurm, A.,...Pickles, A. (2007). Patterns of growth in verbal abilities among children with autism spectrum disorder. *Journal of Consulting and Clinical Psychology, 75*, 594–604.

Asher, S. R. (1978). Referential communication. In G. J. Whitehurst & B. J. Simmerman (Eds.), *The functions of language and cognition*. New York, NY: Academic Press.

Baldwin, D. A. (1991). Infants' contribution to the achievement of joint reference. *Child Development, 62*, 875–890.

Baltaxe, C. (1977). Pragmatic deficits in the language of autistic adolescents. *Journal of Pediatric Psychology, 2*, 176–180.

Baltaxe, C. (1984). The use of contrastive stress in normal, aphasic and autistic children. *Journal of Speech and Hearing Research, 27*, 97–105.

Baltaxe, C., & D'Angiola, N. (1992). Cohesion in the discourse interaction of autistic, specific language-impaired, and normal children. *Journal of Autism and Developmental Disorders, 22*, 1–22.

Baltaxe, C. A. M., & Simmons, J. Q. (1977). Bedtime soliloquies and linguistic competence in autism. *Journal of Speech and Hearing Disorder, 42*, 376–393.

Baron-Cohen, S. (1989). Perceptual role-taking and protodeclarative pointing in autism. *British Journal of Developmental Psychology, 7*, 113–127.

Baron-Cohen, S. (1993). From attention-goal psychology to belief-desire psychology: The development of a theory of mind, and its dysfunction. In S. Baron-Cohen, H. Tager-Flusberg, & D. Cohen (Eds.), *Understanding other minds: Perspectives from autism* (pp. 59–82). Oxford, England: Oxford University Press.

Bartak, L., Rutter, M., & Cox, A. (1975). A comparative study of infantile autism and specific developmental receptive language disorder: I. *The children. British Journal of Psychiatry, 126*, 127–145.

Bartolucci, G., & Albers, R. J. (1974). Deictic categories in the language of autistic children. *Journal of Autism and Childhood Schizophrenia, 4*, 131–141.

Bartolucci, G., Pierce, S. J., & Streiner, D. (1980). Cross-sectional studies of grammatical morphemes in autistic and mentally retarded children. *Journal of Autism and Developmental Disorders, 10*, 39–50.

Bartolucci, G., Pierce, S., Streiner, D., & Tolkin-Eppel, P. (1976). Phonological investigation of verbal autistic and mentally retarded subjects. *Journal of Autism and Childhood Schizophrenia, 6*, 303–315.

Bates, E. (1976). *Language in context.* New York, NY: Academic Press.

Beitchman, J. H., & Inglis, A. (1991). The continuum of linguistic dysfunction from pervasive developmental disorders to dyslexia. *Psychiatric Clinics of North America, 14*, 95–111.

Bekkering, H. (2002). Common mechanisms in the observation and execution of finger and mouth movements. In A. Meltzoff & W. Prinz (Eds.), *The imitative mind: Development, evolution, and brain basis.* (pp. 163–182). Cambridge, England: Cambridge University Press.

Bernard-Opitz, V. (1982). Pragmatic analysis of the communicative behavior of an autistic child. *Journal of Speech and Hearing Disorders, 47*, 99–109.

Bishop, D. V., & Adams, C. (1989). Conversational characteristics of children with semantic-pragmatic disorder: II. What features lead to a judgment of inappropriacy? *British Journal of Disorders of Communication, 24* (3), 241–263.

Bishop, D., Hartley, J., & Weir, F. (1994). Why and when do some language-impaired children seem talkative? A study of initiation in conversations of children with semantic-pragmatic disorder. *Journal of Autism and Developmental Disorders, 24* (2), 177–197.

Bloom, L., & Lahey, M. (1978). *Language development and language disorders.* New York, NY: Wiley.

Boucher, J. (1988). Word fluency in high-functioning autistic children. *Journal of Autism and Developmental Disorders, 18*, 637–645.

Braeutigan, S., Swithenby, S., & Bailey, A. (2008). Contextual integration the unusual way: A magnetoencephalographic study of responses to semantic violations in individuals with autistic spectrum disorders. *European Journal of Neuroscience, 27*, 1026–1036.

Brown, R. (1973). *A first language.* Cambridge, MA: Harvard University Press.

Bruner, J. S. (1975). From communication to language—A psychological perspective. *Cognition, 3*(3), 255–287.

Bruner, J., & Feldman, C. (1993). Theories of mind and the problem of autism. In S. Baron-Cohen, H. Tager-Flusberg, & D. J.

Cohen (Eds.), *Understanding other minds: perspectives from autism.* Oxford, England: Oxford University Press.

Bryson, S. E., Clark, B. S., & Smith, T. M. (1988). First report of a Canadian epidemiological study of autistic syndromes. *Journal of Child Psychology and Psychiatry, 29*, 433–445.

Burgoine, E., & Wing, L. (1983). Identical triplets with Asperger's syndrome. *British Journal of Psychiatry, 143*, 261.

Cantwell, D. P., & Baker, L. (1989). Infantile autism and developmental receptive dysphasia: A comparative follow-up into middle childhood. *Journal of Autism and Developmental Disorders, 19*, 19–30.

Cantwell, D. P., Baker, L., & Mattison, R. E. (1980). Psychiatric disorders in children with speech and language retardation. *Archives of General Psychiatry, 37*, 423–426.

Caplan, R., Guthrie, D., Shields, W. D., & Yudovin, S. (1994). Communication deficits in pediatric complex partial seizure disorders and schizophrenia. *Development and Psychopathology, 6*, 499–517.

Capps, L., Losh, M., & Thurber, C. (2000). "The frog ate the bug and made his mouth sad": Narrative competence in children with autism. *Journal of Abnormal Child Psychology, 28*, 193–204.

Carpenter, M., Nagell, K., & Tomasello, M. (1998). Social cognition, joint attention, and communicative competence from 9 to 15 months of age. *Monographs of the Society for Research in Child Development, 63*(4), 176.

Carpenter, M., Pennington, B., & Rogers, S. (2002). Interrelations among social-cognitive skills in young children with autism. *Journal of Autism and Developmental Disorders, 32*, 91–106.

Carr, E., Shriebman, L., & Lovaas, O. L. (1975). Control of echolalic speech in psychotic children. *Journal of Abnormal Child Psychology, 3*, 331–351.

Cazden, C. (1968). The acquisition of noun and verb inflections. *Child Development, 39*, 443–448.

Centers for Disease Control and Prevention. (2007). Prevalence of ASDs—Autism and Developmental Disabilities Monitoring Network, 14 sites, United States, 2002, Surveillance Summaries. *Morbidity and Mortality Weekly Report, 56* (No. SS-1), 12–28.

Chapman, R. (1981). Exploring children's communicative intents. In J. Miller (Ed.), *Assessing language production in children: Experimental procedures* (pp. 111–138). Baltimore, MD: University Park Press.

Charman, T., Baron-Cohen, S., Swettenham, J., Baird, G., Drew, A., & Cox, A. (2003). Predicting language outcome in infants with autism and pervasive developmental disorder, *International Journal of Language and Communication Disorders, 38*, 265–285.

Charman, T., Drew, A., Baird, C., & Baird, G. (2003). Measuring early language development in preschool children with ASD using the MacArthur Communicative Development Inventory (Infant Form). *Journal of Child Language, 30*, 213–236.

Chiat, S. (1982). If I were you and you were me: The analysis of pronouns in a pronoun-reversing child. *Journal of Child Language, 9*, 359–379.

Cleland, J., Gibbon, F. E., Peppe, S. J. E., O'Hare, A., & Rutherford, M. (2010). Phonetic and phological errors in children with high functioning autism and Asperger syndrome. *International Journal of Speech-Language Phonology*, *12*, 69–76.

Cohen, I. L., Sudhalter, V., Landon-Jimenez, D., & Keogh, M. (1993). A neural network approach to the classification of autism. *Journal of Autism and Developmental Disorders*, *23*, 443–466.

Dahlgren, S. O., & Gillberg, C. (1989). Symptoms in the first two years of life: A preliminary population study of infantile autism. *European Archives of Psychiatric and Neurological Science*, *283*, 169–174.

Darley, F., Aronson, A., & Brown, J. (1975). *Motor speech disorders*. Philadelphia, PA: W.B. Saunders.

Dawson, G., Toth, K., Abbott, R., Osterling, J., Munson, J., Estes, A., & Liaw, J. (2004). Early social attention impairments in autism: Social orienting, joint attention, and attention to distress. *Developmental Psychology*, *40*, 271–283.

Desjardins, R. N., Rogers, J., & Werker, J. F. (1997). An exploration of why preschoolers perform differently than do adults in audiovisual speech perception tasks. *Journal of Experimental Child Psychology*, *66*, 85–110.

Diehl, J. J., & Young, E. C. (2006). Story recall and narrative coherence of high-functioning children with autism spectrum disorders. *Journal of Abnormal Child Psychology*, *34*(1), 83–98.

Dore, J. (1978). Requestive systems in nursery school conversations: Analysis of talk in its social context. In R. Campbell & P. Smith (Eds.), *Recent advances in the psychology of language* (pp. 271–292). New York, NY: Plenum Press.

Doussard-Roosevelt, J., Joe, C., Bazhenova, O., & Porges, S. (2003). Mother–child interaction in autistic and nonautistic children: Characteristics of maternal approach behaviors and child social responses. *Development and Psychopathology*, *15*, 277–295.

Dunn, M., & Bates, J. (2005). Developmental change in neutral processing of words by children with autism. *Journal of Autism and Developmental Disorders*, *35*, 361–370.

Eigsti, I., Bennetto, L., & Dadlani, M. B. (2007). Beyond pragmatics: Morphsyntactic development in autism. *Journal of Autism and Developmental Disorders*, *37*, 1007–1023.

Eigsti, I., Schuh, J., Mencl, E., Schultz, R. T., & Paul P. (2011). The neural underpinnings of prosody in autism. *Child Neuropsychology*, *1*, 1–18.

Elliott, M. J. (1993). *Prelinguistic vocalizations in autistic, developmentally delayed, and normally developing children*. Unpublished master's thesis, University of North Carolina, Greensboro.

Eskes, G. A., Bryson, S. E., & McCormick, T. A. (1990). Comprehension of concrete and abstract words in autistic children. *Journal of Autism and Developmental Disorders*, *20*, 61–73.

Fay, W. (1969). On the basis of autistic echolalia. *Journal of Communication Disorders*, *2*, 38–47.

Fay, W., & Schuler, A. L. (1980). *Emerging language in autistic children*. Baltimore, MD: University Park Press.

Fein, D., & Waterhouse, L. (1979). *Autism is not a disorder of language*. Paper presented at the meeting of the New England Child Language Association, Boston, MA.

Fenson, L., Dale, P., Reznick, J., Bates, E., Thal, D., & Pethick, S. (1994). Variability in early communicative development. *Monographs of the Society for Research in Child Development*, *59* (5, Serial No. 242), i–185.

Fernald, A. (1992). Human maternal vocalizations to infants as biologically relevant signals: An evolutionary perspective. In J. H. Barkow, L. Cosmides, & J. Tooby (Eds.), *The adapted mind: Evolutionary psychology and the generation of culture* (pp. 391–428). New York, NY: Oxford University Press.

Ferrari, V., Gallese, G., Rizzolatti, G., & Fogassi, L. (2003). Mirror neurons responding to the observation of ingestive and communicative mouth actions in the monkey ventral premotor cortex. *European Journal of Neuroscience*, *17*, 1703–1714.

Fraiberg, S., & Fraiberg, L. (1977). *Insights from the blind: Comparative studies of blind and sighted infants*. New York, NY: Basic Books.

Frith, U. (1969). Emphasis and meaning in recall in normal and autistic children. *Language and Speech*, *2*, 29–38.

Frith, U. (1989). *Autism: Explaining the enigma*. New York, NY: Blackwell.

Gaddes, J. (1984). *Probable events and sentence comprehension in autistic children*. Unpublished senior honors thesis, University of Alberta, Edmonton, Alberta.

Gaffrey, M. S., Kleinhans, N. M., Haist, F., Akshoomoff, N., Campbell, A., Courchesne, E., & Miller, R. A. (2007). Atypical participation of visual cortex during word processing in autism: An fMRI study of semantic decision. *Neuropsychologia*, *45*, 1672–1684.

Ghaziuddin, M., & Gerstein, L. (1996). Pedantic speaking style differentiates Asperger syndrome from high-functioning autism. *Journal of Autism and Developmental Disorders*, *26*, 585–595.

Ghaziuddin, M., Tsai, L., & Ghaziuddin, N. (1992). Brief report: A comparison of the diagnostic criteria for Asperger syndrome. *Journal of Autism and Developmental Disorders*, *22*, 643–649.

Goldberg, W., Osann, K., Filipek, P., Laulhere, T., Jarvis, K., Modahl, C., Flodman, P. O., & Spence, M. A. (2003). Language and other regression: Assessment and timing. *Journal of Autism and Developmental Disorders*, *33*, 607–616.

Goldfarb, W., Braunstein, P., & Lorge, I. (1956). A study of speech patterns in a group of schizophrenic children. *American Journal of Orthopsychiatry*, *26*, 544–555.

Goldstein, H. (2002). Communication Intervention for children with autism: A review of treatment efficacy. *Journal of Autism and Developmental Disorders*, *32*, 373–396.

Gopnik, A., & Meltzoff, A. (1987). The development of categorization in the second year and its relation to other cognitive and linguistic developments. *Child Development*, *58*, 1523–1531.

Gray, C. (2000). *The new social story book*. Arlington, TX: Future Horizons.

Grigorenko, E., Klin, A., & Volkmar, F. (2003). Hyperlexia: Disability or superablity? *Journal of Child Psychology and Psychiatry*, *44*, 1079–1091.

Guiraud, J. A., Tomalski, P., Kushnerenko, E., Ribeiro, H., Davies, K., Charman, T., . . . BASIS Team. (2012). Atypical audiovisual speech integration in infants at risk for autism. *PLoS ONE*, *7*, 1–6.

Halliday, M. A. K. (1975). *Learning how to mean: Exploration in the development of language*. London, England: Edward Arnold.

Harris, G. J., Chabris, C. F., Clark, J., Urban, T., Aharon, I., Steele, S., ... Tager-Flusberg, H. (2006). Brain activation during semantic processing in ASDs via functional magnetic resonance imaging. *Brain and Cognition*, *61*, 54–68.

Hellreigel, C., Tao, L., DiLavore, P., & Lord, C. (1995). *The effect of context on nonverbal social behaviors of very young autistic children*. Paper presented at the biannual meetings of the Society for Research in Child Development, Indianapolis, IN.

Hemphill, L., Picardi, N., & Tager-Flusberg, H. (1991). Narrative as an index of communicative competence in mildly mentally retarded children. *Applied Psycholinguistics*, *12*, 263–279.

Herbert, M. R., Harris, G. J., Adrien, K. T., Makris, N., Kennedy, D. N., Lange, N.T., ... Caviness, V. S. (2002). Abnormal asymmetry in language association cortex in autism. *Annals of Neurology*, *52*, 588–596.

Hobson, R. P. (1984). Early childhood autism and the question of egocentrism. *Journal of Autism and Developmental Disorders*, *14*, 85–104.

Hobson, R. P., & Lee, A. (1989). Emotion-related and abstract concepts in autistic people: Evidence from the British Picture Vocabulary Scale. *Journal of Autism and Developmental Disorders*, *19*, 601–623.

Howlin, P. (1984). The acquisition of grammatical morphemes in autistic children: A critique and replication of the findings of Bartolucci, Pierce, and Streiner, 1980. *Journal of Autism and Developmental Disorders*, *14*, 127–136.

Howlin, P. (2003). Outcome in high-functioning adults with autism with and without early language delays: Implications for the differentiation between autism and Asperger syndrome. *Autism and Development Disorders*, *33*, 3–13.

Howlin, P., Goode, S., Hutton, J., & Rutter, M. (2004). Adult outcome for children with autism. *Journal of Child Psychology and Psychiatry*, *45*, 212–229.

Hurtig, R., Ensrud, S., & Tomblin, J. B. (1980). *Question production in autistic children: A linguistic pragmatic perspective*. Paper presented at the University of Wisconsin Symposium on Research in Child Language Disorders, Madison.

Hus, V., Taylor, A., & Lord. C. (2011). Telescoping of caregiver report on the Autism Diagnostic Interview—Revised. *Journal of Child Psychology and Psychiatry*, *52*, 753–760.

Huttenlocher, J. (1974). The origins of language comprehension. In R. L. Solso (Ed.), *Theories in cognitive psychology* (pp. 331–368). Hillsdale, NJ: Erlbaum.

Jarrold, C., Boucher, J., & Russell, J. (1997). Language profiles in children with autism: Theoretical and methodological implications. *Autism*, *1*, 57–76.

Just, M. A., Cherkassky, V. L., Keller, T. A., & Minshew, N. J. (2004). Cortical activation and synchronization during sentence comprehension in high-functioning autism: Evidence of underconnectivity. *Brain*, *127*, 1811–1821.

Kanner, L. (1943). Autistic disturbances of affective contact. *Nervous Child*, *2*, 217–250.

Kanner, L. (1946). Irrelevant and metaphorical language. *American Journal of Psychiatry*, *103*, 242–246.

Kjelgaard, M., & Tager-Flusberg, H. (2001). An investigation of language impairment in autism: Implications for genetic subgroups. *Language and Cognitive Processes*, *16*, 287–308.

Klin, A. (1991). Young autistic children's listening preferences in regard to speech: A possible characterization of the symptom of social withdrawal. *Journal of Autism and Developmental Disorders*, *21*, 29–42.

Klin, A., & Volkmar, F. (1997). Asperger's syndrome. In D. J. Cohen & F. R. Volkmar (Eds.), *Handbook of autism and pervasive developmental disorders* (pp. 94–122). New York, NY: Wiley.

Knaus, T., Silver, A., Lindgren, K., Hadjikhani, N., & Tager-Flusberg, H. (2008). fMRI activation during a language task in adolescents with ASD. *Journal of the International Neuropsychological Society*, *14*, 967–979.

Koning, C., & Magill-Evans, J. (2001). Social and language skills in adolescent boys with Asperger syndrome. *Autism*, *5*(1), 23–36.

Konstantareas, M., Zajdemann, H., Homatidis, S., & McCabe, A. (1988). Maternal speech to verbal and higher functioning versus nonverbal and lower functioning autistic children. *Journal of Autism and Developmental Disorders*, *18*, 647–656.

Krantz, P. J., & McClannahan, L. E. (1998). Social interaction skills for children with autism: A script-fading procedure for beginning readers. *Journal of Applied Behavior Analysis*, *31*, 191–202.

Kurita, H. (1985). Infantile autism with speech loss before the age of 30 months. *Journal of the American Academy of Child Psychiatry*, *24*, 191–196.

Landa, R. (2000). Social language use in Asperger syndrome and high-functioning autism. In A. Klin, F. Volkmar, & S. Sparrow (Eds.), *Asperger syndrome* (pp. 125–155). New York, NY: Guilford Press.

Landry, S. H., & Loveland, K. A. (1989). The effect of social context on the functional communication skills of autistic children. *Journal of Autism and Developmental Disorders*, *19*(2), 283–299.

Le Couteur, A., Bailey, A., Rutter, M., & Gottesman, I. (1989). *Epidemiologically based twin study of autism*. Paper presented at the First World Congress on Psychiatric Genetics, Churchill College, Cambridge, England.

Lee, A., Hobson, R. P., & Chiat, S. (1994). I, you, me and autism: An experimental study. *Journal of Autism and Developmental Disorders*, *24*, 155–176.

Lempert, H. (1978). Extrasyntactic factors affecting passive sentence comprehension in young children. *Child Development*, *49*, 694–699.

Lindgren, K. A., Folstein, S. E., Tomblin, J. B., & Tager-Flusberg, H. (2009). Language and reading abilities of children with autism spectrum disorders and specific language impairment and their first-degree relatives. *Autism Research*, *2*(1), 22–38.

Loban, W. (1976). *Language development: Kindergarten through grade 12*. Urbana, IL: National Council of Teachers of English.

Lopez, B., & Leekam, S. R. (2003). The use of context in children with autism. *Journal of Child Psychology and Psychiatry*, *44*, 285–300.

Lord, C. (1985). Autism and the comprehension of language. In E. Schopler & G. Mesibov (Eds.), *Communication problems in autism* (pp. 257–281). New York, NY: Plenum Press.

Lord, C. (1995). Follow-up of two year-olds referred for possible autism. *Journal of Child Psychology and Psychiatry, 36*, 1365–1382.

Lord, C., Merrin, D. J., Vest, L., & Kelly, K. M. (1983). Communicative behavior of adults with an autistic four-year-old boy and his nonhandicapped twin brother. *Journal of Autism and Developmental Disorders, 13*, 1–17.

Lord, C., & Pickles, A. (1996). Language level and nonverbal social-communicative behaviors in autistic and language-delayed children. *Journal of the American Academy of Child & Adolescent Psychiatry, 35*(11), 1542–1550.

Lord, C., Pickles, A., DiLavore, P. C., & Shulman, C. (1996). *Longitudinal studies of young children referred for possible autism.* Paper presented at the biannual meetings of the International Society for Research in Child and Adolescent Psychopathology.

Lord, C., Risi, S., Lambrecht, L., Cook, E., Leventhal, B., DiLavore, P., . . . Rutter, M. (2000). The Autism Diagnostic Observation Schedule—Generic: A standard measure of social and communication deficits associated with the spectrum of autism. *Journal of Autism and Developmental Disorders, 30*, 205–223.

Lord, C., & Rutter, M. (1994). Autism and pervasive developmental disorders. In M. Rutter, L. Hersov, & E. Taylor (Eds.), *Child and adolescent psychiatry: Modern approaches.* (3rd ed., pp. 569–593). Oxford, England: Blackwell.

Lord, C., Rutter, M., Goode, S., Heemsbergen, J., Jordan, H., Mawhood, L., & Schopler, E. (1989). Autism Diagnostic Observation Schedule: A standardized observation of communicative and social behavior. *Journal of Autism and Developmental Disorders, 19*, 185–212.

Lord, C., Rutter, M., & Le Couteur, A. (1994). Autism Diagnostic Interview—Revised: A revised version of a diagnostic interview for caregivers of individuals with possible pervasive developmental disorders. *Journal of Autism and Developmental Disorders, 24*, 659–685.

Lord, C., Shulman, C., & DiLavore, P. (2004). Regression and word loss in autistic sptectrum disorders. *Journal of Child Psychology and Psychiatry, 45*, 936–955.

Lord, C., Storoschuk, S., Rutter, M., & Pickles, A. (1993). Using the ADI-R to diagnose autism in preschool children. *Infant Mental Health Journal, 14*, 234–252.

Lord, C., & Venter, A. (1992). Outcome and follow-up studies of high-functioning autistic individuals. In E. Schopler & G. Mesibov (Eds.), *High-functioning individuals with autism* (pp. 187–199). New York, NY: Plenum Press.

Loukusa, S., Leinonen, E., Kuusikko, S., Jussila, K., Mattila, M. L., Ryder, N., . . . Moilanen, I. (2007). Use of context in pragmatic language comprehension by children with Asperger syndrome or high-functioning autism. *Journal of Autism and Developmental Disorders, 37*(6), 1049–1059.

Lovaas, O. I. (1977). *The autistic child.* New York, NY: Irvington.

Loveland, K. (1984). Learning about points of view: Spatial perspective and the acquisition of "I/you." *Journal of Child Language, 11*, 535–556.

Loveland, K. A. (1991). Social affordances and interaction: II. Autism and the affordances of the human environment. *Ecological Psychology, 3*, 99–119.

Loveland, K. A., McEvoy, R. E., Tunali, B., & Kelley, M. L. (1990). Narrative story telling in autism and Down's syndrome. *British Journal of Developmental Psychology, 8*, 9–23.

Loveland, K., & Tunali, B. (1993). Narrative language in autism and the theory of mind hypothesis: A wider perspective. In S. Baron-Cohen, H. Tager-Flusberg, & D. J. Cohen (Eds.), *Understanding other minds: Perspectives from autism* (pp. 237–253). Oxford, England: Oxford University Press.

Loveland, K., & Tunali-Kotoski, B. (1997). The school-age child with autism. In D. Cohen & F. Volkmar (Eds.), *Handbook of autism and pervasive developmental disorders* (pp. 283–308). New York, NY: Wiley.

Luyster, R. J., Kadlec, M. B., Carter, A., & Tager-Flusberg, H. (2008). Language assessment and development in toddlers with autism spectrum disorders. *Journal of Autism and Developmental Disorders, 38*(8), 1426–1438.

Luyster, R., Richler, J., Risi, S., Hsu, W. L., Dawson, G., Bernier, R., . . . Lord, C. (2005). Early regression in social communication in autism spectrum disorders: A CPEA Study. *Developmental Neuropsychology, 27*(3), 311–336.

Magiati, I., Moss, J., Charman, T., & Howlin, P. (2011). Patterns of change in children with ASDs who received community based comprehensive interventions in their pre-school years: A seven year follow-up study. *Research in ASDs, 5*, 1016–1027.

Mason, R. A., Williams, D. L., Kana, R. K., Minshew, N., & Just, M. A. (2008). Theory of mind disruption and recruitment of the right hemisphere during narrative comprehension in autism. *Neuropsychologia, 46*, 269–280.

Mayes, L., Volkmar, F., Hooks, M., & Cicchetti, D. (1993). Differentiating pervasive developmental disorder-not otherwise specified from autism and language disorders. *Journal of Autism and Developmental Disorders, 23*, 79–90.

McCann, J., Peppé, S., Gibbon, F. E., O'Hare, A., & Rutherford, M. (2007). Prosody and its relationship to language in school-aged children with high-functioning autism. *International Journal of Language & Communication Disorders, 42*(6), 682–702.

McCleery, J., Ceponiene, R., Burner, K., Townsend, J., Kinnear, M., & Schreibman, L. (2010). Neural correlates of verbal and nonverbal semantic integration in children with autism. *Journal of Child Psychology and Psychiatry, 51*, 277–286.

McEvoy, R. E., Loveland, K. A., & Landry, S. H. (1988). The functions of immediate echolalia in autistic children: A developmental perspective. *Journal of Autism and Developmental Disorders, 18*, 657–668.

McHale, S., Simeonsson, R. J., Marcus, L. M., & Olley, J. G. (1980). The social and symbolic quality of autistic children's communication. *Journal of Autism and Developmental Disorders, 10*, 299–310.

Merewether, F. C., & Alpert, M. (1990). The components and neuroanatomic bases of prosody. *Journal of Communication Disorders, 23*, 325–336.

Mermelstein, R. (1983). *The relationship between syntactic and pragmatic development in autistic, retarded, and normal children*. Paper presented to the Eighth Annual Boston University Conference on Language Development, Boston, MA.

Mitchell, S., Brian, J., Zwaigenbaum, L., Roberts, W., Szatmari, P., Smith, I., & Bryson, S. (2006). Early language and communication development of infants later diagnoses with ASD. *Developmental and Behavioral Pediatrics, 27*, 69–78.

Miller, J., & Chapman, R. S. (1981). The relation between age and mean length of utterance in morphemes. *Journal of Speech and Hearing Research, 24*, 154–162.

Minshew, N. J., & Goldstein, G. (1993). Is autism an amnesic disorder? Evidence from the California Verbal Learning Test. *Neuropsychology, 7*, 209–216.

Mullen, E. (1995). *Mullen Scales of Early Learning*. Circle Pines, MN: American Guidance Service.

Mundy, P., Sigman, M., Ungerer, J., & Sherman, T. (1987). Nonverbal communication and play correlates of language development in autistic children. *Journal of Autism and Developmental Disorders, 17*, 349–364.

Myles, B., Hilgenfeld, T., Barnhill, G., Griswold, D., Hagiwara, T., & Simpson, R. (2002). Analysis of reading skills in individuals with Asperger syndrome. *Focus on Autism & Other Developmental Disabilities, 17*, 1088–3576.

Nation, K. (1999). Reading skills in hyperlexia: A developmental perspective. *Psychological Bulletin, 125*(3), 338–355.

Nation, K., Clarke, P., Wright, B., & Williams, C. (2006). Patterns of reading ability in children with ASD. *Journal of Autism and Developmental Disorders, 36*, 911–919.

Nazzi, T., & Bertoninci, J. (2003). Before and after the vocabulary spurt: Two modes of word acquisition. *Developmental Science, 6*, 136–142.

Norbury, C. F., & Bishop, D. V. (2002). Inferential processing and story recall in children with communication problems: A comparison of specific language impairment, pragmatic language impairment and high-functioning autism. *International Journal of Language and Communication Disorders, 37*, 227–251.

Norbury, C., & Bishop, D. V. M. (2003). Narrative skills of children with communication impairments. *International Journal of Language and Communication Disorders, 38*, 287–314.

Norbury, C. F., Gemmell, T., & Paul, R. (2013, April). Pragmatics abilities in narrative production: A cross-disorder comparison. *Journal of Child Language, 1–26*.

Oberman, L. M., & Ramachandran, V. S. (2007). The simulating social mind: The role of the mirror neuron system and simulation in the social and communicative deficits of autism spectrum disorders. *Psychological Bulletin, 133*(2), 310–327.

Osterling, J., & Dawson, G. (1994). Early recognition of children with autism: A study of first birthday home videotapes. *Journal of Autism and Developmental Disorders, 24*, 247–258.

Ozonoff, S., Pennington, B. F., & Rogers, S. J. (1990). Are there emotion perception deficits in young autistic children? *Journal of Child Psychology and Psychiatry, 31*, 343–362.

Patterson, M. L., & Werker, J. F. (1999). Matching phonetic information in lips and voice is robust in 4.5-month-old infants. *Infant Behavior and Development, 22*, 237–247.

Paul, R. (1985). The emergence of pragmatic comprehension: A study of children's understanding of sentence-structure cues to given/new information. *Journal of Child Language, 12*, 161–179.

Paul, R., Augustyn, A., Klin, A., & Volkmar, F. (2005). Perception and production of prosody by speakers with ASDs. *Journal of Autism and Developmental Disorders, 35*, 205–220.

Paul, R., Chapman, R. S., & Wanska, S. (1980). *The development of complex sentence use*. Paper presented at the meeting of the American Speech and Hearing Association, Detroit, MI.

Paul, R., Chawarska, K., Cicchetti, D., & Volkmar, F. (2008). Langauge outcomes of toddlres with autism spectrum disorders: A two year follow-up. *Autism Research, 1*, 97–107.

Paul, R., Chawarska, K., Fowler, C., Cicchetti, D., & Volkmar, F. (2007). "Listen my children and you shall hear": Auditory preferences in toddlers with ASDs. *Journal of Speech, Langauge, and Hearing Research, 50*, 1350–1364.

Paul, R., Chawarska, K., & Volkmar, F. (2008). Differentiating ASD from DLD in toddlers. *Perspectives on Language Learning Disorders, 15*, 101–111.

Paul, R., & Cohen, D. J. (1984a). Outcomes of severe disorders of language acquisition. *Journal of Autism and Developmental Disorders, 14*, 405–422.

Paul, R., & Cohen, D. J. (1984b). Responses to contingent queries in adults with mental retardation and pervasive developmental disorders. *Applied Psycholinguistics, 349–357*.

Paul, R., & Cohen, D. J. (1985). Comprehension of indirect requests in adults with mental retardation and pervasive developmental disorders. *Journal of Speech and Hearing Research, 28*, 475–479.

Paul, R., Cohen, D. J., & Caparulo, B. K. (1983). A longitudinal study of patients with severe developmental disorders of language learning. *Journal of the American Academy of Child Psychiatry, 22*, 525–534.

Paul, R., & Feldman, C. (1984). *Communication deficits in autism*. Paper presented at the Institute for Communication Deficits in Autistic Youth, Columbia University, New York, NY.

Paul, R., Fischer, M. L., & Cohen, D. (1988). Sentence comprehension strategies in children with autism and specific language disorders. *Journal of Autism and Developmental Disorders, 18*, 669–680.

Paul, R., Fuerst, Y., Ramsay, G., Chawarska, K., & Klin, A. (2010). Out of the mouths of babes: Vocal production in infant siblings of children with ASD. *Journal of Child Psychology and Psychiatry, 52*, 588–598.

Paul, R., Orlovski, S., Marchinko, H., & Volkmar, F. (2009). Conversational behaviors in youth with high-functioning autism and Asperger syndrome. *Journal of Autism and Developmental Disorders, 39*, 115–125.

Paul, R., Shriberg, L. D., McSweeny, J., Cicchetti, D., Klin, A., & Volkmar, F. (2005). Brief report: Relations between prosodic performance and communication and socialization ratings in high functioning speakers with ASDs. *Journal of Autism and Developmental Disorders, 35*, 861–869.

Paul, R., & Weismer, E. S. (in press). Late talking in context: The clinical implications of delayed language development. In L. Rescorla & P. Dale (Eds.), *Late talkers: From research to practice*. New York, NY: Paul H. Brookes.

Perkins, T., Stokes, M., McGillivray, J., & Bittar, R. (2010). Mirror neuron dysfunction in autism spectrum disorders. *Journal of Clinical Neuroscience*, *17*(10), 1239–1243.

Peters, A. (1983). *The units of language acquisition*. New York, NY: Cambridge University Press.

Pierce, S., & Bartolucci, G. (1977). A syntactic investigation of verbal autistic, mentally retarded, and normal children. *Journal of Autism and Childhood Schizophrenia*, *7*, 121–134.

Pinker, S. (1999). How the mind works. *Annals of the New York Academy of Sciences*, *882*, 119–127.

Prizant, B. M. (1983). Echolalia in autism: Assessment and intervention. *Seminars in Speech and Language*, *4*, 63–77.

Prizant, B., & Duchan, J. (1981). The functions of immediate echolalia in autistic children. *Journal of Speech and Hearing Disorders*, *46*, 241–249.

Pronovost, W., Wakstein, M., & Wakstein, D. (1966). A longitudinal study of speech behavior and language comprehension in fourteen children diagnosed as atypical or autistic. *Exceptional Children*, *33*, 19–26.

Ramberg, C., Ehlers, S., Nyden, A., Johansson, M., & Gillberg, C. (1996). Language and pragmatic functions in school-age children on the autism spectrum. *European Journal of Disorders of Communication*, *31*(4), 387–413.

Rapin, I., Dunn, M., Allen, D., Stevens, M., & Fein, D. (2009). Subtypes of language disorders in school-age children with autism. *Developmental Neuropsychology*, *34*, 66–84.

Rice, M. L. (2004). Growth models of developmental language disorders. In M. L. Rice & S. F. Warren (Eds.), *Developmental language disorders: From phenotypes to etiologies* (pp. 207–240). Mahwah, NJ: Erlbaum.

Rice, M. L., Wexler, K., & and Cleave, P. L. (1995). Specific language impairment as a period of extended optional infinitive, *Journal of Speech and Hearing Research*, *38*, 850–863.

Richler, J., Luyster, R., Risi, S., Hsu, W. L., Dawson, G., Bernier, R., ... Lord, C. (2006). Is there a "regressive phenotype" of autism spectrum disorder associated with the measles-mumps-rubella vaccine? A CPEA Study. *Journal of Autism and Developmental Disorders*, *36*(3), 299–316.

Ricks, D. M., & Wing, L. (1976). Language, communication and use of symbols. In L. Wing (Ed.), *Early childhood autism* (pp. 93–134). Oxford, England: Pergamon Press.

Roberts, J., Rice, M., & Tager-Flusberg, H. (2004). Tense marking in children with autism. *Applied Psycholinguistics*, *25*, 429–448.

Rogers, S. (2006). Evidence-based interventions for language development in young children with autism. In T. Charman & W. Stone (Eds.), *Social and communication development in autism spectrum disorders* (pp. 143–179). New York, NY: Guildford Press.

Rojas, D., Bawn, S., Benkers, T., Reite, M., & Rogers, S. (2002). Smaller left hemisphere planum temporale in adults with autistic disorder. *Neuroscience Letters*, *328*, 237–240.

Rumsey, J. M., Rapoport, M. D., & Sceery, W. R. (1985). Autistic children as adults: Psychiatric, social, and behavioral outcomes. *Journal of the American Academy of Child Psychiatry*, *24*, 465–473.

Rutter, M. (1970). Autistic children: Infancy to adulthood. *Seminars in Psychiatry*, *2*, 435–450.

Rutter, M., Le Couteur, A., & Lord, C. (2003). Autism Diagnostic Interview—Revised (ADI-R). Los Angeles, CA: Western Psychological Services.

Rutter, M., & Lord, C. (1987). Language impairment associated with psychiatric disorder. In W. Yule, M. Rutter, & M. Bax (Eds.), *Language development and disorders: Clinic in Developmental Medicine, 101/102* (pp. 206–233). London, England: SIMP/Blackwell Scientific and Lippincott.

Rutter, M., Mawhood, L., & Howlin, P. (1992). Language delay and social development. In P. Fletcher & D. Hall (Eds.), *Specific speech and language disorders in children: Correlates, characteristics and outcomes* (pp. 63–78). London, England: Whurr.

Saalasti, S., Lepistö, T., Toppila, E., Kujala, T., Laakso, M., Nieminem-von Wendt, T., & Jansson-Verkasalo, E. (2008). Language abilities in children with Asperger syndrome. *Journal of Autism and Developmental Disorders*, *38*, 1574–1580.

Saldana, D., & Frith, U. (2007). Do readers with autism make bridging inferences from world knowledge? *Journal of Experimental Child Psychology*, *96*, 310–319

Scarborough, H. S., Rescorla, L., Tager-Flusberg, H., Fowler, A. E., & Sudhalter, V. (1991). The relation of utterance length to grammatical complexity in normal and language-disordered groups. *Applied Psycholinguistics*, *12*, 23–45.

Schoen, E., Paul, R., & Chawarska, K. (2011). Phonology and vocal behaviors in toddlers with ASDs. *Autism Research*, *4*, 177–188.

Seung, H. K. (2007). Linguistic characteristics of individuals with high-functioning autism and Asperger syndrome. *Clinical Linguistics and Phonetics*, *21*, 247–259.

Shapiro, T. (1977). The quest for a linguistic model to study the speech of autistic children: Studies of echoing. *Journal of the American Academy of Child Psychiatry*, *16*, 608–619.

Sheinkopf, S. J., Mundy, P., Oller, D. K., & Steffens, M. (2000). Vocal atypicalities of preverbal autistic children. *Journal of Autism and Developmental Disorders*, *30*(4), 345–354.

Short, C. B., & Schopler, E. (1988). Factors relating to age of onset in autism. *Journal of Autism and Developmental Disorders*, *18*, 207–216.

Shriberg, L., Paul, R., Black, L., & van Santen, J. (2011). The hypothesis of apraxia of speech in children with ASD. *Journal of Autism and Developmental Disorders*, *41*, 405–426.

Shriberg, L., Paul, R., McSweeney, J., Klin, A., Cohen, D., & Volkmar, F. (2001). Speech and prosody characteristics of adolescents and adults with high-functioning autism and AS. *Journal of Speech, Language, and Hearing Research*, *44*, 1097–1115.

Shulman, C., & Guberman, A. (2007). Acquisition of verb meaning through syntactic cues: A comparison of children with autism, children with specific language impairment, and children with normal language development. *Journal of Child Language*, *34*, 411–423.

Siegel, B., Vukicevic, J., Elliott, G., & Kraemer, H. (1989). The use of signal detection theory to assess *DSM-III-R* criteria for autistic disorder. *Journal of the American Academy of Child & Adolescent Psychiatry*, *28*, 542–548.

Sigman, M., & McGovern, C. (2005). Improvement in cognitive and language skills from preschool to adolescence in autism. *Journal of Autism and Developmental Disorders*, *35*, 15–23.

Sigman, M., & Ungerer, J. (1981). Sensorimotor skills and language comprehension in autistic children. *Journal of Abnormal Child Psychology*, *9*, 149–166.

Siller, M., & Sigman, M. (2002). The behaviors of parents of children with autism predict the subsequent development of their children's communication. *Journal of Autism and Developmental Disorders*, *32*, 77–89.

St. James, P. J., & Tager-Flusberg, H. (1994). An observational study of humor in autism and Down syndrome. *Journal of Autism and Developmental Disorders*, *24*, 603–617.

Stone, W. L., & Caro-Martinez, L. M. (1990). Naturalistic observations of spontaneous communication in autistic children. *Journal of Autism and Developmental Disorders*, *20*, 437–453.

Stone, W., Lemanek, K., Fishel, P., Fernandez, M., & Altemeier, W. (1990). Play and imitation skills in the diagnosis of autism in young children. *Pediatrics*, *86*, 267–272.

Stone, W., Ousley, O. Y., & Littleford, C. (1997). Motor imitation in young children with autism: What's the object? *Journal of Abnormal Child Psychology*, *25*, 475–485.

Storoschuk, S., Lord, C., & Jaedicke, S. (1995). *Autism and the use of mental verbs*. Paper presented at the Society for Research in child Development, Indianapolis, IN.

Surian, L., Baron-Cohen, S., & Van der Lely, H. (1996). Are children with autism deaf to Gricean maxims? *Cognitive Neuropsychiatry*, *1*, 55–72.

Tager-Flusberg, H. (1981). Sentence comprehension in autistic children. *Applied Psycholinguistics*, *2*, 5–24.

Tager-Flusberg, H. (1985). The conceptual basis for referential word meaning in children with autism. *Child Development*, *56*, 1167–1178.

Tager-Flusberg, H. (1989). A psycholinguistic perspective on language development in the autistic child. In G. Dawson (Ed.), *Autism: New directions in diagnosis, nature and treatment*, (pp. 92–115). New York, NY: Guilford Press.

Tager-Flusberg, H. (1991). Semantic processing in the free recall of autistic children: Further evidence for a cognitive deficit, *British Journal of Developmental Psychology*, *9*, 417–430.

Tager-Flusberg, H. (1992). Autistic children's talk about psychological states: Deficits in the early acquisition of a theory of mind. *Child Development*, *63*, 161–172.

Tager-Flusberg, H. (1993). What language reveals about the understanding of minds in children with autism. In S. Baron-Cohen, H. Tager-Flusberg, & D. J. Cohen (Eds.), *Understanding other minds: Perspectives from autism* (pp. 138–157). Oxford, England: Oxford University Press.

Tager-Flusberg, H. (1994). Dissociations in form and function in the acquisition of language by autistic children. In H. Tager-Flusberg (Ed.), *Constraints on language acquisition: Studies of atypical children* (pp. 175–194). Hillsdale, NJ: Erlbaum.

Tager-Flusberg, H. (1995). "Once upon a ribbit": Stories narrated by autistic children. *British Journal of Developmental Psychology*, *13*, 45–59.

Tager-Flusberg, H. (2003). Language impairments in children with complex neurodevelopmental disorders: The case of autism. In Y. Levy & J. Schaeffer (Eds.), *Language competence across populations: Toward a definition of specific language impairment* (pp. 297–321). Mahwah, NJ: Erlbaum.

Tager-Flusberg, H., & Anderson, M. (1991). The development of contingent discourse ability in autistic children. *Journal of Child Psychology and Psychiatry*, *32*, 1123–1134.

Tager-Flusberg, H., & Calkins, S. (1990). Does imitation facilitate the acquisition of grammar? Evidence from a study of autistic, Down syndrome and normal children. *Journal of Child Language*, *17*, 591–606.

Tager-Flusberg, H., Calkins, S., Noin, I., Baumberger, T., Anderson, M., & Chadwick-Denis, A. (1990). A longitudinal study of language acquisition in autistic and Down syndrome children. *Journal of Autism and Developmental Disorders*, *20*, 1–22.

Tager-Flusberg, H., & Joseph, R. M. (2003). Identifying neurocognitive phenotypes in autism. *Philosophical Transactions of the Royal Society, Series B*, *358*, 303–314.

Tager-Flusberg, H., & Sullivan, K. (1994). A second look at second-order belief attribution in autism. *Journal of Autism and Developmental Disorders*, *24*, 577–586.

Taylor, A., (2004). *Telescoping in parent reports an milestones in autism*. Unpublished master's thesis, University of Chicago, IL.

Tesink, C. M. J. Y., Buitelaar, J. K., Petersson, K. M., Van der Gaag, R. J., Kan, C. C., Tendolkar, I., & Hagoort, P. (2009). Neural correlates of pragmatic language comprehension in autism spectrum disorders. *Brain*, *132*(7), 1941–1952.

Thurber, C., & Tager-Flusberg, H. (1993). Pauses in the narratives produced by autistic, mentally retarded, and normal children as an index of cognitive demand. *Journal of Autism and Developmental Disorders*, *23*(2), 309–322.

Tomasello, M., & Kruger, A. C. (1992). Joint attention on actions: Acquiring verbs in ostensive and non-ostensive contexts. *Journal of Child Language*, *19*(2), 311–333.

Turner, L. M., Stone, W. L., Pozdol, S. L., & Coonrod, E. E. (2006). Follow-up of children with ASD from age 2 to age 9, *Autism*, *10*, 243–265.

Van Lancker, D., Cornelius, C., & Needleman, R. (1991). Comprehension of verbal terms for emotions in normal, autistic, and schizophrenic children. *Developmental Neuropsychology*, *7*, 1–18.

Ventner, A., Lord, C., & Schopler, D. (1992). A follow-up study of high-functioning autistic children. *Journal of Child Psychology and Psychiatry*, *33*, 489–507.

Volden, J., & Lord, C. (1991). Neologisms and idiosyncratic language in autistic speakers. *Journal of Autism and Developmental Disorders*, *21*, 109–130.

Volkmar, F. R., Klin, A., Siegal, B., Szatmari, P., Lord, C., Campbell, M., . . . Towbin, K. (1994). Field trial for autistic disorder in *DSM-IV*. *American Journal of Psychiatry*, *151*, 1361–1367.

Wahlberg, T., & Magliano, J. P. (2004). The ability of high function individuals with autism to comprehend written discourse. *Discourse Processes*, *38*(1), 119–144.

Wang, A. T., Lee, S. S., Sigman, M., & Dapretto, M. (2006). Neural basis of irony comprehension in children with autism: The role of prosody and context. *Brain*, *129*, 932–943.

Weir, R. (1962). *Language in the crib*. The Hague, The Netherlands: Mouton.

Weismer, S. E., Gernsbacher, M. A., Stronach, S., Karasinski, C., Eernisse, E. R., Venker, C. E., & Sindberg, H. (2011). Lexical and grammatical skills in toddlers on the autism spectrum compared to late talking toddlers. *Journal of Autism and Developmental Disorders, 41*(8), 1065-1075.

Weismer, S. E., Lord, C., & Esler, A. (2010). Early language patterns of toddlers on the autism spectrum compared to toddlers with developmental delay. *Journal of Autism and Developmental Disorders, 40*, 1259–1273.

Wetherby, A. (1986). Ontogeny of communication functions in autism. *Journal of Autism and Developmental Disorders, 16*, 295–316.

Wetherby, A. M., & Prutting, C. A. (1984). Profiles of communicative and cognitive-social abilities in autistic children. *Journal of Speech and Hearing Research, 27*, 364–377.

Whitehouse, A., Maybery, M., & Durkin, K. (2007). Evidence against poor semantic encoding in individuals with autism. *Autism, 11*, 241–254.

Williams, D. L., Goldstein, G., & Minshew, N. J. (2006). Neuropsychologic functioning in children with autism: Further evidence for disordered complex information-processing. *Child Neuropsychology, 12*, 279–298.

Wing, L. (1981). Asperger's syndrome: A clinical account. *Journal of Autism and Developmental Disorders, 9*, 11–29.

Young, G. S., Merin, N., Rogers, S., & Ozonoff, S. (2009). Gaze behavior and affect at 6-months: Predicting clinical outcomes and language development in typically developing infants and infants at-risk for autism. *Developmental Science, 12*, 798–814.

Yule, W., & Rutter, M. (1987). *Language development and disorders*. London, England: MacKeith.

Ziatas, K., Durkin, K., & Pratt, C. (2003). Differences in assertive speech acts produced by children with autism, Asperger syndrome, specific language impairment, and normal development. *Development and Psychopathology, 15*, 73–94.

CHAPTER 11

Play Development in Children With Autism Spectrum Disorders: Skills, Object Play, and Interventions

CONNIE KASARI AND YA-CHIH CHANG

In his case descriptions of autism, Kanner (1943) noted that "children are able to establish and maintain an excellent relationship with objects, that does not threaten to interfere with their aloneness, but are from the start anxiously and tensely impervious to people" (p. 249). Such an observation suggests that children are unimpaired in their engagement with objects; rather the impairment is primarily with people. Researchers and clinicians have debated this observation over the years.

Since Kanner's original observations, much has been written about object engagement in children

with autism spectrum disorders (ASDs), specifically play with objects. Overall, development of play skills proves challenging for children with ASD. However, it is an area of development that is critical to many areas of learning. Children with ASD who play symbolically are more likely to communicate with spoken language and have better peer interactions (Mundy, Sigman, Ungerer, & Sherman, 1987; Sigman & Ruskin, 1999). Therefore, play skills are important to consider in the development of children with autism. In this chapter, we (1) briefly review the nature of play and how it relates to children with autism, (2) describe current interventions for children with autism that target play skills, (3) evaluate the interventions in the past decade, and (4) discuss the implications from these studies with an eye toward remaining gaps in our understanding. We are focusing our review

Note: Preparation of this chapter was supported by the U.S. Department of Health and Human Resources: Autism Intervention Research Network for Behavioral Health (AIR-B) [UA3MC11055], Autism Speaks grant (#7495), and NIH RO1 MH84864.

on object play typically seen during the preschool period, especially functional and symbolic play. Please see Chapter 6, "School-Age Children With ASD," for a detailed description about play with peers, friendship relations, and aspects of play appropriate to the 6- to 12-year period.

PLAY IN TYPICAL DEVELOPMENT

The development of object play skills has been well characterized for typically developing children. According to Piaget, infants start manipulating objects as a means of exploring their environment between 4 and 8 months of age (Ginsburg & Opper, 1988). Exploration of objects becomes more differentiated in the next months when children start to discriminate their actions, such as pushing a button to activate a toy or hitting a stick on a drum. In the second year, children begin to use objects in more differentiated and functional ways. They may push a car, stack blocks or extend familiar actions to dolls (e.g., feeding a doll) (Sigman & Ungerer, 1984). All of these actions use objects in ways in which they were intended, and this developmental phase of play behavior is characterized as *functional play*.

Later, in the second and third years of life, typically developing children will use objects symbolically. During this stage of development, children understand symbols and can perform nonliteral play acts (Casby, 2003). For example, children start using certain objects to represent different objects (i.e., substitution), manipulate and move dolls as if they are capable of actions (i.e., doll as agent), and role-play to pretend as though they are different characters such as mommy and baby (i.e., sociodramatic play) (Rutherford, Young, Hepburn, & Rogers, 2007). Symbolic play can be complex, as children use more spoken language when they are engaged in this type of play.

While object play skills are certainly important, young children generally do not play alone, or in isolation, at least not for very long periods. They often use their play skills and interests to engage in social interactions with others. For young children, this can be a one-on-one play interaction with their caregivers, or it can also be a social interaction with other children. For the purposes of this chapter, we will focus on the social play with objects that develops between children and their caregivers. Social play in which children are able to incorporate objects and people usually emerges between 9 and 15 months of age in typical development, becoming more symbolic, referential, and elaborated throughout the first years of life (Adamson, Bakeman, & Deckner, 2004).

According to Lifter, Mason, and Barton (2011), the central aspect of play consists of spontaneous, naturally occurring activities with objects within a social interaction. The social interaction aspect of play is less emphasized than object play in the literature, but is a foundational part of play that enriches young children's cognitive, language, and social development through social learning processes. Through this process of social engagement, children learn and utilize various skills that can be categorized as functional or symbolic in nature. When children are engaged in a play interaction with a social partner, they might watch their social partner and imitate what the partner does (i.e., imitation of new skills), formulate creative ideas of what to do (i.e., cognitive development), use words to describe what they are doing (i.e., language development), and involve the social partner in the interaction (i.e., social development). Most importantly, social play is fundamentally spontaneous and fun—there is no rubric for play. This inherent fun nature of play provides the motivation to foster subsequent developmental skills.

PLAY CHARACTERISTICS OF CHILDREN WITH AUTISM

Describing children with autism, Kanner (1943) noted that Donald was "constantly happy and busy entertaining himself, but resented being urged to play with certain things. Most of his actions were repetitions carried out in exactly the same way in which they had been performed originally. If he spun a block, he must always start with the same face uppermost" (p. 218). Alfred at 3.5 years, "spotted a train in the toy cabinet, took it out, and connected and disconnected the cars in a slow, monotonous manner. He kept saying many times, 'More train—more train—more train.' He repeatedly counted the windows. He could not in any way be distracted from the trains" (p. 234). "Elaine was very restless but when allowed to look at pictures, play alone with blocks, draw, or string beads, she could entertain herself contentedly for hours" (p. 240). Thus, Kanner noted that the children had intense, repetitive interactions with objects that seemingly caught their attention more than did the people around them. Unlike typical children who often seek others to join their play, children with autism played alone and contentedly for hours with objects. Their play skills generally were not at their expected age level, and they rarely engaged in social play with others. Indeed, they actively pushed people away from their own involvement with objects.

Since Kanner's original descriptions of children with autism, there have been many studies of the play behaviors of children with autism. Play behaviors are typically assessed directly by an examiner, or observed as the child is provided with a range of toys with and without a social partner. The autism field generally has focused on the distinctions between children's expression of functional and symbolic play skills, often from assessments, and less often on spontaneous use of play skills in interactions with others. Social play has been deemphasized (other than general play with peers).

FUNCTIONAL PLAY IN CHILDREN WITH AUTISM: LEVEL, TYPE, AND FREQUENCY

Functional play is defined as the use of objects in ways in which the object is conventionally used, that is, socially defined. For example, a child may push the truck into the garage or put the spoon in the bowl; these are expected actions with the toys. Generally, children with autism are better at playing at a functional level of play than at a symbolic level in which objects are used in imaginative,

pretend ways. There is some debate in the field as to whether functional play skills are preserved or impaired in children with autism. Depending on the comparison sample and the testing context, functional skills may or may not appear impaired. Important considerations in determining whether functional skills are impaired concern how play skills are measured, including the level of functional play, the frequency of play, the type or diversity of functional play acts, whether play skills are measured as spontaneous or in response to a model or prompt, and the overall quality of play. For the purposes of this chapter, we distinguish between level of object play (referring to developmental level of play even within a larger category of play such as functional and symbolic), frequency of object play (how often a play act occurs), and type (i.e., diversity) of object play (refers to multiple play acts within the same level of play that are different from one another). Play can be measured as responsive (especially as children are first learning a new skill) and as spontaneous, when the play act is generated from the child independently. Quality refers to how playful, creative, connected, and fun child behaviors appear to be.

Within functional object play, there are different levels of play including simple (indiscriminate, discriminate, take apart), combination (presentation, general, conventional, physical), and presymbolic (pretend self, child as agent, single scheme) play acts (Kasari, Freeman, & Paparella, 2006; Lifter, Edwards, Avery, Anderson, & Sulzer-Azaroff, 1988). Examining functional object play as a broad category, children with autism can sometimes be comparable to their typical peer counterparts, particularly if these children with autism have high cognitive and language skills. However, the difference between these two groups of children lies within the subcategories of functional object play. For example, Williams, Reddy, and Costall (2001) compared three groups of children of similar mental ages: autism, Down syndrome, and typical development. Even though the children from all three groups spent the same *amount of time* in functional play, there were differences in their subcategorical *levels of functional play*. Children with autism were engaging in more simple play acts, such as pressing a button on a pop-up toy, and the typical children were engaging in more presymbolic play acts, such as extending a miniature cup to self.

While level of functional object play is one issue to examine, type (diversity of play acts) also matters. Children with ASD show limited flexibility in their play acts even within subcategorical levels of play. For example, they may demonstrate multiple instances of the same play act—feeding a doll in the same way, over and over. They may have three frequencies of the behavior, but only one type would be counted for the level of functional play *child as agent* in which the child does some act toward a doll. If the child fed the doll, brushed the doll's hair, and put a hat on the doll's head, the child would have three *frequencies* of child as agent play act, but would also have engaged in three different *types* of child as agent play acts (Ungerer & Sigman, 1981). Frequency of play acts is less important than number of diverse acts, since high frequency may be due to numerous repetitive play acts, while diverse acts indicate flexible and varied play. Showing limited diversity of acts within a level of play suggests that a child may not have completely mastered that level of play.

Similarly, a child may not have mastered a level of play if the child is able to immediately demonstrate a modeled act when asked to imitate (thus, the child responds to the model) but does not initiate the act independently later (showing deferred imitation, for example) or fails to show diversity of play acts at the same play level (e.g., child only feeds the doll, but does not do other acts, such as combing the doll's hair, or putting a hat on the doll that are at the same level of play). In this example, one would want to work on expanding the child's play acts through teaching via multiple strategies (e.g., imitation, modeling, prompting).

The quality of functional play may also appear different for children with autism than for other groups of children. Williams et al. (2001) found that when children with autism engaged in a play act it tended to be a single action play act (e.g., pushing a pop-up toy) without the use of language

or gestures. In contrast, when typically developing children engaged in a play act it was usually in conjunction with language and gestures and directed toward a social partner. In addition to their lack of engagement with their social partners during play, children with autism also show qualitative differences that can include intense scrutiny of an object (e.g., close visual inspection) or acting on the object in unusual ways, such as twisting and spinning the objects over and over, smelling the toy or other unusual behaviors. These actions with objects may be pleasurable to the child, but they may also interfere with engagement with a social partner and learning of functional, appropriate object play skills.

Finally, functional play skills can be measured in two different ways: spontaneous or imitative. Many studies examining play in children with autism have examined the types and frequency of spontaneous functional play acts as a measure of the children's play skills (Kasari et al., 2006; Williams et al., 2001). This type of measurement captures the child's mastered and emerging play skills when an adult is there to provide support. On the other hand, studies have also examined imitative play skills as a form of success for the child. Studies have found that children with autism who are able to imitate object play have better social communication outcomes (Ingersoll, 2008). Whether it is spontaneous or imitative functional play acts, children with autism who have these play skills have better social communication skills.

SYMBOLIC PLAY IN CHILDREN WITH AUTISM

Symbolic play is when children begin to use substitution of an object to represent something else. This requires the child to have mental representations and be able to understand symbols (Ginsburg & Opper, 1988). Similar to functional object play, there are also quantitative and qualitative differences in symbolic play between children with autism, children with other developmental disorders, and typical children (Mundy et al., 1987).

One difference involves onset; the onset of symbolic play in children with autism is delayed relative to other groups (Charman et al., 1997). Also, when children with autism demonstrate symbolic play acts, the *frequency* is diminished relative to typical children and children with Down syndrome (Libby, Powell, Messer, & Jordan, 1998).

Within symbolic play, there are also subcategories: substitution, substitution without object, doll as agent, multischeme sequences, sociodramatic play, and thematic play (Kasari et al., 2006; Lifter et al., 1988). Children with autism rarely demonstrate symbolic play acts, and of the children who do, the most common symbolic play act is object substitution where the child uses one object to represent a different object (Libby et al., 1998). In contrast, typical children matched at the same mental age demonstrated more frequent symbolic play acts and a variety of different types of symbolic play acts (Libby et al., 1998).

THEORIES BEHIND FUNCTIONAL AND SYMBOLIC PLAY SKILL DEFICITS

There are several explanations for the low frequency, level and limited diversity of both functional and symbolic play acts displayed by children with autism. Explanations include (1) a cognitive impairment, (2) a performance deficit, (3) interference due to circumscribed interests, and (4) lack of motivation. The first explanation is that children with autism may have a cognitive deficit that hinders their play abilities (Lifter & Bloom, 1989). Knowledge about objects (i.e., object permanence) and the memory of an object and its functions both contribute to how children play (Lifter & Bloom, 1989). Deficits in functional and symbolic play in children with autism may also be due to a performance deficit (Jarrold, 2003; see Jarrold, Boucher, & Smith, 1993, for a detailed review). For instance, despite the fact that when left on their own, children with autism show reduced generation of symbolic play, they can still carry out pretend play acts when they are given specific play instructions or have been provided with a model of

a play act (Jarold, Boucher, & Smith, 1996; Lewis & Boucher, 1988). This suggests that these children have symbolic play skills but fail to perform unless prompted. Their lack of spontaneous play may be due to factors, such as motivation to "play," difficulties with generation of varying ideas, or an intense interest in specific objects, the third explanation for reductions in frequency and variety of symbolic play acts. For example, if the child has a special interest in cars, the child may have a very well-developed pattern of spinning wheels instead of putting a doll in the toy car and driving it around. The inspection of the object itself in this instance is much more interesting than using the object in a symbolic play routine. The final possibility is that children with autism may lack the motivation to engage in more flexible functional and symbolic play. In other words, children with autism may engage in nonplay acts that can be repetitive and rigid, but inherently pleasurable to them. For example, a child with autism who is fascinated by letters and numbers may like to say the alphabet repeatedly when they see a puzzle of letters, rather than engage in a more functional play act such as placing the alphabet letters in the puzzle board.

SHARED OBJECT PLAY IN CHILDREN WITH AUTISM

Compared to typical children, children with ASD show play skill deficits, but the most noticeable difference may be in the *quality* of their play. In typical development, young children alternate shared positive affect with their caregiver and with objects frequently within the first year of life (Mundy, Kasari, & Sigman, 1992). In contrast, children with autism rarely seek shared affect and object play with others. Instead, they engage in long periods of solitary or object-focused play (Holmes & Willoughby, 2005; Wong & Kasari, 2012). J. A. Hobson, Hobson, Malik, Bargiota, and Caló (2012) found that children with autism would perform the mechanics of play (i.e., functional play acts), but were less playful (e.g., creativity in play, display of positive affect and pleasure) when they were playing with objects and others compared to typical children. The lack of spontaneity and playfulness of play are two qualitative differences that differentiate the play of children with autism and other children (J. A. Hobson et al., 2012; R. P. Hobson, Lee, & Hobson, 2009). Despite the rarity of shared object play in children with autism, they can engage in shared object play if given the appropriate environmental supports (Wong & Kasari, 2012). The implication of this finding is that autism-specific interventions should be helpful for increasing and diversifying object play, both at the level of skills and in social interactions with others. Play skills, however, have infrequently been the focus of targeted interventions, a topic to which we now turn.

INTERVENTIONS TARGETING PLAY SKILLS IN CHILDREN WITH AUTISM

There have been three relatively recent reviews of play interventions for children with autism, describing interventions through 2008. Because more research has been done since these reviews were published, we conducted a review of play interventions between 2001 and the present and evaluated the quality of the study designs using published guidelines. We also attempted to go beyond current reviews that limited their focus to only one type of play (e.g., pretend; Barton & Wolery, 2008) or limited evaluation of outcomes (e.g., no maintenance or generalization; Lang et al., 2009).

Systematic Review of Interventions Targeting Play in Children With Autism

The current review involved a systematic analysis of studies that focused on interventions targeting play in children with autism. A comprehensive search was conducted using the PsychInfo database. The search was limited to peer-reviewed articles in the past decade (2001–present) with the key words *autism*, *play*, and *engagement*. From the initial search, 845 citations were retrieved from the search engine. Studies were only included in the current

review if the study (1) was an experimentally designed intervention study, (2) measured object play pre- and postintervention, and (3) was not a peer-mediated intervention. Based on these criteria, 27 studies were included in the current review.

Most of the intervention studies examining play in children with autism used a single subject design ($n = 18$). Only a few studies were quasi-experimental ($n = 4$) and randomized controlled trials ($n = 5$). Table 11.1 summarizes the (1) participants in the study, (2) type of intervention, (3) play outcomes, (4) maintenance of effects after treatment was withdrawn, and (5) generalization effects.

Participants

Participants in these studies ranged from toddlers (1- to 2-year-olds) to elementary age (7- to 8-year-olds). Forty percent of these studies ($n = 11$) had participants that were elementary aged, 30% had preschoolers, and another 30% had toddlers. Participants varied in their levels of impairment.

Interventions and Outcomes

Of the 27 studies, the majority of the interventions utilized an adult-directed approach that employed applied behavior analysis principles, including prompt hierarchies and reinforcement schedules. The most frequently used intervention model was video modeling ($n = 8$). Children were shown instructional videos on how to play with specific sets of toys, and were able to learn from and reenact what they had seen. Although the video modeling studies found that children with autism increased both functional and symbolic play, only half of these studies demonstrated generalization of play skills with novel toys or new settings (Boudreau & D'Entremont, 2010; Hine & Wolery, 2006; Nikopoulos & Keenan, 2007; Sancho, Sidener, Reeve, & Sidener, 2010). Moreover, MacDonald, Clark, Garrigan, and Vangala (2005) noted that despite the findings that children with autism were able to increase their scripted play acts and verbalizations, they did not show novel play acts. Children who were given different play materials were not able to replicate the same play theme.

TABLE 11.1   Interventions Targeting Play Skills in Children With Autism

Authors	Subjects	Intervention	Play Outcome	Maintenance	Generalization
		Single Subject Design			
Barry and Burlew, 2004	1M, 1F (7–8 yo)	Social stories	Increase in appropriate play		
Boudreau and D'Entremont, 2010	2M (4 yo)	Video modeling	Increase in scripted verbalizations and modeled play acts	X	X
Dykstra, Boyd, Watson, Crais, and Baranek, 2012	2F, 1M (3–5 yo)	Advancing Social-Communication and Play (ASAP)	Increase in functional and symbolic play		
Gillet and LeBlanc, 2007	3M (4–5 yo)	Natural Language Paradigm	Increase in appropriate functional play and decrease in inappropriate play		X
Hine and Wolery, 2006	2F (2–3 yo)	Video modeling	Increase in play skills	X	X
Hume and Odom, 2007	3M (6–20 yo)	Individual work system	Increase in number of play materials utilized	X	
Ingersoll and Schreibman, 2006	5 subjects (2–3 yo)	Contingent imitation, linguistic mapping, modeling play actions	Increase in total pretend play and spontaneous pretend play	X	X
Liber, Frea, and Symon, 2008	3M (5–9 yo)	Time delay (using typical peers)	Learned sequence of play		X
Walberg and Craig-Unkefer, 2010	3 subjects (5–8 yo)	Play themes: describe how to play with toys, how to get your partner's attention, how to share toys	Increase in interactive play		
MacDonald, Clark, Garrigan, and Vangala, 2005	2M (4–7 yo)	Video modeling	Increase in scripted play actions and verbalizations		
MacDonald, Sacramone, Mansfield, Wiltz, and Ahearn, 2009	2M (5–7 yo)	Video modeling	Increase in scripted play actions and verbalizations	X	
Nelson, McDonnell, Johnston, Crompton, and Nelson, 2007	4 subjects (3–4 yo)	Keys to Play	Increase in time spent in play groups and decrease in solitary state	X	
Nikopoulos and Keenan, 2004	3 subjects (7–9 yo)	Video modeling	Increase in reciprocal play skills	X	
Nikopoulos and Keenan, 2007	3 subjects (6–7 yo)	Video modeling	Increase in time engaged in reciprocal play	X	X
Nuzzolo-Gomez, Leonard, Ortiz, Rivera, and Greer, 2002	3 subjects (4–7 yo)	Prompt play with "You do it"	Increase in toy play and decrease in stereotypy		
Ozen, Batu, and Birkan, 2012	3 subjects (9 yo)	Video modeling	Increase in scripted play actions and verbalizations	X	
Paterson and Arco, 2007	2M, 1F (6–7 yo)	Video modeling	Increase in appropriate play behavior and decrease in repetitive play behavior	X	
Sancho, Sidener, Reeve, and Sidener, 2010	1M, 1F (5 yo)	Video modeling	Increase in scripted play acts	X	X
Whalen, Schreibman, and Ingersoll, 2006	3M, 1F (4 yo)	Components of Discrete Trial Training (DTT) and Pivotal Response Training (PRT)	Increase on the Structured Play Assessment	X	

(continued)

TABLE 11.1   *(Continued)*

Quasi-Experimental Design					
Authors	Subjects	Intervention	Play Outcome	Maintenance	Generalization
Bernard-Opitz, Ing, and Kong, 2004	8 subjects (2–3 yo)	Natural Language Paradigm and behavioral modification	Increase on the Symbolic Play Test		
Keen, Rodger, Doussin, and Braithwaite, 2007	14M, 2F (2–3 yo)	Social-pragmatic approach	Increase in symbolic behavior		
Murdock and Hobbs, 2011	12 subjects (4–6 yo)	Picture Me Playing	Increase in unscripted and scripted dialogue		X
Stahmer and Ingersoll, 2004	16M, 4F (m = 2 yo)	Developmentally appropriate practices: incidental teaching, PRT, DTT, structured teaching, floor time	Increase in functional and symbolic play skills		
Randomized Controlled Trials					
Kaale, Smith, and Sponheim, 2012	61 subjects (2–5 yo)	Joint attention	Increase in engagement with teachers and parents		X
Kasari, Freeman, and Paparella, 2006	58 subjects (3–4 yo)	Joint attention and symbolic play intervention	Increase in play level and types of symbolic play		X
Kasari, Gulsrud, Wong, Kwon, and Locke, 2010	38 subjects (1–3 yo)	Joint attention and symbolic play intervention	Increase in types of symbolic play and engagement	X	
Lawton and Kasari, 2012	16 subjects (3–4 yo)	Joint attention and symbolic play intervention	Increase in supported engagement and decrease in object engaged play		
Wong and Kwan, 2010	17 subjects (1–3 yo)	Autism 123 Project	Increase in symbolic play acts		

Video modeling was most common for elementary-aged children with approximately half of the studies (*n* = 6) using these procedures to teach play. An example by MacDonald, Sacramone, Mansfield, Wiltz, and Ahearn (2009) used video modeling to help children increase play verbalization, play acts, and cooperative play. Video models were based on three play sets: an airport, a zoo, and a set of grills. For each set of toys, a script of 14 to 17 sequenced verbalizations was developed with matching play actions. Results indicated an increase in scripted play actions and verbalizations. Other types of intervention that improved play in elementary-aged children included social stories (Barry & Burlew, 2004), prompts (Nuzzolo-Gomez, Leonard, Ortiz, Rivera, & Greer, 2002), and time delays (Liber, Frea, & Symon, 2008). All of these examples were single subject designs.

The intervention methods in the reviewed studies vary by child age. For preschoolers and toddlers, many of the interventions were described as naturalistic behavioral approaches (e.g., Gillet & LeBlanc, 2007; Whalen, Schreibman, & Ingersoll, 2006). These types of interventions focused on following the child's lead, promoting child initiations and spontaneity using natural play activities and events. However, within some of these interventions, more directive adult approaches are also used to elicit verbal responses. For example, the Natural Language Paradigm was described as a naturalistic intervention approach that involved sitting on the floor and facing the child while providing the child with choices. Once the child chose a play set, the adult modeled a play act and prevented access to the chosen play material to elicit prompted or spontaneous vocalization to obtain the toys (Gillet & LeBlanc, 2007). Whalen et al. (2006) used both an adult-directed approach and naturalistic approach to teach play. This particular study divided the play intervention into two phases. The first phase of the intervention was more adult directed, where children were taught to respond appropriately to joint attention bids using discrete trials. This included using hand-over-hand prompt if the child failed to respond. In the second phase of the intervention, the sessions were more naturalistic where the interventionists focused more on child initiations rather than responses. However, as noted in recent reviews of play interventions, some researchers consider spontaneous play to occur if longer than 5 seconds (DiCarlo & Reid, 2004) or 30 seconds after a model (Ingersoll & Schreibman, 2006), while other researchers consider these as examples of prompted (not spontaneous) play (Barton & Wolery, 2008; Luckett, Bundy, & Roberts, 2007). Other studies also have used both child-initiated and adult-directed strategies. These play interventions allowed the child to choose a toy (child initiated) and then allowed for prompting (adult directed) as needed for the child to demonstrate a specific play skill (Kaale, Smith, & Sponheim, 2012; Kasari et al., 2006). For example, Kasari et al. (2006) used both child-initiated developmental strategies (following child's attentional focus, expanding on their toy interests, maintaining developmental level of play, and increasing diversity of play) and adult-directed modeling and prompting (a least to most prompt hierarchy) to increase frequency, diversity, play level, and quality of child play.

Quantitative Play Outcomes

Most studies taught skills or behaviors one at a time and measured their accuracy in response to models or other prompts of the adult or partner. A few studies examined whether novel, nonmodeled play acts were demonstrated in generalization probes. The measured play outcomes varied from discrete skills (such as responding correctly with a play act after it was modeled; e.g., Hine & Wolery, 2006) to more complex behaviors like executing a scripted play sequence (e.g., Boudreau & D'Entremont, 2010) to longer engagement with toy materials (e.g., Barry & Burlew, 2004) to increases in play maturity on

an independent test of play (Whalen et al., 2006) and showing greater diversity of play acts with the parent (e.g., Kasari et al., 2006; Kasari, Paparella, Freeman, & Jahromi, 2008).

An issue for evaluating these studies is the lack of well-defined, commonly accepted definitions of play and common outcome measures. Although play developmental levels are well described in the developmental literature (e.g., Lifter & Bloom, 1998; Ungerer & Sigman, 1981), defining level of play was inconsistent across studies. For example, the description of one child at baseline who "made the animals roar or fight" was interpreted as showing no imaginative play (Liber et al., 2008). However this behavior on most developmental assessments of play would be classified as *doll as agent* (giving life to dolls or animals). Having a commonly accepted metric of play behavior and consistently applied measures would facilitate comparisons across studies.

Other studies focused less on play skill development, and more on sustaining play independently, or engaging with play materials (e.g., Hume & Odom, 2007). While children certainly need to engage themselves independently and appropriately for short periods of time, many children with ASD have not had enough scaffolding of play by adults to develop an understanding of play skills or shared object play with others, and may not have developed an intrinsic pleasure in playing. Children may be less able to independently play if they do not have many play skills; however, this hypothesis needs further testing.

Quality Rating of Research Articles

Twenty-seven intervention studies were evaluated based on their research design: single subject design (SSD), quasi-experimental, and randomized control trials (RCTs). Two independent raters coded reliability for a randomly selected 20% of the articles from each research design. An interrater reliability analysis was performed to determine consistency between raters. Intraclass correlation coefficient for SSDs was 0.92 between the two raters. Due to the small number of quasi-experimental and RCTs, percentage of agreement between the raters was calculated. Two independent coders had 100% agreement on 20% of the randomly selected articles from both quasi-experimental and RCTs.

Single Subject Designs

There were 18 single SSDs in the current review (see Table 11.2). To rate the quality of SSDs, a systematic review process of 14 questions from the American Academy for Cerebral Palsy and Developmental Medicine (AACPDM) was used (Logan, Hickman, Harris, & Heriza, 2005). Based on the amount of affirmative answers to the 14 questions, each study was rated as strong (11–14), moderate (7–10), or weak (<7). In addition to the 14 questions, each study was also evaluated using seven conduct questions. These conduct questions are used to determine the quality of the study in addition to its research method (O'Donnell et al., 2005).

Based on the quality rating scale of AACPM (Logan et al., 2005), most of the single subject designs were evaluated with moderate quality ($n = 11$), and the remaining five articles were evaluated as weak in their research design.

TABLE 11.2   Quality Ratings of Single Subject Research Design Studies

Authors	Quality Rating (American Academy)	Inclusion/ Exclusion Criteria	Well-Defined Sample (i.e., standardized tests)	Replication of Intervention Across Three or More Participants	Generalization/ Maintenance	Blind Assessors	Fidelity of Intervention (Observation Only)
				Quality Components			
Barry and Burlew, 2004	Weak						
Boudreau and D'Entremont, 2010	Weak				x		
Dykstra, Boyd, Watson, Crais, and Baranek, 2012	Moderate	x	x				x
Gillet and LeBlanc, 2007	Moderate				x		
Hine and Wolery, 2006	Moderate				x		x
Hume and Odom, 2007	Moderate	x			x		x
Ingersoll and Schreibman, 2006	Weak		x		x		
Liber, Frea, and Symon, 2008	Weak				x		
MacDonald, Clark, Garrigan, and Vangala, 2005	Weak						
MacDonald, Sacramore, Mansfield, Wiltz, and Ahearn, 2009	Weak				x		
Nelson, McDonnell, Johnston, Crompton, and Nelson, 2007	Weak				x		x
Nikopoulos and Keenan, 2004	Weak				x		
Nikopoulos and Keenan, 2007	Moderate			x	x	x	
Nuzzolo-Gomez, Leonard, Ortiz, Rivera, and Greer, 2002	Moderate	x					
Paterson and Arco, 2007	Moderate	x			x	x	
Sancho, Sidener, Reeve, and Sidener, 2010	Weak	x			x		x
Walberg and Craig-Unkefer, 2010	Weak	x					
Whalen, Schreibman, and Ingersoll, 2006	Weak	x	x		x		

The seven conduct questions revealed many weaknesses in these SSDs: (1) the lack of blind assessors/observers, (2) replication of outcome variables in three or more participants, (3) use of standardized assessments, (4) and fidelity ratings of the intervention.

Only two studies from the 18 SSDs had blind observers or assessors reported in the study (Nikopoulos & Keenan, 2007; Paterson & Arco, 2007). Many of the assessors or observers were reported to be independent but not blind to the intervention of the study. Replication of the effects of the intervention across three of more subjects was another quality indicator that was lacking among the SSDs, particularly if the study had more than one primary outcome variable. In order to receive credit for the replication of the findings, all three participants had to show changes in all the primary outcome variables the study examined. Only one study replicated the findings across three or more participants (Nikopoulos & Keenan, 2007). Description of the characteristics of the sample was another quality indicator that was lacking in many of these studies. Only three of the studies had a detailed description of the sample in which scores of standardized assessments of their participants were reported (Dykstra, Boyd, Watson, Crais, & Baranek, 2012; Ingersoll & Schreibman, 2006; Whalen et al., 2006). In addition to a qualitative description (e.g., vocalizations and one-word utterances) of the children's abilities, these studies also incorporated standardized assessment scores such as the Mullen and the Leiter. Finally, fidelity of treatment implementation was another quality indicator that was lacking in many of these studies. Only five of the studies reported live fidelity ratings. Real-time fidelity ratings (live or video coded) are important to capture objective behaviors of the targets in comparison to self-reports of fidelity that are sometimes reported (and may be subject to bias).

Although none of the SSDs are rated as high quality based on the rating scale, the highest rated moderate quality studies all had positive outcomes in improving participants' functional and/ or symbolic play skills (e.g., Dykstra et al., 2012; Nikopoulos & Keenan, 2007; Whalen et al.,

2006), which is consistent with previous reviews of play interventions (e.g., Lang et al., 2009). Most of the play interventions reported positive results; however, these skills were not generalized to new play materials, settings, or peers.

Quasi-Experimental Designs

There were four quasi-experimental studies in the current review (see Table 11.3). These quasi-experimental designs were evaluated based on the rating criteria by Gersten and colleagues (2005) using a number of essential and desirable quality indicators. Quasi-experimental designs were rated as high quality if the study met all but one of the essential quality indicators and met at least four of the desirable quality indicators. The study was rated as acceptable if the study met all but one of the essential quality indicators and at least one of the desirable quality indicators. For the purpose of this review, all quasi-experimental designs that did not meet criteria for either high quality or acceptable were labeled as unacceptable.

Based on these quality indicators, none of the quasi-experimental designs were of high quality or acceptable quality. All of these quasi-experimental studies used pre- or postdesigns, a design that lacks control for other possible influences on the dependent variable thus prevents the demonstration of causal relations between the intervention and the change. In addition, instead of using multiple measures, these quasi-experimental studies used only one measure to examine play skills (Bernard-Opitz, Ing, & Kong, 2004; Keen, Rodger, Doussin, & Braithwaite, 2007; Murdock & Hobbs, 2011; Stahmer & Ingersoll, 2004). Lastly, none of these studies reported effect sizes.

TABLE 11.3 Quality Ratings of Quasi-Experimental Studies

Authors	Gerstein Quality Assessment
Bernard-Opitz, Ing, and Kong, 2004	Unacceptable
Keen, Rodger, Doussin, and Braithwaite, 2007	Unacceptable
Murdock and Hobbs, 2011	Unacceptable
Stahmer and Ingersoll, 2004	Unacceptable

TABLE 11.4   Quality Ratings of Randomized Controlled Trials

Authors	Quality Rating (American Academy)
Kaale, Smith, and Sponheim, 2012	Strong
Kasari, Gulsrud, Wong, Kwon, and Locke, 2010	Strong
Kasari, Freeman, and Paparella, 2006	Strong
Lawton and Kasari, 2012	Strong

Randomized Controlled Trials

There were five RCTs in the current review (see Table 11.4). These studies used wait list control designs (e.g., Kasari, Gulsrud, Wong, Kwon, & Locke, 2010; Lawton & Kasari, 2012; Wong & Kwan, 2010) or treatment compared to alternative treatment and/or to no treatment community control (e.g., Kaale et al., 2012; Kasari et al., 2006; Kasari et al., 2008). Samples were relatively small to moderate in size (ranging from 16 to 61 participants). Only two studies focused specifically on teaching play skills (Kasari et al., 2006; Kasari et al., 2008; Kasari et al., 2010), while the others used a play measure as an outcome for a treatment focused on social communication skills (Wong & Kwan, 2010) or examined play engagement with an adult as an outcome (Kaale et al., 2012; Kasari et al., 2006; Kasari et al., 2008; Kasari et al., 2010; Lawton & Kasari, 2012).

RCTs were evaluated using the same seven conduct questions that were used to evaluate the quality of SSDs (O'Donnell et al., 2005). Based on the amount of affirmative responses to the seven questions, studies are determined to be strong (6–7), moderate (4–5), or weak (<3).

Based on the seven quality indicators, four of the studies were rated as strong quality and one was rated as moderate quality. The four studies that were rated as strong had a well-defined population of children and provided detailed descriptions of the interventionists who were working the children. These studies also controlled for variables that may affect treatment outcomes such as baseline scores of children in both the control and the treatment groups. In addition, these studies described in detail the treatment of each group whether it was

the control group, alternative treatment group, or treatment group (e.g., Kasari et al., 2006). Lastly, all of these studies had blind assessors to ensure unbiased data collection.

While there have been several RCTs in the past decade, these tend to be small with limited follow-up data. Kasari, Gulsrud, Freeman, Paparella, and Hellemann (2012) followed their original participants in their joint attention and symbolic play intervention from initial assessments at age 3–4 years to 5 years later when children were 8–9 years. This study yielded important predictors from children's initial play abilities to later language development. Initial play level at age 3–4 years predicted language at age 8–9 years and play diversity predicted children's level of cognition as measured by IQ at age 8–9 years. Thus, play level and play diversity would seem to be important intervention targets, but more research is indicated.

CONCLUSIONS AND RECOMMENDATIONS

The study of play and play interventions of children with autism has increased over the past decade. The current review suggests three main conclusions that require further study. First, there are multiple definitions of play in the literature. These range from functional and symbolic play skills (e.g., Dykstra et al., 2012), diversity and level of play (e.g., Kasari et al., 2006), duration of time engaged with play materials (e.g., Barry & Burlew, 2004), engagement in independent play (e.g., Hume & Odom, 2007), and duration of time engaged in social play with parents or teachers (e.g., Kaale et al., 2011). All of these definitions have importance for the study of play in children with ASD; however, it is difficult to generalize across studies when different metrics are used to define different aspects of play—such as what qualifies as symbolic play, or when play is described generally as independent play. Future studies would benefit from more precision in defining the target of study. Likewise there has been little focus on quality of play (e.g., pleasure and creativity in play) and children's motivation in play (Luckett et al., 2007), particularly around social play with others. Given the significant impairment in quality of play for children with ASD, this area of research needs further attention.

Second, studies varied widely in their measurement of play, from experimenter-developed measures to standardized tests. There is no common measure of play that is used across multiple studies. For example, in video-modeling interventions, children's play skills were measured based on an increase in scripted play actions (e.g., MacDonald et al., 2009), whereas other studies used structured experimenter-administered assessments (e.g., Structured Play Assessment; Whalen et al., 2006) to measure more specific play skills.

Finally, intervention research has relied primarily on single subject designs, and the majority of these were characterized as weak in research quality due to limitations in replication of outcomes, use of standardized assessments, and use of blind observers and assessors. However, single subject designs are useful in pinpointing new targets and new intervention approaches for teaching play. Future studies should improve the quality of these designs in order to build new intervention models for teaching play. In particular, these designs may be helpful in testing different active ingredients of intervention that can then be evaluated in group designs.

Based on our current knowledge to date, several recommendations can be made for interventionists and parents. First, play is an important target of intervention that can affect later development in children with ASD (Kasari et al., 2012), and focusing on play targets in early intervention programs is clearly desirable. There are multiple strategies that have been shown to be successful in teaching play, and it may require multiple approaches to help many children improve the quantity and quality of play with objects. Object play that is socially mediated is extremely important to facilitate. Thus, video modeling and prompting may be useful, along with naturalistic strategies that involve environmental arrangement, selection of play targets that are developmentally appropriate for the child, and specific strategies to expand and maintain play engagement with objects and people.

CROSS-REFERENCES

Chapter 5 discusses autism in infants and toddlers; social development is the focus of Chapter 9; imitation is addressed in Chapter 12. Interventions for young children are the focus in Chapter 29.

REFERENCES

Adamson, L., Bakeman, R., & Deckner, D. (2004). The development of symbol-infused joint attention. *Child Development*, *75*, 1171–1187.

Barry, L., & Burlew, S. (2004). Using social stories to teach choice and play skills to children with autism. *Focus on Autism and Other Developmental Disabilities*, *19*, 45–51.

Barton, E., & Wolery, M. (2008). Teaching pretend play to children with disabilities: A review of the literature. *Topics in Early Childhood Special Education*, *28*, 109–125.

Bernard-Opitz, V., Ing, S., & Kong, T. (2004). Comparison of behavioral and natural play interventions for young children with autism. *Autism*, *8*, 319–333.

Boudreau, E., & D'Entremont, B. (2010). Improving the pretend play skills of preschoolers with autism spectrum disorders: The effects of video modeling. *Journal of Developmental and Physical Disabilities*, *22*, 415–431.

Casby, M. W. (2003). The development of play in infants, toddlers, and young children. *Communication Disorders Quarterly*, *24*, 163–174. doi: 10.1177/15257401030240040201

Charman, T., Swettenham, J. S., Baron-Cohen, S., Cox, A., Baird, G., & Drew, A. (1997). Infants with autism: An investigation of empathy, pretend play, joint attention, and imitation. *Developmental Psychology*, *33*, 781–789.

DiCarlo, C. F., & Reid, D. H. (2004). Increasing pretend toy play among 2-year-old children with disabilities in an inclusive setting. *Journal of Applied Behavior Analysis*, *37*, 197–207.

Dykstra, J., Boyd, B., Watson, L., Crais, E., & Baranek, G. (2012). The impact of the Advancing Social-communication And Play (ASAP) intervention on preschoolers with autism spectrum disorder. *Autism*, *16*, 27, 44.

Gersten, R., Fuchs, L., Compton, D., Coyne, M., Greenwood, C., & Innocenti, M. (2005). Quality indicators for group experimental and quasi-experimental research in special education. *Council for Exceptional Children*, *71*, 149–164.

Gillet, J., & LeBlanc, L. (2007). Parent-implemented natural language paradigm to increase language and play in children with autism. *Research in Autism Spectrum Disorders*, *1*, 247–255.

Ginsburg, H. P., & Opper, S. (1988). *Piaget's theory of intellectual development* (3rd ed.). Upper Saddle River, NJ: Prentice-Hall.

Hine, J., & Wolery, M., (2006). Using point-of-view video modeling to teach play to preschoolers with autism. *Topics in Early Childhood Special Education*, *26*, 83–93.

Hobson, J. A., Hobson, R. P., Malik, S., Bargiota, K., & Caló, S. (2012). The relation between social engagement and pretend play in autism. *British Journal of Developmental Psychology*, *31*, 114–127.

Hobson, R. P., Lee, A., & Hobson, J. (2009). Qualities of symbolic play among children with autism: A social-developmental perspective. *Journal of Autism and Developmental Disorders*, *39*, 12–22.

Holmes, E., & Willoughby, T. (2005). Play behavior of children with autism spectrum disorders. *Journal of Intellectual and Developmental Disability*, *30*, 156–164.

Hume, K., & Odom, S. (2007). Effects of an individual work system on the independent functioning of students with autism. *Journal of Autism and Development Disorders*, *37*, 1166–1180.

Ingersoll, B. (2008). The social role of imitation in autism: Implications for the treatment of imitation deficits. *Infants and Young Children*, *21*, 107–119.

Ingersoll, B., & Schreibman, L. (2006). Teaching reciprocal imitation skills to young children with autism using a naturalistic behavioral approach: Effects on language, pretend play, and joint attention. *Journal of Autism and Development Disorders*, *36*, 487–505.

Jarrold, C. (2003). A review of research into pretend play in autism. *Autism*, *7*(4), 379–390.

Jarrold, C., Boucher, J., & Smith, P. (1993). Symbolic play in autism: A review. *Journal of Autism and Development Disorders*, *23*, 281–307.

Jarrold, C., Boucher, J., & Smith, P. (1996). Generativity deficits in pretend play in autism. *British Journal of Developmental Psychology*, *14*, 275–300.

Kaale, A., Smith, L., & Sponheim, E. (2012). A randomized controlled trial of preschool-based joint attention intervention for children with autism. *Journal of Child Psychology and Psychiatry*, *53*, 97–105. doi:10.1111/j.1469-7610.2011.02450.x

Kanner, L. (1943). Autistic disturbances of affective contact. *Nervous Child*, *2*, 217–250.

Kasari, C., Freeman, S., & Paparella, T. (2006). Joint attention and symbolic play in children with autism: A randomized control joint attention intervention. *Journal of Child Psychology and Psychiatry*, *47*, 611–620.

Kasari, C., Gulsrud, A., Freeman, S., Paparella, T., & Hellemann, G. (2012). Longitudinal follow-up of children with autism receiving targeted interventions on joint attention and play. *Journal of the American Academy of Child & Adolescent Psychiatry*, *51*, 487–495.

Kasari, C., Gulsrud, A., Wong, C., Kwon, S., & Locke, J. (2010). Randomized controlled caregiver mediated intervention for toddlers with autism. *Journal of Autism and Development Disorders*, *40*, 1045–1056. doi: 10.1007/s10803-010-0955-5

Kasari, C., Paparella, T., Freeman, S. N., & Jahromi, L. (2008). Language outcome in autism: Randomized comparison of joint attention and play interventions. *Journal of Consulting and Clinical Psychology*, *76*, 125–137.

Keen, D., Rodger, S., Doussin, K., Braithwaite, M. (2007). A pilot study of the effects of a social-pragmatic intervention on the communication and symbolic play of children with autism. *Autism*, *11*, 63–71.

Lang, R., O'Reilly, M., Rispoli, M., Shogren, K., Machalieck, W., Sigafoos, J., & Regester, A. (2009). Review of interventions to increase functional and symbolic play in children with autism. *Education and Training in Developmental Disabilities*, *44*, 481–492.

Lawton, K., & Kasari, C. (2012). Brief report: Teacher-implemented joint attention intervention: Pilot randomized controlled study for preschoolers with autism. *Journal of Counseling and Clinical Psychology*, *30*, 687–693.

Lewis, V., & Boucher, J. (1988). Spontaneous, instructed and elicited play in relatively able autistic children. *British Journal of Developmental Psychology*, *6*, 325–339.

Libby, S., Powell, S., Messer, D., & Jordan, R. (1998). Spontaneous play in children with autism: A reappraisal. *Journal of Autism and Developmental Disorders*, *28*, 487–497.

Liber, D., Frea, W., & Symon, J. (2008). Using time-delay to improve social play skills with peers for children with autism. *Journal of Autism and Development Disorders*, *38*, 312–323.

Lifter, K., & Bloom, L. (1989). Object knowledge and the emergence of language. *Infant Behavior and Development*, *12*, 395–423.

Lifter, K., Edwards, G., Avery, D., Anderson, S. R., & Sulzer-Azaroff, B. (1988). The Developmental Play Assessment (DPA) Instrument. Mini-seminar presented to the Annual Convention of the American Speech Language Hearing Association, Boston, MA, November 1988. Developmental assessment of young children's play: Implications for interventions. Revised July, 1994.

Lifter, K., Mason, E., & Barton, E. (2011). Children's play: Where we have been and where we could go. *Journal of Early Intervention*, *33*, 281–297.

Logan, L., Hickman, R., Harris, S., & Heriza, C. (2005). Single-subject design: recommendations for levels of evidence and quality rating. *Developmental Medicine and Child Neurology*, *50*, 99–105.

Luckett, T., Bundy, A., & Roberts, J. (2007). Do behavioural approaches teach children with autism to play or are they pretending. *Autism*, *11*, 365–388.

MacDonald, R., Clark, M., Garrigan, E., & Vangala, M. (2005). Using video modeling to teach pretend play to children with autism. *Behavioral Interventions*, *20*, 225–238.

MacDonald, R., Sacramone, S., Mansfield, R., Wiltz, K., & Ahearn, W. (2009). Using video modeling to teach reciprocal pretend play to children with autism. *Journal of Applied Behavior Analysis*, *42*, 43–55.

Mundy, P., Kasari, C., & Sigman (1992). Nonverbal communication, affective sharing, and intersubjectivity. *Infant Behavior and Development*, *15*, 377–381.

Mundy, P., Sigman, M., Ungerer, J., & Sherman, T. (1987). Nonverbal communication and play correlates of language development in autistic children. *Journal of Autism and Developmental Disorders*, *17*, 349–364.

Murdock, L., & Hobbs, J. (2011). Picture Me Playing: Increasing pretend play dialogue of children with autism spectrum disorders. *Journal of Autism and Developmental Disorders*, *41*, 870–878.

Nelson, C., McDonell, A., Johnston, S., Crompton, A., & Nelson, A. (2007). Keys to Play: A strategy to increase the social interactions of young children with autism and their typically developing peers. *Education and Training in Developmental Disabilities*, *42*, 165–181.

Nikopoulos, C., & Keenan, M. (2004). Effects of video modeling on social initiations by children with autism. *Journal of Applied Behavior Analysis*, *37*, 93–96.

Nikopoulos, C., & Keenan, M. (2007). Using video modeling to teach complex social sequences to children with autism. *Journal of Autism and Development Disorders, 37,* 678–693.

Nuzzolo-Gomez, R., Leonard, M., Ortiz, E., Rivera, C., & Greer, R. (2002). Teaching children with autism to prefer books or toys over stereotypy or passivity. *Journal of Positive Behavior Interventions, 4,* 80–87.

O'Donnell, M., Darrah, J., Adams, R., Butler, C., Roxborough, L., & Damiano, D. (2005). *AACPDM methodology to develop systematic reviews of treatment interventions (Revision 1.1): 2004 Version.* American Academy for Cerebral Palsy and Developmental Medicine 2005. Retrieved from http://www.aacpdm.org/resources/systematicReviewsMethodology.pdf

Ozen, A., Batu, S., & Birkan, B. (2012). Teaching play skills to children with autism through video modeling: Small group arrangement and observational learning. *Education and Training in Autism and Developmental Disabilities, 47,* 84–96.

Paterson, C., & Arco, L. (2007). Using video modeling for generalizing toy play in children with autism. *Behavior Modification, 31,* 660–681.

Rutherford, M. D., Young, G. S., Hepburn, S., & Rogers, S. J. (2007). A longitudinal study of pretend play in autism. *Journal of Autism and Developmental Disorders, 37,* 1024–1039.

Sancho, K., Sidener, T., Reeve, S., & Sidener, D. (2010). Two variations of video modeling interventions for teaching play skills to children with autism. *Education and Treatment of Children, 33,* 421–442.

Sigman, M., & Ruskin, E. (1999). Social competence in children with Autism, Down syndrome and other developmental delays: A longitudinal study. *Monographs of the Society for Research in Child Development, Serial No. 256, 64*(1). Chicago, IL: University of Chicago Press.

Sigman, M., & Ungerer, J. (1984). Cognitive and language skills in autistic, mentally retarded, and normal children. *Developmental Psychology, 20,* 293–302.

Stahmer, A., & Ingersoll, B. (2004). Inclusive programming for toddlers with autism spectrum disorders: Outcomes form the Children's Toddler School. *Journal of Positive Behavior Intervention, 6,* 67–82.

Ungerer, J., & Sigman, M. (1981). Symbolic play and language comprehension in autistic children. *American Academy of Child Psychiatry, 20,* 318–337.

Walberg, J. L., & Craig-Unkefer, L. (2010). An examination of the effects of a social communication intervention on the play behaviors of children with autism spectrum disorder. *Education and Training in Autism and Developmental Disabilities, 45,* 69–80.

Whalen, C., Schreibman, L., & Ingersoll, B. (2006). The collateral effects of joint attention training on social initiations, positive affect, imitation, and spontaneous speech for young children with autism. *Journal of Autism and Development Disorders, 36,* 655–664.

Williams, E., Reddy, V., & Costall, A. (2001). Taking a closer look at functional play in children with autism. *Journal of Autism and Developmental Disorders, 31,* 67–77.

Wong, C., & Kasari, C. (2012). Play and joint attention of children with autism in preschool special education classroom. *Journal of Autism and Developmental Disorders.* doi: 10.1007/s10803-012-1467-2

Wong, V., & Kwan, Q. (2010). Randomized controlled trial for early intervention for autism: A pilot study of the Autism 1-2-3 Project. *Journal of Autism and Developmental Disorder, 40,* 677–688.

CHAPTER 12

Imitation in Autism Spectrum Disorders

GIACOMO VIVANTI AND ANTONIA HAMILTON

There is a growing body of literature documenting abnormalities in different types of imitative behaviors in autism spectrum disorders (ASDs). As imitation appears to play a critical role in development (Hurley & Chater, 2005; Meltzoff & Prinz, 2002), research in this area has the potential to provide crucial insight into the mechanisms underlying learning difficulties as well as social-cognitive, communicative, and motor disturbances in this population (Carpenter & Tomasello, 2000; Rogers & Williams, 2006).

Difficulties in imitation passed unnoticed by Leo Kanner (1943) and Hans Asperger (1944), although both of their seminal descriptions of autism make reference to a lack of spontaneous learning from others in their patients. The first study that specifically addressed imitation abilities in autism was published in the 1970s (DeMyer et al., 1972); in the following decades interest in the topic increased exponentially, with more than 100 research studies published in the first years of 2000 (Sevlever & Gillis, 2010). Despite the abundance of data

generated by such a research effort, there is still remarkable controversy over a number of critical issues, including (1) whether imitation deficits are universally present in autism, (2) whether there is a profile of intact and impaired imitative abilities that is specific to autism, and (3) whether imitation difficulties are cause, consequence, or comorbid features of the core impairments in autism.

In this chapter, we review data on the development of imitation skills in autism, and consider different theories that could account for abnormal imitation performance. First, we describe the roles of imitation in development and the different strategies that might be used to copy others' behavior, we will then review the literature on imitative behavior in children with ASD, and finally we analyze the possible neurocognitive mechanisms underlying imitative difficulties in ASD, adopting a developmental and neuropsychological perspective. We also discuss remediation strategies focused on imitation.

ROLES OF IMITATION IN DEVELOPMENT

In one of his seminal works on cognitive development, Lev Vygotsky states that imitation is "one of the basic paths of cultural development of the child" (1931/1997, p. 95), emphasizing how children, by imitating adults, can perform tasks that are beyond what they can independently achieve. The role of imitation as a tool for the acquisition of knowledge was detailed in Bandura's social learning theory (1977) and subsequently supported by numerous empirical studies (see Hurley & Chater, 2005). Imitation also serves a social function: Across developmental stages and cultures, humans tend to engage in imitative behaviors in order to establish and strengthen affiliative bonds (Chartrand & Bargh, 1999; Nadel, Baudonniere, & Fontaine, 1985; Over & Carpenter, 2012; Uzgiris, 1981, 1984).

The natural course of imitation development seems to involve an early stage during which infants are capable of a limited number of imitative responses (Heimann, Nelson, & Schaller, 1989; Jones, 2009; Legerstee, 1991; Meltzoff & Prinz, 2002), followed by the emergence and rapid consolidation of synchronic imitation during dyadic exchanges between 18 and 24 months (Nielsen, Suddendorf, & Dissanayake, 2006; Trevarthen, 2001). The subsequent increase in frequency and complexity of imitative behaviors reflects the development of progressively more sophisticated cognitive and social abilities. Indeed, during preschool years, children organize their imitative behavior both on the basis of *rational* considerations (e.g., they imitate actions when they are the most efficient means in pursuing a goal, given the constraints of the situation) and *affective* ones (e.g., they are more likely to imitate actions when they experience social connectedness with the model; Bekkering, Wohlschlager, & Gattis, 2000; Buchsbaum, Gopnik, Griffiths, & Shafto, 2011; Carpenter, 2006; Gergely, Bekkering, & Kiraly, 2002; Nielsen, 2006). Imitation continues to be a central feature in adult social behavior, with research showing that adults copy others' actions both in order to acquire knowledge and to promote feelings of interpersonal closeness (i.e., a desire to conform or to be like others; Henrich & Boyd, 1998; Lakin & Chartrand 2003; Tomasello & Moll, 2010).

The importance of imitation in cultural learning and social-affective relatedness is supported by empirical research showing that early imitative abilities are concurrently associated with social engagement (Masur, 2006; G. S. Young et al., 2011) and predictively associated to nonverbal communication (Heimann et al., 2006), language development (Bates, Bretherton, & Snyder, 1988; Rose, Feldman, & Jankowski, 2009; see also McEwen et al., 2007), social understanding (Olineck & Poulin-Dubois, 2009), and cognitive skills (Strid, Tjus, Smith, Meltzoff, & Heimann, 2006). Thus, imitation is a core human skill, which is critical for the development of both social interaction and practical knowledge.

Types of Copying Behaviors and Tasks to Assess Them

In the scientific study of imitation, it is important to distinguish different types of copying behavior, because different ways of copying others' actions might serve different functions and reflect distinct underlying processes. Recent contributions from comparative psychology have helped to define a taxonomy of copying behaviors (Byrne & Russon, 1998; Want & Harris, 2002) involving the following categories:

1. *Social enhancement.* This phenomenon occurs when the presence of another individual performing an action leads the observer to engage in a different action that would not have otherwise occurred. For example, seeing someone pick up a mug of tea might lead the observer to pour milk into her own tea. The action itself is not copied and the goals might be different but the action occurred as a consequence of observing another individual's behavior.

2. *Stimulus enhancement.* Stimulus enhancement occurs when the observer's attention is drawn to a particular stimulus (or location) by another individual, increasing the probability that the

observer performs a specific action on that stimulus (or that location). For example, the observer might decide to go into a shop to buy something after noticing someone who is leaving the shop with an ice cream in his hands. The action itself is not copied (i.e., the demonstrator is leaving the shop, while the observer enters the shop) and the goals can be different (the observer might decide to buy an item that differs from the demonstrator's), but the observer chose to act on a specific stimulus/location (in the example, the shop) as a consequence of observing the demonstrator acting on the same stimulus/location.

3. *Emulation.* Emulation occurs when the observer copies the goals or the products of an action, but not the means used to achieve the goals. For example, an actor lifts books into a box one at a time; the observer later uses two hands to place a stack of books into the box. This kind of copying involves high fidelity with regard to the goals (the observer wants to achieve the exact same end state achieved by the demonstrator) and low fidelity with regard to the means (different motor acts are used to achieve the same goals).

4. *Imitation* (a.k.a., *true imitation*). Imitation, often called true imitation in comparative literature (Byrne & Russon, 1998; Thorpe, 1956) involves copying both the means and the goals of the actions. For example, the observer learns how to grasp food using chopsticks by replicating the motor acts performed by the demonstrator. This kind of learning involves high fidelity to both observed motor actions and goals.

5. *Mimicry* (a.k.a., *automatic imitation*). Mimicry occurs when the observer spontaneously and unintentionally matches the bodily movements of a model (Moody & McIntosh, 2006). For example, when seeing a happy or a sad facial expression, we may partially match that expression.

These different strategies involve different levels of complexity and require attention to different aspects of the demonstrator's actions. A key distinction here is the difference between the goal of an action and the means by which the goal is achieved. Emulation involves copying a goal, mimicry involves copying the means of an action, while true imitation requires copying of both goals and means (Hamilton, 2008). Another key distinction involves the function of the different copying behaviors. Recent research suggests that mimicry is often driven by the desire to affiliate with or relate to another person (Lakin & Chartrand, 2003) rather than by the desire to learn about objects, whilst emulation appears to reflect an interest in the product and instrumental function of the demonstration (Call, Carpenter, & Tomasello, 2005; Matheson, Moore, & Akhtar, 2012). Nevertheless, the different types of imitation might not be necessarily associated with a clearly distinct function, but rather reflect an interplay between social and instrumental learning processes (Godman, 2012; Uzgiris, 1981).

Different tasks used to study imitation in child development and in ASD put different amounts of emphasis on these different types of imitation. Classifying tasks according to the preceding taxonomy is helpful in defining which aspects of imitation are easy or hard for individuals with autism. Some tasks examine imitation toward a goal or object, or contrast this with imitation of actions that are not directed toward a goal or object. Copying actions on objects (often defined as transitive actions) can be achieved by true imitation, emulation, or stimulus enhancement, as the appreciation of the end state of the demonstrated action (e.g., a box is open) or the specific affordance of the object might be sufficient to elicit a behavior in the observer that is similar to one used by the demonstrator (removing the lid from the box).

Studies of imitation have also compared meaningful and meaningless actions. This factor of meaning is almost inevitably confounded with familiarity—meaningful actions are also often familiar to the participant and may likely have been performed before, while meaningless actions are often novel. Tests of true imitation in the comparative literature almost always use novel (meaningless) actions to ensure that responses are imitative rather than stimulus enhancement.

The meaning or familiarity of an action can be varied independently of object use, because it is possible to demonstrate both meaningful and nonmeaningful actions with and without objects. For example, some imitation paradigms included nonmeaningful actions on objects, that is, transitive actions that do not carry a semantic meaning (e.g., using a lint brush to lift some Play-Doh). The use of pantomime actions, where an actor pretends that an object is present (e.g., pretend to brush your teeth) is also found in autism research. Pantomime actions reduce the problem that participants might just use the object in the most natural way, but the use of pretend might cause difficulties for children with autism independent of their imitation skills. Other imitation paradigms aim to evaluate whether imitative difficulties in autism reflect difficulties in the social versus instrumental function of imitation by manipulating the social demands involved in the task. For example, in some tasks imitation is explicitly demanded in the task instructions, while in others is spontaneously elicited by the social situation and context.

In the next section of this chapter, we review the findings on imitation abilities in ASD across this variety of imitation tasks and processes.

IMITATION IN ASD: FINDINGS

Research in the field has mainly focused on two somewhat different aspects of imitation in ASD, namely, the frequency of spontaneous imitation and the accuracy of imitation performance.

Frequency of Spontaneous Imitation

Spontaneous imitative behavior in individuals with ASD has been investigated using systematic naturalistic observations, parent questionnaires, or paradigms involving nonspecific prompts, (e.g., the demonstrator pats a teddy bear and then gives the teddy to the participant, saying, "You can play"). Most studies document lower rates of spontaneous imitative behavior of actions on objects and gestures in children with ASD, when compared to typically

developing or developmental age-matched control groups (Charman et al., 1997; Colombi et al., 2009; Dawson & Adams, 1984; DeMyer et al., 1972; Ingersoll, 2008a; Knott, Lewis, & Williams, 2007; Lord, 1995; Lord, Storoschuk, Rutter, & Pickles, 1993; Whiten & Brown, 1998). However, counterevidence exists (Brown & Whiten, 2000; Charman & Baron-Cohen, 1994; Rogers, Young, Cook, Giolzetti, & Ozonoff, 2008).

Other studies have investigated spontaneous imitation through the retrospective analysis of home videos of infants later diagnosed with autism, reporting lower rates of spontaneous imitation in the first 2 years of life (Maestro et al., 2001; Osterling & Dawson, 1994; Receveur et al., 2005; Zakian, Malvy, Desombre, Roux, & Lenoir, 2000; but see Mars, Mauk, & Dowrick, 1998). Whilst most of this research has focused on children (from infancy to preadolescence), very little is known about spontaneous imitative behavior in adults with ASD. The notion that individuals with ASD imitate others less frequently than their peers is, however, widely accepted, and many screening and diagnostic instruments include lack of spontaneous imitation as a behavioral marker of early autism (e.g., Social Communication Questionnaire, Rutter, Bailey, & Lord, 2003; Modified Checklist for Autism in Toddlers, Robins, Fein, Barton, & Green, 2001; First Year Inventory, Reznick, Baranek, Reavis, Watson, & Crais, 2007; Childhood Autism Rating Scale, Schopler, Reichler & Renner, 1988; Autism Diagnostic Interview, Lord, Rutter, & Le Couteur, 1994). Some studies have explicitly contrasted imitative behavior in elicited versus naturalistic conditions. These suggest that imitative differences in ASD are more pronounced in a spontaneous versus elicited context (Ingersoll, 2008a; see also McDuffie et al., 2007).

A different way to investigate spontaneous imitation in ASD is through the measurement of rapid and unintentional matching responses to others' actions and facial expressions (i.e., automatic imitation, or mimicry). Using fine-grained measurements of muscular activity, several studies found that individuals with ASD, compared to typically developing controls, show a reduced or delayed automatic motor mimicry response to others' bodily movements and facial expressions (Beall, Moody, McIntosh, Hepburn, & Reed, 2008; McIntosh, Reichmann-Decker, Winkielman, & Wilbarger, 2006; Oberman, Winkielman, & Ramachandran, 2009; Stel, van den Heuvel, & Smeets, 2008). However, other studies documented enhanced (Magnee, de Gelder, van Engeland, & Kemner, 2007) or intact mimicry responses (Bird, Leighton, Press, & Heyes, 2007; Grecucci et al., 2012; Press, Richardson, & Bird, 2010). Given that tasks, stimuli, and measurement strategies vary considerably across studies, more empirical work is needed to solve inconsistencies and clarify the nature of motor mimicry abnormalities in ASD.

Accuracy of Elicited Imitation

Most of the research studies investigating imitation in autism have looked at the accuracy of imitation performance in paradigms involving explicit instructions (e.g., the demonstrator shows an action and then says, "Now you do it" or "Your turn"). The to-be-imitated actions are characterized by the presence or absence of an object (actions on objects versus gestures), by whether the demonstrated actions are directed to a goal (meaningful versus nonmeaningful actions), and whether the actions are simple or complex (single versus sequential actions).

Infants and Toddlers

Using a prospective design, Zwaigenbaum and colleagues (2005) documented difficulties in the imitation of actions on objects in infants with ASD as young as 12 months. Similarly, G. S. Young and colleagues (2011) found difficulties in the imitation of actions on objects, gestures, and oral-facial movements in 12-month-old children subsequently diagnosed with ASD when compared to typically developing peers. However their performance was not different from that of at-risk siblings with developmental delays but no autism. In contrast, studies on toddlers have reported difficulties in

imitation of actions on objects and gestures in participants with ASD when compared to both typically developing and developmental delayed peers (Rogers, Hepburn, Stackhouse, & Wehner, 2003; Rogers, Young, Cook, Giolzetti, & Ozonoff, 2010; Stone, Ousley, & Littleford, 1997).

Several studies investigated the developmental course of imitative behavior in ASD. Employing a prospective design, G. S. Young et al. (2011) showed that imitative abilities in infants with ASD improve between 12 and 24 months, following a similar developmental progression to that of typically developing children. Similarly, Poon and colleagues reported improvements in imitative behavior between 12 and 18 months (Poon, Watson, Baranek, & Poe, 2011); moreover, improvements were documented between 24 and 36 months (Stone et al., 1997; see also Hepburn & Stone, 2006; Vivanti, Hepburn, Philofsky, & Rogers, 2009) and between the ages of 4 and 6 (Heimann & Ullstadius, 1999). However, despite these improvements over time, individuals with autism continue to exhibit imitation deficits at different developmental stages.

Older Children, Adolescents, and Adults

Studies testing older children, adolescents, and adults with ASD using elicited imitation tasks consistently report difficulties in the imitation of nonmeaningful gestures, that is, actions that do not involve objects, do not carry a specific meaning, and can only be described in terms of changes of limb postures in space (e.g., lifting the elbow above the shoulders; Bernier, Dawson, Webb, & Murias, 2007; Jones & Prior, 1985; Rogers, Bennetto, McEvoy, & Pennington, 1996; Stieglitz Ham et al., 2011; Vanvuchelen, Roeyers, & De Weerdt, 2007; Vivanti, Nadig, Ozonoff, & Rogers, 2008). These findings are consistent across developmental age and symptom severity ranges. Given that the familiarity with the demonstrator's goals and means cannot be exploited in this type of task, performance in imitation of nonmeaningful gestures provides the most rigorous test of impairment in true imitation.

Imitation of nonmeaningful oral-facial movements (e.g., lip protrusion, lifting eyebrows while blinking eyes) was also found to be impaired in individuals with ASD across functioning levels and age ranges (Bernier et al., 2007; Freitag, Kleser, & von Gontard, 2006; Page & Boucher, 1998; Rogers et al., 2003). However, most studies investigating imitation of meaningful facial movements (in particular emotional expressions such as smiling, or showing surprise) found normative performance in ASD (Dapretto et al., 2006; Loveland et al., 1994; Stel et al., 2008; but see Grecucci et al., 2012; Grossman & Tager-Flusberg, 2008). This pattern is consistent with the idea that copying action/gestures with a meaning might be easier than copying nonmeaningful movements for individuals with autism.

Research investigating the imitation of meaningful gestures (i.e., conventional gestures that carry a meaning, such as thumbs up or a hammering action without a hammer), also documented ASD-specific deficits across chronological and mental age ranges (Beadle-Brown, 2004; Dewey, Cantell, & Crawford, 2007; Hammes & Langdell, 1981; Mostofsky, et al., 2006; Smith & Bryson, 2007). Nevertheless, several studies that compared performance in different types of tasks suggested that individuals with ASD imitate meaningful gestures better than nonmeaningful ones (Cossu et al., 2012; Oberman, Ramachandran, & Pineda, 2008; Rogers et al., 1996; Vanvuchelen et al., 2007; Wild, Poliakoff, Jerrison, & Gowen, 2011; Zachor, Ilanit, & Ben Itzchak, 2010). Notably, this pattern is seen in typically developing individuals as well (Tessari & Rumiati, 2004).

The notion that imitative performance varies depending on task type is also supported by research involving the imitation of actions on objects (e.g., pressing a button or opening a box). Several studies found that individuals with ASD, across developmental levels and age ranges, have difficulties imitating meaningful actions on objects (Bernier et al., 2007; Colombi et al., 2009; Cossu et al., 2012; Leighton, Bird, Charman, & Heyes, 2008; Rogers et al., 2010; Stieglitz Ham, 2011). Other studies, however, report intact ability to perform this type

of task (Beadle-Brown & Whiten, 2004; Hobson & Hobson, 2008; Rogers et al., 1996), but some of these had results confounded by ceiling effects.

Studies employing both actions on objects and gestures often report that imitation of actions on objects is less impaired than imitation of gestures (DeMyer et al., 1972; Ingersoll & Meyer, 2011a; Vivanti et al., 2008; Zachor et al., 2010). One potential confound in this type of paradigm is that, unlike gestures, actions on objects can sometimes be copied by relying on different social learning strategies (e.g., social enhancement or emulation as opposed to true imitation). For example, if the demonstrator opens a box, the imitator might notice the box and act on it according to the specific affordance or of the object (a closed box invites the action of opening), or to the familiar routine associated to the object (e.g., rocking a baby doll). Actions on objects are also constrained by the features of the object, eliminating some degrees of freedom and scaffolding action imitation performance.

The most stringent test of true imitation of actions on objects involves the use of unconventional or novel actions that do not carry a semantic meaning (nonmeaningful actions on objects; e.g., using a brush to lift some Play-Doh). A number of studies using this type of paradigm reported impairments in ASD across age range and developmental level (Charman et al., 1997; Hammes & Langdell, 1981; Smith & Bryson, 2007). One particularly interesting test of imitation examined how children imitated novel actions on objects (e.g., scrape a stick along a block to make a sound) and whether they imitated the style in which the action was performed (gently or harshly) (Hobson & Lee, 1999; see also Hobson & Hobson, 2008). In the experiment, children with autism accurately imitated the object use and goals but did not imitate the style of the action.

A number of other studies also demonstrate the priority of action goals and outcomes in imitation in ASD. In two different studies, children with autism were successfully able to perform Meltzoff's incomplete intentions task (Aldridge, Stone, Sweeney, & Bower, 2000; Carpenter, Pennington, & Rogers, 2001), in which the child sees an adult attempt but fail to perform a simple action, and then the child is given the chance to perform the same action successfully. Both typical and ASD children imitate the action even though they never saw the adult achieve the goal. Similarly, both children with an ASD and children with typical development show the same characteristic pattern of goal-directed imitation (Hamilton, Brindley, & Frith, 2007). In this task, the demonstrator touches a dot on the right with her left hand (an inefficient action) but both typical and autistic children perform the more efficient action of touching the dot with their right hand, thus copying the action goal but not the means. In another experiment, children with ASD were successful in copying the arbitrary rules to achieve a reward in a categorization game (Subiaul et al., 2007), thus showing sensitivity to the goal/meaning underlying the observed motor actions. Other studies show that children with ASD are more likely to imitate actions on objects that result in relevant/motivating feedback (Ingersoll, Schreibman, & Tran, 2003; Rogers, et al., 2010).

Recent evidence suggests that the tendency to focus on action goals in this population may be driven to some extent by action affordances. In a study based on eye tracking (Vivanti et al., 2011), participants had to complete actions on objects after watching videos in which the demonstrator starts but does not finish the action. The study showed that individuals with ASD tended to complete actions according to the affordances suggested by the objects' properties, rather than relying on the demonstrator's intention (which was conveyed by facial and gaze cues). Difficulties in integrating the social cues provided by the demonstrator are also reported in other studies (e.g., D'Entremont & Yazhek, 2007).

Another dimension that was explored by a number of studies concerns the motor complexity/demand of the demonstrated actions (i.e., single versus sequential actions). The general pattern emerging from available literature is that individuals with ASD, across age range and developmental level, find it more difficult to imitate sequences of actions than singular actions (Libby, Powell, Messer, & Jordan, 1997; Rogers et al., 1996; Smith

& Bryson, 1998; Vanvuchelen et al., 2007). Some studies also document reversal errors during imitation in ASD (i.e., imitation of actions with reversed direction of movement; Carpenter, Tomasello, & Striano, 2005; Stieglitz Ham et al., 2011; Ohta, 1987); however, other studies did not replicate this finding (Vanvuchelen et al., 2007).

Another important issue concerns the universality of the imitation deficit in ASD. If imitation deficits are universal in ASD, these deficits must be present in every individual with ASD, regardless of cognitive ability or severity of ASD symptoms. Remarkable heterogeneity in imitation performance in ASD is reported by a number of studies (e.g., Hobson & Lee, 1999; Rogers et al., 2010; Salowitz et al., 2012; Vanvuchelen, Roeyers, & De Weerdt, 2011; Vivanti et al., 2011), suggesting that imitation difficulties are present in many but not all individuals in the spectrum. For example, in the study by Vanvuchelen and colleagues involving a large sample of toddlers with ASD (2011), imitation deficits were present in around 70% of participants. As most published studies focus on group differences, without reporting on individual variations, more research is needed to gain further knowledge on the issue of universality.

Developmental Correlates of Imitation in ASD

As originally suggested by Rogers and Pennington (1991), the importance of research on imitation in ASD might extend beyond the study of imitative ability per se, as many developmental processes and skills that are relevant in ASD (including communicative, social-cognitive, emotional, and motor-executive abilities) appear to be linked with imitation. A number of studies, for example, found concurrent and predictive correlations between imitation and language in children with ASD (Charman, et al., 2000; Dawson & Adams, 1984; Ingersoll & Meyer, 2011b; McDuffie et al., 2007; Stone & Yoder, 2001; Toth, Dawson, Meltzoff, Greenson, & Fein, 2007; but see Rogers et al., 2003). Other studies found imitative abilities to be correlated with functional and symbolic play (Libby et al., 1997; Stone et al., 1997; Vivanti, Dissanayake, Zierhut, & Rogers, 2013), joint attention (Carpenter, Pennington, & Rogers, 2002; Ingersoll & Schreibman, 2006; Rogers et al., 2003), severity of autistic symptoms (Ingersoll & Meyer, 2011b; Rogers et al., 2003; Zachor et al., 2010), and measures of social reciprocity (McDuffie et al., 2007; G. S. Young et al., 2011), cooperation (Colombi et al., 2009), and theory of mind (Perra et al., 2008; but see Charman et al., 2000). Concurrent correlations between imitation and different measures of praxis and motor abilities are also frequently reported (Mostofsky et al., 2006; Salowitz et al., 2012; Smith & Bryson, 1998; Vanvuchelen et al., 2007).

Summary

In summary, current available evidence suggests that individuals with ASD, as a group, imitate others less frequently and less accurately from infancy, at least when compared to typically developing peers. Despite gains over time in imitative abilities, they continue to show impairments throughout the lifespan. These impairments are more obvious in tasks that measure true imitation, that is, copying the demonstrator's actions and goals without relying on knowledge about the outcomes of the action or the function/use of materials involved in the demonstration. In contrast, individuals with ASD seem to imitate better when tasks involve objects, when they are familiar with the materials involved in the task, when they understand the demonstrator's goals, and when they are interested in the outcome of the action. Moreover, imitation of single actions seems to be easier in this population than imitation of sequences of actions. Differences in imitative behavior appear to be associated to differences in social, communicative, as well as motor skills in this population; however, the nature of these associations is still not clear. Imitative difficulties are unlikely to play a causal role in autism, given that not all individuals in the spectrum show an imitation impairment and at-risk siblings who do not develop autism show a comparable deficit in imitation in infancy (G. S. Young et al., 2011).

In the following section, we review the possible causal mechanisms underlying this complex pattern of imitative abnormalities in ASD.

THEORIES OF IMITATION

In order to understand imitation behavior, it is necessary to consider the underlying cognitive processes that take place during imitation. In information processing terms, imitation is not a single entity, but relies on multiple domain general processes that may contribute to other tasks as well. Here we describe a model of the cognitive components needed for imitation, and then assess how different theories of autism have placed the impairment in different components.

Our earliest models of imitation derive from studies of neuropsychological patients. Rothi & Heilman (1997) proposed a dual route model of imitation, and current research largely supports their ideas. An up-to-date form of the model was presented by Tessari and Rumiati (2004) based on studies of typical adults. In this model (Figure 12.1), an observed action must first be encoded visually (Figure 12.1a). Brain imaging studies link this to MTG/STS (Downing, Peelen, Wiggett, & Tew, 2006). There are then two possible ways in which the action can be processed. A familiar, meaningful action can be matched onto an existing semantic or action knowledge representation (Figure 12.1b). For example, seeing a person pretend to brush her teeth engages the idea of a toothbrush and the motor knowledge of how to brush one's own teeth. This semantic representation can then provide an input to the motor system, allowing the participant to engage the familiar motor plan for teeth brushing and to produce the action (Figure 12.1c). This type of action knowledge and motor planning is commonly associated with IPL (Buxbaum, Kyle, & Menon, 2005; Grafton & Hamilton, 2007).

However, typical individuals also have the ability to imitate actions that are novel and have no preexisting semantic representation. In this case, the visual representation of the observed action must be mapped directly to the motor system. For example, when seeing an unfamiliar hand gesture, the observed shape of the actor's hand must be mapped onto the participant's own hand to allow the participant to produce the same action (Figure 12.1d). In the case of both familiar and

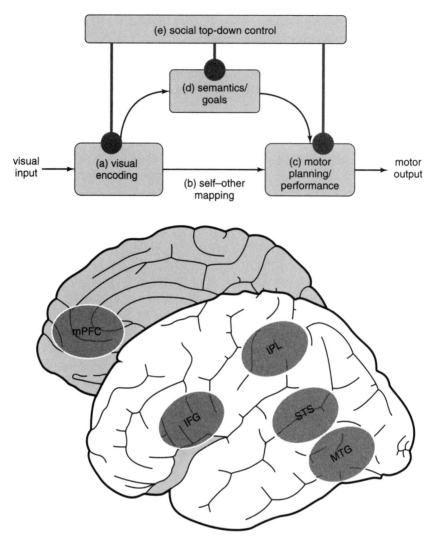

Figure 12.1   Imitation processing and brain systems involved in imitation. (a) Visual encoding of actions involves MTG (middle temporal gyrus) and STS (superior temporal sulcus). (b) Self–other mapping has no clear brain localization. (c) and (d) Motor performance and motor semantics both involve IPL (inferior parietal lobule) and IFG (inferior frontal gyrus), which together comprise the mirror neuron system. (e) Top-down control of imitation involves medial prefrontal cortex (mPFC).

unfamiliar actions, the participant must then have an intact motor system in order to execute the action and show successful imitation (Figure 12.1c). The core of this model (Figure 12.1b, c, and d) comprises the human mirror neuron system (MNS; Rizzolatti & Craighero, 2004).

There are two possible routes through this system: A semantic route allows comprehension of goal and action meaning to contribute to imitation, while a direct route allows imitation of meaningless

gestures. Using both routes together is likely to be necessary for true imitation. This dual route model of imitation has been augmented and elaborated in some recent works (Buxbaum & Kalenine, 2010), but the basic idea of two possible information processing streams for imitation remains a powerful way to understand imitation in a variety of neuropsychological conditions.

The two or more imitation routes present in the MNS (Figure 12.1 a, b, c, and d) together comprise a fundamental visual-motor processing stream, in which visual inputs can be translated into motor outputs. Anatomically, this visuomotor stream is embedded within a much more general visual-motor processing system that receives all visual inputs (not just actions to imitate) and plans and executes appropriate motor responses (Cisek & Kalaska, 2010). The behavior and responsiveness of this system is determined to a large extent by associative learning based on the individual's past experience, rather than being innately specified (Heyes, 2011). This implies that the mirror neuron system is not dedicated purely to imitation but should be considered as part of a broader, more general visual-motor system.

While this dual-route, neuropsychology-based model of imitation has a considerable explanatory power, it has it has recently become clear that there is more to everyday imitation than just this. Typical children and adults imitate far more than they need to just to achieve their everyday goals of moving through the world. Typical toddlers show overimitation (Over & Carpenter, 2012), copying even causally unnecessary components of action sequences, whereas apes do not (Whiten, McGuigan, Marshall-Pescini, & Hopper, 2009). Adults imitate one another's gestures and mannerisms during social interactions, a phenomenon often described as the chameleon effect (Lakin & Chartrand, 2003). The frequency of these additional imitation behaviors is strongly modulated by social cues. For example, toddlers and children overimitate more when they are socially engaged (Brugger, Lariviere, Mumme, & Bushnell, 2007; Nielsen & Blank, 2011) and adults show more unconscious gesture imitation when interacting with someone of high social status or when they have an affiliation goal (Bandura, 1971; Lakin & Chartrand, 2003). These phenomena fall under the broad category of social imitation (Over & Carpenter, 2012).

The existence of social imitation, and the subtle control of this behavior by a variety of social signals, led researchers to augment the basic dual-route imitation model with a top-down control system (Figure 12.1e; Southgate & Hamilton, 2008; Wang & Hamilton, 2012). This system recognizes social cues (eye contact, social status, context, etc.) and based on these signals, can upregulate or down-regulate imitation processing in the visuomotor processing stream. Neuropsychological evidence suggests that the control of imitation is likely to involve the prefrontal cortex. Patients with prefrontal damage often show echolalia or echopraxia, that is, excessive imitation of actions indicative of damaged imitation-control systems (De Renzi, Cavalleri, & Facchini, 1996; Lhermitte, Pillon, & Serdaru, 1986; Luria, 1966; Vendrell et al., 1995). Recent brain imaging studies support this notion. Brass and colleagues showed that medial prefrontal cortex is engaged when participants must inhibit their natural tendency to mimic (Brass, Derrfuss, & von Cramon, 2005). Going further, an functional magnetic resonance imaging (fMRI) study shows that eye contact enhances mimicry and that during this enhancement, medial prefrontal cortex increases its regulation of superior temporal sulcus, which provides inputs to the mirror system (Wang, Ramsey, & Hamilton, 2011). These new information processing models show how imitation behavior involves a subtle interaction of many different brain and cognitive systems. Figure 10.1 provides an overview of the major cognitive processes involved in imitation behavior in typical adults. Different theories of poor imitation in individuals with ASD have posited problems with different components of this model. We review and assess these theories, focusing on one component at a time.

Theories of Poor Visual Encoding

One possibility is that individuals with autism stumble at the first step of the imitation process, that is, they imitate less frequently and less accurately as a consequence of abnormal visual encoding of others' actions (Figure 12.1a). Two bodies of literature support this perspective: first, studies documenting reduced attention to others' actions, and second, studies suggesting atypical perceptual strategies in this population. Individuals with ASD show atypical patterns of attention to both social (Klin, Jones, Schultz, Volkmar, &

Cohen, 2002; Rice, Moriuchi, Jones, & Klin, 2012) and nonsocial stimuli (Anderson, Colombo, & Jill Shaddy, 2006; Sasson, Elison, Turner-Brown, Dichter, & Bodfish, 2011), as well as a lack of interest in people and their actions (Barbaro & Dissanayake, 2013; Kasari, Sigman, Mundy, & Yirmiya, 1990). It is therefore possible that children with ASD fail to imitate because they do not pay attention to actions that are demonstrated to them. This hypothesis was explicitly tested in two eye-tracking studies (Vivanti et al., 2008; Vivanti et al., 2011). Results from these studies indicate that children with autism, across chronological and developmental age groups, show no abnormalities in the amount of attention to actions that are demonstrated to them. However, a reduced attention to the demonstrator's face has been consistently reported. Importantly, this research is based on elicited imitation paradigms; no study, so far, investigated whether differences in visual attention to others' actions explain reduced frequency of spontaneous imitative behavior in this population. Abnormalities in visual encoding in ASD might not be limited to the amount of visual attention, but could possibly involve atypical visual processing (Dakin & Frith, 2005; Simmons et al., 2009). In particular, some studies documented enhanced processing of fine details (possibly at the expenses of the overall picture; Happé & Frith, 2006) and difficulties in the analysis of motion coherence and biological motion (Pellicano, Gibson, Mayberry, Durkin, & Badcock, 2005). However, a recent large-scale study suggests teenagers with ASD process biological motion just like typical individuals (Jones et al., 2011). The nature of these perceptual phenomena is still debated, and there is still no consensus on the role that visual processing abnormalities might play in the development of ASD symptoms (Mottron, Dawson, Soulieres, Hubert, & Burack, 2006; Simmons et al., 2009). No study so far has addressed the possible role of visual processing abnormalities in imitation abilities in ASD.

Overall, eye-tracking research rules out the idea that imitation difficulties in ASD occur as a consequence of lack of attention to the model. It is reasonable to suspect that abnormalities in visual processing of others' actions, both at the quantitative and qualitative level, might affect imitative behavior in ASD. Nevertheless, the idea of a bias toward the subcomponents of the visual stimulus (the demonstration's action units) at the expense of the global meaning of the action (the demonstrator's goal) does not fit with the pattern of strengths and weakness in imitation emerging from the literature, which shows better imitation of goal-directed versus meaningless actions in this population. Furthermore, the initial finding of difficulties in processing biological motion in ASD was not successfully replicated in subsequent research (Jones et al., 2011). More research is needed to investigate the role of atypical visual input processing in imitative performance in ASD. However, available evidence suggests that atypical visual processing of the input does not provide a satisfactory explanation for the range of phenomena documented in ASD imitation research.

Theories of Failed Direct Self–Other Mapping

In their 1991 influential paper, Rogers and Pennington proposed that the imitative deficit in ASD might reflect a specific difficulty with "forming and coordinating specific social representations of self and other" (i.e., self-other mapping) (Figure 12.1b). The construct of self–other mapping, inspired by the work of Stern (1985), refers to the ability to register/appreciate correspondences between own and others' actions (as well as mental and affective states). This process, as reflected in early imitative and affective exchanges, is thought to support the development of a range of social-cognitive skills such as joint attention, symbolic play, and theory of mind, so that an impairment at this level would result in a series of negative developmental sequelae. An updated version of this model proposed by Williams and colleagues in 2001 included the suggestion that the self-other mapping process might be implemented by the MNS, and consequently, that difficulties with self–other mapping might originate from a MNS dysfunction (broken mirrors theory; Williams, Whiten, Suddendorf, & Perrett, 2001).

The mirror neuron system is located in the human inferior parietal and inferior frontal gyrus, and, in typically developing individuals, responds to the self-execution of a given action as well as to the observation of a similar motor act performed by others (Rizzolatti & Craighero, 2004). According to a number of scholars, this distinctive property reflects the implementation of a direct mapping between observed and performed actions, which allows the observer to understand others' actions as if he or she would be doing a similar action (Gallese, 2006). Based on these claims, we illustrate the self–other mapping in Figure 12.1 in terms of the basic link between a visual representation of an action and the motor plan needed to perform the action. After Williams et al.'s original proposal, different versions of the broken mirror theory of autism have been described by several groups (Gallese, Rochat, & Berchio, 2012; Iacoboni & Dapretto, 2006; Ramachandran & Oberman, 2006; Rizzolatti, Fabbri-Destro, & Cattaneo, 2009; Sinigaglia & Sparaci, 2010; Williams, 2008), all sharing the idea that in autism, there is an absence or impairment of a fundamental, low-level mapping between the visual representation of an action performed by another person and a mirrored representation of that same action in the observer's own motor system. This, in turn, disrupts the process of self–other correspondence that enables understanding and reproduction of observed actions.

One specific prediction of the broken mirror model is that mimicry, being a behavioral index of self–other mapping, would be impaired in ASD. As discussed earlier, mimicry in ASD is reported to be reduced in some studies, while other studies report intact or enhanced mimicry; therefore, more research is needed to clarify this issue. Another prediction of the model is that difficulties in imitation would be associated to difficulties in other abilities that are supposedly implemented by self–other mapping (or mirroring) mechanism. These include affect sharing, symbolic play, language, and joint attention (in the original Rogers & Pennington model; see also Pennington, Williams, & Rogers, 2006) as well as goal understanding, theory of

mind and empathy (according to most versions of the broken mirrors model; see Iacoboni, 2009). A number of studies report correlations between imitation and measures of language, joint attention, affect, play, and theory of mind, suggesting that these constructs might reflect some common underlying factors (e.g., Colombi et al., 2009; Ingersoll & Meyer, 2011b). Nevertheless, not all studies confirm these associations (e.g., Johnson, Gillis, & Romanczyk, 2012; Rogers et al., 2003), and more research is needed to understand the causal structure among these variables from a developmental perspective.

A further prediction from the broken mirror model is based on the claim that the mirror neuron system is mainly concerned with goal understanding (Rizzolatti & Sinigaglia, 2010). This implies that participants with autism should have particular difficulties understanding and imitating action goals (Hamilton, 2009). This prediction appears to be inconsistent with the data indicating better imitation of actions with goals versus actions without goals, and better performance in tasks involving emulation versus imitation in ASD (see findings section).

A different approach for testing the broken mirrors model involves the measurement of MNS integrity using neuroimaging techniques during imitation tasks. Surprisingly, most of the studies on MNS activity in ASD have used action-observation tasks rather than imitation tasks, providing little information on the actual role of the putative MNS dysfunction in imitation. The few studies testing MNS activity during imitation task yielded mixed findings. A magnetoencephalography (MEG) study by Nishitani, Avikainen, and Hari (2004) found abnormal MNS activity during an imitation task in ASD. Similarly, a study by Bernier et al. (2007) found a correlation between imitation difficulties and abnormal attenuation of mu-rhythm over the motor cortex during action observation, which is considered an indicator for the action/perception coupling activity (Pineda, 2005) and a specific index of the MNS. Using the same technique, however, Fan, Decety, Yang, Liu, and Cheng (2010), failed to replicate this finding, reporting intact mu-rhythm activity in the presence of impaired imitation. Using fMRI, Dapretto et al. (2006) documented abnormal activity in the frontal component of the MNS during a facial imitation task; this, however, was not associated with imitation performance (which was reported to be intact in the study; however imitative accuracy was not actually measured). In another fMRI study Williams et al. (2006) reported reduced activity in the parietal component of the MNS during an imitation task, which was not correlated to the actual imitative performance. Given the paucity and the inconsistency of the neural processing data gathered during imitation tasks, both in ASD and typical population, more research is necessary to clarify (1) whether the MNS is actually implementing a self-other mapping (mirroring) mechanism underlying imitation and (2) whether a specific deficit in such process is the cause of the range of imitative difficulties observed in ASD. Whilst evidence for the involvement of the MNS in imitation difficulties in ASD is rather spotty (Hamilton, 2013), difficulties with the processing of self–other correspondences might not necessarily be associated with a MNS dysfunction or with a disrupted perception/action matching mechanism. Alternative interpretations of the nature and role of this process in the imitative deficit in ASD are considered in the section on theories of abnormal social top-down control.

Theories of Abnormal Motor and Sensory-Motor Disturbances

A number of studies explored the possibility that poor imitation in ASD might be caused by motor-related disturbances (Figure 12.1c, d). Motor impairments appear to be present in at least a significant subgroup of individuals with ASD and may include deficits in basic fine and gross motor skills as well as difficulties in motor planning and motor learning (Esposito & Vivanti, 2012; Gowen & Hamilton, 2012; Lloyd, Macdonald, & Lord, 2011; Silver & Rapin, 2012). The idea that imitation impairments in ASD reflect deficits in the basic motor operations involved in the execution of the observed actions is supported by studies

documenting an association between motor and imitative performances (McDuffie et al., 2007; Vanvuchelen et al., 2007). However, two recent studies documented that while impaired imitation of gestures in ASD was highly correlated with impairments in basic motor control, the motor impairments did not fully account for impaired imitation (Dowell, Mahone, & Mostofsky, 2009; Dziuk et al., 2007). Several other studies suggested that imitative difficulties distinguish between ASD and other diagnostic groups even when fine and gross motor difficulties are accounted for (Smith & Bryson, 1998; Williams, Whiten, & Singh, 2004).

A number of studies looked at the possibility that poor imitation might be caused by abnormalities in higher motor or sensory-motor processes. Mostofsky and colleagues recently detailed a theory proposing that abnormal imitation in ASD originates from abnormal visual-motor integration (Mostofsky & Ewen, 2011). This is based on the finding that individuals with ASD show a diminished reliance on visual feedback and an increased reliance on proprioceptive feedback when learning novel movements; that is, they tend to use the input from their own internal world rather than visual input from the external world for motor learning. The strength of this bias in ASD was found to be correlated with impairments in imitation (as well as praxis and social interaction difficulties; Haswell, Izawa, Dowell, Mostofsky, Shadmehr, 2009; Izawa et al., 2012).

Overall, theories of abnormal motor or sensory-motor disturbances appear to be supported by a number of findings, including (1) evidence that dyspraxia is common in ASD (Mosconi, Takarae & Sweeney, 2011; Rapin, 1996), (2) evidence that imitation accuracy in this population decreases as the motor demand increases (e.g., in sequential versus single action imitation tasks), (3) evidence of associations between levels of motor and imitation abilities in this population, and (4) evidence of an association between imitation performance and abnormal visual-motor integration specific to ASD (Izawa et al., 2012). Nevertheless, some studies that specifically tested the role of motor versus social factors in imitation performance in ASD found evidence that social factors might be more relevant (e.g., Perra et al., 2008; Zachor et al., 2010). Moreover, neither the general motor planning nor the sensory-motor integration abnormalities hypothesis clearly account for a range of phenomena documented in literature, including evidence that individuals with ASD imitate more in elicited versus naturalistic conditions, the differences in patterns of visual attention to the demonstration, and the difficulties in imitating the affective style versus the goals of the demonstrated actions. More research is necessary to clarify the complex interplay between motor, sensory-motor, and social cognitive functions in relation to imitation in typical development and autism.

Theories of Abnormal Social Top-Down Control

The control of who and when to imitate is not trivial. There are an increasing number of suggestions that abnormal imitation in individuals with autism might be due to failure of top-down control signals or social motivational signals (Figure 12.1e). In typical children and adults, imitation is modulated by social cues such as eye contact (Wang, Newport, & Hamilton, 2011), social interactivity (Brugger et al., 2007), and social status (Cheng & Chartrand, 2003). Failure of this top-down social modulation of imitation could account for many of the imitation differences observed in autism (Southgate & Hamilton, 2008). This model has been termed STORM (social top-down response modulation), and the key claim is that basic imitation mechanisms are intact in autism, while top-down control signals are abnormal or absent in this population (Wang & Hamilton, 2012).

A parallel perspective, building on a different research approach, involves the distinction between *imitation* and *identification* proposed by Hobson (Hobson & Hobson, 2008; Hobson & Lee, 1999), which is based on the idea that a process of identification at the affective level must take place between the observer and the demonstrator for accurate imitation to occur. Hobson proposes that while motor imitation per se is intact in autism, imitative abnormalities reflect a lack of interpersonal-affective identification with others in this population (Hobson, 2010). The construct of interpersonal identification overlaps only in part with the similar notion of self–other mapping (Rogers & Pennington, 1991) as it emphasizes the importance of the propensity/drive to identify with others (supposedly impaired in ASD) rather than the integrity of the visuomotor hardware underlying copying behaviors, which is assumed to be intact (Hobson & Meyer, 2005).

Another, similar, top-down account of abnormal imitation in ASD can be derived from the social motivation theory of autism (Chevallier, Kohls, Troiani, Brodkin, & Schultz, 2012; Dawson, et al., 2005; Mundy & Neal, 2001). According to this perspective, young children with autism, as opposed to their typically developing peers, do not experience social interactions as intrinsically rewarding and do not prioritize social stimuli over nonsocial information, thus failing to develop over time the motivation and the ability to connect to others and maintain social relationships. Evidence from social psychology suggests that unconscious imitation of others is a tool for building and maintaining social relationships (Lakin & Chartrand, 2003), so a lack of social motivation could lead to a lack of imitation. Again, this model predicts that imitation mechanisms themselves are intact in autism but are not appropriately used. One way to test this hypothesis is to study overimitation behavior (the tendency to copy unnecessary actions), which is largely socially motivated. One study found that children with autism do overimitate actions on novel objects (Nielsen, Slaughter, & Dissanayake, 2013), while a second study found that typical children overimitate actions on familiar objects but children with autism do not (Marsh, Pearson, Ropar, & Hamilton, 2013). Further study of the role of social motivation in imitation would be very valuable.

These top-down theories can provide a good explanation of abnormal imitation frequency in ASD. They account for reduced spontaneous imitation (see findings section), especially in response to social cues (Ingersoll, 2008a, 2008b) and also for increased imitation in cases such as echolalia and echopraxia (Grossi, Marcone, Cinquegrana, & Gallucci, 2013; Spengler, Bird, & Brass, 2010). In the latter behaviors, abnormal top-down signals lead to too much imitation or imitation at a socially inappropriate time. The top-down theories are particularly strong in accounting for the widely variable results found in some studies of imitation in ASD, with some studies reporting good performance and others reporting poor performance (see reviews by Hamilton, 2009, and Vivanti, 2013). For example, Hobson and Lee (1999) and Hobson and Hobson (2008) found that children with ASD were able to imitate the goal of an action but did not accurately imitate the style in which the action was performed. Top-down theories suggest that imitation of an action goal is motivated by the nonsocial desire to do the action and does not require social control signals. In contrast, imitation of the action style might only occur if the child identifies with the demonstrator or is socially motivated to engage with them. This latter type of imitation is abnormal in ASD, reflecting failure of social engagement in this population. The eye-tracking studies by Vivanti and colleagues (2008, 2011, 2013) are consistent with the idea that individuals in the spectrum might show reduced sensitivity to the social cues (in particular, referential cues) conveyed by the demonstrator's face, relying instead on the properties of the objects involved in the demonstration or on the demonstrator's actions.

However, few direct tests of the top-down theories of imitation have been conducted. A study by Cook and Bird (2012) examined how mimicry responses are modulated following a conceptual priming manipulation in high-functioning adults with autism. Typical adults show faster mimicry after they performed a task involving unscrambling of pro-social sentences, compared to priming with neutral or anti-social sentences. Adults with autism show the same level of mimicry responses across all three conditions, suggesting that top-down modulation of mimicry is abnormal in this group. Similarly, Grecucci et al. (2012) found normal mimicry of hand actions in autism but a lack of modulation of responses by the presence of an emotional facial expression. A study by Spengler and colleagues (2010) showed that individual differences in activation of medial prefrontal cortex (mPFC) during a theory of mind task predicted individual differences in the control of mimicry, within a sample of high functioning adults with ASD. This suggests that abnormalities in the control of mimicry are linked to abnormalities in brain systems linked to theory of mind, a domain where individuals with autism are known to struggle (Baron-Cohen, Leslie, & Frith, 1985; Senju, 2012). Further studies would be very valuable in testing the top-down control theory of imitation in autism in detail.

One limitation of the STORM theory is that it does not account for reduced accuracy of imitation in ASD. The top-down theory assumes that basic imitation mechanisms are intact in autism, and thus predicts that when imitation does occur, it should be accurate in ASD. There are also several aspects of the top-down theory that are not fully specified. It is not yet clear if failure of top-down control of imitation in ASD is due to difficulties in detecting social cues, or difficulties in implementing control or in a reduced motivation to engage with others. It is not clear if this top-down control applies to other social behaviors beyond imitation, and how it relates to other domains that have been implicated in ASD, including theory of mind and executive function (Pellicano, 2010). Further study on all these possibilities will be very valuable.

INTERVENTION STRATEGIES

Imitation is critical for interventions to help children with ASD because a child who can imitate has a powerful tool for both learning and socialization. A number of strategies have been developed to teach imitative skills in individuals with ASD since the 1960s (Lovaas, Freitag, Nelson, & Whalen, 1967; Metz, 1965). Strategies based on discrete trial teaching involve the use of highly structured settings and external reinforcements (e.g., food) to elicit imitative behavior in response to a predefined fixed series of stimuli. Several studies document that through these procedures individuals with ASD can learn to imitate a number of complex behaviors, including actions on objects (Buffington,

Krantz, McClannahan, & Poulson, 1998; J. M. Young, Krantz, Mcclannahan, & Poulson, 1994), gestures (Buffington et al., 1998), and oral-facial movements (DeQuinzio, Townsend, Sturmey, & Poulson, 2007). Several studies employing behavioral techniques that use peers as models also report positive results (Carr & Darcy, 1990; Ganz, Bourgeois, Flores, & Campos, 2008; Garfinkle & Schwartz, 2002). Video modeling, a behavioral technique that uses video-recorded stimuli rather than live scenarios to model behaviors, has been employed to teach imitation in ASD, with research providing mixed findings (D'Ateno, Mangiapanello, & Taylor, 2003; Rayner, 2011; Rayner, Denholm, & Sigafoos, 2009; Tereshko, MacDonald, & Ahearn, 2010).

In the past decade, developmental research has documented the importance of rewarding social interactions as a framework for learning (Kuhl, 2007). This has informed a new generation of play-based educational programs that places the emphasis on the social context of imitation, as well as the spontaneous use of imitation to learn and to socialize in untrained environments and in the absence of external reinforcement. The reciprocal imitation training model (Ingersoll & Gergans, 2007; Ingersoll, Lewis, & Kroman, 2007) is a naturalistic intervention based on dyadic play exchanges in which the therapist initially imitates the child behavior, thus establishing a turn-taking routine, and then models new actions for the child to imitate. If the child fails to imitate, the therapist prompts the imitative response. All spontaneous imitative behaviors are systematically reinforced through verbal praise. Results from a randomized control trial documented improvements in imitative skills in children undergoing this intervention, as well as gains in joint attention and social functioning (Ingersoll, 2010, 2011).

The Early Start Denver Model (ESDM; Rogers & Dawson, 2010) is a developmental, relationship-based program that employs teaching techniques to foster the development of skills that are foundational to social-cognitive development, including imitation, in young children with ASD. Imitative responses, rather than being taught in isolation, are targeted together with other social (e.g., joint attention, sharing of affect, verbal and nonverbal communication) and nonsocial skills (e.g., fine motor, nonverbal cognitive skills), in the framework of joint activity routines. In these routines the therapist creates a play activity that incorporates the child's choice and involves shared control of the materials and turn-taking exchanges. Instead of following a predetermined schedule, the adult models actions that are meaningful in the context of the play activity (e.g., gestures associated to a song routine, facial expressions to highlight the emotional context of the story in a book, or actions associated to a Play-Doh game), so to motivate the child to produce an imitative response in order to get the activity to continue. A randomized control trial of the ESDM has documented strong positive outcomes in cognitive and adaptive skills (Dawson et al., 2010), and a recent study found frequency of spontaneous imitation to be a positive predictor of outcomes in this intervention model (Vivanti et al., 2013).

The interpersonal synchrony model (Landa, Holman, O'Neill, & Stuart, 2011) focuses on fostering developmental gains in imitation, as well as in other social behaviors such as joint attention and affect sharing, within a group setting. The learning environment involves enhanced opportunities for motivating play-based interactions to promote the spontaneous occurrence of synchronous behavior, including contingent imitative responses to both adults and peers. A randomized control trial documented gains in the treatment group in imitation and other social initiations measures, which were maintained over a 6-month period (Landa et al., 2011). Overall, these studies suggest that including imitation in interventions for ASD is important, but more work is needed to link our theories of imitation to the teaching of imitation skills and to understand the role of imitation learning in driving improvements in social behavior in ASD.

CONCLUSIONS AND FUTURE DIRECTION

Understanding the nature of imitative difficulties in ASD is particularly challenging, as both imitative behavior and autistic behavior might result from a combination of different underlying factors, rather than being the expression of a single linear process or pathway. Different tasks draw on different cognitive processes, and these might be impaired to various degrees in some but not all the individuals in the spectrum. Advances in our understanding of the imitative deficit in ASD will be driven by the increasing recognition of the cognitive systems underlying imitation and of the particular ingredients that make specific imitation tasks difficult for particular individuals in the spectrum.

The findings presented in this chapter suggest that most individuals with ASD struggle more with imitation tasks involving actions that are unfamiliar and do not have a clear goal/outcome. Moreover, imitation performance appears to be poorer as the social-processing and/or motor demands in the task increase. Future research should take into consideration this pattern, rather than testing whether imitation is globally impaired in ASD, and systematically manipulate the different factors associated with the task (e.g., familiarity of the action, opacity of the demonstrator's goal, motor demand) to test the relevance of different candidate mechanisms. Furthermore, individual differences in imitation performance should be mapped into the different neuropsychological profiles of participants, to determine whether the levels of severity of different impairments (e.g., motor planning, goal understanding, or social attention difficulties) predict performance in tasks that pose a particular demand in specific areas.

A more fine-grained understanding of the different imitative behaviors is also needed to advance knowledge in the field. This approach involves a detailed analysis of both the demonstrator's and the imitator's behavior, with a particular attention to the means-end structure of the demonstrated action, the communicative signals conveyed by the demonstrator, the imitator's own goals, the nature of the instructions given, and the social, affective, and physical context in which the demonstration occurs. All these factors are known to affect imitation behavior, not only in terms of the accuracy of performance, but also in terms of the specific learning strategy used by the imitator (Horner &

Whiten, 2005; Over & Carpenter, 2012); however, they are rarely taken into account in ASD research. Finally, as with many phenomena observed in ASD, it is crucial to distinguish between what individuals in the spectrum can do and what they actually do in their everyday life (Klin, Jones, Schultz, & Volkmar, 2003). This requires a new focus on carefully designed observational studies, looking at the factors that drive spontaneous imitative behaviors and the particular copying strategies used by individuals with ASD when they are and are not explicitly instructed to do so. Given that imitation is one of the most powerful tools for learning and socializing, advances in the field can make a significant difference in our ability to facilitate learning and support participation in cultural and social activities in the community for individuals with an ASD.

CROSS-REFERENCES

Chapter 5 focuses on autism in infants and young children. Social development is the focus of Chapter 9, and Chapter 11 focuses on play skills; interventions for young children are the focus in Chapter 29.

REFERENCES

Aldridge, M. A., Stone, K. R., Sweeney, M. H., & Bower, T. G. R. (2000). Preverbal children with autism understand the intentions of others. *Developmental Science*, *3*(3), 294–301

Anderson, C. J., Colombo, J., & Jill Shaddy, D. (2006). Visual scanning and pupillary responses in young children with autism spectrum disorder. *Journal of Clinical and Experimental Neuropsychology*, *28*(7), 1238–1256.

Asperger, H. (1944). Die autistischen psychopathen in Kindersalten. *Archiv fur Psychiatrie und Nervenkrankenheiten*, *117*, 76–136.

Bandura, A. (1971). Analysis of modeling processes. In A. Bandura (Ed.), *Psychological modeling* (pp. 1–62). Chicago, IL: Aldine-Atherton.

Bandura, A. (1977). *Social learning theory*. Oxford, England: Prentice-Hall.

Barbaro, J., & Dissanayake, C. (2013). Early markers of autism spectrum disorders in infants and toddlers prospectively identified in the Social Attention and Communication Study. *Autism*, *17*(1), 64–86.

Baron-Cohen, S., Leslie, A. M., & Frith, U. (1985). Does the autistic child have a "theory of mind"? *Cognition*, *21*(1), 37–46.

Bates, E., Bretherton, I., & Snyder, L. S. (1988). *From first words to grammar: individual differences and dissociable mechanisms.* Cambridge, England, New York, NY: Cambridge University Press.

Beadle-Brown, J. (2004). Elicited imitation in children and adults with autism: the effect of different types of actions. *Journal of Applied Research in Intellectual Disabilities, 17*(1), 37–48.

Beadle-Brown, J. D., & Whiten, A. (2004). Elicited imitation in children and adults with autism: is there a deficit? *Journal of Intellectual & Developmental Disability, 29*(2), 147–163.

Beall, P. M., Moody, E. J., McIntosh, D. N., Hepburn, S. L., & Reed, C. L. (2008). Rapid facial reactions to emotional facial expressions in typically developing children and children with autism spectrum disorder. *Journal of Experimental Child Psychology, 101*(3), 206–223.

Bekkering, H., Wohlschlager, A., & Gattis, M. (2000). Imitation of gestures in children is goal-directed. *Quarterly Journal of Experimental Psychology A, 53*(1), 153–164.

Bernier, R., Dawson, G., Webb, S., & Murias, M. (2007). EEG mu rhythm and imitation impairments in individuals with autism spectrum disorder. *Brain and Cognition, 64*(3), 228–237.

Bird, G., Leighton, J., Press, C., & Heyes, C. (2007). Intact automatic imitation of human and robot actions in autism spectrum disorders. *Proceedings of the Royal Society—Biological Sciences, 274*(1628), 3027–3031.

Brass, M., Derrfuss, J., & von Cramon, D. Y. (2005). The inhibition of imitative and overlearned responses: A functional double dissociation. *Neuropsychologia, 43*(1), 89–98.

Brown, J., & Whiten, A. (2000). Imitation, theory of mind and related activities in autism—An observational study of spontaneous behaviour in everyday contexts. *Autism, 4*, 185–204.

Brugger, A., Lariviere, L. A., Mumme, D. L., & Bushnell, E. W. (2007). Doing the right thing: Infants' selection of actions to imitate from observed event sequences. *Child Development, 78*(3), 806–824.

Buchsbaum, D., Gopnik, A., Griffiths, T. L., & Shafto, P. (2011). Children's imitation of causal action sequences is influenced by statistical and pedagogical evidence. *Cognition, 120*(3), 331–340.

Buffington, D. M., Krantz, P. J., McClannahan, L. E., & Poulson, C. L. (1998). Procedures for teaching appropriate gestural communication skills to children with autism. *Journal of Autism and Developmental Disorders, 28*(6), 535–545.

Buxbaum, L. J., & Kalenine, S. (2010). Action knowledge, visuomotor activation, and embodiment in the two action systems. *Annals of the New York Academy of Sciences, 1191*, 201–218.

Buxbaum, L. J., Kyle, K. M., & Menon, R. (2005). On beyond mirror neurons: Internal representations subserving imitation and recognition of skilled object-related actions in humans. *Cognitive Brain Research, 25*(1), 226–239.

Byrne, R. W., & Russon, A. E. (1998). Learning by imitation: a hierarchical approach. *Behavioral and Brain Sciences, 21*(5), 667–684; discussion 684–721.

Call, J., Carpenter, M., & Tomasello, M. (2005). Copying results and copying actions in the process of social learning: chimpanzees (Pan troglodytes) and human children (Homo sapiens). *Animal Cognition, 8*(3), 151–163.

Carpenter, M. (2006). Instrumental, social, and shared goals and intentions in imitation. In S. J. Rogers & J. H. G. Williams (Eds.), *Imitation and the social mind: Autism and typical development* (pp. 48–70). New York, NY: Guilford Press.

Carpenter, M., Pennington, B. F., & Rogers, S. J. (2001). Understanding of others' intentions in children with autism. *Journal of Autism and Developmental Disorders, 31*(6), 589–599.

Carpenter, M., Pennington, B. F., & Rogers, S. J. (2002). Interrelations among social-cognitive skills in young children with autism. *Journal of Autism and Developmental Disorders, 32*(2), 91–106.

Carpenter, M., & Tomasello, M. (2000). Joint attention, cultural learning, and language acquisition: Implications for children with autism. In A. M. Wetherby & B. M. Prizant (Eds.), *Communication and language issues in autism and pervasive developmental disorder: A transactional developmental perspective* (pp. 31–54). Baltimore, MD: Paul H. Brookes.

Carpenter, M., Tomasello, M., & Striano, T. (2005). Role reversal imitation and language in typically-developing infants and children with autism. *Infancy, 8*(3), 253–278.

Carr, E. G., & Darcy, M. (1990). Setting generality of peer modeling in children with autism. *Journal of Autism and Developmental Disorders, 20*(1), 45–59.

Charman, T., & Baron-Cohen, S. (1994). Another look at imitation in autism. *Development and Psychopathology, 6*(3), 403–413.

Charman, T., Baron-Cohen, S., Swettenham, J., Baird, G., Cox, A., & Drew, A. (2000). Testing joint attention, imitation, and play as infancy precursors to language and theory of mind. *Cognitive Development, 15*(4), 481–498.

Charman, T., Swettenham, J., Baron-Cohen, S., Cox, A., Baird, G., & Drew, A. (1997). Infants with autism: An investigation of empathy, pretend play, joint attention, and imitation. *Developmental Psychology, 33*(5), 781–789.

Chartrand, T. L., & Bargh, J. A. (1999). The chameleon effect: The perception-behavior link and social interaction. *Journal of Personality and Social Psychology, 76*, 893–910.

Cheng, C. M., & Chartrand, T. L. (2003). Self-monitoring without awareness: Using mimicry as a nonconscious affiliation strategy. *Journal of Personality and Social Psychology, 85*(6), 1170–1179.

Chevallier, C., Kohls, G., Troiani, V., Brodkin, E. S., & Schultz, R. T. (2012). The social motivation theory of autism. *Trends in Cognitive Sciences, 16*(4), 231–239.

Cisek, P., & Kalaska, J. F. (2010). Neural mechanisms for interacting with a world full of action choices. *Annual Review of Neuroscience, 33*, 269–298.

Colombi, C., Liebal, K., Tomasello, M., Young, G., Warneken, F., & Rogers, S. J. (2009). Examining correlates of cooperation in autism Imitation, joint attention, and understanding intentions. *Autism, 13*(2), 143–163.

Cook, J. L., & Bird, G. (2012). Atypical social modulation of imitation in autism spectrum conditions. *Journal of Autism and Developmental Disorders, 42*(6), 1045–1051.

Cossu, G., Boria, S., Copioli, C., Bracceschi, R., Giuberti, V., Santelli, E., & Gallese, V. (2012). Motor representation of actions in children with autism. *PLoS ONE, 7*(9), e44779.

Dakin, S., & Frith, U. (2005). Vagaries of visual perception in autism. *Neuron, 48*(3), 497–507.

Dapretto, M., Davies, M. S., Pfeifer, J. H., Scott, A. A., Sigman, M., Bookheimer, S. Y., & Iacoboni, M. (2006). Understanding emotions in others: mirror neuron dysfunction in children with autism spectrum disorders. *Nature Neuroscience, 9*(1), 28–30.

D'Ateno, P., Mangiapanello, K., & Taylor, B. A. (2003). Using video modeling to teach complex play sequences to a preschooler with autism. *Journal of Positive Behavior Interventions, 5*(1), 5–11.

Dawson, G., & Adams, A. (1984). Imitation and social responsiveness in autistic children. *Journal of Abnormal Child Psychology, 12*(2), 209–225.

Dawson, G., Rogers, S., Munson, J., Smith, M., Winter, J., Greenson, J., . . . Varley, J. (2010). Randomized, controlled trial of an intervention for toddlers with autism: The Early Start Denver Model. *Pediatrics, 125*(1), e17–23.

Dawson, G., Webb, S. J., Wijsman, E., Schellenberg, G., Estes, A., Munson, J., & Faja, S. (2005). Neurocognitive and electrophysiological evidence of altered face processing in parents of children with autism: Implications for a model of abnormal development of social brain circuitry in autism. *Development and Psychopathology, 17*(3), 679–697.

DeMyer, M. K., Alpern, G. D., Barton, S., DeMyer, W. E., Churchill, D. W., Hingtgen, J. N., . . . Kimberlin, C. (1972). Imitation in autistic, early schizophrenic, and non-psychotic subnormal children. *Journal of Autism and Childhood Schizophrenia, 2*(3), 264–287.

D'Entremont, B., & Yazhek, A. (2007). Imitation of intentional and accidental actions by children with autism. *Journal of Autism and Developmental Disorders, 37*(9), 1665–1678.

DeQuinzio, J. A., Townsend, D. B., Sturmey, P., & Poulson, C. L. (2007). Generalized imitation of facial models by children with autism. *Journal of Applied Behavior Analysis, 40*(4), 755–759.

De Renzi, E., Cavalleri, F., & Facchini, S. (1996). Imitation and utilisation behaviour. *Journal of Neurology, Neurosurgery, and Psychiatry, 61*(4), 396–400.

Dewey, D., Cantell, M., & Crawford, S. G. (2007). Motor and gestural performance in children with autism spectrum disorders, developmental coordination disorder, and/or attention deficit hyperactivity disorder. *Journal of the International Neuropsychological Society, 13*(2), 246–256.

Dowell, L. R., Mahone, E. M., & Mostofsky, S. H. (2009). Associations of postural knowledge and basic motor skill with dyspraxia in autism: implication for abnormalities in distributed connectivity and motor learning. *Neuropsychology, 23*(5), 563–570.

Downing, P. E., Peelen, M. V., Wiggett, A. J., & Tew, B. D. (2006). The role of the extrastriate body area in action perception. *Society for Neuroscience, 1*(1), 52–62.

Dziuk, M. A., Gidley Larson, J. C., Apostu, A., Mahone, E. M., Denckla, M. B., & Mostofsky, S. H. (2007). Dyspraxia in autism: association with motor, social, and communicative deficits. *Developmental Medicine & Child Neurology, 49*(10), 734–739.

Esposito, G., & Vivanti, G. (2012). Gross motor skills. In Volkmar, F. (Ed.), *The encyclopedia of autism spectrum disorders* (pp. 1459–1462). New York, NY: Springer.

Fan, Y. T., Decety, J., Yang, C. Y., Liu, J. L., & Cheng, Y. W. (2010). Unbroken mirror neurons in autism spectrum disorders. *Journal of Child Psychology and Psychiatry, 51*(9), 981–988.

Freitag, C. M., Kleser, C., & von Gontard, A. (2006). Imitation and language abilities in adolescents with autism spectrum disorder without language delay. *European Child & Adolescent Psychiatry, 15*(5), 282–291.

Gallese, V. (2006). Intentional attunement: A neurophysiological perspective on social cognition and its disruption in autism. *Brain Research, 1079*(1), 15–24.

Gallese, V., Rochat, M. J., & Berchio, C. (2012). The mirror mechanism and its potential role in autism spectrum disorder. *Developmental Medicine & Child Neurology, 55*(1), 15–22.

Ganz, J. B., Bourgeois, B. C., Flores, M. M., & Campos, B. A. (2008). Implementing visually cued imitation training with children with autism spectrum disorders and developmental delays. *Journal of Positive Behavior Interventions, 10*(1), 56–66.

Garfinkle, A. N., & Schwartz, I. S. (2002). Peer imitation: Increasing social interactions in children with autism and other developmental disabilities in inclusive preschool classrooms. *Topics in Early Childhood Special Education, 22*(1), 26–38.

Gergely, G., Bekkering, H., & Kiraly, I. (2002). Rational imitation in preverbal infants. *Nature, 415*(6873), 755.

Godman, M. (2012). Why we do things together: The social motivation for joint action. *Philosophical Psychology.* doi:10.1080/09515089.2012.670905

Gowen, E., & Hamilton, A. (2012). Motor abilities in autism: A review using a computational context. *Journal of Autism and Developmental Disorders, 43*(2), 32.

Grafton, S. T., & Hamilton, A. F. (2007). Evidence for a distributed hierarchy of action representation in the brain. *Human Movement Science, 26*(4), 590–616.

Grecucci, A., Brambilla, P., Siugzdaite, R., Londero, D., Fabbro, F., & Rumiati, R. I. (2012). Emotional resonance deficits in autistic children. *Journal of Autism and Developmental Disorders, 43*(3), 616–628.

Grossi, D., Marcone, R., Cinquegrana, T., & Gallucci, M. (2013). On the differential nature of induced and incidental echolalia in autism. *Journal of Intellectual Disability Research, 57*(10), 903–912.

Grossman, R. B., & Tager-Flusberg, H. (2008). Reading faces for information about words and emotions in adolescents with autism. *Research in Autism Spectrum Disorders, 2*(4), 681–695.

Hamilton, A. F. (2008). Emulation and mimicry for social interaction: A theoretical approach to imitation in autism. *Quarterly Journal of Experimental Psychology, 61*(1), 101–115.

Hamilton, A. F. (2009). Research review: Goals, intentions and mental states: challenges for theories of autism. *Journal of Child Psychology and Psychiatry, 50*(8), 881–892.

Hamilton, A. F. (2013). Reflecting on the mirror neuron system in autism: a systematic review of current theories. *Developmental Cognitive Neuroscience, 3*, 91–105.

Hamilton, A. F. de C., Brindley, R. M., & Frith, U. (2007). Imitation and action understanding in autistic spectrum disorders: How valid is the hypothesis of a deficit in the mirror neuron system? *Neuropsychologia, 45*(8), 1859–1868.

Hammes, J. G., & Langdell, T. (1981). Precursors of symbol formation and childhood autism. *Journal of Autism and Developmental Disorders, 11*(3), 331–346.

Haswell, C. C., Izawa, J., Dowell, L. R., Mostofsky, S. H., & Shadmehr, R. (2009). Representation of internal models of action in the autistic brain. *Nature Neuroscience, 12* (8)970–972.

Happé, F., & Frith, U. (2006). The weak coherence account: Detail-focused cognitive style in autism spectrum disorders. *Journal of Autism and Developmental Disorders, 36*(1), 5–25.

Heimann, M., Nelson, K. E., & Schaller, J. (1989). Neonatal imitation of tongue protrusion and mouth opening: methodological aspects and evidence of early individual differences. *Scandinavian Journal of Psychology, 30*(2), 90–101.

Heimann, M., Strid, K., Smith, L., Tjus, T., Ulvund, S. E., & Meltzoff, A. N. (2006). Exploring the relation between memory, gestural communication, and the emergence of language in infancy: A longitudinal study. *Infant and Child Development, 15*(3), 233–249.

Heimann, M., & Ullstadius, E. (1999). Neonatal imitation and imitation among children with autism and Down syndrome. In J. Nadel & G. Butterworh (Eds.), *Imitation in infancy* (pp. 235–253). Cambridge, England: Cambridge University Press.

Henrich, J., & Boyd, R. (1998). The evolution of conformist transmission and the emergence of between-group differences. *Evolution and Human Behavior, 19*, 215–242.

Hepburn, S. L., & Stone, W. L. (2006). Longitudinal research on motor imitation in autism. In S. J. Rogers & J. H. G. Williams (Eds.), *Imitation and the social mind: Autism and typical development* (pp. 310–329). New York, NY: Guilford Press.

Heyes, C. (2011). Automatic imitation. *Psychological Bulletin, 137*(3), 463–483.

Hobson, R. P. (2010). Explaining autism: Ten reasons to focus on the developing self. *Autism, 14*(5), 391–407.

Hobson, R. P., & Hobson, J. A. (2008). Dissociable aspects of imitation: A study in autism. *Journal of Experimental Child Psychology, 101*(3), 170–185.

Hobson, R. P., & Lee, A. (1999). Imitation and identification in autism. *Journal of Child Psychology and Psychiatry, 40*(4), 649–659.

Hobson, R. P., & Meyer, J. A. (2005). Foundations for self and other: A study in autism. *Developmental Science, 8*(6), 481–491.

Horner, V., & Whiten, A. (2005). Causal knowledge and imitation/emulation switching in chimpanzees (Pan troglodytes) and children (Homo sapiens). *Animal Cognition, 8*(3), 164–181.

Hurley, S. L., & Chater, N. (2005). *Perspectives on imitation: From neuroscience to social science.* Cambridge, MA: MIT Press.

Iacoboni, M. (2009). Imitation, empathy, and mirror neurons. *Annual Review of Psychology, 60*, 653–670.

Iacoboni, M., & Dapretto, M. (2006). The mirror neuron system and the consequences of its dysfunction. *Nature Reviews Neuroscience, 7*(12), 942–951.

Ingersoll, B. (2008a). The effect of context on imitation skills in children with autism. *Research in Autism Spectrum Disorders, 2*(2), 332–340.

Ingersoll, B. (2008b). The social role of imitation in autism—implications for the treatment of imitation deficits. *Infants and Young Children, 21*(2), 107–119.

Ingersoll, B. (2010). Brief report: Pilot randomized controlled trial of reciprocal imitation training for teaching elicited and spontaneous imitation to children with autism. *Journal of Autism and Developmental Disorders, 40*(9), 1154–1160.

Ingersoll, B. (2011). Brief report: Effect of a focused imitation intervention on social functioning in children with autism. *Journal of Autism and Developmental Disorders 42*(8), 1768–1773.

Ingersoll, B., & Gergans, S. (2007). The effect of a parent-implemented imitation intervention on spontaneous imitation skills in young children with autism. *Research in Developmental Disabilities, 28*(2), 163–175.

Ingersoll, B., Lewis, E., & Kroman, E. (2007). Teaching the imitation and spontaneous use of descriptive gestures in young children with autism using a naturalistic behavioral intervention. *Journal of Autism and Developmental Disorders, 37*(8), 1446–1456.

Ingersoll, B., & Meyer, K. (2011a). Do object and gesture imitation skills represent independent dimensions in autism? *Journal of Developmental and Physical Disabilities, 23*(5), 421–431.

Ingersoll, B., & Meyer, K. (2011b). Examination of correlates of different imitative functions in young children with autism spectrum disorders. *Research in Autism Spectrum Disorders, 5*(3), 1078–1085.

Ingersoll, B., & Schreibman, L. (2006). Teaching reciprocal imitation skills to young children with autism using a naturalistic behavioral approach: Effects on language, pretend play, and joint attention. *Journal of Autism and Developmental Disorders, 36*(4), 487–505.

Ingersoll, B., Schreibman, L., & Tran, Q. H. (2003). Effect of sensory feedback on immediate object imitation in children with autism. *Journal of Autism and Developmental Disorders, 33*(6), 673–683.

Izawa, J., Pekny, S. E., Marko, M. K., Haswell, C. C., Shadmehr, R., & Mostofsky, S. H. (2012). Motor learning relies on integrated sensory inputs in ADHD, but over-selectively on proprioception in autism spectrum conditions. *Autism Research, 5*(2), 124–136.

Johnson, A. L., Gillis, J. M., & Romanczyk, R. G. (2012). A brief report: Quantifying and correlating social behaviors in children with autism spectrum disorders. *Research in Autism Spectrum Disorders, 6*(3), 1053–1060.

Jones, C. R. G., Swettenham, J., Charman, T., Marsden, A. J. S., Tregay, J., Baird, G., . . . Happe, F. (2011). No evidence for a fundamental visual motion processing deficit in adolescents with autism spectrum disorders. *Autism Research, 4*(5), 347–357.

Jones, S. S. (2009). The development of imitation in infancy. *Philosophical Transactions of the Royal Society B: Biological Sciences, 364*(1528), 2325–2335.

Jones, V., & Prior, M. (1985). Motor imitation abilities and neurological signs in autistic children. *Journal of Autism and Developmental Disorders, 15*(1), 37–46.

Kanner, L. (1943). Autistic disturbances of affective contact. *The Nervous Child*, *2*, 217–250.

Kasari, C., Sigman, M., Mundy, P., & Yirmiya, N. (1990). Affective sharing in the context of joint attention interactions of normal, autistic, and mentally retarded children. *Journal of Autism and Developmental Disorders*, *20*(1), 87–100.

Klin, A., Jones, W., Schultz, R., & Volkmar, F. (2003). The enactive mind, or from actions to cognition: Lessons from autism. *Philosophical Transactions of the Royal Society B: Biological Sciences*, *358*(1430), 345–360.

Klin, A., Jones, W., Schultz, R., Volkmar, F., & Cohen, D. (2002). Defining and quantifying the social phenotype in autism. *American Journal of Psychiatry*, *159*(6), 895–908.

Knott, F., Lewis, C., & Williams, T. (2007). Sibling interaction of children with autism: Development over 12 months. *Journal of Autism and Developmental Disorders*, *37*(10), 1987–1995.

Kuhl, P. K. (2007). Is speech learning "gated" by the social brain? *Developmental Science*, *10*(1), 110–120.

Lakin, J. L., & Chartrand, T. L. (2003). Using nonconscious behavioral mimicry to create affiliation and rapport. *Psychological Science*, *14*(4), 334–339.

Landa, R. J., Holman, K. C., O'Neill, A. H., & Stuart, E. A. (2011). Intervention targeting development of socially synchronous engagement in toddlers with autism spectrum disorder: A randomized controlled trial. *Journal of Child Psychology and Psychiatry*, *52*(1), 13–21.

Legerstee, M. (1991). The role of person and object in eliciting early imitation. *Journal of Experimental Child Psychology*, *51*(3), 423–433.

Leighton, J., Bird, G., Charman, T., & Heyes, C. (2008). Weak imitative performance is not due to a functional "mirroring" deficit in adults with Autism Spectrum Disorders. *Neuropsychologia*, *46*(4), 1041–1049.

Lhermitte, F., Pillon, B., & Serdaru, M. (1986). Human autonomy and the frontal lobes. Part I: Imitation and utilization behavior: A neuropsychological study of 75 patients. *Annals of Neurology*, *19*(4), 326–334.

Libby, S., Powell, S., Messer, D., & Jordan, R. (1997). Imitation of pretend play acts by children with autism and Down syndrome. *Journal of Autism and Developmental Disorders*, *27*(4), 365–383.

Lloyd, M., Macdonald, M., & Lord, C. (2011). Motor skills of toddlers with autism spectrum disorders. *Autism*, *17*(2), 133–146.

Lord, C. (1995). Follow-up of two-year-olds referred for possible autism. *Journal of Child Psychology and Psychiatry and Allied Disciplines*, *36*(8), 1365–1382.

Lord, C., Rutter, M., & Le Couteur, A. (1994). Autism Diagnostic Interview—Revised: A revised version of a diagnostic interview for caregivers of individuals with possible pervasive developmental disorders. *Journal of Autism and Developmental Disorders*, *24*(5), 659–685.

Lord, C., Storoschuk, S., Rutter, M., & Pickles, A. (1993). Using the ADI-R to diagnose autism in preschool-children. *Infant Mental Health Journal*, *14*(3), 234–252.

Lovaas, O. I., Freitag, L., Nelson, K., Whalen, C. (1967). The establishment of imitation and its use for the establishment of complex behavior in schizophrenic children. *Behaviour Research and Therapy*, *5*, 171–181.

Loveland, K. A., Tunali-Kotoski, B., Pearson, D. A., Brelsford, K. A., Ortegon, J., & Chen, R. (1994). Imitation and expression of facial affect in autism. *Development and Psychopathology*, *6*(3), 433–444.

Luria, A. R. (1966). *Human brain and psychological processes.* New York, NY: Harper & Row.

Maestro, S., Muratori, F., Barbieri, F., Casella, C., Cattaneo, V., Cavallaro, M., . . . Palacio-Espasa F. (2001). Early behavioral development in autistic children: The first 2 years of life through home movies. *Psychopathology*, *34*, 147–152.

Magnee, M. J., de Gelder, B., van Engeland, H., & Kemner, C. (2007). Facial electromyographic responses to emotional information from faces and voices in individuals with pervasive developmental disorder. *Journal of Child Psychology and Psychiatry*, *48*(11), 1122–1130.

Mars, A. E., Mauk, J. E., & Dowrick, P. W. (1998). Symptoms of pervasive developmental disorders as observed in prediagnostic home videos of infants and toddlers. *Journal of Pediatrics*, *132*(3), 500–504.

Marsh, L., Pearson, A., Ropar, D., & Hamilton, A. (2013). Children with autism do not overimitate. *Current Biology*, *23*(7), R266–R268.

Masur, E. F. (2006). Vocal and action imitation by infants and toddlers during dyadic interactions: Evidence about development and speculation about function. In S. J. Rogers & J. H. G. Williams (Eds.), *Imitation and the social mind: Autism and typical development* (pp. 27–47). New York, NY: Guilford Press.

Matheson, H., Moore, C., & Akhtar, N. (2012). The development of social learning in interactive and observational contexts. *Journal of Experimental Child Psychology*, *114*(2), 161–172.

McDuffie, A., Turner, L., Stone, W., Yoder, P., Wolery, M., & Ulman, T. (2007). Developmental correlates of different types of motor imitation in young children with autism spectrum disorders. *Journal of Autism and Developmental Disorders*, *37*(3), 401–412.

McEwen, F., Happé, F., Bolton, P., Rijsdijk, F., Ronald, A., Dworzynski, K., & Plomin, R. (2007). Origins of individual differences in imitation: links with language, pretend play, and socially insightful behavior in two-year-old twins. *Child Development*, *78*(2), 474–492.

McIntosh, D. N., Reichmann-Decker, A., Winkielman, P., & Wilbarger, J. L. (2006). When the social mirror breaks: Deficits in automatic, but not voluntary, mimicry of emotional facial expressions in autism. *Developmental Science*, *9*(3), 295–302.

Meltzoff, A. N., & Prinz, W. (2002). *The imitative mind: Development, evolution, and brain bases.* Cambridge, England, New York, NY: Cambridge University Press.

Metz, J. R. (1965). Conditioning generalized imitation in autistic-children. *Journal of Experimental Child Psychology*, *2*(4), 389–399.

Moody, E., & McIntosh, D. (2006). Imitation in autism findings and controversies. In S. Rogers & J. Williams (Eds.), *Imitation and the social mind: Autism and typical development* (pp. 71–88). New York, NY: Guilford Press.

Mosconi, M. W., Takarae, Y., & Sweeney, J. A. (2011). Motor functioning and dyspraxia in autism spectrum disorders. In D. G. Amaral, G. Dawson, & D. H. Geschwind (Eds.), *Autism* spectrum disorders (pp. 355–380). New York, NY: Oxford University Press

Mostofsky, S. H., Dubey, P., Jerath, V. K., Jansiewicz, E. M., Goldberg, M. C., & Denckla, M. B. (2006). Developmental dyspraxia is not limited to imitation in children with autism spectrum disorders. *Journal of the International Neuropsychological Society*, *12*(3), 314–326.

Mostofsky, S. H., & Ewen, J. B. (2011). Altered connectivity and action model formation in autism is autism. *Neuroscientist*, *17*(4), 437–448.

Mottron, L., Dawson, M., Soulieres, I., Hubert, B., & Burack, J. (2006). Enhanced perceptual functioning in autism: an update, and eight principles of autistic perception. *Journal of Autism and Developmental Disorders*, *36*(1), 27–43.

Mundy, P., & Neal, A. R. (2001). Neural plasticity, joint attention, and a transactional social-orienting model of autism. *International Review of Research in Mental Retardation*, *23*, 139–168.

Nadel, J., Baudonniere, P. M., & Fontaine, A. M. (1985). The social function of reciprocal imitation in 2–3-year-old peers. *Cahiers De Psychologie Cognitive-Current Psychology of Cognition*, *5*(3–4), 405–405.

Nielsen, M. (2006). Copying actions and copying outcomes: Social learning through the second year. *Developmental Psychology*, *42*(3), 555–565.

Nielsen, M., & Blank, C. (2011). Imitation in young children: When who gets copied is more important than what gets copied. *Developmental Psychology*, *47*(4), 1050–1053.

Nielsen, M., Slaughter, V., & Dissanayake, C. (2013). Object-directed imitation in children with high-functioning autism: Testing the motivation hypothesis. *Autism Research*, *6*(1), 23–32.

Nielsen, M., Suddendorf, T., & Dissanayake, C. (2006). Imitation and self- recognition in autism: In search of an explanation. In S. J. Rogers & J. H. G. Williams (Eds.), *Imitation and the social mind: Autism and typical development* (pp. 138–156). New York, NY: Guilford Press.

Nishitani, N., Avikainen, S., & Hari, R. (2004). Abnormal imitation-related cortical activation sequences in Asperger's syndrome. *Annals of Neurology*, *55*(4), 558–562.

Oberman, L. M., Ramachandran, V. S., & Pineda, J. A. (2008). Modulation of mu suppression in children with autism spectrum disorders in response to familiar or unfamiliar stimuli: The mirror neuron hypothesis. *Neuropsychologia*, *46*(5), 1558–1565.

Oberman, L. M., Winkielman, P., & Ramachandran, V. S. (2009). Slow echo: Facial EMG evidence for the delay of spontaneous, but not voluntary, emotional mimicry in children with autism spectrum disorders. *Developmental Science*, *12*(4), 510–520.

Ohta, M. (1987). Cognitive disorders of infantile autism: A study employing the WISC, spatial relationship, conceptualization, and gestural imitations. *Journal of Autism and Developmental Disorders*, *17*(1), 45–62.

Olineck, K. M., & Poulin-Dubois, D. (2009). Infants' understanding of intention from 10 to 14 months: Interrelations among violation of expectancy and imitation tasks. *Infant Behavior and Development*, *32*(4), 404–415.

Osterling, J., & Dawson, G. (1994). Early recognition of children with autism—a study of 1st birthday home videotapes.

Journal of Autism and Developmental Disorders, *24*(3), 247–257.

Over, H., & Carpenter, M. (2012). Putting the social into social learning: Explaining both selectivity and fidelity in children's copying behavior. *Journal of Comparative Psychology*, *126*, 182–192.

Page, J., & Boucher, J. (1998). Motor impairments in children with autistic disorder. *Child Language Teaching and Therapy*, *14*, 233–259.

Pellicano, E. (2010). The development of core cognitive skills in autism: A 3-year prospective study. *Child Development*, *81*(5), 1400–1416.

Pellicano, E., Gibson, L., Maybery, M., Durkin, K., & Badcock, D. R. (2005). Abnormal global processing along the dorsal visual pathway in autism: a possible mechanism for weak visuospatial coherence? *Neuropsychologia*, *43*(7), 1044–1053.

Pennington, B. F., Williams, J. H. G., & Rogers, S. J. (2006). Conclusions. In S. J. Rogers & J. H. G. Williams (Eds.), *Imitation and the social mind: Autism and typical development* (pp. 431–453). New York, NY: Guilford Press.

Perra, O., Williams, J. H. G., Whiten, A., Fraser, L., Benzie, H., & Perrett, D. I. (2008). Imitation and "theory of mind" competencies in discrimination of autism from other neurodevelopmental disorders. *Research in Autism Spectrum Disorders*, *1*, 456–468.

Pineda, J. A. (2005). The functional significance of mu rhythms: Translating "seeing" and "hearing" into "doing." *Brain Research Reviews*, *50*(1), 57–68.

Poon, K. K., Watson, L. R., Baranek, G. T., & Poe, M. D. (2011). To what extent do joint attention, imitation, and object play behaviors in infancy predict later communication and intellectual functioning in ASD? *Journal of Autism and Developmental Disorders*, *42*(6), 1064–1074.

Press, C., Richardson, D., & Bird, G. (2010). Intact imitation of emotional facial actions in autism spectrum conditions. *Neuropsychologia*, *48*(11), 3291–3297.

Ramachandran, V. S., & Oberman, L. M. (2006). Broken mirrors: A theory of autism. *Scientific American*, *295*(5), 62–69.

Rapin, I. (1996). Practitioner review: Developmental language disorders: a clinical update. *Journal of Child Psychology and Psychiatry*, *37*(6), 643–655.

Rayner, C. (2011). Sibling and adult video modelling to teach a student with autism: Imitation skills and intervention suitability. *Developmental Neurorehabilitation*, *14*(6), 331–338.

Rayner, C., Denholm, C., & Sigafoos, J. (2009). Video-based intervention for individuals with autism: Key questions that remain unanswered. *Research in Autism Spectrum Disorders*, *3*(2), 291–303.

Receveur, C., Lenoir, P., Desombre, H., Roux, S., Barthelemy, C., & Malvy, J. (2005). Interaction and imitation deficits from infancy to 4 years of age in children with autism: A pilot study based on videotapes. *Autism*, *9*(1), 69–82.

Reznick, J. S., Baranek, G. T., Reavis, S., Watson, L. R., & Crais, E. R. (2007). A parent-report instrument for identifying one-year-olds at risk for an eventual diagnosis of autism: The First Year Inventory. *Journal of Autism and Developmental Disorders*, *37*(9), 1691–1710.

Rice, K., Moriuchi, J. M., Jones, W., & Klin, A. (2012). Parsing heterogeneity in autism spectrum disorders: Visual scanning of dynamic social scenes in school-aged children. *Journal of the American Academy of Child & Adolescent Psychiatry*, *51*(3), 238–248.

Rizzolatti, G., & Craighero, L. (2004). The mirror-neuron system. *Annual Review of Neuroscience*, *27*, 169–192.

Rizzolatti, G., Fabbri-Destro, M., & Cattaneo, L. (2009). Mirror neurons and their clinical relevance. *Nature Clinical Practice Neurology*, *5*(1), 24–34.

Rizzolatti, G., & Sinigaglia, C. (2010). The functional role of the parieto-frontal mirror circuit: interpretations and misinterpretations. *Nature Reviews Neuroscience*, *11*(4), 264–274.

Robins, D. L., Fein, D., Barton, M. L., & Green, J. A. (2001). The Modified Checklist for Autism in Toddlers: An initial study investigating the early detection of autism and pervasive developmental disorders. *Journal of Autism and Developmental Disorders*, *31*(2), 131–144.

Rogers, S. J., Bennetto, L., McEvoy, R., & Pennington, B. F. (1996). Imitation and pantomime in high-functioning adolescents with autism spectrum disorders. *Child Development*, *67*(5), 2060–2073.

Rogers, S. J., & Dawson, G. (2010). *Early Start Denver Model for young children with autism: Promoting language, learning, and engagement*. New York, NY: Guilford Press.

Rogers, S. J., Hepburn, S. L., Stackhouse, T., & Wehner, E. (2003). Imitation performance in toddlers with autism and those with other developmental disorders. *Journal of Child Psychology and Psychiatry and Allied Disciplines*, *44*(5), 763–781.

Rogers, S. J., & Pennington, B. F. (1991). A theoretical approach to the deficits in infantile autism. *Development and Psychopathology*, *107*, 147–161.

Rogers, S. J., & Williams, J. H. G. (Eds.). (2006). *Imitation and the social mind: Autism and typical development*. New York, NY: Guilford Press.

Rogers, S. J., Young, G. S., Cook, I., Giolzetti, A., & Ozonoff, S. (2008). Deferred and immediate imitation in regressive and early onset autism. *Journal of Child Psychology and Psychiatry*, *49*(4), 449–457.

Rogers, S. J., Young, G. S., Cook, I., Giolzetti, A., & Ozonoff, S. (2010). Imitating actions on objects in early-onset and regressive autism: Effects and implications of task characteristics on performance. *Development and Psychopathology*, *22*(1), 71–85.

Rose, S. A., Feldman, J. F., & Jankowski, J. J. (2009). A cognitive approach to the development of early language. *Child Development*, *80*(1), 134–150.

Rothi, L. J., & Heilman, K. M. (1997). *Apraxia: The neuropsychology of action*. Hove, UK: Psychology Press.

Rutter, M., Bailey, A., & Lord, C. (2003). SCQ: *The Social Communication Questionnaire. Manual*. Los Angeles, CA: Western Psychological Services.

Salowitz, N. M., Eccarius, P., Karst, J., Carson, A., Schohl, K., Stevens, S., . . . Scheidt, R. A. (2012). Brief report: Visuo-spatial guidance of movement during gesture imitation and mirror drawing in children with autism spectrum disorders. *Journal of Autism and Developmental Disorders*, *43*(4), 985–995.

Sasson, N. J., Elison, J. T., Turner-Brown, L. M., Dichter, G. S., & Bodfish, J. W. (2011). Brief report: Circumscribed attention in young children with autism. *Journal of Autism and Developmental Disorders*, *41*(2), 242–247.

Schopler, E., Reichler, J., & Renner, B. (1988). *The Childhood Autism Rating Scale (C.A.R.S.)*. Los Angeles, CA: Western Psychological Services.

Senju, A. (2012). Spontaneous theory of mind and its absence in autism spectrum disorders. *Neuroscientist*, *18*(2), 108–113.

Sevlever, M., & Gillis, J. M. (2010). An examination of the state of imitation research in children with autism: Issues of definition and methodology. *Research in Developmental Disabilities*, *31*(5), 976–984.

Silver, W. G., & Rapin, I. (2012). Neurobiological basis of autism. *Pediatric Clinics of North America*, *59*(1), 45–61, x.

Simmons, D. R., Robertson, A. E., McKay, L. S., Toal, E., McAleer, P., & Pollick, F. E. (2009). Vision in autism spectrum disorders. *Vision Research*, *49*(22), 2705–2739.

Sinigaglia, C., & Sparaci, L. (2010). Emotions in action through the looking glass. *Journal of Analytical Psychology*, *55*(1), 3–29.

Smith, I. M., & Bryson, S. E. (1998). Gesture imitation in autism: I. Nonsymbolic postures and sequences. *Cognitive Neuropsychology*, *15*(6–8), 747–770.

Smith, I. M., & Bryson, S. E. (2007). Gesture imitation in autism: II. Symbolic gestures and pantomimed object use. *Cognitive Neuropsychology*, *24*(7), 679–700.

Southgate, V., & Hamilton, A. F. (2008). Unbroken mirrors: challenging a theory of Autism. *Trends in Cognitive Sciences*, *12*(6), 225–229.

Spengler, S., Bird, G., & Brass, M. (2010). Hyperimitation of actions is related to reduced understanding of others' minds in autism spectrum conditions. *Biological Psychiatry*, *68*(12), 1148–1155.

Stel, M., van den Heuvel, C., & Smeets, R. C. (2008). Facial feedback mechanisms in autistic spectrum disorders. *Journal of Autism and Developmental Disorders*, *38*(7), 1250–1258.

Stern, D. N. (1985). *The interpersonal world of the infant: A view from psychoanalysis and developmental psychology*. New York, NY: Basic Books.

Stieglitz Ham, H., Bartolo, A., Corley, M., Rajendran, G., Szabo, A., & Swanson, S. (2011). Exploring the relationship between gestural recognition and imitation: Evidence of dyspraxia in autism spectrum disorders. *Journal of Autism and Developmental Disorders*, *41*(1), 1–12.

Stone, W. L., Ousley, O. Y., & Littleford, C. D. (1997). Motor imitation in young children with autism: What's the object? *Journal of Abnormal Child Psychology*, *25*(6), 475–485.

Stone, W. L., & Yoder, P. J. (2001). Predicting spoken language level in children with autism spectrum disorders. *Autism*, *5*(4), 341–361.

Strid, K., Tjus, T., Smith, L., Meltzoff, A. N., & Heimann, M. (2006). Infant recall memory and communication predicts later cognitive development. *Infant Behavior and Development*, *29*(4), 545–553.

Subiaul, F., Lurie, H., Romansky, K., Klein, T., Holmes, D., & Terrace, H. (2007). Cognitive Imitation in Autism. *Cognitive Development*, *22*(2), 230.

Tereshko, L., MacDonald, R., & Ahearn, W. H. (2010). Strategies for teaching children with autism to imitate response chains using video modeling. *Research in Autism Spectrum Disorders*, *4*(3), 479–489.

Tessari, A., & Rumiati, R. I. (2004). The strategic control of multiple routes in imitation of actions. *Journal of Experimental*

Psychology: Human Perception and Performance, 30(6), 1107–1116.

Thorpe, W. H. (1956). *Learning and instinct in animals.* London, England: Methuen.

Tomasello, M., & Moll, H. (2010). The gap is social: Human shared intentionality and culture. In P. Kappeler & J. Silk (Eds.), *Mind the gap: Tracing the origins of human universals* (pp. 331–349). Berlin, Germany: Springer.

Toth, K., Dawson, G., Meltzoff, A. N., Greenson, J., & Fein, D. (2007). Early social, imitation, play, and language abilities of young non-autistic siblings of children with autism. *Journal of Autism and Developmental Disorders, 37*(1), 145–157.

Trevarthen, C. (2001). The neurobiology of early communication: Intersubjective regulations in human brain development. In A. F. Kalverboer & A. Gramsbergen (Eds.), *Handbook on brain and behavior in human development* (pp. 841–882). Dordrecht, The Netherlands: Kluwer.

Uzgiris, I. C. (1981). Two functions of imitation during infancy. *International Journal of Behavioral Development, 4*(1), 1–12.

Uzgiris, I. C. (1984). Imitation in infancy—its interpersonal aspects. *Minnesota Symposia on Child Psychology, 17*, 1–32.

Vanvuchelen, M., Roeyers, H., & De Weerdt, W. (2007). Nature of motor imitation problems in school-aged boys with autism: A motor or a cognitive problem? *Autism, 11*(3), 225–240.

Vanvuchelen, M., Roeyers, H., & De Weerdt, W. (2011). Imitation assessment and its utility to the diagnosis of autism: Evidence from consecutive clinical preschool referrals for suspected. *Journal of Autism and Developmental Disorders, 41*(4), 484–496.

Vendrell, P., Junque, C., Pujol, J., Jurado, M. A., Molet, J., & Grafman, J. (1995). The role of prefrontal regions in the Stroop task. *Neuropsychologia, 33*(3), 341–352.

Vivanti, G. (2013). Imitation in autism spectrum disorders: From research to treatment. In D. Riva, S. Bulgheroni, & M. Zappella (Eds.), *Neurobiology, diagnosis and treatment in autism. An update* (pp. 161–165). Mountrouge, France: John Libbey Eurotext.

Vivanti, G., Dissanayake, C., Zierhut, C., & Rogers, S. J. (2013). Brief report: Predictors of outcomes in the Early Start Denver Model delivered in a group setting. *Journal of Autism and Developmental Disorders, 43*(7), 1717–1724.

Vivanti, G., Hepburn, S., Philofsky, A., & Rogers, S. (2009). *The developmental course of imitation deficit in autism.* Proceedings of the 8th International Meeting for Autism Research, Chicago, IL.

Vivanti, G., McCormick, C., Young, G. S., Abucayan, F., Hatt, N., Nadig, A., . . . Rogers, S. (2011). Intact and impaired mechanisms of action understanding in autism. *Developmental Psychology, 47*(3), 841–856.

Vivanti, G., Nadig, A., Ozonoff, S., & Rogers, S. J. (2008). What do children with autism attend to during imitation tasks? *Journal of Experimental Child Psychology, 101*(3), 186–205.

Vygotsky, L. S. (1997). *The collected works of L. S. Vygotsky. Vol. 4. The history of the development of higher mental functions* (M. Hall, Trans.; R. W. Rieber, Ed.). New York, NY: Plenum Press. (Original work published 1931).

Wang, Y., & Hamilton, A. F. (2012). Social top-down response modulation (STORM): A model of the control of mimicry in social interaction. *Frontiers in Human Neuroscience, 6*, 153.

Wang, Y., Newport, R., & Hamilton, A. F. D. (2011). Eye contact enhances mimicry of intransitive hand movements. *Biology Letters, 7*(1), 7–10.

Wang, Y., Ramsey, R., & Hamilton, A. F. C. (2011). The conrol of mimicry by eye contact is mediated by medial prefrontal cortex. *Journal of Neuroscience, 31*(33), 12001–12010.

Want, S. C., & Harris, P. L. (2002). Social learning: Compounding some problems and dissolving others. *Developmental Science, 5*(1), 39–41.

Whiten, A., & Brown, J. (1998). Imitation and the reading of other minds: perspectives from the study of autism, normal children and non-human primates. In S. Braten (Ed.), *Intersubjective communication and emotion in early ontogeny* (pp. 260–280). Cambridge, England: Cambridge University Press.

Whiten, A., McGuigan, N., Marshall-Pescini, S., & Hopper, L. M. (2009). Emulation, imitation, over-imitation and the scope of culture for child and chimpanzee. *Philosophical Transactions of the Royal Society B: Biological Sciences, 364*(1528), 2417–2428.

Wild, K. S., Poliakoff, E., Jerrison, A., & Gowen, E. (2011). Goal-directed and goal-less imitation in autism spectrum disorder. *Journal of Autism and Developmental Disorders, 42*(8): 1739–1749.

Williams, J. H. (2008). Self-other relations in social development and autism: Multiple roles for mirror neurons and other brain bases. *Autism Research, 1*(2), 73–90.

Williams, J. H., Waiter, G. D., Gilchrist, A., Perrett, D. I., Murray, A. D., & Whiten, A. (2006). Neural mechanisms of imitation and 'mirror neuron' functioning in autistic spectrum disorder. *Neuropsychologia, 44*(4), 610–621.

Williams, J. H., Whiten, A., & Singh, T. (2004). A systematic review of action imitation in autistic spectrum disorder. *Journal of Autism and Developmental Disorders, 34*(3), 285–299.

Williams, J. H., Whiten, A., Suddendorf, T., & Perrett, D. I. (2001). Imitation, mirror neurons and autism. *Neuroscience & Behavioral Reviews, 25*(4), 287–295.

Young, G. S., Rogers, S. J., Hutman, T., Rozga, A., Sigman, M., & Ozonoff, S. (2011). Imitation from 12 to 24 months in autism and typical development: A longitudinal Rasch analysis. *Developmental Psychology, 47*(6), 1565–1578.

Young, J. M., Krantz, P. J., Mcclannahan, L. E., & Poulson, C. L. (1994). Generalized imitation and response-class formation in children with autism. *Journal of Applied Behavior Analysis, 27*(4), 685–697.

Zachor, D. A., Ilanit, T., & Ben Itzchak, E. (2010). Autism severity and motor abilities correlates of imitation situations in children with autism spectrum disorders. *Research in Autism Spectrum Disorders, 4*(3), 438–443.

Zakian, A., Malvy, J., Desombre, H., Roux, S., & Lenoir, P. (2000). Early signs of autism: A new study of family home movies. *Encephale-Revue De Psychiatrie Clinique Biologique Et Therapeutique, 26*(2), 38–44.

Zwaigenbaum, L., Bryson, S., Rogers, T., Roberts, W., Brian, J., & Szatmari, P. (2005). Behavioral manifestations of autism in the first year of life. *International Journal of Developmental Neuroscience, 23*(2–3), 143–152.

CHAPTER 13

Neuropsychological Characteristics of Autism Spectrum Disorders

KATHERINE D. TSATSANIS AND KELLY POWELL

Autism spectrum disorders (ASDs) are neurodevelopmental disorders that primarily involve disruptions of social development, impaired verbal and nonverbal communication, and behavioral disturbances. A puzzling aspect of ASDs continues to be their etiology. There are numerous competing theories to account for pathways of development in autism, with evidence for differences in gene expression, brain architecture, and possibly environmental influences. The mechanisms that lead to ASDs are not fully understood; in the face of substantial phenotypic heterogeneity, the identification of the variant expressions of the disorder would seem to be relevant to studies of its pathogenesis.

Note: This chapter has been adapted from the previous *Handbook* (2005) chapter and a chapter entitled "Neuropsychological Characteristics of Asperger Syndrome" from *Asperger Syndrome*, second edition (New York, NY: Guilford Press).

Research in the psychological literature generally divides into the study of specific social cognitive and general perceptual cognitive and learning mechanisms (Volkmar, Lord, Bailey, Schultz, & Klin, 2004). Within each branch, there are specific skills and processes proposed to have causal explanatory value, including joint attention and face processing skills on the one hand, and sensory perception, attention, memory, and executive function on the other. An approach to understanding autism that puts faith in the explanatory power of a single construct is, of course, highly suspect. At the very least, the complexity and variability of expression of the syndrome argues against a unitary cause. Moreover, the proposed constructs are themselves neither unitary nor fully explicated. Although individual researchers may emphasize different components of functioning and use a distinct language, they are alike in fundamental ways. Each of their theories represents an attempt to characterize how individuals with autism acquire and process information and in turn form an internal representation of the world. Core deficits in regulation, integration, and flexibility are represented in these models.

Reviewing neuropsychological factors in autism spectrum disorders presents several challenges, as the literature is expansive and diverse. Psychological models that have dominated the field include theory of mind, central coherence, and executive functions, with related research findings interpreted and integrated into these specific constructs. Because these models are reviewed elsewhere in this volume they will not be critically evaluated here. Social cognitive mechanisms and language development also fall within the domain of neuropsychological function but each is addressed in a separate chapter. In this chapter, focus is placed on specific cognitive learning mechanisms later positioned in the context of a broader discussion of relevant issues in the field.

Despite the noted quantity of research, methodological issues present a special challenge in this review as they render findings among studies equivocal and limit general conclusions. A major source of variability lies in subject selection. This includes age, level of functioning, choice of control groups, and number of subjects. The possibility of clinical heterogeneity within and between groups of individuals with ASD is a crucial concern that highlights the need for a well-characterized sample and appropriate controls. When clinical groups have been distinguished, research findings are specified as pertaining to individuals with autism or Asperger syndrome (AS). In addition, a more clearly systematic approach to the investigation of these domains of functioning will advance understanding.

One unequivocal characteristic of ASD is clinical variability; children with autism spectrum disorders may share many core features, but their individual pathways to learning or cognitive profiles will have unique characteristics. Treatment approaches are enhanced when the core areas of strength and vulnerability for individuals with

autism are identified and evaluated across stages of development. In the current discussion, the specific assets and deficits identified are in most cases neither specific to nor characteristic of all individuals with autism. They do represent meaningful areas for clinical consideration and recognize significant programs of research.

SENSORY PERCEPTION

Assessment of the sensory perceptual systems has particular significance for developmental disorders such as ASD with onset in early childhood. If an individual has basic impairments in one or more sensory perceptual systems early in development, developmental consequences may ensue over time. The cumulative effects of deficient information processing through a particular sensory modality may result in not having the type or amount of stored information by which to readily judge current or incoming information (Rourke, van der Vlugt, & Rourke, 2002). As such, the early templates that serve as a foundation for higher order skills/processes may not be well formed. In addition, experiences may be fragmented in a very fundamental way if information received through one sensory perceptual modality must be shared with another modality in order to learn and complete complex tasks.

Sensory Perceptual Features and Theories Associated With ASD

The ubiquitous nature of abnormal sensory features in individuals with autism dates back to Kanner's (1943) account of observed sensory differences (e.g., auditory and visual sensitivities and fascinations). Currently, more than 96% of children with autism are reported to have hypo- and hyper-responsivities in multiple domains (e.g., visual, tactile, auditory) (Marco, Hinkley, Hill, & Nagarajan, 2011). Similar to the range of phenotypic expression of social communication deficits found in individuals with autism, sensory disturbance differences also exist on a continuum from mild to severe. In early emerging cognitive theories of autism, sensory disturbances were well documented and viewed as a primary area of deficit. Ornitz and Ritvo (1968a) detailed the range of hypo- and hyper-sensitivities affecting each of the senses in over 150 cases of autism. Based on their observations, they postulated that an inability to adequately modulate sensory input in children with autism manifests itself in alternating states of excitement (e.g., spinning, hand flapping, hypersensitivity to stimuli) and inhibition (e.g., nonresponsiveness) and that this state of dysregulation, or *homeostatic imbalance*, in turn leads to *perceptual inconstancy*. From this account, inadequate modulation of sensory input in autism produces inconsistent and disordered perceptions of external events. The (lack of) coherence of these children's perceptions is considered to impact upon early developmental achievements including social relating and communication (Ornitz, 1974, 1983; Ornitz & Ritvo, 1968a, 1968b, 1976).

Descriptions of unusual responses to sensory stimuli are also readily found in first-person accounts of autism. For example, Temple Grandin (1992) makes note of her profound hypersensitivity to touch and sound. The repetitive behaviors that are manifest in autism also often appear to involve a sensory stimulatory component (e.g., visual fascination with spinning wheels, fans, string), and it is argued that disturbances of movement, such as hand flapping and whirling, may in fact provide wanted sensory input through visual and proprioceptive channels (Ornitz, 1983). Although repetitive behaviors are oftentimes interfering, they may be functional in regulating arousal levels for children with autism with comorbid sensory processing vulnerabilities (Gabriels et al., 2008; Liss, Saulnier, Fein, & Kinsbourne, 2006). Repetitive behaviors may act as a coping strategy to help regulate high levels of arousal (hyperarousal) or reduce anxiety. On the other hand, in relation to hypoarousal, repetitive behaviors may help increase sensory stimulation (Leekam, Prior, & Uljarevic, 2011). Grandin (1995) makes a connection between her own problems in sensory reactivity and her unresponsive affect (or shutting down) and fearful states.

As such, one approach to the presence of these sensory disturbances has been to appreciate more fully their connection with levels of arousal, attention, emotional regulation, and action or adaptive goal-directed behavior (Anzalone & Williamson, 2000; Laurent & Rubin, 2004). Ornitz and Ritvo (1968b; Ornitz, 1983, 1988) also proposed neurological substrates for a disturbance in the modulation of sensory input in autism. Their earlier writings pointed to the reticular activating system and vestibular system. Ornitz (1988) has also emphasized a role for the thalamus. In their seminal paper, Damasio and Maurer (1978) concluded that multiple brain regions are involved in autism, including the mesial frontal lobes, mesial temporal lobes, basal ganglia, and thalamus (specifically, dorsomedial and anterior nuclear groups). The thalamus has traditionally been referred to as the sensory gateway of the cortex, but a current perspective of this structure suggests that it is involved in multiple processes that permit the transmission, tuning, and integrated processing of information in the brain. An MRI study of the thalamus in individuals with autism indicated that despite increases in cortical size, the thalamus does not appear to develop to the expected degree in individuals with autism (Tsatsanis et al., 2003). Others have explored the neurophysiological responses to sensory (e.g., auditory, visual, tactile, and multimodal) stimuli utilizing a variety of neuroimaging techniques; however, findings are generally varied and contradictory. These issues are reviewed in detail in Chapter 16 of this *Handbook*.

Sensory Perceptual Research in ASD

An abnormal response to sensory stimulation has been consistently found to differentiate between children with autism and developmentally matched controls in studies of early behavioral characteristics (Adrien et al., 1992; Dahlgren & Gillberg, 1989; Osterling & Dawson, 1994; Stone, 1997). This cluster of behaviors includes empty gaze; visual fascination with patterns and movements; failure to react to sounds/appears deaf; hyposensitivity to pain, cold, or heat; hypersensitivity to taste; and inappropriate use of objects (e.g., interest in the sensory aspects of objects, such as licking/mouthing, peering, or interest in texture). Abnormal sensory reactivity appears to differentiate children with autism from typical and mixed developmentally delayed groups by 2.5 years of age, although children with fragile X syndrome also show increased sensory symptoms (Rogers, Hepburn, & Wehner, 2003).

Studies using parent questionnaires also indicate severe and/or frequent sensory symptoms in young children (3 through 6 years of age; Cohen et al., 2010; Watling, Deitz, & White, 2001) and school-aged children (Kientz & Dunn, 1997) with ASD. Tomchek and Dunn (2007) found that in a sample of 281 children with autism aged 3 to 10 years, 95% demonstrated sensory processing dysfunction as measured on the Short Sensory Profile (SSP; McIntosh, Miller, & Shyu, 1999). Leekam, Nieto, Libby, Wing, and Gould (2007) found similar results; in a sample of 33 children with autism, over 90% had sensory abnormalities as reported on the Diagnostic Interview for Social and Communication Disorders (DISCO). Parents of children with AS also reported sensory symptoms starting at young ages and similar to those found in children with autism (Dunn, Myles, & Orr, 2002).

The preceding findings of atypical sensory responses are based on *observation* of behaviors manifest in everyday functioning. Psychophysical studies of tactile perception have also been used to examine whether atypical sensory responses are present in this modality. Several studies have confirmed increased sensitivity to tactile stimulation, specifically vibration, in small samples of adults with AS and AS/high-functioning autism (HFA; Blakemore et al., 2006; Cascio et al., 2008). When rating the *perception* of tactile stimulation, the adults with AS also showed tactile hypersensitivity, rating both externally and self-produced touch as more intense than the control group (Blakemore et al., 2006). The AS group showed a typical perceptual response with regard to attenuation of self- versus externally produced touch. Thresholds for detecting light touch and mild warmth and

cool were found to be similar in the mixed ASD group as compared to controls (Cascio et al., 2008). Sensitivity to thermal pain was increased; that is, thresholds for cold and heat pain sensitivity were lower in the AS/HFA group.

The direct assessment of perceptual processes using traditional neuropsychological instruments is more equivocal as to areas of deficit and/or distinction in the way tactile information is processed. In a traditional neuropsychological assessment, tactile, visual, and auditory perceptual functioning are generally assessed at elementary levels, such as basic sensory perception/imperception, as well as higher levels of perceptual ability, such as finger agnosia and form or coin recognition in the tactile domain. A retrospective review of medical, psychiatric, and assessment records indicated that out of 101 children (91 with a diagnosis of AS), 42 had auditory perceptual and 36 tactile perceptual dysfunction, with 21 children showing combined deficits (Sturm, Fernell, & Gillberg, 2004). In a study of preschool children with AS and HFA, the two clinical groups did not differ in their performance on measures of stereognosis (perception of form/object through touch) and finger localization, but notably 70% of the sample diagnosed with Asperger syndrome scored below the average range on the former and 40% on the latter (Iwanaga, Kawasaki, & Tsuchida, 2000). Performance in this domain of functioning (tactile perception) was not correlated with intelligence scores. This finding was not replicated in a small sample of 8- to 14-year-olds with AS when their performance was compared to a typically developing control group. Measures of tactile perception such as finger agnosia and fingertip writing tasks as well as memory, location, or time to completion on the Tactile Performance Test were not found to discriminate between children with AS and typically developing controls (Ryburn, Anderson, & Wales, 2009).

The visual perceptual characteristics of individuals with autism have been interpreted to indicate a detail-focused processing bias and a relative challenge seeing the big picture or abstracting the gestalt form when processing incoming information for meaning (Frith, 1989; Happé & Booth, 2008;

Happé & Frith, 2006). Using simple local–global stimuli (e.g., large number composed of smaller numbers), the visual processing of local versus global information was compared in autism, AS, and controls (Rinehart, Bradshaw, Moss, Brereton, & Tonge, 2000). The results indicated no difference between the clinical groups with both groups showing disrupted processing of global stimuli when the local information was incongruent, a result not found in the control group. The findings were interpreted to support an "absence of global precedence" as originally proposed by Mottron and Belleville (1993) wherein global processing or apprehension of the *whole* does not take priority over processing of local features or the *parts*. Additionally, it was proposed that the interference effect of local on global processing could be consistent with deficits in inhibition and shifting set associated with dysfunction in the frontal systems, and/or right hemispheral functioning associated with global processing. Adults with AS and autism were found to show a preference for local features specifically when there was an emphasis on the processing of interelemental spatial relationships (Rondan & Deruelle, 2007).The latter finding supports the notion that enhanced local processing may arise as the demand for configural analysis increases.

A similar conclusion was reached when perceptual organizational processes were analyzed using the Rey-Osterrieth Complex Figure Test (ROCF), a standard neuropsychological test that requires the analysis and reproduction of an unfamiliar, nonmeaningful figure (Tsatsanis et al., 2011). The individuals with ASD appeared to rely on a part-oriented strategy to cope with the complexity of the task; organizational processes affecting whether they perceived the pieces of information as connected to one another appeared to further impact later recall of the features. The ASD group did not show superiority for attending to, copying, and recalling the details of the ROCF figure; rather, they were likely to process complex information by parsing it into its component parts. The latter findings are more consistent with Kanner's (1943) language on this topic, with specific reference to

how the individual with ASD may experience the world; that is, as made up of elements, challenged to experience wholes without full attention to the constituent parts.

Different aspects of auditory perception and processing have also been examined, often using event-related potential (ERP) methods. Research on language functioning has typically focused on the pragmatic aspects of language and communication, a characteristic deficit area in ASD. In a recent comprehensive investigation of language abilities in school-aged children with AS, measures of phonological processing and nonword repetition as well as sentence comprehension in background noise were included in the assessment battery (Saalasti et al., 2008). The results indicated that the AS group did not perform differently than the typically developing (TD) control group on these measures, although there was a trend toward lower performance overall on the phonological processing task. (The AS group did perform significantly more poorly than the controls on a language comprehension task also included in the language battery.)

Using ERP paradigms, Lepistö et al. (2006) found a diminished involuntary orienting response to speech pitch and phoneme changes, but not to corresponding changes in nonspeech sounds. Despite the relative preservation of their language development, the children with AS differed from controls and were similar to children with autism in their sound-discrimination and orienting response at the cortical level as measured through ERP. Consistent with expectations, impairments were specific to the socially relevant versus nonsocial information; neural response to nonspeech changes appeared to be enhanced.

In addition to auditory hypo- and hypersensitivities, understanding speech in noisy environments may be problematic for individuals with ASD. When assessed using speech reception thresholds, a significant difference was found specifically for background sounds containing temporal or spectro-temporal dips (Alcantara, Weisblatt, Moore, & Bolton, 2004). It was proposed that a reduced ability to integrate information from the fragments present in temporal dips in noise may be a factor contributing to difficulties understanding speech in noisy environments. Segregation of concurrent stream sounds may also contribute to such challenges; ERP recordings indicated differences for conditions requiring stream segregation but not simple feature detection for children with AS compared to their age-matched controls (Lepistö et al., 2009).

A handful of studies have examined the link between sensory abnormalities and other core features of ASD. A significant association was not found when the relationship between sensory symptom severity and severity of autism symptomatology (e.g., social communication skill deficits) was examined (Kientz & Dunn, 1997; Rogers et al., 2003), but degree of abnormal sensory responsivity and impairments in adaptive behavior were related (Rogers et al., 2003). A study using older children with HFA found at least moderate correlations between sensory dysfunction, as assessed using the Sensory Profile, and social competence, as measured using the Social Responsiveness Scale (SRS; Constantino & Gruber, 2005), indicating that sensory processing may be a function of the severity of the social disability (Hilton, Graver, & LaVesser, 2007).

Children with autism who experience unusual sensory sensitivities also appear to evidence more repetitive behaviors (Baker, Lane, Angley, & Young, 2008; Chen, Rodgers, & McConachie, 2009). In their review of the literature on repetitive behaviors in autism over the last decade, Leekam and colleagues (2011) found that hyper- or hypoarousal may act as a key trigger for unusual patterns of behavior. Individuals with William syndrome (WS) are also reported to have sensory processing abnormalities (John & Mervis, 2010) and evidence repetitive behaviors (Davies, Udwin, & Howlin, 1998). Riby, Janes, and Rodgers (2013) found a significant direct relationship between sensory processing abnormalities and repetitive behaviors in individuals with WS. Taken together, the results suggest a possible link between sensory abnormalities and repetitive behaviors across neurodevelopmental disorders that may merit further investigation.

Summary

There is evidence from behavioral report, neuropsychological measures, and ERP paradigms for atypical sensory and perceptual processing in ASD. When comparisons are made between individuals with autism and AS, few discrepancies are found between the clinical groups. Despite the prevalence of sensory perceptual differences in ASD, this domain of functioning was understudied in comparison to higher order levels of cognition, such as executive functioning, and core features of the disorders, such as social and communication impairments. This has begun to change, and with the addition of this symptom to the fifth edition of the *Diagnostic and Statistical Manual of Mental Disorders* (*DSM-5*; American Psychiatric Association [APA], 2013) diagnostic criteria for ASD, this is a feature of the disorder that may begin to receive greater attention. Given that integrated higher order functioning generally builds from simple perceptual discrimination to more complex levels of perceptual organization, a better understanding of the role of sensory perception and modulation from earliest development might also help to elucidate whether there are basic impairments in one or more sensory perceptual systems with ensuing downstream effects. Although differences between ASD and TD groups are a consistent finding, it is not clear what, if any, the association is between the results from behavioral report, performance on neuropsychological measures, and response at the cortical level as measured through ERP. Further study to identify whether atypicalities in the sensory perceptual domain bear any relationship to arousal, emotional regulation, and reward/salience systems, as well as core impairments in social functioning is warranted. As pursued in other domains of functioning, it would also be interesting to examine whether there are differences in sensory perceptual processing in response to social versus nonsocial stimuli. From a clinical standpoint, sensory disturbances may be associated with regulatory difficulties and parents may express concern when their child encounters everyday stimuli and reacts quite differently from peers or siblings.

Additionally, sensory input (e.g., tactile, auditory, olfactory, vestibular, etc.) would appear to be an integral part of the social and relational experience from the earliest days of development; impairments and/or atypicalities in this domain could reasonably impact the formation of coherent percepts as well as ability to plan and coordinate an appropriate social response.

ATTENTION

Attention is a core capacity that is central to the processes of information reduction, response selection, and preparation for eventual action. Talsma, Senkowski, Soto-Faraco, and Woldorff (2010) define attention as "a relatively broad cognitive concept that includes a set of mechanisms that determine how particular sensory input, perceptual objects, trains of thought, or courses of action are selected for further processing from an array of concurrent possible stimuli, objects, thoughts and actions" (p. 400). New information arrives in the form of a continuous flow of both internal and external stimuli, and individuals develop an increasing capacity to override the impulse to attend to what is most striking or novel or desired, in order to anticipate, direct, or guide attention based on prior knowledge and internal goals.

Although perhaps difficult to isolate, it is important to examine the domain of attention before consideration is given to more complex undertakings and levels of processing. Measures of attention by necessity include a perceptual processing component (e.g., visual, auditory, tactile). The clinical assessment may include specific measures of sustained, selective, and divided attention. In addition, during a comprehensive assessment, an individual is typically required to process information under conditions that tap and tax attentional capacities to different degrees; behavioral observations and results from across a number of heterogeneous tasks may be compared to draw conclusions about the individual's attentional capacities.

Attentional Features and Associated Theories in ASD

The early emphasis on the role of sensory modulation systems in ASD was later supplanted by an emphasis on the role of attention on cognitive processing. The focus moved away from response to sensory input to the processes involved in the identification and selection of relevant information in general. This was reflected in deficit terminology such as stimulus overselectivity, directed attention, and attentional shifts. In addition, at least one group of researchers proposed that attention was a central deficit in autism and the neocerebellum an important structure in the coordination of attention and arousal systems, presenting evidence for its abnormal development in autism (Courchesne, 1995; Courchesne, Saitoh, et al., 1994; Courchesne, Townsend, et al., 1994b; Courchesne, Yeung-Courchesne, Press, Hesselink, & Jernigan, 1988; Murakami, Courchesne, Press, Yeung-Courchesne, & Hesselink, 1989).

Behavioral qualities of individuals with autism often include an intense focus on unusual features of objects and repetitive activities, attention to non-salient aspects of the environment, and difficulty shifting focus or transitioning from one activity to the next. Allen and Courchesne (2001) proposed that behavioral indicators, such as tantrums, in response to sensory sensitivities, such as sound, may also be related to neurobehavioral driven distractibility. Attention is purported to influence each stage of sensory modulation (Marco et al., 2011). Therefore, the consideration of sensory features in autism would be insufficient without the discussion of the attentional systems.

Various brain regions, including the superior colliculus, the cerebellum, and the frontal lobes, have been implicated in processing, modulating, and integrating sensory information (Courchesne, Akshoomoff, Townsend & Saitoh, 1995; Stein & Meredith, 1990). When the pathophysiology is compared, both shared abnormalities in brain function (fronto-striato-parietal activation) and disorder-specific abnormalities (more severe dorsolateral prefrontal dysfunction in attention-deficit/hyperactivity disorder [ADHD], fronto-striato-cerebellar dysregulation in autism) during sustained attention have been found (Christakou et al., 2013).

Marco and colleagues (2011) purport that the multidirectional flow of information is impaired for individuals with autism. Furthermore, they suggest that the inability of individuals with autism to attend to their environment in flexible, productive, and meaningful ways is impacted by this disruption in cortical communication. However, there are aspects of attention that are noted to be spared in individuals with autism, notably sustained attention. Deviation occurs on more complex tasks, as discussed in the following.

Attention Research in ASD

Sustained attention for simple repetitive visual information is generally intact in individuals with autism compared to developmentally matched controls, as measured by continuous performance tasks (Buchsbaum et al., 1992; Casey, Gordon, Mannheim, & Rumsey, 1993; Garretson, Fein, & Waterhouse, 1990; Goldstein, Johnson, & Minshew, 2001; Minshew, Goldstein, & Siegel, 1997; Pascualvaca, Fantie, Papgeorgiou, & Mirsky, 1998). In contrast, deficits in attention for more complex tasks requiring filtering of information, selective attention, and shifts in attention are indicated (Casey et al., 1993; Ciesielski, Courchesne, & Elmasian, 1990; Courchesne, Townsend, et al., 1994b; Frazier et al., 2001; McGrath, Joseph, Tadevosyan, Folstein, & Tager-Flusberg, 2002; Townsend, Harris, & Courchesne, 1996; Wainwright-Sharp & Bryson, 1996). Researchers who place this deficit at a higher order level suggest that it is part of a more general difficulty with executive control originating from frontal lobe dysfunction, as evidenced by specific deficits on measures of attention that require cognitive flexibility or shifting between categories, sets or rules (Goldstein et al., 2001; Ozonoff et al., 2004; Pascualvaca et al., 1998).

There have been comparatively few studies to assess attention directly or systematically in children with AS despite the presence of associated behavioral features of inattention and distractibility. Attention deficits were indicated on a battery of tests used to assess sustained attention, selective attention, and the ability to shift attention (Nydén, Gillberg, Hjelmquist, & Heiman, 1999). For all three clinical groups in this study (AS, ADHD, and reading and writing disorder), performance was significantly lower than that of the TD control group on the majority of measures; no specific marker of attention/executive function deficits emerged to distinguish the three groups. The children with AS made few omission or commission errors but showed lengthier reaction times, particularly in the auditory condition, as well as large variability in response time on the go-no-go tasks and conflict conditions, which were presented as measures of the sustain and focus-execute components of attention. In a preliminary study of attention in AS, an inconsistent or variable response pattern to stimuli on a sustained visual attention task was also reported (Schatz, Weimer, & Trauner, 2002). In the Nydén et al. (1999) study, the AS group did not differ from TD controls on the shift dimension, as measured using the Wisconsin Card Sorting Test (WCST) variables, including number of categories sorted, perseverative errors, and failure to maintain set. When the requirement to shift attention was measured using a task involving moving from processing a detail to a whole (Rinehart, Bradshaw, Moss, Brereton, & Tonge, 2001), the AS group again did not show a deficit; the autism group was significantly slower than controls, a finding that is consistent with other reports of impairment in shifting attention in autism. Others find evidence for a more basic deficiency in broadening the spread of visual attention (e.g., the attentional spotlight) and report difficulty switching attention from local to global processing in individuals with ASD (Katagiri, Kasai, Kamio, & Murohashi, 2013; Mann & Walker, 2003).

Of the comorbid psychiatric disorders described in individuals with ASD, the diagnosis of ADHD is of particular interest; symptoms of inattention and overactivity were identified in the *DSM-IV-TR* (APA, 2000) as associated features of Asperger syndrome, and it was noted that an ADHD diagnosis frequently precedes a diagnosis of AS in children. Significant problems with attention, hyperactivity, and/or impulse control in children with AS have been identified on parent-report behavioral measures (Holtmann, Bölte, & Poustka, 2005; Thede & Coolidge, 2007), through retrospective review of medical/psychiatric records (Sturm et al., 2004), and through retrospective self-report by adults with AS (Tani et al., 2006). When rates of comorbidity were examined in children with ASD (e.g., Ehlers & Gillberg, 1993; Ghaziuddin, Weidmer-Mikhail, & Ghaziuddin, 1998; Leyfer et al., 2006; Sturm et al., 2004), a high rate of comorbid ADHD was found. Yet, when a group of children with HFA were directly compared to a group of children with ADHD, the HFA group showed no deficits in sustained attention, as measured by their performance on a go-no-go task, and the ADHD group showed clear deficits (Johnson et al., 2007). Given a very large sample of individuals with ASD (1,838 children and adolescents), less than 16% were found to meet clinically significant levels of ADHD symptoms, per parent report, and when both parent and teacher reports were considered, the comorbidity rate was lower, at 2 % (Hanson et al., 2013).

The role of attention in academic attainment for children with ASD has also been examined (May, Rinehart, Wilding, & Cornish, 2013). No differences were found between school-aged children with ASD and age- and gender-matched typical children on measures of mathematics, reading, attentional switching, or sustained attention, with full scale IQ controlled. However, difficulties with attentional switching were associated with poorer mathematics performance in the group of children with ASD.

Summary

Taken together, these findings raise questions whether observations of inattention, distractibility, and/or overactivity in children with ASD reflect the presence of a comorbid condition such as ADHD, vulnerabilities in emotional functioning (anxiety, depression), and/or the primary disability itself (e.g., social functioning). From the latter perspective, individuals with ASD show deficits in attending to or processing the most salient information from their environment (Klin, Jones, Schultz, & Volkmar, 2003) and attending to the shared aspects of a situation (Klin, 2000), both of which are of great relevance to the daily lives of individuals with autism. Developmentally, a related concept is, of course, joint attention. These acts of coordinating attention between interactive social partners and environmental stimuli are a distinguishing deficit area for children with autism (considered in more depth elsewhere). Orienting to the social overtures of others requires that specific information is registered, attended to, and has meaning. Ongoing systematic and comprehensive study is needed. The clinical implications are significant as they relate to differential diagnosis; academic, behavioral, and adaptive functioning; and treatment approach.

MEMORY

Very few aspects of higher cognitive function and learning could operate successfully without some memory contribution. Memory is often treated as a unitary construct but is thought to be comprised of multiple interrelated systems. Divisions include working, implicit, and explicit memory, with the latter further subdivided into two subsystems, semantic and episodic memory. As with the other domains discussed earlier, memory functioning, too, can be assessed in a variety of modalities (e.g., auditory, visual, auditory-visual, tactile, etc.). Memory and learning are also inextricably connected, as early emerging deficits in memory impact how an individual learns, which subsequently affects development, both neurobiological and behavioral maturation.

Memory Features and Associated Theories in ASD

The behavioral and neuropsychological research evidence suggests the usefulness of considering different aspects of memory functioning in autism. Some individuals with ASD show extraordinary memory for discrete domains of knowledge, accumulating a wealth of factual information on a narrow topic. At the same time, they are observed to have tremendous difficulty navigating their daily environment, such as remembering where objects and belongings are located, or remembering their schedule of classes and activities or morning routine. Further, the capacity of higher functioning individuals to provide a reliable account of the day's activities or to recollect personal experiences is more limited than might be predicted based on level of language or cognitive functioning alone.

There have been a small number of researchers who speculated that at least some of the characteristics of autism could be explained in terms of a memory deficit. Some postulated that autism may in part arise from developmental amnesia associated with hippocampal or diencephalic brain aberrations (Boucher & Warrington, 1976; DeLong, 1978; Rimland, 1964). Boucher (1981a; Boucher & Warrington, 1976) suggested that the pattern of memory performance of autistic individuals is similar to that of patients with medial temporal lobe amnesic disorder; however, the cumulative research evidence does not support this proposal. DeLong (1992) speculated that autism is the developmental syndrome of hippocampal dysfunction in the young child and proposed that individuals with autism are not able to benefit from experiential learning (i.e., integrating past and present experiences to create a structure of meaning), which may account for a typically rote or rigid manner when engaged in events and interactions and the need for explicit preparation when entering a novel context or social situation. Powell & Jordan (1993) discussed a role for episodic memory and its implications for teaching autistic individuals how to learn.

There is also some support for abnormalities in brain regions identified as central to memory functions. Notably, the pathophysiology of autism has implicated regions including the hippocampal formation, amygdala, and cerebellum (Abell et al., 1999; Aylward et al., 1999; Bachevalier 1994; Bachevalier & Merjanian, 1994; Bauman &

Kemper, 1994; Courchesne et al., 1988; Kemper & Bauman, 1993; Schultz, Romanski, & Tsatsanis, 2000). In regard to declarative memory, various neural substrates have been associated with this process, including the disconnectivity of primary sensory and association areas; dysfunctions of medial prefrontal cortex, hippocampus, or posterior parietal lobe; or combinations of these associated with neural disconnectivity (Boucher, Mayes, & Bigham, 2012). Clinical (e.g., executive function) studies support a role for frontal lobe dysfunction in autism. The pattern of memory function in ASD, that is, impairments in episodic memory, retrieval, and subjective organization, are suggestive of frontal lobe dysfunction. One hypothesis for memory deficit is related to limbic-prefrontal pathways (e.g., Ben-Shalom, 2003). Evidence of underconnectivity between perceptual and memory regions has been revealed in neuroimaging studies (e.g., Just, Cherkassky, Keller, & Minshew, 2004; Koshino et al., 2005).

Memory Research in ASD

Most memory tasks comprise both implicit and explicit learning components. Implicit memory does not require conscious or intentional recollection of experiences although they have an effect on current performance. When perceptual processing tasks have been used to examine implicit memory in ASD, no evidence of impairment has been found (Bowler, Matthews, & Gardiner, 1997; Gardiner, Bowler, & Grice, 2003; Heaton, Williams, Cummins, & Happé, 2007; Renner, Klinger, & Klinger, 2000; Toichi, 2008).

Explicit memory, also referred to as declarative memory, is considered with reference to two subsystems defined by Tulving (1972) as episodic and semantic memory. Episodic memory refers to the system involved in recollecting particular experiences, whereas semantic memory refers to factual knowledge or knowledge of the world. It is consistently found that individuals with autism show intact digit span and intact immediate recall for semantically unrelated lists of words relative to ability-matched and, in some cases, normal controls

(Bennetto, Pennington, & Rogers, 1996; Bowler, Limoges, & Mottron, 2009; Goldstein et al., 2001; Lincoln, Allen, & Kilman, 1995). There is also evidence to suggest well-developed associative learning mechanisms (Boucher & Warrington, 1976; Minshew & Goldstein, 2001; Minshew, Goldstein, Muenz, & Payton, 1992).

For individuals with AS, strengths are obtained on measures of factual and lexical knowledge on individual subtests of the Wechsler scales (e.g., Ehlers et al., 1997; Ghaziuddin & Mountain-Kimchi, 2004; Mayes & Calhoun, 2003), which is reminiscent of accounts of exceptional stores of factual information in these individuals. Performance is lower on Wechsler subtests involving attention to and mental manipulation of (numerical) information; these results may be consistent with the findings reported above suggestive of inconsistent attentional focus.

Overall performance on the immediate recall of semantically *related* lists of words is impaired for participants with autism relative to ability-matched TD controls (Boucher & Warrington, 1976; Bowler, Gaigg, & Gardiner, 2008; Bowler, Gardiner, Grice, & Saavalainen, 2000b; Tager-Flusberg, 1991). When a cued recall paradigm was used, the participants with autism benefited from the provision of semantic cues suggesting a deficit in retrieval versus encoding processes. Individuals with autism may equally encode the meanings of the words presented but be deficient in their ability to employ a strategic search to assist their retrieval of the unrecalled semantically related words. This suggests that individuals with autism may not spontaneously use semantic relations to augment verbal memory; however, when cued, they are able to utilize semantic meaning to aid recall (Boucher et al., 2012).

The results of similar list learning tasks also offer some support for inefficiency in the ability to actively organize information during learning and retrieval for individuals with autism, reflected, for example, in an impaired serial position effect or failure to group words into conceptual categories (Bennetto et al., 1996; Minshew et al., 1992; Minshew & Goldstein, 1993; Renner et al., 2000). This last effect was also found in adults with AS

(Bowler et al., 1997). Tasks requiring a greater level of semantic organization also appear to impact the memory performance of autistic subjects, which may reflect a more general deficiency related to complexity of the material to be remembered (Fein et al., 1996; Minshew & Goldstein, 2001).

Adults with AS also failed to capitalize on semantic or phonological information to aid free recall to the extent that was seen in the typical control group; cued recall support led to performance at the same level as the control group but training at the time of learning (to enhance relational encoding) did not (Bowler et al., 1997; Smith, Gardiner, & Bowler, 2007). The results lead to a similar conclusion as reported in autism; individuals with AS too may be challenged to recall information when they have to develop complex organizing strategies to help in their recall. A subsequent study further indicated that patterns of organization tended not to converge in the adults with AS, suggesting that they did not utilize a shared system of organization but rather may have organized the information in more idiosyncratic ways. Convergence was seen in the control participants who were likely to have used a conventional semantic system (Bowler et al., 2008).

Episodic memory function has been examined in people with ASD, although not always as the stated focus of study. Boucher (1981a) compared the performance of children with ASD and ability-matched controls on a test of immediate recall of a series of word lists. There was no significant difference between the total recall scores of the two groups; however, there was a significant difference between their primacy and recency scores. The children with autism showed significantly poorer recall of the first three words of the lists (primacy effect) but comparable recall of the last three words (recency effect). It is proposed that the last three words in the list are maintained in the articulatory loop of the working memory system. This account is consistent with the results of Russell, Jarrold, and Henry's (1996) study indicating that the articulatory loop is intact in individuals with ASD. In contrast, recall of the first three words of the study episode requires the individual to consciously recollect and reexamine the study list, thereby drawing upon episodic memory.

More recently, Renner and colleagues (2000) examined this phenomenon in children with autism and found that individuals with autism showed a lack of the usual primacy effect on a single-trial recall. Additionally, Bowler and colleagues (2009) found that although there was a noted increase in the primacy effect for adults with autism over repeated trials, the rate was slower compared to controls.

Boucher (1981b) also examined memory for recent events in three groups of children who ranged in age from 10 to 16 years. They included children with autism, children with intellectual disability (ID), and those with TD. The children were present for a 1- to 2-hour session, during which they participated in a variety of activities. At the end of the session, the materials were cleared away and the children were asked to recall the session's events. Single word responses and gestures were acceptable. Boucher reported a significant difference between the recall scores of all three groups. The children with autism recalled significantly fewer events relative to both comparison groups. In addition, the performance of the mentally retarded children was poorer than that of the normal controls. It is argued that this type of task also assesses episodic memory, as it requires the children to think back to and reexperience a prior subjective event. Notably, Boucher (1981b) observed that the autistic children's recall improved when they were provided with cueing strategies. Again, the deficit appears to lie in retrieval (e.g., making use of context dependent cues) versus encoding processes.

The results of a second related study appear to support this interpretation (Boucher & Lewis, 1989). In this case, children were asked to recall activities that they had taken part in several months earlier. The performance of children with autism was compared to learning disabled controls under free recall (e.g., open questions) and cued recall (e.g., leading questions) conditions. Whereas the free recall scores differed significantly, the cued recall scores were not significantly different between the two groups. Although the children with autism engaged in little self-cueing, they were able to benefit from cues provided by the examiner.

Bennetto et al. (1996) examined whether individuals with autism display a pattern of deficits that is similar to patients with frontal lesions. Measures of temporal order memory, source memory, and working memory were administered. The subjects consisted of high-functioning children with autism and children with learning disabilities. A comparison of the performance of the two groups showed that the children with autism were significantly impaired on all tasks. Notably, the autistic group also displayed significantly more intrusion errors on a list-learning task, which was interpreted as a deficit in source memory. Bennetto et al. observed that the children with autism in their study displayed a pattern of memory function that is similar to that of patients with frontal lesions and interpreted their findings in terms of a general deficit in working memory. However, the tasks that they employed in their study appeared more consistent with a usual approach to the assessment of episodic memory. On the Sentence and Counting Span tasks, subjects were required to process information, but they were not asked to simultaneously store that information. Rather, the subjects were asked to recall their responses at the end of the task. Wheeler, Stuss, and Tulving (1997) identified three types of tests that assess episodic memory. One approach is to assess aspects of the learning episode that are not central to the target information. The Sentence and Counting Span tasks appear to fulfill this requirement. The items requested for recall on these tasks would be recoverable only through a conscious recollection of the study episode. In addition, Wheeler et al. identified tests of memory for source and memory for temporal order, specifically Corsi's task, as measures of episodic memory. Again, these appear to be precisely the kinds of instruments employed in the Bennetto et al. (1996) study.

Bowler and colleagues have examined episodic memory function in adults with AS in a series of studies and reported impairments in source memory as well as greater reliance on "knowing" and less reliance on "remembering" relative to controls (e.g., Bowler, Gardiner, & Grice, 2000; Gardiner et al., 2003). Their findings suggest a subtle yet persistent weakness of episodic memory paired with abnormalities in processing semantically meaningful information. A subsequent study confirmed the hypothesis that with source support or cueing, the performance of individuals with AS was comparable to that of controls (Bowler, Gardiner, & Berthollier, 2004). Individuals with AS may show impairments in episodic memory, but consistent with findings from studies in autism, the deficit appears to be at the level of retrieval versus encoding.

When memory performance in relation to witnessing an everyday experience was examined in a group of children with AS (McCrory, Henry, & Happé, 2007), a similar result was obtained. That is, compared to their peers, the children with AS freely recalled less information, but questioning to cue their recall did yield a similar level of recall as the control group. In addition, the AS group was less likely to mention the most salient or gist elements of the event, and was less focused on a socially salient subscene; again, however, their recall was aided by general questioning yielding a comparable pattern of recall. Impairment at the level of retrieval was suggested; the authors in turn raised the question whether organizing strategies or a representational deficit with respect to semantic, relational, and contextual properties accounted for the differences in free recall. Notably, whereas recall performance was significantly positively correlated with performance on two (verbal) executive functioning tasks in the AS group, this relationship was not significant in the peer group. Taken together, the results indicated that the AS group may not have accessed gist-based organizational strategies and rather relied on other more broad-based cognitive processes.

Socially oriented stimuli have also been found to be an important factor as relates to the memory of individuals with autism. O'Shea, Fein, Cillessen, Klin, and Schultz (2005) investigated fact and socially relevant source memory in children with autism and typically developing controls. For this study, the children were read stories and then asked to recognize elements from the stories as well as elements from the social context (e.g., the clothing of the reader, the face of the reader). The children with autism performed similar to controls on the fact recognition measure, but their performance on the source memory task, which involved social context, was significantly lower. Similarly, Williams, Goldstein, and Minshew (2005, 2006a, 2006b) found that individuals with autism performed as well as controls on immediate and delayed memory for word pairs and stories, but the group with autism was impaired on immediate and delayed recall of faces and common social scenes. These findings implicate contributions of the social deficit on memory in real-life situations.

Bowler and colleagues further examined the question whether episodic remembering in adults with AS is qualitatively similar to normal controls (Bowler, Gardiner, & Gaigg, 2007). A *quantitative* impairment in performance on episodic memory tasks was found, but it was concluded that the performance of the adults with AS was not *qualitatively* different than typical individuals; that is, the capacity for recalling past events in a spatiotemporal context and for recalling the self-referential aspects of the episode was demonstrated, although to a lesser extent.

Adults with AS differed from control participants when required to retrieve a memory of a personal experience in response to a word cue; the AS group generated fewer specific memories in response to positive, negative, and neutral cues (e.g., the word *leisure*), and they were also slower overall to retrieve specific memories to cues (Goddard, Howlin, Dritschel, & Patel, 2007). When presented with a social problem-solving task, they were equally able to access a relevant personal experience as well as categorical information. However, their solutions were less effective, less detailed, and showed less appreciation that some solutions to problems evolve over a time course (versus a focus on the here-and-now solution). Notably, in the AS group, retrieval of specific memories on the *cueing* task was significantly related to problem-solving performance but memory during problem solving was not; in contrast, whether or not past experiences were retrieved *during* problem solving was related to the problem-solving performance of the TD control group. Individuals with AS may possess a store of past experiences but not see the relevance of applying these past experiences to solve a particular problem.

As suggested by the results of several of the studies described previously, organization has a role in memory as do other executive control processes. Working memory is a component of memory function that is often considered within the domain of executive function as it requires the ability to simultaneously attend to, recall, and act upon information held in an online state. Working memory is often needed for completion of more complex problem solving tasks. Research on working memory in ASD yields equivocal results (Boucher et al., 2012). Although deficits in working memory may be found in ASD, they do not appear to be specific to the disorder. When presented with working memory capacity tasks, both children with autism and children with moderate learning difficulties performed significantly more poorly than the normal controls on all three tasks (Russell et al., 1996). There was no difference, however, in the performance between the two comparison groups. The authors concluded that working memory deficits are not specific to autism but are likely related to a general deficit in information processing (marked by level of intellectual functioning). Ozonoff and Strayer (2001) also reported no autism-specific impairments in working memory in the context of a significant association between IQ and age and performance on working memory tasks. Bennetto and colleagues (1996) ostensibly found a different set of results, but a careful consideration of the tasks used in their study is more suggestive of an evaluation of episodic versus working memory processes (see later discussion). Other studies, however, which have looked at working memory in different modalities, have found that individuals with autism have intact verbal working memory yet deficits in spatial working memory (Goldberg et al., 2005; Steele, Minshew, Luna, & Sweeney, 2007; Williams, Goldstein, Carpenter & Minshew, 2005). A deficit in spatial working memory has also been reported in a small sample of adults with AS (Morris et al., 1999). Generally, tests of working memory including immediate, serial-order free recall of a sequence of unstructured items show intact abilities in individuals with ASD (Boucher et al., 2012).

Summary

The research to date suggests intact implicit memory, a deficit in spatial working memory, impairments at the level of retrieval versus encoding for new learning, and quantitative (both in amount and speed of retrieval) but not qualitative differences in episodic memory. The profile of memory functioning in AS is similar to that found in autism. Episodic memory in particular has been comprehensively examined in AS, although replication with a larger subject sample size and wider age range (the studies have typically employed adults) is suggested. Other divisions of memory such as semantic and working memory have been less exhaustively studied in AS specifically; comparisons made across modalities (e.g., tactile, verbal, visual, spatial, etc.) are also lacking more generally.

Individuals with autism appear to learn through rote memory, classical conditioning (e.g., stimulus–response learning), and procedural mechanisms, but show a more limited capacity for flexibility, abstraction, and generalization. Given the specific deficits in retrieval of information on learning tasks, simple repetition alone cannot be counted on to facilitate recall of new information; rather, the provision of specific context cues is suggested. Consideration should also be given to how information is organized for the person with ASD; information may be organized but in an idiosyncratic way. When creating meaning from experiences, individuals with ASD may have difficulty connecting past and present experiences to create a structure by which to guide their social behavior. Information about a relevant past event may be stored but not readily applied to solve a problem; individuals with ASD may be less likely than their TD peers to call up relevant information from a past experience for problem-solving a current situation. Learning and problem solving may be advanced through direct support for connecting a current learning episode with prior concepts or events as well as explicit preparation as to what is salient information, particularly before entering a social situation.

EXECUTIVE FUNCTIONS

Executive functioning (EF) is comprised of a set of processes that contribute to maintaining an appropriate problem-solving set to guide future behaviors. These include inhibition, set shifting, planning, self-monitoring, organization, flexibility, and working memory. Although there is overlap between the aspects of executive functioning and other neuropsychological domains—namely, attention and memory—distinct measures, concepts, and neuroanatomical regions characterize this literature, especially pertaining to function in the prefrontal cortex and measures developed to assess such function.

EF Features and Associated Theories in ASD

Several behavioral characteristics of individuals with ASD are reminiscent of the kinds of impairments seen in patients with prefrontal cortical damage. These include response perseveration, disinhibition, narrow range of interests, failure to plan, difficulty taking the perspective of others, and lack of self-monitoring. A failure to generalize newly learned concepts is also ascribed to deficits in higher cognitive functioning. Ozonoff (1995) and others (Hughes, 2001; Russell, 1997) argued for the contributions of executive functions in understanding the range of impairments in autism. Frontal lobe abnormalities in autism were also hypothesized, since executive functions are considered to be mediated by regions of the frontal lobes. Two regions in the prefrontal cortex are distinguished: Damage to dorsolateral regions is associated with impairment in high-level cognitive ability, whereas damage to orbital regions is associated with disturbances in social and affective behavior (e.g., Damasio, 1985). Ozonoff (1995) noted that since the frontal cortex is central to the regulation of both

higher cognitive and social-emotional behavior, and individuals with ASD display deficits in both of these domains, then frontal lobe dysfunction may be able to account for the impairments seen in autism. The function of the prefrontal cortex, according to Goldman-Rakic (1987), is to guide behavior by internal representations of the outside world, without direct stimulation from the environment. These deficits, then, may be related more generally to an inability to disengage from immediate environmental cues and be guided by internal rules or mental representations.

Concrete thinking and limited abstraction abilities have long been observed in individuals with ASD (Adams & Sheslow, 1983; Rutter, 1978; Tsai, 1992) and can be related to overall developmental or intellectual level. However, another relevant dichotomy when thinking about concrete versus abstract/conceptual ability is that of internally controlled processes or generative demands and externally generated problem-solving strategies and external structures (e.g., the solution is inherent in or constrained by the problem). This latter question is reminiscent of Klin et al.'s (2003) discussion of open domain and closed domain tasks in the context of social environment as well as research suggesting intact rule categorization in the face of impaired formation of prototypic mental representations when a concrete rule is not available on cognitive tasks (e.g., Klinger & Dawson, 2001). In both instances, individuals with autism appear to be more capable of knowing through a set of rules versus knowing through learning formed from repeated experience. It is not surprising, then, that intervention approaches emphasize consistency; routine; predictability, through the use of visual supports for planning events across the day; preparing for challenging situations; making the implicit rules of engagement explicit; and teaching generalization (e.g., applying the rules in naturalistic situations).

EF Research in ASD

Research generally suggests that both adults and children with ASD exhibit difficulties in executive functioning, including planning (Hughes, Russell, & Robbins, 1994), mental flexibility (Ozonoff & Jensen, 1999; Prior & Hoffman, 1990), response inhibition (Robinson, Goddard, Dritschel, Wisley, & Howlin, 2009), and generativity (Hill, 2004), when compared to typically developing controls. From studies of traditional EF tasks, such as the Wisconsin Card Sorting Test, it is observed that for individuals with autism, the capacity to deal with complex information or new situations is limited by deficits in cognitive flexibility and/or an incomplete understanding of novel/abstract concepts (Bennetto et al., 1996; Goldstein et al., 2001; Minshew, Meyer, & Goldstein 2002; Ozonoff & McEvoy, 1994; Ozonoff, Pennington, & Rogers, 1991; Ozonoff & Strayer, 1997; Ozonoff, Strayer, McMahon, & Filloux, 1994; Rumsey & Hamburger, 1990; Szatmari, Tuff, Finlayson, & Bartolucci, 1990). Individuals with autism have also been shown to evidence deficits on the switching conditions within subtests from the Delis-Kaplan Executive Function System (D-KEFS), such as trails, color-word interference, and design fluency (Kleinhans, Akshoomoff, & Delis, 2005). For all of these tasks, individuals are required to exhibit cognitive flexibility. Conceptual flexibility versus perceptual or attentional flexibility (or simple inhibitory control) appears to be the predominant deficit in higher functioning individuals (Goldstein et al., 2001; Ozonoff et al., 1994; Ozonoff et al., 2004; Ozonoff & Strayer, 1997). Additionally, rule learning and shifting within a rule or category are within the range of normal function (Berger et al., 1993; Minshew et al., 2002; Ozonoff et al., 2004). Higher functioning individuals with autism show some capacity to learn rules and procedures as well as identify concepts, but are challenged to abstract information to attain concepts or develop flexible strategies for problem solving, which may be evidenced most directly by perseverative errors or persisting in a strategy even when it is not successful.

Strong group differences in performance have also been found on the Tower of Hanoi and modified versions of this task (Bennetto et al., 1996; Hughes et al., 1994; Ozonoff et al., 1994; Ozonoff

et al., 2004; Ozonoff, Pennington, et al., 1991; Szatmari et al., 1990). These tests are commonly used measures of executive function that require the individual to solve a problem by planning before acting and identifying the subgoals needed to reach a target goal. The task also typically taps rule following and procedural learning. Ozonoff, Pennington, et al. (1991) reported that the Tower of Hanoi provided the highest discriminatory power between groups of high-functioning children with autism and matched controls, relative to other measures (e.g., theory of mind, memory, emotion perception, and visual spatial tasks). This finding was particularly interesting because the control group consisted of children who might also be expected to show EF deficits (e.g., 25% of the control sample met criteria for ADHD). It is proposed that the challenge for higher functioning individuals is related to planning efficiency (Ozonoff et al., 2004) and resolving goal–subgoal conflicts (Goldstein et al., 2001).

While several studies have investigated EF profiles in ASD, fewer have examined its developmental course. Deficits have been reported at both lower and higher levels of IQ in individuals with autism across the age range of 6 to 47 years (Ozonoff et al., 2004). In a 3-year follow-up study, the expected age-related improvement in planning efficiency was not found in adolescents with autism, again suggesting that EF difficulties persist over time (Ozonoff & McEvoy, 1994). A similar finding was reported in preschoolers with autism on a measure of cognitive flexibility (e.g., Griffith, Pennington, Wehner, & Rogers, 1999). However, more recent evidence from a cross-sectional (Happé, Booth, Charlton, & Hughes, 2006) and longitudinal (Pellicano, 2010) study indicate EF deficits become less marked with age, a finding that may be specific to higher functioning or cognitively able children with ASD.

The executive functioning profile and degree of impairment in children with AS has generally been found to be similar to that of high functioning individuals with autism (Kenworthy et al., 2005; Klin, Volkmar, Sparrow, Cicchetti, and Rourke, 1995; Manjiviona & Prior, 1999; Miller & Ozonoff,

2000; Ozonoff, Pennington, et al., 1991; Verté, Geurts, Roeyers, Oosterlaan, & Sergeant, 2006) with exceptions (e.g., Szatmari et al., 1990). The findings from studies of EF functioning in adults with AS yield a more varied set of conclusions. Hill and Bird (2006) reported no differences between adults with AS and TD controls on traditional measures of inhibition, set shifting, cognitive flexibility, and verbal fluency. Rather, the greatest area of impairment overall was on measures of response initiation, intentionality, and planning; that is, the ability to engage and disengage actions in the service of overarching goals. Towgood and colleagues (Towgood, Meuwese, Gilbert, Turner, & Burgess, 2009), using the same measures, found deficits for response initiation and suppression but not planning. Slowed processing/motor speed was also characteristic of the AS groups in both studies. Towgood et al. observed that variability in performance was the most defining feature in the AS group. Ambery et al. (2006) reported preserved response inhibition but impairments in set shifting, word generation, and flexibility. Intact response inhibition (upon direct measurement) appears to be one consistent finding across studies. Of note, when inhibitory control was assessed using five task levels increasing in cognitive load, deficits in inhibitory control as cognitive load increased (e.g., with the addition of a set-shifting component) were found in the group with HFA as well as more response variability than the AS group whose performance did not differ from that of the control participants in any of the conditions (Rinehart, Bradshaw, Tonge, Brereton, & Bellgrove, 2002). Employing tests from the D-KEFS in a small sample of adults with ASD, Kleinhans et al. (2005) also found that performance was not impaired for the higher order conditions involving inhibition or inhibition and switching; rather, the degree of inherent structure was seen as a variable that was relevant to performance across the different tasks. When cognitive switching and initiation of efficient retrieval strategies were required, deficits were found in the verbal domain specifically.

Preliminary evidence for an association between measures of EF and rating measures of autistic symptomatology (Autism Spectrum Quotient and Communication Checklist) was also reported (Hill & Bird, 2006). They did not find a relationship between EF performance and autistic symptomatology (as measured by the Autism Spectrum Quotient) but did report a significant association between the amount of individual variability on the tests and the social and communication subscales of the Autism Diagnostic Observation Schedule (ADOS).

Ratings on *behavioral* measures of EF identify significant concerns for this area of functioning in the daily functioning of children with ASD. Parental ratings of children and adolescents with AS yielded significantly more behaviors associated with a dysexecutive syndrome than TD controls (Channon, Charman, Heap, Crawford, & Rios, 2001), with flexibility and planning/organization as particular concerns. When HFA and AS groups were compared on a parent report measure of executive function challenges in day-to-day behavior, the overall results indicated more frequent concerns for attention and working memory in the HFA versus AS group (Kenworthy et al., 2005). This finding was interpreted to reflect differences in language abilities and response to spoken information, as there were no differences between the groups on, for example, their measured attention on a visual continuous performance task. Flexibility and planning/organization were pervasive concerns in both groups. On a parent report neurobehavioral measure, children and adolescents with HFA and AS showed significant elevations on the executive function scales relative to controls (Thede & Coolidge, 2007). The clinical group was elevated on the EF deficits scale overall and for the decision-making difficulties, metacognitive problems, and social inappropriateness subscales. Consistent with the finding obtained using EF performance measures, an association has been reported between behavioral ratings of EF and levels of adaptive functioning in children and adolescents with ASD (Gilotty, Kenworthy, Sirian, Black, & Wagner, 2002). Specifically, deficits in metacognitive skills, in particular working memory and initiation, were important contributors to adaptive functioning impairments.

Although executive functioning deficits are often found in individuals with ASD, executive functioning deficits are not unique to autism. Other clinical groups, most notably ADHD, also demonstrate deficits in executive functions. Nonetheless, there are some unique patterns between these two groups. As compared to ADHD groups, individuals with ASD display deficits in the area of planning and cognitive flexibility, whereas more marked deficits in inhibition are reported in the ADHD comparison groups (Geurts, Verté, Oosterlaan, Roeyers, & Sergeant, 2004; Gioia, Isquith, Kenworthy, & Barton, 2002; Kleinhans et al., 2005; Ozonoff & Jensen, 1999). A study based on parent report showed similar findings; the HFA group was distinguished by deficits in flexibility, whereas the ADHD (combined) group exhibited more severe deficits in inhibitory control (Gioia et al., 2002). When compared across young and old age groups, Happé et al. (2006) reported less severe and persistent deficits in individuals with ASD compared to ADHD. Happé et al. (2006) reported group differences for the domains of response selection and planning but not flexibility. Specifically, the ADHD group showed marked deficits for response selection/inhibition and planning on a spatial working memory task; the ASD group showed poorer performance on a measure of response selection/monitoring. The older ASD group (11 to 16 years) performed better than their younger counterparts (8 to 10 years, 11 months) and showed far less impairment relative to the older ADHD sample, suggesting an age-related improvement in EF functioning in ASD. EF performance was also related to adaptive functioning in the communication and socialization domains of the Vineland Adaptive Behavior Scales, and the relationship was stronger in the ASD as compared to the ADHD group.

In school-aged children, EF (specifically on the higher order Tower task) and theory of mind abilities were reported to explain significant variance in communication symptoms in children with autism (Joseph & Tager-Flusberg, 2004). No mediating role for EF ability with regard to theory of mind task performance was found once the shared effects of nonverbal ability and language level were controlled; the exception was a specific process related to inhibitory control and working memory and the ability to represent epistemic mental states (e.g., knowledge and belief). EF performance (on measures of working memory, working memory and inhibitory control, and planning) was not found to be related to core social interaction or repetitive behavior symptoms once the effects of language were controlled (Joseph & Tager-Flusberg, 2004).

Higher level executive functions and a representational understanding of mind appear to be related to severity of communication impairments in autism. Joseph and Tager-Flusberg (2004) hypothesized that social perceptual skills (e.g., information communicated through eye gaze, facial expressions, vocal intonation, etc.) would be more closely related to impairments in social reciprocity. The relationship between language and EF ability was also examined in a subsequent study of school-aged children with autism; deficits in EF performance were found in the autism group, but performance was not related to level of language functioning (with nonverbal ability controlled). Language and executive function were significantly positively correlated in control participants. The results were interpreted to suggest that executive dysfunction and language impairment are not directly related in autism, with support for the hypothesis that there may instead be a deficit in the use of (internal) language in the service of executive control (Joseph, McGrath, & Tager-Flusberg, 2005). A similar conclusion was drawn from the results of a study on the effects of inner speech disruption on EF task performance, which was diminished in TD adolescents but not in the high-functioning ASD group (Wallace, Silvers, Martin, & Kenworthy, 2009).

Lopez, Lincoln, Ozonoff, and Lai (2005) reported impairments in cognitive flexibility and planning in their adult HFA participants, with similar performance to controls on measures of response inhibition and working memory. A model inclusive of strengths in response inhibition and working memory and deficits in cognitive flexibility accounted for a significant portion of the variance in restricted, repetitive behavior symptoms. Partial support was found for a relationship between EF performance (again using the WCST as a measure of cognitive flexibility) and repetitive behaviors in children and adolescents (South, Ozonoff, & McMahon, 2007).

Overall group effects may also mask individual differences within the ASD group. Behavioral impairments in regulatory and metacognitive functioning characterize many but not all children with ASD (Ventola, Tirrell, Levine, Akbar, & Tsatsanis, under review). There appears to be a subset of children for whom these challenges are present to a significant degree, independent of IQ and ASD symptom severity. This raises the question whether EF behaviors represent another dimension by which to characterize subgroups of ASD and whether there are implications for neurobiological mechanisms and the genetics of the disorder. As found in other studies, there were significant differences in adaptive functioning, as measured using the Vineland Adaptive Behavior Scales, Second Edition (VABS-II), with the group with greater EF impairments having lower adaptive skills. From a clinical standpoint, the level of impairment in this group and the significant relationship to adaptive functioning underscore the need to focus on this domain of behaviors when assessing and treating children with ASD.

Summary

On neuropsychological measures of executive functioning, response inhibition appears to be in tact in ASD, whereas deficits in the area of cognitive flexibility and planning are reported. When compared across young and old age groups, Happé et al. (2006) report less severe and persistent deficits in individuals with ASD as compared to ADHD with the caveat that the study is cross-sectional in nature. Two studies of adults with AS indicate few differences from TD controls on traditional EF measures of inhibition, set shifting, and cognitive flexibility, and rather identify specific deficits in response initiation and suppression on newer EF tasks. Children with ASD have difficulty on measures requiring them to resolve goal–subgoal

conflicts and develop effective problem-solving strategies; for adults with ASD, the ability to engage and disengage actions in the service of overarching goals may be specifically challenging. In both cases, advance preparation and external support may be needed to break down tasks that are more abstract, novel/ambiguous, and/or involve multiple steps, also drawing on any strengths in visual or verbal abilities to effectively support problem solving and planning. The EF profile in groups with AS is not very distinct from autism groups; flexibility and planning/organization are identified concerns for both ASD groups on behavioral ratings and neuropsychological measures. Exceptions include behavioral ratings of attention and working memory, which are found to be significant for individuals with autism alone, interpreted to reflect differences in language abilities. Behavioral ratings of EF indicate significant challenges in day-to-day behavior. There is a relationship between EF functioning as measured through both behavioral ratings and performance on neuropsychological tests and level of adaptive functioning; EF impairment is associated with adaptive impairment. In autism, EF ability may be associated with communication symptoms but not language impairment; the evidence for an association to repetitive behaviors has been mixed.

INTELLECTUAL ABILITY PROFILES

Level of cognitive functioning for individuals with ASD spans the entire range, from profound mental retardation to superior intellect. The terms *low functioning* (IQ <70) and *high functioning* (IQ >70) autism are often used in the literature to denote subgroups based on differences in level of intellectual ability. This distinction has also been applied to the children described by Kanner (1943) and Asperger (1944). Whereas Kanner's description is consistent with the classically autistic or lower functioning child with autism, Asperger's description has been associated with the less impaired, more verbal, and older child with autism (Klin & Volkmar, 1997).

The intellectual profiles of individuals with autism have also been studied extensively, and it is typically found that visual and visual-spatial processing are well preserved and are frequently a strength relative to verbal abilities (e.g., Ghaziuddin & Mountain-Kimchi, 2004; Rumsey, 1992; see Barnhill, Hagiwara, Myles, & Simpson, 2000; Lincoln et al., 1995; Mayes & Calhoun, 2003, for a review). Siegel, Minshew, and Goldstein (1996) examined intellectual profiles in autism and found that in the majority of studies they reviewed, performance IQ (PIQ) scores were higher than verbal IQ (VIQ) scores. This is consistent with the observations of Temple Grandin (1992), who emphasizes her own visually mediated approach to learning and making sense of the world. Selected verbal subtests, such as comprehension (assessing understanding or commonsense reasoning and social judgment) on the Wechsler scales are typically significantly impaired relative to subtests involving visual perceptual or spatial analysis and integration, such as block design and object assembly. The discrepancy between verbal and nonverbal abilities in autism needs to be further understood in the context of factors such as age and overall level of ability.

Using the third edition of the Wechsler Intelligence Scale for Children (WISC-III), Mayes and Calhoun (2003) found strengths in lexical knowledge relative to verbal reasoning in both high- and low-IQ groups of older children, but a selective strength in visual spatial ability in their low-IQ group. Within the younger age group, assessed using the Stanford-Binet: IV, relative strengths in visual processing were found for both IQ groups, as well as a strength in rote memory. The disparity between verbal and nonverbal abilities observed in the younger group was not obtained in the group of older children, representing an increase in Verbal IQ versus change in nonverbal ability. Ghaziuddin and Mountain-Kimchi (2004) also found no difference in WISC-III VIQ and PIQ scores overall in their sample of subjects with HFA (mean age 12.42 years).

Uneven patterns of abilities have been noted within the verbal and nonverbal domains. For example, among verbal abilities, individuals with autism tend to show intact or well-developed rote verbal memory skills (e.g., digit span) and evidence greater difficulty on more abstract verbal problem solving tasks (e.g., comprehension) (Siegel et al., 1996). Similar discrepancies within nonverbal abilities exist including visual spatial strengths (e.g., block design) with greater impairments on picture arrangement or coding (Rumsey & Hamburger, 1988; Szatmari et al., 1990). Although not universal in autism, many individuals with autism appear to have greater difficulty on nonverbal tasks that are conceptual versus perceptual or visuospatial (Kuschner, Bennetto, & Yost, 2007).

Whereas the Wechsler scales are recommended for more able and verbally proficient children with autism, the Leiter International Performance Scale—Revised (Leiter-R) can be valuable for the larger group of children with autism who have more profound communication, attentional, and behavioral difficulties. The Leiter-R measures nonverbal cognitive functioning. In a group of children who presented with significant language limitations and obtained a Vineland expressive communication age equivalent score at or below 3 years of age, Leiter-R scores indicated higher nonverbal IQ scores with strengths on subtests drawing primarily on visualization skills and particularly spatial reasoning (Tsatsanis et al., 2003). Kuschner and colleagues (2007) also examined uneven cognitive profiles of young children with autism using the Leiter-R and found a relative strength in perceptual abilities (e.g., tasks of disembedding and detail-focused processing [figure ground and form completion]) and weaknesses in nonverbal conceptual abilities (e.g., tasks of abstraction and concept formation [repeated patterns and sequential order]) as compared to groups of typical and developmentally delayed children.

Current knowledge regarding cognitive abilities in individuals with autism is at minimum consistent for a scattered profile, suggesting that cognitive function may not be well integrated, yielding isolated strengths and a broad range of deficits. Longitudinal studies are needed to test evidence of continuity and discontinuity pertaining to cognitive profiles over time and whether specific performance profiles (versus overall level of ability) on measures of cognitive functioning predict outcome on measures of autistic symptomatology or social ability and disability.

Several studies have investigated the intellectual profiles of individuals diagnosed with AS, as opposed to HFA. Although diagnostic criteria and validity of the AS diagnosis are a matter of debate, these studies report a pattern of better verbal relative to poorer perceptual organizational skills overall (Ehlers et al., 1997; Ghaziuddin & Mountain-Kimchi, 2004; Lincoln, Courchesne, Allen, Hanson, & Ene, 1998; Ozonoff, South, & Miller, 2000). Intragroup analyses indicated significantly higher global IQ scores and a significant split between verbal and performance IQ with VIQ > PIQ on average for AS as a group relative to HFA. In consideration of these findings, a particular neuropsychological model, nonverbal learning disability (NLD; Rourke, 1989), has been proposed as a source of external validity for AS (Klin et al., 1995; Klin & Volkmar, 1997). In brief, the NLD profile involves a pattern of functioning of better developed verbal relative to visual, tactile, and complex motor skills as well as better reading and spelling skills relative to arithmetic.

Individuals with AS and/or NLD may share similar difficulties including trouble with social reciprocity, nonverbal communication, pragmatic language, and visual-spatial skill deficits (Gunter, Ghaziuddin, & Ellis, 2002). Furthermore, as mentioned, on assessments of cognitive functioning, researchers have noted that children with AS and NLD evidence stronger verbal as compared to nonverbal abilities (Klin et al., 1995). However, although some symptoms may be shared, children with AS are reported to evidence the stereotyped and restricted patterns of interest and the need to adhere to routines, which is absent in children with NLD (Semrud-Clikeman, 2007). Klin et al. (1995) also reported that deficits that were predictive of AS were fine motor skills, visual motor integration, visual-spatial perception, nonverbal concept formation, gross motor skills, and visual

memory. Deficits that were identified as not predictive of AS included articulation, verbal output, auditory perception, vocabulary, and verbal memory. This finding was reflected more generally in the pattern of IQ scores in the two groups as the AS group showed a significant and unusually large verbal–performance discrepancy (higher VIQ compared to PIQ score), whereas no such discrepancy was exhibited by the HFA group.

Preserved verbal memory skills, relative to individuals with HFA and relative to their own abilities, have been reported by others (e.g., Gunter et al., 2002; Ozonoff, Rogers, & Pennington, 1991). In addition, better reading/decoding relative to mechanical arithmetic skills is found (Griswold, Barnhill, Myles, Hagiwara, & Simpson, 2002). However, this was an area of debate complicated by differences in diagnostic approaches that made it difficult to compare studies (Klin & Volkmar, 2003), especially in the context of variability in the cognitive profiles within each group. Additionally, the restrictive onset criteria for AS relative to HFA (leading to differences in early language abilities) was considered by some to represent another confound. Whereas these profiles may not be relevant to diagnostic distinctions, these results may point to important implications for intervention, as different supports or strategies (e.g., verbally mediated strategies as compared to visual supports) may be preferred or better suited for children and adolescents with a given cognitive profile.

Other studies have not supported the finding of an NLD profile (Ambery, Russell, Perry, Morris, & Murphy, 2006). In the latter study, it was observed that a significant VIQ–PIQ discrepancy, irrespective of direction, was more common in the sample of AS adults as compared to the general population. Although the VIQ > PIQ intellectual profile is often considered to typify individuals with AS, another report indicated that this profile is also found in children and adults with HFA with some frequency (Williams, Goldstein, Kojkowski, & Minshew, 2007).

Joseph, Tager-Flusberg, and Lord (2002) examined the cognitive profiles of children with ASD and found that large discrepancies in either direction were more frequent in the ASD group relative to controls, although patterns in the cognitive profiles differed between school age and preschool groups. The direction of the discrepancy was significantly correlated with symptom severity; specifically, enhanced nonverbal abilities were associated with greater severity of autistic symptoms. It was further proposed that this disparity in cognitive abilities may reflect a significant disturbance in brain development and organization. In a subsequent study, Tager-Flusberg and Joseph (2003) found a significant inverse relationship between magnitude of the discrepancy (nonverbal abilities greater than verbal) and both head circumference and brain volume; that is, the subgroup of children with autism with discrepantly high nonverbal cognitive abilities also showed enlarged head circumference and brain volume. These studies provided evidence that isolating distinct cognitive profiles in ASD is relevant to expression of the disorder and may provide a path to identifying specific neurobiological mechanisms and possibly associated genes.

A high degree of unevenness in the cognitive profiles of individuals with ASD often seems to be the rule rather than the exception clinically and may be the most consistent finding to emerge from the research. As such, the traditional approach to identifying group differences—a comparison of group means—may in fact obscure some important findings. Widely discrepant interindividual as well as intra-individual scores are potentially masked by group averages. Indeed, when both group and single-case study methods were employed in a sample of adults diagnosed with AS, group-level analyses alone inadequately characterized the cognitive profiles (Towgood et al., 2009).

FUTURE DIRECTIONS

Although a syndrome that is defined primarily in behavioral terms, there has been considerable research devoted to the various cognitive impairments that characterize individuals with ASD. In association with these findings, competing theories have arisen over the decades concerning the primacy of a specific deficit in explaining the disorder. The complexity and clinical heterogeneity that typifies autism spectrum disorders is reflected not only in these accounts but also in differences in subject characteristics. With fundamental disparities in subject selection and diagnostic assignment, questions remain regarding the neuropsychological phenotype in ASD, including aspects of the phenotype that are specific to the disorder, changes in the phenotype with development, and how these constructs might explain response to treatment.

The most defining characteristic of cognitive profiles in ASD may be the pattern of marked variability both within and across individuals. Heterogeneity is a fact of these disorders; therefore, it is also reasonable to assume that a particular impairment (or strength) will be characteristic of only a fraction of children. If so, the question arises, what do these points of convergence and divergence signify with regard to expression of the disorder as well as adaptive functioning, presence of comorbid affective disorders, differences in regulatory functioning, treatment (e.g., impact of having impairments on one or more dimensions), brain development, and genetic susceptibility? Identifying the points of divergence may be relevant to the complexity and diversity of expression of the disorder as well as relevant to uncovering etiologic pathways. The points of convergence may represent the intersection of co-presenting disorders. It may be equally important to take a dimensional approach and examine the intersection points of different processes, that is, to determine the implications of co-variation among the different dimensions of interest.

One important implication for research methodology is consideration not only of the group but of individuals within the group. Overall group effects may represent the extreme performance of a subset of children or the average of two extremes. Group means may mask individual differences within the group and also the fact that many children may in fact be performing in the normal range. This might be addressed simply by reporting the percentage of the sample showing a significant strength or weakness or clinical elevation on a measure, ranges and frequencies of performance levels, and/or comparisons of variance in scores between clinical groups and controls. More sophisticated approaches include the application of, for example, the multiple case series approach employed by Hill and Bird (2006) and Towgood et al. (2009). It may be the case that variability is not only an index by which to separate groups but also the measured variable and construct of interest.

Another approach has been to identify specific aspects of the broader autism phenotype, such as measurable components not detected by the unaided eye that might fall along the pathway between disease and distal genotype (e.g., endophenotypes; Gottesman & Gould, 2003). Reciprocally, identification of the genes involved in the disorder may also help define the phenotype. This latter approach places a stronger emphasis on dimensionality and the measurement of continuously distributed traits. The challenge has been to identify and develop such measures. Innovative behavioral and neurofunctional methodologies have been used to assess salient social constructs and suggest that dimensionality can be achieved if we focus on processes that are very early emerging (Klin et al., 2003; Volkmar et al., 2004).

Given the amount of inherent structure available in the examination or research framework, subtle impairments in problem solving, organization, and behavioral activation may not be easily revealed. Yet, the fundamental deficit for individuals with autism is that of initiating complex behavior in unstructured settings. This investigative focus requires a movement away from externally controlled or constrained tasks toward gaining access to internally controlled experientially driven mechanisms. A mutual consideration of ASD as a complex heterogeneous disorder is that understanding will be increased through multiple levels of analysis and the integration of tools and information from other disciplines (e.g., genetic and brain research). Global features of brain function are far more likely to be bound up in the coordination and relation among things (cooperating to form coherent patterns) than they are to be revealed in an approach where one level of analysis has priority

over any other. Mediators of outcome through longitudinal associations and the mapping of developmental trajectories from the earliest stages of development using the simultaneous examination of social and neuropsychological processes may serve not only to identify diagnostic pathways but also to study fundamental mechanisms of social development and their relationship to cognitive and neurobiological factors.

A further approach might be to consider whether there are protective factors, for example, particular components of functioning that if intact contribute to a positive outcome. Finally, a developmental approach is crucial; by mapping the continuities and discontinuities of the central features of a developmental disability from first detection early in childhood, there is the potential to clarify syndrome expression and diagnostic pathways at the level of developmental processes as well as disentangle what leads to social disabilities from the effects of having such disabilities. Diagnostic validity depends on finding differences in etiology and identifying meaningful group distinctions. By examining the early dimensions along which diagnostic groups differ, the timing of their emergence, and the contributions of these dimensions to later diagnostic outcome, we may obtain some clues as to the beginning of different developmental pathways for ASDs.

CROSS-REFERENCES

Chapter 25 discusses diagnostic instruments relevant to autism spectrum disorders; Chapter 26 addresses multidisciplinary intervention, and Chapters 27 and 29 address communication and behavioral interventions, respectively.

REFERENCES

Abell, F., Krams, M., Ashburner, J., Passingham, R., Friston, K., Frackowiak, R., . . . Frith, U. (1999). The neuroanatomy of autism: A voxel-based whole brain analysis of structural scans. *Neuroreport, 10,* 1647–1651.

Adams, A. V., & Sheslow, B. V. (1983). A developmental perspective of adolescence. In E. Schopler & G. B. Mesibov (Eds.), *Autism in adolescents and adults* (pp. 11–36). New York, NY: Plenum Press.

Adrien, J. L., Barthelemy, C., Perrot, A., Roux, S., Lenoir, P., Hameury, L., & Sauvage, D. (1992). Validity and reliability of the Infant Behavioral Summarized Evaluation (IBSE): A rating scale for the assessment of young children with autism and developmental disorders. *Journal of Autism and Developmental Disorders*, *22*, 375–394.

Alcantara, J. I., Weisblatt, E. J. L., Moore, B. C. J., & Bolton, P. F. (2004). Speech-in-noise perception in high-functioning individuals with autism or Asperger's syndrome. *Journal of Child Psychology and Psychiatry*, *45*, 1107–1114.

Allen, G., & Courchesne, E. (2001). Attention function and dysfunction in autism. *Frontiers in Bioscience*, *6*, D105–D119.

Ambery, F. Z., Russell, A. J., Perry, K., Morris, R., & Murphy, D. G. M. (2006). Neuropsychological functioning in adults with Asperger syndrome. *Autism*, *10*, 551–564.

American Psychiatric Association. (2000). *Diagnostic and statistical manual of mental disorders* (4th ed., text rev.). Washington, DC: Author.

American Psychiatric Association. (2013). *Diagnostic and statistical manual of mental disorders* (5th ed.). Arlington, VA: American Psychiatric Publishing.

Anzalone, M. E., & Williamson, G. G. (2000). Sensory processing and motor performance in autism spectrum disorders. In A. M. Wetherby & B. M. Prizant (Eds.), *Autism spectrum disorders: A transactional developmental perspective*. Baltimore, MD: Paul H. Brookes.

Asperger, H. (1944). Die "Autistischen Psychopathen" im kindersalter. *Archive fur Psychiatrie und Nervenkrankheiten*, *117*, 76–136.

Aylward, E. H., Minshew, N. J., Goldstein, G., Honeycutt, N. A., Augustine, A. M., Yates, K. O.,...Pearlson, G. D. (1999). MRI volumes of amygdala and hippocampus in non-mentally retarded autistic adolescents and adults. *Neurology*, *53*, 2145–2150.

Bachevalier, J. (1994). Medial temporal lobe structures and autism: A review of clinical and experimental findings. *Neuropsychologia*, *32*, 627–648.

Bachevalier, J., & Merjanian, P. (1994). The contribution of medial temporal lobe structures in infantile autism: A neurobehavioral study in primates. In M. L. Bauman & T. L. Kemper (Eds.), *The neurobiology of autism* (pp. 146–169). Baltimore, MD: Johns Hopkins University Press.

Baker, A. E., Lane, A., Angley, M. T., & Young, R. L. (2008). The relationship between sensory processing patterns and behavioural responsiveness in autistic disorder: A pilot study. *Journal of Autism and Developmental Disorders*, *38*, 867–875.

Barnhill, G., Hagiwara, T., Myles, B. S., & Simpson, R. L. (2000). Asperger syndrome: A study of the cognitive profiles of 37 children and adolescents. *Focus on Autism and Other Developmental Disabilities*, *15*, 146–153.

Bauman, M. L., & Kemper, T. L. (1994). Neuroanatomic observations of the brain in autism. In M. L. Bauman & T. L. Kemper (Eds.), *The neurobiology of autism* (pp. 119–145). Baltimore, MD: Johns Hopkins University Press.

Bennetto, L., Pennington, B. F., & Rogers, S. J. (1996). Intact and impaired memory functions in autism. *Child Development*, *67*, 1816–1835.

Ben-Shalom, D. (2003). Memory in autism: Review and synthesis. *Cortex*, *39*, 1129–1138.

Berger, H., van Spaendonck, K., Horstink, M., Buytenhuijs, E., Lammers, P., & Cools, A. (1993). Cognitive shifting as a predictor of progress in social understanding in high-functioning adolescents with autism: A prospective study. *Journal of Autism and Developmental Disorders*, *23*, 341–359.

Blakemore, S. J., Tavassoli, T., Calò, S., Thomas, R. M., Catmur, C., Frith, U., & Haggard, P. (2006). Tactile sensitivity in Asperger syndrome. *Brain and Cognition*, *61*, 5–13.

Boucher, J. (1981a). Immediate free recall in early childhood autism: Another point of behavioral similarity with the amnesic syndrome. *British Journal of Psychology*, *72*, 211–215.

Boucher, J. (1981b). Memory for recent events in autistic children. *Journal of Autism and Developmental Disorders*, *11*, 293–301.

Boucher, J., & Lewis, V. (1989). Memory impairments and communication in relatively able autistic children. *Journal of Child Psychology and Psychiatry*, *30*, 99–122.

Boucher, J., Mayes, A., & Bigham, S. (2012). Memory in autistic spectrum disorder. *Psychological Bulletin*, *138*(3), 458–496.

Boucher, J., & Warrington, E. K. (1976). Memory deficits in early infantile autism: Some similarities to the amnesic syndrome. *British Journal of Psychology*, *67*, 73–87.

Bowler, D. M., Gaigg, S. B., & Gardiner, J. M. (2008). Effects of related and unrelated context on recall and recognition by adults with high-functioning autism spectrum disorder. *Neuropsychologia*, *46*, 993–999.

Bowler, D. M., Gardiner, J. M., & Berthollier, N. (2004). Source memory in adolescents and adults with Asperger's syndrome. *Journal of Autism and Developmental Disorders*, *34*, 533–542.

Bowler, D. M., Gardiner, J. M., & Gaigg, S. B. (2007). Factors affecting conscious awareness in the recollective experience of adults with Asperger's syndrome. *Consciousness and Cognition*, *16*, 124–143.

Bowler, D. M., Gardiner, J. M., & Grice, S. J. (2000). Episodic memory and remembering in adults with Asperger syndrome. *Journal of Autism and Developmental Disorders*, *30*(4), 295–304.

Bowler, D. M., Gardiner, J. M., Grice, S., & Saavalainen, P. (2000b). Memory illusions: False recall and recognition in high functioning adults with autism. *Journal of Abnormal Psychology*, *109*, 663–672.

Bowler, D. M., Limoges, E., & Mottron, L. (2009). Different verbal learning strategies in autism spectrum disorder: Evidence from the Rey Auditory Verbal Learning Test. *Journal of Autism and Developmental Disorders*, *39*(6), 910–915.

Bowler, D. M., Matthews, N. J., & Gardiner, J. M. (1997). Asperger's syndrome and memory: Similarity to autism but not amnesia. *Neuropsychologia*, *35*, 65–70.

Buchsbaum, M. S., Siegel, B. V., Jr., Wu, J. C., Hazlett, E., Sicotte, N., & Haier, R. (1992). Brief report: Attention performance in autism and regional brain metabolic rate assessed by positron emission tomography. *Journal of Autism and Developmental Disorders*, *22*, 115–125.

Cascio, C., McGlone, F., Folger, S., Tannan, V., Baranek, G., Pelphrey, K. A., & Essick, G. (2008). Tactile perception in adults with autism: A multidimensional psychophysical study. *Journal of Autism and Developmental Disorders*, *38*, 127–137.

Casey, B. J., Gordon, C. T., Mannheim, G. B., & Rumsey, J. M. (1993). Dysfunctional attention in autistic savants. *Journal of Clinical and Experimental Neuropsychology*, *15*, 933–946.

Channon, S., Charman, T., Heap, J., Crawford, S., & Rios, P. (2001). Real-life-type problem-solving in Asperger's syndrome. *Journal of Autism and Developmental Disorders*, *31*, 461–469.

Chen, Y., Rodgers, J., & McConachie, H. (2009). Restricted and repetitive behaviours, sensory processing and cognitive style in children with autism spectrum disorders. *Journal of Autism and Developmental Disorders*, *39*(4), 635–642.

Christakou, A., Murphy, C. M., Chantiluke, K., Cubillo, A. I., Smith, A. B., Giampietro, V., ... Rubia, K. (2013). Disorder-specific functional abnormalities during sustained attention in youth with Attention Deficit Hyperactivity Disorder (ADHD) and with Autism. *Molecular Psychiatry*, *18*, 236–244.

Ciesielski, K. T., Courchesne, E., & Elmasian, R. (1990). Effects of focused selective attention tasks on event-related potentials in autistic and normal individuals. *Electroencephalography and Clinical Neurophysiology*, *75*, 207–220.

Cohen, I. L., Gomez, T. R., Gonzalex, M. G., Lennon, E. M., Karmel, B. Z., & Gardner, J. M. (2010). Parent PDD behavior inventory profiles of young children classified according to Autism Diagnostic Observation Schedule—Generic and Autism Diagnostic Interview—Revised criteria. *Journal of Autism and Developmental Disorders*, *40*, 246–254.

Constantino, J. N., & Gruber, C. P. (2005). *Social responsiveness scale*. Los Angeles, CA: Western Psychological Services.

Courchesne, E. (1995). New evidence of cerebellar and brainstem hypoplasia in autistic infants, children, and adolescents: The MR imaging study by Hashimoto and colleagues. *Journal of Autism and Developmental Disorders*, *25*, 19–22.

Courchesne, E., Akshoomoff, N. A., Townsend, J., & Saitoh, O. (1995). A model system for the study of attention and the cerebellum: Infantile autism. *Electroencephalography and Clinical Neurophysiology*, *44*, 315–325.

Courchesne, E., Saitoh, O., Yeung-Courchesne, R., Press, G. A., Lincoln, A. J., Haas, R. H., & Schreibman, L. (1994). Abnormality of cerebellar vermian lobules, VI & VII in patients with infantile autism: Identification of hypoplastic and hyperplastic subgroups with MR imaging. *American Journal of Roentgenology*, *162*, 123–130.

Courchesne, E., Townsend, J., Akshoomoff, N. A., Saitoh, O., Yeung-Courchesne, R., Lincoln, A. J., ... Lau, L. (1994b). Impairment in shifting attention in autistic and cerebellar patients. *Behavioral Neuroscience*, *108*, 848–865.

Courchesne, E., Yeung-Courchesne, R., Press, G. A., Hesselink, J. R., & Jernigan, T. L. (1988). Hypoplasia of cerebellar vermal lobules VI & VII in autism. *New England Journal of Medicine*, *318*, 1349–1354.

Dahlgren, S. O., & Gillberg, C. (1989). Symptoms in the first two years of life: A preliminary population study of infantile autism. *European Archives of Psychiatry and Neurological Sciences*, *238*, 169–174.

Damasio, A. R. (1985). The frontal lobes. In K. M. Heilman & E. Valenstein (Eds.), *Clinical neuropsychology* (2nd ed., pp. 339–375). New York, NY: Oxford University Press.

Damasio, A. R., & Maurer, R. G. (1978). A neurological model for childhood autism. *Archives of Neurology*, *35*, 777–786.

Davies, M., Udwin, O., & Howlin, P. (1998). Adults with Williams syndrome: Preliminary study of social, emotional, and behavioural difficulties. *British Journal of Psychiatry*, *172*, 273–276.

DeLong, G. R. (1978). A neuropsychological interpretation of infantile autism. In M. Rutter & E. Schopler (Eds.), *Autism* (pp. 207–218). New York, NY: Plenum Press.

DeLong, G. R. (1992). Autism, amnesia, hippocampus, and learning. *Neuroscience and Biobehavioral Reviews*, *16*, 63–70.

Dunn, W., Myles, B. S., & Orr, S. (2002). Sensory processing issues associated with Asperger syndrome: A preliminary investigation. *American Journal of Occupational Therapy*, *56*(1), 97–102.

Ehlers, S., & Gillberg, C. (1993). The epidemiology of Asperger syndrome: A total population study. *Journal of Child Psychology and Psychiatry*, *34*, 1327–1350.

Ehlers, S., Nydén, A., Gillberg, C., Dahlgren-Sandberg, A., Dahlgren, S.-O., Hjelmquist, E., & Odén, A. (1997). Asperger syndrome, autism, and attention disorders: A comparative study of the cognitive profiles of 120 children. *Journal of Child Psychology and Psychiatry*, *38*, 207–217.

Fein, D., Dunn, M. A., Allen, D. M., Aram, R., Hall, N., Morris, R., & Wilson, B. C. (1996). Neuropsychological and language data. In I. Rapin (Ed.), *Preschool children with inadequate communication: Developmental language disorder, autism, low IQ* (pp. 123–154). London: Mac Keith Press.

Frazier, J. A., Beiderman, J., Bellordre, C. A., Garfield, S. B., Geller, D. A., Coffey, B. J., & Faraone, S. V. (2001). Should the diagnosis of attention deficit/hyperactivity disorder by considered in children with pervasive developmental disorder? *Journal of Attention Disorders*, *4*, 203–211.

Frith, U. (1989). *Autism: Explaining the enigma*. Oxford, UK: Blackwell.

Gabriels, R. L., Agnew, J. A., Miller, L. J., Gralla, J., Pan, Z., Goldson, E., ... Hooks, E. (2008). Is there a relationship between restricted, repetitive, stereotyped behaviours and interests and abnormal sensory response in children with autism spectrum disorders? *Research in Autism Spectrum Disorders*, *2*, 660–670.

Gardiner, J. M., Bowler, D. M., & Grice, S. J. (2003). Further evidence for preserved priming and impaired recall in adults with Asperger syndrome. *Journal of Autism and Developmental Disorders*, *33*, 259–269.

Garretson, H. B., Fein, D., & Waterhouse, L. (1990). Sustained attention in children with autism. *Journal of Autism and Developmental Disorders*, *20*, 101–114.

Geurts, H. M., Verté, S., Oosterlaan, J., Roeyers, H., & Sergeant, J. A. (2004). How specific are executive functioning deficits in attention deficit hyperactivity disorder and autism? *Journal of Child Psychology and Psychiatry*, *45*, 836–854.

Ghaziuddin, M., & Mountain-Kimchi, K. (2004). Defining the intellectual profile of Asperger syndrome: Comparison with high-functioning autism. *Journal of Autism and Developmental Disorders*, *34*, 279–284.

Ghaziuddin, M., Weidmer-Mikhail, E., & Ghaziuddin, N. (1998). Comorbidity of Asperger syndrome: A preliminary report. *Journal of Intellectual Disability Research*, *42*, 279–283.

Gilotty, L., Kenworthy, L., Sirian, L., Black, D. O., & Wagner, A. E. (2002). Adaptive skills and executive function in autism spectrum disorders. *Child Neuropsychology*, 8, 241–248.

Gioia, G. A., Isquith, P. K., Kenworthy, L., & Barton, R. M. (2002). Profiles of everyday executive function in acquired and developmental disorders. *Child Neuropsychology*, 8, 121–137.

Goddard, L., Howlin, P., Dritschel, B., & Patel, T. (2007). Autobiographical memory and social problem-solving in Asperger syndrome. *Journal of Autism and Developmental Disorders*, *37*, 291–300.

Goldberg, M. C., Mostofsky, S. H., Cutting, L. E., Mahone, E. M., Astor, B. C., Denkla, M., B., & Landa, R. J. (2005). Subtle executive functioning impairment in children with autism and children with ADHD. *Journal of Autism and Developmental Disorders*, *35*, 279–293.

Goldman-Rakic, P. S. (1987). Circuitry of primate prefrontal cortex and regulation of behavior by representational memory. In V. B. Mountcastle, F. Plum, & S. R. Geiger (Eds.), *Handbook of physiology: The nervous system* (pp. 373–417). Bethesda, MD: American Physiological Society.

Goldstein, G., Johnson, C. R., & Minshew, N. J. (2001). Attentional processes in autism. *Journal of Autism and Developmental Disorders*, *31*, 433–440.

Gottesman, I., & Gould, T. D. (2003). The endophenotype concept in psychiatry: Etymology and strategic intentions. *American Journal of Psychiatry*, *160*, 636–645.

Grandin, T. (1992). An inside view of autism. In E. Schopler & G. B. Mesibov (Eds.), *High functioning individuals with autism* (pp. 105–126). New York, NY: Plenum Press.

Grandin, T. (1995). How people with autism think. In E. Schopler & G. B. Mesibov (Eds.), *Learning and cognition in autism* (pp. 137–156). New York, NY: Plenum Press.

Griffith, E. M., Pennington, B. F., Wehner, E. A., & Rogers, S. J. (1999). Executive functions in young children with autism. *Child Development*, *70*, 817–832.

Griswold, D. E., Barnhill, G. P., Myles, B. S., Hagiwara, T., & Simpson, R. L. (2002). Asperger syndrome and academic achievement. *Focus on Autism and Other Developmental Disabilities*, *17*, 94–102.

Gunter, H. L., Ghaziuddin, M., & Ellis, H. D. (2002). Asperger syndrome: Tests of right hemisphere functioning and interhemispheric communication. *Journal of Autism and Developmental Disorders*, *32*, 263–281.

Hanson E., Cerban, B. M., Slater, C. M., Caccamo, L. M., Bacic, J., & Chan, E. (2013). Brief report: Prevalence of attention deficit/hyperactivity disorder among individuals with an autism spectrum disorder. *Journal of Autism and Developmental Disorders*, *43*, 1459–1464.

Happé, F. G. H., & Booth, R. D. L. (2008). The power of the positive. *Revisiting weak coherence in autism spectrum disorders. Quarterly Journal of Experimental Psychology*, *61*, 50–63.

Happé, F. G. E., Booth, R., Charlton, R., & Hughes, C. (2006). Executive function deficits in autism spectrum disorders and attention-deficit/hyperactivity disorder: Examining profiles across domains and ages. *Brain and Cognition*, *61*, 25–39.

Happé, F., & Frith, U. (2006). The weak coherence account: Detail-focused cognitive style in autism spectrum disorders. *Journal of Autism and Developmental Disorders*, *36*(1), 5–25.

Heaton, P., Williams, K., Cummins, O., & Happé, F. (2007). Beyond perception: Musical representation and on-line processing in autism. *Journal of Autism and Developmental Disorders*, *37*, 1355–1360.

Hill, E. L. (2004). Evaluating the theory of executive dysfunction in autism. *Developmental Review*, *24*, 189–233.

Hill, E. L., & Bird, C. M. (2006). Executive processes in Asperger syndrome: Patterns of performance in a multiple case series. *Neuropsychologia*, *44*, 2822–2835.

Hilton, C., Graver, K., & LaVesser, P. (2007). Relationship between social competence and sensory processing in children with high functioning autism spectrum disorders. *Research in Autism Spectrum Disorders*, *1*, 164–173.

Holtmann, M., Bölte, S., & Poustka, F. (2005). ADHD, Asperger syndrome, and high-functioning autism. *Journal of the American Academy of Child & Adolescent Psychiatry*, *44*, 1101.

Hughes, C. (2001). Executive dysfunction in autism: Its nature and implications for everyday problems experienced by individuals with autism. In J. Burack, T. Charman, N. Yirmiya, & P. Zelazo (Eds.), *The development of autism: Perspectives from theory and research* (pp. 255–275). Mahwah, NJ: Erlbaum.

Hughes, C., Russell, J., & Robbins, T. W. (1994). Evidence for executive dysfunction in autism. *Neuropsychologia*, *32*, 477–492.

Iwanaga, R., Kawasaki, C., & Tsuchida, R. (2000). Brief report: Comparison of sensory-motor and cognitive function between autism and Asperger syndrome in preschool children. *Journal of Autism and Developmental Disorders*, *30*, 169–174.

John, A. E., & Mervis, C. B. (2010). Sensory modulation impairments in children with Williams syndrome. *American Journal of Medical Genetics Part C*, *154C*, 266–276.

Johnson, K. A., Robertson, I. H., Kelly, S., Silk, T., Barry, E., Daibhis, A., … Bellgrove, M. A. (2007). Dissociation in performance of children with ADHD and high-functioning autism on a task of sustained attention. *Neuropsychologia*, *45*, 2234–2245.

Joseph, R. M., McGrath, L. M., & Tager-Flusberg, H. (2005). Executive dysfunction and its relation to language ability in verbal school-age children with autism. *Developmental Neuropsychology*, *27*, 361–378.

Joseph, R. M., & Tager-Flusberg, H. (2004). The relationship between theory of mind and executive functions to symptom type and severity in children with autism. *Development and Psychopathology*, *16*, 137–155.

Joseph, R. M., Tager-Flusberg, H., & Lord, C. (2002). Cognitive profiles and social-communicative functioning in children with autism spectrum disorders. *Journal of Child Psychology and Psychiatry*, *43*, 807–821.

Just, M. A., Cherkassky, V. L., Keller, T. A., & Minshew, N. J. (2004). Cortical activation and synchronization during sentence comprehension in high-functioning autism: Evidence of underconnectivity. *Brain*, *127*, 1811–1821.

Kanner, L. (1943). Autistic disturbances of affective contact. *Nervous Child*, *2*, 217–250.

Katagiri, M., Kasai, T., Kamio, Y., & Murohashi, H. (2013). Individuals with Asperger's disorder exhibit difficulty in switching attention from a local level to a global level. *Journal of Autism and Developmental Disorders*, *43*, 395–403.

Kemper, T. L., & Bauman, M. L. (1993). The contribution of neuropathologic studies of the understanding of autism. *Neurologic Clinics*, *11*, 175–186.

Kenworthy, L. E., Black, D. O., Wallace, G. L., Ahluvalia, T., Wagner, A. E., & Sirian, L. M. (2005). Disorganization: The forgotten executive dysfunction in high-functioning autism (HFA) spectrum disorders. *Developmental Neuropsychology*, *28*, 809–827.

Kientz, M. A., & Dunn, W. (1997). A comparison of the performance of children with and without autism on the Sensory Profile. *American Journal of Occupational Therapy*, *51*(7), 530–537.

Kleinhans, N., Akshoomoff, N., & Delis, D. C. (2005). Executive functions in autism and Asperger's Disorder: Flexibility, fluency, and inhibition. *Developmental Neuropsychology*, *27*, 379–401.

Klin, A. (2000). Attributing social meaning to ambiguous visual stimuli in higher functioning autism and Asperger syndrome: The Social Attribution Task. *Journal of Child Psychology, Psychiatry and Allied Disciplines*, *33*, 763–769.

Klin, A., Jones, W., Schultz, R. T., & Volkmar, F. R. (2003). The enactive mind: From actions to cognition: Lessons from autism. *Philosophical Transactions of the Royal Society, Biological Sciences*, *358*, 345–360.

Klin, A., & Volkmar, F. R. (1997). Asperger's syndrome. In D. J. Cohen & F. R. Volkmar (Eds.), *Handbook of autism and pervasive developmental disorders* (2nd ed., pp. 94–122). New York, NY: Wiley.

Klin, A., & Volkmar, F. R. (2003). Asperger syndrome: Diagnosis and external validity. *Child and Adolescent Psychiatric Clinics of North America*, *12*, 1–13.

Klin, A., Volkmar, F. R., Sparrow, S. S., Cicchetti, D. V., & Rourke, B. P. (1995). Validity and neuropsychological characterization of Asperger syndrome. *Journal of Child Psychology, Psychiatry, and Allied Disciplines*, *36*, 1127–1140.

Klinger, L. G., & Dawson, G. (2001). Prototype formation in autism. *Development and Psychopathology*, *13*(1), 111–124.

Koshino, H., Carpenter, P. A., Minshew, N. J., Cherkassky, V. L., Keller, T. A., & Just, M. A. (2005). Functional connectivity in an fMRI working memory task in high-functioning autism. *Neuroimage*, *24*, 810–821.

Kuschner, E., Bennetto, L., & Yost, K. (2007). Patterns of nonverbal cognitive functioning in young children with autism spectrum disorders. *Journal of Autism and Developmental Disorders*, *37*, 795–807.

Laurent, A. C., & Rubin, E. (2004). Emotional regulation challenges in Asperger syndrome and high functioning autism. *Topics in Language Disorders*, *24*(4), 286–297.

Leekam, S. R., Nieto, C., Libby, S. J., Wing, L., & Gould, J. (2007). Describing the sensory abnormalities of children and adults with autism. *Journal of Autism and Developmental Disorders*, *37*, 894–910.

Leekam, S. R., Prior, M. R., & Uljarevic, M. (2011). Restrictive and repetitive behaviours in autism spectrum disorders: A review of research in the last decade. *Psychological Bulletin*, *137*(4), 562–593.

Lepistö, T., Kuitunen, A., Sussman, E., Saalasti, S., Jansson-Verkasalo, E., Nieminen-von Wendt, T., & Kujala, T. (2009). Auditory stream segregation in children with Asperger syndrome. *Biological Psychology*, *82*, 301–307.

Lepistö, T., Silokallio, S., Nieminen-von Wendt, T., Alku, P., Naatanen, R., & Kujala, T. (2006). Auditory perception and attention as reflected by the brain event-related potential in children with Asperger syndrome. *Clinical Neurophysiology*, *117*, 2161–2171.

Leyfer, O. T., Folstein, S. E., Bacalman, S., Davis, N. O., Dinh, E., Morgan, J., . . . Lainhart, J. E. (2006). Comorbid psychiatric disorders in children with autism: Interview development and rates of disorders. *Journal of Autism and Developmental Disorders*, *36*, 849–861.

Lincoln, A. J., Allen, M. H., & Kilman, A. (1995). The assessment and interpretation of intellectual abilities in people with autism. In E. Schopler & G. B. Mesibov (Eds.), *Learning and cognition in autism* (pp. 89–117). New York, NY: Plenum Press.

Lincoln, A., Courchesne, E., Allen, M., Hanson, E., & Ene, M. (1998). Neurobiology of Asperger syndrome: Seven case studies and quantitative magnetic resonance imaging findings. In E. Schopler & G. B. Mesibov (Eds.), *Asperger syndrome or high-functioning autism? Current issues in autism* (pp. 145–163). New York, NY: Plenum Press.

Liss, M., Saulnier, C., Fein, D., & Kinsbourne, M. (2006). Sensory and attention abnormalities in autistic spectrum disorders. *Autism*, *10*, 155–172.

Lopez, B. R., Lincoln, A. J., Ozonoff, S., & Lai, Z. (2005). Examining the relationship between executive functions and restricted, repetitive symptoms of autistic disorder. *Journal of Autism and Developmental Disorders*, *35*, 445–460.

Manjiviona, J., & Prior, M. (1999). Neuropsychological profiles of children with Asperger syndrome and autism. *Autism*, *3*, 327–356.

Mann, T. A., & Walker, P. (2003). Autism and a deficit in broadening the spread of visual attention. *Journal of Child Psychology and Psychiatry and Allied Disciplines*, *44*, 274–284.

Marco, E. J., Hinkley, L. B., Hill, S. S., & Nagarajan, S. S. (2011). Sensory processing in autism: a review of neurophysiologic findings. *Pediatric Research*, *69*(5, Pt 2), 48R–54R.

May T., Rinehart N., Wilding J., & Cornish K. (2013). The role of attention in the academic attainment of children with autism spectrum disorder. *Journal of Autism and Developmental Disorders*, *43*, 2147–2158.

Mayes, S. D., & Calhoun, S. L. (2003). Analysis of WISC-III, Stanford-Binet, IV, & academic achievement test scores in children with autism. *Journal of Autism and Developmental Disorders*, *33*, 329–341.

McCrory, E., Henry, L. A., & Happé, F. (2007). Eye-witness memory and suggestibility in children with Asperger syndrome. *Journal of Child Psychology and Psychiatry*, *48*, 482–489.

McGrath, L., Joseph, R., Tadevosyan, O., Folstein, S., Tager-Flusberg, H. (2002, November). Overlapping ADHD symptoms in autism: Relationship to executive functioning. Poster presentation at the International Meeting for Autism Research, Orlando, FL.

McIntosh, D. N., Miller, L. J., & Shyu, V. (1999). Development and validation of the Short Sensory Profile. In W. Dunn (Ed.), *Sensory Profile Manual* (pp. 59–63). San Antonio, TX: Psychological Corporation.

Miller, J. N., & Ozonoff, S. (2000). The external validity of Asperger disorder: Lack of evidence from the domain of neuropsychology. *Journal of Abnormal Psychology, 109,* 227–238.

Minshew, N. J., & Goldstein, G. (1993). Is autism an amnesic disorder? Evidence from the California Verbal Learning Test. *Neuropsychology, 7,* 209–216.

Minshew, N. J., & Goldstein, G. (2001). The pattern of intact and impaired memory functions in autism. *Journal of Child Psychology and Psychiatry and Allied Disciplines, 42,* 1095–1101.

Minshew, N. J., Goldstein, G., Muenz, L. R., & Payton, J. B. (1992). Neuropsychological functioning in nonmentally retarded autistic individuals. *Journal of Clinical and Experimental Neuropsychology, 14,* 749–761.

Minshew, N. J., Goldstein, G., & Siegel, D. J. (1997). Neuropsychologic functioning in autism: Profile of a complex information processing disorder. *Journal of the International Neuropsychological Society, 3,* 303–316.

Minshew, N. J., Meyer, J., & Goldstein, G. (2002). Abstract reasoning in autism: A dissociation between concept formation and concept identification. *Neuropsychology, 16,* 327–334.

Morris, R. G., Rowe, A., Fox, N., Feigenbaum, J. D., Miotto, E. C., & Howlin, P. (1999). Spatial working memory in Asperger's syndrome and in patients with focal frontal and temporal lobe lesions. *Brain and Cognition, 41,* 9–26.

Mottron, L., & Belleville, S. (1993). A study of perceptual analysis in a high-level autistic subject with exceptional graphic abilities. *Brain and Cognition, 23,* 279–309.

Murakami, J. W., Courchesne, E., Press, G. A., Yeung-Courchesne, R., & Hesselink, J. R. (1989). Reduced cerebellar hemisphere size and its relationship to vermal hypoplasia in autism. *Archives of Neurology, 46,* 689–694.

Nydén, A., Gillberg, C., Hjelmquist, E., & Heiman, M. (1999). Executive function/attention deficits in boys with Asperger syndrome, Attention Disorder, and Reading/Writing Disorder. *Autism, 3,* 213–228.

Ornitz, E. M. (1974). The modulation of sensory input and motor output in autistic children. *Journal of Autism and Childhood Schizophrenia, 4,* 197–215.

Ornitz, E. M. (1983). The functional neuroanatomy of infantile autism. *International Journal of Neuroscience, 19,* 85–124.

Ornitz, E. M. (1988). Autism: A disorder of directed attention. *Brain Dysfunction, 1,* 309–322.

Ornitz, E. M., & Ritvo, E. R. (1968a). Neurophysiological mechanisms underlying perceptual inconstancy in autistic and schizophrenic children. *Archives of General Psychiatry, 19,* 22–27.

Ornitz, E. M., & Ritvo, E. R. (1968b). Perceptual inconstancy in early infantile autism: The syndrome of early infant autism and its variants including certain cases of childhood schizophrenia. *Archives of General Psychiatry, 18,* 76–98.

Ornitz, E. M., & Ritvo, E. R. (1976). The syndrome of autism: A critical review. *American Journal of Psychiatry, 133,* 609–622.

O'Shea, A. G., Fein, D. A., Cillessen, A. H. N., Klin, A., & Schultz, R. T. (2005). Source memory in children with autism spectrum disorders. *Developmental Neuropsychology, 27,* 337–360.

Osterling, J., & Dawson, G. (1994). Early recognition of children with autism: A study of first- birthday home videotapes. *Journal of Autism and Developmental Disorders, 24,* 247–257.

Ozonoff, S. (1995). Executive functions in autism. In E. Schopler & G. B. Mesibov (Eds.), *Learning and cognition in autism* (pp. 199–219). New York: Plenum Press.

Ozonoff, S., Cook, I., Coon, H., Dawson, G., Joseph, R. M., Klin, A., . . . Wrathall, D. (2004). Performance on Cambridge Neuropsychological Test Automated Battery subtests sensitive to frontal lobe function in people with autistic disorder: Evidence from the Collaborative Programs of Excellence in Autism Network. *Journal of Autism and Developmental Disorders, 34,* 139–150.

Ozonoff, S., & Jensen, J. (1999). Brief report: Specific executive function profiles in three neurodevelopmental disorders. *Journal of Autism and Developmental Disorders, 29,* 171–177.

Ozonoff, S., & McEvoy, R. E. (1994). A longitudinal study of executive function and theory of mind development in autism. *Development and Psychopathology, 6,* 415–431.

Ozonoff, S., Pennington, B. F., & Rogers, S. J. (1991). Executive function deficits in high- functioning autistic individuals: Relationship to theory of mind. *Journal of Child Psychology and Psychiatry, 32,* 1081–1105.

Ozonoff, S., Rogers, S., & Pennington, B. (1991). Asperger's syndrome: Evidence of an empirical distinction. *Journal of Child Psychology and Psychiatry, 32,* 1107–1122.

Ozonoff, S., South, M., & Miller, J. N. (2000). *DSM-IV*-defined Asperger syndrome: Cognitive, behavioral and early history differentiation from high-functioning autism. *Autism, 4,* 29–46.

Ozonoff, S., & Strayer, D. L. (1997). Inhibitory function in nonretarded children with autism. *Journal of Autism and Developmental Disorders, 27,* 59–77.

Ozonoff, S., & Strayer, D. L. (2001). Further evidence of intact working memory in autism. *Journal of Autism and Developmental Disorders, 31,* 257–263.

Ozonoff, S., Strayer, D. L., McMahon, W. M., & Filloux, F. (1994). Executive function abilities in autism and Tourette syndrome: An information processing approach. *Journal of Child Psychology and Psychiatry, 35,* 1015–1032.

Pascualvaca, D. M., Fantie, B. D., Papageorgiou, M., & Mirsky, A. F. (1998). Attentional capacities in children with autism: Is there a general deficit in shifting focus? *Journal of Autism and Developmental Disorders, 28,* 467–478.

Pellicano, E. (2010). The development of core cognitive skills in autism: A 3-year prospective study. *Child Development, 81,* 1400–1416.

Powell, S. D., & Jordan, R. R. (1993). Being subjective about autistic thinking and learning to learn. *Educational Psychology, 13,* 359–370.

Prior, M. R., & Hoffmann, W. (1990). Brief report: Neuropsychological testing of autistic children through an exploration with frontal lobe tests. *Journal of Autism and Developmental Disorders, 20,* 581–590.

Renner, P., Klinger, L. G., & Klinger, M. R. (2000). Implicit and explicit memory in autism: Is autism an amnesic disorder? *Journal of Autism and Developmental Disorders, 30,* 3–14.

Riby, D. M., Janes, E., & Rodgers, J. (2013). Brief report: Exploring the relationship between sensory processing and repetitive behaviours in Williams syndrome. *Journal of Autism and Developmental Disorders, 43,* 478–482.

Rimland, B. (1964). *Infantile autism.* New York, NY: Appleton–Century–Crofts.

Rinehart, N., Bradshaw, J. L., Moss, S. A., Brereton, A. V., & Tonge, B. J. (2000). Atypical interference of local detail on global processing in high-functioning autism and Asperger's disorder. *Journal of Child Psychology and Psychiatry, 41,* 769–778.

Rinehart, N., Bradshaw, J. L., Moss, S. A., Brereton, A. V., & Tonge, B. J. (2001). A deficit in shifting attention present in high-functioning autism but not Asperger's disorder. *Autism, 5,* 67–80.

Rinehart, N., Bradshaw, J. L., Tonge, B. J., Brereton, A. V., & Bellgrove, M. A. (2002). A neurobehavioral examination of individuals with high-functioning autism and Asperger's disorder using a fronto-striatal model of dysfunction. *Behavioral and Cognitive Neuroscience Reviews, 1,* 164–177.

Robinson, S., Goddard, L., Dritschel, B., Wisley, M., & Howlin, P. (2009). Executive functions in children with Autism spectrum disorders. *Brain and Cognition, 71,* 362–368.

Rogers, S., Hepburn, S., & Wehner, E. (2003). Parent reports of sensory symptoms in toddlers with autism and those with other developmental disorders. *Journal of Autism and Developmental Disorders, 33*(6), 631–642.

Rondan, C., & Deruelle, C. (2007). Global and configural visual processing in adults with autism and Asperger syndrome. *Research in Developmental Disabilities, 28,* 197–206.

Rourke, B. P. (1989). *Nonverbal learning disabilities: The syndrome and the model.* New York, NY: Guilford Press.

Rourke, B. P., van der Vlugt, H., & Rourke, S. B. (2002). *Practice of child-clinical neuropsychology: An introduction.* Lisse, The Netherlands: Swets & Zeitlinger.

Rumsey, J. M. (1992). Neuropsychological studies of high-level autism. In E. Schopler & G. B. Mesibov (Eds.), High-functioning individuals with autism (pp. 41–64). New York: Plenum Press.

Rumsey, J. M., & Hamburger, S. D. (1988). Neuropsychological findings in high-functioning men with infantile autism residual state. *Journal of Clinical and Experimental Neuropsychology, 10,* 201–221.

Rumsey, J. M., & Hamburger, S. D. (1990). Neuropsychological divergence of high-level autism and severe dyslexia. *Journal of Autism and Developmental Disorders, 20,* 155–168.

Russell, J. (1997). How executive disorders can bring about an inadequate "theory of mind." In J. Russell (Ed.), *Autism as an executive disorder* (pp. 256–304). Oxford, England: Oxford University Press.

Russell, J., Jarrold, C., & Henry, L. (1996). Working memory in children with autism and with moderate learning difficulties. *Journal of Child Psychology, Psychiatry, and Allied Disciplines, 37,* 673–686.

Rutter, M. (1978). Diagnosis and definitions of childhood autism. *Journal of Autism and Childhood Schizophrenia, 8,* 139–161.

Ryburn, B., Anderson, V., & Wales, R. (2009). Asperger syndrome: How does it relate to non-verbal learning disability? *Journal of Neuropsychology, 3,* 107–123.

Saalasti, S., Lepistö, T., Toppila, E., Kujala, T., Laakso, M., Nieminen-von Wendt, T., von Wendt, L., & Jansson-Verkasalo, E. (2008). Language abilities of children with Asperger syndrome. *Journal of Autism and Developmental Disorders, 38,* 1574–1580.

Schatz, A. M., Weimer, A. K., & Trauner, D. A. (2002). Brief report: Attention differences in Asperger syndrome. *Journal of Autism and Developmental Disorders, 32,* 333–336.

Schultz, R. T., Romanski, L. M., & Tsatsanis, K. D. (2000). Neurofunctional models of Autistic Disorder and Asperger syndrome: Clues from neuroimaging. In A. Klin, F. R. Volkmar, & S. S. Sparrow (Eds.), *Asperger syndrome* (pp. 172–209). New York, NY: Guilford Press.

Semrud-Clikeman, M. (2007). *Social competence in children.* New York, NY: Springer.

Siegel, D. J., Minshew, N. J., & Goldstein, G. (1996). Wechsler IQ profiles in diagnosis of high-functioning autism. *Journal of Autism and Developmental Disorders, 26*(4), 389–406.

Smith, B. J., Gardiner, J. M., & Bowler, D. M. (2007). Deficits in free recall persist in Asperger's syndrome despite training in the use of list-appropriate learning strategies. *Journal of Autism and Developmental Disorders, 37,* 445–454.

South, M., Ozonoff, S., & McMahon, W. M. (2007). The relationship between executive functioning, central coherence, and repetitive behaviors in the high-functioning autism spectrum. *Autism, 11,* 437–451.

Steele, S. D., Minshew, N. J., Luna, B., & Sweeney, J. A. (2007). Spatial working memory deficits in autism. *Journal of Autism and Developmental Disorders, 37,* 605–612.

Stein, B. E., & Meredith, M. A. (1990). Multisensory integration: Neural and behavioral solutions for dealing with stimuli from different sensory modalities. *Annals of the New York Academy of Sciences, 608,* 51–65.

Stone, W. L. (1997). Autism in infancy and early childhood. In D. J. Cohen & F. R. Volkmar (Eds.), *Handbook of autism and pervasive developmental disorders* (2nd ed., pp. 266–282). New York, NY: Wiley.

Sturm, H., Fernell, E., & Gillberg, C. (2004). Autism spectrum disorders in children with normal intellectual levels: Associated impairments and subgroups. *Developmental Medicine and Child Neurology, 46,* 444–447.

Szatmari, P., Tuff, L., Finlayson, M. A. J., & Bartolucci, G. (1990). Asperger's syndrome and autism: Neurocognitive aspects. *Journal of the American Academy of Child & Adolescent Psychiatry, 29,* 130–136.

Tager-Flusberg, H. (1991). Semantic processing in the free recall of autistic children: Further evidence for a cognitive deficit. *British Journal of Developmental Psychology, 9,* 417–430.

Tager-Flusberg, H., & Joseph, R. M. (2003). Identifying neurocognitive phenotypes in autism. *Philosophical Transactions of the Royal Society B: Biological Sciences, 358,* 303–314.

Talsma, D., Senkowski, D., Soto-Faraco, S., & Woldorff, M. G. (2010). The multifaceted interplay between attention and multisensory integration. *Trends in Cognitive Sciences, 14,* 400–410.

Tani, P., Lindberg, N., Appelberg, B., Nieminen-von Wendt, T., von Wendt, L., & Porkka-Heiskanen, T. (2006). Childhood inattention and hyperactivity symptoms self-reported by adults with Asperger syndrome. *Psychopathology, 39,* 49–54.

Thede, L. L., & Coolidge, F. L. (2007). Psychological and neurobehavioral comparisons of children with Asperger's Disorder versus high-functioning autism. *Journal of Autism and Developmental Disorders, 37,* 847–854.

Toichi, M. (2008). Episodic memory, semantic memory, and self- awareness in high-functioning autism. In J. Boucher & D. Bowler (Eds.), *Memory in autism: Theory and evidence* (pp. 143–165). Cambridge, England: Cambridge University Press.

Tomchek, S., & Dunn, W. (2007). Sensory processing in children with and without autism: A comparative study using the Short Sensory Profile. *American Journal of Occupational Therapy, 61,* 190–200.

Towgood, K. J., Meuwese, J. D. I., Gilbert, S. J., Turner, M. S., & Burgess, P. W. (2009). Advantages of the multiple case series approach to the study of cognitive deficits in autism spectrum disorder. *Neuropsychologia, 47,* 2981–2988.

Townsend, J., Harris, N. S., & Courchesne, E. (1996). Visual attention abnormalities in autism: Delayed orienting to location. *Journal of the International Neuropsychological Society, 2,* 541–550.

Tsai, L. Y. (1992). Diagnostic issues in high-functioning autism. In E. Schopler & G. B. Mesibov (Eds.), *High-functioning individuals with autism* (pp. 11–40). New York, NY: Plenum Press.

Tsatsanis, K. D., Dartnall, N., Cicchetti, D., Sparrow, S., Klin, A., & Volkmar, F. R. (2003). A comparison of performance on the Leiter and Leiter-R in low-functioning children with autism. *Journal of Autism and Developmental Disorders, 33*(1), 23–30.

Tsatsanis, K. D., Noens, I. L. J., Illmann, C. L., Pauls, D. L., Volkmar, F. R., Schultz, R. T., & Klin, A. (2011). Managing complexity: Impact of organization and processing style on nonverbal memory in autism spectrum disorders. *Journal of Autism and Developmental Disorders, 41,* 135–147.

Tulving, E. (1972). Episodic and semantic memory. In E. Tulving & W. Donaldson (Eds.), *Organization of memory* (pp. 381–403). New York, NY: Academic Press.

Ventola, P., Tirrell, J., Levine, M., Akbar, M., & Tsatsanis, K. (under review). Executive functioning profiles and their relation to social and adaptive skills in children with autism spectrum disorders. *Journal of Autism and Developmental Disorders.*

Verté, S., Geurts, H. M., Roeyers, H., Oosterlaan, J., & Sergeant, J. A. (2006). Executive functioning in children with an autism spectrum disorder: Can we differentiate within the spectrum. *Journal of Autism and Developmental Disorders, 36,* 351–372.

Volkmar, F. R., Lord, C., Bailey, A., Schultz, R. T., & Klin, A. (2004). Autism and pervasive developmental disorders. *Journal of Child Psychology and Psychiatry, 45,* 135–170.

Wainwright-Sharp, J. A., & Bryson, S. E. (1996). Visual-spatial orienting in autism. *Journal of Autism and Developmental Disorders, 26,* 423–438.

Wallace, G. L., Silvers, J. A., Martin, A., & Kenworthy, L. E. (2009). Brief Report: Further Evidence for inner speech deficits in autism spectrum disorders. *Journal of Autism and Developmental Disorders, 39,* 1735–1739.

Watling, R. L., Deitz, J., & White, O. (2001). Comparison of Sensory Profile score of young children with and without autism spectrum disorders. *American Journal of Occupational Therapy, 55*(4), 416–423.

Wheeler, M. A., Stuss, D. T., & Tulving, E. (1997). Toward a theory of episodic memory: The frontal lobes and autonoetic consciousness. *Psychological Bulletin, 121,* 331–354.

Williams, D. L., Goldstein, G., Carpenter, P. A., & Minshew, N. (2005a). Verbal and spatial working memory in autism. *Journal of Autism and Developmental Disorders, 35,* 747–756.

Williams, D. L., Goldstein, G., Kojkowski, N., & Minshew, N. (2007). Do individuals with high-functioning autism have the IQ profile associated with nonverbal learning disability? *Research in Autism Spectrum Disorders, 1,* 1–9.

Williams, D. L., Goldstein G., & Minshew, N. J. (2005b). Impaired memory for faces and social scenes in autism: Clinical implications of the memory disorder. *Archives of Clinical Neuropsychology, 20,* 1–15.

Williams, D. L., Goldstein, G., & Minshew, N. J. (2006a). Neuropsychologic functioning in children with autism: Further evidence disordered complex information processing. *Child Neuropsychology, 12,* 279–298.

Williams, D. L., Goldstein, G., & Minshew, N. J. (2006b). The profile of memory function in children with autism. *Neuropsychology, 20,* 21–29.

CHAPTER 14

Autism and Emotion

R. PETER HOBSON

The characteristic of autism that most impressed Kanner (1943) about his 11 cases of children with "autistic disturbances of affective contact," was their "inability to relate themselves in the ordinary way to people and situations from the beginning of life" (p. 242). In the course of his case histories, Kanner recorded a variety of clinical features that reflected the children's seeming unawareness of the people around them and their imperviousness to the human significance of the surrounding world. He concluded that "further study of our children may help to furnish concrete criteria regarding the still diffuse notions about the constitutional components of emotional reactivity" (p. 250).

It has taken several decades to disentangle Kanner's original take on autism from another and quite separate thesis about the disorder—that it might be caused by cold or otherwise pathological mothering. For a long time it seemed that only by positing a primary linguistic or cognitive disorder could one reject the suggestion that this is a psychogenic disturbance, or avoid the implication that the children's characteristic and severely restricting limitations in creative and context-sensitive

thinking are somehow incidental or of secondary importance. Now freed from this constraint, we can acknowledge that social-affective engagement may be disrupted by constitutional abnormalities that have potentially far-reaching developmental repercussions.

This is a change that brings fresh grounds for unease, however. Is there really going to be a *test* of whether perceptual, cognitive, motivational or affective deficits are primary in the pathogenesis of the syndrome? Is any one of these theoretical options likely to lead to a satisfactory explanation of autism? Or are we framing our questions in the wrong way?

CONCEPTUAL ISSUES

Kanner (1943) did not restrict himself to commenting on the children's limited affective engagement with people, pivotal though this seemed. He also referred to their ways of relating to things, for example by showing repetitive and often highly restricted interests. One aspect of this disorder that has attracted much attention in the subsequent literature is the way in which children with autism have a paucity of symbolic play; another is their relative inflexibility in adjusting language to the context in which it is used, and especially, according to meanings that depend on the psychological orientations of speakers and listeners. Such impairments are *not* considered to be emotional, for obvious reasons. If children with autism are unable to engage in creative symbolic play, even when they seem to be trying their best to use play materials, one hardly wants to say that they are prevented by emotional or motivational factors; if they are simply at a loss when trying to communicate, it would be wrong (not to say perverse) to attribute this to their feelings about the situation.

And yet these apparently clear examples may lead us to become overconfident about the conceptual boundaries that separate cognitive, conative, and affective domains of psychological functioning. Not only is there the deep philosophical issue about what (if not something like feelings or experiences) connects humans and our thoughts with what those thoughts are about—the representations of a computer are *not* like thoughts, because they do not have this natural aboutness and have to be interpreted by humans—but also there is the developmental issue of what thoughts, feelings, and motivations develop *out of*. It is at least plausible that certain qualities of our thinking, for example, some of the ways we discriminate this from that, or generalize from one object or situation or event to another, are dependent on the ways that things affect us or lend themselves to actions that have meaning because of accompanying feelings. In this sense, at least, there are emotional bases for thinking. Or again, there are forms of feeling perception: to see a smile as a smile *is* to have a propensity to react with feelings, and it may be only because we have the capacity to perceive and relate to others' expressions in this way that we come to understand smiles as expressive of inner states, and ultimately come to comprehend the nature of people with minds (R. P. Hobson, 1993a, 1993b). More radically still, if one person can only share experiences with someone else because of affective

coordination between the two, and if sharing of this kind is required for a range of transactions that occur *between* people—for example, an adult pointing out things to a child, or negotiating those forms of symbolic meaning embodied in language and creative play—then the cognitive implications of supposedly emotion-specific impairments are wide-ranging indeed (R. P. Hobson, 2002).

Therefore once one adopts a developmental perspective, one can no longer assume that psychological categories which seem to function fairly well when applied to adults are also applicable to earlier phases of development. What have become paradigmatic cases of *thinking* or *willing* or *perceiving* in adults, and seemingly separable from feelings, may have originated in infantile states that implicated each of these functions as inseparable *aspects* of the infant's relations with the world (R. P. Hobson, 2008). If so, the challenge may become one of distinguishing among different modes of infant relatedness. In this case, we shall need to respect how *intersubjective* modes of relatedness that occur between infants and other people, sometimes in relation to a shared world, are not only heavily imbued with affect and motivational force (especially, through the pull of other people's attitudes), but also transformational for the growing child's ability to achieve a kind of mental space required for symbolic thinking.

Given that there are a number of things we want to know about the role of emotion in the pathogenesis and expression of autism, it is not surprising that methods have evolved to investigate the domain from various standpoints. Each method has its own strengths and limitations, and each its own standards for methodological adequacy. There are important insights to be gained from individual case descriptions, from clinical accounts of groups of children, from systematic observational studies, from interviews with informants such as parents, from quasi-experimental investigations, from more strictly controlled experiments on specific aspects of the disorder, and from family and related studies elucidating the role of genetic and environmental factors in pathogenesis. As we shall see, there is also value in studying atypical forms of autism; and neurofunctional studies are bringing new insights. Some of these studies yield results that increase our knowledge of what is or is not characteristic of autism; some are more concerned with the degree to which given deficits are specific to the emotional domain; others again point to alternative pathways of abnormal development. In what follows, I shall present a less than comprehensive sample of studies from the voluminous literature.

Case descriptions comprise the most difficult part of that literature to summarize. As my one example, the following excerpt from Kanner (1943) illustrates just how much we stand to gain by paying close attention to clinical detail. It concerns 6-year-old Frederick attending Kanner's clinic for the first time:

> He was led into the psychiatrist's office by a nurse, who left the room immediately afterward. His facial expression was tense, somewhat apprehensive, and gave the impression of intelligence. He wandered aimlessly about for a few moments, showing no sign of awareness of the three adults present. He then sat down on the couch, ejaculating unintelligible sounds, and then abruptly lay down, wearing throughout a dreamy-like smile.... Objects absorbed him easily and he showed good attention and perseverance in playing with them. He seemed to regard people as unwelcome intruders to whom he paid as little attention as they would permit. When forced to respond, he did so briefly and returned to his absorption in things. When a hand was held out before him so that he could not possibly ignore it, he played with it briefly as if it were a detached object. (p. 224)

I shall leave this vivid portrayal to linger in the mind, as we turn to systematic controlled studies of socio-emotional impairments in children and adolescents with autism.

SYSTEMATIC STUDIES OF THE EARLY YEARS

Parental Reports

Parental reports afford an important perspective on the early clinical features of autism. Among a range of studies (e.g., Dahlgren & Gillberg, 1989; Lord, Storoschuk, Rutter, & Pickles, 1993; Stone & Lemanek, 1990; Vostanis et al., 1998; Wing, 1969), one by Wimpory and colleagues (Wimpory, Hobson, Williams, & Nash, 2000) offers an especially clear view of emotional aspects of what has been reported.

Wimpory et al. (2000) interviewed parents of very young children who were referred to a child development center with difficulties in relating to and communicating with others. At the time of interview, the undiagnosed children were between 32 and 48 months old, and it was only subsequently that 10 children diagnosed with autism were compared with 10 children, matched for age and developmental level, who did not have autism. This meant that when parents were asked about the children's behavior in the first 2 years of life, they were recalling events from only 6 to 24 months previously, and their memories were not distorted by knowledge of autism.

The parents' reports indicated that as infants, not one of those with autism had shown frequent and intense eye contact, engaged in turn taking with adults, or used noises communicatively, whereas half of the control children were reported to show each of these kinds of behavior. There were also fewer infants with autism who greeted or waved to their parents, who raised their arms to be picked up, who directed feelings of anger and distress towards people, who were sociable in play, or who enjoyed and participated in lap games. In each of these respects, there were clear limitations in their affective engagement with others.

These interviews also revealed group differences in the infants' ways of relating to other people with reference to objects and events in the environment. For example, not one of the infants with autism but at least half the infants in the control group were reported to offer, give, or point to objects to others in the first 2 years of life. Here we seem to be moving beyond what is paradigmatically emotional—yet it is very plausible that emotional engagement with other people's bodily expressed attitudes is what drives offering, giving, and so on. One could say that the children's lack of interpersonal engagement extends to circumstances in which they might share experiences of the world with other people. They not only appear to be less connected with other people for their own sake, but also less connected with or able to share others' affective attitudes to a shared world (Kasari, Sigman, Mundy, & Yirmiya, 1990).

Observational and Experimental Studies

Some studies have employed diagnostic instruments alongside direct observations of young children with autism. For example, Lord (1995; see also Stone, Hoffman, Lewis, & Ousley, 1994) assessed thirty 2-year-old children referred for possible autism using a modified version of the Autism Diagnostic Interview along with a rating scale for direct observations, and reassessed them 1 year later in order to ascertain which children received a diagnosis of autism at this later stage. On reexamining the data from the earlier assessment, she concluded that the 2-year-olds with autism differed from the other children with developmental disorders in specific aspects of (a) communicative behavior: their lack of response to another person's voice, absence of pointing, and failure to understand gesture; (b) social reciprocity: lack of seeking to share their enjoyment, failure to greet, unusual use of others' bodies, lack of initiative in directing visual attention, and lack of interest in children; and (c) restricted, repetitive behavior: hand and finger mannerisms and unusual sensory behavior.

What about the very earliest months of life? Studies of infant siblings of children with autism have revealed that by 12 months of age, many but not all of those who go on to develop autism show clinical features that include atypicalities in eye contact and social interest and affect (e.g., Bryson et al., 2007; Zwaigenbaum et al., 2005). On the other hand, up to the present the evidence for social-affective abnormalities over the 1st year of life is patchy, and even in the ensuing period, there are individual differences as the clinical picture unfolds. As Rogers (2009, p. 133) concludes from her review of this body of research, "Lack of differentiating symptoms at 6 months suggests

a discontinuity to social development, with early sociability supported by different underlying mechanisms than toddler sociability.... Certainly the number of studies and number of measures used thus far is small, and the use of other risk markers may reveal clearer differences." The jury is out, on at least two counts: firstly, whether or not the majority of infants who develop autism have limitations in socioemotional functioning over the earliest period of infancy (and here I would be looking for the infants' capacity to *initiate* and spontaneously *sustain* emotional engagement, and to be emotionally moved by others); and secondly, whether the emotional deficits that become prominent thereafter are of pivotal importance for shaping other features of the syndrome.

Returning to children in the years just beyond infancy, the following controlled studies begin to tease out some of the characteristics of their emotional relations.

Interpersonal Coordination of Affect

Kasari et al. (1990) employed videotapes of semistructured child–experimenter interactions to assess how matched autistic and nonautistic developmentally delayed 3- to 6-year-olds, and mental age-matched typically developing children with a mean age of 2 years, expressed affect toward the experimenter in the contexts of joint attention and requesting. Participants' facial expressions were coded second by second for a total of 8 minutes, using a standardized coding instrument (the Maximally Discriminative Movement Coding System designed by Izard, 1979). Although the children with autism showed uniformly low levels of positive affect toward the adult, they diverged most markedly in their decreased level of positive feeling during situations of joint attention. These were the situations in which the typically developing children smiled most of all, sharing their feelings with the other person.

This evidence of autism-specific abnormality in face-to-face affective coordination is supported by three further studies. In the first, Snow, Hertzig, and Shapiro (1987) videotaped 10 autistic children aged between 2.5 and 4 years, and 10 age- and nonverbal mental age-matched developmentally delayed children, as they interacted with their mother, a child psychiatrist, and a nursery school teacher who were told to behave just as they normally would in a comfortable room stocked with toys. Twenty 15-second intervals of child interaction with each partner were coded using a checklist of emotionally expressive actions such as smiles and laughter. Whereas almost all the positive affect of the children without autism was expressed toward the other person, the less frequent displays of affect by children with autism were as likely to occur at seemingly random, self-absorbed moments, as in the context of social interaction. In a similar vein, from videotaped interactions as well as parental reports of preschool children with autism compared with matched children with Down syndrome, Reddy, Williams, and Vaughan (2002) found evidence that despite similarity in overall frequencies of laughter, the children with autism rarely smiled at or attempted to join in others' laughter, or to re-elicit laughter through acts of clowning. Instead, preschoolers with autism showed higher frequencies of *unshared* laughter.

In the third study, by Dawson, Hill, Spencer, Galpert, and Watson (1990), 16 autistic children aged 2 to 6 years and 16 typically developing children matched for receptive language were videotaped interacting with their mothers in three different contexts: free play, a more structured situation in which the mother asked the child to help her to put away some toys, and a face-to-face situation over snack time. (It is important to note that this kind of comparison with typically developing children leaves some uncertainty whether differences in the autistic children's behavior might reflect mental retardation rather than autism per se.) The findings were interesting not only for the group differences that emerged, but also for the fact that there were no significant group differences in the children's frequency or duration of gaze at the mother's face, nor differences in the frequency or duration of smiles in the face-to-face interaction over a snack. However, children with autism were much less likely than typically developing children to combine their smiles with eye contact

in a single act that seemed to convey an intent to communicate feelings. Not only this, but whereas 10 out of 14 typically developing children with codable data smiled in response to their mother's smile, only 3 out of 15 autistic children ever did so. It was also observed that the mothers of the children with autism were less likely to smile in response to their children's smiles, which after all were rarely combined with sustained eye contact. One might question how much sharing or coordination of affective states was taking place between the mothers and children.

Further studies from the UCLA group (Sigman, Kasari, Kwon, & Yirmiya, 1992) have examined other forms of interpersonal coordination of affect. Participants were 30 young autistic children with a mean age of under 4 years, and closely matched nonautistic retarded and typically developing children. The technique was to code these children's behavior when an adult pretended to hurt herself by hitting her finger with a hammer, simulated fear toward a remote-controlled robot, and pretended to be ill by lying down on a couch for a minute, feigning discomfort. In each of these situations, children with autism were unusual in rarely looking at or relating to the adult. When the adult pretended to be hurt, for example, children with autism often appeared unconcerned and continued to play with toys. When a small remote-controlled robot moved toward the child and stopped about four feet away, the parent and the experimenter, who were both seated nearby, made fearful facial expressions, gestures, and vocalizations for 30 seconds. Almost all the nonautistic children looked at an adult at some point during this procedure, but fewer than half the children with autism did so, and then only briefly. The children with autism were not only less hesitant than the nonautistic children in playing with the robot, but they also played with it for substantially longer periods of time. It seemed that they were less influenced by the fearful attitudes of those around them. Here again we find evidence that autistic children are relatively unengaged, not only in one-to-one interpersonal-affective transactions, but also with another person's emotional attitudes toward objects and events in the world.

These studies inspired investigations of 20-month-olds by Charman and colleagues (1997). Children's videotaped reactions to an investigator's feigned hurt revealed that only 4 out of 10 children with autism but every one of the nonautistic children looked to the investigator's pained face. When a potentially anxiety-provoking toy (e.g., a robot) was placed on the floor a short distance from the child, the children with autism very rarely switched their gaze between toy and adult to check out the toy (and see Bacon, Fein, Morris, Waterhouse, & Allen, 1998, for related results with somewhat older children). In each respect, these very young children seemed unconnected with the feelings of others.

The preceding research illustrates how young children with autism have characteristic abnormalities in reciprocal and mutual social engagement, and shared affective relatedness with the surrounding world. Although there is much to be said for studying such interpersonal relations in context, it has also proved instructive to analyze young children's expression and perception of emotion in experimental settings that allow for more precise definition of specific profiles of impairment. It is to these that I now turn.

Emotional Expressiveness

Ricks (1975, 1979) tape-recorded six 3- and 4-year-old nonverbal children with autism, six nonverbal developmentally delayed children of the same age but without autism, and six typically developing infants aged between 8 and 11 months, in four situations. The first was a requesting situation, when the child was hungry and his favorite meal was prepared and shown to him; the second was an occasion of frustration, when the meal was withheld for a few moments; the third was one of greeting, when the child saw his mother on waking in the morning, or when she returned to the room after an absence; and in the fourth, involving pleased surprise, the child was presented with a novel and interesting stimulus, the blowing up of a balloon or the lighting of a sparkler firework. The recordings of the children's vocalizations in each of these situations were edited, and played back

to the mothers of the children. The mother's task was to identify in which context each vocalization had been recorded, to identify her own child, and to identify the child without autism. The second set of recordings comprised the request vocalizations of all six autistic children, and the task was for the mother to identify her own child.

When this kind of procedure was conducted with recordings of typically developing infants' vocalizations, the mothers could easily identify the message of each signal of every infant, but found difficulty in identifying which signals came from their own child. When the tapes of the remaining participants were presented to the mothers of the children with autism, these mothers, too, could recognize the contexts from which their own autistic child's vocalizations had been derived, and they could also identify the signals of the one developmentally delayed child without autism (often explaining that he "sounded normal"). What they were unable to do was to recognize the contexts associated with the vocalizations of autistic children other than their own. Each of these children's signals seemed to be idiosyncratic. Correspondingly, and in contrast with the parents of typically developing children, they could readily and unerringly identify their own child from the various vocalizations. Ricks concluded that whereas typically developing infants seem to have an unlearned set of emotionally communicative vocalizations, autistic children either do not develop these signals or, having reached the age of 3 to 5, they no longer use them. On the other hand, their idiosyncratic signals do have emotional meanings.

Yirmiya, Kasari, Sigman, and Mundy (1989) studied videotapes of semistructured child–experimenter interactions involving activated toys, a song-and-tickle social game, a turn-taking activity, and a balloon-blowing episode. The children's facial expressions were coded second by second, using the anatomically based scheme of Izard (1979). The principal findings were that children with autism were more flat or neutral in affective expressions than were control children, but more important than this, they displayed a variety of unique and ambiguous expressions that were not displayed by any of the other children. Although the authors described these in terms of negative and incongruous blends of expression, for example, of fear with anger or anger with joy, it is uncertain whether what might normally serve as reliable indices of fear, anger, and so on had the same meanings here. The evidence suggests that for autistic children, the intrapersonal coordination of expressions might be abnormal, with obvious implications for the patterning of the children's personal and interpersonal affective experiences.

LATER CHILDHOOD AND ADOLESCENCE

With children beyond their early years, it is possible to complement naturalistic and quasi-naturalistic studies with additional kinds of experimental investigation, including neurofunctional research. Although it is somewhat arbitrary to divide up aspects of emotional relations, when the perception, expression, and experience of feelings are so closely bound together along with tendencies to action, this may be helpful for purposes of exposition. It is fitting to begin this section with a focus on interpersonal relations, and to come full circle when we return to consider so-called self-conscious or social emotions.

Emotional Engagement and Empathy

Just as in the case of young children with autism, systematic studies with older children and adolescents as well as adults reveal what it means to have limited interpersonal engagement with, and empathy for, other people.

Attwood, Frith, and Hermelin (1988) observed adolescents with autism and with Down syndrome interacting with their peers for a total of twenty 30-second periods in the playground and at the dinner table. All 15 participants with Down syndrome interacted socially during the period of observation, but only 11 of the 18 autistic children did so. Although the mean number of gestures per interaction did not distinguish the groups, there were differences in the kinds of gestures employed.

Both groups used simple pointing gestures and gestures to prompt behavior, such as those to indicate "Come here" or "Be quiet"; but whereas 10 out of 15 individuals with Down syndrome used at least one expressive gesture such as giving a hug of consolation, making a thumbs-up sign, or covering the face in embarrassment, not one such gesture was seen among the participants with autism.

Hobson and Lee (1998) videotaped children and adolescents greeting an unfamiliar person and later taking their leave. Compared with matched developmentally delayed participants without autism, only half as many of the children and adolescents with autism gave spontaneous expressions of greeting, and many failed to respond even after prompting. All the young people without autism made eye contact, but a third of those with autism failed to do so; no fewer than 17 of the former group smiled, but only 6 of those with autism did so. In the farewell episode, half the individuals without autism but only three of those with autism made eye contact and said a goodbye. Fewer than half as many participants with as without autism waved in response to a final prompt, and their waves were strangely uncoordinated and limp.

Yet in a way, it is only indirectly that such studies of children's expressive conduct, even in interpersonal settings, tell us about the subjective experience of *engagement*. In fact, in the hello-goodbye study of Hobson and Lee (1998), the raters were asked to look at the videotaped episode up to the time the children sat down at the table and to rate the degree of personal engagement with each person they were greeting. It turned out that different raters who made these ratings independently were in good agreement with each other, which meant the subjective ratings were objective. The results were that 14 participants without autism but only 2 with autism were judged to be in the most strongly engaged category and only 2 without autism but 13 with autism were in the least engaged category.

So, too, García-Pérez, Lee, and Hobson (2007) rated videotaped conversations between an adult and participants with autism for two *relational* characteristics: participants' degree of affective engagement with the interviewer and the flow of the dyadic exchange. The results were striking for the discrepancy between the very marked group differences that appeared on subjective (but objectively reliable) judgments of affective engagement and interactive flow between the conversational partners, and what seemed to be either absent, or subtle but modest, group differences on behavioral measures of amounts of looking, smiling, and head-nods/shakes. It is not just that affective engagement can be measured. There is also evidence that it is important for other aspects of communication. In particular, affective engagement correlates with speaker–listener *cognitive engagement* in conversation (R. P. Hobson, Hobson, García-Pérez, & DuBois, 2012).

One critically important expression of interpersonal engagement is empathy. We have already seen evidence of limited empathy in toddlers with autism, so what about older children and adolescents? Here we can examine whether any restrictions in empathy amount to a failure to perceive and/or respond to affective expressions, or reflect more far-reaching limitation in the children's propensity to experience and orientate to other persons as centers of subjectivity.

With this question in mind, J. A. Hobson, Harris, García-Pérez, and Hobson (2009), tested 16 school-age children and adolescents with autism and 16 children without autism of similar age and verbal ability for showing concern toward another person whose drawing was torn by a second tester. The children were between the ages of 8 and 16 years, with a mean verbal mental age of about 7 years. In this study, the tester whose drawing was torn did not show any overt emotional reaction to the event, although she did witness its occurrence. Therefore it could not be the case that her observable emotional display played a role in triggering participants' responses.

Two testers invited each child individually to play a game. The child was seated beside one tester and across from the other. Everyone drew an animal. The tester seated beside the child ascertained that the child knew who drew the turtle (the tester seated across) and then proceeded to tear this drawing in two. Both testers maintained a neutral facial expression. On another day, 6 months later, a similar scenario was repeated with the exception that the drawing torn was a blank note card.

Videotapes of the episodes were given to two raters unaware of participant diagnoses who were asked to find each look to the tester whose drawing was torn, and then evaluate which of those looks expressed concern. These were looks in which the child appeared to become involved with the tester whose drawing was torn, apparently taking on her psychological stance (becoming upset on her behalf), experiencing concern for her feelings, or showing a sense of discomfort about her position (e.g., through nervous laughter). The raters had excellent agreement on the quality of such looks. The results were that when the blank index card was torn, the children rarely looked at the tester seated across the table. When it was the tester's drawing that was torn, however, some of the children with autism but especially those without autism looked at her during or immediately after the event. More importantly, on the torn drawing condition, similar numbers of individuals in each group showed at least one nonconcerned look; but whereas 67% of the nonautistic children with learning disability showed at least one *concerned* look, only 15% of participants with autism did so. Global ratings of concern also distinguished the two groups. This synopsis of the findings fails to convey how charged an atmosphere was generated by the procedure—albeit not for the participants with autism—nor how swiftly many children without autism cast concerned looks to the injured party.

Such quasi-naturalistic studies are complemented by other methodological approaches adopted with older and more able individuals. In a study by Yirmiya, Sigman, Kasari, and Mundy (1992), high-functioning young adolescents with autism scored lower than control participants in reporting empathic feelings in response to videotapes of emotional scenarios, an ability correlated with full-scale IQ only for the group with autism. This suggested to the authors that the children might have been employing cognitive strategies in interpreting social situations. A program of studies designed to tap into aspects of empathizing and systemizing in able people with autism and Asperger syndrome, for example, through self-report questionnaires (see Baron-Cohen et al., 2005), has yielded evidence that they have a relative deficit in the former but not latter respect.

Experiments on Emotional Expression

Observations of spontaneous social engagement among older children and adolescents are complemented by the work of investigators who have asked participants to pose emotionally expressive faces and voices. In an early experiment conducted by Langdell (1981), for example, judges rated children's attempts to make happy and sad faces as more inappropriate than those of matched developmentally delayed children without autism. In a more elaborate study by Macdonald and colleagues (1989), raters judged that high-functioning participants with autism posed facial and vocal expressions were more odd than those of control subjects, and the (photographed) faces were also less easily classified with respect to the emotions expressed; and when Loveland et al. (1994) tested children's ability to imitate as well as produce expressions of facial affect on instruction, the children with autism not only found difficulty but also produced more bizarre and mechanical expressions. In deliberate as well as spontaneous expressions of emotion, therefore, the evidence points to qualitative as well as quantitative abnormalities in individuals with autism.

I have already remarked how in the realm of interpersonal relations, the perception of people and what they express is only partly dissociable from the emotional experience that such perception engenders in the heart (and the I) of the beholder. Correspondingly, investigations of emotion perception are not divorced from the other studies we have been considering.

Experiments on Emotion Perception

There has been controversy over the behavioral evidence for emotion recognition deficits among individuals with autism. I shall come to consider how complementary forms of evidence promise to resolve disputes in this domain, but first I illustrate insights that can be gained when the design of experiments succeeds in highlighting as well as delineating atypicalities in how participants with autism perceive emotional expressions. Readers who wish to have an overview of the now extensive literature are referred to summary tables provided by Harms, Martin, and Wallace (2010) on facial emotion recognition and Gaigg (in press) on perception of emotion in other modalities.

To begin with, it is important to be clear what these studies are aiming to achieve, and the methods that are needed to address those aims (R. P. Hobson, 1991). It is not expected that experiments will provide a *quantitative* estimate of the size of real-life group differences in emotion perception, for a number of reasons that include the effects of matching procedures (to match by verbal ability is to match by a partial index of social coordination that may be emotion-dependent, thereby controlling out some of the group difference one is trying to examine), the artificiality of the test materials and test situation (which may be more manageable for children with autism than real-life emotional exchanges), and the possibility that successful judgments may be made with superficial understanding of emotion itself. For example, suppose some children with autism were to apply abnormal perceptual strategies and identify a smile as an upturned mouth (which is not the usual way to apprehend a smile!). To be confident that one is testing the ability to register the subjective emotional meanings of expressions, one needs to devise task materials that are difficult to interpret *unless* one perceives emotional meaning.

In this respect, consider the study of Ozonoff, Pennington, and Rogers (1991), who tested a group of high-functioning autistic individuals and a heterogeneous control sample who were matched for age and verbal IQ on a battery of tests, including one of emotion perception. A photograph of a face displaying an emotional expression served as the target, and the participant was asked to choose one out of four photographs that "felt the same way." Correct choices varied from the target in the identity of the model and the intensity of the expressed affect. There were 34 items, half of which contained distractor photographs that shared similar perceptual features with correct choices; for example, a face expressing fear was used as a distractor for the target emotion of surprise, since both emotions share the feature of an open mouth. Nine emotions were depicted, four simple emotions (happiness, sadness, anger, and fear) and five complex emotions (surprise, shame, disgust, interest, and contempt). Participants with autism performed significantly less well than those in the control group in matching both simple and complex emotions, and made a higher number of errors on items with an obvious perceptual foil. The authors considered that perhaps they were using a different, more perceptually driven matching strategy.

The most important (but frequently neglected) point here is that in order to reveal something about the processes that underlie given levels of performance, one needs appropriate control tasks in order to examine profiles of scores across tests that do and do not require emotion recognition. No wonder that some of the most persuasive evidence for autism-specific deficits has come from studies that have compared closely matched participants on tests of judging emotion-related and emotion-unrelated materials such as photographs, drawings, or videotape and audiotape recordings of people vis-à-vis nonpersonal objects (e.g., R. P. Hobson, Ouston, & Lee, 1988a, for cross-modal matching of facial and vocal expressions vis-à-vis cross-modal matching of appearances and sounds of things and actions; R. P. Hobson, Ouston, & Lee, 1989, for naming emotions in faces and voices vis-à-vis naming photographs and sounds of nonemotional stimuli; and R. P. Hobson & Lee, 1989, for naming emotional vis-à-vis nonemotional pictures that appear in a standard IQ test).

The following two studies illustrate what may be learned from controlled studies. The first was designed by R. P. Hobson, Ouston, and Lee (1988b; and see Celani, Battachi, & Arcidiacono, 1999, for a related approach) to test whether individuals with autism who were matched for verbal ability with nonautistic people might be impaired in matching people's faces according to (a) happy, unhappy, angry, and afraid emotions and (b) identities. The task was to match emotions expressed by different individuals, and to match people's identities although they were expressing different emotions. In order to explore the possibility that autistic children might perform well by applying some form of nonemotional perceptual analysis, we repeated the two forms of the task with modifications: Firstly, the faces on the cards to be sorted had blanked-out mouths, and secondly, they had blanked-out mouths and foreheads. Our intention was to retain the feel of the emotions even in these latter materials (to establish an advantage for emotion-sensitive subjects) while at the same time to reduce the availability of non-emotion-related cues (to thwart alternative strategies of sorting). In a final condition, the standard photographs and the full faces for sorting were each presented upside-down, to tilt the balance in the opposite direction in favor of participants with abnormal strategies of face perception.

The first result was that whereas on the identities task, the performance of the two groups showed a similar steady decline as the photographs became increasingly blanked-out, on the emotions task the performance of autistic subjects worsened more abruptly than that of control subjects as cues to emotion were progressively reduced. It seemed that the children with autism were relatively unable to use the feel in the faces to guide performance. Not only this, but correlations between individuals' scores on the identity and emotion tasks were higher for participants with autism, again suggesting that they might have been sorting the expressive faces by nonemotional perceptual strategies. Secondly, whereas the performance of control participants slumped in sorting upside-down faces, the children with autism became significantly superior to the control group on matching both identities and emotions (also Langdell, 1978; and for later studies of recognizing emotion in the eyes, see, e.g., Baron-Cohen, Wheelwright, & Jolliffe, 1997; Baron-Cohen, Wheelwright, Hill, Raste, & Plumb, 2001).

A second approach to defeating abnormal perceptual strategies concerns judgments of gestural expressions of emotion (Moore, Hobson, & Lee, 1997; and see Jennings, 1973, and Weeks & Hobson, 1987, for equally strong evidence for group differences between language-matched groups in judging emotion in facial expressions). Here, children and adolescents with and without autism—again, matched for verbal ability as well as age, and also comparable in the productivity of what they said during the task—were shown videotape sequences of people's moving bodies depicted merely by dots of light attached to the trunk and limbs. As a stringent control task, we tested the children's abilities to judge actions such as digging or pushing. Firstly, we presented separate 5-second sequences of the point-light person enacting in turn the gestures of surprise, sadness, fear, anger, and happiness. In the surprise sequence, for example, the person walked forward and suddenly checked his stride and jerked backward with his arms thrown out to the side, and gave a sigh of relief; in the sad sequence, the person walked forward with a stooped posture, paused, and sighed, then raised his arms out slowly and allowed them to drop to his sides, and finally seated himself in a slumped manner and put his head in his hands. In each case, adults who saw the videotapes were 100% accurate in judging the expressions.

The children were told, "You're going to see some bits of film of a person moving. I want you to tell me about this person. Tell me what's happening." In response, all but one of the nonautistic children made a spontaneous comment about the person's emotional state for at least one presentation, and most referred to emotions on two or more of the five sequences. In contrast, 10 of the 13 children with autism *never* referred to emotional states, whether correctly or incorrectly. In the case of the children and adolescents with autism, it was the person's movements and actions rather than feelings that were reported. For example, the sad figure was described as "walking and sitting down on a chair," "walking and flapping arms and bent down," and "walking and waving his arms and kneeling down... hands to face." Almost none of

the responses were wrong, but very few referred to feelings.

A final task was designed to explore how accurately the children and adolescents could name actions and emotions when explicitly asked to do so. We added five new emotionally expressive sequences to the five already described. These showed the point-light person in states of itchiness, boredom, tiredness, cold, and hurt. When these sequences were shown, one by one, we said, "I want you to tell me what the person is feeling." Alongside this test involving emotions and other attitudes, there was a test for the recognition of nonemotional actions: lifting, chopping, hopping, kicking, jumping, pushing, digging, sitting, climbing, and running. Here the instructions were, "I want you to tell me what the person is doing." The tasks were adjusted to exclude items on which there were ceiling or floor effects, and to equate tasks for level of difficulty. The participants with autism were not significantly different in their scores on the actions task (mean score 5 out of 8 correct, compared with 6 out of 8 for the control group); but on the emotions task, where once again the control group achieved a mean score of 6 out of 8 correct, the children with autism had a mean score of only 2 out of 8 correct. Here is striking evidence of a *specific* limitation in recognizing emotions in children carefully matched for verbal ability and linguistic productivity.

If these highly selected illustrations are far from exceptional in pointing to atypical emotion perception among participants with autism, there are also many studies (summarized in the review by Harms et al., 2010) that have suggested they achieve similar *levels* of performance on certain tests of emotion recognition. It is here that complementary avenues of research have added depth to the interpretation of the findings. For example, a number of eye-tracking studies (e.g., Pelphrey et al., 2002; Corden, Chilvers, & Skuse, 2008) have shown that when looking at emotionally expressive faces, high-functioning individuals with autism pay relatively little attention to the eye regions and instead look to more peripheral features (Bal et al., 2010; Hernandez et al., 2009).

Neurofunctional studies (Ashwin, Chapman, Colle, & Baron-Cohen, 2006; Dapretto et al., 2006; Pelphrey, Morris, McCarthy, & LaBar, 2007) have yielded evidence for reduced amygdala activity when participants view emotionally expressive faces, whereas other regions of the brain appear to be recruited instead (e.g., Wang, Dapretto, Hariri, Sigman, & Bookheimer, 2004). So it is that at the end of a lengthy review of evidence from behavioral, eye-tracking, electrophysiological, and brain imaging studies of facial emotion recognition, Harms et al. (2010, p. 317) conclude as follows: "The studies reviewed here provide evidence that individuals with ASD decode facial expressions differently than TD individuals...the fact that nearly all the eye-tracking, neuroimaging, and ERP studies have found group differences suggests that mixed findings in behavioral studies may be due to limits in the sensitivity of certain types of behavioral measures (e.g., faces depicting prototypical emotional expressions) to detect group differences." These authors also note that when participants with autism perform well in behavioral studies, they may be drawing on compensatory mechanisms such as verbal mediation or feature-based learning (e.g., Grossman, Klin, Carter, & Volkmar, 2000).

There remain outstanding issues to do with the specificity of *emotion* recognition in facial, vocal, and other expressions (e.g., Boucher, Lewis, & Collis, 1998; Klin et al., 1999). Here it is important to note that even if certain perceptual processing deficits extend beyond the emotional domain, which is perfectly possible for at least some individuals with autism, the most significant developmental implications might arise through an impact on specifically socioemotional perception and the interpersonal relations for which such perception is needed.

Self-Conscious or Social Emotions

Thus far, we have concentrated on so-called simple emotions, which are often presumed to be less cognitively elaborated than feelings such as coyness, guilt, pride, or shame. One aspect of the latter emotions is that they appear to implicate self-consciousness. Bosch (1970) remarked how the child with autism often seems to lack a sense of self-consciousness and shame, and to be missing something of the "'self-involvement,' the acting with, and the identification with the acting person" (p. 81). This process of identifying with others may be critical for establishing the ability to reflect on oneself from a somewhat distanced, outside position, in that *through* others, we come to assume attitudes toward ourselves. Similar processes may also establish conditions for developing attitudes of approval and disapproval toward oneself, or indeed a range of self-reflective attitudes.

What, then, have controlled studies revealed about self-conscious feelings in individuals with autism? And is there evidence that they may be limited in the degree to which they identify with others?

There have been several approaches to studying self-consciousness among children with autism. For instance, young children with autism who are not severely cognitively impaired do remove rouge from their faces when they perceive themselves in a mirror (Dawson & McKissick, 1984; Neuman & Hill, 1978; Spiker & Ricks, 1984). What most do *not* show are the signs of coyness typical of young typically developing and nonautistic retarded children. Thus the autistic child can make use of his own reflection to register what it means to have his own body marked, and he is likely to act accordingly in trying to remove the mark from his face. What is far less certain, is whether such behavior is motivated by a concern with the way he looks to other people and with the evaluative attitudes that others may entertain in seeing him marked in an unusual manner (R. P. Hobson, 1990). And indeed, a controlled study of coy behavior (R. P. Hobson, Chidambi, Lee, & Meyer, 2006) yielded evidence that it is especially in sustained engagement with someone else that one distinguishes a relative lack of coyness among children with autism.

This notion receives some support from a study conducted by Kasari, Sigman, Baumgartner, and Stipek (1993) with young autistic and nonautistic learning disabled children (mean age 42 months) and mental age-matched typically developing children (mean age 23 months). Each participant completed a puzzle, and the investigator and parent reacted neutrally; then the child completed a second puzzle, and after 3 seconds, both adults gave praise. Although children with autism were like mentally retarded and typically developing children in being inclined to smile when they succeeded with the puzzles, autistic children were less likely to draw attention to what they had done or to look up to an adult, and less likely to show pleasure in being praised. Their pride assumed a strangely asocial form. In assessments of pride in high-functioning children and adolescents with autism (Capps, Yirmiya, & Sigman, 1992; Kasari, Chamberlain, & Bauminger, 2001), the children could cite situations eliciting pride, but provided instances that were less personal and in some ways more stereotyped (e.g., finishing one's homework or winning games) than was the case with control children.

So, too, with regard to guilt. Kasari et al. (2001) describe how high-IQ children with autism can report feeling guilt, but compared with control children they provide fewer self-evaluative statements and are more likely to describe situations in terms of rule breaking, disruptiveness, and damage to property, rather than those of causing physical or emotional harm to others. The researchers conclude that for children with autism, guilt appears to be defined in terms of memorizable rules and actions such as taking toys from school, stealing cookies, running away, and so on, rather than in interpersonal, empathic terms. R. P. Hobson et al. (2006) conducted an experimental study in which children with autism were less likely to respond to a potentially guilt-inducing event and to show a guilty looks pattern of engagement.

Similar results emerge when the focus turns to embarrassment. According to Capps et al. (1992) and Kasari et al. (2001), children with autism are liable to give examples of embarrassing situations that are external and uncontrollable, whereas matched typically developing children often give more specific and personal examples that are related to controllable events. Especially frequent are reports of feeling embarrassment because of

teasing by others, but references to the presence of an audience are relatively infrequent.

Parental reports of younger adolescents and children illustrate something more about the specificity of the children's atypicality in these respects. Hobson et al. (2006) conducted a semistructured interview with parents of children with autism, and parents of children without autism of similar age (6–13 years) and verbal mental age (3.5–9 years). Most of the questions concerned whether the children showed social emotions such as jealousy, guilt, and concern. We inquired after specific instances of each emotion. Parents of both groups of children reported that their offspring showed feelings such as happiness, distress, and anger (although we did not inquire closely on the person-directedness of the anger). They also reported that their children were affected by the moods of other people, and here it was clearly *not* the case that the children with autism were globally unresponsive.

On the other hand, when parents were asked about their children's emotions of pity, concern, and guilt, there were marked group differences. A majority of children without autism were said to show *clear* manifestations of these feelings. In the case of the children with autism, a majority showed *possible* or *atypical* signs of pity and concern, but only one was reported to show clear instances of these feelings. In the case of guilt, moreover, 7 out of 10 children with autism, but not a single one of those without autism, were said not to show guilt at all.

An especially interesting result concerned the emotion of jealousy. The question about jealousy was, "Have you observed jealousy in your child—that is, resenting the attention you or someone else is giving to other individuals?" Here there was close *similarity* between the groups, and over half the parents of children with autism reported clear signs of jealousy. This finding is in keeping with those from a study by Bauminger (2004), who reported that in two jealousy-eliciting conditions—one in which the child's parent praised another child's picture while ignoring his or her own child's, and another in which the parent engaged in affectionate play exclusively with the other child—the majority of children with autism displayed clear indications of jealousy, and there was not a group difference from control participants in this respect. On the other hand, the children with autism tended to express themselves by acting toward the parent, rather than looking at him or her. In separate tests, the children with autism were less proficient in recognizing jealousy in a picture, and only half could produce personal and affective (as opposed to social-cognitive) examples of jealousy, whereas all the control children could do so.

How are we to interpret this pattern of results? It is relevant to note that children with autism form attachments (Rogers, Ozonoff, & Maslin-Cole, 1991; Shapiro, Sherman, Calamari, & Koch, 1987; Sigman & Mundy, 1989; Sigman & Ungerer, 1984). Therefore although there is ample evidence that the children are atypical in the patterns of their social relatedness, aspects of their relationships are relatively typical in certain respects. It seems that the biologically based processes that underlie human and probably other animals' propensities to form attachments and to manifest jealousy are dissociable from other processes that lead humans to experience and respond to—and in due course, think about—other-person-centered emotional states. To be more specific, attachments and jealousy may not require a human to have much by the way of intersubjective engagement or identification with other persons. On the other hand, emotions such as pity, concern, and guilt, at least when fully organized and differentiated, do depend on the capacity to identify with the emotions of others as the states of other people with whom one is emotionally connected and from whom one is differentiated. The evidence from autism highlights how among children without autism, emotional experience and behavior are organized in a particular way that yields the capacity to feel for someone else.

Having said this, it is obvious that emotional dimensions of interpersonal engagement are important for someone's experience of relationships. When Lee and Hobson (1998) conducted self-understanding interviews, they found that children with autism were not only restricted in the feelings they expressed about themselves, but also failed to mention friends or being members of a social group. Bauminger and Kasari (2000) described how children with autism spoke of loneliness but failed to refer to the affective dimension of being left out of close intimate relationships. As Bauminger (2004) suggests, children with autism appear to find difficulty in considering interpersonal relationships when reflecting on their emotional experiences.

The upshot of these studies is that we cannot presume which aspects of emotion, even supposedly complex emotion, are or are not absent in autism. Nor can we assume that even seemingly complex feelings depend on sophisticated cognitive abilities. Therefore when such feelings are atypical in autism, we should not jump to the conclusion that this is for reasons of cognitive (e.g., theory of mind) impairment.

Finally, but importantly, we must not neglect the fact that in many of the studies cited, there are a number of children with autism who do seem to register others' feelings, both toward themselves and toward a shared world, and who manifest a range of emotions, sometimes in a manner centered on the other person—and this, too, needs investigation.

FURTHER PERSPECTIVES

This overview has emphasized social-relational aspects of emotional behavior and experience among individuals with autism. We need to clarify what underlies the observed social-affective atypicalities, whether on psychological, physiological, or neurofunctional levels, and how far any atypicalities are characteristic of all or only some affected individuals.

One line of investigation is to study families in which there is a person with autism. There is uncertainty quite how far the variable social-emotional difficulties of first-degree relatives of individuals with autism correspond with those of the individuals themselves, but a lack of interest, reciprocity, and affection in social interaction as well as related aloof personality traits are not uncommon (see Bailey, Palferman, Heavey, & Le Couteur, 1998). This is also the case among monozygotic twins without autism (Le Couteur et al., 1996). There may well be a genetic component to emotion-related abnormalities among many persons with autism.

Atypicalities in emotional functioning may extend beyond the specifically social domain. For instance, Bird and colleagues have been exploring the possible role of alexithymia in autism. Alexithymia is a term that refers to difficulties in recognizing, distinguishing, and describing feelings from the bodily sensations of emotional arousal. Thus far, there is evidence that degree of alexithymia relates to anterior insula activity when empathizing with the pain of others (Bird et al., 2010), as well as fixations to the eye and mouth area (Bird, Press, & Richardson, 2011). It has even been suggested that alexithymia might underlie participants' deficits in recognizing emotion in the face (Cook, Brewer, Shah, & Bird, 2013). Although it is contentious to claim that some individuals with autism have comorbid alexithymia, as well as to equate alexithymic features in autism with those expressed among people without autism, further research promises to clarify such issues.

There is a connection between these studies and research into emotional responsiveness to music. In particular, Allen, Davis, and Hill (2012; also Heaton et al., 2012) reported that groups of high-functioning adults with autism spectrum disorder were not distinctive in their physiological responsiveness to music, but their lesser ability to verbalize their emotions was also reflected in their alexithymia score. However one wishes to explain this latter relation, any theory of emotion in autism needs to encompass the fact that such adults with autism *do* respond emotionally to music (Allen, Hill, & Heaton, 2009; Heaton, Allen, Williams, Cummins, & Happé, 2008).

In due course, we may also learn much from intervention studies that are intended to improve specific aspects of (for example) emotion perception, or to facilitate emotional engagement between autistic children and others (e.g., Bauminger, 2002; Rogers, 2000). Personally, and despite the

optimism of other researchers (e.g., Golan et al., 2010; Harms et al., 2010), I am doubtful whether teaching how to interpret emotional expressions will achieve much of clinical value, especially because of failures to generalize any benefits in a meaningful way to real-life settings. On the other hand, approaches designed to foster interpersonal relations among persons with autism may not only promote substantial change, but may also reveal how affected individuals' *potential* for emotional engagement may be realized (Gutstein, Burgess, & Montfort, 2007; J. A. Hobson, Tarver, Beurkens, & Hobson, 2013; Mahoney & Perales, 2003).

Views From Neuroscience

It seems that for some researchers as well as laypeople, neuroscientific perspectives promise to yield *the* most important evidence about the nature of emotion-related impairments in autism. There is some justification for such a view. Neurofunctional correlates of emotional experience and even empathy, both in typically developing individuals (e.g., Decety & Chaminade, 2003) and in those with autism (e.g., Schulte-Rüther et al., 2011), are important and revealing, and we have already noted how neuroscientific research may clarify ambiguities in behavioral data. It is very likely that the large majority of children who develop autism have primary abnormality in brain function, and we need to know in what such abnormality consists and how consistent or variable it is from one affected individual to another.

Having said this, the pathogenesis of autism is going to require complexly interwoven neurological *and* psychological levels of explanation over the course of an affected person's life. It must be borne in mind that experience shapes brains, as well as the other way round (Bachevalier & Loveland, 2006; Pelphrey, Shultz, Hudac, & Vander Wyk, 2011). The neural functioning of individuals in older childhood and beyond may *result from* and reflect, as well as underlie, psychological abilities and disabilities. It will take longitudinal studies from early in life to tease out which abnormalities in neurological functioning are at the source of autism in some or most affected children, and which result from the developmental implications of other neurological or psychological impairment.

Here I make reference to three important avenues of research: investigations of dysfunction in the social brain, studies of mirror neurone functioning in persons with autism, and, broadening the range of measures beyond brain scanning, research on physiological responsiveness.

In the first respect, there is a relative consensus that among individuals with autism past childhood, there are abnormalities in the functioning of parts of the brain that are critically involved in emotional aspects of experience and behavior. Among brain regions affected are the amygdala and cingulate cortex of the limbic system, parts of the cortex of the temporal lobes (in particular, the superior temporal sulcus, fusiform gyrus, and temporal poles), and medial prefrontal and orbitofrontal areas, as well as interconnections among these structures (see, for example, complementary reviews by Bachevelier & Loveland, 2006: Minshew & Keller, 2010; and Neuhaus, Beauchaine, & Bernier, 2010; also Critchley et al., 2000). It is important to note that such findings set socioemotional dimensions center stage in the psychopathology of autism.

The second avenue of research has been prompted by the idea that human beings (and in some respects, certain nonhuman primates) have a neuronal system that serves to map what is perceived as the actions and feelings of other people on to one's own motor and affective system. Through this mechanism, a person might be engaged with the subjective life of others without the need for prior cognitions or theory of mind. There is indeed some evidence that such resonating or mimicking of feelings is limited among people with autism (McIntosh, Reichmann-Decker, Winkielman, & Wilbarger, 2006), and earlier we considered evidence for impairments in intersubjective engagement.

However, it remains uncertain whether the neurological source of this psychological deficit lies in the mirroring system. Although there is some evidence, both from fMRI findings (e.g., Dapretto et al., 2006) and electroencephalography (EEG)

patterns of mu frequency suppression (Oberman et al., 2005) that such functioning may be atypical among children with autism, the claims of the mirror neuron theory of autism (Williams, Whiten, Suddenforf, & Perrett, 2001) are disputed on both empirical and theoretical grounds (e.g., Southgate & Hamilton, 2008). There is much yet to discover in these respects.

Third, studies that have employed physiological measures such as those of skin conductance or heart rate suggest that individuals with autism spectrum disorder may have reduced physiological responsiveness to some although perhaps not all forms of emotional input (e.g., Bal et al., 2010; Blair, 1999; Corona, Dissanayake, Arbelle, Wellington, & Sigman, 1998; Hubert, Wicker, Monfardini, & Deruelle, 2009). Extending such observations to the interpersonal domain, there is evidence that adults with Asperger syndrome show limited corticospinal response to another person's perceived pain (Minio-Paluello, Baron-Cohen, Avenanti, Walsh, & Aglioti, 2009).

Congenitally Blind Children and Romanian Orphans

I have been presenting the case, as much by illustration as by logical argument, that there is developmental continuity between aspects of typically developing infants' emotional life, and qualities of infants' subsequent social and cognitive relations that appear less obviously emotional in nature. I have also implied that some of these lines of development may be discerned through the specific profile of social and cognitive (and perceptual and motivational) impairments and limitations in individuals with autism. Especially important here is the idea that through emotional engagement with other people, typically developing infants are moved to assume the psychological orientation of others; and that by means of this process of identification in the context of triadic person-person-world relations, they are lifted out of their one-track, inflexible perspective to apprehend things and events "according to the other." In my view (R. P. Hobson, 1993a, 1993b, 2002), this process is not only disrupted in children with autism, but it is also critically important for the development of context-sensitive symbolic thinking.

This theoretical perspective locates the final common pathway to autism in what fails to happen *between* people and in their mutual relations with the surroundings. Insofar as this perspective is valid, one might be led to investigate whether there are a variety of routes by which the pivotal experiences of identifying with, and being moved by, someone else's attitudes to a shared world could be impaired. In this context, studies of atypical autism may be specially revealing. Here I shall consider two such cases: congenital blindness and Romanian orphans.

When colleagues and I became intrigued by the social impairments of congenitally blind children, there were already clinical reports suggesting that both autistic features and the syndrome of autism might be more prevalent in children who suffer congenital blindness (e.g., Fraiberg, 1977; Keeler, 1958; Rogers & Newhart-Larson, 1989). It seemed to us that congenital blindness might deprive an infant of something essential in the domain of emotional relatedness: the ability to perceive, be moved by, and identify with the attitudes of someone else *as these are directed towards objects and events in a visually shared world.* Whereas sighted children with autism are not moved by others' feelings because they do not experience typical forms of feeling perception toward the expressions of others, so congenitally blind children are not only restricted in the expressions they perceive, but are also deprived of the insight that different attitudes may be directed to the same visually specified object or event—and therefore that objects and events may have multiple (context-sensitive, person-dependent, even symbolic) meanings. In other words, congenital blindness might predispose (but not predetermine) a child to develop autism, for the reason that blindness unhinges the very fulcrum of early development that is said to be lacking in sighted children with autism.

In order to establish whether the evidence was in keeping with this hypothesis, Brown, Hobson, Lee, and Stevenson (1997) tested children who had

been totally or near-totally blind from birth, aged between 3 and 9 years of age and with no identifiable disorder of the nervous system, available in six schools for visually impaired children. The children's behavior was rated over at least three periods of 20 minutes at free play, in the classroom during a lesson, and in a session of language testing, and the results were complemented by teacher reports. It turned out that no fewer than 10 of the 24 children satisfied the clinical criteria for autism.

In a subsequent study (R. P. Hobson, Lee, & Brown, 1999), nine of the blind children who met the criteria for autism were compared with nine sighted children with autism who matched for age and IQ. The two groups were similar in many respects, but there were indications that the blind children were not so impaired in their emotional expressions and that their relations with people were better. The majority gave the impression of being less severely autistic. In the clinical judgment of the child psychiatrist investigator, only two of the nine blind children displayed the *quality* of social impairment that was characteristic of the sighted but autistic children, a quality that involves the special feel one has of a lack in emotional contact. It seems that when children are blind from birth, they are predisposed to autism even if their social impairment is somewhat less profound than in sighted children with autism. Their lack of vision plays a role in causing the picture of autism, even when their intrinsic social disability is not so severe. Accordingly, we predicted that the natural history of blind and sighted children with autism would be different, and at 8-year follow-up (Hobson & Lee, 2010), only one of the nine blind children whom we studied still satisfied the diagnostic criteria for autism.

We also predicted that even among those children whose social relations were less affected by blindness, there would be some indication of autistic-like problems. In order to test this prediction, we compared the children who were *not* autistic with sighted children from mainstream schools who were similar in age and IQ. Not one of the mainstream children showed any autistic-like behavior, whereas every one of the blind children did so. The two groups differed in several respects, including relating to people, responses to objects, communication of all kinds, motor coordination, and interactive play. Only the blind children had a tendency to echo back what other people said—arguably, a revealing index of their difficulty in identifying with a person-anchored linguistic perspective that shifts from person to person.

The message from these studies of blind children is that there may be more than one way to develop autism. The reason is that there may be more than one kind of barrier to experiencing personal relations toward other people—people with whose attitudes to a shared world one can identify.

Evidence that bears on this thesis comes from another, initially unexpected quarter: studies by Rutter and colleagues (1999) of 4- to 6-year-olds who had been placed in Romanian orphanages early in the first year of life and moved to the United Kingdom in their first or second years. In a nutshell, about 1 in 16 of the children showed a picture that closely resembled that of autism, and a further 1 in 16 presented with milder autistic features. Severely affected children displayed problems with social relationships and impoverished reciprocal communication with others, lack of empathy toward others, poverty of eye-to-eye gaze and gestures in social exchanges, and limited language and to-and-fro conversation. A majority of the children had preoccupations with sensations and intense interests of unusual kinds. Yet there was something atypical about the autism, for example, when the children made spontaneous efforts to communicate with sign language or other kinds of social approach. As with the blind, although there were fewer children showing quasi-autistic patterns at follow-up when they were aged 11–12 years, there was also a substantial degree of persistence (Rutter et al., 2007).

It seems that particular forms of very severe deprivation of emotionally patterned interpersonal experience—whether this occurs through constitutional abnormalities in the child' that restrict the effective social environment and weaken or deflect emotional pushes and pulls that occur between people, or through specific forms of perceptual

handicap, or even through appalling privation of social input—may have autism-related social and cognitive implications. We may be drawing closer to an account that accords due weight to social-emotional factors in the pathogenesis of autism.

CONCLUSIONS

It remains to step back and reflect on autism and emotion—and to consider how reshaping our concepts of emotion may help us to understand autism, and how investigations of autism may help us rethink emotion. We should not underestimate the value of clinical observations of autism for our understanding of typical early development, for the reason that they alert us to the profound developmental significance of the coordination of subjective states between individuals; and we should not overestimate the decisive contribution of any particular methodological approach to determining the specific bases of autism, when the pathogenesis of autism appears to be complex and, to some extent, different in different children.

Any explanation of autism will need to trace the origins and repercussions of what Kanner (1943) called the children's abnormality in affective contact with others. We should pay special attention to the quality of emotional impairment in the interpersonal domain, for it would seem to be in the interpersonal domain—and specifically, in respect of sharing subjective states and coordinating attitudes with other people vis-à-vis the world, as in episodes of joint attention—that a critical abnormality is to be found. To be sure, nearly all children with autism have constitutional abnormalities, but these may be of diverse kinds and arise on the bases of diverse aetiologies; and not all of these may be characterized as primarily emotional in nature, as the example of congenital blindness testifies. Yet perhaps each cause operates through a final common pathway that implicates abnormality in the patterned coordination of affectively configured subjective states between the affected child and others. Affected children appear to have a restricted propensity to *identify with* other people, to move toward and (in part) assimilate the other person's attitude and psychological orientation to the world.

As we have seen, not all complex features of social life depend on cognitive sophistication, and the ways in which biology structures typical social-emotional experience may be vulnerable to disruption prior to the onset of symbolic (or metarepresentational) abilities (also Chevallier, Kohls, Troiani, Brodkin, & Schultz, 2012).

It seems doubtful whether the quintessentially *inter*personal abnormality that characterizes autism will prove to be the result of some single perceptual or cognitive deficit. As in the case of congenital blindness, lower-level domain-general deficits will play a pathogenic role in at least some cases. From a complementary perspective, it seems doubtful that we shall arrive at an adequate theory of the syndrome of autism unless we accord this special form of interpersonal disorder—one that prevents or derails the coordination of subjective states involving feelings—a pivotal place within our multilevel explanatory scheme.

CROSS-REFERENCES

Chapters 5 through 9 address aspects of autism over the lifespan; psychopharmacological interventions are addressed in Chapter 23; social skills interventions are the focus in Chapter 37.

REFERENCES

Allen, R., Davis, R., & Hill, E. (2012). The effects of autism and alexithymia on physiological and verbal responsiveness to music. *Journal of Autism and Developmental Disorders, 43*, 432–444.

Allen, R., Hill, E., & Heaton, P. (2009). "Hath charms to soothe . . .": An exploratory study of how high-functioning adults with ASD experience music. *Autism, 13*, 21–41.

Ashwin, C., Chapman, E., Colle, L., & Baron-Cohen, S. (2006). Impaired recognition of negative basic emotions in autism: A test of the amygdala theory. *Social Neuroscience, 1*, 349–363.

Attwood, A., Frith, U., & Hermelin, B. (1988). The understanding and use of interpersonal gestures by autistic and Down's syndrome children. *Journal of Autism and Development Disorders, 18*, 241–257.

Bachevalier, J., & Loveland, K. (2006). The orbito-frontal-amygdala circuit and self-regulation of social-emotional behavior in autism. *Neuroscience and Biobehavioral Reviews, 30*, 97–117.

Bacon, A. L., Fein, D., Morris, R., Waterhouse, L., & Allen, D. (1998). The responses of autistic children to the distress of others. *Journal of Autism and Developmental Disorders, 28*, 129–142.

Bailey, A., Palferman, S., Heavey, L., & Le Couteur, A. (1998). Autism: The phenotype in relatives. *Journal of Autism and Developmental Disorders, 28*, 369–392.

Bal, E., Harden, E., Lamb, D., Vaughan van Hecke, A., Denver, J. W., & Porges, S. W. (2010). Emotion recognition in children with autism spectrum disorders: Relations to eye gaze and autonomic state. *Journal of Autism and Developmental Disorders, 40*, 358–370.

Baron-Cohen, S., Wheelwright, S., Hill, J., Raste, Y., & Plumb, I. (2001). The "reading the mind in the eyes test" revised version: A study with normal adults, and adults with Asperger syndrome or high-functioning autism. *Journal of Child Psychology and Psychiatry, 42*, 241–251.

Baron-Cohen, S., Wheelwright, S., & Jolliffe, T. (1997). Is there a "language of the eyes"? Evidence from normal adults, and adults with autism or Asperger syndrome. *Visual Cognition, 4*, 311–331.

Baron-Cohen, S., Wheelwright, S., Lawson, J., Griffin, R., Ashwin, C., Billington, J., & Chakrabarti, B. (2005). Empathizing and systemizing in autism spectrum conditions. In F. Volkmar, R. Paul, A. Klin, & D. Cohen (Eds.), *Handbook of autism and pervasive developmental disorders* (Vol. *1*, pp. 628–639). Hoboken, NJ: Wiley.

Bauminger, N. (2002). The facilitation of social-emotional understanding and social interaction in high-functioning children with autism: Intervention outcomes. *Journal of Autism and Developmental Disorders, 32*, 283–298.

Bauminger, N. (2004). The expression and understanding of jealousy in children with autism. *Development and Psychopathology, 16*, 157–177.

Bauminger, N., & Kasari, C. (2000). Loneliness and friendship in high-functioning children with autism. *Child Development, 71*, 447–456.

Bird. G., Press, C., & Richardson, D. C. (2011). The role of alexithymia in reduced eye-fixation in autism spectrum conditions. *Journal of Autism and Developmental Disorders, 41*, 1556–1564.

Bird, G., Silani, G., Brindley, R., White, S., Frith, U., & Singer, T. (2010). Empathic brain responses in insula are modulated by levels of alexithymia but not autism. *Brain, 133*, 1515–1525.

Blair, R. J. R. (1999). Psychophysiological responsiveness to the distress of others in children with autism. *Personality and Individual Differences, 26*, 477–485.

Bosch, G. (1970). *Infantile autism* (D. Jordan & I. Jordan, Trans.). New York, NY: Springer-Verlag.

Boucher, J., Lewis, V., & Collis, G. (1998). Familiar face and voice matching and recognition in children with autism. *Journal of Child Psychology and Psychiatry, 39*, 171–181.

Brown, R., Hobson, R. P., Lee, A., & Stevenson, J. (1997). Are there "autistic-like" features in congenitally blind children? *Journal of Child Psychology and Psychiatry, 38*, 693–703.

Bryson, S. E., Zwaigenbaum, L., Brian, J., Roberts, W., Szatmari, P., Rombough, V., & McDermott, C. (2007). A prospective case series of high-risk infants who developed autism. *Journal of Autism and Developmental Disorders, 37*, 12–24.

Capps, L., Yirmiya, N., & Sigman, M. (1992). Understanding of simple and complex emotions in non-retarded children with autism. *Journal of Child Psychology and Psychiatry, 33*, 1169–1182.

Celani, G., Battacchi, M. W., & Arcidiacono, L. (1999). The understanding of the emotional meaning of facial expressions in people with autism. *Journal of Autism and Developmental Disorders, 29*, 57–66.

Charman, T., Swettenham, J., Baron-Cohen, S., Cox, A., Baird, G., & Drew, A. (1997). Infants with autism: An investigation of empathy, pretend play, joint attention, and imitation. *Developmental Psychology, 33*, 781–789.

Chevallier, C., Kohls, G., Troiani, V., Brodkin, E. S., Schultz, R. T. (2012). The social motivation theory of autism. *Trends in Cognitive Sciences, 16*, 231–239.

Cook, R., Brewer, R., Shah, P., & Bird, G. (2013). Alexithymia, not autism, predicts poor recognition of emotional facial expressions. *Psychological Science, 24*, 723–732.

Corden, B., Chilvers, R., & Skuse, D. (2008). Avoidance of emotionally arousing stimuli predicts social-perceptual impairment in Asperger's syndrome. *Neuropsychologia, 46*, 137–147.

Corona, R., Dissanayake, C., Arbelle, S., Wellington, P., & Sigman, M. (1998). Is affect aversive to young children with autism? Behavioral and cardiac responses to experimenter distress. *Child Development, 6*, 1494–1502,

Critchley, H., Daly, E., Bullmore, E., Williams, S., Van Amelsvoort, T., Robertson, D., . . . Murphy, D. (2000). The functional anatomy of social behavior: Changes in cerebral blood flow when people with autistic disorder process facial expression. *Brain, 123*, 2203–2212.

Dahlgren, S. O., & Gillberg, C. (1989). Symptoms in the first two years of life: A preliminary population study of infantile autism. *European Archives of Psychiatry and Neurological Sciences, 238*, 169–174.

Dapretto, M., Davies, M. S., Pfeifer, J. H., Scott, A. A., Sigman, M., Bookheimer, S. Y., & Iacoboni, M. (2006). Understanding emotions in others: Mirror neuron dysfunction in children with autism spectrum disorders. *Nature Neuroscience, 9*, 28–30.

Dawson, G., Hill, D., Spencer, A., Galpert, L., & Watson, L. (1990). Affective exchanges between young autistic children and their mothers. *Journal of Abnormal Child Psychology, 18*, 335–345.

Dawson, G., & McKissick, F. C. (1984). Self-recognition in autistic children. *Journal of Autism and Development Disorders, 14*, 383–394.

Decety, J., & Chaminade, T. (2003). Neural correlates of feeling sympathy. *Neuropsychologia, 41*, 127–138.

Fraiberg, S. (1977). *Insights from the blind*. London, England: Souvenir.

Gaigg, S. B. (in press). The interplay between emotion and cognition in Autism Spectrum Disorder: Implications for developmental theory. *Frontiers in Integrative Neuroscience.*

García-Pérez, R. M., Lee, A., & Hobson, R. P. (2007). On intersubjective engagement: A controlled study of nonverbal communication in autism. *Journal of Autism and Developmental Disorders, 37*, 1310–1322.

Golan, O., Ashwin, E., Granader, Y., McClintock, S., Day, K., Leggett, V., & Baron-Cohen, S. (2010). Enhancing emotion recognition in children with autism spectrum conditions: An intervention using animated vehicles with real emotional faces. *Journal of Autism and Developmental Disorders, 40*, 269–279.

Grossman, J. B., Klin, A., Carter, A. S., & Volkmar, F. R. (2000). Verbal bias in recognition of facial emotions in children with Asperger syndrome. *Journal of Child Psychology and Psychiatry, 41*, 369–379.

Gutstein, S., Burgess, A. F., & Montfort, K. (2007). Evaluation of the Relationship Development Intervention Program. *Autism, 11*, 397–411.

Harms, M. B., Martin, A., & Wallace, G. L. (2010). Facial emotion recognition in autism spectrum disorders: A review of behavioral and neuroimaging studies. *Neuropsychology Review, 20*, 290–322.

Heaton, P., Allen, R., Williams, K., Cummins, O., & Happé, F. (2008). Do social and cognitive deficits curtail musical understanding? Evidence from autism and Down syndrome. *British Journal of Developmental Psychology, 26*, 171–182.

Heaton, P., Reichenbacher, L., Sauter, D., Allen, R., Scott, S., & Hill, E. (2012). Measuring the effects of alexithymia on perception of emotional vocalizations in autistic spectrum disorder and typical development. *Psychological Medicine, 42*, 2453–2459. doi: 10.1017/S0033291712000621

Hernandez, N., Metzger, A., Magné, R., Bonnet-Brilhaut, F., Roux, S., Barthelemy, C., & Martineu, J. (2009). Exploration of core features of a human face by healthy and autistic adults analyzed by visual scanning. *Neuropsychologia, 47*, 1004–1012.

Hobson, J. A., Harris, R., García-Pérez, R., & Hobson, R. P. (2009). Anticipatory concern: A study in autism. *Developmental Science, 12*, 249–263.

Hobson, J. A., Tarver, L., Beurkens, N., & Hobson, R. P. (2013). The relation between severity of autism and caregiver–child interaction: A study in the context of relationship-oriented intervention. (Manuscript submitted for publication).

Hobson, R. P. (1990). On the origins of self and the case of autism. *Development and Psychopathology, 2*, 163–181.

Hobson, R. P. (1991). Methodological issues for experiments on autistic individuals' perception and understanding of emotion. *Journal of Child Psychology and Psychiatry, 32*, 1135–1158.

Hobson, R. P. (1993a). *Autism and the development of mind*. Hillsdale, NJ: Erlbaum.

Hobson, R. P. (1993b). The emotional origins of social understanding. *Philosophical Psychology, 6*, 227–249.

Hobson, R. P. (2002). *The cradle of thought*. London, England: Pan Macmillan.

Hobson, R. P. (2008). Interpersonally situated cognition. *International Journal of Philosophical Studies, 6*, 377–397.

Hobson, R. P., Chidambi, G., Lee, A., & Meyer, J. (2006). Foundations for self-awareness: An exploration through autism. *Monographs of the Society for Research in Child Development, 284*, 71, 1–165.

Hobson, R. P., Hobson, J. A., García-Pérez, R., & Du Bois, J. (2012). Dialogic linkage and resonance in autism. *Journal of Autism and Developmental Disorders, 42*, 2718–2728. doi: 10.1007/s10803-012-1528-6

Hobson, R. P., & Lee, A. (1989). Emotion-related and abstract concepts in autistic people: Evidence from the British Picture Vocabulary Scale. *Journal of Autism and Developmental Disorders, 19*, 601–623.

Hobson, R. P., & Lee, A. (1998). Hello and goodbye: A study of social engagement in autism. *Journal of Autism and Developmental Disorders, 28*, 117–126.

Hobson, R. P., & Lee, A. (2010). Reversible autism in congenitally blind children? *Journal of Child Psychology and Psychiatry, 51*, 1235–1241.

Hobson, R. P., Lee, A., & Brown, R. (1999). Autism and congenital blindness. *Journal of Autism and Developmental Disorders, 29*, 45–56.

Hobson, R. P., Ouston, J., & Lee, A. (1988a). Emotion recognition in autism: coordinating faces and voices. *Psychological Medicine, 18*, 911–923.

Hobson, R. P., Ouston, J., & Lee, A. (1988b). What's in a face? The case of autism. *British Journal of Psychology, 79*, 441–453.

Hobson, R. P., Ouston, J., & Lee, A. (1989). Naming emotion in faces and voices: Abilities and disabilities in autism and mental retardation. *British Journal of Developmental Psychology, 7*, 237–250.

Hubert, B. E., Wicker, B., Monfardini, E., & Deruelle, C. (2009). Electrodermal reactivity to emotion processing in adults with autism spectrum disorder. *Autism, 13*, 9–19.

Izard, C. E. (1979). *The maximally discriminative facial movement coding system (MAX)*. Newark: University of Delaware Instructional Resources Center.

Jennings, W. B. (1973). *A study of the preference for affective cues in autistic children*. Unpublished doctoral dissertation, Memphis State University, Memphis, TN.

Kanner, L. (1943). Autistic disturbances of affective contact. *Nervous Child, 2*, 217–250.

Kasari, C., Chamberlain, B., & Bauminger, N. (2001). Social emotions and social relationships: Can children with autism compensate? In J. A. Burack, T. Charman, N. Yirmiya, & P. R. Zelazo (Eds.), *The development of autism* (pp. 309–323). Mahwah, NJ: Erlbaum.

Kasari, C., Sigman, M. D., Baumgartner, P., & Stipek, D. J. (1993). Pride and mastery in children with autism. *Journal of Child Psychology and Psychiatry, 34*, 352–362.

Kasari, C., Sigman, M., Mundy, P., & Yirmiya, N. (1990). Affective sharing in the context of joint attention interactions of normal, autistic and mentally retarded children. *Journal of Autism and Developmental Disorders, 20*, 87–100.

Keeler, W. R. (1958). Autistic patterns and defective communication in blind children with retrolental fibroplasias. In P. H. Hoch & J. Zubin (Eds.), *Psychopathology of communication* (pp. 64–83). New York, NY: Grune & Stratton.

Klin, A., Sparrow, S. S., de Bildt, A., Cicchetti, D. V., Cohen, D. J., & Volkmar, F. R. (1999). A normed study of face recognition in autism and related disorders. *Journal of Autism and Developmental Disorders, 29*, 499–508.

Langdell, T. (1978). Recognition of faces: An approach to the study of autism. *Journal of Child Psychology and Psychiatry, 19*, 255–268.

Langdell, T. (1981). *Face perception: An approach to the study of autism*. Unpublished doctoral dissertation, University College, London.

Le Couteur, A., Bailey, A., Goode, S., Pickles, A., Robertson, S., Gottesman, I., & Rutter, M. (1996). A broader phenotype of autism: The clinical spectrum in twins. *Journal of Child Psychology and Psychiatry, 37*, 785–801.

Lee, A., & Hobson, R. P. (1998). On developing self-concepts: A controlled study of children and adolescents with autism. *Journal of Child Psychology and Psychiatry, 39*, 1131–1141.

Lord, C. (1995). Follow-up of two-year-olds referred for possible autism. *Journal of Child Psychology and Psychiatry, 36*, 1365–1382.

Lord, C., Storoschuk, S., Rutter, M., & Pickles, A. (1993). Using the ADI-R to diagnose autism in preschool children. *Infant Mental Health Journal, 14*, 234–252.

Loveland, K. A., Tunali-Kotoski, B., Pearson, D. A., Brelsford, K. A., Ortegon, J., & Chen, R. (1994). Imitation and expression of facial affect in autism. *Development and Psychopathology, 6*, 433–444.

Macdonald, H., Rutter, M., Howlin, P., Rios, P., Le Couteur, A., Evered, C., & Folstein, S. (1989). Recognition and expression of emotional cues by autistic and normal adults. *Journal of Child Psychology and Psychiatry, 30*, 865–877.

Mahoney, G., & Perales, F. (2003). Using relationship-focused intervention to enhance the social-emotional functioning of young children with autism spectrum disorders. *Topics in Early Childhood Special Education, 23*, 77–89.

McIntosh, D. N., Reichmann-Decker, A., Winkielman, P., & Wilbarger, J. L. (2006). When the social mirror breaks: Deficits in automatic, but not voluntary, mimicry of emotional facial expressions in autism. *Developmental Science, 9*, 295–302.

Minio-Paluello, I., Baron-Cohen, S., Avenanti, A., Walsh, V., & Aglioti, S. M. (2009). Absence of embodied empathy during pain observation in Asperger syndrome. *Biological Psychiatry, 65*, 55–62.

Minshew, N. J., & Keller, T. A. (2010). The nature of brain dysfunction in autism: Functional brain imaging studies. *Current Opinion in Neurology, 23*, 124–130.

Moore, D., Hobson, R. P., & Lee, A. (1997). Components of person perception: An investigation with autistic, nonautistic retarded and normal children and adolescents. *British Journal of Developmental Psychology, 15*, 401–423.

Neuhaus, E., Beauchaine, T. P., & Bernier, R. (2010). Neurobiological correlates of social functioning in autism. *Clinical Psychology Review, 30*, 733–748.

Neuman, C. J., & Hill, S. D. (1978). Self-recognition and stimulus preference in autistic children. *Developmental Psychobiology, 11*, 571–578.

Oberman, L. M., Hubbard, E. M., McCleery, J. P., Altschuler, E. L., Ramachandran, V., & Pineda, J. A. (2005). EEG evidence for mirror neuron dysfunction in autism spectrum disorders. *Cognitive Brain Research, 24*, 190–198.

Ozonoff, S., Pennington B. F., & Rogers S. J. (1991). Executive function deficits in high-functioning autistic children: Relationship to theory of mind. *Journal of Child Psychology and Psychiatry, 32,* 1081–1105.

Pelphrey, K. A., Morris, J. P., McCarthy, G., & LaBar, K. S. (2007). Perception of dynamic changes in facial affect and identity in autism. *Scan, 2,* 140–149.

Pelphrey, K. A., Sasson, N. J., Reznick, J. S., Paul, G., Goldman, B. D., & Piven, J. (2002). Visual scanning of faces in autism. *Journal of Autism and Developmental Disorders, 32,* 249–261.

Pelphrey, K. A., Shultz, S., Hudac, C. M., & Vander Wyk, B. C. (2011). Research review: Constraining heterogeneity: the social brain and its development in autism spectrum disorder. *Journal of Child Psychology and Psychiatry, 52,* 631–644.

Reddy, V., Williams, E., & Vaughan, A. (2002). Sharing humour and laughter in autism and Down's syndrome. *British Journal of Psychology, 93,* 219–242.

Ricks, D. M. (1975). Vocal communication in pre-verbal normal and autistic children. In N. O'Connor (Ed.), *Language, cognitive deficits, and retardation* (pp. 75–80). London, England: Butterworths.

Ricks, D. M. (1979). Making sense of experience to make sensible sounds. In M. Bullowa (Ed.), *Before speech* (pp. 245–268). Cambridge, England: Cambridge University Press.

Rogers, S. J. (2000). Interventions that facilitate socialization in children with autism. *Journal of Autism and Developmental Disorders, 30,* 399–409.

Rogers, S. J. (2009). What are infant siblings teaching us about autism in infancy? *Autism Research, 2,* 125–137.

Rogers, S. J., & Newhart-Larson, S. (1989). Characteristics of infantile autism in five children with Leber's congenital amaurosis. *Developmental Medicine and Child Neurology, 31,* 598–608.

Rogers, S. J., Ozonoff, S., & Maslin-Cole, C. (1991). A comparative study of attachment behaviour in young children with autism or other psychiatric disorders. *Journal of the American Academy of Child & Adolescent Psychiatry, 30,* 483–488.

Rutter, M., Andersen-Wood, L., Beckett, C., Bredenkamp, D., Castle, J., Groothues, C., ... the English and Romanian Adoptees (ERA) Study Team. (1999). Quasi-autistic patterns following severe early global privation. *Journal of Child Psychology and Psychiatry, 40,* 537–549.

Rutter, M., Kreppner, J., Croft, C., Murin, M., Colver, E., Beckett, C., Castle, J., & Sonuga-Barke, E. (2007). Early adolescent outcomes of institutionally deprived and non-deprived adoptees. III. Quasi-autism. *Journal of Child Psychology and Psychiatry, 48,* 1200–1207.

Schulte-Rüther, M., Greimel, E., Markowitsch, H. J., Kamp-Becker, I., Remschmidt, H., Fink, G. R., & Piefke, M. (2011). Dysfunctions in brain networks supporting empathy: An fMRI study in adults with autism spectrum disorders. *Social Neuroscience, 6,* 1–21.

Shapiro, T., Sherman, M., Calamari G., & Koch, D. (1987). Attachment in autism and other developmental disorders. *Journal of the American Academy of Child & Adolescent Psychiatry, 26,* 485–490.

Sigman, M., & Mundy, P. (1989). Social attachments in autistic children. *Journal of the American Academy of Child & Adolescent Psychiatry, 28,* 74–81.

Sigman M., & Ungerer, J. A. (1984). Attachment behaviors in autistic children. *Journal of Autism and Developmental Disorders, 14,* 231–243.

Sigman, M. D., Kasari, C., Kwon, J. H., & Yirmiya, N. (1992). Responses to the negative emotions of others by autistic, mentally retarded, and normal children. *Child Development, 63,* 796–807.

Snow, M. E., Hertzig, M. E., & Shapiro, T. (1987). Expression of emotion in autistic children. *Journal of the American Academy of Child & Adolescent Psychiatry, 26,* 836–838.

Southgate, V., & Hamilton, A. F. de C. (2008). Unbroken mirrors: challenging a theory of autism. *Trends in Cognitive Sciences, 12,* 225–229.

Spiker, D., & Ricks, M. (1984). Visual self-recognition in autistic children: Developmental relationships. *Child Development, 55,* 214–225.

Stone, W. L., Hoffman, E. L., Lewis, S. E., & Ousley, O. Y. (1994). Early recognition of autism: Parental reports vs. clinical observation. *Archives of Pediatrics and Adolescent Medicine, 148,* 174–179.

Stone, W. L., & Lemanek, K. L. (1990). Parental report of social behaviors in autistic preschoolers. *Journal of Autism and Developmental Disorders, 20,* 513–522.

Vostanis, P., Smith, B., Corbett, J., Sungum-Paliwal, R., Edwards, A., Gingell, K., ... Williams, J. (1998). Parental concerns of early development in children with autism and related disorders. *Autism, 2,* 229–242.

Wang, A. T., Dapretto, M., Hariri, A. R., Sigman, M., & Bookheimer, S. Y. (2004). Neural correlates of facial affect processing in children and adolescents with autism spectrum disorder. *Journal of the Academy of Child & Adolescent Psychiatry, 43,* 481–490.

Weeks, S. J., & Hobson, R. P. (1987). The salience of facial expression for autistic children. *Journal of Child Psychology and Psychiatry, 28,* 137–152.

Williams, J. H. G., Whiten, A., Suddendorf, T., & Perrett, D. I. (2001). Imitation, mirror neurons and autism. *Neuroscience & Biobehavioral Reviews, 25,* 287–295.

Wimpory, D. C., Hobson, R. P., Williams, J. M., & Nash, S. (2000). Are infants with autism socially engaged? A study of recent retrospective parental reports. *Journal of Autism and Developmental Disorders, 30,* 525–536.

Wing, L. (1969). The handicaps of autistic children — A comparative study. *Journal of Child Psychology and Psychiatry, 10,* 1–40.

Yirmiya, N., Kasari, C., Sigman, M., & Mundy, P. (1989). Facial expressions of affect in autistic, mentally retarded and normal children. *Journal of Child Psychology and Psychiatry, 30,* 725–735.

Yirmiya, N., Sigman, M. D., Kasari, C., & Mundy, P. (1992). Empathy and cognition in high-functioning children with autism. *Child Development, 63,* 150–160.

Zwaigenbaum, L., Bryson, S., Rogers, T., Roberts, W., Brian, J., & Szatmari, P. (2005). Behavioral manifestations of autism in the first year of life. *International Journal of Developmental Neuroscience, 23,* 143–152.

CHAPTER 15

Motor Control and Motor Learning Processes in Autism Spectrum Disorders

STEFANIE BODISON AND STEWART MOSTOFSKY

A significant body of research has well documented the existence of disordered motor behavior in children with autism spectrum disorders (ASDs). Studies have demonstrated impairments in postural control (Chang, Wade, Stoffregen, Hsu, & Pan, 2010; Fournier, Kimberg, et al., 2010; Memari et al., 2013; Minshew, Sung, Jones, & Furman, 2004; Molloy, Dietrich, & Bhattacharya, 2003; Travers, Powell, Klinger, & Klinger, 2012), gait (Nayate et al., 2012; Nobile et al., 2011; Rinehart, Tonge, Iansek, et al., 2006; Rinehart, Tonge, Bradshaw, et al., 2006; Jansiewicz et al., 2006), the attainment of fine and gross motor skills (David et al., 2009; David, Baranek, Wiesen, Miao, & Thorpe, 2012; Dewey, Cantell & Crawford, 2007; Green et al., 2009), and specific functional skills such as handwriting (Beversdorf et al., 2001; Fuentes, Mostofsky, & Bastian, 2009; Fuentes, Mostofsky, & Bastian, 2010; Hellinckx, Roeyers, & Van Waelvelde, 2013). In addition, research has suggested that motor impairments in children with ASD may be present early enough to serve

as a marker for future inclusion into the diagnostic group (Baranek, 1999; Bolton, Golding, Emond, & Steer, 2012; Esposito, Venuti, Maestro, & Muratori, 2009; Flanagan, Landa, Bhat, & Bauman, 2012; Landa & Garrett-Mayer, 2006; Mulligan & White, 2012; Ozonoff et al., 2008), that their attainment is delayed and may never reach typical levels in adulthood (Lloyd, MacDonald, & Lord, 2011; Minshew et al., 2004; Nayate et al., 2012), and that mechanisms underlying motor impairments may similarly contribute to the disordered development of socialization and communication skills that are the core features of autism (Dziuk et al., 2007; Haswell, Izawa, Dowell, Mostofsky, & Shadmehr, 2009). Clinically, motor impairments in ASD are often a concern for parents and educators who find that the child's ability to access his or her educational environment, engage in play and leisure activities with family and peers, and independently participate in activities of daily living are negatively impacted by motor delays. The disciplines regularly involved in the care of children with ASD, including neurology, psychiatry, occupational therapy, speech-language pathology, psychology, education, and physical therapy, work as interdisciplinary teams to develop intervention programs designed to improve the overall functioning of the child with ASD, which often include recommendations for interventions focused on motor skill development.

Historically, much of the early research on motor behavior in ASD focused on documenting the incidence and nature of motor impairments to advocate that they should routinely be considered a hallmark feature of the disorder. A number of these studies used standardized and clinical assessments of motor function including the Movement Assessment Battery for Children (Henderson, Sugden, & Barnett, 2007), the Bruninks-Osterestky Test of Motor Performance (Bruininks & Bruininks, 2005), the Bayley Scales of Infant Development (Bayley, 2005), the Peabody Developmental Motor Scales (Folio & Fewell, 2000), and the Physical and Neurological Examination of Subtle Signs (PANESS) (Denckla, 1985). While these early studies did not specifically link motor impairments to underlying neural processes, they did substantiate that individuals with ASD, including those identified as low-functioning, high-functioning, verbal and nonverbal, do in fact demonstrate significant motor impairments across multiple domains (for reviews, see Appendix 15.1, this chapter; Bhat, Landa, & Galloway, 2012; Downey & Rapport, 2012; Fournier, Hass, Naik, Lodha, & Cauraugh, 2010; Gowen & Hamilton, 2013; Stackhouse, 2010).

Over time, as the specificity of research related to motor differences in ASD has expanded, findings have further solidified that individuals with ASD show particular difficulty with motor imitation and dyspraxia, where impaired execution of skilled movements or gestures is out of proportion to, and not wholly explained by, basic motor impairment or perceptual-motor impairment (Mostofsky et al., 2006; Rogers, Bennetto, McEvoy, & Pennington, 1996). While the term *apraxia* is traditionally used in the adult literature to refer to an acquired impairment in the ability to carry out skilled movements in the absence of fundamental sensorimotor, language, or general cognitive impairment sufficient

to preclude it, *developmental dyspraxia* is more encompassing, as unlike acquired adult-onset apraxia, coexisting sensory and basic motor problems may also be present (Ayres, 2011; Mostofsky & Ewen, 2011; Steinman, Mostofsky, & Denckla, 2010). For instance, Dziuk and colleagues (2007) reported that, while performance on measures of praxis were strongly correlated with basic motor skill (i.e., times to complete repetitive limb movements on standardized motor exam), children with ASD continued to demonstrate poorer performance on praxis exam as compared to typically developing (TD) children, even after accounting for basic motor skill. A thorough examination of praxis involves careful assessment of the types of errors made by the individual (transitive versus intransitive) and the means used to elicit these errors (Heilman & Gonzalez Rothi, 2003). Transitive actions refer to pantomimed tool use to command (i.e., brushing hair), intransitive actions are symbolic (i.e., waving goodbye, saluting), and imitative transitive actions include imitation of meaningless body and hand postures (i.e., touching your nose, linking your pinky fingers to form an *x*). Several studies have suggested a more pervasive deficit in praxis (not just limited to imitation), with documented impairments in performance of gestures to *command and with actual tool use* comparable to those of imitation (Dowell, Mahone, & Mostofsky, 2009; Dziuk et al., 2007; Mostofsky et al., 2006). Common to all three aspects of praxis examination is the ability to access parietal representations of skilled movement necessary to guide proper movement selection/sequencing mediated by the premotor cortex (Heilman & Gonzalez Rothi, 2003).

As evidence for specificity of dyspraxia in autism, Dewey et al. (2007) reported that while children with ASD, attention-deficit/hyperactivity disorder (ADHD), and developmental coordination disorder (DCD) plus ADHD all showed impairments in basic motor development, only children with ASD showed deficits in gestural performance. Consistent with these findings, MacNeil and Mostofsky (2012) recently found that while both children with ADHD and children with ASD showed impaired basic motor skill performance, impaired gestural performance on praxis examination was specific to children with ASD (who showed high significant impairment compared both to children with ADHD and TD children).

Furthermore, in two fairly distinct samples of subjects, these pervasive praxis deficits were shown to be correlated with the core behavioral features of ASD, including social and communicative impairments as measured by the Autism Diagnostic Observation Schedule (ADOS; Dowell et al., 2009; Dzuik et al., 2007). Additionally, these core behavioral features of ASD (as measured by the ADOS) were predicted not only by impaired imitation, but also by impaired performance of gestures to command and tool use. As such, it appears that multiple areas of praxis abnormalities are associated with some of the defining features of ASD. These findings have led to the suggestion that for some with autism, a "dyspraxia for social skills" may contribute to the core social/communicative features of the disorder (Mostofsky & Ewen, 2011), such that disordered development of internal action models underlying gestural representation result in impaired execution of a wide range of skills—both motor and social—as well as impaired ability to recognize/interpret these actions as performed by others. To further explore this concept, the ability to correctly identify gestures as performed by others (postural knowledge) have been examined in children with ASD, with findings revealing children with ASD show impaired representational knowledge of skilled gestures and that this postural knowledge is correlated with impaired performance of skilled gestures on praxis examination (Dowell et al., 2009; MacNeil & Mostofsky, 2012).

The findings revealing both impaired praxis and postural knowledge suggest that autism may be associated with dysfunction within the parietal-premotor networks necessary to both execution and understanding of a wide range of skilled behavior. To further expand our understanding of the nature of these impairments and provide a model upon which to increase our knowledge, we advocate that the literature on motor control and motor learning theories from various fields and

disciplines be bridged with the current research related to motor impairments in ASD. Given the developmental nature of autism, a focus on motor learning is particularly crucial. An understanding of the phenomenology and neural basis of how children are impaired in their ability to acquire and subsequently generate skilled actions, and by extension, their ability to interpret the actions of others, can provide a basis for the development of novel interventions targeting not only generalized motor impairments, but the social/communicative skill deficits that define the disorder.

Multiple fields have contributed to an understanding of motor control and motor learning in typical human systems, including neurophysiology, psychology, physical education, kinesiology, engineering, robotics, and computational neuroscience (see Schmidt & Lee, 2011, for a review). In parallel to research on typically developing human systems have been translational efforts by neurology, psychology, occupational therapy, physical therapy, and speech language pathology, which have helped inform the clinical picture of impaired motor behaviors across a range of acquired and developmental conditions. Clinicians involved in the rehabilitation of children with ASD have conceptualized and theorized about the underlying problems in motor control and motor learning, in an effort to both (1) improve understanding of the neural basis of autism and (2) develop interventions aimed at increasing the individual's ability to independently participate in skilled behaviors necessary to motor, as well as social and communicative, function. While the literature on motor control and motor learning processes in typical and atypical human systems across disciplines appears, at least at first glance, quite disparate, an in-depth review and rigorous analysis reveals that many concepts are overlapping and interrelated, with slightly different terminology often used to represent similar constructs. With this in mind, we seek to provide a broad view of the current state of motor control and motor learning theories as they relate to the available research on motor impairments in individuals with ASD, with the unitary goal of informing the development and refinement of clinical interventions. To do this, the chapter will be organized into the following three sections: (1) overview of motor control and motor learning processes; (2) bridging theories of motor control and motor learning with research in ASD; and (3) recommendations for clinical interventions and future directions.

OVERVIEW OF MOTOR CONTROL AND MOTOR LEARNING PROCESSES

For the purposes of our discussion, we have chosen to include the constructs of motor control and motor learning into one overarching conceptual model (see Figure 15.1); this being consistent with findings from lesion, imaging, and brain stimulation studies showing substantial overlap in neural regions/systems underlying motor execution/control and its perquisite learning (Ayres, 1979, 2005; Gowen & Hamilton, 2013; Schmidt & Lee, 2011; Shadmehr & Krakauer, 2008; Shadmehr, Smith, & Krakauer, 2010; Shumway-Cook & Woollacott, 2007; Wolpert, Diedrichsen, & Flanagan, 2011; Wolpert, Gharamani & Jordan, 1995). While we recognize that there are extensive

fields of study devoted to each, our goal is simply to provide as comprehensive a conceptual framework as possible within which to situate the ever-growing research on motor impairments in ASD. It is not our intention to cover each concept in great detail or provide an extensive review of the supporting foundational research. This lies outside the nature and scope of this chapter.

As we begin our overview of the motor control and motor learning processes, we submit the following definitions to provide a basis for our discussion. Schmidt and Lee (2011) and Shumway-Cook and Woollacott (2007), define *motor control* as the central nervous system's ability to orchestrate and direct the mechanisms essential to movement. *Motor learning* is the process of acquiring the *capacity* (both neurologically and behaviorally) to produce skilled movements, which spurs relatively permanent changes in the human system's ability to perform increasingly more complex skilled motor behaviors over time (Kandel, Schwartz & Jessell, 2000; Schmidt & Lee, 2011). With these definitions in place, we provide an example of a typically developing 15-month-old girl learning to use a spoon to self-feed cereal and milk to illustrate these concepts in total.

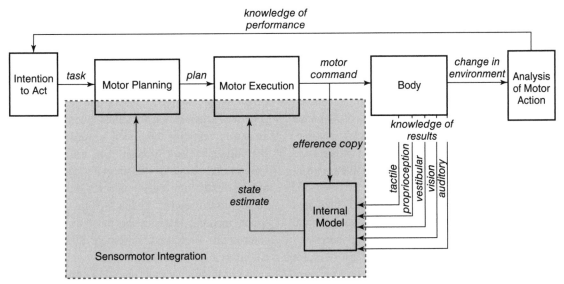

Figure 15.1 Conceptualization of motor control and motor learning processes (developed in collaboration with Terence D. Sanger).

Let us assume that the young child about whom we are thinking is positioned in a developmentally appropriate seating arrangement and can sit independently without external support. As she is presented with a spoon and a bowl of cereal with milk, her *intention to act on the environment* is spurred by her desire to eat. She automatically starts to *gather task-relevant sensory data*—including visual information about the location of the bowl, its relative distance to her arm and mouth; tactile and proprioceptive information about the spoon and its changing weight as she loads the spoon with cereal and milk—and she will continue to receive streams of sensory data across these different modalities throughout the task as she moves her arm forward and back, scoops the food, and places it into her mouth. As the sensory data collection continues, the central nervous system *filters and processes* that information so it can be integrated into a unified *state estimate* that will provide insight into the relative position of the child's hand on the spoon, the arm near the bowl or mouth, and so on. Then, as proposed by Shadmehr & Krakauer (2008), when the child generates a motor action, the expected sensory feedback is combined with the actual sensory feedback resulting in "sensorimotor maps that transform the internal belief about states into motor commands" (p. 362). In our example, this occurs when the goal of picking up the spoon, scooping the food, and bringing it to the mouth are all transformed into a series of *motor plans* and *motor commands*, which produce motor movements and ultimately, a *change in the environment* as anticipated (successful scooping of food and bringing to mouth). As is depicted in the highlighted area in Figure 15.1, *sensorimotor integration* involves a series of interactions involving individual components of motor control. From a neural system perspective, this sensorimotor integration has its basis in an integrated neural network involving, at a cortical level, frontal premotor-posterior (parietal) network necessary to generating and storing these sensory-motor maps, and subcortical input involving the cerebellum and basal ganglia (both via the thalamus),

crucial to respective error-based and reward-based modulation of intended actions.

During the execution of each movement, there are series of motor learning processes that influence the refinement and adaptation of the motor performance. The first of these processes relates to the types of *feedback during and after the movement*. One type of *internal feedback* relates directly to the sensory receptors that monitor the ongoing movement and provide updates as things progress—the child feels the weight of the spoon, uses visual and kinesthetic feedback to balance the cereal and milk, and so on. But because this type of internal feedback is limited by delays in transmission of the sensory data and potential noise in the system, additional internal feedback occurs as the motor commands are generated producing *efferent copies* that monitor the motor output and predict their sensory consequences. In our example, as the child scoops each bite of cereal and brings it to her mouth, she is receiving constant updates from the sensory receptors and at the same, her central nervous system is predicting what her movements should feel and look like so that if an error occurs, such as pronation of the arm that causes the cereal to spill, she can adjust the motor commands as needed. In tandem with this internal feedback, the child also receives *external or explicit feedback* about her performance. Most obvious is her knowledge of results, which specifically relates to whether or not she is able to successfully get the cereal into her mouth (the intended goal). The second type of explicit feedback, knowledge of performance, relates to the movement pattern she generates when trying to achieve the end goal. If, as she is bringing the spoon toward her mouth, she simultaneously pronates her arm so that the spoon turns upside down, she will begin to couple that particular movement pattern and the subsequent proprioceptive feedback with unsuccessful spoon feeding, learning the need to consciously control this unwanted movement until it can be automatically controlled.

Additionally, motor learning processes are influenced by the various *strategies used to aid the motor learning process* (see Wolpert et al., 2011). Cerebellar-mediated *error-based learning* occurs when the motor system compares the predicted sensory outcome to the actual movement. During this type of learning, the motor system not only provides information about whether the target or goal was missed, but the specific way the target or goal was missed (i.e., pronation of arm during elbow flexion when bringing spoon to mouth causes spillage). This error-based mechanism allows the motor system to make adjustments so that motor behaviors can be well calibrated and become increasingly more refined. *Reinforcement learning* seeks to provide increased information about the errors being made during movement and assigns credit or blame, possibly through explicit feedback mechanisms. The final learning mechanism, *use-dependent learning*, simply suggests that the motor system can be positively or negatively changed and adapted through the repetition of movement.

A quick review of the neural structures at work during these motor control and motor learning processes finds key roles for frontal-parietal connections, cerebellum, and basal ganglia circuitry (see Shadmehr & Krakauer, 2008, for a comprehensive review). The cerebellum assists in adaptation and error correction during movement as described by the learning processes above by constantly comparing competing copies of predicted sensory feedback and actual sensory feedback so that rapid changes in motor performance can be made as needed. The basal ganglia circuitry contributes to the learning process by providing rewards and estimating expected costs of each movement. With each successful motor interaction (i.e., specific motor movements support successful scooping of food that enters the child's mouth), the basal ganglia triggers a dopaminergic surge that (perhaps via projections to GABAergic cortical interneurons) reinforces the specific motor response so that there is an increased likelihood it will be repeated. Frontal-parietal connections integrate the predicted multimodal sensory outcomes with actual sensory feedback to form an internal belief about the state

of the body and the environment. These engrams or internal states are stored in this part of the brain and available for comparison with each new movement. Finally, the functions of the frontal premotor cortices are to transform the sensory predictions (or belief about internal state) into motor commands to be executed. It is the overarching transfer of sensory data to motor responses that is considered to be a process of sensorimotor integration.

A final note about our example simply reflects what has *not* been included in our discussion of the theories on motor control and motor planning. As articulated by Shumway-Cook and Woollacott (2007), the acquisition of motor skills and their adaptation within the human motor system does not occur in isolation. Specifically, all movement, and its subsequent adaptation, is influenced not only by the individualized components of the human system, but by the elements of the task itself and the environment within which the particular human system is operating. We have primarily highlighted for discussion the aspects within and about the individual, and so our emphasis will rest there. But no understanding of motor control and motor learning is complete without at least some recognition that the nature of the task and the changing environment can significantly alter motor performance and contribute to its development over time (for review see Ayres 2005, 2011; Shumway-Cook & Woollacott, 2007).

BRIDGING THEORIES OF MOTOR CONTROL AND MOTOR LEARNING WITH RESEARCH IN ASD

Within the framework of this model, we have organized our discussion of the motor impairments in ASD around three distinct processes that have been studied in autism: *goal directed reaching*, *postural stability*, and *motor learning*. For each process we discuss the findings in the context of the proposed model. As will be discussed below, the findings in autism warrant a particular emphasis on sensorimotor integration. Theories around the concepts of sensory integration and sensorimotor integration in autism have a long history, the discussion of which is beyond the scope of this chapter. Crucially, our discussion on sensory and motor integration will center on how sensory feedback is used to guide motor control and learning, as proposed in models of computational motor control (Shadmehr & Krakauer, 2008; Wolpert et al., 1995; Wolpert et al., 2011). Using this conceptualization, we propose that sensorimotor integration has its basis in an integrated neural network involving, at a cortical level, frontal premotor-posterior parietal network necessary to generating and storing of sensory-motor maps, and subcortical input involving the cerebellum and basal ganglia (both via the thalamus), crucial to respective error-based and reward-based modulation of intended actions. Disordered integration across this network can lead to anomalous patterns of internal model formation that may serve as a foundation for the varying types of motor impairments noted in ASD. Due to the nature of research on motor impairments in ASD to date, we acknowledge that not all aspects of motor control and/or motor learning processes have been explored and recognize that future work may expand our understanding of the complex nature of movement and their associated impairments in ASD.

Goal-Directed Reaching

In a line of research designed to explore how children assemble different motor acts into a coherent motor action, Cattaneo et al. (2007) and Fabbri-Destro, Cattaneo, Boria, and Rizzolatti (2009) implemented a series of studies to investigate the influence of the demands of a task, or the expected motor outcome, on global motor planning behavior. Using electromyography (EMG) techniques, Cattaneo et al. (2007) measured the activity of the mylohyoid (MH) muscle (used when opening the mouth) when children with ASD and their TD controls either grasped an object to eat or grasped an object to place into a container mounted on the shoulder. In the TD group, the MH muscle

showed EMG activity when the children reached for the object to eat, but not when they reached for the object to place into the container. This finding suggests that in TD children, the global motor plan and subsequent neural organization of the motor commands are informed by the intention and outcome of the movement to allow for an efficient and timely motor response. In contrast, the MH muscle of the children with ASD in this study did not show activation at the initiation of reach to either the condition of grasping the object to eat or grasping the object to place into the container. In fact, the children with ASD only showed MH activity as the object to eat was coming toward the mouth, indicating that they lacked the ability to construct a global motor plan and, instead, initiated each motor act as a separate action in the chain of movements. Fabbri-Destro et al. (2009) showed similar results using an experimental reach, grasp and place task where the final placement of the object was predetermined to go into one of two different sizes of containers. In this study, researchers measured the reach time and placing time of children with ASD compared TD age-matched controls. In the TD children, both reach time and placing time were significantly different across the two conditions as these children altered their motor plans to reflect the different sizes of the opening of the container into which they needed to place an object. This result suggests that the TD children were able to plan a visually guided motor action globally, before moving, rather than as a sequence of independent steps. In stark contrast, only the placing times differed in the children with ASD, not the reaching times, indicating that they made no changes to the planning of the reach and grasp components of the motor sequence irrespective of the size of the opening of the container. They only slowed down at the end of the motor sequence when some care was needed to get the object into a smaller opening, suggesting that children with ASD may be unable to organize their actions as a chain of motor acts because they have difficulty integrating the visual information about the task and environment and, instead, program single motor acts independently from each other. This inability to plan a sequence of movements with a global plan in mind based on an intended outcome could be detrimental to the child's ability to learn increasingly more complex series of actions over time, especially if the construction of single motor acts takes increasingly longer periods of time as the tasks become more complex.

In Dowd, McGinley, Taffe, and Rhinehart (2012), the upper-limb movement kinematics of children with HFA were explored during a point-to-point movement paradigm. While the children with ASD, on average, took a similar amount of time to perform the reach and grasp task as TD, they demonstrated increased variability in movement time preparation, sometimes giving less time to plan their movements, sometimes more. In another compelling finding from this study, Dowd et al. (2012) performed additional trials of the point-to-point movement task where they provided a visual distractor and instructed participants to ignore the extraneous visual data while completing the task. For the TD children, the addition of the visual distractor caused more variability in the time taken to plan their movements, decreased speed in movement execution and more variable time to peak acceleration than the children with ASD who, when faced with the same visual distractor, showed no real difference in movement planning or execution compared to trials without a visual distractor. This finding is significant because it suggests that TD children consider all sensory data (in this case, visual information) when planning and executing movements while children with ASD may not (essentially ignoring the visual information provided). This supports the notion that children with ASD may have difficulty accurately integrating visual sensory data into successful motor actions during goal-directed reaching movements.

It is imperative to note that across the studies exploring goal-directed reaching differences in children with ASD, the findings have relied on comparisons exclusively involving age-matched TD children. This makes it difficult to determine if the differences noted among children with ASD are specific to this population alone. It will be necessary for future investigations to include clinical comparison groups of children with other developmental disabilities, including specific language impairment, intellectual disability, DCD, and ADHD, in order to understand the extent to which disordered sensorimotor integration in goal-directed reaching is specific to ASD.

Postural Stability

The ability to maintain upright posture in humans is a fundamental skill, the components of which are well understood. Postural stability has been defined as the ability to maintain the projected center of mass within the base of support (Shumway-Cook & Woollacott, 2007) and requires precise integration between the somatosensory feedback generated by the forces of the ground and the reactionary motor responses of the body, the vestibular feedback generated by the pull of gravity, and the incoming visual information that provides feedback about the head and body position relative to the environment. Across the ASD literature, several researchers have contributed to our understanding of the postural stability issues in individuals with ASD by documenting their existence and specificity (Chang et al., 2010; Fournier, Hass, et al., 2010; Gepner, Mestre, Masson, & de Schonen, 1995; Kohen-Raz, Volkmar, & Cohen, 1992; Travers et al., 2012). While there may be multiple factors influencing the development of postural control, a few studies have demonstrated that the observed postural anomalies in individuals with ASD may be the result of impaired sensorimotor mechanisms, either with the individual with ASD relying too heavily on one sense over the other, or problems in effectively integrating all inputs to aid in precise postural control.

In one of the earliest examinations of the relative contributions of visual, somatosensory, and vestibular inputs on postural control, Molloy et al. (2003) examined the postural stability of boys with ASD to age-matched TD peers under varying conditions of somatosensory and visual input.

Under all conditions in which vision was occluded, the postural control of the children with ASD was significantly poorer than that of the TD children. There was not a significant difference in postural control between groups when participants stood on either the stable surface or foam pad with their eyes open, suggesting that the children with ASD in this study overrelied on visual cues to maintain their balance possibly due to deficits in the integration of somatosensory input.

Minshew et al. (2004) assessed the postural stability of children with high-functioning autism (HFA) compared to TD individuals under varying conditions where both somatosensory and visual information was altered. Using a commercially available dynamic posturography system (NeuroCom International, Clackamas, Oregon, USA), participants were required to maintain their balance with either eyes open or eyes closed during varying conditions where the floor plates were either stable or moving; or where the visual environment was either stable or moving. Results suggested that individuals with HFA presented with reduced postural stability, especially when the somatosensory input was disrupted by altering the actions of the footplates. In addition to these basic findings about postural control, Mishew et al. (2004) also explored the effect of age on the acquisition of postural mechanisms. Results suggested that, unlike their typically developing peers whose balance improved steadily from 5 years to 15–20 years of age, where it plateaued at adult-like levels, the individuals with HFA did not begin to show improved postural responses until the age of 12, and their overall postural responses never reached TD adult-like levels.

Recently, a group of investigators (Greffou et al., 2012) were able to undertake a detailed assessment of the role of vision in postural reactivity. They examined younger and older individuals with ASD using a fully immersive virtual environment where the dynamicity of the visual environment was manipulated. All participants stood in an upright position on a stable surface while immersed in a virtual tunnel where the walls of the tunnel were either stable or oscillated at various frequencies. As the participants looked straight ahead at a red-dot on the horizon, their body-sway and postural perturbations were measured using a motion tracking system. Both age groupings of ASD participants were able to translate and integrate the sensory information into an appropriate postural response under most experimental conditions, except when the processing and integration of fast visual stimuli was required. Specifically, the younger individuals with ASD were hyporeactive to the fast, oscillating visual environment such that they did not demonstrate the same level of postural perturbations as their typically developing peers. These results suggest that children with ASD may have a visual motion integration deficit such that the atypical postural reactivity observed in ASD may be specific to fast moving visual stimulation and a delay in the integration of visual, somatosensory, and vestibular inputs.

In sum, the findings from studies of postural control in autism are somewhat conflicting, with some suggesting an over reliance on visual feedback to compensate for poor integration of somatosensory and vestibular inputs during postural tasks on both stable and unstable surfaces; while a more recent study suggesting that children with ASD are underresponsive to visual feedback during postural control. Additionally, as was the case with research studies involving goal-directed reaching, the specificity of these findings is yet to be determined, and future studies of postural control would benefit from inclusion of clinical control groups of children with other developmental disabilities.

Motor Learning

In neuroscience, internal models have been conceptualized by Shadmehr and Mussa-Ivaldi (1994) and Shadmehr and Krackauer (2008) as the central nervous system's ability to monitor the motor output produced by the individual and predict the sensory consequences of that motor output so that motor performance can be quickly adjusted depending on the task and the environment. In this model, the cerebellum is thought to play a role in predicting the sensory consequences of motor commands, while the parietal cortex combines the expected sensory feedback with the actual sensory feedback to compute a belief about the current state of the system. In occupational therapy, the concept of internal models and state estimates is closely linked to the development of body schema as multisensory inputs are integrated in the postparietal cortex to establish sensory maps or engrams upon which motor plans can be generated (Ayres, 1979, 2005).

Examination of upper-limb motor control in ASD has revealed fundamental differences in the way children with ASD form internal models of action necessary to learning novel movement patterns. The findings have principally come from examination of motor adaptation, that is, the ability to adjust motor output based on a perceived sensory change. Studies using a wide range of adaptation tasks reveal that children with ASD are able to adapt their motor output by forming a predictive internal model, with rates of acquisition and decay that, by-and-large, are not different from those of TD children (Gidley Larson, Bastian, Donchin, Shadmehr, & Mostofsky, 2008; Mostofsky, Bunoski, Morton, Goldberg, & Bastian, 2004). However, studies suggest that despite the normal rate of acquisition, children with ASD show a fundamental difference in the pattern of sensorimotor integration underlying learning—specifically, that they show a bias toward reliance on proprioceptive, as opposed to visual, feedback to guide motor adaption. In one such study, Haswell et al. (2009), children used a novel tool (a robotic arm) and learned to compensate for force perturbations produced by the robotic device. Analysis of the patterns of generalization revealed that in learning an internal model of the novel tool, children with ASD showed an abnormal bias for reliance on proprioceptive, rather than visual, feedback to guide motor learning. That is, the sense of proprioception and its association with motor commands, which is mediated by connections between primary motor and somatosensory cortices, appeared to be abnormally up-regulated. In contrast, the association

between visual input and motor commands, which is mediated by longer-range connections between premotor and posterior parietal cortices, appeared to be abnormally down-regulated. The findings are consistent with those from a study of prism adaptation revealing that, in contrast to children with developmental delay and TD controls, children with autism appeared to rely on proprioceptive rather than visual feedback to adapt arm movement (Masterson & Biederman, 1983). Demonstrated specificity for this anomalous bias in sensorimotor integration was revealed in a follow up study in which children with ADHD showed a pattern of generalization consistent with that of TD children and significantly different than that of children with ASD (Izawa et al., 2012). Perhaps most relevant, in both the Haswell et al. (2009) and follow-up Izawa et al. (2012) studies, it was observed that the bias toward reliance on proprioceptive rather than visual feedback was a robust predictor of impaired motor imitation, praxis, and basic motor skill in children with autism, as well as measures of the core social/communicative features of autism.

These altered patterns of motor learning and disordered sensorimotor integration in ASD may have their basis in altered patterns of neural connectivity (Mostofsky & Ewen, 2011). Several lines of evidence in autism point to abnormal patterns of cerebral connectivity (Belmonte et al., 2004; Casanova et al., 2006; Herbert et al., 2004), with an overgrowth of localized connectivity between neighboring regions, including primary motor and somatosensory cortices necessary to encoding proprioceptive-motor feedback, and decreased long-range connectivity that would include parietal-premotor connections necessary to encoding visual-motor feedback. Data derived from magnetoencephalography techniques in individuals with ASD, in fact, reveal enlarged somatotopic cortical representations of the thumb and lip in individuals within the somatosensory cortex (Coskun et al., 2009). Additionally, increased white matter volume within primary sensorimotor cortex was found to predict impaired basic motor skill performance in children with ASD, in contrast to TD children and children with ADHD for whom increased volume predicted better motor skill function (Mostofsky et al., 2006).

Alternatively, disordered sensorimotor integration during motor learning in autism may be due to dysfunction within the cerebellum. Functional MRI has revealed that children with ASD show increased activation in anterior cerebellar regions involved in somatosensorimotor integration (Allen, Muller, & Courchesne, 2004) with simple finger movements and decreased activation of posterior cerebellar regions important for visuomotor integration during performance of a more complex skilled finger sequencing task (Mostofsky et al., 2009). The findings, which are consistent with the known predilection for Purkinje cell loss in posterior cerebellum (Bauman & Kemper, 2005), suggest a possible cerebellar basis for the observed bias for reliance on proprioceptive rather than visual feedback.

In sum, a review of the literature in ASD across the various categories described here lend support to the hypothesis that children with ASD show disordered sensorimotor integration, specifically demonstrating a bias toward use of proprioception, rather than the use of vision, to guide upper-limb motor control. In considering the acquisition of motor skills as a developmental process whereby the learning of motor skills is optimized by accurate internal models, it is not surprising then that children with ASD display delays in the attainment of many motor skills and development of various complex abilities, including those related to communication and socialization. As we consider the overall findings related to sensorimotor integration, it provides a basis to better understand the oft observed problems with imitation and praxis, especially related to understanding others. Specifically, if children with ASD have an impaired ability to integrate the visual information from the environment into successful motor plans involving limb control, it will prove difficult for them to acquire internal models of action through imitation of others. This could contribute

to delayed and atypical development of motor skills necessary to engaging in motor, as well as social and communicative, behavior.

RECOMMENDATIONS FOR CLINICAL INTERVENTIONS AND FUTURE DIRECTIONS

As stated at the outset, our review of the motor control and motor learning processes relative to the literature on motor impairments in ASD would not be complete without some tie to the clinical interventions currently being employed by clinicians and those under development. Our comprehensive review, especially related to motor planning (Gidley Larson et al., 2008; Haswell et al., 2009; Izawa et al., 2012), suggests a core feature of motor dysfunction in autism may be a lack of efficient integration of visual feedback with a bias towards increased reliance on proprioceptive feedback. This may provide a basis for understanding the consistent findings of impaired performance of skilled gestures on praxis examination, with associated deficits in motor imitation reliant on visual-motor integration, contributing to delayed and atypical formation of internal action models necessary to both performance skilled motor (as well as social and communicative) gestures as well as to understanding the intention of others' actions. Given these findings, we suggest that one possible strategy when targeting improvements in motor behavior may be to exploit the relative proprioceptive strengths demonstrated by children with ASD to assist in the development of motor skills. Using this "play to the strengths" conceptualization has a long history in occupational therapy, where a classic model of intervention guided by a focus on sensorimotor integration has been regularly employed with children with ASD showing promising results (Pfeiffer, Koenig, Kinnealey, Sheppard, & Henderson, 2011; Schaaf, Benevides, Kelly, & Mailloux-Maggio, 2012). That said, the mechanisms by which one acquires action models necessary to both performing and understanding others' social behavior is likely dependent on motor imitation, and therefore necessitating efficient use of visual feedback in guiding motor control and learning. Given this, it will be imperative for future investigations to explore the role of applying Hebbian principles to engaging neuroplasticity such that children with ASD are better able to incorporate visual feedback for sensorimotor integration necessary to acquiring motor skills important for engaging in social and communicative behavior. As suggested by Lainé, Rauzy, Tardif, and Gepner (2011), given that the difficulty with visual-motor integration in ASD may be related to difficulty with efficient transcoding of biological motion, behavioral training involving the simplification of visual stimuli, for instance, slowing down the speed of presentation, may have some initial efficacy for improving motor imitation in autism. Alternatively, up-regulation of neural networks necessary to visual-motor connectivity could involve either brain stimulation, for instance, using transcranial direct current stimulation (tDCS) or behavioral training focusing on engagement in tasks requiring repeated practice of motion prompted by increasingly complex visual input, including biological motion.

We hope the review offered in this chapter has provided a model within which to view the motor impairments of ASD, and we anticipate that future research efforts will provide additional insight into the further specificity of these impairments. As research into the effectiveness of clinical interventions related to social, communication, and motor impairments expands, we turn to a recent consensus report to evaluate the effectiveness of interventions for children with ASD for recommendations to guide future research efforts. The Agency for Healthcare Research and Quality (AHRQ) report (Warren et al. 2011) summarized an extensive review of the effectiveness of multiple interventions for children with ASD, including early intensive behavioral and developmental, educational, medical, allied health, and complementary and alternative medicine. While the review found that most of the literature to date across these interventions is insufficient to truly evaluate their effectiveness, one of the most significant outcomes of this report is recommendations for researchers and clinicians about ways in which to conduct future studies measuring the effectiveness of interventions. Specifically, this report highlighted the need for substantial improvements in methodologic rigor for all therapies in the field such that manuals specifying the intervention procedures under study be standardized and measures taken to ensure fidelity to the prescribed intervention. In addition, the AHRQ report recommended that future intervention studies consider multisite trials, so that replication of intervention results can be measured across sites. Finally, and most importantly relative to the population of children with ASD, the AHRQ report summarized the need for better characterization of children, both phenotypically and genotypically, to move toward personalization of treatments for improved outcomes. When considering the motor impairments in ASD and varied history of impairments documented over time, it is imperative that future research move to characterize these impairments within a framework of motor control and motor learning theories so that interventions can be developed that target the underlying neural circuitry rather than the discrete motor skills. By doing so, we argue that improvements in motor control, which may serve as a foundation of support for communication and socialization skills, will be generalizable across multiple contexts and activities and support the growth and development of the whole child.

CROSS-REFERENCES

Issues of imitation are discussed in Chapter 12 and neuropsychological functioning in Chapter 13. Chapter 16 addresses sensory features in autism. Aspects of multidisciplinary intervention are discussed in Chapter 26. Comprehensive treatment programs are addressed in Chapter 30 and evidence-based treatments in Chapter 42.

APPENDIX 15.1: SUMMARY OF THE LITERATURE ON MOTOR IMPAIRMENTS IN AUTISM SPECTRUM DISORDERS

First Author (Year)	Research Goals or Questions	Subjects			Assessments		Findings Related to Specific Area of Motor Impairment
		Groups	N	Mean Age	Motor	Other	
Dyspraxia							
Dewey (2007)	To determine the extent to which deficits in gesture reflect impairment in motor skill in children with DCD, ASD, ADHD, and DCD+ADHD. Also, to examine the differences between the disorders in specific types of gestural errors.	ASD DCD ADHD DCD+ ADHD TD	49 46 27 38 78	10.2 y 11.7 y 12.0 y 11.3 y 11.3 y	BOT2-S MABC DCDQ GT	ADI-R CARS	Children with ASD, DCD, and ADHD all display deficits in motor skills compared to TD. However, not all children with ADHD displayed impairments in motor functioning. Overall, children with ASD were substantially more impaired than children with specific motor skills deficits. And although children with ASD, DCD and DCD+ADHD displayed impairments in motor skill relative to TD, only the children with ASD showed deficits in the performance of gestures.
Dowell (2009)	To determine whether dyspraxia in ASD is associated with impaired representational (postural) knowledge and to examine the contributions of postural knowledge and basic motor skill on dyspraxia in ASD.	ASD TD	37 50	10.26 y 10.55 y	FAB PANESS	ADOS ADI-R DICA WISC	Children with ASD show significant impairments on praxis examinations, even after accounting for age, IQ, basic motor skill, and postural knowledge. Both measures of basic motor skill and postural knowledge were significant predictors of praxis performance. Performance on the praxis examination was correlated with the behavioral characteristics of ASD as measured by the ADOS.
Dziuk (2007)	To examine the correlation between performance on a praxis exam and basic motor skill in ASD versus TD. Also to explore associations between praxis skills and ADOS scores.	ASD TD	47 47	10.7 y 10.6 y	FAB-R PANESS	ADOS ADI-R	After accounting for age and FSIQ, there was a significant effect of basic motor skill on praxis performance. In the children with ASD, the level of impairment on the praxis exam significantly correlated with total ADOS score, which suggests that the impaired performance of skilled gestures may contribute to impaired social interaction and communication skills.
Gidley Larson (2008)	To investigate the ability of HFA to acquire internal models of action when compared to TD across three well-studied protocols of motor adaptation.	HFA TD	21 20	None listed!	Motor adaptation tasks	ADI-R ADOS WISC DICA	Children with HFA showed similar extent and time course of adaptation, and similar postadaptation aftereffects to TD. Results suggest that children with HFA improved their performances through formation of predictive internal models, with rates of acquisition and forgetting similar to TD.
Ham (2011)	To examine praxis skills in ASD by assessing gesture recognition and imitation using transitive, intransitive, and pantomime gestures.	ASD TD	19 23	12.1 y 12.0 y	VMI WMTBC	ADOS SCQ WASI	Results revealed that in all tasks of recognition and imitation, the ASD group performed significantly worse than TD. Intransitive gesture recognition was the most difficult task, followed by pantomime and object recognition.
MacNeil (2012)	To explore the specificity of impaired basic motor control, postural knowledge, and praxis performance in ASD compared to TD and ADHD.	ASD ADHD TD	24 24 24	9.69 y 9.73 y 10.33	PANESS FAB-R PKT	ADI-R DICA WISC	Children with ASD exhibited impairments in basic motor skill, postural knowledge, and praxis performance. Children with ADHD exhibited impairments in basic motor skill. ASD showed impaired recognition and performance of skilled gestures.

Study	Purpose	Group	N	Age	Measure	Measure	Findings
Mostofsky (2000)	To investigate judgment of explicit time intervals and procedural learning in participants with AUT and TD.	AUT TD	11 17	13.3 y 12.5 y	SRTT JTT	ADI-R ADOS	Compared to TD, AUT had impaired ability to acquire procedural knowledge based on a lack of significant reduction in response time on specific trials of the SRTT and a significantly lower rebound in reaction time. AUT demonstrated normal ability to judge explicit time intervals.
Mostofsky (2006)	To determine whether the pattern of dyspraxia errors in children with ASD differ from TD and to examine the associations of praxis with age.	ASD TD	21 24	10.6 y 10.6 y	FAB-R	ADOS ADI-R DICA WISC	Children with ASD showed impaired performance of gestures not only with imitation, but in response to verbal command and with tool use. Findings suggest that neural processes specific to imitation cannot entirely account for impaired performance. Correlation of dyspraxia errors with age suggest delayed rather than disordered development of gestural skills.

Gross and Fine Motor Skills

Study	Purpose	Group	N	Age	Measure	Measure	Findings
Freitag (2007)	To compare the simple and complex nonadaptive motor movements, adaptive motor skills, and associated movements of individuals with HFA/AS versus TD.	HFA/AS TD	16 16	16.4 y 17. 9 y	ZNA	ADI-R ADOS WISC CBCL	The motor performance of the HFA/AS individuals versus TD was impaired, specifically with regard to dynamic balance skills and diadochokinesis. In addition, poor motor performance was strongly associated with the CBCL social withdrawal subscore in the HFA/AS group.
Green (2009)	To measure the prevalence of movement impairments in ASD and to examine the association between severity of movement impairment and adaptive behavior, independent of IQ.	ASD	101	11.4 y	MABC DCDQ	WISC VABS	Movement problems were nearly universal in the subgroup of ASD with an IQ below 70, but they occurred in only two thirds of ASD with an IQ of 70 or more. Movement impairments were not associated with everyday adaptive behavior once the effect of IQ was accounted for. The DCDQ performed moderately well as a screen for movement impairments compared to the MABC.
Hilton (2012)	Is motor impairment present in unaffected siblings (UAS) of children with ASD? What is the relationship between degree of motor impairment and autistic severity in children with ASD?	ASD ASD Sib UAS	67 29 48	9.8 y 9.11 y 9.11 y	BOT2 DCDQ	ADI SRS	In ASD, motor proficiency was impaired and the degree of motor impairment correlated with the degree of social impairment. Motor proficiency was not impaired in UAS. The DCDQ showed moderately strong correlations (.79) with the BOT2 suggesting that it could serve as a proxy measure for motor impairment when direct measurement of motor skills is not feasible.
Jansiewicz (2006)	To examine the full range of subtle neurological signs in motor control of ASD; to determine if there are any motor distinctions between HFA and AS; to assess the discriminative strength of the PANESS.	ASD TD	40 55	11.4 y 11.6 y	PANESS	ADI ADOS DICA WISC	No significant motor differences were found between HFA and AS on the PANESS. Compared to TD, children with ASD showed impaired performance on the PANESS including balance and gait, slower speed and more dysrhythmia with timed movements of the hands and feet, and overflow during performance of timed movements. PANESS variables were powerful enough to effectively distinguish between ASD and TD.

(continued)

APPENDIX 15.1 (Continued)

Gross and Fine Motor Skills

First Author (Year)	Research Goals or Questions	Subjects			Assessments		Findings Related to Specific Area of Motor Impairment
		Groups	N	Mean Age	Motor	Other	
Lloyd (2011)	To describe and compare the gross and fine motor skills of ASD 12–36 months of age; to describe the gross and fine motor skills of ASD over two time periods, 6 months apart.	ASD	162	20.4 m 27.7 m 33.3 m	MSEL	ADI-R ADOS	Results suggested that the gross and fine motor skills of young children with ASD are delayed and become progressively more delayed with age, even when controlling for nonverbal problem-solving skills. Motor deficits should not be a secondary concern when planning and implementing early intervention programs for young children with ASD.
Ming (2007)	To describe the prevalence of motor deficits (hyportonia, motor apraxia, reduced ankle mobility, history of gross motor delay, and toe-walking) in ASD and the improvement of these symptoms with age.	ASD	154	6 y	Physical exam Denver II	ADI-R ADOS CARS	The distribution of motor impairments across ASD subtypes did not appear to be significantly different. Sixty-three percent of ASD aged 2–6 years and 38% of HFA aged 7–18 years presented with hypotonia. 41% of ASD aged 2–6 years and 27% of HFA aged 7–18 years presented with apraxia. Nineteen percent of all ASD exhibited toe-walking for an estimated minimum of 6 months during the child's life. Nine percent of all ASD had a history of gross motor delay.
Noterdaeme (2010)	To compare the cognitive profile, language, motor performance, and psychosocial functioning of children with AS and HFA.	AS HFA	57 55	11.2 y 10.6 y	Neurological exam	ADOS ADI-R	Motor problems were identified in 53% of children with AS and 47% of children with HFA. The main difference between AS and HFA was the presence of an early language delay. Seventy percent of AS and 74% of HFA in this simple were at least moderately to severely impaired with respect to psychosocial functioning.
Papadopoulos (2011)	To investigate the neuromotor profile of HFA and AS in relation to emotional-behavioral disturbance.	AS HFA LFA TD	22 23 8 20	9.10 y 9.4 y 9.9 y 9.10 y	MABC DBC-P	ADI CARS WISC WASI	Results suggested that HFA and AS are associated with different neuromotor profiles. The degree of motor impairment experienced by HFA and AS may help predict the degree of emotional behavioral disturbance.
Staples (2010)	To compare the performance of fundamental movement skills in children with ASD to three groups of TD children matched on chronological age (TDCA), movement skill development (TDDEV), and cognitive development (TDMA).	ASD TDCA TDDEV TDMA	25 21 18 16	11.1 y 11.1 y 5.87 y 7.75 y	TGMD	ADOS SRS Leiter	ASD demonstrated poor motor performance compared to TDCA, and had particular difficulty coordinating movements that involved both sides of their body or both arms and legs. Many children with ASD had difficulty controlling the force and direction when throwing or kicking a ball. On the TGMD, ASD performed similarly to TDDEV who were half their age, suggesting a significant delay in development. When compared to TDMA, ASD's poor motor performance cannot be attributed to cognition.

Author (year)	Aim	Group	N	Age	Task	Tests	Findings
Travers (2010)	To examine motor-linked implicit learning in persons with ASD under conditions that minimized the influence of explicit learning processes.	ASD TD	15 18	19.0 y 19.0 y	SRTT	ADI-R ADOS SRS	ASD and TD showed similar amounts of learning of a 12-step sequence. Results suggested that motor-linked implicit learning is likely intact with ASD. No significant correlations between motor-linked implicit learning and symptom severity in ASD were found.

Motor Planning

Author (year)	Aim	Group	N	Age	Task	Tests	Findings
Cattaneo (2007)	Is there is a difference between TD children and those with ASD in their ability to respond to the observation of actions performed by others and also in the organization of their own actions?	ASD TD	7 8	6.2 y 6.5 y	Reach to grasp experimental task EMG	ADOS ADI-R WISC WPPSI	During the observation of eating action, a marked increase of oral motor muscle activity was seen in TD children during the reaching phase. This increase became more evident during grasping and persisted during bringing to the mouth. No increase of oral motor muscle activity was present during the observation of the placing action. In contrast, the children with autism did not show any oral motor muscle activation during either the observation of eating or placing actions, suggesting they disordered motor planning.
Dowd (2012)	To investigate the motor planning and execution patterns of young children with ASD using kinematics.	ASD TD	11 12	6.2 y 6.6 y	Kinematics	DBC-P WISC WPPSI	Children with ASD demonstrated increased variability in the time taken to prepare point-to-point movements compared to TD. ASD had greater variability in movement preparation, sometimes giving less time to plan their movements, sometimes more.
Fabbri-Destro (2009)	What is the influence of the demands of the task on motor behavior in children with ASD? Can children with ASD assemble different motor acts into a coherent action?	ASD TD	12 14	10.0 y 7.6 y	Reach to grasp experimental task	ADOS WISC	In TD children, the difficulty of the final motor act in a sequence of motor actions influenced the movement time of the first one in the chain so that reaching time increases with the difficulty of the final motor act. Children with ASD were unable to translate their motor intention into an action. They programed single motor acts independently, one from another.
Rinehart, Bellgrove (2006)	Do children with HFA and AS show qualitatively different motor planning deficits but intact movement execution?	HFA AS	12 12	8.1 y 12.0 y	Kinematics	ADI WPPSI WISC WAIS	Both children with HFA and AS had deficits at the motor planning, rather than motor execution stage. Children with HFA had more consistently impaired motoric preparation/initiation than individuals with AS.

(continued)

APPENDIX 15.1 (Continued)

First Author (Year)	Research Goals or Questions	Subjects			Assessments		Findings Related to Specific Area of Motor Impairment
		Groups	N	Mean Age	Motor	Other	

Postural Control and Gait

First Author (Year)	Research Goals or Questions	Groups	N	Mean Age	Motor	Other	Findings Related to Specific Area of Motor Impairment
Chang (2010)	To examine the influence of suprapostural visual tasks on the postural control of TD children and those with ASD.	ASD TD	16 22	8.75 y 8.93 y	Kinematics	None	Overall magnitude of postural sway during upright stance was greater among children with ASD than TD. Both ASD and TD children reduced the postural variability of their head and torso during visual tasks requiring participants to search a block of text for designated target letters while standing.
Fournier, Kimberg (2010)	Do children with ASD have postural control impairments during both static and dynamic postural challenges?	ASD TD	13 12	11.1 y 12.9 y	Force plates	ADOS SCQ CARS	Children with ASD demonstrated increased postural sway in quiet stance and postural instabilities associated with the dynamic task of gait initiation.
Memari (2013)	To examine if children with ASD have a propensity to sway more than their TD peers in all of the sway parameters.	ASD TD	21 30	11.5 y 11.6 y	Force plates	ADI-R ATEC AQ	Children with ASD showed differing patterns of postural sway in mediolateral versus anteroposterior directions compared to TD. In addition, the results suggested that autism symptom severity was related to the amount of postural sway in children with ASD.
Nayate (2012)	In AUT, AS, and TD, to investigate gait control by manipulating walking speed; the effects of cuing strategies to improve gait; and high-level information processing in the context of gait.	AUT AS TD	11 11 11	12.9 y 11.9 y 13.4 y	Gait analysis	ADI WISC WAIS	Results show a distinction in gait patterning associated with AUT and AS. In AUT, wide base of support was consistently found across the preferred-, fast-, and slow-speed walking conditions. In AS, variable base of support was present only during preferred walking. In AUT, results also revealed increased stride length at any given cadence when compared to TD.
Nobile (2011)	To gather data on the locomotion system of non-mentally impaired and drug-naive children with ASD.	ASD TD	16 16	10.5 y 9.9 y	Gait analysis	ADOs ADI-R WISC	ASD showed impaired performance on a variety of motor parameters including upper body kinematics, walk orientation, and smoothness. Data suggested the presence of a pervasive impairment in movements involving not only basic motor skills (linear gait parameters) but also motor control strategies based on processing and integration of sensorimotor information.
Rinehart, Tonge, Iansek (2006)	To assess whether newly diagnosed children with AUT show variable stride length together with variable stride duration.	AUT TD	11 11	5.10 y 5.9 y	Gait analysis	ADI-R DBC WPPSI WISC	AUT children in this sample had greater difficulty walking in a straight line, reduced stride irregularity with increased variability in velocity, and the coexistence of variable stride length and duration. Results suggested that gait variables might be useful for clinical definition of the disorder.

Study	Objective	Group	N	Age	Task	Measures	Findings
Rinehart, Tonge, Bradshaw (2006)	To conduct a gait study comparing normally intelligent individuals with HFA and AS to TD controls.	HFA AS TD	10 10 10	126 m 129 m 128 m	Gait analysis	ADI	HFA showed increased stride-length variability in gait compared to TD across all three walking conditions. HFA did not show reduced stride length or show any improvements in gait function with additional external cues. No significant differences were found between HFA and AS on direct comparison of gait measures.
Travers (2012)	Examination of postural stability and postural symmetry in ASD versus TD. Examination of relationship between ASD symptom severity and postural stability and symmetry.	ASD TD	26 26	21.8 y 21.3 y	Nintendo Wii	ADOS ADI-R RBS-R SRS WASI	Participants with ASD lost balance significantly earlier than TD during one-legged stance. ASD participants demonstrated more drift and more waver during one-legged stance. During two-legged stance, the ability to stand symmetrically with eyes closed and postural waver were positively related to ASD symptom severity.

Reaching, Grasping, Tool Use, Handwriting

Study	Objective	Group	N	Age	Task	Measures	Findings
Beversdorf (2001)	To explore if individuals with ASD exhibit larger handwriting than TD children.	ASD TD	10 13	30.8 y 30.6 y	Handwriting Samples	WAIS	Adults with ASD exhibited macrographia when handwriting samples were compared with age-matched TD, even when covaried with educational level.
David (2009)	To explore if children with HFA have abnormalities in temporal coordination of grip and load forces during precision grip.	HFA TD	13 13	11.2 y 10.8 y	EHI GD	SCQ	Children with HFA displayed significantly different temporal dyscoordination between grip and load forces while performing a precision grip task when compared with TD. One weakness highlighted was fact that there was no comparative diagnostic group. See David 2012.
David (2012)	What are the developmental correlates of motor coordination in children with ASD? To what extent are motor coordination deficits unique to ASD? What is the association between motor coordination variables and FM skills?	ASD DD TD	24 11 30	54.0 m 54.5 m 47.3 m	EHI GD MSEL VABS	ADOS ADI-R CARS LIPS-R	No statistically significant associations found between fine motor skills and any of the four motor coordination variables assessed experimentally with the grasping device. Mental age (MA) appears to be an important variable in predicting motor performance across groups, especially for grip to load force onset latencies and time to peak grip force. ASD and developmentally delayed (DD) groups could not be differentiated on their motor performance during the precision grasp tasks, suggesting that temporal coordination deficits found are most likely due to MA and not unique to ASD.
Fuentes (2009)	Do children with ASD show handwriting impairments and if so, are they in specific qualitative categories?	ASD TD	14 14	10.2 y 11.1 y	MHA PANESS	ADOS ADI-R WASI WISC	No significant difference between groups in age, PRI, or block design score. Motor performance predicted overall handwriting quality as well as performance on some subtests of MHA. Therapies targeting motor control are the best approach to improve handwriting in ASD.

(continued)

APPENDIX 15.1 (Continued)

First Author (Year)	Research Goals or Questions	Groups	N	Mean Age	Motor	Other	Findings Related to Specific Area of Motor Impairment
		Subjects			Assessments		
Reaching, Grasping, Tool Use, Handwriting							
Fuentes, Mostofsky, and Bastian (2010)	Do adolescents with ASD show handwriting impairments and if so, are they in specific qualitative categories?	ASD TD	14 14	10.2 y 11.1 y	MHA PANESS	ADOS ADI-R WASI WISC	No significant difference between groups in age, full-scale IQ, verbal comprehension index, or PRI. Significant differences noted between TD and ASD on PANESS, MHA total, and MHA spacing. PRI predicted handwriting scores in ASD group.
Hellinckx (2013)	To what extent do demographic, perceptual, motor, and cognitive variables predict handwriting quality and speed in children with ASD?	ASD TD	69 61	10.9 y 10.3 y	MABC-2 SSH VMI	FSIQ OMRT	In children with ASD, age, gender, and visual-motor integration skills predicted handwriting quality; whereas age, reading abilities, and manual dexterity predicted writing speed.
Schmitz (2003)	To examine how anticipatory postural adjustments develop in children with ASD during a bimanual load-lifting task.	ASD TD	8 16	7.9 y 6.0 y	Force, elbow rotation and EMG	CARS	In children with ASD, the muscular event enabling postural stabilization during bimanual load-lifting tasks was not anticipated as in TD, but corresponded to a feedback response. For these children, they slow down their motor responses to give themselves time to react rather than predict the movement.
Sensorimotor Integration							
Abu-Dahab (2012)	To examine motor and tactile-perceptual impairments in children within three age groups (young, middle, older) with HFA versus TD. Evaluation of motor skills was limited to grip strength, motor speed, and coordination.	*HFA* young middle older *TD* young middle older	12 23 38 2 26 37	6.69 y 9.92 y 14.9 y 6.74 y 10.4 y 15.0 y	Dynamometer FTT Grooved pegboard	ADOS ADI-R Luria Reitan-Klove	The individuals with HFA demonstrated lower motor skills compared to TD and had lower levels of tactile-perceptual skills on the tests of stereognosis and finger recognition skills. Weakness in grip strength appears to be present from a young age for children with HFA and persists through adolescence and early adulthood. Findings also indicated that HFA performed significantly worse than TD on motor speed and that the difference increased with age. Results suggested that incoordination problems in HFA appear to decrease with age.
Fuentes (2011)	To establish whether there are proprioceptive differences in ASD on a peripheral level or in how the information is neurally represented and integrated with efferent information.	ASD TD	12 12	14.4 13.8	PANESS KINARM EMG	ADOS ADI-R SP	Participants with ASD showed comparable proprioceptive accuracy and precision on the KINEARM tasks compared to TD. Based on performance on the PANESS and specific difficulties noted on the SP, the ASD participants in this study demonstrated movement-related sensory and motor execution impairments. Combined with the findings on the KINEARM tasks, results suggested that the movement processing impairments did not arise from peripheral proprioceptive deficits.

Author (year)	Aim/Question	Group	N	Age	Task	Assessment	Findings
Greffou (2012)	Postural reactivity and stability was measured in two age groups of ASD versus TD children to assess the visual and vestibular components of posture activity.	ASD TD ASD TD	8 11 8 23	13.0 y 13.6 y 21.0 y 23.0 y	FIVE	ADOS ADI-R WISC	ASD demonstrated similar postural behaviors to TD under most conditions, except when the processing and integration of fast visual stimuli was required. Findings suggested that atypical postural behavior observed in ASD may be due to integrative deficits between the vestibular and visual and/or somatosensory input.
Haswell (2009)	Is there a fundamental difference in how children with ASD build associations between their motor commands and the sensory feedback received during a motor action?	ASD TD	14 13	10.5 y 10.4 y	Reach adaptation task PANESS	ADOS ADI-R WISC SRS	When children with ASD learn a motor task, the internal models they form create a stronger than normal association between the self-generated motor commands and proprioception. See Izawa 2012, for a follow-up study including an additional diagnostic group.
Izawa (2012)	When compared to TD children and those with ADHD, do children with ASD uniquely demonstrate an altered motor learning pattern with a bias for relying on joint position rather than visual feedback?	ASD ADHD TD	23 17 20	10.4 y 10.8 y 10.9 y	Reach adaptation task PANESS	ADOS ADI-R DICA WIAT WISC CPRSR SRS	During adaptation of reaching movements that acquired motor memory, children with ASD showed atypical generalization patterns when compared to children with ADHD and TD. Specifically, children with ASD strongly relied on propricoceptive information over visual feedback. The generalization patterns of the children with ADHD were indistinguishable from the TD children suggesting that the anamalous pattern is specific to ASD.
Jasmin (2009)	To assess the association of sensory responses and motor skills with daily living skills of preschool children with.	ASD	35	44.1 m	PDMS-2	ADOS ADI-R SSP VABS WeeFIM	Preschool children with ASD presented with atypical sensory responses, motor difficulties, and difficulties with daily-living skills compared to TD. Several significant correlations were found between sensory processing and daily-living skills, suggesting that atypical somatosensory responses may explain difficulties with gross motor skills and be related to motor planning.
Mari (2003)	To examine the movement of children with ASD during reach-to-grasp movements.	ASD TD	20 20	9.0-13.1 y 8.0-12.5 y	Kinematics	WISC	The reach-to-grasp patterns exhibited by adolescents with ASD suggested that they had difficulty initiating, switching, efficiently performing, or continuing ongoing motor actions.
Minshew (2004)	In individuals with ASD without intellectual disability, are there impairments in postural stability and any age effects?	HFA TD	79 61	17.0 y 16.7 y	EquiTest	ADOS ADI	ASD subjects have reduced postural stability, especially under conditions in which somatosensory input was disrupted. In the ASD subjects, postural control did not begin to improve until age 12 and never achieved adult levels. In TD, postural control improved steadily from age 5-15or 20, when it plateaued at adult levels.

(continued)

APPENDIX 15.1 (Continued)

First Author (Year)	Research Goals or Questions	Subjects Groups	N	Mean Age	Motor	Assessments Other	Findings Related to Specific Area of Motor Impairment
Sensorimotor Integration							
Molloy (2003)	Postural stability of children with ASD versus TD and the relative contribution of sensory information to postural control.	ASD TD	8 8	124 m 126 m	AccuSway	ADOS ABC	Children with ASD overly relied on visual cues to reduce sway and maintain balance. Under conditions where vision was occluded, children with ASD had increased sway area when compared with TDs, whether or not somatosensory input was altered.
Paton (2012)	To explore unimodal and multimodal sensory and proprioceptive processing in HFA versus TD.	HFA TD	17 17	32.0 y 27.0 y	RHI Grasping task	DSM-IV	HFA displayed less general proprioceptive drift toward the rubber hand than TD. Patterns of acceleration in a reach trial reflected the presence of the RHI in both groups, but HFA had the reverse pattern of acceleration compared to TD.
Siaperas (2012)	To investigate motor and sensory performance in children with AS and to examine whether performance was affected by development.	AS TD	50 50	10.7 y 10.8 y	MABC-2 SIPT	ADI-R WASI CAST	AS had significant impairments across the sensorimotor and motor tests versus TD, suggesting that movement performance in AS may be underlined by problems with sensory integration. Findings also suggest that movement and sensory processing problems persist into later childhood.

KEY TO ABBREVIATIONS USED IN APPENDIX

ABC: Autism Behavior Checklist; **AccuSway**: Commercially purchased force platform system; **ADOS**: Autism Diagnostic Schedule; **ADI-R**: Autism Diagnostic Interview–Revised; **AQ**: Autism Quotient Checklist; **AS**: Asperger; **ATEC**: Autism Treatment Evaluation Checklist; **AUT**: autism; **BOT2**: Bruininks-Oseretsky Test of Motor Proficiency; **BOT2-S**: Bruininks-Oseretsky Test of Motor Proficiency–Short Form; **CARS**: Childhood Autism Rating Scale; **CAST**: Childhood Asperger Syndrome Test; **CBCL**: Child Behavior Checklist; **CPRSR**: Connor's Parent Rating Scale–Revised; **CTRSR**: Connor's Teacher Rating Scale–Revised; **DBC-P**: Developmental Behavior Checklist–Primary Caregiver; **DCDQ**: Development Coordination Disorder Questionnaire; **DICA**: Diagnostic Interview for Children and Adolescents; **EHI**: Edinburgh Handedness Inventory; **EMG**: electromyographic activity; **EquiTest**: commercially available standardized, dynamic posturography test; **FAB**: Florida Apraxia Battery; **FAB-R**: Florida Apraxia Battery–Revised for children; **FIVE**: Fully immersive virtual environment; **FSIQ**: Full-Scale Intelligence Quotient; **FTT**: finger tapping test; **GD**: experimental grasping device; **JTT**: Judgment of Timing Test based on Ivry, Keele, and Diener, 1988; **KINARM**: commercially available robotic arm that allows individually applied torques to elbow and shoulder joints; **LIPS-R**: Leiter International Performance Scale–Revised; **Luria**: Luria-Nebraska tests of simple touch, sharp-dull discrimination, positions sense and stereognosis; **m**: months; **MA**: Mental Age; **MABC-2**: Movement Assessment Battery for Children, second edition; **MHA**: Minnesota Handwriting Assessment; **MSEL**: Mullen Scales of Early Learning; **OMRT**: One Minute Reading Test; **PANESS**: Revised Physical and Neurological Examination for Subtle (Motor) Signs; **PKT**: Postural Knowledge Test; **PDMS-2**: Peabody Developmental Motor Scales, second edition; **PPVTR**: Peabody Picture Vocabulary Test–Revised; **PRI**: Perceptual Reasoning Index; **RBS-R**: Repetitive Behavior Scale–Revised; **RHI**: rubber hand illusion; **Reitan-Klove**: test of finger recognition based on tactile stimulation; **SIPT**: Sensory Integration and Praxis Test; **SCQ**: Social Communication Questionnaire; **SP**: Sensory Profile; **SRS**: Social Responsiveness Scale; **SRTT**: Serial Response Time Task based on Nissen and Bullemer, 1987; **SSH**: Dutch Systematic Screening of Handwriting; **SSP**: Short Sensory Profile; **TGMD**: Test of Gross Motor Development; **VABS**: Vineland Adaptive Behavior Scale; **VMI**: Developmental Test of Visual Motor Integration; **WAIS-R**: Wechsler Adult Intelligence Scale–Revised; **WASI**: Wechsler Abbreviated Scale of Intelligence; **WIAT**: Wechsler Individual Achievement Test; **WISC**: Wechsler Intelligence Scale for Children; **WeeFIM**: Functional Independence Measure for children; **WMTBC**: Working Memory Test Battery for Children; **WPPSI**: Weschsler Preschool and Primary Scale of Intelligence; **y**: years; **ZNA**: Zurich Neuromotor Assessment

REFERENCES

Abu-Dahab, S. M., Skidmore, E. R., Holm, M. B., Rogers, J. C., & Minshew, N. J. (2012). Motor and tactile-perceptual skill differences between individuals with high-functioning autism and typically developing individuals ages 5–21. *Journal of Autism and Developmental Disorders*, *43*(10), 2241–2248.

Allen, G., Muller, R., & Courchesne, E. (2004). Cerebellar function in autism: Functional magnetic resonance image activation during a simple motor task. *Biological Psychiatry*, *56*(4), 269–278.

Ayres, A. J. (1979). *Sensory integration and learning disabilities*. Los Angeles, CA: Western Psychological Services.

Ayres, A. J. (2005). *Sensory integration and the child: Understanding hidden sensory challenges*. Los Angeles, CA: Western Psychological Services.

Ayres, A. J. (2011). *Ayres dyspraxia monograph: 25th anniversary edition*. Torrance, CA: Pediatric Therapy Network.

Baranek, G. T. (1999). Autism during infancy: A retrospective video analysis of sensory-motor and social behaviors at 9–12 months of age. *Journal of Autism and Developmental Disorders*, *29*(3), 213–224.

Bauman, M. L., & Kemper, T. L. (2005). Neuroanatomic observations of the brain in autism: A review and future directions. *International Journal of Developmental Neuroscience*, *23*(2–3), 183–187.

Bayley, N. (2005). *Bayley Scales of Infant Development* (3rd ed.). San Antonio, TX: Pearson Assessments.

Belmonte, M. K., Allen, G., Beckel-Mitchener A., Boulanger L. M., Carper, R. A., & Webb, S. J. (2004). Autism and abnormal development of brain connectivity. *Journal of Neuroscience*, *24*, 9228–9231.

Beversdorf, D. Q., Anderson, J. M., Manning, S. E., Anderson, S. L., Nordgren, R. E., Felopulos, G. J., & Bauman, M. L. (2001). Brief report: Macrographia in high-functioning adults with autism spectrum disorder. *Journal of Autism and Developmental Disorders*, *31*(1), 97–101.

Bhat, A. N., Landa, R. J., & Galloway, J. C. (2012). Current perspectives on motor functioning in infants, children, and adults with autism spectrum disorders. *Physical Therapy*, *91*(7), 1116–1129.

Bolton, P. F., Golding, J., Emond, A., & Steer, C. D. (2012). Autism spectrum disorder and autistic traits in the Avon Longitudinal Study of Parents and Children: Precursors and early signs. *Journal of the American Academy of Child & Adolescent Psychiatry*. Retrieved from http://www.sciencedirect.com/science/article/pii/S0890856711011439

Bruininks, R. H., & Bruininks, B. D. (2005). *Bruininks-Osteretsky Test of Motor Proficiency* (2nd ed.). Circle Pines, MN: American Guidance Services.

Casanova, M. F., van Kooten, I. A., Switala, A. E., van Engeland, H., Heinsen, H., Steinbusch, H. W., ... Schmitz, C. (2006). Minicolumnar abnormalities in autism. *Acta Neuropathologica (Berl)*, *112*, 287–303.

Cattaneo, L., Fabbri-Destro, M., Boria, S., Pieraccini, C., Monti, A., Cossu, G., & Rizzolatti, G. (2007). Impairment of actions chains in autism and its possible role in intention understanding. *Proceedings of the National Academy of Sciences, USA*, *104*(45), 17825–17830.

Chang, C. H., Wade, M. G., Stoffregen, T. A., Hsu, C. Y., & Pan, C. Y. (2010). Visual tasks and postural sway in children with and without autism spectrum disorders. *Research in Developmental Disabilities*, *31*(6), 1536–1542.

Coskun, M. A., Varghese, L., Reddoch, S., Castillo, E. M., Pearson, D. A., Loveland, K. A., ... Sheth, B. R. (2009). How somatic cortical maps differ in autistic and typical brains. *NeuroReport*, *20*(2), 175–179.

David, F. J., Baranek, G. T., Giuliani, C. A., Mercer, V. S., Poe, M. D., & Thorpe, D. E. (2009). A pilot study: Coordination of precision grip in children and adolescents with high functioning autism. *Pediatric Physical Therapy*, *21*(2), 205.

David, F. J., Baranek, G. T., Wiesen, C., Miao, A. F., & Thorpe, D. E. (2012). Coordination of precision grip in 2–6 years-old children with autism spectrum disorders compared to children developing typically and children with developmental disabilities. *Frontiers in Integrative Neuroscience*, *6*. Retrieved from http://www.ncbi.nlm.nih.gov/pmc/articles/PMC3533230/

Denckla, M. B. (1985). Revised neurological examination for subtle signs. *Psychopharmacology Bulletin*, *21*, 772–800.

Dewey, D., Cantell, M., & Crawford, S. G. (2007). Motor and gestural performance in children with autism spectrum disorders, developmental coordination disorder, and/or attention deficit hyperactivity disorder. *Journal of the International Neuropsychological Society*, *13*(02), 246–256.

Dowd, A. M., McGinley, J. L., Taffe, J. R., & Rinehart, N. J. (2012). Do planning and visual integration difficulties underpin motor dysfunction in autism? A kinematic study of young children with autism. *Journal of Autism and Developmental Disorders*, *42*, 1539–1548.

Dowell, L. R., Mahone, E. M., & Mostofsky, S. H. (2009). Associations of postural knowledge and basic motor skill with dyspraxia in autism: Implication for abnormalities in distributed connectivity and motor learning. *Neuropsychology*, *23*(5), 563.

Downey, R., & Rapport, M. J. (2012). Motor activity in children with autism: A review of current literature. *Pediatric Physical Therapy*, *24*, 2–20.

Dziuk, M. A., Larson, J. C., Apostu, A., Mahone, E. M., Denckla, M. B., & Mostofsky, S. H. (2007). Dyspraxia in autism: Association with motor, social, and communicative deficits. *Developmental Medicine & Child Neurology*, *49*(10), 734–739.

Esposito, G., Venuti, P., Maestro, S., & Muratori, F. (2009). An exploration of symmetry in early autism spectrum disorders: Analysis of lying. *Brain and Development*, *31*(2), 131–138.

Fabbri-Destro, M., Cattaneo, L., Boria, S., & Rizzolatti, G. (2009). Planning actions in autism. *Experimental Brain Research*, *192*(3), 521–525.

Flanagan, J. E., Landa, R., Bhat, A., & Bauman, M. (2012). Head lag in infants at risk for autisma preliminary study. *American Journal of Occupational Therapy*, *66*(5), 577–585.

Folio, M. R., & Fewell, R. R. (2000). *Peabody Developmental Motor Scales*. Austin, TX: PRO-ED.

Fournier, K. A., Hass, C. J., Naik, S. K., Lodha, N., & Cauraugh, J. H. (2010). Motor coordination in autism spectrum disorders a synthesis and meta-analysis. *Journal of Autism and Developmental Disorders*, *40*(10), 1227–1240.

Fournier, K. A., Kimberg, C. I., Radonovich, K. J., Tillman, M. D., Chow, J. W., Lewis, M. H., ... Hass, C. J. (2010). Decreased static and dynamic postural control in children with autism spectrum disorders. *Gait & Posture*, *32*(1), 6–9.

Freitag, C. M., Kleser, C., Schneider, M., & Von Gontard, A. (2007). Quantitative assessment of neuromotor function in adolescents with high functioning autism and Asperger syndrome. *Journal of Autism and Developmental Disorders*, *37*(5), 948–959.

Fuentes, C. T., Mostofsky, S. H., & Bastian, A. J. (2009). Children with autism show specific handwriting impairments. *Neurology*, *73*(19), 1532–1537.

Fuentes, C. T., Mostofsky, S. H., & Bastian, A. J. (2010). Perceptual reasoning predicts handwriting impairments in adolescents with autism. *Neurology*, *75*(20), 1825–1829.

Fuentes, C. T., Mostofsky, S. H., & Bastian, A. J. (2011). No proprioceptive deficits in autism despite movement-related sensory and execution impairments. *Journal of Autism and Developmental Disorders*, *41*(10), 1352–1361.

Gepner, B., Mestre, D., Masson, G., & de Schonen, S. (1995). Postural effects of motion vision in young autistic children. *NeuroReport*, *6*, 1211–1214.

Gidley Larson, J. C., Bastian, A. J., Donchin, O., Shadmehr, R., & Mostofsky, S. H. (2008). Acquisition of internal models of motor tasks in children with autism. *Brain*, *131*(11), 2894–2903.

Gowen, E., & Hamilton, A. (2013). Motor abilities in autism: A review using a computational context. *Journal of Autism and Developmental Disorders*, *43*, 323–344.

Green, D., Charman, T., Pickles, A., Chandler, S., Loucas, T., Simonoff, E., & Baird, G. (2009). Impairment in movement skills of children with autistic spectrum disorders. *Developmental Medicine & Child Neurology*, *51*(4), 311–316.

Greffou, S., Bertone, A., Hahler, E. M., Hanssens, J. M., Mottron, L., & Faubert, J. (2012). Postural hypo-reactivity in autism is contingent on development and visual environment: A fully immersive virtual reality study. *Journal of Autism and Developmental Disorders*, *42*(6), 961–970.

Ham, H. S., Bartolo, A., Corley, M., Rajendran, G., Szabo, A., & Swanson, S. (2011). Exploring the relationship between gestural recognition and imitation: Evidence of dyspraxia in autism spectrum disorders. *Journal of Autism and Developmental Disorders*, *41*, 1–12.

Haswell, C. C., Izawa, J., Dowell, L. R., Mostofsky, S. H., & Shadmehr, R. (2009). Representation of internal models of action in the autistic brain. *Nature Neuroscience*, *12*(8), 970–972.

Heilman, K. M., & Gonzalez Rothi, L. J. (2003). *Apraxia*. New York, NY: Oxford University Press.

Hellinckx, T., Roeyers, H., & Van Waelvelde, H. (2013). Predictors of handwriting in children with Autism spectrum disorder. *Research in Autism Spectrum Disorders*, *7*(1), 176–186.

Henderson, S. E., Sugden, D. A., & Barnett, A. (2007). *Movement Assessment Battery for Children* (2nd ed.). San Antonio, TX: Pearson.

Herbert, M. R., Ziegler, D. A., Makris N., Filipek, P. A., Kemper, T. L., Normandin, J. J., ... Caviness, V. S. (2004). Localization of white matter volume increase in autism and developmental language disorder. *Annals of Neurology*, *55*, 530–540.

Hilton, C. L., Zhang, Y., Whilte, M. R., Klohr, C. L., & Constantino, J. (2012). Motor impairment in sibling pairs concordant and discordant for autism spectrum disorders. *Autism*, *16*(4), 430–441.

Ivry, R., Keele, S., & Diener, H. C. (1988). Dissociation of the lateral and medial cerebellum in movement timing and movement execution. *Experimental Brain Research*, *73*, 167–180.

Izawa, J., Pekny, S. E., Marko, M. K., Haswell, C. C., Shadmehr, R., & Mostofsky, S. H. (2012). Motor learning relies on integrated sensory inputs in ADHD, but over-selectivity on proprioception in autism spectrum conditions. *Autism Research*, *2*, 124–135.

Jansiewicz, E. M., Goldberg, M. C., Newschaffer, C. J., Denckla, M. B., Landa, R., & Mostofsky, S. H. (2006). Motor signs distinguish children with high functioning autism and Asperger's syndrome from controls. *Journal of Autism and Developmental Disorders*, *36*(5), 613–621.

Jasmin, E., Couture, M., McKinley, P., Reid, G., Fombonne, E., & Gisel, E. (2009). Sensorimotor and daily living skills of preschool children with autism spectrum disorders. *Journal of Autism and Developmental Disorders*, *39*(2), 231–241.

Kandel, E. R., Schwartz, J. H., & Jessell, T. M. (2000). *Principles of neural science* (4th ed.). New York, NY: McGraw-Hill.

Kohen-Raz, R., Volkmar, F. R., Cohen, D. J. (1992). Postural control in children with autism. *Journal of Autism and Developmental Disorders*, *22*, 419–432.

Lainé, F., Rauzy, S., Tardif, C., & Gepner, B. (2011). Slowing down the presentation of facial and body movements enhances imitation performance in children with severe autism. *Journal of Autism and Developmental Disorders*, *41*(8), 983–996.

Landa, R., & Garrett-Mayer, E. (2006). Development in infants with autism spectrum disorders: A prospective study. *Journal of Child Psychology and Psychiatry*, *47*(6), 629–638.

Lloyd, M., MacDonald, M., & Lord, C. (2011). Motor skills of toddlers with autism spectrum disorders. *Autism*. Retrieved from http://aut.sagepub.com/content/early/2011/05/19/1362 361311402230.short

MacNeil, L. K., & Mostofsky, S. H. (2012). Specificity of dyspraxia in children with autism. *Neuropsychology*, *26*(2), 165.

Mari, M., Castiello, U., Marks, D., Marraffa, C., Prior, M., Mari, M., ... Prior, M. (2003). The reach-to-grasp movement in children with autism spectrum disorder. *Philosophical Transactions of the Royal Society of London. Series B: Biological Sciences*, *358*(1430), 393–403.

Masterson, B., & Biederman, G. (1983). Proprioceptive versus visual control in autistic children. *Journal of Autism and Developmental Disorders*, *13*(2), 141–152.

Memari, A. H., Ghanouni, P., Gharibzadeh, S., Eghlidi, J., Ziaee, V., & Moshayedi, P. (2013). Postural sway patterns in children with autism spectrum disorder compared with typically developing children. *Research in Autism Spectrum Disorders*, *7*, 325–332.

Ming, X., Brimacombe, M., & Wagner, G. C. (2007). Prevalence of motor impairment in autism spectrum disorders. *Brain and Development*, *29*, 565–570.

Minshew, N. J., Sung, K. B., Jones, B. L., & Furman, J. M. (2004). Underdevelopment of the postural control system in autism. *Neurology*, *63*(11), 2056–2061.

Molloy, C. A., Dietrich, K. N., & Bhattacharya, A. (2003). Postural stability in children with autism spectrum disorder. *Journal of Autism and Developmental Disorders*, *33*(6), 643–652.

Mostofsky, S. H., Bunoski, R., Morton, S., Goldberg, M. C., & Bastian, A. (2004). Children with autism adapt normally during a catching task implicating the cerebellum. *Neurocase 2004*, 59, 257–264.

Mostofsky, S. H., Dubey, P., Jerath, V. K., Jansiewicz, E. M., Goldberg, M. C., & Denckla, M. B. (2006). Developmental dyspraxia is not limited to imitation in children with autism spectrum disorders. *Journal of the International Neuropsychological Society, 12*(3), 314–326.

Mostofsky, S. H., & Ewen, J. B. (2011). Altered connectivity and action model formation in autism is autism. *Neuroscientist, 17*(4), 437–448.

Mostofsky, S. H., Goldberg, M. C., Landa, R. J., & Denckla, M. B. (2000). Evidence for a deficit in procedural learning in children and adolescents with autism: Implications for cerebellar contribution. *Journal of the International Neuropsychological Society, 6*(7), 752–759.

Mostofsky, S. H., Powell, S. K., Simmonds, D. J., Goldberg, M. C., Caffo, B., & Pekar, J. J. (2009). Decreased connectivity and cerebellar activity in autism during motor task performance. *Brain, 132*(9), 2413–2425.

Mulligan, S., & White, B. P. (2012). Sensory and motor behaviors of infant siblings of children with and without autism. *American Journal of Occupational Therapy, 66*(5), 556–566.

Nayate, A., Tonge, B. J., Bradshaw, J. L., McGinley, J. L., Iansek, R., & Rinehart, N. J. (2012). Differentiation of high-functioning autism and Asperger's disorder based on neuromotor behaviour. *Journal of Autism and Developmental Disorders, 42*(5), 707–717.

Nissen, M., & Bullemer, P. (1987). Attentional requirements of learning: Evidence from performance measures. *Cognitive Psychology, 19*, 1–32.

Nobile, M., Perego, P., Piccinini, L., Mani, E., Rossi, A., Bellina, M., & Molteni, M. (2011). Further evidence of complex motor dysfunction in drug naïve children with autism using automatic motion analysis of gait. *Autism, 15*(3), 263–283.

Noterdaeme, M., Wriedt, E., & Höhne, C. (2010). Asperger's syndrome and high-functioning autism: Language, motor and cognitive profiles. *European Child & Adolescent Psychiatry, 19*(6), 475–481.

Ozonoff, S., Young, G. S., Goldring, S., Greiss-Hess, L., Herrera, A. M., Steele, J., . . . Rogers, S. J. (2008). Gross motor development, movement abnormalities, and early identification of autism. *Journal of Autism and Developmental Disorders, 38*(4), 644–656.

Papadopoulos, N., McGinley, J., Tonge, B., Bradshaw, J., Saunders, K., Murphy, A., & Rinehart, N. (2011). Motor proficiency and emotional/behavioural disturbance in autism and asperger's disorder: Another piece of the neurological puzzle? *Autism, 19*(6), 627–640.

Paton, B., Hohwy, J., & Enticott, P. G. (2012). The rubber hand illusion reveals proprioceptive and sensorimotor differences in autism spectrum disorders. *Journal of Autism and Developmental Disorders, 42*(9), 1870–1883.

Pfeiffer, B., Koenig, K., Kinnealey, M., Sheppard, M., & Henderson, L. (2011). Effectiveness of sensory integration interventions in children with autism: A pilot study. *American Journal of Occupational Therapy, 65*, 76–85.

Rinehart, N. J., Bellgrove, M. A., Tonge, B. J., Brereton, A. V., Howells-Rankin, D., & Bradshaw, J. L. (2006). An examination of movement kinematics in young people with high-functioning autism and Asperger's disorder: Further evidence for a motor planning deficit. *Journal of Autism and Developmental Disorders, 36*(6), 757–767.

Rinehart, N. J., Tonge, B. J., Bradshaw, J. L., Iansek, R., Enticott, P. G., & McGinley, J. (2006). Gait function in high-functioning autism and Asperger's disorder. *European Child & Adolescent Psychiatry, 15*(5), 256–264.

Rinehart, N. J., Tonge, B. J., Iansek, R., McGinley, J., Brereton, A. V., Enticott, P. G., & Bradshaw, J. L. (2006). Gait function in newly diagnosed children with autism: Cerebellar and basal ganglia related motor disorder. *Developmental Medicine & Child Neurology, 48*(10), 819–824.

Rogers, S. J., Bennetto, L., McEvoy, R., & Pennington, B. F. (1996). Imitation and pantomime in high-functioning adolescents with autism spectrum disorders. *Child Development, 67*(5), 2060–2073.

Schaaf, R. C., Benevides, T. W., Kelly, D., & Mailloux-Maggio, Z. (2012). Occupational therapy and sensory integration for children with autism: A feasibility, safety, acceptability and fidelity study. *Autism, 16*(3), 321–327.

Schmidt, R. A., & Lee, T. D. (2011). *Motor control and motor learning: A behavior emphasis* (5th ed.). Champaign, IL: Human Kinetics.

Schmitz, C., Martineau, J., Barthelemy, C., & Assaiante, C. (2003). Motor control and children with autism: Deficit of anticipatory function? *Neuroscience Letters, 348*, 17–20.

Shadmehr, R., & Krakauer, J. W. (2008). A computational neuroanatomy for motor control. *Experimental Brain Research, 185*, 359–381.

Shadmehr, R., & Mussa-Ivaldi, F. A. (1994). Adaptive representation of dynamics during learning of a motor task. *Journal of Neuroscience, 14*, 3208–3224.

Shadmehr, R., Smith, M. A., & Krakauer, J. W. (2010). Error correction, sensory prediction, and adaptation in motor control. *Annual Review of Neuroscience, 33*, 89–108.

Shumway-Cook, A., & Woollacott, M. H. (2007). *Motor control: Translating research into clinical practice* (3rd ed.). Philadelphia, PA: Lippincott, Williams, & Wilkins.

Siaperas, P., Ring, H. A., McAllister, C. J., Henderson, S., Barnett, A., Watson, P., & Holland, A. J. (2012). Atypical movement performance and sensory integration in Asperger's syndrome. *Journal of Autism and Developmental Disorders, 42*(5), 718–725.

Stackhouse, T. M. (2010). Motor differences in the autism spectrum disorders. In H. Miller Kuhaneck & R. Watling (Eds.), *Autism: A comprehensive occupational therapy approach* (3rd ed.). Bethesda, MD: AOTA Press.

Staples, K. L., & Reid, G. (2010). Fundamental movement skills and autism spectrum disorders. *Journal of Autism and Developmental Disorders, 40*(2), 209–217.

Steinman, K. J., Mostofsky, S. H., & Denckla, M. B. (2010). Toward and narrower, more pragmatic view of developmental dyspraxia. *Journal of Child Neurology, 25*(1), 71–81.

Travers, B. G., Klinger, M. R., Mussey, J. L., & Klinger, L. G. (2010). Motor-linked implicit learning in persons with autism spectrum disorders. *Autism Research, 3*(2), 68–77.

Travers, B. G., Powell, P. S., Klinger, L. G., & Klinger, M. R. (2012). Motor difficulties in autism spectrum disorder: Linking symptom severity and postural stability. *Journal of Autism and Developmental Disorders, 43*, 1568–1583.

Warren, Z., McPheeters, M. L., Sathe, N., Foss-Fieg, J. H., Glasser, A., & Veenstra-VanderWeele, J. (2011). A systematic review of early intensive intervention for autism spectrum disorders. *Pediatrics, 127*(5), 1303–1311.

Wolpert, D. M., Diedrichson, J., & Flanagan, J. R. (2011). Principles of sensorimotor learning. *Neuroscience, 12*, 739–751.

Wolpert, D. M., Ghahramani, Z., & Jordan, M. I. (1995). An internal model for sensorimotor integration. *Science, 269*, 1880–1882.

CHAPTER 16

Sensory Features in Autism Spectrum Disorders

GRACE T. BARANEK, LAUREN M. LITTLE, L. DIANE PARHAM,
KARLA K. AUSDERAU, AND MAURA G. SABATOS-DeVITO

INTRODUCTION

Sensory features have been noted in persons with autism spectrum disorders (ASDs) dating back to the earliest case studies on record (Kanner, 1943), and these intriguing behaviors continue to perplex parents, clinicians, and researchers today.

We thank Dr. Sarah Schipul for her thoughtful review and comments on this chapter. We also appreciate the detailed administrative assistance of Lauren DeMoss, Alicia Chen, and Anna Pincus at the Sensory Experiences Project laboratory (R01-HD42168) at the University of North Carolina at Chapel Hill. We also acknowledge the contributions of Dr. Jim Bodfish in our earlier chapter in the previous edition of this *Handbook*.

Kanner's case studies described both sensory fascinations (e.g., watching light reflecting from mirrors) that provided seemingly endless joy, as well as heightened sensitivities (e.g., covering ears to shield against noise) that caused distress in some children with ASD. Following several decades of scant research on sensory features, these issues have gained prominence in recent literature with the advent of new technologies, theories, and methods that have (a) more comprehensively characterized sensory phenotypes; (b) clarified associations with other features of ASD; (c) better addressed questions of pathogenesis, development, and impact; and (d) informed clinical assessment and intervention approaches. Thus, we are pleased to contribute this chapter to the *Handbook* and highlight new findings regarding sensory features in ASD.

DESCRIPTION, PREVALENCE, AND SPECIFICITY OF SENSORY FEATURES

Myriad terms have been used in the literature to describe the vast array of sensory experiences reported and/or behavioral manifestations evidenced by individuals with ASD. These include, but are not limited to under-, over-, and fluctuating responsiveness to various sensory stimuli (O'Neill & Jones, 1997; Schoen, Miller, & Green, 2008); hypo- and hypersensitivities (e.g., Baron-Cohen, Ashwin, Ashwin, Tavassoli, & Chakrabarti, 2009); sensory avoidances or aversions (e.g., Baranek, 2002; Dunn 2001); sensory overload (O'Neill & Jones, 1997); sensory seeking or craving behaviors (e.g., Dunn, 2001; Miller, Anzalone, Lane, Cermak, & Osten, 2007); fascinations or preoccupations with sensory aspects of the environment (e.g., Cesaroni & Garber, 1991); superior acuities or enhanced perceptions (e.g., Mottron, Burack, Iarocci, Belleville, & Enns, 2003); sensory integration deficits (e.g., Schaaf et al., 2010); sensory-perceptual distortions (Minshew & Hobson, 2008); and synesthesias and other paradoxical reactions to sensory stimuli (Asher et al., 2009; Cytowic, 2002; Iarocci & McDonald, 2006). Many phenomenological accounts (e.g., Cesaroni & Garber, 1991; Grandin & Scariano, 1986; Jones, Quigney, & Huws, 2003; Tammet, 2006; D. Williams, 1994) and empirical studies (e.g., Baranek, David, Poe, Stone, & Watson, 2006; Hirstein, Iverson, & Ramachandran, 2001; Leekam, Nieto, Libby, Wing, & Gould, 2007; Watson et al., 2011) have demonstrated that sensory features are evidenced across all modalities, including auditory, visual, somatosensory, gustatory, olfactory, and vestibular systems, and are thought to reflect underlying differences in uni- and multisensory processing, and/or integration functions. Because sensory processing functions are vital to higher order perceptual and cognitive processes, research

in this area may inform theories regarding these unusual sensory features as well as other central characteristics of the disorder such as impaired social cognition and language development.

A major challenge in the ASD literature is reconciling terminology and translating across disparate fields from the basic neurosciences through more clinically applied behavioral fields. In this chapter we use the term *features* (rather than *symptoms*) to describe specific behavioral manifestations that may reflect enhancements as well as deficits in sensory processing abilities. Furthermore, although we present largely convergent findings and generalizations across behavioral and neurophysiological studies that may help to explain the pathogenesis and development of sensory features, we recognize that sensory experiences in the real world are individualized and varied. Sensory features may present differently across people with ASD, as well as across time and contexts within the same person, presumably as a result of individual capacities transacting with challenges/affordances encountered in complex physical and social environments.

Sensory features are common in persons with ASD at all ages. Although there are no epidemiological studies, smaller studies of preschool/school-aged samples have reported prevalence of sensory features ranging from ~40% to >90% (Baranek et al., 2006; Kern et al., 2006; Kientz & Dunn, 1997; Le Couteur et al., 1989; Leekam et al., 2007; O'Donnell, Deitz, Kartin, Nalty, & Dawson, 2012; Ornitz, Guthrie, & Farley, 1977; Tomchek & Dunn, 2007; Volkmar, Cohen, & Paul, 1986; Watling, Deitz, & White, 2001). Fewer studies report rates of sensory features in very young children (e.g., Ben-Sasson et al., 2007; Wiggins, Robins, Bakeman, & Adamson, 2009) or older adolescents/adults with ASD (e.g., Crane, Goddard, & Pring, 2009; Kern, Trivedi, et al., 2007).

Modality Specific Descriptions of Sensory Features

Among the most commonly reported sensory features in ASD are auditory processing problems, particularly hyperacusis (Bettison, 1996; Grandin & Scariano, 1986; Greenspan & Wieder, 1997; Reynolds & Lane, 2008; Talay-Ongan & Wood, 2000; Volkmar et al., 1986). Higher functioning individuals with ASD often report trouble filtering out background noise during conversations. It is not clear whether auditory sensitivities are more common than sensitivities in other modalities, or whether distressing auditory stimuli are less avoidable in naturalistic environments and thus more salient to observers. Differentiating auditory hypersensitivities from anxiety and fears of specific objects or situations (Green & Ben-Sasson, 2010; Pfeiffer, Kinnealey, Reed, & Herzberg, 2005) is challenging, especially since stressful situations exacerbate physiological arousal. Auditory talents including superior pitch recognition, discrimination of musical tones, or enhanced perception of specific frequencies of sounds that are not easily discernible by others (e.g., Bonnel et al., 2003) are also reported. (Psychophysical/physiological studies are presented in later sections.) Paradoxically, despite the high prevalence of hypersensitivities to sound, hyporesponsiveness (i.e., absent, delayed, or inconsistent response) to auditory stimuli, particularly spoken language, is considered a hallmark sign of ASD in young children and often results in a clinical referral. Although hearing is generally intact (Gravel, Dunn, Lee, & Ellis, 2006; Klin, 1993; Tharpe et al., 2006), conductive, sensorineural, or mixed hearing loss can co-occur with ASD (Jure, Rapin, & Tuchman, 1991; Rosenhall, Nordin, Sandström, Ahlsen, & Gillberg, 1999).

In the visual domain, a variety of strengths (e.g., detection of small details) and deficits (e.g., reduced global perception; decreased motion processing) are noted. Visual fascinations and stereotypies (e.g., wiggling fingers near eyes; watching objects flicker/spin) as well as peripheral sighting (e.g., looking out the corner of the eyes) are commonly reported (e.g., Lord, Rutter, & Le Couteur, 1994; Mottron et al., 2007). Much research has been conducted on gaze aversion due to its presumed relevance to social deficits in ASD, especially poor eye contact (see Simmons et al., 2009, for review). Studies measuring visual acuity (Kaplan, Rimland,

& Edelson, 1999; Scharre & Creedon, 1992) indicate that 18% to 50% of children with ASD have difficulties with near and far acuity, fixation, binocularity, and/or strabismus; however, these deficits are insufficient to fully explain the wide-ranging visual sensitivities, fascinations, and stereotypies. One study noted enhanced visual acuity for low-level (i.e., threshold) processing (Ashwin, Ashwin, Rhydderch, Howells, & Baron-Cohen, 2009). Experiments testing luminance and texture contrast have suggested strengths in the parvocellular system (i.e., ventral visual stream that is sensitive to temporal resolution, and identification of colors, textures, and patterns; often referred to as the "what" system) and deficits in the magnocellular system (i.e., dorsal visual stream that is sensitive to spatial resolution and motion—often referred to as the "where" system) in ASD (e.g., Bertone, Mottron, Jelenic, & Faubert, 2005; Bölte, Holtmann, Poustka, Scheurich, & Schmidt, 2007; Davis, Brockbrader, Murphy, Hetrick, & O'Donnell, 2006; Milne et al., 2002; Mottron et al., 2003; Plaisted, Swettenham, & Rees, 1999; Tsermentseli, O'Brien, & Spencer, 2008; Vandenbroucke, Scholte, van Engelund, Lamme, & Kemner, 2008).

Unusual responses to somatosensory stimuli (e.g., tactile defensiveness, withdrawal from social touch, aberrant responses to pain) are central to autobiographical accounts of high-functioning persons with ASD (Grandin & Scariano, 1986; Jones et al., 2003). Despite such reports, experimental studies of tactile perception in ASD are limited in comparison to those in auditory and visual modalities, and results are mixed (see later sections for psychophysical/ neurophysiological findings). In the gustatory/olfactory modality there is even less systematic research; however, picky eating is a commonly reported behavior that may reflect both oral (taste, texture, smell) functions as well as cognitive rigidities (see Ledford & Gast, 2006, for review).

Sensory Response Patterns Across Modalities

Although experimental research often targets unimodal sensory processes, sensory features in ASD are well documented across all sensory modalities and may aggregate into response patterns (e.g., Baranek et al., 2006; Dunn, 1997; Miller et al., 2007). Recognizing that other patterns may exist, we categorize sensory features into four distinct behavioral patterns that have been most commonly reported and empirically validated across modalities: (1) hyporesponsiveness; (2) hyperresponsiveness; (3) sensory interests, repetitions, and seeking behaviors; and (4) enhanced perception. Grouping features by behavioral response patterns may elucidate pathogenesis and facilitate understanding of generalized mechanisms supporting multimodal sensory processes, as well as inform intervention planning.

Hyporesponsiveness is characterized by a lack of, less intense, or delayed response to sensory stimuli (e.g., Baranek et al., 2006; Ben-Sasson et al., 2007; Dunn, 1997). For example, a child may show no behavioral orienting to a novel sound or may have a diminished response to pain. Hyperresponsiveness is characterized by an exaggerated, aversive, or avoidant response to sensory stimuli (e.g., Baranek, Boyd, Poe, David, & Watson, 2007; Dunn, 1997; Reynolds & Lane, 2008). For example, a child may show discomfort to grooming activities or cover ears in response to certain sounds. Sensory interests, repetitions, and seeking behaviors are characterized by a fascination with or craving of sensory stimulation, which is intense and may be repetitive in nature (e.g., Ausderau et al., in revision; Dunn, 1997; Freuler, Baranek, Watson, Boyd, & Bulluck, 2012). For example, a child may show a fascination with flickering lights or rubbing textures. Enhanced perception is characterized by superior acuity, awareness, and/or discrimination of specific sensory stimuli or specific elements of stimuli (e.g., Happé & Frith, 2006; Mottron, Dawson, Soulières, Hubert, & Burack, 2006).

While these four sensory patterns are distinct, they may coexist with significant heterogeneity (Baranek et al., 2006; Ben-Sasson et al., 2007; Ben-Sasson et al., 2009; Hilton, Graver, & LaVesser, 2007; Lane, Young, Baker, & Angley, 2010; Liss, Saulnier, Fein, & Kinsbourne, 2006). Phenomenological reports (Cesaroni & Garber, 1991; Grandin & Scariano, 1986; D. Williams,

1994) have provided corroborating evidence of fluctuating and coexisting sensory response patterns in some persons with ASD. For example, an individual may show distress to certain sounds, textures, or sights, while ignoring other stimuli that appear more intense in their psychophysical properties. Studies have particularly noted the co-occurrence of hypo- and hyperresponsiveness in children with ASD (e.g., Ben-Sasson et al., 2007). For example, Baranek et al. (2006) reported that 38% children with ASD, ages 2–6.5 years, evidenced significantly high levels of both coexisting patterns, and this was in contrast to a group of children with developmental disabilities that showed only 2% with high levels of both hyper- and hyporesponsiveness. Both sensory patterns are associated with sensory seeking behaviors, which may serve some arousal modulation functions (Dunn, 1997; Liss et al., 2006). Hyporesponsiveness appears to be a very early developing feature (e.g., Freuler et al., 2012) and is thought to be more unique to ASD as compared to neurotypical and developmental disabilities control groups (Baranek et al., 2013; Ben-Sasson et al., 2009; Greenspan & Wieder, 1997; Hirstein et al., 2001; Rogers & Ozonoff, 2005), particularly at lower mental ages and verbal abilities. Enhanced perception is not significantly correlated with hyporesponsiveness (Ausderau et al., in revision), but is hypothesized to lead to hyperresponsiveness (aversion, avoidance, distress) perhaps due to sensory overload (Mottron et al., 2006). Enhanced perception tasks distinguish high functioning adolescents/adults with ASD when compared with neurotypical controls (Mottron et al., 2006; Mottron, Dawson, & Soulières, 2009); however, this pattern is difficult to measure and detect in very young or nonverbal children.

Unusual sensory features are associated with a variety of conditions, including other developmental disabilities (e.g., Ermer & Dunn, 1998; Rogers, Hepburn, & Wehner, 2003), which challenges the specificity of sensory features to ASD. Utilizing appropriate developmental controls to sort out characteristics uniquely associated with ASD from those associated with intellectual disability in general, some studies (Baranek et al., 2006;

Lord, 1995; Rogers et al., 2003) found that parents endorsed sensory symptoms at a significantly higher rate for preschoolers with ASD than for those with nonspecific developmental delays, whereas others (Stone & Hogan, 1993) did not. Further differentiating results by sensory patterns helps to clarify that sensory hyporesponsiveness (versus hyperresponsiveness) may be more specific to children with ASD than to children with other developmental disabilities (Baranek et al., 2006; Ben-Sasson et al., 2007; Rogers et al., 2003). The large heterogeneity of sensory features represented in persons with ASD and the co-occurrence of seemingly paradoxical sensory response patterns has led some researchers to investigate the existence of specific subtypes among children with ASD (Ausderau et al., under review; Lane et al., 2010; Liss et al., 2006). Subtypes may provide more homogeneous sensory phenotypes that could be useful to elucidate the pathogenesis of co-occurring features, as well as potentially inform more specific interventions.

NEUROPSYCHOLOGICAL PERSPECTIVES ON SENSORY FEATURES

Although theories of social cognition and theory of mind (e.g., Adolphs, 2001; Baron-Cohen, Leslie, & Frith, 1985) have provided reasonable explanations of deficits in social interaction and communication in ASD, they have not sufficiently explained the presence of unusual sensory features. Executive dysfunction theories propose that certain behavioral characteristics (e.g., rigidities, compulsive behaviors, rituals, etc.) may be due to poor cognitive flexibility, including planning, inhibition, and set-shifting components (Ozonoff, Strayer, McMahon, & Filloux, 1994). Although some sensory features are related to behavioral rigidities (e.g., Baranek, Foster, & Berkson, 1997; Boyd et al., 2010), one study found no significant associations between sensory features and measures of executive function (Boyd, McBee, Holtzclaw, Baranek, & Bodfish, 2009). Specific problems with attention disengagement

and attention shifting have also been implicated in ASD (Allen & Courchesne, 2001; Courchesne et al.,1994; Landry & Bryson, 2004; Van der Geest, Kemner, Camfferman, Verbaten, & van Engelund, 2001) and provide explanations for why some children overfocus on certain sensory stimuli and fail to respond to other sensory stimuli, but more research is needed.

Other neuropsychological approaches have focused on how sensory-perceptual functions may impact generalized cognitive processes. For example, weak central coherence theory gives one plausible explanation for the strong detail (as opposed to gestalt) oriented processing style demonstrated in individuals with ASD (Happé & Frith, 2006). Other researchers have clarified that people with ASD are capable of global processing, but have superior local processing, or enhanced perception (Mottron et al., 2006; Mottron & Burack, 2001). Complexity of stimuli may be another source of variation across studies with some researchers arguing that persons with ASD display heightened abilities with lower level sensory-perceptual tasks, but as stimuli become increasingly complex, performance becomes more disrupted (e.g., Bertone, Mottron, Jelenic, & Faubert, 2003; D. L. Williams, Goldstein, & Minshew, 2006). Although these theories may account for some sensory features (e.g., heightened sensitivities; intense focus on sensory aspects) in ASD, they do not fully explain the wide heterogeneity across individuals or co-occurrence of sensory response patterns.

PSYCHOPHYSICAL AND PHYSIOLOGICAL PERSPECTIVES ON SENSORY FEATURES

Diverse methods are used in ASD to examine the underlying physical events and hypothesized neural substrates that may account for unusual behavioral responses to sensory stimuli. Psychophysical methods are used to study the detection, discrimination, and integration of sensory information as it affects perception and behavior. Electrophysiological methods are used to examine the perception, regulation, and integration of sensory information in the brain. Electrodermal responses (EDR) and cardiac measures are used to evaluate the effect of sensory stimuli on the body's arousal and self-regulation systems. We focus on generalized mechanisms (psychophysical, psychophysiological, and neurophysiological) that may particularly explain constellations of similar types of sensory features across modalities (i.e., sensory response patterns). One caveat is that much more physiological research has been conducted on auditory, visual, and multisensory processing than on touch, smell, or taste in ASD (see Marco, Hinkley, Hill & Nagarajan, 2011, for review).

Stimulus Detection

A number of psychophysical studies examined sensory thresholds (i.e., lowest intensity level at which the participant perceives the stimulus) in persons with ASD. Studies of taste and smell detection thresholds have not found significant group differences between groups with ASD and controls (Bennetto, Kuschner, & Hyman, 2007; Suzuki, Critchley, Rowe, Howlin, & Murphy, 2003; Tavassoli & Baron-Cohen, 2012a). In the tactile modality, findings have varied and depend upon the specific types of stimuli and ages of samples studied. Some researchers failed to find significant differences between children with ASD and typically developing controls for ability to detect and discriminate roughness of textures (O'Riordan & Pasetti, 2006) or tactile vibratory input (Güçlü, Tanidir, Mukaddes &, Unal, 2007). Cascio et al. (2008) found that adults with ASD showed more sensitivities to vibration and thermal pain (forearm and palm) than neurotypical controls, but light touch detection thresholds, nonnoxious warm/cool detection, and pleasantness ratings for textures were similar between groups. Contrastingly, Blakemore et al. (2006) reported that adults with ASD had superior detection of some high frequency (not low frequency) vibratory stimuli as compared to neurotypical controls. More research is needed to reconcile discrepancies across studies, particularly the extent to which reported problems in stimulus detection reflect peripheral, subcortical, and/or cortical processing differences.

Detection of auditory stimuli is measured by auditory brainstem response (ABR), also known as brainstem auditory evoked response (occurring within ~20 ms after presentation of a rapid series of clicks), provides a method for determining whether auditory information is being detected by the central nervous system at the entry point into the brainstem (de Regnier, 2008). Evidence in ASD is inconsistent (e.g., Courchesne, Courchesne, Hicks, & Lincoln, 1985; Kwon, Kim, Choe, Ko, & Park, 2007; Rosenhall, Nordin, Brantberg, & Gillberg, 2003; Tharpe et al., 2006) and depends somewhat upon the type of stimuli presented, namely, simple nonspeech stimuli such as clicks (e.g., Klin, 1993; Rapin & Dunn, 2003) versus more complex stimuli such as speech (e.g., Russo, Nicol, Trommer, Zecker, & Kraus, 2009). For individuals with ASD who have average intelligence and language skills, ABRs elicited by clicks appeared normal, but deficient brainstem encoding was evident in subgroups of school-aged children for speech sounds with noise and varied pitch contours (Russo et al., 2008). Other evidence from young (24–45 months) children with ASD revealed significantly prolonged latencies to click stimuli compared to normative data (Roth, Muchnik, Shabtai, Hidesheimer, & Henkin, 2012). Longitudinal studies are needed to test neurodevelopmental hypotheses that early sensory processing differences for simple sensory stimuli may attenuate over time but nonetheless have potentially negative and cascading effects for processing of more complex speech stimuli.

Sensory Discrimination

Sensory discrimination studies focus on a person's ability to differentiate between distinct sensory stimuli with respect to their stimulus characteristics (e.g., frequency, duration, location, intensity). Higher order perceptual processes (e.g., object and speech recognition) and cognitive functions depend upon intact lower level sensory processing functions (Bomba & Pang, 2004; Fitch & Tallal, 2003); thus many ASD studies have investigated the integrity of sensory discrimination functions across modalities. Findings depend upon the modalities tested, and the age and intellectual levels of the participants included. For example, children with ASD were found to be less accurate than controls in olfactory discrimination tasks (Suzuki et al., 2003) as well as taste discrimination tasks for sour and bitter (but not sweet and salty) (Bennetto et al., 2007). However, for high-functioning adults with ASD, olfactory adaptation following prolonged exposure to an odor was found to be normal (Tavassoli & Baron-Cohen, 2012b). Heightened sensory discrimination abilities have been noted in several experiments for auditory (Bonnel et al., 2003; Heaton, Davis & Happé, 2008), visual (e.g., Ashwin et al., 2009), and tactile (e.g., Blakemore et al., 2006; Cascio et al., 2008) modalities, at least for high-functioning adolescents/adults with ASD. Tommerdahl, Tannan, Cascio, Baranek, and Whitsel (2007) found heightened baseline tactile sensitivities with concomitant deficits in vibrotactile spatial adaptation and temporal order judgments among adults with ASD, suggesting aberrant short-range (cortico-cortical) connectivity within the somatosensory cortex (see Mountcastle, 2005). Taken together, findings related to perceptual enhancements may reflect overconnected local processing networks (short range) in individuals with ASD, perhaps sometimes at the expense of impaired long range neural connectivity that is important to more integrative functions and attention (e.g., Gomot et al., 2006; O'Riordan, Plaisted, Driver, & Baron-Cohen, 2001).

Evoked potentials and event-related potentials (ERPs) are electroencephalography (EEG) measures that record sequential cortical activity across time following presentation of sensory, cognitive, or motor events (de Regnier, 2008). Short-latency ERP components usually reflect modality-specific early sensory neural processing, whereas long-latency ERPs reflect higher-level cognitive processes that may involve multisensory integration (Bomba & Pang, 2004). EEG studies with persons with ASD have mostly examined the auditory modality (for reviews see Marco et al., 2011; Samson, Mottron, Jemel, Belin, & Ciocca, 2006). Although

behavioral findings suggest that high-functioning children and adolescents with ASD demonstrate relative strengths in processing simple auditory stimuli such as pure tones (e.g., Bonnel et al., 2003; Heaton, 2003), EEG studies have generally demonstrated weaknesses in selective attention and processing, particularly for complex auditory input with multiple sound sources as required for language processing (e.g., Jansson-Verkasalo et al., 2003; Teder-Salejarvi, Pierce, Courchesne, & Hillyard, 2005). The most consistently reported finding is a decreased P3 amplitude to novel auditory stimuli (e.g., Čeponienė et al., 2003; G. Dawson, Finley, Phillips, Galpert, & Lewy, 1988; Donkers et al., in press; Kemner, Verbaten, Cuperus, Camfferman, & van Engeland, 1995; Lincoln, Courchesne, Harms, & Allen, 1993); this is hypothesized to reflect differences in attention allocation or salience evaluation. More studies are needed to determine to what extent early sensory processing differences (e.g., attenuation of P1/N1 to standard tones) found in some EEG studies (e.g., Bruneau, Roux, Adrien, &, Barthélémy, 1999; Donkers et al., under review) may impact later processing functions (discrimination, attention allocation, etc.), and/or multisensory integration.

EEG studies also use mismatch negativity (MMN) paradigms to measure automatic change detection independent of voluntary attention; this method is passive and thus well suited for young children or less verbal populations such as ASD. In MMN studies, subjects are exposed to a series of repeating, identical stimuli with distinct, mismatching stimuli interspersed occasionally to determine if deviant sounds are distinguishable from the identical ones. Reports of MMN amplitude and latency in response to auditory stimuli in children with ASD are conflicting. Some studies have indicated higher MMN amplitudes and shorter latencies (e.g., Ferri et al., 2003), supporting the idea that children with autism have some heightened sensitivities. Others reported lower MMN amplitudes and longer latencies (Seri, Cerquiglini, Pisani, & Curatolo, 1999), which may support deficits in auditory memory encoding needed for accurate discrimination (e.g., Oram Cardy, Flagg, Roberts, & Roberts, 2005).

Relatively few EEG studies have examined visual discrimination in ASD. In contrast to findings in the auditory domain, P3 amplitude differences were generally not found between ASD and neurotypical controls during simple visual target detection tasks (Ciesielski, Courchesne, & Elmasian,1990; Courchesne et al., 1985; Pritchard, Raz, & August, 1987); however, studies using oddball paradigms have shown either abnormally small occipital P3 responses (e.g., Kemner, Verbaten, Cuperus, Camfferman, & van Engeland, 1994; Kemner et al., 1995) or prolonged latencies (right hemisphere) to novel visual stimuli (Sokhadze et al., 2009) in persons with ASD. The prolonged latencies may reflect right hemisphere cortical over-processing, which was also suggested in an EEG study of short-latency somatosensory evoked potentials following median nerve electrical stimulation (Miyazaki et al., 2007).

Sensory Gating

Sensory gating refers to the brain's capacity to regulate its sensitivity to stimuli (Davies, Chang, & Gavin, 2009) and is commonly measured through either prepulse inhibition (PPI) (i.e., attenuation of the startle response to an intense auditory, visual, or tactile stimulus, usually preceded by a weaker stimulus) (Yuhas et al., 2011), or P50 ERP suppression (i.e., stimulus filtering, or a reduced response to sensory input presented following an initial conditioning stimulus, which can be intra- or cross-modal) (Kisley, Noecker, & Guinther, 2004; Oranje, Geyer, Bocker, Kenemans, & Verbaten, 2006). When sensory gating fails, processing of irrelevant or distracting stimuli may occur, leading to sensory overload, and disrupting attention and higher order cognitive processing (Seri, Pisani, Thai, & Cerquiglini, 2007). The degree of inhibition reflects the degree of sensorimotor gating, thus hypo- and hyperresponsive behavioral patterns could be related to ineffective gating. Adults with ASD have demonstrated reduced PPI, supporting a hypothesis of hyperresponsiveness to auditory stimuli (McAlonan et al., 2002). Adolescents with ASD have shown significantly prolonged startle latencies, but fewer impairments in PPI as compared to adolescents with fragile X syndrome with and without autism (Yuhas et al., 2011). Evidence from P50 suppression studies have failed to find evidence of sensory gating abnormalities in individuals with ASD compared to typical controls across age groups (e.g., Kemner, Oranje, Verbaten, & van Engeland, 2002; Magnée, Oranje, van Engeland, Kahn, & Kemner, 2009; Myles-Worsley et al., 1996; Orekhova et al., 2008). More studies are needed to resolve discrepancies in findings of sensory gating studies, explicate developmental factors influencing maturation of sensory gating mechanisms, and examine potential associations with clinical/behavioral measures of sensory response patterns in ASD.

Multisensory Integration and Perception

Most naturally occurring environmental stimuli engage multiple senses at any given moment. Multisensory integration (MSI) refers to the process of condensing and managing information from multiple modalities, and is integral to a person's ability to experience perceptual coherence and generate appropriate responses within the ongoing stream of environmental events (e.g., Iarocci & McDonald, 2006). Persons with ASD are reported to have a variety of sensory features that appear to implicate differences in MSI (e.g., Russo et al., 2010; Russo, Mottron, Burack, & Jemel, 2012), such as difficulty processing and using visual feedback in environments with excessive auditory stimulation (Iarocci, Rombough, Yager, Weeks, & Chua, 2010), synesthesias (i.e., stimulation of one sensory modality results in an experience perceived by a second sensory pathway, such as perceiving musical tones as different colors) (Cytowic, 2002), and deficits integrating interoceptive (e.g., proprioceptive) and exteroceptive (e.g., visual) feedback (e.g., Mostofsky & Ewen, 2011). MSI functions may be different or more effortful in children than adults as a function of cortico-cortical development that supports more automatic processing (Brandwein et al. 2011; Molholm et al., 2002).

Several groups have proposed that some sensory features in ASD may be the result of difficulties simultaneously filtering and processing sensory information from multiple modalities (Foss-Feig et al., 2010; Iarocci & McDonald, 2006; O'Neill & Jones, 1997; Russo et al., 2010). The extent to which simple versus complex (e.g., Bebko, Weiss, Denmark, & Gomez, 2006; Minshew, Goldstein, & Siegel, 1997) and amodal (e.g., spatial pattern) versus modality-specific (e.g., color, sound frequency) (e.g., Bahrick & Lickliter, 2004) aspects of sensory stimuli are being integrated and processed efficiently by individuals with ASD is debated. Individuals with ASD have demonstrated deficits in higher level MSI using complex auditory-visual stimuli, such as the McGurk effect (which involves the ability to combine visual lip reading and auditory phoneme perception stimuli) (Bebko et al., 2006; Mongillo et al., 2008). E. G. Smith and Bennetto (2007) reported that, even when trained to use the visual feedback provided by lip reading in the McGurk task, children with ASD still failed to integrate visual with auditory speech stimuli. In contrast, some studies of basic-level MSI revealed typical integration abilities in children with ASD for nonlinguistic, simple stimuli (Bebko et al., 2006; van der Smagt, van Engeland, & Kemner, 2007). Likewise, studies of low-level MSI using the flash-beep illusion (i.e., pairing of presentations of multiple auditory tones with one visual stimulus to create an illusory perceptual experience of multiple visual flashes) showed no differences between children with ASD and typically developing controls (van der Smagt et al., 2007), although, one study (Foss-Feig et al., 2010) found that children with ASD had a wider temporal window in which the illusion continued to be produced (as compared to typical controls). Also, there are neurophysiological reports of timing differences between ASD and controls in integrative auditory-somatosensory tasks (Russo et al., 2010). New advances in technology, particularly with functional neuroimaging, are rapidly increasing our knowledge of these issues in persons with ASD, at least for high-functioning, verbal, and older populations. More research is needed with young children and less verbal populations.

Among individuals with ASD, integrative processing that requires an extended period of time may reflect inefficient MSI, leading to problems responding to specific modalities in the presence of input from other modalities, particularly when stimuli in either modality are rapidly changing. These findings also reinforce the neuropsychological theories described earlier with respect to a local rather than global processing bias in ASD, perhaps due to a failure to integrate multisensory information in the brain. A plausible explanation is provided by the temporal-binding hypothesis (i.e., that the timing of cross-modal integration of sensory and spatiotemporal information from the same event or contexts is impaired in ASD) (Alcantara, Weisblatt, Moore, & Bolton, 2004; J. Brock, Brown, Boucher, & Rippon, 2002; E. G. Smith & Bennetto, 2007), which may be related to neural underconnectivity (e.g., Just, Cherkassky, Keller, Kana, & Minshew, 2007).

Researchers have also investigated a hypothesized association between MSI and attention in autism, with some findings in support (e.g., Talsma & Woldorff, 2005) and some against (e.g., Zimmer & Macaluso, 2007). Results may vary depending upon whether tasks involve selective versus divided attention, with MSI problems more apparent during divided attention tasks in persons with ASD (Koelewijn, Bronkhorst, & Theeuwes, 2010; Magnée, de Gelder, van Engeland, & Kemner, 2011). This finding does not support a primary MSI deficit in ASD, but instead suggests difficulty in dividing attention across multiple modalities of information.

Autonomic Responses

The autonomic nervous system, comprised of the sympathetic (SNS; arousal and fight-flight) and parasympathetic (PNS; homeostasis and recovery) branches, promotes adaptation and self-regulation in response to internal and external sensory stimuli. Sensory hyper- or hyporesponsive behavioral patterns among individuals with ASD are often hypothesized to reflect excessive or inadequate SNS activation (Schoen et al., 2008) and/or difficulty restoring homeostasis after a stressor (deficit in PNS functions) (Schaaf, Miller, Seawell, & O'Keefe, 2003). Electrodermal response (EDR; skin conductance) measures detect changes in SNS activation via sweat gland activity (M. E. Dawson, Schell, & Filion, 2007). Studies have consistently found EDR/skin conductance differences between individuals with ASD in relative to neurotypical controls; however, results are inconsistent with respect to the prevalence of overresponse and difficulty habituating to repeated stimuli (e.g., Barry & James, 1988; Chang et al., 2012) versus underresponse indicated by low or delayed responses to stimuli (e.g., Schoen, Miller, Brett-Green, & Nielson, 2009; Stevens & Gruzelier, 1984; van Engeland, 1984). Schoen and colleagues (2008, 2009) found that high-functioning children with ASD demonstrated significantly lower electrodermal responses than control groups (neurotypical children and those with sensory modulation disorders) across all sensory domains (auditory, visual, tactile, olfactory, vestibular). However, EDR findings were not significantly correlated with clinical sensory features as measured by the Sensory Profile (Dunn, 1999), a parent questionnaire. Additional analyses suggested two subgroups within ASD, including a high-arousal group (higher skin conductance/electrodermal magnitudes, faster latencies, and slower habituation) that was more hyperresponsive behaviorally, and a low-arousal group (lower skin conductance/electrodermal magnitudes, slower latencies, and faster habituation) that was behaviorally more hyporesponsive. In contrast, Chang et al. (2012) found that high-functioning children with ASD (relative to controls) had higher skin conductance at baseline and recovery, and demonstrated significantly higher EDR to presentations of a standard auditory tone, but not to a siren recording. Among the group with ASD, electrodermal measures were positively, significantly correlated with caregiver report of hyper- and hyporesponsiveness as measured by the Sensory Processing Measure Home Form (Parham, Ecker, Miller-Kuhaneck, Henry, & Glennon, 2007). The contrasting findings across EDR studies might be due to the presence of subgroups (e.g., overresponsive versus underresponsive) or perhaps general

dysregulation of sensory modulation processes among children with ASD (Chang et al., 2012).

Vagal tone, also known as respiratory sinus arrhythmia, is estimated from measures of heart rate variability adjusted for respiratory rate, and taps PNS activity via vagal nerve (Fox & Stifter, 1989). High PNS activity as measured by variability in heart rate is indicative of an ability to adapt and cope with changing stimuli, whereas low PNS activity is related to a poor ability to physiologically adapt to changes. Very little is known about vagal tone patterns of children with ASD. One study found low vagal tone and cardiac baroreflex sensitivity at rest, suggesting parasympathetic deficits, along with high heart rate and blood pressure at rest, suggesting sympathetic overactivity (Ming, Julu, Brimacombe, Connor, & Daniels, 2005). In contrast, another study found no differences in vagal tone or EDR among children with ASD, compared to typical controls, following exposure to a social stressor (Levine et al., 2012). Considering the evidence pointing to heterogeneity of sympathetic responses among children with ASD, it seems reasonable to expect subgroups of parasympathetic responsiveness as well in this population.

Further studies are needed to unravel the complexities presented in physiological studies of children with ASD, particularly with regard to how parent-report and behavioral measures of sensory response patterns are associated with physiological findings. Few studies have investigated how physiological findings may be aligned or associated with caregiver report and behavioral measures of sensory features among individuals with ASD. Chang et al. (2012) found that caregiver-reported hypo- and hyperresponsiveness were associated with EDR, while Donkers et al. (in press) demonstrated that sensory seeking behaviors (as measured by clinical behavioral assessments) were associated with atypical EEG response (i.e., attenuation of P1/N1 to standard tones). Discrepancies across studies may reflect differences in stimulus types (e.g., tones versus speech), or be a result of unimodal versus panmodal investigations. Additionally, inconsistent findings may be due to differences in sampling characteristics such as language ability or IQ (Samson et al., 2006) or potential subtypes of individuals with ASD. Methods that require individuals with ASD to withstand demands related to physiological measures (e.g., EEG) or require increased cognitive abilities (e.g., provide pain ratings) may not be feasible in children with extreme sensory features (Donkers et al., in press) or those that are lower functioning, leading to the exclusion of children with stronger neurophysiological disruptions.

DEVELOPMENTAL PERSPECTIVES ON SENSORY FEATURES

Although sensory systems (e.g., auditory, tactile, vestibular) have formed by the second gestational trimester, and basic sensory functions (e.g., reflexes to touch, hearing higher pitched sounds, visual detection of motion and light sensitivity) are reliably evidenced in newborns (e.g., Simion, Regolin, & Bulf, 2008; Starr, Amlie, Martin, & Sanders, 1977), the sensory systems continue to mature at varying rates, and refine their functional integration and differentiation throughout childhood via meaningful engagement with the physical and social environment (e.g., Gottlieb, 1976; Turkewitz & Kenny, 2004). Sensory processing is dependent upon the integrity of neural systems, and is essential to support lower order (e.g., sensory) as well as higher order cognitive functions (e.g., perception, action, learning) (e.g., Budinger, Heil, Hess, Scheich, 2006; Woldorff et al., 1993). Developmental timing in cortical maturation of certain sensory functions may have adaptive advantages. For example, young infants' visual responsiveness is limited to low spatial frequencies, which may help to organize their responses to their sensory environment (i.e., reduce total amount of stimulation to be processed), thereby supporting the development of more efficient perceptual and cognitive integration capacities (see Lewkowicz, 2002, for a review of intersensory perceptual development). Thus, if infants' sensory experiences are either too limited or too unrestricted during sensitive periods of development, a sensory system may fail to develop optimally (Turkewitz & Kenny,

2004). This may lead to atypical sensory responsiveness, which may transact with other domains of development and contribute to a variety of risk processes that have cascading effects over time.

Neurobiological accounts of ASD suggest that there are disruptions in neural architecture that may arise very early in utero, and result in changes in short-range and long-range neural connectivity (e.g., Belmonte et al., 2004) that is important for adequate processing of sensory information as well as many other social and cognitive functions. These neurodevelopmental disruptions may reflect multiple risk factors (e.g., genetics, neurophysiology, environment) that transact with various developmental risk processes over time (e.g., altered engagement and social interactions) (G. Dawson, 2008), and potentially give rise to a variety of phenotypic expressions (including sensory features) in ASD that may manifest differently at different points in development. Several researchers have posited that impairments in earlier developing systems (e.g., sensory orienting), particularly during very sensitive periods of brain development, may have secondary consequences in later developing systems (e.g., joint attention, language) (e.g., Baranek et al., in press; Loveland, 2001; Mundy & Neal, 2001; Waterhouse, Fein, & Modahl, 1996). Further, co-occurring deficits (e.g., in social and nonsocial domains) may reciprocally influence each other over time (G. Dawson, 2008; E. Williams, Costall, & Reddy, 1999), but it is difficult to empirically test such transactions, particularly longitudinally.

Attentional processes play a role in several stages of sensory processing, including selection of, filtering of, and switching to relevant sensory stimuli. Components of visual attention, including alertness, orienting, executive attention, and sustained attention, develop significantly in the first few years of life as a result of the maturation of the underlying subcortical and cortical neural substrates that support these skills (see Colombo, 2001, for a review). In particular, attentional orienting to stimuli seems to be slower and less flexible in ASD (e.g., Courchesne et al., 1994; Landry & Bryson, 2004; Renner, Klinger, & Klinger, 2006;

Wainwright & Bryson, 1996), as early as 9 to 12 months of age (Bryson et al., 2007; Osterling & Dawson, 1994; Zwaigenbaum et al., 2005). The overlap in timelines between the development of the orienting/executive attention networks and the emergence of behavioral manifestations of sensory features (particularly hyporesponsiveness) may have implications for understanding pathogenesis of these features.

The emergence, developmental course, and stability of sensory features across the lifespan for individuals with ASD are not well understood. The earliest manifestations of sensory features during infant development have been detected through various methods including retrospective parental reports or clinical case studies (e.g., Dahlgren & Gillberg, 1989; Watson et al., 2007), retrospective video analysis studies (e.g., Baranek, 1999a; Freuler et al., 2012; Osterling & Dawson, 1994), and prospective studies usually with high-risk samples such as infant siblings of children with ASD (Bryson et al., 2007; Zwaigenbaum et al., 2005). These studies have shown that both high-risk infant siblings and infants from low-risk samples later diagnosed with ASD show predominantly hyporesponsive sensory patterns (e.g., failure to orient to social and nonsocial stimuli, low activity levels) and some unusual sensory focused behaviors and repetitions (e.g., rubbing hands repetitively on an object, unusual mouthing/sniffing, visual fixations) by 6 to 12 months of age (e.g., Bryson et al., 2007; Dahlgren & Gillberg, 1989; Freuler et al., 2012; Guinchat et al., 2012; Osterling & Dawson, 1994; Zwaigenbaum et al., 2005), and that these behaviors may even precede some of the social and communication features of ASD in some cases. Hyperresponsive behaviors (e.g., touch aversion, intense reactions to stimuli) are also occasionally noted by 9–12 months (Baranek, 1999a; Bryson et al., 2007; Zwaigenbaum et al., 2005), but seem to increase in their frequency of being reported/observed in the early toddler and preschool years (e.g., Guinchat et al., 2012; Zwaigenbaum et al., 2005), potentially as a result of parents becoming more aware of their atypicality and/or association with a clinical diagnosis (Lord, 1995).

It is difficult to separate out sensory features from regulatory and temperamental differences in infancy since these constructs are related (M. E. Brock et al., 2012; Clifford et al., 2012; Garon et al., 2009). Unusual sensory reactivity, particularly hyperresponsiveness, is often reflected in more difficult temperament (e.g., withdrawal from stimuli; negative affect) and in self-regulation problems (e.g., sleep disturbances; inconsolable crying), all of which have been commonly recalled by parents of children with ASD in the first 2 years of life (e.g., Bryson et al., 2007; Dahlgren & Gillberg, 1989; Greenspan & Wieder, 1997; Guinchat et al., 2012; Werner, Dawson, Munson & Osterling, 2005; Wing, 1969; Young, Brewer, & Pattison, 2003), even in cases with late-onset or regressive autism (Werner & Dawson, 2005). Collectively, these infant studies indicate that a pattern of behavioral hyporesponsiveness to sensory stimuli and regulatory difficulties may be emerging in the first year of life, followed closely by, or perhaps in tandem with, hyperresponsive and sensory seeking patterns.

Correlational studies provide some evidence for maturational development impacting the degree to which sensory features manifested behaviorally. Some reported that hyperresponsiveness may become more prominent (e.g., Liss et al., 2006; Talay-Ongan & Wood, 2000) as a function of increasing chronological age; others suggested hyperresponsiveness may decrease with greater mental abilities irrespective of chronological age (Baranek et al., 2007). Hyporesponsiveness has been found to decrease as a function of age (particularly mental age) in preschool/school age samples (Baranek et al., 1997; Baranek et al., in press; Kern, Trivedi, et al., 2007; Kern, Garver, et al., 2007). It is also possible that development is nonlinear, and changes reflect different functions at different developmental periods. A recent meta-analysis suggested that severity of sensory features, specifically hyperresponsiveness and sensory-seeking patterns, increases with chronological age from toddlerhood through the early school years, and subsequently decreases (Ben-Sasson et al., 2009). Although the severity of sensory features may vary over time depending on many other factors to be further explored (e.g., cortical maturation, intervention effects, coping abilities, etc.), there is evidence that sensory differences among individuals with ASD persist throughout life (Ben-Sasson et al., 2009; Kern et al., 2006). Crane and colleagues (2009) reported that although the modality affected and the severity level of symptoms varies, 94.4% of adults with ASD indicate some sensory features. The nature and direction of change over time in sensory features remains uncertain due to limitations in research design (e.g., cross-sectional rather than longitudinal) and differences in measurement tools (e.g., measures of general development or autism symptoms rather than sensory symptoms per se). More longitudinal studies are needed to expand our understandings of the developmental nature of sensory features and their transactions with other aspects of development including social, emotional, language, motor, and cognitive skills.

ASSOCIATIONS WITH OTHER FEATURES OF ASD

Studies have linked specific sensory features to social-communication deficits, the presence of restricted and repetitive behaviors, and atypical motor features among individuals with ASD. Often these co-occurring features are conflated and difficult to unravel experimentally.

Social-Communication

Sensory features are evident across social and nonsocial contexts for persons with ASD (Baranek et al., in press; Hilton et al., 2007; Liss et al., 2006). Some studies indicate that verbal and nonverbal communication deficits in children with ASD may overshadow some of their difficulties with sensory experiences. For example, Nader, Oberlander, Chambers, and Craig (2004) found that although caregivers often perceived children with ASD as being hyporesponsive to pain, detailed observational scales coded during routine venipuncture procedures revealed that these children had heightened pain responses relative to typically developing children.

Several studies have shown negative correlations between the degree of sensory features, particularly hyporesponsiveness, and social-communication abilities (Lane et al., 2010; Watson et al., 2011). Specifically, difficulty orienting to both social and nonsocial sensory stimuli, often reported in very young children with ASD, may negatively impact development of joint attention (Baranek et al., in press; G. Dawson et al., 2004) and subsequent opportunities for language acquisition (e.g., Watson et al., 2011). Deficits found in temporal processing of complex auditory stimuli (Jansson-Verkasalo et al., 2003; Teder-Salejarvi et al., 2005), auditory memory encoding (Seri et al., 1999), and temporal synchrony (Bahrick, Lickliter, & Flom, 2004) may have particular implications for language functions.

Phenomenological accounts from highly verbal individuals with ASD (e.g., Grandin & Scariano, 1986; D. Williams, 1994) also provide insights into how complex multisensory environments, particularly in social situations, may become overstimulating, resulting in decreased ability to filter relevant information from conversations and increasing tendencies for social withdrawal. Laboratory studies indicating physiological overarousal (Barry & James, 1988; McAlonan et al., 2002), heightened sensitivities (Cascio et al., 2012; Gomot, Giard, Adrien, Barthélémy, & Bruneau, 2002), and/or deficits in multisensory integration (e.g., Hardan et al., 2008) provide some support for such interpretations, but few have shown correlations with clinical measures of hyperresponsiveness (e.g., Chang et al., 2012). Tactile hyperresponsiveness has also been documented in several behavioral (Baranek et al., 1997) and physiological studies (Cascio et al., 2008), and has been linked with social withdrawal. One theory posits that early neurodevelopmental disruptions in an affiliative social touch system involving C-touch (CT) afferents (i.e., unmyelinated tactile mechanoreceptors distributed primarily in the hairy skin) may be implicated (Olausson et al., 2002; Vallbo, Olausson, & Wessberg, 1999; Wessberg, Olausson, Fernstrom, & Vallbo, 2003), but studies directly testing these hypotheses are needed (Cascio et al., 2008).

Restricted and Repetitive Behaviors

Restricted and repetitive behaviors (RRBs) are conflated and difficult to parse out from sensory features, particularly for the category of sensory seeking behaviors that may be intense, repetitive, and overfocused on sensory feedback from object manipulations (e.g., sighting closely while twiddling string) or body movements (e.g., body rocking). Furthermore, sensory features, especially hyperresponsiveness to sensory stimuli (Green & Ben-Sasson, 2010), as well as RRBs (Turner, 1999), have been linked to hyperarousal, perhaps to serve a homeostatic function or to alleviate anxiety. Moreover, studies have shown correlations with developmental maturation such that lower IQ or lower mental age is associated with both RRBs (Bishop, Reichler, & Lord, 2006; Bodfish, Symons, Parker, & Lewis, 2000) and sensory features (Baranek et al., 2007; Boyd et al., 2010) in ASD. To deal with these issues, studies have begun to adjust for IQ and remove duplicate questionnaire items, yet they still find that degree of sensory features is associated with the severity of RRBs among children with ASD (Boyd et al., 2009; Chen, Rodgers, & McConachie, 2009; Gabriels et al., 2008). With regard to specific sensory response patterns, hyperresponsiveness has been correlated with rigid and inflexible behaviors (Baranek et al., 1997) as well as stereotypies, compulsions, and rituals/sameness behaviors (Boyd et al., 2010), while sensory-seeking behaviors positively correlated only with rituals/sameness behavior (Boyd et al., 2010). Contrasting findings suggest that RRBs are associated with hyporesponsiveness (in the tactile modality) and sensory seeking (Foss-Feig, Heacock, & Cascio, 2012). More research is needed to uncover shared mechanisms that may underlie the manifestation of both sensory features and RRBs.

Motor Features

Atypical motor features such as difficulties with postural control, dyspraxia, and dyscoordination (David et al., 2009; Dziuk et al., 2007; Gepner, Mestre, Masson, & de Schonen, 1995) are common in ASD but are not considered as core impairments. Evidence that motor difficulties may be linked with deficits in higher order sensory processing (i.e., integration of multisensory information in complex neural systems, rather than simple detection by unimodal first-order analysis of sensory information in the brain) includes studies that have found compromised postural stability among individuals with ASD compared with typical controls, particularly under conditions when one sensory system (e.g., somatosensory input) is altered (Minshew, Sung, Jones, & Furman, 2004; Molloy, Dietrich, & Bhattacharya, 2003). Typical development of postural stability emerges as the integration of vestibular, proprioceptive, and visual information become refined with experience and maturation (Shumway-Cook & Woolacott, 1985).

Dyspraxia is likely related to impairments in imitation of body positions and movements in individuals with ASD (I. M. Smith & Bryson, 1994), which may reflect disturbances in the integration of somatosensory (i.e., tactile and proprioceptive) with visual information. Research suggests that imitation of body movements is more impaired than object imitation in young children with ASD (DeMyer et al., 1972; Stone, Ousely, & Littleford, 1997); thus, generating or using internal somatosensory representations of visually modeled actions may be more difficult than reproducing actions that provide ongoing visual cues. However, recent findings suggested that accuracy of proprioceptive learning (i.e., decoding of elbow position) was similar for adolescents with ASD and neurotypical controls, indicating that peripheral proprioceptive signals or lower level neural representations of limb positions did not account for motor coordination difficulties in ASD (Fuentes, Mostofsky, & Bastian, 2011). A more plausible explanation for motor difficulties may be impairment in higher level integration of proprioceptive with other sensory information, such as visual, vestibular, and tactile sensations as they change in time and space. In support, Izawa et al. (2012) found that children with ASD had an abnormal bias toward reliance on internal proprioceptive feedback over external visual feedback, which may have implications for learning novel movements, as well as acquiring internal models of action from social imitation.

FUNCTIONAL IMPACT AND ADAPTIVE OUTCOMES

Adaptive functioning (e.g., daily-living skills, social skills, school functioning, etc.) is often compromised among individuals with ASD (Baker, Lane, Angley, & Young, 2008; O'Donnell, Deitz, Kartin, Nalty, & Dawson, 2012), even in the presence of average cognitive ability (e.g., Klin et al., 2007). Research suggests that the overall degree of sensory features (Rogers et al., 2003) as well as specific sensory response patterns (Ashburner, Ziviani, & Rodger, 2008; Baranek et al., 1997) or subtypes (e.g., Ausderau et al., under review; Lane et al., 2010) may be related to difficulties with adaptive functioning. Specifically, sensory hyporesponsiveness and sensory-seeking patterns have been associated with maladaptive behavior (Baker et al., 2008; Liss et al., 2006; Reynolds, Bendixen, Lawrence, & Lane, 2011).

Participation in activities in the home and community (e.g., helping prepare meals, attending school clubs, visiting neighbors) promotes development and learning (Dunst, Bruder, Trivette, Raab, & McLean, 2001; Humphry & Wakeford, 2006). Research suggests that children with ASD participate less frequently, with less variety, and with fewer individuals in activities as compared to typically developing children and those with other developmental disabilities (e.g., Hilton, Crouch, & Israel, 2008; Orsmond & Kou, 2011); however, studies demonstrating how specific sensory features affect participation, either negatively (Bagby, Dickie, & Baranek, 2012; Hochhauser & Engel-Yeger, 2010; Schaaf, Toth-Cohen, Outten, Johnson, & Madrid, 2011) or positively (Little, 2012), are just emerging. For example, enhanced perception abilities may contribute to success in some tasks, such as doing puzzles, among children with autism (Little, 2012).

Studies have reported that hyperresponsive sensory patterns especially interfere with activities in the home (e.g., mealtimes, grooming) and community (e.g., going out to restaurants, entertainment venues) for families of children with ASD (Baranek et al., 1997; Dickie, Baranek, Schultz, Watson & McComish, 2009; Hochhauser & Engel-Yeger, 2010; Jasmin, Courture, McKinley, Fombonne, & Gisel, 2009; Lane et al., 2010; Little, 2012; Marquenie, Rodger, Mangohig, & Cronin 2010). Although a number of studies have focused on the limited social participation among school-age children and adolescents with ASD (Potvin, Snider, Prelock, Kehayia, & Wood-Dauphinee, 2012; Solish, Perry, & Minnes, 2010), it may be that the unpredictability of sensory stimuli in unfamiliar social contexts, coupled with children's social-communication limitations, impacts their participation. Sensory stimuli associated with activities in the home versus community may be more predictable and manageable for families (Bagby et al., 2012; Schaaf et al., 2011). Furthermore, children's maturational levels and autism severity likely interact with sensory features to impact activity participation (Little, 2012), lending support for a transactional view of the complexities involved in children's participation across contexts.

APPROACH TO CLINICAL ASSESSMENT

Professionals across a wide range of disciplines (e.g., occupational therapists, physical therapists, speech-language pathologists, audiologists, psychologists, and physicians, etc.) may assess sensory processing abilities (e.g., modulation, discrimination, or integrative functions) in individuals with ASD across contexts such as home, school, work environment, and clinic. Various tools are available, depending on the purpose of the assessment (e.g., initial assessment/diagnosis, eligibility for services, intervention planning, progress monitoring, and outcome evaluation). Although most individuals with ASD do not have a primary sensory deficit such as a hearing or vision loss, the appropriate professionals should assess these functions, resolving any concerns before further evaluating sensory processing functions. The assessment of sensory features among individuals with ASD necessitates a thorough understanding of the purpose of the assessment, nature of concerns, and potential impact of the disorder on important areas of functioning (e.g., social communication, adaptive behavior, etc.). Specific behavioral manifestations of sensory features, including strengths and weaknesses, need to be assessed appropriately if such concerns appear to be impacting daily functioning or social participation.

A top-down approach (American Occupational Therapy Association, 2002; Coster, 1998) would begin by focusing on the most global level of assessment such as social participation, which is an essential consideration for individuals with ASD and their families. This approach would then systematically address more specific aspects of engagement (i.e., activities and tasks) and followed by specific impairments (e.g., sensory processing deficits). Use of sensory assessment tools in a strictly bottom-up approach runs the risk of focusing on sensory deficits while neglecting the transactional relationship between the impairment level (i.e., sensory processing deficits) and the more global participation level. A combination of interviews (client and caregiver), structured and unstructured skilled clinical observations, and standardized assessments may provide a holistic perspective and guide an individualized and contextually relevant intervention plan.

Clinical Assessments/Behavioral Measures

A number of clinical caregiver report measures and behavioral assessments have been developed to characterize sensory features in individuals with ASD and/or other populations, and these assessments are often aligned with specific sensory processing conceptual frameworks. Theoretical perspectives that inform the clinical assessment of sensory features among individuals with ASD include but are not limited to the Optimal Engagement Band (Baranek, Reinhartsen, & Wannamaker, 2000), Dunn's Model of Sensory Processing

(Dunn, 1997), and Miller and colleagues' Proposed Nosology of Sensory Integration (2007). Although assessment measures may aid in understanding strengths and weaknesses for diagnostic purposes or intervention planning, few have been developed or tested systematically for their sensitivity to change (positive or negative) and validity as outcome measures of intervention. Goal attainment scaling (GAS) is one method used to set individualized goals in collaboration with family members, and can be monitored over time to assess progress (Mailloux et al., 2007). Systematic monitoring of meaningful goals aligns with current recommendations of the American Academy of Pediatrics (2012) regarding therapies for children with developmental and behavioral disorders.

A comprehensive assessment of sensory features may obtain an inventory of sensory experiences across modalities and/or patterns, or focus on a specific construct (e.g., hyperresponsiveness) or modality (e.g., tactile). An exhaustive review of the psychometric properties of clinical caregiver report measures and behavioral assessments is beyond the scope of this chapter (see Baranek, Parham, & Bodfish, 2005, for more details). Clinical caregiver report measures (presented in alphabetical order) include the Sensory Experiences Questionnaire Version 3.0 (SEQ-3.0; Baranek, 2009), a 105-item assessment developed for children with ASD and other developmental disorders, ages 2 through 12 years. The SEQ-3.0 measures the frequency of behaviors associated with four sensory response patterns (i.e., hyporesponsiveness; hyperresponsiveness; sensory interests, repetitions, and seeking behaviors; and enhanced perception) as well as modalities (i.e., auditory, visual, tactile, gustatory, vestibular) across social or nonsocial contexts. In addition to using a Likert scale (i.e., 1 = never/almost never to 5 = always/almost always) of frequency of behaviors, the SEQ-3.0 has eight items that allow the caregiver to provide qualitative responses related to their children's sensory features. The Sensory Processing Measure (SPM; Parham et al., 2007) is a norm-referenced questionnaire for parents or teachers of children ages 5–12 years. It is designed to detect atypical behaviors in sensory processing, praxis, and social participation. A preschool version, the SPM-P, is for children ages 2–5 years (Miller-Kuhaneck, Ecker, Parham, Henry, & Glennon, 2010), which provides scores for social participation, praxis, five sensory systems (visual, auditory, tactile, proprioceptive, and vestibular), and a total sensory composite. The Sensory Profile (SP; Dunn, 1999), normed with typically developing children aged 3 to 10 years, is a 125-item questionnaire that uses a 5-point Likert scale (i.e., 1 = never/almost never to 5 = always/almost always) to measure reactions to various sensory situations and some behavioral/emotional consequences of sensory reactivity. An Infant/Toddler SP (Dunn, 2002), Adolescent/Adult SP (self-report) (Brown & Dunn, 2002), and a short form (SSP; McIntosh, Miller, Shyu, & Dunn, 1999) are also available. Scores are obtained for four quadrants: low registration, sensory seeking, sensory sensitivity, and sensory avoiding.

A variety of behavioral assessments are available for testing specific sensory features or processing; however, few were developed for assessment of sensory features among individuals with ASD, and the psychometric properties of many continue to be investigated. The Sensory Integration and Praxis Tests (SIPT; Ayres, 1989) include 17 subtests designed to detect dysfunctional sensory processes (e.g., visual perception, tactile perception, vestibular-proprioceptive functions) in children ages 4 to 9 years. The Sensory Over-Responsivity Scales: Assessment and Inventory (SensOR; Schoen et al., 2008) measures sensory overresponsivity in seven sensory domains (i.e., tactile, auditory, visual, proprioceptive, olfactory, gustatory, vestibular) in ages 3 through 55 years through both an examiner-administered performance evaluation ($n = 53$ items) and a caregiver self-rating scale ($n = 76$ items). The Sensory Processing Assessment (SPA; Baranek, 1999b) is a brief behavioral measure designed to assess sensory response patterns for children with ASD and related developmental disorders ages 9 months through 6 years. The SPA uses a semistructured play-based format to assess approach-avoidance patterns with sensory

toys, orienting responses to social and nonsocial sensory stimuli, and habituation to repeated stimuli. The Tactile Defensiveness and Discrimination Test—Revised (TDDT-R; Baranek, 1998) is a structured behavioral assessment with five subtests administered in a game-like fashion to measure tactile processing in preschool and school-aged children.

CONSIDERATIONS FOR INTERVENTION

Intervention approaches should be highly individualized and aim to maximize engagement in meaningful activities and social participation in the community that are critical to support long-term health, wellness, and quality of life (e.g., Bober, Humphry, Carswell, & Core, 2001). Individualized interventions ideally should align with the goals of the client or family, consider strengths as well as weaknesses, and be contextually relevant, theoretically sound, and congruent with existing clinical and empirical evidence.

A variety of intervention approaches (e.g., sensory-based therapies, parent-mediated interventions, developmental/behavioral programs, alternative therapies) targeting sensory features in children with ASD have proliferated in clinical settings. There is much less research conducted on efficacy of interventions for sensory processing issues relative to interventions for other core features of ASD (e.g., social-communication skills), and very few large-scale randomized controlled trials exist. Furthermore, although these intervention approaches differ with respect to structure, process, and intended outcomes, they are often discussed as if they are equivalent (e.g., sensory-based therapy is often erroneously labeled as "sensory integration therapy"). Thus, practitioners and families are often confronted with making therapeutic decisions in the face of a limited evidence base and surrounding controversies in the literature (American Academy of Pediatrics, 2012; May-Benson & Koomar, 2010). A systematic critique is presented elsewhere (see Baranek, 2002); however, we describe some of the more common sensory-based approaches below and acknowledge that many other approaches are available. Regardless of the intervention used, interventionists should consider the evidence base for the interventions and systematically evaluate outcomes (positive and negative) for their clients. Due to the heterogeneous nature of ASD, children's responses to differential treatments are likely to be quite individualized and varied.

Sensory stimulation approaches involve administration of specific protocols or activities, controlled by an intervener, in a time-limited manner (e.g., wearing a weighted vest for touch pressure input, swinging for vestibular input, sitting on a therapy ball for proprioceptive input, or brushing for tactile input). Expected outcomes usually focus on improving attention, decreasing self-stimulatory behavior, and increasing self-regulation; these have been studied using single-system research designs or alternating treatment group designs, resulting in mixed findings and usually for short-term effects (e.g., Devlin, Healy, Leader, & Hughes, 2010; Fertal-Daly, Bedell, & Hinojosa, 2001; Schilling & Schwartz, 2004; Van Rie & Heflin, 2009). Two randomized controlled trials (RCTs) using a massage protocol reported some improvements in tactile modulation and reductions in problem behaviors, perhaps related to improved sleep after massage (Escalona, Field, Singer-Strunck, Cullen, & Harshorn, 2001; Field et al., 1997). A small RCT used the Grandin Hug Machine (touch pressure) for 6 weeks and reported some reduction in self-perceived anxiety and decreased arousal/reactivity in children with ASD (Edelson, Edelson, Kerr & Grandin, 1999). Auditory integration programs involve complex applications of auditory stimuli (e.g., filtered auditory input delivered through headphones or other listening systems) and target a variety of outcomes including sensory modulation, improved language, and adaptive functioning; these have been tested in small scaled group comparison designs or RCTs, with mixed and/or inconclusive findings reported (e.g., Bettison, 1996; May-Benson & Teasdale, 2012; Mudford et al., 2000; Rimland & Edelson, 1995; for reviews see Baranek, 2002; Dawson & Watling, 2000).

In contrast to intervener-imposed sensory stimulation protocols, an alternative approach uses teaching and/or coaching individuals with ASD (usually with mental ages over 8 years) to cognitively notice their behavioral states and use sensory strategies to manage self-regulation (e.g., Alert Program; M. S. Williams & Shellenberger, 1994); however little research is available. Another approach is to modify sensory environments to improve performance, but studies with ASD samples are rare. Kinnealey et al. (2012) conducted a single subject study ($n = 4$ adolescents; 3 with ASD) and reported some positive effects of sound absorption and softer light modifications on attention to academic tasks and self-reported comfort in the classroom.

Ayres's sensory integration therapy (Ayres, 1972, 2005; Parham & Mailloux, 2010) is a long-term, individualized therapy that requires specialized training (usually by occupational therapists) to elicit active child engagement through "just-right challenges." It is delivered in individual 30–60 minute sessions, one to two times per week, for 6–12 months' duration and takes place in a large therapy room containing multisensory equipment such as swings, climbing structures, and textured materials. A fidelity instrument is available (Parham et al., 2011). Aims are to directly enhance sensory integration and praxis abilities in order to impact broader, developmental social participation and adaptive outcomes. ASD studies have primarily used single-subject designs or alternating treatments group designs (Case-Smith & Bryan, 1999; Linderman & Stewart, 1999; Smith, Press, Koenig, & Kinnealey, 2005; Watling & Dietz, 2007), with mixed evidence regarding improvements in various outcomes (e.g., engagement, play, socialization, behavior regulation, stereotypic behavior). RCT studies with children with ASD are emerging (Pfeiffer, Koenig, Kinnealey, Sheppard, & Henderson, 2011; Schaaf, Hunt, & Benevides, 2012); these limited studies report some individualized gains using goal attainment scaling as well as standardized measures.

Recent trends involve moving intervention out of the clinic to natural contexts. These caregiver-mediated approaches coach caregivers to recognize children's sensory features and problem-solve the dilemmas that arise in daily routines when living with a person with ASD (e.g., Baranek et al., in preparation; Dunn, Cox, Foster, Mische-Lawson, & Tanquary, 2012). Engagement in school- or community-based activity programs, such as exercise, yoga, swimming, martial arts, or horseback riding, are recommended by some clinicians to supplement intervention programs in an effort to enrich sensory or movement experiences that may enhance self-regulation or improve behavior. As with other interventions, efficacy research is limited (Hartshorn et al., 2001; Koenig, Buckley-Reen, & Garg, 2012).

In summary, interventions to address sensory features in ASD differ greatly in format, process, and intended outcomes. Although emergent research has validated the potentially detrimental effects of sensory processing problems for persons with ASD and their families, more research using rigorous designs and with larger samples is needed to test and compare effects of specific approaches. Future studies should clearly identify and carefully describe the specific intervention being tested, as well as the rationale for the expected outcomes. Skills that are not directly addressed and integrated meaningfully in the context of natural daily routines are less likely to improve. The dearth of efficacy studies warrants that practitioners select and monitor interventions for sensory processing problems carefully and target meaningful outcomes (e.g., functional activities, social participation, etc.) that are specific to each individual with ASD.

CONCLUSIONS

Sensory features in ASD have gained prominence in the literature over the past decade, and the field is burgeoning with more descriptive, correlational, and experimental studies to elucidate the nature of these issues. Research in the areas of attention, perception, and multisensory integration has enhanced our understanding of sensory processing differences (both strengths and weaknesses) that

manifest in persons with ASD, and could facilitate the discovery of specific endophenotypes underlying both sensory features and other core features of ASD. The ubiquity of sensory features across the lifespan, and evidence of strong associations with social-communication deficits as well we repetitive behaviors in ASD, further supports their inclusion in current diagnostic nosologies as core features. Unlike the fourth edition of the *Diagnostic and Statistical Manual of Mental Disorders* (*DSM-IV*; American Psychiatric Association [APA], 2000), which largely excluded sensory features (i.e., sensory symptoms were considered associated features), the *DSM-5* (APA, 2012) includes sensory symptoms (i.e., hyper-or hyporeactivity to sensory input or unusual interest in sensory aspects of environment) as diagnostic features of ASD.

We recognize that sensory features are early developing, pervasive, and panmodal, and they affect people with ASD individually and differentially throughout their lifetimes. Yet, there is still a need for more rigorous and systematic research, particularly with respect to issues of pathogenesis, heterogeneity, developmental trajectories, and functional impact of sensory processing problems. More studies are required to determine neural mechanisms underlying specific sensory response patterns, and how sensory processes transact with other domains over time to enhance or inhibit development. We need to further differentiate the extent to which sensory processing abilities in persons with ASD are similar or different from other clinical disorders or to typically developing individuals at different stages of development. Intriguing questions also remain with regard to the overlap of seemingly paradoxical sensory response patterns; thus more research on subtypes and their neurobiological and genetic linkages is required. Very few studies include physiological and behavioral/clinical methods concurrently, and those that do have had difficulty fully reconciling discrepant findings. Finally, there has been limited progress on developing valid assessment tools and translating scientific findings into more effective interventions to address sensory processing issues in ways that are most beneficial in people's lives.

New methodological and technological advances show promise to advance research in this area; however, progress continues to be hampered by limited funding, inconsistent terminologies, professional controversies, and insufficient collaborations among basic and clinical science disciplines, as well as among researchers and practitioners. It is important to move forward sensibly, strategically, and collaboratively, involving all stakeholders (individuals with ASD, families, primary care providers, therapists, educators, advocates, and researchers including basic scientists, neuroscientists, applied and translational scientists, as well as funding agencies, etc.) in evolving the theoretical, scientific, and clinical knowledge base in this field.

CROSS-REFERENCES

Chapters 4 and 5 address issues of autism in infants and young children and school-age children, respectively. Chapter 15 addresses motor control and learning. Aspects of multidisciplinary intervention are discussed in Chapter 26. Comprehensive treatment programs are addressed in Chapter 30 and evidence-based treatments in Chapter 42.

REFERENCES

Adolphs, R. (2001). The neurobiology of social cognition. *Current Opinion in Neurobiology, 11*, 231–239.

Alcantara, J. I., Weisblatt, E. J. L., Moore, B. C. J., & Bolton, P. F. (2004). Speech-in-noise perception in high-functioning individuals with autism or Asperger's syndrome. *Journal of Child Psychology and Psychiatry, 45*, 1107–1114.

Allen, G., & Courchesne, E. (2001). Attention function and dysfunction in autism. *Frontiers in Bioscience, 6*, 105–119.

American Academy of Pediatrics. (2012). Policy statement: Sensory integration therapies for children with developmental and behavioral disorders. *Pediatrics, 129*, 1186–1189.

American Occupational Therapy Association. (2002). Occupational therapy practice framework: Domain and process. *American Journal of Occupational Therapy, 56*(6), 609–639.

American Psychiatric Association. (2000). *Diagnostic and Statistical Manual of Mental Disorders* (4th ed., text rev.). Washington, DC: Author.

American Psychiatric Association. (2012). *Autism spectrum disorder*. Retrieved from http://www.dsm5.org/proposed revisions/pages/proposedrevision.aspx?rid=94

Ashburner, J., Ziviani, J., & Rodger, S. (2008). Sensory processing and classroom, emotional, behavioral, and educational outcomes in children with autism spectrum disorder. *American Journal of Occupational Therapy, 62*(5), 564–573.

Asher, J. E., Lamb, J. A., Brocklebank, D., Cazier, J. B., Maestrini, E., Addis, L.,...Monaco, A. P. (2009). A whole-genome scan and fine-mapping linkage study of auditory-visual synesthesia reveals evidence of linkage to chromosomes 2q24, 5q33, 6p12, and 12p12. *American Journal of Human Genetics, 84*, 279–285.

Ashwin, E., Ashwin, C., Rhydderch, D., Howells, J., & Baron-Cohen, S. (2009). Eagle-eyed visual acuity: An experimental investigation of enhanced perception in autism. *Biological Psychiatry, 65*(10), 17–21.

Ausderau, K. K., Furlong, M., Sideris, J., Little, L. M., Bulluck, J., Watson, L. R.,...Baranek, G. T. (under review). *Sensory subtypes in children with ASD: Latent profile transition analysis using a national survey of sensory features.*

Ausderau, K., Sideris, J., Furlong, M., Little, L. M., Bulluck, J., & Baranek, G. T. (in revision). *National survey of sensory features of children with ASD: Factor structure of the Sensory Experience Questionnaire.*

Ayres, A. J. (1972). *Sensory integration and learning disorders.* Los Angeles, CA: Western Psychological Services.

Ayres, A. J. (1989). *Sensory Integration and Praxis Tests.* Los Angeles, CA: Western Psychological Services.

Ayres, A. J. (2005). *Sensory integration and the child: Understanding hidden sensory challenges* (2nd ed.). Los Angeles, CA: Western Psychological Services.

Bagby, M., Dickie, V., & Baranek, G. T. (2012). How sensory experiences in children with and without autism affect family occupations. *American Journal of Occupational Therapy, 66*, 78–86.

Bahrick, L. E., & Lickliter, R. (2004). Infants' perception of rhythm and tempo in unimodal and multimodal stimulation: A developmental test of the intersensory redundancy hypothesis. *Cognitive, Affective and Behavioral Neuroscience, 4*, 137–147.

Bahrick, L. E., Lickliter, R., & Flom, R. (2004). Intersensory redundancy guides the development of selective attention, perception, and cognition in infancy. *Current Directions in Psychological Science, 13*, 99–102.

Baker, A., Lane, A., Angley, M., & Young, R. (2008). The relationship between sensory processing patterns and behavioural responsiveness in autistic disorder: A pilot study. *Journal of Autism and Developmental Disorders, 38*(5), 867–875. doi:10.1007/s10803-007-0459-0

Baranek, G. T. (1998). *Tactile Defensiveness and Discrimination Test—Revised (TDDT-R).* Unpublished manuscript, University of North Carolina at Chapel Hill.

Baranek, G. T. (1999a). Autism during infancy: A retrospective video analysis of sensory motor and social behaviors at 9–12 months of age. *Journal of Autism and Developmental Disorders, 29*(3), 213–224.

Baranek, G. T. (1999b). *Sensory Processing Assessment for Young Children (SPA).* Unpublished manuscript, University of North Carolina at Chapel Hill.

Baranek, G. T. (2002). Efficacy of sensory and motor interventions for children with autism. *Journal of Autism and Developmental Disorders, 32*, 397–422.

Baranek, G. T. (2009). *Sensory experiences questionnaire version 3.0.* Unpublished manuscript.

Baranek, G. T., Boyd, B. A., Poe, M. D., David, F. J., & Watson, L. R. (2007). Hyperresponsive sensory response patterns in young children with autism, developmental delay, and typical development. *American Journal on Mental Retardation, 112*(4), 233–245.

Baranek, G. T., David, F. J., Poe, M. D., Stone, W. L., & Watson, L. R. (2006). Sensory Experiences Questionnaire: Discriminating sensory features in young children with autism, developmental delays, and typical development. *Journal of Child Psychology and Psychiatry, 47*(6), 591–601.

Baranek, G. T., Foster, L. G., & Berkson, G. (1997). Tactile defensiveness and stereotyped behaviors. *American Journal of Occupational Therapy, 51*(2), 91–95.

Baranek, G. T., Parham, D. L., & Bodfish, J. W. (2005). Sensory and motor features in autism: Assessment and intervention. In F. Volkmar, R. Paul, A. Klin, & D. Cohen (Eds.), *Handbook of autism and pervasive developmental disorders: Vol. 2. Assessment, interventions, and policy* (pp. 831–857). Hoboken, NJ: Wiley.

Baranek, G. T., Reinhartsen, D. B., & Wannamaker, S. W. (2000). Play: Engaging children with autism. In R. Heubner (Ed.), *Sensorimotor interventions in autism* (pp. 311–351). Philadelphia, PA: F. A. Davis.

Baranek, G. T., Turner Brown, L., Watson, L. R., Field, S. H., Crais, E. R., Wakeford, C. L., ... Reznick, S. (in preparation). *A randomized controlled trial of Adapted Responsive Teaching for infants at-risk for autism spectrum disorder in a community sample.*

Baranek, G. T., Watson, L. R., Boyd, B. A., Poe, M. D., David, F. J., & McGuire, L. (2013). Hyporesponsiveness to social and nonsocial sensory stimuli in children with autism, children with developmental delays, and typically developing children. *Development and Psychopathology, 25*(2), 307–320. doi:10.1017/S0954579412001071

Baron-Cohen, S., Ashwin, E., Ashwin, C., Tavassoli, T., & Chakrabarti, B. (2009). Talent in autism: Hyper-systemizing, hyper-attention to detail and sensory hypersensitivity. *Philosophical Transactions of the Royal Society, 364*, 1377–1383.

Baron-Cohen, S., Leslie, A. M., & Frith, U. (1985). Does the autistic child have a "theory of mind"? *Cognition, 21*, 37–46.

Barry, R. J., & James, A. L. (1988). Coding of stimulus parameters in autistic, retarded, and normal children: Evidence for a two-factor theory of autism, *International Journal of Psychophysiology, 6*(2), 139–149. doi:10.1016/0167-8760(88)90045-1

Bebko, J. M., Weiss, J. A., Denmark, J. L., & Gomez, P. (2006). Discrimination of temporal synchrony in intermodal events by children with autism and children with developmental disabilities without autism. *Journal of Child Psychology and Psychiatry, 47*(1), 88–98.

Belmonte, M. K., Allen, G., Beckel-Mitchener, A., Boulanger, L. M., Carper, R. A., & Webb, S. J. (2004). Autism and abnormal development of brain connectivity. *Journal of Neuroscience, 24*, 9228–9231.

Bennetto, L., Kuschner, E. S., & Hyman, S. L. (2007). Olfaction and taste processing in autism. *Biological Psychiatry, 62*, 1015–1021. doi:10.1016/j.biopsych.2007.04.019

Ben-Sasson, A., Cermak, S. A., Orsmond, G. I., Tager-Flusberg, H., Cater, A. S., Kadlec, M. B., & Dunn, W. (2007). Extreme sensory modulation behaviors in toddlers with autism spectrum disorders. *American Journal of Occupational Therapy, 61*(5), 584–592.

Ben-Sasson, A., Hen, L., Fluss, R., Cermak, S., Engel-Yeger, B., & Gal, E. (2009). A meta-analysis of sensory modulation symptoms in individuals with autism spectrum disorders. *Journal of Autism and Developmental Disorders, 39*, 1–11.

Bertone, A., Mottron, L., Jelenic, P., & Faubert, J. (2003). Motion perception in autism: A "complex" issue. *Journal of Cognitive Neuroscience, Neurosurgery, and Psychiatry, 15*(2), 218–225.

Bertone, A., Mottron, L., Jelenic, P., & Faubert, J. (2005). Enhanced and diminished visuo-spatial information processing in autism depends on stimulus complexity. *Brain, 128*(10), 2430–2440.

Bettison, S. (1996). The long-term effects of auditory training on children with autism. *Journal of Autism and Developmental Disorders, 26*(3), 361–374. doi:10.1007/BF02172480

Bishop, S., Reichler, J., & Lord, C. (2006). Association between restricted and repetitive behaviors and nonverbal IQ in children with autism spectrum disorders. *Child Neuropsychology, 12*, 247–267.

Blakemore, S. J., Tavassoli, T., Calo, S., Thomas, R. M., Catmur, C., Frith, U., & Haggard, P. (2006). Tactile sensitivity in Asperger syndrome. *Brain and Cognition, 61*, 5–13.

Bober, S. J., Humphry, R., Carswell, H. W., & Core, A. J. (2001). Toddlers' persistence in the emerging occupations of functional play and self-feeding. *American Journal of Occupational Therapy, 55*, 369–376.

Bodfish, J., Symons, F., Parker, D., & Lewis, M. (2000). Varieties of repetitive behavior in autism: Comparisons to mental retardation. *Journal of Autism and Developmental Disorders, 30*(3), 237–243. doi:10.1023/A:1005596502855

Bölte, S., Holtmann, M., Poustka, F., Scheurich, A., & Schmidt, L. (2007). Gestalt perception and local–global processing in high-functioning autism. *Journal of Autism and Developmental Disorders, 37*(8), 1493–1504.

Bomba, M. D., & Pang, E. W. (2004). Cortical auditory evoked potentials in autism: A review. *International Journal of Psychophysiology, 53*(3), 161–169.

Bonnel, A., Mottron, L., Peretz, I., Trudel, M., Gallun, E., & Bonnel, A. M. (2003). Enhanced pitch sensitivity in individuals with autism: A signal detection analysis. *Journal of Cognitive Neuroscience, 15*(2), 226–235.

Boyd, B. A., Baranek, G. T., Sideris, J., Poe, M. D., Watson, L. R., Patten, E., & Miller, H. (2010). Sensory features and repetitive behaviors in children with autism and developmental delays. *Autism Research, 3*, 78–87.

Boyd, B. A., McBee, M., Holtzclaw, T., Baranek, G. T., & Bodfish, J. W. (2009). Relationships among repetitive behaviors, sensory features, and executive functions in high functioning autism. *Research in Autism Spectrum Disorders, 3*, 959–966.

Brandwein, A. B., Foxe, J. J., Russo, N. N., Altschuler, T. S., Gomes, H., & Molholm, S. (2011). The development of audiovisual multisensory integration across childhood and early adolescence: A high-density electrical mapping study. *Cerebral Cortex, 21*(5), 1042–1055.

Brock, J., Brown, C. C., Boucher, J., & Rippon, G. (2002). The temporal binding deficit hypothesis of autism. *Developmental Psychopathology, 14*(2), 209–224.

Brock, M. E., Freuler, A., Baranek, G. T., Watson, L. R., Poe, M. D., & Sabatino, A. (2012). Temperament and sensory features of children with autism. *Journal and autism and developmental disorders, 42*(11), 2271–2284.

Brown, C. E., & Dunn, W. (2002). *Adolescent/Adult Sensory Profile: User's manual*. Antonia, TX: Psychological Corporation.

Bryson, S. E., Zwaigenbaum, L., Brian, J., Roberts, W., Szatmari, P., Rombough, V., & McDermott, C. (2007). A prospective case series of high-risk infants who developed autism. *Journal of Autism and Developmental Disorders, 37*(1), 12–24.

Bruneau, N., Roux, S., Adrien, J., & Barthélémy, C. (1999). Auditory associative cortex dysfunction in children with autism: Evidence from late auditory evoked potentials (N1 wave–T complex). *Clinical Neurophysiology, 110*(11), 1927–1934. doi:10.1016/S1388-2457(99)00149-2

Budinger, E., Heil, P., Hess, A., Scheich, H. (2006). Multisensory processing via early cortical stages: Connections of the primary auditory cortical field with other sensory systems. *Neuroscience, 143*(4), 1065–1083.

Cascio, C., McGlone, F., Folger, S., Tannan, V., Baranek, G., Pelphrey, K. A., & Essick, G. (2008). Tactile perception in adults with autism: A multi-dimensional psychophysical study. *Journal of Autism and Developmental Disorders, 38*(1), 127–137.

Cascio, C. J., Moana-Filho, E. J., Guest, S., Nebel, M. B., Weisner, J., Baranek, G. T., & Essick, G. K. (2012). Perceptual and neural response to affective tactile texture stimulation in adults with autism spectrum disorders. *Autism Research, 5*, 231–244.

Case-Smith, J., & Bryan, T. (1999). The effects of occupational therapy with sensory integration emphasis on preschool-age children with autism. *American Journal of Occupational Therapy, 53*, 489–497.

Čeponienė, R., Lepistö, T., Shestakova, A., Vanhala, R., Alku, P, Näätänen, R., & Yaguchi, K. (2003). Speech-sound-selective auditory impairment in children with autism: They can perceive but do not attend. *Proceedings of the National Academy of Sciences, USA, 100*(9), 5567–5572. doi:10.1073/pnas .0835631100

Cesaroni, L., & Garber, M. (1991). Exploring the experience of autism through firsthand accounts. *Journal of Autism and Developmental Disorders, 21*(3), 303–313.

Chang, M. C., Parham, L. D., Blanche, E. I., Schell, A., Chou, C. P., Dawson, M., & Clark, F. (2012). Autonomic and behavioral responses of children with autism to auditory stimuli. *American Journal of Occupational Therapy, 66*, 567–576. doi:10.5014/ajot.2012.004242

Chen, Y. H., Rodgers, J., & McConachie, H. (2009). Restricted and repetitive behaviors, sensory processing and cognitive style in children with autism spectrum disorders. *Journal of Autism and Developmental Disorders, 39*, 635–42.

Ciesielski, K., Courchesne, E., & Elmasian, R. (1990). Effects of focused selective attention tasks on event-related potentials in autistic and normal individuals. *Electroencephalography and Clinical Neurophysiology, 75*(3), 207–220.

Clifford, S. M., Hundry, K., Elsabbagh, M., Charman, T., Johnson, M. H., & the BASIS Team. (2012). Temperament in the first 2 years of life in infants at high-risk for autism spectrum disorders. *Journal of Autism and Developmental Disorders*. Advance online publication. doi:10.1007/s10803-012-1612-y

Colombo, J. (2001). The development of visual attention in infancy. *Annual Review of Psychology, 52*, 337–367.

Coster, W. (1998). Occupation-centered assessment of children. *American Journal of Occupational Therapy, 52*(5), 337–334.

Courchesne, E., Courchesne, R. Y., Hicks, G., & Lincoln, A. J. (1985). Functioning of the brain stem auditory pathway in non-retarded autistic individuals. *Electroencephalography and Clinical Neurophysiology, 51*, 491–501.

Courchesne, E., Townsend, J., Akshoomoff, N., Saitoh, O., Yeung-Courchesne, R., Lincoln, A.,...Lau, L. (1994). Impairment in shifting attention in autistic and cerebellar patients. *Behavioral Neuroscience, 108*(5), 848–865. doi:10.1037/0735-7044.108.5.848

Crane, L., Goddard, L., & Pring, L. (2009). Sensory processing in adults with autism spectrum disorders. *Autism, 13*(3), 215–228.

Cytowic, R. E. (2002). *Synesthesia: A union of the senses* (2nd ed.). Cambridge, MA: MIT Press.

Dahlgren, S., & Gillberg, C. (1989). Symptoms in the first two years of life: A preliminary population study of infantile autism. *European Archives of Psychiatry & Neurological Sciences, 238*(3), 169–174. doi:10.1007/BF00451006

David, F. J., Baranek, G. T., Giuliani, C. A., Mercer, V. S., Poe, M. D., & Thorpe, D. E. (2009). A pilot study: Coordination of precision grip in children and adolescents with high functioning autism. *Pediatric Physical Therapy, 21*(2), 205–211.

Davies, P. L., Chang, W. P., & Gavin, W. J. (2009). Maturation of sensory gating performance in children with and without sensory processing disorders. *International Journal of Psychophysiology, 72*(2), 187–197.

Davis, R. A., Bockbrader, M. A., Murphy, R. R., Hetrick, W. P., & O'Donnell, B. F. (2006). Subjective perceptual distortions and visual dysfunction in children with autism. *Journal of Autism and Developmental Disorders, 36*, 199–210.

Dawson, G. (2008). Early behavioral intervention, brain plasticity, and the prevention of autism spectrum disorder. *Development and Psychopathology, 20*(3), 773–803.

Dawson, G., Finley, C., Phillips, S., Galpert, L., & Lewy, A. (1988). Reduced P3 amplitude of the event-related brain potential: Its relationship to language ability in autism. *Journal of Autism and Developmental Disorders, 18*(4), 493–504.

Dawson, G., Toth, K., Abbott, R., Osterling, J., Munson, J., Estes, A., & Liaw, J. (2004). Early social attention impairments in autism: Social orienting, joint attention, and attention to distress. *Developmental Psychology, 40*, 271–283.

Dawson, G., & Watling, R. (2000). Interventions to facilitate auditory, visual, and motor integration in autism: A review of the evidence. *Journal of Autism and Developmental Disorders, 30*(5), 415–421. doi:10.1023/A:1005547422749

Dawson, M. E., Schell, A. M., & Filion, D. L. (2007). The electrodermal system. In J. T. Cacioppo, L. G. Tassinary, &

G. G. Berntson (Eds.), *Handbook of psychophysiology* (3rd ed., pp. 159–181). New York, NY: Cambridge University Press.

DeMyer, M., Alpern, G., Barton, S., DeMyer, W., Churchill, D., Hingtgen, J.,... Kimberlin, C. (1972). Imitation in autistic, early schizophrenic, and non-psychotic subnormal children. *Journal of Autism and Childhood Schizophrenia, 2*(3), 264–287. doi:10.1007/BF01537618

de Regnier, R. A. (2008). Neurophysiological evaluation of brain function in extremely premature newborn infants. *Seminars in Perinatology, 32*, 2–10.

Devlin, S., Healy, O., Leader, G., & Hughes, B. M. (2010). Comparison of behavioral intervention and sensory-integration therapy in the treatment of challenging behavior. *Journal of Autism and Developmental Disorders.* Advance online publication. doi:10.1007/s10803-010-1149-x

Dickie, V. A., Baranek, G. T., Schultz, B., Watson, L. R., & McComish, C. S. (2009). Parent reports of sensory experiences of preschool children with and without autism: A qualitative study. *American Journal of Occupational Therapy, 63*(2), 172–181.

Donkers, F., Schipul, S., Baranek, G., Cleary, K., Willoughby, M., Evans, A.,... Belger, A. (in press). Attenuated auditory event-related potentials and associations with atypical sensory response patterns in children with autism. *Journal of Autism and Developmental Disorders.*

Dunn, W. (1997). The impact of sensory processing abilities on the daily lives of young children and their families: A conceptual model. *Infants and Young Children, 9*(4), 23–35.

Dunn, W. (1999). *Sensory Profile.* San Antonio, TX: Psychological Corporation.

Dunn, W. (2001). The sensations of everyday life: Empirical, theoretical, and pragmatic considerations. *American Journal of Occupational Therapy, 55*, 608–620.

Dunn, W. (2002). *Infant/Toddler Sensory Profile manual.* San Antonio, TX: Psychological Corporation.

Dunn, W., Cox, J., Foster, L., Mische-Lawson, L., & Tanquary, J. (2012). Impact of a contextual intervention on child participation and parent competence among children with autism spectrum disorders: A pretest-posttest repeated-measure design. *American Journal of Occupational Therapy, 66*, 520–528. doi:10.5014/ajot.2012.004119

Dunst, C. J., Bruder, M. B., Trivette, C. M., Raab, M., & McLean, M. (2001). Characteristics and consequences of everyday natural learning opportunities. *Topics in Early Childhood Special Education, 21*, 68–92.

Dziuk, M. A., Gidley Larson, J. C., Apostu, A., Mahone, E. M., Denckla, M. B., & Mostofsky, S. H. (2007). Dyspraxia in autism: Association with motor, social, and communicative deficits. *Developmental Medicine and Child Neurology, 49*, 734–739. doi:10.1111/j.1469-8749.2007.00734

Edelson, S. M., Edelson, M. G., Kerr, D. C., & Grandin, T. (1999). Behavioral and physiological effects of deep pressure on children with autism: A pilot study evaluating the efficacy of Grandin's Hug Machine. *American Journal of Occupational Therapy, 53*(2), 145–152.

Ermer, J., & Dunn, W. (1998). The sensory profile: A discriminant analysis of children with and without disabilities. *American Journal of Occupational Therapy, 52*(4), 283–290.

Escalona, A., Field, T., Singer-Strunck, R., Cullen, C., & Harshorn, K. (2001). Brief report: Improvements in the behavior of children with autism following massage therapy. *Journal of Autism and Developmental Disorders, 31*(5), 513–516.

Ferri, R., Elia, M., Agarwal, N., Lanuzza, B., Musumeci, S. A., & Pennisi, G. (2003). The mismatch negativity and the P3a components of the auditory event-related potentials in autistic low-functioning subjects. *Clinical Neurophysiology, 114*, 1671–1680.

Fertal-Daly, D., Bedell, G., & Hinojosa, J. (2001). Effects of a weighted vest on attention to task and self-stimulatory behaviors in preschoolers with pervasive developmental disorders. *American Journal of Occupational Therapy, 55*(6), 629–640.

Field, T., Lasko, D., Mundy, P., Henteleff, T., Kabat, S., Talpins, S., & Dowling, M. (1997). Brief report: Autistic children's attentiveness and responsivity improve after touch therapy. *Journal of Autism and Developmental Disorders, 27*, 333–338.

Fitch, H., & Tallal, P. (2003). Neural mechanisms of language-based learning impairments: Insights from human populations and animal models. *Behavioral and Cognitive Neuroscience Reviews, 2*(3), 155–178.

Foss-Feig, J. H., Heacock, J. L., & Cascio, C. J. (2012). Tactile responsiveness patterns and their association with core features in autism spectrum disorders. *Research in Autism Spectrum Disorders, 6*, 337–344.

Foss-Feig, J. H., Kwakye, L. D., Cascio, C. J., Burnette, C. P., Kadivar, H., Stone, W. L., & Wallace, M. T. (2010). An extended multisensory temporal binding window in autism spectrum disorders. *Experimental Brain Research, 203*, 381–389.

Fox, N. A., & Stifter, C. A. (1989). Biological and behavioral differences in infant reactivity and regulation. In G. A. Kohnstamm, J. E. Bate, & M. K. Rothbart (Eds.), *Temperament in childhood* (pp. 169–183). New York, NY: Wiley.

Freuler, A., Baranek, G., Watson, L., Boyd, B., & Bulluck, J. (2012). Brief report: Precursors and trajectories of sensory features: Qualitative analysis of infant home videos. *American Journal of Occupational Therapy, 66*, e81–e84. doi: 10.5014/ajot.2012.004465

Fuentes, C., Mostofsky, S., & Bastian, A. (2011). No proprioceptive deficits in autism despite movement-related sensory and execution impairments. *Journal of Autism and Developmental Disorders, 41*(10), 1352–1361. doi: 10.1007/s10803-010-1161-1

Gabriels, R. L., Agnew, J. A., Miller, L. J., Gralla, J., Pan, Z., Goldson, E.,... Kooks, E. (2008). Is there a relationship between restricted, repetitive, stereotyped behaviors and interests and abnormal sensory response in children with autism spectrum disorders? *Research in Autism Spectrum Disorders, 2*(4), 660–670.

Garon, N., Bryson, S. E., Zwaigenbaum, L., Smith, I. M., Brian, J., Roberts, W., & Szatmari, P. (2009). Temperament and its relationship to autistic symptoms in a high-risk infant sib cohort. *Journal of Abnormal Child Psychology, 37*, 59–78.

Gepner, B., Mestre, D., Masson, G., & de Schonen, S. (1995). Postural effects of motion vision in young autistic children. *NeuroReport, 6*, 1211–1214.

Gomot, M., Bernard, F., Davis, M., Belmonte, M., Ashwin, C., Bullmore, E., & Baron-Cohen, S. (2006). Change detection in children with autism: An auditory event-related fMRI study. *Neuroimage*, 29(2), 475–484.

Gomot, M., Giard, M. H., Adrien, J. L., Barthélémy, C., & Bruneau, N. (2002). Hypersensitivity to acoustic change in children with autism: Electrophysiological evidence of left frontal cortex dysfunctioning. *Psychophysiology*, 39(5), 577–584. doi:10.1017.S0048577202394058

Gottlieb, G. (1976).The roles of experience in the development of behavior and the nervous system. In G. Gottlieb (Ed.), *Neural and behavioral plasticity* (pp. 25–54). New York, NY: Academic Press.

Grandin, T., & Scariano, M. M. (1986). *Emergence: Labeled autistic*. Novato, CA: Arena Press.

Gravel, J., Dunn, M., Lee, W., & Ellis, M. (2006). Peripheral audition of children on the autism spectrum. *Ear and Hearing*, 27(3), 299–312. doi:10.1097/01.aud.0000215979.65645.22

Green, S. A., & Ben-Sasson, A. (2010). Anxiety disorders and sensory over-responsivity in children with autism spectrum disorders: Is there a causal relationship? *Journal of Autism and Developmental Disorders*, 40(12), 1495–1504.

Greenspan, S., & Wieder, S. (1997). Developmental patterns and outcomes in infants and children with disorders in relating and communicating: A chart review of 200 cases in children with autistic spectrum disorders. *Journal of Developmental and Learning Disorders*, 1(1), 1–38.

Güçlü, B., Tanidir, C., Mukaddes, N. M., & Unal, F. (2007). Tactile sensitivity of normal and autistic children. *Somatosensory and Motor Research*, 24(1–2), 21–33.

Guinchat, V., Chamak, B., Bonniau, B., Bodeau, N., Perisse, D., Cohen, D., & Danion, A. (2012). Very early signs of autism reported by parents include many concerns not specific to autism criteria. *Research in Autism Spectrum Disorders*, 6(2), 589–601.

Hardan, A. Y., Minshew, N. J., Melhem, N. M., Srihari, S., Jo, B., Bansal, R., ... Stanley, J. A. (2008). An MRI and proton spectroscopy study of the thalamus in children with autism. *Psychiatry Research: Neuroimaging*, 163(2), 97–105.

Happé, F., & Frith, U. (2006). The weak coherence account: Detail focused cognitive style in autism spectrum disorders. *Journal of Autism and Developmental Disorders*, 36(1), 5–25.

Hartshorn, K., Olds, L., Field, T., Delage, J., Cullen, C., & Escaloa, A. (2001). Creative movement therapy benefits children with autism. *Early Child Development and Care*, 166, 1–5. doi:10.1080/0300443011660101

Heaton, P. (2003). Pitch memory, labeling, and disembedding in autism. *Journal of Child Psychology and Psychiatry*, 44(4), 543–551. doi:10.1111/1469-7610.00143

Heaton, P., Davis, R. E., & Happé, F. G. (2008). Research note: exceptional absolute pitch perception for spoken words in an able adult with autism. *Neuropsychologia*, 46, 2095–2098.

Hilton, C., Graver, K., & LaVesser, P. (2007). Relationship between social competence and sensory processing in children with high-functioning autism spectrum disorders. *Research in Autism Spectrum Disorders*, 1(2), 164–173.

Hilton, C. L., Crouch, M. C., & Israel, H. (2008). Out-of-school participation patterns in children with high-functioning

autism spectrum disorders. *American Journal of Occupational Therapy*, 62, 554–563.

Hirstein, W., Iverson, P., & Ramachandran, V. S. (2001). Autonomic responses of autistic children to people and objects. *Proceedings of the Royal Society*, 268, 1883–1888. doi: 10.1098/rspb.2001.1724

Hochhauser, M., & Engel-Yeger, B. (2010). Sensory processing abilities and the relation to participation in leisure activities among children with high-functioning autism spectrum disorder. *Research in Autism Spectrum Disorders*, 4, 746–754.

Humphry, R., & Wakeford, L. (2006). An occupation-centered discussion of development and implications for practice. *American Journal of Occupational Therapy*, 60, 358–267.

Iarocci, G., & McDonald, J. (2006). Sensory integration and the perceptual experience of persons with autism. *Journal of Autism and Developmental Disorders*, 36, 77–90.

Iarocci G., Rombough, A., Yager, J., Weeks, D. J., & Chua, R. (2010). Visual influences on speech perception in children with autism. *Autism*, 14, 305–320.

Izawa, J., Pekny, S. E., Marko, M. K., Haswell, C. C., Shadmehr, R., & Mostofsky, S. H. (2012). Motor learning relies on integrated sensory inputs in ADHD, but overselectively on proprioception in autism spectrum conditions. *Autism Research*, 5, 124–136, 2012b.

Jasmin, E., Couture, M., McKinley, P., Fombonne, E., & Gisel, E. (2009). Sensorimotor and daily living skills of preschool children with autism spectrum disorders. *Journal of Autism and Developmental Disorders*, 39(2), 231–241.

Jansson-Verkasalo, E., Ceponiene, R., Kielinen, M., Suominen, K., Jäntti, V., Linna, S. L., ... Näätänen, R. (2003). Deficient auditory processing in children with Asperger syndrome, as indexed by event-related potentials. *Neuroscience Letters*, 338(3), 197–200.

Jones, R. S. P., Quigney, C., & Huws, J. C. (2003). First-hand accounts of sensory perceptual experiences in autism: A qualitative analysis. *Journal of Intellectual and Developmental Disability*, 28, 112–121.

Jure, R., Rapin, I., & Tuchman, R. F. (1991). Hearing-impaired autistic children. *Developmental Medicine and Child Neurology*, 33, 1062–1072.

Just, M., Cherkassky, V., Keller, T., Kana, R., & Minshew, N. (2007). Functional and anatomical cortical underconnectivity in autism: Evidence from an fMRI study of an executive function task and corpus callosum morphometry. *Cerebral Cortex*, 17(4), 951–961. doi: 10.1093/cercor/bhl006

Kanner, L. (1943). Autistic disturbances of affective contact. *Nervous Child*, 2, 217–250.

Kaplan, M., Rimland, B., & Edelson, S. M. (1999). Strabismus in autism spectrum disorder. *Focus on Autism and other Developmental Disabilities*, 14(2), 101–105.

Kemner, C., Oranje, B., Verbaten, M., & van Engeland, H. (2002). Normal P50 gating in children with autism. *Journal of Clinical Psychiatry*, 63(3), 214–217.

Kemner, C., Verbaten, M. N., Cuperus, J. M., Camfferman, G., & Van Engeland, H. (1994). Visual and somatosensory event-related brain potentials in autistic children and three different control groups. *Electroencephalography and Clinical Neurophysiology*, 92, 225–237.

Kemner, C., Verbaten, M. N., Cuperus, J. M., Camfferman, G., & van Engeland, H. (1995). Auditory event-related brain potentials in autistic children and three different control groups. *Biological Psychiatry, 38*, 150–165.

Kern, J. K., Garver, C. R., Carmody, T., Andrews, A. A., Trivedi, M. H., & Mehta, J. A. (2007). Examining sensory quadrants in autism. *Research in Autism Spectrum Disorders, 1*(2), 185–193.

Kern, J. K., Trivedi, M. H., Garver, C. R., Grannemann, B. D., Andrews, A. A., Savla, J. S.,…Schroeder J. L. (2006). The pattern of sensory processing abnormalities in autism. *Autism, 10*(5), 480–494.

Kern, J. K., Trivedi, M. H., Grannemann, B. D., Garver, C. R., Johnson, D. G., Andrews, A. A.,…Schroeder J. L. (2007). Sensory correlations in autism. *Autism, 11*(2), 123–134.

Kientz, M. A., & Dunn, W. (1997). A comparison of the performance of children with and without autism on the Sensory Profile. *American Journal of Occupational Therapy, 51*(7), 530–537.

Kinnealey, M., Pfeiffer, B., Miller, J., Roan, C., Shoener, R., & Ellner, M. (2012). Effect of classroom modification on attention and engagement of students with autism or dyspraxia. *American Journal of Occupational Therapy, 66*, 511–519.

Kisley, M., Noecker, T., & Guinther, P. (2004). Comparison of sensory gating to mismatch negativity and self-reported perceptual phenomena in healthy adults. *Psychophysiology, 41*, 604–612.

Klin, A. (1993). Auditory brainstem responses in autism: Brainstem dysfunction or peripheral hearing loss? *Journal of Autism and Developmental Disorders, 23*(1), 15–35. doi:10.1007/BF01066416

Klin, A., Saulnier, C., Sparrow, S., Cicchetti, D., Volkmar, F., & Lord, C. (2007). Social and communication abilities in higher functioning individuals with autism spectrum disorders: The Vineland and the ADOS. *Journal of Autism and Developmental Disorders, 37*(4), 748–759. doi:10.1007/s10803-006-0229-4

Koelewijn, T., Bronkhorst, A., & Theeuwes, J. (2010). Attention and the multiple stages of multisensory integration: A review of audiovisual studies. *Acta Psychologica, 134*(3), 372–384.

Koenig, K. P., Buckley-Reen, A., & Garg, S. (2012). Efficacy of the Get Ready to Learn yoga program among children with autism spectrum disorders: A pretest-posttest control group design. *American Journal of Occupational Therapy, 66*, 538–546. doi:ajot.2012.004390

Kwon, S., Kim, J., Choe, B., Ko, C., & Park, S. (2007). Electrophysiologic assessment of central auditory processing by auditory brainstem responses in children with autism spectrum disorders. *Journal of Korean Medical Science, 22*(4), 656–659. doi:10.3346/jkms.2007.22.4.656

Landry, R., & Bryson, S. (2004). Impaired disengagement of attention in young children with autism. *Journal of Child Psychology and Psychiatry, 45*(6), 1115–1122. doi:10.1111/j.1469-7610.2004.00304.x

Lane, A. E., Young, R. L., Baker, A. Z., & Angley, M. T. (2010). Sensory processing subtypes in autism: Association with adaptive behavior. *Journal of Autism and Developmental Disorders, 40*, 112–122.

Le Couteur, A., Rutter, M., Lord, C., Rios, P., Robertson, S., Holdgrafer, M., & McLennan, J. D. (1989). Autism Diagnostic Interview: A semistructured interview for parents and caregivers of autistic persons. *Journal of Autism and Developmental Disorders, 19*(3), 363–387.

Ledford, J. R., & Gast, D. L. (2006). Feeding problem in children with autism spectrum disorders: A review. *Focus on Autism and other Developmental Disabilities, 21*, 153–166.

Leekam, S., Nieto, C., Libby, S., Wing, L., & Gould, J. (2007). Describing the sensory abnormalities of children and adults with autism. *Journal of Autism and Developmental Disorders, 37*, 894–910. doi:10.1007/s10803-006-0218-7

Levine, T., Sheinkopf, S., Pescosolido, M., Rodino, A., Elia, G., & Lester, B. (2012). Physiologic arousal to social stress in children with autism spectrum disorders: A pilot study. *Research in Autism Spectrum Disorders, 6*(1), 177–183. doi:10.1016/j.rasd.2011.04.003

Lewkowicz, D. J. (2002). Heterogeneity and heterochrony in the development of intersensory perception. *Cognitive Brain Research, 14*(1), 41–63.

Lincoln, A. J., Courchesne, E., Harms, L., & Allen, M. (1993). Contextual probability evaluation in autistic, receptive developmental language disorder, and control children: Event-related brain potential evidence. *Journal of Autism and Developmental Disorders, 23*(1), 37–58.

Linderman, T. M., & Stewart, K. B. (1999). Sensory-integrative-based occupational therapy and functional outcomes in young children with pervasive developmental disorders: A single-subject study. *American Journal of Occupational Therapy, 53*, 207–213.

Liss, M., Saulnier, C., Fein, D., & Kinsbourne, M. (2006). Sensory and attention abnormalities in autistic spectrum disorders. *Autism, 10*, 155–171.

Little, L. M. (2012). Home and community activities: Dimensions and associations with patterns of sensory response among children with autism spectrum disorders. Unpublished dissertation, University of North Carolina at Chapel Hill.

Lord, C. (1995). Follow-up of two-year-olds referred for possible autism. *Journal of Child Psychology and Psychiatry, 36*, 1365–1382.

Lord, C., Rutter, M., & Le Couteur, A. (1994). Autism Diagnostic Interview–Revised: A revised version of a diagnostic interview for caregivers of individuals with possible pervasive developmental disorders. *Journal of Autism and Developmental Disorders, 24*(5), 659–685.

Loveland, K. A. (2001). Toward an ecological theory of autism. In J. A. Burack, T. Charman, N. Yirmiya, & P. R. Zelazo (Eds.), *The development of autism: Perspectives from theory and research* (pp. 17–37). Mahwah, NJ: Erlbaum.

Magnée, M., de Gelder, B., van Engeland, H., & Kemner, C. (2011). Multisensory integration and attention in autism spectrum disorder: Evidence from event-related potentials. *PLoS ONE, 6*(8), e24196. doi:10.1371/journal.pone.0024196

Magnée, M., Oranje, B., van Engeland, H., Kahn, R., & Kemner, C. (2009). Cross-sensory gating in schizophrenia and autism spectrum disorder: EEG evidence for impaired brain connectivity. *Neuropsychologia, 47*(7), 1728–1732. doi:10.1016/j.neuropsychologia.2009.02.012

Mailloux, Z. K., May-Benson, T. A., Summers, C. A., Miller, L. J., Brett-Green, B., Burke, J. P.,…Schoen, S. A. (2007). Goal attainment scaling as a measure of meaningful outcomes for children with sensory integration disorders. *American Journal of Occupational Therapy, 61,* 254–259.

Marco, E., Hinkley, L., Hill, S., & Nagarajan, S. (2011). Sensory processing in autism: A review of neurophysiologic findings. *Pediatric Research, 69*(5), 48R–54R. doi: 10.1203/PDR.0b013e3182130c54

Marquenie, K., Rodger, S., Mangohig, K., & Cronin, A. (2010). Dinnertime and bedtime routines and rituals in families with a young child with an autism spectrum disorder. *Australian Occupational Therapy Journal, 58*(3), 145–154.

May-Benson, T., & Teasdale, A. (2012). *The effectiveness of the home-based Integrated Listening System (iLs) Program for children with autism.* Retrieved from http://www.integra tedlistening.com / wp-content/ils-files//2012/08/Spiral-Study -Results.pdf

May-Benson, T. A., & Koomar, J. A. (2010). Systematic review of the research evidence examining the effectiveness of interventions using a sensory integrative approach for children. *American Journal of Occupational Therapy, 64,* 403–414. doi:10.5014/ajot.2010.09071

McAlonan, G., Daly, E., Kumari, V., Critchley, H., van Amelsvoort, T., Suckling, J., . . . Murphy, D. (2002). *Brain, 127,* 1594–1606. doi:10.1093/brain/awf150

McIntosh, D. N., Miller, L. J., & Shyu, V., & Dunn, W. (1999). Overview of the Short Sensory Profile (SSP). In W. Dunn (Ed.), *The Sensory Profile* (pp. 59–74). San Antonio, TX: Psychological Corporation.

Miller, L. J., Anzalone, M. E., Lane, S. J., Cermak, S. A., & Osten, E. T. (2007). Concept evolution in sensory integration: A proposed nosology for diagnosis. *American Journal of Occupational Therapy, 61*(2), 135–140.

Miller-Kuhaneck, H., Ecker, C. E., Parham, L. D., Henry, D. A., & Glennon, T. J. (2010). *Sensory Processing Measure-Preschool (SPM-P): Manual.* Los Angeles, CA: Western Psychological Services.

Milne, E., Swettenham, J., Hansen, P., Campbell, R., Jeffries, H., & Plaisted, K. (2002). High motion coherence thresholds in children with autism. *Journal of Child Psychology and Psychiatry, 43*(2), 255–263.

Ming, X., Julu, P. O., Brimacombe, M., Connor, S., & Daniels, M. L. (2005). Reduced cardiac parasympathetic activity in children with autism. *Brain and Development, 27*(7), 509–516.

Minshew, N., Goldstein, G., & Siegel, D. (1997). Neuropsychologic functioning in autism: Profile of a complex informational processing disorder. *Journal of the International Neuropsychological Society, 3*(4), 303–316.

Minshew, N., Sung, K., Jones, B., & Furman, J. (2004). Underdevelopment of the postural control system in autism. *Neurology, 63*(11), 2056–2061. doi:10.1212/01.WNL.0000145771 .98657.62

Minshew, N. J., & Hobson, J. A. (2008). Sensory sensitivities and performance on sensory perceptual tasks in high-functioning individuals with autism. *Journal of Autism and Developmental Disorders, 38*(8), 1485–1498.

Miyazaki, M., Fujii, E., Saijo, T., Mori, K., Hashimoto, T., Kagami, S., & Kuroda, Y. (2007). Short-latency somatosensory evoked potentials in infantile autism: Evidence of hyperactivity in the right primary somatosensory area.

Developmental Medicine & Child Neurology, 49(1), 13–17. doi:10.1017/S0012162207000059.x

Molholm S., Ritter, W., Murray, M. M., Javitt, D. C., Schroeder, C. E., & Foxe, J. J. (2002). Multisensory auditory–visual interactions during early sensory processing in humans: A high-density electrical mapping study. *Cognitive Brain Research, 14,* 115–128.

Molloy, D., & Dietrich, K. Bhattacharya, A. (2003). Postural stability in children with autism spectrum disorder. *Journal of Autism and Developmental Disorders, 33*(6), 643–652.

Mongillo, E. A., Irwin, J. R., Whalen, D. H., Klaiman, C., Carter, A. S., & Schultz, R. T. (2008). Audiovisual processing in children with and without autism spectrum disorders. *Journal of Autism and Developmental Disorders, 38*(7), 1349–1358.

Mostofsky, S. H., & Ewen, J. B. (2011). Altered connectivity and action model formation in autism is autism. *Neuroscientist, 17*(4), 437–448.

Mottron, L., & Burack, J. (2001). Enhanced perceptual functioning in the development of autism. In J. A. Burack, T. Charman, N. Yirmiya, & P. R. Zelazo (Eds.), *The development of autism: Perspectives from theory and research* (pp. 131–148). Mahwah, NJ: Erlbaum.

Mottron, L., Burack, J. A., Iarocci, G., Belleville, S., & Enns, J. T. (2003). Locally oriented perception with intact global processing among adolescents with high-functioning autism: Evidence from multiple paradigms. *Journal of Child Psychology and Psychiatry, 44*(6), 904–913.

Mottron, L., Dawson, M., & Soulières, I. (2009). Enhanced perception in savant syndrome: Patterns, structure and creativity. *Philosophical Transactions of the Royal Society B: Biological Sciences, 364*(1522), 1385–1391.

Mottron, L., Dawson, M., Soulières, I., Hubert, B., & Burack, J. (2006). Enhanced perceptual functioning in autism: An update, and eight principles of autistic perception. *Journal of Autism and Developmental Disorders, 36*(1), 27–43.

Mottron, L., Mineau, S., Martel, G., St.-Charles Bernier, C., Berthiaume, C., Dawson, M., . . . Faubert, J. (2007). Lateral glances toward moving stimuli among young children with autism: Early regulation of locally oriented perception? *Development and Pscyhopathology, 19,* 23–36.

Mountcastle, V. B. (2005). *The sensory hand: Neural mechanisms in somatic sensation.* London, England: University Press.

Mudford, O. C., Cross, B. A., Breen, S., Cullen, C., Reeves, D., Gould, J., & Douglas, J. (2000). Auditory integration training for children with autism: No behavioral benefits detected. *American Journal on Mental Retardation, 105*(2), 118–129.

Mundy, P., & Neal, R. (2001). Neural plasticity, joint attention and autistic developmental pathology. *International Review of Research in Mental Retardation, 23,* 139–168.

Myles-Worsley, M., Coon, H., Byerley, W., Waldo, M., Young, D., & Freedman, R. (1996). Developmental and genetic influences on the p50 sensory gating phenotype. *Biological Psychiatry, 39*(4), 289–295. doi:10.1016/0006-3223(95)00134-4

Nader, R., Oberlander, T., Chambers, C., & Craig, K. (2004). Expression of pain in children with autism. *Clinical Journal of Pain, 20*(2), 88–97.

O'Donnell, S., Deitz, J., Kartin, D., Nalty, T., & Dawson, G. (2012). Sensory processing, problem behavior, adaptive behavior, and cognition in preschool children with autism spectrum disorders. *American Journal of Occupational Therapy, 66*, 586–594.

Olausson, H., Lamarre, Y., Backlund, H., Morin, C., Wallin, B. G., Starck, G.,... Bushnell, M. C. (2002). Unmyelinated tactile afferents signal touch and project to insular cortex. *Nature Neuroscience, 5*(9), 900–904.

O'Neill, M., & Jones, R. (1997) Sensory-perceptual abnormalities in autism—a case for more research? *Journal of Autism and Developmental Disorders, 27*, 283–293.

Oram Cardy, J. E., Flagg, E. J., Roberts, W., & Roberts, T. P. (2005). Delayed mismatch field for speech and non-speech sounds in children with autism. *NeuroReport, 16*(5), 521.

Oranje, B., Geyer, M., Bocker, K., Kenemans, J., & Verbaten, M. (2006). Prepulse inhibition and P50 suppression: Commonalities and dissociations. *Psychiatry Research, 143*, 147–158. doi:10.1016/j.psychres.2005.11.002

Orekhova, E., Stroganova, T., Prokofyev, A., Nygren, G., Gillberg, C., & Elam, M. (2008). Sensory gating in young children with autism: Relation to age, IQ, and EEG gamma oscillations. *Neuroscience Letters, 434*, 218–223. doi:10.1016/j.neulet.2008.01.066

O'Riordan, M., & Passetti, F. (2006). Discrimination in autism within different sensor modalities. *Journal of Autism and Developmental Disorders, 36*(5), 665–675.

O'Riordan, M., Plaisted, K., Driver, J., & Baron-Cohen, S. (2001). Superior visual search in autism. *Journal of Experimental Psychology: Human Perception and Performance, 27*(3), 719–730. doi: 10.1037//0096-1523.27.3.719

Ornitz, E., Guthrie, D., & Farley, A. (1977). The early development of autistic children. *Journal of Autism and Developmental Disorders, 7*(3), 207–229. doi:10.1007/BF01538999

Orsmond, G. I., & Kou, Y. (2011). The daily lives of adolescents with an autism spectrum disorder: Discretionary time use and activity partners. *Autism, 15*(2), 1–21.

Osterling, J., & Dawson, G. (1994). Early recognition of children with autism: A study of first birthday home videotapes. *Journal of Autism and Developmental Disorders, 24*(3), 247–257. doi: 10.1007/BF02172225

Ozonoff, S., Strayer, D. L., McMahon, W. M., & Filloux, F. (1994). Executive function abilities in autism and Tourette syndrome: An information processing approach. *Journal of Child Psychology and Psychiatry, 35*, 1015–1037.

Parham, L. D., Ecker, C., Miller-Kuhananeck, H., Henry, D. A., & Glennon, T. (2007). *Sensory Processing Measure (SPM) manual.* Los Angeles, CA: Western Psychological Services.

Parham, L. D., & Mailloux, Z. (2010). Sensory integration. In J. Case-Smith & A. Allen (Eds.), *Occupational therapy for children* (6th ed., pp. 325–372). St. Louis, MO: Mosby Elsevier.

Parham, L. D., Roley, S. S., May-Benson, T., Koomar, J., Brett-Green, B., Burke, J. P.,... Schaaf, R. C. (2011). Development of a fidelity measure for research on Ayres sensory integration. *American Journal of Occupational Therapy, 65*, 133–142. doi:10 .5014/ajot.2011.000745

Pfeiffer, B., Kinnealey, M., Reed, C., & Herzberg, G. (2005). Sensory modulation and affective disorders in children and adolescents with Asperger's disorder. *American Journal of Occupational Therapy, 59*, 335–345.

Pfeiffer, B. A., Koenig, K., Kinnealey, M., Sheppard, M., & Henderson, L. (2011). Effectiveness of sensory integration interventions in children with autism spectrum disorders: A pilot study. *American Journal of Occupational Therapy, 65*, 76–85. doi:10.5014/ajot.2011.09205

Plaisted, K., Swettenham, J., & Rees, L. (1999). Children with autism show local precedence in a divided attention task and global precedence in a selective attention task. *Journal of Child Psychology and Psychiatry, 40*(5), 733–742.

Potvin, M., Snider, L., Prelock, P., Kehayia, E., & Wood-Dauphinee, S. (2012). Recreational participation of children with high functioning autism. *Journal of Autism and Developmental Disorders*, 1–13. doi:10.1007/s10803-012-1589-6

Pritchard, W. S., Raz, N., & August, G. J. (1987). Visual augmenting/ reducing and P300 in autistic children, *Journal of Autism and Developmental Disorders, 17*, 231–241.

Rapin, I., & Dunn, M. (2003). Review article: Update on the language disorders of individuals on the autism spectrum. *Brain & Development, 25*(3), 166–172.

Renner, P., Klinger, L. G., & Klinger, M. R. (2006). Exogenous and endogenous attention orienting in autism spectrum disorders. *Child Neuropsychology, 12*, 361–382.

Reynolds, S., Bendixen, R. M., Lawrence, T., & Lane, S. J. (2011). A pilot study examining activity participation, sensory responsiveness, and competence in children with high functioning autism spectrum disorder. *Journal of Autism and Developmental Disorders, 41*, 1496–1506.

Reynolds, S., & Lane, S. J. (2008). Diagnostic validity of sensory over-responsivity: a review of the literature and case reports. *Journal of Autism and Developmental Disorders, 38*(3), 516–529.

Rimland, B., & Edelson, S. E. (1995). Brief report: A pilot study of auditory integration training in autism. *Journal of Autism and Developmental Disabilities, 25*, 61–70.

Rogers, S. J., Hepburn, S., & Wehner, E. (2003). Parent reports of sensory symptoms in toddlers with Autism and those with other developmental disorders. *Journal of Autism and Developmental Disorders, 33*(6), 631–642. doi:10.1023/B:JADD.0000006000.38991.a7

Rogers, S. J., & Ozonoff, S. (2005). Annotation: What do we know about sensory dysfunction in autism? A critical review of the empirical evidence. *Journal of Child Psychology and Psychiatry, 46*(12), 1255–1268. doi:10.1111/j.1469-7610.2005.01431.x

Rosenhall, U., Nordin, V., Brantberg, K., & Gillberg, C. (2003). Autism and auditory brainstem responses. *Ear and Hearing, 24*, 206–214.

Rosenhall, U., Nordin, V., Sandström, M., Ahlsen, G., & Gillberg, C. (1999). Autism and hearing loss. *Journal of Autism and Developmental Disorders, 29*(5), 349–357.

Roth, D. A., Muchnik, C., Shabtai, E., Hildesheimer, M., & Henkin, Y. (2012). Evidence for atypical auditory brainstem responses in young children with suspected autism spectrum disorders. *Developmental Medicine & Child Neurology, 54*, 23–29. doi:10.1111/j.1469-8749.2011.04149.x

Russo, N. M., Bradlow, A. R., Skoe, E., Trommer, B. L., Nicol, T., Zecker, S., & Kraus, N. (2008). Deficient brainstem encoding of pitch in children with autism spectrum disorders. *Clinical Neurophysiology*, *119*, 1720–1731.

Russo, N., Foxe, J. J., Brandwein, A. B., Altschuler, T., Gomes, H., & Molholm, S. (2010). Multisensory processing in children with autism: high density electrical mapping of auditory–somatosensory integration. *Autism Research*, *3*(5), 253–267.

Russo, N., Mottron, L., Burack, J. A., & Jemel, B. (2012). Parameters of semantic multisensory integration depend on timing and modality order among people on the autism spectrum: Evidence from event-related potentials. *Neuropsychologia*, *50*(9), 2131–2141.

Russo, N., Nicol, T., Trommer, B., Zecker, S., & Kraus, N. (2009). Brainstem transcription of speech is disrupted in children with autism spectrum disorders. *Developmental Science*, *12*, 557–567. doi:10.1111/j.1467-7687.2008.00790.x

Samson, F., Mottron, L., Jemel, B., Belin, P., & Ciocca, V. (2006) Can spectro-temporal complexity explain the autistic pattern of performance on auditory tasks? *Journal of Autism and Developmental Disorders*, *36*(1), 65–76.

Schaaf, R. C., Benevides, T., Blanche, E., Brett-Green, B., Burke, J. P., Cohn, E. S., … Schoen, S. A. (2010). Parasympathetic functions in children with Sensory Processing Disorder. *Frontiers in Integrative Neuroscience*, *4*, 1–11. doi:10.3389/fnint.2010.00004B

Schaaf, R. C., Hunt, J., & Benevides, T. (2012). Occupational therapy using sensory integration to improve participation of a child with autism: A case report. *American Journal of Occupational Therapy*, *66*, 547–555. doi:10.5014/ajot.2012.004473

Schaaf, R. C., Miller, L., Seawell, D., & O'Keefe, S. (2003). Children with disturbances in sensory processing: A pilot study examining the role of the parasympathetic nervous system. *American Journal of Occupational Therapy*, *57*, 442–449. doi:10.5014/ajot.57.4.442

Schaaf, R. C., Toth-Cohen, S., Outten, G., Johnson S., & Madrid, G. (2011). The everyday routines of families of children with autism: Examining the impact of sensory processing difficulties on the family. *Autism Research*, *15*(3), 373–389.

Scharre, J., & Creedon, M. (1992). Assessment of visual function in autistic children. *Optometry and Vision Science*, *69*(6), 433–439.

Schilling, D. L., & Schwartz, I. S. (2004). Alternative seating for young children with autism Spectrum disorder: Effects on classroom behavior. *Journal of Autism and Developmental Disorders*, *34*, 423–432. doi:10.1023/B:JADD.0000037418.48587.f4

Schoen, S. A., Miller, L., Brett-Green, B., & Nielsen, D. (2009). Physiological and behavioral differences in sensory processing: A comparison of children with Autism Spectrum Disorder and Sensory Modulation Disorder. *Frontier in Integrative Neuroscience*, *3*, 1–11.

Schoen, S. A., Miller, L. J., & Green, K. E. (2008). Pilot study of the sensory over-responsivity scales: Assessment and inventory. *American Journal of Occupational Therapy*, *62*, 393–406.

Seri, S., Cerquiglini, A., Pisani, F., & Curatolo, P. (1999). Autism in tuberous sclerosis: Evoked potential evidence for a deficit in auditory sensory processing. *Clinical Neurophysiology*, *110*(10), 1825–1830.

Seri, S., Pisani, F., Thai, J. N., & Cerquiglini, A. (2007). Pre-attentive auditory sensory processing in autistic spectrum disorder. Are electromagnetic measurements telling us a coherent story? *International Journal of Psychophysiology*, *63*, 159–163.

Shumway-Cook, A., & Woollacott, M. H. (1985). The growth of stability: Postural control from a developmental perspective. *Journal of Motor Behavior*, *17*, 131–147.

Simion, F., Regolin, L., & Bulf, H. (2008). A predisposition for biological motion in the newborn baby. *Proceedings of the National Academy of Sciences, USA*, *105*(2), 809–813.

Simmons, D. R., Robertson, A. E., McKay, L. S., Toal, E., McAleer, P., & Pollick, F. E. (2009). Vision in autism spectrum disorders. *Vision Research*, *49*, 2705–2739.

Smith, E. G., & Bennetto, L. (2007). Audiovisual speech integration and lipreading in autism. *Journal of Child Psychology and Psychiatry*, *48*(8), 813–821.

Smith, I. M., & Bryson, S. E. (1994). Imitation and action in autism: A critical review. *Psychological Bulletin*, *116*(2), 259.

Smith, S. A., Press, B., Koenig, K. P., & Kinnealey, M. (2005). Effects of sensory integration intervention on self-stimulating and self-injurious behaviors. *American Journal of Occupational Therapy*, *59*, 418–425.

Sokhadze, E., Baruth, J., Tasman, A., Sears, L., Mathai, G., El-Baz, A., & Casanova, M. F. (2009). Event-related potential study of novelty processing abnormalities in autism. *Applied Psychophysiology and Biofeedback*, *34*, 37–51. doi:10.1007/s10484-009-9074-5

Solish, A., Perry, A., & Minnes, P. (2010). Participation of children with and without disabilities in social, recreational and leisure activities. *Journal of Applied Research in Intellectual Disabilities*, *23*, 226–236.

Starr, A., Amlie, R. N., Martin, W. H., & Sanders, S. (1977). Development of auditory function in newborn infants revealed by auditory brainstem potentials. *Pediatrics*, *60*(6), 831–839.

Stevens, S., & Gruzelier, J. (1984). Electrodermal activity to auditory stimuli in autistic, retarded, and normal children. *Journal of Autism and Developmental Disorders*, *14*(3), 245–260. doi:10.1007/BF02409577

Stone, W., & Hogan, K. (1993). A structured parent interview for identifying young children with autism. *Journal of Autism and Developmental Disorders*, *23*(4), 639–652. doi:10.1007/BF01046106

Stone, W. L., Ousely, O. Y., & Littleford C. D. (1997). Motor imitation in young children with autism: What's the object? *Journal of Abnormal Child Psychology*, *25*(6), 475–485. doi:10.1023/A:1022685731726

Suzuki, Y., Critchley, H., Rowe, A., Howlin, P., & Murphy, D. (2003). Impaired olfactory identification in Asperger's syndrome. *Journal of Neuropsychiatry and Clinical Neuroscience*, *15*, 105–107.

Talay-Ongan, A., & Wood, K. (2000). Unusual sensory sensitivities in autism: A possible crossroads. *International Journal of Disability, Development, and Education*, *47*(2), 201–212.

Talsma, D., & Woldorff, M. (2005). Selective attention and multisensory integration: Multiple phases of effects on the evoked brain activity. *Journal of Cognitive Neuroscience*, *17*(7), 1098–1114.

Tammet, D. (2006). *Born on a blue day: A memoir of Aspergers and an extraordinary mind*. London, England: Hodder & Stoughton.

Tavassoli, T., & Baron-Cohen, S. (2012a). Taste identification in adults with autism spectrum conditions. *Journal of Autism and Developmental Disorders*, *42*(7), 1–6.

Tavassoli, T., & Baron-Cohen, S. (2012b). Olfactory detection thresholds and adaptation in adults with autism spectrum condition. *Journal of Autism and Developmental Disorders*, *42*(6), 905–909.

Teder-Salejarvi, W., Pierce, K., Courchesne, E., & Hillyard, S. (2005). Auditory spatial localization and attention deficits in autistic adults. *Cognitive Brain Research*, *23*, 221–234. doi:10.1016/j.cogbrainres.2004.10.021

Tharpe, A., Bess, F., Sladen, D., Schissel, H., Couch, S., & Schery, T. (2006). Auditory characteristics of children with autism. *Ear & Hearing*, *27*(4), 430–441.

Tomchek, S. D., & Dunn, W. (2007). Sensory processing in children with and without autism: A comparative study using the Short Sensory Profile. *American Journal of Occupational Therapy*, *61*(2), 190–200.

Tommerdahl, M., Tannan, V., Cascio, C. J., Baranek, G. T., & Whitsel, B. L. (2007). Vibrotactile adaptation fails to enhance spatial localization in adults with autism. *Brain Research*, *1154*, 116–123.

Tsermentseli, S., O'Brien, J. M., & Spencer, J. V. (2008). Comparison of form and motion coherence processing in autistic spectrum disorders and dyslexia. *Journal of Autism and Developmental Disorders*, *38*(7), 1201–1210.

Turkewitz, G., & Kenny, P. A. (2004). Limitation on input as a basis for neural organization and perceptual development: A preliminary theoretical statement. *Developmental Psychobiology*, *15*(4), 357–368.

Turner, M. (1999). Repetitive behavior in autism: a review of psychological research. *Journal of Child Psychology and Psychiatry*, *40*, 839–849.

Vallbo, A. B., Olausson, H., & Wessberg, J. (1999). Unmyelinated afferents constitute a second system coding tactile stimuli of the human hairy skin. *Journal of Neurophysiology*, *81*, 2753–2763.

Vandenbroucke, M. W. G., Scholte, H. S., van Engeland, H., Lamme, V. A. F., & Kemner, C. (2008). Coherent versus component motion perception in autism spectrum disorder. *Journal of Autism and Developmental Disorders*, *38*, 941–949.

Van der Geest, J. N., Kemner, C., Camfferman, G., Verbaten, M. N., & van Engeland, H. (2001). Eye movements, visual attention and autism: A saccadic reaction time study using the gap and overlap paradigm. *Biological Psychiatry*, *50*, 614–619.

van der Smagt, M., van Engeland, H., & Kemner, C. (2007). Brief report: Can you see what is not there? Low-level auditory-visual integration in autism spectrum disorder. *Journal of Autism and Developmental Disorders*, *37*, 2014–2019. doi:10.1007/s10803-006-0346-0

van Engeland, H. (1984). The electrodermal orienting response to auditive stimuli in autistic children, normal children, mentally retarded children, and child psychiatric patients. *Journal of Autism and Developmental Disorders*, *14*(3), 261–279. doi:10.1007/BF02409578

Van Rie, G. L., & Heflin, L. J. (2009). The effect of sensory activities on correct responding for children with autism spectrum disorders. *Research in Autism Spectrum Disorders*, *3*, 783–796. doi:10.1016/j.rasd.2009.03.001

Volkmar, F., Cohen, D., & Paul, R. (1986). An evaluation of *DSM-III* criteria for infantile autism. *Journal of the American Academy of Child Psychiatry*, *25*(2), 190–197.

Wainwright, J. A., & Bryson, S. E. (1996): Visual-spatial orienting in autism. *Journal of Autism and Developmental Disorders*, *26*, 423–438.

Waterhouse, L., Fein, D., & Modahl, C. (1996). Neurofunctional mechanisms in autism. *Psychological Review*, *103*(3), 457–489.

Watling, R. L., & Dietz, J. (2007). Immediate effect of Ayres's sensory integration-based occupational therapy intervention on children with autism spectrum disorders. *American Journal of Occupational Therapy*, *61*, 574–583.

Watling, R. L., Deitz, J., & White, O. (2001). Comparison of sensory profile scores of young children with and without autism spectrum disorders. *American Journal of Occupational Therapy*, *55*(4), 416–423.

Watson, L., Baranek, G., Crais, E., Reznick, S., Dykstra, J., & Perryman, T. (2007). The first year inventory: retrospective parent responses to a questionnaire designed to identify one-year-olds at risk for autism. *Journal of Autism and Developmental Disorders*, *37*, 49–61. doi:10.1007/s10803-006-0334-4

Watson, L., Patten, E., Baranek, G. T., Poe, M., Boyd, B., Freuler, A., & Lorenzi, J. (2011). Differential associations between sensory response patterns and language, social, and communication measures in children with autism or other developmental disabilities. *Journal of Speech, Language, and Hearing Research*, *54*, 1562–1576.

Werner, E., & Dawson, G. (2005). Validation of the phenomenon of autistic regression using home videotapes. *Archives of General Psychiatry*, *62*(8), 889–895. doi:10.1001/archpsyc.62.8.889

Werner, E., Dawson, G., Munson, J., & Osterling, J. (2005). Variation in early developmental course in autism and its relation with behavioral outcome at 3–4 years of age. *Journal of Autism and Developmental Disorders*, *35*(3), 337–350.

Wessberg, J., Olausson, H., Fernstrom, K. W., & Vallbo, Å. B. (2003). Receptive field properties of unmyelinated tactile afferents in the human skin. *Journal of Physiology*, *89*(3), 1567–1575. doi:10.1152/jn.00256.2002

Wiggins, L., Robins, D., Bakeman, R., & Adamson, L. (2009). Brief report: Sensory abnormalities as distinguishing symptoms of autism spectrum disorders in young children. *Journal of Autism and Developmental Disorders*, *39*, 1087–1091. doi:10.1007/s10803-009-0711-x

Williams, D. (1994). *Somebody somewhere*. New York, NY: Doubleday.

Williams, D. L., Goldstein, G., & Minshew, N. J. (2006). The profile of memory function in children with autism. *Neuropsychology*, *20*, 21–29.

Williams, E., Costall, A., & Reddy, V. (1999). Children with autism experience problems with both objects and people.

Journal of Autism and Developmental Disorders, 29(5), 367–378. doi: 10.1023/A:1023026810619

Williams, M. S., & Shellenberger, S. (1994). *"How does your engine run": A leader's guide to the Alert Program for Self-Regulation.* Albuquerque, NM: TherapyWorks.

Wing, L. (1969). The handicaps of autistic children—a comparative study. *Journal of Child Psychology and Psychiatry, 10*(1), 1–40.

Woldorff, M. G., Gallen, C. G., Hampson, S. A., Hillyard, S. A., Pantev, C., Sobel, D., & Bloom, F. E. (1993). Modulation of early sensory processing in human auditory cortex during auditory selective attention *Neurobiology, 90,* 8722–8726.

Young, R. L., Brewer, N., & Pattison, C. (2003). Parental identification of early behavioural abnormalities in children with autistic disorder. *Autism, 7*(2), 125–143.

Yuhas, J., Cordeiro, L., Tassone, F., Ballinger, E., Schneider, A., Long, J., . . . Hessl, D. (2011). Brief report: Sensorimotor gating in idiopathic autism and autism associated with fragile x syndrome. *Journal of Autism and Developmental Disorders, 41*(2), 248–253. doi:10.1007/s10803-010-1040-9

Zimmer, U., & Macaluso, E. (2007). Processing of multisensory spatial congruency can be dissociated from working memory and visuo-spatial attention. *European Journal of Neuroscience, 26,* 1681–1691. doi:10.1111/j.1460-9568.2007.05784.x

Zwaigenbaum, L., Bryson, S., Rogers, T., Roberts, W., Brian, J., & Szatmari, P. (2005). Behavioral manifestations of autism in the first year of life. *International Journal of Developmental Neuroscience, 23,* 143–152.

SECTION III

Neurobiology and Medical Issues

In the past decade we have witnessed important advances both in understanding the neurobiology of autism and in appreciation of autism as a disorder affecting the entire person with associated medical features. The chapters in this section detail many of these advances and together represent the state of the art in the systems biology of autism. Rutter and Thapar (Chapter 17) kick off this section with an incisive review of genetic findings. They begin with a critical discussion of changing concepts and constructs in the field of autism. This allows us to understand new genetic findings in the context of the shifting landscape of diagnostic systems and a broadening definition of autism. Far from identifying genes specific to autism, the recent surge of genetic findings presents us with the challenge of understanding shared genetic liability, with overlap in genetic mechanisms among neurodevelopmental disorders being the rule as opposed to the exception. These challenges notwithstanding, the field has now demonstrated convincingly that: (a) autism is not explained by disruption in any single specific gene; (b) genetic risk factors have probabilistic effects being neither necessary nor sufficient to result in autism; and (c) relatives of those affected and unaffected controls can be carriers of genetic risk variants and yet appear to be phenotypically unaffected.

Complementing the chapter on genetic risks, Lyall, Schmidt, and Hertz-Picciotto (Chapter 18) review research on environmental risk factors in autism. A growing number of environmental factors are being investigated in association with autism, including air pollution, chemicals used in housing materials and consumer goods, metals,

and pesticides. Further, *environment* is now conceptualized and studied more broadly as being all nongenetic factors, from viruses to chemical and physical agents and social and cultural influences. Like the genetic studies, research on environmental factors has led to a greater recognition of the etiologic complexity of autism. The current thinking is that multiple causes are likely operating in any individual and can include several or many genes, and similarly for environmental factors.

As surveyed by Anderson (Chapter 19), biochemical biomarker studies of individuals with autism identify biochemical alterations that advance our understanding of atypical brain development as a result of genetic and environmental factors and their joint action. Biochemical measures offer promising endophenotypes in themselves; their relationships to behavioral, cognitive, and neuroimaging endophenotypes are also worthy of investigation. There is also great promise that biochemical biomarkers might be useful in predicting risk and in identifying relatively homogeneous subgroups of individuals with autism, thereby parsing the considerable heterogeneity in this etiologically and phenotypically complex disorder.

McPartland and colleagues (Chapter 20) bridge the gap between genes and cognition with an overview of social neuroscience findings generated from noninvasive neuroimaging and electrophysiological techniques. Given the predominance and universality of social deficits in the autistic phenotype, dysfunction in brain systems subserving social perception has become a key focus in autism research. This chapter reviews our understanding of the neural systems involved in the processing of social information and its disruption in autism while highlighting recent advances. In addition, work investigating an alternative interpretation of autistic dysfunction, problems with interconnectivity, and consequent difficulties with sophisticated information processing is addressed.

Neuroimaging and electrophysiological techniques provide critical insight into the neural-systems-level correlates of autism, but a mechanistic understanding of the disorder requires studies at the neuronal level of analysis. Casanova (Chapter 21) provides a masterful review of neuropathological findings in autism. While critical discoveries have been made in this area of autism research—for example, the identification of minicolumn pathology—progress has been hampered by the relative scarcity of brain tissue. Coordinated efforts are now under way to increase brain bank donations so that the research can better reflect the heterogeneity of this disorder and capture key developmental transitions.

In Chapter 22, Volkmar and colleagues remind us that autism affects the entire person, while addressing critical issues in the medical care of individuals with autism. Two of the major challenges in autism—difficulties with communication and social interaction—pose significant challenges for provision of health care. Difficulties with social interaction and sensitivity to change may mean a child does not like to be touched or will refuse to cooperate when being examined and even the most minor procedures can pose challenges. To better meet these challenges, these authors present numerous recommendations for best practice and preventive care. They review a number of key topics, including medical conditions that are overrepresented in individuals with autism and age-related health issues, and conclude with a discussion of the role of the primary care provider and medical home model.

Scahill, Tillberg, and Martin (Chapter 23) provide a comprehensive review of psychopharmacology for autism. While commonly employed in clinical practice, empirical evidence concerning several medications used in clinical practice remains limited. This chapter reviews the empirical support and clinical applications of the major drug categories that are commonly used in the treatment of children and adults with autism, including atypical antipsychotics, serotonin reuptake inhibitors, stimulants, and nonstimulant medications for hyperactivity in autism. The authors then evaluate data concerning the use of anticonvulsants and glutamate antagonists. Encouraging advances in early drug development and directions for future research are also presented.

CHAPTER 17

Genetics of Autism Spectrum Disorders

MICHAEL RUTTER AND ANITA THAPAR

At first sight, it might be supposed that a review of the literature on genetic influences on autism spectrum disorders (ASD) should be quite straightforward. All that should be needed is a search of the literature on this topic. Unfortunately, that was not possible because of the major changes in the concept of autism that have been necessitated as a result of empirical research findings (Rutter, 2013). Accordingly, we begin by a brief discussion of some of those changes that are most particularly relevant for discussing genetic influences. Second, the past decade has seen a substantial broadening of genetic concepts. Accordingly, these are briefly reviewed as they apply to psychopathology in general, before we turn to specific findings on ASD. Third, there is a growing number of claims regarding the identification of common molecular genetic variants that could explain most of the risk for autism (e.g., Klei et al., 2012).

We are deeply grateful to Joanna Martin for her thorough and thoughtful search of the literature on genetic findings with regard to ASD.

Such claims tend to assume that there can be a single figure (usually derived from some form of risk ratio). However, it is very evident that there are major differences among the concepts of relative risk, absolute risk, and population-attributable risk. Accordingly, we summarize these differences.

CHANGING CONCEPTS OF AUTISM

Traditional diagnostic concepts assume that each diagnosis is separate from all others, with overlap patterns being relatively rare. It is now clear that this assumption is unsound (Rutter, 2013). Thus, it has been found that some 20%–50% of children with attention-deficit/hyperactivity disorder (ADHD) also meet the criteria for an autism spectrum disorder, and conversely 30%–80% of children with ASD meet the criteria for ADHD (Rommelse, Franke, Geurts, Hartman, & Buitelaar, 2010). Initial attention focused on the overlap between autism and ADHD, but research findings have shown that ASD is associated with a broader range of psychopathology that extends well beyond ADHD (Simonoff et al., 2008). Research has also shown that there is substantial shared genetic liability between ASD, learning disorders, and ADHD (Lichtenstein, Carlström, Råstam, Gillberg, & Anckarsäter, 2010). Early social cognition research postulated that an impaired theory of mind was relatively specific to autism (Frith, 1989); (Happé & Frith, 1996) but somewhat similar deficits are also found in schizophrenia (Biedermann, Frajo-Apor, & Hofer, 2012; Sprong, Schothorst, Vos, Hox, & Van Engeland, 2007).

Considerable interest was aroused by research findings on the importance of copy number variations (CNVs)—meaning submicroscopic deletions or duplications of segments of DNA. These have been found, however, to be associated not only with autism (Sebat et al., 2007), but with schizophrenia (The International Schizophrenia Consortium, 2008) and ADHD (Williams et al., 2010), as well as with intellectual disability (B. de Vries et al., 2005).

Happé and Ronald (2008) argued for a fractionable autism triad in which social interaction, communication, and restricted/repetitive behaviors and interests are viewed as genetically separable and therefore better studied independently rather than as part of an overall cohesive syndrome (see also Leekham, Prior, & Uljarevic, (2011)). This is a provocative hypothesis in that, if proven correct, it would undermine the utility of studying genetic influences on the syndrome of autism as a whole. However, one attempt to look at that directly (Ronald et al., 2010) using a genome-wide association study was not very supportive of the hypothesis.

Finally, twin and family studies have clearly shown the reality of a broader phenotype of autism that goes beyond the traditional diagnosis but in which the social communication and behavioral abnormalities are very similar in quality to those found in autism (Le Couteur et al., 1996). The limited available evidence suggests that this broader phenotype involves the same genetic liability as found for autism as traditionally diagnosed. However, researchers have been very slow to develop reliable and valid measures of broader phenotype

features, and up to now there is no evidence that the available measures (Dawson et al., 2007) can differentiate mild autistic features from social anxiety or schizotypal features. That is a crucial limitation because it is obvious that autism cannot possibly account for all major problems in social relationships, and any adequate measure would have to be able to differentiate between those that are, and those that are not, associated with autism. That has not been done as yet.

GENETIC ADVANCES

In the past 5 years there has been a rapid escalation in molecular genetic studies. The aims have been to investigate the contribution of common and rare genetic variation to autism. Capturing relevant genetic variation is challenging. The studies we will discuss later have utilized a number of different techniques that have changed over the years as new technologies have become available and affordable. The types of genetic variants examined have included ones that are common (>5%), as well as rare (<1% frequency), have involved alterations in DNA sequence (e.g., single nucleotide polymorphisms—SNPs) and structure (e.g., CNVs) and have been localized in specific selected genes of interest or have represented initial attempts to capture variation across the whole genome. Many studies, especially the earliest ones, focused on variants in specific candidate genes that were selected either on the basis of their chromosomal location or because of their function, whilst more recent studies have set out to identify common risk variants and rare CNVs across the genome. These have included genome-wide association studies (GWAS) of common SNPs as well as investigation of rare CNVs (submicroscopic chromosomal deletions and duplications).

The SNPs investigated in GWAS have been physically located across the genome including intergenic regions as well as within genes that include coding (exons) and noncoding regions (introns) and previously known regulatory regions. They have essentially been considered to be an "anonymous" set of SNPs that "tag" a proportion of common genetic variation. More recently, studies have attempted to also capture rare variants in exomes (the coding region of genes) using DNA sequencing. We will discuss these findings in turn.

It is important to realize two important methodological points. First, it is not a trivial matter to capture all types of genetic variation in terms of DNA sequence and structure. Future whole genome sequencing theoretically provides this possibility, although huge sample sizes would be needed to carry out such large scale testing and that (among other difficulties) is a serious challenge for neuropsychiatric disorders such as autism. Second, it is difficult to define what is meant by *relevant genetic variation*; we now know that knowledge of gene sequence and where genes are physically located is insufficient for providing insights into the etiology of disorders including ASD. We need to understand genomic function if we are to make mechanistic links with disease risk.

DNA is transcribed into mRNA (messenger RNA) that in turn provides the code for generating proteins. This process is not simply dictated by DNA sequence within genes. The Encyclopedia of DNA Elements (ENCODE) project (Muers, 2012) has set out to identify all functional elements encoded in the human genome. This work is ongoing (http://genome.ucsc.edu/ENCODE/), but findings so far suggest that at least 80% of the genome has a biochemical role. This dismisses the idea that the majority of the human genome is junk DNA because it lies outside protein-coding genes. The results show that the human genome contains vast numbers of elements that regulate genes. There are some key take-home findings from the results so far published. The majority of GWAS SNPs that have shown significant association with a phenotype (e.g., Crohn's disease) have been located outside genes coding for proteins. The emerging ENCODE studies find that these GWAS SNPs are enriched for ENCODE functional elements thereby suggesting that these functional elements that lie outside genes are important in terms of disease risk. This suggests that exome sequencing will not be adequate for capturing disease relevant

genetic variation. The ENCODE data and future ongoing findings will provide a way of interpreting genetic association findings. Findings from the project also highlight that identifying associated genetic variants is only a start point; the challenge is in interpreting the biological meaning of findings. Then these findings have to be linked to the clinical picture.

Bearing in mind these challenges, some key findings are starting to emerge from molecular genetic studies of ASD that we will first highlight broadly before considering them in greater detail. First, ASD is not explained by disruption in any single specific gene; multiple genes and multiple genetic variants are involved. Second, associated genetic risk variants are no different from other risk factors for complex disorders in that they have probabilistic effects; that is, they are neither necessary nor sufficient to result in ASD. Also, it is well-established that relatives of those affected and unaffected controls can be carriers of genetic risk variants and yet appear to be phenotypically unaffected or minimally affected. Third, molecular genetic findings are in keeping with twin studies in showing shared genetic risk influences operate across different forms of psychopathology. Single gene syndromes and genetic variants that are associated with increased risk of ASD have been linked to a very wide range of psychiatric disorders. That is, these genetic risks appear to be pleiotropic. Again, the nonspecific link between risk factor and phenotypic manifestation is typical of other risk factors for complex diseases. For example, thus far the most consistent findings in relation to autism suggest the involvement of rare genetic variants, notably large, rare copy number variants that have included submicroscopic deletions and duplications (Ben-David & Shifman, 2012).

Fourth, there has been considerable debate about whether the genetic architecture of autism and other neuropsychiatric disorders is better explained by rare variants. Although there has been increased interest in rare variants (<1% frequency), indirect evidence suggests that the genetic architecture of ASD and other psychiatric disorders is best explained by multiple variants that have a spectrum of frequencies, from rare to common (Sullivan, Daly, & O'Donovan, 2012). An interesting fifth observation, that we will discuss again later, is that there is now consistent evidence that many rare mutations including CNVs arise as de novo mutations, that is, the parents of the affected individual do not carry the mutation, although other mutations are inherited from parents. De novo mutations would contribute to heritability estimates observed in twin studies but would not explain the familial transmission of ASD. Interestingly, increased maternal and especially paternal age appear to be associated with the rate of de novo mutations (Kong et al., 2012). Advanced parental age has previously been found to be associated with ASD (Durkin et al., 2008), and there has been much discussion on the possible mechanisms involved that could include male germ line mutations, an accumulation of environmental exposures in both parents, and pregnancy complications in mothers. The genetic findings so far (Kong et al. 2012), suggest that an increased rate of paternal mutations is one plausible explanation. There is a puzzle as to why disorders with markedly low fecundity—such as autism and schizophrenia—do not die out as there should be strong selection effects (Power et al., 2012). One plausible explanation is the emergence of new mutations, although there are likely other mechanisms that at present remain unknown.

QUANTIFYING EFFECTS

There are widespread misunderstandings about how to quantify size of effects. In the Academy of Medical Sciences working group report (Academy of Medical Sciences, 2007), Down syndrome was used as an illustration of this. High maternal age is a well demonstrated feature that greatly increases a woman's chance of having a baby with Down syndrome. For women over the age of 40 years the likelihood is some 16 times higher than that for women aged 20–25 years—an absolutely huge increase in relative risk, but the same data show that the absolute risk is very low. That is, the chance of a woman over the age of 40 years

having a Down syndrome baby is a mere 1%. Note that this is simply another way of expressing the size of effects, and the Academy of Medical Sciences working party recommended that all publications should include absolute risk as well as, or instead of, relative risk. The contrast is even more striking with respect to the population attributable risk—meaning the absolute increase in risk due to the specified causal factor. Continuing with the Down syndrome example, that is very low because it is hugely influenced by the population frequency of the causal factor. In the population as a whole the average IQ of a person with Down syndrome is some 60 points below the general population mean—a massive causal effect, but this does not translate into a high population attributable risk because the majority of babies with Down syndrome are born to young mothers. That is because young mothers are much more common than older mothers. These differences in concept are clearly relevant to the quantification of genetic influences.

TWIN STUDIES

The first clear evidence of a substantial genetic influence on the liability to autism came from Folstein & Rutter's (1977a, 1977b) twin study. The sample studied was small but it did reflect a nationwide search for twins in which one or both twins had autism. A follow-up by Bailey et al. (1995) reassessed the same twins and an additional sample of twins was identified using the same methods. The findings showed that very few twins had been missed in the original sampling, and this provided confidence in the robustness of the findings. Two key features were evident. First, the heritability was high, being estimated at 90%, and second, the genetic liability extended well beyond the traditional diagnosis (Le Couteur, et al., 1996).

In the past decade, there have been a substantial number of further twin studies (Ronald & Hoekstra, 2011). There have been four recent twin studies on autism spectrum disorders as such. First, Taniai, Nishiyama, Miyachi, Imaeda, and Sumi (2008) used a Japanese sample based on child screening systems as well as clinical referrals. Case vignettes on 45 twin pairs were used for diagnosis on a continuous childhood autism rating scale. The findings showed a heritability of 73% for males and 87% for females. Second, Rosenberg et al. (2009) used a voluntary online database to obtain 277 twin pairs. The concordance in monozygotic pairs was 77% and 31% within dizygotic pairs, thus giving rise to a high heritability. This is not a very satisfactory way of sampling, despite the advantage of giving rise to a large sample size. Nevertheless, the twin concordances (88% from monozygotic twin pairs and 31% from dizygotic pairs again show a high heritability. A third study by Lichtenstein et al. (2010) used the Swedish twin registry for sampling to obtain 117 twin pairs. The estimated heritability was 80%. None of the first three twin studies used well-accepted, standardized diagnostic measures but there was general agreement that the heritability is high, albeit with a concordance rate in dizygotic twins that was higher than in the early studies.

The last study was that by Hallmayer et al. (2011), which is the least satisfactory because of its 17% participation rate and its total ignoring of the findings from other twin studies, all of which differed markedly from their own conclusion that the heritability was only 38%.

In addition, there have been studies of autistic traits in the general population based on the Missouri twin sample (Constantino & Todd, 2000, 2003, 2005), the U.K. twins early development study (TEDS) (Ronald et al., 2006; Ronald et al., 2010; Ronald, Happé, & Plomin, 2005, 2008), and samples in the United Kingdom studied by Skuse, Mandy, and Scourfield (2005); a Dutch sample of 380 twin pairs from the Netherlands Twin Register; a Boston University twin sample of very young twins (Edelson & Saudino, 2009); and a representative sample from the Wisconsin twin panel (Stilp, Gernsbacher, Schweigert, Arneson, & Goldsmith, 2010). Firm conclusions are tricky, if only because the several different reports using the same sample have often disagreed substantially. Nevertheless, what the findings do show is that autism seems to function as a continuously distributed trait with heritability mainly in the range between 60% and 90%.

Finally, there have been a small number of twin studies concerned with psychiatric comorbidity between autistic features and other forms of psychopathology. Reiersen, Constantino, Grimmer, Martin, and Todd (2008) found a genetic correlation between autistic traits and ADHD behaviors of 0.72. Ronald, Simonoff, Kuntsi, Asherson, and Plomin (2008) found similar genetic correlations, albeit slightly lower (0.54–0.57). Lichtenstein et al. (2010) found high genetic correlations between autism spectrum disorders and all the neuropsychiatric disorders studied (ADHD, developmental incoordination, tic disorder, and learning disorders). The genetic overlap was highest between ASD and ADHD. By contrast, Hallett, Ronald, and Happé (2009) and Hallett, Ronald, Rijsdijk, and Happé (2010) found only a very low genetic correlation between autistic traits and anxiety-related behaviors, although (Hoekstra, Bartels, Hudziak, Van Beijsterveldt, & Boomsma, 2007) found a genetic correlation between autistic traits and withdrawn behavior of 0.56.

SINGLE GENE DISORDERS AND THEIR POSSIBLE REVERSIBILITY

Zoghbi & Bear (2012) provided an excellent review of key syndromic disorders associated with autism and intellectual disability that are characterized by penetrant mutations in genes that have been shown in animal models to disrupt synaptic function (see also Ameis & Szatmari, 2012). Grafodatskaya, Chung, Szatmari, and Weksberg (2010) have indicated that dysregulated epigenetic mechanisms are involved in several of the syndromic disorders. The pathophysiology of both autism and intellectual disability has raised the possibility of therapeutic interventions to bring synapses into a normal operating range. Here we focus on just three of these syndromes: fragile X syndrome, tuberous sclerosis, and Rett syndrome. All three illustrate the value of animal models based on a mutant gene (rather than trying to create a model based on behavioral similarities). The three examples chosen, however, differ in key respects.

Rett Syndrome

Although the disorder was originally described by Rett (1966), it became much more widely recognized when Hagberg and colleagues published a description of 35 cases in 1983 (Hagberg, Aicardi, Dias, & Ramos, 1983). Girls with Rett syndrome appeared to develop normally up to 6 to 18 months of age but, then, head growth typically decelerates, leading to microcephaly by the second or third year of life. The children lose purposeful use of their hands and develop stereotypic hand wringing or washing movements. Often, in early childhood, there are social features that appear a little bit like autism. Epileptic seizures often start about the age of 4 years but tend to decrease in severity in adulthood. It was found that mutations in the X-linked methyl-CpG-binding protein 2 (MeCP2) cause the syndrome (Amir et al., 1999; Neul et al., 2008). It is striking that mutations that partially compromise the function of MeCP2 lead to a surprisingly diverse range of phenotypes. Mice lacking functional MeCP2 reproduce features of Rett syndrome (Chen, Akbarian, Tudor, & Jaenisch, 2001; Guy, Hendrich, Holmes, Martin, & Bird, 2001). Strikingly, despite the devastating neurological phenotypes, the brain appears normal with the exception of microcephaly, a decrease in dendritic spine density, and dendritic swelling (Belichenko et al., 2009). Although Rett syndrome functions as a progressive neurodegenerative disorder, genetic and pharmacological studies provide hope that the disease might be reversible (Giacometti, Luikenhuis, Beard, & Jaenisch, 2007; Guy, Gan, Selfridge, Cobb, & Bird, 2007). The results show that neuronal connectivity is actually intact and that the neurons and glia are not permanently damaged from MeCP2 loss (Tropea et al., 2009). It is usually thought that the gene reversal has led to reversal of a neurodegenerative disorder, but actually that does not seem the most appropriate way of viewing it. Rather, in line with the relatively normal brain

findings, reversal or partial reversal points to the disorder being the result of postnatal malfunction. That is indeed highly encouraging but it remains most uncertain how far this could be seen as a more general possibility.

Fragile X Syndrome

Martin and Bell (1943) first described a family in which intellectual deficits segregated as an X-linked trait. Lubs (1969) subsequently observed a constriction on the long arm of the X chromosome in some males with intellectual disability and went on to describe many physical features (such as large testes, large low-set ears, and asymmetric facial features). Common behavioral features include hyperactivity, anxiety, and autistic-like features involving gaze avoidance. Postmortem neuropathological studies reveal structural abnormalities of dendritic spines. Fu et al. (1991) and Verkerk et al. (1991) showed that expansions of a CGG repeat in the fragile X gene (FMR1) cause the syndrome. Obviously, fragile X differs strikingly from Rett syndrome in the presence of brain abnormalities and numerous physical anomalies. Nevertheless, mouse and fly fragile X models in which the genes homologous to FMR1 have been knocked out have led to an understanding of the pathophysiology of the disease. It seems that excessive protein synthesis downstream from mGluR5 is pathogenic. This has led to the undertaking of trials of negative mGluR5 regulators. Preliminary findings only are available and they are only slightly encouraging. An additional approach has been the focus on impaired GABAergic inhibition (Levenga, de Vrij, Oostra, & Willemsen, 2010).

Tuberous Sclerosis

This is a neurocutaneous, dominantly inherited, multisystem disorder characterized by the presence of benign tumors (hamartomas) that occur in many organs but especially in the brain, skin, eyes, kidneys, and heart (Curatolo, Bombardieri, & Jozwiak, 2008). Tuberous sclerosis is caused by mutations in two distinct genes. Clearly, there is no way in which all these changes could be reversed. It is not surprising that brain development will be altered by tumor growth and seizures during early life (Numis et al., 2011). What is new, however, is the growing appreciation that substantial brain dysfunction occurs independently of tumor formation and epilepsy (P. J. de Vries, 2010). This suggestion received a major boost with the development of rodent models of tuberous sclerosis. The treatment of mutant mice with the immune-suppressive drug rapamycin has been found to ameliorate several phenotypes. This suggests that some synaptic and behavioral phenotypes might be due to ongoing pathophysiological processes, rather than an irreversible derailment of development. Insofar as that is the case, pathophysiological changes might be correctable with drugs.

Somewhat similar approaches have been adopted in relation to the SHANK2 gene. Mice carrying a mutation identical to the ASD-associated micro-deletion in humans exhibit ASD-like behaviors including reduced social interaction, a reduced social communication by ultrasonic vocalizations, and repetitive jumping. It has been claimed that direct stimulation of glutamate receptors with D-cycloserine normalizes glutamate receptor function and improves social interaction in mice (Won et al., 2012). Similar findings have been shown for neuroligin-3 knockout mice (Baudouin et al., 2012).

MOLECULAR GENETICS FINDINGS

A decade ago the main research strategy was provided by genetic linkage analyses using an affected sibling-pair design in multiplex families. These have been productive in the sense of giving rise to replicated linkage peaks from two or more independent studies (Abrahams & Geschwind, 2008; Freitag, Staal, Klauck, Duketis, & Waltes, 2010). These have been found on chromosomes 1, 2, 3, 5, 7, 9, 11, and 17, with the evidence strongest with respect to 7 and 17. The independent replications provide confidence that these are not chance findings or false positive findings but, at least so far, they

have not resulted in the identification of individual susceptibility genes. Because of a concern over likely genetic heterogeneity, there have been multiple attempts to reduce heterogeneity by focusing on samples according to specific phenotypes, or by refining phenotypic definition according to sex of proband, language, autistic regression, or behavioral inflexibility (see Abrahams & Geschwind, 2008). Obviously, more could be done by using additional features such as macrocephaly or the presence of seizures. The endeavor was certainly worthwhile, but although there have been some claims of the value of this approach (Miles, 2011), none of these approaches has resulted in finding individual genes with a replicable effect. Accordingly, attention has to some extent shifted to the possibility of using genetic findings to identify key biological pathways (Geschwind, 2011), as discussed later.

An important step forward was provided by the discovery of rare ASD-associated mutations in neuroligins 3 and 4 (Jamain et al., 2003) and in SHANK 3 (Durand et al., 2006; Moessner et al., 2007). The discoveries came about because cost-effective resequencing made it possible to build on cytogenetic studies (Abrahams & Geschwind, 2008). The importance of these rare mutations lies in the implications for possible biological pathways. However, not only do such mutations account for only a tiny proportion of cases of autism, none is specific for autism. Rather, they give rise to a wide range of neurobehavioral phenotypes particularly including intellectual disability and language impairment. Accordingly, questions need to be raised with respect to the implications of the findings for nonsyndromic autism.

GWAS became possible through advances in technology. The strength of GWAS lies in the ability to cover the whole genome without having to rely on the identification of particular candidate genes. The downside, however, is that there is an inevitably high rate of false positives. Although appropriate ways of dealing with this issue have been put forward—see Burton et al. (2007)—no entirely satisfactory answer has been obtained. One of the difficulties is that there needs to be identification of controls without the disorder being investigated. That is always tricky, but it becomes much more difficult if the genetic effects apply across a range of different syndromes and disorders. Unfortunately, that is exactly what the results tend to show (Talkowski et al., 2012).

Anney and colleagues (2010, 2012) have published findings on a particularly large sample (2,705 families), finding that individual common variants exert only weak effects on the risk for autism spectrum disorders. Unfortunately, none of the positive SNPs have achieved genome-wide statistical significance and none has been independently replicated (Sullivan et al., 2012).

GENETIC LEADS ON BIOLOGICAL PATHWAYS TO ASD

Locating genes is of very little value in itself unless it is known what the genes do. Peñagarikano & Geschwind (2012) have argued that the integration of multiple research approaches, from human studies to animal models, converge to inform functional biology that could lead to novel treatment development. They use the example of the CNTNAP2 gene. They note that the forkhead box P2 (FOXP2), which is associated with speech and language disorders, directly binds intron 1 of the CNTNAP2 gene and regulates its expression. However, the FOXP2 gene's association with language disorders is much more complex than suggested, in that the individuals in the family that gave rise to the discovery have multiple deficits, of which language is only one. It is argued, too, that the CNTNAP2 knockout mouse is a good model for autism because treatment of the mice with risperidone rescues the increased repetitive behavior but not the social deficits. Others might suggest that this might indicate the value of the model for stereotyped repetitive behavior but not for autism.

Voineagu (2012) has argued that gene expression data may be helpful in identifying common molecular pathways dysregulated in autism. However, so far the biological understanding deriving from this approach has been rather small. Ben-David & Shifman (2012) constructed a gene coexpression network based on a widespread survey of gene expression in the human brain. In brief, the approach was to consider whether autism genes identified through GWAS or by the study of rare mutations were coexpressed in relation to what is known on gene expression in the human brain, with respect to genes concerned with protein interactions. It was found that the coexpressed modules included genes involved in synaptic and neuronal plasticity and expressed in areas associated with learning, memory, and sensory perception. The findings suggested that both common and rare variants contributed to ASD.

Kou, Betancur, Xu, Buxbaum, and Ma'Ayan (2012) used a support vector machine to compare genes identified on the basis of a possible etiological role in ASD and those derived from protein–protein interactions (PPI) data from published databases. Both the PPI-based classifiers and the autism attribute–based classifiers discriminated between ASD and intellectual disability genes, and other genes, but the PPI performed only slightly better and all classifiers reported a relatively high degree of false positives.

O'Roak et al. (2012) sequenced all coding regions of the genome (the exome) for parent–child trios exhibiting sporadic ASD (i.e., with only one child in the family having ASD). These were compared with the exomes of 50 unaffected siblings. The findings showed that de novo point mutations were overwhelmingly paternal in origin (with a 4 to 1 bias)—see also Iossifov et al. (2012)—and positively correlated with paternal age. Two fifths of the most severe or disruptive mutations mapped to a highly interconnected β-catenin/chromatin remodeling protein network. Combined with CNV data, the results indicated extreme locus heterogeneity.

Guilmatre et al. (2009) found that most of the CNVs that were significantly associated with autism involved genes involved in neurotransmission or in synapse formation and maintenance, and that they were similarly present in schizophrenia and mental retardation, supporting the existence of shared biological pathways in these neurodevelopmental disorders. State and Levitt (2011) similarly noted the marked lack of diagnostic specificity.

Note the potential importance of the discovery that there are three genes found on GWAS that have genome-wide significance (Anney et al., 2010; Wang et al., 2009; Weiss, Arking, Daly, & Chakravarti, 2009), but a caution is needed in that each study has so far failed to replicate the findings from either of the others and a joint evaluation of all three decreased the evidence for association for all of the identified risk alleles (Devlin, Melhem, & Roeder, 2011). With respect to diagnostic specificity, as shown in numerous studies, State & Levitt (2011) suggested that this could arise as a combination of pleiotropy and locus heterogeneity, but they emphasized that convincing answers have yet to be obtained.

In summary, a range of different methods have been used to try to identify biological pathways associated with genes relevant to the liability to autism. All depend on what is known about the functions of the relevant genes. It is clear that somewhat similar, if not identical, biological pathways concern a diverse mixture of disorders. Hence, the understanding of the relevance to autism as such remains uncertain and no firm conclusions are as yet possible. The goal is undoubtedly a good one, but the conceptual and methodological problems involved are considerable. The biggest challenge will probably be the very marked diversity of the biological features associated with the identified genes. The findings do not seem to suggest any clear-cut meaningful biological pathway but, in addition, there is the substantial diagnostic lack of specificity. It may be that there are genetic influences on liability to psychopathology more generally as well as rather different genetic influences that are specific to particular disorders. It is reasonable to go ahead with hope but that needs to be accompanied by substantial caution and the avoidance of premature claims.

ENVIRONMENTAL INFLUENCES

Both Landrigan (2011) and Hertz-Picciotto (2011) have summarized the available research findings on possible environmental factors, and Rodier (2011) has done the same with respect to toxins and teratogenic agents. There are a variety of possibly useful leads, but evidence is lacking on proven environmental influences as they operate with respect to nonsyndromic autism. There was a suggestion that either the measles, mumps, rubella vaccine (MMR), or Thimerosal, a mercury preservative, might have led to an epidemic of autism, but the research findings have been consistently negative.

CLINICAL IMPLICATIONS

The evidence that genetic influences are very important in the liability to autism spectrum disorders was certainly important in the past in leading to a rejection of the general assumption that autism was a psychogenic disorder. Nevertheless, the evidence has also shown that, in the great majority of cases, autism is a multifactorial disorder—leading to the expectation that not only will there be multiple genetic factors, but also that important environmental influences are to be anticipated. It may also be expected that there will be gene–environment interplay involving a genetic moderation of environmental effects, and vice versa. Unfortunately, in the absence of sound data on environmental causes, this is a probability to be borne in mind when thinking about the issues but it is not yet one that is of any practical importance in dealing with individual patients.

Genetic influences are of more direct importance in the case of syndromic autism, but these account for a small minority of cases—probably less than 10%. Nevertheless, the proven association with fragile X syndrome has pointed to the need for there to be routine screening for fragile X in the case of individuals with a possible autism spectrum disorder. Similarly, known association with tuberous sclerosis has meant that routine medical assessments should involve the use of Wood's light in order to detect the skin features that are diagnostic of tuberous sclerosis. Genetic counseling is also indicated in cases of syndromic autism.

What remains much more problematic is genetic counseling of the families with a child whose autism is not associated with an identifiable syndrome. Family studies have made clear that there is a raised rate of the broader phenotype in family members, but at present, adequate proven measures of the broader phenotype have yet to be developed. It is not that there are no measures available but, rather, that such measures have not been tested as to whether they can differentiate between social and other features of the broader autism phenotype from social problems associated with, say, schizophrenia or anxiety disorders. There is no shortcut that avoids the need for a careful clinical assessment of family members for whom the possibility arises of having the broader autism phenotype.

The other consideration that arises out of the genetic findings is the high frequency with which autism spectrum disorders are associated with other forms of psychopathology—perhaps particularly involving ADHD. Again, clinicians need to be alert to this possibility when taking account of it with respect to both diagnostic assessment and treatment.

Undoubtedly the situation will alter in a major way once there is identification of the relevant susceptibility genes for autism liability, or when the mode of inheritance is known, and when there are better measures of the broader phenotype. In this chapter we have considered the various possibilities of genetic findings casting light on the relevant biological causal pathways and, again, once these have been identified with replicable findings, the situation will change. Accordingly, by the time of the next edition of the *Handbook*, it is quite likely that genetic findings will have more direct clinical value, but that day has not yet arrived.

CROSS-REFERENCES

Issues of diagnosis in autism and related conditions are addressed in Chapter 1 and aspects of the broader autism phenotype in Chapter 2. Medical care (including clinical genetic assessment) is addressed in Chapter 22.

REFERENCES

Abrahams, B. S., & Geschwind, D. H. (2008). Advances in autism genetics: On the threshold of a new neurobiology. *Nature Reviews Genetics*, 9(5), 341–355.

Academy of Medical Sciences. (2007). *Identifying the environmental causes of disease: How should we decide what to believe and when to take action?* London, England: Author.

Ameis, S. H., & Szatmari, P. (2012). Imaging-genetics in autism spectrum disorder: Advances, translational impact, and future directions. *Frontiers in Psychiatry*, 3, 1–13.

Amir, R., Van den Veyver, I., Wan, M., Tran, C., Francke, U., & Zoghbi, H. (1999). Rett syndrome is caused by mutations in X-linked MeCP2, encoding methyl-CpG-binding protein 2. *Nature Genetics*, 23(2), 185–188.

Anney, R., Klei, L., Pinto, D., Almeida, J., Bacchelli, E., Baird, G., . . . Bourgeron, T. (2012). Individual common variants exert weak effects on risk for autism spectrum disorders. *Human Molecular Genetics*, 21, 1–23.

Anney, R., Klei, L., Pinto, D., Regan, R., Conroy, J., Magalhaes, T. R., . . . Hallmayer, J. (2010). A genome-wide scan for common alleles affecting risk for autism. *Human Molecular Genetics*, 19, 4072–4082. doi:10.1093/hmg/ddq307

Bailey, A., Le Couteur, A., Gottesman, I., Bolton, P., Simonoff, E., Yuzda, E., & Rutter, M. (1995). Autism as a strongly genetic disorder: Evidence from a British twin study. *Psychological Medicine*, 25, 63–77.

Baudouin, S. J., Gaudias, J., Gerharz, S., Hatstatt, L., Zhou, K., Punnakkal, P., . . . De Zeeuw, C. I. (2012). Shared synaptic pathophysiology in syndromic and nonsyndromic rodent models of autism. *Science*, 338, 128–132.

Belichenko, P. V., Wright, E. E., Belichenko, N. P., Masliah, E., Li, H. H., Mobley, W. C., & Francke, U. (2009). Widespread changes in dendritic and axonal morphology in MeCP2-mutant mouse models of Rett syndrome: Evidence for disruption of neuronal networks. *Journal of Comparative Neurology*, 514(3), 240–258.

Ben-David, E., & Shifman, S. (2012). Networks of neuronal genes affected by common and rare variants in autism spectrum disorders. *PLoS Genetics*, 8(3), e1002556.

Biedermann, F., Frajo-Apor, B., & Hofer, A. (2012). Theory of mind and its relevance in schizophrenia. *Current Opinion in Psychiatry*, 25, 71–75.

Burton, P. R., Clayton, D. G., Cardon, L. R., Craddock, N., Deloukas, P., Duncanson, A., . . . Samani, N. J. (2007). Genome-wide association study of 14,000 cases of seven common diseases and 3,000 shared controls. *Nature*, 447(7145), 661–678.

Chen, R. Z., Akbarian, S., Tudor, M., & Jaenisch, R. (2001). Deficiency of methyl-CpG binding protein-2 in CNS neurons results in a Rett-like phenotype in mice. *Nature Genetics*, 27(3), 327–331.

Constantino, J. N., & Todd, R. D. (2000). Genetic structure of reciprocal social behavior. *American Journal of Psychiatry*, 157(12), 2043–2045.

Constantino, J. N., & Todd, R. D. (2003). Autistic traits in the general population: A twin study. *Archives of General Psychiatry*, 60(5), 524.

Constantino, J. N., & Todd, R. D. (2005). Intergenerational transmission of subthreshold autistic traits in the general population. *Biological Psychiatry*, 57(6), 655–660.

Curatolo, P., Bombardieri, R., & Jozwiak, S. (2008). Tuberous sclerosis. *The Lancet*, 372, 657–668.

Dawson, G., Estes, A., Munson, J., Schellenberg, G., Bernier, R., & Abbott, R. (2007). Quantitative assessment of autism symptom-related traits in probands and parents: Broader phenotype autism symptom scale. *Journal of Autism and Developmental Disorders, 37*, 523–536.

Devlin, B., Melhem, N., & Roeder, K. (2011). Do common variants play a role in risk for autism? Evidence and theoretical musings. *Brain Research, 1380*, 78–84.

de Vries, B., Pfundt, R., Leisink, M., Koolen, D. A., Vissers, L. E. L. M., Janssen, I. M.,...Leeuw, N. (2005). Diagnostic genome profiling in mental retardation. *American Journal of Human Genetics, 77*(4), 606–616.

de Vries, P. J. (2010). Targeted treatments for cognitive and neurodevelopmental disorders in tuberous sclerosis complex. *Neurotherapeutics, 7*(3), 275–282.

Durand, C. M., Betancur, C., Boeckers, T. M., Bockmann, J., Chaste, P., Fauchereau, F.,...Anckarsäter, H. (2006). Mutations in the gene encoding the synaptic scaffolding protein SHANK3 are associated with autism spectrum disorders. *Nature Genetics, 39*(1), 25–27.

Durkin, M. S., Maenner, M. J., Newschaffer, C. J., Lee, L. C., Cunniff, C. M., Daniels, J. L.,...Zahorodny, W. (2008). Advanced parental age and the risk of autism spectrum disorder. *American Journal of Epidemiology, 168*(11), 1268–1276.

Edelson, L. R., & Saudino, K. J. (2009). Genetic and environmental influences on autistic-like behaviors in 2-year-old twins. *Behavior Genetics, 39*(3), 255–264.

Folstein, S., & Rutter, M. (1977a). Genetic influences and infantile autism. *Nature, 265*(5596), 726–728.

Folstein, S., & Rutter, M. (1977b). Infantile autism: A genetic study of 21 twin pairs. *Journal of Child Psychology and Psychiatry, 18*, 297–321.

Freitag, C. M., Staal, W., Klauck, S. M., Duketis, E., & Waltes, R. (2010). Genetics of autistic disorders: Review and clinical implications. *European Child & Adolescent Psychiatry, 19*(3), 169–178.

Frith, U. (1989). *Autism: Explaining the Enigma.* Malden, MA: Blackwell.

Fu, Y. H., Kuhl, D., Pizzuti, A., Pieretti, M., Sutcliffe, J. S., Richards, S.,...Warren, S. T. (1991). Variation of the CGG repeat at the fragile X site results in genetic instability: Resolution of the Sherman paradox. *Cell, 67*(6), 1047–1058.

Geschwind, D. H. (2011). Genetics of autism spectrum disorders. *Trends in Cognitive Sciences, 15*(9), 409–416.

Giacometti, E., Luikenhuis, S., Beard, C., & Jaenisch, R. (2007). Partial rescue of MeCP2 deficiency by postnatal activation of MeCP2. *Proceedings of the National Academy of Sciences, USA, 104*, 1931–1936. doi: 10.1073/pnas.0610593104

Grafodatskaya, D., Chung, B., Szatmari, P., & Weksberg, R. (2010). Autism spectrum disorders and epigenetics. *Journal of the American Academy of Child & Adolescent Psychiatry, 49*(8), 794–809.

Guilmatre, A., Dubourg, C., Mosca, A. L., Legallic, S., Goldenberg, A., Drouin-Garraud, V.,...Bonnet-Brilhault, F. (2009). Recurrent rearrangements in synaptic and neurodevelopmental genes and shared biologic pathways in schizophrenia, autism, and mental retardation. *Archives of General Psychiatry, 66*(9), 947.

Guy, J., Gan, J., Selfridge, J., Cobb, S., & Bird, A. (2007). Reversal of neurological defects in a mouse model of Rett syndrome. *Science, 315*, 1143–1147.

Guy, J., Hendrich, B., Holmes, M., Martin, J. E., & Bird, A. P. (2001). A mouse MeCP2-null mutation causes neurological symptoms that mimic Rett syndrome. *Nature Genetics, 27*, 322–326.

Hagberg, B., Aicardi, J., Dias, K., & Ramos, O. (1983). A progressive syndrome of autism, dementia, ataxia, and loss of purposeful hand use in girls: Rett's syndrome: Report of 35 cases. *Annals of Neurology, 14*(4), 471–479.

Hallett, V., Ronald, A., & Happé, F. (2009). Investigating the association between autistic-like and internalizing traits in a community-based twin sample. *Journal of the American Academy of Child & Adolescent Psychiatry, 48*(6), 618–627.

Hallett, V., Ronald, A., Rijsdijk, F., & Happé, F. (2010). Association of autistic-like and internalizing traits during childhood: A longitudinal twin study. *American Journal of Psychiatry, 167*(7), 809–817.

Hallmayer, J., Cleveland, S., Torres, A., Phillips, J., Cohen, B., Torigoe, T.,...Risch, N. (2011). Genetic heritability and shared environmental factors among twin pairs with autism. *Archives of General Psychiatry, 68*, 1905–1102.

Happé, F., & Frith, U. (1996). The neuropsychology of autism. *Brain, 119*(4), 1377–1400.

Happé, F., & Ronald, A. (2008). The "fractionable autism triad": A review of evidence from behavioural, genetic, cognitive and neural research. *Neuropsychological Review, 18*, 287–304. doi: 10.1007/s11065-008-9076-8

Hertz-Picciotto, I. (2011). Environmental risk factors in autism: Results from large-scale epidemiologic studies. In D. G. Amaral, G. Dawson, & D. Geschwind (Eds.), *Autism Spectrum Disorders* (pp. 827–862). New York, NY: Oxford University Press.

Hoekstra, R. A., Bartels, M., Hudziak, J. J., Van Beijsterveldt, T. C. E. M., & Boomsma, D. I. (2007). Genetic and environmental covariation between autistic traits and behavioral problems. *Twin Research and Human Genetics, 10*(6), 853–860.

International Schizophrenia Consortium. (2008). Rare chromosomal deletions and duplications increase risk of schizophrenia. *Nature, 455*(7210), 237–241.

Iossifov, I., Ronemus, M., Levy, D., Wang, Z., Hakker, I., Rosenbaum, J.,...Leotta, A. (2012). De novo gene disruptions in children on the autistic spectrum. *Neuron, 74*(2), 285–299.

Jamain, S., Quach, H., Betancur, C., Råstam, M., Colineaux, C., Gillberg, I. C.,...Gillberg, C. (2003). Mutations of the X-linked genes encoding neuroligins NLGN3 and NLGN4 are associated with autism. *Nature Genetics, 34*(1), 27–29.

Klei, L., Sanders, S. J., Murtha, M. T., Hus, V., Lowe, J. K., Willsey, A. J.,...Geschwind, D. (2012). Common genetic variants, acting additively, are a major source of risk for autism. *Molecular Autism, 3*(1), 9.

Kong, A., Frigge, M. L., Masson, G., Besenbacher, S., Sulem, P., Magnusson, G.,...Jonasdottir, A. (2012). Rate of de novo mutations and the importance of father/'s age to disease risk. *Nature, 488*(7412), 471–475.

Kou, Y., Betancur, C., Xu, H., Buxbaum, J. D., & Ma'Ayan, A. (2012). Network- and attribute-based classifiers can prioritize genes and pathways for autism spectrum disorders and intellectual disability. *American Journal of Medical Genetics Part C: Seminars in Medical Genetics, 160c*, 130–142.

Landrigan, P. (2011). Environment and autism. In E. Hollander, A. Kolevzon, & J. T. Coyle (Eds.), *Textbook of autism spectrum disorders* (pp. 247–264). Washington, DC: American Psychiatric Publishing.

Le Couteur, A., Bailey, A., Goode, S., Pickles, A., Robertson, S., Gottesman, I., & Rutter, M. (1996). A broader phenotype of autism: The clinical spectrum in twins. *Journal of Child Psychology and Psychiatry, 37*(7), 785–801.

Leekam, S., Prior, M., & Uljarevic, M. (2011). Restricted and repetitive behaviors in autism spectrum disorders: A review of research in the last decade. *Psychological Bulletin, 137*, 562–593.

Levenga, J., de Vrij, F., Oostra, B. A., & Willemsen, R. (2010). Potential therapeutic interventions for fragile X syndrome. *Trends in Molecular Medicine, 16*(11), 516–527.

Lichtenstein, P., Carlström, E., Råstam, M., Gillberg, C., & Anckarsäter, H. (2010). The genetics of autism spectrum disorders and related neuropsychiatric disorders in childhood. *American Journal of Psychiatry, 167*, 1357–1363.

Lubs, H. A. (1969). A marker X chromosome. *American Journal of Human Genetics, 21*(3), 231.

Martin, J. P., & Bell, J. (1943). A pedigree of mental defect showing sex-linkage. *Journal of Neurology and Psychiatry, 6*(3–4), 154.

Miles, J. H. (2011). Autism subgroups from a medical genetics perspective. In D. G. Amaral, G. Dawson, & D. H. Geschwind (Eds.), *Autism Spectrum Disorders* (pp. 705–721). New York, NY: Oxford University Press.

Moessner, R., Marshall, C. R., Sutcliffe, J. S., Skaug, J., Pinto, D., Vincent, J., . . . Szatmari, P. (2007). Contribution of SHANK3 mutations to autism spectrum disorder. *American Journal of Human Genetics, 81*(6), 1289–1297.

Muers, M. (2012). Human genetics: Fruits of exome sequencing for autism. *Nature Reviews Genetics, 13*(6), 377–377.

Neul, J. L., Fang, P., Barrish, J., Lane, J., Caeg, E. B., Smith, E. O., . . . Glaze, D. G. (2008). Specific mutations in methyl-CpG-binding protein 2 confer different severity in Rett syndrome. *Neurology, 70*(16), 1313–1321.

Numis, A. L., Major, P., Montenegro, M. A., Muzykewicz, D. A., Pulsifer, M. B., & Thiele, E. A. (2011). Identification of risk factors for autism spectrum disorders in tuberous sclerosis complex. *Neurology, 76*(11), 981–987.

O'Roak, B. J., Vives, L., Girirajan, S., Karakoc, E., Krumm, N., Coe, B. P., . . . Eichler, E. E. (2012). Sporadic autism exomes reveal a highly interconnected protein network of de novo mutations. *Nature, 485*(7397), 246–250.

Peñagarikano, O., & Geschwind, D. H. (2012). What does CNTNAP2 reveal about autism spectrum disorder? *Trends in Molecular Medicine, 18*, 1–8.

Power, R. A., Kyaga, S., Uher, R., MacCabe, J. H., Langstrom, N., Landen, M., . . . Svensson, A. C. (2012). Fecundity of patients with schizophrenia, autism, bipolar disorder, depression, anorexia nervosa, or substance abuse vs their unaffected siblings. *JAMA Psychiatry, 70*(1), 22–30.

Reiersen, A. M., Constantino, J. N., Grimmer, M., Martin, N. G., & Todd, R. D. (2008). Evidence for shared genetic influences on self-reported ADHD and autistic symptoms in young adult Australian twins. *Twin Research and Human Genetics, 11*(6), 579.

Rett, A. (1966). On a unusual brain atrophy syndrome in hyperammonemia in childhood. *Wiener Medizinische Wochenschrift (1946), 116*(37), 723.

Rodier, P. M. (2011). Environmental exposures that increase the risk of autism spectrum disorders. In D. Amaral, G. Dawson, & D. Geschwind (Eds.), *Autism spectrum disorders* (pp. 863–974). Oxford, England: Oxford University Press.

Rommelse, N., Franke, B., Geurts, H., Hartman, C., & Buitelaar, J. (2010). Shared heritability of attention-deficit/ hyperactivity disorder and autism spectrum disorder. *European Child & Adolescent Psychiatry, 19*, 281–295.

Ronald, A., Butcher, L. M., Docherty, S., Davis, O. S. P., Schalkwyk, L. C., Craig, I. W., & Plomin, R. (2010). A genome-wide association study of social and non-social autistic-like traits in the general population using pooled DNA, 500 K SNP microarrays and both community and diagnosed autism replication samples. *Behavior Genetics, 40*, 31–45.

Ronald, A., Happé, F., Bolton, P., Butcher, L. M., Price, T. S., Wheelwright, S., . . . Plomin, R. (2006). Genetic heterogeneity between the three components of the autism spectrum: A twin study. *Journal of the American Academy of Child & Adolescent Psychiatry, 45*(6), 691–699.

Ronald, A., Happé, F., & Plomin, R. (2005). The genetic relationship between individual differences in social and nonsocial behaviours characteristic of autism. *Developmental Science, 8*(5), 444–458.

Ronald, A., Happé, F., & Plomin, R. (2008). A twin study investigating the genetic and environmental aetiologies of parent, teacher and child ratings of autistic-like traits and their overlap. *European Child & Adolescent Psychiatry, 17*(8), 473–483.

Ronald, A., & Hoekstra, R. A. (2011). Autism spectrum disorders and autistic traits: A decade of new twin studies. *American Journal of Medical Genetics Part B: Neuropsychiatric Genetics, 156*(3), 255–274.

Ronald, A., Simonoff, E., Kuntsi, J., Asherson, P., & Plomin, R. (2008). Evidence for overlapping genetic influences on autistic and ADHD behaviours in a community twin sample. *Journal of Child Psychology and Psychiatry, 49*(5), 535–542.

Rosenberg, R. E., Law, J. K., Yenokyan, G., McGready, J., Kaufmann, W. E., & Law, P. A. (2009). Characteristics and concordance of autism spectrum disorders among 277 twin pairs. *Archives of Pediatrics & Adolescent Medicine, 163*(10), 907.

Rutter, M. (2013). Changing concepts and findings on autism. *Journal of Autism and Developmental Disorders, 43*, 1749–1757.

Sebat, J., Lakshmi, B., Malhotra, D., Troge, J., Lese-Martin, C., Walsh, T., . . . Kendall, J. (2007). Strong association of de novo copy number mutations with autism. *Science, 316*, 445–449.

Simonoff, E., Pickles, A., Charman, T., Chandler, S., Loucas, T., & Baird, G. (2008). Psychiatric disorders in children with autism spectrum disorders: Prevalence, comorbidity, and associated factors in a population-derived sample. *Journal of the American Academy of Child & Adolescent Psychiatry, 47*(8), 921–929.

Skuse, D. H., Mandy, W. P. L., & Scourfield, J. (2005). Measuring autistic traits: Heritability, reliability and validity of the Social and Communication Disorders Checklist. *British Journal of Psychiatry*, *187*(6), 568–572.

Sprong, M., Schothorst, P., Vos, E., Hox, J., & Van Engeland, H. (2007). Theory of mind in schizophrenia: Meta-analysis. *British Journal of Psychiatry*, *191*(1), 5–13.

State, M. W., & Levitt, P. (2011). The conundrums of understanding genetic risks for autism spectrum disorders. *Nature Neuroscience*, *14*, 1–8.

Stilp, R. L. H., Gernsbacher, M. A., Schweigert, E. K., Arneson, C. L., & Goldsmith, H. H. (2010). Genetic variance for autism screening items in an unselected sample of toddler-age twins. *Journal of the American Academy of Child & Adolescent Psychiatry*, *49*(3), 267–276.

Sullivan, P. F., Daly, M. J., & O'Donovan, M. (2012). Genetic architectures of psychiatric disorders: The emerging picture and its implications. *Nature Reviews Genetics*, *13*(8), 537–551.

Talkowski, M. E., Rosenfeld, J. A., Blumenthal, I., Pillalamarri, V., Chiang, C., Heilbut, A., . . . Lindgren, A. M. (2012). Sequencing chromosomal abnormalities reveals neurodevelopmental loci that confer risk across diagnostic boundaries. *Cell*, *149*, 1–13.

Taniai, H., Nishiyama, T., Miyachi, T., Imaeda, M., & Sumi, S. (2008). Genetic influences on the broad spectrum of autism: Study of proband-ascertained twins. *American Journal of Medical Genetics Part B: Neuropsychiatric Genetics*, *147*(6), 844–849.

Tropea, D., Giacometti, E., Wilson, N. R., Beard, C., McCurry, C., Fu, D. D., . . . Sur, M. (2009). Partial reversal of Rett syndrome-like symptoms in MeCP2 mutant mice. *Proceedings of the National Academy of Sciences, USA*, *106*(6), 2029–2034.

Verkerk, A. J., Pieretti, M., Sutcliffe, J. S., Fu, Y. H., Kuhl, D. P., Pizzuti, A., . . . Zhang, F. P. (1991). Identification of a gene (FMR-1) containing a CGG repeat coincident with a breakpoint cluster region exhibiting length variation in fragile X syndrome. *Cell*, *65*(5), 905.

Voineagu, I. (2012). Gene expression studies in autism: Moving from the genome to the transcriptome and beyond. *Neurobiology of Disease*, *45*(1), 69–75.

Wang, K., Zhang, H., Ma, D., Bucan, M., Glessner, J. T., Abrahams, B. S., . . . Sleiman, P. M. A. (2009). Common genetic variants on 5p14. 1 associate with autism spectrum disorders. *Nature*, *459*(7246), 528–533.

Weiss, L. A., Arking, D. E., Daly, M. J., & Chakravarti, A. (2009). A genome-wide linkage and association scan reveals novel loci for autism. *Nature*, *461*(7265), 802–808. doi: 10.1038/nature08490

Williams, N., Zaharieva, I., Martin, A., Langley, K., Mantripragada, K., Fossdal, R., . . . Thapar, A. (2010). Rare chromosomal deletions and duplications in attention-deficit hyperactivity disorder: A genome-wide analysis. *The Lancet*, *376*, 1401–1408. doi: 10.1016/s0140-6736(10)61109-9

Won, H., Lee, H. R., Gee, H. Y., Mah, W., Kim, J. I., Lee, J., . . . Cho, Y. S. (2012). Autistic-like social behaviour in Shank2-mutant mice improved by restoring NMDA receptor function. *Nature*, *486*(7402), 261–265.

Zoghbi, H. Y., & Bear, M. F. (2012). Synaptic dysfunction in neurodevelopmental disorders associated with autism and intellectual disabilities. *Cold Spring Harbor Perspectives in Biology*, *4*(3), 1–22.

CHAPTER 18

Environmental Factors in the Preconception and Prenatal Periods in Relation to Risk for ASD

KRISTEN LYALL, REBECCA J. SCHMIDT, AND IRVA HERTZ-PICCIOTTO

INTRODUCTION

As early as the 1970s, possibly the first environmental risk factor for autism was identified when congenital rubella, a viral infection, was noted to have a strong link to autistic behaviors. Over the next few decades, the importance of genetics was demonstrated through twin studies and recurrence rates in siblings of affected children, both suggesting high heritability. While the magnitude of the contribution from environment was originally thought to be low based on remarkably high monozygotic twin concordance in earlier small studies (Folstein & Rutter, 1977; Steffenburg et al., 1989), over time, as sample sizes grew, estimates of the contribution from environmental factors have increased. Most recently, in the largest twin study to date, Hallmayer and colleagues found that environment accounted for 55% of the variance in autism risk (Hallmayer et al., 2011).

Both genetic and environmental lines of research have led to recognition of the etiologic complexity of this disorder. Current thinking is that multiple causes are likely operating in any individual, and can include several or many genes and environmental factors. Moreover, the environmental exposures may operate at different stages in brain development, including formation and closure of the neural tube, cell differentiation and migration, formation of structures such as cortical mini-columns, synaptogenesis, and myelination. These processes are likely to be influenced through the interaction of environmental factors with genes. For example, at the molecular level, signaling pathways may involve epigenetics (chemical and physical alterations of DNA structure that do not affect the genetic code itself), leading to changes in gene expression; additionally, genes may alter the metabolism, receptors, and activity of xenobiotic chemicals, thereby altering the biochemistry and potentially inducing a pathophysiologic aberration of the central nervous system (CNS). Immune dysregulation, metabolism of xenobiotic chemicals to induce oxidative stress, and deficiencies in nutrients or essential fatty acids may also play a pathogenic role. Evidence that de novo (i.e., not inherited) changes to DNA, such as copy number variants (where segments of DNA are deleted, or duplicated, sometimes producing a large number of copies), are associated with autism risk suggests yet another pathway of environmentally initiated damage that can lead, at an early stage, to aberrant CNS development.

A growing number of environmental factors are being investigated in association with autism spectrum disorders (ASDs). Recent epidemiologic studies have addressed air pollution, chemicals used in housing materials and consumer goods, metals, and pesticides. However, the environment can be defined more broadly as all nongenetic factors, from viruses to medications, and from chemical and physical agents to social and cultural influences. Further, environmental factors affect pathophysiology by acting during key windows of developmental susceptibility. A transgenerational effect has also been hypothesized.

This chapter discusses modifiable environmental exposures that may alter risk for autism or severity of core symptoms, with a focus on exogenous agents that act during the preconception and prenatal periods. The rationale for highlighting modifiable factors is that human behaviors at the individual or the societal level could change the levels of exposure, and thereby potentially reduce the incidence of autism. Ultimately, the identification of such causes has as its ultimate goal the primary prevention of ASD. The emphasis on events and exposures prior to birth stems from evidence of strong risk factors during the prenatal period, from neuropathologic findings in the brains of persons with autism that suggest anatomical changes likely to originate during organogenesis and fetal CNS development, and from experimental models of features of autism. Exposures have been grouped as (1) environmental chemicals, (2) maternal lifestyle factors, and (3) medically related factors. A fourth category consists of factors that are unlikely to be causes per se, but may serve as proxies for causative agents.

Though findings from neuroanatomic, epidemiologic, and animal studies support prenatal origins of autism (Courchesne, Yeung-Courchesne, Press, Hesselink, & Jernigan, 1988; Herbert et al., 2005; Hultman, Sparen, & Cnattingius, 2002; H. J. Larsson et al., 2005; Rodier, Ingram, Tisdale, Nelson, & Romano, 1996; Shi, Fatemi, Sidwell, & Patterson, 2003), the timing implicated varies by mechanism or by risk factor (Figure 18.1). Thus, the critical period of increased susceptibility for ASD remains unclear and may extend from preconception through the first few years of life. Additional research on the effects of timing of these and other environmental exposures is needed.

A final cautionary note is that many factors discussed in this chapter share associations with other neurodevelopmental disorders, that is, they may not be specific to autism or ASD. In particular, obstetric complications, maternal nutrition, smoking and alcohol use, and certain environmental chemicals have been associated with a range of issues such as cognitive impairment or attention deficits. These factors may therefore activate pathways that can lead to a number of related outcomes, including autism.

Methodologic Considerations

The most reliable and, hence, the primary source of information regarding causes of autism is human studies. Evidence from experimental animals can suggest potential exposures of concern and can clarify mechanisms for neurodevelopmental toxicity, but problems in extrapolation across species dictate the central role of human epidemiology. This chapter begins with a brief discussion of key methodologic issues for the design and conduct

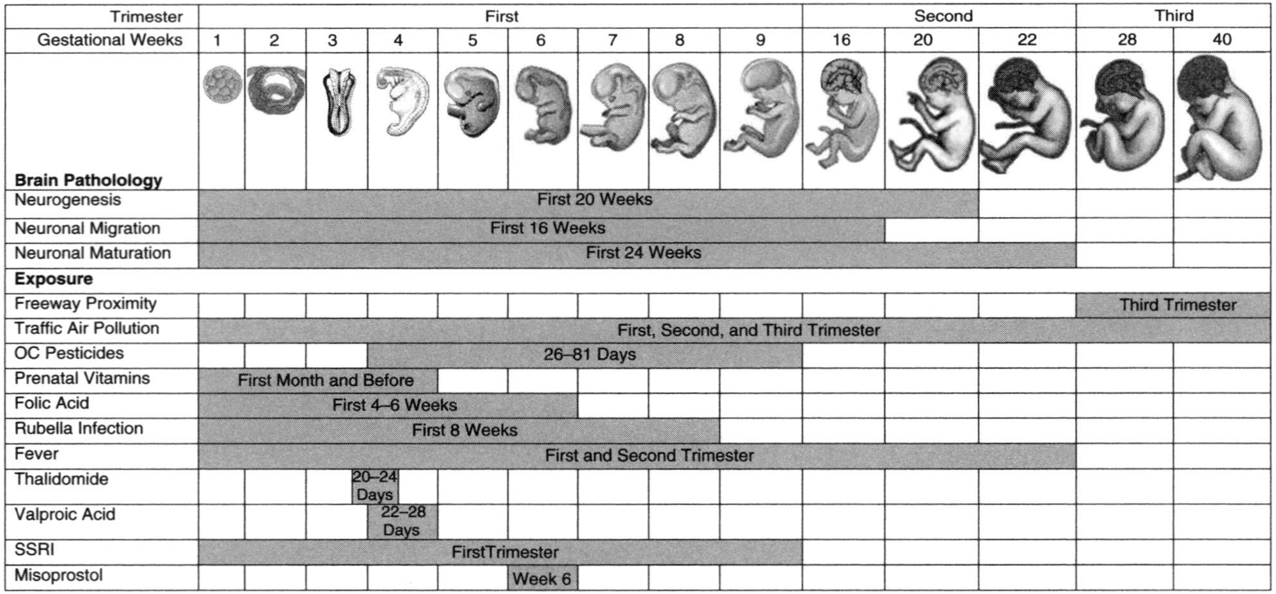

Figure 18.1 Critical periods of susceptibility indicated from studies of autism spectrum disorders.

Neuropathology (autopsy and imaging) studies of brains of individuals with autism spectrum disorders found evidence of dysregulated neurogenesis, neuronal migration, and neuronal maturation compared to brains of typically developed individuals, processes that generally occur in the first half of pregnancy. Evidence from epidemiological studies of environmental exposures that demonstrated an association with autism spectrum disorders and examined windows of higher risk within pregnancy have variable results, but tend to congregate in the first half of pregnancy. Days = Fetal days after conception. Figure adapted from those in *The Developing Human: Clinically Oriented Embryology*, 6th edition, by K. Moore and T. Persaud, 1998, Philadelphia, PA: W.B. Saunders. Adapted with permission.

of epidemiologic investigations on causes and contributing factors for autism. It then reviews the epidemiologic research on environmental contributions to autism, highlights strengths and weaknesses in this body of evidence, and suggests directions for further work that could markedly advance identification of modifiable risk factors.

Epidemiologic Design and Analysis for Studies of Autism Risk Factors

Conducting large-scale epidemiologic studies that are entirely free of bias is virtually impossible. Bias and imprecision can arise during all three phases of the design, data collection, and statistical analysis. While a randomized trial provides the strongest evidence of causation, for a great many environmental exposures, such trials would be unethical and may also be infeasible. In lieu of such human experiments, the next best evidence derives from observational studies on samples of individuals that are either (a) representative of the population at risk for developing a condition—cohort studies; or (b) selected to represent both the affected group and the population that gave rise to those affected—case-control studies. In the case-control design, exposure information is most often retrospectively obtained for the prediagnostic period. In contrast, the cohort approach begins by collecting information on individuals beginning before or during periods when the biologic changes that lead to the condition occur, and then determines who does and does not become a case. The case-control study provides a more economical design well suited for relatively rare outcomes or developmental conditions, and also permits investigation of multiple contributing factors. The cohort design can be far more expensive, as it requires a lengthy follow-up period and a large sample size for rare outcomes, since the vast majority of the individuals will not develop as cases. However, cohort studies have the advantage of eliminating inaccuracies and biases that are often introduced when exposure information is collected retrospectively. It is also possible to conduct retrospective cohort studies, and to improve the exposure assessment of case-control

studies by using preexisting databases (e.g., medical records) or archived environmental samples or specimens, when available, for documenting exposures of the past.

Until recently, many papers on environmental contributors to autism used an ecologic study design, which does not analyze data on individuals, but rather uses summary information for both exposures *and* outcomes. These summary data apply to large groups: for example, *average* emissions of a pollutant is used to predict *rates* of autism, using areas defined by political or administrative boundaries (e.g., counties or school districts). Such studies are considered the weakest design in terms of the potential for causal inference. Fortunately, cohort and case-control designs with individual-level data are becoming the norm.

Several methodological issues are of special concern for epidemiologic studies of autism. For valid inference in case-control studies, the choice of control group is paramount. In studying etiologic factors, the purpose of a control group is to provide the best estimate of the distribution of the exposures under study in the population from which the cases arose. Thus, defining that population is critical. An inappropriate control group can lead easily to invalid results when the likelihood or the level of the exposure of interest among participating controls differs from that in the population from which cases arose. For example, children with other developmental disorders may be an inappropriate comparison group for understanding the contribution of factors like air pollutants, nutrition, or maternal infections, as these factors may also increase risk of a broader class of delays. Likewise, use of sibling controls would tend to obscure the influence of maternal factors that would be correlated among pregnancies of the same woman, such as hypertension or body mass index. Friend controls would similarly be inappropriate when examining any exposure that is associated with, for instance, socioeconomic status or geography, since friendships tend to cluster by these factors (Wacholder, Silverman, McLaughlin, & Mandel, 1992). These examples illustrate how a skewed control group may yield an exposure distribution that does not represent the true referent population, thereby biasing toward the null any measure of association with autism.

Specific considerations during fieldwork include the need to (a) ensure that the team obtaining exposure data or conducting laboratory analyses of samples is unaware of the disease status of the participants (i.e., is blinded), and (b) take measures that minimize the influence on reporting that stems from an interviewer's or parents' knowledge of their child's diagnosis (or lack of diagnosis; often controls report less information or less accurate information). Notably, these biases can arise through omission and/or commission in data collection, but also in the analysis (e.g., when participants fail to report information and thereby are excluded due to missing data items). Explicit conceptual models can serve to guide analysis, and directed acyclic graphs have highlighted the underappreciated bias introduced by inappropriate adjustment for intermediate or marker variables (Hernán, Hernández-Diaz, Werler, & Mitchell, 2002). Analysis of mediating variables is widely used in the field of psychology (MacKinnon, Fairchild, & Fritz, 2007), though only under certain defined conditions will this strategy provide a valid measure of the direct association between the upstream exposure and the final outcome (MacKinnon et al., 2007; Petersen, Sinisi, & Van der Laan, 2006; Robins & Greenland, 1992; VanderWeele, 2009).

Paramount for robust study results is the degree to which investigators have adhered to sound epidemiologic principles, transcended mere significance testing, given proper relative weight to random versus systematic error and to different sources of systematic error (confounding, information, or measurement bias; nondifferential or differential participation or follow-up), and distinguished the small from large biases. Additional caution is required for generalizing results beyond the source population studied. In fact, understanding of the conditions that must be met to ensure generalizability is fundamental to interpreting virtually any study and its broad applicability. The preceding principles provide context and guidance for an evaluation of the scientific evidence on autism risks from environmental chemicals, maternal lifestyle, and medical factors.

ENVIRONMENTAL CHEMICALS

Background

Exposures to chemicals in air, food, water, and personal care or household products represent a potential hazard for the developing organism. This is in part because regulations for testing adverse health effects have been weak with regard to neurodevelopment. In the early 1960s, the finding that thalidomide caused phocomelia (absent or severely stunted limbs) in humans ignited concern over exposures with teratogenic potential (the ability to induce physical malformations during organogenesis). Yet, federal requirements that substances be tested for long-term behavioral aberrations or cognitive or functional deficits caused by prenatal exposures have been slow to evolve. Even decades after effects from low-level lead exposure on child brain development were demonstrated (Needleman & Leviton, 1979), lead-containing products, including ones specifically targeted for children like lunch boxes and Halloween costumes, still commonly enter the market (http://consumerist.com/2012/10/16/pirate-costumes-rendered-decidedly-more-scary-due-to-high-levels-of-lead/; http://www.komonews.com/news/10731686.html; Norman, Hertz-Picciotto, Salmen, & Ward, 1997). Other well-known neurodevelopmental toxins such as methylmercury and organophosphate pesticides have been recognized for their stronger impact on fetuses or young children as compared with adults (National Research Council, 2000; U.S. Environmental Protection Agency, 2002). Evidence also suggests deleterious neurobehavioral effects from polychlorinated biphenyls (Boucher, Muckle, & Bastien, 2009) and other endocrine-disrupting compounds (Weiss, 2011). Very few of the tens of thousands of compounds that are present in consumer products, general commerce, or industrial settings have been regulated at either the federal or U.S. state level, and states vary considerably in what and how they regulate environmental chemicals that are of concern for adverse effects on neurodevelopment (Zajac, Sprecher, Landrigan, & Trasande, 2009). In some cases, such as for mercury or organophosphates, regulations are designed to reduce rather than eliminate exposures. In others, persistence in the environment and long half-lives in the body have demonstrated that even decades after banning production, as in the case of polychlorinated biphenols (PCBs), human exposure has not been eliminated.

The list of suspect etiologic agents for autism begins with known neurotoxins and neurodevelopmental toxins, but also extends to a range of compounds that operate via mechanisms initiated outside the CNS, wherein other tissues interact with neurons: immune dysregulation, altered lipid metabolism, and mitochondrial dysfunction, among others. Finally, chemicals of concern are those having widespread contact with human populations. Not surprisingly, therefore, many of the factors discussed below are common in everyday environments, for example, at home, work, and places where people gather. When exposures are highly prevalent, even though their effects are modest on an individual basis, their public health impact can be great. A summary of environmental chemicals potentially associated with autism is provided in Table 18.1.

TABLE 18.1   Summary of Environmental Chemicals Potentially Associated With Autism

Environmental Factor	State of the Evidence	Reviews or Influential References
Air pollution	Associated with increased risk of autism in several studies. Exposure measures have included(a) modeled estimates by Census tract; (b) proximity of geocoded home address to freeway; (c) estimated levels of NO_2, $PM_{2.5}$, and PM_{10} at geocoded home address based on monitoring and land use regression. Results for specific air pollutants not entirely consistent.	Windham, Zhang, Gunier, and Croen, 2006; Kalkbrenner et al., 2010; Volk, Hertz-Picciotto, Delwiche, Lurmann, and McConnell, 2011; Volk, Lurmann, Penfold, Hertz-Picciotto, & McConnell, 2013; Becerra, Wilhelm, Olsen, Cockburn, and Ritz, 2013
Endocrine disruptors: polybrominated diphenyl ethers (PBDEs)	No human evidence on ASD risk. Evidence of epigenetic effect of BDE-47 in an MeCP2 mouse model (a Rett syndrome model). Thyroid hormones influenced by some BDEs; endocrine disruption is a hypothesized mechanism for ASD.	Woods et al., 2012; Zota et al., 2011
Endocrine disruptors: phthalates	One study showed association with vinyl flooring in the home, a major indoor contributor to phthalates. Another found higher measured urinary metabolites in ASD cases than in typical controls, but finding may not be relevant to etiology given the short half-life of phthalates.	M. Larsson, Weiss, Janson, Sundell, and Bornehag, 2009; Testa et al., 2012
Endocrine disruptors: PCBs	No studies have examined an association with ASD. Rodent studies show effects on social behaviors. Non-dioxin-like PCBs can influence neuronal dendritic development. Thyroid hormone homeostasis considered a strong candidate for mechanisms of neurodevelopmental toxicity.	Park et al., 2010; Forns et al., 2012; Wayman et al., 2012; Jolous-Jamshidi, Cromwell, McFarland, and Meserve, 2010
Pesticides: Organophosphates	Three studies provide evidence. Two cohort studies reported associations between prenatal exposure to organophosphates and symptoms of pervasive developmental disorder (PDD). One obtained direct measures of chlorpyrifos in plasma (cord or maternal); the other measured metabolites in urine. A case-control study linked proximity to agricultural applications of organophosphates with risk for autism.	Rauh et al., 2011; Eskenazi et al., 2007; E. M. Roberts et al., 2007
Pesticides: Other	A case-control study found diagnoses of ASD to be strongly associated with nearby applications of organochlorines during the first trimester; association also observed with applications of a pyrethroid, bifenthrin, which degrades slowly in the environment.	E. M. Roberts et al., 2007

Air Pollution and Proximity to Freeways

Reports on the relation between air pollution and risk of autism, using individual-level data, are now appearing regularly, and have incorporated a variety of methods for estimating exposure (Kalkbrenner et al., 2010; Palmer, Blanchard, & Wood, 2009; Volk, Hertz-Picciotto, Delwiche, Lurmann, & McConnell, 2011; Volk, Lurmann, Penfold, Hertz-Picciotto, & McConnell, 2013; Windham, Zhang, Gunier, Croen, & Grether, 2006). Windham and colleagues conducted the first analysis of air pollution that avoided an ecologic design, by using individual-level data on outcomes and confounders, though exposure was estimated at the group level. For 284 children with autism and 657 controls, exposure was estimated using U.S. EPA-derived census tract-based estimates of 19 hazardous air pollutants (HAPs) (Windham et al., 2006). In the adjusted analyses, an elevated risk for autism was found for those children whose residences were in census tracts falling in the top quartile of exposure to chlorinated solvents and heavy metals. Specific compounds significantly associated with autism were trichloroethylene and vinyl chloride, as well as cadmium, mercury, and nickel. Diesel particulate matter was also significantly associated with autism (odds ratio (OR) for top quartile = 1.44, 95% confidence interval (CI): 1.03–2.02). Exposures in this study were based on modeled estimates of HAPs in the census tract of the birth residence, derived for those locations 2 years after the birth; thus, it is unclear how adequately these models captured prenatal exposure.

Two recent studies have replicated several of the preceding findings. An analysis of 325 cases and 22,000 controls from the Nurses' Health Study II (which includes participants across the United States) also found significant associations for risk of maternally reported autism spectrum disorder with diesel, nickel, mercury, and cadmium (A. Roberts et al., 2013). This study thus replicated several of the key findings from Windham et al. (2006) but used U.S. Environmental Protection Agency modeled levels of HAPs for the year of birth rather than at age 2. The significant associations were primarily observed in boys. A study of North Carolina and West Virginia children also found significantly elevated risk of autism for a number of air pollutants, including diesel, mercury, nickel, styrene, and beryllium in unadjusted but not in adjusted analyses (Kalkbrenner et al., 2010). However, the range of concentrations for certain pollutants was small, the exposure assessment corresponded to the year of birth for only a fraction of the children, and no statistically significant associations were found when adjusting for demographic factors.

Two large and rigorous studies of air pollution have been published. One involved analyses of 304 autism cases and 259 controls from a large population-based case control study in California, the Childhood Autism Risks from Genetics and the Environment (CHARGE) study (Hertz-Picciotto et al., 2006), which used residential proximity to a major freeway during pregnancy as a surrogate for exposure. Exposure was assigned at the individual level by calculating the shortest distance to a freeway from the geocoded residence for each mother at time of delivery (Volk et al., 2011). Exposure groups were then defined as the closest 10%, the next 15%, and the next 25% of the distribution of distance from freeway, with the referent group being the remaining 50% (those nearly a mile away or farther). After adjustment for sociodemographic factors and maternal smoking, residence within 309 meters of a freeway at time of delivery (as compared with greater than 1,419 meters distance from a freeway) was linked with nearly a doubling in odds of having a child with autism (OR = 1.86, 95% CI: 1.04–3.45), while residence in third trimester for the same contrast in distance was associated with an OR = 2.22 (95% CI: 1.16–4.42). Intermediate distances were not associated with autism, nor was proximity to smaller roadways, which is consistent with the established high concentration of pollutants near major freeways and a decline in particulate matter to background levels beyond 300 meters from a major freeway. Further analyses utilizing estimates of traffic-related pollution using the CALINE4 line-source air-quality dispersion model, and regional air pollutant measures based on EPA's Air Quality System data, also demonstrated significant associations with autism from higher exposures to NO_2 and both fine and coarse particle concentrations in ambient air (Volk, Lurmann, Penfold, Hertz-Picciotto, & McConnell, 2013). The CHARGE study was the only air pollution analysis in which all diagnoses were confirmed using standardized instruments.

An exceptionally large study with careful exposure assessment utilized data for Los Angeles County, analyzing 7,603 cases that were linked to their birth records, and 10 controls per case matched on birth year and sex, and having a gestation at least as long as the case (Becerra, Wilhelm, Olsen, Cockburn, & Ritz, 2013). Residences at the time of delivery were geocoded and linked to air pollutant monitoring data on ozone, carbon dioxide, fine and coarse particulate matter, and several oxides of nitrogen; these data were supplemented with land-use regression for both nitrogen dioxide (NO_2) and nitric oxide. The authors showed small but significant associations with risk for autism for estimated ozone and NO_2 exposure during the entire pregnancy, in models adjusted for a range of sociodemographic confounders (education, maternal age, ethnicity, parity, birth year, child sex, etc.). Odds ratios increased when models with two pollutants were fit. The strongest associations were for those in the lowest educational stratum, who also were the most likely to have the higher levels of exposures.

Thus, as summarized in Table 18.1, a growing body of work suggests potential associations between air pollutants and autism risk, although residual confounding from sociodemographic or other factors cannot be excluded. Understanding the impact of specific chemicals will be difficult, because air pollution is a highly complex and variable mixture of particles of different sizes, metals, and volatile organic compounds, and, moreover, many of these constituents correlate with one another. Additionally, consideration should be given to possible confounding effects from noise pollution, which is often associated with high traffic density. While no studies have addressed associations with autism, noise pollution has been linked with disturbances of sleep and concentration, hypertension, and social behaviors, and in children, with impaired reading comprehension and loss of memory (Stansfeld & Matheson, 2003).

The associations seen between chemicals in air pollution and autism may be explained by a number of potential biological pathways, which may involve direct effects on CNS development, an immune-mediated pathway, or compromise in the normal protection of the brain during early development so as to allow other chemicals to access neural tissue. Studies have shown alterations in blood-brain barrier signaling through oxidative stress and inflammation in mice exposed to diesel particulates (Hartz, Bauer, Block, Hong, & Miller, 2008). Rats exposed prenatally to ozone, benzo[a]pyrene, and other HAPs have been found to have a range of neurological aberrations with relevance to autism, including alterations in neural circuitry, decreased neuronal plasticity, reduced glutamate receptor development, reduced expression of serotonin receptors, and behavioral deficits (Bouayed et al., 2009; Brown et al., 2007). These animal studies add biologic plausibility to the hypothesis of a causal relationship between high levels of air pollution exposure and increased autism risk.

Persistent Organic Pollutants

Since the 1960s, a number of organic compounds have been identified that are persistent (remaining intact for years), widely distributed throughout the environment (air, soil, bodies of water) by natural processes, and toxic to both wildlife and human health. These compounds, designated as POPs (persistent organic pollutants), became the target of efforts for elimination, restricted production, and overall reduction through an international organization originally convened in 2001, known as the Stockholm Convention. POPs include certain pesticides, industrial chemicals, and by-products of industrial processes. Some of the listed POPs have demonstrated adverse effects on neurodevelopment and therefore deserve consideration for possible contributions to increased risk of autism spectrum disorder. Although concern is high for POPs, not all compounds deleterious to neurodevelopment are persistent; short-lived compounds could also have detrimental effects.

Several POPs have been found to be endocrine-disrupting chemicals (EDCs). A mechanism by which EDCs may influence neurodevelopment is via disruption of thyroid hormones. Dioxins, PCBs (Goldey & Crofton, 1998), PBDEs (Ren & Guo, 2012), and two classes of nonpersistent EDCs—Bisphenol A (BPA; Chevrier et al., 2013) and phthalates (Meeker & Ferguson, 2011)—have all shown potential to disrupt thyroid function, in addition to other types of toxicity. The fetus depends on maternal thyroid hormones (T3 and T4) during the first part of pregnancy. Adequate levels are required for fetal neurodevelopment, including neuronal growth, cell migration and differentiation in the hippocampus, cerebral cortex, and cerebellum (Boas, Feldt-Rasmussen, & Main, 2012). In cell cultures from mouse cerebellum, changes in thyroid hormone levels affected dendritic development of Purkinje cells (Kimura-Kuroda, Nagata, & Kuroda, 2007), notable given that one of the most highly replicated findings in autism, from autopsy studies, is Purkinje cell loss (Amaral, Schumann, & Nordahl, 2008). The only data directly pertaining to autism found that *very* low levels of thyroid hormones at birth were associated with autism (Hoshiko, Grether, Windham, Smith, & Fessel, 2011). For the above reasons, EDC disruption of thyroid hormones during pregnancy has been hypothesized to be a potential pathway for autism etiology (Roman, 2007).

There are a number of other routes by which EDCs could affect neurodevelopment. They may alter molecular signaling, including calcium (Shafer, Meyer, & Crofton, 2005; Wong, Joy, Albertson, Schantz, & Pessah, 1997), or have direct effects on neural development or the placental or blood-brain barriers. Additionally, the strong male:female ratio in autism of over 4:1 could be a clue that effects of EDCs on steroid hormones or early sexual differentiation of the brain might play a role in autism etiology, as both testosterone and estradiol influence fetal brain development. Finally,

EDCs may interact in combination with genes to influence autism risk. Animal studies indicate that PBDE exposure disrupts levels of brain-derived neurotrophic factor (BDNF) (Viberg, Mundy, & Eriksson, 2008), and BDNF gene polymorphisms have been linked with autism. To date, very little research has addressed the influence of environment on epigenetics or on gene expression relevant to neurodevelopment. Similarly, there have been few assessments of interaction, that is, modification of environmental effects on neurodevelopment by genotype, one form of gene-by-environment interaction.

Thus, a wide array of mechanisms relevant to EDCs or other POPs have potential to alter brain development so as to increase risk for the set of behaviors that define autism spectrum disorder. Very few studies, however, have been conducted to examine EDC or POP associations with autism risk.

Polybrominated Diphenyl Ethers (PBDEs)

PBDEs are a class of POPs that have been added as flame retardants to polyurethane foam used in furniture, textiles, and children's clothing (penta-BDEs), as well as plastic casings of electronic products such as TVs, printers, and computers (octa- and deca-BDEs). While penta- and octa- forms of PBDEs are no longer produced in the United States, deca- formulations continue to be manufactured. Beginning in the 1990s, concentrations in environmental samples and human tissues were observed to rise dramatically. This increase, similar to many other POPs, is due to bioaccumulation through the food chain. Levels of PBDEs in the U.S. population are much higher than in Europe, and the highest levels of PBDEs are consistently found in the youngest individuals (Rose et al., 2010). In addition, PBDEs easily cross the placenta (Frederiksen, Vorkamp, Mathiesen, Mose, & Knudsen, 2010). In rodent studies, PBDEs have been shown to produce hyperactivity and altered motor behavior and development (Gee & Moser, 2008; Suvorov et al., 2009).

The only epidemiologic study that examined PBDEs in relation to autism did not address maternal exposures. Plasma concentrations from samples collected in children aged 2–5, after their diagnoses, did not differ between cases and controls, in this pilot sample (Hertz-Picciotto et al., 2011). That diet noticeably influences PBDE levels (Rose et al., 2010), and that children's food consumption changes markedly between birth and age 2–5, together suggest that despite somewhat long half-lives of some PBDE congeners, measurements relevant to etiology need to be taken during pregnancy or at early postnatal time points. In investigations of other neurodevelopmental outcomes, one cohort study showed higher cord blood concentrations of PBDEs were associated with lower scores on mental and psychomotor development tests (including the Bayley Mental Development Index and the Wechsler IQ test) at 12–48 and 72 months of age (Herbstman et al., 2010), while another study related maternal blood serum PBDEs to decreased fine motor skills and increased attention problems at school age (Roze et al., 2009). Investigation of PBDEs during critical time periods of fetal and infant development and subsequent risk of ASD is warranted.

An epigenetic mechanism involving PBDEs, and of potential relevance to autism, was explored in a MeCP2 mouse model. MECP2 is the gene involved in Rett syndrome, a pervasive neurodevelopmental disorder characterized by severe cognitive and motor impairment, as well as behavioral similarities to ASD. The methyl-CpG binding protein 2 (MeCP2) gene codes for methyl-CpG binding protein 2, which acts epigenetically to bind methyl groups and is critical for nerve development; mutations in the gene for MeCP2 are responsible for Rett syndrome. In this MeCP2 mouse model, perinatal treatment with one of the most abundant PBDEs, BDE-47, resulted in hypomethylation of adult brain DNA, with accompanying reduced sociability that was independent of genotype (Woods et al., 2012). This demonstration of perinatal PBDE effects on social behaviors in genetically predisposed mice suggests potential relevance to ASD in humans carrying certain genetic susceptibilities.

Nonpersistent Organic Pollutants

Several nonpersistent organic pollutants have been found to disrupt production of endocrine hormones. BPA is a plasticizer found in plastic drink containers, the lining of food cans and plastic food wrappings, dental appliances and resins, and baby bottles, among other products. BPA has estrogenic properties and has been linked to obesity (Trasande, Attina, & Blustein, 2012), diabetes (Silver, O'Neill, Sowers, & Park, 2011), and coronary heart disease and elevated liver enzymes (Melzer, Rice, Lewis, Henley, & Galloway, 2010), but this work has been cross-sectional. In a prospective study, maternal BPA metabolites measured from urine samples collected before 16 weeks gestation were associated with an increase in externalizing problem behaviors (Braun et al., 2009).

Another class of chemicals, phthalates, has also been shown to be endocrine disrupting. Phthalates are used in cosmetics, lotions, and fragrances, have antiandrogenic properties (Sharpe, 2008), and their urinary metabolites correlate with body size in a cross-sectional study of adults (Hatch, Nelson, Stahlhut, & Webster, 2010). In children, prospective research has shown associations of some of the metabolites with body size (Teitelbaum et al., 2012), conduct disorder or attention problems (Engel et al., 2010), and social deficits (Miodovnik et al., 2011). With regard to autism risk, a recent Swedish study investigating indoor environmental factors found an unexpected doubling of risk for autism in children whose homes had vinyl (PVC) flooring in the child and parent bedrooms (M. Larsson, Weiss, Janson, Sundell, & Bornehag, 2009); PVC flooring is a significant source of airborne phthalates. Replication and continued investigation of these short-lived endocrine-disrupting chemicals in association with neurodevelopment and autism in particular is needed.

Pesticides

Pesticides are typically designed to damage the nervous systems of the targeted species, and often act on neurotransmission. Further, several pesticides have been classified as POPs (http://chm.pops.int/Convention/ThePOPs/tabid/673/Default.aspx) and/or have endocrine disrupting properties (Korrick & Sagiv, 2008), suggesting similar mechanisms to those discussed previously. In the 1950s, organochlorine pesticides (DDT, heptachlor) were widely used in major efforts aimed at the eradication of malaria through mosquito control. Establishment of persistence of these compounds and adverse effects on wildlife led to development of less persistent compounds, such as the organophosphates. Nevertheless, some organochlorines continue to be used, and one of the first reports on pesticides and autism, a case-control study, found a strong association with residential proximity to agricultural applications of endosulfan and dicofol during the first trimester (Roberts et al., 2007). No other epidemiologic evidence on organochlorines and autism has emerged, though it does not appear that further studies have been conducted.

Other classes of pesticides have been investigated further, including organophosphates. They have been widely used in both agricultural and residential applications, with production of residential products banned by the U.S. EPA in 2001. In a cohort study that began during pregnancy and was conducted in a farm worker community, poorer scores on a subscale of the Child Behavior Checklist measuring symptoms for PDD were associated with urinary levels of organophosphate pesticide metabolites during pregnancy (Eskenazi et al., 2007). In a cohort from New York City, higher umbilical cord blood plasma concentrations of chlorpyrifos, one of the most commonly used organophosphates, were also associated with PDD symptoms in early childhood (Rauh et al., 2006). Organophosphates were also related, in other epidemiologic investigations, to deficits in motor coordination, visuospatial performance, and memory (Harari et al., 2010), and decrements in cognitive development, particularly perceptual reasoning (Engel et al., 2011), with evidence that a gene involved in metabolizing these chemicals, paraoxonase 1 (PON1), may be a susceptibility factor.

Organophosphates continue to be used in commercial applications, while in the household product market, pyrethroid pesticides have become increasingly common (Williams, Helmer, Duncan, Peat, & Mellis, 2008). As of 2009, over 3,500 registered products contained synthetic pyrethroids or their naturally derived counterparts, pyrethrins (U.S. Environmental Protection Agency, 2010). Despite relatively short half-lives in humans, pyrethroid metabolites have been found in over 70% of adults in the United States (Barr et al., 2010), likely due to their common usage and ubiquitous presence in household products. Other pesticides of concern include imidacloprid and fipronil, both used in insecticide gels, flea sprays, and other products to eliminate pests.

Depending on the type of compound, pesticides could influence neurodevelopment through a variety of mechanisms, recently reviewed by Shelton and colleagues (Shelton, Hertz-Picciotto, & Pessah, 2012). These include interference with establishment of serotonergic systems; changes in activity of monoamine oxidase or acetylcholinesterase, or altered gamma-aminobutyric acid (GABA) function potentially leading to dysregulation of neural stem cell proliferation, differentiation, and migration; reduced expression of GABA receptors; mitochondrial dysfunction, endocrine disruption (Roman, 2007), immune dysregulation, and altered lipid metabolism; and, like PBDEs, pesticides have also been associated with calcium signaling (Lawrence & Casida, 1983; Malaviya, Husain, & Seth, 1993).

MATERNAL LIFESTYLE FACTORS

Interpregnancy Interval

Short interpregnancy intervals have been associated with schizophrenia, congenital anomalies, preterm birth, and low birth weight (Shachar & Lyell, 2012), and two recent investigations found that short interpregnancy interval (defined as the time between consecutive birth dates minus the gestational age of the later born sibling) is also associated with increased risk for ASD (Cheslack-Postava, Liu,

& Bearman, 2011; Dodds et al., 2011). A linked database cohort study of 129,733 children (924 children with autism diagnosis) born between 1990 and 2002 in Nova Scotia, by Dodds et al. (2011) demonstrated increased risk for autism in children whose mothers became pregnant earlier than 18 months after their previous delivery. These results persisted after adjustment for other associated maternal and infant risk factors.

Similar findings were found in a study of 662,730 pairs of first and second born single-ton siblings identified from all California births 1992 to 2002 (Cheslack-Postava et al., 2011). Autism diagnoses among the second-born children were obtained from the California Department of Developmental Services system. As interpregnancy interval increased, autism diagnoses decreased in a dose-response manner, with odds ratios (95% confidence intervals) for <12, 12 to 23, and 24 to 35 months, as compared with 36 months or greater, of 3.39 (3.00–3.82), 1.86 (1.65–2.10), and 1.26 (1.10–1.45), respectively. Sociodemographic characteristics were adjusted for, and further adjustment for mediators such as preterm birth and low birth weight did not change the results.

These associations have been attributed to depletion of maternal nutrient reserves after the preceding birth. Essential nutrients are preferentially distributed to the developing fetus, resulting in depleted stores of the mother, a state that remains for some time after delivery. Folate has been a nutrient of primary interest (Smits & Essed, 2001; van Eijsden, Smits, van der Wal, & Bonsel, 2008) because folate levels decrease during unsupplemented pregnancies (Milman, Byg, Hvas, Bergholt, & Eriksen, 2006) and remain low for at least 12 months postpartum (O'Rourke, Redlinger, & Waller, 2000). Depletion of other nutrients, including iron or polyunsaturated fatty acids, or factors unrelated to nutrition, like family planning or other lifestyle factors, could also play a role in the association with short interpregnancy intervals.

Maternal Nutrition

Though maternal nutrition is known to be essential to fetal brain development, relatively little research has directly explored maternal dietary factors in association with risk of ASD in the offspring. Nutrient and mineral deficiencies during early development can result in adverse structural, cognitive, and neurobehavioral outcomes. Pregnant women are particularly vulnerable to nutritional deficiencies because of the increased metabolic demands imposed by pregnancy that affect a growing placenta, fetus, and maternal tissues (Institute of Medicine, 1990; Picciano, 2003).

Folate and Other B Vitamins

Folate, an essential B vitamin, is the focus of much of the literature on nutrition and neurodevelopment, given the protective effect of folic acid (synthetic folate) near the time of conception on the neural tube as it transforms into the brain and spinal cord. Folic acid supplements taken before or during the first trimester have been established to protect against the occurrence of neural tube defects, with estimates of reductions of 50–70% (Czeizel, 2000; MRC Vitamin Study Research Group, 1991). Perhaps less well known are the associations with fewer behavioral problems in children at 18 months of age (Roza et al., 2010); improved scores on measures of verbal skills, verbal-executive function, social competence, and attention at 4 years (Julvez et al., 2009); and lower scores for childhood hyperactivity and peer problems at 8 years (Schlotz et al., 2010). Though maternal folate levels have yet to be assessed in relation to risk for autism in the child, recent work suggests a potential protective effect of folic acid–containing supplements, especially in combination with gene polymorphisms leading to inefficient folate metabolism. In an investigation of a large population-based case-control study, Schmidt and colleagues (Schmidt et al., 2011) reported significantly reduced risk for autism (OR = 0.62, 95% CI: 0.42–0.93) and ASD (OR = 0.59, 95% CI: 0.41–0.84) in children whose mothers reported taking prenatal vitamins supplements, after adjustment for maternal education and the child's birth year. The study also described significant gene-environment interactions, with risk for autism in children whose mothers did not take prenatal vitamins periconceptionally being particularly elevated, if they or their mothers also carried gene variants leading to less efficient folate- and B vitamin–dependent one-carbon metabolism.

Extending these results, Schmidt and colleagues (Schmidt et al., 2012) quantified total folic acid from reported intake of prenatal vitamins, multivitamins, folic acid–specific vitamins, other supplements, and breakfast cereals. Mean total folic acid intake in the first month of pregnancy was significantly greater for mothers of typically developing children ($n = 278$) than for mothers of children who later developed ASD ($n = 429$), and the associated risk of having delivered children diagnosed with ASD decreased as mean daily folic acid intake increased ($P_{trend} = 0.001$). However, reported intake of 600 mcg or more folic acid (the recommended daily intake for pregnant women in the United States) was only protective when either the mother or the child carried a common variant in the methylenetetrahydrofolate reductase gene, MTHFR 677 C > T, that leads to less efficient folate metabolism.

Recently, the finding of lower risk for autistic disorder associated with periconceptional folic acid supplements (typically containing 400 mcg) was replicated in a Norwegian cohort study (Suren et al., 2013). Self-reported maternal folic acid supplement intake for the period 6 weeks before and after the estimated date of conception was examined for 85,176 children, of which 270 were diagnosed with ASD (114 were diagnosed with autistic disorder). The effect size, with nearly a 40% reduction in risk for autistic disorder, was similar to that observed in the study by Schmidt and colleagues (Schmidt et al., 2012). These studies are among the first to suggest that modifiable factors could reduce risk of autism.

The period near conception that was associated with the greatest protective effect of folic acid–containing supplements on autism risk correlates with the critical period when maternal folic acid supplements are protective against the other adverse neurodevelopmental outcomes described earlier, suggesting possible common mechanisms (Julvez et al., 2009; MRC Vitamin Study Research Group, 1991; Roza et al., 2010; Schlotz et al.,

2010). One such mechanism could involve methylation (the addition of a one-carbon group) of proteins, neurotransmitters, and DNA, which then influences their expression or activity. Folate and other B-complex vitamins (betaine, choline, vitamins B6 and B12, and methionine) provide a major source of these methyl groups. Around implantation, mammalian embryos undergo extensive DNA demethylation, or the removal of these one-carbon groups, followed by reestablishment of methylation patterns (Reik & Walter, 2001). Although the exact purpose of these stages is unclear, methylation capacity in children with autism and in their mothers was found to be impaired in comparison with typically developing children and their mothers (James et al., 2010). Methylation is one of several types of changes in the genome that do not affect the underlying DNA code; such alterations collectively are called epigenetic effects. Other evidence also supports a role for epigenetics in autism etiology, probably through changes in gene expression (Schanen, 2006). Maternal periconceptional folic acid supplementation increases methylation in specific gene regions of the child (Steegers-Theunissen et al., 2009), which alters regulation of expression of those genes. Though not shown directly, these types of epigenetic changes could result in differential neurodevelopmental paths.

Maternal Fatty Acid Intake

Omega-3 fatty acids are known to be central in brain development, and the developing fetus requires maternal stores of these fats. Maternal fatty acids may also be relevant to autism, though findings are preliminary. Only one study to date has examined maternal fat and fatty acid intake during pregnancy in association with autism (Lyall, Munger, O'Reilly, Santangelo, & Ascherio, 2013). Lyall and colleagues used prospectively collected dietary data from validated food frequency questionnaires in a subgroup of the large, ongoing Nurses' Health Study II cohort. The authors found that mothers with higher intake of polyunsaturated fatty acids (PUFA) before and during pregnancy had reduced risk of having a child with ASD relative to mothers with the lowest PUFA intake.

In addition, mothers with extremely low intake of omega-3 fatty acids (the lowest 5% of the distribution of intake) had increased risk of having a child with ASD relative to mothers in the middle 90% of the distribution.

Maternal fish intake may also be relevant to neurodevelopment and autism, both as a source of fatty acids (which may confer protective effects) and as a potential source of mercury (which is deleterious to fetal brain development). As reviewed by Oken and Bellinger (Oken & Bellinger, 2008), the majority of studies examining maternal fish intake and child neurodevelopmental outcomes have suggested higher maternal fish intake is associated with higher child development scores, though type of fish and mercury levels need to be taken into account. The only study to date to have examined maternal fish intake in association with autism specifically did not find any relationship (Lyall, Munger, et al., 2013). However, variation in fish intake was limited in this study, and the number of women with reported fish intake during pregnancy was small. More work is needed in this area to determine the potential contributions of fatty acids to autism risk, taking account mercury, when fish is the major source.

Maternal Vitamin D

Low maternal vitamin D levels have also been hypothesized as a risk factor for developmental disorders and ASD specifically (Grant & Soles, 2009). The circumstantial evidence for this hypothesis includes increased rates of autism among children of dark-skinned immigrant mothers who moved to high latitudes (Dealberto, 2011) and reports on seasonality of birth or conception. Fernell and colleagues (Fernell et al., 2010) compared serum 25-hydroxyvitamin D, measured in the spring and autumn, amongst four groups of mothers in Sweden ($n = 12$ to 17 in each group): (1) mothers of Somali origin with at least one child with autism, (2) mothers of Somali origin without a child with autism, (3) mothers of Swedish origin with at least one child with autism, and (4) mothers of Swedish origin without a child with autism. Both groups of mothers of Somali origin had lower serum 25-hydroxyvitamin D levels than both groups of mothers of Swedish origin. However, no significant differences in serum 25-hydroxyvitamin D were found comparing mothers of children with autism to mothers of children without autism among either the Somalis or Swedes. The study was limited by small sample size and the timing of vitamin D measurements which was not during gestation.

More recently, Whitehouse and colleagues conducted the first study examining associations between maternal 25-hydroxyvitamin D concentrations measured in serum collected at the 18th week of pregnancy and the child's Autism-Spectrum Quotient (AQ) scores in early adulthood for 406 offspring from the Raine Study in Perth, Australia (Whitehouse et al., 2012). They did not find associations with total AQ scores, or four of the five AQ subscales (social skills, communication, attention to detail, and imagination), but they did find evidence for poorer attention switching (the fifth subscale) in children whose mothers were in the lowest tertile of 25-hydroxyvitamin D. Only three children were clinically diagnosed with ASD, and their mother's vitamin D concentrations were not low (above the mean for the overall cohort).

Nevertheless, there is ample biological plausibility for a relationship between autism risk and maternal vitamin D, given the role of vitamin D in neuronal differentiation, the metabolism of neurotrophic factors and neurotoxins, protection from brain inflammation, endocrine functions, and fetal brain growth. The importance of vitamin D during neurodevelopment has been demonstrated in animal studies, with rats born to vitamin D–deficient dams having profound alterations in the brain at birth (Eyles, Brown, Mackay-Sim, McGrath, & Feron, 2003). Maternal vitamin D insufficiency has also been linked with impaired language development of the child at ages 5 and 10 years (Whitehouse et al., 2012). Because no study to date has directly examined the relationship between maternal or gestational vitamin D and ASD diagnosis, further research is needed to understand the relevance of vitamin D to autism etiology.

Alcohol

Maternal alcohol consumption is well known to be deleterious to fetal development. ASD has been reported in association with prenatal alcohol exposure and fetal alcohol syndrome (Aronson, Hagberg, & Gillberg, 1997; Harris, MacKay, & Osborn, 1995; Landgren, Svensson, Stromland, & Andersson Gronlund, 2010; Nanson, 1992), but the quality of the reports precludes any inferences (case reports; uncontrolled confounding from living in orphanages in Eastern Europe or foster homes). Surprisingly, few rigorous studies have been conducted on relationships between maternal alcohol use or alcoholism and autism risk. Published results for maternal alcoholism and autism have been conflicting (Bolton, Pickles, Murphy, & Rutter, 1998; Daniels et al., 2008; DeLong & Dwyer, 1988; Lobascher, Kingerlee, & Gubbay, 1970; Miles, Takahashi, Haber, & Hadden, 2003; Piven et al., 1991), including a pedigree analysis of families having a child with autism suggested an association between reported alcoholism of females among first and second degree relatives (Miles et al., 2003), and a nested case-control study in Sweden that found no association between autism and alcohol and drug addiction/abuse (Daniels et al., 2008).

Turning from alcoholism to the topic of alcohol consumption, Eliasen and colleagues conducted the largest study of prenatal alcohol exposure and the risk of ASD using a population-based prospective design with 80,552 children and their mothers (Eliasen et al., 2010). Alcohol consumption was obtained by self-report during pregnancy for participants enrolled in the Danish National Birth Cohort study from 1996 to 2002. Four hundred and one children from the Danish Central Psychiatry Register had an ASD diagnosis, including 157 with infantile autism. No association was found between either ASD or infantile autism and average alcohol consumption, and no trend was observed with increasing number of drinks (0, 0.5–1.5, 2–3.5, or 4+ per week) or binge episodes (5 or more drinks on one occasion) during pregnancy. A likely spurious association between a single binge

episode and lower ASD risk was found. However, the participation rate in the study (~30%) was low, potentially resulting in selection bias, which may have influenced the lack of association with heavy alcohol drinking. Reporting bias could have also occurred despite the prospective data collection if reporting inaccuracies of either alcohol consumption (underreporting) or of timing of the last menstrual period were associated with underlying risk factors/confounders. Because of its prospective design and large size (and the serious deficiencies in other studies), the suggestion of no increased ASD risk from light to moderate maternal alcohol use from this study is the best evidence to date on maternal alcohol intake and ASD. However, obtaining accurate information on alcohol consumption is challenging in any epidemiologic study. Given that high prenatal alcohol exposure impairs neurodevelopment in humans (Eliasen et al., 2010; Jacobson & Jacobson, 2002) and in animal studies produces social avoidance (Middleton, Varlinskaya, & Mooney, 2012) and structural brain anomalies congruent with those observed in children with ASD (Casanova, 2007), further research on the impact of high maternal alcohol exposure on ASD is warranted.

Cigarette Smoking

Several longitudinal studies have linked maternal cigarette smoking and risk for psychiatric sequelae and behavioral disorders, including social problems in the child (Button, Maughan, & McGuffin, 2007). A number of studies have assessed maternal smoking in association with autism, each with limitations. Several investigations lacked adjustment for socioeconomic factors that are probable confounders given associations of high socioeconomic status (SES) with both ASD diagnosis (Thomas et al., 2011) and lower prevalence of smoking during pregnancy (Kalkbrenner et al., 2012). Thus, the inconsistency of findings from these studies is difficult to interpret: an inverse association in two studies; a null association in one (Larsson et al., 2005); and positive associations with maternal smoking in three studies (Hultman et al., 2002;

Hvidtjørn et al., 2011; Williams, Oliver, Allard, & Sears, 2003) and with second-hand smoke in another (Zhang et al., 2010).

Of the studies that *did* adjust for socioeconomic factors, two found evidence for a positive association with maternal smoking. In the first, a small population-based prospective study of 84 adolescents at 14 years (Indredavik, Brubakk, Romundstad, & Vik, 2007), maternally reported smoking during pregnancy was strongly associated with social problems as measured by the Autism Spectrum Screening Questionnaire (ASSQ; Ehlers, Gillberg, & Wing, 1999). The second, a Danish study of indoor environmental contributions including 72 children with ASD among 4,779 children aged 6–8 years, found a significant association between maternal smoking and parentally reported ASD (M. Larsson et al., 2009).

The remaining studies that adjusted for socioeconomic factors produced null findings regarding an association of maternal cigarette smoking and risk for ASD. Two of these studies (Burstyn, Sithole, & Zwaigenbaum, 2010; Maimburg & Vaeth, 2006) adjusted for potentially mediating variables (i.e., birth weight and other effects of the exposure), calling to question the validity of the adjusted estimates. However, a third study (Lee et al., 2012) did not share this problem; these authors appropriately controlled for sociodemographic characteristics (parental education, income, and occupation) and not for potential intermediates in a register-based Swedish study that used a nested design of 3,958 ASD cases and 38,983 controls. In their fully adjusted analyses, no association was observed between maternal smoking during pregnancy and ASD, although a significant association and a dose-response trend was found in unadjusted analyses and after adjustment for a smaller set of covariates (parental age and parity), underscoring the importance of adjusting for SES. Other strengths were a multisource case ascertainment system likely to capture most cases, and prospective reporting of smoking that would not be subject to recall bias.

Kalkbrenner and colleagues (Kalkbrenner et al., 2012) provided additional evidence for no association between maternal smoking and ASD after adjustment for SES and other confounders, but (appropriately) not for mediating variables. Information on maternal smoking and other factors was obtained from the birth certificates of 633,989 children in 11 U.S. states who were in four waves of the U.S. Centers for Disease Control and Prevention's Autism and Developmental Disabilities Monitoring (ADDM) network, including 3,315 children with ASD. They found a slightly increased risk between maternal smoking and ASD not otherwise specified (likely higher functioning autism), but no association with classically defined autism. Strengths of this study include its large sample size, population-based design with standardized identification of ASD cases, and inclusion of sensitivity analyses to assess outcome misclassification. Nevertheless, lack of validity of birth certificate data on smoking is well documented and varies considerably by education level (Land et al., 2012).

Mechanisms by which maternal smoking might alter risk for ASD and other neurobehavioral outcomes include reduced blood flow to the brain due to placental insufficiency and oxygen deprivation (Albuquerque, Smith, Johnson, Chao, & Harding, 2004), alteration of gene expression in the fetal brain (Luck, Nau, Hansen, & Steldinger, 1985), and alteration of nicotinic receptors that develop in the first trimester of pregnancy (Williams et al., 1998) and influence brain development. Prenatal nicotine exposure has been shown to lead to changes in neurotransmitter activity and turnover that can persist into adulthood (Muneoka et al., 2001; Roy & Sabherwal, 1998). An interaction between maternal smoking and both catechol O-methyltransferase and serotonin transporter genes in relation to ASD symptoms of children with attention-deficit/hyperactivity disorder (ADHD) may support an effect of maternal smoking on neurotransmitters (Nijmeijer et al., 2010). In addition, in some mothers, prenatal smoking may be an indicator of underlying psychological problems that themselves could influence risk in the offspring (Fergusson, Woodward, & Horwood, 1998).

Despite past conflicting results for an association between maternal smoking and autism, the best evidence thus far does not support maternal cigarette smoking as a strong risk factor for ASD. However, biologic plausibility for an effect of nicotine on the developing fetal brain, limitations in even the methodologically stronger studies particularly with regard to exposure assessment, and some evidence for a harmful effect in smaller well-conducted investigations indicate that it is premature to draw conclusions from the extant research regarding cigarette smoking during gestation and risk for autism. Also, because smoking has shown a propensity for gene by environment interaction effects (Honein, Paulozzi, & Moore, 2000; van Rooij et al., 2001), investigation of maternal smoking in combination with genetic susceptibility, and potential epigenetic effects of components in cigarette smoke, may be a fruitful avenue for research. Smoking and other maternal lifestyle factors are summarized in Table 18.2.

MEDICALLY RELATED FACTORS

Pregnancy Complications and Obstetric Factors

Obstetric Suboptimality

Obstetric suboptimality is a general term used to define a range of obstetric and pregnancy complications occurring during the pre- and perinatal periods. Many studies used summary scales/scores such as the Gillberg Optimality Scale (Gillberg & Gillberg, 1983), which sums a range of complications in a single score. Factors commonly included in these scores are pregnancy complications such as hypertension and gestational diabetes, advanced maternal age, prior stillbirths and miscarriages, Cesarean delivery, twin/multiple birth, child low APGAR scores, premature birth, and others. Overall, the literature suggests an association between the general class of obstetric complications and autism, as well as other neurodevelopmental disorders, and greater risk with increasing number

TABLE 18.2   Summary of Maternal Lifestyle Factors Associated With Autism

Environmental Factor	State of Evidence	Reviews and Influential References
Interpregnancy interval	Shorter intervals associated with autism in two studies. One was very large and showed a dose-response relationship. Association could be a result of maternal nutrient depletion.	Cheslak-Postava, Liu, and Bearman, 2011; Dodds et al., 2011
Maternal prenatal vitamin use	Associated with decreased risk for ASD if taken before or near conception in one large case-control study, especially in combination with certain one-carbon metabolism genotypes.	Schmidt et al., 2011
Maternal folic acid	Higher folic acid intake in first month of pregnancy associated with reduced risk for ASD in one large case-control study, especially if mother or child has methylenetetrahydrofolate reductase T-allele. Folic acid supplements taken 6 weeks before and after conception associated with decreased risk for autism in a large cohort study.	Schmidt et al., 2012; Surén et al., 2013
Maternal fat intake	One preliminary study reported decreased risk with increased maternal polyunsaturated fat intake, in particular omega-6 fatty acids. Very low omega-3 intake was associated with increased risk.	Lyall, Munger, O'Reilly, Santangelo, and Ascherio, 2013
Maternal vitamin D	Maternal serum levels (18 weeks gestation) were not associated with offspring autism phenotypes in a general population study; a weak association was found with the attention switching subscale.	Whitehouse et al., 2012
Maternal alcohol consumption	No increased risk from light to moderate maternal alcohol consumption; subject to potential inaccuracies of self-reported use.	Eliasen et al., 2010
Maternal smoking	Evidence is inconsistent, though a number of studies do not support maternal cigarette smoking as a strong risk factor for ASD. Further studies investigating high-functioning ASD and potential gene x environment interactions, and utilizing objective markers of cigarette smoking are needed to rule out an effect.	Burstyn, Sithole, and Zwaigenbaum, 2010; Kalkbrenner et al., 2012; Lee et al., 2012

of complications (Gardener, Spiegelman, & Buka, 2009; Lyall, Pauls, Spiegelman, Ascherio, & Santangelo, 2012). For instance, in the Nurses' Health Study II cohort, women with pregnancy complications (defined as preeclampsia, pregnancy-induced hypertension, or gestational diabetes) had 1.49 times the odds of having a child with ASD relative to those with no such complications. When examining obstetric scores, women with four or more of a broader class of obstetric complications had 2.76 times the odds of having a child with ASD relative to those without suboptimality factors (95% CI: 2.04, 3.74) (Lyall et al., 2012). Other studies utilizing suboptimality scores observed similar patterns (Gillberg & Gillberg, 1983; Juul-Dam, Townsend, & Courchesne, 2001; Steffenburg et al., 1989), or noted a clustering of multiple complications in mothers of children with ASD (Brimacombe, Ming, & Lamendola, 2007).

Although a few studies have not seen increased risk of ASD with higher suboptimality scores (Burd, Severud, Kerbeshian, & Klug, 1999), or have suggested that the association between obstetric complications and autism no longer persists after accounting for factors like birth order, parity, and maternal age (Lord, Mulloy, Wendelboe, & Schopler, 1991; Piven et al., 1993), these investigations were limited by small sample sizes, resulting in low power. Many other studies have taken the approach of assessing pre- and perinatal variables individually, rather than creating a summary score, and shown specific factors that are included in suboptimality scores to have significant associations with ASD (Glasson et al., 2004; Hultman et al., 2002; Larsson et al., 2005; Maimburg & Vaeth, 2006). On the whole, however, findings for specific individual complications, discussed in this section, have been less consistent than for results for the overall class of complications.

Multiple Births

Multiple gestation, including twin and higher order births, has been linked to higher risk for autism in a number of reports. In a meta-analysis of peri- and neonatal factors, inconsistencies were noted in the findings from 10 studies identified that

examined twin/multiple births in association with autism (Gardener, Spiegelman, & Buka, 2011). Specifically, five reports (all finding no association) were limited by very small numbers and/or only assessed crude associations; two large Norwegian registry-based studies found no association in unadjusted analyses (Hultman et al., 2002; Larsson et al., 2005), while two other studies (one moderate-sized and the other the largest study on this association to date) did find increased risk of autism with multiple births as compared to singletons, in adjusted analyses (Brimacombe et al., 2007; Croen, Grether, & Selvin, 2002). Another large study reported higher prevalence of multiple births in the autism group, but did not take into account account potential confounders (Wier, Yoshida, Odouli, Grether, & Croen, 2006). The meta-analysis summary estimate suggested a significant 77% increased risk of autism among twin/multiple births (OR = 1.77, 95% 1.23, 2.55). Another investigation not included in the meta-analysis also noted a significant positive association with multiple birth in adjusted analyses (Williams et al., 2008).

The mechanisms underlying the relation between multiple births and autism could be related to the twinning process, sharing of the in-utero environment, or other factors that often occur as a result of multiple births and also are associated with autism. For example, multiple gestation is associated with increased risk of pregnancy complications, low birth weight, and preterm birth, as well as poorer neonatal outcomes more broadly (Qazi, 2011). Thus, while the sum of the available evidence to date from large studies does suggest autism is slightly more common in multiple births, it is not clear whether the twinning process itself may increase autism risk, or, rather, the associations are mediated through correlated perinatal complications.

Gestational Diabetes

Another individual complication associated with autism in a number of studies is gestational diabetes. A recent large population-based case control study found a significant increase in autism risk in children of mothers with any of the following metabolic conditions during pregnancy: obesity, type 2 diabetes, gestational diabetes, or hypertension (Krakowiak et al., 2012). In addition, a large cohort study in the United States identified nearly a doubling in risk of autism in offspring of mothers having gestational diabetes (Lyall, Pauls, Santangelo, Spiegelman, & Ascherio, 2011), as did a meta-analysis (Gardener et al., 2009), though other studies found no association (Dodds et al., 2011; Hultman et al., 2002).

The mechanisms relating gestational diabetes to autism have not been clearly defined, though some have hypothesized a metabolic pathway, by which hyperinsulinemia in the fetus may lead to increased oxygen metabolism and chronic hypoxia that affects the developing brain (Krakowiak et al., 2012). This mechanism is consistent with some literature on other potential hypoxia-related conditions. Other hypothesized pathways are through nutritional status related to diabetes, including decreased micronutrient availability, or possible associations with hormone levels, which have also been suggested as relevant in autism (Baron-Cohen, Lutchmaya, & Knickmeyer, 2004; Lyall et al., 2011). In addition, gestational diabetes is often associated with Cesarean section delivery and low infant blood sugar at birth (Eidelman & Samueloff, 2002), perinatal risk factors that could play a mediating role in the association.

Gestational Bleeding

Bleeding during pregnancy may be the result of, or an indicator for, various pregnancy complications, especially placental problems, particularly when the bleeding occurs in the third trimester. Almost every study that has examined the association has suggested a slight to moderate increase in autism with maternal gestational bleeding, though statistical significance is achieved in only a few reports (Gardener et al., 2009). In a large Swedish case-control study (Hultman et al., 2002), the risk of autism after gestations in which the mother experienced bleeding was nonsignificantly elevated, though analyses included adjustment for potentially downstream factors, including birth weight and mode of delivery, therefore potentially biasing results. Two case-control investigations

reported strong increases in risk associated with bleeding (Brimacombe et al., 2007; Juul-Dam et al., 2001), but neither adjusted for potential confounding factors, and both were based on comparison to population rates. Three other larger studies, including a population-based registry study and two case-control investigations, found no significant association in adjusted analyses (Glasson et al., 2004; Stein, Weizman, Ring, & Barak, 2006; M. K. Williams et al., 2008); another large case-control study also found no association; however, the comparison group was sibling controls, which may not be appropriate given the genetics of autism (Mason-Brothers et al., 1990).

In the meta-analysis of prenatal risk factors for autism, which included the studies described earlier, the summary estimate suggested a significant 81% increase in risk of autism in offspring of mothers who experienced bleeding during pregnancy (Gardener et al., 2009); however, the results from Juul-Dam and colleagues (2001), which suggested an OR > 10, may have unduly influenced the summary estimate. More recently, a large investigation found no significant association after adjusting for potentially confounding factors (Dodds et al., 2011). The observed associations between gestational bleeding and autism in some studies may be related to fetal hypoxia, which has been purported to influence brain development.

Maternal Obesity

Recently, maternal weight, obesity, and/or body mass index (BMI, defined as weight in kilograms divided by height in meters squared) have been associated with autism. Higher prepregnancy weight was associated with autism in one study, as was increased weight gain during pregnancy (Dodds et al., 2011); weight gain remained significant in adjusted analyses taking into account prepregnancy weight, suggesting each factor may contribute independently to autism risk. In a large population-based case control study, maternal prepregnancy obesity (defined as a BMI of 30 or higher) was associated with a 70% increase in odds of autism when compared to typically developing controls (Krakowiak et al., 2012). An additional study found an association with high maternal BMI during late adolescence (age 18), rather than at a time closer to pregnancy, in association with risk of having a child with autism (Lyall et al., 2011). Associations with BMI or weight may be due to relationships with insulin (described earlier), or perhaps alterations in hormone levels, nutrition, or some other as-yet unidentified mechanism.

Other Obstetric Factors

Obstetric variables with the strongest evidence for no association with autism, according to a review of prenatal factors through 2009, include prior fetal loss, maternal hypertension, swelling, and toxemia/preeclampsia (Gardener et al., 2011). However, the meta-analysis did not exclude studies based on methodologic weakness, and since factors like study heterogeneity, small sample sizes, use of control groups affected by another condition, and analyses that did not take into account potential confounders may have limited prior findings, some of these factors may require further study. More recently, a large study including 87,677 births from South Carolina Medicaid data (including 472 children with autism) did suggest a significant association between preeclampsia and increased risk of autism (Mann, McDermott, Bao, Hardin, & Gregg, 2010). The association was slightly attenuated after accounting for birth weight but remained statistically significant for a moderate increase in risk; however, such adjustment for a factor downstream of preeclampsia might introduce bias. These newer results suggest that additional methodologically rigorous studies are needed to confirm whether toxemia/preeclampsia represents a risk factor for autism.

Other pre- and perinatal obstetric factors appear to have been examined in one study only, which reported no association with autism. These factors include chronic maternal diseases, venous thrombosis, frequency of intercourse during pregnancy, exposure to X-rays, amniocentesis, chorionic villus sampling, and month of initiation of prenatal care (Dodds et al., 2011; Gardener et al., 2009). Additionally, these factors have been found to have no association with autism in two studies to date: prenatal ultrasounds (Dodds et al., 2011; Grether, Li, Yoshida, & Croen, 2010), maternal oral contraceptive use, maternal menstrual cycle characteristics, and prior stillbirths or spontaneous abortions (Gardener et al., 2009; Juul-Dam et al., 2001; Lyall et al., 2012). Nevertheless, at this time, the research has been insufficient to draw conclusions about these factors. For some, (e.g., prenatal ultrasound), further development of methodology for measurement or estimation of exposure may be required before definitive work can be undertaken.

A number of labor complications, including Cesarean delivery, have been consistently associated with ASD. Neonatal complications, including preterm birth and low birth weight, have also been associated with autism; however, a review of these and other neonatal risk factors for autism is beyond the scope of this chapter. Medical factors reviewed here are summarized in Table 18.3.

Potential Mechanisms

Associations between obstetric complications and autism could arise from (a) a causal association, that is, the complications act biologically to directly increase risk of autism; (b) a common upstream cause of both complications and autism, perhaps by genetic/familial factors; (c) the result of the underlying pathology of autism, rather than a cause of it; or (d) interactions between genetic or other environmental factors and the complications lead to autism (in a type of two-hit pathway). Each of these explanations has plausibility, and different explanations likely apply to different complications, subgroups of individuals with autism, or studies. With regard to confounding, birth order and maternal age should be taken into account in studies of obstetric factors, because some complications occur more frequently in those born first, others in those of higher birth order, and many are more common among older mothers.

Direct evidence of mechanisms explaining associations between complications and autism is lacking. However, insights about potential pathways can be gained from certain investigations of familial factors. One study found that increased number of pre-, peri-, and neonatal complications in autistic probands was associated with a greater number of unaffected family members having the

TABLE 18.3   Summary of Medical Factors Associated With Autism

Factor	Summary of Evidence	Influential References or Reviews
Thalidomide	From case reports, increased prevalence of autism in children whose mothers were given these drugs during pregnancy. Due to low prevalence of use, none of these factors can account for more than a small percentage of autism cases today.	Stromland, Nordin, Miller, Akerstrom, and Gillberg, 1994
Valproic acid/ antiepileptic drugs		Moore et al., 2000; Rodier, Ingram, Tisdale, Nelson, and Romano, 1996
Misopristol		Bandim, Ventura, Miller, Almeida, and Costa, 2003
Other medications	Insufficient research on different types of medications. Studies that have grouped a broad range of medications have yielded inconsistent findings. Suggested association with maternal SSRI use in one study, with strongest effect seen in first trimester.	Croen, Grether, Yoshida, Odouli, and Hendrick, 2011; Gardener, Spiegelman, and Buka, 2009 (review)
Infertility	Higher prevalence of infertility in case mothers noted in a few early reports. Two recent large studies saw no association with infertility; one study found association only for multiple births.	Grether et al., 2012; Hvidtjørn et al., 2011; Lyall, Pauls, Spiegelman, Ascherio, and Santangelo, 2012
Infertility treatments	Inconsistent findings from a handful of small studies; most have reported either no association or modest increases in risk for infertility treatments and ASD or broader neurodevelopmental outcomes. No association of assisted reproductive technologies (including IVF) with ASD in multiple large studies. Suggestive association with infertility medications in multiple births only in recent report, and with ovulation drugs only in subgroup analyses (advanced maternal age, female offspring) of two larger studies.	Grether et al., 2012; Hvidtjørn et al., 2011; Lyall et al., 2012; Lyall, Baker, Hertz-Picciotto, and Walker, 2013
Pregnancy complications/obstetric suboptimality	Inconsistent findings for individual complications. Overall association with increased number of complications/increased suboptimality in case mothers commonly seen.	Gardener et al., 2009 (review); Lyall et al., 2012; Juul-Dam, Townsend, and Courchesne, 2001; Brimacombe, Ming, and Lamendola, 2007
Gestational diabetes	Associated with increased risk of autism in recent large studies. Earlier, smaller studies yielded inconsistent results. Whether controlled versus uncontrolled diabetes alters association has not been examined.	Krakowiak et al., 2012; Lyall et al., 2012
Maternal infections during pregnancy	Congenital rubella, cytomegalovirus, and maternal fever and influenza during pregnancy each associated with autism in a number of studies and in meta-analysis.	Chess, 1971; Zerbo et al., 2012; Gardener et al., 2009 (review)
Season of birth or conception	Results of a few studies conflicting, but autism births most consistently associated with winter months. Season of conception (winter) associated with autism in two recent large studies. This association could be an indicator of a role of infection, maternal nutrition, or other environmental factor that varies by season and location, such as pesticide use.	Zerbo, Iosif, Delwiche, Walker, and Hertz-Picciotto, 2011

broader autism phenotype (i.e., milder, autistic symptoms) (Bolton et al., 1997). A similar association between familial broader autism phenotype and obstetric complications was also noted in another study (Zwaigenbaum et al., 2002). These findings may be consistent with a number of the explanations provided above, but suggest overlap between family history of obstetric complications and either autism or even perhaps liability to developmental problems overall. In particular, it is worth highlighting that obstetric complications have been associated with other psychiatric and neurodevelopmental disorders (Eaton, Mortensen, Thomsen, & Frydenberg, 2001; Glasson et al., 2004; Halmoy, Klungsoyr, Skjaerven, & Haavik, 2012; Hultman et al., 2002; Larsson et al., 2005; Maimburg & Vaeth, 2006). Thus, complications in the pre-, peri-, and neonatal periods may be general markers of or predictors for vulnerabilities to a broad range of neurodevelopmental problems.

Infections

Infectious agents provided some of the earliest clues about nongenetic etiologic factors in autism. In an epidemic of rubella in the 1960s, children whose mothers were infected during pregnancy had a remarkably high autism prevalence of 4%–7% (Chess, 1971; Chess, Fernandez, & Korn, 1978). Congenital cytomegalovirus exposure has also been associated with autism (Sweeten, Posey, & McDougle, 2004; Yamashita, Fujimoto, Nakajima, Isagai, & Matsuishi, 2003). These investigations highlighted gestation as a critical period of susceptibility to aberrant brain development in autism, and a role for viral infections in that process.

Maternal infections of relevance to today's children have also been linked to increased autism risk. Maternal fever and influenza have been associated with autism in some, but not all, studies (Gardener et al., 2009). The summary estimate from a meta-analysis of prenatal factors suggested a significantly increased risk of autism with maternal infection (OR = 1.82, 95% CI: 1.01, 3.30), although limitations in many earlier studies (including lack of control for potential confounders) raise the possibility of bias in this estimate. Recently, maternally reported untreated fever, as well as influenza, during pregnancy were associated with increased odds of autism in large population-based case-control study; however, there was no association with fever among those who took medication to control the fever (Zerbo et al., 2012). These findings and two other lines of evidence suggest a potential role of the maternal immune response during pregnancy. First, rodent models using poly I:C (viral) injections during pregnancy, which do not cause an actual infection, induce several autistic-like behaviors in the pups (Boksa, 2010; Smith, Li, Garbett, Mirnics, & Patterson, 2007). Second, maternal autoantibodies to fetal brain proteins have been demonstrated in a subset of mothers of children with autism but not in mothers of typically developing children (Braunschweig et al., 2008; Braunschweig et al., 2012; Braunschweig & Van de Water, 2012). Other evidence bearing on the infection/immune hypothesis

comes from the literature on seasonality, discussed previously.

Maternal Medications

Early Investigations

Thalidomide, a medication used primarily for morning sickness during the 1950s and 1960s, was found to increase risk of having a child with autism in mothers using the drug at days 20–24 postconception (Stromland, Nordin, Miller, Akerstrom, & Gillberg, 1994). Among 100 mothers using thalidomide, four of their children had autism (Lotter, 1966), an occurrence 100 times higher than the estimate of 4 in 10,000 from that era (Fombonne, 2009). Valproic acid, an antiepileptic drug, has also been associated with a substantial increase in autism risk, though concerns regarding increased risk need to be weighed against the need to treat maternal seizures. In mothers using this drug during pregnancy, prevalence of autism increased to approximately 5%–8% in two separate clinical investigations (Moore et al., 2000; Rasalam et al., 2005). These studies also suggested a high prevalence of developmental delays or broadly defined autistic behaviors (60%–77%) in children whose mothers used this and other antiepileptic drugs. Though maternal use of valproic acid and thalidomide cannot account for a large proportion of autism cases today or in the past, these associations demonstrate that pharmacologic agents acting during fetal brain development have the potential to initiate a pathway to autism. In particular, as both of these are antifolate drugs, one mechanism that may underlie the association is through effects on folic acid.

Maternal Vaccinations

Concern surrounding potential associations between maternal vaccinations during pregnancy arose largely due to speculation that mercury preservatives in vaccines may influence neurodevelopment. Maternal Rh status and prenatal RhIg injections (used to treat maternal-fetal Rh incompatibility) in particular have been examined in association with risk of offspring autism

(Table 18.3). A relatively large study found no association between prenatal anti-D immunoglobulin exposure/RhIg injections, or Rh negative status, and risk of autism (Croen, Matevia, Yoshida, & Grether, 2008).

Maternal Medication Use

Although numerous reports suggest a higher prevalence of the broad category of maternal medication use during pregnancy in cases with autism as compared to controls (Deykin & MacMahon, 1980; Gillberg & Gillberg, 1983; Piven et al., 1993), other studies saw no differences (Maimburg & Vaeth, 2006; Matsuishi et al., 1999). More to the point, inclusion of a broad range of medications having no common biologic mechanisms of action in study designs is not likely to be informative. Further, most studies of maternal medications have not considered timing of use. In one study that did examine a specific medication and time period in detail, a twofold increase in risk of autism was seen with maternal selective serotonin reuptake inhibitor (SSRI) use within 1 year prior to the child's birth (Croen, Grether, Yoshida, Odouli, & Hendrick, 2011). A stronger association was seen for use during the first trimester. Another large study, conducted in Sweden and including over 4,000 cases of ASD, also found an association with antidepressant use during pregnancy, as well as with maternal depression (Rai et al., 2013). When stratified by intellectual disability (ID), the association with antidepressants was seen only in cases without ID. More broadly, SSRIs and antidepressants have been suggested to be related to altered psychomotor development in a case-control study ("SSRI Antidepressants: Altered Psychomotor Development Following Exposure in Utero?," 2013), as well as to preterm birth, low birth weight, small for gestational age, though results for these factors are conflicting (Malm, 2012). Table 18.3 briefly summarizes the major findings on maternal medications as risk factors for autism.

A particular concern in studying effects of medications is the potential role of the underlying condition being treated: that is, whether there is confounding by indication. If the indication for use of such medications has an independent relationship to autism risk, a spurious association with the medication may be seen. Several psychiatric conditions in family members have been associated with ASD. In a large Danish nested case-control study with nearly 700 cases, autism was significantly associated with both parental schizophrenia-like psychosis and affective disorders, but not with parental substance abuse, which often occurs as a response to these conditions (H. J. Larsson et al., 2005). Maternal depression has also been reported to be associated with autism (Daniels et al., 2008; H. J. Larsson et al., 2005; Lauritsen, Pedersen, & Mortensen, 2005; Wallace, Anderson, & Dubrow, 2008). This may indicate that, at least in some families, there may be a shared genetic predisposition to neurologic or psychiatric disease, or biologic similarity between conditions. Little research, as of this writing, has attempted to tease apart the separate and joint contributions to risk for ASD from psychotropic medications and from underlying psychiatric morbidity.

Infertility and Fertility Therapies

Parallel rises in prevalence of autism and use of infertility therapies has led to a number of studies examining the potential relationship between these factors. Biological pathways that could link the two include alteration of methylation patterns and imprinting of genes, which have been demonstrated in animal studies of in vitro fertilization (IVF) and ovulation induction (Fernández-Gonzalez et al., 2004; Sato, Otsu, Negishi, Utsunomiya, & Arima, 2007). Mechanisms underlying infertility could also plausibly affect autism risk. The first investigations of infertility treatments and autism (reviewed in Hvidtjørn et al., 2011) were limited by small numbers of cases, lack of adjustment for confounders, and reliance on retrospective reporting. In addition, many early studies combined autism with a broader group of developmental or psychiatric conditions, and therefore did not examine associations with autism specifically. The definition used for assisted reproductive technologies (ART), and the types of therapies investigated, has also differed across studies.

Table 18.3 summarizes the epidemiologic literature on fertility and infertility treatments in relation to risk for autism. Recently, three methodologically rigorous studies have suggested modest associations between infertility treatments and autism. However, significant associations were only found in subgroup analyses, and the subgroup identified differed for each. In the largest sample examined for this association to date, including nearly 4,000 cases and over 33,000 exposed births from Denmark, no increased risk of autism was found following ART (Hvidtjørn et al., 2011). However, a moderate association with ovulation-inducing drugs was seen in subgroup analyses of female offspring only. A smaller study conducted in the United States also did not observe a significant association between ART and autism, and also demonstrated a significant association with ovulation-inducing drugs, though in this report the association was significant only among mothers of advanced maternal age (≥ 35) (Lyall et al., 2012). Heterogeneity by maternal age was not evaluated within the Danish study. Another case-control investigation relying on medical record data found an association between autism and infertility treatments broadly, as well as infertility medications, only in children from multiple births (Grether et al., 2012).

Confounding by indication of underlying infertility is also a possible explanation for associations seen with treatments; however, research from the two largest samples evaluating maternal infertility—described above with regard to infertility treatments—did not find an association with autism (Hvidtjørn et al., 2011; Lyall et al., 2012). The third recent study did report a significantly elevated risk for autism with maternal history of infertility and infertility evaluation at index pregnancy for multiple births only (Grether et al., 2012), though confidence intervals were wide and numbers small. Limited research exists examining specific infertility diagnoses, potential underlying pathways, and rarer specific therapies, though a recent investigation conducted within the CHARGE case-control study examined these topics (Lyall, Baker, Hertz-Picciotto, & Walker,

2013). No significant associations were found in that report, though power for rarer diagnoses and treatments was limited. The study also provides a review of the topic of infertility, its treatments, and ASD, noting suggestions for future work.

PROXIES FOR ENVIRONMENTAL EXPOSURES

Some factors serve as markers of higher risk, rather than being specific identifiable exposures of interest. Although these types of factors are not directly modifiable, studying them has provided clues about potentially causal exposures that can be altered. For example, associations with older maternal age could result from age-related increases in pregnancy complications, accumulated toxins over time, or higher rates of autoimmune conditions. Paternal age, which has been linked to de novo copy number variation (O'Roak et al., 2012), could be a marker of age-related decline in DNA repair efficiency, changes in epigenetic regulation, or cumulative exposures.

Similarly, season provides an intriguing example of an easily measured proxy variable for a variety of environmental exposures, such as influenza or other infections, sunlight/vitamin D, and pesticides. Seasonality of birth or conception has been associated with increased risk of autism in several studies (Hebert, Miller, & Joinson, 2010; Kolevzon et al., 2006; Zerbo, Iosif, Delwiche, Walker, & Hertz-Picciotto, 2011) (Table 18.3). The largest rigorous study of seasonality and autism to date, which included nearly 20,000 autism cases and over 6 million births over a 12-year period in California, found a small but statistically significant increase in risk of autism (adjusted OR = 1.06, 95% CI: 1.02–1.10) for children conceived in the winter months (December, January, February, March) compared to the summer (Zerbo et al., 2011). Another recent study, including data from the same region but shorter time frame, used a different methodology, focusing on clusters over time in which autism conceptions showed unusually high peaks, and reported November episodes in several years (Mazumdar, Liu, Susser, & Bearman, 2012). Conception marks the initiation of a well-defined trajectory of precisely timed processes, but itself could be a proxy, for instance, an association between winter conceptions and ASD could really represent a link to second trimester exposures occurring during late spring or early summer.

Previous studies focused primarily on season of *birth* rather than *conception*, and were inconsistent in their findings, some reporting no association (Hultman et al., 2002; Kolevzon et al., 2006), and others suggesting a higher autism risk with birth in March or other months (Barak, Ring, Sulkes, Gabbay, & Elizur, 1995; Mouridsen, Nielsen, Rich, & Isager, 1994). However, the shorter gestations of autism cases as compared with the general population (Lampi et al., 2012; Leavey, Zwaigenbaum, Heavner, & Burstyn, 2012) introduces uncertainty to the meaning of birth date in relation to intrinsic biologic processes, and the resulting misclassification of exposure would tend to obscure an association, particularly if a seasonally changing cause operated within a precise developmental window in gestation. Other explanations for variation in results may be small sample sizes, different time periods and regions studied, inappropriate comparison group, or inadequate control of confounding.

As influenza epidemics, nutritional factors, air pollution, and use of pesticides vary both seasonally and by location, discrepancies in seasonality studies could also stem from such spatiotemporal variability in exposure (pesticides applied in different calendar months in California versus Iowa). Moreover, multiple seasonal factors might amplify risk by exerting effects at different critical periods in early development.

SUMMARY AND FUTURE DIRECTIONS

Recently, considerable progress has been made in uncovering clues about environmental contributions to autism. A growing body of evidence supports potential roles for preconception or prenatal maternal nutrition, lifestyle, infection, medications, and exposures to environmental chemicals such as pesticides and constituents of ambient air pollution. It is clear that there is no single or universal cause of autism; rather, many environmental and genetic factors are likely involved, and the specific subsets of factors that are operating will vary across different individuals.

As noted, many of the factors reviewed here have associations with a broader class of neurodevelopmental or psychiatric conditions, and therefore may not be unique risk factors for autism. Genetic factors or critical time periods may influence how these xenobiotics or noninherited conditions alter brain connectivity and determine whether the exposure results in autism as opposed to other deficits. Large gene-by-environment studies are therefore required to capture the complexity of this disorder, as is increased focus on identifying specific environmental factors and time periods of vulnerability. Promising directions for future research include determination of critical etiologic windows for environmental exposures (which likely vary by type of exposure; see Figure 18.1); continued investigation into maternal nutritional, obstetric, metabolic and other factors during the preconception, prenatal and perinatal periods; and disentangling the role of maternal and paternal influences, including the environmental influences on de novo mutations that are predominant in paternally contributed genes (O'Roak et al., 2012). Parallel mechanistic investigations using both toxicologic and molecular epidemiologic approaches are also critical to unraveling the pathways by which exogenous factors might alter the course of brain development and contribute to autism. Although the preconception and prenatal periods likely have the strongest impact, continued plasticity of the central nervous system implies that further insults or protective factors in the first year or two of life may also contribute to the phenotypic development of the child and concomitant risk for autism.

CROSS-REFERENCES

Issues of diagnosis in autism and related conditions are addressed in Chapter 1. Chapter 17 discusses genetic aspects of ASD. Medical care (including clinical genetic assessment) is addressed in Chapter 22.

REFERENCES

Albuquerque, C. A., Smith, K. R., Johnson, C., Chao, R., & Harding, R. (2004). Influence of maternal tobacco smoking during pregnancy on uterine, umbilical and fetal cerebral artery blood flows. *Early Human Development, 80*(1), 31–42.

Amaral, D. G., Schumann, C. M., & Nordahl, C. W. (2008). Neuroanatomy of autism. *Trends in Neuroscience, 31*(3), 137–145.

Aronson, M., Hagberg, B., & Gillberg, C. (1997). Attention deficits and autistic spectrum problems in children exposed to alcohol during gestation: A follow-up study. *Developmental Medicine & Child Neurology, 39*(9), 583–587.

Bandim, J. M., Ventura, L. O., Miller, M. T., Almeida, H. C., & Costa, A. E. (2003). Autism and Möbius sequence: An exploratory study of children in northeastern Brazil. *Arquivos de Neuro-Psiquiatria, 61*(2A), 181–185.

Barak, Y., Ring, A., Sulkes, J., Gabbay, U., & Elizur, A. (1995). Season of birth and autistic disorder in israel. *American Journal of Psychiatry, 152*(5), 798–800.

Baron-Cohen, S., Lutchmaya, S., & Knickmeyer, R. (2004). *Prenatal testosterone in mind.* Cambridge, MA: MIT Press.

Barr, D. B., Olsson, A. O., Wong, L. Y., Udunka, S., Baker, S. E., Whitehead, R. D., . . . Needham, L. L. (2010). Urinary concentrations of metabolites of pyrethroid insecticides in the general U.S. population: National health and nutrition examination survey 1999–2002. *Environmental Health Perspectives, 118*(6), 742–748.

Becerra, T. A., Wilhelm, M., Olsen, J., Cockburn, M., & Ritz, B. (2013). Ambient air pollution and autism in Los Angeles County, California. *Environmental Health Perspectives, 121*(3), 380–386.

Boas, M., Feldt-Rasmussen, U., & Main, K. M. (2012). Thyroid effects of endocrine disrupting chemicals. *Molecular and Cellular Endocrinology, 355*(2), 240–248.

Boksa, P. (2010). Effects of prenatal infection on brain development and behavior: A review of findings from animal models. *Brain, Behavior, and Immunity, 24*(6), 881–897.

Bolton, P. F., Murphy, M., MacDonald, H., Whitlock, B., Pickles, A., & Rutter, M. (1997). Obstetric complications in autism: Consequences or causes of the condition? *Journal of the American Academy of Child & Adolescent Psychiatry, 36*(2), 272–281.

Bolton, P. F., Pickles, A., Murphy, M., & Rutter, M. (1998). Autism, affective and other psychiatric disorders: Patterns of familial aggregation. *Psychological Medicine, 28*(2), 385–395.

Bouayed, J., Desor, F., Rammal, H., Kiemer, A. K., Tybl, E., Schroeder, H., . . . Soulimani, R. (2009). Effects of lactational exposure to benzo[alpha]pyrene (b[alpha]p) on postnatal neurodevelopment, neuronal receptor gene expression and behaviour in mice. *Toxicology, 259*(3), 97–106.

Boucher, O., Muckle, G., & Bastien, C. H. (2009). Prenatal exposure to polychlorinated biphenyls: A neuropsychologic analysis. *Environmental Health Perspectives, 117*(1), 7–16.

Braun, J. M., Yolton, K., Dietrich, K. N., Hornung, R., Ye, X., Calafat, A. M., & Lanphear, B. P. (2009). Prenatal bisphenol A exposure and early childhood behavior. *Environmental Health Perspectives, 117*(12), 1945–1952. doi: 10.1289/ehp.0900979

Braunschweig, D., Ashwood, P., Krakowiak, P., Hertz-Picciotto, I., Hansen, R., Croen, L. A., . . . Van de Water, J. (2008). Autism: Maternally derived antibodies specific for fetal brain proteins. *Neurotoxicology, 29*(2), 226–231.

Braunschweig, D., Duncanson, P., Boyce, R., Hansen, R., Ashwood, P., Pessah, I. N., . . . Van de Water, J. (2012). Behavioral correlates of maternal antibody status among children with autism. *Journal of Autism and Developmental Disorders, 42*(7), 1435–1445.

Braunschweig, D., & Van de Water, J. (2012). Maternal autoantibodies in autism. *Archives of Neurology, 69*(6), 693–699.

Brimacombe, M., Ming, X., & Lamendola, M. (2007). Prenatal and birth complications in autism. *Maternal and Child Health Journal, 11*(1), 73–79.

Brown, L. A., Khousbouei, H., Goodwin, J. S., Irvin-Wilson, C. V., Ramesh, A., Sheng, L., . . . Hood, D. B. (2007). Down-regulation of early ionotrophic glutamate receptor subunit developmental expression as a mechanism for observed plasticity deficits following gestational exposure to benzo(a)pyrene. *Neurotoxicology, 28*(5), 965–978.

Burd, L., Severud, R., Kerbeshian, J., & Klug, M. G. (1999). Prenatal and perinatal risk factors for autism. *Journal of Prenatal Medicine, 27*, 441–450.

Burstyn, I., Sithole, F., & Zwaigenbaum, L. (2010). Autism spectrum disorders, maternal characteristics and obstetric complications among singletons born in Alberta, Canada. *Chronic Diseases and Injuries in Canada, 30*(4), 125–134.

Button, T. M., Maughan, B., & McGuffin, P. (2007). The relationship of maternal smoking to psychological problems in the offspring. *Early Human Development, 83*(11), 727–732.

Casanova, M. F. (2007). The neuropathology of autism. *Brain Pathology, 17*(4), 422–433.

Cheslack-Postava, K., Liu, K., & Bearman, P. S. (2011). Closely spaced pregnancies are associated with increased odds of autism in California sibling births. *Pediatrics, 127*(2), 246–253.

Chess, S. (1971). Autism in children with congenital rubella. *Journal of Autism and Childhood Schizophrenia, 1*(1), 33–47.

Chess, S., Fernandez, P., & Korn, S. (1978). Behavioral consequences of congenital rubella. *Journal of Pediatrics, 93*(4), 699–703.

Chevrier, J., Gunier, R. B., Bradman, A., Holland, N. T., Calafat, A. M., Eskenazi, B., & Harley, K. G. (2013). Maternal urinary bisphenol A during pregnancy and maternal and neonatal thyroid function in the CHAMACOS study. *Environmental Health Perspectives, 121*(1), 138–144.

Courchesne, E., Yeung-Courchesne, R., Press, G. A., Hesselink, J. R., & Jernigan, T. L. (1988). Hypoplasia of cerebellar vermal lobules vi and vii in autism. *New England Journal of Medicine, 318*(21), 1349–1354.

Croen, L. A., Grether, J. K., & Selvin, S. (2002). Descriptive epidemiology of autism in a california population: Who is at risk? *Journal of Autism and Developmental Disorders, 32*(3), 217–224.

Croen, L. A., Grether, J. K., Yoshida, C. K., Odouli, R., & Hendrick, V. (2011). Antidepressant use during pregnancy and childhood autism spectrum disorders. *Archives of General Psychiatry, 68*(11), 1104–1112.

Croen, L. A., Matevia, M., Yoshida, C. K., & Grether, J. K. (2008). Maternal Rh D status, anti-D immune globulin exposure during pregnancy, and risk of autism spectrum disorders. *American Journal of Obstetrics & Gynecology, 199*(3), 234, e231–236.

Czeizel, A. E. (2000). Primary prevention of neural-tube defects and some other major congenital abnormalities: Recommendations for the appropriate use of folic acid during pregnancy. *Pediatric Drugs, 2*(6), 437–449.

Daniels, J. L., Forssen, U., Hultman, C. M., Cnattingius, S., Savitz, D. A., Feychting, M., & Sparen, P. (2008). Parental psychiatric disorders associated with autism spectrum disorders in the offspring. *Pediatrics, 121*(5), e1357–1362.

Dealberto, M. J. (2011). Prevalence of autism according to maternal immigrant status and ethnic origin. *Acta Psychiatrica Scandinavia, 123*(5), 339–348.

DeLong, G. R., & Dwyer, J. T. (1988). Correlation of family history with specific autistic subgroups: Asperger's syndrome and bipolar affective disease. *Journal of Autism and Developmental Disorders, 18*(4), 593–600.

Deykin, E. Y., & MacMahon, B. (1980). Pregnancy, delivery, and neonatal complications among autistic children. *American Journal of Diseases of Children, 134*(9), 860–864.

Dodds, L., Fell, D. B., Shea, S., Armson, B. A., Allen, A. C., & Bryson, S. (2011). The role of prenatal, obstetric and neonatal factors in the development of autism. *Journal of Autism and Developmental Disorders, 41*(7), 891–902.

Eaton, W. W., Mortensen P. B., Thomsen, P. H., & Frydenberg, M. (2001). Obstetric complications and risk for severe psychopathology in childhood. *Journal of Autism and Developmental Disorders, 31*(3), 279–285.

Ehlers, S., Gillberg, C., & Wing, L. (1999). A screening questionnaire for asperger syndrome and other high-functioning autism spectrum disorders in school age children. *Journal of Autism and Developmental Disorders, 29*(2), 129–141.

Eidelman, A. I., & Samueloff, A. (2002). The pathophysiology of the fetus of the diabetic mother. *Seminars in Perinatology, 26*(3), 232–236.

Eliasen, M., Tolstrup, J. S., Nybo Andersen, A. M., Gronbaek, M., Olsen, J., & Strandberg-Larsen, K. (2010). Prenatal alcohol exposure and autistic spectrum disorders—A population-based prospective study of 80,552 children and their mothers. *International Journal of Epidemiology, 39*(4), 1074–1081.

Engel, S. M., Miodovnik, A., Canfield, R. L., Zhu, C., Silva, M. J., Calafat, A. M., & Wolff, M. S. (2010). Prenatal phthalate exposure is associated with childhood behavior and executive functioning. *Environmental Health Perspectives, 118*(4), 565–571.

Engel, S. M., Wetmur, J., Chen, J., Zhu, C., Barr, D. B., Canfield, R. L., & Wolff, M. S. (2011). Prenatal exposure to organophosphates, paraoxonase 1, and cognitive development in childhood. *Environmental Health Perspectives, 119*(8), 1182–1188.

Eskenazi, B., Marks, A. R., Bradman, A., Harley, K., Barr, D. B., Johnson, C., . . . Jewell, N. P. (2007). Organophosphate pesticide exposure and neurodevelopment in young Mexican-American children. *Environtal Health Perspectives, 115*(5), 792–798.

Eyles, D., Brown, J., Mackay-Sim, A., McGrath, J., & Feron, F. (2003). Vitamin D3 and brain development. *Neuroscience, 118*(3), 641–653.

Fergusson, D. M., Woodward, L. J., & Horwood, L. J. (1998). Maternal smoking during pregnancy and psychiatric adjustment in late adolescence. *Archives of General Psychiatry, 55*(8), 721–727.

Fernández-Gonzalez, R., Moreira, P., Bilbao, A., Jiménez, A., Pérez-Crespo, M., Ramérez, M. A., . . . Gutiérrez-Adán, A. (2004). Long-term effect of in vitro culture of mouse embryos with serum on mRNA expression of imprinting genes, development, and behavior. *Proceedings of the National Academy of Sciences, USA, 101*(16), 5880–5885.

Fernell, E., Barnevik-Olsson, M., Bagenholm, G., Gillberg, C., Gustafsson, S., & Saaf, M. (2010). Serum levels of 25-hydroxyvitamin D in mothers of Swedish and of Somali origin who have children with and without autism. *Acta Paediatrica, 99*(5), 743–747.

Folstein, S., & Rutter, M. (1977). Infantile autism: A genetic study of 21 twin pairs. *Journal of Child Psychology and Psychiatry, 18*(4), 297–321.

Fombonne, E. (2009). Epidemiology of pervasive developmental disorders. *Pediatric Research, 65*(6), 591–598.

Forns, J., Torrent, M., Garcia-Esteban, R., Grellier, J., Gascon, M., Julvez, J., . . . Sunyer, J. (2012). Prenatal exposure to polychlorinated biphenyls and child neuropsychological development in 4-year-olds: An analysis per congener and specific cognitive domain. *Science of the Total Environment, 432*, 338–343.

Frederiksen, M., Vorkamp, K., Mathiesen, L., Mose, T., & Knudsen, L. E. (2010). Placental transfer of the polybrominated diphenyl ethers BDE-47, BDE-99 and BDE-209 in a human placenta perfusion system: An experimental study. *Environmental Health, 9*, 32.

Gardener, H., Spiegelman, D., & Buka, S. L. (2009). Prenatal risk factors for autism: Comprehensive meta-analysis. *British Journal of Psychiatry, 195*(1), 7–14.

Gardener, H., Spiegelman, D., & Buka, S. L. (2011). Perinatal and neonatal risk factors for autism: A comprehensive meta-analysis. *Pediatrics, 128*(2), 344–355.

Gee, J. R., & Moser, V. C. (2008). Acute postnatal exposure to brominated diphenylether 47 delays neuromotor ontogeny and alters motor activity in mice. *Neurotoxicology and Teratology, 30*(2), 79–87.

Gillberg, C., & Gillberg, I. C. (1983). Infantile autism: A total population study of reduced optimality in the pre-, peri-, and neonatal period. *Journal of Autism and Developmental Disorders*, *13*(2), 153–166.

Glasson, E. J., Bower, C., Petterson, B., de Klerk, N., Chaney, G., & Hallmayer, J. F. (2004). Perinatal factors and the development of autism: A population study. *Archives of General Psychiatry*, *61*(6), 618–627.

Goldey, E. S., & Crofton, K. M. (1998). Thyroxine replacement attenuates hypothyroxinemia, hearing loss, and motor deficits following developmental exposure to Aroclor 1254 in rats. *Toxicological Sciences*, *45*(1), 94–105.

Grant, W. B., & Soles, C. M. (2009). Epidemiologic evidence supporting the role of maternal vitamin D deficiency as a risk factor for the development of infantile autism. *Dermato-Endocrinology*, *1*(4), 223–228.

Grether, J. K., Li, S. X., Yoshida, C. K., & Croen, L. A. (2010). Antenatal ultrasound and risk of autism spectrum disorders. *Journal of Autism and Developmental Disorders*, *40*(2), 238–245.

Grether, J. K., Qian, Y., Croughan, M. S., Wu, Y. W., Schembri, M., Camarano, L., & Croen, L. A. (2012). Is infertility associated with childhood autism? *Journal of Autism and Developmental Disorders*, *43*(3), 663–672.

Hallmayer, J., Cleveland, S., Torres, A., Phillips, J., Cohen, B., Torigoe, T.,...Risch, N. (2011). Genetic heritability and shared environmental factors among twin pairs with autism. *Archives of General Psychiatry*, *68*(11), 1095–1102.

Halmoy, A., Klungsoyr, K., Skjaerven, R., & Haavik, J. (2012). Pre- and perinatal risk factors in adults with attention-deficit/hyperactivity disorder. *Biological Psychiatry*, *71*(5), 474–481.

Harari, R., Julvez, J., Murata, K., Barr, D., Bellinger, D. C., Debes, F., & Grandjean, P. (2010). Neurobehavioral deficits and increased blood pressure in school-age children prenatally exposed to pesticides. *Environmental Health Perspectives*, *118*(6), 890–896.

Harris, S. R., MacKay, L. L., & Osborn, J. A. (1995). Autistic behaviors in offspring of mothers abusing alcohol and other drugs: A series of case reports. *Alcohol: Clinical and Experimental Research*, *19*(3), 660–665.

Hartz, A. M., Bauer, B., Block, M. L., Hong, J. S., & Miller, D. S. (2008). Diesel exhaust particles induce oxidative stress, proinflammatory signaling, and P-glycoprotein up-regulation at the blood-brain barrier. *FASEB Journal*, *22*(8), 2723–2733.

Hatch, E. E., Nelson, J. W., Stahlhut, R. W., & Webster, T. F. (2010). Association of endocrine disruptors and obesity: Perspectives from epidemiological studies. *International Journal of Andrology*, *33*(2), 324–332.

Hebert, K. J., Miller, L. L., & Joinson, C. J. (2010). Association of autistic spectrum disorder with season of birth and conception in a UK cohort. *Autism Research*, *3*(4), 185–190.

Herbert, M. R., Ziegler, D. A., Deutsch, C. K., O'Brien, L. M., Kennedy, D. N., Filipek, P. A.,...Caviness, V. S., Jr. (2005). Brain asymmetries in autism and developmental language disorder: A nested whole-brain analysis. *Brain*, *128*(Pt 1), 213–226.

Herbstman, J. B., Sjodin, A., Kurzon, M., Lederman, S. A., Jones, R. S., Rauh, V.,...Perera, F. (2010). Prenatal exposure to PBDEs and neurodevelopment. *Environmental Health Perspectives*, *118*(5), 712–719.

Hernán, M. A., Hernéndez-Diaz, S., Werler, M. M., & Mitchell, A. A. (2002). Causal knowledge as a prerequisite for confounding evaluation: An application to birth defects epidemiology. *American Journal of Epidemiology*, *155*(2), 176–184.

Hertz-Picciotto, I., Bergman, A., Fangstrom, B., Rose, M., Krakowiak, P., Pessah, I.,...Bennett, D. H. (2011). Polybrominated diphenyl ethers in relation to autism and developmental delay: A case-control study. *Environmental Health*, *10*(1), 1.

Hertz-Picciotto, I., Croen, L. A., Hansen, R., Jones, C. R., van de Water, J., & Pessah, I. N. (2006). The CHARGE study: An epidemiologic investigation of genetic and environmental factors contributing to autism. *Environmental Health Perspectives*, *114*(7), 1119–1125.

Honein, M. A., Paulozzi, L. J., & Moore, C. A. (2000). Family history, maternal smoking, and clubfoot: An indication of a gene-environment interaction. *American Journal of Epidemiology*, *152*(7), 658–665.

Hoshiko, S., Grether, J. K., Windham, G. C., Smith, D., & Fessel, K. (2011). Are thyroid hormone concentrations at birth associated with subsequent autism diagnosis? *Autism Research*, *4*(6), 456–463.

Hultman, C. M., Sparen, P., & Cnattingius, S. (2002). Perinatal risk factors for infantile autism. *Epidemiology*, *13*(4), 417–423.

Hvidtjørn, D., Grove, J., Schendel, D., Schieve, L. A., Svaerke, C., Ernst, E. (2011). Risk of autism spectrum disorders in children born after assisted conception: A population-based follow-up study. *Journal of Epidemiology and Community Health*, *65*(6), 497–502.

Indredavik, M. S., Brubakk, A. M., Romundstad, P., & Vik, T. (2007). Prenatal smoking exposure and psychiatric symptoms in adolescence. *Acta Paediatrica*, *96*(3), 377–382.

Institute of Medicine. (1990). *Nutrition during pregnancy 1990*. Washington, DC: National Academies Press.

Jacobson, J. L., & Jacobson, S. W. (2002). Effects of prenatal alcohol exposure on child development. *Alcohol Research and Health*, *26*(4), 282–286.

James, S. J., Melnyk, S., Jernigan, S., Pavliv, O., Trusty, T., Lehman, S.,...Cleves, M. A. (2010). A functional polymorphism in the reduced folate carrier gene and DNA hypomethylation in mothers of children with autism. *American Journal of Medical Genetics*, *153B*(6), 1209–1220.

Jolous-Jamshidi, B., Cromwell, H. C., McFarland, A. M., & Meserve, L. A. (2010). Perinatal exposure to polychlorinated biphenyls alters social behaviors in rats. *Toxicology Letters*, *199*(2), 136–143.

Julvez, J., Fortuny, J., Mendez, M., Torrent, M., Ribas-Fito, N., & Sunyer, J. (2009). Maternal use of folic acid supplements during pregnancy and four-year-old neurodevelopment in a population-based birth cohort. *Paediatric and Perinatal Epidemiology*, *23*(3), 199–206.

Juul-Dam, N., Townsend, J., & Courchesne, E. (2001). Prenatal, perinatal, and neonatal factors in autism, pervasive developmental disorder-not otherwise specified, and the general population. *Pediatrics*, *107*(4), E63.

Kalkbrenner, A. E., Braun, J. M., Durkin, M. S., Maenner, M. J., Cunniff, C., Lee, L. C.,...Daniels, J. L. (2012). Maternal smoking during pregnancy and the prevalence of autism spectrum disorders, using data from the autism and developmental disabilities monitoring network. *Environmental Health Perspectives, 120*(7), 1042–1048.

Kalkbrenner, A. E., Daniels, J. L., Chen, J. C., Poole, C., Emch, M., & Morrissey, J. (2010). Perinatal exposure to hazardous air pollutants and autism spectrum disorders at age 8. *Epidemiology, 21*(5), 631–641.

Kimura-Kuroda, J., Nagata, I., & Kuroda, Y. (2007). Disrupting effects of hydroxy-polychlorinated biphenyl (PCB) congeners on neuronal development of cerebellar Purkinje cells: A possible causal factor for developmental brain disorders? *Chemosphere, 67*(9), S412–420.

Kolevzon, A., Weiser, M., Gross, R., Lubin, G., Knobler, H. Y., Schmeidler, J., … Reichenberg, A. (2006). Effects of season of birth on autism spectrum disorders: Fact or fiction? *American Journal of Psychiatry, 163*(7), 1288–1290.

Korrick, S. A., & Sagiv, S. K. (2008). Polychlorinated biphenyls, organochlorine pesticides and neurodevelopment. *Current Opinion in Pediatrics, 20*(2), 198–204.

Krakowiak, P., Walker, C. K., Bremer, A. A., Baker, A. S., Ozonoff, S., Hansen, R. L., & Hertz-Picciotto, J. (2012). Maternal metabolic conditions and risk for autism and other neurodevelopmental disorders. *Pediatrics, 129*(5), e1121–e1128.

Lampi, K. M., Lehtonen, L., Tran, P. L., Suominen, A., Lehti, V., Banerjee, P. N., … Sourander, A. (2012). Risk of autism spectrum disorders in low birth weight and small for gestational age infants. *Journal of Pediatrics, 161*(5), 830–836.

Land, T. G., Landau, A. S., Manning, S. E., Purtill, J. K., Pickett, K., Wakschlag, L., & Dukic, V. M. (2012). Who underreports smoking on birth records: A Monte Carlo predictive model with validation. *PLoS One, 7*(4), e34853.

Landgren, M., Svensson, L., Stromland, K., & Andersson Gronlund, M. (2010). Prenatal alcohol exposure and neurodevelopmental disorders in children adopted from Eastern Europe. *Pediatrics, 125*(5), e1178–1185.

Larsson, H. J., Eaton, W. W., Madsen, K. M., Vestergaard, M., Olesen, A. V., Agerbo, E., … Mortensen, P. B. (2005). Risk factors for autism: Perinatal factors, parental psychiatric history, and socioeconomic status. *American Journal of Epidemiology, 161*(10), 916–925; discussion 926–928.

Larsson, M., Weiss, B., Janson, S., Sundell, J., & Bornehag, C. G. (2009). Associations between indoor environmental factors and parental-reported autistic spectrum disorders in children 6–8 years of age. *Neurotoxicology, 30*(5), 822–831.

Lauritsen, M. B., Pedersen, C. B., & Mortensen, P. B. (2005). Effects of familial risk factors and place of birth on the risk of autism: A nationwide register-based study. *Journal of Child Psychology and Psychiatry, 46*(9), 963–971.

Lawrence, L. J., & Casida, J. E. (1983). Stereospecific action of pyrethroid insecticides on the gamma-aminobutyric acid receptor-ionophore complex. *Science, 221*(4618), 1399–1401.

Leavey, A., Zwaigenbaum, L., Heavner, K., & Burstyn, I. (2012). Gestational age at birth and risk of autism spectrum disorders in Alberta, Canada. *Journal of Pediatrics, 162*(2), 361–368.

Lee, B. K., Gardner, R. M., Dal, H., Svensson, A., Galanti, M. R., Rai, D., … Magnusson, C. (2012). Brief report: Maternal smoking during pregnancy and autism spectrum disorders. *Journal of Autism and Developmental Disorders, 42*(9), 2000–2005.

Lobascher, M. E., Kingerlee, P. E., & Gubbay, S. S. (1970). Childhood autism: An investigation of aetiological factors in twenty-five cases. *British Journal of Psychiatry, 117*(540), 525–529.

Lord, C., Mulloy, C., Wendelboe, M., & Schopler, E. (1991). Pre- and perinatal factors in high-functioning females and males with autism. *Journal of Autism and Developmental Disorders, 21*(2), 197–209.

Lotter, V. (1966). Epidemiology of autistic conditions in young children: Some characteristics of the parents and children. *Social Psychiatry, 1*, 124–137.

Luck, W., Nau, H., Hansen, R., & Steldinger, R. (1985). Extent of nicotine and cotinine transfer to the human fetus, placenta and amniotic fluid of smoking mothers. *Developmental Pharmacology and Therapeutics, 8*(6), 384–395.

Lyall, K., Baker, A., Hertz-Picciotto, I., & Walker, C. K. (2013). Infertility and its treatments in association with autism spectrum disorders: A review and results from the CHARGE study. *International Journal of Environmental Research and Public Health, 10*(8), 3715–3734.

Lyall, K., Munger, K. L., O'Reilly, E. J., Santangelo, S., & Ascherio, A. (2013). Maternal dietary fat intake in association with autism spectrum disorders. *American Journal of Epidemiology, 178*(2), 209–220.

Lyall, K., Pauls, D. L., Santangelo, S. L., Spiegelman, D., & Ascherio, A. (2011). Maternal early life factors associated with hormone levels and the risk of having a child with an autism spectrum disorder in the Nurses' Health Study II. *Journal of Autism and Developmental Disorders, 41*(5), 618–627.

Lyall, K., Pauls, D. L., Spiegelman, D., Ascherio, A., & Santangelo, S. L. (2012). Pregnancy complications and obstetric suboptimality in association with autism spectrum disorders in children of the Nurses' Health Study II. *Autism Research, 5*(1), 21–30.

MacKinnon, D. P., Fairchild, A. J., & Fritz, M. S. (2007). Mediation analysis. *Annual Review of Psychology, 58*, 593–614.

Maimburg, R. D., & Vaeth, M. (2006). Perinatal risk factors and infantile autism. *Acta Psychiatrica Scandinavia, 114*(4), 257–264.

Malaviya, M., Husain, R., & Seth, P. K. (1993). Perinatal effects of two pyrethroid insecticides on brain neurotransmitter function in the neonatal rat. *Veterinary and Human Toxicology, 35*(2), 119–122.

Malm, H. (2012). Prenatal exposure to selective serotonin reuptake inhibitors and infant outcome. *Therapeutic Drug Monitoring, 34*(6), 607–614.

Mann, J. R., McDermott, S., Bao, H., Hardin, J., & Gregg, A. (2010). Pre-eclampsia, birth weight, and autism spectrum disorders. *Journal of Autism and Developmental Disorders, 40*(5), 548–554.

Mason-Brothers, A., Ritvo, E. R., Pingree, C., Petersen, P. B., Jenson, W. R., McMahon, W. M., … Ritvo, A. (1990). The UCLA-University of Utah epidemiologic survey of autism:

Prenatal, perinatal, and postnatal factors. *Pediatrics*, *86*(4), 514–519.

Matsuishi, T., Yamashita, Y., Ohtani, Y., Ornitz, E., Kuriya, N., Murakami, Y.,... Yamashita, F. (1999). Brief report: Incidence of and risk factors for autistic disorder in neonatal intensive care unit survivors. *Journal of Autism and Developmental Disorders*, *29*(2), 161–166.

Mazumdar, S., Liu, K. Y., Susser, E., & Bearman, P. (2012). The disappearing seasonality of autism conceptions in California. *PLoS One*, *7*(7), e41265

Meeker, J. D., & Ferguson, K. K. (2011). Relationship between urinary phthalate and bisphenol a concentrations and serum thyroid measures in U.S. adults and adolescents from the National Health and Nutrition Examination Survey (NHANES) 2007–2008. *Environmental Health Perspectives*, *119*(10), 1396–1402.

Melzer, D., Rice, N. E., Lewis, C., Henley, W. E., & Galloway, T. S. (2010). Association of urinary bisphenol A concentration with heart disease: Evidence from NHANES 2003/06. *PLoS One*, *5*(1), e8673.

Middleton, F. A., Varlinskaya, E. I., & Mooney, S. M. (2012). Molecular substrates of social avoidance seen following prenatal ethanol exposure and its reversal by social enrichment. *Developmental Neuroscience*, *34*(2–3), 115–128.

Miles, J. H., Takahashi, T. N., Haber, A., & Hadden, L. (2003). Autism families with a high incidence of alcoholism. *Journal of Autism and Developmental Disorders*, *33*(4), 403–415.

Milman, N., Byg, K. E., Hvas, A. M., Bergholt, T., & Eriksen, L. (2006). Erythrocyte folate, plasma folate and plasma homocysteine during normal pregnancy and postpartum: A longitudinal study comprising 404 Danish women. *European Journal of Haematology*, *76*(3), 200–205.

Miodovnik, A., Engel, S. M., Zhu, C. B., Ye, X. Y., Soorya, L. V., Silva, M. J.,... Wolff, M. S. (2011). Endocrine disruptors and childhood social impairment. *Neurotoxicology*, *32*(2), 261–267.

Moore, S. J., Turnpenny, P., Quinn, A., Glover, S., Lloyd, D. J., Montgomery, T., & Dean, J. C. (2000). A clinical study of 57 children with fetal anticonvulsant syndromes. *Journal of Medical Genetics*, *37*(7), 489–497.

Mouridsen, S. E., Nielsen, S., Rich, B., & Isager, T. (1994). Season of birth in infantile autism and other types of childhood psychoses. *Child Psychiatry & Human Development*, *25*(1), 31–43.

MRC Vitamin Study Research Group. (1991). Prevention of neural tube defects: Results of the Medical Research Council Vitamin Study. *The Lancet*, *338*(8760), 131–137.

Muneoka, K., Ogawa, T., Kamei, K., Mimura, Y., Kato, H., & Takigawa, M. (2001). Nicotine exposure during pregnancy is a factor which influences serotonin transporter density in the rat brain. *European Journal of Pharmacology*, *411*(3), 279–282.

Nanson, J. L. (1992). Autism in fetal alcohol syndrome: A report of six cases. *Alcohol: Clinical and Experimental Research*, *16*(3), 558–565.

National Research Council, Committee on the Toxicological Effects of Methylmercury. (2000). *Toxicological effects of methylmercury*. Washington, DC: National Academies Press.

Needleman, H. L., & Leviton, A. (1979). Neurologic effects of exposure to lead. *Journal of Pediatrics*, *94*(3), 505–506.

Nijmeijer, J. S., Hartman, C. A., Rommelse, N. N., Altink, M. E., Buschgens, C. J., Fliers, E. A.,... Hoekstra, P. J. (2010). Perinatal risk factors interacting with catechol O-methyltransferase and the serotonin transporter gene predict ASD symptoms in children with ADHD. *Journal of Child Psychology and Psychiatry*, *51*(11), 1242–1250.

Norman, E. H., Hertz-Picciotto, I., Salmen, D. A., & Ward, T. H. (1997). Childhood lead poisoning and vinyl miniblind exposure. *Archives of Pediatrics and Adolescent Medicine*, *151*(10), 1033–1037.

O'Roak, B. J., Vives, L., Girirajan, S., Karakoc, E., Krumm, N., Coe, B. P.,... Eichler, E. E. (2012). Sporadic autism exomes reveal a highly interconnected protein network of de novo mutations. *Nature*, *485*(7397), 246–250.

O'Rourke, K. M., Redlinger, T. E., & Waller, D. K. (2000). Declining levels of erythrocyte folate during the postpartum period among Hispanic women living on the Texas-Mexico border. *Journal of Women's Health and Gender-Based Medicine*, *9*(4), 397–403.

Oken, E., & Bellinger, D. C. (2008). Fish consumption, methylmercury and child neurodevelopment. *Current Opinion in Pediatrics*, *20*(2), 178–183.

Palmer, R. F., Blanchard, S., & Wood, R. (2009). Proximity to point sources of environmental mercury release as a predictor of autism prevalence. *Health Place*, *15*(1), 18–24.

Park, H. Y., Hertz-Picciotto, I., Sovcikova, E., Kocan, A., Drobna, B., & Trnovec, T. (2010). Neurodevelopmental toxicity of prenatal polychlorinated biphenyls (PCBs) by chemical structure and activity: A birth cohort study. *Environmental Health*, *9*, 51.

Petersen, M. L., Sinisi, S. E., & van der Laan, M. J. (2006). Estimation of direct causal effects. *Epidemiology*, *17*(3), 276–284.

Picciano, M. F. (2003). Pregnancy and lactation: Physiological adjustments, nutritional requirements and the role of dietary supplements. *Journal of Nutrition*, *133*(6), 1997S–2002S.

Piven, J., Chase, G. A., Landa, R., Wzorek, M., Gayle, J., Cloud, D., & Folstein, S. (1991). Psychiatric disorders in the parents of autistic individuals. *Journal of the American Academy of Child & Adolescent Psychiatry*, *30*(3), 471–478.

Piven, J., Simon, J., Chase, G. A., Wzorek, M., Landa, R., Gayle, J., & Folstein, S. (1993). The etiology of autism: Pre-, peri- and neonatal factors. *Journal of the American Academy of Child & Adolescent Psychiatry*, *32*(6), 1256–1263.

Qazi, G. (2011). Obstetric and perinatal outcome of multiple pregnancy. *Journal of College of Physicians and Surgeons Pakistan*, *21*(3), 142–145.

Rai, D., Lee, B. K., Dalman, C., Golding, J., Lewis, G., & Magnusson, C. (2013). Parental depression, maternal antidepressant use during pregnancy, and risk of autism spectrum disorders: Population based case-control study. *British Medical Journal*, *346*, f2059.

Rasalam, A. D., Hailey, H., Williams, J. H., Moore, S. J., Turnpenny, P. D., Lloyd, D. J., Dean, J. C. (2005). Characteristics of fetal anticonvulsant syndrome associated autistic disorder. *Developmental Medicine & Child Neurology*, *47*(8), 551–555.

Rauh, V., Arunajadai, S., Horton, M., Perera, F., Hoepner, L., Barr, D. B., & Whyatt, R. (2011). Seven-year neurodevelopmental scores and prenatal exposure to chlorpyrifos, a common agricultural pesticide. *Environmental Health Perspectives*, *119*(8), 1196–1201.

Rauh, V. A., Garfinkel, R., Perera, F. P., Andrews, H. F., Hoepner, L., Barr, D. B., . . . Whyatt, R. W. (2006). Impact of prenatal chlorpyrifos exposure on neurodevelopment in the first 3 years of life among inner-city children. *Pediatrics*, *118*(6), e1845–e1859.

Reik, W., & Walter, J. (2001). Genomic imprinting: Parental influence on the genome. *Nature Reviews Genetics*, *2*(1), 21–32.

Ren, X. M., & Guo, L. H. (2012). Assessment of the binding of hydroxylated polybrominated diphenyl ethers to thyroid hormone transport proteins using a site-specific fluorescence probe. *Environmental Science & Technology*, *46*(8), 4633–4640.

Roberts, A., Lyall, K., Hart, J. E., Laden, F., Just, A. C., Bobb, J. F., . . . Weisskopf, M. G. (2013). Perinatal air pollutant exposures and autism spectrum disorder in the children of Nurses' Health Study II participants. *Environmental Health Perspectives*, *121*(8), 978–984.

Roberts, E. M., English, P. B., Grether, J. K., Windham, G. C., Somberg, L., & Wolff, C. (2007). Maternal residence near agricultural pesticide applications and autism spectrum disorders among children in the California Central Valley. *Environmental Health Perspectives*, *115*(10), 1482–1489.

Robins, J. M., & Greenland, S. (1992). Identifiability and exchangeability for direct and indirect effects. *Epidemiology*, *3*(2), 143–155.

Rodier, P. M., Ingram, J. L., Tisdale, B., Nelson, S., & Romano, J. (1996). Embryological origin for autism: Developmental anomalies of the cranial nerve motor nuclei. *Journal of Comparative Neurology*, *370*(2), 247–261.

Roman, G. C. (2007). Autism: Transient in utero hypothyroxinemia related to maternal flavonoid ingestion during pregnancy and to other environmental antithyroid agents. *Journal of the Neurological Sciences*, *262*(1–2), 15–26.

Rose, M., Bennett, D. H., Bergman, A., Fangstrom, B., Pessah, I. N., & Hertz-Picciotto, I. (2010). PBDEs in 2-5 year-old children from california and associations with diet and indoor environment. *Environmental Science & Technology*, *44*(7), 2648–2653.

Roy, T. S., & Sabherwal, U. (1998). Effects of gestational nicotine exposure on hippocampal morphology. *Neurotoxicology and Teratology*, *20*(4), 465–473.

Roza, S. J., van Batenburg-Eddes, T., Steegers, E. A., Jaddoe, V. W., Mackenbach, J. P., Hofman, A., . . . Tiemeier, H. (2010). Maternal folic acid supplement use in early pregnancy and child behavioural problems: The Generation R study. *British Journal of Nutrition*, *103*(3), 445–452.

Roze, E., Meijer, L., Bakker, A., Van Braeckel, K. N., Sauer, P. J., & Bos, A. F. (2009). Prenatal exposure to organohalogens, including brominated flame retardants, influences motor, cognitive, and behavioral performance at school age. *Environmental Health Perspectives*, *117*(12), 1953–1958.

Sato, A., Otsu, E., Negishi, H., Utsunomiya, T., & Arima, T. (2007). Aberrant DNA methylation of imprinted loci in superovulated oocytes. *Human Reproduction*, *22*(1), 26–35.

Schanen, N. C. (2006). Epigenetics of autism spectrum disorders. *Human Molecular Genetics*, *15* (Spec. No. 2), R138–R150.

Schlotz, W., Jones, A., Phillips, D. I., Gale, C. R., Robinson, S. M., & Godfrey, K. M. (2010). Lower maternal folate status in early pregnancy is associated with childhood hyperactivity and peer problems in offspring. *Journal of Child Psychology and Psychiatry*, *51*(5), 594–602.

Schmidt, R. J., Hansen, R. L., Hartiala, J., Allayee, H., Schmidt, L. C., Tancredi, D. J., . . . Hertz-Picciotto, I. (2011). Prenatal vitamins, one-carbon metabolism gene variants, and risk for autism. *Epidemiology*, *22*(4), 476–485.

Schmidt, R. J., Tancredi, D. J., Ozonoff, S., Hansen, R. L., Hartiala, J., Allayee, H. (2012). Maternal periconceptional folic acid intake and risk of autism spectrum disorders and developmental delay in the CHARGE (CHildhood Autism Risks from Genetics and Environment) case-control study. *American Journal of Clinical Nutrition*, *96*(1), 80–89.

Shachar, B. Z., & Lyell, D. J. (2012). Interpregnancy interval and obstetrical complications. *Obstetrical and Gynecological Survey*, *67*(9), 584–596.

Shafer, T. J., Meyer, D. A., & Crofton, K. M. (2005). Developmental neurotoxicity of pyrethroid insecticides: Critical review and future research needs. *Environmental Health Perspectives*, *113*(2), 123–136.

Sharpe, R. M. (2008). "Additional" effects of phthalate mixtures on fetal testosterone production. *Toxicological Sciences*, *105*(1), 1–4.

Shelton, J. F., Hertz-Picciotto, I., & Pessah, I. N. (2012). Tipping the balance of autism risk: Potential mechanisms linking pesticides and autism. *Environmental Health Perspectives*, *120*(7), 944–951.

Shi, L., Fatemi, S. H., Sidwell, R. W., & Patterson, P. H. (2003). Maternal influenza infection causes marked behavioral and pharmacological changes in the offspring. *Journal of Neuroscience*, *23*(1), 297–302.

Silver, M. K., O'Neill, M. S., Sowers, M. R., & Park, S. K. (2011). Urinary bisphenol A and type-2 diabetes in U.S. adults: Data from NHANES 2003–2008. *PLoS One*, *6*(10), e26868.

Smith, S. E., Li, J., Garbett, K., Mirnics, K., & Patterson, P. H. (2007). Maternal immune activation alters fetal brain development through interleukin-6. *Journal of Neuroscience*, *27*(40), 10695–10702.

Smits, L. J., & Essed, G. G. (2001). Short interpregnancy intervals and unfavourable pregnancy outcome: Role of folate depletion. *The Lancet*, *358*(9298), 2074–2077.

SSRI antidepressants: Altered psychomotor development following exposure in utero? (2013). *Prescrire International*, *22*(135), 43–44.

Stansfeld, S. A., & Matheson, M. P. (2003). Noise pollution: Non-auditory effects on health. *British Medical Bulletin*, *68*, 243–257.

Steegers-Theunissen, R. P., Obermann-Borst, S. A., Kremer, D., Lindemans, J., Siebel, C., Steegers, E. A., . . . Heijmans, B. T. (2009). Periconceptional maternal folic acid use of 400 microg per day is related to increased methylation of the IGF2 gene in the very young child. *PLoS One*, *4*(11), e7845.

Steffenburg, S., Gillberg, C., Hellgren, L., Andersson, L., Gillberg, I. C., Jakobsson, G., & Bohman, M. (1989). A twin study of autism in Denmark, Finland, Iceland, Norway and Sweden. *Journal of Child Psychology and Psychiatry, 30*(3), 405–416.

Stein, D., Weizman, A., Ring, A., & Barak, Y. (2006). Obstetric complications in individuals diagnosed with autism and in healthy controls. *Comprehensive Psychiatry, 47*(1), 69–75.

Stromland, K., Nordin, V., Miller, M., Akerstrom, B., & Gillberg, C. (1994). Autism in thalidomide embryopathy: A population study. *Developmental Medicine & Child Neurology, 36*(4), 351–356.

Surén, P., Roth, C., Bresnahan, M., Haugen, M., Hornig, M., Hirtz, D., . . . Stoltenberg, C. (2013). Association between maternal use of folic acid supplements and risk of autism spectrum disorders in children. *JAMA, 309*(6), 570–577.

Suvorov, A., Girard, S., Lachapelle, S., Abdelouahab, N., Sebire, G., & Takser, L. (2009). Perinatal exposure to low-dose BDE-47, an emergent environmental contaminant, causes hyperactivity in rat offspring. *Neonatology, 95*(3), 203–209.

Sweeten, T. L., Posey, D. J., & McDougle, C. J. (2004). Brief report: Autistic disorder in three children with cytomegalovirus infection. *Journal of Autism and Developmental Disorders, 34*(5), 583–586.

Teitelbaum, S. L., Mervish, N., Moshier, E. L., Vangeepuram, N., Galvez, M. P., Calafat, A. M., . . . Wolff, M. S. (2012). Associations between phthalate metabolite urinary concentrations and body size measures in New York City children. *Environmental Research, 112*, 186–193.

Testa, C., Nuti, F., Hayek, J., De Felice, C., Chelli, M., Rovero, P., Latini, G., & Papini, A. M. (2012). Di-(2-ethylhexyl) phthalate and autism spectrum disorders. *ASN Neuro, 4*(4), 223–229.

Thomas, P., Zahorodny, W., Peng, B., Kim, S., Jani, N., Halperin, W., & Brimacombe, M. (2011). The association of autism diagnosis with socioeconomic status. *Autism, 16*(2), 201–213.

Trasande, L., Attina, T. M., & Blustein, J. (2012). Association between urinary bisphenol A concentration and obesity prevalence in children and adolescents. *JAMA, 308*(11), 1113–1121.

U.S. Environmental Protection Agency. (2002). *Organophosphate pesticides: Revised cumulative risk assessment*. Retrieved from http://www.epa.gov/opp00001/cumulative/rra-op/

U.S. Environmental Protection Agency. (2010, August). *Reevaluation: Pyrethrins and pyrethroids. Pesticides: Regulating pesticides*. Retrieved from http://www.epa.gov/oppsrrd1/reevaluation/pyrethroids-pyrethrins.html

VanderWeele, T. J. (2009). Marginal structural models for the estimation of direct and indirect effects. *Epidemiology, 20*(1), 18–26.

van Eijsden, M., Smits, L. J., van der Wal, M. F., & Bonsel, G. J. (2008). Association between short interpregnancy intervals and term birth weight: The role of folate depletion. *American Journal of Clinical Nutrition, 88*(1), 147–153.

van Rooij, I. A., Wegerif, M. J., Roelofs, H. M., Peters, W. H., Kuijpers-Jagtman, A. M., Zielhuis, G. A., . . . Steegers-Theunissen, R. P. (2001). Smoking, genetic polymorphisms in biotransformation enzymes, and nonsyndromic oral

clefting: A gene-environment interaction. *Epidemiology, 12*(5), 502–507.

Viberg, H., Mundy, W., & Eriksson, P. (2008). Neonatal exposure to decabrominated diphenyl ether (PBDE 209) results in changes in BDNF, CaMKII and GAP-43, biochemical substrates of neuronal survival, growth, and synaptogenesis. *Neurotoxicology, 29*(1), 152–159.

Volk, H. E., Hertz-Picciotto, I., Delwiche, L., Lurmann, F., & McConnell, R. (2011). Residential proximity to freeways and autism in the CHARGE study. *Environmental Health Perspectives, 119*(6), 873–877.

Volk, H. E., Lurmann, F., Penfold, B., Hertz-Picciotto, I., & McConnell, R. (2013). Traffic related air pollution, particulate matter, and autism. *Archives of General Psychiatry*, 1–7.

Wacholder, S., Silverman, D. T., McLaughlin, J. K., & Mandel, J. S. (1992). Selection of controls in case-control studies. II. Types of controls. *American Journal of Epidemiology, 135*(9), 1029–1041.

Wallace, A., Anderson G., & Dubrow, R. (2008). Obstetric and parental psychiatric variables as potential predictors of autism severity. *Journal of Autism and Developmental Disorders, 38*(8), 1542–1554.

Wayman, G., Yang, D., Bose, D. D., Lesiak, A., Ledoux, V., Bruun, D., Pessah, I. N., & Lein, P. J. (2012). PCB-95 promotes dendritic growth via ryanodine receptor-dependent mechanisms. *Environmental Health Perspectives, 120*(7), 997–1002.

Weiss, B. (2011). Endocrine disruptors as a threat to neurological function. *Journal of the Neurological Sciences, 305*(1–2), 11–21.

Whitehouse, A. J., Holt, B. J., Serralha, M., Holt, P. G., Hart, P. H., & Kusel, M. M. (2012). Maternal vitamin D levels and the autism phenotype among offspring. *Journal of Autism and Developmental Disorders, 43*(7), 1495–1504.

Wier, M. L., Yoshida, C. K., Odouli, R., Grether, J. K., & Croen, L. A. (2006). Congenital anomalies associated with autism spectrum disorders. *Developmental Medicine & Child Neurology, 48*(6), 500–507.

Williams, K., Helmer, M., Duncan, G. W., Peat, J. K., & Mellis, C. M. (2008). Perinatal and maternal risk factors for autism spectrum disorders in New South Wales, Australia. *Child: Care, Health and Development, 34*(2), 249–256.

Williams, G., Oliver, J. M., Allard, A., & Sears, L. (2003). Autism and associated medical and familial factors: A case control study. *Journal of Developmental and Physical Disabilities, 15*(4), 335–349.

Williams, G. M., O'Callaghan, M., Najman, J. M., Bor, W., Andersen, M. J., & Richards, D. (1998). Maternal cigarette smoking and child psychiatric morbidity: A longitudinal study. *Pediatrics, 102*(1), e11.

Williams, M. K., Rundle, A., Holmes, D., Reyes, M., Hoepner, L. A., Barr, D. B., & Whyatt, R. M. (2008). Changes in pest infestation levels, self-reported pesticide use, and permethrin exposure during pregnancy after the 2000–2001 U.S. Environmental Protection Agency restriction of organophosphates. *Environmental Health Perspectives, 116*(12), 1681–1688. doi: 10.1289/ehp.11367 [doi]

Windham, G., Zhang, L., Gunier, R., Croen, L., & Grether, J. (2006). Autism spectrum disorders in relation to distribution of hazardous air pollutants in the San Francisco Bay area. *Environmental Health Perspectives, 114*(9), 1438–1444.

Wong, P. W., Joy, R. M., Albertson, T. E., Schantz, S. L., & Pessah, I. N. (1997). Ortho-substituted 2,2′,3,5′,6-pentachloro biphenyl (PCB 95) alters rat hippocampal ryanodine receptors and neuroplasticity in vitro: Evidence for altered hippocampal function. *Neurotoxicology, 18*(2), 443–456.

Woods, R., Vallero, R. O., Golub, M. S., Suarez, J. K., Ta, T. A., Yasui, D. H.,... LaSalle, J. M. (2012). Long-lived epigenetic interactions between perinatal PBDE exposure and Mecp2308 mutation. *Human Molecular Genetics, 21*(11), 2399–2411.

Yamashita, Y., Fujimoto, C., Nakajima, E., Isagai, T., & Matsuishi, T. (2003). Possible association between congenital cytomegalovirus infection and autistic disorder. *Journal of Autism and Developmental Disorders, 33*(4), 455–459.

Zajac, L., Sprecher, E., Landrigan, P. J., & Trasande, L. (2009). A systematic review of US state environmental legislation and regulation with regards to the prevention of neurodevelopmental disabilities and asthma. *Environmental Health, 8,* 9.

Zerbo, O., Iosif, A. M., Delwiche, L., Walker, C., & Hertz-Picciotto, I. (2011). Month of conception and risk of autism. *Epidemiology, 22*(4), 469–475.

Zerbo, O., Iosif, A. M., Walker, C., Ozonoff, S., Hansen, R. L., & Hertz-Picciotto, I. (2012). Is maternal influenza or fever during pregnancy associated with autism or developmental delays? Results from the CHARGE (CHildhood Autism Risks from Genetics and Environment) study. *Journal of Autism and Developmental Disorders, 43*(1), 25–33.

Zhang, X., Lv, C. C., Tian, J., Miao, R. J., Xi, W., Hertz-Picciotto, I., & Qi, L. (2010). Prenatal and perinatal risk factors for autism in China. *J Autism Dev Disord, 40*(11), 1311–1321.

Zota, A. R., Park, J.-S., Wang, Y., Petreas, M., Zoeller, R. T., & Woodruff, T. J. (2011). Polybrominated diphenyl ethers, hydroxylated polybrominated diphenyl ethers, and measures of thyroid function in second trimester pregnant women in California. *Environmental Science & Technology, 45*(18), 7896–7905.

Zwaigenbaum, L., Szatmari, P., Jones, M. B., Bryson, S. E., MacLean, J. E., Mahoney, W. J.,... Tuff L. (2002). Pregnancy and birth complications in autism and liability to the broader autism phenotype. *Journal of the American Academy of Child & Adolescent Psychiatry, 41*(5), 572–579.

CHAPTER 19

Biochemical Biomarkers for Autism Spectrum Disorder

GEORGE M. ANDERSON

INTRODUCTION

The behavioral, emotional, and cognitive symptoms presented by individuals categorized as having autism spectrum disorder (ASD) clearly indicate that central nervous system (CNS) functioning is altered in ASD. The early onset, pervasive nature, and chronicity of ASD also point directly to brain neurodevelopmental atypicality. Furthermore, twin and family studies strongly suggest that ASD has a genetic basis (Cook, 2001; Folstein & Piven, 1991; Lauritsen & Ewald, 2001; Lotspeich & Ciaranello, 1993; Rutter & Schopler, 1987; State & Levitt, 2011). Although the relative proportion of the genetic and environmental contributions to ASD risk has been the subject

of recent discussion and debate (Anderson, 2012; Grabrucker, 2012; Hallmayer et al. 2011; Szatmari, 2011), most researchers believe that genetic factors predominate.

Biochemical biomarker studies of ASD individuals have been undertaken in order to identify biochemical alterations that might advance the understanding of the atypical neurodevelopment seen in ASD. In addition, there is the promise that biochemical biomarkers might be useful in predicting risk and in subtyping. Most of the studies to date have examined neurochemical biomarkers related to neural transmission in the central and peripheral nervous systems. The search for neurochemical alterations and causes in ASD is given impetus by the rapid advance of basic neuroscience and the success of neuropharmacology in the relatively specific treatment of a range of neurological and psychiatric disorders and symptoms. Areas of increasing ASD biochemical biomarker research include the omics approach, as well as endocrine, oxidative stress, and immune-related measures. There is an increasing recognition that autism or ASD is polygenetic and heterogenetic, and that its neurobiology may be best approached by examining the component and continuous traits that combine in a particular individual to produce autism (Anderson & Cohen, 2002; Folstein & Rosen-Sheidley, 2001; McBride, Anderson, & Shapiro, 1996). Biochemical measures offer promising endophenotypes in themselves; their relationship to behavioral, cognitive, and neuroimaging endophenotypes are also worthy of investigation.

A wide range of biochemical systems has been examined. In this chapter, I first deal with neurochemical studies measuring levels of neurotransmitters, their metabolites, and associated enzymes in blood, urine, and cerebrospinal fluid (CSF). Separate sections cover serotonin, dopamine, and stress response systems (including the central noradrenergic, sympathoadrenomedullary, and the hypothalamic-pituitary-adrenal axis systems). Following sections review research on melatonin, sex hormones, neuropeptides including oxytocin, amino acids and acetylcholine, purines and related compounds, immune-related measures, oxidative stress/redox status, and omics research.

A number of prior reviews have covered the biochemical research of autism, with a tendency to focus on the neurochemical (Anderson, 2002; Anderson, Horne, Chatterjee, & Cohen, 1990; Cohen & Young, 1977; Cook, 1990; DeMyer, Hingtgen, & Jackson, 1981; McBride, Anderson, & Mann, 1990; Ritvo, 1977; J. G. Young, Kavanagh, Anderson, Shaywitz, & Cohen, 1982; Yuwiler, Geller, & Ritvo, 1985). More recent reviews or theoretical considerations of the broad area of biochemical biomarkers in autism/ASD are also available (Hu, 2012; Mizejewski, 2012; Ratajczak, 2011; Veenstra-VanderWeele & Blakely, 2012; Walsh, Elsabbagh, Bolton, & Singh, 2011;

Wang, Angley, Gerber, & Sorich, 2011; Yerys & Pennington, 2011).

SEROTONIN

Serotonin (5-hydroxytryptamine; 5-HT) is an important neurotransmitter in the central nervous system, where it is involved in controlling a number of important functions and behaviors, including sleep, mood, body temperature, appetite, and hormone release (Iverson & Iverson, 1981; Lucki, 1998). Cell bodies of most central neurons utilizing 5-HT as a neurotransmitter are located in the midbrain; however, the neurons make connections throughout the brain and spinal cord. Serotonin is synthesized from its amino acid precursor, tryptophan (TRP), by hydroxylation and decarboxylation; it is predominately metabolized to 5-hydroxyindoleacetic acid (5-HIAA) by the enzyme monoamine oxidase (MAO).

Serotonin is the neurotransmitter that has stimulated the most neurochemical research in autism. Initial interest in the possible role of 5-HT in autism arose from a consideration of its role in perception. The powerful effects of serotonergic hallucinogens, such as lysergic acid diethylamide (LSD) and psilocybin, stimulated speculation around 5-HT and led to early studies of platelet 5-HT in autism (Schain & Freedman, 1961). Although much of the work has focused on the platelet hyperserotonemia of autism, a number of other observations have contributed to the increasing interest in 5-HT. Reports of a critical role for 5-HT during embryogenesis (Bonnin et al., 2011; Buznikov, 1984) and in the development of the central nervous system (Janusonis, Gluncic, & Rakic, 2004; Lauder, 1990; Waage-Baudet et al., 2003; Whitaker-Azmitia, 2001; Whitaker-Azmitia, Druse, Walker, & Lauder, 1996; Zhou, Auerbach, & Azmitia, 1987) have made 5-HT of special interest in neurodevelopmental disorders. An increasing appreciation of 5-HT's growth factor–like actions in the periphery (Anderson, Cook, & Blakely, 2009; Berger, Gray, & Roth, 2009; Brand & Anderson, 2011), coupled with observations of brain and body overgrowth in ASD (Chawarska et al., 2011), also contribute to the continued interest.

Early studies of serotonergic drugs as possible therapeutic agents were not particularly promising. The 5-HT-releasing agent fenfluramine, despite initial enthusiasm, also has not been found to be of much use in treating autistic symptoms. However, the wide use of 5-HT selective reuptake inhibitors (SSRIs) in ASD and a number of small treatment studies of SSRIs—including clomipramine, fluvoxamine, and fluoxetine—have suggested that manipulation of the serotonergic system might be of some benefit (Posey & McDougle, 2000). Although a large multicenter study did not find citalopram to be useful for treating irritability in ASD (King et al., 2009), patient selection criteria, target symptoms, and outcome measures might be crucial to determining whether the SSRIs are clinically useful.

To assess central and peripheral 5-HT function in autism, researchers have measured CSF and urine levels of the major metabolite of 5-HT, 5-HIAA, and blood and urine levels of 5-HT itself. Initial brain imaging studies attempted to examine 5-HT synthesis rates in autism (Chugani et al., 1999); however methodological issues (Shoaf et al., 2000) make interpretation of reported differences difficult. The neurochemical studies, along with those examining the metabolism as well as the behavioral and neuroendocrine effects of the 5-HT precursors, TRP and 5-hydroxytryptophan (5-HTP), are reviewed next.

Blood 5-HT

The greatest number of 5-HT studies in autism concern the measurement of blood levels of 5-HT. A general consensus has been reached, dating from Schain and Freedman's original observation in 1961, that group mean levels of blood (platelet) 5-HT are increased in autism (McBride et al., 1998). Much of the 5-HT-related research in autism has been directed toward further characterizing the elevation and attempting to elucidate the causes. In a more recent study of a large and relatively homogeneous group, it was reported that platelet 5-HT is bimodally distributed in autism and pervasive developmental disorder (PDD; Mulder et al., 2004). It now appears that hyperserotonemia might be able to be rationally defined and that approximately half of individuals with ASD can be placed in this category. Careful examination of those hyperserotonemic individuals in the upper mode should facilitate research in this area. The association of the hyperserotonemia with specific aspects of the ASD phenotype is also warranted (Kolevzon et al., 2010; Leventhal, Cook, Morford, Ravitz, & Freedman, 1990).

A major line of research has focused on trying to identify the physiological mechanism of the elevation. Serotonin in blood derives from that synthesized in the wall of the gut; it is stored in platelets while circulating and is catabolized to 5-HIAA by MAO after uptake into lung, liver, and capillary endothelium (Anderson, Stevenson, & Cohen, 1987). These aspects of blood 5-HT, and the factor(s) that might cause the increase in autism, have been discussed in detail (Anderson, 2002; Anderson et al., 1990; Hanley, Stahl, & Freedman, 1977; Veenstra-VanderWeele & Anderson, 2010).

Research on the platelet storage and handling of 5-HT has been extensive. At first it appeared that there might be differences between normal and autistic subjects in terms of the number of platelets (Ritvo et al., 1970) and in the platelet efflux of 5-HT (Boullin, Coleman, O'Brien, & Rimland, 1971). However, it appears that these platelet indices, as well as the number of platelet 5-HT uptake sites, are normal in autism (Anderson, Minderaa, van Bentem, Volkmar, & Cohen, 1984; Boullin et al., 1982; Yuwiler et al., 1975). A study of hyperserotonemic relatives of children with autism found some suggestive differences in platelet 5-HT uptake and the numbers of platelet 5-HT-type 2 receptors in subgroups of the relatives (Cook et al., 1993). Taken together, studies on platelet uptake indicate that transport rates do not differ (Anderson et al., 1990). However, a neuroimaging report of decreased central serotonin transporter (SERT) binding (Nakamura et al., 2010), a human SERT gain of function mutation with associated autism-related behaviors (Ozaki et al., 2003), genetic associations with SERT variants (Prasad, Steiner, Sutcliffe, & Blakely, 2009; Sutcliffe et al., 2005), and findings from an animal gain of function model (Veenstra-VanderWeele et al., 2012) have all increased interest in the possible role of the transporter in ASD.

It should also be noted that no differences in platelet levels of the catabolic enzyme MAO have been found in autism (Giller et al., 1980; J. G. Young et al., 1982). Unfortunately, because 5-HT is principally metabolized by MAO-A rather than the form found in platelets (MAO-B), these studies of MAO are not definitive. Studies of 5-HT synthesis include those examining urine levels of 5-HIAA and 5-HT, and those in which TRP was administered.

Urine 5-HIAA and 5-HT

Because most 5-HT produced in the body is eventually metabolized to and excreted as 5-HIAA (Udenfriend, Titus, Weissbach, & Peterson, 1959), urine levels of 5-HIAA are a good indicator of the rate of 5-HT synthesis, at least as long as routes of metabolism and elimination are not altered significantly. There have been relatively few studies of urine 5-HIAA excretion in autistic subjects. One major study reported elevated levels (6.08 versus 3.23 mg/day) of 5-HIAA in autistic subjects compared to mentally retarded individuals (Hanley et al., 1977). In addition, a greater increase in 5-HIAA was seen for autistic subjects after a TRP load (12.9 versus 6.5 mg/day). Two previous studies (Partington, Tu, & Wong, 1973; Schain & Freedman, 1961) had not detected differences in urine 5-HIAA excretion between autistic and typically developing individuals, although in one of the studies hyperserotonemic autistic subjects did have elevated urine 5-HIAA levels. Urinary excretion of 5-HIAA in a group of individuals with autism who were not receiving medication was observed to be very similar to that seen in an age-matched control group (Minderaa, Anderson, Volkmar, Akkerhuis, & Cohen, 1987). Furthermore, no correlation between urine 5-HIAA and whole blood 5-HT levels was observed in autistic or typically developing subjects, although hyperserotonemic

autistic individuals may have had slightly higher urine levels of 5-HIAA compared to other autistic subjects or to controls. These data regarding 5-HIAA suggest that normal amounts of 5-HT are produced in autistic individuals. In a subsequent study, no differences in urinary excretion of 5-HT itself were seen between autistic and control subjects (Anderson, Minderaa, Cho, Volkmar, & Cohen, 1989), and in other related studies, no group differences were seen for free plasma levels of 5-HT (Anderson, Hertzig, & McBride, 2012; Cook, Leventhal, & Freedman, 1988). Taken together, these observations indicate that the platelet of autistic individuals is exposed to normal levels of 5-HT. This in turn suggests that there is an alteration in the platelet's handling of 5-HT, at least in the hyperserotonemic subgroup.

Tryptophan Metabolism

Tryptophan, an essential amino acid, is the dietary precursor of 5-HT and of the vitamin nicotinic acid. It has been shown that the level of TRP in the brain is determined to some extent by plasma levels of free (nonprotein-bound) TRP. Hoshino, Yamamoto, et al. (1984) determined plasma free and total TRP levels and blood serotonin levels simultaneously and reported that both plasma free TRP and blood 5-HT levels were significantly higher in autistic children than in normal control subjects. In addition, there tended to be a significant correlation between the plasma free TRP level and several clinical rating scales in autistic children, although there was no correlation between blood 5-HT and free TRP levels in these children. In contrast, Anderson, Volkmar, et al. (1987) reported that whole blood TRP concentrations tended to be slightly (but not significantly) lower in unmediated autistics compared to nor mal controls, while Takatsu, Onizawa, and Nakahato (1965) had previously reported that total plasma TRP was reduced in autism.

Several investigators have attempted to demonstrate metabolic alterations in the serotonin metabolism of autistic children by administering large oral doses of L-tryptophan (L-TRP). Schain and Freedman (1961) performed TRP (one gram) loading tests in autistic and mildly intellectually disabled children but found no differences in blood 5-HT and urinary 5-HIAA concentration between the two groups. On the other hand, Hanley et al. (1977) reported that TRP (1g) loading raised urinary 5-HT levels in hyperserotonemic autistic children but lowered urinary 5-HT levels in mildly retarded children having normal levels of blood serotonin. In both groups the TRP load caused a slight decrease of blood 5-HT and a marked increase of urinary 5-HIAA excretion. In a later study (Cook et al., 1992), an oral TRP load was not observed to increase blood 5-HT levels in relatives of autistic individuals. However, depletion of plasma TRP by the use of an amino acid drink has been reported to exacerbate symptoms in autism (McDougle et al., 1996).

Neuroendocrine Studies of Serotonergic Functioning

Several groups (Hoshino et al., 1983; Hoshino, Tachibana, et al., 1984; Sverd, Kupretz, Winsberg, Hurwic, & Becker, 1978) have examined the effect of L-5-HTP on serotonin metabolism and hypothalamo-pituitary function in autistic children. Hoshino and colleagues (Hoshino et al., 1983; Hoshino, Tachibana, et al., 1984) administered L-5-HTP to autistic children and normal controls and measured chronological changes of blood serotonin, plasma human growth hormone (HGH), and prolactin (PRL). After loading, blood serotonin showed a smaller increase compared with normal controls, although the baseline levels of blood serotonin were significantly higher in autistic children. The levels of plasma HGH observed after 5-HTP-stimulated release were similar in the groups studied, as were baseline HGH concentrations. However, lower baseline levels of prolactin and a blunted prolactin response to 5-HTP were present in the autistic group (Hoshino et al., 1983; Hoshino, Tachibana, et al., 1984). These results might be explained on the basis of diminished central serotonergic functioning or enhanced activity of tuberoinfundibular dopamine neurons known to exert a powerful inhibitory control on prolactin release. In contrast, other researchers have found normal baseline levels of plasma prolactin and have observed an apparently normal increase in prolactin after chronic treatment with dopamine blockers (Anderson et al., 2007; Minderaa et al., 1989). In a detailed study of the neuroendocrine response to the serotonergic agent fenfluramine, McBride and colleagues (1989) found that autistic subjects had a blunted prolactin response (with normal baseline prolactin levels). This was interpreted to suggest that central 5-HT type-2 receptor functioning might be reduced in autism. Simultaneous studies of the responsivity of the platelet 5-HT type-2 receptor also showed a blunted response in the autistic subjects. These findings are consistent with two recent neuroimaging studies: a SPECT study in adults with Asperger's syndrome (Murphy et al., 2006) and a PET study in parents of children with autism (J. Goldberg et al., 2009) both have described lower central 5-HT type-2 receptor binding.

CSF 5-HIAA

Levels of 5-HIAA and other monoamine metabolites have been widely measured in CSF in order to estimate brain turnover of the parent neurotransmitters (Garelis, Young, Lal, & Sourkes, 1974). Nearly all 5-HT is metabolized to 5-HIAA before elimination from the brain, and a substantial route for egress of brain 5-HIAA is through the CSF (Aizenstein & Korf, 1979; Meek & Neff, 1973). It is clear that certain drugs and treatments known to affect brain 5-HT turnover have corresponding effects on levels of CSF 5-HIAA (Kirwin et al., 1997; S. N. Young, Anderson, & Purdy, 1980), and it has been shown that CSF 5-HIAA is not contaminated with 5-HT or 5-HIAA arising elsewhere in the body. The invasiveness of the lumbar puncture required has limited the number of studies carried out with autistic individuals. Three studies have been performed using probenecid to block the transport of 5-HIAA and other acidic compounds out of CSF. In two of the studies, levels of 5-HIAA were observed to be similar (Cohen, Shaywitz, Johnson, & Bowers, 1974) or slightly lower (Cohen, Caparulo, Shaywitz, & Bowers, 1977) in autistic subjects compared to nonautistic psychotic children. In a third probenecid study, no control groups were used; however, a few of the autistic subjects did not show the expected increase in 5-HIAA after probenecid administration (Winsberg, Sverd, Castells, Hurwic, & Perel, 1980). In studies of baseline levels of CSF 5-HIAA, no significant differences have been observed between autistic and control subjects (C. Gillberg & Svennerholm, 1987; C. Gillberg, Svennerholm, & Hamilton-Hellberg, 1983; Narayan, Srinath, Anderson, & Meundi, 1993). In summary, the CSF studies suggest that if central 5-HT metabolism is altered in autism, the alteration does not involve a widespread or marked change in 5-HT turnover.

DOPAMINE

The cell bodies of most dopamine (DA) containing neurons lie in the midbrain. Dopaminergic neurons appear to be especially important in the control of motor function, in cognition, and in regulating hormone release. Dopamine is synthesized from the dietary amino acids, phenylalanine or tyrosine, by hydroxylation and decarboxylation. Dopamine can be subsequently converted to norepinephrine and epinephrine by the action of the enzymes dopamine-β-hydroxylase and phenylethanolamine-N-methyltransferase. Once released from the neuron, DA is enzymatically degraded by MAO and catechol-O-methyltransferase (COMT) to homovanillic acid (HVA) and 3,4-dihydroxyphenylacetic acid (DOPAC).

The DA blockers (the neuroleptics or major tranquilizers) have been observed to be effective in treating some aspects of autism. This, and the fact that certain symptoms of autism—such as stereotypies and hyperactivity—can be induced in animals by increasing DA function, has suggested that central DA neurons may be overactive in autism. Central dopamine function has been assessed in humans by several methods, including postmortem measurements of DA, its metabolites, and receptors in brain tissue; positron emission tomography (PET scanning); CSF measurements

of HVA and DOPAC; and blood or urine measures of DA, HVA, and DOPAC.

CSF HVA

Studies in humans and in animals have indicated that changes in central dopamine turnover are reflected to some extent in CSF levels of the principal dopamine metabolite, HVA (Garelis et al., 1974). In previously discussed studies of CSF 5-HIAA in autistic individuals, measurements of HVA also were made. In two of the three studies using probenecid to block transport of the acid metabolites out of CSF (Cohen et al., 1974; Cohen et al., 1977), no significant group differences were observed between autistic children and various comparison groups. Comparison groups included nonautistic psychotic, aphasic, motor disordered, and neurologically disordered (contrast) children. In both studies, CSF HVA did tend to be lower in autistic children compared to nonautistic psychotic children, and in one of the studies (Cohen et al., 1974), HVA values were reported to be lower in the more disturbed autistic individuals. A third study employing the probenecid technique did not include measurements made in comparison groups; however, the increases in CSF HVA seen after probenecid appeared normal (Winsberg et al., 1980).

In later CSF studies, probenecid was not administered. In a study carried out in Sweden, the baseline, unperturbed, concentrations of CSF HVA were observed to be elevated approximately 50% in the autistic group compared to an age- and sex-matched control group of neurologically disordered children (C. Gillberg et al., 1983; C. Gillberg & Svennerholm, 1987). However, two other studies of baseline CSF HVA in autism have not seen significant elevations in autistic individuals compared to controls (Narayan, Srinath, et al., 1993; Ross, Klykylo, & Anderson, 1985). This question of whether CSF levels are increased in autism has been the subject of debate (C. Gillberg, 1993; Narayan, Srinath, et al., 1993; Narayan, Anderson, & Srinath, 1993). Taken together, the CSF studies do not appear to provide strong support for the idea that central DA turnover is increased in autism.

Plasma and Urine Measures of Dopamine Function

Unfortunately, the relationship of peripheral measures of DA, HVA, and DOPAC to central DA function is tenuous at best. It has been estimated that approximately 25% of blood or urine HVA is of central origin (Elchisak, Polinsky, Ebert, Powers, & Kopin, 1978; Maas, Hattox, Greene, & Landis, 1980). On the other hand, peripheral DA itself is known to arise almost completely from the adrenal, kidney, and the sympathetic nervous system, rather than from the brain. In the one study of plasma HVA levels in autism, no differences were observed between unmedicated autistic subjects and normal controls (Minderaa et al., 1989). In two studies examining baseline plasma levels of prolactin, a hormone under powerful tonic inhibitory control by dopaminergic tuberoinfidibular neurons, no group differences have been seen (McBride et al., 1989; Minderaa et al., 1989). Although several groups have reported that the urinary excretion of HVA is increased in autism, in a large study of urinary DA and HVA no differences were observed between autistic and control groups in the rate of urinary excretion of these compounds (Minderaa et al., 1989). Studies of the catabolic enzyme COMT, which along with MAO converts DA to HVA, have found similar activities in red blood cells of autistic and control subjects (Giller et al., 1980; O'Brien, Semenuk, & Spector, 1976). A study of CSF levels of one form of tetrahydrobiopterin, a cofactor in the synthesis of DA, has found lower levels in autistic subjects (Tani, Fernell, Watanbe, Kanai, & Langstrom, 1994).

Neuroendocrine Studies of Dopamine Functioning

Ritvo et al. (1971) designed a small ($n = 4$) study to assess neurochemical, behavioral, and neuroendocrine effects of L-Dopa administration. Results indicated a significant decrease in blood 5-HT concentrations and a significant increase in platelet counts. Urinary excretion of 5-HIAA decreased significantly in one patient, and a similar trend was noted in others. However, no changes were observed in the clinical course of the disorder, the amount of motility disturbances (stereotypic behavior), percentages of rapid eye movement (REM) sleep time, or in measures of endocrine function (plasma LH and FSH levels). In a study of the effects of L-dope on the secretion of growth hormone (HGH), Realmuto and colleagues (Realmuto, Jensen, Reeve, & Garfinkel, 1990) found that, while autistic subjects had normal peak responses in plasma HGH, they had a delayed response compared to controls. As mentioned, normal baseline levels of prolactin and normal increase seen after dopamine-blockers in ASD also are consistent with normal functioning of the dopaminergic tuberinfindibular system (Anderson et al., 2007; Minderaa et al., 1989).

STRESS RESPONSE SYSTEM

The noradrenergic-sympatho-adrenomedullary system and the hypothalamic-pituitary-adrenal (HPA) axis are the two major components of the stress response system (Chrousos & Gold, 1992). The system is of interest in autism due to the hyperarousal, hyperactivity, and the overreactivity to novel situations often seen in autism. Most central norepinephrine-containing neurons have their cell bodies localized in one section of the hindbrain, the locus coeruleus. These neurons project in a diffuse manner to many areas of the brain and spinal cord and are crucial in processes related to arousal, anxiety, stress responses, and memory. Drugs that lessen central norepinephrine neuronal activity, such as clonidine, have been used to treat withdrawal symptoms (Redmond & Huang, 1979). Other agents that increase central noradrenergic functioning, such as yohimbine and desipramine, increase arousal or serve as antidepressants. Norepinephrine also serves as the major neurotransmitter in peripheral postganglionic sympathetic nervous neurons. These neurons serve to control autonomic functions and are balanced against cholinergic neurons that enervate the same organs. When sympathetic system activity predominates, the characteristic flight-or-fight response is elicited.

Functioning of the sympatho-adrenomedullary system has been assessed through measurements of norepinephrine (NE) and epinephrine (EPI) in plasma or urine. In addition, plasma

TABLE 19.1   Stress Response Systems in Autism/ASD: Sympatho-Adrenomedullary Function

Sample/ Measure	Finding[*]	Reference
Measures of Basal Functioning		
Urine		
Norepinephrine	NC	Launay et al., 1987; Martineau, Barthelemy, Jouve, Muh, and Lelord, 1992; Minderaa, Anderson, Volkmar, Akkerhuis, and Cohen, 1994
	↓	J. G. Young, Cohen, Brown, and Caparulo, 1978
	↑	Barthelemy et al., 1988
Epinephrine	NC	Minderaa et al., 1994
MHPG	NC	Launay et al., 1987; Minderaa et al., 1994
	↓	Barthelemy et al., 1988; J. G. Young et al., 1981
VMA	NC	Minderaa et al., 1994
Plasma/Serum		
MHPG	NC	J. G. Young et al., 1981; Minderaa et al., 1994
DBH	NC	Lake, Ziegler, and Murphy, 1977; J. G. Young, Kyprie, Ross, and Cohen, 1980
Cerebrospinal Fluid		
MHPG	NC	J. G. Young et al., 1981; C. Gillberg and Svennerholm, 1987
Measures of Acute Response		
Plasma		
Norepinephrine	↑	Lake et al., 1977; LeBoyer et al., 1992; Leventhal, Cook, Morford, Ravitz, and Freedman, 1990
Cardiovascular		
BP/heart rate	↑	Hirstein, Iversen, and Ramachandran, 2001; Kootz and Cohen, 1981; Tordjman et al., 2009

[*]**Key**: ↑ increased in autism; ↓ decreased in autism; NC no change or difference in autism/ASD
Abbreviations: BP blood pressure; DBH dopamine-β-hyroxylase; MHPG methoxyhydroxyphenylethyleneglycol; VMA vanillylmandelic acid

and urine levels of the major NE metabolites, 3-methoxy-4-hydroxyphenylethylglycol (MHPG) and vanillylmandelic acid (VMA) have been determined. Serum levels of dopamine-β-hydroxylase, the synthetic enzyme secreted along with NE from sympathetic neurons, have also been studied. As seen in Table 19.1, indices reflecting basal functioning of the sympathetic/adrenomedullary system generally have been found to be normal in patients with autism (including plasma MHPG, serum DBH and the various urine measures). On the other hand, most of the studies measuring indices of acute stress response (including plasma NE, heart rate, and blood pressure) have found elevations in patients with autism. Taken together, the data support the idea that autistic patients are not in a chronic state of hyperarousal, but that the sympathetic/adrenomedullary system is hyperresponsive when individuals with autism are stressed (Minderaa et al., 1994). Findings from studies of HPA axis function are in general consistent with this idea and support the same conclusions (Tordjman et al., 1997). The apparent increased response to stressors could be due to a difference in the level of perceived stress, to an overelicitation of the physiological response, or to an abnormality in the stress response systems themselves. The observation of a normal dirurnal rhythm in urinary excretion of NE and EPI (Minderaa et al., 1994) argues somewhat against the last possibility, at least with respect to the sympatho-adrenomedullary system.

MELATONIN

The most compelling rationale for investigating melatonin production in ASD comes from several empirical studies that have found markedly lower group mean plasma melatonin levels and lower urinary excretion of melatonin sulfate (MEL-S, also referred to as 6-sulfatoxymelatonin) in individuals with autism/ASD (Rossignol & Frye, 2011; Tordjman, Anderson, Pichard, Charbuy, & Touitou, 2005; Tordjman et al., 2012). Melatonin's important influence on the sleep-wake cycle and circadian rhythms (Morris, Aeschbach, & Scheer, 2012), its involvement in fetal development and neurodevelopment (Kennaway, 2000), its use in the treatment of sleep problems (Andersen, Kaczmarska, McGrew, & Malow, 2008; Lord, 1998; Sivertsen, Posserud, Gillberg, Lundervold, & Hysing, 2012), and its emerging role in gut function and physiology (Bubenik, 2002) provide a strong theoretical basis for studying melatonin in autism/ASD. Given melatonin's powerful antioxidant properties (Reiter et al., 2007; Tan et al., 2002), alterations in melatonin can be suggested to contribute to observations of increased oxidative stress or compromised redox status in autism. Although the prevalence of gastrointestinal (GI) problems in ASD is not clear (Black, Kaye, & Jick, 2002; Erickson et al., 2005; Wang, Tancredi, & Thomas, 2011), a possible role for melatonin is worth considering. The intestinal wall is the main peripheral source of both 5-HT and nonpineal melatonin, and lower Mel-S excretion in hyperserotonemic ASD individuals has been recently reported (Mulder et al., 2010).

As has been recently reviewed (Tordjman et al., 2012), all prior studies have reported abnormalities in the melatonin production in ASD (Kulman et al., 2000; Melke et al., 2008; Mulder et al., 2010; Nir et al., 1995; Ritvo et al., 1993; Tordjman et al., 2005). With one exception (Ritvo et al., 1993), plasma levels of melatonin and urinary MEL-S excretion have been observed to be lower in ASD than in typically developing control subjects. It is noted that MEL-S is the predominant metabolite of melatonin and that urinary excretion of MEL-S has been shown to be highly correlated with integrated (AUC) plasma melatonin concentration and to give an excellent index of melatonin production (Bojkowski, Arendt, Shih, & Markey, 1987; Graham, Cook, Kavet, Sastre, & Smith, 1998). In one of the largest studies, nighttime excretion of MEL-S was substantially lower in prepubertal individuals with ASD compared to age-matched controls (Tordjman et al., 2005). More recently it has been shown that both nighttime and daytime MEL-S excretion rates are lower in postpubertal individuals with ASD (Tordjman et al., 2012). The results demonstrate that there is a deficit in melatonin production in a substantial proportion of individuals with autism and this deficit is present at night and during the day, indicating that both pineal and extra-pineal production of melatonin is lower in autism. As mentioned, daytime melatonin appears to be mainly derived from the gut wall, where the compound has been reported to have important cytoprotective and antioxidant properties (Bubenik, 2002; Reiter et al., 2007).

SEX AND THYROID HORMONES

Sex Hormones

It has been suggested that differences in early androgen exposure may influence the expression of autism (Auyeung et al., 2012; Manning, Baron-Cohen, Wheelwright, & Sanders, 2001; Tordjman, Ferrari, Sulmont, Duyme, & Roubertoux, 1997). The proposal is based on conjecture that autism represents an extreme form of male behavior, on findings of an association between amniotic testosterone levels and autism traits assessed on follow-up, and on reports of elevated rates of testosterone-related disorders in women with ASD and in mothers of ASD children. The use of sexually dimorphic traits such as digit length ratios in assessing this possibility has been suggested (Hönekopp, 2012; Manning et al., 2001). The hypothesis has been subject to considerable theorizing and debate, and it has served to increase interest in the general area of sex hormone research in ASD (Baron-Cohen, 2012; Baron-Cohen, Auyeung, Ashwin, & Knickmeyer, 2009).

The adrenal steroids dehydroepiandrosterone (DHEA) and androstenedione serves as precursors to testosterone and estradiol. In addition, DHEA has important direct effects on several neurotransmitter receptors and has been termed a *neurosteroid*. In younger subjects (7–10 years old), measurement of DHEA-sulfate and androstenedione provide a good index of adrenarchal status. Two groups have reported unaltered plasma levels of DHEA-sulfate in autism (Ruta, Ingudomnukul, Taylor, Chakrabarti, & Baron-Cohen, 2011; Tordjman et al., 1995), and there is one report of decreased plasma DHEA-sulfate levels in autism (Strous et al., 2005). In the only published study of plasma androstenedione in ASD, increased levels were observed in male and female individuals with ASD (Ruta et al., 2011). Mean plasma levels of testosterone and estradiol in males with ASD have been reported to be similar (Ruta et al., 2011; Tordjman et al., 1995) or lower (Croonenberghs et al., 2010) in ASD compared to controls, while there is one report of higher levels of free testosterone in females with ASD (Schwarz et al., 2011). There do not appear to be any published reports of plasma progesterone levels in ASD.

Thyroid Hormone

Aspects of thyroid function in infantile autism and the efficacy of triiodothyronine (T3) treatment of autistic children have been studied by several investigators (M. Campbell, Small, et al., 1978; Sherwin, Flach, & Stokes, 1958). Kahn (1970) reported diminished values of T3 uptake in 45 of 62 autistic children. On the other hand, Abbassi, Linscheid, and Coleman (1978) and Cohen, Young, Lowe, and Harcherik (1980) have investigated T3, T4, and TSH (thyroid stimulating hormone, thyrotropin) concentrations in 13 autistic children and found no clinical evidence for hypothyroidism, reporting that all had levels within the normal range. M. Campbell, Small, et al. (1978) have conducted a placebo-controlled crossover study of behavioral effects of T3 in 30 young, clinically euthyroid autistic children and reported that T3 did not differ from placebo, although, as a group the lower IQ autistic children responded to T3. M. Campbell, Hollander, et al. (1978) performed the thyrotropin-releasing hormone (TRH) test in psychotic children. After administering synthetic TRH intravenously to 10 young psychotic children, plasma T3, TSH, and prolactin (PRL) were measured over time. In general, there was an elevated response to TSH and a delayed or blunted response of T3 in psychotic children. Suwa et al. (1984) examined hypothalamo-pituitary function by means of the TRH test in four children with autism. Hyperresponse of PRL to TRH was observed in one of the children with autism. Moreover, three of the four autistic children showed a hyperresponse of TSH to TRH. Similarly, Hoshino et al. (1983) reported that

six autistic children showed an elevated response of TSH to TRH. Unlike Suwa et al. (1984), they found a blunted response of PRL to TRH. In contrast, Hashimoto and colleagues (1991) found a blunted TSH response to TRH in a large group ($n = 41$) of children with autism and others have observed normal hormone responses to TRH. Congenital hypothyroidism has been described in a number of patients with autism (C. Gillberg & Coleman, 1992; I. C. Gillberg, Gillberg, & Koop, 1992; Ritvo et al., 1990).

OXYTOCIN AND OTHER NEUROPEPTIDES

The important role of peptides in central neurotransmission and neuromodulation is well established. Neuropeptides have been shown to be crucial to processes related to emotion, appetite, pain perception, and sexual behavior. Measurement of CSF, plasma, and urine levels of specific or uncharacterized peptides in schizophrenia and depression has not clearly indicated whether peptides have etiological significance in these disorders. In autism, the work can be divided into studies of specific opioid peptides, oxytocin, and more general studies of peptide excretion patterns.

Opioid Peptides

The enkephalins and the endorphins appear to be endogenous ligands for receptors activated by morphine and related compounds. Several investigators have theorized that the opioid peptides are involved in producing at least some of the symptoms of autism (Colette, 1978; Panksepp, 1979; Sandman, 1991, 1992). In particular, similarities between behaviors seen in opiate-injected animals and those displayed in autistic subjects (decreased pain perception, behavioral persistence, self-injurious behavior, poor social relations) have suggested that the opioid peptides are hyperfunctional in autism. As an aside, it should be noted that pain perception and sensitivity are probably unaltered in ASD; rather, there are differences in how the perception of pain is expressed (Tordjman et al.,

2009). The opioid hypothesis has been tested by measuring levels of opioids in plasma and CSF, and by administering the opiate antagonist, naloxone, to self-injurious and autistic subjects.

Previous research on the plasma opioids yielded somewhat inconsistent results, with some investigators finding elevations in autism, while others have found little difference between groups (Barrett, Feinstein, & Hole, 1989; Bernstein, Hughes, Mitchell, & Thompson, 1987; Coid, Allolio, & Rees, 1983; LeBoyer, Bouvard, & Dupes, 1988; Sandman, Barron, Chicz-Demet, & Demet, 1990; Weizman et al., 1984). A study examining B-endorphin fragments in plasma has reported an extreme elevation in C-terminal fragments in autistic individuals (LeBoyer et al., 1994); further work on this aspect is warranted. Studies of CSF opioids have reported increased levels of met-enkephalin (C. Gillberg, Terenius, & Lonnerholm, 1985; Ross, Klykylo, & Hitzeman, 1987) and increased or unaltered (Nagamitsu, 1993) B-endorphin in autistic subjects. It should be noted that while CSF opioids are presumably derived from central sources, plasma B-endorphin has a peripheral origin. In fact, B-endorphin appears to be released along with adrenocorticotropic hormone (ACTH) and probably should be considered a human stress hormone.

Initial tests of the effect of naloxone on self-injurious behavior in mentally retarded individuals were promising (Sandman et al., 1983). This result supported the idea of a hyperfunctional opioid system, at least with respect to this one dimension of behavior. However, further studies of naloxone's effects did not tend to demonstrate clear clinical effects of the opioid antagonists in treating autism (M. Campbell et al., 1990; Herman, 1991; LeBoyer et al., 1992).

Urinary Neuropeptides

The urinary excretion of unidentified peptides and peptide complexes in autism has been described in a qualitative manner in several reports (C. Gillberg, Trygstad, & Foss, 1982; Israngkun, Newman, Patel, Duruibe, & Abou-Issa, 1986; Reichelt et al., 1981; Reichelt, Saelid, Lindback, & Boler, 1986). Distinctive patterns of urinary peptides have been reported to occur in several childhood neuropsychiatric illnesses, including autism. Although there have been a number of reports of differences between autistic and control subjects in terms of their patterns of peptide excretion, the studies are far from definitive. The relatively nonspecific nature of the analytical separations and detection processes employed and the nonquantitative aspect of the studies hindered interpretation. In a collaborative study (Le Couteur, Trygstad, Evered, Gillberg, & Rutter, 1988), researchers did not find reproducible differences between autistic and control subjects' urinary excretion of peptides. Although differences in peptide handling continued to be hypothesized to be involved in autism (Reichelt & Knivsberg, 2003), the use of highly specific mass spectrometric methods has now definitively demonstrated that the prior reports of alterations in urinary opiod peptide excretion in autism are in error (Cass et al., 2008; Dettmer, Hanna, Whetstone, Hansen, & Hammock; 2007). Research along these lines that has found differences in peptides in neonatal blood spots of autistic children is also questionable given the lack of disorder specificity and (more importantly) the failure to replicate the underlying methodology (Nelson et al., 2001).

Oxytocin

The neuropeptide oxytocin (OT) is important in social learning and affiliative behavior in animals (Ferguson et al., 2000; Ferguson, Aldag, Insel, & Young, 2001; Insel, O'Brien, & Leckman, 1999; Probe, Pearson, Defense, Bolivar, & Young, 2012; L. J. Young, Murphy Young, & Hammock, 2005) and humans (Turner, Altemus, Enos, Cooper, & McGuinness, 1999). OT facilitates eye gaze (Guastella, Mitchell, & Dadds, 2008), enhances activation to biological motion (A. Perry et al., 2010), and increases social motivation (Geenen et al., 1988), while reducing amygdala activation to emotional faces (Domes, Heinrichs, Michel, Berger, & Herpertz, 2007). Regions hypoactive in response to social rewards in ASD have a high density of OT receptors. Variants of the OT receptor gene OXTR and a deficiency in the OXTR have been reported to be associated with ASD (D. B. Campbell et al., 2011; Gregory et al., 2009; Jacob et al., 2007; Lerer et al., 2008; Wu et al., 2005; Yrigollen et al., 2008), and significant associations between the degree of OXTR methylation and brain activity evoked by the perception of animacy have been reported (Jack, Connelly, & Morris, 2012). Increased urinary oxytocin excretion has been reported as a response to several forms of affiliative interaction (Feldman, Gordon, & Zagoory-Sharon, 2011; Nagasawa, Kikusui, Onaka, & Ohta, 2009). There also have been reports of altered plasma levels of OT in autism (Al-Ayadhi, 2005; Green et al., 2001; Jansen et al., 2006; Modahl et al., 1998) and in social anxiety (Hoge, Pollack, Kaufman, Zak, & Simon, 2008). Several promising studies using intranasal OT to treat ASD associated symptoms have been reported (reviewed in Anagnostou et al., 2012), although a recent study of 38 male youths (7–16 years old) with ASD did not observe benefits of subacute intranasal oxytocin (M. Dadds, personal communication, 2013). A recent study reported that platelet 5-HT and plasma OT concentrations were negatively correlated in humans and in mice (Hammock et al., 2012).

AMINO ACIDS AND ACETYLCHOLINE

A number of inborn errors of amino acid metabolism have been identified, and several of these disorders, such as phenylketonuria, histidinemia, and homocystinuria, affect the central nervous system and have severe behavioral consequences (Scriver & Rosenberg, 1973).

Sylvester, Jorgensen, Mellerup, and Rafaelsen (1970) surveyed amino acid excretion in 178 children suffering from different psychiatric disorders, including psychosis, neurosis, character disorder, mental deficiency, and other functional disturbances. In no case was a specific hyperaminoaciduria found. Johnson, Wiersema, and Kraft (1974) analyzed amino acid composition of hair protein and found no significant differences

between autistic and control children. In 1978, T. L. Perry, Hansen, and Christie measured amino compounds and organic acids in CSF, plasma, and urine of autistic and control children. Similar levels of most compounds were observed in the two groups; however, the mean concentration of ethanolamine in CSF was significantly higher in autistic children than in control subjects. Based on this finding, they suggested that a subgroup of autistic children possibly may have a brain disorder involving ethanolamine metabolism.

Kotsopoulos and Kutty (1979) and Rutter and Bartak (1971) have reported cases showing features of infantile autism who exhibited histidinemia, with histidine blood levels several times higher than normal. It is not clear whether coexistence of autism and histidinemia is coincidental, if not histidinemia may have constituted a necessary but not sufficient factor leading to the clinical condition of autism. An association between phenylketonceria and autism has been noted (Friedman, 1969). In a subsequent study, Lowe, Tanaka, Seashore, Young, and Cohen (1980) surveyed 65 children with pervasive developmental disturbance (autism and atypical childhood psychosis) using standard urinary amino acid screening methods and found three children exhibiting phenylketonuria (PKU). The children were treated with low phenylalanine diets and showed improvement in functioning and developmental level after treatment. The study underlined the relevance of urinary amino acid screening for children being evaluated for serious developmental disturbances of childhood. Other work on aromatic amino acid precursors of the catecholamines (phenylalanine) and the indoleamines (TRP) found that autistic subjects had reduced intestinal absorption of the compounds (Naruse, Hayashi, Takesada, Nakane, & Yamazaki, 1989). Although an attempt was made to relate these peripheral findings to some central alteration in monoamine metabolism, this relationship is not at all clear.

Abnormalities in plasma glutamate and gamma-aminobutyric acid (GABA) have been reported in autism (Aldred, Moore, Fitzgerald, & Waring, 2003; Dhossche et al., 2002; Shimmura et al., 2011) and postmortem brain studies have observed differences in hippocampal GABA receptor density and alterations in the synthetic enzyme that converts glutamate to GABA (glutamic acid decarboxylase) (Blatt et al., 2001; Fatemi et al., 2002). The neurochemical findings, as well as apparent association of GABA receptor genes with autism risk, indicate that further research in this area is warranted (Blatt & Fatemi, 2011).

The general area of cholinergic mechanisms in autism has been relatively neglected due to difficulties in assessing central and peripheral cholinergic metabolism and functioning. However, findings of altered cholinergic receptors in cortical regions of postmortem brain specimens obtained from patients with autism (Lee at al., 2002; E. K. Perry et al., 2001), along with reported alterations of in vivo brain choline levels and acetylcholinesterase activity (Sokol, Dunn, Edwards-Brown, & Feinberg, 2002; Suzuki, Sugihara, et al., 2011), have stimulated considerable interest in this area. Further neurobiological research is clearly called for and some consideration has been given to the possible utility of cholinergic agents in the treatment of autism.

PURINES AND RELATED COMPOUNDS

A good deal of attention has been paid to the role of cyclic AMP (adenosine-3', 5'-cyclic monophosphate) as a second messenger in the mechanism of neural transmission. The enzymes involved in brain synthesis (adenylate cyclase) and decomposition (phosphodiesterase) of cyclic AMP are more active in the brain than in other body organs. Norepinephrine, among other neurotransmitters, elevates intracellular cyclic AMP after interacting with membrane receptors; the elevation of cyclic AMP appears crucial to the subsequent neuronal firing. Cyclic GMP (guanosine-3', 5'-cyclic monophosphate) is a nucleotide related to cyclic AMP and also has second messenger properties.

Winsberg et al. (1980) measured cyclic AMP in CSF of autistic children and reported that levels were increased in all by probenecid administration; however, no comparison to control groups was made. Hoshino et al. (1979) found that plasma cyclic AMP levels were higher in autistic and hyperkinetic intellectually disabled children compared to typically developing children and were positively correlated with the hyperactivity score. Goldberg, Hattab, Meir, Ebstein, and Belmaker (1984) reported that plasma cyclic AMP was significantly elevated by over 100% in groups of patients with childhood-onset psychoses compared with controls, although plasma cyclic GMP was not elevated. The origin of plasma cyclic AMP remains unclear; the compound has been assumed to be derived from peripheral organs, such as the liver, kidneys, lungs, and adrenals, as well as the brain. Sankar (1971) reported that ATPase activity in red blood cell Iyzates was significantly higher in autistic-like schizophrenic children compared to normal controls.

Uric acid is the final end-product of all purine pathways and increased urinary excretion of uric acid (hyperuricosuria) has been reported to occur in up to one quarter of the autistic children studied in the United States and France (Page & Coleman, 2000; Rosenberger-Debiesse & Coleman, 1986). These observations warrant further investigation, given the high proportion of patients suggested to be so affected (though elevated rates of gout have not been reported in autism). A more specific form of uric acid alteration has been reported by Nyhan, James, Teberg, Sweetman, and Nelson (1969). They described a 3-year-old boy with unusual autistic behavior, who was shown to have an excessive rate of uric acid synthesis due to an increase in the purine enzyme phosphoribosylpyrophosphate synthetase in his fibroblasts (Becker, Raivio, Bakay, Adams, & Nyhan, 1980). Other children with this enzyme abnormality have been reported (Christen, Hanfeld, Duley, & Simmonds, 1992; Simmonds, Webster, Lingham, & Wilson, 1985). Jaeken and Van den Berghe (1984) reported that succinyladenosine and succinylaminoimidazole carboxamide riboside were found in body fluids (CSF, plasma, and urine) in three children with severe infantile autism. Their presence indicates a deficiency of the enzyme adenylosuccinase, which is involved in both de novo synthesis of purines and the formation of adenosine monophosphate from inosine monophosphate. Moreover, according to their report, assays in one patient revealed markedly decreased adenylosuccinase activity in the liver and absence of activity in the kidney. They suggested that the accumulation of both succinylpurines in the CSF implies that there is also a deficiency of this enzyme in the brain and that this may be the basic defect in a subgroup of children with autism. This work was followed up with a study of autistic siblings having a markedly lowered Vmax of adenylosuccinase (Barshop, Alberts, & Gruber, 1989). The molecular basis of the three cases of severe retardation with autistic features has been identified; the affected children are homozygous for a point mutation while their family members are heterozygous (Stone et al., 1992). The point mutation in the purine nucleotide biosynthetic enzyme, adenylosuccinate lyase, thus segregates with the disorder.

IMMUNE-RELATED MEASURES

A possible role for immune alteration and dysfunction in autism/ASD has been proposed based on epidemiological studies finding increased immune-related problems in mothers of ASD children, reported neuroinflamatory states in postmortem brain, reported alterations of immune-related measures including cytokines in ASD, findings of associations between ASD and immune-related genes, and results from animal models with altered immune response (Careaga, Van de Water, & Ashwood, 2010; Onore, Careaga, & Ashwood, 2012; Van Gent, Heijnen, & Treffers, 1997). Most of the biochemical research has focused on the cytokines, including the peptides and proteins of the interleukin and interferon families. Overall, the cytokine research has indicated that ASD is associated with an elevated immune response. However, at this point, the cytokine research has not been sufficiently consistent to point to specific cytokines or patterns of alteration that could serve as biomarkers (Abdallah

et al., 2013; Cohly & Panja, 2005; Napolioni et al., 2013; Suzuki, Matsuzaki, et al., 2011). The intriguing connection between serotonin (both central and peripherally acting 5-HT) and the immune system has been recently discussed in the context of ASD and other neuropsychiatric disorders (Baganz & Blakely, 2013). Future research will attempt to resolve discrepancies between the published studies. It also seems worthwhile to address the issues of whether subtypes based on particular types of altered immune function can be defined and whether associations with particular aspects or dimensions of ASD are related to immune dysfunction (Napolioni et al., 2013; Singh, 2009).

OXIDATIVE STRESS/REDOX STATUS

As recently reviewed (Frustaci et al., 2012; Rossignol & Frye, 2012; Villagonzalo et al., 2010), there are over 50 clinical reports indicating that redox status is altered or oxidative stress is increased in individuals diagnosed with ASD (e.g., Chauhan, Chauhan, Brown, & Cohen, 2004; Deth, Muratore, Benzecry, Power-Charnitsky, & Waly, 2008; Ming et al., 2005). Very few negative or nonreplicating studies have been reported. More than one third of the studies have focused on measuring plasma glutathione, with most researchers observing lower levels of reduced glutathione (GSH) and higher oxidized glutathione (GSSG) levels in ASD (Main, Angley, O'Doherty, Thomas, & Fenech, 2012). Plasma indices of oxidative stress, including biomarkers of lipid oxidation, have also been consistently reported to be increased in ASD (Frustaci et al., 2012; James et al. 2004; Lakshmi Priya & Geetha, 2011). In addition to the research on the plasma measures, several studies of postmortem brain tissue have also reported increased levels of oxidative stress markers in ASD (Chauhan, Audhya, & Chauhan, 2012; Rose et al., 2012; Sajdel-Sulkowska, Xu, McGinnis, & Koibuchi, 2011). As previously mentioned, the reported deficits in melatonin production in ASD can be speculated to be playing a role in the apparent altered redox status and increased oxidative stress (Galano, Tan, & Reiter, 2011; Reiter et al., 2007).

OMIC RESEARCH

Omic research is concerned with the simultaneous measurement of a large numbers of analytes. Broad categories include transcriptomics (measurement of RNA species), proteomics (measurement of peptides and proteins), and metabolomics (measurement of all other compounds, generally of molecular weight of less than 1,000 Daltons [grams/mole]). The usual approach is to ratio the amounts of the analyte seen in two comparison groups in attempt to detect species that are either significantly increased or decreased; the results are often reported as fold-change for specific (though oftentimes unidentified) analytes. The advantages of the approach are the unbiased appraisal of possible group differences, the ability to discern patterns of alterations, and the potential for unanticipated discovery. The diadvantages are the unfocused nature of the approach and the difficulties involved in analyzing the large amounts of data produced.

Although an early proteomics effort in autism involving two-dimensional gel electrophoresis was mentioned over two decades ago (Anderson et al., 1990; Levenson, Anderson, Cohn, & Blackshear, 1990), the first productive proteomic application appears to the work of Pevsner and colleagues (Purcell, Jeon, Zimmerman, Blue, & Pevsner, 2001), who found a group difference in the AMPA glutamate subtype in postmortem brain. Around the same time the possible utility of proteomics in autism was reviewed by Junaid and Pullarkat, 2001. The pace of omics research in autism/ASD has recently accelerated with improvements in the available methodologies and the successful application of omics research in other areas of biomedicine. Several recent reviews have discussed the potential for the omic approach in ASD research (Dudley, Hässler, & Thome, 2011; Maurer, 2012; Voineagu, 2012). There are several recent studies of the transcriptome in ASD examining both brain tissue (Garbett et al., 2008; Voineagu et al., 2011;

Ziats & Rennert, 2013) and blood elements (Kong et al., 2012; Luo et al., 2012). Proteomic studies have also examined both brain (Junaid et al., 2004; Purcell et al., 2001) and whole blood, serum, or plasma (Corbett et al., 2007; Glatt et al., 2012; Kong et al., 2012; Momeni et al., 2012; Schwarz et al., 2011; Shen et al., 2011; Taurines et al., 2010). To date, the metabolomic research in autism has compared urinary excretion of metabolites in ASD and typically developing individuals (Ming, Stein, Barnes, Rhodes, & Guo, 2012; Wang et al., 2011; Yap et al., 2010) and has examined lipid profiles (lipidomics) in plasma (El-Ansary, Ben Bacha, & Al-Ayahdi, 2011; Pastural et al., 2009). At this time, most of the omics research is in need of replication in terms of the specific transcripts (mRNAs), proteins, or compounds that have been identified as altered in autism and with respect to the discriminant power that has been claimed for observed patterns of alteration. As pointed out by Voineagu (2012), an especially powerful approach might be to integrate the genomic, transcriptomic, proteomic and metablomic observations.

CONCLUSION

On surveying the field of biochemical research in autism, it is notable how few replicated differences have been found between individuals with autism/ASD and typically developing individuals. The studies reporting similarities between the groups should not be considered negative studies as they have served to narrow the field of investigation. The relatively few differences that have been reported tend to stand out. Most robust and well replicated is the increase in platelet 5-HT seen in autism. However, replicated abnormalities also have been reported in melatonin production, stress response system responsivity, plasma glutamate, uric acid excretion, and central gabaergic receptors.

Certainly an elucidation of the factor(s) causing the elevation of blood 5-HT would be of interest. Additional studies of hormone release, oxytocin levels, oxidative stress, amino acid, and purine metabolism seem warranted, given the reported abnormalities, their possible relevance to central neurotransmitter function, and the compounds' physiological importance. Finally, the general area of diurnal rhythms appears to be a potentially fruitful area of research.

The direction of future research on the biochemical basis of autism no doubt will be influenced by advances in the basic neurosciences, by genetic findings, and by parallel studies in the biological psychiatry of other mental disorders. In general, the availability of postmortem tissue should enhance assessment of central biochemistry and neurochemistry in autism. In the future, a greater consensus should be reached as to just which aspects of central functioning are abnormal in autism. The application of improved methods of biochemical assessment including the omic techniques also should allow a more complete picture to be drawn.

CROSS-REFERENCES

Issues of diagnosis in autism and related conditions are addressed in Chapter 1. Chapter 17 discusses genetic aspects of ASD. Medical care (including clinical genetic assessment) is addressed in Chapter 22. Pharmacological interventions are discussed in Chapter 23.

REFERENCES

Abbassi, V., Linscheid, T., & Coleman, M. (1978). Triiodothyronine (T3) concentration and therapy in autistic children. *Journal of Autism and Childhood Schizophrenia, 8*, 383–387.

Abdallah, M. W., Larsen, N., Grove, J., Bonefeld-Jørgensen, E. C., Nørgaard-Pedersen, B., Hougaard, D. M., & Mortensen, E. L. (2013). Neonatal chemokine levels and risk of autism spectrum disorders: Findings from a Danish historic birth cohort follow-up study. *Cytokine, 61*(2), 370–376.

Aizenstein, M. L., & Korf, J. (1979). On the elimination of centrally formed 5-hydroxy-indoleacetic acid by cerebrospinal fluid and urine. *Journal of Neurochemistry, 32*, 1227–1233.

Al-Ayadhi, L. Y. (2005). Altered oxytocin and vasopressin levels in autistic children in Central Saudi Arabia. *Neurosciences (Riyadh), 10*(1), 47–50.

Aldred, S., Moore, K. M., Fitzgerald, M., & Waring, R. H. (2003). Plasma amino acid levels in children with autism and their families. *Journal of Autism and Developmental Disorders, 33*, 93–97.

Anagnostou, E., Soorya, L., Chaplin, W., Bartz, J., Halpern, D., Wasserman, S., . . . Hollander, E. (2012). Intranasal oxytocin versus placebo in the treatment of adults with autism spectrum disorders: a randomized controlled trial. *Molecular Autism, 3*(1), 16.

Andersen, I. M., Kaczmarska, J., McGrew, S. G., & Malow, B. A. (2008). Melatonin for insomnia in children with autism spectrum disorders. *Journal of Child Neurology, 23*, 482–485.

Anderson, G. M. (2002). Genetics of childhood disorders: XLV. Autism, Part 4: Serotonin in autism. *Journal of the American Academy of Child & Adolescent Psychiatry, 41*, 1513–1516.

Anderson, G. M. (2012). Twin studies in autism: What might they say about genetic and environmental influences. *Journal of Autism and Developmental Disorders, 42*(7), 1526–1527.

Anderson, G. M., & Cohen, D. J. (2002). Neurochemistry of childhood psychiatric disorders. In M. Lewis (Ed.), *Child and adolescent psychiatry: A comprehensive textbook* (3rd ed., pp. 47–60). Baltimore, MD: Williams & Wilkins.

Anderson, G. M., Cook, E. H., Jr., & Blakely, R. D. (2009). Serotonin rising. *New England Journal of Medicine, 360*, 2580.

Anderson, G. M., Hertzig, M. E., & McBride, P. A. (2012). Platelet-poor plasma serotonin in autism. *Journal of Autism and Developmental Disorders, 42*, 1510–1514.

Anderson, G. M., Horne, W. C., Chatterjee, D., & Cohen, D. J. (1990). The hyperserotonemia of autism. *Annals of the New York Academy of Sciences, 600*, 333.

Anderson, G. M., Minderaa, R. B., Cho, S. C., Volkmar, F. R., & Cohen, D. J. (1989). The issue of hyperserotonemia and platelet serotonin exposure: A preliminary study. *Journal of Autism and Developmental Disorders, 19*, 349–351.

Anderson, G. M., Minderaa, R. B., van Bentem, P.-P. G., Volkmar, F. R., & Cohen, D. J. (1984). Platelet imipramine binding in autistic subjects. *Psychiatry Research, 11*, 133–141.

Anderson, G. M., Scahill, L., McCracken, J. T., McDougle, C. J., Aman, M. G., Tierney, E., . . . Vitiello, B. (2007). Effects of short- and long-term risperidone treatment on prolactin levels in children with autism. *Biological Psychiatry, 61*(4), 545–550.

Anderson, G. M., Stevenson, J. M., & Cohen, D. J. (1987). Steady-state model for plasma free and platelet serotonin in man. *Life Sciences, 41*, 1777–1785.

Anderson, G. M., Volkmar, F. R., Hoder, E. L., McPhedran, P., Minderaa, R. B., Young, J. G., . . . Cohen, D. J. (1987). Whole blood serotonin in autistic and normal subjects. *Journal of Child Psychiatry and Psychology, 28*, 885–900.

Auyeung, B., Ahluwalia, J., Thomson, L., Taylor, K., Hackett, G., O'Donnell, K. J., & Baron-Cohen, S. (2012). Prenatal versus postnatal sex steroid hormone effects on autistic traits in children at 18 to 24 months of age. *Molecular Autism, 3*(1), 17.

Baganz, N. L., & Blakely, R. D. (2013). A dialogue between the immune system and brain, spoken in the language of serotonin. *ACS Chemical Neuroscience, 4*(1), 48–63.

Baron-Cohen, S. (2012). Empathizing, systemizing, and the extreme male brain theory of autism. *Progress in Brain Research, 186*, 167–175.

Baron-Cohen, S., Auyeung, B., Ashwin, E., & Knickmeyer, R. (2009). Fetal testosterone and autistic traits: A response to three fascinating commentaries. *British Journal of Psychology*, *100*(Pt 1), 39–47.

Barrett, P. R., Feinstein, C., & Hole, W. T. (1989). Effects of naloxone and naltrexone on self-injury: A double-blind placebo-controlled analysis. *American Journal of Mental Retardation*, *93*, 644–651.

Barshop, B. A., Alberts, A. S., & Gruber, H. E. (1989). Kinetic studies of mutant human adenylosuccinase. *Biochemica et Biophysica Acta*, *999*, 19–23.

Barthelemy, C., Bruneau, N., Cottet-Eymard, J. M., Domenech-Jouve, J., Garreau, B., Lelord, G., ... Peyrin, L. (1988). Urinary free and conjugated catecholamines and metabolites in autistic children. *Journal of Autism and Developmental Disorders*, *18*, 583–591.

Becker, M. A., Raivio, K. O., Bakay, B., Adams, W. B., & Nyhan, W. L. (1980). Variant human phosphoribosylpyrophosphate synthetase altered in regulatory and catalytic functions. *Journal of Clinical Investigations*, *65*, 109–120.

Berger, M., Gray, J. A., & Roth, B. L. (2009). The expanded biology of serotonin. *Annual Review of Medicine*, *60*, 355–366.

Bernstein, G. A., Hughes, J. R., Mitchell, J. E., & Thompson, T. (1987). Effects of narcotic antagonist on self-injurious behavior: A single case study. *Journal of the American Academy of Child & Adolescent Psychiatry*, *26*, 886–889.

Black, C., Kaye, J. A., & Jick, H. (2002). Relation of childhood gastrointestinal disorders to autism: nested case–control study using data from the UK General Practice Research Database. *British Medical Journal*, *325*(7361), 419–421.

Blatt, G. J., Fatemi, S. H. (2011). Alterations in GABAergic biomarkers in the autism brain: research findings and clinical implications. *Anatomical Record*, *294*(10), 1646–1652.

Blatt, G. J., Fitzgerald, C. M., Guptill, J. T., Booker, A. B., Kemper, T. L., & Bauman, M. L. (2001). Density and distribution of hippocampal neurotransmitter receptors in autism: An autoradiographic study. *Journal of Autism and Developmental Disorders*, *31*, 537–543.

Bojkowski, C. J., Arendt, J., Shih, M. C., & Markey, S. P. (1987). Melatonin secretion in humans assessed by measuring its metabolite, 6-sulfatoxymelatonin. *Clinical Chemistry*, *33*, 1343–1348.

Bonnin, A., Goeden, N., Chen, K., Wilson, M. L., King, J., Shih, J. C., ... Levitt, P. (2011). A transient placental source of serotonin for the fetal forebrain. *Nature*, *472*(7343), 347–350.

Boullin, D. J., Coleman, M., O'Brien, R. A., & Rimland, B. (1971). Laboratory predictions of infantile autism based on 5-hydroxytryptamine efflux from blood platelets and their correlation with the Rimland E-2 score. *Journal of Autism and Childhood Schizophrenia*, *1*, 63–71.

Boullin, D. J., Freeman, B. J., Geller, E., Ritvo, E., Rutter, M., & Yuwiler, A. (1982). Toward the resolution of conflicting findings. *Journal of Autism and Developmental Disorders*, *12*, 97–98.

Brand, T., & Anderson, G. M. (2011). The measurement of platelet-poor plasma serotonin: A systematic review of prior reports and recommendations for improved analysis. *Clinical Chemistry*, *57*(10), 1376–1386.

Bubenik, G. A. (2002). Gastrointestinal melatonin: Localization, function, and clinical relevance. *Digestive Diseases & Sciences*, *47*, 2336–2348.

Buznikov, G. A. (1984). The action of neurotransmitters and related substances on early embryogenesis. *Pharmacology and Therapeutics*, *25*, 23–59.

Campbell, D. B., Datta, D., Jones, S. T., Batey Lee, E., Sutcliffe, J. S., Hammock, E. A., & Levitt, P. (2011). Association of oxytocin receptor (OXTR) gene variants with multiple phenotype domains of autism spectrum disorder. *Journal of Neurodevelopmental Disorders*, *3*, 101–112.

Campbell, M., Anderson, L. T., Small, A. M., Locascio, J. J., Lynch, N. S., & Choroco, M. C. (1990). Naltrexone in autistic children: A double-blind and placebo controlled study. *Psychopharmacology Bulletin*, *26*, 130–135.

Campbell, M., Hollander, C. S., Ferris, S., & Greene, L. W. (1978). Response to thyrotropin-releasing hormone stimulation in young psychotic children: A pilot study. *Psychoneuroendocrinology*, *3*, 195–201.

Campbell, M., Small, A. M., Hollander, C. S., Korein, J., Cohen, 1. L., Kalmijn, M., & Ferris, S. (1978). A controlled crossover study of triiodothyronine in autistic children. *Journal of Autism and Childhood Schizophrenia*, *8*, 371–381.

Careaga, M., Van de Water, J., & Ashwood, P. (2010). Immune dysfunction in autism: A pathway to treatment. *Neurotherapeutics*, *7*, 283–292.

Cass, H., Gringras, P., March, J., McKendrick, I., O'Hare, A. E., Owen, L., & Pollin, C. (2008). Absence of urinary opioid peptides in children with autism. *Archives of Disease in Childhood*, *93*(9), 745–750.

Chauhan, A., Audhya, T., & Chauhan, V. (2012). Brain region-specific glutathione redox imbalance in autism. *Neurochemical Research*, *37*(8), 1681–1689.

Chauhan, A., Chauhan, V., Brown, W. T., & Cohen I. (2004). Oxidative stress in autism: Increased lipid peroxidation and reduced serum levels of ceruloplasmin and transferrin—the antioxidant proteins. *Life Sciences*, *75*, 2539–2549.

Chawarska, K., Campbell, D., Chen, L., Shic, F., Klin, A., & Chang, J. (2011). Early generalized overgrowth in boys with autism. *Archives of General Psychiatry*, *68*(10), 1021–1031.

Christen, H. J., Hanfeld, F., Duley, J. A., & Simmonds, H. A. (1992). Distinct neurological syndrome in two brothers with hyperuricaemia. *The Lancet*, *340*, 1167–1168.

Chrousos, G. P., & Gold, P. W. (1992). The concepts of stress and stress system disorders. Overview of physical and behavioral homeostasis. *JAMA*, *267*(9), 1244–1252.

Chugani, D. C., Muzik, O., Behen, M. E., Rothermal, R., Janisse, J. J., Lee, J., & Chugani, H. T. (1999). Developmental changes in brain serotonin synthesis capacity in autistic and non-autistic children. *Annals of Neurology*, *45*, 287–295.

Cohen, D. J., Caparulo, B. K., Shaywitz, B. A., & Bowers, M. B., Jr. (1977). Dopamine and serotonin metabolism in neuropsychiatrically disturbed children: CSF homovanillic acid and 5-hydroxyindoleacetic acid. *Archives of General Psychiatry*, *34*, 545–550.

Cohen, D. J., Shaywitz, B. A., Johnson, W. T., & Bowers, M. B., Jr. (1974). Biogenic amines in autistic and atypical children: Cerebrospinal fluid measures of homovanillic acid and

5-hydroxyindoleacetic acid. *Archives of General Psychiatry, 31*, 845–853.

Cohen, D. J., & Young, J. G. (1977). Neurochemistry and child psychiatry. *Journal of the American Academy of Child Psychiatry, 16*, 353–411.

Cohen, D. J., Young, J. G., Lowe, T. L., & Harcherik, D. (1980). Thyroid hormone in autistic children. *Journal of Autism and Developmental Disorders, 10*, 445–450.

Cohly, H. H., & Panja, A. (2005). Immunological findings in autism. *International Review of Neurobiology, 71*, 317–341.

Coid, J., Allolio, B., & Rees, L. H. (1983). Raised plasma metenkephlin in patients who habitually mutilate themselves. *The Lancet, 2*, 545.

Colette, J. W. (1978). Speculation on similarities between autism and opiate addiction. *Journal of Autism and Childhood Schizophrenia, 8*, 477–479.

Cook, E. H. (1990). Autism: Review of neurochemical investigation [review]. *Synapse, 6*, 292–308.

Cook, E. H. (2001). Genetics of autism. *Child & Adolescent Psychiatric Clinics in North America, 10*, 333–350.

Cook, E. H., Anderson, G. M., Heninger, G. R., Fletcher, K. E., Freedman, D. X., & Leventhal, B. L. (1992). Tryptophan loading in hyperserotonemic and normoserotonemic adults. *Biological Psychiatry, 31*, 525–528.

Cook, E. H., Arora, R. C., Anderson, G. M., Berry-Kravis, E. M., Yan, S., Yeoh, H. C.,... Leventhal, B. L. (1993). Platelet serotonin in hyperserotonemic relatives of children with autistic disorder. *Life Sciences, 52*, 2005–2015.

Cook, E. H., Leventhal, B. L., & Freedman, D. X. (1988). Free serotonin in plasma: Autistic children and their first degree relatives. *Biological Psychiatry, 24*, 488–491.

Corbett, B. A., Kantor, A. B., Schulman, H., Walker, W. L., Lit, L., Ashwood, P.,... Sharp, F. R. (2007). A proteomic study of serum from children with autism showing differential expression of apolipoproteins and complement proteins. *Molecular Psychiatry (3)*, 292–306.

Croonenberghs, J., Van Grieken, S., Wauters, A., Van West, D., Brouw, L., Maes, M., Deboutte, D. (2010). Serum testosterone concentration in male autistic youngsters. *Neuroendocrinology Letters, 31*, 483–488.

DeMyer, M. K., Hingtgen, J. N., & Jackson, R. K. (1981). Infantile autism reviewed: A decade of research. *Schizophrenia Bulletin, 7*, 388–451.

Deth, R., Muratore, C., Benzecry, J., Power-Charnitsky, V. A., & Waly M. (2008). How environmental and genetic factors combine to cause autism: A redox/methylation hypothesis. *Neurotoxicology, 29*, 190–201.

Dettmer, K., Hanna, D., Whetstone, P., Hansen, R., & Hammock, B. D. (2007). Autism and urinary exogenous neuropeptides: development of an on-line SPE-HPLC-tandem mass spectrometry method to test the opioid excess theory. *Analytical and Bioanalytical Chemistry, 388*(8), 1643–1651.

Dhossche, D., Applegate, H., Abraham, A., Maertens, P., Bland, L., Bencsath, A., & Martinez, J. (2002). Elevated plasma gamma-aminobutyric acid (GABA) levels in autistic youngsters: stimulus for a GABA hypothesis of autism. *Medical Science Monitor, 8*, PR1–6.

Domes, G., Heinrichs, M., Michel, A., Berger, C., & Herpertz, S. C. (2007). Oxytocin improves "mind-reading" in humans. *Biological Psychiatry, 61*, 731–733.

Dudley, E., Hässler, F., & Thome, J. (2011). Profiling for novel proteomics biomarkers in neurodevelopmental disorders. *Expert Review of Proteomics, 8*(1), 127–136.

El-Ansary, A. K., Ben Bacha, A. G., & Al-Ayahdi, L. Y. (2011). Impaired plasma phospholipids and relative amounts of essential polyunsaturated fatty acids in autistic patients from Saudi Arabia. *Lipids in Health and Disease, 10*, 63.

Elchisak, M. A., Polinsky, R. J., Ebert, M. H., Powers, J., & Kopin, I. J. (1978). Contribution of plasma homovanillic acid (HVA) to urine and CSF HVA in the monkey and its pharmacokinetic disposition. *Life Sciences, 23*, 2339–2348.

Erickson, C. A., Stigler, K. A., Corkins, M. R., Posey, D. J., Fitzgerald, J. F., & McDougle, C. J. (2005). Gastrointestinal factors in autistic disorder: a critical review. *Journal of Autism and Developmental Disorders, 35*, 713–727.

Fatemi, S. H., Halt, A. R., Stary, J. M., Kanodia, R., Schulz, S. C., & Realmuto, G. R. (2002). Glutamic acid decarboxylase 65 and 67 kDa proteins are reduced in autistic parietal and cerebellar cortices. *Biological Psychiatry, 52*, 805–810.

Feldman, R., Gordon, I., & Zagoory-Sharon, O. (2011). Maternal and paternal plasma, salivary, and urinary oxytocin and parent-infant synchrony: considering stress and affiliation components of human bonding. *Developmental Science, 14*, 752–761.

Ferguson, J. N., Aldag, J. M., Insel, T. R., & Young, L. J. (2001). Oxytocin in the medial amygdala is essential for social recognition in the mouse. *Journal of Neuroscience, 21*, 8278–8285.

Ferguson, J. N., Young, L. J., Hearn, E. F., Matzuk, M. M., Insel, T. R., & Winslow, J. T. (2000). Social amnesia in mice lacking the oxytocin gene. *Nature Genetics, 25*, 284–288.

Folstein, S. E., & Piven, J. (1991). Etiology of autism: Genetic influences. *Pediatrics, 87*, 767–773 (supplement).

Folstein, S. E., & Rosen-Sheidley, B. (2001). Genetics of autism: Complex aetiology for a heterogeneous disorder. *Nature Reviews Genetics, 2*, 943–955.

Friedman, E. (1969). The "autistic syndrome" and phenylketonuria. *Schizophrenia, 1*, 249–261.

Frustaci, A., Neri, M., Cesario, A., Adams, J. B., Domenici, E., Dalla Bernardina, B., & Bonassi, S. (2012). Oxidative stress-related biomarkers in autism: Systematic review and meta-analyses. *Free Radical Biology & Medicine, 52*(10), 2128–2124.

Galano, A., Tan, D. X., & Reiter, R. J. (2011). Melatonin as a natural ally against oxidative stress: A physicochemical examination [Review]. *Journal of Pineal Research, 51*, 1–16.

Garbett, K., Ebert, P. J., Mitchell, A., Lintas, C., Manzi, B., Mirnics, K., & Persico, A. M. (2008). Immune transcriptome alterations in the temporal cortex of subjects with autism. *Neurobiology of Disease, 30*(3), 303–311.

Garelis, E., Young, S. N., Lal, S., & Sourkes, T. L. (1974). Monoamine metabolites in lumbar CSF: The question of their origin in relation to clinical studies. *Brain Research, 79*, 1–8.

Geenen, V., Adam, F., Baro, V., Mantanus, H., Ansseau, M., Timsit-Berthier, M., & Legros, J. J. (1988). Inhibitory influence of oxytocin infusion on contingent negative variation and some memory tasks in normal men. *Psychoneuroendocrinology, 13*, 367–375.

Gillberg, C. (1993). Comment on CSF HVA. *Biological Psychiatry, 34,* 746.

Gillberg, C., & Coleman, M. (1992). *The biology of the autistic syndromes* (2nd ed.). London, England: Mac Keith Press.

Gillberg, C., & Svennerholm, L. (1987). CSF monoamines in autistic syndromes and other pervasive developmental disorders of early childhood. *British Journal of Psychiatry, 151,* 89–94.

Gillberg, C., Svennerholm, L., & Hamilton-Hellberg, C. (1983). Childhood psychosis and monoamine metabolites in spinal fluid. *Journal of Autism and Developmental Disorders, 13,* 38–96.

Gillberg, C., Terenius, L., & Lonnerholm, G. (1985). Endorphin activity in childhood psychosis. *Archives of General Psychiatry, 42,* 780–783.

Gillberg, C., Trygstad, O., & Foss, J. (1982). Childhood psychosis and urinary excretion of peptides and protein-associated peptide complexes. *Journal of Autism and Developmental Disorders, 12,* 229–241.

Gillberg, I. C., Gillberg, C., & Koop, S. (1992). Hypothyroidsim and autism spectrum disorders. *Journal of Child Psychology and Psychiatry and Allied Disciplines, 33,* 531–542.

Giller, E. L., Young, J. G., Breakefield, X. O., Carbonari, C., Braverman, M., & Cohen, D. J. (1980). Monoamine oxidase and catechol-O-methyltransferase activities in cultured fibroblasts and blood cells from children with autism and the Gilles de la Tourette syndrome. *Psychiatry Research, 2,* 187–197.

Glatt, S. J., Tsuang, M. T., Winn, M., Chandler, S. D., Collins, M., Lopez, L., . . . Courchesne, E. (2012). Blood-based gene expression signatures of infants and toddlers with autism. *Journal of the American Academy of Child & Adolescent Psychiatry, 51*(9), 934–944.e2.

Goldberg, J., Anderson, G. M., Zwaigenbaum, L., Hall, G. B., Nahmias, C., Thompson, A., & Szatmari, P. (2009). Cortical serotonin type-2 receptor density in parents of children with autism spectrum disorders. *Journal of Autism and Developmental Disorders, 39,* 97–104.

Goldberg, M., Hattab, J., Meir, D., Ebstein, R. P., & Belmaker, R. H. (1984). Plasma cyclic AMP and cyclic GMP in childhood-onset psychoses. *Journal of Autism and Developmental Disorders, 14,* 159–164.

Grabrucker, A. M. (2012). Environmental factors in autism. *Frontiers in Psychiatry, 3,* 118.

Graham, C., Cook, M. R., Kavet, R., Sastre, A., & Smith, D. K. (1998). Prediction of nocturnal plasma melatonin from morning urinary measures. *Journal of Pineal Research, 24,* 230–238.

Green, L., Fein, D., Modahl, C., Feinstein, C., Waterhouse, L., & Morris, M. (2001). Oxytocin and autistic disorder: Alterations in peptide forms. *Biological Psychiatry, 50,* 609–613.

Gregory, S. G., Connelly, J. J., Towers, A. J., Johnson, J., Biscocho, D., Markunas, C. A., . . . Pericak-Vance, M. A. (2009). Genomic and epigenetic evidence for oxytocin receptor deficiency in autism. *BMC Medicine, 7,* 62.

Guastella, A. J., Mitchell, P. B., & Dadds, M. R. (2008). Oxytocin increases gaze to the eye region of human faces. *Biological Psychiatry, 63,* 3–5.

Hallmayer, J., Cleveland, S., Torres, A., Phillips, J., Cohen, B., Torigoe, T., . . . Risch, N. (2011). Genetic heritability and shared environmental factors among twin pairs with autism. *Archives of General Psychiatry, 68*(11), 1095–1102.

Hammock, E., Veenstra-VanderWeele, J., Yan, Z., Kerr, T. M., Morris, M., Anderson, G. M, . . . Jacob, S. (2012). Examining autism spectrum disorders by biomarkers: example from the oxytocin and serotonin systems. *Journal of the American Academy of Child & Adolescent Psychiatry, 51,* 712–721.

Hanley, H. G., Stahl, S. M., & Freedman, D. X. (1977). Hyperserotonemia and amine metabolites in autistic and retarded children. *Archives of General Psychiatry, 34,* 521–531.

Hashimoto, T., Aihara, R., Tayama, M., Miyazaki, M., Shirakawa, Y., & Kuroda, Y. (1991). Reduced thyroid-stimulating hormone response to thyrotropin-releasing hormone in autistic boys. *Developmental Medicine & Child Neurology, 33,* 313–319.

Herman, B. H. (1991). Effects of opioid receptor antagonists on the treatment of autism and self-injurious behavior. In J. J. Ratey (Ed.), *Mental retardation: Developing pharmacotherapies, progress in psychiatry* (Vol. 32, pp. 107–137). Washington, DC: American Psychiatric Press.

Hirstein, W., Iversen, P., & Ramachandran, V. S. (2001). Autonomic responses of autistic children to people and objects. *Proceedings of the Royal Society of London, Series B: Biological Sciences, 268,* 1883–1888.

Hoge, E. A., Pollack, M. H., Kaufman, R. E., Zak, P. J., & Simon, N. M. (2008). Oxytocin levels in social anxiety disorder. *CNS Neuroscience & Therapeutics, 14*(3), 165–170.

Hönekopp, J. (2012). Digit ratio 2D:4D in relation to autism spectrum disorders, empathizing, and systemizing: A quantitative review. *Autism Research, 5*(4), 221–230.

Hoshino, Y., Kumashiro, H., Kaneko, M., Numata, Y., Honda, K., Yashima, Y., . . . Watanabe, M. (1979). Serum serotonin, free tryptophan and plasma cyclic AMP levels in autistic children with special reference to their relation to hyperkinesia. *Fukushima Journal of Medical Science, 26*(3–4), 79–91.

Hoshino, Y., Tachibana, R., Watanabe, M., Murata, S., Yokoyama, F., Kaneko, M., . . . Kumashiro, H. (1984). Serotonin metabolism and hypothalamic-pituitary function in children with infantile autism and minimal brain dysfunction. *Japanese Journal of Psychiatry, 26,* 937–945.

Hoshino, Y., Watanabe, M., Tachibana, R., Murata, S., Kaneko, M., Yashima, Y., & Kumashiro, H. (1983). A study of the hypothalamus-pituitary function in autistic children by the loading test of 5HTP, TRH and LH-RH. *Japanese Journal of Brain Research, 9,* 94–95.

Hoshino, Y., Yamamoto, T., Kaneko, M., Tachibana, R., Watanabe, M., Ono, Y., & Kumashiro, H. (1984). Blood serotonin and free tryptophan concentration in autistic children. *Neuropsychobiology, 11,* 22–27.

Hu, V. W. (2012). Subphenotype-dependent disease markers for diagnosis and personalized treatment of autism spectrum disorders. *Disease Markers, 33*(5), 277–288.

Insel, T. R., O'Brien, D. J., & Leckman, J. F. (1999). Oxytocin, vasopressin, and autism: Is there a connection? *Biological Psychiatry, 45*(2), 145–157.

Israngkun, P. P., Newman, H. A., Patel, S. T., Duruibe, V. A., & Abou-Issa, H. (1986). Potential biochemical markers for infantile autism. *Neurochemical Pathology, 5,* 51–70.

Iverson, S. D., & Iverson, L. L. (1981). *Behavioral pharmacology* (2nd ed.). New York, NY: Oxford University Press.

Jack, A., Connelly, J. J., & Morris, J. P. (2012, October 10). DNA methylation of the oxytocin receptor gene predicts neural response to ambiguous social stimuli. *Frontiers in Human Neuroscience, 6*, 280. Epub.

Jacob, S., Brune, C. W., Carter, C. S., Leventhal, B. L., Lord, C., & Cook, E. H., Jr. (2007). Association of the oxytocin receptor gene (OXTR) in Caucasian children and adolescents with autism. *Neuroscience Letters, 417*, 6–9.

Jaeken, J., & Van den Berghe, G. (1984). An infantile autistic syndrome characterized by the presence of succinylpurines in body fluids. *The Lancet, 2*, 1058–1061.

James, S. J., Cutler, P., Melnyk, S., Jernigan, S., Janak, L., Gaylor, D. W., & Neubrander, J. A. (2004). Metabolic biomarkers of increased oxidative stress and impaired methylation capacity in children with autism. *American Journal of Clinical Nutrition, 80*(6), 1611–1617.

Jansen, L. M., Gispen-de Wied, C. C., Wiegant, V. M., Westenberg, H. G., Lahuis, B. E., & van Engeland, H. (2006). Autonomic and neuroendocrine responses to a psychosocial stressor in adults with autistic spectrum disorder. *Journal of Autism and Developmental Disorders, 36*, 891–899.

Janusonis, S., Gluncic, V., & Rakic, P. (2004). Early serotonergic projections to Cajal-Retzius cells: Relevance for cortical development. *Journal of Neuroscience, 7*, 1652–1659.

Johnson, R. J., Wiersema, V., & Kraft, 1. A. (1974). Hair amino acids in childhood autism. *Journal of Autism and Childhood Schizophrenia, 4*, 187–188.

Junaid, M. A., Kowal, D., Barua, M., Pullarkat, P. S., Sklower Brooks, S., & Pullarkat, R. K. (2004). Proteomic studies identified a single nucleotide polymorphism in glyoxalase I as autism susceptibility factor. *American Journal of Medical Genetics Part A, 131*(1), 11–17.

Junaid, M. A., & Pullarkat, R. K. (2001). Proteomic approach for the elucidation of biological defects in autism. *Journal of Autism and Developmental Disorders, 31*(6), 557–560.

Kahn, A. A. (1970). Thyroid dysfunction. *British Medical Journal, 4*, 495.

Kennaway, D. J. (2000). Melatonin and development: physiology and pharmacology. *Seminars in Perinatology, 24*, 258–266.

King, B. H., Hollander, E., Sikich, L., McCracken, J. T., Scahill, L., Bregman, J. D., . . . STAART Psychopharmacology Network. (2009). Lack of efficacy of citalopram in children with autism spectrum disorders and high levels of repetitive behavior: Citalopram ineffective in children with autism *Archives of General Psychiatry, 66*, 583–590.

Kirwin, P. D., Anderson, G. M., Chappell, P. D., Saberski, L., Leckman, J. F., Geracioti, T. D., . . . McDougle, C. (1997). Assessment of diurnal variation of cerebrospinal fluid tryptophan and 5-hydrxyindoleacetic acid in healthy human females. *Life Sciences, 60*, 899–907.

Kolevzon, A., Newcorn, J. H., Kryzak, L., Chaplin, W., Watner, D., Hollander, E., . . . Silverman, J. M. (2010). Relationship between whole blood serotonin and repetitive behaviors in autism. *Psychiatry Research, 175*, 274–276.

Kong, S. W., Collins, C. D., Shimizu-Motohashi, Y., Holm, I. A., Campbell, M. G., Lee, I. H., . . . Kohane, I. S. (2012). Characteristics and predictive value of blood transcriptome signature in males with autism spectrum disorders. *PLoS One, 7*(12), e49475.

Kootz, J. P,, & Cohen, D. J. (1981). Modulation of sensory intake in autistic children: Cardiovascular and behavioral indices. *Journal of the American Academy of Child & Adolescent Psychiatry, 20*(4), 692–701.

Kotsopoulos, S., & Kutty, K. M. (1979). Histidinemia and infantile autism. *Journal of Autism and Developmental Disorders, 9*, 55–60.

Kulman, G., Lissoni, P., Rovelli, F., Roselli, M. G., Brivio, F., & Sequeri, P. (2000). Evidence of pineal endocrine hypofunction in autistic children. *Neuroendocrinology Letters, 21*, 31–34.

Lake, R., Ziegler, M. G., & Murphy, D. L. (1977). Increased norepinephrine levels and decreased DBH activity in primary autism. *Archives of General Psychiatry, 35*, 553–556.

Lakshmi Priya, M. D., & Geetha A. (2011). A biochemical study on the level of proteins and their percentage of nitration in the hair and nail of autistic children. *Clinica Chimica Acta, 412*(11–12), 1036–1042.

Lauder, J. M. (1990). Ontogeny of the serotonergic system in the rat: Serotonin as a developmental signal. *Annals of the New York Academy of Sciences, 600*, 297–313.

Launay, J. M., Bursztejn, C., Ferrari, P., Dreux, C., Braconnier, A., Zarifian E., . . . Fermanian, J. (1987). Catecholamines metabolism in infantile autism: A controlled study of 22 autistic children. *Journal of Autism and Developmental Disorders, 17*, 333–347.

Lauritsen, M. B., & Ewald, H. (2001). The genetics of autism. *Acta Psychiatrica Scandinavica, 103*, 411–427.

LeBoyer, M., Bouvard, M. P., & Dupes, M. (1988). Effects of naltrexone on infantile autism. *The Lancet, 1*, 715.

LeBoyer, M., Bouvard, M. P., Launay, J. M., Tabuteau, F., Waller, D., Dugas, M., . . . Panksepp, J. (1992). Brief report: A double-blind study of naltrexone on infantile autism. *Journal of Autism and Developmental Disorders, 22*, 309–319.

LeBoyer, M., Bouvard, M. P., Recasens, C., Philippe, A., Guilloud-Bataille, M., Bondoux, D., . . . Launay, J. M. (1994). Differences between plasma N- and C-terminally directed beta-endorphin immunoreactivity in infantile autism. *American Journal of Psychiatry, 151*, 1797–1801.

Le Couteur, A., Trygstad, O., Evered, C., Gillberg, C., & Rutter, M. (1988). Infantile autism and urinary excretion of peptides and protein-associated peptide complexes. *Journal of Autism and Developmental Disorders, 18*, 181–190.

Lee, M., Martin-Ruiz, C., Graham A., Court J., Jaros, E., Perry, R., . . . Perry, E. (2002). Nicotinic receptor abnormalities in the cerebellar cortex in autism. *Brain, 125*, 1483–1495.

Lerer, E., Levi, S., Salomon, S., Darvasi, A., Yirmiya, N., & Ebstein, R. P. (2008). Association between the oxytocin receptor (OXTR) gene and autism: relationship to Vineland Adaptive Behavior Scales and cognition. *Molecular Psychiatry, 13*, 980–988.

Levenson, R. M., Anderson, G. M., Cohn, J. A., & Blackshear, P. J. (1990). Giant two-dimensional gel electrophoresis: Methodological update and comparison with intermediate-format gel systems. *Electrophoresis, 11*, 269–279.

Leventhal, B. L., Cook, E. H., Jr., Morford, M., Ravitz, A., & Freedman, D. X. (1990). Relationships of whole blood serotonin and plasma norepinephrine within families. *Journal of Autism and Developmental Disorders, 20*, 499–511.

Lord C. (1998). What is melatonin? Is it a useful treatment for sleep problems in autism? *Journal of Autism and Developmental Disorders, 28*, 345–346.

Lotspeich, L. J., & Ciaranello, R. D. (1993). The neurobiology and genetics of infantile autism. *International Review of Neurobiology, 35*, 87–129.

Lowe, T. L., Tanaka, K., Seashore, M. R., Young, J. G., & Cohen, D. J. (1980). Detection of phenylketonuria in autistic and psychotic children. *Journal of the American Medical Association, 243*, 126–128.

Lucki, I. (1998). The spectrum of behaviors influenced by serotonin. *Biological Psychiatry, 44*, 151–162.

Luo, R., Sanders, S. J., Tian, Y., Voineagu, I., Huang, N., Chu, S. H., . . . Geschwind, D. H. (2012). Genome-wide transcriptome profiling reveals the functional impact of rare de novo and recurrent CNVs in autism spectrum disorders. *American Journal of Human Genetics, 91*(1), 38–55.

Maas, J. W., Hattox, S. E., Greene, N. M., & Landis, B. H. (1980). Estimates of dopamine and serotonin synthesis by the awake human brain. *Journal of Neurochemistry, M 34*, 1547–1549.

Main, P. A., Angley, M. T., O'Doherty, C. E., Thomas, P., & Fenech, M. (2012). The potential role of the antioxidant and detoxification properties of glutathione in autism spectrum disorders: A systematic review and meta-analysis. *Nutrition & Metabolism, 9*, 35.

Manning, J. T., Baron-Cohen, S., Wheelwright, S., & Sanders, G. (2001). The 2nd to 4th digit ratio and autism. *Developmental Medicine & Child Neurology, 43*, 160–164.

Martineau, J., Barthelemy, C., Jouve, J., Muh, J. P., & Lelord, G. (1992). Monoamines (serotonin and catecholamines) and their derivatives in infantile autism: Age-related changes and drug effects. *Developmental Medicine & Child Neurology, 34*, 593–603.

Maurer, M. H. (2012). Genomic and proteomic advances in autism research. *Electrophoresis, 33*(24), 3653–3658.

McBride, P. A., Anderson, G. M., Hertzig, M. E., Snow, M. E., Thompson, S. M., Khait, V. D., . . . Cohen, D. J. (1998). Effects of diagnosis, race, and pubertal status on platelet serotonin levels in autism and mental retardation. *Journal of the American Academy of Child & Adolescent Psychiatry, 37*, 767–779.

McBride, P. A., Anderson, G. M., Hertzig, M. E., Sweeney, J. A., Kream, J., Cohen, D. J., & Mann, J. J. (1989). Serotonergic responsivity in male young adults with autistic disorder. *Archives of General Psychiatry, 46*, 213–221.

McBride, P. A., Anderson, G. M., & Mann, J. J. (1990). Serotonin in autism. In E. F. Coccaro & D. L. Murphy (Eds.), *Serotonin in major psychiatric disorders* (pp. 47–68). Washington, DC: American Psychiatric Press.

McBride, P. A, Anderson, G. M., & Shapiro, T. (1996). Autism research: Bringing together approaches to pull apart the disorder. *Archives of General Psychiatry, 53*, 980–983.

McDougle, C. J., Naylor, S. T., Cohen, D. J., Aghajanian, G. K., Heninger, G. R., & Price, L. H. (1996). Effects of tryptophan depletion in drug-free adults with autistic disorder. *Archives of General Psychiatry, 53*, 993–1000.

Meek, J. L., & Neff, N. H. (1973). Is cerebrospinal fluid the major avenue for the removal of 5-hydroxyindoleacetic acid from the brain? *Neuropharmacology, 12*, 497–499.

Melke, J., Goubran, B. H., Chaste, P., Betancur, C., Nygren, G., Anckarsater, H., . . . Bourgeron, T. (2008). Abnormal melatonin synthesis in autism spectrum disorders. *Molecular Psychiatry, 13*, 90–98.

Minderaa, R. B., Anderson, G. M., Volkmar, F. R., Akkerhuis, G. W., & Cohen, D. J. (1987). Urinary 5-HIAA and whole blood 5-HT and tryptophan in autism and normal subjects. *Biological Psychiatry, 22*, 933–940.

Minderaa R. B., Anderson, G. M., Volkmar, F. R., Akkerhuis, G. W., & Cohen D. J. (1994). Noradrenergic and adrenergic functioning in autism. *Biological Psychiatry, 36*, 237–241.

Minderaa, R. B., Anderson, G. M., Volkmar, F. R., Harcherik, D., Akkerhuis, C. W., & Cohen, D. J. (1989). Neurochemical study of dopamine functioning in autistic and normal subjects. *Journal of the American Academy of Child & Adolescent Psychiatry, 28*, 200–206.

Ming, X., Stein, T. P., Barnes, V., Rhodes, N., & Guo, L. (2012). Metabolic perturbance in autism spectrum disorders: A metabolomics study. *Journal of Proteome Research, 11*(12), 5856–5862.

Ming, X., Stein, T. P., Brimacombe, M., Johnson, W. G., Lambert, G. H., & Wagner, G. C. (2005). Increased excretion of a lipid peroxidation biomarker in autism. *Prostaglandins Leukotrienes & Essential Fatty Acids, 73*, 379–384.

Mizejewski, G. J. (2012). Biomarker testing for suspected autism spectrum disorder in early childhood: is such testing now feasible? *Biomarkers in Medicine, 6*(4), 503–506.

Modahl, C., Green, L., Fein, D., Morris, M., Waterhouse, L., Feinstein, C., & Levin, H. (1998). Plasma oxytocin levels in autistic children. *Biological Psychiatry, 43*, 270–277.

Momeni, N., Bergquist, J., Brudin, L., Behnia, F., Sivberg, B., Joghataei, M. T., & Persson, B. L. (2012). A novel blood-based biomarker for detection of autism spectrum disorders. *Translational Psychiatry, 2*, e91.

Morris, C. J., Aeschbach, D., & Scheer, F. A. (2012). Circadian system, sleep and endocrinology. *Molecular and Cellular Endocrinology, 349*, 91–104.

Mulder, E. J., Anderson, G. M., Kema, I. P., de Bildt, A., van Lang, N. D., den Boer, J. A., & Minderaa, R. B. (2004). Platelet serotonin levels in pervasive developmental disorders and mental retardation: Diagnostic group differences, within-group distribution, and behavioral correlates. *Journal of the American Academy of Child & Adolescent Psychiatry, 43*, 491–499.

Mulder, E. J., Anderson, G. M., Kemperman, R. F., Oosterloo-Duinkerken, A., Minderaa, R. B., & Kema, I. P. (2010). Urinary excretion of 5-hydroxyindoleacetic acid, serotonin and 6-sulphatoxymelatonin in normoserotonemic and hyperserotonemic autistic individuals. *Neuropsychobiology, 61*, 27–32.

Murphy, D. G., Daly, E., Schmitz, N., Toal, F., Murphy, K., Curran, S., . . . Travis, M. (2006). Cortical serotonin 5-HT2A receptor binding and social communication in adults with Asperger's syndrome: an in vivo SPECT study. *American Journal of Psychiatry, 163*, 934–936.

Nagamitsu, S. (1993). CSF beta-endorphin levels in pediatric neurologic disorders. *Kurume Medical Journal, 40*, 223–241.

Nagasawa, M., Kikusui, T., Onaka, T., & Ohta, M. (2009). Dog's gaze at its owner increases owner's urinary oxytocin during social interaction. *Hormones and Behavior, 55,* 434–441.

Nakamura, K., Sekine, Y., Ouchi, Y., Tsujii, M., Yoshikawa, E., Futatsubashi, M.,...Mori, N. (2010). Brain serotonin and dopamine transporter bindings in adults with high-functioning autism. *Archives of General Psychiatry, 67,* 59–68.

Napolioni, V., Ober-Reynolds, B., Szelinger, S., Corneveaux, J. J., Pawlowski, T., Ober-Reynolds, S.,...Huentelman, M. J. (2013). Plasma cytokine profiling in sibling pairs discordant for autism spectrum disorder. *Journal of Neuroinflammation, 10*(1), 38.

Narayan, M., Anderson, G. M., & Srinath, S. (1993). CSF HVA in autism (in reply). *Biological Psychiatry, 34,* 746–747.

Narayan, M., Srinath, S., Anderson, G. M., and Meundi, D. B. (1993). Cerebrospinal fluid levels of homovanillic acid and 5-hydroxyindoleacetic acid in autism. *Biological Psychiatry, 33,* 630–635.

Naruse, H., Hayashi, T., Takesada, M., Nakane, A., & Yamazaki, K. (1989). Metabolic changes in aromatic amino acids and monoamines in infantile autism and development of new treatment related to the finding. *No to Hattatsu [Brain and Development], 21,* 181–189.

Nelson, K. B., Grether, J. K., Croen, L. A., Dambrosia, J. M., Dickens, B. F., Jelliffe, L. L.,...Phillips, T. M. (2001). Neuropeptides and neurotrophins in neonatal blood of children with autism or mental retardation. *Annals of Neurology, 49*(5), 597–606.

Nir, I., Meir, D., Zilber, N., Knobler, H., Hadjez, J., & Lerner, Y. (1995). Brief report: circadian melatonin, thyroid-stimulating hormone, prolactin, and cortisol levels in serum of young adults with autism. *Journal of Autism and Developmental Disorders, 25*(6), 641–654.

Nyhan, W. L., James, J. A., Teberg, A. J., Sweetman, L., & Nelson, L. G. (1969). A new disorder of purine metabolism with behavioral manifestations. *Journal of Pediatrics, 74*(1), 20–27.

O'Brien, R. A., Semenuk, G., & Spector, S. (1976). Catechol-O-methyltransferase activity in erythrocytes of children with autism. In E. Coleman (Ed.), *The autistic syndromes* (pp. 43–49). Amsterdam, The Netherlands: North-Holland.

Onore, C., Careaga, M., & Ashwood, P. (2012). The role of immune dysfunction in the pathophysiology of autism. *Brain, Behavior, and Immunity, 26*(3), 383–392.

Ozaki, N., Goldman, D., Kaye, W., Plotnikov, K., Greenberg, B., Rudnick, G., & Murphy, D. L. (2003). A missense mutation in the serotonin transporter is associated with a complex neuropsychiatric phenotype. *Molecular Psychiatry, 11,* 8933–8936.

Page, T., & Coleman, M. (2000). Purine metabolism abnormalities in a hyperuricosuric subclass of autism. *Biochimica et Biophysica Acta, 1500,* 291–296.

Panksepp, J. (1979). A neurochemical theory of autism. *Trends in Neuroscience, 2,* 174–177.

Partington, M. W., Tu, J. B., & Wong, C. Y. (1973). Blood serotonin levels in severe mental retardation. *Developmental Medicine and Child Neurology, 15,* 616–627.

Pastural, E., Ritchie, S., Lu, Y., Jin, W., Kavianpour, A., Khine Su-Myat, K.,...Goodenowe, D. B. (2009). Novel plasma phospholipid biomarkers of autism: mitochondrial dysfunction as a putative causative mechanism. *Prostaglandins Leukot Essent Fatty Acids, 81*(4), 253–264.

Perry, A., Bentin, S., Shalev, I., Israel, S., Uzefovsky, F., Bar-On, D., & Ebstein, R. P. (2010). Intranasal oxytocin modulates EEG mu/alpha and beta rhythms during perception of biological motion. *Psychoneuroendocrinology, 35,* 1446–1453.

Perry, E. K., Lee, M. L., Martin-Ruiz, C. M., Court, J. A., Volsen, S. G., Merrit, J.,...Wenk, G. L. (2001). Cholinergic activity in autism: Abnormalities in the cerebral cortex and basal forebrain. *American Journal of Psychiatry, 158,* 1058–1066.

Perry, T. L., Hansen, S., & Christie, R. G. (1978). Amino compounds and organic acids in CSF, plasma, and urine of autistic children. *Biological Psychiatry, 13,* 575–586.

Posey, D. J., & McDougle, C. J. (2000). The pharmacotherapy of target symptoms associated with autistic disorder and other pervasive developmental disorders. *Harvard Review of Psychiatry, 8,* 45–63.

Prasad, H. C., Steiner, J. A., Sutcliffe, J. S., & Blakely, R. D. (2009). Enhanced activity of human serotonin transporter variants associated with autism. *Philosophical Transactions of the Royal Society of London B: Biological Sciences, 364,* 163–173.

Probe, R. L., Pearson, B. L., Defense, E. B., Bolivar, V. J., Young, W. S., III, Lee, H. J.,...Blanchard, R. J. (2012). Oxytocin receptor knockout mice display deficits in the expression of autism-related behaviors. *Hormones and Behavior, 61,* 436–444.

Purcell, A. E., Jeon, O. H., Zimmerman, A. W., Blue, M. E., & Pevsner, J. (2001). Postmortem brain abnormalities of the glutamate neurotransmitter system in autism. *Neurology, 57,* 1618–1628.

Ratajczak, H. V. (2011). Theoretical aspects of autism: Biomarkers—a review. *Journal of Immunotoxicology, 8*(1), 80–94.

Realmuto, G. M., Jensen, J. B., Reeve, E., & Garfinkel, B. D. (1990). Growth hormone response to L-dopa and clonidine in autistic children. *Journal of Autism and Developmental Disorders, 20,* 455–465.

Redmond, D. E., Jr., & Huang, Y. W. (1979). New evidence for a locus coeruleus-norepinephrine connection with anxiety. *Life Sciences, 25,* 2149–2162.

Reichelt, K. L., Hole, K., Hamberger, A., Saelid, G., Edminson, P. D., Braestrup, C. B.,...Orbeck, H. (1981). Biologically active peptide-containing fractions in schizophrenia and childhood autism. *Advances in Biochemistry and Psychopharmacology, 28,* 627–643.

Reichelt, K. L., & Knivsberg, A. M. (2003). Can the pathophysiology of autism be explained by the nature of the discovered urine peptides? *Nutritional Neuroscience, 6,* 19–28.

Reichelt, K. L., Saelid, G., Lindback, T., & Boler, J. B. (1986). Childhood autism: A complex disorder. *Biological Psychiatry, 21,* 1279–1290.

Reiter, R. J., Tan, D. X., Manchester, L. C., Pilar Terron, M., Flores, L. J., & Koppisepi, S. (2007). Medical implications of melatonin: receptor-mediated and receptor-independent actions. *Advances in Medical Sciences, 52,* 11–28.

Ritvo, E. R. (1977). Biochemical studies of children with the syndromes of autism, childhood schizophrenia and related developmental disabilities: A review. *Journal of Child Psychology and Psychiatry, 13,* 373–379.

Ritvo, E. R., Mason-Brothers, A., Freeman, B. J., Pingree, C., Jenson, W. R., McMahon, W. M., . . . Ritvo, A. (1990). The UCLA–University of Utah epidemiologic survey of autism: The etiologic role of rare diseases. *American Journal of Psychiatry, 147,* 1614–1621.

Ritvo, E. R., Ritvo, R., Yuwiler, A., Brothers, A., Freeman, B. J., & Plotkin, S. (1993). Elevated daytime melatonin concentrations in autism: A pilot study. *European Child and Adolescent Psychiatry, 2,* 75–78.

Ritvo, E. R., Yuwiler, A., Geller, E., Kales, A., Rashkis, S., Schicor, A., . . . Howard, C. (1971). Effects of L-dopa in autism. *Journal of Autism and Childhood Schizophrenia, 1,* 190–205.

Ritvo, E. R., Yuwiler, A., Geller, E., Ornitz. E. M., Saeger, K., & Plotkin, S. (1970). Increased blood serotonin and platelets in early infantile autism. *Archives of General Psychiatry, 23,* 566–572.

Rose, S., Melnyk, S., Pavliv, O., Bai, S., Nick, T. G., Frye, R. E., & James, S. J. (2012). Evidence of oxidative damage and inflammation associated with low glutathione redox status in the autism brain. *Translational Psychiatry, 10*(2), e134.

Rosenberger-Diesse, J., & Coleman, M. (1986). Brief report: Preliminary evidence for multiple etiologies in autism. *Journal of Autism and Developmental Disorders, 16,* 385–392.

Ross, D. L., Klykylo, W. M., & Anderson, G. M. (1985). Cerebrospinal fluid indoleamine and monoamine effects in fenfluramine treatment of autism. *Annals of Neurology, 18,* 394.

Ross, D. L., Klykylo, W. M., & Hitzeman, R. (1987). Reduction of elevated CSF beta-endorphin by fenfluramine in infantile autism. *Pediatric Neurology, 3,* 83–86.

Rossignol, D. A., & Frye, R. E. (2011). Melatonin in autism spectrum disorders: A systematic review and meta-analysis. *Developmental Medicine & Child Neurology, 53,* 783–792.

Rossignol, D. A., & Frye, R. E. (2012). A review of research trends in physiological abnormalities in autism spectrum disorders: Immune dysregulation, inflammation, oxidative stress, mitochondrial dysfunction and environmental toxicant exposures. *Molecular Psychiatry, 17,* 389–401.

Ruta, L., Ingudomnukul, E., Taylor, K., Chakrabarti, B., & Baron-Cohen, S. (2011). Increased serum androstenedione in adults with autism spectrum conditions. *Psychoneuroendocrinology, 36,* 1154–1163.

Rutter, M., & Bartak, L. (1971). Causes of infantile autism: Some considerations from recent research. *Journal of Autism and Childhood Schizophrenia, 1,* 20–32.

Rutter, M., & Schopler, E. (1987). Autism and pervasive developmental disorders: Concepts and diagnostic issues. *Journal of Autism and Developmental Disorders, 17,* 159–186.

Sajdel-Sulkowska, E. M., Xu, M., McGinnis, W., & Koibuchi, N. (2011). Brain region-specific changes in oxidative stress and neurotrophin levels in autism spectrum disorders (ASD). *Cerebellum, 10,* 43–48.

Sandman, C. A. (1991). The opiate hypothesis in autism and self-injury. *Journal of Child and Adolescent Psychopharmacology, 1,* 237–248.

Sandman, C. A. (1992). Various endogenous opioids and autistic behavior: A response to Gillberg. *Journal of Autism and Developmental Disorders, 22,* 132–133.

Sandman, C. A., Barron, J. L., Chicz-Demet, A., & Demet, E. M. (1990). Plasma ß-endorphin levels in patients with self-injurious behavior and stereotypy. *American Journal of Mental Retardation, 95,* 84–92.

Sandman, C. A., Patta, P. C., Banon, J. Hoehler, F. K., Williams, C., Williams, C., & Swanson, J. M. (1983). Naloxone attenuates self-abusive behavior in developmentally disabled clients. *Applied Research in Mental Retardation, 4,* 5–11.

Sankar, D. V. S. (1971). Studies on blood platelets, blood enzymes, and leukocyte chromosome breakage in childhood schizophrenia. *Behavioral Neuropsychiatry, 2,* 2–10.

Schain, R. J., & Freedman, D. X. (1961). Studies on 5-hydroxyindole metabolism in autistic and other mentally retarded children. *Journal of Pediatrics, 58,* 315–320.

Schwarz, E., Guest, P. C., Rahmoune, H., Wang, L., Levin, Y., Ingudomnukul, E., . . . Bahn S. (2011). Sex-specific serum biomarker patterns in adults with Asperger's syndrome. *Molecular Psychiatry, 16*(12), 1213–1220.

Scriver, C. R., & Rosenberg, L. E. (1973). *Amino acid metabolism and its disorders.* Philadelphia, PA: W. B. Saunders.

Shen, C., Zhao, X. L., Ju, W., Zou, X. B., Huo, L. R., Yan, W., . . . Zhong N. (2011). A proteomic investigation of B lymphocytes in an autistic family: A pilot study of exposure to natural rubber latex (NRL) may lead to autism. *Journal of Molecular Neuroscience, 43*(3), 443–452.

Sherwin, A. C., Flach, F. F., & Stokes, P. E. (1958). Treatment of psychoses in early childhood with triiodothyronine. *American Journal of Psychiatry, 115,* 166–167.

Shimmura, C., Suda, S., Tsuchiya, K. J., Hashimoto, K., Ohno, K., Matsuzaki, H., . . . Mori N. (2011). Alteration of plasma glutamate and glutamine levels in children with high-functioning autism. *PLoS One, 6*(10), e25340.

Shoaf, S. E., Carson, R. E., Hommer, D., Williams, W. A., Higley, J. D., Schmall, B., . . . Linnoila, M. (2000). The suitability of 11C-alpha-methyl-L-tryptophan as a tracer for serotonin synthesis. *Journal of Cerebral Blood Flow & Metabolism, 20*(20), 244–252.

Simmonds, H. A., Webster, D. R., Lingham, S., & Wilson, J. (1985). An inborn error of purine metabolism, deafness and neurodevelopmental abnormality. *Neuropediatrics, 16,* 106–108.

Singh, V. K. (2009). Phenotypic expression of autoimmune autistic disorder (AAD): A major subset of autism. *Annals of Clinical Psychiatry, 21*(3), 148–161.

Sivertsen, B., Posserud, M. B., Gillberg, C., Lundervold, A. J., & Hysing, M. (2012). Sleep problems in children with autism spectrum problems: A longitudinal population-based study. *Autism, 16,* 139–150.

Sokol, D. K., Dunn, D. W., Edwards-Brown, M., & Feinberg, J. (2002). Hydrogen proton magnetic resonance spectroscopy in autism: preliminary evidence of elevated choline/creatine ratio. *Journal of Child Neurology, 17,* 245–249.

State, M. W., & Levitt, P. (2011). The conundrums of understanding genetic risks for autism spectrum disorders. *Nature Neuroscience, 14*(12), 1499–506.

Stone, R. L., Aimi, J., Barshop, B. A., Jaeken, J., Van den Berghe, G., Zalkin, H., & Dixon, J. E. (1992). A mutation in adenylosuccinate lyase associated with mental retardation and autistic features. *Nature Genetics*, *1*, 59–63.

Strous, R. D., Golubchik, P., Maayan, R., Mozes, T., Tuati-Werner, D., Weizman, A., & Spivak, B. (2005). Lowered DHEA-S plasma levels in adult individuals with autistic disorder. *European Neuropsychopharmacology*, *15*, 305–309.

Sutcliffe, J. S., Delahanty, R. J., Prasad, H. C., McCauley, J. L., Han, Q., Jiang, L., . . . Blakely, R. D. (2005). Allelic heterogeneity at the serotonin transporter locus (SLC6A4) confers susceptibility to autism and rigid-compulsive behaviors. *American Journal of Human Genetics*, *77*, 265–279.

Suwa, S., Naruse, H., Ohura, T., Tsuruhara, T., Takesoda, M., Yamazaki, K., & Mikuni, M. (1984). Influence of pimozide on hypothalamo-pituitary function in children with behavioral disorders. *Psychoneuroendocrinology*, *9*, 37–44.

Suzuki, K., Matsuzaki, H., Iwata, K., Kameno, Y., Shimmura, C., Kawai, S., . . . Mori, N. (2011). Plasma cytokine profiles in subjects with high-functioning autism spectrum disorders. *PLoS One*, *6*(5), e20470.

Suzuki, K., Sugihara, G., Ouchi, Y., Nakamura, K., Tsujii, M., Futatsubashi, M., . . . Mori, N. (2011). Reduced acetylcholinesterase activity in the fusiform gyrus in adults with autism spectrum disorders. *Archives of General Psychiatry*, *68*(3), 306–313.

Sverd, J., Kupretz, S. S., Winsberg, B. G., Hurwic, M. J., & Becker, L. (1978). Effect of L-5-hydroxytryptophan in autistic children. *Journal of Autism and Childhood Schizophrenia*, *8*, 171–180.

Sylvester, O., Jorgensen, E., Mellerup, T., & Rafaelsen, O. J. (1970). Amino acid excretion in urine of children with various psychiatric diseases. *Danish Medical Bulletin*, *17*, 166–170.

Szatmari, P. (2011). Is autism, at least in part, a disorder of fetal programming? *Archives of General Psychiatry*, *68*(11), 1091–1092.

Takatsu, T., Onizawa, J., & Nakahato, M. (1965). Tryptophan metabolism disorder and therapeutic diet in children with infantile autism. *Amino Acids*, *5*, 13–14.

Tan, D. X., Reiter, R. J., Manchester, L. C., Yan, M. T., El-Sawi, M., Sainz, R. M., . . . Hardeland, R. (2002). Chemical and physical properties and potential mechanisms: melatonin as a broad spectrum antioxidant and free radical scavenger. *Current Topics in Medicinal Chemistry*, *2*, 181–198.

Tani, Y., Fernell, E., Watanbe, Y., Kanai, T., & Langstrom, B. (1994). Decrease in 6R-5, 6, 7, 8-tetrahydrobiopterin content in cerebrospinal fluid of autistic patients. *Neuroscience Letters*, *181*, 169–172.

Taurines, R., Dudley, E., Conner, A. C., Grassl, J., Jans, T., Guderian, F., . . . Thome, J. (2010). Serum protein profiling and proteomics in autistic spectrum disorder using magnetic bead-assisted mass spectrometry. *European Archives of Psychiatry and Clinical Neuroscience*, *260*(3), 249–255.

Tordjman, S., Anderson, G. M., Bellissant, E., Botbol, M., Charbuy, H., Camus, F., . . . Touitou, Y. (2012). Day and nighttime excretion of 6-sulphatoxymelatonin in adolescents and young adults with autistic disorder. *Psychoneuroendocrinology*, *37*, 1990–1997.

Tordjman, S., Anderson, G. M., Brailly-Tabard, S., Perez-Diaz, F., Graignic, R., Carlier, M., . . . Roubertoux, P. (2009). Pain reactivity and plasma β-endorphin in children and adolescents with autistic disorder. *PLoS One*, *4*(8), e5289.

Tordjman, S., Anderson, G. M., McBride, P. A., Hertzig, M. E., Snow, M. E., Hall, L. M., . . . Cohen, D. J. (1995). Plasma androgens in autism. *Journal of Autism and Developmental Disorders*, *25*, 295–304.

Tordjman, S., Anderson, G. M., McBride, P. A., Hertzig, M. E., Snow, M. E., Hall, L. M., . . . Cohen, D. J. (1997). Plasma beta-endorphin, adrenocorticotropin hormone, and cortisol in autism. *Journal of Child Psychology and Psychiatry*, *38*, 705–715.

Tordjman, S., Anderson, G. M., Pichard, N., Charbuy, H., & Touitou, Y. (2005). Nocturnal excretion of 6-sulphatoxymelatonin in children and adolescents with autistic disorder. *Biological Psychiatry*, *57*, 134–138.

Tordjman, S., Ferrari, P., Sulmont, V., Duyme, M., & Roubertoux, P. (1997). Androgenic activity in autism. *American Journal of Psychiatry*, *154*, 1626–1627.

Turner, R. A., Altemus, M., Enos, T., Cooper, B., & McGuinness, T. (1999). Preliminary research on plasma oxytocin in normal cycling women: Investigating emotion and interpersonal distress. *Psychiatry*, *62*, 97–113.

Udenfriend, S., Titus, E., Weissbach, H., & Peterson, R. E. (1959). Biogenesis and metabolism of 5-hydroxyindole compounds. *Journal of Biological Chemistry*, *219*, 335–344.

Van Gent, T., Heijnen, C. J., & Treffers, P. D. (1997). Autism and the immune system. *Journal of Child Psychology and Psychiatry*, *38*(3), 337–349.

Veenstra-VanderWeele J., & Anderson, G. M. (2010). The serotonin system in autism. In E. Hollander, A. Kolevzon, & J. T. Coyle (Eds.), *Textbook of autism spectrum disorders* (pp. 315–322). Arlington, VA: American Psychiatric Publishing.

Veenstra-VanderWeele, J., & Blakely, R. D. (2012). Networking in autism: Leveraging genetic, biomarker and model system findings in the search for new treatments. *Neuropsychopharmacology*, *37*(1), 196–212.

Veenstra-VanderWeele, J., Muller, C. L., Iwamoto, H., Sauer, J. E., Owens, W. A., Shah, C. R., . . . Blakely, R. D. (2012). Autism gene variant causes hyperserotonemia, serotonin receptor hypersensitivity, social impairment and repetitive behavior. *Proceedings of the National Academy of Sciences, USA*, *109*(14), 5469–5474.

Villagonzalo, K. A., Dodd, S., Dean, O., Gray, K., Tonge, B., & Berk, M. (2010). Oxidative pathways as a drug target for the treatment of autism. *Expert Opinion on Therapeutic Targets*, *14*, 1301–1310.

Voineagu, I. (2012). Gene expression studies in autism: moving from the genome to the transcriptome and beyond. *Neurobiology of Disease*, *45*(1), 69–75.

Voineagu, I., Wang, X., Johnston, P., Lowe, J. K, Tian, Y., Horvath, S., . . . Geschwind, D. H. (2011). Transcriptomic analysis of autistic brain reveals convergent molecular pathology. *Nature*, *474*(7351), 380–384.

Waage-Baudet, H., Lauder, J. M., Dehart, D. B., Kluckman, K., Hiller, S., Tint, G. S., & Sulik, K. K. (2003). Abnormal serotonergic development in a mouse model for the Smith-Lemli-Opitz syndrome: Implications for autism.

International Journal of Developmental Neuroscience, *21*(8), 451–459.

Walsh, P., Elsabbagh, M., Bolton, P., & Singh, I. (2011). In search of biomarkers for autism: Scientific, social and ethical challenges. *Nature Reviews Neuroscience,* *12*(10), 603–612.

Wang, L., Angley, M. T., Gerber, J. P., & Sorich, M. J. (2011). A review of candidate urinary biomarkers for autism spectrum disorder. *Biomarkers,* *16*(7), 537–552.

Wang, L. W., Tancredi, D. J., & Thomas, D. W. (2011). The prevalence of gastrointestinal problems in children across the United States with autism spectrum disorders from families with multiple affected members. *Journal of Development & Behavioral Pediatrics,* *32*, 351–360.

Weizman, R., Weizman, A., Tyrano, S., Szekely, B., Weissman, B. A., & Sarne, Y. (1984). Humoral-endorphin blood levels in autistic, schizophrenic and healthy subjects. *Psychopharmacology,* *82*, 368–370.

Whitaker-Azmitia, P. M. (2001). Serotonin and brain development: Role in human developmental diseases. *Brain Research Bulletin,* *56*, 479–485.

Whitaker-Azmitia, P. M., Druse, M., Walker, P., & Lauder, J. M. (1996). Serotonin as a developmental signal. *Behavioural Brain Research,* *73*, 19–29.

Winsberg, B. G., Sverd, J., Castells, S., Hurwic, M., & Perel, J. M. (1980). Estimation of monoamine and cyclic-AMP turnover and amino acid concentrations of spinal fluid in autistic children. *Neuropediatrics,* *11*, 250–255.

Wu, S., Jia, M., Ruan, Y., Liu, J., Guo, Y., Shuang, M., . . . Zhang, D. (2005). Positive association of the oxytocin receptor gene (OXTR) with autism in the Chinese Han population. *Biological Psychiatry,* *58*(1), 74–77.

Yap, I. K., Angley, M., Veselkov, K. A., Holmes, E., Lindon, J. C., & Nicholson, J. K. (2010). Urinary metabolic phenotyping differentiates children with autism from their unaffected siblings and age-matched controls. *Journal of Proteome Research,* *9*(6), 2996–3004.

Yerys, B. E., & Pennington, B. F. (2011). How do we establish a biological marker for a behaviorally defined disorder? Autism as a test case. *Autism Research,* *4*(4), 239–241.

Young, J. G., Cohen, D. J., Brown, S. L., & Caparulo, B. K. (1978). Decreased urinary free catecholamines in childhood autism. *Journal of the American Academy of Child Psychiatry,* *17*, 671–678.

Young, J. G., Cohen, D. J., Kavanagh, M. E., Landis, H. D., Shaywitz, B. A., & Maas, J. W. (1981). Cerebrospinal fluid, plasma, and urinary MHPG in children. *Life Sciences,* *28*, 2837–2845.

Young, J. G., Kavanagh, M. E., Anderson, G. M., Shaywitz, B. A., & Cohen, D. J. (1982). Clinical neurochemistry of autism and associated disorders. *Journal of Autism and Developmental Disorders,* *12*, 147–165.

Young, J. G., Kyprie, R. M., Ross, N. T., & Cohen, D. J. (1980). Serum dopamine-beta-hydroxylase activity: Clinical applications in child psychiatry. *Journal of Autism and Developmental Disorders,* *10*(1), 1–14.

Young, L. J., Murphy Young, A. Z., & Hammock, E. A. (2005). Anatomy and neurochemistry of the pair bond. *Journal of Comparative Neurology,* *493*, 51–57.

Young, S. N., Anderson, G. M., & Purdy, W. C. (1980). Indoleamine metabolism in rat brain studied through measurements of tryptophan, 5-hydroxyindoleactic acid and indoleactic acid in cerebrospinal fluid. *Journal of Neurochemistry,* *34*, 309–315.

Yrigollen, C. M., Han, S. S., Kochetkova, A., Babitz, T., Chang, J. T., Volkmar, F. R., . . . Grigorenko, E. L. (2008). Genes controlling affiliative behavior as candidate genes for autism. *Biological Psychiatry,* *63*, 911–916.

Yuwiler, A., Geller, A., & Ritvo, E. (1985). Biochemical studies of autism. In E. Lajtha (Ed.), *Handbook of neurochemistry* (pp. 671–691). New York, NY: Plenum Press.

Yuwiler, A., Ritvo, E. R., Geller, E., Glousman, R., Schneiderman, G., & Matsuno, D. (1975). Uptake and efflux of serotonin from platelets of autistic and nonautistic children. *Journal of Autism and Childhood Schizophrenia,* *5*, 83–98.

Zhou, E. C., Auerbach, S., & Azmitia, E. C. (1987). Denervation of serotonergic fibers in the hippocampus induced a trophic factor which enhance the maturation of transplanted serotonergic neurons but not norepinephrine neurons. *Journal of Neuroscience Research,* *17*, 235–246.

Ziats, M. N., & Rennert, O. M. (2013). Aberrant expression of long noncoding RNAs in autistic brain. *Journal of Molecular Neuroscience,* *49*(3), 589–593.

CHAPTER 20

The Social Neuroscience of Autism Spectrum Disorder

JAMES C. McPARTLAND, RACHAEL M. TILLMAN, DANIEL Y.-J. YANG,
RAPHAEL A. BERNIER, AND KEVIN A. PELPHREY

INTRODUCTION

Autism spectrum disorder (ASD) is an early-onset neurodevelopmental disorder marked by impairments in reciprocal social interaction, communication, and the presence of repetitive or restricted interests and behaviors (American Psychiatric Association, 2000). Despite great phenotypic heterogeneity and etiologic diversity in ASD, social dysfunction has been the hallmark and unifying feature of ASD since its original description (Kanner, 1943), affecting both simple (e.g., shared gaze) and complex social behaviors (e.g., back-and-forth conversations). Unlike repetitive behaviors or language problems, which are present in numerous disorders (e.g., expressive language impairment or obsessive compulsive disorder), early developing abnormalities in social perception are unique to ASD. They are documented in both nonverbal and verbal domains spanning multiple sensory modalities (Hubbard et al., 2012; Pelphrey et al.,

2003) and emerge within the first years of life (Chawarska, Macari, & Shic, 2013; Elsabbagh, Mercure, et al., 2012). This chapter focuses on understanding the neural systems involved in the processing of social information and its disruption in ASD by reviewing conceptual background and highlighting recent advances. In addition, work investigating an alternative interpretation of autistic dysfunction, problems with interconnectivity, and consequent difficulties with sophisticated information processing are addressed.

NEURAL SYSTEMS FOR SOCIAL PERCEPTION, ACTION UNDERSTANDING, AND MENTAL STATE REASONING

Social Perception

Given the predominance and universality of social deficits in the autistic phenotype, dysfunction in brain systems subserving social perception has become a key focus in autism research. The theoretical framework for understanding development in ASD posits that (a) specific brain systems evolved to process information pertaining to humans (Brothers, 1990) and (b) autistic dysfunction originates in these brain systems, exerting cascading, peripheral impacts throughout development. The social motivation hypothesis builds upon this framework and suggests that reduced social drive leads to inattention to people and consequent failure of developmental specialization in experience-expectant brain systems, such as the face perception system (Dawson, Webb, & McPartland, 2005). Diminished social motivation in ASD might stem from deficits in forming representations of and categorizing the reward value of social information. Individuals with ASD show less activation in reward circuits when viewing social rewards (i.e., faces) than controls (Kohls, Chevallier, Troiani, & Schultz, 2012; Scott-Van Zeeland, Dapretto, Ghahremani, Poldrack, & Bookheimer, 2010). It is still unclear whether these impairments reflect a general reward processing deficit (Dichter & Adolphs, 2012) or abnormalities in specialized neural systems subserving social reward.

Three specific neural systems and corresponding neuroanatomical regions have been hypothesized to comprise the neural underpinnings for social behavior (LeDoux, 1994). First, the social perception system, evolutionarily conserved and shared with other primates, refers to the initial stages in social information processing and consists of five key nodes: (1) the superior temporal sulcus (STS), involved in the decoding of nonverbal social signals such as gaze direction and facial expression (Pelphrey et al., 2003); (2) the fusiform gyrus (FFG), or the fusiform face area (FFA), associated with face perception and recognition (Pelphrey et al., 2003); (3) the extrastriate body area in lateral occipitotemporal cortex (EBA), responsible for visual perception and recognition of the human body (Downing, Jiang, Shuman, & Kanwisher, 2001); (4) the amygdala and limbic system, involved in perception of emotional states and salient emotional experiences (Adolphs, Tranel, Damasio, & Damasio, 1995; LeDoux,

1994); and (5) the orbitofrontal cortex (OFC) and ventrolateral prefrontal cortex (VLPFC), involved in social reward and reinforcement (Bechara, Damasio, Damasio, & Anderson, 1994; Cools, Clark, Owen, & Robbins, 2002). Second, the mirror neuron system, also an evolutionarily conserved system, involves the inferior frontal gyrus and the inferior parietal lobe (IPL), both of which play an important role in action perception, understanding, and prediction (Iacoboni et al., 1999; Rizzolatti & Craighero, 2004). Finally, the mental state reasoning system, also known as theory of mind and perhaps the only system unique to humans, consists of two key nodes: the temporo-parietal junction (TPJ), responsible for reasoning about others' thoughts, and the medial prefrontal cortex (MPFC) (Carrington & Bailey, 2009). Rather than a collection of modules, these systems reflect distinct networks with some degree of specialization at individual nodes and emergent functionality via integrated processing across nodes.

In the social perception system, the perceptual processing of nonverbal social behavior, such as gaze direction or facial expression, enables people to form accurate representations of the mental states and intentions of other individuals. This system plays a predominant role in communication during the first year of life, in which human infants primarily rely on nonverbal signals to learn from their environment and interact with caregivers. Brain imaging research demonstrates the existence of this system across major sensory modalities (visual, auditory, and somatosensory) and its disruption in ASD.

In the visual domain, researchers have employed point-light displays to reflect the essential information of biological motion. Typically developing adults are able to infer complex attributes from these sparse stimuli such as the identity and the emotional states (e.g., happy versus sad) of the person exhibiting the actions (Dittrich, Troscianko, Lea, & Morgan, 1996). These stimuli are independent of visual experience and even during the first few days of life, human infants differentiate and preferentially attend to coherent versus scrambled biological motion (Simion, Regolin, & Bulf, 2008).

Distinction of biological motion occurs rapidly; by 200 milliseconds, the brain distinguishes biological motion from other forms of movement (Hirai, Fukushima, & Hiraki, 2003; Jokisch, Daum, Suchan, & Troje, 2005). Behavioral studies have shown that from very early in life, children with ASD display reduced sensitivity to biological motion (Klin, Lin, Gorrindo, Ramsay, & Jones, 2009). Neuroimaging evidence also supports that perception of biological motion is impaired in ASD. Compared to typical peers and unaffected siblings, children with ASD showed hypoactivation in the FFG, amygdala, VLPFC, and STS when they were shown biological motion stimuli versus scrambled motion stimuli (Kaiser et al., 2010).

Face processing and face and affect recognition are also well-studied social functions in ASD (e.g., Baker, Haltigan, & Messinger, 2010; Philip et al., 2010; Schultz, 2005). Humans preferentially attend to faces and recognize individual faces in early infancy (Johnson, Dziurawiec, Ellis, & Morton, 1991). Neural specialization for face perception is evident by 3 months of age (de Haan, Johnson, & Halit, 2003) and throughout the lifespan (de Haan, Pascalis, & Johnson, 2002; Nelson, 2001). While children with ASD may exhibit reduced (Maestro et al., 2002) or atypical patterns of visual attention to faces in the first year of life (Elsabbagh, Gliga, et al., 2012; Key & Stone, 2012), measures of early brain function show atypical face processing when compared to neurotypical infants (Key & Stone, 2012), and this neural pattern persists throughout childhood (Webb, Dawson, Bernier, & Panagiotides, 2006) and adulthood (Schultz, 2005). Reduced activity in the FFA during free viewing of faces in individuals with ASD (Schultz, 2005; Schultz et al., 2000) may reflect underlying differences in visual attention, that is, that people with autism tend to fixate on different parts of the faces, such as the mouth rather than the eyes (Dalton et al., 2005). Individuals with ASD also show slowed processing of faces (McPartland, Dawson, Webb, Panagiotides, & Carver, 2004), a finding that has also been observed in parents of children with ASD (Kanwisher, McDermott, & Chun, 1997) and infants at risk for ASD (McCleery, Akshoomoff,

Dobkins, & Carver, 2009). Face perceptual anomalies in ASD are heterogeneous (Apicella, Sicca, Federico, Campatelli, & Muratori, 2012; Dawson, Webb, Carver, Panagiotides, & McPartland, 2004; Wong, Fung, Chua, & McAlonan, 2008). Although variability between studies in stimulus, task, attention, gaze control, age, and cognitive abilities renders comparisons difficult, diffuse impairments in integrating social information conveyed by faces are evident across studies (Wong et al., 2008; Wright et al., 2012). Attentional factors likely contribute to these differences, as individuals with ASD show reduced attentional modulation of face perception (Churches, Wheelwright, Baron-Cohen, & Ring, 2010).

A matter of debate regarding face perception difficulties in ASD is whether they reflect a specific problem with social perception or a wider perceptual problem (Behrmann, Thomas, & Humphreys, 2006). For example, slowed processing of faces could be interpreted as a reflection of atypical social perception or a broader problem with connectivity among visual areas. Evidence in support of the former account has been provided by recent work contrasting analogous brain networks involved in perception of social and nonsocial information. Like faces, letters from an alphabet in which one is literate elicit a rapid event-related potential (ERP) component (N170) over occipitotemporal scalp (Wong, Fung, McAlonan, & Chua, 2009). McPartland and colleagues (2011) presented high-functioning individuals with ASD and typical controls with letters of the Roman alphabet and a confabulated alphabet of pseudoletters. Although individuals with ASD displayed a characteristic delay in neural response to faces, they did not demonstrate delays in the analogous response to letters, drawing upon a comparably complex neural network. These findings provide strong evidence that the nature of social information, per se, is relevant in understanding the brain bases of ASD.

In the auditory domain, human nonspeech sounds (e.g., laughing or crying), which convey information about mental states, also activate the STS region more than nonhuman nonspeech sounds (e.g., animal cries; Belin, Zatorre, Lafaille, Ahad,

& Pike, 2000). Within human nonspeech sounds, the STS region responds more strongly to communicative (e.g., laughter) versus noncommunicative (e.g., coughing) sounds, supporting the role of decoding the communicative intent in this system. Furthermore, neuroimaging demonstrates that the STS region is hypoactive in individuals with ASD versus typical peers when hearing vocal sounds (Gervais et al., 2004).

Finally, for somatosensory signals, affective touch to the arm activates a class of unmyelinated, slow-conducting, afferent fibers, as well as the STS, OFC, mPFC, insula, and amygdala, suggesting that people use this system to process the intentions and psychological dispositions of the touch provider. Strikingly, individuals with more autistic traits tend to have reduced activation in OFC and STS in response to affective touch (Gordon et al., 2013).

Action Understanding

The action-perception system's role in imitation deficits in ASD has also received considerable attention in the literature. Imitative deficits in individuals with autism are consistently observed (Rogers, 2007; Rogers, Bennetto, McEvoy, & Pennington, 1996; Rogers, Hepburn, Stackhouse, & Wehner, 2003; Sevlever & Gillis, 2010; Williams, Whiten, & Singh, 2004; Williams, Whiten, Suddendorf, & Perrett, 2001) and are considered one of the core impairments of autism (Williams et al., 2004). It has been speculated that imitation impairments in ASD stem from a deficit in self–other mapping (Rogers et al., 1996) and that this deficit may be a consequence of dysfunction of an action observation-execution matching system, or mirror neuron system (Williams et al., 2001) disrupted in ASD (Bernier, Dawson, Webb, & Murias, 2007; Dapretto et al., 2006; Hadjikhani, Joseph, Synder, & Tager-Flusberg, 2006; Martineau, Cochin, Magne, & Barthelemy, 2008; Oberman et al., 2005; Oberman et al., 2013; Theoret et al., 2005; Williams et al., 2006).

Transcranial magnetic stimulation has revealed reduced excitability in people with ASD compared to controls in the primary motor cortex during the observation of meaningless hand movements (Theoret et al., 2005). Functional MRI (fMRI) studies have found less activation of putative mirror neuron system regions in children with ASD when imitating or observing facial expressions or finger movements (Dapretto et al., 2006; Williams et al., 2006), and structural MRI has indicated decreased gray matter in related brain regions, with cortical thinning in mirror neuron system regions correlating with ASD symptom severity (Hadjikhani et al., 2006). Electroencephalography (EEG) studies of attenuation in mu rhythm (8–13 Hz), the neural EEG signal subserving the action execution-observation matching system, suggest atypical function of the action-perception domain in ASD. Unlike typical counterparts, who display attenuation of mu rhythm during both execution and observation of hand movements, several studies have shown mu suppression during execution but not observation of actions in individuals with ASD (Bernier et al., 2007; Martineau et al., 2008; Oberman et al., 2005; Oberman et al., 2013).

Action-perception has also been shown to relate to imitation (Bernier et al., 2007) as well as familiarity of the observed individual in ASD; a group of children with ASD showed typical mu wave attenuation when observing a grasping action performed by their mothers but atypical attenuation when observing actions by a stranger (Oberman, Ramachandran, & Pineda, 2008). However, these findings have not been universally replicated; some studies using EEG (Bernier, Aaronson, & McPartland, in press; Fan, Decety, Yang, Liu, & Cheng, 2010; Raymaekers, Wiersema, & Roeyers, 2009) and magnetoencephalography (MEG) (Avikainen, Kulomaki, & Hari, 1999) have indicated activity comparable to typical individuals during action-observation. Of note, follow-up analysis of the sample employed in the MEG study revealed differences between individuals with ASD and typical adults at later stages of the action-perception process, specifically in the inferior frontal gyrus (Nishitani, Avikainen, & Hari, 2004).

The heterogeneity in these findings may be attributed to variability in imitation skills suggesting that the EEG mu rhythm reflects neural activity underlying social cognitive skills often impaired in ASD (Bernier et al., in press). While no differences in EEG mu attenuation were found between a well-characterized sample of children with ASD and an age- and gender-matched group with typical development, findings revealed that individual differences in mu wave attenuation were linked to impairments in aspects of social cognition, such as imitation. These findings implicate imaging and electrophysiological indices of action-perception in autism and highlight the relevance of action-perception in the social neuroscience of autism.

Mental State Reasoning

Both the social perception system and the mirror neuron system enable individuals to interpret the actions and mental states of others based on the individual's perspective. However, the ability to understand another's perspective, that people act on the basis on their own beliefs and representations of reality, is referred to as theory of mind. For example, a child might pretend a banana to be a telephone, and to understand such pretense requires the perceiver to hold two separable versions of reality: the child's own versus the perceiver's own. Another typical example often studied is false-belief understanding (e.g., Baron-Cohen, Leslie, & Frith, 1985). In brief, this ability is for reasoning about others' thoughts in line with the world others subjectively perceive it to be, even when it might be incongruent with one's own understanding of the reality, and the ability appears to be unique to humans (Call & Tomasello, 1999). The corresponding neural system is often referred to as a mental state reasoning system and has been found to be impaired among individuals with ASD (Baron-Cohen et al., 1985; Koster-Hale, Saxe, Dungan, & Young, 2013; Tager-Flusberg, 2001).

The TPJ is a key node for mental state reasoning (Aichhorn et al., 2009; Saxe & Kanwisher, 2003; Yamada et al., 2012), which is anatomically close to but functionally distinct from the STS region, located in a slightly posterior and dorsal region relative to the STS (Saxe, Whitfield-Gabrieli,

Scholz, & Pelphrey, 2009). The TPJ region has been found to be activated when people need to infer others' intentions in line with others' thoughts; for example, during comprehension of narratives (Mason & Just, 2009), understanding others' unintentionality in an embarrassing event that violates social norms (Berthoz, Armony, Blair, & Dolan, 2002), understanding others' unintentionality in accidental physical harms (Young & Saxe, 2009), as well as understanding others' actions of pretense (German, Niehaus, Roarty, Giesbrecht, & Miller, 2004). A body of behavioral work demonstrates that individuals with ASD tend to judge more harshly for others' accidental harms (Moran et al., 2011), are less able to spontaneously predict others' behaviors in line with others' false beliefs (Senju, Southgate, White, & Frith, 2009), and are less able to understand the appropriateness of well-intentioned social pretense, known as social acting, routinely produced in an in-group setting (Yang & Baillargeon, 2013). Individuals with ASD display hypoactivation in the TPJ region when reasoning about dissimilar others' thoughts (e.g., asking British participants to estimate how likely the British Queen is to think that keeping a diary is important; Lombardo, Chakrabarti, Bullmore, & Baron-Cohen, 2011).

CONNECTIVITY IN NEURAL SYSTEMS FOR SOCIAL INFORMATION PROCESSING

Interconnectivity theories of ASD, in contrast to social information processing theories, have been put forward as an alternative account for the clinical impairments observed in ASD. These theories suggest the presence of abnormal interactions between functionally linked brain regions in ASD (Minshew & Williams, 2007) and emphasize nonspecific brain processes in which the nature of information processing is relevant only insofar as it requires distributed brain function (Horwitz, Rumsey, Grady, & Rapoport, 1988; Just, Cherkassky, Keller, & Minshew, 2004). For example, perhaps complex and distributed information processing is impaired in ASD due to poor long range connectivity, while simple, low-information processing demands are intact (Minshew & Williams, 2007). Because social interactions tend to be complex, they may be particularly underserved by long-range connectivity and reflect the social deficits found in ASD. Additionally, ASD is associated with a wide range of difficulties beyond social impairments (i.e., perceptual, cognitive), and disruption in neural connectivity has been suggested as a parsimonious account for the varied findings (Belmonte, Allen, et al., 2004; Belmonte, Cook, et al., 2004). Several studies have demonstrated atypical patterns of connective tissue in ASD via direct imaging of white matter tracts connecting different brain regions (Barnea-Goraly et al., 2004; Herbert et al., 2004; Keller, Kana, & Just, 2007); however, most evidence for atypical interconnectivity in ASD has relied on fMRI to examine covariation in activity in distal brain regions. In utilizing this approach, atypical connectivity was found at rest (Cherkassky, Kana, Keller, & Just, 2006; Di Martino et al., 2009) and during a variety of paradigms: face perception (Bird, Catmur, Silani, Frith, & Frith, 2006; Kleinhans et al., 2008; Koshino et al., 2008; Welchew et al., 2005), attribution of mental states during viewing of animations (Castelli, Frith, Happé, & Frith, 2002; Kana, Keller, Cherkassky, Minshew, & Just, 2008), language processing (Just et al., 2004; Kana, Keller, Cherkassky, Minshew, & Just, 2006), executive function (Just, Cherkassky, Keller, Kana, & Minshew, 2007; Koshino et al., 2005), visual-motor action (Mizuno, Villalobos, Davies, Dahl, & Muller, 2006; Turner, Frost, Linsenbardt, McIlroy, & Muller, 2006; Villalobos, Mizuno, Dahl, Kemmotsu, & Muller, 2005), and response inhibition (Kana, Keller, Minshew, & Just, 2007). The collective results from this body of research have yielded inconsistent trends across studies, including underconnectivity, overconnectivity, and typical patterns of connectivity. It is still unclear what role connectivity plays in ASD and whether connectivity abnormalities are a universal feature of ASD (Kleinhans et al., 2008).

The developmental nature of connectivity problems in ASD has remained largely unexplored.

Given the import of network feedback in developing long-range brain connections, localized problems in early development could manifest as connectivity issues. Bosl, Tierney, Tager-Flusberg, and Nelson (2011) provided initial evidence for a role of connectivity in early development. The authors contrasted EEG complexity (using multiscale entropy, a metric of complexity in biological systems) in infants at risk for ASD and normal risk controls, revealing reduced complexity in infants at risk. Though this study suggests the role of connectivity in early development in ASD risk, diagnostic outcome was not available for infants in this study, so it is unclear whether connectivity reflects an early marker of disease or autism-risk. Catarino, Churches, Baron-Cohen, Andrade, and Ring (2011) applied similar methods to demonstrate reduced complexity during a visual recognition task in adults with ASD.

An area of growth for connectivity research in ASD will be increased application of imaging measures with high temporal resolution to enable the study of effective connectivity, in contrast to functional connectivity. Functional connectivity studies test the null hypothesis that activity in two regions shares no mutual information; they are thus model free, largely data driven, and without power to specify directionality of influence (L. Lee, Harrison, & Mechelli, 2003). In contrast, effective connectivity examines the direct influence of one neural system on another by testing a causal model, with theoretically constrained connections (in terms of neuroanatomical, neurofunctional, and neuropsychological considerations) specified in advance (Buchel & Friston, 2000; Friston, Frith, Liddle, & Frackowiak, 1993). Because current models of effective connectivity feature rapid and transient integration of information at both the local and distal level, fMRI studies lack requisite temporal resolution to test effective connectivity (Rippon, Brock, Brown, & Boucher, 2007). Several recent studies have applied the technique to electrophysiological brain data, which yields the significant benefit of approximating the time scale of actual brain processes (Astolfi et al., 2004; Astolfi et al., 2005). MEG studies have employed effective connectivity to specify a neural path during typical face perception that flows from the occipital lobe to the superior temporal sulcus, inferior parietal lobe, inferior frontal gyrus, and then motor cortex (Nishitani & Hari, 2000, 2002), highlighting the role of brain regions involved in face processing (fusiform gyrus; Itier & Taylor, 2002) and action-perception (inferior parietal lobe, inferior frontal gyrus; Iacoboni, 2005). Wicker and colleagues (2008) examined effective connectivity in ASD compared to typical controls, revealing patterns of atypical connectivity among social brain regions during emotional face perception. Groups were not matched on cognitive ability, and thus it cannot be determined to what degree functional differences reflected ASD, per se, versus general cognitive impairment or nonspecific developmental disturbance. This nascent area of research suggests that future work investigate effective connectivity using imaging methods, such as EEG and MEG, with acute temporal resolution.

The appeal of the underconnectivity notion lies partly in the fact that it appears to offer a systems-level model of brain dysfunction that purports to account for the specific symptoms of ASD as well as the heterogeneity of etiology, behaviors, and cognition (Geschwind & Levitt, 2007). Key goals for underconnectivity research include explaining the developmental emergence of atypical connectivity in ASD and distinguishing connectivity patterns in ASD from other neurodevelopmental disorders also characterized by underconnectivity.

An understanding of the development of connectivity in ASD is complicated by a bias in the literature toward research in adults. To date, few fMRI studies have tested *children* with ASD (e.g., Brito et al., 2009; P. S. Lee et al., 2009), and they have yielded inconsistent results. For instance, P. S. Lee and colleagues (2009) examined functional connectivity in data collected during a go/no-go task in samples of 8- to 12-year-old children with and without an ASD. They focused on the connectivity values between the left and right inferior frontal cortices (IFC; BA 47) and regions of the respective frontal, striatal, and parietal cortices.

The two groups of children did not differ in their functional connectivity. Intriguingly, in the ASD group, there was a significant negative correlation between age and two long-range IFC correlation pairs: the right IFC ↔ bilateral presupplementary motor area (BA 6) and right IFC ↔ right caudate. These findings indicate normal prefrontal cortical functional connectivity in school-age children with ASD, but also suggest that some functional connections may abnormally decrease with age in the children with ASD. In other words, the brains of these children become more disconnected over time instead of starting that way.

More information is also required about the specificity of reduced functional connectivity for ASD relative to other neurodevelopmental and neuropsychiatric disorders. Reduced functional connectivity, including reductions in the long-range frontal ↔ temporal cortical and frontal ↔ parietal cortical connections, have been reported in a variety of disparate neurological, neuropsychiatric, and neurodevelopmental disorders and conditions including Alzheimer's disease (e.g., Supekar, Menon, Rubin, Musen, & Greicius, 2008), schizophrenia (e.g., Esslinger et al., 2009; Friston & Frith, 1995), adolescent depression (Cullen et al., 2009), chronic heroin use (Liu et al., 2009), posttraumatic stress disorder (Shaw et al., 2009), and dyslexia (e.g., Richards & Berninger, 2008). One study of Romanian orphans reported prominent effects on brain connectivity from the experience of profound, early, and severe socioemotional deprivation. Eluvathingal and colleagues (2006) examined, using diffusion tensor imaging (DTI) tractography, the integrity of white matter tracts that connect limbic and paralimbic structures, including the orbital frontal gyrus, infralimbic prefrontal cortex, hippocampus/amygdala, lateral temporal cortex, and the brainstem. These regions were selected a priori on the basis of a prior positron emission tomography (PET) study that identified glucose hypometabolism in each of these neuroanatomical structures in children with ASD (Chugani et al., 2001). The children exhibited relatively mild specific cognitive impairment and impulsivity, but they did not have an ASD. Fractional anisotropy values in the left uncinate fasciculus (which connects the gyri of the frontal lobe with the anterior end of the temporal lobe) were decreased significantly in the early deprivation group compared with typically developing (TD) comparison children. This finding highlights the possibility that the observed findings of reduced long-range functional connectivity in adults with ASD are actually the *result* of the ASD. If individuals with an ASD lack the necessary, early developing mechanisms for social engagement that ensure normative social development, then opportunities for social interaction are inherently reduced, particularly experiences sought out by the individual.

TRANSLATIONAL DIRECTIONS

Identifying Early Biological Markers of Risk for ASD

The social difficulties that characterize ASD are observed with their developmental emergence of social and communicative behaviors. For this reason, it is presumed that behaviorally unobservable problems in social function may precede these overt signs. Developing sensitive predictors of ASD prior to the emergence of behavioral symptoms is a key translational objective of social neuroscientists. Detecting autism earlier could reduce the typical delay to treatment onset by several years. To understand the trajectory of autistic development, prospective longitudinal studies of infant siblings of children with ASD use a comparison group of infant siblings without familial risks (the normal-risk group) to gather longitudinal information about developmental trajectories across the first 3 years of life, followed by clinical diagnosis at 36 months. Although recent study suggests behavioral indicators of abnormal attention as early as 6 months (Chawarska et al., 2013), most behavioral work to date has not revealed reliable behavioral indicators of atypical social development in the first months of life (Rogers, 2009). Recent research using infant-appropriate neuroimaging methods suggests that investigation at the neural systems level may reveal distinctions inaccessible to behavioral assays alone. Electrophysiological brain responses to dynamic eye gaze shifts during the first year predict diagnostic outcomes at 36 months (Elsabbagh, Gliga, et al., 2012). An aim of social neuroscience research in ASD is to apply such findings to develop noninvasive, brain-based screening methods that could detect differences prior to behavioral emergence in an affordable and highly efficient manner (Zwaigenbaum et al., 2005).

Improving Social Brain Function With Oxytocin

Animal and human studies have implicated the neuropeptide oxytocin in several aspects of social behavior including attachment, social memory, and parenting (e.g., Atzil, Hendler, Zagoory-Sharon, Winetraub, & Feldman, 2012; Ferguson et al., 2000; Guastella, Mitchell, & Mathews, 2008; Y. Liu & Wang, 2003). Oxytocin also plays a key role in social reward systems and might modulate the dopamine reward pathway during social interaction (Baskerville & Douglas, 2010). Emerging research suggests a possible link between oxytocin function and social motivation and consequently, the potential to ameliorate symptoms in ASD.

While behavioral studies in which oxytocin is administered intranasally have revealed some enhancement of social behaviors in typically developing individuals (e.g., Ditzen et al., 2009; Domes, Heinrichs, Michel, Berger, & Herpertz, 2007) and in individuals with ASD (e.g., Andari et al., 2010; Guastella et al., 2010), the influence of oxytocin on neural mechanisms is not yet well understood. In typically developing male participants, amygdala activation is attenuated in response to faces (Domes, Heinrichs, Glascher, et al., 2007; Kirsch et al., 2008; Petrovic, Kalisch, Singer, & Dolan, 2008); however, typically developing female participants exhibit the opposite pattern (Domes et al., 2010). Another study found that oxytocin significantly increased ventral tegmental area (VTA) activation in response to face cues signaling reward (friendly face) or punishment (angry face), implicating the VTA as a node where oxytocin processes socially relevant cues (Groppe et al., 2013). Electrophysiological studies further support the role of oxytocin in recruiting cortical resources for salient social information. Typically developing female adults presented with point-light displays of continuous biological motion showed significantly more mu suppression in the oxytocin condition compared to the placebo condition (Perry et al., 2010).

Even though the majority of extant literature highlights the involvement of oxytocin in prosocial behaviors in both typical individuals and individuals with ASD, the specific function of oxytocin in the dopaminergic system and its effects in social information processing have yet to be clarified. Additionally, many positive findings in oxytocin studies are mediated by individual differences and specific contexts in both typically and atypically developing participants (Bartz, Zaki, Bolger, & Ochsner, 2011; Feldman, Gordon, Influs, Gutbir, & Ebstein, 2013; Hirosawa et al., 2012; Riem, Bakermans-Kranenburg, Huffmeijer, & van Ijzendoorn, 2013). Characterizing the spatiotemporal substrates of oxytocin function in the brain can elucidate the mechanism by which oxytocin influences social cognition and behavior and help orient the neuropeptide's role within a larger theoretical framework (e.g., social motivation hypothesis). This is crucial if we are to understand the relationship between oxytocin in ASD and adequately integrate behavioral interventions and oxytocin administration as treatment for ASD (Stravropoulos & Carver, 2013).

Future Directions

Some of the previously discussed findings have yet to be replicated, and some have failed to replicate universally across samples. In part, these issues reflect the etiological diversity and heterogeneity in brain function and behavioral phenotype in ASD. The research presented here underscores the necessity of multimethod, longitudinal studies of development (i.e., including behavioral measures and spatial and temporal imaging) to reveal meaningful differences that may be evident only in trajectory. This integrated research approach harnesses the informative variance inherit in ASD

and exploits the strengths of each investigative method to enable profiling of function across levels and at distinct stages of processing, thereby improving the ability to tailor treatments to the individual. For example, individuals exhibiting deficits at processing associated with low-level perception would naturally require different intervention approaches from those showing problems with subsequent, higher-order processes. We envision an extension of these same principles to create detailed individual profiles of brain-behavior performance not only for more effective treatment selection, but also for more accurate subcategorization (e.g., for genetic analysis), and better prediction of treatment response. The viability of this approach is evidenced by preliminary findings showing that individuals presenting with behavioral and brain markers of difficulties with emotion regulation improve in both measures after cognitive-behavioral therapy targeted to their specific domain of impairment (Sukhodolsky et al., 2011).

CONCLUSION

Social neuroscience research in ASD suggests specificity of dysfunction to brain systems subserving social perception and information processing with preserved function in parallel systems processing nonsocial information. It remains unclear whether connectivity problems reflect developmental effects of anomalies in social brain systems or core brain dysfunction and whether problems with connectivity are specific to ASD or reflective or generic developmental perturbation in the context of neurodevelopmental disorder. Key objectives for social neuroscience research include developing assays for early detection of atypical brain function, formulating treatments to specifically target the brain systems hypothesized to underlie social and communicative impairments, and more accurately describing phenotypic heterogeneity in ASD.

CROSS-REFERENCES

Issues of diagnosis in autism and related conditions are addressed in Chapter 1, and Chapter 2 discusses the broader autism phenotype. Chapter 13 is concerned with neuropsychological assessments. Social development is the focus of Chapter 9. Chapter 17 discusses genetic aspects of ASD.

REFERENCES

Adolphs, R., Tranel, D., Damasio, H., & Damasio, A. R. (1995). Fear and the human amygdala. *Journal of Neuroscience, 15,* 5879–5891.

Aichhorn, M., Perner, J., Weiss, B., Kronbichler, M., Staffen, W., & Ladurner, G. (2009). Temporo-parietal junction activity in theory-of-mind tasks: Falseness, beliefs, or attention. *Journal of Cognitive Neuroscience, 21,* 1179–1192.

American Psychiatric Association. (2000). *Diagnostic and statistical manual of mental disorders* (4th ed., text rev.). Washington, DC: Author.

Andari, E., Duhamel, J. R., Zalla, T., Herbrecht, E., Leboyer, M., & Sirigu, A. (2010). Promoting social behavior with oxytocin in high-functioning autism spectrum disorders. *Proceedings of the National Academy of Sciences, USA, 107,* 4389–4394.

Apicella, F., Sicca, F., Federico, R. R., Campatelli, G., & Muratori, F. (2012). Fusiform gyrus responds to neutral and emotional faces in children with autism spectrum disorders: A high density ERP study. *Behavioral Brain Research.* doi: 10.1016/j.bbr.2012.10.040

Astolfi, L., Cincotti, F., Babiloni, C., Carducci, F., Basilisco, A., Rossini, P. M., ... Babiloni, F. (2005). Estimation of the cortical connectivity by high-resolution EEG and structural equation modeling: simulations and application to finger tapping data. *IEEE Transactions on Biomedical Engineering, 52*(5), 757–768.

Astolfi, L., Cincotti, F., Mattia, D., Salinari, S., Babiloni, C., Basilisco, A., ... Babiloni, F. (2004). Estimation of the effective and functional human cortical connectivity with structural equation modeling and directed transfer function applied to high-resolution EEG. *Magnetic Resonance Imaging, 22,* 1457–1470.

Atzil, S., Hendler, T., Zagoory-Sharon, O., Winetraub, Y., & Feldman, R. (2012). Synchrony and specificity in the maternal and the paternal brain: Relations to oxytocin and vasopressin. *Journal of the American Academy of Child & Adolescent Psychiatry, 51,* 781–811.

Avikainen, S., Kulomaki, T., & Hari, R. (1999). Normal movement reading in Asperger subjects. *NeuroReport, 10,* 3467–3470.

Baker, J., Haltigan, J. D., & Messinger, D. S. (2010). Non-expert ratings of infant and parent emotion: Concordance with expert coding and relevance to early autism risk. *International Journal of Behavioral Development, 34,* 88–95.

Barnea-Goraly, N., Kwon, H., Menon, V., Eliez, S., Lotspeich, L., & Reiss, A. L. (2004). White matter structure in autism: Preliminary evidence from diffusion tensor imaging. *Biological Psychiatry, 55,* 323–326.

Baron-Cohen, S., Leslie, A. M., & Frith, U. (1985). Does the autistic child have a theory of mind? *Cognition, 21,* 37–46.

Bartz, J. A., Zaki, J., Bolger, N., & Ochsner, K. N. (2011). Social effects of oxytocin in humans: Context and person matter. *Trends in Cognitive Science, 15,* 301–309.

Baskerville, T. A., & Douglas, A. J. (2010). Dopamine and oxytocin interactions underlying behaviors: Potential contributions to behavioral disorders. *CNS Neuroscience & Therapeutics, 16,* 92–123.

Bechara, A., Damasio, A. R., Damasio, H., & Anderson, S. W. (1994). Insensitivity to future consequences following damage to human prefrontal cortex. *Cognition, 50*(1–3), 7–15.

Behrmann, M., Thomas, C., & Humphreys, K. (2006). Seeing it differently: Visual processing in autism. *Trends in Cognitive Sciences, 10*(6), 258–264.

Belin, P., Zatorre, R. J., Lafaille, P., Ahad, P., & Pike, B. (2000). Voice-selective areas in human auditory cortex. *Nature, 403*(6767), 309–312.

Belmonte, M. K., Allen, G., Beckel-Mitchener, A., Boulanger, L. M., Carper, R. A., & Webb, S. J. (2004). *Journal of Neuroscience, 24,* 1614–1624.

Belmonte, M. K., Cook, E. H., Jr., Anderson, G. M., Rubenstein, J. L., Greenough, W. T., Beckel-Mitchener, A., ... Tierney, E. (2004). Autism as a disorder of neural information processing: Directions for research and targets for therapy. *Molecular Psychiatry, 9,* 646–663.

Bernier, R., Aaronson, B., & McPartland, J. (in press). The role of imitation in the observed heterogeneity in EEG mu rhythm in autism spectrum disorders. *Brain and Cognition.*

Bernier, R., Dawson, G., Webb, S., & Murias, M. (2007). EEG mu rhythm and imitation impairments in individuals with autism spectrum disorder. *Brain Cognition, 64,* 228–237.

Berthoz, S., Armony, J. L., Blair, R. J. R., & Dolan, R. J. (2002). An fMRI study of intentional and unintentional (embarrassing) violations of social norms. *Brain, 125,* 1696–1708.

Bird, G., Catmur, C., Silani, G., Frith, C., & Frith, U. (2006). Attention does not modulate neural responses to social stimuli in autism spectrum disorders. *Neuroimage, 31,* 1614–1624.

Bosl, W., Tierney, A., Tager-Flusberg, H., & Nelson, C. (2011). EEG complexity as a biomarker for autism spectrum disorder risk. *BMC Medicine, 9,* 18.

Brito, A. R., Vasconcelos, M. M., Domingues, R. C., Hygino da Cruz, L. C., Jr., Rodrigues, L. de S., Gasparetto, E. L., & Calcada, C. A. (2009). Diffusion tensor imaging findings in school-aged autistic children. *Journal of Neuroimaging, 19,* 337–343.

Brothers, L. (1990). The social brain: A project for integrating primate behavior and neurophsyiology in a new domain. *Concepts in Neuroscience, 1,* 27–51.

Buchel, C., & Friston, K. (2000). Assessing interactions among neuronal systems using functional neuroimaging. *Neural Networks, 13,* 871–882.

Call, J., & Tomasello, M. (1999). A nonverbal false belief task: The performance of children and great apes. *Child Development, 70,* 381–395.

Carrington S. J., & Bailey, A. J. (2009). Are there theory of mind regions in the brain? A review of the neuroimaging literature. *Human Brain Mapping, 30,* 2313–2335.

Castelli, F., Frith, C., Happé, F., & Frith, U. (2002). Autism, Asperger syndrome and brain mechanisms for the attribution of mental states to animated shapes. *Brain, 125,* 1839–1849.

Catarino, A., Churches, O., Baron-Cohen, S., Andrade, A., & Ring, H. (2011). Atypical EEG complexity in autism spectrum conditions: A multiscale entropy analysis. *Clinical Neurophysiology, 122,* 2375–2383.

Chawarska, K., Macari, S., & Shic, F. (2013). Decreased spontaneous attention to social scenes in 6-month-old infants later diagnosed with autism spectrum disorders. *Biological Psychiatry.* Advance online publication. doi: 10.1016/j.biopsych.2012.11.022

Cherkassky, V. L., Kana, R. K., Keller, T. A., & Just, M. A. (2006). Functional connectivity in a baseline resting-state network in autism. *NeuroReport, 17,* 1687–1690.

Chugani, H. T., Behen, M. E., Muzik, O., Juhasz, C., Nagy, F., & Chugani, D. C. (2001). Local brain functional activity following early deprivation: A study of postinstitutionalized Romanian orphans. *Neuroimage, 14,* 1290–1301.

Churches, O., Wheelwright, S., Baron-Cohen, S., & Ring, H. (2010). The N170 is not modulated by attention in autism spectrum conditions. *NeuroReport, 21,* 399–403.

Cools, R., Clark, L., Owen, A. M., & Robbins, T. W. (2002). Defining the neural mechanisms of probabilistic reversal learning using event-related functional magnetic resonance imaging. *Journal of Neuroscience, 22,* 4563–4563.

Cullen, K. R., Gee, D. G., Klimes-Dougan. B., Gabbay, V., Hulvershorn, L., Mueller, B. A.,...Milham, M. P. (2009). A preliminary study of functional connectivity in comorbid adolescent depression. *Neuroscience Letters, 460,* 227–231.

Dalton, K. M., Nacewicz, B. M., Johnstone, T., Schaefer, H. S., Gernsbacher, M. A., Goldsmith, H. H., & Davidson, R. J. (2005). Gaze fixation and the neural circuitry of face processing in autism. *Nature Neuroscience, 8,* 519–526.

Dapretto, M., Davies, M. S., Pfeifer, J. H., Scott, A. A., Sigman, M., Bookheimer, S. Y., & Iacoboni, M. (2006). Understanding emotions in others: Mirror neuron dysfunction in children with autism spectrum disorders. *Nature Neuroscience, 9,* 28–30.

Dawson, G., Webb, S. J., Carver, L., Panagiotides, H., & McPartland, J. (2004). Young children with autism show atypical brain responses to fearful versus neutral facial expressions of emotion. *Developmental Science, 7,* 340–359.

Dawson, G., Webb, S. J., & McPartland, J. (2005). Understanding the nature of face processing impairment in autism: insights from behavioral and electrophysiological studies. *Developmental Neuropsychology, 27,* 403–424.

de Haan, M., Johnson, M. H., & Halit, H. (2003). Development of face-sensitive event-related potentials during infancy: A review. *International Journal of Psychophysiology, 51,* 45–58.

de Haan, M., Pascalis, O., & Johnson, M. H. (2002). Specialization of neural mechanisms underlying face recognition in human infants. *Journal of Cognitive Neuroscience, 14,* 199–209.

Dichter, G., & Adolphs, R. (2012). Reward processing in autism: A thematic series. *Journal of Neurodevelopmental Disorders, 4,* 20.

Di Martino, A., Shehzad, Z., Kelly, C., Roy, A. K., Gee, D. G., Uddin, L. Q.,...Milham, M. P. (2009). Relationship between cingulo-insular functional connectivity and autistic traits in neurotypical adults. *American Journal of Psychiatry, 166,* 891–899.

Dittrich, W. H., Troscianko, T., Lea, S. E., & Morgan, D. (1996). Perception of emotion from dynamic point-light displays represented in dance. *Perception, 25,* 727–738.

Ditzen, B., Schaer, M., Gabriel, B., Bodenmann, G., Ehlert, U., & Heinrichs, M. (2009). Intranasal oxytocin increases positive communication and reduces cortisol levels during couple conflict. *Biological Psychiatry, 65,* 728–731.

Domes, G., Heinrichs, M., Glascher, J., Buchel, C., Braus, D. F., & Herpertz, S. C. (2007). Oxytocin attenuates amygdala responses to emotional faces regardless of valence. *Biological Psychiatry, 62,* 1187–1190.

Domes, G., Heinrichs, M., Michel, A., Berger, C., & Herpertz, S. C. (2007). Oxytocin improves "mind-reading" in humans. *Biological Psychiatry, 61,* 731–733.

Domes, G., Lischke, A., Berger, C., Grossmann, A., Hauenstein, K., Heinrichs, M., & Herpertz, S. C. (2010). Effects of intranasal oxytocin on emotional face processing in women. *Psychoneuroendocrinology, 35,* 83–93.

Downing, P. E., Jiang, Y., Shuman, M., & Kanwisher, N. (2001). A cortical area selective for visual processing of the human body. *Science, 293,* 2470–2473.

Elsabbagh, M., Gliga, T., Pickles, A., Hudry, K., Charman, T., Johnson, M. H., & The BASIS Team. (2012). The development of face orienting mechanisms in infants at-risk for autism. *Behavioral Brain Research.* doi: 10.1016/j.bbr.2012.07.030

Elsabbagh, M., Mercure, E., Hudry, K., Chandler, S., Pasco, G., Charman, T.,...Johnson, M. H. (2012). Infant neural sensitivity to dynamic eye gaze is associated with later emerging autism. *Current Biology, 22,* 338–342.

Eluvathingal, T. J., Chugani, H. T., Behen, M. E., Juhasz, C., Muzik, O., Maqbool, M.,...Makki, M. (2006). Abnormal brain connectivity in children after early severe socioemotional deprivation: A diffusion tensor imaging study. *Pediatrics, 117,* 2093–2100.

Esslinger, C., Walter, H., Kirsch, P., Erk, S., Schnell, K., Arnold, C.,...Meyer-Lindenberg, A. (2009). Neural mechanisms of a genome-wide supported psychosis variant. *Science, 324,* 605.

Fan, Y. T., Decety, J., Yang, C. Y., Liu, J. L., & Cheng, Y. (2010). Unbroken mirror neurons in autism spectrum disorders. *Journal of Child Psychology and Psychiatry, 51,* 981–988.

Feldman, R., Gordon, I., Influs, M., Gutbir, T., & Ebstein, R. P. (2013). Parental oxytocin and early caregiving jointly shape children's oxytocin response and social reciprocity. *Neuropsychopharmacology.* doi: 10.1038/npp.2013.22

Ferguson, J. N., Young, L. J., Hearn, E. F., Matzuk, M. M., Insel, T. R., & Winslow, J. T. (2000). Social amnesia in mice lacking the oxytocin gene. *Nature Genetics, 25,* 284–288.

Friston, K. J., & Frith, C. D. (1995). Schizophrenia: A disconnection syndrome? *Clinical Neuroscience, 3,* 89–97.

Friston, K. J., Frith, C. D., Liddle, P. F., & Frackowiak, R. S. (1993). Functional connectivity: The principal-component analysis of large (PET) data sets. *Journal of Cerebral Blood Flow and Metabolism, 13,* 5–14.

German, T. P., Niehaus, J. L., Roarty, M. P., Giesbrecht, B., & Miller, M. B. (2004). Neural correlates of detecting pretense: Automatic engagement of the intentional stance under covert conditions. *Journal of Cognitive Neuroscience,* *16*, 1805–1817.

Gervais, H., Belin, P., Boddaert, N., Leboyer, M., Coez, A., Sfaello, I., . . . Zilbovicius, M. (2004). Abnormal cortical voice processing in autism. *Nature Neuroscience, 7,* 801–802.

Geschwind, D. H., & Levitt, P. (2007). Autism spectrum disorders: Developmental disconnection syndromes. *Current Opinion in Neurobiology, 17,* 103–111.

Gordon, I., Voos, A. C., Bennett, R. H., Bolling, D. Z., Pelphrey, K. A., & Kaiser, M. D. (2013). Brain mechanisms for processing affective touch. *Human Brain Mapping, 34,* 914–922.

Groppe, S. E., Grossen, A., Rademacher, L., Hahn, A., Westphal, L., Grunder, G., & Spreckelmeyer, K. N. (2013). Oxytocin influences processing of socially relevant cues in the ventral tegmental area of the human brain. *Biological Psychiatry.* doi: 10.1016/j.biopsych.2012.12.023

Guastella, A. J., Einfeld, S. L., Gray, K. M., Rinehart, N. J., Lambert, T. J., & Hickie, I. B. (2010). Intranasal oxytocin improves emotion recognition for youth with autism spectrum disorders. *Biological Psychiatry, 67,* 692–694.

Guastella, A. J., Mitchell, P. B., & Mathews, F. (2008). Oxytocin enhances the encoding of positive social memories in humans. *Biological Psychiatry, 64,* 256–258.

Hadjikhani, N., Joseph, R. M., Snyder, J., & Tager-Flusberg, H. (2006). Anatomical differences in the mirror neuron system and social cognition network in autism. *Cerebral Cortex, 16,* 1276–1282.

Herbert, M. R., Ziegler, D. A., Makris, N., Filipek, P. A., Kemper, T. L., Normandin, J. J., . . . Caviness, V. S., Jr. (2004). Localization of white matter volume increase in autism and developmental language disorder. *Annals of Neurology, 55,* 530–540.

Hirai, M., Fukushima, H., & Hiraki, K. (2003). An event-related potentials study of biological motion perception in humans. *Neuroscience Letters, 344,* 41–44.

Hirosawa, T., Kikuchi, M., Higashida, H., Okumura, E., Ueno, S., Shitamichi, K., . . . Minabe, Y. (2012). Oxytocin attenuates feelings of hostility depending on emotional context and individuals' characteristics. *Scientific Reports, 384.* doi:10.1038/srep00384

Horwitz, B., Rumsey, J. M., Grady, C. L., & Rapoport, S. I. (1988). The cerebral metabolic landscape in autism. Intercorrelations of regional glucose utilization. *Archives of Neurology, 45,* 749–755.

Hubbard, A. L., McNealy, K., Scott-Van Zeeland, A. A., Callan, D. E., Bookheimer, S. Y., & Dapretto, M. (2012). Altered integration of speech and gesture in children with autism spectrum disorders. *Brain and Behavior, 5,* 606–619.

Iacoboni, M. (2005). Neural mechanisms of imitation. *Current Opinion in Neurobiology, 15,* 632–637.

Iacoboni, M., Woods, R. P., Brass, M., Bekkering, H., Mazziotta, J. C., & Rizzolatti, G. (1999). Cortical mechanisms of human imitation. *Science, 286,* 2526–2528.

Itier, R. J., & Taylor, M. J. (2002). Inversion and contrast polarity reversal affect both encoding and recognition processes of unfamiliar faces: A repetition study using ERPs. *Neuroimage, 15,* 353–372.

Johnson, M. H., Dziurawiec, S., Ellis, H., & Morton, J. (1991). Newborns' preferential tracking of face-like stimuli and its subsequent decline. *Cognition, 40,* 1–19.

Jokisch, D., Daum, I., Suchan, B., & Troje, N. F. (2005). Structural encoding and recognition of biological motion: Evidence from event-related potentials and source analysis. *Behavioural Brain Research, 157,* 195–204.

Just, M. A., Cherkassky, V. L., Keller, T. A., Kana, R. K., & Minshew, N. J. (2007). Functional and anatomical cortical underconnectivity in autism: Evidence from an FMRI study of an executive function task and corpus callosum morphometry. *Cerebral Cortex, 17,* 951–961.

Just, M. A., Cherkassky, V. L., Keller, T. A., & Minshew, N. J. (2004). Cortical activation and synchronization during sentence comprehension in high-functioning autism: Evidence of underconnectivity. *Brain, 127,* 1811–1821.

Kaiser, M. D., Hudac, C. M., Shultz, S., Lee, S. M., Cheung, C., Berken, A. M., . . . Pelphrey, K. A. (2010). Neural signatures of autism. *Proceedings of the National Academy of Sciences, USA, 107,* 21223–21228.

Kana, R. K., Keller, T. A., Cherkassky, V. L., Minshew, N. J., & Just, M. A. (2006). Sentence comprehension in autism: Thinking in pictures with decreased functional connectivity. *Brain, 129,* 2484–2493.

Kana, R. K., Keller, T. A., Cherkassky, V. L., Minshew, N. J., & Just, M. A. (2008). Atypical frontal-posterior synchronization of Theory of Mind regions in autism during mental state attribution. *Social Neuroscience, 3,* 1–18.

Kana, R. K., Keller, T. A., Minshew, N. J., & Just, M. A. (2007). Inhibitory control in high-functioning autism: Decreased activation and underconnectivity in inhibition networks. *Biological Psychiatry, 62,* 198–206.

Kanner, L. (1943). Autistic disturbances of affective contact. *Nervous Child, 2,* 217–250.

Kanwisher, N., McDermott, J., & Chun, M. M. (1997). The fusiform face area: A module in human extrastriate cortex specialized for face perception. *Journal of Neuroscience, 17,* 4302–4311.

Keller, T. A., Kana, R. K., & Just, M. A. (2007). A developmental study of the structural integrity of white matter in autism. *NeuroReport, 18,* 23–27.

Key, A. P., & Stone, W. L. (2012). Same but different: 9-month-old infants at average and high risk for autism look at the same facial features but process them using different brain mechanisms. *Autism Research, 5,* 253–266.

Kirsch, P., Esslinger, C., Chen, Q., Mier, D., Lis, S., Siddhanti, S., . . . Meyer-Lindenberg, A. (2008). Oxytocin modulates neural circuitry for social cognition and fear in humans. *Journal of Neuroscience, 25,* 11489–11493.

Kleinhans, N. M., Richards, T., Sterling, L., Stegbauer, K. C., Mahurin, R., Johnson, L. C., . . . Aylward, E. (2008). Abnormal functional connectivity in autism spectrum disorders during face processing. *Brain, 131,* 1000–1012.

Klin, A., Lin, D. J., Gorrindo, P., Ramsay, G., & Jones, W. (2009). Two-year-olds with autism orient to non-social contingencies rather than biological motion. *Nature, 459,* 257–261.

Kohls, G., Chevallier, C., Troiani, V., & Schultz, R. T. (2012). Social "wanting" dysfunction in autism: Neurobiological underpinnings and treatment implications.

Journal of Neurodevelopmental Disorders, 4, 10. doi: 10.1186/1866-1955-4-10

Koshino, H., Carpenter, P. A., Minshew, N. J., Cherkassky, V. L., Keller, T. A., & Just, M. A. (2005). Functional connectivity in an fMRI working memory task in high-functioning autism. *Neuroimage, 24*, 810–821.

Koshino, H., Kana, R. K., Keller, T. A., Cherkassky, V. L., Minshew, N. J., & Just, M. A. (2008). fMRI investigation of working memory for faces in autism: Visual coding and underconnectivity with frontal areas. *Cerebral Cortex, 18*, 289–300.

Koster-Hale, J., Saxe, R., Dungan, J., & Young, L. L. (2013). Decoding moral judgments from neural representations of intentions. *Proceedings of the National Academy of Sciences, USA, 110*, 5648–5653.

LeDoux, J. E. (1994). Emotion, memory and the brain. *Scientific American, 270*, 50–57.

Lee, L., Harrison, L. M., & Mechelli, A. (2003). A report of the functional connectivity workshop, Dusseldorf 2002. *Neuroimage, 19*, 457–465.

Lee, P. S., Yerys, B. E., Della Rosa, A., Foss-Feig, J., Barnes, K. A., James, J. D., ... Kenworthy, L. E. (2009). Functional connectivity of the inferior frontal cortex changes with age in children with autism spectrum disorders: An fcMRI study of response inhibition. *Cerebral Cortex, 19*, 1787–1794.

Liu, J., Liang, J., Qin, W., Tian, J., Yuan, K., Bai, L., ... Gold, M. S. (2009). Dysfunctional connectivity patterns in chronic heroin users: an fMRI study. *Neuroscience Letters, 460*, 72–77.

Liu, Y., & Wang, Z. X. (2003). Nucleus accumbens oxytocin and dopamine interact to regulate pair bond formation in female prairie voles. *Neuroscience, 121*, 537–544.

Lombardo, M. V., Chakrabarti, B., Bullmore, E. T., & Baron-Cohen, S. (2011). Specialization of right temporo-parietal junction for mentalizing and its relation to social impairments in autism. *Neuroimage, 56*, 1832–1838.

Maestro, S., Muratori, F., Cavallaro, M. C., Pei, F., Stern, D., Golse, B., & Palacio-Espasa, F. (2002). Attentional skills during the first 6 months of age in autism spectrum disorder. *Journal of the American Academy of Child & Adolescent Psychiatry, 41*, 1239–1245.

Martineau, J., Cochin, S., Magne, R., & Barthelemy, C. (2008). Impaired cortical activation in autistic children: Is the mirror neuron system involved? *International Journal of Psychophysiology, 68*, 35–40.

Mason, R. A., & Just, M. A. (2009). The role of the theory-of-mind cortical network in the comprehension of narratives. *Language and Linguistics Compass, 3*, 157–174.

McCleery, J. P., Akshoomoff, N., Dobkins, K. R., & Carver, L. J. (2009). Atypical face versus object processing and hemispheric asymmetries in 10-month-old infants at risk for autism. *Biological Psychiatry, 66*, 950–957.

McPartland, J., Dawson, G., Webb, S. J., Panagiotides, H., & Carver, L. J. (2004). Event-related brain potentials reveal anomalies in temporal processing of faces in autism spectrum disorder. *Journal of Child Psychology and Psychiatry, 45*, 1235–1245.

McPartland, J. C., Wu, J., Bailey, C. A., Mayes, L. C., Schultz, R. T., & Klin, A. (2011). Atypical neural specialization for social percepts in autism spectrum disorder. *Social Neuroscience, 6*, 436–451.

Minshew, N. J., & Williams, D. L. (2007). The new neurobiology of autism: cortex, connectivity, and neuronal organization. *Archives of Neurology, 64*, 945–950.

Mizuno, A., Villalobos, M. E., Davies, M. M., Dahl, B. C., & Muller, R. A. (2006). Partially enhanced thalamocortical functional connectivity in autism. *Brain Research, 1104*, 160–174.

Moran, J. M., Young, L. L., Saxe, R., Lee, S. M., O'Young, D., Mavros, P. L., & Gabrieli, J. D. (2011). Impaired theory of mind for moral judgment in high- functioning autism. *Proceedings of the National Academy of Sciences, USA, 108*, 2688–2692.

Nelson, C. A. (2001). The development and neural bases of face recognition. *Infant and Child Development, 10*, 3–18.

Nishitani, N., Avikainen, S., & Hari, R. (2004). Abnormal imitation-related cortical activation sequences in Asperger's syndrome. *Annals of Neurology, 55*, 558–562.

Nishitani, N., & Hari, R. (2000). Temporal dynamics of cortical representation for action. *Proceedings of the National Academy of Sciences, USA, 97*, 913–918.

Nishitani, N., & Hari, R. (2002). Viewing lip forms: Cortical dynamics. *Neuron, 36*, 1211–1220.

Oberman, L. M., Hubbard, E. M., McCleery, J. P., Altschuler, E. L., Ramachandran, V. S., & Pineda, J. A. (2005). EEG evidence for mirror neuron dysfunction in autism spectrum disorders. *Cognitive Brain Research, 24*, 190–198.

Oberman, L. M., McCleery, J. P., Hubbard, E. M., Bernier, R., Wiersema, J. R., ... Pineda, J. A. (2013). Developmental changes in mu suppression to observed and executed actions in autism spectrum disorders. *Social Cognitive Affective Neuroscience, 8*, 300–304.

Oberman, L. M., Ramachandran, V. S., & Pineda, J. A. (2008). Modulation of mu suppression in children with autism spectrum disorders in response to familiar or unfamiliar stimuli: The mirror neuron hypothesis. *Neuropsychologia, 46*, 1558–1565.

Pelphrey, K. A., Mitchell, T. V., McKeown, M. J., Goldstein, J., Allison, T., & McCarthy, G. (2003). Brain activity evoked by the perception of human walking: Controlling for meaningful coherent motion. *Journal of Neuroscience, 23*, 6819–6825.

Perry, A., Bentin, S., Shalev, I., Israel, S., Uzefovsky, F., Bar-On, D., & Ebstein, R. P. (2010). Intranasal oxytocin modulates EEG mu/alpha and beta rhythms during perception of biological motion. *Psychoneuroendocrinology, 35*, 1446–1453.

Petrovic, P., Kalisch, R., Singer, T., & Dolan, R. J., (2008). Oxytocin attenuates affective evaluations of condition faces and amygdala activity. *Journal of Neuroscience, 28*, 6607–6615.

Philip, R. C., Whalley, H. C., Stanfield, A. C., Sprengelmeyer, R., Santos, I. M., Young, A. W., ... Hall, J. (2010). Deficits in facial, body movement and vocal emotional processing in autism spectrum disorders. *Psychological Medicine, 40*, 1919–1929.

Raymaekers, R., Wiersema, J. R., & Roeyers, H. (2009). EEG study of the mirror neuron system in children with high functioning autism. *Brain Research, 1304*, 113–121.

Richards, T. L., & Berninger, V. W. (2008). Abnormal fMRI connectivity in children with dyslexia during a phoneme task:

Before but not after treatment. *Journal of Neurolinguistics, 21*, 294–304.

Riem, M. M., Bakermans-Kranenburg, M. J., Huffmeijer, R., & van Ijzendoorn, M. H. (2013). Does intranasal oxytocin promote prosocial behavior to an excluded fellow player? A randomized-controlled trial with Cyberball. *Psychoneuroendocrinology, 38*, 1418–1425.

Rippon, G., Brock, J., Brown, C., & Boucher, J. (2007). Disordered connectivity in the autistic brain: Challenges for the "new psychophysiology." *International Journal of Psychophysiology, 63*, 164–172.

Rizzolatti, G., & Craighero, L. (2004). The mirror-neuron system. *Annual Review of Neuroscience, 27*, 169–192.

Rogers, S. (2007). Nature of motor imitation problems in school-aged males with autism. *Developmental Medicine and Child Neurology, 49*, 5.

Rogers, S. J. (2009). What are infant siblings teaching us about autism in infancy? *Autism Research, 3*, 125–137.

Rogers, S. J., Bennetto, L., McEvoy, R., & Pennington, B. F. (1996). Imitation and pantomime in high-functioning adolescents with autism spectrum disorders. *Child Development, 67*, 2060–2073.

Rogers, S. J., Hepburn, S. L., Stackhouse, T., & Wehner, E. (2003). Imitation performance in toddlers with autism and those with other developmental disorders. *Journal of Child Psychology and Psychiatry, 44*, 763–781.

Saxe, R., & Kanwisher, N. (2003). People thinking about thinking people. The role of the temporo-parietal junction in "theory of mind." *Neuroimage, 19*, 1835–1842.

Saxe, R., Whitfield-Gabrieli, S., Scholz, J., & Pelphrey, K. A. (2009). The development of brain regions for perceiving and reasoning about other people. *Child Development, 80*, 1197–1209.

Schultz, R. T. (2005). Developmental deficits in social perception in autism: The role of the amygdala and fusiform face area. *International Journal of Developmental Neuroscience, 23*, 125–141.

Schultz, R. T., Gauthier, I., Klin, A., Fullbright, R., Anderson, A., Volkmar, F., . . . Gore, J. C. (2000). Abnormal ventral temporal cortical activity during face discrimination among individuals with autism and Asperger syndrome. *Archives of General Psychiatry, 57*, 331–340.

Scott-Van Zeeland, A. A., Dapretto, M., Ghahremani, D. G., Poldrack, R. A., & Bookheimer, S. Y. (2010). Reward processing in autism. *Autism Research, 3*, 53–67.

Senju, A., Southgate, V., White, S., & Frith, U. (2009). Mindblind eyes: An absence of spontaneous theory of mind in Asperger Syndrome. *Science, 325*, 883–885.

Sevlever, M., & Gillis, J. M. (2010). An examination of the state of imitation research in children with autism: Issues of definition and methodology. *Research in Developmental Disabilities, 31*, 976–984.

Shaw, M. E., Moores, K. A., Clark, R. C., McFarlane, A. C., Strother, S. C., Bryant, R. A., . . . Taylor, J. D. (2009). Functional connectivity reveals inefficient working memory systems in post-traumatic stress disorder. *Psychiatry Research, 172*, 235–241.

Simion, F., Regolin, L., & Bulf, H. (2008). A predisposition for biological motion in the newborn baby. *Proceedings of the National Academy of Sciences, USA, 105*, 809–813.

Stravropoulous, K. K., & Carver, L. J. (2013). Research review: Social motivation and oxytocin in autism—implications for joint attention, development, and intervention. *Journal of Child Psychology and Psychiatry*. Advance online publication. doi:10.1111/jcpp.12061

Sukhodolsky, D. G., Bolling, D. Z., Wu, J., Crowley, M., McPartland, J., Scahill, L., & Pelphrey, K. A. (2011). *Cognitive behavior therapy for irritability in high-functioning ASD: Pilot study of neurobiological mechanisms*. Paper presented at the International Meeting for Autism Research, San Diego, CA.

Supekar, K., Menon, V., Rubin, D., Musen, M., & Greicius, M. D. (2008). Network analysis of intrinsic functional brain connectivity in Alzheimer's disease. *PLoS Computational Biology, 6*, doi: 10.1371/journal.pcbi.1000100

Tager-Flusberg, H. (2001). A reexamination of the theory of mind hypothesis of autism. In J. A. Burack, T. Charman, N. Yimiya, & P. R. Zelazo (Eds.), *The development of autism: Perspectives from development and theory* (pp. 173–193). Mahwah, NJ: Erlbaum.

Theoret, H., Halligan, E., Kobayashi, M., Fregni, F., Tager-Flusberg, H., & Pascual-Leone, A. (2005). Impaired motor facilitation during action observation in individuals with autism spectrum disorders. *Current Biology, 15*, R84–85.

Turner, K. C., Frost, L., Linsenbardt, D., McIlroy, J. R., & Muller, R. A. (2006). Atypically diffuse functional connectivity between caudate nuclei and cerebral cortex in autism. *Behavioral and Brain Functions, 2*, 34.

Villalobos, M. E., Mizuno, A., Dahl, B. C., Kemmotsu, N., & Muller, R. A. (2005). Reduced functional connectivity between V1 and inferior frontal cortex associated with visuomotor performance in autism. *Neuroimage, 25*, 916–925.

Webb, S. J., Dawson, G., Bernier, R., & Panagiotides, H. (2006). ERP evidence of atypical face processing in young children with autism. *Journal of Autism and Developmental Disorders, 36*, 881–890.

Welchew, D. E., Ashwin, C., Berkouk, K., Salvador, R., Suckling, J., Baron-Cohen, S., & Bullmore, E. (2005). Functional disconnectivity of the medial temporal lobe in Asperger's syndrome. *Biological Psychiatry, 57*, 991–998.

Wicker, B., Fonlupt, P., Hubert, B., Tardif, C., Gepner, B., & Deruelle, C. (2008). Abnormal cerebral effective connectivity during explicit emotional processing in adults with autism spectrum disorder. *Social Cognitive Affective Neuroscience, 3*, 135–143.

Williams, J. H., Waiter, G. D., Gilchrist, A., Perrett, D. I., Murray, A. D., & Whiten, A. (2006). Neural mechanisms of imitation and "mirror neuron" functioning in autistic spectrum disorder. *Neuropsychologia, 44*, 610–621.

Williams, J. H., Whiten, A., & Singh, T. (2004). A systematic review of action imitation in autistic spectrum disorder. *Journal of Autism and Developmental Disorders, 34*, 285–299.

Williams, J. H., Whiten, A., Suddendorf, T., & Perrett, D. I. (2001). Imitation, mirror neurons and autism. *Neuroscience Biobehavioral Reviews, 25*, 287–295.

Wong, T. K., Fung, P. C., Chua, S. E., & McAlonan, G. M. (2008). Abnormal spatiotemporal processing of emotional facial expressions in childhood autism: Dipole source analysis of event-related potentials. *European Journal of Neuroscience, 28*, 407–416.

Wong, T. K., Fung, P. C., McAlonan, G. M., & Chua, S. E. (2009). Spatiotemporal dipole source localization of face processing ERPs in adolescents: a preliminary study. *Behavioral and Brain Functions, 5*, 16.

Wright, B., Alderson-Day, B., Prendergast, G., Bennett, S., Jordan, J., Whitton, C.,...Green G. (2012). Gamma activation in young people with autism spectrum disorders and typically-developing controls when viewing emotions on faces. *PLoS One, 7*, e41326. doi: 10.1371/journal.pone.0041326

Yamada, M., Camerer, C. F., Fujie, S., Kato, M., Matsuda, T., Takano, H.,...Takahashi, H. (2012). Neural circuits in the brain that are activated when mitigating criminal sentences. *Nature Communications, 3*, 759. doi:10.1038/ncomms1757

Yang, D. Y.-J., & Baillargeon, R. (2013). Difficulty in understanding social acting (but not false beliefs) mediates the link between autistic traits and ingroup relationships. *Journal of Autism and Developmental Disorders, 43*(9), 2199–2206.

Young, L., & Saxe, R. (2009). Innocent intentions: A correlation between forgiveness for accidental harm and neural activity. *Neuropsychologia, 47*, 2065–2072.

Zwaigenbaum, L., Bryson, S., Rogers, T., Roberts, W., Brian, J., & Szatmari, P. (2005). Behavioral manifestations of autism in the first year of life. *International Journal of Developmental Neuroscience, 23*, 143–152.

CHAPTER 21

The Neuropathology of Autism

A noticeable aspect of the history of brain research on autism is the scant number of neuropathological studies and the small number of autopsied cases reported within them. It is possible that the scarcity of cases has been due to the conception of autism as a psychogenic disorder; one whose etiology is rooted in the mind rather than the brain. In the 1800s mental disorders were attributed to diseases of the mind therefore lacking in a structural substrate (Winslow, 1854). In the case of autism the feeling persisted unquenched for the next 100 years. It has been argued that when psychiatry stood back from neuropathology it allowed for the recruitment of other disciplines, such as psychoanalysis, in order to better understand mental illnesses (Lishman,

I wish to acknowledge the generous bequeath of tissue to different brain banks and honor the memory of the donors. Without the precious gift from these individuals no research into the neuropathological underpinnings of autism would have been possible. I would also like to recognize the formative role of my mentors (and source of inspiration) within the field of neuropathology: Donald Price, Arthur Clark, Juan Troncoso, and Tom Kemper.

1992; 1995). With this mind-set it is not surprising, according to Corsellis (1972), that psychiatrists had little time for either the anatomy or pathology of the nervous system.

In 1969 the British Neuropathological Society conducted a survey of 171 psychiatric hospitals exploring their ties to pathology services (Corsellis, 1972). One hundred and twenty-seven hospitals replied, canvassing a total of 140,000 patients. From that figure it was calculated that approximately 10% of the patients died each year but that only one in six of these cases were autopsied. Performed autopsies were often made under the authority of the coroner to comply with the legal mandate of establishing the immediate cause of death. Seldom was a thorough study of the nervous system attempted. The survey concluded that it was doubtful whether 1 in 50 of the autopsied brains was examined by a neuropathologist and more rarely so by microscopy (Corsellis, 1972). The fostered lackadaisical attitude was alarming as a significant number of patients at psychiatric hospitals suffered from a known or suspected physical condition. By way of illustration, at the Maudsely neuropsychiatric clinic almost half of referred patients suffered from clear organic psychosyndromes and an added 20% comprised a group of patients whose symptoms gave rise to uncertainties about an organic or nonorganic disorder (Lishman, 1992).

The salient exception to the schism between psychiatry and neuropathology was Germany, where practitioners of the 19th century combined the disciplines of psychiatry, neurology, and neuropathology. Indeed, Wilhelm Griesinger, who at one time headed an institution for mentally handicapped children, stated that "mental diseases are brain diseases" (Lishman, 1995, p. 285). Before his death in 1868 he famously professed, "Psychiatry and neuropathology are not merely two closely related fields; they are but one field in which only one language is spoken and the same laws rule" (Zilboorg & Henry, 1941, p. 436). Unfortunately, even in Germany, early researchers had to waddle their way through confusing terminology and classification schemes. Published articles variously referred to autism as childhood psychosis, *dementia praecoccisima*, *dementia infantilis*, or childhood schizophrenia. Furthermore, patients with autism were often embedded within series of intellectually disabled or epileptic patients wherein their intrinsic findings were diluted and ultimately lost to posterity.

Both the mental attitude and confusing terminology certainly played a major role in limiting the number of neuropathology reports on autism during the 20th century. Another major determinant was the small number of cases being recognized or diagnosed. It was the Swiss psychiatrist Bleuler who first introduced the term *autism* in 1911 while describing the extreme withdrawal of some schizophrenic patients. In 1943 Kanner borrowed the term to emphasize the lack of affective contact he observed in 11 children (Kanner, 1943). Two decades later a review of the literature by Bernard Rimland found only one autopsied case with scant documentation (Rimland, 1964). By 1997 the literature indicated the existence of less than 30 brains with detailed postmortem examinations

(Rapin, 1999). The numbers would only slightly increase by the next decade, that is, $n = 40$ in 2004 (Palmen, Van Engeland, Hof, & Schmitz, 2004). Further reducing the total number of cases is the fact that, having been reused from established brain collections, some reported cases were duplicates.

In order to facilitate brain research the National Alliance for Autism Research (NAAR) established an initiative in 1998 geared toward collecting postmortem tissue. The initiative, called the Autism Tissue Program (ATP), was later taken over by Autism Speaks when these organizations merged in 2006. The ATP is not a brain bank per se but works directly with the Harvard Tissue Resource Center in Boston, Massachusetts, to serve as its tissue repository. As of February 2012 the ATP listed 539 cases for all banks or private collections that have been noted as used in projects (Jane Pickett, personal communication, 2012). In all, the ATP has supplied tissue for 122 projects in 15 countries yielding 100 published articles since 2001. A striking endeavor of the ATP has been the creation of a histological atlas comparing whole brain serial sections of 13 individuals with autism and an equal number of age-matched controls (Wegiel et al., 2010). A data access system provides information on existing tissues to allow investigators sorting of cases (e.g., age, medication, hospitalization, seizure history). The information can be found at www.atpportal.org (Briacombe, Pickett, & Pickett, 2007; Pickett & London, 2005).

EARLY HISTORY

Within reported series, early findings tended to be nonspecific (i.e., changes that were also seen in controls) or probably the result of postmortem artifacts and of agonal/preagonal conditions. Several authors made claims of combing through the literature for autopsied cases, but the resultant handful of cases added little information to the prevailing wisdom and failed to motivate clinicians. Among the early studies the most comprehensive review was performed by John Darby during his tenure as the director of research and education at the Scott and White Hospital and Clinic in Texas. In 1976, Darby expanded on a review of the literature that started with an annotated bibliography of over 1,700 references of cases diagnosed as either childhood psychosis, childhood schizophrenia, or autism (Bellak, 1958; Bellak & Loeb, 1969; Darby, 1976; Goldfarb & Dorsen, 1956). In addition to the existing bibliography, Darby performed a Medlar search of the literature, made inquiries to interested clinicians, and corresponded with higher academic institutions having pathology services. The resultant exploration provided for 33 cases with severe psychotic syndrome associated with autism (Darby, 1976). Twenty-nine of the cases had been previously reported; only four cases were new to the literature and obtained through the author's inquiries. Six cases comprised three pairs of siblings (Malamud, 1959) and two had tuberous sclerosis. Clinical data and availability of tissue was sparse for many of the cases. Some reports originated from brain biopsies or had only one slide available for pathological examination.

The neuropathology in Darby's (1976) series led to few conclusions. Overall, reported cases had variable age of onset and differed significantly in regards to their clinical presentation. The brain specimens at gross examination were unremarkable. The most common finding by microscopy was cerebral lipidosis, a term that in the absence of an inheritance pattern or suggestive clinical findings (e.g., progressive spastic paralysis, blindness) made reference to lipofuscin accumulation. The pigmentary or fuscous degeneration of neurons consisted of accumulation within vacuoles of a golden-yellow substance that turned black with osmic acid and was associated in advanced cases with cell death (so-called pigmentary atrophy). The reported finding is of arguable significance and could be compatible with normal aging. However, a more recent study doing a quantitative analysis of the size of lipofuscin aggregates revealed significantly greater number of pigmented cells in Brodmann areas 22 and 39 of individuals with autism. The authors believed that the findings were consistent with accelerated neuronal death

or increased oxidative stress (López-Hurtado & Prieto, 2008).

Darby (1976) concluded that the constellation of disturbed behaviors observed in autism were the expression of a number of disorders. The espoused concept reminds us of the "final common pathway" of Bellak (1958) in regard to the nature of schizophrenia wherein a variety of insults are somehow funneled to provide similar phenotypic expressions. A modern version of this concept is the "lowest common denominator of autism," proposed by E. L. Williams and Casanova (2011), which suggests that the phenotypic commonalities of the condition lie not at the genetic level of comparison but at the molecular and neuroanatomical levels.

Aarkrog (1968) added to the literature the microscopic analysis of a frontal lobe biopsy. The results showed a slight thickening of the arterioles, a slight increase in connective tissue in the leptomeninges and some cell increase. More recently, R. S. Williams, Hauser, Purpura, DeLong, and Swisher (1980) examined the brains of four individuals who exhibited documented features of autism. Age range varied from 4 to 33 years of age. Two of the patients had associated disorders; one had phenylketonuria and the other probably had Rett's syndrome. Within the body of the article one of the patients is confusingly reported as having died at either 12 or 14 years of age. Three of the patients were males. One of the brains was perfused with embalming fluid and later used for both electron microscopy and rapid Golgi impregnation. Gyral pattern was judged to be normal in all patients. Multiple areas were sampled with some of the tissue embedded in either paraffin or celloidin. Neuropathological findings, including microscopy of Golgi impregnated tissue sections, were unremarkable.

Coleman, Romano, Lapham, and Simon (1985) were the first to report cell counts for neurons (pyramidal and others) and glia in the cerebral cortex of a patient with autism and two age- and sex-matched controls. Areas explored included those involved with the perception and production of speech, including primary auditory cortex, Broca's speech area, and the auditory association cortex. Tissues were embedded in celloidin and serial sections stained with hematoxylin-eosin, cresyl violet, Luxol fast blue, and Bodian silver impregnation. Cell counts were done with an oil immersion objective at 100× magnification. The eyepiece had a grid inserted in it to ensure systematic counting of cells through 70 μm wide strips of cortex extending from the pia to the white matter. Five adjacent strips were examined per slide. A total of 17,689 cells were manually counted and categorized. Results showed a smaller glia/neuron ratio than the average of the two controls in all regions examined; however, all comparison failed to reach statistical significance. Small pockets of eosinophilic neurons were frequently found in the depths of sulci. The pattern of changes reminded this author (MFC) of that seen in ulegyria. Reduced perfusion from hypotension may preferentially damage the deep sulcal cortex (Janzer & Friede, 1979). The pathological findings are in agreement with the presumed cause of death for the patient, that is, infection and/or shock leading to disseminated intravascular coagulation (DIC). Given the widespread damage evidenced at pathological examination, the suitability of this brain for a cell count study is questioned.

The review by Darby (1976) and the reports of R. S. Williams et al. (1980) and Coleman et al. (1985) punctuate the early history of neuropathological studies in autism. The efforts of these authors provided valuable leads for future studies. Some of the key points can be summarized as follows:

1. After substantial perusal of archived pathological records and published studies (<1985) only a few cases were uncovered. The recent revival of interest and increased number of publications involving postmortem studies can be attributed primarily to the efforts of the Autism Tissue Program in facilitating tissues to interested researchers.
2. There is an inherited tendency in autism as shown by sibling pairs within reported autopsy series.
3. Autism can be divided into those cases that are *idiopathic* (of unknown cause) and those

secondary to other conditions, so-called double syndromes (Ozonoff, 1997). Idiopathic cases comprise the majority of cases. Among secondary cases, genetic conditions (e.g., tuberous sclerosis) appear to be common.
4. Given the heterogeneity in clinical presentations it is not surprising that multiple brain sites were implicated. However, the cerebral cortex was favored when considering clinicopathological correlations to autism.
5. Gross examination of the brain is usually normal. The gyral pattern appears to be unremarkable and ventricles are of normal size.
6. Early investigators questioned the significance of some pathological (microscopic) findings as artifacts due to delayed tissue fixation or their nonspecificity. As an example, a prolonged postmortem interval to tissue fixation was blamed for the observed diminutions in the number of dendritic spines seen in autism as well as in other mental disorders (R. S. Williams et al., 1980).
7. A significant percentage of neuropathological reports either came or were drafted by ill-qualified individuals. Not many neuropathologists lent their expertise to the systematic study of autism.
8. Early investigators emphasized the need for appropriate tissue processing in order to minimize preparation artifacts. The use of celloidin in cell counts studies and cytoarchitectural work was preferred over paraffin embedding.
9. It was difficult to judge the significance of some reported findings when compared against appropriate controls. In the cell count study of Coleman et al. (1985), data on the case with autism differed from one control less so than the data between the two controls.

MODERN HISTORY

Bauman and Kemper

The most extensive and best known studies dealing with the neuropathology of autism are those of

Figure 21.1   Margaret Bauman and Thomas Kemper have been involved in autism research since 1983. They were the first investigators to report neuropathological changes in autism involving neuronal circuits of importance to learning, emotion, and behavior.

Bauman and Kemper (Bauman, 1991; Bauman & Kemper, 1985, 1996, 2005; Kemper & Bauman, 1993; Raymond, Bauman, & Kemper, 1996). It is widely regarded that the published studies by this pair of researchers marks the beginning of the modern history of neuropathological studies in autism (Figure 21.1). Their laborious research entailed the systematic study of serial full-hemisphere sections spanning the rostrocaudal extent of the brain. Their first case report was published in 1985 and corresponded to the autopsies of a 29-year-old individual with autism and a 25-year-old male control (Bauman & Kemper, 1985). The patient with autism achieved normal milestones until 2.5 years when speech development stopped, regressed, and from then onward never spoke more than two-word phrases. His attention span was short, he showed no eye contact, he exhibited rocking and stereotypical behaviors, and he inconsistently responded to his name. During adolescence he was treated with chlorpromazine, trifluoperazine, and diazepam in an unsuccessful attempt to improve his behavior. He had his first major motor seizure at 21 years of age. An electroencephalogram (EEG) examination revealed a photoconvulsive pattern and a pneumoencephalogram showed mild ventricular dilation. He was variously treated for his epilepsy with phenytoin, primidone, and phenobarbital. He died by accidental drowning at the age of 29.

A detailed autopsy report of the incept case by Bauman and Kemper (1985) concluded that the topography of brain areas showing pathology comprised interrelated circuits of the hippocampal complex (i.e., hippocampus and subiculum), entorhinal cortex, and two areas directly related to it, the septum and mammillary bodies. Other brain areas deemed pathological were confined to the central, medial and cortical nuclei of the amygdala. Outside of the forebrain abnormalities included bilateral and symmetric loss of Purkinje and granule cells in the neocerebellum with lack of glial cell hyperplasia. The authors recognized that the history of seizures and use of phenytoin could have contributed to the loss of Purkinje cells. However, the lack of concomitant gliosis and absence of retrograde olivary cell loss led them to believe that Purkinje cell loss was more consistent with an early lesion during brain development. This conclusion was unfortunately based on qualitative observations of Nissl stained slides.

Since their initial case report Bauman and Kemper have added an additional nine cases to their series, one of them with a diagnosis of Asperger's (Bauman, 1991; Bauman & Kemper, 1985, 2005; Kemper & Bauman, 1993; Raymond et al., 1996). Eight of the 10 brains were cut midsagitally leaving only one hemisphere available for microscopic examination. Two of the 10 brains had both hemispheres available for study. Brains were embedded in celloidin and cut coronally at 35 microns. Every 20th section was stained for Nissl substance and for each 100th section an adjacent slide was stained for myelin by the Loyez method. Selected sections of the cerebellum, hippocampus, amygdala, septum, and hypothalamus were stained with hematoxylin-eosin (H-E).

Age range and intelligence varied widely in these patients. The subjects with autism included six children (five boys and one girl) aged 7–12 years, and three men aged 22–29 years. The single male Asperger patient was 21 years old upon his death. The initial examination of the brains was performed with a Zeiss comparison light microscope wherein the split window allowed corresponding brain areas to be viewed simultaneously side by side at the same magnification. The technique avoided having to rely on the observer's memory when comparing different series of objects under a conventional light microscope. The initial survey of the slides was qualitative with areas of presumed abnormalities being further examined by quantitating the number of neurons per unit volume (packing density) and neuronal cell size. Quantitation was achieved by using an optical reticle at the magnification of 160×. More recent studies by the group have used computerized stereological techniques.

At least 4 of the 10 patients reported by Bauman and Kemper (see earlier) had seizures and had been treated with anticonvulsants. There were no abnormalities at gross examination. Myelin staining was judged unremarkable. The slides were reviewed by the author (MFC) who believes that the quality, preparation, and preservation of the available material made it hard to draw firm conclusions about the cerebral cortex. Many of the difficulties stemmed from transferring the huge pieces of tissue into the glass slides. Folds, uneven staining, drying, and other artifacts limited the regions of interest from where reliable information could be obtained. Not surprisingly, most significant observations came from subcortical nuclei and only minor changes were reported for the cerebral cortex. Findings in the cerebral cortex included individual cases showing either an indistinct laminar pattern in the anterior cingulate gyrus or a minor malformation in the orbitofrontal cortex (Bauman & Kemper, 1987; Kemper & Bauman, 1998).

Microscopy in Bauman and Kemper's series suggested reduced neuronal size and increased density in the amygdala (primarily the medial, central, and cortical nuclei), hippocampal complex, subiculum, entorhinal cortex, medial septal nuclei, and mammillary bodies (Bauman & Kemper, 2005). In the nucleus of the diagonal band of Broca, neurons were larger in the brains of younger patients. All cases had abnormalities in the cerebellum with Purkinje cell loss and lack of retrograde abnormalities in the olivary nucleus. In their three younger individuals with autism, the neurons of the olivary nuclei were enlarged

but normal in number and appearance while in their three older patients neurons were pale and smaller. The authors suggested that the described abnormalities had an antenatal origin evidencing the persistence of a fetal olivary-dentate circuit, which typically regresses by 30 weeks of gestation.

In addition to the aforementioned brain regions, Bauman and Kemper used their brain collection to conduct a systematic screening of the striatum, pallidum, hypothalamus, and basal forebrain (Bauman & Kemper, 2005). No histologic abnormalities were found in these areas. However, a preliminary study by this group on the ventral lateral thalamic nuclei in the brains of two subjects with autism showed small cell size and increased packing density in comparison to controls (Schultz, Bauman, & Kemper, 1999). The topography of thalamic abnormalities described by Schultz et al. (1999) differs from the one described by Weidenheim et al. (2001) in two cases of secondary autism due to neuroaxonal dystrophy. In Weidenheim's cases spheroids were seen in thalamic nuclei connected to the limbic system, including anterior, dorsomedial, and midline nuceli, but not in those nuclei related to sensory functions, for example, ventralposterolateral.

Bauman and Kemper added to their impressive cumulus of work an analysis of the hippocampus by impregnating tissue with the rapid Golgi technique (Raymond et al., 1996). The case report included two patients with autism: one boy aged 9 who died of unknown cause and one girl aged 7 who died by accidental drowning. Control patients were 8 and 13 years old, of undetermined gender, whose cause of death was not defined. Neither the anatomical level of the hippocampus used for sampling nor the number of slides taken for analysis was specified. The Golgi method allowed for visualization of good CA4 neuronal staining in only one of the cases with autism, while both patients had adequate staining of the CA1 pyramidal cells. Neurons were drawn with a camera lucida at 1000× magnification and dendritic arborization determined by using concentric circles of Sholl (1956). Perikaryal area measurements were taken with a digital planimeter. The results showed decreased size of neuronal perikaryon in CA4 of one child with autism and decreased complexity of dendritic arborization in the CA1 and CA4 subfields of both children with autism as compared to controls. The authors indicated that the findings were consistent with their previous observations of reduced neuronal size and increased cell packing density of the hippocampus using routine stains. However, the capriciousness of the Golgi impregnation, lack of methodological detail, and small number of patients limits interpretation of the data. A previous attempt at using the Golgi method reported a reduction in dendritic spine counts within neocortical areas as being the result of a prolonged postmortem interval (R. S. Williams et al., 1980). A more recent study using the Golgi impregnation to quantify dendritic density of pyramidal cells was performed by Hutsler and Zhang (2010). Regions of interest included frontal (BA9), temporal (BA21), and parietal lobe (BA7). In this study average spine densities across the three cortical regions were higher in the subjects with autism as compared to controls.

Density of interneuronal subsets of cells within the anterior hippocampus was explored by immunocytochemistry using calbindin (CB), calretinin (CR), and parvalbumin (PV). The sample consisted of five individuals with autism (two died from seizures, one from cardiopulmonary arrest, another from a pancreatic blood clot, and one of unknown cause) and an equal number of age-matched controls. Alternating sections were sampled at an interval of 2500 μm in order to create a 5000 μm counting interval with a minimum of seven slides counted per case. Sections were taken from frozen blocks and cut at 50 μm on a freezing microtome. Results showed topographical selectivity with increased density of CB immunoreactive neurons in the dentate gyrus, increase CR positive interneurons in area CA1, and an increase in PV interneurons in the CA1 and CA3 subfields of the hippocampus of individuals with autism. The authors did not discuss any possible correlations between their results and the agonal/preagonal condition of the patients (e.g., seizures), medication usage, nor did they examine for concomitant gliosis (e.g., glial fibrillary acid protein [GFAP]).

The significance of this and other studies using similar methodology should be cautiously considered. Unbiased quantitation on human postmortem immunocytochemistry (itself a biased technique) may provide spurious results (Casanova & Kleinman, 1990). The antibody-antigen reaction does not form covalent bonds and its equilibrium in human postmortem tissue may be influenced by factors such as the preagonal state of the patient, postmortem interval, type of fixative, length of fixation, and tissue processing.

RECENT STUDIES

Based primarily on Bauman and Kemper's studies, a recent review of the neuropathology of autism by Palmen et al. (2004) found that 9 out of 14 studied cases showed increased cell-packing density and smaller neuronal (soma) size in the limbic system. Other investigators have been unable to reproduce these findings. Bailey et al. (1998) found no consistent differences between cases with and without autism in the various CA subfields examined. Counts in one particular case were below the control range (case 5); however, the finding was explained by the patient's diagnosis of epilepsy. Only one individual with autism (case 3) exhibited elevated counts in all CA subfields as compared to a control.

Using an optical fractionator, Stereoinvestigator software, and a detailed description of anatomical guidelines to define subdivisions of the human amygdala, Schumann and Amaral (2005, 2006) were unable to corroborate the presence of decreased neuronal size or increased cell-packing density in autism. The study included amygdalae of nine individuals with autism and 10 age-matched controls focusing on the following subdivisions: (a) lateral nucleus, (b) basal nucleus, (c) accessory basal nucleus, (d) central nucleus, and (e) the remaining nuclei. The investigators reported no group differences in the volume of the total amygdala or its nuclei; however, cell counts revealed significantly fewer neurons in individuals with autism ($10.74 \times 10^6 \pm 1.47 \times 10^6$ mean $\pm$ s.d.)

as compared to controls ($12.21 \times 10^6 \pm 1.28 \times 10^6$; $p = 0.032$). Thus, design based stereology gave opposite results to what had been previously reported based on qualitative observations (Amaral, Schumann, & Nordahl, 2008). A difference between the series of Schuman and Amaral (2006) and Bauman and Kemper (1994, 2005) was the exclusion in the former of individuals with seizures.

Several years after the work by Bauman and Kemper was published, Bailey et al. (1998) reported a comprehensive neuropathological study on the brains of six mentally handicapped patients with autism. In this seminal study Bailey et al. (1998) found olivary nuclei abnormalities in three of five patients who had available slides. Studies of a single cross section of the hippocampus revealed increased packing density in only one out of five cases with autism. Other brainstem abnormalities noted by Bailey et al. (1998) involved the medulla, pons, locus coeruleus, stria medullaris, and arcuate nuclei. Two of Bailey et al.'s (1998) patients had neuronal ectopias and an increased number of individual neurons within the white matter. Two cases showed an increased number of individual neurons within the white matter, that is, neurons not clustering into patches. One additional case showed subpial gliosis, which was curiously tabulated as a pathological finding of the white matter. According to Bailey et al. (1998) the reported observations did not support previous claims of localized neurodevelopmental abnormalities; rather, they pointed to the involvement of the cerebral cortex in autism.

Other neuropathological studies in autism have involved case reports or the analysis of specific neuronal elements, for example, axons. Hof, Knabe, Bovier, and Bouras (1991) provided a descriptive study of a microcephalic patient with autism and premature closure of the cranial sutures. At 7 years of age the patient developed a very serious form of self-injurious behavior characterized by head hitting, head banging, eye gouging, and self-biting. Repeated head and eye trauma made the patient blind from bilateral retinal detachment and dullness of the cornea. The brain exhibited generalized gross cerebral atrophy but a normal gyral and sulcal pattern. At autopsy, neurofibrillary tangles were found in clusters preferentially within the superficial layers of the perirhinal and entorhinal cortex. Neurofibrillary tangles were found in the cortex primarily in layers II and III. There were no concomitant senile plaques or amyloid deposits. Given the seriousness of the patient's self-injurious behavior, the authors believed that the neurofibrillary tangles were the results of traumatic brain injury similar to those observed in dementia pugilistica, or "punch drunk syndrome." The authors did not comment on any neuropathological changes that could be ascribed to autism.

Guerin et al. (1996) reported a case of a 16-year-old female with autism and severe psychomotor retardation who died from pulmonary infection. The case was published without details regarding postmortem interval to fixation, tissue processing or staining, nor regions of interest sampled. A neuropathologist was not apparently involved in the case report. The main findings came from the gross examination: microencephaly, ventricular dilation, and a thin corpus callosum. A few microglial nodules in the brainstem were regarded as the remnants of prior encephalitis. The authors explained their findings as a result of excessive axonal elimination during brain development. The possibility of axonal pathology leading to disrupted neural communication in autism has been further pursued by several independent investigators (see later discussion).

Axonal pathology was described in two unrelated cases of neuroxonal dystrophy with secondary autism (Weidenheim et al., 2001). Spheroids were abundant in catecholaminergic and serotonergic nuclei with diencephalic projections. The topographic distribution of spheroids suggested that pathology of the limbic and deep gray matter structures play an important role in the etiopathology of autistic behaviors.

The density of axons and the thickness of axons and myelin sheaths were investigated using unbiased quantitative stereology by Zikopoulos and Barbas (2010). The study involved five people with autism (one female) and four age-matched controls (two females). Postmortem intervals (PMI) differed significantly among the comparison groups given the prolonged interval of one subject with autism (99 hours). Within the reported case series some of the individuals with autism were diagnosed as having seizure disorder, depression, and/or schizophrenia. Regions of interest included the white matter below the anterior cingulate cortex,

(a)   (b)

Figure 21.2   The number of serotonergic axons appears increased in the temporal cortex of a 29-year-old individual with autism (b) as compared to his 25-year-old control (a). The supernumerary axons were described as dystrophic. In the study by Azmitia, Singh, Hou, and Wegiel (2011) statistical analysis revealed a correlation between abnormal axons and age: Fibers appear increased at the youngest age examined (2.8 years) and stay elevated during adolescent when the serotonergic fibers begin to degenerate. The highest level of dystrophic axons was found in a young teenager who died of the serotonergic syndrome. (Photographs courtesy of Efraim Azmitia).

the orbitofrontal cortex, and the lateral prefrontal cortex. Below the anterior cingulate cortex there was an excessive number of thin axons while axons in the orbitofrontal cortex had decreased myelin thickness. The white matter in the lateral prefrontal cortex appeared normal. The results provide an anatomical counterpart to other pathological studies suggesting excessive short-range connectivity and reduced strength of long-distance connections in autism (Casanova et al., 2006b).

Immunocytochemical evidence of dystrophic serotonergic axons was reported by Azmitia, Singh, Hou, and Wegiel (2011) in the brains of 13 individuals with autism (aged 2.8 to 29 years) and 9 controls (ages 2 to 29 years) (Figure 21.2). Five of the subjects had experienced seizures, and three displayed aggression/self-injurious behaviors. Regions of interest included the temporal lobe hemispheres and telecephalic subcortical structures from where two major ascending serotonergic tracts corresponding to the medial and lateral forebrain bundles were identified. A Methods section is curiously missing from the article and important details regarding the quantitation are lacking. Serotonergic immunorective fibers were more abundant in the brains of individuals with autism as compared to controls. The increase in serotonergic axons was noted for the medial and lateral bundles, as well as for the amygdala, piriform, superior temporal, and parahippocampal cortices. The significance of the findings is limited as length of fixation and postmortem interval were not provided or considered when evaluating the results.

BRAIN WEIGHT

Brain weight is only a crude indicator of pathology whose significance increases when the reported values fall at the tail ends of the spectrum. Macro- or microencephaly refers to brains whose weights are more than two standard deviations outside the mean for age, sex, race, and gestation. Approximately 2% of the population has macrocephaly. Investigation of such individuals may show an abnormality causing increased head size; however, the majority of individuals are normal with a familial tendency towards a large head (Fenichel, 2005).

Both macrocephaly and microcephaly, using head circumference as an index, are found in higher proportions than expected in children with autism. A recent series of 126 individuals from the southwest of France revealed macrocephaly (head circumference above the 97th percentile) in 16.7% of the population and microcephaly (head circumference below the 3rd percentile) in 15.1% of the sample (Fombonne, Rogé, Claverie, Courty, & Frémolle, 1999). Macrocephaly was not associated to gender, developmental level, the presence of epilepsy or the severity of autistic symptomatology. Microcephaly was significantly associated with the presence of medical disorders. Although common in autism, macrocephaly is not usually present at birth. Lainhart et al. (1997) reported that rates of head growth were abnormal in early and middle childhood in some (37%) children with autism. The macrocephaly of autism therefore differs from so-called true macroencephaly, which is a proliferative disorder of embryonic origin where abnormal brain weight is noticeable at term (Menkes & Sarnat, 2000).

Most reported data on postmortem brain weights should be considered estimates. Details disclosing the manner in which brain weight was acquired (e.g., fresh versus fixed) are seldom reported in the postmortem literature of autism. Formalin fixation typically provides for increased brain weights with estimates that vary according to the age of the patients. According to Quester and Schröder (1997), there is a 7% to 13.4% gain in weight of the cerebrum primarily between 1 and 5 days of fixation. Higher gains may be seen at lower concentrations of fixative (Itabashi, Andrews, Tomiyasu, Erlich, & Sathyavagiswaran, 2007). In adults the gain in brain weight approximates 8.8% (Finkbeiner, Ursell, & Davis, 2004) and higher gains (10% to 14.1%) are reported in children, (Larroche, 1977; Ludwig, 2002). The findings parallel the water content of the brain. At birth 90% of the brain consists of water, in contrast to only 70%–75% for the adult brain (Nelson, 2003).

Useful clinical indices to keep in mind when considering the validity of brain weights include cause of death, duration of terminal illness, and terminal state of hydration (Itabashi et al., 2007). At a minimum postmortem brain weight studies should ensure that the same autopsy procedures are in place to standardize the presence or stripping of leptomeninges and brainstem structures. A possible source of variation between series is the PMI or death to autopsy interval. There is a rapid increase in brain weight during the first 12 hours postmortem that may account for changes in ventricular and sulcal size (Appel & Appel, 1942a, 1942b; Sarwar & McCormick, 1978). Relying on histological assessment as a measure of postmortem edema is inaccurate. There are large variations in postmortem water content that go undetected on histologic examination for edema (Yates, Thelmo, & Pappius, 1975).

Studies on postmortem brain weight or case series reporting this parameter are summarized in the next few paragraphs. Thus far most of these postmortem series have failed to disclose relevant details that may have helped clarify the significance of their reported findings. More specifically, the narrative for gross findings invariably fails to describe any evidence of atrophy or swelling, and discussions of findings almost never take into consideration the agonal and preagonal conditions of the patients.

In R. S. Williams et al.'s (1980) study of four subjects with autism brain weights were reported as 1,200 g for the 4-year-old; 1,430 g for the 14-year-old; 1,240 g for the 27-year-old; and 1,520 g for the 33-year-old. All four subjects were within two standard deviations of the mean for age. The subject in the Hof et al. (1991) case died at 24 years of age and her brain weighed 773 g. The patient was diagnosed as microcephalic at her first physical examination. She also presented with micophthalmos and enophthalmos. Bauman and Kemper (1994) collected fresh brain weights from 12 children with autism, aged 5 to 13 years, and 8 adults with autism, aged 18–54 years. The investigators compared the data with that of controls from a published series (Dekaban & Sadowsky, 1978) and concluded that the majority of the children's brains were significantly heavier than expected for age and sex, by 100 g–200 g. The authors also suggested the data was in agreement with other reports of the literature indicating that relative to controls brain development in autism is associated with accelerated growth early in life which is later followed by an apparent deceleration.

I analyzed the tabulated data of Bauman and Kemper (1994) and compared the same against normative brain fresh brain weights reported by Dekaban and Sadowsky (1978). There were three evident outliers as seen in a plot of deviation from mean brain weight versus age (Figure 21.3). Two of the cases had unusually high brain weights, and one individual was nearly twice the age of any other person in the sample. The remaining data showed a clear trend toward a continuous diminution in brain weight with aging.

Bailey et al. (1993) reported heavier brain weight in three of four brains of individuals with autism but without an obvious increase in neuronal density. At death the ages of the patients were 4, 22, 24, and 27 years. The clustering and small number of cases prevented generalizing conclusions regarding brain weight and age. Qualitative microscopic examination revealed no obvious increase in neuronal density, suggesting that megalencephaly was associated with an excessive number of neurons. Two additional cases were later added to the series (Bailey et al., 1998). The brains corresponded to those of men 20 and 23 years old. There is a note within the case reports that during the revision of the manuscript the brain of a cachectic 41-year-old with autism became available for study. The brain weighed 1,233 g. The figure may be lower than expected due to malnutrition (Brown, 1966). The authors also mentioned that postmortem findings, but not tissue, were available for a further 14 individuals with a clinical diagnosis of autism. Brain weights were recorded in four young adult males (1,530 g; 1,450 g; 1,400 g; and 1,300 g), one young adult female (1400 g), and one 16-year-old female (1,330 g). It is difficult to ascribe any significance to the added cases as they lacked both in terms of history and tissue examination.

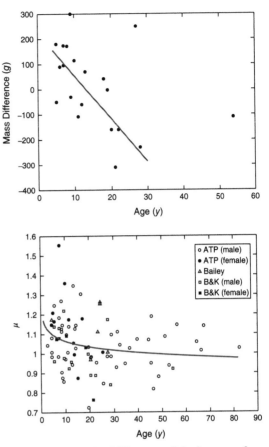

Figure 21.3 (Left) Difference of brain mass from expected brain mass, as a function of age, as reported by Bauman and Kemper (2005). Three clear outliers are visible, including two cases of unusually high brain weight (1,670 g and 1,690 g) and one individual 54 years old, nearly twice the age of any other person in the sample. The remaining data show a clear trend, which was quantified by fitting a line to all data using least median of squares, with the result that deviation = 224 g – 17 g × (age/1 y). (Right) Ratio of brain mass to expected brain mass, as a function of age. Data are abstracted from Bailey et al. (1998), "Bailey"; Bauman and Kemper (2005), "B&K"; and the ATP portal, "ATP." The relationship of mass ratio with age was modeled as a power law: $\mu = 1.17 \times (\text{age}/1 \text{ y})^{-0.0415}$.

The study by Bailey et al. (1998) has been the only one to report the ratio of total brain to brainstem and cerebellar weight. Out of the six brains described by Bailey et al. (1998), three showed evidence of swelling without herniation (brain weights 1,600 g; 1,805 g; and 1,820 g). One brain in particular evidenced signs of putrefaction: soft to the touch and containing numerous bacteria. The reported findings suggest that increased brain weight in some cases within Bailey et al.'s (1998) series was the result of an artifact, that is, postmortem edema.

Guerin et al. (1996) case report was that of a microencephalic 16-year-old patient with height retardation (1.37 m, 4.46 standard deviations below mean for age). Fresh brain weights reported by Weidenheim et al. (2001) for her two cases of secondary autism due to neuroaxonal dystrophy were 1125 g (expected weight 1,260 g ± 40 g for an 11-year-old) and 1,473 g (expected wright 1445 g ± 20 g for a 20-year-old man). Hutsler, Love, and Zhang (2007) reported 8 autism spectrum disorder cases ages 10–45 (mean of 29 years) and an equal number of controls, ages 11–51 (mean of 30.13 years). Two of their autism spectrum disorder (ASD) patients had brain weights in excess of one standard deviation of published norms (1,710 g and 1,720 g). Mean brain weight for their postmortem ASD cases was 1,378.75 g and 1,455.00 g for their controls. In Santos et al. (2011) study of Von Economo neurons in the frontoinsular cortex of children with autism there were no reported difference in brain weight ($p = 0.489$) or postmortem interval ($p = 0.721$). Brain weight for the four children with autism (mean age 7 years) was 1,425 g and 1,355 g for the 3 controls (mean age 8.7 years).

Courchesne, Müller, and Saitoh (1999) reported on brain weights at autopsy for 5 new cases and 16 previously reported, and compared them with 6 normative series. Of the 21 individuals with autism, brain weights were within normal range in 17 occasions, 3 were reported as megalencephalic, and 1 as microencephalic. The authors concluded that brain weights in most postmortem cases of autism are normal with rare cases of megalencephaly. In this study brain weights were reported as taken at autopsy but it was not clarified as to whether they were fresh or whether they had been taken after fixation. Two cases of putative megalencephaly had been previously reported by Bailey et al. (1998) and may have been artifacts of postmortem edema (see earlier discussion).

Courchesne pursued his initial findings with a metanalysis of fresh postmortem brain weight data on 55 specimens (Courchesne et al., 1999; Redcay & Courchesne, 2005). The study showed a significant effect of age with younger individuals (2–5 years) having the greatest deviation from normal (Redcay & Courchesne, 2005). In six of the reported cases, data were derived by doubling the weight of single hemispheres (Casanova, Buxhoeveden, Switala, & Roy, 2002b). Several other cases had postmortem edema or putrefaction (Bailey et al., 1998). There is a scarcity of brain material to prove Courchesne's view that the brain of individuals with autism is smaller at birth (Redcay & Courchesne, 2005). Brain weight at birth for subjects with autism was less than one standard deviation below average. In this regard, the study of Gillberg and de Souza (2002) provides almost the same percentage difference in head circumference as the percentage difference in brain volumes noted by Courchesne (Redcay & Courchesne, 2005).

Redcay and Courchesne's (2005) meta-analysis of 15 studies of head circumference and brain volume, the latter obtained via MRI, in autistic disorder modeled the difference D from the neurotypical case. The difference was expressed as a percentage, a sum of two decaying exponentials

$$D = -Ae^{-t/t_r} + Be^{-t/t_f}$$

where t is age in years, and the least squares parameter estimates were $A = 21.18\%$, $B = 13\%$, $t_r = 0.297$ years, and $t_f = 8.31$ years. (The original article expressed the estimates in terms of $1/t_r$ and $1/t_f$ instead.) They concluded that brain size in autism normalizes as patients approach adulthood. However, they did not report any alternative models to the best fit, whose functional form practically guarantees that D will go to zero later in life. The simplest alternative is to add a nonzero asymptote to the model of Redcay and Courchesne (2005):

$$D = -Ae^{-t/t_r} + Be^{-t/t_f} + D_0$$

Upon fitting this model to the data, the least squares estimate for D_0 was 0.511%, not significantly different from 0 ($F_{1,18} = 0.0617$, p = 0.807).

Moreover, this alternative is actually a worse fit in an information theoretic sense, with corrected Akaike information criterion $AIC_C = -548$, while the original model, fit using the same procedure, had $AIC_C = -551$. The conclusion of Redcay and Courchesne (2005) appears to be justified and brain weights/volumes of individuals with and without autism appear to converge later in life (Figure 21.3).

A final note to this section, meant to emphasize possible stumbling blocks for postmortem brain weight studies: Investigators should be aware of updates to databases as clerical mistakes are corrected. A donor formerly coded as B6115 (now AN02338) was listed on the ATP portal with a diagnosis of Asperger syndrome and a brain weight of 1,158 g. This 17-year-old female is now classified as with autism, and revision of the autopsy report indicates that the fresh brain weight, prior to fixation, was 1,580 g. The specimen, used in some neuropathological studies, could greatly alter study findings related to brain weight analysis.

GLIOSIS

Gliosis involves the production of excess glia within damaged areas of the central nervous system. In stroke or trauma, the lesion itself, the ischemic environment, the presence of dysoria (i.e., break down of the blood brain barrier), inflammatory response, as well as the oxidative load, all affect the extent of reactive gliosis (Pekny & Nilsson, 2005). In autism the presence of seizures or the common occurrence of ischemic agonal events may promote a gliotic response readily evident at autopsy (see later section, Expected Pathology). Otherwise classic descriptions of inflammatory processes involve a vascular component leading to the accumulation of cells and fluid within the extravascular space. In this regard autopsy series of subjects with autism have shown that their brains lack a vascular component and a classic inflammatory response (Casanova, 2007).

Coleman et al. (1985) provided neuronal and glial cell counts in the cerebral cortex of an individual with autism and two age- and sex-matched controls. Results showed a smaller glia/neuron ratio than the average of the two controls in all regions examined. In area 21 the ratio was 2.35 for controls, 1.30 for the brain of the individual with autism; in area 41, 1.475 for controls, 0.80 for cases with autism; in area 44, 2.025 for controls and 1.70 for cases with autism. Although all areas followed the same trend toward smaller glia/neuron ratios differences proved nonsignificant.

Bailey et al. (1998) found cerebral subpial gliosis in two of their cases. Similar changes have been reported in epilepsy, frontotemporal dementia, Alzheimer's disease, and mitochondrial encephalopathy (Doherty, Rostad, Kraemer, Vossler, & Haltiner, 2007; Hulkova, Druga, Ondejovic, & Elleder, 2008; Lanska et al., 1998; Mann, 1998). Two areas of gliosis in one of their cases may have been the result of childhood trauma that resulted in a depressed right frontal fracture.

López-Hurtado, DeFelipe, and Prieto (2002) reported the presence of marked microglia and astroglia activation in the brains of seven patients with autism. The study was done using GFAP as a marker suggesting reactive gliosis and an ongoing process at the time of death. The work was presented as an abstract at an international meeting and details about patients' demographics, tissue processing, and quantitation procedures are not available. A subsequent study by the same group was done on eight patients with autism (mean age 21 years) and seven controls (mean age 33 years) (López-Hurtado & Prieto, 2008). All of the patients were male. The study examined language-related cortices including Brodmann areas 22, 39, and 44. An optical fractionator method was employed to estimate cell density. Results showed increased density of glial cells in all regions examined and a reduction in density of neurons in areas 22 and 39. The authors failed to divulge the medical history of the patients for which no details, except age and sex, are provided. Besides lacking matched controls, results were never analyzed for the possible effects of seizures or other deleterious preagonal conditions.

Using MAP2 immunocytochemical staining, Mukaetova-Ladinska, Arnold, Jaros, Perry, and

Perry (2004) found no overall difference in density of glial cells in the frontal cortex of two individuals with autism. The findings were not altered when the data was corrected using the Abercrombie constant. Analysis of glial cells by individual cortical layers showed a gradual increase in density in the deeper laminae. The increase in glia was most prominent for the frontal subcortical white matter where the two cases with autism exhibited a glial cell density 1.85 times that of controls ($F_{1,6} = 5.954; p = 0.050$). The authors indicate that the findings of subcortical white matter gliosis should be interpreted with caution as one of their subjects with autism suffered from long-standing epilepsy. Indeed, when the data was analyzed by individual patient, the subject with epilepsy had a 1.84-fold higher glial density than the other individual with autism, and 2.40-fold higher density than the mean of the controls. According to the authors, "This suggests that in autism unaffected by additional pathology because of epilepsy, glial cells may be unaltered in the subcortical white matter. However, this observation needs to be explored further in a large sample" (Mukaetova-Ladinska et al., 2004, p. 621).

Neuroglial activation was examined in brain tissues from cerebellum, midfrontal, and cingulate gyrus from fixed tissue in 11 individuals with autism and 6 controls (Vargas, Nascimbene, Krishnan, Zimmerman, & Pardo, 2005). No mention was made of specific cytoarchitectural regions or subdivision of the cerebellar hemisphere sampled. According to the demographics (Vargas et al., 2005, Table 1), there appears to be a difference in postmortem intervals between patients with autism (PMI = 26.9 hours) and controls (PMI = 18.4 hours). Six of the individuals with autism suffered from epilepsy. Cause of death was reported for five patients with autism as drowning (no mention of resuscitation), and for an additional four others was reported as undefined (either sudden death or unknown). GFAP immunostaining was increased in all three regions studied, that is, cerebellum, midfrontal, and cingulate gyrus. Astrogliosis was characterized histologically by increased volume of the soma and glial processes. Western blotting of GFAP expression showed significant increased

expression in all areas examined in individuals with autism as compared to controls. Microglial activation seemed to follow the same pattern as the astrocytosis and appeared to be significantly elevated in those patients with epilepsy. In the cerebellum occasional microglial nodules were seen in the granule cell layer and white matter. Guerin et al. (1996) had previously reported the presence of perivascular lymphocytic infiltrates and a few microglial nodules in the brainstem of a subject with autism. The latter authors attributed the microglial nodules to a prior history of encephalitis. In discussing their analysis Vargas et al. (2005) did not take into consideration differences in PMI or cause of death. Further studies are needed to examine whether the results are either indicative of how the patients died, comorbidity (e.g., seizures), or a core characteristic of autism.

Microglia activation within a single brain parcellation (dorsolateral prefrontal cortex) was assessed by immunocytochemistry in 13 people with autism and 9 controls (Morgan et al., 2010). The researchers used ionized calcium binding adapter molecule 1 as a marker and stereological estimates of density and average somal volume. A major limitation, and a design flaw of the study, is that tissue processing and sectioning followed two different protocols at independent laboratories. Eight cases ($n = 5$ with autism and $n = 3$ controls) were sectioned at 80 μm and 16 cases ($n = 10$ with autism and $n = 6$ controls) at 50 μm. Many of the studied parameters were statistically related to the tissue processing technique. Results showing a dependence as to the where and how the tissue had been sectioned, rather than to a core pathology of autism, included grey matter microglial somal volume, white matter microglial somal volume, and white matter microglial density. Although expected, the study failed to disclose a correlation between any microglial-related measures and seizures. The brain of one of the cases with autism weighed a phenomenal 1,990 g. There is no mention in this or other cases as to the probable presence of postmortem edema. Eight of the 13 autism cases died of drowning but no further description as to those who may have been rescued and resuscitated.

Survival of a drowning event (near drowning) can lead to serious secondary complications from hypoxia reperfusion injury.

The patient population in Morgan et al.'s (2010) article was used again to study the spatial relationship of microglia (immunocytochemically positive to ionized calcium-binding adapter molecule-1) and neurons in the dorsolateral prefrontal cortex (Morgan et al., 2012). Microglia were more frequently located near neurons in individuals with autism at distance intervals of 25 μm, 75 μm, and 100 μm. No significant differences were present at 50 μm. The authors were unclear as to the meaning of the microglia-neuron interaction, for example, protective, pro-healing, or deleterious effects.

BRAINSTEM

Rodier, Ingram, Tisdale, Nelson, and Romano (1996) examined sections through the brainstem (lower cranial nuclei) in a single patient with autism. The authors reported multiple abnormalities including a shortened distance between landmarks in the trapezoid body and the inferior olive. Both the superior olivary and facial nuclei were absent. The authors concluded that some type of injury occurred around the time of neural tube closure or 4 weeks of fetal development. Not coincidentally, the timing corresponds to the teratogenicity of thalidomide exposure during pregnancy (Miller et al., 2005; Rodier & Hyman, 1998). Patients exposed to thalidomide during gestation who later develop an autism phenotype also exhibit an external ear malformation and an uncommon form of strabismus (Duane syndrome) but no malformations of their extremities. Timing of these malformations suggests a time window of vulnerability during the embryonic period early in gestation (20–24 days) (Arndt, Stodgell, & Rodier, 2005; Rodier, 2002).

Following the lead of Rodier et al. (1996) other investigators screened the superior olivary nuclei for pathology. The superior olivary complex is the first station where auditory information from both ears is compared. In humans the olivary complex is comprised of eight distinct nuclei, the two principal divisions being its medial and lateral components. Given Rodier et al.'s (1996) report of a complete absence of the superior olivary complex in a patient with autism, Kulesza and Mangunay (2008) examined the architecture of the medial superior olive in the brains of five subjects with autism (ages 8 to 32 years) and two controls (ages 26 and 29 years). The controls did not match the ages of the younger individuals with autism (8 and 13 years). Identification of the individual cases at the ATP portal reveled that one of them (Aut05 in publication or AN13835 at the ATP portal) had a diagnosis of fragile X syndrome. Another of the cases is difficult to identify: 26-year-old with brain weight of 1,610 g (identified in publication as Aut01). The ATP has a case of a brain weighing 1,610 g but age 23 (IBR-93–01). Otherwise, if the brain weight is 1,310 g and the age of the patient is 26 years, then AN14829 (chromosome 15q duplication) would match it. The results showed significant differences in the morphology of medial superior olivary neurons in each of the five autistic cases. Differences were noted in cell body area, cell body shape (circularity), and orientation as defined by the longitudinal axis of the cells. I examined many of the brainstem slides used in the study and judged them to be of poor quality for the purpose of quantitation. More recent work by Thevarkunnel, Martchek, Kemper, Bauman, and Blatt (2004) has shown the presence of the superior olivary and facial nuclei in the brains of individuals with autism. Details of the latter work remain unknown as the original abstract presentation has never been published in a peer-reviewed journal.

Another area of the brain stem that has been paid close attention is the locus coeruleus. Out of the six cases reported by Bailey et al. (1998), one had a widely dispersed locus coeruleus while another one was described as having loosely grouped neurons. Some years later, in a study of five male patients with autism and an equal number of non-age-matched controls Martchek, Thevarkunnel, Bauman, Blatt, and Kemper (2006) used stereological methods to examine neuronomorphometric parameters of this nuclei. Average age of controls was 41.2 years and 29.2 years for the cohort with autism. In the study only hemisections through the brainstem were available allowing analysis of only one side of this structure. In four out of their five control cases the right side was available, while in four out of the five individuals with autism the left side was available. Brain stems were cryoprotected, flash frozen, and serially sectioned at 50 μm. Every 20th section was stained with cresyl violet. The fractionator scheme was used with random sampling using an optical dissector box. There were no significant between group differences in total cell counts, volume of the locus coeruleus, or numerical density.

CEREBELLUM

One of the more often reported findings in autism is reduced number of Purkinje cells. This finding has not been universally reproduced. Furthermore the same group that initially ascribed the cell loss to an early defect during embryogenesis later reassessed their views. Initially, the lack of retrograde loss of inferior olivary neurons was used to suggest a prenatal onset to the observed Purkinje cell loss. It was claimed that since olivary climbing fibers synapse with Purkinje cells in a transitory zone (*lamina dissecans*) that disappears between 29 and 30 weeks of gestation, cell loss occurred at or before this time (Bauman & Kemper, 2005). However, observations regarding the number of inferior olivary neurons were subjective and never pursued with stereology. A later study by the same group comparing immunocytochemistry and Nissl staining indicated that possible agonal circumstances and postmortem handling could have accounted for inadequate Nissl staining and lower Purkinje cell counts in their previous studies. The researchers concluded that Purkinje cell loss seemingly occurs after they have migrated to their proper location. The time frame corresponds to a period during late gestation or postnatal life (Whitney, Kemper, Rosene, Bauman, & Blatt, 2009). Recent studies using GFAP immunocytochemistry reveal a reactive gliotic response to Purkinje cell loss (Bailey et al., 1998;

Vargas et al., 2005) that is actively occurring at time of death. While different abnormalities in the nuclei of the brainstem and cerebellum may denote a migrational abnormality (Kemper, 2009), the weight of the evidence clearly indicates that Purkinje cell loss is an acquired phenomenon possibly related to seizures or ischemic preagonal events. The following paragraphs describe some of the available neuropathological studies of the cerebellum in autism.

R. S. Williams et al. (1980) in a study of four brains found a reduced number of cells in one subject having an inherited metabolic disorder but not in two subjects with idiopathic autism or in another one with phenylketonuria (PKU). In the one subject having reduced cell numbers electron micrographs of the cerebellar cortex were of poor quality because of marked distortion of nuclei and membranous cytoplasmic structures. Ritvo et al. (1986) found reduced Purkinje cell counts in the cerebellar hemispheres and vermis in all four patients of their study as compared to controls. Although the results were statistically significant, counts between subjects were highly variable and called attention to the importance of using total cell counts. In Guerin et al.'s (1996) case report histological examination of the cerebellum revealed Purkinje cells that were normal in size and number.

Bauman and Kemper noted variable loss of Purkinje and granule cells as well as involvement of the deep cerebellar and the inferior olivary nuclei (Arin, Bauman, & Kemper, 1991). Purkinje cell loss was prominent throughout the cerebellar hemispheres primarily involving the posterolateral neocerebellar and archicerebellar cortices. Only two individuals with autism showed staining pallor for granule cells, and both occurred in areas of marked reductions in the numbers of Purkinje cells. Bauman and Kemper have indicated that contrary to neuroimaging studies of vermal abnormalities in autism, no corresponding histological abnormality has been found in this region (Arin et al., 1991; Bauman & Kemper, 1996).

Bauman and Kemper also reported the presence of small clusters of mineralized heterotopic neurons in the cerebellar molecular layer (Bauman &

Kemper, 1987; Kemper & Bauman, 1998). The nutritional status of the latter patient is unknown. Nutritional encephalomalacia produced by a diet low in vitamin E targets the molecular layer of the cerebellum. In these cases mineralization is commonly seen albeit involving macrophages and astrocytes (Hassan, Jönsson, & Hakkarainen, 1985).

Tantam, Evered, and Hersov (1990) reported three subjects with Asperger's syndrome and a Marfanoid habitus, connective tissue disorder, and ligamentous laxity. The relationship of autism to Ehlers-Danlos syndrome was first discussed by Sieg (1992). Soon afterward the autopsy report of a 19-year-old man with early infantile autism, mental retardation, and Ehlers-Danlos type 2 syndrome was documented by Fehlow, Bernstein, Tennstedt, and Walther (1993). The patient died of a mechanical ileus and a megacolon due to excessive aerophagia. Autopsy findings showed significant rarefaction and marked reduction in the number of Purkinje cells as well as cells of the *stratum granulare* in cerebellar lobules VI and VII. No other studies have pursued the possible comorbidity of Ehlers-Danlos and autism.

Bailey et al. (1998) reported the cerebellar findings in their series as evidence of acquired pathology. The number of Bergman glia and GFAP staining were concomitantly increased in three of their six cases. They reported no empty baskets; however, it is difficult to surmise how long baskets would persist following Purkinje cell loss. As pointed out by Harding and Copp (1997) and later on by Bailey et al. (1998), any substantial loss of Purkinje cells before 32 weeks of gestation is associated with hypoplastic cerebellar folia. The normal development of cerebellar folia in autism therefore suggests an acquired pathology. Bailey et al. (1998) also reported the presence of Purkinje cell inclusions seen in one of their patients (case 1, 4 years of age). The inclusions occurred in multiple numbers within cells (mean number 2 but ranging up to six per cell) and stained homogenously with Luxol fast blue and cresyl violet. Similar intracytoplasmic inclusions have been documented in children diagnosed with various conditions (e.g., 7q

deletion, cerebral palsy, ataxia-telagiectasia) and normative individuals (Zherebitskiy & Del Bigio, 2009). Electron microscopy of the inclusions suggests that they are trapped within the lumen of smooth endoplasmic reticulum. Their presence in younger individuals, both neurotypicals and others variously diagnosed, and absence in degenerative conditions, suggests that they are transient phenomena probably related to growth and/or repair (Zherebitskiy & Del Bigio, 2009).

Cerebellar atrophy was present in two cases with an unusual variant of neuroaxonal dystrophy but associated with spheroids in only one of the cases (Weidenheim et al., 2001). In contrast to the findings previously reported by Bauman and Kemper (1996), Weidenheim et al. (2001) reported diffuse vermian atrophy, with lobule VII being more severely affected in one of their patients. In another case by the authors, diagnosed with Asperger syndrome, autopsy findings failed to reveal convincing findings within the cerebellum (Weidenheim, Escobar, & Rapin, 2012). Both vermis and cerebellar hemispheres exhibited the normal complement of Purkinje cells. There was generalized gliosis within the cerebellar sections. The architecture and cellularity of the dentate nucleus was normal. A microscopic focus of heterotopia was reported in the roof of the fourth ventricle near the midline.

Autopsy findings in two cases with autism revealed decreased number of Purkinje cells (Lee et al., 2002). Both patients were mentally retarded, and one had a diagnosis of epilepsy. The authors reported concomitant white matter thinning of the cerebellum and demyelination in one of the cases. Contemporaneously to Lee et al.'s (2002) effort, Fatemi et al. (2002) did a quantitative comparison of size and density of Purkinje cells in the cerebellum of five subjects with autism and an equal number of age-matched controls. Frozen, unfixed samples were cut with a microtome and stained with 1% cresyl violet. There is no mention of cryoprotection or postfixation of slides. Only two slides per brain were selected for quantitation, each separated by a variable distance without apparent regard to anatomical level. Cells were counted at a magnification of 20× [*sic*]. The authors do not mention whether only cells with visible nucleoli were counted or measured. The final cell count was uncorrected (e.g., section thickness, split particles) (Casanova & Kleinman, 1990). Results showed that the average cross section of Purkinje cells was smaller in the autism group as compared to controls by 24%. No difference in Purkinje cell density was observed between groups. Differences in cell size could be accounted by findings in two of the autism patients for which the authors fail to report the presence or absence of seizures. Wegiel (2004) used whole brain serial sections imbedded in cellodin to define cellular and volumetric abnormalities in the cerebellum of individuals with autism. The sample consisted of eight with autism and eight age-matched controls that were collected by Autism Speaks as part of their Human Brain Atlas project. Purkinje cells in autism were described as smaller than normal and decreased in number (i.e., 41% reduction) throughout the entire cerebellum. Cerebellar total volumes were reduced by 19% (cerebellar white matter by 30%, molecular layer by 17%, and granule cell layer by 11%). No mention was made of total brain volume for comparison. The volume and number of neurons in the inferior olivary nucleus, as well as in the dentate nucleus, did not reveal significant changes.

Neuroglial activation was assessed by immunocytochemistry in the brains of individuals with autism as compared to neurotypicals by Vargas et al. (2005). The most prominent histological changes were noted in the cerebellum. Loss of Purkinje and granule cells was reported in 9 of 10 cerebella examined. The most severe loss was observed in a 25-year-old male patient with epilepsy. Only one cerebellum failed to show evidence of Purkinje cell loss. Areas of Purkinje cell loss were punctuated by marked reactivity of Bergman glia. Concomitant microglial activation was noted in the cerebellar white matter of patients with autism and a history of epilepsy ($p = .025$ using Mann-Whitney U test) as compared to those without epilepsy.

A recent study comparing different stains revealed significantly lower counts in 2 of 10 specimens when using Nissl but none with calbindin (Whitney, Kemper, Bauman, Rosene, & Blatt, 2008). The results suggested to the authors that possible agonal chances and postmortem handling could have accounted for inadequate Nissl staining and lower Purkinje cell counts in previous studies. The same group followed their initial observations by assessing the density of cerebellar basket and stellate cells. The study used immunocytochemistry for parvalbumin in serial sections from the posterior cerebellar lobe of six individuals with autism and four controls (Whitney et al., 2009). Prior Purkinje cell counts were available to calculate their relationship to basket and stellate cells (Whitney et al., 2008). No significant between-group differences were noted neither in the total number of basket and stellate cells nor in their relation to Purkinje cells. The authors concluded that the evidence supported the model wherein Purkinje cell loss occurred after they were generated and migrated to their proper layer. The authors believed that Purkinje cell loss occurred in the latter part of the gestational period and could persists into postnatal life. The same group also used immunocytochemistry for peripherin as a marker for climbing fibers in olivocerebellar projections (Yip, Marcon, Kemper, Bauman, & Blatt, 2005). Measurements were made in six adults with autism and an equal number of age-matched controls. The authors found that the innervation of Purkinke cells by olivocerebellar climbing fibers was similar in cases with and without autism.

CEREBRAL CORTEX

In the modern history of neuropathological studies of autism, Bailey et al. (1998) were the first to clearly call attention to possible abnormalities within the cerebral cortex. Their published observations showed abnormalities of neuronal density and lamination of the frontal cortex in four out of their six patients. Bailey et al. (1998) also described an increased number of neurons in layer I of one case and disordered cortical laminar architecture in three of their patients. One patient showed temporal lobes that were enlarged and hyperconvoluted.

Among the cortical abnormalities reported by Bauman and Kemper (1994) was included an indistinct lamination of the anterior cingulate gyrus in five out of their six cases. These poorly laminated areas also exhibited smaller cells and altered cell-packing density (Kemper & Bauman, 1993, 1998). In order to better document any possible neuronomorphometric abnormalities, the same group of researchers instituted a systematic study using modern stereological principles to quantitatively assess the anterior cingulate gyrus in nine male patients with autism and four male cases that were matched for age range. The age range of the four controls was 20 to 55 years, and that of cases with autism was 15 to 54 years. Mean age for both populations was 38.8 years for the controls and 27.9 years for the cases with autism. The hemisphere side was not available in two of the controls and was the right side in the remaining cases. Seven hemispheres for the patients with autism were from the left side and only two from the right side. Blocks of brain tissue fixed in 10% formalin were cryoprotected and flash frozen. Slides were defatted and dehydrated though graded alcohols before staining in thionin. A qualitative assessment revealed irregular lamination in three of the nine cases with autism. Quantitative results showed a significant decrease in cell size in layers I–III and layers V–VI of area 24b and in cell packing density in layers V–VI of area 24c. There was increased density of neurons in the subcortical white matter (without clustering) in two brains of patients with autism. The significance of the study is arguable as the comparison groups were not matched for age or side of hemisphere sampled.

The orbitofrontal cortex was conspicuously involved in both of the autopsied patients reported by Weidenheim et al. (2001) and was the site of polymicrogyria in a brain reported by Kemper and Bauman (1998). There was an anomalous gyrus in the temporal lobe in one of the two specimens reported by Weidenheim et al. (2001). The superior temporal gyrus of an Asperger's patient was unusual in having prominent tertiary sulci running in a vertical direction. The resultant gyri acquired a radial configuration around the Sylvian fissure (Weidenheim et al., 2012). The gyral configuration has been reported in cases of congenital hydrocephalus and in the mantle surrounding porencephalic cysts, none of which were described in this case.

Simms, Kemper, Timbie, Bauman, and Blatt (2009) took sections through the anterior cingulate gyrus to perform a preliminary study on the density and size of von Economo neurons (VEN). The study revealed no between group differences for any of the parameters studied. Despite the lack of significance differences the authors undertook post hoc analysis to define subgroups of patients with autism: three brains with increased and six cases with reduced VEN density. The authors believe that their results reflect at a larger scale the heterogeneity in clinical presentation of individuals with autism. However, it may be questionable to provide for data dredging when between groups comparisons were nonsignificant. Other studies on von Economo neurons have provided unremarkable results. Allman, Watson, Tetreault, and Hakeem (2005) did a preliminary study in two brains of patients with autism noting a large concentration of these cells in the white matter that extended into layers VI and V. Results from an independent group showed no significant differences in VEN (spindle cell) density within the frontoinsular cortex of subjects with autism as compared to controls (D. P. Kennedy, Semendeferi, & Courchesne, 2007). The study was the first to offer quantitative stereological data on spindle cell number in autism.

A significant higher ratio of VEN to pyramidal cells in cases with autism as compared to controls was reported by Santos et al. (2011). In this study cells were quantitated using stereology in the frontoinsular cortex of four children with autism (mean age 7 years, two males) and three controls (mean age 8.7 years, two males). Brains were divided in the midsagittal plane with only one hemisphere available for study. Average section thickness for the tissue sections was 200 µm from cases with autism. Controls were variously quantitated in 200 µm and 500 µm sections with an average thickness of 300 µm for the sections examined. The total number of pyramidal neurons did not differ significantly between groups; however, the patients with autism had significantly higher ratio of VEN to pyramidal cells (3.53 ± 0.55 mean ± s.d.) than controls (2.30 ± 0.34; $p = 0.020$). The Santos et al. (2011) study differed from previous ones in having a higher number of subjects under the age of 16 years (one subject in Simms et al, 2009, and two subjects in D. P. Kennedy et al., 2007). It may be the case that pooling together the results of subjects with widely different age ranges may have diluted the effects of younger patients. However, it is difficult to draw meaningful conclusions from the small samples in the aforementioned studies and the absence of precise matching for age, sex, and hemisphere.

The dorsolateral prefrontal cortex of two individuals with autism (both males, 29 and 31 years of age) and two controls (one male aged 19 and one female aged 34 years) were examined using Nissl staining and MAP2 immunohistochemistry (Mukaetova-Ladinska et al., 2004). The length of fixation varied from 3 to 8 months for the patients with autism and from 40 to 47 months for the control subjects. Blocks of tissue containing BA9 and BA10 were embedded in paraffin and sectioned at 10 μm thickness. Sections were stained with Cresyl Fast Violet (Nissl) for cytoarchitectural detail and MAP2 immunocytochemistry for dendritic complexity. Only a single section through the frontal lobe was used for the purpose of manual quantitation of images acquired using Image-Pro 4.0 software. The results showed ill-defined cortical layers and a reduced level of MAP2 expression in neuronal soma and dendrites of the two individuals with autism relative to controls.

Hutsler et al. (2007) evaluated thickness and lamination as proxy measurements of cortical organization in eight postmortem ASD patients and eight age- and sex-matched controls. All cases met ADI-R (Autism Diagnostic Interview–Revised) diagnostic criteria for autism with the exception of one case that did not meet the cutoff score in the area of communication and was classified as Asperger's syndrome. Two quantitatively parallel methods were used to assess cortical layering and thickness, including structural MRIs and

histological sections of eulaminate cortex, for example, superior frontal gyrus (BA9), superior parietal lobule (BA7), and the middle temporal gyrus (BA21). Average cortical thickness for each lobe for ASD cases was never greater than 3% those of controls. The exception was that of the temporal lobes where thickness values exceeded 5% but were still considered nonsignificant. Qualitative examination revealed evidence of cell clustering and supernumerary cell in lamina I and subplate (boundary of layer VI and the white matter). The findings did not indicate a defect in the laminar pattern typically found for the cerebral cortex.

Several years after Hutsler's initial study in 2007, Avino and Hutsler (2010) used the same series of patients and regions of interests to expand on the abnormal cell patterning at the gray-white matter boundary that Hutsler had previously described. Quantification of the transition zone between the cortical gray and the underlying white matter used overlaying sigmoid functions in binary images. Regions were selected semirandomly by a lack of cortical folding while the operator was blind to diagnosis. Sections selected for sampling were chosen according to stereological principles. In all three regions examined (see earlier discussion) the slope of the sigmoid curves was shallower in the ASD subjects as compared to neurotypicals. The results indicate an indistinct boundary between layer VI and the white matter reflecting the presence of supernumerary neurons beneath the cortical plate. The authors believed that the presence of supernumerary neurons was the result of either migrational defects or failed apoptosis within the subplate region.

Hutsler used the density of spines as an expression of the quantity and distribution of connections onto individual neurons in the cerebral cortex of 10 individuals with autism and 15 controls (Hutsler & Zhang, 2010). Pyramidal cells were studied in both the superficial and deep cortical layers using Golgi impregnation. Regions of interest included frontal (BA9), temporal (BA21), and parietal lobe (BA7). The selection process for individual neurons was biased given the capricious nature of the Golgi technique. Cells were thus selected based on the quality of staining. Average spine densities across the three cortical regions were higher in the cases with autism as compared to controls. Increased spine density was most apparent in superficial layers (II) of all three cortical regions. The alteration in spine density observed in cases with autism was not related to the presence of seizures. In this particular study spine density was increased in the lowest functioning subgroup of individuals with autism. The findings are contrary to the expected association of spine loss with mental retardation. The results shed interesting insights into the connectivity pattern of the brain as the superficial cortical layers establish their synaptic connections during the postnatal period and are predominantly involved in intrahemispheric corticocortical connections. One could therefore argue that these intracortical connections are being remodeled during postnatal life in the brains of individuals with autism.

Neuron number and size was analyzed in the prefrontal cortex of seven children with autism and six controls by Courchesne et al. (2011). Regions of interest included the dorsolateral and mesial prefrontal cortex from serial whole hemisphere coronal brain sections obtained through the Human Brain Atlas Project of the Autism Tissue Program. Methods followed stereological procedures for quantitation. Neurons were distinguished from other cells by the presence of a prominent nucleoli and high cytoplasm-to-nucleus ratio thus leaving unaccounted interneurons. Most of the children with autism died of acute global ischemia. Children with autism had 67% more neurons (79% more in the dorsolateral and 29% in the mesial prefrontal cortex) as compared to controls. There were no differences in size of the soma. It was claimed that the increased cell density was not apparent at low or high magnification by light microscopy. This could be due to the thickness of the tissue. An interesting observation was that patients with autism had more neurons than predicted from their large brain weights.

Prior to Courchesne et al.'s (2011) stereological study neuronal density in the dorsolateral prefrontal cortex had been described as higher

(34%) in individuals with autism as compared to controls (Casanova et al., 2006b). The latter study found that the higher density was not circumscribed to the frontal lobe. In addition, contrary to Courchesne's et al. (2011) findings, Casanova et al. (2006b) found a reduction of pyramidal cell size. The authors explained their findings based on an increased number of cell minicolumns. A decrease in size of pyramidal cells would constrain formation of longer range, metabolically expensive projections biasing neuronal networks towards local connections, a so-called intrahemispheric modus operandi (Casanova, El-Baz, & Switala, 2011). Smaller pyramidal neurons but no differences in density or layer volume have also been found in Brodmann areas 44 and 45 of individuals with autism (Jacot-Descombes et al., 2012). The authors believe that the smaller neurons may be the result of immaturity or atrophy.

Cortical Minicolumnarity

In order to determine whether minicolumnar abnormalities were present in autism, Casanova et al. (2002b) examined the configuration of this modular structure with the use of a computerized image analysis system. The study involved nine individuals with autism (mean age 12 years) and nine age-matched controls (mean age 15 years) collected by the Autism Research Foundation. Three brain regions were studied (Brodmann areas 9, 21, and 22) from whole hemisphere celloidin imbedded Nissl stained sections cut at 35 μm. Photomicrographs were obtained and analyzed from lamina III of each sampled area. Columnarity was assessed by an algorithm using an Euclidean minimum spanning tree. A threshold function was used to eliminate smaller neurons (interneurons), glia, and other spurious anatomical elements. The parameters defined by this algorithm were modeled against three-dimensional measurements and corrected for false positive counts (i.e., neurons counted for a minicolumn as they stranded from an adjacent structure) (Casanova & Switala, 2005). The authors found significant differences in the horizontal spacing that separated minicolumns and in the relative dispersion of cells for all areas examined. More specifically, minicolumns in the brains of individuals with autism were smaller, more numerous, and less compact in their cellular configuration with reduced neuropil space at their peripheries.

The presence of minicolumnar abnormalities in autism was corroborated using the Gray Level Index method of Schlaug, Schleicher, and Zilles (1995). Patient population ($n = 9$) and tissue samples were the same as used in their initial study with the exception that control samples were increased to include 11 individuals (Casanova, Buxhoeveden, Switala, & Roy, 2002c). Photomicrographs were taken with a 10× objective of lamina III from each region of interest. The Gray Level Index (GLI) was computed in windows 11 μm wide and 110 μm tall. These profiles were smoothed leading to a profile that was analyzed for their peaks and troughs. The authors concluded that in autism an increased number of minicolumns combined with the greater dispersion of cells per minicolumn results in no global difference in neuronal density as measured by GLI. The study failed to consider the possibility of increased cell density with neurons of smaller cell bodies.

The initial results suggesting a minicolumnopathy in autism have been reproduced in two independent samples. The first was a study of two subjects with autism (average age 22 years) and five controls (average age 35 years) (Buxhoeveden et al., 2006). Two of the control cases were embedded in paraffin, cut at 20 μm, and stained with a silver impregnation method. The rest of the series were cryoprotected, cut at 80 μm and Nissl stained. The significance of the study is arguable given the small sample and differences in tissue processing, slide thickness, and staining among their own sample. Studies by Pakkenberg (1966) and Robins, Smith, and Eydt (1956) suggest that the tissue processed for paraffin would have a tissue linear shrinkage of 36%, a 74% volume reduction, as compared to the cryoprotected tissues. Despite major limitations in the study the results reproduced the initial findings of reduced minicolumnar width in subjects with autism (Casanova et al., 2002b). The average minicolumnar width was reported to be 46.8 μm for $n = 9$ patients with autism and 52.8 μm for $n = 9$ controls in the Casanova et al. (2002b) study and 45.5 μm and 56.2 μm in cases with autism and controls, respectively, in Buxhoeveden et al. (2006).

A second study reproducing the presence of a minicolumnopathy in autism was the result of an international effort sponsored by the Autism Tissue Program (Casanova et al., 2006b). This study used four cortical regions in a series of six age-matched cases with autism and neurotypical individuals to produce indices of minicolumnar morphometry. In this study computerized image analysis of slides was done blind to diagnosis. Minicolumns in individuals with autism were thinner, neuronal density greater, and mean neuron and nucleolar cross-sections smaller in subjects with autism as compared to controls. A Delaunay triangulation suggested that the increased cell density was the result of a larger number of minicolumns; otherwise the number of cells per minicolumns was normal. Findings were reproduced using the GLI method of Schlaug et al. (1995). The authors concluded that in autism the smaller cell bodies and nucleoli of pyramidal cells provide a bias in connectivity favoring short connections (e.g., arcuate fibers) at the expense of longer ones (e.g., commisural connections) (see also Casanova & Trippe, 2009).

The postmortem study on the radial organization of pyramidal cell arrays in autism has centered on cortical lamina III. Casanova et al. (2006a; Casanova, El-Baz, Vanbogaert, Narahari, & Switala, 2010) used image analysis of digitized photomicrographs to compare different minicolumnar morphometric parameters across different lamina in nine brain regions (Brodmann areas 3b, 4, 9, 10, 11, 17, 24, 43, and 44). The study used six pairs of people with autism and age matched controls. Subjects with autism had the smallest minicolumns, the greatest difference being identified in area 44. The authors suggested that the diminished cortical width across different lamina probably reflects involvement of an anatomical element in common among the different layers. Two possible, not mutually exclusive agents were discussed as possible culprits: inhibitory elements within the peripheral neuropil space of the minicolumn and reductions in the soma of pyramidal cells.

Postmortem studies in autism have shown evidence of cortical abnormalities manifested as a minicolumnopathy (Casanova, Buxhoeveden, Switala, & Roy, 2002a; Casnova et al., 2006b). The increased number of minicolumns can be traced to supernumerary symmetric divisions of perventricular germinal cells. The core of the minicolumn is composed of pyramidal cells and their projections (i.e., apical dendritic bundles and axonal bundles) while their periphery is made, among other anatomical elements, of inhibitory cells. Compartmentalization of this module in subjects with and without autism has shown that reductions in width are confined primarily to the peripheral neuropil space, site of the so-called shower curtain of inhibition for the minicolumn (Casanova et al., 2002b). The findings on cortical

modularity suggest that in autism heterochronic divisions of periventricular germinal cells cause neuroblasts (future pyramidal cells), arriving at the cortical plate to mature asynchronously to the available complement of tangentially migrating inhibitory neurons (Casanova, 2013; Casanova, Buxhoeveden, & Gomez, 2003) (Figure 21.4). This excitatory/inhibitory imbalance is capable of explaining many clinical features of autism including sensorimotor abnormalities and seizures.

ASPERGER SYNDROME

A preliminary study examining the hippocampal complex in a single patient with Asperger's syndrome revealed a generalized reduction in neuronal cell size and increased cell-packing density (Bauman & Kemper, 2005). The changes were considered similar to those previously described in autism (Bauman & Kemper, 2005). Also, similar to autism, Purkinje cell loss has been described throughout the cerebellar hemispheres (Bauman & Kemper, 2005).

Two individuals with Asperger syndrome were studied for evidence of minicolumnar abnormalities in three different brain regions (Brodmann 9, 21, 22) (Casanova et al., 2002a). The series included results for 3 control cases from the Autism Research Foundation and 15 additional controls from the Yakovlev-Haleem collection. Brains were imbedded in celloidin and cut in 35 μm thick sections. Minicolumnar abnormalities were reported in the three areas studied. More specifically, minicolumns were smaller and their component cells more dispersed than normal. The findings were similar to those described in autism, but with reduced severity (Casanova et al., 2002a). The authors concluded that despite clinical differences both autism and Asperger stem from related minicolumnar abnormalities.

A thorough autopsy was recently documented in a gifted mathematician who died at 63 years of age devoid of any additional comorbidity including seizures. There was no history of chronic medication usage. The patient did not receive a diagnosis

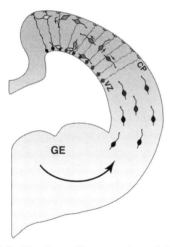

Figure 21.4   The figure illustrates the radial migration of neuroblasts from the germinal layer of the ventricular zone (VZ) to the cortical plate (CP). These cells will provide for pyramidal (excitatory) cell arrays within the core of minicolumns. A tangential mode of migration is shown as originating, among several places, in the ganglionic eminence (GE). These cells give rise to interneurons (i.e., inhibitory neurons). When properly coupled, both migratory elements provide a balance between excitatory and inhibitory influences in the cortex. Illustration from Yokota et al. (2007) used in accordance with the Creative Commons Attribution License.

during life; however, the history provided by a close family member was in keeping with the diagnosis of Asperger. Only the right cerebral hemisphere was available for examination. According to the authors, autopsy examination revealed "no convincing morphological signature detectable with routine neuropathologic technology" (Weidenheim et al., 2012, p. 460).

EXPECTED PATHOLOGY

A recent survey of tissue collected by the Autism Tissue Program showed a total of 35 brain donations from subjects with autism the significant majority of which had suffered from hypoxic/ischemic deficits and/or reperfusion injury during their preagonal period (Casanova, 2007). Eleven of the patients drowned (31.4% of the total, PMI 21.0 h ± 12 h), 1 stated no cause of death, and 23 were listed as having died from diverse causes (PMI 23.7 h ± 16.7 h), including seizures, circulatory failure, sepsis, anoxic encephalopathy, and acute respiratory distress. Of the 11 drowning victims, 3 were missing medical history and autopsy findings. Two drowning victims received CPR and survived for an indeterminate amount of time. The short survey clearly indicates that most of the available brain tissues used for anatomical/neuropathological studies of autism have suffered, to variable degrees, a hypoxic insult.

For the purpose of neuropathological studies, the almost universal presence of preagonal conditions causing hypoxia/ischemia in subjects with autism is compounded by the high prevalence of seizures in this patient population (Bolton et al., 2011). About one third of individuals with autism have suffered at least two seizures by the time they get to puberty. In autism the available cadre of brains in tissue repositories is therefore likely to exhibit pathology related to hypoxia/ischemia superimposed on those core attributes of the condition. Some of those hypoxic/ischemic changes relate to selective cellular, laminar, and regional vulnerabilities.

Hypoxia and ischemia in adults preferential affect anatomical elements of the gray matter, while cases with reperfusion injury may preferential damage the white matter. Preagonal and agonal conditions therefore help explain many of the reported findings in autism, for example, Purkinje cell loss and gliosis of the white matter. Furthermore, ischemia temporarily induces amyloid peptide overexpression in neurons, glia, and the extracellular space (i.e., secondary or reactive amyloidosis) that may be confused as pathological (Pluta, 2002). A recent article suggests a higher prevalence of amyloid β accumulation in subjects with autism and dup(15) as compared to subjects with idiopathic autism (Wegiel et al., 2012). The dup(15) autism cohort associated with the highest percentage of neurons accumulating α-secretase product had microcephaly, very early onset seizures, intractable seizures, and a high prevalence of unexpected death in epilepsy (SUDEP). The study supports the link between epilepsy and alterations in the proteolytic cleavage of the amyloid β precursor protein (Wegiel et al., 2012).

Cause of death may have also played a major role in the rather inconclusive postmortem studies investigating apoptotic markers in autism. Seizures, suffocation, and drowning promote anoxia/hypoxia which has been shown to trigger suppression of Bcl-2 thorough an NFκB-dependent manner and accumulation of p53 (Graeber et al., 1994; Matsushita et al., 2000). This possible confound remains unaccounted in the results of the Araghi-Niknam and Fatemi (2003) and Sheikh et al. (2010) studies.

Cells that express a selective vulnerability after hypoxic insults include the CA1 pyramidal neurons along with the Purkinje cells of the cerebellum. Apart from these cell populations others may be affected depending on the length and severity of the insult. These populations include layers III, V, and VI of the neocortex, the reticular neurons of the thalamus, and the medium-sized neurons of the striatum (Busl & Greer, 2010). Within the white matter the anatomy of arterioles (i.e., linear with few anastomoses) predisposes the adjacent tissue to hypoxic ischemic injury. The insult is compounded by the fact that within the vasculature of the deeper white matter lays an internal border zone (Ginsberg, Hedley-Whyte, & Richardson, 1976).

After resuscitation from a purely hypoxic deficit the resulting encephalopathy is often referred to as hypoxic-ischemic. Cardiovascular collapse when combined with hypoxia leads to severe brain injury and worsened prognosis (Busl & Greer, 2010). Cell damage can appear within a few hours, with longer durations of insults leading to a shorter delay in manifestation (Lipton, 1999). Hyperglycemia may worsen the concomitant acidosis by increasing the amounts of lactic acid. Chronic hyperglycemia (within the preagonal state) is associated with increased ischemic damage and mortality (Hoxworth, Xu, Zhou, Lust, & LaManna, 1999). All of these confounds need to be taken into account when interpreting reported neuropathological findings in autism.

Drowning needs special consideration as it is listed as the cause of death in a significant number of donors having been diagnosed with autism. Near drowning is defined as temporary survival after aspiration of fluid into the lungs. Increased public awareness of cardiopulmonary resuscitation has resulted in many more near drowning victims. Restoration of circulation after an ischemic period results in hyperemia with loss of vasoreactivity, disruption of the blood brain barrier, inflammation, and oxidative damage. Free radicals develop in the newly perfused tissue, which, along with catabolic enzymes, destroy structural proteins, membrane lipids, and other cellular contents. The extent of the resultant neuronal loss and membrane damage depends on the severity of the underlying insult. Both astrocytosis and microglial activation appear abundant primarily within the white matter of the brain (Vargas et al., 2005). In effect, brain slice experiments indicate that the white matter is particularly vulnerable to free radical formation (Omata et al., 2003), which themselves are toxic to oligodendrocytes (Husain & Juurlink, 1995).

A TRIPLE HIT HYPOTHESIS

Recent articles suggest that we cannot explain away the rising prevalence of autism as artifacts based on increased public awareness and changing diagnostic criteria (Weintraub, 2011). Studies indicate that only one half of the increase in prevalence can be attributed to changes in diagnostic criteria and other practices (Hertz-Picciotto & Delwiche, 2009; King & Bearman, 2009). As of 2007 this left unexplained a threefold increase in the prevalence of autism (Hertz-Picciotto, 2012). Furthermore, in the passing years since these studies were performed, the disparity between known and unknown causes has continued to widen (Hertz-Picciotto, 2012).

The old model of autism as highly heritable has given rise to a more balanced appraisal, one involving the interaction of both genes and environmental factors during brain development. Hundreds of different genes involving many potential changes in DNA (e.g., deletion, duplications, translocation, inversion) are now identified as causing some type of susceptibility to the disorder although not necessarily to the same degree (Marshal et al., 2008). Each gene may vary in its degree of influence and in what aspects of the phenotype they control. A recent study on 3,400 8-year-old twin pairs completing the Childhood Asperger Syndrome Test underwent genetic model fitting of categorical and continuous data on the triad of impairments (social, communication, restricted behaviors, and interests) that define autism (Ronald et al., 2006). Results indicate the heterogenous influence of different genes on the triad of impairments.

The most recent and largest series of twins ($n = 192$ pairs) indicates that although 38% of the diagnostic concordance was explained by genetic factors, a significantly larger percentage (58%) was due to shared environmental factors (Hallmayer et al., 2011). According to the authors these shared environmental factors were, most possibly, of prenatal and perinatal origin. Autism is therefore a complex or multifactorial disorder that clusters in families without having a clear-cut pattern of inheritance. In keeping with the earlier evidence I and my colleagues have postulated that manifestations in autism supervene when three factors impinge on a particular infant (a triple hit hypothesis): (1) an underlying vulnerability (genetic predisposition), (2) exogenous stressor(s) (e.g., infection, drugs), and (3) a critical period of brain development (Casanova, 2007; E. L. Williams & Casanova, 2010). This hypothesis is meant to account for the diverse composition and severity of signs/symptoms in autism that lack a simple association to genetic markers. Thus, polygenetic factors provide vulnerability for autism but they need additional intervening agents to start its progression. It has been suggested that the same genes,

in the absence of environmental stressors, may lead to normal outcomes or, in some instances, to actual advantages (Pliszka, 2004).

Different contributions among the three factors of the triple hit hypothesis may account for the heterogeneity of autism and related spectrum disorders (Figure 21.5). The hypothesis calls for variability in clinical presentation along a severity gradient rather than discrete clusters of phenotypes. A recent study using complete linkage hierarchical cluster analysis on the 50 features examined in the Autism Spectrum Quotient in 333 individuals with autism spectrum disorder is consistent within this unitary spectrum model (Ring, Woodbury-Smith, Watson, Wheelwright, & Baron-Cohen, 2008).

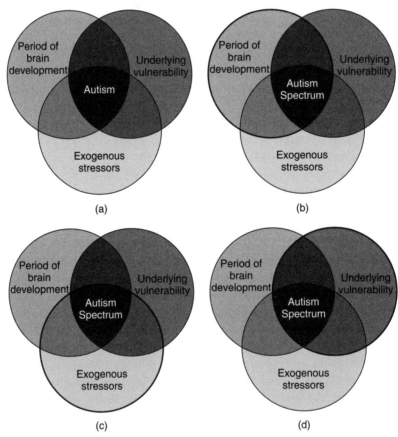

Figure 21.5 Venn diagrams showing possible relations between different elements of the triple hit hypothesis in autism: (1) a selective vulnerability, (2) exogenous factor(s), and (3) a time window during development. Unequal contribution toward pathology is marked by thickening of the circumference as shown in (b), (c), and (d). The central compartment denotes cases of classical autism. Variability between these influences may help account for the heterogeneity of clinical presentations observed in autism.

A *LOCUS MINORIS RESISTENTIAE*

Locus minoris resistentiae is a Latin phrase that means the place of least resistance. It is an expression commonly used in medicine to indicate an area described as a weak link for pathogen invasion. In Alzheimer's disease the term has been applied to the hippocampus in order to emphasize its universal involvement in autopsies of affected patients (Ball, 2006; Ball et al., 1985). In this regard it makes reference to a lesion necessary for disease development and progression.

A summary of the neuropathological literature suggests that periventricular germinal cells offer a *locus minoris resistentiae* to autism (Figure 21.6). The asymmetrical division of periventricular germinal cells provides for the migration of neuroblasts (daughter cells) to the cortical plate. Lower layer

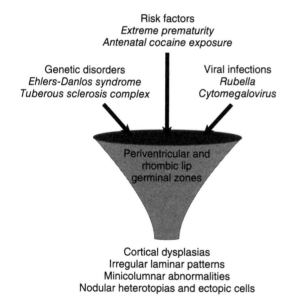

Autism

Figure 21.6 Germinal zones of the developing brain may provide a *locus minoris resistentiae* for autism. These zones or matrices are populated by stem cells with little connective tissue support and a loose network of thin-walled blood vessels. Cytokines, a group of pleotrophic proteins, orchestrate many of the functions of the germinal zone including the renewal of neuroepithelial/radial glia cells and the shift from neuro- to gliogenesis.

neurons of the cortical plate stem from the ventricular zone, while upper layer neurons derive from the subventricular zone. The outer subventricular zone is a primate-specific germinal zone that generates a significant portion of projection neurons participating in interareal networks (H. Kennedy & Dehay, 2012). Laminar fate of the progeny is determined by the cell cycle of periventricular cells and modulatory extrinsic factors (Dehay & Kennedy, 2007). Research on minicolumnar morphometry suggests that in autism exogenous factors provide for heterochronic divisions of periventricular cells and an uncoupling of the radially migrating neurons (pyramidal cells) from those migrating tangentially (interneurons) (Casanova, 2013; Casanova et al., 2003).

Migratory defects of neuronal migration involve several different steps: (1) onset of migration from precursor field (germinal matrix), (2) ongoing migration through the future white matter (intermediate zone), (3) penetration through the subplate, (4) progression through the cortical plate, and (5) stopping at the pial-glial barrier (Monuki & Ligon, 2004). In autism migrational abnormalities are suggested from accounts of cortical dysplasias, thickening of the cortex, variations in neuronal density, minicolumnar alterations, the presence of neurons in the molecular layer as well as in the white matter, irregular laminar patters, poor gray-white matter differentiation, and ectopic foci of cells (Schmitz & Rezaie, 2008). Neuronal migratory defects have been linked to abnormalities in brain growth and cortical organization both of which are closely tied to gyrification.

When neurons do not migrate from the periventricular germinal zone they form nodular heterotopias. These are unorganized islands of neurons present under the ependyma of the ventricles. When they migrate half way, they end up in clusters within the white matter. Contrary to genetic conditions that provide for bilateral and generalized heterotopias (e.g., mutations of the filamin A, alpha [FLNA] gene) heterotopias in autism tend to be focal and asymmetrical (Wegiel et al., 2010). This has given rise to their appellation as *epigenetic* heterotopias (Monuki & Ligon, 2004).

Bailey et al. (1998) reported widespread cortical dysgenesis in five of seven cases and increased numbers of white matter neurons in four out of seven brain specimens. Similar to Bailey et al. (1998), Hutsler et al. (2007) described supernumerary cells within the subcortical white matter. These cells were never arranged in islands or clusters as described by Bailey et al. (1998). Hutsler et al. (2007) attributed the difference between the studies as due to the nonuniversality of the findings and the limited white matter sampling in their own study. All nine cases with autism reported by Bauman and Kemper (2005) showed abnormal clustering of neurons in the inferior olive and in one case an ectopic cluster adjacent to the inferior peduncle. All of the ectopic neurons are derived from a germinal zone in the rhombic lip present during the 8th through the 20th week of gestation (Sidman & Rakic, 1982; Kemper, 2009).

Nodular heterotopias of the periventricular region (Figure 21.7) have been reported in idiopathic and secondary autism (e.g., Ehlers-Danlos syndrome) (Sheen & Walsh, 2005; Sieg, 1992; Wegiel et al., 2010). This type of abnormality is especially common in tuberous sclerosis. Approximately 40%–45% of patients with tuberous sclerosis meet criteria for autism or pervasive

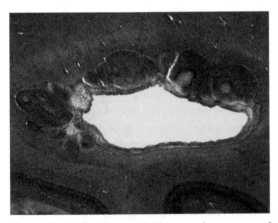

Figure 21.7   The photograph illustrates the presence of periventricular nodular heterotopias in the occipital horn of the lateral ventricle in an patient with autism. The heterotopias indicate an inability of neuroblasts to migrate away from the germinal layer of the ventricular neuropepithelium. (Photograph courtesy of Jerzy Wegiel).

developmental disorders not otherwise specified (Smalley, 1998). Brains of patients with tuberous sclerosis often exhibit smooth, rounded projections into the ventricles that because of their appearance have been given the name of candle guttering.

Evidence of periventricular germinal cell involvement in the pathogenesis of autism is also derived from congential viral conditions and other risk factors (e.g., extreme prematurity, antenatal cocaine exposure) for the condition. During pregnancy, different viral infections exhibit neurotropism for the periventricular matrix. Cases of congenital cytomegalovirus and rubella infection that exhibit symptoms of typical autism have the commonality of germinal cysts (Yamashita, Fujimoto, Nakajima, Isagai, & Matsuishi, 2003). The first description of the possible association between cytomegalovirus (CMV) and autism was by Stubbs in 1978. Since then a total of approximately eight cases have been reported in the literature (Ivarsson, Bjerre, Vegfors, & Ahlfors, 1990; Markowitz, 1983; Stubbs, 1978; Stubbs, Ash, & Williams, 1984; Yamashita et al., 2003). The article by Yamashita et al. (2003) is of particular importance as it was the first to describe subependymal cysts in those patients with congenital CMV that developed autism.

Extremely premature children (born more than 3 months before expected date of delivery) have double the prevalence rate of autism. In a recent study 21% of extremely premature children (27 weeks of gestation or less) tested positive for possible autism when given the Modified Checklist for Autism in Toddlers (M-CHAT) at age 2 (Kuban et al., 2009). Similar results have been obtained in independent samples using different screening instruments (e.g., Social Communication Questionnaire) (Johnson et al., 2010) and high rates have been recorded in adolescents with a birth weight of <2,000 g (Pinto-Marin et al., 2011). Extreme prematurity is commonly accompanied by germinal matrix hemorrhages/infarction and periventricular leukomalacia (Volpe, 1997).

Cocaine is the number one illicit drug of choice among pregnant women (Davis et al., 1992). A retrospective study of children exposed in utero to cocaine revealed significant neurodevelopmental abnormalities including language delay (94%) and an extremely high prevalence of autism (11.4%) (Davis et al., 1992). According to the authors, the high rate of autism is not known to occur in children exposed to alcohol or opiates thus suggesting a specific cocaine effect. In animal models used to capture the features of recreational usage in human, cocaine selectively alters the proliferative cell types of the subventricular zone (Patel, Booze, & Mactutus, 2012). Furthermore, cocaine has significant sex effects with females showing higher nestin (+) expression as compared to males.

SUMMARY

Postmortem work is often characterized as being tedious, laborious, and offering uncertain rewards to interested researchers. These types of studies are usually done using small series of patients, employing tissues of less than optimal quality and whose statistical analysis has to consider a large number of variables imposed by the use of medication, comorbidities, and the preagonal/agonal conditions of the patients. The inability to overcome many of these challenges means that findings related to core aspects of the condition are often hidden behind confusing findings in the literature. In many occasions studies lacking in adequate control series (e.g., not age matched) or whose tissues differed in the way they were processed, sectioned, or stained, should be interpreted taking these limitations into consideration. Other articles summarizing results of quantitative immunocytochemistry or Golgi impregnation in human postmortem material should be cautiously considered. Using stereology in quantiating results does not counteract the capriciousness of the employed techniques, especially when the same is applied to human postmortem material. Finally, results that can be explained by the agonal/preagonal conditions of the patients (e.g., seizures) but fail to take these into consideration, as well as those based solely on subjective observations, should be confirmed or disproven in studies using better designs.

A noncritical review of the literature would lead some to conclude that the most commonly reported finding in autism is Purkinje cell loss. This statement needs to be qualified as the presence of a reactive glial response to Purkinje cell loss clearly indicates an acquired phenomenon. The fact that in such cases astrocytic cell somas are plump and GFAP positive differentiates this process from chronic gliosis in which there is a scarcity of cell bodies and a mesh of phosphotungstic acid-haematoxylin (PTAH) or Holzer staining fibers. Thus, Purkinje cell loss in autism is a process that happens postnatally and is ongoing at the time of death. Since seizures cause both Purkinje cell loss and reactive astrocytosis it is unsurprising that immunocytochemical studies using GFAP describe the most striking gliosis in those patients with autism having the additional diagnosis of epilepsy. In this regard Purkinje cell loss does not appear to be related to the core pathology of the autistic disorder.

The most commonly reported finding that may bear significance to the neuropathology of autism is abnormalities of the cerebral cortex. Described findings are clearly dysplastic in nature and take place during brain development. These findings include effacement of the normal lamination pattern, minicolumnar abnormalities, and variations in neuronal density. All of the aforementioned neuropathological processes, as well as the presence of heterotopias, can be explained as the result of a migratory defect stemming from supernumerary divisions of periventricular germinal cells.

The presence of pathology within periventricular germinal cells in cases of idiopathic and secondary autism (e.g., tuberous sclerosis, Ehlers-Danlos, congenital cytomegalovirus, extreme prematurity) makes this a weak link or a *locus minoris resistentiae* to the condition. Heterochronic division of germinal cell may account for dysplastic changes in nuclei of the brainstem, cerebellum, and the cerebral cortex. The large span of time during which these structures develop emphasizes the equally broad span during which an exogenous factor(s) may provide its noxious effect (triple hit hypothesis). Heterochronic divisions of germinal cells also account for migratory abnormalities such as nodular heterotopias and clusters of cells within the white matter. These heterotopias differ in quantity and location among subjects with autism and can be classified as epigenetic in origin. It has been hypothesized that this migratory disturbance provides for desynchronization in the maturation of radially migrating derived neuroblasts (pyramidal cells) from those that migrate tangentially (interneurons). The end effect is an excitatory-inhibitory bias in the cortex of individuals with autism. Thus, although the basic mechanisms underlying autism are presently being unraveled; the pertinent story has enlarged to include genetics, environmental factors, and timing of brain development. Variability in these components may account for the clinical heterogeneity of autism.

CROSS-REFERENCES

Chapter 19 discusses the biochemistry of autism and Chapter 20 the neuroscience of social disability. Chapter 22 focuses on medical care issues and Chapter 23 on psychopharmacology.

REFERENCES

Aarkrog, T. (1968). Organic factors in infantile psychoses and borderline psychoses: Retrospective study of 45 cases subjected to pneumoencephalography. *Danish Medical Bulletin*, *15*, 283–288.

Allman, J. M., Watson, K. K., Tetreault, N. A., & Hakeem, A. Y. (2005). Intuition and autism: A possible role for von Economo neurons. *Trends in Cognitive Sciences*, *9*, 367–373.

Amaral, D. G., Schumann, C. M., & Nordahl, C. W. (2008). Neuroanatomy of autism. *Trends in Neurosciences*, *31*, 137–145.

Appel, F. W., & Appel, E. M. (1942a). Intracranial variation in the weight of the human brain. *Human Biology*, *14*, 48–68.

Appel, F. W., & Appel, E. M. (1942b). Intracranial variation in the weight of the brain (concluded). *Human Biology*, *14*, 235–250.

Araghi-Niknam, M., & Fatemi, S. H. (2003). Levels of Bcl-2 and P53 are altered in superior frontal and cerebellar cortices of autistic subjects. *Cellular and Molecular Neurobiology*, *23*, 945–952.

Arin, D. M., Bauman, M. L., & Kemper, T. L. (1991). The distribution of Purkinje cell loss in the cerebellum in autism. *Neurology*, *41*(3 Suppl. 1), 307.

Arndt, T. L., Stodgell, C. J., & Rodier, P. M. (2005). The teratology of autism. *International Journal of Developmental Neuroscience*, *23*, 189–199.

Avino, T. A., & Hutsler, J. J. (2010). Abnormal cell patterning at the cortical gray-white matter boundary in autism spectrum disorders. *Brain Research*, *1360*, 138–146.

Azmitia, E. C., Singh, J. S., Hou, X. P., & Wegiel, J. (2011). Dystrophic serotonin axons in postmortem brains from young autism patients. *The Anatomical Record*, *294*, 1653–1662.

Bailey, A., Luthert, P., Bolton, P., Le Couteur, A., Rutter, M., & Harding, B. (1993). Autism and megalencephaly. *The Lancet*, *341*, 1225–1226.

Bailey, A., Luthert, P., Dean, A., Harding, B., Janota, I., Montgomery, M., ... Lantos, P. (1998). A clinicopathological study of autism. *Brain*, *121*, 889–905.

Ball, M. J. (2006). The essential lesion of Alzheimer disease: A surprise in retrospect. *Journal of Alzheimer's Disease*, *9*(Suppl. 3), 29–33.

Ball, M. J., Hachinski, V., Fox, A., Kirshen, A. J., Fisman, M., Blume, W., ... Merskey, H. (1985). A new definition of Alzheimer's disease: A hippocampal dementia. *The Lancet*, *325*, 14–16.

Bauman, M. L. (1991). Microscopic neuroanatomic abnormalities in autism. *Pediatrics*, *87*, 791–796.

Bauman, M., & Kemper, T. L. (1985). Histoanatomic observations of the brain in early infantile autism. *Neurology*, *35*, 866–874.

Bauman, M. L., & Kemper, T. L. (1987). Limbic involvement in a second case of early infantile autism. *Neurology*, *37*(Suppl. 1), 147.

Bauman, M. L., & Kemper, T. L. (1994). Neuroanatomical observations of the brain in autism. In M. L. Bauman & T. L. Kemper (Eds.), *The neurobiology of autism* (pp. 119–145). Baltimore, MD: Johns Hopkins University Press.

Bauman, M. L., & Kemper, T. L. (1996). Observations on the Purkinje cells in the cerebellar vermis in autism. *Journal of Neuropathology and Experimental Neurology*, *55*, 613.

Bauman, M. L., & Kemper, T. L. (2005). Structural brain anatomy in autism: What is the evidence? In M. L. Bauman & T. L. Kemper (Eds.), *The neurobiology of autism* (2nd ed., pp. 121–135). Baltimore, MD: Johns Hopkins University Press.

Bellak, L. (1958). *Schizophrenia: A review of the syndrome*. New York, NY: Logos Press.

Bellak, L., & Loeb, L. (1969). *Childhood schizophrenia: The schizophrenic syndrome*. New York, NY: Grune & Stratton.

Bolton, P. F., Carcani-Rathwell I., Hutton, J., Goode, S., Howlin, P., & Rutter, M. (2011). Epilepsy in autism: Features and correlates. *British Journal of Psychiatry*, *198*, 289–294.

Briacombe, M. B., Pickett, R., & Pickett, J. (2007). Autism postmortem neuroinformatic resource: The autism tissue program (ATP) informatics portal. *Journal of Autism and Developmental Disorders*, *37*, 574–579.

Brown, R. E. (1966). Organ weight in malnutrition with special reference to brain weight. *Developmental Medicine and Child Neurology*, *8*, 512–522.

Busl, K. M., & Greer, D. M. (2010). Hypoxic-ischemic brain injury: Pathophysiology, neuropathology and mechanisms. *NeuroRehabilitation*, *26*, 5–13.

Buxhoeveden, D. P., Semendeferi, K., Buckwalter, J., Schneker, N., Switzer, R, & Courchesne, E. (2006). Reduced minicolumns in the frontal cortex of patients with autism. *Neuropathology and Applied Neurobiology, 32*, 483–491.

Casanova, M. F. (2007). The neuropathology of autism. *Brain Pathology, 17*, 422–433.

Casanova, M. F. (2013). The minicolumnopathy of autism. In J. Buxbaum & P. Hof (Eds.), *The neuroscience of autism spectrum disorders* (pp. 327–333). Amsterdam, The Netherlands: Elsevier.

Casanova, M. F., Buxhoeveden, D., & Gomez, J. (2003). Disruption in the inhibitory architecture of the cell minicolumn: Implications for autism. *The Neuroscientist, 9*, 496–507.

Casanova, M. F., Buxhoeveden, D. P., Switala, A. E., & Roy, E. (2002a). Asperger's syndrome and cortical neuropathology. *Journal of Child Neurology, 17*, 142–145.

Casanova, M. F., Buxhoeveden, D. P., Switala, A. E., & Roy, E. (2002b). Minicolumnar pathology in autism. *Neurology, 58*, 428–432.

Casanova, M. F., Buxhoeveden, D. P., Switala, A. E., & Roy, E. (2002c). Neuronal density and architecture (gray level index) in the brains of autistic patients. *Journal of Child Neurology, 17*, 515–521.

Casanova, M. F., El-Baz, A., & Switala, A. (2011). Laws of conservation as related to brain growth, aging, and evolution: Symmetry of the minicolumn. *Frontiers in Neuroanatomy, 5*, 66.

Casanova, M. F., El-Baz, A., Vanbogaert, E., Narahari, P., & Switala, A. (2010). A topographic study of minicolumnar core width by lamina comparison between autistic subjects and controls: Possible minicolumnar disruption due to an anatomical element in-common to multiple laminae. *Brain Pathology, 20*, 451–458.

Casanova, M. F., & Kleinman, J. E. (1990). The neuropathology of schizophrenia: A critical assessment of research methodologies. *Biological Psychiatry, 27*, 353–362.

Casanova, M. F., & Switala, A. E. (2005). Minicolumnar morphometry: Computerized image analysis. In M. F. Casanova (Ed.), *Neocortical modularity and the cell minicolumn* (pp. 161–180). New York, NY: Nova Biomedical.

Casanova, M., & Trippe, J. (2009). Radial cytoarchitecture and patterns of cortical connectivity in autism. *Philosophical Transactions of the Royal Society B, 364*, 1433–1436.

Casanova, M. F., Van Kooten I., Switala, A. E., Van Engeland H., Heinsen, H., Steinbusch, H. W. M., . . . Schmitz, C. (2006a). Abnormalities of cortical minicolumnar organization in the prefrontal lobes of autistic patients. *Clinical Neuroscience Research, 6*, 127–133.

Casanova, M. F., Van Kooten, I. A. J., Switala, A. E., Van Engeland H., Heinsen, H., Steinbusch, H. W. M., . . . Schmitz, C. (2006b). Minicolumnar abnormalities in autism. *Acta Neuropathologica, 112*, 287–303.

Coleman, P., Romano, J., Lapham, L., & Simon, W. (1985). Cell counts in cerebral cortex of an autistic patients. *Journal of Autism and Developmental Disorders, 15*, 245–255.

Corsellis, J. A. N. (1972). Neuropathology and psychiatry. *Psychological Medicine, 2*, 329–331.

Courchesne, E., Mouton, P. R., Calhoun, M. E., Semendeferi, K., Ahrens-Barbeau, C., Hallet, M. J., . . . Pierce, K. (2011). Neuron number and size in prefrontal cortex of children with autism. *JAMA, 306*, 2001–2010.

Courchesne, E., Müller, R. A., & Saitoh, O. (1999). Brain weight in autism: Normal in the majority of cases, megalencephalic in rare cases. *Neurology, 52*, 1057–1059.

Darby, J. K. (1976). Neuropathologic aspects of psychosis in children. *Journal of Autism and Childhood Schizophrenia, 6*, 339–352.

Davis, E., Fennoy, I., Laraque, N., Kanem, N., Brown, G., & Mitchell, J. (1992). Autism and developmental abnormalities in children with perinatal cocaine exposure. *Journal of the National Medical Association, 84*, 315–319.

Dehay, C., & Kennedy, H. (2007). Cell-cycle control and cortical development. *Nature Reviews Neuroscience, 8*, 438–450.

Dekaban, A. S., & Sadowsky, D. (1978). Changes in brain weights during the span of human life: Relation of brain weights to body heights and body weights. *Annals of Neurology, 4*, 345–356.

Doherty, M. J., Rostad, S. W., Kraemer, D. L., Vossler, D. G., & Haltiner, A. M. (2007). Neocortical gliosis in temporal lobe epilepsy: Gender-based differences. *Epilepsia, 48*, 1455–1459.

Fatemi, S. H., Halt, A. R., Realmuto, G., Earle, J., Kist, D. A., Thuras, P., & Merz, A. (2002). Purkinje cell size is reduced in cerebellum of patients with autism. *Cellular and Molecular Neurobiology, 22*, 171–175.

Fehlow, P., Bernstein, K., Tennstedt, A., & Walther, F. (1993). Autismus infantum und exzessive Aerophagie mit symptomatischem Megakolon und Ileus bei einem Fall von Ehlers-Danlos-Syndrom. *Pädiatrie und Grenzgebiete, 31*, 259–267.

Fenichel, G. M. (2005). *Clinical pediatric neurology: A signs and symptoms approach* (5th ed.). Philadelphia, PA: Elsevier Saunders.

Finkbeiner, W. E., Ursell, P. C., & Davis, R. L. (2004). *Autopsy, pathology: A manual and atlas*. Philadelphia, PA: Churchill Livingston.

Fombonne, E., Rogé, B., Claverie, J., Courty, S., & Frémolle, J. (1999). Microcephaly and macrocephaly in autism. *Journal of Autism and Developmental Disorders, 29*, 113–119.

Gillberg, C., & de Souza, L. (2002). Head circumference in autism, Asperger syndrome, and ADHD: A comparative study. *Developmental Medicine and Child Neurology, 44*, 296–300.

Ginsberg, M. D., Hedley-Whyte, E. T., & Richardson, E. P. (1976). Hypoxic-ischemic leukoencephalopathy in man. *Archives of Neurology, 33*, 5–14.

Goldfarb, W., & Dorsen, M. M. (1956). *Annotated bibliography of childhood schizophrenia and related disorders*. New York, NY: Basic Books.

Graeber, T. G., Peterson, J. F., Tsai, M., Monica, K., Fornace, A. J., Jr., & Giaccia, A. J. (1994). Hypoxia induces accumulation of p53 protein, but activation of a G1-phase checkpoint by low-oxygen conditions is independent of p53 status. *Molecular and Cellular Biology, 14*, 6264–6277.

Guerin, P., Lyon, G., Barthelemy, C., Sostak, E., Chevrollier, V., Garreau, B., & Lelord, G. (1996). Neuropathological study of a case of autistic syndrome with severe mental retardation. *Developmental Medicine and Child Neurology, 38*, 203–211.

Hallmayer, J., Cleveland, S., Torres, A., Phillips, J., Cohen, B., Torigoe, T.,... Risch, N. (2011). Genetic heritability and shared environmental factors among twin pairs with autism. *Archives of General Psychiatry, 68*, 1095–1102.

Harding, B., & Copp, A. J., (1997). Malformations. In D. I. Graham & P. L. Lantos (Eds.), *Greenfield's neuropathology* (pp. 397–533). London, England: Arnold.

Hassan, S., Jönsson, L., & Hakkarainen, J. (1985). Morphological studies on nutritional encephalomalacia in chicks, with special reference to mineralization deposits in the cerebellum. *Zentralblatt für Veterinärmedizin Reihe A, 32*, 662–675.

Hertz-Picciotto, I. (2012, January 3). Commentary on the *LA Times* series on autism. *Autism Speaks official blog.* Retrieved from http://blog.autismspeaks.org/2012/01/03/commentary-on-the-la-times-series-on-autism

Hertz-Picciotto, I., & Delwiche, L. (2009). The rise in autism and the role of age at diagnosis. *Epidemiology, 20*, 84–90.

Hof, P. R., Knabe, R., Bovier, P., & Bouras, C. (1991). Neuropathological observations in a case of autism presenting with self-injury behavior. *Acta Neuropathologica, 82*, 321–326.

Hoxworth, J. M., Xu, K., Zhou, Y., Lust, W. D., & LaManna J. C. (1999). Cerebral metabolic profile, selective neuron loss, and survival of acute and chronic hyperglycemic rats following cardiac arrest and resuscitation. *Brain Research, 82*, 467–479.

Hulkova, H., Druga, R., Ondejovic, P., & Elleder, M. (2008). Subpial astrocytosis and focal leptomeningeal angiotropic asatrocytosis leading to vascular compression: Observations made in a case of mitochondrial encephalopathy. *Acta Neuropathologica, 116*, 667–669.

Husain, J., & Juurlink, B. H. (1995). Oligodendroglial precursor cell susceptibility to hypoxia is related to poor ability to cope with reactive oxygen species. *Brain Research, 698*, 86–94.

Hutsler, J. J., Love, T., & Zhang, H. (2007). Histologic and magnetic resonance imaging assessment of cortical layering and thickness in autism spectrum disorders. *Biological Psychiatry, 61*, 449–457.

Hutsler, J. J., & Zhang, H. (2010). Increased dendritic spine densities on cortical projection neurons in autism spectrum disorders. *Brain Research, 1309*, 83–94.

Itabashi, H. H., Andrews, J. M., Tomiyasu, U., Erlich, S. S., & Sathyavagiswaran, L. (2007). *Forensic neuropathology: A practical review of the fundamentals.* New York, NY: Elsevier.

Ivarsson, S. A., Bjerre, I., Vegfors, P., & Ahlfors, K. (1990). Autism as one of several disabilities in two children with congenital cytomegalovirus infection. *Neuropediatrics, 21*, 102–103.

Jacot-Descombes, S., Uppal, N., Wicinski, B., Santos, M., Schmeidler, J., Giannakopoulos, P.,... Hof, P. R. (2012). Decreased pyramidal neuron size in Brodmann areas 44 and 45 in patients with autism. *Acta Neuropathologica, 124*, 67–70.

Janzer, R. C., & Friede, R. L. (1979). Perisulcal infarcts: Lesions caused by hypotension during increased intracranial pressure. *Annals of Neurology, 6*, 399–404.

Johnson, S., Hollis, C., Kochhar, P., Henessy, E., Wolke, D., & Marlow, N. (2010). Autism spectrum disorders in extremely preterm children. *Journal of Pediatrics, 156*, 525–531.

Kanner, L. (1943). Autistic disturbances of affective contact. *Nervous Child, 2*, 217–250.

Kemper, T. L. (2009). The developmental neuropathology of autism. In G. J. Blatt (Ed.), *The neurochemical basis of autism* (pp. 69–82). New York, NY: Springer.

Kemper, T. L., & Bauman, M. L. (1993). The contribution of neuropathologic studies to the understanding of autism. *Neurologic Clinics, 11*, 175–187.

Kemper, T. L., & Bauman, M. L. (1998). Neuropathology of infantile autism. *Journal of Neuropathology and Experimental Neurology, 57*, 645–652.

Kennedy, D. P., Semendeferi, K., & Courchesne, E. (2007). No reduction of spindle neuron number in frontoinsular cortex in autism. *Brain and Cognition, 64*, 124–129.

Kennedy, H., & Dehay, C. (2012). Self-organization and interareal networks in the primate cortex. *Progress in Brain Research, 195*, 341–360.

King, M., & Bearman, P. (2009). Diagnostic change and the increased prevalence of autism. *International Journal of Epidemiology, 38*, 1224–1234.

Kuban, K. C. K., O'Shea, T. M., Allred, E. N., Tager-Flusberg, H., Goldstein, D. J., & Leviton, A. (2009). Positive screening on the Modified Checklist for Autism in Toddlers (M-CHAT) in extremely low gestational age newborns. *Journal of Pediatrics, 154*, 535–540.e1.

Kulesza, R. J., & Mangunay, K. (2008). Morphological features of the medial superior olive in autism. *Brain Research, 1200*, 132–137.

Lainhart, J., Piven, J., Wzorek, M., Landa, R., Santangelo, D. L., Coon, H., & Folstein, S. E. (1997). Macrocephaly in children and adults with autism. *Journal of the American Academy of Child & Adolescent Psychiatry, 36*, 282–290.

Lanska, D. J., Markesbery, W. R., Cochran, E., Bennett, D., Lanska, M. J., & Cohen, M. (1998). Late-onset sporadic progressive subcortical gliosis. *Journal of the Neurological Sciences, 157*, 143–147.

Larroche, J. C. (1977). *Developmental pathology of the neonate.* Amsterdam, The Netherlands: Excerpta Medica.

Lee, M., Martinez-Ruiz C., Graham, A., Court, J., Jaros, E., & Perry, R. (2002). Nicotinic receptor abnormalities in the cerebellar cortex in autism. *Brain, 125*, 1483–1495.

Lipton, P. (1999). Ischemic cell death in brain neurons. *Physiological Reviews, 79*, 1431–1568.

Lishman, W. A. (1992). What is neuropsychiatry? *Journal of Neurology, Neurosurgery and Psychiatry, 55*, 983–985.

Lishman, W. A. (1995). Psychiatry and neuropathology: The maturing of a relationship. *Journal of Neurology, Neurosurgery and Psychiatry, 58*, 284–292.

López-Hurtado E., DeFelipe J., & Prieto, J. J. (2002). A microscopical study on the neuroanatomical abnormalities of language related cortical areas in autistic patients. *IMFAR Program Booklet & Abstracts, 2.* Retrieved from http://www.brainbankforautism.org.uk/abstracts/neuroanatomical_abnormalities_of_language.html

López-Hurtado, E., & Prieto, J. J. (2008). A microscopic study of language-related cortex in autism. *American Journal of Biochemistry and Biotechnology, 4*, 130–145.

Ludwig, J. (2002). *Handbook of autopsy practice.* Totowa, NJ: Humana Press.

Malamud, M. (1959). Heller's disease and childhood schizophrenia. *American Journal of Psychiatry, 116*, 215–219.

Mann, D. M. (1998). Dementia of frontal type and dementias with subcortical gliosis. *Brain Pathology, 8*, 325–338.

Markowitz, P. I. (1983). Autism in a child with congenital cytomegalovirus infection. *Journal of Autism and Developmental Disorders, 13*, 249–253.

Marshal, C. R., Noor, A., Vincent, J. B., Lionel, A. C., Feuk, L., Skaug, J., . . . Scherer, S. W. (2008). Structural variation of chromosomes in autism spectrum disorder. *American Journal of Human Genetics, 82*, 477–488.

Martchek, M., Thevarkunnel, S., Bauman, M., Blatt, G., & Kemper, T. (2006). Lack of evidence of neuropathology in the locus coeruleus in autism. *Acta Neuropathologica, 111*, 497–499.

Matsushita, H., Morishita, R., Nata, T., Aoki, M., Nakagami, H., Taniyama, Y., . . . Oqihara, T. (2000). Hypoxia-induced endothelial apoptosis through nuclear factor-kappaB (NF-kappaB)-mediated bcl-2 suppression: In vivo evidence of the importance of NF-kappaB in endothelial cell regulation. *Circulation Research, 86*, 974–981.

Menkes, J. H., & Sarnat, H. B. (2000). *Child neurology.* Philadelphia, PA: Lippincott Williams and Wilkins.

Miller, M. T., Storyland, K., Ventura, L, Johansson, M., Bandim, J. M., & Gillberg, C. (2005). Autism associated with conditions characterized by developmental errors in early embryogenesis: A mini review. *International Journal of Developmental Neuroscience, 23*, 201–219.

Monuki, E. S., & Ligon, K. L. (2004). Cerebral heterotopia. In J. A. Golden & B. N. Harding (Eds.), *Developmental neuropathology* (pp. 52–60). Basel: ISN Neuropathology Press.

Morgan, J. T., Chana, G., Abramson, I., Semendeferi, K., Courchesne, E., & Everall, I. P. (2012). Abnormal microglial-neuronal spatial organization in the dorsolateral prefrontal cortex in autism. *Brain Research, 1456*, 72–81.

Morgan, J. T., Chana, G., Pardo, C. A., Achim, C., Semendeferi, K., Buckwalter, J., . . . Everall, I. P. (2010). Microglial activation and increased microglial density observed in the dorsolateral prefrontal cortex in autism. *Biological Psychiatry, 68*, 368–376.

Mukaetova-Ladinska, E. B., Arnold, H., Jaros, E., Perry, R., & Perry, E. (2004). Depletion of *MAP2* expression and laminar cytoarchitectonic changes in dorsolateral prefrontal cortex in adult autistic individuals. *Neuropathology and Applied Neurobiology, 30*, 615–623.

Nelson, J. S. (2003). *Principles and practice of neuropathology* (2nd ed.). New York, NY: Oxford University Press.

Omata, N., Murata, T., Muruoka, N., Fujibayashi, Y., Yonekura, Y., & Wada, Y. (2003). Different mechanisms of hypoxic injury on white matter and gray matter as revealed by dynamic changes in glucose metabolism in rats. *Neuroscience Letters, 353*, 148–152.

Ozonoff, S. (1997). Causal mechanisms of autism: Unifying perspective from an information processing framework. In D. J. Cohen & F. R. Volkmar (Eds.), *Handbook of autism and pervasive developmental disorders* (2nd ed., pp. 868–879). New York, NY: Wiley.

Pakkenberg, H. (1966). The number of cells in the cerebral cortex of man. *Journal of Comparative Neurology, 128*, 17–20.

Palmen, S. J., Van Engeland, H., Hof, P. R., & Schmitz, C. (2004). Neuropathological findings in autism. *Brain, 127*, 2572–2584.

Patel, D. A., Booze, R. M., & Mactutus, C. F. (2012). Prenatal cocaine exposure alters progenitor cell markers in the subventricular zone of the adult rat brain. *International Journal of Developmental Neuroscience, 30*, 1–9.

Pekny, M., & Nilsson, M. (2005). Asctrocyte activation and reactive gliosis. *Glia, 50*, 427–434.

Pickett, J., & London, E. (2005). The neuropathology of autism: A review. *Journal of Neuropathology and Experimental Neurology, 64*, 925–935.

Pinto-Marin, J. A., Levy, S. E., Feldman, J. F., Lorenz, J. M., Paneth, N., & Whitaker, A. H. (2011). Prevalence of autism spectrum disorders in adolescents born weighing <2000 grams. *Pediatrics, 128*, 883–891.

Pliszka, S. R. (2004). *Neuroscience for the mental health clinician.* New York, NY: Guilford Press.

Pluta, R. (2002). Astroglial expression of the β-amyloid in ischemia-reperfusion brain injury. *Annals of the New York Academy of Sciences, 977*, 102–108.

Quester, R., & Schröder, R. (1997). The shrinkage of the human brain stem during formalin fixation and embedding in paraffin. *Journal of Neuroscience Methods, 75*, 81–89.

Rapin, I. (1999). Autism in search of a home in the brain. *Neurology, 52*, 902–904.

Raymond, G. V., Bauman, M. L., & Kemper, T. L. (1996). Hippocampus in autism: A Golgi analysis. *Acta Neuropathologica, 91*, 117–119.

Redcay, E., & Courchesne, E. (2005). When is the brain enlarged in autism? A metaanalysis of all brain size reports. *Biological Psychiatry, 58*, 1–9.

Rimland, B. (1964). *Infantile autism.* New York, NY: Appleton-Century-Crofts.

Ring, H., Woodbury-Smith, M., Watson, P., Wheelwright, S., & Baron-Cohen, S. (2008). Clinical heterogeneity among people with high functioning autism spectrum conditions: Evidence favouring a continuous severity gradient. *Behavioral and Brain Functions, 4*, 11.

Ritvo, E. R., Freeman, B. J., Scheibel, A. B., Duong, T., Robinson, H., Guthrie, D., & Ritvo, A. (1986). Lower Purkinje cell counts in the cerebella of four autistic subjects: Initial findings of the UCLA–NSAC Autopsy Research Report. *American Journal of Psychiatry, 143*, 862–866.

Robins, E., Smith, E. E., & Eydt, K. M. (1956). The quantitative histochemistry of the cerebral cortex. *Journal of Neurochemistry, 1*, 54–67.

Rodier, P. M. (2002). Converging evidence for brain stem injury in autism. *Development and Psychopathology, 14*, 537–557.

Rodier, P. M., & Hyman, S. L. (1998). Early environmental factors in autism. *Mental Retardation and Developmental Disabilities Research Reviews, 4*, 121–128.

Rodier, P. M., Ingram, J. L., Tisdale, B., Nelson, S., & Romano, J. (1996). Embryological origins for autism: Developmental abnormalities of the cranial nerve motor nuclei. *Journal of Comparative Neurology, 370*, 247–261.

Ronald, A., Happé, F., Butcher, L. M., Price, T. S., Wheelwright, S., Baron-Cohen, S., & Plomin, R. (2006). Genetic heterogeneity between the three components of the autism spectrum: A twin study. *Journal of the American Academy of Child & Adolescent Psychiatry, 45,* 691–699.

Santos, M., Uppal, N., Butti, C., Wicinski, B., Schmeidler, J., Giannakopoulos, P., . . . Hof, P. R. (2011). Von Economo neurons in autism: A stereological study of the frontoinsular cortex in children. *Brain Research, 1380,* 206–217.

Sarwar, M., & McCormick, W. F. (1978). Decrease in ventricular and sulcal size after death. *Radiology, 127,* 409–411.

Schlaug, G., Schleicher, A., & Zilles, K. (1995). Quantitative analysis of the columnar arrangement of neurons in the human cingulate cortex. *Journal of Comparative Neurology, 351,* 441–452.

Schmitz, C., & Rezaie, P. (2008). The neuropathology of autism: Where do we stand? *Neuropathology and Applied Neurobiology, 34,* 4–11.

Schultz, J. E., Bauman, M. L., & Kemper, T. L. (1999). Histoanatomic observations in the dentatothalamic pathway in the brains of two autistic males. *Neurology, 52*(Suppl. 2), A47.

Schumann, C. M., & Amaral, D. G. (2005). Stereological estimation of the number of neurons in the human amygdaloid complex. *Journal of Comparative Neurology, 491,* 320–329.

Schumann, C. M., & Amaral, D. G. (2006). Stereological analysis of amygdala neuron number in autism. *Journal of Neuroscience, 26,* 7674–7679.

Sheen, V. L., & Walsh, C. A. (2005). Periventricular heterotopia: New insights into Ehlers-Danlos syndrome. *Clinical Medical Research, 3,* 229–233.

Sheikh, A. M., Malik, M., Wen, G., Chauhan, A., Chauhan, V., Gong, C. X., . . . Li, X. (2010). BDNF-Akt-Bcl2 antiapoptotic signaling pathway is compromised in the brain of autistic individuals. *Journal of Neuroscience Research, 88,* 2641–2647.

Sholl, D. A. (1956). *The organization of the cerebral cortex.* New York, NY: Wiley.

Sidman, R. L., & Rakic, P. (1982). Development of the human nervous system. In W. Haymaker & R. D. Adams (Eds.), *Histology and histopathology of the nervous system* (pp. 3–145). Springfield, IL: Charles C. Thomas.

Sieg, K. G. (1992). Autism and Ehlers-Danlos syndrome. *Journal of the American Academy of Child & Adolescent Psychiatry, 31,* 173.

Simms, M. L., Kemper, T. L., Timbie, C. M., Bauman, M. L., & Blatt, G. J. (2009). The anterior cingulate cortex in autism: Heterogeneity of qualitative and quantitative cytoarchitectonic features suggests possible subgroups. *Acta Neuropathologica, 118,* 673–684.

Smalley, S. L. (1998). Autism and tuberous sclerosis. *Journal of Autism and Developmental Disorders, 28,* 407–414.

Stubbs, E. G. (1978). Autistic syndromes in a child with congenital cytomegalovirus infection. *Journal of Autism and Childhood Schizophrenia, 8,* 37–43.

Stubbs, E. G., Ash, E., & Williams, C. P. S. (1984). Autism and congenital cytomegalovirus. *Journal of Autism and Childhood Schizophrenia, 14,* 183–189.

Tantam, D., Evered, C., & Hersov, L. (1990). Asperger's syndrome and ligamentous laxity. *Journal of the American Academy of Child & Adolescent Psychiatry, 29,* 892–896.

Thevarkunnel, S., Martchek, M. A., Kemper, T. L., Bauman, M. L., & Blatt, G. J. (2004). A neuroanatomical study of the brainstem nuclei in autism. *Abstracts: Society for Neuroscience, 1028.*10.

Vargas, D. L., Nascimbene, C., Krishnan, C., Zimmerman, A. W., & Pardo, C. A. (2005). Neuroglial activation and neuroinflammation in the brain of patients with autism. *Annals of Neurology, 57,* 67–81.

Volpe, J. (1997). Brain injury in the premature infant: Neuropathology, clinical aspects, pathogenesis, and prevention. *Clinics in Perinatology, 24,* 567–587.

Wegiel, J. (2004). Neuronal deficits in the motor system of people with autism with less pronounced pathology in the memory system. Abstract in the proceedings of the Integrating the Clinical and Basic Sciences of Autism: A Developmental Biology Workshop, Fort Lauderdale, FL, November 12–13.

Wegiel, J., Frackowiak, J., Mazur-Kolecka, B., Schanen, N. C., Cook, E. H., Jr., Sigman, M., . . . Wisniewski, T. (2012). Abnormal intracellular accumulation and extracellular A β deposition in idiopathic and Dup 15q11.2-q13 autism spectrum disorders. *PLOS one, 7,* e35414.

Wegiel, J., Kuchna, I., Nowicki, K., Imaki, H., Wegiel, J., Marchi, E., . . . Wisnieski, T. (2010). The neuropathology of autism: Defects of neurogenesis and neuronal migration, and dysplastic changes. *Acta Neuropathologica, 119,* 755–770.

Weidenheim, K. M., Escobar, A., & Rapin, I. (2012). Brief report: Life history and neuropathology of a gifted man with Asperger syndrome. *Journal of Autism and Developmental Disorders, 42,* 460–467.

Weidenheim, K. M., Goodman, L., Dickson, D. W., Gillberg, C., Rastam, M., & Rapin, I. (2001). Etiology and pathophysiology of autistic behavior: Clues from two cases with an unusual variant of neruoaxonal dystrophy. *Journal of Child Neurology, 16,* 809–819.

Weintraub, K. (2011). The prevalence puzzle: Autism counts. *Nature, 479,* 22–24.

Whitney, E. R., Kemper, T. L., Bauman, M. L., Rosene, D. L., & Blatt, G. J. (2008). Cerebellar Purkinje cells are reduced in a subpopulation of autistic brains: A stereological experiment using calbindin-D28K. *Cerebellum, 7,* 406–416.

Whitney, E. R., Kemper, T. L., Rosene, D. L., Bauman, M. L., & Blatt, G. J. (2009). Density of cerebellar basket and stellate cells in autism: Evidence for a late developmental loss of Purkinje cells. *Journal of Neuroscience Research, 87,* 2245–2254.

Williams, E. L., & Casanova, M. F. (2010). Potential teratogenic effects of ultrasound on corticogenesis: Implications for autism. *Medical Hypotheses, 75,* 53–58.

Williams, E. L., & Casanova, M. F. (2011). Above genetics: Lessons from cerebral development in autism. *Translational Neuroscience, 2,* 106–120.

Williams, R. S., Hauser, S. I., Purpura, D. P., DeLong, G. R., & Swisher, C. N. (1980). Autism and mental retardation: Neuropathologic studies performed in four retarded persons with autistic behavior. *Archives of Neurology, 37,* 749–753.

Winslow, F. (1854). *Lettsomiam lectures in insanity.* London, England: John Churchill.

Yamashita, Y., Fujimoto, C., Nakajima, E., Isagai, T., & Matsuishi, T. (2003). Possible association between congenital cytomegalovirus infection and autistic disorder. *Journal of Autism and Developmental Disorders, 33,* 455–459.

Yates, A. J., Thelmo, W., & Pappius, H. M. (1975). Postmortem changes in the chemistry and histology of normal and edematous brains. *American Journal of Pathology*, *79*, 555–564.

Yip, J., Marcon, R., Kemper, T., Bauman, M., & Blatt, G. (2005). The olivocerebellar projection in autism: Using the intermediate protein peripherin as a marker for climbing fibers. *IMFAR Program Booklet & Abstracts*, *4*, 49.

Yokota, Y., Ghashgaei, H. T., Han, C., Watson, H., Campbell, K. J., & Anton, E. S. (2007). Radial glia dependent and independent dynamics of interneuronal migration in the developing cerebral cortex. *PLoS One*, *2*, e794.

Zherebitskiy, V., & Del Bigio, M. R. (2009). Eosionophilic intracytoplasmic inclusions in Purkinje neurons in children. *Neuropathology*, *29*, 9–12.

Zikopoulos, B., & Barbas, H. (2010). Changes in prefrontal axons may disrupt the network in autism. *Journal of Neuroscience*, *30*, 14595–14609.

Zilboorg, G., & Henry, G. W. (1941). *A history of medical psychology*. London, England: Allen & Unwin.

CHAPTER 22

Medical Care in Autism and Related Conditions

FRED R. VOLKMAR, JUSTIN ROWBERRY, OANA DE VINCK-BAROODY,
ABHA R. GUPTA, JENNIFER LEUNG, JUDITH MEYERS, NITA VASWANI,
AND LISA A. WIESNER

CHALLENGES IN PROVIDING HEALTHCARE FOR INDIVIDUALS WITH ASD

Not surprisingly, two of the major challenges for individuals with autism—difficulties with

From the Child Study Center and Department of Pediatrics Yale University School of Medicine. Portions of this chapter were adapted from Volkmar and Wiesner, *A Practical Guide to Autism* (Hoboken, NJ: Wiley, 2009), Chapter 8.

communication and social interaction—also pose significant challenges for provision of health care. In the person with limited verbal ability acute disease may actually present in various ways, such as irritability, decreased appetite or refusal to eat, acute weight loss, or behavioral changes such as head banging or self-injury. Difficulties with social interaction and sensitivity to change may mean a child will not cooperate when being examined and even the most minor procedures can pose challenges. The rapid pace of medical care and the sometimes numerous individuals in the health care system can further exacerbate these difficulties. Unfortunately this only seems to increase over time—and may make examination more difficult—particularly in situations where the care provider is unfamiliar with the individual or where the environment is unfamiliar and over stimulating (e.g., the emergency room). For persons with autism, the long-term goal is to help the individual participate as much as possible in the process of getting good health care and leading a healthy lifestyle. Having a health-care provider who takes an interest in making this happen are very helpful in this process (Volkmar & Wiesner, 2009).

Preventive care is particularly important for individuals with autism. Routine screening by physical exam and laboratory testing are important to detect problems early—when treatments can be helpful and prevent more severe or permanent conditions. Participation in regular well-child visits and later periodic physical examinations helps the provider and patient get to know each other. This facilitates care provision when the individual is ill. Regular screening for common health problems and immunizations are also part of this process.

In addition to challenges arising from caring for a child with autism other challenges arise given our complex health-care system. These issues can come about through difficulties with insurance, for example, finding providers who accept certain insurance plans or, for adults, finding an insurance provider. Other issues arise given the tendency for health care to be delivered by different providers, for example, specialists like a psychiatrist, neurologist, psychologist, or speech pathologist. One important way to prevent this problem, as we discuss subsequently, is having a medical home with a provider or provider group who takes a leadership role in integrating care and services.

In this chapter, we discuss some of the issues involved in providing quality health care to individuals on the autism spectrum. We review a number of topics, including medical conditions more frequent in individuals with autism spectrum disorders (ASDs), coping with hospitalization, and other special situations. We also discuss a number of age-related health issues and conclude with a discussion of the role of the primary care provider and medical home model. While a review of the relevant literature is presented, it should be noted that there is a dearth of literature in some areas such as health care for adults (Piven, Rabins, & Autism-in-Older Adults Working Group, 2011); also see Howlin (Chapter 4, this *Handbook*) and Chapters 24, 42, and 44 on screening, evidence-based treatments, and practice guidelines.

MEDICAL CONDITIONS FREQUENTLY ASSOCIATED WITH AUTISM

Over time our understanding of the medical conditions associated with autism has shifted dramatically. Early on in the literature, case reports linked autism with a veritable host of conditions (e.g., Gillberg & Coleman, 1992). Over time it became clear that an overreliance on case reports was problematic given the publication bias for only positive associations to be published, the tendency to republish the same case(s), and the general lack of more epidemiological data to put the results in context. Rutter and colleagues (Rutter, Bailey, Bolton, & Le Couteur, 1994) pointed out the important issue was not whether an association was *ever* reported but if it was significantly more frequent than would be expected given chance alone. In their review Rutter and colleagues note that the list of stronger than expected associations of medical conditions is relatively short and includes epilepsy (recurrent seizures) and several genetic conditions—these associations may be relevant to understanding more basic issues of etiology in autism.

Epilepsy and Autism

Epilepsy involves recurrent seizures—children are typically diagnosed with epilepsy after having more than two unprovoked seizures. The prevalence of epilepsy in childhood in the general population is estimated to be 0.4% to 1%, while in children with autism, a prevalence rate as high as 42% has been reported (Peake, Notghi, & Philip, 2006). By the time patients with autism become adults, one third of them will develop epilepsy (Levisohn, 2004). Further, patients with autism without seizures often are found to have abnormalities on electroencephalogram (EEG) (Ekinci, Arman, Isik, Bez, & Berkem, 2010; Peake et al., 2006). Seizure disorders are some of the most frequently encountered complications associated with autism, and they are noted more frequently than in other neurodevelopmental conditions, such as learning problems or intellectual disability (Peake et al., 2006).

Children with autism can exhibit various seizure types and EEG abnormalities. There is a relationship between autism and temporal lobe dysfunction, where EEG abnormalities are most commonly found (Peake et al., 2006). Although this association between autism and epilepsy has been well established and has supported the organic nature of autism, the underlying pathophysiology has not been elucidated at this time and needs further investigation. It is also unclear at this time how the seizure disorder or EEG abnormalities affects the behavioral phenotype in children with autism. Although an underlying genetic etiology is often accepted to be part of the syndrome and several specific genetic conditions, including tuberous sclerosis, Angelman syndrome, and Rett syndrome are linked with both autism and an increased risk of seizures, the genetic etiology is often not determined with only 10%–20% cases of autism being secondary to a known disorder (Tuchman & Rapin, 2002). Further, it is unclear how the seizures or EEG abnormalities affect the clinical presentation, and controlling the seizures may not result in improvement in the symptoms of autism.

Epilepsy has a bimodal onset in children with autism, with a peak occurring in children under 5 years of age and then again in adolescence. In children with autism, several risk factors have been identified including having intellectual disability,

motor disabilities, more significant autistic features, and severe language disorders, particularly receptive language difficulties (Levisohn, 2004; Peake et al., 2006; Volkmar & Nelson, 1990). Seizures are particularly common in children with autism and intellectual disability.

Physicians need to consider a seizure disorder diagnosis in children with autism when the patient exhibits symptoms that are suspicious of a seizure and when there has been a regression in the child's behavior and development. About 20% of children with autism will exhibit a regression in their development as reported by their parents (Volkmar & Wiesner, 2009). Some of these children may have an abnormal EEG and/or epilepsy; however, in these situations it is unclear if the regression and the developmental phenotype is caused by the seizure activity or EEG abnormalities. This relationship between seizures and autism in children with regression continues to need clarification.

In children with autism who have experienced a developmental or behavioral regression, a prolonged sleep EEG is recommended to evaluate for conditions such as nonconvulsive status epilepticus and Landau-Kleffner syndrome (Peake et al., 2006). Landau-Kleffner syndrome is a condition that typically involves regression in language skills at an older age than is typically seen in typical autistic regression, usually at 3 to 5 years of age (compared to 18 to 24 months of age in autistic regression) and seizures or epileptiform activity on EEG. Treating the seizures in Landau-Kleffner syndrome, may or may not reverse the developmental and behavioral symptoms (Levisohn, 2004). Since this condition is very rare, further study is necessary in order to understand if anticonvulsant treatment can affect the disease course (Tuchman, 2004).

Treatment of epilepsy in children with autism is essentially analogous to treatment of children with epilepsy alone, although children with autism often have comorbid conditions that complicate their treatment, including behavioral difficulties such as aggression, hyperactivity, and mood symptoms that may require multiple medications for treatment (Volkmar & Wiesner, 2009).

Fragile X Syndrome

This genetic condition is fairly frequently associated with autism, and is the most common form of inherited intellectual disability (Van Esch, 2012). This X-linked disorder is caused by decreased or absent fragile X mental retardation protein, or FMRP, secondary to mutation of the fragile X mental retardation 1 gene (FMR1) found at Xq27.3. Typically this results from a loss of function mutation due to an unstable expansion of a trinucleotide repeat (CGG). More than 200 repeats of this trinucleotide are referred to as full mutations and will result in silencing of the FMR1 gene and resultant absence of FMRP causing the fragile X syndrome phenotype. Of note, individuals can also experience mutations between 50 and 200 repeats that are referred to as permutations. These individuals may experience a spectrum of clinical findings. Since this is an X-linked condition, males with the full mutation are typically severely affected while females experience a range of severity.

The diagnosis of fragile X syndrome is made via genetic testing and requires a high index of suspicion as more specific features of the disorder may not be apparent until the child is older and early intervention and family planning are important in the overall management and support of the family. Frequently a diagnosis of fragile X syndrome is delayed and a quarter of families have had a second child with the disorder before the first child is diagnosed (Van Esch, 2012).

Several phenotypic features are observed. In terms of physical examination children with fragile X syndrome classically will exhibit relative macrocephaly, long face, large ears, prominent forehead, hypotonia, arched palate, and testicular enlargement. However, these features may not be noticeable in a child and will become most apparent in adolescence. Medical problems include seizures, mitral valve prolapse, hypotonia, and frequent ear infections and sinusitis as well as learning disabilities and/or moderate intellectual disability (Van Esch, 2012). The degree of intellectual impairment correlates with the FMRP produced by the individual (Visootsak, Warren, Anido, & Graham, 2005). On psychological testing weaknesses in mathematics, visuospatial abilities, attention, and executive functioning and visual-motor coordination are observed, and sometimes intellectual and adaptive functioning decline over time (Van Esch et al., 2012). Children with fragile X syndrome also have language and speech disorders and about 10% will be nonverbal.

The behavioral features of fragile X syndrome include social anxiety (often suggestive of autism or ASD) and features of attention-deficit/hyperactivity disorder (ADHD). Children may have poor eye contact, gaze aversion, tactile sensitivities, extreme shyness, and perseverative speech (Visootsak et al., 2005). Some cases will meet criteria for autistic disorder (Hagerman et al., 2009), although the striking gaze avoidance and perseverative speech are more marked than in autism alone (Moss, Oliver, Arron, Burbidge, & Berg, 2009). As a single gene disorder this condition may represent a potential target for pharmacological intervention.

Tuberous Sclerosis

Tuberous sclerosis is found in 1% to 4% of children with autism, although 25% to 50% of children with tuberous sclerosis (TS) are noted to have autism or some features of autism (Wiznitzer, 2004). Children with tuberous sclerosis are particularly at risk to develop autism when they have temporal lobe tubers (Peake et al., 2006). Additionally, more severe intellectual disability and seizure disorder or EEG abnormalities (particularly infantile spasms) increase risk of autism (Levisohn, 2004). In contrast to the usual male predominance in autism, in tuberous sclerosis the male-to-female ratio in the affected population is approximately equal (Wiznitzer, 2004). Children with tuberous sclerosis and autism spectrum disorders tend to have more severe cognitive impairment compared to children with only tuberous sclerosis, with 75% of children with tuberous sclerosis and autism having cognitive impairment, usually in the moderate to severe range. Additionally, 75% to 100% of these children also have a history of seizure disorder. However, there are also patients with tuberous sclerosis and autism that do not have cognitive impairments and/or seizure disorder.

Tuberous sclerosis is a neurocutaneous disorder potentially impacting many organ systems, including the skin, brain, eyes, heart, and kidney. The diagnosis of tuberous sclerosis is made clinically, and the expression or severity of the disease can vary widely between patients (see Roach & Sparagana, 2004, for a review). Diagnosis is made based on certain clinical criteria and definite diagnosis includes two major features or one major and two minor features (Roach & Sparagana, 2004). Examples of major features include facial angiofibromas, renal angiomyolipoma, cortical tubers, subependymal modules, cardiac rarhabdomyoma, more than three hypomelanotic macules, and so forth; minor features include bone cysts, fibromas in the gingiva, nonrenal hamartoma, and multiple renal cysts, among others (see Roach & Sparagana, 2004).

Tuberous sclerosis is an autosomal dominant condition caused by an abnormality of the TSC-1 or TSC-2 genes; usually this occurs as a de novo mutation. Genetic testing is not required for diagnosis, but 60% to 89% of patients who meet diagnostic criteria for tuberous sclerosis will exhibit a disease-causing mutation on testing (Plon & Owens, 2012). The TSC-1 gene codes to the 9q34 chromosome for the hamartin protein and TSC-2 gene codes to the 16p13.3 chromosome encoding for the tuberin protein. The tuberin and hamartin proteins form a complex, and it is possible that they function as tumor suppressor genes.

Clinically, the spectrum of presentation of tuberous sclerosis can vary widely even within the same family from normal to severely impaired cognitive function. The classic Vogt triad of tuberous sclerosis of seizures, intellectual disability, and facial angiofibromas is only present in less than one third of patients with tuberous sclerosis (Plon & Owens, 2012). Therefore, when considering this diagnosis, a high index of suspicion is recommended with attention to the major and minor criteria and particular focus on the skin and neurological examinations. Although this is a clinical diagnosis,

genetic testing is often recommended to confirm the diagnosis and also to identify if other family members carry the mutation. Of note, however, if a patient does not have a mutation on testing, this does not exclude the diagnosis.

This disorder is progressive with different features across the lifetime. In early childhood, many of the clinical features may not be apparent, and often the most common initial symptoms at this age are seizures or cardiac rhabdomyosarcoma. During childhood is when most of the dermatologic features and also neurologic abnormalities (such as learning disability, cognitive impairment, etc.) become apparent, and it is when most cases of tuberous sclerosis are diagnosed. The diagnosis is occasionally also made in adults, especially after the diagnosis of a child in the family in parent who is a mosaic for a TSC mutation.

In terms of clinical features of the disease, most patients will have one of characteristic dermatologic findings, with the most common finding being the hypopigmented macules. The dermatologic findings develop at different ages with the hypopigmented macules and forehead plaques being among the earliest findings that may even be apparent in infants. Additionally, neurologic abnormalities are another common finding, with epilepsy affecting 79% to 90% and intellectual disability affecting 44% to 65% of patients with tuberous sclerosis (Plon & Owens, 2012). Oftentimes seizures begin in the first year of life and are the most common presenting concern. Infantile spasms occur in 36% to 69% of patients (Plon & Owens, 2012). Additionally, patients with tuberous sclerosis also present with cardiac, renal, pulmonary, and ophthalmic abnormalities, and are at increased risk of invasive malignancy. Periodic surveillance is an important part of the management of patients with tuberous sclerosis and included brain neuroimaging, renal ultrasonography and subspecialist involvement and assessments.

The reason for the co-occurrence of tuberous sclerosis and autism has not been explained at this time although several hypotheses have been generated. For example, it is plausible that the TSC genes themselves are causative of the autism symptoms, that the effects of tuberous sclerosis on the brain cause the autism symptoms (location of tubers, seizures, etc.) or possibly a linkage of the TSC genes and the genes causing autism. Further research is needed to better understand this relationship.

Awareness of the association of TS and autism should prompt screening for the other condition if one is present, for example, use of Wood's lamp and assessment for other criteria of tuberous sclerosis and monitoring for symptoms of an autism spectrum disorder in those with TS. Additionally, a child with tuberous sclerosis who experiences an autistic regression should have an EEG to test for concomitant seizure disorder that may be aggravating the course.

Children with tuberous sclerosis and autism spectrum disorder should have ongoing monitoring by a specialist familiar with both disease processes and potentially may require the support of several subspecialists. Although it is noted that patients with both conditions and other concomitant disorders such as cognitive impairment and seizure disorder may have poorer response to intervention than those who have autism spectrum disorder alone, all should receive appropriate educational and behavioral interventions through the school system. Seizure disorders should be promptly treated due to the potential effects on symptom course, including both cognitive functioning and autism symptoms.

Other Genetic Conditions

Additional genetic conditions that have been found to have an increased rate of autism include Angelman syndrome, Down syndrome, phenylketonuria, and Smith-Lemli-Opitz syndrome. The significance of such associations remains unclear. As noted subsequently careful consideration of genetic conditions/evaluation should be part of an initial comprehensive medical assessment.

FREQUENT MEDICAL ISSUES AND PROBLEMS

Nutrition/Eating Issues

Children with autism can have a number of problems with eating and food, including unusual food preferences and sensitivities (which can lead to a restricted diet) and pica (Volkmar & Wiesner, 2009). Difficulties with change further complicate the introduction of new and varied foods in the diets of children with autism, thus the child may have a highly idiosyncratic diet with resultant implications for physical growth and development (Strickland, 2009). Table 22.1 summarizes the important role of nutrients important in certain body functions (adapted from Strickland, 2009).

Strategies for coping with a child with unusual food preferences and restricted diet include the following (Volkmar & Wiesner, 2009):

- Attempt a very, very *gradual* change in introducing new foods (including the use of blenders and food processors as needed)
- Vary the way in which food is presented (e.g., freezing pureed vegetables into popsicles)
- Engage the child in helping prepare the food with photos or visual approaches for recipes
- Involve the child in grocery shopping to spark interest in new foods

TABLE 22.1   Nutrients and Their Functions

Body Function	Nutrient
Brain development and function	Vitamins, minerals, amino acids, essential fatty acids
Detoxification process	Zinc, selenium, magnesium, beta carotene, vitamin A, vitamin E, choline
Gastrointestinal health	Amino acid glutamate, vitamins, minerals
Immune system function	Vitamin C, vitamin A, vitamin E, vitamin D, B vitamins, iron, selenium, zinc, bioflavonoids
Erythropoiesis	Iron, vitamin B6, copper, folate, vitamin B12, vitamin C, vitamin E

Various professionals can be of help, including speech-language pathologists (SLPs), occupational therapists, dieticians, behavioral psychologists, as well as experienced teachers and parents (Volkmar & Wiesner, 2009). Behavioral psychologists may help design a plan for gradually introducing new foods and expanding the child's dietary range. Moreover, registered dieticians have specific training in diet and nutrition, and can help design a better diet for the child, sometimes working in conjunction with the child's behavioral program. Information on diet and accredited dietetic professionals is provided on American Dietetic Association's website (www.eatright.org). Lastly, SLPs or occupational therapists may help develop ways to help the child become more tolerant of a greater range of textures or help with other aspects of presentation of foods (Volkmar & Wiesner, 2009). Children with pica (mouthing or consuming nonfood items) should be screened for high lead levels (Volkmar & Wiesner, 2009).

Dietary interventions are among the most common alternative/complementary therapies employed by parents (see Chapter 46). Special diets used include the gluten-free, casein-free; Feingold; antifungal; and specific carbohydrate diets. There is little scientific research support for their efficacy (Strickland, 2009).

Gastrointestinal Problems

Comorbidities in ASDs include behavioral disorders, mood disorders, sleep abnormalities, seizures, metabolic conditions, and gastrointestinal dysfunction. There is a great deal of heterogeneity in patient presentation (Bill & Geschwind, 2009; Coury et al., 2012) and considerable controversy regarding the significance of reported associations.

In recent years there has been considerable interest in gastrointestinal problems in autism (the "gut connection"). A recent consensus report reviewed gastrointestinal (GI) disturbances in ASDs relevant to clinical care (Buie et al., 2010) and noted that chronic constipation, resultant encopresis, and abdominal pain (with or without

diarrhea) were frequently reported. Various factors (lack of exercise, limited diet, and poor diet) may contribute to such problems. Other GI problems observed have included gastroesophageal reflux disease, abdominal bloating, and disaccharides deficiencies. Abnormalities of the enteric nervous system and gastrointestinal tract inflammation have also been noted. Primary areas of concern in children with ASDs afflicted by gastrointestinal disease include constipation, diarrhea, reflux, and nutrition (Coury et al., 2012). Although case reports of GI problems in autism began to appear in the 1970s, little systematic work was done until the 1990s (Horvath & Perman, 2002b). The data vary widely, reflecting major differences in approach (e.g., reliance of parent survey data) and results (the latter presumably reflecting the former). In one survey of 412 children with autism, parents did not recollect the age at which children first had gastrointestinal symptoms, but reported that they were noticed since birth or began approximately when behavior dysregulation was first noted (Horvath & Perman, 2002a). Parents reported significantly more gastrointestinal problems in children with ASDs compared with their unaffected siblings (42% versus 12%) (Wang, Tancredi, & Thomas, 2011). Documentation from pediatric gastroenterologists showed gastrointestinal symptoms in 46% to 84% of children with ASDs (Kuddo & Nelson, 2003). A report by Coury et al. (2012) mentions the prevalence of gastrointestinal disorders in children with ASDs ranging from 9% to 91%, with abdominal pain or discomfort ranging from 2% to 41%, constipation from 6% to 45%, diarrhea from 3% to 77%, and persistent diarrhea from 8% to 19%. However, the British Medical Research Council suggests that there are no epidemiological data documenting the incidence and prevalence of gastrointestinal disturbances in children with ASDs (Medical Research Council, 2001).

Constipation and diarrhea appear to be the most frequently reported gastrointestinal symptoms in children with autism in a study with 589 children with familial ASD and 163 unaffected siblings in the control group (Wang et al., 2011). In a group of 15,500 children born from 1992 to 1995, in which 18.8% of autistic children experienced gastrointestinal symptoms, 9.4% experienced constipation (Fombonne & Chakrabarti, 2001). Afzal et al. in 2003 found moderate or severe constipation to be more common in the autism group than in the controls (36% versus 10%). Use of milk was the strongest predictor but stool frequency, gluten consumption, soiling, and abdominal pain were factors not predictive of constipation. In a study by Atladóttir et al. in 2009, with 121 autistic children and 242 control subjects, autistic children were more likely to be diagnosed with constipation. However, a study conducted in the United Kingdom on healthy children in the age group of 4–7 years reported constipation in 34% of the subjects (Loening-Baucke, 1998). A study of 137 autistic children ranging from 24 months to 96 months of age showed diarrhea was the most common symptom, reported in 17% of patients (Molloy & Manning-Courtney, 2003). It has been noted that GI problems may predispose to other difficulties, for example, sleep problems (Horvath & Perman, 2002b) or irritability.

While many areas appear worthy of further work (Coury et al., 2012) it will be important that future research addresses a number of important limitations of current research. These include lack of control groups, referral bias, retrospective approach, reliance on parent report, and heterogeneity of populations studied (Buie et al., 2010; Coury et al., 2012). Evidence-based guidelines are currently not available for gastrointestinal disease in children with ASDs and so standard levels of practice should prevail.

Sleep Problems

Difficulties with sleep are very common in children with ASD, with prevalence estimates ranging from a 40% up to 86% (Cortesi, Giannotti, Ivaneko, & Johnson 2010; Liu, Hubbard, Fabes, & Adam 2006; Richdale, 1999). In a study of 160 children with ASD from 2 to 18 years old, 52% of the children were found to have sleep disorders consisting of sleep initiation that was delayed by at least 1 hour, daily nighttime awakenings for 10 or more minutes, a total sleep time of less than 6 hours per night, or sleep disordered breathing (Ming, Brimacombe, Caaban, Zimmerman-Bier, & Wagner 2008). Sleep problems in children with ASD have been shown to be related to a combination of factors commonly found in ASD including comorbid epilepsy, ADHD, gastrointestinal symptoms, asthma, sensory hypersensitivities, use of medications, and cosleeping (Liu et al., 2006). Though some of those factors, such as hypersensitivity and gastrointestinal symptoms, are thought to be causative of some degree of sleep difficulty; other factors, such as cosleeping, may be the result of the child's sleep disorder.

Though the neurobiological mechanisms for sleep disorders in children with ASD are not yet completely understood, it has been hypothesized that it is contributed to by abnormalities in the neurotransmitter systems involving gamma-aminobutyric acid (GABA), serotonin, and melatonin; and abnormalities in the regulation of circadian rhythms by the hypopituitary- pituitary-adrenal axis (Cortesi et al., 2010; Levitt, Eagleson, & Powell 2004). Sleep disorders in children with ASD are often medically treated, despite the lack of Food and Drug Administration (FDA) approved medications for pediatric insomnia. Often, the first medication used is melatonin, for delayed sleep onset, or melatonin controlled release for sleep maintenance. Both preparations of melatonin have shown efficacy and minimal side effects in small sample trials (Giannotti, Cortesi, Cerquiglini, & Bernabei 2006). Other medication types frequently used to treat sleep disorders in children with ASD include alpha-agonists, atypical antipsychotics, and highly sedative antidepressants. Often these medications are used for a combination of their primary effect—such as Risperidone, which is FDA approved for aggression and self-injurious behavior in children with ASD—and their sedative effect (Johnson & Malow, 2008). Various behavioral resources to treat sleep disorders are available as well (see Volkmar & Wiesner, 2009, for a review).

Accidents, Injuries, and Safety

Accidents and safety issues are major concerns in autism and related disorders. The Centers for Disease Control and Prevention (CDC) has reported unintentional injury to be the leading cause of hospitalizations and deaths in children 18 and younger, and several studies have noted increased risk of injury in children with developmental disabilities including ASD (CDC, 2010, 2011). In a recent study based on nationwide cross-sectional data of 3- to 5-year-old children, those with ASD were found to have over twice the annual prevalence of injury requiring medical attention (24.2% versus 11.6% for unaffected controls) after adjusting for the child's sex, age, race, poverty level, and the number of children in the family (Lee, Harrington, Chang, & Connors, 2008). Compared to typically developing peers, children with ASD are at approximately 1.5 times greater risk for head, face, and neck injuries (McDermott, Zhou, & Mann, 2008).

The increased risk of injury and poisoning in children with ASD is consistent with the decreased awareness of risk and increased level of impulsivity often found in children with ASD. Self-injurious behaviors are also frequently seen in more severely affected children with autism. The decreased risk of injuries due to strains and sprains are likely due to the decreased participation in organized sports and activities that predispose to these types of injuries. We discuss specific age-related safety issues subsequently.

AGE-RELATED HEALTH-CARE ISSUES

Infancy and Early Childhood

Challenges for health care in this age group include (a) screening and initial diagnostic evaluations, (b) relevant medical evaluations (genetic, hearing, and so forth), (c) facilitating provision of treatment, and (d) beginning a collaboration with parents/family in the long-term provision of health care. For young parents the task of dealing with

the challenge of having a child with any special needs are significant and health-care providers have an important opportunity to facilitate the parents long-term coping and adaptation.

Fortunately, over the past 10 years, educational campaigns, parent organizations, and the development and implementation of early screening instruments have resulted in an increased number of children under the age of 3 identified and beginning early intervention.

As identification moves to younger children, it should be noted that children under age 2 years differ in their presentation of symptoms in comparison to preschoolers and older children. Additionally, in the current *Diagnostic and Statistical Manual of Mental Disorders—DSM-5*—revisions will provide severity ratings that may be more useful toward the younger age groups, as differentiation within the spectrum is challenging in younger children (Steiner, Goldsmith, Snow, & Chawarska, 2012), although issues around the applicability of *DSM-5* in young children have also been raised (Barton, Robins, Jashar, Brenna, & Fein, in press; Matson, Kozlowski, Hattier, Horovitz, & Sipes, 2012).

It seems likely (although this remains the focus of some debate) that in many if not most cases, the earliest signs of ASDs occur between 6 and 12 months of life (see Chapter 5). Prior to that, eye contact and social smile are apparently much less likely to be experienced as abnormal. By 1 year of age, some children exhibit decreased response to name, social ability, and nonverbal communication, as well as repetitive behaviors, atypical object exploration, and language delays. Current research has not yet lead to established guidelines within this age group for diagnosis of ASDs. If delays are noted on screening and surveillance, appropriate services should be provided and there should be a reevaluation in 3–6 months. It is important to emphasize how important it is to take parental concern (or observation of concerning behaviors) seriously given the growing body of work on the significant impact of early intervention. By the second year of life, stability of the ASD diagnosis increase substantially and ranges from 80% to

100%. Those who are higher functioning and have milder social symptoms are less likely to retain the diagnosis (Steiner et al., 2012; see also Chapter 5).

Screening for autism is performed on two tiers. Level 1 screening is intended to be used for all children and identifies a wide spectrum of developmental issues. Children identified to be at risk on level 1 screening should undergo a more extensive evaluation, using a level 2 screener, which differentiates ASDs from other developmental disorders. Level 1 screeners include the Child Development Inventories (CDIs), Ages and Stages Questionnaire (ASQ), Parents Evaluation of Developmental Status (PEDS), Modified Checklist for Autism in Toddlers (M-CHAT), Pervasive Developmental Disorders Screening Test–Stage 1 (PDDST-Stage 1), and so on. Level 2 screeners include interview instruments such as the Gilliam Autism Rating Scale (GARS), Autism Diagnostic Interview–Revised (ADI-R), the Parent Interview for Autism (PIA), and Pervasive Developmental Disorders Screening Test–Stage 3 (PDDST-Stage 3); observation instruments such as the Childhood Autism Rating Scale (CARS), the Screening Tool for Autism in Two-Year-Olds (STAT), and Autism Diagnostic Observation Schedule–2 (ADOS-2); and clinical diagnosis (Filipek et al., 1999) (see Chapter 24).

Diagnosis of an ASD should be comprehensive, exploring verbal and nonverbal developmental skills, social communication and interaction, motor and sensory behaviors, adaptive functioning, medical history, developmental history, and family history. Medical evaluation should consist of a genetic screening (genetics of autism is discussed in a separate chapter), neurological examination, assessment of vision, and hearing exam as indicated. Additional focus should be invested in problems with attention, attachment, and anxiety. Developmental delays in young children with ASDs do not fully account for their deficits in adaptive functioning. The Vineland Adaptive Behavior Scales, Second Edition (VABS-II) has emerged as the gold standard for measuring adaptive skills in infants and toddlers. It consists of an interview or parent rating form divided into a three domain

structure addressing communication, daily living, and socialization (Steiner et al., 2012).

Delays in diagnosis remain common—particularly for less classic cases (particularly those with Asperger's). These delays may reflect inadequate screening, parent unfamiliarity with symptoms, and a delay in evaluation (Steiner et al., 2012). In a study regarding geographic access to health services and diagnosis with an ASD, it was reported that median ages at diagnosis were 3–16 months earlier for children living in areas with many psychologists, physician specialists, and medical schools, and no shortage of health professionals; however, children living in areas with many primary care physicians or in close proximity to Division of Treatment and Education of Autistic and Related Communication Handicapped Children agencies or Children's Developmental Services agencies were diagnosed 4 to 5 months later (Kalkbrenner et al., 2011).

The Autism Diagnostic Observation Schedule–Generic (ADOS-G) is the most extensively used instrument for diagnostic assessment, but in younger children (under age 2) the ADOS-G may overestimate children with low adaptive function and underestimate children with high-functioning ASDs. The ADOS-2 is the newly redesigned ADOS, which includes revised algorithms for Modules 1–3 and the feature of a comparison score that allows for comparison of children's symptoms to others of the same age and language skills. Specifically for toddlers, to improve the sensitivity and specificity of assessment, the Autism Diagnostic Observation Schedule—Toddler (ADOS-T) module was developed by Luyster et al. (2009) and is part of the ADOS-2. Children with a nonverbal mental age of at least 12 months, motor skills that allow them to cruise, and a chronological age of less than 30 months can be assessed using the ADOS-T (Steiner et al., 2012).

The ADI-R is a useful parent interview measure to assess ASDs (Huerta & Lord, 2012). The ADI-R tends to suffer from the same limitations as the ADOS-G in the sense that children more severely affected are overdiagnosed, and children who are higher functioning are underdiagnosed. The ADI-R is more effective for children over 4 years of age in comparison with younger children (Volkmar, Chawarska, & Klin, 2005). A toddler version has been developed to address these limitations. However, its lengthy administration time and administrator training requirement remain drawbacks of use (Huerta & Lord, 2012).

Hearing

As of 2007, the CDC's Early Hearing Detection and Intervention (EHDI) program's universal newborn hearing screen was practiced for 97% of U.S. births (CDC, 2007). The age of the initial diagnosis of hearing loss has decreased from 19–36 months to 3–6 months (Myck-Wayne, Robinson, & Henson, 2011). A formal audiological evaluation is recommended if autism is suspected; some children with autism may be misdiagnosed with peripheral hearing loss. Frequency-specific auditory brainstem response (ABR) is the best procedure for evaluating hearing thresholds (Filipek et al., 2000).

Myck-Wayne et al. (2011) followed four children with a dual diagnosis of hearing loss and ASD, and retrospectively reviewed screening, services, and interventions based on parent report. Deaf and hard of hearing (D/HH) diagnosis was made first, followed by a diagnosis of ASD several months to years later. Lack of an improvement following early intervention for hearing loss is an indicator for the need for autism screening. Additionally, a concerted effort by all service providers involved leads to a better outcome. Research in children with a dual diagnosis of hearing loss and ASD is limited. In the 2004–2005 Annual Survey of Deaf and Hard of Hearing Children and Youth, 1% of children had both hearing loss and ASD. Over the years, the incidence of this dual diagnosis has progressively increased to 1.6% on the 2007–2008 survey. Hearing loss and ASD have overlapping symptoms (e.g., not responding to name, communication impairments), which presents as a diagnostic challenge. Each diagnosis should receive focused intervention as treatments differ for these groups (Myck-Wayne et al., 2011).

Genetic Testing

The medical evaluation of all individuals with an ASD should include a clinical genetics evaluation for several reasons. The identification of a known genetic syndrome can be consequential if there is additional organ involvement; it may also allow a clinician to provide anticipatory guidance to a family. A positive test can have implications for genetic counseling, especially if a mutation is found to be inherited. Identifying a genetic etiology can prove helpful in obtaining needed services for the individual with ASD. A family can also avoid pursuing further diagnostic tests. However, exactly which tests should be performed has been a topic of debate over the years. Although it is well established in the field that genetic factors contribute strongly to the etiology of ASD, there is no one gene test for ASD. There are likely hundreds of genes involved, a subset of which interacts to help produce the phenotype in any one individual (State & Levitt, 2011).

Various academic societies have differed in their recommendations as to the most appropriate tests, and due to rapid advancements in genomic technologies, recommendations become outdated relatively quickly. The American Academy of Child and Adolescent Psychiatry (AACAP) practice parameters from 1999 recommended that specific laboratory testing be guided by history and examination—fragile X DNA testing would be typically indicated given the significant overlap between this condition and ASD (Volkmar, Cook, Pomeroy, Realmuto, & Tanguay, 1999). These recommendations will be modified in the pending update (Volkmar, Woodbury-Smith, King, McCracken, & State, in press). American Academy of Neurology practice parameters from 2000 recommended high-resolution karyotype and fragile X DNA testing in the presence of intellectual disability (ID), family history of fragile X or undiagnosed ID, or dysmorphic features (Filipek et al., 2000). The American Academy of Pediatrics published a clinical report in 2007, which also recommended high-resolution karyotype and fragile X DNA testing in the presence of ID (Johnson, Meyers,

& American Academy of Pediatrics Council on Children With Disabilities, 2007).

Most recently the American College of Medical Genetics (ACMG) provided guidelines for the clinical genetics evaluation of ASD (Schaefer, Mendelsohn, & Professional Practice and Guidelines Committee, 2013). These guidelines reflect the revolution in genetics of high-throughput techniques, which allow for surveying the entire genome of an individual for mutations at a fine scale. Therefore, the ACMG proposes two tiers of tests, with those in the first tier expected to have a higher diagnostic yield. If the first tier tests are negative, clinicians are directed to a second tier of tests.

The ACMG recommends that clinical geneticists focus first on the detection of a known genetic syndrome or metabolic disorder, guided by history and physical examination and confirmed by the relevant specific diagnostic criteria. If a condition that has a well-established association with ASD is diagnosed, the investigation can be considered complete. The ACMG lists these conditions as follows: 22q11.2 deletion syndrome, Angelman syndrome, CHARGE syndrome, de Lange syndrome, fragile X, MED12 disorders, Prader-Willi syndrome, PTEN-associated disorders, Rett syndrome, Smith-Lemli-Opitz syndrome, Smith-Magenis syndrome, Sotos syndrome, and tuberous sclerosis. Otherwise, the clinician should proceed to chromosomal microarray analysis (CMA). The previous ACMG practice guidelines from 2008 recommended a high-resolution karyotype, consistent with other academic societies (Schaefer et al., 2013). However, the International Standard Cytogenomic Array Consortium published a consensus statement that CMA should replace karyotypes (Miller et al., 2010). The consortium found that CMA has a much higher diagnostic yield (15%–20%) in patients with idiopathic ID, ASD, or multiple congenital anomalies than G-banded karyotyping (3%). They also justify this switch by pointing out that, although CMA misses balanced chromosomal rearrangements and low-level mosaicism, these abnormalities are rare (<1%) in these patients. Also included as a first-tier test is fragile X DNA testing for all male patients and for select female patients (those with clinical features suggestive of fragile X; family history positive for X-linked neurodevelopmental disorders; or premature ovarian insufficiency, ataxia, or tremors in close relatives).

If all first-tier tests are negative, clinical geneticists can consider second tier tests. These include MECP2 gene testing in all female patients with ASD. In addition to being the primary etiology of Rett syndrome, MECP2 mutations have been identified in 4% of females with idiopathic ASD (Schaefer et al., 2013). MECP2 testing should be considered in males with ASD and clinical features of MECP2 duplication (drooling, recurrent respiratory infections, hypotonic facies). PTEN gene testing should be considered in patients with ASD and a head circumference > 2.5 standard deviations above the mean. Finally, brain MRI should be performed in patients with history or examination concerning for indicators such as microcephaly, regression, seizures, and lethargy.

For idiopathic ASD, it is reasonable that a minimal clinical genetics evaluation consist of CMA and fragile X testing, which would have a combined diagnostic yield of 10%–15%. Summing up the expected diagnostic yields of all the tests in the two-tiered approach, the ACMG estimates that a comprehensive clinical genetics evaluation will identify an etiology in 30%–40% of individuals with ASD. Notably, the ACMG does not endorse the use of the various autism gene panels that are now commercially available. These panels often screen a list of genes that have widely varying levels of evidence for association with ASD. Some have been found to be mutated at very low frequencies (<1%) in ASD. The current state of the science in autism genetics does not support the clinical testing of individual genes other than FMR1, MECP2, and PTEN at this time. However, as researchers continue to dissect the genetic etiology of ASD, the clinical genetics evaluation will obviously evolve as to the most appropriate tests to order. It is reasonable to expect that an autism gene panel will be validated for diagnostic purposes sometime in the future.

Regression

Loss of skills is frequently reported in autism (Bernabi, Cerquiglini, Cortesi, & D'Ardia, 2007). Developmental regression can be defined as "Loss of both language and social skills" or "Loss of either language or social skills," according to a study by Hansen et al. (2008). Another study by Luyster et al. (2005) defined regression based on the presence, for a minimum of 3 months, spontaneous, meaningful words used daily followed by a loss (at least for 1 month) of all spontaneous words or the presence of multiple prosocial behaviors before the age of 24 months not usually seen in young children with autism, followed by the loss of multiple of these skills. The prevalence rates of regression in children with ASDs have been reported to range from 15.6% to 50%. This wide range can be accounted for in part by inconsistent definitions and sampling methods (Hansen et al., 2008). In one study of several hundred cases, parental report of regression was noted to not reflect significant developmental delays noted by parents but not appreciated as such; in that study only a small number of cases (1%–2%) had clearly documented histories of regression (Siperstein & Volkmar, 2004).

The most characteristic aspect of regression is loss of vocabulary as well as loss of nonverbal communicative, interactive, cognitive and symbolic abilities. Typically the onset of regression is between 10 and 42 months and peak incidence is approximately 18 months. There are two reported scenarios for regression to occur. One is the situation in which a child who is developmentally delayed loses some abilities between 12 and 18 months. The other situation is less commonly observed in which a child with typical development experiences regression. Children experiencing regression have poorer cognitive development outcomes in comparison with children who do not experience regression (Bernabi et al., 2007). Consistent with the observation of Siperstein and Volkmar (2004), over 50% of children with autism and regression exhibit early social delays within the first year of life, well before regression is noted (Ozonoff, Williams, & Landa, 2005).

In a multicenter study by Luyster et al. (2005) of 351 children with ASDs, 21 children with developmental delays, and 31 children with typical development, there were considerable differences in early course of development and minor differences in behavior, associated with regression. In a retrospective study done by Bernabi et al. (2007) consisting of 40 children, where children who regressed were compared with a nonregressed group, children with regression were delayed in expressive and receptive language, communication and request modalities, and play activities, but there was no difference between the groups in acquisition of motor skills. Hansen et al. (2008) reported that children with ASD who regressed had lower communication scores on the Vineland Adaptive Behavior Scales, lower expressive language scores on the Mullen Scales of Early Learning, and higher lethargy scores on the Aberrant Behavior Checklist compared with an early onset of autism group. A majority (82%) of the regression group lost social interest and engagement behaviors, and 54% lost language skills. Regression has an impact on subsequent development, with a global delay in the course and the manner in which the skills are acquired (Bernabi et al., 2007).

Early Intervention

Provision of an evidence-based intervention program once a diagnosis is established is critically important. A number of such programs have been developed, and with increased awareness and screening, more and more children are referred at increasingly younger ages (see Chapter 29). Consistent with federal mandates the intervention program should be individualized, the National Research Council Report (2001) noted that a minimum of 25 hours per week of intervention was associated with program efficacy. The intervention program should address developmental needs and parent training, and should be modified depending on progress (Steiner et al., 2012). It is important for health-care providers to ensure that children are not only referred for intervention but that intervention programs are put into place. A number of models of intervention are now available (see NRC, 2001; Volkmar & Wiesner, 2009). Recent work has shown not only behavioral but also brain-based changes in response to treatments with several of these interventions (e.g., Voos et al., 2013). Important issues of dose and intensity of program and of matching children to best treatment approaches remain (see Chapter 29). It is important to note that although overall improvement in outcome (see Chapter 4) appears to occur with earlier identification and intervention, it is the case that some children, even in apparently good intervention programs, fail to dramatically improve. Future research efforts should be concentrated on these children in order to determine how to tailor early intervention programs to meet their needs, especially toward teaching social skills to younger children (Volkmar et al., 2005).

Safety

Preschool children with ASD are probably at greater than expected risk for accidents and injury. Parents should be counseled regarding household safety and be aware of common household poisons and first aid procedures. Younger and more developmentally delayed children can have problems with mouthing objects as well as with pica. Parents should be sure lead-based paint is not used in the home, and children's lead levels should be checked periodically. With the elimination of lead in indoor paint this is less of a problem, but older homes may still present possibilities for exposure.

SCHOOL-AGED CHILDREN

Within the school setting the school nurse will often be the person at school who is most knowledgeable about the child's medical problems. She or he may be involved daily if the child needs to take medication while at school. The school nurse should know about changes in medication (including doses) to be on the lookout for side effects. The nurse and teachers should have a plan in place in advance to deal

with any emergencies—anticipated (e.g., allergies) or unanticipated (accidents and falls).

As with younger children a major emphasis should be on preventing health-care problems (obesity and so forth), monitoring side effects of medication (often increasingly used as children become older), and counseling parents on effective use of resources. Children with specific medical problems, for example, seizures obviously require specific interventions and follow-up.

Preventive care is particularly important for children with autism—both because it tries to prevent problems that may be even more difficult to deal with in a child with an ASD and because it helps give the child and health-care provider an opportunity to know each other apart from times when the child is ill. Routine screening by physical exam and laboratory testing are important to detect problems early—when treatments can be helpful and prevent more severe or permanent conditions. Poor growth, dental problems, sensory impairments, curved spine (scoliosis), and high blood pressure are a few of the other disorders that might be found at a routine preventive care exam. Follow-up care is especially important if a child is on regular medications. Immunizing children against many previously common infectious diseases is an important part of preventive care.

As with younger children safety issues are important. Accidents are the leading cause of death in individuals with autism; this risk begins in early childhood and then continues in the school years. The increased risk reflects lack of appreciation of danger, impulsivity, limited social and communication skills, unusual sensory interests—all in the face of motor skills often being relatively preserved. The child who is otherwise fearful of new things or situations may seem driven to explore a new construction site, or the child who is otherwise afraid of the water may be preoccupied with a neighbor's swimming pool.

Wandering is a major potential risk factor as is bolting (i.e., darting away from caregivers). At home parents can use special locks that are harder to open, or for younger children, hook-and-eye type locks well out of their reach. Another choice is to put alarms on the windows or doors that go off when they are opened, alerting parents to a child's trying to leave the house. If the child has a tendency to wander help her learn to wear a MedicAlert bracelet. A recent study (Anderson et al., 2012) suggests that almost 50% of children with autism bolt from home and even more in community settings (Anderson et al., 2012). Although sometimes impulsive, at other times bolting can seem much more premeditated. As always there is a balance between wanting to encourage appropriate adaptive skills and maintaining safety. For children for whom this is known to be a problem it is important to maintain constant adult supervision with the child always visible to the teacher, staff member, or parent and with continued observation of the area. A behavioral plan for dealing with the behavior should be developed (see Volkmar & Wiesner, 2009).

Safety issues at school are complex. The presence of other students can lead to potential difficulties, and areas where typically developing children are less supervised (recess, gym, even the cafeteria) may be much more likely to surface as trouble spots for children on the autism spectrum. Transition times are, in particular, times when children with autism may be more likely to have trouble. Teachers should all be trained in basic safety issues and simple first aid. In situations where there are potential danger areas (e.g., if there is a pool at school or if there is access to potentially toxic materials), children should never be left unsupervised. As children acquire more understanding of language, teaching safety concepts can be directly incorporated in curricula.

For older and more able children there is significant potential for teasing and social ostracism and bullying—this increases in adolescence (Dubin, 2007). For younger children use of an assigned peer buddy during recess can be helpful. A similar procedure can be used with older and more able children, for example, giving the child on the spectrum a task he can engage in with an assigned peer during recess.

ADOLESCENTS AND ADULTS

Adolescents and adults on the autism spectrum experience a number of challenges relative to health care. As with younger individuals the social nature of autism, difficulties with cognitive functioning, communication, and organizational skills can pose challenges even for the most cognitively able individual. Unfortunately, knowledge about autism and related conditions in health-care professionals typically dealing with adults is highly limited (Stoddart, Burke, & King, 2012), as is the available literature on the topic. Individuals with ASD become an orphan population, falling between cracks in the health-care system and often having difficulties accessing the most basic of services. As noted previously, morbidity and mortality are high in this population—and in this age group—particularly in more cognitively disabled individuals (Shavelle, Strauss, & Pickett, 2001). There is remarkably little work on autism in aging (as a practical matter, one of the few papers on this topic points out that there is essentially no research in this group!) (Piven et al., 2011). Supports and relevant services for adults are often lacking—this is especially true for the most cognitively able individuals. Paradoxically, it is this group that, with support, might be most likely to be self-sufficient in society.

Risks for health problems in adolescents and adults arise from several sources. Medication use is high with attendant exposure to untoward effects. Long-term effects of medication use are often underappreciated, and the increasingly common use of psychotropic agents, particularly the antipsychotics, raises concerns about subsequent metabolic and other problems. Other issues arise given the frequent difficulties seen in autism, for example, with sensory issues and communication problems (which may delay diagnosis of relevant health problems). Even the more cognitively able individual may have difficulties in accessing and appropriately utilizing various supports (Stoddart et al., 2013); sometimes the evident cognitive ability leads to a failure to appreciate the severity of adaptive and executive functioning skills. In addition social interaction difficulties are a tremendous problem for effective utilization of a highly demanding health care system. Finally, difficulties with anxiety and depression (which are apparently more common in individuals with ASD in adolescent and adulthood) may themselves pose obstacles for effective access of the health-care system.

The health-care system itself, at least to date, poses other challenges. As with other chronic disorders of childhood onset, there may be little appreciation of the needs of (and supports available to) individuals on the autism spectrum. Providers for adults may be less knowledgeable about appropriate accommodations than pediatric providers, and may fail to take developmental level into account. Relatively few physicians for adults have received training in ASD (Bruder, Kerins, Mazzarella, Sims, & Stein, 2012).

Sexuality

Issues of sexuality can pose significant challenges for adolescents and adults on the autism spectrum—as they do for typically developing children, who also must deal with changes in body, issues of sexuality and sexual orientation, but who do so with the great advantage of sophisticated social skills and social relationships that can help them negotiate these tasks. Issues of sexual development and sexuality can pose significant problems for individuals on the autism spectrum. Some adolescents with autism will have strong sexual feelings; others will not. Issues of gender identification may emerge (Williams, Allard, & Sears, 1996). Some children, particularly higher functioning children, may be very motivated to have a girlfriend or boyfriend, and sometimes this extra motivation helps the child make important gains. Sexual feelings can sometimes be quite intense—for lower and higher functioning children alike. Unfortunately, one of the prime sources

of information available to typically developing children (i.e., their peers) is not so readily available to the child with an ASD. With better intervention and improving outcome more people with ASDs are having meaningful relationships—sometimes including sexual relationships. A range of resources are available for teaching about sexuality (see Volkmar & Wiesner, 2009, for a review).

Bullying

The experience of being bullied can be a major problem in adolescence (and young adulthood). Often beginning before high school, bullying tends to increase in frequency—particularly for more cognitively able students. This is unfortunate for many reasons, including the fact that it is just this group who are most likely to be mainstreamed. Factors predisposing to bullying include problems in reading social cues and in dealing with the fast pace of social interaction. Unusual interests may make the student with ASD stand out from peers—at a point in development when standing out is generally not a good thing. Language issues—particularly social language issues—may be a problem as challenges in dealing with more sophisticated language and figures of speech may lead to confusion. It is typical for the teenager with ASD to say something that is perceived as funny by peers (even if this was not intentioned); conversely the attempt to actually make a joke may go over like a lead balloon. As a result the more able individuals with ASD may frequently have the experience of seeming to be laughed at (for reasons not apparent to him or her). Strong connections to sport and other social group can also present a challenge and, at times, deciding what bullying is or is not (e.g., the teacher who uses sarcasm or ridicule) can be difficult.

Bullying can be an isolated instance but can also be ongoing and frequent. Types of bullying vary with developmental level so that notes that younger children are more likely to exhibit physical or verbal aggression toward same-sex peers, while in early adolescence social bullying become more common. In later adolescence, sexual aspects of bullying may be more prominent. Severity of social difficulties, social isolation, and difficulties with social language use apparently increase risk. Individuals who have idiosyncratic styles of relating/communication are also at increased risk (Volkmar & Wiesner, 2009).

Individuals with Asperger's or the nonverbal learning disability (NLD) profile have a four-fold increase in bullying. Bullying can lead to stress-related problems as well as anxiety and depression. It may also precipitate aggression. Bullying is probably most common in situations without adequate adult monitoring (unfortunately, just the situations where the individuals with an ASD will have more trouble). Bullying can also happen in nonschool settings. Unfortunately, some of the same problems that contribute to bullying in the first place also make it less likely that the more able child with an ASD will report the bullying. The child may be afraid of retaliation/payback, or may not understand the motivation of the bullying, and he may not even think about asking adults for help. An awareness of teachers and parents that bullying is occurring may only come after some incident or after a child's anxiety, depression, or school avoidance prompt a careful search for contributing factors (Cappadocia, Weiss, & Pepler, 2012).

Although a policy of zero tolerance of bullying might, at first blush, seem to be a good solution, it carries its own problems (e.g., relative to children who have been repeatedly bullied but then act out); zero tolerance also may potentially discourage reporting. Having an explicit discussion with all students and an established school code of conduct can be helpful. An effective bullying prevention program will also include sensible strategies for helping students being bullied and those who bully (sometimes there is overlap of the two groups). Various resources to prevent and deal with bullying are provided by Heinrichs (2003) and Dubin (2007).

HELPING MEDICAL VISITS BE SUCCESSFUL

Both parents and the doctor and his staff can take steps to make visits to the office successful. Routine visits are important for many reasons. Having the child become familiar with the doctor's office and procedures when she is well also makes cooperation during an illness much more likely. Routine visits also offer the chance for preventative care. Several steps can be taken to facilitate medical visits. These include (a) preparation of the child for the visit, (b) being sensible about visit schedules and waiting time, (c) planning activities to help keep the child occupied, and (d) giving extra time for examination to enable the child to be more familiar with procedures and the examiner (see Volkmar & Wiesner, 2009, for a review).

Dental Care

Prevention is a critically important aspect of dental care and one that is often overlooked or avoided given the multiple difficulties of a child with ASD. Children who have inadequate prevention are at risk for major problems as they age, for example, dental pain may cause self-injurious behavior and untreated dental problems can lead to other medical problems—sometimes severe ones. A growing body of work on dental care for children with autism is available (see Volkmar and Wiesner, 2009 for a review). One recent large survey (Kopycka-Kedzierawski & Auinger, 2008) assessed dental status and needs of large nationally representative sample of children and adolescents with and without autism. About half of the children and adolescents with autism were reported to have excellent or good dental status (as compared to nearly 70% of typically developing children). Given the increased rates of accident/injury, it is not surprising that traumatic dental injuries may be even more likely in children with ASD.

Guidelines for working with patients with autism for dental professionals are available (e.g., Green

& Flanagan, 2008) as are suggestions for parents to encourage successful dental visits (see Marshall, Sheller, Williams, Mancl, & Cowan, 2007; Volkmar & Wiesner, 2009). As with visits to the family doctor or pediatrician a variety of procedures may be used to prepare the child.

Special Health-Care Situations: Emergency Department and Hospital Stays

The fast pace of medical care, particularly in emergency settings, can present challenges for the child with ASD. A lack of familiarity with ASD on the part of emergency department (ED) staff may also complicate the situation, sometimes further worsening the child's anxiety or behavior. Parents can be both effective advocates and a comforting presence. The primary care provider should be contacted if at all possible and certainly should be included in any follow-up.

Although some literature exists for ED staff on children with disabilities in general (e.g., Grossman, Richards, Anglin, & Hutson, 2000), specific information on autism for such professionals has been minimal. This lack of information (and training) can also be a problem for emergency responders. Schools should have basic information needed for emergency situations and use of a MedicAlert bracelet can be helpful in indicating allergies, medications, conditions, and so on. On the side of the ED, it is important to avoid overstimulation of the individual, to keep the pace of interaction somewhat slower than usual, and to listen to reports of parents or school staff who will know the child best. Obviously in some truly urgent situations this is not possible, and the bare minimum of facts may be all that can be conveyed. Guidelines for parents are available (e.g., Volkmar & Wiesner, 2009). The more cognitively able individual may present special sources of confusion for ED staff who should be helped to understand the nature of the social disability present (Raja & Azzoni, 2001).

Unlike visits to the ED, hospitalizations are usually planned in advance. This gives an opportunity for preparation with a tour and engagement with child-life staff (if they are available). In some cases procedures can be done so that the child is discharged the same day. The individual's health-care provider can facilitate the process of hospitalization. Various steps can be taken to minimize the individual's anxiety and make the hospital stay as pleasant (and short) as possible. Familiar activities, videos, toys, and so forth may help lessen the child's anxiety, as will the presence of familiar family members. As much as possible the child's routines should be followed—including school work if possible. Hospital staff should be aware of the child's difficulties and take extra precautions around safety issues.

For surgical and other procedures, careful explanation should be provided if possible. For elective surgery there is often an opportunity for patient and parents to meet the staff, see the recovery room, and so forth (Volkmar & Wiesner, 2009). If necessary, medications can be used to reduce pain and anxiety.

IMMUNIZATIONS AND AUTISM

Over the past century the advent of immunizations to prevent communicable disease has been a major medical accomplishment. Unfortunately a single paper published some years ago in *The Lancet* (Wakefield et al., 1998) set off a wave of concern that immunization (in this case, for measles) might increase risk for developing autism. Other concerns were raised regarding the use of mercury continuing preservative (thimerisol) in some vaccines. These concerns were increased by extensive media coverage, but these issues have been extensively examined and a link between immunization and autism has been discounted (Fombonne, 1999; Smith, Ellenberg, Bell, & Rubin, 2008). Unfortunately considerable concern lingers in the minds of many parents who avoid immunizations or try to minimize them (Offit,

2008). As more children remain unimmunized there is growing concern of the potential for the return of the various preventable (and sometimes severe) childhood illnesses like measles, mumps, and rubella, and occasional outbreaks of these conditions now occur. It is important for the health of the child and of the public that immunizations be provided to all children. The primary care provider can be a good source of information on the benefits and risks associated with immunization.

THE ROLE OF THE PRIMARY CARE PROVIDER AND THE MEDICAL HOME MODEL

The emerging best practice model for pediatric primary care is the medical home. The American Academy of Pediatrics (AAP) originally developed the medical home model to address the needs of children and youth with special health care needs (AAP, 2002). A medical home is a primary care practice that provides health care that is: comprehensive including preventive, acute and chronic care; coordinated across primary and specialty care; accessible; continuous from birth through the transition to adulthood; family-centered; compassionate; and culturally sensitive. A further elaboration of the characteristics of a medical home as defined by the AAP along with the American Academy of Family Physicians, the American Osteopathic Association, and the American College of Physicians includes the following (Holt, Esquivel, & Pariseau, 2010):

- A partnership between the family and the child's/youth's primary health-care professional
- Relationships based on mutual trust and respect
- Connections to supports and services to meet the nonmedical and medical needs of the child/youth and their family
- Respect for a family's cultural and religious beliefs
- After-hour and weekend access to medical consultation
- Families who feel supported in caring for their child

- Primary health-care professionals coordinating care with a team of other care providers

The medical home model is now seen as the standard of care for all children but is an approach that is especially effective for those with special needs. A review of 33 studies supports the fact that when children with special health care needs receive their primary health care through a medical home, their health status, timeliness of care, family centeredness, and family functioning are improved (Homer et al., 2008).

Because of the particular complexity of conditions experienced by children with autism spectrum disorder (ASD), the medical home model of health care delivery is especially tailored to meet their needs. These children are reported to have less comprehensive and coordinated care and greater unmet needs, when compared to the broader cohort of children and youth with special health care needs. Several studies based on national survey data found that parents of children with autism were less likely to report care consistent with that in a medical home such as family-centered, comprehensive or coordinated, and less satisfaction with their children's primary care than were parents of children with other special health care needs regardless of severity of condition, personal characteristics or insurance status (Brachlow, Ness, McPheeters & Gurney, 2007; Carbone, Behl, Azor & Murphy, 2010). They were more likely to report difficulty in accessing subspecialty care, and less likely to be offered help with education, therapy or support groups.

When receiving care through a medical home, however, families report improved health and decreased financial burdens (Golnik, Scal, Wey, & Gaillard, 2012). The functions of a medical home that are central to health care for children with ASD include developmental screening to identify signs and symptoms at the earliest point in time, referral for more comprehensive evaluation and intervention, coordination of care with specialists and all other agencies and professionals involved, ongoing monitoring and management of ASD and coexisting medical problems, medication management and support, education for families in seeking interventions including complementary and alternative medicine, and transition to adult services.

According to the screening guidelines established by AAP, in addition to general developmental screening for children at 9, 18, and 30 months of age, screening for ASD should be incorporated into well child visits at 18 and 24 months of age. The challenges to universal screening for ASD include concerns about the accuracy of existing validated instruments, the time and costs involved, comfort in managing children with ASD before other services and supports are in place, and limited resources in the community once the diagnosis is made (Hyman & Johnson, 2012). The Modified Checklist for Autism in Toddlers (M-CHAT) is the most commonly used structured screening tool, though its predictive value with specific recommended follow-up questions has been reported to be as low as 57% (Hyman & Johnson, 2012). The early identification of autism through the use of structured screening tools, however, surpasses that of developmental surveillance alone.

Child health providers report several barriers to serving children with ASD that include lack of necessary skills such as recognizing signs and symptoms and addressing the medical and behavioral comorbid conditions, lack of time and resources to provide extensive care coordination, and lack of familiarity with local resources unique to children with ASD (Williams et al., 2012).

Because of the special challenges in treating children with autism, specific efforts may be needed to assure optimal care is provided in a medical home model. Golnik et al. (2012) evaluated a primary care medical home designed specifically to address the needs of children with ASD at the Fairview Children's Clinic in Minneapolis. Elements of this medical home included individualized care plans, care coordination that included ASP-specific resources including dentists, tools to improve patient visits including ASD-specific toys, longer visits, pictures and stories written in tailored format. They found that designing a medical home specifically to address the unique needs of children with ASD results in an increased likelihood of children receiving care that meets medical home criteria as well as increased satisfaction among parents of children with ASD. In a qualitative study that included focus groups with pediatricians, the following resources were cited as helpful to them in providing a medical home for children with ASD: a website of community resources, evidence-based guidelines for younger children with ASDs, and insurance reimbursed care coordinators (Carbone et al., 2010).

There are an increasing number of tools and initiatives to assist providers in treating and managing children with ASD (AAP, 2013). However, even with the national and state efforts, pediatricians still report feeling unprepared to provide the needed care. Further education for providers and parents about the medical home model along with changes in the broader health care system to promote and support a more integrated approach across medical, educational and community systems and sufficient resources to meet the treatment and support needs for the increasing number of children identified through universal screening are needed (Carbone et al., 2010).

SUMMARY

In this chapter we have addressed some of the challenges individuals with autism/ASD face in accessing medical care. Sadly, along with the rest of the population, insurance coverage is inconsistent, medical care can be fragmented, and knowledgeable practitioners difficult to find. This situation becomes worse as children age. Adults with autism are, in some sense, an orphan population with limited knowledge of health care providers and surprisingly little systematic research. On the other hand there has been an increased concern with health (and mental health) issues in this population, and awareness is growing. A number of excellent resources are available and guides to evidence based practice have appeared as have various practice guidelines (see Chapters 42 and 44). We hope that the growing awareness of autism on the part of parents and health-care practitioners and new changes in mandates for service will bring additional attention (and resources).

CROSS-REFERENCES

Issues of diagnosis are discussed in Chapter 1; Chapters 5 through 8 address developmental aspects of autism. Drug treatments are discussed in Chapter 23 and screening approaches in Chapter 24. Chapter 42 focuses on evidence-based interventions and Chapter 44 on practice guidelines.

REFERENCES

Afzal, N., Murch, S., Thirrupathy, K., Berger, L., Fagbemi, A., & Heuschkel, R. (2003). Constipation with acquired megarectum in children with autism. *Pediatrics, 112*, 939–942.

American Academy of Pediatrics, Medical Home Initiatives for Children With Special Needs Project Advisory Committee. (2002). Policy Statement: The medical home. *Pediatrics, 110*, 184–186.

American Academy of Pediatrics Autism Expert Panel. (2013). *Autism: Caring for children with autism spectrum disorders: A resource toolkit for clinicians* (2nd ed.). Elk Grove, IL: American Academy of Pediatrics.

Anderson, C., Law, J. K., Daniels, A., Rice, C., Mandell, D. S., Hagopian, L., & Law, P. A. C. (2012). Occurrence and family impact of elopement in children with autism spectrum disorders. *Pediatrics, 130*(5), 870–877.

Atladóttir, H. O., Pedersen, M. G., Thorsen, P., Mortensen, P. B., Deleuran, B., Eaton, W. W., & Parner, E. T. (2009). Association of family history of autoimmune diseases and autism spectrum disorders. *Pediatrics, 124*(2), 687–694.

Barton, M. L., Robins, D., Jashar, D., Brenna, L., & Fein, D. (in press). Sensitivity and specificity of proposed DSM-5 criteria for autism spectrum disorder in toddlers. *Journal of Autism and Developmental Disorders*.

Bernabei, P., Cerquiglini, A., Cortesi, F., & D'Ardia, C. (2007). Regression versus no regression in the autistic disorder: Developmental trajectories. *Journal of Autism and Developmental Disorders, 37*(3), 580–588.

Bill, B. R., & Geschwind, D. H. (2009). Genetic advances in autism: Heterogeneity and convergence on shared pathways. *Current Opinion in Genetics & Development, 19*, 271–278.

Brachlow, A. E., Ness, K. K., McPheeters, M. L., & Gurney, J. G. (2007). Comparison of indicators for a primary care medical home between children with autism or asthma and other special health care needs: National Survey of Children's Health. *Archives of Pediatrics and Adolescent Medicine, 161*(4), 399–405.

Bruder, M. B., Kerins, G., Mazzarella, C., Sims, J., & Stein, N. (2012). Brief report: The medical care of adults with autism spectrum disorders: Identifying the needs. *Journal of Autism and Developmental Disorders, 42*(11), 2498–2504.

Buie, T., Campbell, D. B., Fuchs, G. J., III, Furuta, G.T., Levy, J., VandeWater, J., ... Winter, H. (2010). Evaluation, diagnosis, and treatment of gastrointestinal disorders in individuals with ASDs: A consensus report. *Pediatrics, 125*(Suppl. 1), S1–S18.

Cappadocia, M., Weiss, J. A., & Pepler, D. (2012). Bullying experiences among children and youth with autism spectrum disorders. *Journal of Autism and Developmental Disorders, 42*(2), 266–277.

Carbone, P. S., Behl, D. D., Azor, V., & Murphy, N. A. (2010). The medical home for children with autism spectrum disorders: Parent and pediatrician perspectives. *Journal of Autism and Developmental Disorders, 40*(3), 317–324.

Centers for Disease Control and Prevention. (2007). *Hearing loss in children: Data and statistics*. Retrieved from http://www.cdc.gov/ncbddd/ehdi/data.htm#2007

Centers for Disease Control and Prevention, National Center for Injury Prevention and Control. (2010). *Ten leading causes of death, 2010, United States*. Retrieved from http://www.cdc.gov/injury/wisqars/fatal_injury_reports.html

Centers for Disease Control and Prevention, National Center for Injury Prevention and Control. (2011). *Ten leading causes of nonfatal injury, 2011, United States*. Retrieved from http://webappa.cdc.gov/sasweb/ncipc/nfilead2001.html

Cortesi, F., Giannotti, F., Ivanenko, A., & Johnson, K. (2010). Sleep in children with autistic spectrum disorder. *Sleep medicine, 11*(7), 659–664.

Coury, D. L., Ashwood, P., Fasano, A., Fuchs, G., Geraghty, M., Kaul, A., ... Jones N. E. (2012). Gastrointestinal conditions in children with autism spectrum disorder: Developing a research agenda. *Pediatrics, 130*(Suppl 2), S160–168.

Dubin, N. (2007). *Asperger syndrome and bullying: Strategies and solutions*. London, England: Jessica Kingsley.

Ekinci, O., Arman, A. R., Isik, U., Bez, Y., & Berkem, M. (2010). EEG abnormalities and epilepsy in autistic spectrum disorders: Clinical and familial correlates. *Epilepsy and Behavior, 17*, 178–182.

Filipek, P. A., Accardo, P. J., Ashwal, S., Baranek, G. T., Cook, E. H., Dawson, G., ... Volkmar, F. R. (2000). Practice parameter: Screening and diagnosis of autism: Report of the quality standards subcommittee of the American Academy of Neurology and the Child Neurology Society. *Neurology, 55*, 468–479.

Filipek, P. A., Accardo, P. J., Baranek, G. T., Cook, E. H., Jr., Dawson, G., Gordon, B., ... Volkmar, F. R. (1999). The screening and diagnosis of autistic spectrum disorders. *Journal of Autism and Developmental Disorders, 29*, 439–484.

Fombonne, E. (1999). Are measles infections or measles immunizations linked to autism? *Journal of Autism and Developmental Disorders, 29*(4), 349–350.

Fombonne, E., & Chakrabarti, S. (2001). No evidence for a new variant of measlesmumps-rubella-induced autism. *Pediatrics, 108*, E58.

Giannotti, F., Cortesi, F., Cerquiglini, A., & Bernabei, P. (2006). An open-label study of controlled-release melatonin in treatment of sleep disorders in children with autism. *Journal of Autism and Developmental Disorders, 36*(6), 741–752.

Gillberg, C., & Coleman, M. (1992). *The biology of the autistic syndromes*. London, England: Mac Keith Press.

Golnik, A., Scal, P., Wey, A., & Gaillard, P. (2012). Autism-specific primary care medical home intervention. *Journal of Autism and Developmental Disorders*, *42*(6), 1087–1093.

Green, D., & Flanagan, D. (2008). Understanding the autistic dental patient. *General Dentistry, 56*(2), 167–171.

Grossman, S. A., Richards, C. F., Anglin, D., & Hutson, H. R. (2000). Caring for the patient with mental retardation in the emergency department. *Annals of Emergency Medicine, 35*(1), 69–76.

Hagerman, R. J., Berry-Kravis, E., Kaufmann, W. E., Ono, M. Y., Tartaglia, N., Lachiewicz, A., ... Tranfaglia, M. (2009). Advances in the treatment of fragile X syndrome. *Pediatrics, 123*, 378–390.

Hansen, R. L., Ozonoff, S., Krakowiak, P., Angkustsiri, K., Jones, C., Deprey, L. J., ... Hertz-Picciotto, I. (2008). Regression in autism: Prevalence and associated factors in the CHARGE study. *Ambulatory Pediatrics, 8*, 25–31.

Heinrichs, R. R. (2003). A whole-school approach to bullying: Special considerations for children with exceptionalities. *Interventions in School and Clinic, 38*, 195–204.

Holt, J., Esquivel, M., & Pariseau, C. (2010). *Medical home competencies for LEND trainees.* Association of University Centers on Disabilities. Retrieved from http://www.aucd.org/template/page.cfm?id=633

Homer, C., Klatka, K., Romm, D., Kuhlthau, K., Bloom, S., Newacheck, P., ... Perrin, J. M. (2008). A review of the evidence for the medical home for children with special health care needs. *Pediatrics, 122*, e922–e937.

Horvath, K., & Perman, J. A. (2002a). Autism and gastrointestinal symptoms. *Current Gastroenterology Reports, 4*(3), 251–258.

Horvath, K., & Perman, J. A. (2002b). Autistic disorder and gastrointestinal disease. *Current Opinion in Pediatrics, 14*, 583–587.

Huerta, M., & Lord, C. (2012). Diagnostic evaluation of autism spectrum disorders *Pediatric Clinics of North America, 59*(1), 103–111.

Hyman, S. L., & Johnson, J. K. (2012). Autism and pediatric practice: Toward a medical home. *Journal of Autism and Developmental Disorders, 42*(6), 1156–1164.

Johnson, K. P., & Malow, B. A. (2008). Assessment and pharmacologic treatment of sleep disturbance in autism. *Child and Adolescent Psychiatric Clinics of North America, 17*(4), 773–785.

Johnson, C. P., Myers, S. M., & American Academy of Pediatrics Council on Children With Disabilities. (2007). Identification and evaluation of children with autism spectrum disorders. *Pediatrics, 120*(5), 1183–1215.

Kalkbrenner A. E., Daniels J. L., Emch M., Morrissey J., Poole C., & Chen J. C. (2011). Geographic access to health services and diagnosis with an autism spectrum disorder. *Annals of Epidemiology, 21*(4), 304–310.

Kopycka-Kedzierawski, D. T., & Auinger, P. (2008). Dental needs and status of autistic children: results from the National Survey of Children's Health. *Pediatric Dentistry, 30*(1), 54–58.

Kuddo, T., & Nelson, K. B. (2003). How common are gastrointestinal disorders in children with autism? *Current Opinion in Pediatrics, 15*, 339–343.

Lee, L. C., Harrington, R. A., Chang, J. J., & Connors, S. L. (2008). Increased risk of injury in children with developmental disabilities. *Research in Developmental Disabilities, 29*(3), 247–255.

Levisohn, P. (2004). Electroencephalography findings in autism: Similarities and differences from Landau-Kleffner Syndrome. *Seminars in Pediatric Neurology, 11*(3), 218–224.

Levitt, P., Eagleson, K. L., & Powell, E. M. (2004). Regulation of neocortical interneuron development and the implications for neurodevelopmental disorders. *Trends in Neurosciences, 27*(7), 400–406.

Liu, X., Hubbard, J. A., Fabes, R. A., & Adam, J. B. (2006). Sleep disturbances and correlates of children with autism spectrum disorders. *Child Psychiatry and Human Development, 37*(2), 179–191.

Loening-Baucke, V. (1998). Constipation in Children. *New England Journal of Medicine, 339*, 1155–1156.

Luyster, R., Gotham, K., Guthrie, W., Coffing, M., Petrak, R., Pierce, K., ... Lord, C. (2009). The Autism Diagnostic Observation Schedule-toddler module: A new module of a standardized diagnostic measure for autism spectrum disorders. *Journal of Autism and Developmental Disorders, 39*(9), 1305–1320.

Luyster, R., Richler, J., Risi, S., Hsu, W. L., Dawson, G., Bernier, R., ... Lord, C. (2005). Early regression in social communication in autism spectrum disorders: A CPEA study. *Developmental Neuropsychology, 27*(3), 311–336.

Marshall, J., Sheller, B., Williams, B. J., Mancl, L., & Cowan, C. (2007). Cooperation predictors for dental patients with autism. *Pediatric Dentistry, 29*(5), 369–376.

Matson, J. L., Kozlowski, A. M., Hattier, M. A., Horovitz, M., & Sipes, M. (2012). DSM-IV vs DSM-5 diagnostic criteria for toddlers with autism. *Developmental Neurorehabilitation, 15*(3), 185–190.

McDermott, S., Zhou, L., & Mann, J. (2008). Injury treatment among children with autism or pervasive developmental disorder. *Journal of Autism and Developmental Disorders, 38*, 626–633.

Medical Research Council. (2001). *MRC review of autism research: Epidemiology and causes.* Retrieved from http://www.mrc.ac.uk/Utilities/Documentrecord/index.htm?d=MRC002394

Miller, D. T., Adam, M. P., Aradhya, S., Biesecker, L. G., Brothman, A. R., Carter, N. P., ... Ledbetter, D. H. (2010). Consensus statement: Chromosomal microarray is a first-tier clinical diagnostic test for individuals with developmental disabilities or congenital anomalies. *American Journal of Human Genetics, 86*(5), 749–764.

Ming, X., Brimacombe, M., Chaaban, J., Zimmerman-Bier, B., & Wagner, G. C. (2008). Autism spectrum disorders: Concurrent clinical disorders. *Journal of Child Neurology, 23*(1), 6–13.

Molloy, C. A., & Manning-Courtney, P. (2003). Prevalence of chronic gastrointestinal symptoms in children with autism and autistic spectrum disorders. *Autism, 7*(2), 165–171.

Moss, J., Oliver, C., Arron, K., Burbidge, C., & Berg, K. (2009). The prevalence and phenomenology of repetitive behavior in genetic syndromes. *Journal of Autism and Developmental Disorders, 39*(4), 572–588.

Myck-Wayne, J., Robinson, S., & Henson, E. (2011). Serving and supporting young children with a dual diagnosis of hearing loss and autism: the stories of four families. *American Annals of the Deaf*, *156*(4), 379–390.

National Research Council. (2001). *Educating young children with autism*. Washington, DC: National Academies Press.

Offit, P. (2008). *Autism's False Prophets*. New York, NY: Columbia University Press.

Ozonoff, S., Williams, B. J., & Landa, R. (2005). Parental report of the early development of children with regressive autism: The delays-plus-regression phenotype. *Autism: The International Journal of Research and Practice*, *9*(5), 461–486.

Peake, D., Notghi, L. M., & Philip, S. (2006). Management of Epilepsy in Children with Autism. *Current Paediatrics*, *16*(7), 489–494.

Piven, J., Rabins, P., & Autism-in-Older Adults Working, Group. (2011). Autism spectrum disorders in older adults: Toward defining a research agenda. *Journal of the American Geriatrics Society*, *59*(11), 2151–2155. doi: http://dx.doi.org/10.1111/j.1532–5415.2011.03632.x DOI:10.1111/j.1532-5415.2011.03632.x

Plon, S., & Owens, J. (2012). Tuberous sclerosis complex: Genetics, clinical features, and diagnosis. *UpToDate*, 1–32. Retrieved from http://www.uptodate.com/contents/tuberous-sclerosis-complex-genetics-clinical-features-and-diagnosis?detectedLanguage=en&source=search_result&search=tuberous+sclerosis+complex%3A+Genetics%2C+clinical+features&selectedTitle=1%7E150&provider=noProvider

Raja, M., & Azzoni, A. (2001). Asperger's disorder in the emergency psychiatric setting. *General Hospital Psychiatry*, *23*(5), 285–293.

Richdale, A. L. (1999). Sleep problems in autism: prevalence, cause, and intervention. *Developmental Medicine & Child Neurology*, *41*(01), 60–66.

Roach, E. S., & Sparagana, S. P. (2004). Diagnosis of tuberous sclerosis complex. *Journal of Child Neurology*, *19*(9), 643–649.

Rutter, M., Bailey, A., Bolton, P., & Le Couteur, A. (1994). Autism and known medical conditions: myth and substance. *Journal of Child Psychology and Psychiatry*, *35*(2), 311–322.

Schaefer, G. B., Mendelsohn, N. J., & Professional Practice and Guidelines Committee. (2013). Clinical genetics evaluation in identifying the etiology of autism spectrum disorders: 2013 guideline revisions. *Genetics in Medicine*, *15*(5), 399–407.

Shavelle, R. M., Strauss, D. J., & Pickett, J. (2001). Causes of death in autism. *Journal of Autism and Developmental Disorders*, *31*(6), 569–576.

Siperstein, R., & Volkmar, F. (2004). Brief report: Parental reporting of regression in children with. *Journal of Autism and Developmental Disorders*, *34*(6), 731–734.

Smith, M. J., Ellenberg, S. S., Bell, L. M., & Rubin, D. M. (2008). Media coverage of the measles-mumps-rubella vaccine and autism controversy and its relationship to MMR immunization rates in the United States. *Pediatrics*, *121*(4), e836–e843.

State, M. W., & Levitt, P. (2011). The conundrums of understanding genetic risks for autism spectrum disorders. *Nature Neuroscience*, *14*(12), 1499–1506.

Steiner, A. M., Goldsmith, T. R., Snow, A. V., & Chawarska, K. (2012). Practitioner's guide to assessment of autism spectrum disorders in infants and toddlers. *Journal of Autism and Developmental Disorders*, *42*, 1183–1196.

Stoddart, K. P., Burke, L., & King, R. (2012). *Asperger syndrome in adulthood: A comprehensive guide for clinicians*. New York, NY: W. W. Norton.

Stoddart, K. P., Burke, L., Muskat, J., Duhaime, S., Accardi, C., Burnh Riosa, P., & Bradley, E. A. (2013). *Diversity in Ontario's youth and adults with autism spectrum disorders: Complex needs in unprepared systems* (p. 52). Toronto, Ontario: The Redpath Centre.

Strickland, E. (2009). *Eating for autism: The revolutionary 10-step nutrition plan to help treat your child's autism, Asperger's, or ADHD*. Cambridge, MA: Da Capo Press, 1–4.

Tuchman, R. F. (2004). AEDs and psychotropic drugs in children with autism and epilepsy. *Mental Retardation and Developmental Disabilities Research Reviews*, *10*, 135–138.

Tuchman, R., & Rapin, I. (2002). Epilepsy in autism. *Lancet Neurology*, *1*, 352–358.

Van Esch, H. (2012). Fragile X syndrome: Clinical features and diagnosis in children and adolescents. *UpToDate*, 1–16. Retrieved from http://www.uptodate.com/contents/fragile-x-syndrome-clinical-features-and-diagnosis-in-children-and-adolescents

Visootsak, J., Warren, S. T., Anido, A., & Graham, J. M. (2005). Fragile X syndrome: An update and review for the primary pediatrician. *Clinical Pediatrics*, *44*, 374–381.

Volkmar, F., Chawarska, K., & Klin, A. (2005). Autism in infancy and early childhood. *Annual Review of Psychology*, *56*, 315–336.

Volkmar, F. R., Cook, E. H. J., Pomeroy, J., Realmuto, G., & Tanguay, P. (1999). Practice parameters for the assessment and treatment of children, adolescents, and adults with autism and pervasive developmental disorders. *Journal of the American Academy of Child & Adolescent Psychiatry*, *38*, 32S–54S.

Volkmar, F. R., & Nelson, D. S. (1990). Seizure disorders in autism. *Journal of the American Academy of Child & Adolescent Psychiatry*, *29*(1), 127–129.

Volkmar, F., & Wiesner, L. (2009). *A practical guide to autism: What every parent, family member, and teacher needs to know*. Hoboken, NJ: Wiley.

Volkmar, F. R., Woodbury-Smith, M., King, B. H., McCracken, J., & State, M. (in press). Practice Paramters for the assessment and treatment of children and adolescents with autism and pervasive developmental disorders. *Journal of the American Academy of Child & Adolescent Psychiatry*.

Voos, A. C., Pelphrey, K. A., Tirrell, J., Bolling, D. Z., Vander Wyk, B., Kaiser, M. D., . . . Ventola, P. (2013). Neural mechanisms of improvements in social motivation after pivotal response treatment: Two case studies. *Journal of Autism and Developmental Disorders*, *43*(1), 1–10.

Wakefield, A. J., Murch, S. H., Anthony, A., Linnell, J., Casson, D. M., Malik, M., . . . Walker-Smith, J. A. (1998). RETRACTED: Ileal-lymphoid-nodular hyperplasia, nonspecific colitis, and pervasive developmental disorder in children. *The Lancet*, *351*(9103), 637–641.

Wang, L. W., Tancredi, D. J., & Thomas, D. W. (2011). The prevalence of gastrointestinal problems in children across the United States with autism spectrum disorders from families with multiple affected members. *Journal of Developmental & Behavioral Pediatrics, 32*(5), 351–360.

Williams, P. G., Allard, A. M., & Sears, L. (1996). Case study: Cross-gender preoccupations with two male children with autism. *Journal of Autism and Developmental Disorders, 26*(6), 635–642.

Williams, P., Tomchek, S., Grau, R., Bundy, M., Davis, D., & Kleinert, H. (2012). Parent and physician perceptions of medical home care for children with autism spectrum disorders in the state of Kentucky. *Clinical Pediatrics, 51*(11), 1071–1078.

Wiznitzer, M. (2004). Autism and tuberous sclerosis. *Journal of Child Neurology, 19*, 675–679.

CHAPTER 23

Psychopharmacology

LAWRENCE SCAHILL, CAITLIN S. TILLBERG, AND ANDRÉS MARTIN

INTRODUCTION

Psychopharmacological treatment of children and adults with autism is common in clinical practice (Coury et al., 2011; Oswald & Sonenklar 2007; Rosenberg et al., 2010). Although there has been steady increase in findings from large-scale, multisite trials over the past decade, empirical support for several medications used in clinical practice

remains limited (McPheeters et al., 2011). This chapter reviews the major drug categories that are commonly used in the treatment of children and adults with autism spectrum disorder (ASD). The chapter is divided into six sections according to the drug category: (1) atypical antipsychotics, (2) serotonin reuptake inhibitors, (3) stimulants, and (4) nonstimulant medications for hyperactivity in ASD. Each of these sections includes a brief

This work was supported in part by the following federal grants to Yale University: RUPP-MH70009-04 and RUPP-PI MH 66762-02; STAART U54-MH066494; and the CTSA Award (RR024139) from the National Center for Research Resources 514 (NCRR).

The authors acknowledge the advice and collaboration of Drs. Michael G. Aman, PhD; Christopher J. McDougle, MD; James T. McCracken, MD; Bryan King, MD; Ben Vitiello, MD; L. Eugene Arnold, MD, MEd; and James Dziura, PhD.

background on the class of compound, the empirical support and clinical applications for patients with autism spectrum disorders. The fifth section briefly reviews data from several chemically unrelated compounds, including anticonvulsants and glutamate antagonists. The final section examines compounds in early drug development and directions for future research.

ATYPICAL ANTIPSYCHOTICS

Atypical antipsychotics (AAPs), including clozapine, risperidone, olanzapine, quetiapine, ziprasidone, aripiprazole, paliperidone, and asenapine, have garnered considerable interest in the treatment of children and adults with autism spectrum disorder. These compounds are frequently used for treating severe maladaptive behaviors and symptoms associated with ASD and have largely replaced traditional antipsychotics such as haloperidol in this population. The target problems for pharmacotherapy with AAPs typically include aggression, tantrums, or self-injury in any combination. Support for the concept that these agents may be useful for these target problems in ASD derives from the line of research with haloperidol done by Campbell and colleagues (Anderson et al., 1989; Campbell et al., 1997). The AAPs, however, offer distinct advantages over the typical antipsychotics exemplified by haloperidol. Importantly, the AAPs have a lower risk of neuromotor adverse effects and, presumably, a lower risk of tardive dyskinesia as well. In addition, based on the promise that these newer compounds could also improve negative symptoms in adults of schizophrenia, there has been great interest in whether the AAPs may also improve core symptoms of autism such as social withdrawal and lack of spontaneous interaction (Scahill, Hallett, et al., 2012). The fact that the AAPs are also effective in the treatment of tics (Scahill, Erenberg, et al., 2006) with a similar magnitude of effect as the high potency traditional antipsychotics, suggests that the AAPs could also reduce stereotypic behaviors in patients with ASDs.

The reduced occurrence of dyskinesias and the purported improvement in negative symptoms of schizophrenia may be related to the dual action of 5-HT to dopamine (DA) receptor blockade (Meltzer, 1999). Alternatively, it has been shown that the AAPs do not bind as tightly to postsynaptic dopamine receptors, permitting them to be displaced by endogenous dopamine in striatum (Kapur & Seeman, 2001).

Clozapine

Clozapine was the first atypical antipsychotic to be introduced in the United States (Baldessarini & Frankenburg, 1991). The drug's ability to block 5-HT_{2A}, 5-HT_{2C}, 5-HT_3, and DA $D_1\text{-}D_4$ receptors has been proposed as its mechanism of action. Two reports have described the use of clozapine in autism. In the first study, 3 children who displayed marked hyperactivity, fidgetiness, or aggression were treated for up to 8 months with doses ranging from 200 to 450 mg per day (Zuddas, Ledda, Fratta, Muglia, & Cianchetti, 1996). Two of the 3 children showed sustained improvement, though the third had a return of symptoms to baseline levels after an initial response. More recently, Chen, Bedair, McKay, Bowers, and Mazure (2001) reported the case of a 17-year-old male with autism and severe mental retardation who showed a significant reduction in signs of overt tension, hyperactivity, and repetitive motions in response to clozapine 275 mg per day, during a 15-day hospitalization. The low use of clozapine in autism probably reflects concern about the risk of agranulocytosis and seizures that are associated with the drug. Additionally, the requirement for frequent blood draws can be challenging to obtain in children with autism.

Risperidone

Risperidone has high affinities for DA $D_2\text{-}D_4$, 5-HT_{1D}, 5-HT_{2A}, 5-HT_{2C} receptors (Leysen et al., 1988). Multiple open-label reports and case series, as well as double-blind, placebo-controlled trials in children and adolescents and adults have described the beneficial effects of risperidone in individuals with autism and other ASDs. The Research Units in Pediatric Psychopharmacology (RUPP) Autism Network completed a multisite trial to evaluate the short- and long-term safety and efficacy of risperidone in children and adolescents with autism accompanied by severe tantrums, aggression, and/or self-injurious behavior (RUPP Autism Network, 2002). The *first phase* of the study was an 8-week, randomized, double-blind trial of risperidone versus placebo. The primary outcome measures were the 15-item Irritability subscale of the Aberrant Behavior Checklist (ABC) and the Improvement item of the Clinical Global Impression scale (CGI-I). The Irritability subscale is rated from 0 to 3 (not a problem to severe). In school-age children, a score of 18 is often used as a threshold for clinically meaningful severity (Brown, Aman, & Havercamp, 2002).The Improvement item on the CGI is a 7-point scale ranging from *very much improved* (score of 1) through *no change* (score of 4) to *very much worse* (score of 7).

One hundred and one (101) children were recruited into the study (82 boys and 19 girls, mean age 8.8 years). Of these, 49 were randomized to risperidone and 52 to placebo. Eight weeks of risperidone treatment (mean dose, 1.8 mg/day in divided doses) resulted in a 57% reduction on the ABC Irritability score, compared to a 14% decrease for the placebo group ($t = 6.4$, $p < .0001$ effect size = 1.2). Based on an a priori definition of response (at least a 25% reduction on the Irritability score and a score of *much improved* or *very much improved* on the CGI-I), the improvement rate was 69.4% (34 of 49) on risperidone and 11.5% (6 of 52) on placebo (Chi square = 32.9; p < .0001).

Risperidone was associated with an average weight gain of 2.7 kg after 8 weeks, compared to 0.8 kg for placebo ($t = 3.7$; $p = .0004$). Parents reported increased appetite, fatigue, drowsiness, tremor, and drooling at higher rates than parents of children in the placebo group. In general, these adverse effects were typically in the mild to moderate range and most were transient. The largest difference was the parent-reported increase in appetite. Just below 25% of children in the

risperidone group was cited by parents with a new and moderate problem of increased appetite compared to 4% in the placebo group.

The *second phase* of the study was a 4-month open-label extension in 63 subjects who showed a positive response during the 8-week trial (nonresponders to placebo who were treated openly joined the extension phase following evidence of positive response). The positive effects of risperidone were remarkably stable, and it was not necessary to raise the dose above the average dose of 1.8 mg per day established at the start of the extension phase. The open-label extension was followed by a *third phase* in which subjects were randomly assigned to continue active medication at the same maintenance dose, or to a gradual withdrawal to placebo over a 3-week period. The rate of medication withdrawal was roughly 25% per week. The maximum observation period in this final phase of the study was 8 weeks, but relapse marked the end of the study for any given subject. Relapse was defined as a 25% or greater increase on the Irritability subscale of the Aberrant Behavior Checklist and two consecutive ratings of *much worse* or *very much worse* on the CGI-I. The investigators also developed a *stopping rule* for this phase of the study. A planned interim analysis after 32 subjects (16 per group) showed that the relapse rate was significantly greater in the placebo group compared to the group that continued on risperidone, leading to study termination (RUPP Autism Network, 2005b). Two of 16 (12.5%) subjects in the risperidone maintenance group relapsed compared to 10 of 16 (62.5%) in the group assigned to placebo-discontinuation (Chi square = 6.53; $p = .01$). Although the difference in the relapse rate was significant, the fact that 6 of 16 subjects who withdrew to placebo did not relapse suggests that some children may be safely withdrawn from the medication after 6 months.

The large magnitude of treatment effect (43% difference in the mean change from baseline between risperidone and placebo on the ABC Irritability scale) is striking. By contrast, past studies of haloperidol in autism showed differences in the 15% to 20% range, depending on the behavioral measure used (Anderson et al., 1989).

Another important contrast is the rate and severity of adverse effects. Haloperidol was associated with sedation in 31 of 40 subjects (77.5%), compared with generally mild sedation in about half of the subjects in the risperidone group. Acute dystonic reactions occurred in 25% of haloperidol-treated patients, compared to none in this risperidone trial.

The positive results of the RUPP Autism Network risperidone trial and the replicated findings in a subsequent industry trial (Shea et al., 2004) resulted in the approval of risperidone by the Food and Drug Administration (FDA) in 2006. Bristol-Myers Squibb initiated a drug program with aripiprazole focused on the same target symptoms and obtained approval for aripiprazole in 2009 (see later discussion).

The focus on severe behavior problems leaves an open question about possible additive effects of medication and behavior therapy. For example, the improvement in serious behavior problems associated with risperidone may enable a child to make fuller use of psychoeducational interventions directed at improving academic and daily-living skills. The addition of behavior therapy might also permit the successful discontinuation of risperidone without relapse. To test these questions, the RUPP Autism Network conducted a 6-month study of risperidone alone ($n = 49$) compared to risperidone plus a structured parent training program ($n = 75$) in children with ASDs and serious behavioral problems. The randomization was deliberately unbalanced on the assumption that most parents would prefer the combined treatment. Consistent with the first study, risperidone was effective in reducing tantrums, aggression, and self-injury in both groups. However, after 6 months of treatment, children assigned to combined treatment showed small, but significantly greater reductions in serious behavioral problems compared to risperidone treatment alone (Aman et al., 2009). In addition, the combined treatment group showed greater gains in socialization and communication on a measure of adaptive functioning in everyday life (Vineland Adaptive Behavior Scales; Scahill, McDougle, et al., 2012; Sparrow, Balla, & Cicchetti, 1984).

Olanzapine

Olanzapine has high affinity for DA D_1, D_2, and D_4 receptors, for 5-HT_{2A}, 5-HT_{2C}, and 5-HT_3 receptors (Bymaster et al., 1996). To date, it has only been studied in relatively small open-label trials and one small randomized, placebo-controlled study in children or adults with ASDs. Rubin (1997) described a 17-year-old male with autistic disorder who demonstrated decreased agitation on olanzapine 30 mg per day. A 10-year-old boy with autism, mental retardation, and bipolar disorder not otherwise specified showed reduced aggression following the addition of olanzapine 20 mg per day to ongoing treatment with lithium (Horrigan, Barnhill, & Courvoisie, 1997). Heimann (1999) treated a hospitalized 14-year-old boy with autism accompanied by psychotic symptoms. Following an ineffective trial with risperidone, olanzapine up to 40 mg per day resulted in substantial improvement and the child's return to school. In a study employing a randomized, parallel groups design, 12 children with autism (mean age, 7.8 ± 2.1 years) were randomized to either 6 weeks of open-label treatment with olanzapine or haloperidol (Malone, Cater, Sheikh, Choudhury, & Delaney, 2001). Mean final dosages were 7.9 ± 2.5 mg per day for olanzapine and 1.4 ± 0.7 mg per day for haloperidol. Both groups showed symptom reduction. Five of six subjects in the olanzapine group and three of six in the haloperidol group were rated as positive responders on the CGI-I. Weight gain from baseline to the end of treatment was significantly higher in the olanzapine group (mean, 9.0 ± 3.5 lbs) than in the haloperidol group (mean, 3.2 ± 4.9 lbs). One subject in the haloperidol group demonstrated mild rigidity, but no subjects in the olanzapine group showed neuromotor side effects. Results from an open-label trial olanzapine monotherapy in children, adolescents, and adults with ASDs ($n = 7$) were generally positive, though significant weight gain did occur (Potenza, Holmes, Kanes, & McDougle, 1999). Hollander and colleagues (2006) evaluated the effects of olanzapine in an 8-week, randomized trial with placebo in 11 subjects with ASDs (6 to 14 years).

In this small study, olanzapine showed a higher rate of positive response on the CGI-I than placebo. Weight increased 7.5 pounds in the active treatment group compared to 1.5 pounds in placebo. These results and several reports of drug-induced glucose dysregulation and diabetes in adults treated with olanzapine suggest that olanzapine should be used with caution in children with ASDs (Citrome, Holt, Walker, & Hoffmann, 2011).

Quetiapine

Quetiapine has a relatively low to moderate affinity for D_1 and D_2 receptors, moderate affinity for $5HT_{2A}$ receptors, and higher affinity for alpha$_1$-adrenergic, H_1-histaminic (Hirsch, Link, Goldstein, & Arvanitis, 1996). In the only published report of its use in ASD, six males with autism and mental retardation, ages 6 to 15 years (mean, 10.9 ± 3.3), entered a 16-week open-label study (mean daily dose, 225 ± 108 mg; range, 100–350 mg). Two subjects were considered responders, but there was no statistically significant improvement for the group on various rating scales. The other four subjects dropped out due to lack of response and sedation ($n = 3$) and a possible drug-induced seizure during the fourth week of treatment ($n = 1$). Other side effects included behavioral activation, increased appetite, and weight gain (range, 2 to 18 lbs). The authors concluded that quetiapine was poorly tolerated and ineffective in their sample, with the caveat that the sample size was small (Martin, Koenig, Scahill, & Bregman, 1999).

Ziprasidone

Ziprasidone is potent antagonist of $5HT_{2A}$ and D_2 receptors, though it has relatively greater affinity for $5HT_{2A}$ receptors. In contrast to quetiapine, it has low affinity for adrenergic and histaminergic receptors (Seeger et al., 1995). In the one published report of ziprasidone use in the ASDs, McDougle, Kem, and Posey (2002) conducted a preliminary evaluation of its safety and effectiveness in children, adolescents, and young adults with autism. Twelve patients (mean age = 11.6 ± 4.38 years;

range, 8–20 years) with autism ($n = 9$) or pervasive developmental disorder not otherwise specified ($n = 3$) received open-label treatment with ziprasidone (mean daily dose, 59.2 ± 34.76 mg; range, 20–120 mg). Treatment ranged from 6 to 30 weeks (mean = 14.1 ± 8.29). Six (50%) of the 12 patients were considered responders based on a CGI-I rating of *much improved* or *very much improved*. Transient sedation was the most common side effect. No cardiovascular side effects, including chest pain, tachycardia, palpitations, dizziness, or syncope, were observed or reported. The mean change in body weight for the group was −5.8 ± 12.52 pounds (range, −35 to +6 pounds). This range may reflect weight loss following discontinuation of the drug used prior to treatment with ziprasidone.

Another open-label study with ziprasidone was conducted by Malone, Delaney, Hyman, and Cater (2007). The 6-week study enrolled 12 subjects (mean age 14.5 years) using doses ranging from 20 to 160 mg per day (mean = 98 ± 40 mg). Nine of 12 subjects were rated as *much improved* or *very much improved* on the CGI-I, and there was no weight gain. There was a 14.7 msec increase in the QTc on average. Taken together, these data indicate lack of consensus on dosing. Although ziprasidone appears to be weight neutral, QT prolongation remains a concern.

Aripiprazole

Aripiprazole is reported to have a novel mechanism of action and is classified as a partial dopamine agonist (Tamminga, 2002). This term refers to the fact that aripiprazole has the capacity to bind (affinity) with presynaptic dopamine receptors, but has a lower biological effect that dopamine itself. Thus, it is presumed to have an overall antidopamine or antagonist effect. In addition, aripiprazole has serotonin blocking properties at the 5 HT2 site. As with the other AAPs, studies in adults with schizophrenia have shown that aripiprazole is an effective antipsychotic medication with a low risk of neurological side effects (rigidity, dystonia, and dyskinesia) (Kane et al., 2002). There was no difference in weight gain across active treatment and placebo groups. This profile of action suggests that aripiprazole has features in common with other AAPs, but may also be fundamentally different.

Following the completion of two large-scale trials (Marcus et al., 2009; Owen et al., 2009), aripiprazole was approved by the FDA for the treatment of irritability in children with autism age 5 to 17. In the first study, 218 subjects (age 5 to 17) were randomly assigned to 5, 10, or 15 mg of aripiprazole or placebo for 8 weeks (Marcus et al., 2009). The study used essentially the same entry criteria as used in the RUPP Autism Network (2002) study with risperidone. For example, the subjects had to have a diagnosis of autism, be medication-free, and have at least moderate level of tantrums, aggression, and/or self-injury. On the CGI-I, approximately 35% of placebo-treated subjects were rated *much improved* or *very much improved* compared to 55% in each of the active dose groups. Across the three dose levels of aripiprazole, the most commonly reported adverse events were sedation (17% to 28%), tremor (7% to 11%); drooling (4% to 14%). Twenty-one aripiprazole-treated subjects exited the study due to adverse events compared to zero in placebo.

In the second study, 98 subjects were randomly assigned to flexibly dosed aripiprazole or placebo for 8 weeks. The dose schedule started at 2 mg and went up to 5, 10, or 15 mg over the first 5 weeks as tolerated. Aripiprazole was superior to placebo on the parent-rated ABC Irritability subscale. Two thirds of the children in the aripiprazole group were rated as *much improved* or *very much improved* on the CGI-I compared to 16% in the placebo group. Using this flexible dose strategy the most common doses for the aripiprazole group were 5 and 10 mg, with nearly three fourths of the sample treated at these dose levels. The rate of neuromotor adverse events appeared low. The most common adverse events associated with aripiprazole were increased appetite (15%), vomiting (15%), somnolence (17%), and fatigue (21%). Five subjects (just over 10%) withdrew from the aripiprazole group due to adverse events. Weight gain of 2 kg was significantly greater in the aripiprazole group compared to 0.8 kg for placebo. In contrast to the RUPP

Autism Network (2002) trial with risperidone, 75% of subjects in the active treatment group were rated *much improved* or *very much improved*. The average weight gain with risperidone was 2.7 kg. The results of these two aripiprazole trials suggest that it is safe and effective for treating serious behavioral problems in children with autism. The magnitude of benefit appears slightly lower than risperidone. Aripiprazole is not weight neutral, but the magnitude of weight gain is less than risperidone (Maayan & Correll, 2011).

Paliperidone

Paliperidone, the first metabolite of risperidone, was evaluated in 25 subjects with autistic disorder (21 males and 4 females, age 12 to 21 years) in an 8-week open-label study (Stigler, Mullett, Erickson, Posey, & McDougle, 2012). The study entry criteria were similar to the RUPP Autism Network (2002) risperidone trial and the Owen et al. (2009) aripiprazole trial. The flexible dose strategy started at 3 mg per day with scheduled 3 mg dose increases each week to a maximum of 12 mg. The average dose was 7.1 mg per day. Twenty-one of 25 subjects were rated as *much improved* or *very much improved*, and there was an over 50% drop in the ABC Irritability subscale. On average, there was a 2.2 kg weight gain, but some subjects actually lost weight (perhaps related to discontinuation of a prior medication that promoted weight gain). The newer atypical antipsychotic, asenapine, has not been carefully studied in children with ASDs.

SEROTONIN REUPTAKE INHIBITORS

Serotonin reuptake inhibitors (SRIs) such as clomipramine, fluoxetine, fluvoxamine, sertraline, paroxetine, citalopram, escitalopram, and vilazodone are a group of chemically unrelated compounds that potently inhibit the reuptake of serotonin (5-hydroxytryptamine, 5-HT) at the presynaptic transporter site. Clomipramine is a tricyclic antidepressant (TCA) that inhibits the reuptake of both norepinephrine and serotonin. The other compounds are more selective in their action and are collectively termed *selective* serotonin reuptake inhibitors (SSRI). Although commonly used in clinical practice (Coury et al., 2011; Oswald & Sonenklar, 2007) the SRIs have not been well studied in the ASD.

Clomipramine

In a pair of studies, Gordon and colleagues first compared clomipramine to desipramine in seven subjects with autism in a crossover design (Gordon, Rapoport, Hamburger, State, & Mannheim, 1992). In that study, clomipramine was superior to desipramine in reducing repetitive behaviors and stereotypies. The second study was a double-blind crossover study that compared clomipramine to desipramine and to placebo (Gordon, State, Nelson, Hamburger, & Rapoport, 1993). Twenty-four subjects with a mean age of 9.7 years (range, 6 to 18 years) were included in the study. Of these, 12 were randomly assigned to clomipramine and desipramine in a crossover design, and the other 12 to clomipramine and placebo in a crossover design. Clomipramine was superior to both desipramine and placebo in reducing autistic symptoms (as measured by the 14-item Children's Psychiatric Rating Scale), as well as repetitive, obsessive-compulsive disorder (OCD)-like symptoms (as measured by a global measure of OCD). One subject treated with clomipramine had a seizure; other adverse effects of clomipramine included prolonged QT interval in one subject and tachycardia in another.

Four open-label studies of clomipramine, which included both children and adults, reported beneficial effects in mixed populations of ASD patients (Brasic et al., 1994; Brodkin, McDougle, Naylor, Cohen, & Price, 1997; Garber, McGonigle, Slomka, & Monteverde, 1992; McDougle et al., 1992). However, a fifth study, composed solely of prepubertal subjects ($n = 8$, 3.5–8.7 years old) showed a generally poor response to clomipramine (Sanchez et al., 1996). Indeed, only one subject showed even moderate improvement. Adverse effects, including urinary retention, drowsiness, aggressive behavior, and mood instability, were common.

Clomipramine was compared to haloperidol and placebo in a three-arm crossover trial in 36 subjects with autistic disorder (age range 10 to 36 years) (Remington, Sloman, Konstantareas, Parker, & Gow, 2001). Each treatment was 6 weeks in duration with a 1-week washout. The dose schedules for the active drugs were somewhat aggressive (25 mg increments of clomipramine every 2 days; 0.25 mg of haloperidol every 2 days). No maximum dose was described in the report, and the dose schedule appeared to be the same for children and adults. Attrition was significantly higher in the clomipramine group (12 of 32 subjects in this arm completed the trial compared to 23 of 33 for haloperidol and 21 of 32 for placebo). Haloperidol was superior to placebo on the ABC Irritability subscale, but no other benefits were detected for either clomipramine or haloperidol compared to placebo.

In conclusion, concerns about lowered seizure threshold in the ASD population, the need for electrocardiographic and blood level monitoring, and the unconvincing results to date raise fundamental questions about the use of clomipramine in patients with ASD.

Fluvoxamine

A double-blind, placebo-controlled trial of fluvoxamine in adults with autism showed that 8 of 15 were judged *much improved* or *very much improved* on the Improvement scale of the Clinical Global Impression scale, as compared to 0 of 15 in the placebo group (McDougle et al., 1996). Improvements included reduced compulsive behavior and aggression, and increased prosocial behavior. Based on these encouraging results, McDougle and colleagues conducted a placebo-controlled study in 34 children and adolescents (age range 5 to 18 years) with ASD. In stark contrast to the positive findings in the adult study, only 1 of 16 patients showed a positive response to fluvoxamine (C. McDougle, personal communication). Behavioral activation characterized by hyperactivity, disinhibition, insomnia, and aggression occurred in 12 of 16 subjects, resulting in discontinuation of the trial. The dose of fluvoxamine ranged from

2.5 to 3.0 mg/kg, which is lower than the average fluvoxamine dose of 4.4 mg/kg used in a multisite study of typically developing children with anxiety disorders (RUPP Anxiety Group, 2001). At this higher dose level, the RUPP investigators observed behavioral activation in 27% of those on fluvoxamine, compared to 12% on placebo. Taken together, these findings suggest that children with ASD may be at higher risk for SSRI-induced behavioral activation than adults with ASD and typically developing children with anxiety disorders.

Martin, Koenig, Anderson, and Scahill (2003) conducted a pilot study of fluvoxamine in 18 children and adolescents with ASD and anxiety symptoms. One aim of the study was to examine age-related differences in response to fluvoxamine suggested by the two prior studies. In order to reduce to risk of behavioral activation in youngsters with ASD, the investigators used even lower doses of fluvoxamine (1.5 mg/kg/day) than the dose used in the McDougle et al. study. The subjects had a mean age of 11.3 ± 3.6 years (range, 8 to 16 years). Fluvoxamine was started at either 12.5 or 25 mg daily (for subjects weighing less or more than 40 kg, respectively). In the absence of significant side effects, medication was adjusted weekly in increments of 12.5 or 25 mg until the maximum dosage was reached (1.5 mg/kg/day, rounded to the nearest 12.5 mg dose), given on a bid schedule. This dose showed clear evidence of effective serotonin reuptake inhibition as measured by blockade at the platelet membrane level (see Epperson et al., 2001). Fourteen children (78%) completed the 10-week study; premature discontinuation due to behavioral activation occurred in three subjects. This finding suggests that SSRI activation is indeed related to starting dose and the pace of dose escalation. Although there were no significant benefits for the group as a whole, eight subjects (including all four females) showed a positive response (Martin et al., 2003).

Sertraline

No controlled studies of sertraline in subjects with autistic disorder or other ASDs have been published, although a number of open-label reports have appeared. In a 28-day trial of sertraline (at doses of 25 mg to 150 mg daily) in nine adults with mental retardation (five of whom had autistic disorder), significant decreases in aggression and self-injurious behavior occurred in eight as rated on the CGI severity scale (Hellings, Kelley, Gabrielli, Kilgore, & Shah, 1996). In a case series of nine autistic children (ages 6 to 12 years) treated with sertraline (25 mg to 50 mg daily), eight showed significant improvement in anxiety, irritability, and ability to manage transitions (Steingard, Zimnitzky, DeMaso, Bauman, & Bucci, 1997). Two children exhibited agitation when the dose was raised to 75 mg daily.

A 12-week, open-label, prospective study of 42 adults with ASDs (including patients with autistic disorder, Asperger's disorder, and ASD not otherwise specified) reported that sertraline (mean dose, 122 mg per day) was effective for improving aggression and repetitive behavior (McDougle et al., 1998). On the CGI-I, 15 of 22 subjects with autistic disorder, none of 6 with Asperger's disorder, and 9 of 14 with pervasive developmental disorder not otherwise specified (PDD-NOS) were categorized as responders. Three of the 42 subjects dropped out of the study due to activation.

Paroxetine

Only a few reports, none of them controlled, have appeared on the use of paroxetine in autistic disorder. Paroxetine 20 mg per day decreased self-injurious behavior in a 15-year-old boy with high-functioning autistic disorder (Snead, Boon, & Presberg, 1994). In another report, paroxetine was effective for a broader range of symptoms, including irritability, temper tantrums, and preoccupations in a 7-year-old boy with autistic disorder (Posey, Litwiller, Koburn, & McDougle, 1999). The optimal dose of paroxetine was 10 mg daily; an increase of paroxetine to 15 mg per day was associated with activation. A retrospective case analysis found paroxetine to be effective in approximately 25% of adults with PDD NOS (Branford, Bhaumik, & Naik, 1998).

Fluoxetine

An early open-label study of fluoxetine in 23 patients with autism ranging in age from 7 to 28 years of age showed promising effects on repetitive behaviors. At doses ranging from 10 to 80 mg per day, 15 of 23 subjects were classified as responders on a global measure of severity (Cook, Rowlett, Jaselskis, & Leventhal, 1992). Although the primary outcome measure was crude, the study provided hints of age-related effects on therapeutic response. In the younger age group (subjects less than 15 years of age), 6 of 11 were classified as responders. By contrast, 9 of 12 subjects older than 15 years were classified as responders. Cook and colleagues (1992) also observed symptoms of activation, including hyperactivity, restlessness, agitation, elation, irritability, and insomnia in 6 of 23 subjects. Whether these symptoms of behavioral activation were more common in the younger age group was not reported.

In a retrospective study of fluoxetine in 37 young children with autism not selected for any specific set of target symptoms, DeLong, Teague, and McSwain Kamran (1998) reported that 22 of 37 subjects improved in core symptoms of autism. The children ranged in age from 2 to 7 years of age (mean, 4.5 years). The dose of fluoxetine was not reported. In addition, the characteristics of the sample were not provided. Among nonresponders, a high (though unspecified) percentage of children showed signs of activation as evidenced by hyperactivity, insomnia, agitation, and, occasionally, aggression. Thus, the results of this trial are useful for hypothesis generation, but offer little guidance to clinicians regarding the use of fluoxetine in children with autism.

Hollander and colleagues (2005) conducted a crossover trial with fluoxetine and placebo in 39 subjects with ASDs (age range 5 to 16 years; 30 boys and 9 girls). Thirty-five subjects met criteria for autistic disorder and four with Asperger's disorder. Subjects were randomly assigned to receive either 8 weeks of fluoxetine followed by a 2-week washout and 8 weeks of placebo, or the reverse order. The primary outcome measure was a clinician-rated instrument of repetitive behavior (Compulsion scales of the Children's Yale-Brown Obsessive-Compulsive Scales). The investigators used a conservative dosing schedule—beginning with 2.5 mg per day of liquid fluoxetine followed by gradual increases (mean dose was 10 mg/day). This conservative approach apparently prevented the occurrence of activation in this trial. The crossover design hinders the assessment of benefit in this trial. Focusing just on the first 8 weeks (fluoxetine versus placebo), there was a 10% decline in repetitive behavior for fluoxetine compared to a 4% decrease in the placebo group, suggesting minimal benefit for the active drug.

Fluoxetine was evaluated in a relatively large 14-week placebo-controlled trial with parallel groups by the neuropharm company. The company developed a melt-in-the-mouth tablet and pursued a drug program to obtain FDA approval for the treatment of repetitive behavior in children with autism. The study enrolled 158 subjects (age 5 to 17 years) across several sites in the United States. After 14 weeks of treatment, there was no difference between fluoxetine and placebo on the clinician-rated Children's Yale-Brown Obsessive-Compulsive Scales –modified for autism spectrum disorder (CYBOCS-ASD). This study also used a relatively conservative dosing schedule, which seemed to limit the occurrence of activation. The company announced on its website that there was no difference between the drug and placebo on repetitive behavior as measured on the CYBOCS-ASD (Autism Speaks, 2009).

To date, there is one placebo-controlled trial of fluoxetine in 34 adults with ASD (Hollander et al., 2012). In this trial, 21 subjects were randomly assigned to fluoxetine and 13 to placebo for 12 weeks. The average age of the sample (26 males and 11 females) was 34.3 years. The dose was started at 10 mg per day with gradual increases in first 10 mg and then 20 mg increments to a maximum of 80 mg per day. The primary outcomes were on the Compulsion scale of the Yale-Brown Obsessive-Compulsive Scales (YBOCS) and the CGI-I. Thirty percent of the subjects randomly assigned to fluoxetine were rated *much improved* or *very much improved* on the CGI-I compared to 0% in the placebo group. Given this sample size, this was not a significant difference. On the YBOCS, there was a 16% drop in the fluoxetine group (mean dose = 64.8 mg/day) compared to a 4% decline for placebo. This small difference was reported as statistically significant. In light of the modest rate of 30% for positive response on the CGI-I, however, this difference on the YBOCS seems clinically insignificant. The drug was well tolerated, with no reports of activation.

Citalopram

A multisite study of citalopram in children with ASD targeting repetitive behavior was conducted by the federally funded Studies To Advance Autism Research and Treatment (STAART) centers. In that study, 149 subjects (age 5 to 17) were randomly assigned to citalopram ($n = 73$) or placebo ($n = 76$) for 12 weeks. The primary outcome measures were the CGI-I and the CYBOCS-ASD (Scahill, McDougle, et al., 2006). The medication dose began with 2.5 mg per day and was increased gradually over 8 weeks. The dose schedule was slightly more conservative for younger children. The treating clinician was free to delay a scheduled increase or to reduce the dose to manage adverse effects. After 12 weeks of treatment, the average dose of citalopram was about 16 mg per day—slightly less than the maximum for the study of 20 mg per day (King et al., 2009).

There was no difference between groups on the rate of positive response on the CGI-I: 33% of subjects in the citalopram group were rated *much improved* or *very much improved* on the CGI-I compared to 34% for placebo. Similarly, there was no difference between groups on the CYBOCS-ASD. The only difference between groups was the rate of activation (e.g., increased energy, insomnia, hyperactivity), which was greater in the citalopram group compared to placebo. Although the rate of activation was higher in the citalopram group, it contributed to attrition in only about 10% of cases. The study showed that activation can often be managed by holding the dose for 1 day and resuming at 50% of the prior dose.

Escitalopram

Escitalopram is a single isomer in contrast to the racemic compound, citalopram. It was examined in 28 subjects with ASD (6 to 17 years of age; 25 boys, 3 girls) in a 10-week open trial. The drug dose began at 2.5 mg with planned weekly increases to 20 mg per day. However, 17 of 28 subjects were unable to tolerate more than 10 mg per day due to activation side effects (disinhibition, hyperactivity). Surprisingly, sleep disturbance was not observed. As in prior citalopram and fluoxetine trials, activation was often managed by dose decrease, but two subjects exited the trial due to activation. On average there were significant reductions on several Aberrant Behavior Checklist subscales (Irritability, Social Withdrawal, and Hyperactivity).

In summary, available evidence provides only limited support for the use of SSRIs for repetitive behavior in children with ASD. To date, only fluoxetine and citalopram have been evaluated in large-scale placebo-controlled trials, and neither drug was superior to placebo. Given the consistently demonstrated efficacy of the SSRIs in the treatment of typically developing children with OCD, the lack of efficacy in these trials suggests that repetitive behavior in ASD may be different than repetitive behavior in OCD. Despite the meager evidence, however, the SSRIs are commonly used in children and adolescents with ASD. Children with ASD appear to be especially vulnerable to activation and the risk may be greater in younger children. The details on adverse events in the Neuropharm fluoxetine trial have not yet been published. Results from the Hollander et al. (2005) and King et al. (2009) trials, however, suggest that starting with low doses followed by gradual increase lowers the risk of activation. Thus, clinicians who initiate treatment for other indications such as anxiety or depression can make use of this clinical approach.

STIMULANTS

The stimulants, methylphenidate, d-amphetamine, and d,l-amphetamine are standard medications for the treatment of attention-deficit/hyperactivity disorder (ADHD) in typically developing children. The results of the National Institute of Mental Health (NIMH) sponsored Multimodal Treatment of ADHD (MTA Group, 1999) provide strong evidence that the stimulants are effective for the treatment of ADHD. Newer formulations offer additional options for once a day administration and the potential for more even behavioral control across the day. The efficacy and safety of stimulants in the ASDs, however, have been less well studied.

The fourth edition of the *Diagnostic and Statistical Manual of Mental Disorders* (*DSM-IV*; American Psychiatric Association [APA], 2000) advises against adding the diagnosis of ADHD in children with ASDs. *DSM-5* (APA, 2013), however, takes a different approach and offers no such caution. Whether the symptoms of motor restlessness, overactivity, distractibility, and disruptive behavior seen in ADHD and ASD share a common neural pathway is not clear. Nonetheless, these symptoms are common in children with ASD and children with developmental disorders. Stimulants are commonly used in children with ASD (Cortese, Castelnau, Morcillo, Roux, & Bonnet-Brilhault, 2012; Oswald & Sonenklar, 2007). Despite their common use in clinical practice, the rate of positive response appears to be lower and the frequency of side effects may be higher in developmentally disabled populations (see Aman, Buican, & Arnold, 2003, for a review). Of particular concern in this population is the apparently higher rate of adverse effects such as stereotypies, tics, social withdrawal, and irritability.

STIMULANT TREATMENT STUDIES OF ADHD IN DEVELOPMENTALLY DISABLED POPULATIONS

Aman, Marks, Turbott, Wilsher, and Merry (1991) compared the efficacy of methylphenidate (MPH) with that of thioridazine in a sample of 30 children and adolescents with mental retardation and disruptive behavior disorders. In this double-blind, crossover trial, MPH (but not thioridazine) significantly reduced ADHD symptoms on standard teacher rating scales and significantly improved performance on a continuous performance task (CPT). Parents, however, did not report much improvement with either medication. Clinical benefit from methylphenidate was observed in subjects with IQ scores above 45.

In a series of double-blind, crossover investigations, Handen and colleagues (Handen, Breaux, Gosling, Ploof, & Feldman, 1990; Handen, Feldman, Lurier, & Murray, 1999; Handen, Johnson, & Lubetsky, 2000) showed that MPH was successful in reducing hyperactivity, irritability, inattention, and off-task behavior among two thirds to three quarters of subjects with ADHD and mild to moderate mental retardation. One of these trials included subjects with autism (Handen et al., 2000). A dosage of 0.6 mg/kg was more effective than a dosage of 0.3 mg/kg on some measures, but increased frequency of irritability, social withdrawal, and tics was associated with the higher dose (Handen et al., 2000; Handen, Feldman, Gosling, Breaux, & McAuliffe, 1991). Pearson et al. (2003) reported similar observations in a sample of 24 children with mental retardation and ADHD treated with 0.15, 0.3, and 0.6 mg/kg/dose and placebo in a crossover design. Taken together, data from these studies suggest that children with intellectual disability with ADHD are at higher risk for adverse effects from the stimulants than typically developing children with ADHD. The rate of responders and the mean percentage of improvement are somewhat lower than those observed in typically developing children with ADHD.

The RUPP Autism Network (2005a) conducted a placebo-controlled trial of immediate-release methylphenidate in 66 children (age 5 to 14 years) with ASD and hyperactivity. The subjects had a mental age of at least 18 months, met criteria for an ASD (PDD-NOS, Asperger's disorder, or autistic disorder), and had at least a moderate level of hyperactivity. The 4-week crossover trial included three dose levels of MPH and placebo each given for one week in random order. The medication (or placebo) was administered in identically appearing capsules three times per day (breakfast, noon, and 4 p.m.); the 4 p.m. dose was roughly half the strength of the other two doses. The low, medium, and high dose levels of MPH were 0.125 mg/kg/morning dose, 0.25 mg/kg/morning dose, and 0.5 mg/kg/morning dose, respectively. The primary outcome measure was the ABC Hyperactivity subscale rated by parents. Subjects who met prespecified criteria for positive response (e.g., 30% improvement on parent rating and *much improved* or *very much improved* on the clinician-rated CGI-I) were treated for 8 additional weeks on the best of the three active doses to evaluate the stability of response.

Thirty-five of the 66 patients showed a positive response to a least one dose of methylphenidate (RUPP Autism Network, 2005a). All three active doses were superior to placebo, but the magnitude of response was small to medium. For example, the improvement over placebo on parent ratings ranged from 12% for the low dose and 20% for the medium and highest dose levels (effect sizes ranged from 0.3 to .05). Contrary to expectation, IQ did not moderate response. Compared to typically developing children with ADHD, children with ASD and hyperactivity are less likely to show a positive response and the magnitude of response is lower. In addition, 7 of the 66 (10.6%) participants in the double-blind crossover stopped treatment due to adverse effects, which is much higher than the percentage of children who terminated prematurely in the MTA study. The most common adverse event leading to discontinuation in the RUPP Autism Network trial was irritability. Other adverse effects included appetite suppression, insomnia, increased stereotypies, or motor tics.

The results of this study show that methylphenidate can be effective for children with ASD and hyperactivity. In contrast to typically developing children with ADHD, however, the magnitude of benefit may not be large. The initial dose should be conservative and increased incrementally to avoid adverse effects. Parent and teacher ratings may be useful to monitor treatment response.

NONSTIMULANT MEDICATIONS FOR HYPERACTIVITY IN ASD

Alpha 2 Agonists

Clonidine and guanfacine are alpha 2 adrenergic agonists developed to treat hypertension. They were introduced in child psychiatry over 30 years ago for the treatment of Tourette syndrome and ADHD and, more recently, for children with ASD. New extended release formulations of clonidine and guanfacine have been approved by the U.S. Food and Drug Administration for the treatment of children with ADHD (Scahill, 2012).

The reduction in blood pressure is presumed to be caused by a stimulating effect on alpha 2 receptors in the locus coeruleus. These neurons play a role in arousal, heart rate, and blood pressure. The stimulating effect of the alpha 2 agonists reduces the firing of these neurons resulting in slower heart rate and decreased blood pressure. Clonidine, which is more potent than guanfacine, is often associated with sedation due its action at alpha 2 receptors in the thalamus. Preclinical evidence accumulated over the past 25 years shows that guanfacine also stimulates alpha 2 receptors in the prefrontal cortex (PFC). This action may have positive effects on attention and impulse control (Arnsten & Pliszka, 2011).

Although the clonidine and guanfacine are commonly used in clinical practice, neither compound has been well studied in children with ASD. Early studies with clonidine in children with autism encountered recurring problems with sedation, which has limited use of this drug in clinical practice. The promise of less sedation with guanfacine prompted interest in several clinical populations (Scahill, 2012).

Guanfacine was evaluated in 25 subjects (23 boys and 2 girls, age 5 to 14 years) with ASD and hyperactivity in an 8-week open-label, multisite trial (Scahill, Aman, et al., 2006). The dose of immediate-release guanfacine ranged from 1.0 to 3.0 mg per day in two or three divided doses. After 8 weeks of treatment, mean scores on a parent rating of hyperactivity showed a 40% improvement over baseline. Although of lower magnitude, teacher ratings also showed a significant improvement. There were no serious adverse events and the drug was generally well tolerated (4 of 25 subjects withdrew from the trial because of adverse effects). The most common adverse events were sedation, irritability, sleep disturbance (e.g., insomnia or midsleep awakening), increased aggression, or self-injury in a few subjects. One subject reported perceptual disturbance (visual distortion of size and distance). Most of these adverse events were managed by dose adjustment (e.g., lowering the dose or changing the time of the dose). On average, systolic blood pressure declined 7 points at Week 4, but returned to baseline by Week 8. Diastolic blood pressure remained stable throughout the trial and there were no clinically significant changes from baseline in the electrocardiogram (Scahill, Aman, et al., 2006).

Handen, Sahl, and Hardan (2008) examined the efficacy and safety of guanfacine in 11 children (10 boys and 1 girl; ages 5 to 9 years) with developmental disabilities (ASD = 6; intellectual disability without ASD = 5), as well as prominent symptoms of ADHD in an unbalanced crossover study. Subjects were randomly assigned to receive guanfacine for 4 weeks followed by a 1-week washout and another week of placebo. Alternatively, subjects received placebo for 1 week followed by 4 weeks of guanfacine and then the 1-week washout. The target dose was 3 mg per day (range 1–3 mg) given in three divided doses (morning, noon, and late afternoon). After subtracting the effects of placebo, the 35% mean decrease on a parent-rated measure of hyperactivity was significant. Drowsiness occurred in five subjects and limited upward dose adjustment in three subjects. When using the immediate release compound, gradual dose escalation with repeat dosing every 6 hours might result in fewer adverse effects. To determine the safety and efficacy of guanfacine in children with ASD accompanied by hyperactivity and impulsiveness, large-scale trials are needed.

Extended-Release Guanfacine

A new formulation of guanfacine was approved by the FDA for the treatment of typically developing children with ADHD in fall 2009 (Biederman et al., 2008). Sallee and colleagues (2009) examined the long-term efficacy and tolerability of extended-release guanfacine (ERG) in a 2-year open-label trial in 259 subjects with ADHD (6 to 17 years of age; 188 boys and 71 girls). Approximately half of the sample dropped out by the end of the first year due to waning benefit or adverse effects. The most common adverse effects were somnolence (33% of subjects) and headache (25% of subjects). To date, there are no placebo-controlled trials on the use of this new formulation in children with ASD. The convenience of single day dosing is likely to prompt clinicians to try this medication in children with ASD and hyperactivity. Based on these results in typically developing children with ADHD, weekly increases in 1 mg increments as in the Biederman et al. trial (2008) may not be well tolerated in children with PDD—especially younger children.

Atomoxetine

Atomoxetine is approved for the treatment of typically developing children with ADHD (Michelson et al., 2003). This mechanism of action, selective norepinephrine (NE) reuptake inhibition, is shared with the tricyclic antidepressants, such as desipramine. Although desipramine has shown superiority to placebo for children with ADHD and tic disorders (Spencer et al., 2002), it has fallen out of use due to the need for cardiograms, drug plasma levels, and vulnerability of the tricyclics for drug–drug interaction. The tricyclics also lower the seizure threshold, which is a concern in children with ASD.

In an 8-week open-label trial of atomoxetine in 16 high-functioning youth with ASD (mean age 7.7 ± 2.2 years) accompanied by ADHD symptoms, Posey and colleagues (2006) reported that 75% ($n = 12$) of the subjects were rated *much improved* or *very much improved* on the CGI-I. Beneficial effects were observed on parent and teacher ratings. Atomoxetine was given in a wide dose range from 0.4 to 1.3 mg/kg/day in two divided doses. Two subjects withdrew early due to irritability (Posey et al., 2006). Another open trial was conducted by Troost and colleagues (2006) in 12 children with ASD (6 to 14 years) with mild to moderate levels of hyperactivity were treated with 0.49 to 1.7 mg/kg/day of atomoxetine (mean = 1.19 mg/kg/day) given in a single dose for up to 10 weeks. Five subjects withdrew from the trial due to adverse effects (nausea in two subjects; anxiety, increased aggression, and anorexia with weight loss each in one subject). Other common adverse effects included decreased appetite, irritability, and sleep problems. The seven subjects who completed the trial showed improvement in ADHD symptoms.

Arnold and colleagues (2006) enrolled 16 children with ASD (ages 5 to 15) in a crossover trial in which subjects were randomized to atomoxetine followed by placebo or the reverse. The 6-week treatment phases were separated by a 1-week washout. The medication was gradually increased to 1.4 mg/kg/day given in divided doses. Of the 16 subjects, 9 responded to atomoxetine and 4 responded to placebo. Atomoxetine was superior to placebo on parent ratings of hyperactivity—but the magnitude of response was modest. Common adverse events included gastrointestinal (GI) complaints (nausea, abdominal discomfort, constipation), decreased appetite, and tachycardia. One subject was hospitalized for violent behavior while on atomoxetine.

The largest placebo-controlled study of atomoxetine to date enrolled 97 children (ages 6 to 17 years) with ASD and ADHD symptoms in an 8-week trial (Harfterkamp et al., 2012). The primary outcomes were the investigator rated ADHD Rating Scale and the CGI-I. The active drug was gradually increased over the first few weeks to a fixed dose of 1.2 mg/kg/day given in a single morning. After 8 weeks of treatment atomoxetine was superior to placebo on the dimensional measure (ADHD Rating Scale). On the CGI-I, however, there was no difference between active medication and placebo. In the atomoxetine group, 21% of subjects were rated *much improved* or *very much improved* (conventional definition of positive response) compared to 9% for placebo. Moreover, the 21% positive response rate is modest and not a strong vote of confidence for atomoxetine in the population. The drug was well tolerated, with only one subject exiting the study due to an adverse effect. The most common adverse effects associated with atomoxetine were nausea, decreased appetite, abdominal pain, and early morning awakening.

Taken together, these results suggest that atomoxetine may be useful for treating ADHD symptoms in children with ASD. Although serious adverse effects are rare, the adverse effect burden is relatively high, appears to be dose related and appears to be higher when the drug is given in a single daily dose. The available data on atomoxetine in children with ASD fit the pattern observed with stimulants. Dosing should start low and move up gradually. The magnitude of benefit is likely to be lower than what has been reported in studies of typically developing children with ADHD. In addition, children with ASD appear to be a greater risk for adverse effects when treated with atomoxetine—compared to typically developing children with ADHD.

MISCELLANEOUS COMPOUNDS

Over the past 40 years, several other medications have been evaluated in the treatment of children with ASD including fenfluramine (Ritvo et al., 1986), naltrexone (Campbell et al., 1993; Feldman, Kolmen, & Gonzaga, 1999; Kolmen, Feldman, Handen, & Janosky, 1997), buspirone (Buitelaar, van der Gaag, & van der Hoeven, 1998), and secretin (Williams, Wray, & Wheeler, 2012). Initial reports of open-label studies with naltrexone in autism seemed promising (Campbell et al., 1989; Panksepp & Lensing, 1991), but results of subsequent placebo-controlled studies were disappointing (Campbell et al., 1993; Feldman et al., 1999; Kolmen et al., 1997). Fenfluramine and secretin were introduced with high expectations for improving core features of autism, but neither drug has shown persuasive evidence for benefit. Indeed, fenfluramine has been removed from the market due to its association with cardiopulmonary complications (Ioannides-Demos, Proietto, Tonkin, & McNeil, 2006). Secretin has been evaluated in 16 randomized clinical trials involving some 900 children with ASD and is no better than placebo (see Williams et al., 2012, for detailed review).

Mirtazapine

The atypical antidepressant mirtazapine (an agent with both serotonergic and noradrenergic properties) was evaluated in an open-label study in 26 children (mean age 10.1 + 4.8 years) with autism or other ASDs (Posey, Guenin, Kohn, Swiezy, & McDougle, 2001). In doses ranging from 7.5 to 45 mg per day (mean 30.3 + 12.6 mg), 25 of 26 subjects completed at least 4 weeks of treatment. Nine subjects were medication free at baseline and 17 were taking at least one concomitant psychotropic medication. Nine of the 26 (34.6%) were rated *much improved* or *very much improved* on the CGI-I based on improvement in a variety of symptoms including aggression, self-injury, irritability, hyperactivity, anxiety, depression, and insomnia. Mirtazapine did not improve core symptoms of social or communication impairment. Adverse effects were minimal and included increased appetite, irritability, and transient sedation. In summary, mirtazapine was well tolerated, but the heterogeneous nature of the sample does not offer much guidance on how to use this drug in practice. Nonetheless, these preliminary results suggest that mirtazapine may deserve more study for the treatment for the treatment of anxiety in youngsters with ASDs.

Anticonvulsants

Anticonvulsant medications have not been well studied in children with ASD. In addition to antiseizure properties, this class of compounds has been evaluated in few case series and small open-label trials for the treatment of aggression and behavioral dyscontrol associated with autism. Hollander and colleagues (2010) conducted a 12-week placebo-controlled trial of valproate in 27 subjects (ages 5 to 17 years). The study used a gradually increasing dose schedule in the first 4 weeks. For example, children less than 40 kg started with 125 mg per day with an increase to 125 twice a day on Day 5 and then increase stepwise to 250 mg twice a day with subsequent increases based on blood level (target 50 mcg/ml) and tolerability. Ten of 16 children randomly assigned to valproate were rated as *much improved* or *very much improved* on the CGI-I compared to 1 of 11 subjects in the placebo group (p < .01). After accounting for the change in the placebo group, there was a 4-point improvement in the Irritability subscale of the Aberrant Behavior Checklist. This difference (20% from baseline) was statistically significant, but reflects only modest improvement. The drug was well tolerated with only one subject dropping out due to adverse effects.

A study of lamotrigine in 28 children with autism (Belsito, Law, Kirk, Landa, & Zimmerman, 2001) showed no separation between active drug and placebo on any of the outcome measures used. The higher rates of adverse skin reactions in children compared to adults (including exfoliative dermatolysis and Stevens Johnson syndrome) provide further caution on the use of this agent in the treatment of children with autism (Messenheimer, 1998).

Memantine, Amantadine

Amantadine and memantine are noncompetitive NMDA glutamate receptor antagonists. Glutamate is of interest in autism because it plays a role in learning and memory. In addition, accumulating preclinical data implicate dysregulation of glutamate in the pathophysiology of fragile X, which is assocaited with autism in some cases (Dolen & Bear, 2008).

Results from an open-label study in 24 typically developing children with ADHD suggested that amantadine might be effective in treating impulsiveness and hyperactivity (Donfrancesco, Calderoni, & Vitiello, 2007). Thus far, there is only one placebo-controlled trial of amantadine in children with ASD. King and colleagues (2001) conducted a 4-week placebo-controlled trial in 39 subjects and reported that amantadine (5 mg/kg/day) was not superior to placebo on the parent-rated ABC Irritability or Hyperactivity subscales.

Memantine is a newer NMDA antagonist that is approved for the treatment of Alzheimer's disease. Information on memantine in patients with ASD is also limited. Results from an open-label trial in 16 typically developing children (age 6 to 12 years) with ADHD suggests that memantine at doses from 10 to 20 mg is tolerable. In general, scores on ADHD rating scales went down—but the magnitude of benefit was modest (Findling et al., 2007). An open-label study in 14 children with ASD showed 50% reduction on the Hyperactivity subscale of the ABC (Owley et al., 2006). Despite this encouraging reduction on average, 5 subjects showed increased hyperactivity. In an open-label trial (duration 1 to 20 months) of 151 children with ASD, Chez (2007) reported no benefit on hyperactivity. The dose ranged from 2.5 to 30 mg per day (given in a single or in two divided doses). Twenty-two subjects (15%) discontinued treatment due to increased hyperactivity, irritability, or both; 5 discontinued due to lack of efficacy. Taken together, these results suggest that more information is needed on subject selection and dosing of memantine in children with ASD.

FUTURE DIRECTIONS

Several compounds aimed at treating the core symptoms of ASD have moved into the foreground over the past decade. One of the barriers in drug development in this population is the dearth of reliable and valid outcome measures for core features of ASD. The modified Children's Yale-Brown Obsessive Compulsive Scales (CYBOCS-ASD) has demonstrated reliability, validity, and sensitivity to change with treatment (McDougle et al., 2005; Scahill, McDougle, et al, 2006). Given the demonstrated reliability and validity of the CYBOCS-ASD, the negative findings in the citalopram study are trustworthy. To evaluate social disability, a few studies have used the Social Withdrawal subscale of the Aberrant Behavior Checklist (Jacquemont et al., 2011; Scahill, Hallett, et al., 2012; Veenstra-VanderWeele et al., 2011). This measure reflects the degree to which the individual initiates interaction and responds to interaction initiated by others. Although this measure is not diagnosis-specific, it appears to capture the severity of social disability and it is sensitive to change (Scahill, Hallett, et al., 2012). Trustworthy outcome measures of prosocial behavior, adaptive behavior, anxiety and depression would be welcomed contributions to promote drug development.

Oxytocin

Oxytocin is a peptide comprised of nine amino acids produced by the hypothalamus. Its role in parturition and lactation are well-established (Lee, Macbeth, Pagani, & Young, 2009). A rich literature from animal studies has shown that oxytocin (OT) also plays a role in mother–infant attachment, grooming, and pair bonding (Insel, 1997; Young, 2008). Beginning with healthy adults, several investigators have evaluated the effects of single dose intranasal OT. In the laboratory setting, single doses of OT reportedly enhance trust and attention to social cues in healthy adults (Kosfeld, Heinrichs, Zak, Fischbacher, & Fehr, 2005). These preliminary results led to a series of single-dose studies of intranasal OT versus placebo in adults and, more recently, in youth with ASD (see Guastella & MacLeod, 2012, for detailed review). The usual dose of OT given was 24 IU (e.g., three squirts per nostril) at one visit and placebo on the other visit—in random order. In general, these studies consistently showed small but often significantly improved performance on tasks reflecting social interaction. To date, only a few studies have examined the effects of multiple doses. Anagnostou and colleagues (2012) enrolled 19 adults with high-functioning autism or Asperger's disorder into a 6-week trial of twice daily OT (24 IU per dose) versus placebo under double-blind conditions. The drug was well tolerated. Two subjects reported increased irritability. Three of 10 subjects randomly assigned to OT were rated *much improved* or *very much improved* on the CGI-I compared one of nine subjects in the placebo group. There were modest improvements on measures of repetitive behavior. This study provides new information on repeat doses of OT. However, the small sample size limits interpretation. Using a step-wise approach to drug development, intermediate size trials with more encouraging results are needed before undertaking a large-scale trial.

Biopterin

Biopterin is a cofactor in several metabolic pathways such as the production of monoamines and nitric oxide and the breakdown of phenylalanine. Under the trade name Kuvan, it is approved for the treatment of phenylketonuria (PKU). Based on the possibility that biopterin may play a role in abnormal metabolic pathways in ASD, Klaimen, Huffman, Masaki, and Elliott (2013) conducted a 16-week, placebo-controlled of biopterin in 46 children (age 3 to 7 years). On the primary outcome measure, the CGI-I, the positive response rate was 25% and 14% for active treatment group and placebo, respectively. The report included results from several secondary analyses and showed evidence of benefit on measures of language and social disability. The entry criteria for the trial did not specify pretreatment threshold scores on any measure and several measures showed wide variation by group at baseline. Given the relatively rare occurrence of PKU, biopterin is prohibitively expensive. Nonetheless, if the mechanism is supported by further study, new variants of the compound may be developed.

N-acetylcysteine (NAC)

NAC is an amino acid supplement that is sold over the counter as an antioxidant. It is also used in the treatment of acetaminophen overdose to offset drug-induced liver damage. The rationale for using NAC in autism is based on the proposed imbalance of excitatory and inhibitory signaling may play a role in autism (Oberman, 2012). Glutamate is the primary excitatory neurotransmitter in the brain and gamma aminobutiric acid (GABA) is the primary inhibitory neurotransmitter. NAC is believed to reduce glutamate transmission. A 12-week, randomized trial of 29 children (age 3 to 12 years) was conducted by Hardan and colleagues (2012). The primary outcome measure was the Irritability subscale of the ABC. After 12 weeks of treatment, subjects on NAC showed an average decline of 57% on the ABC Irritability subscale compared to 11% drop for placebo. Despite this marked improvement on the ABC Irritability subscale, only 36% (5 of 14 subjects) in the NAC group were rated *much improved* on the CGI-I compared to 13% (2 of 15) in the placebo group. This suggests that clinicians considering the larger clinical picture were not seeing overall improvement. The dosing schedule was set for gradual increase to 900 mg three times a day. The actual dose was not reported. The drug was associated with complaints of nausea and vomiting in the NAC group, but no serious adverse effects.

Arbaclofen

Arbaclofen is the active enantiomer of racemic baclofen. Baclofen, which is currently marketed as a muscle relaxant, is a GABA B receptor agonist. This action, either directly, indirectly or both, boosts the inhibitory action of GABA—thereby restoring the presumed excitatory and inhibitory balance. Arbaclofen has been examined in a trial of 63 subjects (age 6 to 40 years) with fragile X syndrome in a crossover design (Berry-Kravis et al., 2012). Subjects were randomly assigned to arbaclofen ($n = 30$) or placebo ($n = 33$) for 4 weeks. Following a 2-week washout, subjects crossed over to the other condition. The results showed no difference between groups on the primary outcome measure (Irritability subscale of the ABC). There was improvement on the ABC Social Withdrawal subscale with subjects in the arbaclofen group showing a 25% decrease in the Social Withdrawal subscale compared to no change in the placebo group. The drug was well tolerated with no differences in the pattern of adverse effects across the two treatment conditions. An open pilot study in adults with autism has also provided some encouraging preliminary results (Veenstra-VanderWeele et al., 2011). Taken together, these results suggest that arbaclofen and drugs with a similar mechanism warrant further study in ASD.

mGluR Antagonists

The mGluR (metabotropic glutamate receptor) story begins with exciting findings in fragile X. Fragile X is a genetic form of intellectual disability affecting an estimated 1 in every 2,500 births with the full mutation (Sansone et al., 2012). The mutation results in an expansion of the CGG repeat on the fragile X mental retardation 1 (FMR1) gene, resulting in a significant reduction or absence of the FMR1 protein. This protein regulates glutamate signaling (Dolen & Bear, 2008; Jin & Warren, 2003). The failure to regulate glutamate signaling has a negative impact on synaptic plasticity and dendritic maturation. The mGluR appears to play a role in this dysregulation. The use of an mGluR antagonist may regulate glutamate signaling even in the absence of FMR1 protein. Elegant preclinical work supports this possibility (Dolen & Bear, 2008; Jin & Warren, 2003). Several companies have an mGluR antagonist in development and they are beginning to be used in clinical trials (Jacquemont et al., 2011).

An estimated one third of children with fragile X meet criteria for ASD. Thus, these preclinical findings in fragile X are of interest in ASD. To date, there is one pilot trial of an mGluR antagonist in fragile X, none in ASD (Jacquemont et al., 2011). In that study, 30 adults with fragile X were randomly assigned to the mGluR antagonist (AFQ056) ($n = 16$) or placebo ($n = 14$) for 3 weeks followed by a 2-week taper, 1-week washout, and 3 weeks of treatment in the other condition. There was no difference between groups on the primary outcome measure (ABC total score). The choice of this metric as the primary outcome measure makes it difficult to interpret these findings.

The ABC is a 58-item factor-analyzed measure that includes five factors. In addition to the Irritability and Social Withdrawal subscales mentioned previously, there are three other subscales (Hyperactivity, Stereotypy, and Inappropriate Speech). The factor analysis shows that these subscales measure separate behavioral domains. A given subject could be high on Social Withdrawal and low on Hyperactivity; another subject could show a reverse pattern of scores—but the total score may be the same. Thus, the total score was a less than optimal choice as a primary outcome measure and the finding of no difference is not informative. However, at doses of 150 mg twice daily, the drug was well tolerated. For future studies in fragile X and in ASD, subject selection and choice of the primary outcome measure warrant careful consideration.

CONCLUSIONS

There have been considerable advances in the pharmacological treatment of ASD over the past decade. There are a growing number of randomized clinical trials that inform clinical practice. Several additional studies are ongoing. Federal support for networks such as Research Units on Pediatric Psychopharmacology Autism Network and other treatment consortia has played an important role in these recent advancements. The pharmaceutical industry has also contributed to testing of existing drugs (e.g., aripiprazole), new formulations

(Neuropharm study of fluoxetine) and novel compounds (mGluR antagonists). Continued support by the federal government for multisite trials, voluntary organizations for pilot trials, and industry will be necessary to guide drug development in ASD. In the next decade, it is likely that the field will become more involved in studying drugs that are not yet on the market (e.g., arbaclofen and the mGluR antagonist described earlier).

Risperidone and aripiprazole were approved based on the Irritability subscale of the ABC. Although irritability is not a core feature of ASD, the approval of these drugs provides a potential pathway for FDA approval. The modified CYBOCS and Social Withdrawal subscales of the ABC have also been used successfully as outcome measures in randomized drug treatment trials in subjects with ASD and appear to be well-positioned for use FDA registration trials. There is a pressing need for additional reliable and valid outcome measures that are sensitive to change. Outcomes of interest include aggression, anxiety, adaptive functioning, cognition, and subdomains of social behavior. Given the common language and cognitive delays in children with ASD, simply adapting outcome measures used in typically developing children is unlikely to be a winning strategy.

To be successful, drug development needs to be stepwise. Pilot trials designed to learn more about feasibility, tolerability, and dosing of a new drug should not be encumbered with the need to show superiority of the active drug over placebo. This requirement may result in premature discard of a useful compound. At the same time, a rapid jump from promising pilot to large-scale randomized trial runs a risk of spending significant resources in a poorly selected candidate drug. Whenever possible, early studies should incorporate evaluation or confirmation of the possible drug mechanism of action. Early study results may show promise for the mechanism—even if a specific compound has liabilities, other compounds that share this mechanism may be worth pursuing.

CROSS-REFERENCES

The biochemistry of autism is addressed in Chapter 19; medical care issues are the focus of Chapter 22; Chapter 44 focuses on practice guidelines.

REFERENCES

Aman, M. G., Buican, B., & Arnold, L. E. (2003). Methylphenidate treatment in children with borderline IQ and mental retardation: Analysis of three aggregated studies. *Journal of Child and Adolescent Psychopharmacology*, *13*, 29–40.

Aman, M. G., Marks, R. E., Turbott, S. H., Wilsher, C. P., & Merry, S. N. (1991). Methylphenidate and thioridazine in the treatment of intellectually subaverage children: Effects on cognitive-motor performance. *Journal of the American Academy of Child & Adolescent Psychiatry*, *30*, 816–824.

Aman, M. G., McDougle, C. J., Scahill, L., Handen, B., Arnold, L. E., Johnson, C., . . . Research Units on Pediatric Psychopharmacology Autism Network. (2009). Medication and parent training in children with pervasive developmental disorders and serious behavior problems: Results from a randomized clinical trial. *Journal of the American Academy of Child & Adolescent Psychiatry*, *48*(12), 1143–1154.

American Psychiatric Association. (2000). *Diagnostic and statistical manual of mental disorders* (4th ed., text rev.). Washington, DC: Author.

American Psychiatric Association. (2013). *Diagnostic and statistical manual of mental disorders* (5th ed.). Arlington, VA: American Psychiatric Publishing.

Anagnostou, E., Soorya, L., Chaplin, W., Bartz, J., Halpern, D., Wasserman, S., . . . Hollander, E. (2012). Intranasal oxytocin versus placebo in the treatment of adults with autism spectrum disorders: a randomized controlled trial. *Molecular Autism*, *3*(16), 2040–2392.

Anderson, L. T., Campbell, M., Adams, P., Small, A. M., Perry, R., & Shell, J. (1989). The effects of haloperidol on discrimination learning and behavioral symptoms in autistic children. *Journal of Autism and Developmental Disorders*, *19*, 227–239.

Arnold, L. E., Aman, M. G., Cook, A. M., Witwer, A. N., Hall, K. L., Thompson, S., & Ramadan, Y. (2006). Atomoxetine for hyperactivity in autism spectrum disorders: Placebo-controlled crossover pilot trial. *Journal of the American Academy of Child & Adolescent Psychiatry*, *45*(10), 1196–1205.

Arnsten, A. F. T., & Pliszka, S. R. (2011). Catecholamine influences on prefrontal cortical function: Relevance to treatment of attention deficit/hyperactivity disorder and related disorders. *Pharmacology, Biochemistry and Behavior*, *99*, 211–216.

Autism Speaks. (2009). *Autism Speaks reports Neuropharm's SOFIA results*. Retrieved from http://esciencenews.com/articles/2009/02/18/autism.speaks.reports.neuropharms.sofia.results

Baldessarini, R. J., & Frankenburg, F. R. (1991). Clozapine: A novel antipsychotic agent. *New England Journal of Medicine, 324*, 746–754.

Belsito, K. M., Law, P. A., Kirk, K. S., Landa, R. J., & Zimmerman, A. W. (2001). Lamotrigine therapy for autistic disorder: A randomized, double-blind, placebo-controlled trial. *Journal of Autism and Developmental Disorders, 31*, 175–181.

Berry-Kravis, E. M., Hessl, D., Rathmell, B., Zarevics, P., Cherubini, M., Walton-Bowen, K., & Hagerman, R. J. (2012). Effects of STX209 (arbaclofen) on neurobehavioral function in children and adults with fragile X syndrome: A randomized, controlled, phase 2 trial. *Science Translational Medicine. 4*(152), 152ra127

Biederman, J., Melmed, R. D., Patel, A., McBurnett, K., Konow, J., Lyne, A., Scherer, N., & SPD503 Study Group. (2008). A randomized, double-blind, placebo-controlled study of guanfacine extended release in children and adolescents with attention-deficit/hyperactivity disorder. *Pediatrics, 121*(1), e73–e84.

Branford, D., Bhaumik, S., & Naik, B. (1998). Selective serotonin re-uptake inhibitors for the treatment of perseverative and maladaptive behaviours of people with intellectual disability. *Journal of Intellectual Disability Research, 42*, 301–306.

Brasic, J. R., Barnett, J. Y., Kaplan, D., Sheitman, B. B., Aisemberg, P., Lafargue, R. T., ... Young, J. G. (1994). Clomipramine ameliorates adventitious movements and compulsions in prepubertal boys with autistic disorder and severe mental retardation. *Neurology, 44*, 1309–1312.

Brodkin, E. S., McDougle, C. J., Naylor, S. T., Cohen, D. J., & Price, L. H. (1997). Clomipramine in adults with pervasive developmental disorders: A prospective open-label investigation. *Journal of Child and Adolescent Psychopharmacology, 7*, 109–121.

Brown, E. C., Aman, M. G., & Havercamp, S. M. (2002). Factor analysis and norms for parent ratings on the Aberrant Behavior Checklist—Community for young people in special education. *Research in Developmental Disabilities, 23*(1), 45–60.

Buitelaar, J. K., van der Gaag, R. J., & van der Hoeven, J. (1998). Buspirone in the management of anxiety and irritability in children with pervasive developmental disorders: Results of an open-label study. *Journal of Clinical Psychiatry, 59*, 56–59.

Bymaster, F. P., Calligaro, D. O., Falcone, J. F., Marsh, R. D., Moore, N. A., Tye, N. C., ... Wong, D. T. (1996). Radioreceptor binding profile of the atypical antipsychotic olanzapine. *Neuropsychopharmacology, 14*, 87–96.

Campbell, M., Anderson, L. T., Small, A. M., Adams, P., Gonzalez, N. M., & Ernst, M. (1993). Naltrexone in autistic children: behavioral symptoms and attentional learning. *Journal of the American Academy of Child & Adolescent Psychiatry, 32*, 1283–1291.

Campbell, M., Armenteros, J. L., Malone, R. P., Adams, P. B., Eisenberg, Z. W., & Overall, J. E. (1997). Neuroleptic-related dyskinesias in autistic children: a prospective, longitudinal study. *Journal of the American Academy of Child & Adolescent Psychiatry, 36*, 835–843.

Campbell, M., Overall, J. E., Small, A. M., Sokol, M. S., Spencer, E. S., Adams, P., ... Roberts, E. (1989). Naltrexone in autistic children: an acute open dose range tolerance trial. *Journal of the American Academy of Child & Adolescent Psychiatry, 28*, 200–206.

Chen, N. C., Bedair, H. S., McKay, B., Bowers, M. B., Jr., & Mazure, C. (2001). Clozapine in the treatment of aggression in an adolescent with autistic disorder. *Journal of Clinical Psychiatry, 62*, 479–480.

Chez, M. G. (2007). Memantine as adjunctive therapy in children diagnosed with autistic spectrum disorders: An observation of initial clinical response and maintenance tolerability. *Journal of Child Neurology, 22*(5), 574–579.

Citrome, L., Holt, R. I., Walker, D. J., & Hoffmann, V. P. (2011). Weight gain and changes in metabolic variables following olanzapine treatment in schizophrenia and bipolar disorder. *Clinical Drug Investigation, 31*(7), 455–482.

Cook, E. H., Jr., Rowlett, R., Jaselskis, C., & Leventhal, B. L. (1992). Fluoxetine treatment of children and adults with autistic disorder and mental retardation. *Journal of the American Academy of Child & Adolescent Psychiatry, 31*, 739–745.

Cortese, S., Castelnau, P., Morcillo, C., Roux, S., & Bonnet-Brilhault, F. (2012). Psychostimulants for ADHD-like symptoms in individuals with autism spectrum disorders. *Expert Review of Neurotherapeutics, 12*(4), 461–473.

Coury, D. L., Anagnostou, E., Manning-Courtney, P., Reynolds, A., Cole, L., McCoy, R., ... Perrin, J. M. (2011). Use of psychotropic medication in children and adolescents with autism spectrum disorders. *Journal of Child and Adolescent Psychopharmacology, 21*(6), 571–579.

DeLong, G. R., Teague, L. A., & McSwain Kamran, M. (1998). Effects of fluoxetine treatment in young children with idiopathic autism. *Developmental Medicine & Child Neurology, 40*, 551–562.

Dolen, G., & Bear, M. (2008). Role for metabotropic glutamate receptor 5 (mGluR5) in the pathogenesis of fragile X syndrome. *Journal of Physiology, 586*(6), 1503–1508.

Donfrancesco, R., Calderoni, D., & Vitiello, B. (2007). Open-label amantadine in children with attention-deficit/hyperactivity disorder. *Journal of Child & Adolescent Psychopharmacology, 17*(5), 657–664.

Epperson, N., Czarkowski, K. A., Ward-O'Brien, D., Weiss, E., Gueorguieva, R., Jatlow, P., & Anderson, G. M. (2001). Maternal sertraline treatment and serotonin transport in breast-feeding mother-infant pairs. *American Journal of Psychiatry, 158*, 1631–1637.

Feldman, H. M., Kolmen, B. K., Gonzaga, A. M. (1999). Naltrexone and communication skills in young children with autism. *Journal of the American Academy of Child & Adolescent Psychiatry, 38*, 587–593.

Findling, R. L., McNamara, N. K., Stansbrey, R. J., Maxhimer, R., Periclou, A., Mann, A., & Graham, S. M. (2007). A pilot evaluation of the safety, tolerability, pharmacokinetics, and effectiveness of memantine in pediatric patients with attention-deficit/hyperactivity disorder combined type.

Journal of Child and Adolescent Psychopharmacology, *17*(1), 19–33.

Garber, H. J., McGonigle, J. J., Slomka, G. T., & Monteverde, E. (1992). Clomipramine treatment of stereotypic behaviors and self-injury in patients with developmental disabilities. *Journal of the American Academy of Child & Adolescent Psychiatry, 31,* 1157–1160.

Gordon, C. T., Rapoport, J. L., Hamburger, S. D., State, R. C., & Mannheim, G. B. (1992). Differential response of seven subjects with autistic disorder to clomipramine and desipramine. *American Journal of Psychiatry, 149,* 363–366.

Gordon, C. T., State, R. C., Nelson, J. E., Hamburger, S. D., & Rapoport, J. L. (1993). A double-blind comparison of clomipramine, desipramine, and placebo in the treatment of autistic disorder. *Archives of General Psychiatry, 50,* 441–447.

Guastella, A. J., & MacLeod, C. (2012). A critical review of the influence of oxytocin nasal spray on social cognition in humans: evidence and future directions. *Hormones & Behavior, 61*(3), 410–418.

Handen, B. L., Breaux, A. M., Gosling, A., Ploof, D. L., & Feldman, H. (1990). Efficacy of methylphenidate among mentally retarded children with attention deficit hyperactivity disorder. *Pediatrics, 86,* 922–930.

Handen, B. L., Feldman, H., Gosling, A., Breaux, A. M., & McAuliffe, S. (1991). Adverse side effects of methylphenidate among mentally retarded children with ADHD. *Journal of the American Academy of Child & Adolescent Psychiatry, 30,* 241–245.

Handen, B. L., Feldman, H. M., Lurier, A., & Murray, P. J. (1999). Efficacy of methylphenidate among preschool children with developmental disabilities and ADHD. *Journal of the American Academy of Child & Adolescent Psychiatry, 38,* 805–812.

Handen, B. L., Johnson, C. R., & Lubetsky, M. (2000). Efficacy of methylphenidate among children with autism and symptoms of attention-deficit hyperactivity disorder. *Journal of Autism and Developmental Disorders, 30,* 245–255.

Handen, B. L, Sahl, R., & Hardan, A. Y. (2008). Guanfacine in children with autism and/or intellectual disabilities. *Journal of Developmental & Behavioral Pediatrics, 29*(4), 303–308.

Hardan, A. Y., Fung, L. K., Libove, R. A., Obukhanych, T. V., Nair, S., Herzenberg, L. A.,...Tirouvanziam, R. (2012). *Biological Psychiatry, 71*(11), 956–961.

Harfterkamp, M., van de Loo-Neus, G., Minderaa, R. B., van der Gaag, R. J., Escobar, R., Schacht, A.,...Hoekstra, P. J. (2012). A randomized double-blind study of atomoxetine versus placebo for attention-deficit/hyperactivity disorder symptoms in children with autism spectrum disorder. *Journal of the American Academy of Child & Adolescent Psychiatry, 51*(7), 733–741.

Heimann, S. W. (1999). High-dose olanzapine in an adolescent. *Journal of the American Academy of Child & Adolescent Psychiatry, 38,* 496–498.

Hellings, J. A., Kelley, L. A., Gabrielli, W. F., Kilgore, E., & Shah, P. (1996). Sertraline response in adults with mental retardation and autistic disorder. *Journal of Clinical Psychiatry, 57,* 333–336.

Hirsch, S. R., Link, C. G., Goldstein, J. M., & Arvanitis, L. A. (1996). ICI 204,636: A new atypical antipsychotic drug. *British Journal of Psychiatry—Supplementum, 29,* 45–56.

Hollander, E., Chaplin, W., Soorya, L., Wasserman, S., Novotny, S., Rusoff, J.,... Anagnostou, E. (2010). Divalproex sodium vs. placebo for the treatment of irritability in children and adolescents with autism spectrum disorders. *Neuropsychopharmacology, 35*(4), 990–998.

Hollander, E., Phillips, A., Chaplin, W., Zagursky, K., Novotny, S., Wasserman, S., Iyengar, R. (2005). A placebo controlled crossover trial of liquid fluoxetine on repetitive behaviors in childhood and adolescent autism. *Neuropsychopharmacology, 30*(3), 582–589.

Hollander, E., Soorya, L., Chaplin, W., Anagnostou, E., Taylor, B. P., Ferretti, C. J.,...Settipani, C. (2012). A double-blind placebo-controlled trial of fluoxetine for repetitive behaviors and global severity in adult autism spectrum disorders. *American Journal of Psychiatry, 169*(3), 292–299 [*Erratum American Journal of Psychiatry, 169*(5), 540]

Hollander, E., Wasserman, S., Swanson, E. N., Chaplin, W., Schapiro, M. L., Zagursky, K., Novotny, S. (2006). A double-blind placebo-controlled pilot study of olanzapine in childhood/adolescent pervasive developmental disorder. *Journal of Child and Adolescent Psychopharmacology, 16*(5), 541–548.

Horrigan, J. P., Barnhill, L. J., & Courvoisie, H. E. (1997). Olanzapine in PDD. *Journal of the American Academy of Child & Adolescent Psychiatry, 36,* 1166–1167.

Insel, T. R. (1997). A neurobiological basis of social attachment. *American Journal of Psychiatry, 154,* 726–735.

Ioannides-Demos, L. L., Proietto, J., Tonkin, A. M., & McNeil, J. J. (2006). Safety of drug therapies used for weight loss and treatment of obesity. *Drug Safety, 29*(4), 277–302.

Jacquemont, S., Curie, A., des Portes, V., Torrioli, M. G., Berry-Kravis, E., Hagerman, R.,...Gomez-Mancilla, B. (2011). Epigenetic modification of the FMR1 gene in fragile X syndrome is associated with differential response to the mGluR5 antagonist AFQ056. *Science Translational Medicine, 3*(64), 64ra1.

Jin, P., & Warren, S. T. (2003). New insights into fragile X syndrome: From molecules to neurobehaviors. *Trends in Biochemical Sciences, 28*(3), 152–158.

Kane, J. M., Carson, W. H., Saha, A. R., McQuade, R. D., Ingenito, G. G., Zimbroff, D. L., & Ali, M. W. (2002). Efficacy and safety of aripiprazole and haloperidol versus placebo in patients with schizophrenia and schizoaffective disorder. *Journal of Clinical Psychiatry, 63,* 763–771.

Kapur, S., & Seeman, P. (2001). Does fast dissociation from the dopamine d(2) receptor explain the action of atypical antipsychotics? A new hypothesis. *American Journal of Psychiatry, 158,* 360–369.

King, B. H., Hollander, E., Sikich, L., McCracken, J. T., Scahill, L., Bregman, J. D.,...STAART Psychopharmacology Network. (2009). Lack of efficacy of citalopram in children with autism spectrum disorders and high levels of repetitive behavior: Citalopram ineffective in children with autism. *Archives of General Psychiatry, 66*(6), 583–590.

King, B. H., Wright, D. M., Handen, B. L., Sikich, L., Zimmerman, A. W., McMahon, W.,...Cook, E. H., Jr. (2001). Double-blind, placebo-controlled study of amantadine hydrochloride in the treatment of children with autistic disorder. *Journal of the American Academy of Child & Adolescent Psychiatry, 40,* 658–665.

Klaiman, C., Huffman, L., Masaki, L., & Elliott, G. R. (2013). Tetrahydrobiopterin as a treatment for autism spectrum disorders: A double-blind, placebo-controlled trial. *Journal of Child and Adolescent Psychopharmacology, 23*(5), 320–328.

Kolmen, B. K., Feldman, H. M., Handen, B. L., & Janosky, J. E. (1997). Naltrexone in young autistic children: Replication study and learning measures. *Journal of the American Academy of Child & Adolescent Psychiatry, 36,* 1570–1578.

Kosfeld, M., Heinrichs, M., Zak, P. J., Fischbacher, U., & Fehr, E. (2005). Oxytocin increases trust in humans. *Nature, 435,* 673–676.

Lee, H. J., Macbeth, A. H., Pagani, J. H., Young, W. S., III. (2009). Oxytocin: The great facilitator of life. *Progress in Neurobiology, 88*(2), 127–151.

Leysen, J. E., Gommeren, W., Eens, A., de Chaffoy de Courcelles, D., Stoof, J. C., & Janssen, P. A. (1988). Biochemical profile of risperidone, a new antipsychotic. *Journal of Pharmacology and Experimental Therapeutics, 247,* 661–670.

Maayan, L., & Correll, C. U. (2011). Weight gain and metabolic risks associated with antipsychotic medications in children and adolescents. *Journal of Child and Adolescent Psychopharmacology, 21*(6), 517–535.

Malone, R. P., Cater, J., Sheikh, R. M., Choudhury, M. S., & Delaney, M. A. (2001). Olanzapine versus haloperidol in children with autistic disorder: An open pilot study. *Journal of the American Academy of Child & Adolescent Psychiatry, 40,* 887–894.

Malone, R. P., Delaney, M. A., Hyman, S. B., & Cater, J. R. (2007). Ziprasidone in adolescents with autism: An open-label pilot study. *Journal of Child and Adolescent Psychopharmacology, 17*(6), 779–790.

Marcus, R. N., Owen, R., Kamen, L., Manos, G., McQuade, R. D., Carson, W. H., & Aman, M. G. (2009). A placebo-controlled, fixed-dose study of aripiprazole in children and adolescents with irritability associated with autistic disorder. *Journal of the American Academy of Child & Adolescent Psychiatry, 48*(11), 1110–1119.

Martin, A., Koenig, K., Anderson, G. M., & Scahill, L. (2003). Low-dose fluvoxamine treatment of children and adolescents with pervasive developmental disorders: A prospective, open-label study. *Journal of Autism and Developmental Disorders, 33,* 77–85.

Martin, A., Koenig, K., Scahill, L., & Bregman, J. (1999). Open-label quetiapine in the treatment of children and adolescents with autistic disorder. *Journal of Child and Adolescent Psychopharmacology, 9,* 99–107.

McDougle, C. J., Brodkin, E. S., Naylor, S. T., Carlson, D. C., Cohen, D. J., & Price, L. H. (1998). Sertraline in adults with pervasive developmental disorders: a prospective open-label investigation. *Journal of Clinical Psychopharmacology, 18,* 62–66.

McDougle, C. J., Kem, D. L., & Posey, D. J. (2002). Case series: Use of ziprasidone for maladaptive symptoms in youths with autism. *Journal of the American Academy of Child & Adolescent Psychiatry, 41,* 921–927.

McDougle, C. J., Naylor, S. T., Cohen, D. J., Volkmar, F. R., Heninger, G. R., & Price, L. H. (1996). A double-blind, placebo-controlled study of fluvoxamine in adults with autistic disorder. *Archives of General Psychiatry, 53,* 1001–1008.

McDougle, C. J., Price, L. H., Volkmar, F. R., Goodman, W. K., Ward-O'Brien, D., Nielsen, J., ... Cohen, D. J. (1992). Clomipramine in autism: Preliminary evidence of efficacy. *Journal of the American Academy of Child & Adolescent Psychiatry, 31,* 746–750.

McDougle, C. J., Scahill, L., Aman, M. G., McCracken, J. T., Tierney, E., Davies, M., ... Vitiello, B. (2005). Risperidone for the core symptom domains of autism: Results from the RUPP Autism Network Study. *American Journal of Psychiatry, 162,* 1142–1148.

McPheeters M. L., Warren Z., Sathe N., Bruzek J. L., Krishnaswami S., Jerome R. N., & Veenstra-Vanderweele, J. (2011). A systematic review of medical treatments for children with autism spectrum disorders. *Pediatrics, 127*(5), e1312–1321.

Meltzer, H. Y. (1999). The role of serotonin in antipsychotic drug action. *Neuropsychopharmacology, 21,* 106S–115S.

Messenheimer, J. A. (1998). Rash in adult and pediatric patients treated with lamotrigine. *Canadian Journal of Neurological Sciences, 25,* S14–S18.

Michelson, D., Adler, L., Spencer, T., Reimherr, F. W., West, S. A., Allen, A. J., ... Milton, D. (2003). *Atomoxetine in adults with ADHD: Two randomized, placebo-controlled studies. Biological Psychiatry, 53*(2), 112–120.

MTA Group. (1999). A 14-month randomized clinical trial of treatment strategies for attention-deficit/hyperactivity disorder. The MTA Cooperative Group. Multimodal Treatment Study of Children with ADHD. *Archives of General Psychiatry, 56,* 1073–1086.

Oberman, L. M. (2012). mGluR antagonists and GABA agonistis as novel pharmacological agents for the treatment of autism spectrum disorders. *Expert Opinion Investigational Drugs, 21*(2), 1819–1825.

Oswald D. P., & Sonenklar, N. A. (2007). Medication use among children with autism spectrum disorders. *Journal of Child & Adolescent Psychopharmacology, 17*(3), 348–355.

Owen, R., Sikich, L., Marcus, R., Corey-Lisle, P., Manos, G., McQuade, R. D., ... Findling, R. L. (2009). A multicenter, double-blind, randomized, placebo-controlled, flexible-dose, parallel-group study of aripiprazole in the treatment of irritability in children and adolescents (6–17 years) with autistic disorder. *Pediatrics, 124,* 1533–1540.

Owley, T., Salt, J., Guter, S., Grieve, A., Walton, L., Ayuyao, N., ... Cook, E. H., Jr. (2006). A prospective, open-label trial of memantine in the treatment of cognitive, behavioral, and memory dysfunction in pervasive developmental disorders. *Journal of Child and Adolescent Psychopharmacology, 16*(5), 517–524.

Panksepp, J., & Lensing, P. (1991). Brief report: A synopsis of an open-trial of naltrexone treatment of autism with four children. *Journal of Autism and Developmental Disorders, 21,* 243–249.

Pearson, D. A., Santos, C. W., Roache, J. D., Casat, C. D., Loveland, K. A., Lachar, D., ... Cleveland, L. A. (2003). Treatment effects of methylphenidate on behavioral adjustment in

578   Psychopharmacology

children with mental retardation and ADHD. *Journal of the American Academy of Child & Adolescent Psychiatry, 42*, 209–216.

Posey, D. J., Guenin, K. D., Kohn, A. E., Swiezy, N. B., & McDougle, C. J. (2001). A naturalistic open-label study of mirtazapine in autistic and other pervasive developmental disorders. *Journal of Child and Adolescent Psychopharmacology, 11*, 267–277.

Posey, D. J., Litwiller, M., Koburn, A., & McDougle, C. J. (1999). Paroxetine in autism. *Journal of the American Academy of Child & Adolescent Psychiatry, 38*, 111–112.

Posey, D. J., Wiegand, R. E., Wilkerson, J., Maynard, M., Stigler, K. A., & McDougle, C. J. (2006). Open-label atomoxetine for attention-deficit/hyperactivity disorder symptoms associated with high-functioning pervasive developmental disorders. *Journal of Child and Adolescent Psychopharmacology, 16*(5), 599.

Potenza, M. N., Holmes, J. P., Kanes, S. J., & McDougle, C. J. (1999). Olanzapine treatment of children, adolescents, and adults with pervasive developmental disorders: An open-label pilot study. *Journal of Clinical Psychopharmacology, 19*, 37–44.

Remington, G., Sloman, L., Konstantareas, M., Parker, K., & Gow, R. (2001). Clomipramine versus haloperidol in the treatment of autistic disorder: A double-blind, placebo-controlled, crossover study. *Journal of Clinical Psychopharmacology, 21*(4), 440–444.

Ritvo, E. R., Freeman, B. J., Yuwiler, A., Geller, E., Schroth, P., Yokota, A., . . . Leventhal, B. (1986). Fenfluramine treatment of autism: UCLA collaborative study of 81 patients at nine medical centers. *Psychopharmacology Bulletin, 22*(1), 133–140.

Rosenberg, R. E., Mandell, D. S., Farmer, J. E., Law, J. K., Marvin, A. R., & Law, P. A. (2010). Psychotropic medication use among children with autism spectrum disorders enrolled in a national registry, 2007–2008. *Journal of Autism and Developmental Disorders, 40*, 342–351.

Rubin, M. (1997). Use of atypical antipsychotics in children with mental retardation, autism, and other developmental disabilities. *Psychiatric Annals, 27*, 219–221.

RUPP Anxiety Group. (2001). Fluvoxamine for the treatment of anxiety disorders in children and adolescents. *The Research Unit on Pediatric Psychopharmacology Anxiety Study Group. New England Journal of Medicine, 344*, 1279–1285.

RUPP Autism Network. (2002). Risperidone in children with autism and serious behavioral problems. *New England Journal of Medicine, 347*, 314–321.

RUPP Autism Network. (2005a). Randomized, controlled, crossover trial of methylphenidate in pervasive developmental disorder. *Archives of General Psychiatry, 62*, 1266–1274.

RUPP Autism Network. (2005b). Risperidone treatment of autistic disorder: Longer term benefits and blinded discontinuation after six months. *American Journal of Psychiatry, 162*(7), 1361–1369.

Sallee, F. R., Lyne, A., Wigal, T., & McGough, J. J. (2009). Long-term safety and efficacy of guanfacine extended release in children and adolescents with attention-deficit/hyperactivity disorder. *Journal of Child and Adolescent Psychopharmacology, 19*, 215.

Sanchez, L. E., Campbell, M., Small, A. M., Cueva, J. E., Armenteros, J. L., & Adams, P. B. (1996). A pilot study of clomipramine in young autistic children. *Journal of the American Academy of Child & Adolescent Psychiatry, 35*, 537–544.

Sansone, S. M., Widaman, K. F., Hall, S. S., Reiss, A. L., Lightbody, A., Kaufmann, W. E., . . . Hessl, D. (2012). Psychometric study of the Aberrant Behavior Checklist in fragile X syndrome and implications for targeted treatment, *Journal of Autism and Developmental Disorders, 42*, 1377–1392.

Scahill, L. (2012). Adrenergic agents in child and adolescent psychiatry. In D. R. Rosenberg & S. Gershon (Eds.), *Pharmacotherapy of child and adolescent psychiatric disorders* (3rd ed., pp. 341–363). Oxford, England: Wiley.

Scahill, L., Aman, M. G., McDougle, C. J., McCracken, J. T., Tierney, E., Dziura, J., . . . Vitiello, B. (2006). A prospective open trial of guanfacine in children with pervasive developmental disorders. *Journal of Child and Adolescent Psychopharmacology, 16*(5), 589–598.

Scahill, L., Erenberg, G., Berlin, C. M., Budman, C., Coffey, B. J., Jankovic, J., . . . Walkup, J. (2006). Contemporary assessment and pharmacotherapy of Tourette syndrome. *NeuroRx, 3*, 192–206.

Scahill, L., Hallett, V., Aman, M., McDougle, C. J., Arnold, L. E., McCracken, J. T., . . . Vitiello, B. (2012). Brief report: Social disability in autism spectrum disorder: Results from Research Units on Pediatric Psychopharmacology (RUPP) Autism Network Trials. *Journal of Autism and Developmental Disorders, 43*(3), 739–746.

Scahill, L., McDougle, C. J., Aman, M. G., Johnson, C., Handen, B., Bearss, K., . . . Research Units on Pediatric Psychopharmacology Autism Network. (2012). Effects of risperidone and parent training on adaptive functioning in children with a pervasive developmental disorders and serious behavioral problems. *Journal of the American Academy of Child & Adolescent Psychiatry, 51*(2), 136–146.

Scahill, L., McDougle, C. J., Williams, S. K., Dimitropoulos, A., Aman, M. G., McCracken, J., . . . Vitiello, B. (2006). The Children's Yale-Brown Obsessive Compulsive Scales modified for pervasive developmental disorders. *Journal of the American Academy of Child & Adolescent Psychiatry, 45*(9), 1114–1123.

Seeger, T. F., Seymour, P. A., Schmidt, A. W., Zorn, S. H., Schulz, D. W., Lebel, L. A., . . . Heym, J. (1995). Ziprasidone (CP-88,059): a new antipsychotic with combined dopamine and serotonin receptor antagonist activity. *Journal of Pharmacology and Experimental Therapeutics, 275*, 101–113.

Shea, S., Turgay, A., Carroll, A., Schulz, M., Orlik, H., Smith, I., & Dunbar, F. (2004). Risperidone in the treatment of disruptive behavioral symptoms in children with autistic and other pervasive developmental disorders. *Pediatrics, 114*(5), e634–41.

Snead, R. W., Boon, F., & Presberg, J. (1994). Paroxetine for self-injurious behavior. *Journal of the American Academy of Child & Adolescent Psychiatry, 33*, 909–910.

Sparrow, S. S., Balla, D. A., & Cicchetti, D. V. (1984). Vineland Adaptive Behavior Scales: Survey form manual. Circle Pines, MN: American Guidance Service.

Spencer, T., Biederman, J., Coffey, B., Geller, D., Crawford, M., Bearman, S., . . . Faraone, S. (2002). A double-blind comparison of desipramine and placebo in children and adolescents with chronic tic disorder and comorbid attention-deficit/hyperactivity disorder. *Archives of General Psychiatry, 59*(7), 649.

Steingard, R. J., Zimnitzky, B., DeMaso, D. R., Bauman, M. L., & Bucci, J. P. (1997). Sertraline treatment of transition-associated anxiety and agitation in children with autistic disorder. *Journal of Child and Adolescent Psychopharmacology, 7*, 9–15.

Stigler, K. A., Mullett, J. E., Erickson, C. A., Posey, D. J., & McDougle, C. J. (2012). Paliperidone for irritability in adolescents and young adults with autistic disorder. *Psychopharmacology, 223*(2), 237–245.

Tamminga, C. A. (2002). Partial dopamine agonists in the treatment of psychosis. *Journal of Neural Transmission, 109*, 411–420.

Troost, P. W., Steenhuis, M. P., Tuynman-Qua, H. G., Kalverdijk, L. J., Buitelaar, J. K., Minderaa, R. B., & Hoekstra, P. J. (2006). Atomoxetine for attention-deficit/hyperactivity disorder symptoms in children with pervasive developmental disorders: A pilot study. *Journal of Child and Adolescent Psychopharmacology, 16*(5), 611–619.

Veenstra-VanderWeele, J., King, B., Erickson, C., Ginsberg, L., Melman, R., Scahill, L., . . . Wang, P. (2011). An open label trial of arbaclofen in autism spectrum disorder shows improvements in multiple symptom domains. Poster presentation, NCDEU meeting, June 13–16, Boca Raton, FL.

Williams, K., Wray, J. A., & Wheeler, D. M. (2012). Intravenous secretin for autism spectrum disorders (ASD). *Cochrane Database Systematic Reviews, 4*, CD003495.

Young, S. N. (2008). The neurobiology of human social behaviour: An important but neglected topic. *Journal of Psychiatry & Neuroscience, 33*, 391–392.

Zuddas, A., Ledda, M. G., Fratta, A., Muglia, P., & Cianchetti, C. (1996). Clinical effects of clozapine on autistic disorder. *American Journal of Psychiatry, 153*, 738.

Author Index

Subject Index

Aberrant Behavior Checklist (ABC), 544, 558, 561, 562, 565, 567, 570, 571, 572, 573, 574

Academics. *See* Education and academic achievement

Academy of Medical Sciences, 414

Accidents, injuries and safety issues, 540, 545–546

Acetylcholine, 469

Adaptive functioning:
  executive function relationship to, 320
  infant and toddler, 130
  interventions improving, 204
  pharmacological treatments impacting, 559
  sensory development impacting, 392

ADHD Rating Scale, 569

Adolescents with ASD:
  bullying and victimization of, 177, 547–548
  college transition for, 183–185
  education and academic achievement of, 118, 176–183, 183–186
  emotional expression and response in, 179, 338–345
  employment preparation in, 118, 180, 183, 184
  friend and peer relations in, 177, 180–182, 183, 185
  functional curriculum transition for, 182–183
  future research on, 185–186
  health care issues among, 546–548
  imitation in, 282–284
  intelligence level in, 182
  interventions and treatment for, 176, 177, 178–183, 185, 546

language and communication in, 179, 182–183, 238

mental health issues in, 177, 488, 547, 548

nonverbal communication in, 179, 182–183, 338, 339–343

overview of, 118, 176–177

peer-mediated interventions for, 181–182

pharmacological treatment of, 546

pivotal response treatment for, 178

priming for, 178–179

self-management for, 179–180

sexuality in, 547

social development and interaction in, 180–182, 183, 185

social event interventions for, 182, 185

video modeling for, 180–181

Adult Asperger Assessment (AAA), 195–196

Adults with ASD:
  aggression or hostility in, 109, 197, 202–203
  childhood predictors for, 101–102, 221–222
  clinical issues in, 194–200
  deterioration and improvement in, 108–110, 192
  developmental course in, 192–193
  education/college attendance among, 98, 100, 193–194, 201
  elderly, 2, 20, 111–112, 206
  employment among, 98, 100, 103–106, 107, 110–111, 192, 194, 200–201
  epilepsy in, 107, 108
  family situations of, 102, 194, 203
  friendship development among, 98, 100, 101, 110, 111
  gender of, 101, 196